SACRED REALMS

ESSAYS IN RELIGION, BELIEF, AND SOCIETY

Richard Warms
Texas State University—San Marcos

James Garber
Texas State University—San Marcos

Jon McGee
Texas State University—San Marcos

New York   Oxford
OXFORD UNIVERSITY PRESS
2004

Oxford University Press

Oxford   New York
Auckland   Bangkok   Buenos Aires   Cape Town   Chennai
Dar es Salaam   Delhi   Hong Kong   Istanbul   Karachi   Kolkata
Kuala Lumpur   Madrid   Melbourne   Mexico City   Mumbai   Nairobi
São Paulo   Shanghai   Taipei   Tokyo   Toronto

Published by Oxford University Press, Inc.
198 Madison Avenue, New York, New York 10016
www.oup.com

Oxford is a registered trademark of Oxford University Press

Cover photo: © Stephen Swintek/Getty Images

Library of Congress Cataloging-in-Publication Data

Sacred realms : essays in religion, belief, and society / [compiled by] Richard Warms,
James Garber, Jon McGee.
    p. cm.
   Includes bibliographical references and index.
   ISBN 0-19-517550-6 (soft cover)
     1. Religion. 2. Religions. I. Warms, Richard L. II. Garber, James. III. McGee, R.
Jon, 1955– .

BL48.S223 2004
200—dc22   2003061622

Printing number: 9 8 7 6 5 4 3 2 1

Printed in the United States of America
on acid-free paper

BRIEF CONTENTS

CONTENTS

PREFACE

Sacred Realms is the result of the editors' experiences teaching the anthropology of religion. Over the past fifteen years, each of the editors has taught yearly sections of a very popular class on the anthropology of religion at Texas State University–San Marcos (formerly Southwest Texas State University). In that time, more than twenty thousand students have taken the course. Though we have had the opportunity to use many different textbooks, we have never found one that captures the excitement and breadth of the study of religion, is accessible to undergraduate students, and represents the best of current academic work in the field. The current volume is an attempt to fill that vacuum.

OVERVIEW AND APPROACH

Sacred Realms is designed to give students the tools to understand and analyze religion as well as to consider its important role in current world affairs. It does so by employing a variety of techniques:

- *Strong introductory material. Sacred Realms* begins with an introductory essay describing and defining religion in broad, nonevaluative terms. The introductory essay is designed to encourage students to think about religion as a general human experience rather than from the perspective of their own background and upbringing. The essay helps students reflect on the ways in which their religious experiences are similar to and different from others' experiences.

- *Sections representing the major topics in the study of religion.* This book is divided into sections that reflect the ways religion courses are usually structured. Topics such as religion and society, ritual specialists, altered states of consciousness, healing, and death, as well as many others, each have their own section.

- *Current essays chosen for both their scholarly content and their appeal to students and instructors.* We include essays by classic authors such as Bronislaw Malinowski, Victor Turner, and Anthony F. C. Wallace, but our emphasis has been on choosing articles published since the late 1980s written by authors of diverse ethic and national backgrounds.

- *Vivid ethnographic examples.* We have combed the literature to find essays that illustrate key points in the study of religion by focusing on vividly portrayed examples drawn from field studies of individual cultures. All areas of the world, including the United States and Europe, are represented by the essays. Some essays focus on religious rituals and beliefs of great age; others take up new practices.

- *World religions section.* No treatment of religion can afford to ignore the important current and historic roles played by the major world religions. We believe that students are hungry for basic, reliable, nonbiased information about the world's largest religions. We further think that they need such information to be able to evaluate current events. To these ends we have written brief, engaging summaries of five of the world's numerically and historically most important religions. While not all instructors include such material in their courses, this section provides a valuable, accessible, and reliable reference source for students.

- *Eclectic, anthropologically based perspective.* Though the editors of *Sacred Realms* are anthropologists and the viewpoint this volume takes is anthropological, we have incorporated insights and essays from history, sociology, social work, and many other perspectives. This results in an exciting selection of essays that will interest students and instructors alike. It also shows how anthropological knowledge is applied and the interrelationships between anthropology and other fields of study. Its broad, eclectic approach makes this book appropriate for classes not only in anthropology but in many other disciplines as well.

PEDAGOGY

Sacred Realms is rooted in the extensive classroom experience of its editors and is designed with student instruction in mind. The essays were chosen to capture the attention and interest of students, and the pedagogical techniques are designed to focus their attention and sharpen their ability to draw useful information from the readings.

- Each part of *Sacred Realms* opens with a photo and caption designed to draw students into the material.

- Each section opens with an introduction clearly listing the title of each essay in the section along with the year of its original publication.

- The subject of the section is given a brief introduction stating a few critical facts or raising some important issues. This introduction is followed by a series of bulleted points that provide essential background information for understanding the essays and raise issues of concern for the general study of religion. The writing style is direct, concise, and easily accessible.

- Each essay is introduced by a headnote of 300 to 500 words. The headnotes place each article in context, provide a brief summary of its critical points, and include a series of questions for students to consider as they read. This approach focuses student attention and helps them understand what they are reading.

SUPPLEMENTS

Instructor's Manual/Test Bank: An indispensable instructor supplement, prepared by Andrew Buckser, Purdue University, features chapter outlines, key terms, and a complete test bank.

ACKNOWLEDGMENTS

Sacred Realms has been several years in the making and has required the help, patience, forbearance, and wisdom of many people. First and foremost we wish to thank our families, who put up with us as we worked on this manuscript. We also thank the friends and colleagues who shared their opinions and advice as we chose the essays for this volume. This volume would not have been possible without the unflagging administrative support from the Department of Anthropology at Texas State University–San Marcos and our students Kiyomi Appleton and Heather Bohac, who copied articles, ran errands, and offered criticism and advice on our work.

We also wish to thank the reviewers who helped with this project. We appreciate their time and efforts, and their feedback has been critical to shaping this project. The reviewers are Dr. David Jones, *University of Central Florida;* Dr. William Leons, *University of Toledo;* Clay Robarchek, *Wichita State University;* Terry N. Simmons, *Paradise Valley Community College;* and Phillips Stevens, Jr., Ph.D., *SUNY at Buffalo.*

We especially wish to thank Jan Beatty, formerly of Mayfield Publishing, with whom we worked out the original plan for *Sacred Realms,* and our editor Kevin Witt of McGraw-Hill, who took over the project after Mayfield was purchased by McGraw-Hill and whose advice and support have been essential to this project. Our thanks to Christine Walker, our project manager at McGraw-Hill.

Introduction:
What Is Religion?

Religion has been a key concern of the social sciences since their early years. In his 1871 book *Primitive Culture,* Sir Edward Burnett Tylor, whom many consider a founder of anthropology, laid out his theories about culture—but his primary goal was to explain the development of religious thought. He believed it originated in universal human experiences, such as dreams, and had followed an evolutionary path from primitive superstition to enlightened nineteenth-century Christianity. Today, while honoring much of Tylor's work, scholars reject his notions about the evolution of religion.

Many other important figures in the history of social science have also been critically concerned with religion. Émile Durkheim examined how religions model the social worlds of their members. Karl Marx sought the meaning of religion in its role in supporting the social order and the position of the privileged of society. Max Weber explored the relationship between the emergence of Protestantism and capitalism. Sigmund Freud saw religious origins in the psychodynamics of family and group life. Claude Lévi-Strauss looked for universal messages hidden in the myths and sacred stories of all people. Victor Turner examined religious rituals, exploring their structure and function. These and many other individuals have created a wealth of knowledge about the nature of religion and the role it plays in society.

The goal of this introduction is to introduce you to some of the critical ideas and definitions in the study of religion. The sections of *Sacred Realms* explore these concepts, providing examples of the beliefs and practices of people from many different cultures.

Anthropologists generally consider religion to be a human universal. While the beliefs of individuals within cultures certainly vary, all cultures have religious traditions and no group of people could be said to be truly without religion. However, as is the case for many other critical concepts, defining religion in a way that accounts for all religious variation within and between cultures is a daunting task. Most of our common attempts at definition fail. For example, when most Americans think about religion, they probably think about an institution. That is, they think about their membership (or lack of membership) in a particular organization such as the Evangelical Lutheran Church or the Union of American Hebrew Congregations. They further think of such groups as having a physical presence: buildings, clergy, officers, and so on. Thus, we tend to think of religions as being composed of institutions and of ourselves as being members of those institutions. But defining religion as an institution to which people belong clearly won't work across all cultures. For example, anthropological research shows us that many cultures of the world, particularly groups organized as bands or tribes, lack institutions in the

sense in which we generally use the term—there are no religious organizations to which the individuals belong, and no one chooses among different possible religious groups. Instead, in these cultures, religious identity and practice are simply part of ethnic identity. Consequently, a member of such a group who is asked what their religion is, what "church" they belong to, would probably not understand the question.

It is also tempting to define religion as beliefs about the supernatural. But this, too, is deceptive and may reveal more about our own assumptions than about people's religion. Most members of Western societies divide the world into the "natural" and the "supernatural." When we say that something is "natural," we generally mean that it is normal and logical, that it obeys laws of nature that are (at least in principle) discoverable, and that rational people may be expected to accept and understand it. On the other hand, when we say that something is "supernatural," we generally mean that it is neither normal nor logical, and that it defies rational understanding. By extension, we generally think that people who believe in the "supernatural" are superstitious and irrational. We very rarely use the term *supernatural* when talking about our own beliefs and religions.

This attitude can get in the way of our understanding of religion. For example, suppose I don't believe in the supernatural. I am walking down the street one afternoon and I hear the voice of God. I physically hear it, not as a thought in my mind but rather I have the sensation of having physically heard a voice, in the same way I would hear a person's voice. If this were to happen, for me, it would clearly be "supernatural." But because I do not believe in the "supernatural," I would most likely think it had a natural cause . . . perhaps I had a high fever, or had eaten something bad for lunch, or was going insane. In other words, I would look for a "natural" cause. On the other hand, suppose that, like many Americans, I believe in a very personal God who frequently talks to humans. Then, when I, walking down the same street, have the same experience of hearing God's voice, how do I react? Perhaps I stop, listen, and obey (or perhaps not). In either event, I understand the event as part of my expected world and therefore "natural." I don't look for further cause in my diet or my psychological state. The implication of this is that for me, God speaking is "natural," not "supernatural." Thus, to define religion as society's mechanism for dealing with the "supernatural" misses the experience of certain kinds of believers. Further, it suggests that we consider religion (at least other people's religion) irrational.

Even though no simple universal definition of religion has ever been agreed upon, there is a way out of this dilemma. Rather than try to define religion, we can come up with a series of characteristics that virtually all religions have in common. In that way, we can characterize religion without taking a position on belief. The following seven characteristics seem to be shared by nearly all religions.

1. Religions are composed of stories.
2. Religions posit the existence of nonempirical beings, powers, states, places, and qualities.
3. Religions make common use of symbols and symbolism.
4. Religions include rituals.
5. Religions have clerics. Following the eminent anthropologist Morton Klass, we use the term *cleric* in the broadest sense to refer to practitioners of all sorts: leaders, authorities, officiants, formal and informal officeholders, not just members of Christian religious orders.[1]
6. Religions frequently make use of altered states of consciousness.
7. The practice of religion changes over time.

Religions Are Composed of Stories

At some level, every religion is simply a collection of stories told by members of a group. Some elements of these stories may be objectively verifiable, but many are not. For example, most scholars believe that Siddhartha Guatama, the founder of Buddhism, was indeed an historic personage: that there was an Indian prince by that name who lived in the sixth or fifth century B.C.E. However, whether he became the Buddha by achieving enlightenment while sitting under a banyan tree is much less subject to empirical evaluation.

Although there is probably no single subject that is dealt with by all the world's religions, there are many subjects that are quite common. Most religions have stories about where human beings came from and where they go after they die. Many have stories about where the world itself came from. The deeds of religious founders, heroes, prophets, saints, gods, and spirits are also the subject of religious narrative. The disasters typically faced by preindustrial people, such as famine, drought, flood, fire, and earthquake, also loom large in religious stories.

One way of understanding religious stories is as sacred narratives. Such stories are more than simply tales told round a campfire. For believers, the stories are held to reveal profound truths and provide both guidance and commandment for action in the world. In some cases, the actual words themselves are held to be sacred, having been dictated directly by God or by other powerful forces. However, not all religious stories are equally sacred. Consider the stories that surround the Christian celebrations of Christmas and Easter. Almost all Christians hold that the story of Jesus' Crucifixion and Resurrection is both literally true and extremely sacred—that there really was a historical individual named Jesus, that he was the

son of God, that he was crucified, that he rose from the dead, and that these acts enabled the salvation of humankind. There is far less consensus about the stories that surround Christmas. Did three kings really follow a star to Bethlehem and present gifts of gold, incense, and myrrh? Some Christians believe that this is literally true; many do not. It is clear that the story of the Crucifixion and Resurrection is much more central to Christianity than the Christmas stories.

It has been common in religious studies to refer to religious stories as myths, but this is a term that we should use with great caution. In some senses the word *myth* is appropriate. When we think of myth, we think of stories of great deeds, stories that explain the origins of the world, or of particular practices in it, stories of heroes such as Athena or Hercules, stories where time is compressed or expanded and reality is composed of many levels. These are indeed characteristics of religious stories. However, in English the word *myth* most commonly also carries the idea of a story that people believed in the past (as in Greek and Roman myths) or that people of different religions believe today (as in American Indian myths). In these cases, the use of the term suggests that we know better—that these stories are not literally true or, to modern enlightened people, spiritually important. This is simple prejudice. American Indians hold their stories to be as true as Christians, Jews, and Muslims hold theirs. Ancient Greeks and Romans held their stories to be sacred as well. And all of these stories typify the characteristics of myth listed above. Modern scholars of religion do not usually talk about "the myth of Jesus" or "the myth of Moses." They should be similarly cautious in talking about American Indian or Greek "myths." These are all simply religious stories, and at least some of them are held to be literally true, sacred, and of central importance.

Religions Posit the Existence of Supernatural Beings, Powers, States, Places, and Qualities

Religions are almost endlessly diverse. Some propose that there is no God, some propose that there are a great many gods. Some fill the world with animate beings, spirits, and objects; others insist that humans alone are possessed of consciousness and a soul. Some propose that humans live once and are judged on their actions during that life; others insist that humans live repeatedly until they are able to perfect themselves. Is there any commonality that binds all of these beliefs together? The answer is yes, but this commonality is broad and general. All religions claim that there is something that is, in a scientific sense, nonempirical, but which nonetheless exists. (By "nonempirical" we mean something that we cannot measure, either directly or by technological means.) This is, perhaps, an understanding of God and other aspects of religion upon which both the religious and nonreligious might agree.

Consider, for a moment, this question: Does God exist? We can construct many philosophical arguments about this question, but there really is only one scientific way to answer it: we would have to build a device, call it a "god-o-meter" (pronounced to rhyme with *speedometer*), to empirically measure the existence of God. However, two objections immediately interpose, one found in many religious traditions, the other found in all. The first is that in the Jewish, Christian, and Islamic traditions (as well as many others), a critical characteristic of God is that God is infinite. By definition, something that is infinite cannot be measured. Therefore, our attempt to build a god-o-meter must fail. The second objection is more powerful still. The god-o-meter must measure the physical presence of something. But what? What could members of all religious traditions, the nonreligious as well as the religious, agree upon to measure to show the presence of God?

Members of a single religious tradition might believe that the truth of their beliefs is proven by the existence of a physical object. For example, some Muslims might believe that the black stone housed in the Kaaba in Mecca is physical proof of the existence of God and the truth of Islam. However, members of other religious traditions do not believe such objects prove anything at all. Members of many religious traditions claim that what they see as the beauty and perfection of life on Earth could not be a matter of chance or the workings of impersonal natural laws. They insist that the world itself proves the existence of a divine Creator (this is called the argument from design). Most scientists, on the other hand, are convinced that it is precisely the workings of natural law that have produced the Earth and all life on it.

Thus, it seems clear that people of different religious and nonreligious understandings cannot agree on what might be observed and measured to prove the existence of God or how such a thing might be observed and measured. Further, they are extremely unlikely to come to any such agreement in the future. Consequently, our attempt to build a god-o-meter must fail.

In our attempt to build a god-o-meter, we considered the Jewish, Christian, and Muslim understanding of God. However, we can pose the same problem in every religious tradition. It is similarly impossible to build a device to measure the existence of ancestors, spirits, heaven, hell, the power contained in a religious object, the state of enlightenment, the magical power of a phrase, and so on, in a way that members of different traditions will agree upon. Yet all religious traditions are built around and incorporate some of these elements.

Have we now begun a book about religion with an attempt to disprove the existence of God and other aspects of religion? Certainly not. What our god-o-meter experiment shows is that science can provide no answer to questions about the existence (or lack thereof) of God or other nonempirical aspects of religion. But that is very different from saying that these do not exist. We deal comfortably with nonempirical qualities all of the time. For example, few of us doubt the existence of beauty, and most of us have experienced beauty, but beauty is nonempirical. That is to say, no machine has ever been invented (or likely will ever be invented) that can, in a scientific sense, show how much beauty an individual, a painting, or a sunset possesses. Similarly, we believe in good and we believe in truth. In fact, some religions, such as the Society for Ethical Culture, devote themselves to the pursuit of good and truth. However, for several thousand years philosophers have been searching for ways to observe, measure, and quantify these, without any notable success.

Religions Make Common Use of Symbols and Symbolism

One important aspect of religion is the use of symbols. A symbol is simply something that stands for something else. Symbols have *conventional* meanings. In other words, the meanings of symbols are created by agreement. An object, word, or other kind of symbol has no intrinsic meaning but rather gains meaning from common usage. All symbols, but religious symbols in particular, have several critical features. First, they store information. Humans in all cultures pass information to each other and between generations by the use of symbols. Religious symbols encapsulate critical religious ideas and help people remember religious stories. Second, symbols are *multivalent.* That is, they carry many different meanings. Consider, for example, the cross, a common religious symbol with which virtually everyone is familiar. Now, what is the meaning of the cross? The question is virtually impossible to answer—or to answer completely, in any case. The problem is that the cross has so many possible meanings, both to Christians and non-Christians, that any attempt to explain its meanings would be very long, and ultimately incomplete.

The fact that symbols can pack so many meanings makes them particularly useful in religion. In religious observances, symbols can be shown, manipulated, discussed, and even, in some cases, desecrated. By performing these actions, worshipers create and manipulate meaning. Seeing a religious symbol brings to mind the many different ideas and emotions connected with it. Treating symbols in certain ways actualizes these ideas and emotions. Consider the Christian observance of communion. In communion, the believer symbolically consumes the body and blood of Jesus. Note that, for our purposes, it makes no difference if the wine and wafer are symbolic themselves (as most Protestants believe) or become the actual physical body and blood of Jesus (as the Catholic doctrine of transubstantiation claims). In either case, receiving communion is a profound symbolic event. As with other symbolic events, it is impossible to say what communion means, for it means a great many different things. However, in receiving communion, Christians declare simultaneously their belief, their membership in the church, and their religious identity. Thus, the symbolic act of communion forges and reinforces community membership, demands and demonstrates belief, and displays commitment, at least theoretically, to a series of precepts and practices.

A third characteristic of symbols is well worth considering. Victor Turner, a very influential anthropologist who studied symbols, claimed that symbols illustrate what he called "polarization of meaning." He said that symbols have both an ideological and a sensory pole. By this he meant that any symbol has a field of meaning that refers to the physical world—to blood, earth, pain, pleasure, or other sensations or objects. But symbols also have a field of meaning that refers to the social and moral principles that underlie the structure of the society in which they are found. One example of this used by Turner was the Mudyi tree found frequently in ritual among the Ndembu, an African people. Turner wrote that the white sap of the Mudyi tree was at the same time a symbol for breast milk and a symbol of the principle of matrilineality (descent following the mother's line).[2] We can easily see how the principle of polarity of meaning would operate in a symbol such as the cross, which at one pole might stand for blood and suffering, and at the other for salvation and resurrection. However, it is not clear that all symbols in all traditions exhibit this characteristic.

Religions Include Rituals

In one sense, a ritual is simply any stylized repetitive action. However, this definition is entirely too broad to be of much use. Brewing a morning cup of coffee, brushing one's teeth, and saying grace before meals are all clearly stylized repetitive actions, but equally clearly only one of them is religious.

Two characteristics mark religious ritual as different from rituals of other kinds. First, religious ritual involves interface with the supernatural. In other words, in religious ritual, individuals and groups address, are addressed by, or attempt to in some way come into contact with whatever supernatural character or quality they perceive as playing an important role in their current situation. In religious ritual, people attempt to forge a link between themselves and gods, spirits, ancestors, enlightenment, the good, or any other nonempirical facet of the world as they understand it.

Second, religious ritual centers fundamentally around the notion that events that occur in ritual are not pretense, but truly happen. Because of this, believers understand ritual as able to effect changes in the world. A good way to understand this is to contrast religious ritual with plays, movies, and novels. All of these forms tell stories and make assertions about the world. In our society movies, plays, and novels often deal with religious subjects, telling stories about gods, spirits, ancestors, and the like. They may contain rich moral instruction and serve to educate and entertain (all characteristics of many religious rituals). However, there is a fundamental difference between these and religious ritual. Plays, movies, and novels are about suspension of disbelief. That is, when we go to a play or movie, we agree to pretend.

We know that the characters, even if historical, are not real. For example, if we go to see Shakespeare's play *Richard the Third*, we know that there was a historical King Richard but we would never think we had actually seen him (after all, he died in 1485). We see an actor playing the part of Richard, and, if the play is performed well enough, we're drawn into the fantasy for a few hours and willfully forget that we're watching an actor, not the real Richard. Thus, if the play or movie is good, we pretend that what we see is real while we watch the show. But we are aware that plays and movies are products of an author's imagination as well as that of the people who stage them.

Religion involves no such pretense, no such awareness. For believers, what happens in a ritual really and truly happens. Consider, for example, a ritual to contact the ancestors and seek their protection. In such a ritual, believers do not pretend to contact the ancestors, but actually do so (or understand themselves as doing so). If the ritual is successful, the blessings of the ancestors are actually received. There is no play-acting involved. Similarly, a preacher who, in a charismatic Christian ritual, says "the spirit of God is with us now" does not mean "Let's pretend that God is present among us" but rather that the Spirit of God is literally (though nonempirically) present.

Because believers understand the actions of religious ritual as truly happening, such ritual can have a vital effect on the world. In one sense this is simply obvious. A ritual in which two people are married changes their social (and in some cases legal and economic) status. A ritual that initiates a member into a secret society gives them rights and responsibilities as well as access to hidden knowledge. A second sense is more subtle. Ritual may change our understanding and hence change our actions. Individuals who believe themselves purified by religious ritual may behave differently than those who have not taken part in such a ritual. Individuals who believe that the gods or ancestors have blessed or forbidden a particular undertaking bring a different state of mind to it than those who do not believe this, and this may affect their chances for success.

Religions Have Clerics

In all communities, there are individuals who are particularly knowledgeable about religion and who perform religious rituals for other members of their group. The general term for such individuals is *cleric*. Anthropologists have conventionally divided such clerics into two broad classes, *priests* and *shamans*.

There is a lively and often vitriolic debate about the precise meaning and the usefulness of these terms. Briefly, some anthropologists hold that the word *shaman* is only properly used in referring to clerics within the religious traditions of specific groups in Northeastern Siberia. The term originated among these groups, and the precise attributes to which it applies exist only there.[3] Other anthropologists (probably the majority, although we do not know of any survey done on this question) believe that the term should apply to a wide variety of clerics with some similar characteristic who exist in cultures all over the world.

The debate is interesting, because it reflects a larger dispute that has existed from at least the late nineteenth century. Since then, anthropology has been divided into those who believe that the primary goal of the discipline should be to provide accurate and insightful descriptions of the cultures of different groups of people and those who believe that anthropologists should be concerned with formulating general principles of culture that can be applied to many different groups of people. People sympathetic to the first of these goals will lean toward a very restricted use of the term *shaman;* those who favor the second are likely to subscribe to a broad notion of shamanism.

One of our goals in this book (and indeed in this definition of religion) is to draw your attention to commonalities among the world's religious traditions, so we favor a very broad definition of shamanism. We believe that this highlights fundamental similarities, not only in religious experience but in the organization of social behavior in societies throughout the world.

Probably no single criterion separates priests from shamans in all cases, but the best single indicator of whether a cleric might be considered priest or shaman is the nature of their employment. Priests are officeholders in institutionalized religions, whereas shamans are essentially independent operators. That is to say, priests hold offices that exist independently of themselves and are certified by the institutions to which they belong and they are answerable to those institutions. A good example is the minister at your local Methodist church. The minister holds an office. A minister who leaves (by choice, death, or the choice of the congregation) will be replaced by another. The individual is able to hold the office because she or he has a diploma from a theological seminary and is certified by the church to authentically represent it. If the minister professes beliefs or commits actions that are at great variance with those of the organization, he or she can be dismissed and replaced. The oracle at Delphi, in ancient Greece, is a more exotic example. The oracle was a priestess of Apollo who stood in a small enclosure at the temple to Apollo at Delphi. She would fall into a trance by inhaling vapors emanating from the walls of her chamber (probably methane and ethane gas that came from the rock lying beneath the site).[4] In trance the oracle would thrash wildly and utter words that were interpreted as predicting the future. Despite the exotic aspects of the oracle, she was an officeholder in an ancient religion, authorized and certified by high-ranking priests of Apollo. If she died or became incapacitated, she was replaced by another individual who similarly held the office Oracle at Delphi and played the same role within the organization of ancient Greek religion and society.

A shaman, on the other hand, holds no office and represents no institution. Shamans are individuals who claim, and are understood by their followers, to be able to use power from whatever nonempirical source they perceive to be effective in the world to achieve particular ends, such as curing or cursing an individual, determining guilt or innocence of someone accused of a crime, or predicting future events. Shamans understand their powers to be a direct function of their ability to contact (and frequently to travel in) the world of gods, spirits, ancestors, and powers. They are certainly part of the traditions of their culture, but they are individual operators. A shaman who chooses to leave, or dies, or is rejected by his or her community is not replaced in the same sense as a priest is. Other rival shamans might assume the first shaman's position, or it may be taken over by a younger relative, but this individual would have to prove his or her ability to effectively contact the nonempirical world.

Though ecstasy, trance, and other experiences of direct contact with the nonempirical are common among both priests and shamans, there are many examples of priests who do not have ecstatic religious experiences—whereas virtually all shamans have such experiences. Priests' authority comes ultimately from the institution they represent, so direct evidence of religious experience is not always required for followers to believe that the priest is authentic. Priests might experience religious ecstasy and trance. They might use mind-altering substances. However, a priest's authority ultimately stems from their position and not from their ecstatic experiences. For example, in Catholicism, individuals perform confession, are given penance (duties they must perform, usually in the form of prayer), and, if they do these properly, receive God's forgiveness for their sins. While a priest must hear confession and assign penance, God alone can forgive; and whether or not the priest has had a personal experience of God, or even believes such is possible, is not relevant to receiving God's forgiveness for sin. Ancient Mayan priests let their own (and others') blood to nourish the gods. Aided by trance, they visited the otherworld to commune with gods and ancestors. However, their right to do so came from their position in the Mayan political and religious hierarchy, and their revelations were endorsed and promoted by that hierarchy.

The shaman, on the other hand, claims direct contact with the nonempirical without any intercession from a bureaucratic hierarchy. Therefore, shamans must demonstrate their ability by communicating with, traveling in, or being possessed by the nonempirical. Their power to perform acceptable ritual rests upon public acceptance of claims of their ability. Therefore, shamanic practice will almost always include demonstrations of ecstatic religious states.

Religions Make Frequent Use of Altered States of Consciousness

In every religion, at least some people have experiences that they understand as direct contact with the nonempirical. For individuals who have them, and for others as well, these experiences generally verify the central truths of their beliefs—the existence of God, spirits, ancestors, powers, enlightenment, and so on. For reasons we detailed at the start of this introduction, we can never know, in objective way, if these experiences are authentic. However, though we cannot know whether the soul truly meets the supernatural during such experiences, we can know what happens in the body during them. When people have such experiences, their bodies and their brains show measurable changes. In a purely physical sense, they experience altered states of consciousness.

Religious techniques to alter states of consciousness vary widely. Methods such as meditation, contemplation, the use of mantras, or repeated prayers and song are common in the Jewish, Christian, and Muslim traditions, with which most readers are familiar. Other techniques are less familiar to us. People in many societies use powerful hallucinogenic drugs as part of religious rituals; such drug use is particularly common among aboriginal groups of Central and South America. People in many places also achieve altered states through physical trauma—suspending themselves from cords in a Sun Dance or, like the European flagellants (members of a Christian sect in the thirteenth and fourteenth centuries), whipping and beating themselves into religious frenzy. Today, *Los Hermano Penitentes,* a Catholic men's society located primarily in New Mexico, continues the practice of inducing religious ecstasy through whipping.[5]

Much research remains to be done on the specific brain effects of various religious practices, but we do have considerable knowledge of the neural pathways through which these techniques work. For example, meditation, contemplation, and repetitive prayer seem to affect an area of the superior parietal lobe. This brain region is involved in the perception of orientation and location. The sense of timelessness and oneness that people often report during religious experiences induced by these methods seems directly related to effects on this region of the brain.[6] Similarly, studies on physical trauma, intense physical activity, or powerful emotional experiences show that these result in the release of endorphins, neurohormones that activate opiate receptors in the brain and produce feelings of euphoria and well-being.

Both naturally occurring hallucinogens and synthetics like LSD seem to have strong effects on both the cerebral cortex and the locus ceruleus. This latter brain region is interesting because it is heavily implicated in states of consciousness and responses to novelty, including anxiety and panic.

While the new research on the relationship of brain chemistry to religion is fascinating, the critical aspect of religious states of altered consciousness is not how they are generated or the specific areas of the brain they affect, but how they are interpreted. Religious experience—whether generated by chant, fast, meditation, dance, physical trauma, exertion, hallucinogen, or any other technique—is largely dependent on the context in which it happens. Cultural background, religious stories, and individual expectations play a much greater role in determining the nature of religious experience than do the specifics of different religious techniques. Experiences of timelessness, transformation, visual or auditory encounters with nonempirical entities, travel across vast distances, and states of both euphoria and terror are reported by people using many different conscious-altering techniques.

Religious Belief and Practice Change over Time

Scholars within different religious traditions may argue about the authenticity of particular practices. They may suggest that religion itself is eternal, though imperfectly practiced by human beings. Such matters generally are not amenable to objective verification. However, what is clear is that the ways in which human societies practice religions change greatly over time. New styles of worship, new rituals, ceremonies, and beliefs are constantly developing while old rituals and beliefs disappear.

Religious change has many possible sources. Some innovations are undoubtedly the idiosyncratic inspirations of particular individuals. People in or out of altered states of consciousness may have new ideas about their beliefs and practices. Other religious changes may be inspired by events in the natural world. For example, some scholars believe that the flood story of the Bible has its basis in a historical fact. They hypothesize that about 7,600 years ago, at the end of the Ice Age, sea level rose by several hundred feet. The Black Sea had been separated from the Mediterranean by the Bosporus, a relatively low ridge of land. Over time, much of this land eroded and the Mediterranean poured in, raising the water level by about five hundred feet in a bit less than a year, and permanently flooding the settlements that lined the lake.[7] Volcanic eruptions, earthquakes, and hurricanes or other large storms may be the sources of many religious stories and changes in religion.

Though there are many sources of religious change, perhaps the most important sources are social and economic change. Invasions, revolutions, conquests, and enslavement have always been fertile generators of religious change. This has been particularly true in the past five hundred years, a period when today's wealthy nations, largely centered in Europe and North America, spread their influence across the globe—sometimes through trade but more often through conquest, sometimes through peaceful means but more often through violence. It is hard to overstate the effects of this expansion. It created the world we know: a world of contact between cultures, rapid communication, and constant swift change.

Culture contact and conquest caused religious change in many ways. In some cases, the religion of the conquerors was simply imposed on the conquered. In others, missionaries sent from powerful and wealthy countries persuaded people to alter their beliefs and practices—sometimes using the power of their words and the example of their lives, sometimes using more coercive techniques such as the offering or withholding of medical aid, education, or trade items as well as threats of temporal penalties and eternal damnation. But even beyond the effects of missionaries, conquest—and the epidemics of fatal diseases that often accompanied conquest in the Americas and the Pacific Islands—undermined the cultures and beliefs of those conquered. Religion is, in some sense, a model of the meaning of the world, a way of understanding oneself and one's place in society. As conquest radically changed the world, many religious models no longer worked, and new practices and beliefs emerged.

Cultures have never been static, but today we live in a world of constant and rapid change. This change has its sources in technology, in the massive social and economic inequities within and among nations, and in the older sources—conquest, enslavement, and rebellion. Religious movements interact with these sources of change, sometimes dampening their effects, sometimes catalyzing and accelerating them. The position of religion, at the forefront of or in reaction to many social movements, makes the anthropological study of religion both fascinating and important to understanding the world.

THE ORGANIZATION OF THIS BOOK

The readings in this book explore many of the facets of religion that we've just described. They provide examples of some of the best recent work about religion as well as a scattering of classic works in the field. Our goal has been to select cutting-edge essays that introduce and analyze important theoretical ideas through the use of vivid ethnographic examples. Though the essays can be read in any order, the book progresses from speculative essays on the origins of religion and essays that situate religion with respect to society and the environment to an increasingly more detailed focus, such as some of the various aspects of life in which religious beliefs and practices are manifested. The essays in Part 6 describe some of the world's major religious traditions. Our goal in this organization is to provide a wealth of information that will help readers think about religion at a wide variety of levels—from the origins of religion, to relationships between religious and social forms, to religious experiences. To this end, we include essays from many different theoretical positions.

Each of the six parts of *Sacred Realms* opens with a brief introduction that provides background and context for the readings in that part. There is also a brief introduction to each reading that highlights its major points and suggests some questions for the reader to consider.

Part One, "Introducing Religion," establishes the groundwork for understanding religion. In it you will find essays that explore the origins of religion, myths, and sacred stories, as well as the ways religion articulates with other aspects of society, particularly social structure and environment. Part Two, "Ritual, Religion, and the Supernatural," explores the various structures of religions themselves. The readings in this section examine the worlds of supernatural beings and powers, the roles of religious practitioners such as priests and shamans, and both the nature and structure of religious ritual. Parts Three and Four invite you to consider the nature of religious experience. These essays focus on describing religious experiences and situating these with respect to the societies in which they occur. Part Three, "Journeys of the Soul," examines altered states of consciousness and death. Part Four, "Sickness and Health," describes the connections among religion, health, and sickness and includes essays on the use of religion in both causing and curing illness. Part Five, "New Religious Movements," explores the changing nature of religion and society in the modern world. Religions both change society and are changed by society. This results not only in the creation of new understandings and practices within religions but in the creation of new religions. The book concludes with Part Six, "World Religions," a collection of essays we have written for this volume to describe some of the world's major religions: Hinduism, Buddhism, Judaism, Christianity, and Islam.

NOTES

1. Morton Klass, *Ordered Universes: Approaches to the Anthropology of Religion* (Boulder: Westview, 1995).

2. Victor Turner, *The Forest of Symbols: Aspects of Ndembu Ritual* (Ithaca, N.Y.: Cornell University Press, 1967).

3. See Alice Beck Kehoe, *Shamans and Religion: An Anthropological Exploration in Critical Thinking* (Prospect Heights, Ill.: Waveland, 2000).

4. J. Z. deBoer, J. R. Hale, and J. Chanton, "New Evidence for the Geological Origins of the Ancient Delphic Oracle (Greece)," *Geology* 29, no. 8 (2001): 707–710.

5. Michael Wallace and Craig Varjabedian, *En Divina Luz: The Penitente Moradas of New Mexico* (Albuquerque: University of New Mexico Press, 1994).

6. A. Newberg, E. D'Aquili, and V. Rause, *Why God Won't Go Away: Brain Science and the Biology of Belief* (New York: Ballantine Books, 2001).

7. William Ryan and Walter Pitman, *Noah's Flood: The New Scientific Discoveries about the Event That Changed History* (New York: Simon & Schuster, 1998).

PART ONE

Introducing Religion

The Pyramid of Kukulcan (or Castillo) at Chitzen Itza is one of the most famous religious sites in the Americas. This massive building, almost eighty feet tall, combines themes of power, ritual observance, and astronomical observation. It dominates the jungle around it, an awe inspiring monument to the power of the Mayan Kings whose rituals were celebrated on its summit. Staircases of 91 steps ascend each of the pyramid's four sides. These, combined with an additional step at the top give a total of 365 steps, the number of days in the solar year. Indeed, observances at the pyramid seem to have been linked to the calendar. The principal stairway is constructed so that during the spring and fall equinoxes, a shadow moves down the stairs giving the appearance of the Serpent God Kukulcan undulating down the stairs toward a sacred cenote, or sacrificial well.

1

The Origins of Religion

Where did religion come from? Human beings have wrestled with the question of the origins of religion for centuries. For many, the notion that their religion exists because a divine being gave it to them is a sufficient answer. However, since the nineteenth century, philosophers, anthropologists, and psychologists have proposed answers to this question that are grounded in archaeological evidence (including Paleolithic cave burials and artwork), observations of religious customs in other societies, or, more recently, studies of the brain and altered states of consciousness. The three essays in this section use such approaches to tackle the question of how religion began. As you read the essays in this section, keep the following points in mind:

- E. B. Tylor, one of the leading British anthropologists of the nineteenth century, proposed that modern religions evolved from a belief that living things and some objects had a spirit that was separate from their physical form. Tylor called this notion "animism" and proposed that it was founded in the experience of dreams, trance states, and other paranormal experiences.

- Some modern theories of the evolution of religion propose that religion is an inherent human characteristic, the result of natural selection and human evolution. James McClenon's article falls into this category. McClenon links the origins of religion to hypnosis, or the ability to enter an altered state of consciousness. He proposes that a propensity for entering hypnotic trance increases the likelihood of experiencing a paranormal event, and that such events provided the foundation upon which prehistoric shamanism was built. In its reliance on trance states and paranormal experience, McClenon's explanation is quite close to Tylor's. One critical difference is that McClenon links these states to religious healing; Tylor did not.

- Some evangelical Christian worshipers believe themselves to be possessed by the Holy Spirit, speak in tongues, and engage in behaviors such as passing their hands through flame without harm. All of these behaviors have strong parallels to the shamanic practices described in McClenon's essay. In fact, the quest for altered states of consciousness in the form of religious ecstasy is something found in virtually all religions. Could the fact that these behaviors are found all around the world be evidence of an evolutionary process that selected for these behaviors in the human population?

- Many theories of religion describe religious rituals as responses to belief systems. Graber proposes exactly the opposite scenario. His theory on the origin of religion is based on the psychologist B. F. Skinner's work on conditioning. Graber argues that religious rituals originated as conditioned responses to things such as the environment and danger, and that beliefs that rationalized the rituals arose much later.

- Until the late nineteenth and early twentieth centuries, anthropologists generally considered non-Western religious beliefs to be examples of irrational superstition and mythology. Many anthropologists of the early twentieth century fought against these beliefs. They argued that the religions of non-Western people were simply different from Western religions, and that the people who held such beliefs were neither more nor less rational or superstitious than Westerners. Bronislaw Malinowski was an anthropologist who devoted much of his life's work to showing that "primitives" were as logical and rational as others. In his essay in this section, he points out that the Trobriand islanders are as rational as any European and that their use of magic is eminently reasonable. He proposes that people turn to magical or religious rituals in situations where logic does not, or cannot, be applied. Compare this essay to Gmelch's essay in Section 7 and you will see that Malinowski's reasoning works very well in our own society.

How Religion Began:
Human Evolution and the Origin of Religion

James McClenon

Although the founding events of many specific religions are well documented, how can the prehistoric origin of religion as a pan-human cultural phenomenon be explained? How did religion start? What evidence is available to shed light on events from our distant past? In this essay, James McClenon attempts to explain the origin of religion through a "ritual healing theory." Briefly, McClenon proposes that early hominids practiced therapeutic rituals. He then argues that evolutionary development selected humans with a predisposition to hypnotic suggestion because those who are easily hypnotized are more easily cured with ritualized, or shamanic, forms of healing. Because hypnotizability correlates with a tendency on the part of test subjects to report paranormal experiences—such as seeing apparitions, extrasensory perception, and out-of-body experiences—McClenon concludes that these experiences were the basis for the earliest forms of shamanic activity and that the first religious systems developed out of shamanic practices. In his essay he provides firsthand descriptions of shamanic performances and discusses the role of hypnotic trance in these performances. McClenon then discusses his own research that supports a link between hypnotizability, paranormal experiences, and "wondrous" healing events described by people all around the world.

Ultimately, the answer to the question tackled in McClenon's essay remains out of reach. There is no way to directly recover the thoughts and beliefs of the first humans to practice religion. Neither is there agreement about when the first religious activity might have occurred. However, McClenon's broad multidisciplinary approach provides thought-provoking links among hypnosis, paranormal experiences, and forms of shamanic healing and opens one avenue for future research on this question.

As you read, consider these questions:
1. What is meant by the term *shamanic performance,* and how does shamanic performance relate to healing?
2. What is ritual healing theory, and how does it relate to the development of religion and ritual?
3. What is the basis for beliefs in spirits, souls, and life after death?

People have puzzled over the origins of religion for many centuries. The *ritual healing theory* argues that hominid use of therapeutic rituals selected for genes providing the physiological basis for religious experience and sentiment. Religion is not merely a cultural product, as assumed by many social scientists. Studies of twins indicate that modern people have a genetically-based religious propensity (Waller et al. 1990). According to evolutionary theory, this physiological basis must have evolved through some series of stages.

We might imagine a scene within hominid history. Our *Homo erectus* ancestors, unable to speak in a modern manner, chanted songs while sitting around their fires. They were part of the evolutionary progression leading to *Homo sapiens'* capacity for rapid speech. One *Homo erectus* female, skillful at modulating her voice, devised repetitive songs that the group often adapted. These pre-linguistic songs were made up of tonal chants, lacking "words" in the modern sense.

The hominids stared at the fire, "singing" the hypnotic, wordless tunes together for hour after hour: "Hey, hey, hey . . . hey, hey, hey . . . hey, hey, hey," the males chanted. "Whoo, Whoo, Whoo . . . Whoo, Whoo, Whoo . . . Whoo, whoo, whoo," the females responded. As they sang, two sick children lay on the ground, waiting with anticipation. The creative female strongly hoped they would recover. She closed her eyes and felt caught up by the chanting. For her, normal life disappeared. The song took her into an altered state of consciousness, a world where she joined the fire. She rose, danced toward the coals, and walked safely over the embers. The group was transfixed by her behavior. A strange sensation flowed through her hands as she touched the sick children. They knew she was trying to help them.

One child relaxed, his eyelids fluttering. He felt a powerful force enter his body. By the morning, his fever had declined. The other child remained frightened. He died the next day. To the degree that their mental abilities allowed it, the hominids pondered these events: How had the female danced safely over the hot coals? Why had one child died while the other recovered?

This wondrous healing ritual, and others like it, contributed to the beginning of religion. The ritual healing theory proposes that ancient hominids practiced rudimentary therapeutic rituals. Many rituals had repetitive qualities, associated with hypnotic processes, such as trances, hallucinations, and other altered states of consciousness. The Homo erectus child who was more suggestible recovered, grew up, and passed on his genes to future generations. He, and other survivors, were ancestors of modern people. The child who was less suggestible left no offspring. The result was that genotypes related to hypnotizability, and associated propensities, became prevalent among modern *Homo sapiens*.

When *Homo sapiens* developed language, their healing rituals become even more therapeutic since altered states of consciousness were coupled with verbal suggestions. Those who were hypnotizable gained the greatest benefits. Because hypnotizability is linked to certain experiences generating specific religious beliefs, this process created a foundation for shamanism, the first religious form. These experiences, which include apparitions, extrasensory perceptions, out-of-body experiences, sleep paralysis, and psychokinesis (mind over matter), occur in all cultures. Such episodes create belief in spirits, souls, life after death, and magical abilities, the basis for shamanism.

Although controversial, the ritual healing theory is subject to empirical evaluation within the fields of anthropology, folklore studies, animal behavior (ethology), ancient medical history, neurophysiology, and the social-psychology of religion and medicine. This chapter cites evidence gathered by anthropologists who find that spiritual healing has a degree of effectiveness, ethologists who view animal rituals as functional, historians who document the link between ancient medicine and religion, and psychologists who find that measures of hypnotizability are correlated with the frequency of experiences leading to religious belief. My research over the past two decades implies that spiritual healing practices all over the world have common features, intrinsically connected with anomalous experience and that certain types of people benefit from these practices to a greater degree than others. Example cases illustrate the ritual healing theory.

BANGKOK, THAILAND, 1985

Wilasinee, an attractive former school teacher, found she could go into trance, allowing spirits to speak through her. She came to believe that these spirits could heal (McClenon 1994: 87–89). At first they healed Wilasinee's relatives and neighbors, but when word spread of their success, the spirits devised a healing ceremony which attracted people from all over Thailand. Wilasinee told me that the treatments were most suitable for "people doctors cannot help."

A crowd assembled each Saturday, seeking to be healed. Wilasinee went into trance, allowing a male spirit to speak. He proclaimed his ability to overcome infirmities and demonstrated his power by having Wilasinee extinguish a huge bundle of glowing incense on the palm of her hand. When she revealed that her hand was uninjured, the audience gasped in amazement. With the help of an assistant, she inserted silver needles through her cheeks, tongue, arm, and hand. With a huge needle passing through her tongue, she told jokes, making the audience laugh at her slurred speech

and clownish behavior. She flirted with an elderly woman in the front row. "She is possessed by a spirit who loves women," someone explained to me, laughing. The incongruity of the situation captured people's attention. Wilasinee showed no discomfort and none of her wounds bled.

After the needles were removed, the spirit speaking through Wilasinee interviewed each supplicant, asking about medical and personal problems. The spirit maintained a professional, yet concerned demeanor. Sometimes he seemed to know of a person's infirmity without being told. Wilasinee's extended family also performed, waving knives about people's infirmities to cut away their problems. Her brother-in-law rapped rhythmically on a table with a special stone. This caused one man to writhe about on the floor until the demon thought to possess him departed. "He suffers from a mental disorder or maybe a devil," someone told me. "This treatment is designed to take care of those things." The high point of the performance was the final healing ceremony. Wilasinee again went into trance and the supplicants were brought before her. She placed her foot on a red hot iron plate and then on each person's afflicted body part. Her foot remained unharmed.

I talked with audience members afterward. They agreed that the rituals had been successful and some described previous healings. "Last year, I was virtually blind," one woman told me. "After Wilasinee's ceremony, my sight completely returned. Now I come to tell my story and to see the healing of others." Although others told similarly wondrous stories, I noticed that the arthritic woman beside me had not gained greater range of motion in her hands and fingers. Others also appeared "unhealed," no matter what they claimed. "Only some people benefit," I thought.

Wilasinee's ceremony illustrates a shamanic performance. Shamanism is a religious system in which the shaman, or spiritual practitioner, goes into trance in order to contact spirits thought to affect living people. Shamanism is the oldest religion, the basis for all later religious forms (Winkelman 2000). Shamans may fly spiritually (mentally travel to a distant place), allow their bodies to be taken over by spirits (trance possession or mediumship), demonstrate heat immunity (handle or walk over burning coals), exhibit pain denial (pierce or cut their bodies), and perform spiritual healing or cursing. The most typical forms of shamanic performance involve a practitioner going into trance, communicating with spirits, and gaining remedies or effecting cures for those seeking aid.

Shamanic performances generally include therapeutic suggestions, often inferred. We might speculate that the blind Thai woman suffered from a psychological problem that prevented her brain from processing signals received from her eyes. Wilasinee's ceremony probably triggered cognitive and even physiological changes allowing her brain to begin normal functioning. As a result of suggestion, her vision returned.

People sometimes refer to such methods as "faith healing." Those believing in a ritual gain benefits due to their faith. Wilasinee's ceremony illustrates how shamanic performances can stimulate faith. It is clear she has special talents. Not everyone can go into trance, extinguish burning incense on their palm, puncture their skin without bleeding, or touch a red hot iron grill without blistering. Her performance captures people's attention and they assume that the spirits allowing such phenomena can heal.

Two well-established processes help explain spiritual healing: placebos and hypnosis. These two mechanisms overlap, yet differ. Placebos are defined as actions or substances, devoid of pharmacological effect, given for psychological effect. Placebos require belief and are based on expectation. A person who believes that a ritual is curative gains benefits from participating. Placebos can cause release of endorphins in the brain, a natural opiate that reduces pain. Hypnosis differs from placebos since it depends on the trait, hypnotizability. Hypnosis is "a psychophysiological condition in which attention is so focused that there occurs a relative reduction of both peripheral awareness and critical analytic mentation, leading to distortions in perception, mood, and memory which in turn produce significant behavioral and biological changes" (Wickramasekera 1987: 12). Hypnotizability, the trait allowing certain people to respond to ritual suggestions, can be measured using standardized tests. Hypnotic treatments can be successful even if the person does not believe and is not in trance. Hypnotic reduction of pain is not dependent on endorphins, but hypnosis can induce belief and expectation, and, as a result, create placebo effects (Spiegel and Albert 1983; Van Dyck and Hoogduin 1990). Both placebos and hypnosis can cause physiological results: they can thwart bleeding from a wound or blistering after exposure to heat. If the Thai woman's sight disorder was psychologically based, as seems likely, a hypnotist could cure her. Researchers in the field of psychoneuroimmunology note that emotional factors affect health and that psychological treatments, such as those provided by Wilasinee, can have physiological effects.

I have observed shamanic performances in Thailand, Sri Lanka, Taiwan, Korea, Philippines, Okinawa, and the United States. Everywhere these healers appear to use hypnotic processes to induce trance, to demonstrate heat and pain resistance, and to effect cures. Anthropologists have observed similar rituals all over the world, suggesting that shamanism has physiological basis associated with specific altered states of consciousness (Winkelman 2000). I argue that hypnotic processes explain many of the effects associated with shamanic performance and healing. Those who are more open to hypnotic suggestion are better able to perform as shamans and also more likely to be ritually healed. Although some scholars argue that hypnosis is merely culturally-constructed role playing, researchers have found that hypnotizability is genetically based and relatively stable throughout one's life (Morgan 1973; Morgan and Hilgard 1973). Although hypnotizable people need not be in trance to respond to suggestions, ritual inductions facilitate their response (Hilgard and Tart 1966).

Anthropologists have observed effective spiritual healing in a wide variety of settings over many decades (Kleinman 1980; 1986: 130; McClenon 1994a). Evaluative studies suggest that this effectiveness is due, in part, to placebo and hypnotic effects (Kleinman and Sung 1979; McClenon 1997b; Schumaker 1995). As a result, shamanic practices over the past 30,000 years have selected for genotypes associated with hypnotizability and related traits. For example, the Thai woman cured of blindness would be more likely to attract a husband and to rear her children successfully as a result of her cure. She and the others healed would be more likely to pass on their genes to future generations than those not healed. Over time, the frequency of genotypes related to hypnotizability would increase. Even if only 1% of a community were cured by a shamanic healing system, this degree of effectiveness would have a major impact over thousands of years. Stebbins (1982: 15) illustrates this point by describing a hypothetical mouse-sized animal increasing in size by natural selection at a rate of one tenth of one percent of the mean weight within each generation—an increase so small that it could not be detected by human observers within their lifetimes. Using these mathematical assumptions, he demonstrated that the animal could reach the size of an elephant within 12,000 generations, increasing from 40 grams (mouse size) to an average weight of 6,457,400 grams (elephant size) during a period of about 60,000 years. Since hominids evolved into *Homo sapiens* during 7 million years and Neanderthals left behind evidence of rudimentary forms of ritual about 60,000 years ago (as well as indications that they cared for their injured), there was sufficient time for ritual healing systems to have had evolutionary impact. The "seeds" for religious sentiment, those experiences related to hypnosis which cause belief in spirits, souls, life after death, and magical abilities, could have grown figuratively from "mouse size" to "elephant size" during the human evolutionary time-span.

ANOMALOUS EXPERIENCES IN NORTH CAROLINA, U.S.A.

Each semester since 1988, I have had my Introduction to Anthropology students at Elizabeth City State University in North Carolina interview their friends, relatives, and neighbors. They ask, "If you have had a very unusual experience, would you describe it?" Between 1988 and 1996, I collected 1,446 anomalous experience narratives. The purpose of this research was not to prove that supernatural or religious claims are valid but to determine the types of experience that people talk about and the degree that these experiences are universal.

The stories indicate that the majority of unusual experiences occur spontaneously, outside of ritual environments. For example, one student transcribed his grandmother's account:

> I was involved in an accident that left me partially paralyzed. Because I was in my late forties, the doctors said the bone

tissue wouldn't heal properly so I probably would never walk again. After that, all the days seemed to run into one drab routine because I was not able to do most of the things that I always took for granted. But after several months of what seemed like darkness, the sun finally shone again. I awoke to a familiar voice calling me from the next room. I sat up in my bed and the voice seemed to get louder. It was my late husband calling me from the next room. I sprang out of my bed and ran into the room where the voice was coming from, but by the time I got there it had stopped. So I began searching the entire house but still I came up with nothing. Then it happened: I passed by a mirror and caught the reflection of myself, then once again the voice appeared and said, "See, honey, I knew you could do it!"

Although it is possible that the grandmother's husband actually communicated with her, the student interviewer provided a more scientific interpretation:

My grandmother is convinced that anything is possible if you just believe. Maybe that's true, but in my opinion it was her fear that paralyzed her, not the accident. Therefore, in the instant that she heard my grandfather's voice her fears were taken over by a comforting voice.

This story illustrates the connection between wondrous experience and wondrous healing. Those reporting many anomalous experiences are more likely to experience healings and to become healers themselves. Although it is possible that the woman heard her husband's actual voice, it is likely that a second person, present in the grandmother's house, would not have heard anything. For most anomalous experiences to occur, unconscious perceptions must "bubble up" into consciousness. In a "reverse" process, spiritual healing requires reaction to a suggestion—a command effectively passes into the unconscious mind and has a physiological effect. For spiritual healing to occur, suggestions must affect physiological processes which are normally controlled outside of consciousness. Some people seem to have "thinner" cognitive barriers and, as a result, allow greater flow of information in both directions across cognitive barriers (Hartmann 1991). These people tend to be more hypnotizable. I would predict that the woman had "thin" cognitive boundaries. This allowed her unconscious and conscious minds to interact in a manner that caused her to hear her husband's voice and to stand and walk as a result.

An alternate hypothesis is that a supernatural force, such as her husband's spirit, directly healed the woman. Although this supernatural theory cannot be evaluated scientifically, it does not exclude the previous hypothesis. Both supernatural and natural processes could occur simultaneously. People perceiving anomalous events seemingly require special cognitive capacities since not everyone has these experiences.

Between 1982 and 1986, I interviewed dozens of spiritual healers throughout Asia (McClenon 1994). All described unusual experiences which had shaped their beliefs, leading them to eventually become healers. Most typically, these episodes involved apparitions, extrasensory percep-

tions, out-of-body experiences, and psychokinesis. Researchers have found that the frequency of these episodes, as well as typical "religious" experiences, are correlated with hypnotizability (Hood 1973; McClenon 1997a). People who perceive many anomalous experiences tend to be hypnotizable and it is from this sample of the population that spiritual healers emerge. Those who perceive frequent anomalous episodes develop the profound beliefs required of shamanic performers to heal.

Much evidence supports this argument. I have surveyed diverse groups and compared stories of apparitions, paranormal dreams, waking extrasensory perceptions, out-of-body experience, and sleep paralysis gathered from various cultures: 339 elite North American scientists (1981), 314 dormitory residents at three colleges in Xi'an, China (1986), 214 dormitory residents at the University of Maryland, College Park (1987), 391 students at Elizabeth City State University, North Carolina (1988), 132 students at Tsukuba University, Japan (1989), and 532 students at the University of North Carolina, Greensboro (1990). Respondents within each sample described similar forms of anomalous experience and all groups contained individuals reporting frequent episodes (McClenon 1994). The common forms (apparitions, paranormal dreams, waking extrasensory perceptions, sleep paralysis, and out-of-body experience) have cross-culturally consistent features. This suggests that these types of experience have physiological basis since elements within people's reports are similar even though cultures varied widely.

Respondents in Northeastern North Carolina report the same forms of anomalous experience. Table 1 summarizes the categories into which their accounts can be classified. *Apparitions* consist of perceptions, thought to be exterior to the observer, having anomalous qualities. *Paranormal dreams* include information, gained anomalously while dreaming, later verified as valid. *Waking extrasensory perceptions* entail gaining information anomalously during an awake state. *Psychokinesis* involves perception of physical action lacking normal explanation. The *spiritual healing* category includes accounts describing the restoration of physical, mental, emotional, or spiritual health ostensibly through occult, supernatural, or paranormal means. *Occult events* refer to magical practices or rituals undertaken to influence events or to produce anomalous experiences (root-lore, which may produce occult events, was classified separately). *Rootlore,* a specific form of occult practice associated with African-American traditions, refers to magical rituals with African origins producing anomalous results. *Synchronistic experiences* entail the perception, not regarded as ESP, that two seemingly unrelated events coincide in an improbable manner, such as an omen predicting an event. *Out-of-body experiences* entail an awake person feeling separate from his or her body. *Sleep paralysis* experiences refer to the perception of awakening, being unable to move, and perceiving unusual sensations. *Unidentified flying*

TABLE 1   Incidence of Narrative Types

| | Anomalous Experience Memorates: | | | |
| | Prominence within Narrative | | | |
	primary	secondary	total	total
Apparition	496	147	643	34.4%
Paranormal dream	157	22	179	9.6
Psychokinesis	96	73	169	9.0
Healing	85	29	114	6.1
Rootlore	87	6	93	5.0
Sleep paralysis	71	16	87	4.7
Waking ESP	59	22	81	4.3
Synchronistic events	42	17	59	3.2
Misc. paranormal	33	11	44	2.4
Occult event	30	13	43	2.3
Out-of-body experience	30	5	35	1.9
Unidentified Flying Object	29	2	31	1.7
Total anomalous types:	1,215	363	1,578	84.4
Other Types of Report:				
Folklore	91	38	129	6.9
Normal dream	75	18	93	5.0
Oral history	65	5	70	3.7
Total other types:	231	61	292	15.6
Column totals:	1,446	424	1,870	100.0

objects (UFOs) must be described as moving in the sky or else they are classified as apparitions. *Miscellaneous paranormal events* include all other phenomena labeled by informants as being unexplained by normal means. Accounts were classified by independent judges. Those which were not regarded as within any of these categories were classified as *folklore* (a story which involved anomalous events but was not a first or second hand account), *normal dream* (a dream which was not regarded as anomalous), or *oral history* (stories not containing anomalous elements). Because some narratives contained more than one experience, the "second most significant" experience was coded as *secondary.*

Although the incidence of these types of experience vary among societies, all cultures seemingly contain people reporting these episodes. Some people report that their experiences powerfully affected their beliefs—their unusual perceptions caused them to gain profound faith in spirits, souls, life after death, and magical abilities. Frequent experiencers often feel compelled to perform healing rituals, associated with their faith.

Experiential types reveal similar motifs, themes, and patterns in all cultures. For example, extrasensory and apparition stories often pertain to family and death:

All of a sudden my eyes were open and there was this figure. . . . At the foot of my bed stood Grandma Helen! . . . Grandma Helen walked to the side of the bed and looked at me, with a smile on her face. Then she turned around and left. The next day my family woke up and sat down to breakfast. I began telling them about the strange occurrence the night before. My entire family sat there in disbelief and shock because all of them had the same exact dream, except Grandma Helen had gone to their rooms instead. After we verbalized our dreams, the phone rang. There was complete silence. I felt as if the world just stopped; it was the hospital. Last night Grandma Helen had suffered a stroke and died in her sleep. We were all flabbergasted!

Such stories do not "prove" the existence of supernatural phenomena but reveal cross-culturally consistent features. Although many accounts are linked to death in an anomalous manner, the improbability of this connection cannot be determined precisely. In 1894, members of the British Society for Psychical Research calculated the ratio of the apparition-death coincidences within their collection to be 30 out of about 1,300 cases (1/43). They calculated that the incidence of death coincidences was 440 times the probability of any particular person dying, a statistic that should not be attributed to chance (Sidgwick and Committee 1894). The North Carolina collection revealed a ratio similar to that of the British: 1/36 of apparition accounts were simultaneous with a death. Other forms of anomalous experience also revealed high coincidence of death coincidence: 1/18 of paranormal dreams, 1/13 of waking ESP, 1/44 of PK, and 1/8 of synchronistic experiences occurred while someone was dying. Although it is not possible to calculate the actual improbability of these coincidences (since we do not know what percentage of people were aware that the person in question might die), these cases allow us to understand why people who have frequent experiences devise and accept religious explanations involving life after death.

Extrasensory accounts (waking ESP, paranormal dreams, and apparitions providing information) reveal special structural features:

1. Information tends to pertain to family members.

2. Information frequently involves a death.

3. Paranormal dreams tend to refer to future events while waking ESP more often pertains to the present.

4. Waking ESP tends to be associated with greater conviction (indicated by the person taking action), while paranormal dreams are associated with less conviction.

5. Paranormal dreams tend to provide more data (number of details, person or event identified) than apparitions or waking ESP.

6. The quality and amount of information gained during a paranormal dream is negatively correlated with the severity of event (death being most serious and other events less so).

7. Apparitions all over the world reveal particular "abnormal features of perception"
   (a) images disappearing or fading out,
   (b) insubstantial images,
   (c) glowing images,
   (d) special white and dark clothing,
   (e) sickly or horrible appearance,
   (f) partial bodies,
   (g) abnormal walking,
   (h) abnormal sounds (McClenon 2000).

These patterns suggest that these anomalous episodes have physiological bases, subject to shaping by evolutionary processes.

TESTING THE RITUAL HEALING THEORY

The ritual healing theory allows testable hypotheses: (1) Shamanic healing is effective, in part, due to hypnotic/placebo processes; as a result, its effectiveness is correlated with hyp-

notizability. (2) Hypnotizability has a genetic component. (3) Shamanic healing has been practiced for sufficient time to have affected the prevalence of genes related to hypnotizability. (4) Hypnotizability is correlated with the propensity to perceive anomalous experience. (5) Anomalous experiences generate belief in spirits, souls, life after death, and magical abilities. These hypotheses can be evaluated within the fields of anthropology, folklore, history, physiology, social-psychology, and medicine. Much evidence already exists supporting these hypotheses.

Anthropology

Many anthropologists have observed indigenous spiritual healers' use of hypnotic/placebo processes (Schumaker 1995; McClenon 2002). Further research could extend these studies. Anthropologists and sociologists could devise questionnaires for identifying clients who would most benefit from a particular spiritual healing method. Elements within Hartmann's (1991) boundary questionnaire might prove useful for this purpose. Those with "thin" cognitive boundaries are hypothesized to gain greater benefits from ritual healing. Culturally specific tests of hypnotizability, absorption, and dissociative tendencies could also be devised and could prove useful for identifying people most likely to benefit from ritual healing. Applied studies could improve health care delivery systems.

Folklore Studies

Folklore data from many societies indicate that apparitions, paranormal dreams, extrasensory perceptions, out-of-body experiences, synchronistic events, and sleep paralysis have cross-culturally consistent narrative features, suggesting physiological basis. These perceptions generate belief in spirits, souls, life after death, and magical abilities. Extrasensory perception accounts from Finland, Germany, England, USA, Japan, and China share similar structural features (McClenon 1994, 2000, 2002). Content analysis of folk healing narratives from North Carolina indicate that folk healing methods alleviate the same types of symptoms treatable through hypnotherapy (McClenon 1997b). These findings could be replicated using data from any society.

The History of Medicine and Religion

The ritual healing theory hypothesizes that all ancient medical systems had religious basis. Evidence from ancient Mesopotamia, Egypt, Greece, India, and China supports this argument (Sigerist 1987a,b).

The ritual healing scenario coincides with what we know of pre-historical eras. Hunter and gatherer societies were the only human social system during the millions of years of the Paleolithic era. Paleolithic evidence indicates that ritual burial of the dead occurred as early as 50,000 years ago and shamanic rituals probably took place as far back as 30,000 years ago. Paleolithic painting and artifacts suggest that rituals involved altered states of consciousness (Lewis-Williams and Dowson 1988). All modern hunter and gatherer societies observed by anthropologists have shamanic religious systems and later religious/healing systems reflect increasing cultural complexity. This suggests that shamanism provided the foundation for all later religions (Winkelman 1992, 2000). These findings are subject to further anthropological analysis.

Animal Behavior

Ethologists note that many animals engage in rituals, that these activities provide benefits, and that evolutionary processes shaped these behaviors. Studies indicate that the impact of stress on animals' immune systems varies within a species (McClenon 2002). Researchers could measure animals' physiological responses during ritual behaviors to determine the nature of the benefits derived.

Certain animal propensities may constitute "seeds" from which human religiosity developed. One trait, the *Totstell reflect,* often labeled *animal hypnosis,* refers to the propensity for some animals to become paralyzed when threatened or disturbed in a particular manner. This reaction could be the evolutionary origin of human hypnotizability.

Primates reveal altered states of consciousness related to hypnosis, hypothesized to be the basis for religiosity. They demonstrate depressed immune systems when subjected to chronic stress and use rituals to alleviate the effects of stress. Researchers could investigate the physiological processes related to animal mind/body relationships, seeking to understand how human hypnotizability evolved.

Neurophysiology

Neurological studies shed light of altered states of consciousness. Researchers have found that the temporal lobe region of the brain plays a particularly important role in facilitating anomalous experiences (Persinger and Makarec 1987; Persinger and Valliant 1985). Tiller and Persinger (1994) have stimulated a sense of spiritual "presence" by firing magnetic fields (1–2 microT) into the temporal lobe area. They argue that the information flow between hemispheres creates the awareness of spiritual entities that some people perceive (those with "thin" boundaries experience greater flow). Research indicates that temporal lobe lability (measured both by EEG and by questionnaire; Makarec and Persinger 1990) is correlated with the propensity for anomalous and religious experience as well as hypnotizability (Makarec and Persinger 1990; Persinger and Makarec 1987).

Genetics

As hypothesized by the ritual healing theory, twin studies indicate that hypnotizability has a genetic basis (Morgan 1973). The ritual healing theory also hypothesizes that thinness of cognitive boundaries (measured by Hartmann's questionnaire) and propensity for anomalous experience have genetic basis, assertions subject to empirical evaluation.

Social-Psychology of Religion

Schumaker (1995) reviews the evidence indicating that religious practices are interwoven with hypnotic processes. Gibbons and De Jarnette (1972) conducted a study illustrating the connection between religious experience and hypnotizability. They interviewed 185 undergraduates who had been administered the Harvard Group Scale of Hypnotic Susceptibility and found that ". . . all of the high-susceptibles who professed having been 'saved' reported that the experience was characterized by profound experiential changes, while none of the low-susceptible group reported such phenomena" (Gibbons and De Jarnette 1972: 152). This evidence suggests that the "spontaneous" experience of being "born again" is shaped by hypnotic susceptibility. In general, people who report religious experience tend to be more hypnotizable (Hood 1973) and to reveal greater temporal lobe lability (Persinger 1984). These findings are subject to replication. . . .

The ritual healing theory has practical applications specifying ways to improve modern health care systems. Researchers could devise questionnaires that help identify patients with a propensity for anomalous experience who are most likely to benefit from psychological/spiritual healing. For more information on this topic, see McClenon (2002).

The ritual healing theory is more amenable to empirical testing than are traditional theories of religion. Freudian and Durkheimian theorists provide few (or no) testable hypotheses and, as a result, cannot convert those opposed to their positions. Although established social scientists may defend accepted social scientific paradigms, their efforts will inevitably prove unsuccessful. Dennett (1995: 63) has characterized Darwin's idea as like a "universal acid," so powerful that it eats through whatever vessel attempts to contain it. Discoveries within the fields of evolutionary anthropology, physiology, genetics, animal behavior, and evolutionary social-psychology will continually carve away at academic domains thought safe from Darwinian intrusion. As knowledge of evolutionary social-psychology increases, understanding of the processes by which humans became religious will also increase.

REFERENCES

Dennett, Daniel C. 1995. *Darwin's Dangerous Idea: Evolution and the Meanings of Life.* New York: Simon and Schuster.

Gibbons, Don and James De Jarnette. 1972. Hypnotic Susceptibility and Religious Experience. *Journal for the Scientific Study of Religion* 11: 152–156.

Hartmann, Ernest. 1991. *Boundaries in the Mind: A New Psychology of Personality.* New York: Basic Books.

Hilgard, Ernest R. and Charles T. Tart. 1966. Responsiveness to Suggestions Following Waking and Imagination Instructions and Following Induction of Hypnosis. *Journal of Abnormal Psychology* 71: 196–208.

Hood, Ralph W. 1973. Hypnotic Susceptibility and Reported Religious Experience. *Psychological Reports* 33: 549–550.

Kleinman, Arthur. 1980. *Patients and Healers in the Context of Culture: An Exploration of the Borderland Between Anthropology, Medicine, and Psychiatry.* Berkeley, CA: University of California Press.

Kleinman, Arthur. 1986. *Rethinking Psychiatry: From Cultural Category to Personal Experience.* New York: The Free Press.

Kleinman, Arthur and L. H. Sung. 1979. Why Do Indigenous Practitioners Successfully Heal? A Follow-up Study of Indigenous Practice in Taiwan. *Social Science and Medicine* 13B: 7–26.

Lewis-Williams, J. David and Thomas A. Dowson. 1988. The Signs of All Times: Entoptic Phenomena in Upper Paleolithic Art. *Current Anthropology* 29: 201–245.

Makarec, Katherine and Michael A. Persinger. 1990. Electroencephalographic Validation of a Temporal Lobe Signs Inventory in a Normal Population. *Journal of Research in Personality* 24: 323–337.

McClenon, James. 1994. *Wondrous Events: Foundations of Religious Belief.* Philadelphia: University of Pennsylvania Press.

McClenon, James. 1997a. Shamanic Healing, Human Evolution, and the Origin of Religion. *Journal for the Scientific Study of Religion* 36: 345–354.

McClenon, James. 1997b. Spiritual Healing and Folklore Research: Evaluating the Hypnosis/Placebo Theory. *Alternative Therapies in Health and Medicine* 3: 61–66.

McClenon, James. 2000. Content Analysis of an Anomalous Memorate Collection: Testing Hypotheses Regarding Universal Features. *Sociology of Religion* 61: 155–169.

McClenon, James. 2002. *Wondrous Healing: Shamanism, Human Evolution, and the Origin of Religion.* DeKalb, IL: Northern Illinois University Press.

Morgan, Arlene H. 1973. The Heritability of Hypnotic Susceptibility in Twins. *Journal of Abnormal and Social Psychology* 82: 55–61.

Morgan, Arlene and Ernest R. Hilgard. 1973. Age Differences in Susceptibility to Hypnosis. *International Journal of Clinical and Experimental Hypnosis* 21: 78–85.

Persinger, Michael A. 1984. People Who Report Religious Experiences May Display Enhanced Temporal Lobe Signs. *Perceptual and Motor Skills* 58: 963–975.

Persinger, Michael A. and Katherine Makarec. 1987. Temporal Lobe Epileptic Signs and Correlative Behaviors Displayed by Normal Populations. *Journal of General Psychology* 114: 179–195.

Persinger, Michael A. and P. M. Vallient, 1985. Temporal Lobe Signs and Reports of Subjective Paranormal Experiences in a Normal Population: A Replication. *Perceptual and Motor Skills* 60: 903–909.

Schumaker, John F. 1995. *The Corruption of Reality: A Unified Theory of Religion, Hypnosis, and Psychopathology.* Amherst, NY: Prometheus Books.

Sidgwick, Henry and Committee. 1894. Report on the Census of Hallucinations. *Proceedings of the Society for Psychical Research* 10: 25–422.

Sigerist, Henry E. 1987a. *A History of Medicine: Vol. 1, Primitive and Archaic Medicine.* New York: Oxford University Press (originally published in 1951, New York: Oxford University Press).

Sigerist, Henry E. 1987b. *A History of Medicine: Vol. 2, Early Greek, Hindu, and Persian Medicine.* New York: Oxford University Press (originally published in 1961, New York: Oxford University Press).

Spiegel, David and L. H. Albert. 1983. Naloxone Fails to Reverse Hypnotic Alleviation of Chronic Pain. *Psychopharmacology* 81: 140–143.

Stebbins, G. L. 1982. *Darwin to DNA, Molecules to Humanity.* San Francisco: W. H. Freeman.

Tiller, S. G. and M. A. Persinger. 1994. Elevated Incidence of a Sensed Presence and Sexual Arousal During Partial Sensory Deprivation and Sensitivity to Hypnosis: Implications for Hemisphericity and Gender Differences. *Perceptual and Motor Skills* 79: 1527–1531.

Van Dyck, Richard and Kees Hoogduin. 1990. Hypnosis: Placebo or Nonplacebo? *American Journal of Psychotherapy* 44: 396–404.

Waller, Niels G., Brian A. Kojetin, Thomas J. Bouchard, Jr., David T. Lykken, and Auke Tellegen. 1990. Genetic and Environmental Influences on Religious Interests, Attitudes, and Values: A Study of Twins Reared Apart and Together. *Psychological Science* 1: 138–142.

Wickramasekera, Ian E. 1987. Risk Factors Leading to Chronic Stress-Related Symptoms. *Advances: Journal of the Institute for the Advancement of Health* 4: 9–35.

Winkelman, Michael. 1992. *Shamans, Priests and Witches: A Cross-Cultural Study of Magico-Religious Practitioners.* Tempe, AZ: Arizona State University Anthropological Research Papers No. 44.

Winkelman, Michael. 2000. *Shamanism: The Neural Ecology of Consciousness and Healing.* Westport, CT: Bergin and Garvey.

Ritual, Consciousness, Belief:
A Speculation on the Origin of Religion

Robert Bates Graber

What can we know about the origins of religion? In the previous essay McClenon speculated that hypnotizability was positively related to paranormal experiences, and that these experiences in turn formed the foundation for shamanic ritual that led to religion. In this essay Graber argues that ritualized behavior and supernatural beliefs are the product of reinforcement and simply follow fundamental principles of psychological conditioning outlined by B. F. Skinner in the 1940s. He further argues that if the observational data from primate studies are correct, and studying primate behavior can provide insights into the behavior of the evolutionary ancestors of humans, then it is likely that ritual preceded religious beliefs, possibly by millions of years. As our hominid ancestors developed the capability for language and symbolic thought, Graber says, they could have invented beliefs to explain the behavioral rituals that had developed through reinforcement.

The basis of Graber's proposition is taken from studies of animal behavior conducted by psychologists and anthropologists and the psychological principle of "accidental" or "partial" reinforcement. Studies demonstrate how ritualized behaviors, such as a chimpanzee "rain dance," can be related to environmental phenomena such as thunderstorms. When the ritualized behavior (in Graber's case, chimps waving tree branches in the rain) occurs in conjunction with, or is soon followed by, a desirable result (the end of the thunderstorm), then the ritualized behavior may become associated with the desired result through accidental reinforcement. Psychological links established through partial reinforcement are highly resistant to extinction. In other words, once established they are very hard to change. According to Graber, this explains why magico-religious behaviors seem to last much longer than other cultural phenomena and allows personal practices such as prayer or good luck rituals (see Gmelch's essay "Baseball Magic" in section 7) to survive long periods of apparent failure, waiting only to be reinforced anew by the next chance convergence of ritual and event.

Graber's view on the origins of religion are derived from well-established principles of human psychology and years of research on animal behavior. Although his view ultimately is speculative, its scientific foundation makes it an attractive line of thought to those who do not find supernatural explanations of religion satisfying.

As you read, consider these questions:
1. What is accidental reinforcement, and how does it relate to the formation of ritual behavior?
2. How did the author reach his conclusion that ritual precedes belief?
3. How does the "ritual behavior" of pigeons and chimps compare to ritual behavior of humans?

It has been good scholarly form, for many years now, to dismiss the entire problem of religion's historical origin on the grounds that anything said would be mere speculation. All speculations, however, are not created equal; a more informed one surely is preferable to a less informed one. In fact, selected results from the last several decades of behavioristic experimentation and ethological observation suggest a reconstruction of religion's origin which, if still speculative, is better grounded in empirical evidence than were the ingenious classical efforts of Edward B. Tylor (1871), Sigmund Freud (1958, 1961), and lesser luminaries.[1] In the course of moving from the evidence to a speculation based thereon, the old question of which came first, ritual or belief, will be answered.

"SUPERSTITION" IN THE PIGEON

A classic paper by B. F. Skinner (1948) demonstrated that what is called "accidental reinforcement" can strengthen and maintain idiosyncratic, objectively pointless" behavior in lower organisms. Eight untrained pigeons were brought to a stable hunger condition, at 75 percent of well-fed body weight. Each bird then was placed singly in a cage equipped with a machine that automatically presented a food hopper every 15 seconds, *"with no reference whatsoever to the bird's behavior"* (Skinner 1948:168, emphasis in original).

What happened? Six of the eight pigeons soon were filling the 15-second intervals with behaviors as stereotyped and well-defined as they were strange:

One bird was conditioned to turn counterclockwise about the cage, making two or three turns between reinforcements. Another repeatedly thrust its head into one of the upper corners of the cage. A third developed a 'tossing' response, as if placing its head beneath an invisible bar and lifting it repeatedly. Two birds developed a pendulum motion of the head and body, in which the head was extended forward and swung from right to left with a sharp movement followed by a somewhat slower return. The body generally followed the movement and a few steps might be taken when it was extensive. Another bird was conditioned to make incomplete pecking or brushing movements directed toward but not touching the floor. (Skinner 1948:168)

Why did this happen? Whatever a bird happened to be doing immediately prior to the first appearance of the food became more likely to be repeated one or more times in the ensuing seconds. If it happened still to be repeating that behavior when the food reappeared, the behavior grew even more likely to be repeated. Were it doing something different when the food reappeared, however, the process would not necessarily have been derailed; rather, that new behavior might have continued, to be reinforced by the third "reward." For six of the eight birds, then, an incidental behavior in this way came under the control of accidental reinforcement. Two of the birds for some reason failed to develop any such pattern. Significantly, in none of the six was the behavior noticeable prior to the accidental reinforcement. Therefore, although the behavior's very first occurrence was not due to the accidental reinforcement, its development into a repetitive, definite pattern was.

Most of the behaviors, interestingly enough, were oriented to the environment:

> With the exception of the counter-clockwise turn, each response was almost always repeated in the same part of the cage, and it generally involved an orientation toward some feature of the cage. The effect of the reinforcement was to condition the bird to respond to some aspect of the environment rather than merely to execute a series of movements. (Skinner 1948:169). Accidentally reinforced behaviors, once established, prove very resistant to "extinction": one bird repeated its behavior more than 10,000 times after food had entirely stopped appearing (Skinner 1948:170).

Does all this have any relation to human behavior? Skinner believed that it does:

> The experiment might be said to demonstrate a sort of superstition. The bird behaves as if there were a causal relation between its behavior and the presentation of food, although such a relation is lacking. There are many analogies in human behavior. Rituals for changing one's luck at cards are good examples. A few accidental connections between a ritual and favorable consequences suffice to set up and maintain the behavior in spite of many unreinforced instances. . . . These behaviors have, of course, no real effect upon one's luck . . . just as in the present case the food would appear as often if the pigeon did nothing—or, more strictly speaking, did something else. (Skinner 1948:171).

Though Skinner refers here only to individual "rituals," an anthropologist can scarcely overlook points of resemblance between the pigeons' behavior and social ritual. The absence of any real ability of the behaviors to bring about their (apparent) aim; their clearly defined, repetitive form;

their orientation to places and objects in the environment; their persistence in the face of failure: resemblances as impressive as these could be taken to indicate that human ritual—in the form of critical rites, at least—is not merely analogous to the behavior of the pigeons, but is virtually the same kind of thing.

Accepting the pigeons' behavior as ritual, or at least proto-ritual, would seem to decide the old question of the temporal priority of ritual and belief firmly in favor of the former—unless, that is, one wants to entertain the idea that pigeons are capable of belief. This is by no means absurd; the birds do, after all, behave as if they believed that their actions were bringing food. I think, however, that most of us would prefer to regard beliefs as, by definition, symbolically constituted and, as such, possible only for creatures possessing symbols.

Yet there remains a rather good reason to reject the conclusion that the pigeons' behavior is ritual or even proto-ritual. One may, after all, regard ritual as the kind of thing that, by definition, has meaning for its participants; and it appears reasonable to believe that pigeons are not sufficiently complex, cognitively, for their own behavior to have meaning for them. This, however, is to raise the vexed problem of consciousness, and its place in the origin of religion; to explore this it is appropriate to turn to a species far more like ourselves.

"RAIN DANCE" IN THE CHIMPANZEE

Jane Goodall has described the usual reaction to rain among free-living chimpanzees (Pan troglodytes—evidently our closest living relatives, from whose evolutionary line our own split between five and fifteen million years ago):

> At the onset of a heavy shower or deluge the chimpanzees normally stopped whatever they were doing, at least temporarily. Sometimes they moved under overhanging tree trunks or thick tangles of foliage at the start of a storm, but as the rain began to penetrate their shelters they usually moved out and sat in 'huddled' positions. . . . Infants often ran to the embrace of their mothers. During heavy rain the chimpanzees sometimes walked bipedally, holding one wrist with the other hand or with both hands held close together in front of them. (Goodall 1968:172).

Occasionally something quite surprising transpired:

> At other times, however, male chimpanzees, at the start of a rain storm, performed vigorous and rhythmic branch-waving and -dragging displays . . . sometimes for as long as 3 or 4 min. (On one occasion a female gave a brief display of this type during rain.) Often, too, infants and juveniles played wildly when it was raining, jumping and swinging through the trees either alone or with a companion. One juvenile turned somersault after somersault through the mud as he followed in the wake of a branch-waving mature male. Whatever the motivation of the displaying of mature individuals or the playing of youngsters during rain there can be no doubt that

they are warmed up by the activity. On occasions it seemed very cold during or after rain, particularly if there were a wind. After heavy rainfall of long duration, especially when this was at night, chimpanzees were seen to shiver violently: they frequently showed the symptoms of bad colds during the rainy season. (Goodall 1968:172).

Goodall's technical accounts, of which this is the longer, are restrained (see also Goodall 1986:335); her popular writings, however, call such displays the "rain dance" (1988:54), and she confesses to have conjured up "primitive men displaying their strength and defying the elements" (Goodall 1967:77).

I have been unable to determine the usual lapse of time between the end of these displays and the stopping of the rain. Sometimes it would be considerable, because the storms may last over two hours; it may be, however, that brief showers are common enough to create a natural—rather than experimental—case of recurrent accidental reinforcement. That is, whenever the rain happens to stop during, or shortly following, the "dance, the latter may be said to have been reinforced by removal of an "aversive stimulus" (rain) (Ferster and Skinner 1957:723). As with Skinner's pigeons, then, we again have "coincidence of a performance and a reinforcer" in the absence of any "contingent relationship between the organism's performance and the reinforcer"—i.e., *accidental reinforcement* (Ferster and Culbertson 1982:367). Reinforcement, accidental or not, makes a behavior more probable when the stimulus (in this case, a rainstorm) recurs; probably, then, the display is a behavioral pattern maintained at least in part by accidental reinforcement. It may also be maintained, as Goodall noted, by the reinforcing effect of having warmed up a bit; and perhaps, too by the psychobiologically reinforcing effect of having "let off steam" (cf. Homans 1941).

The claim that this behavior has no meaning to the participants, plausible enough for Skinner's pigeons, is highly implausible for Goodall's chimps. Ingenious experiments by Jonathan Schull and J. David Smith, too recent to have appeared in print, indicate that even monkeys and dolphins—but not rats—are sufficiently "metacognitive" to recognize their own uncertainty when two tones become too similar for them to differentiate (Breslin 1992:9). Chimpanzees, moreover, exhibit self-awareness by recognizing their own reflection (unlike pigeons or, for that matter, housecats). And it probably is self-awareness, in turn, that makes possible "deception, attribution, empathy, and other higher forms of social cognition" (de Waal 1992:87). The evidence of deception among primates is especially copious and compelling. Primate deception definitely appears to be a matter of intentionality rather than mere conditioning. As de Waal writes in his recent overview:

> There is no reason why animals capable of understanding the effects of their own communication could not learn to achieve certain effects through voluntary control over signals. Instead of being mere reflections of internal states, signals would thus

become tools to manipulate the social environment for the benefit of the performer. (de Waal 1992:86).

It seems vanishingly improbable, then, that the "rain dance" has no meaning to its performers. What might that meaning be? It would be interesting to show a film of the rain dance to chimps knowing sign language, and try to elicit an interpretation from them. Short of that, however, we have evidence that (1) chimpanzees dislike rain; (2) much of the rain dance consists of aggressive display-type behavior; and (3) a sympathetic observer, also a hominoid, spontaneously compared the behavior to—and even named it after—ritual in her own species. This all points to one simple conclusion: the chimpanzee rain dance is a ritual aimed at stopping the rain. And it is probably maintained, like "critical rites" among humans, in large part by the mechanism of accidental reinforcement.

I do not know precisely how this connects with the evolution of consciousness. It is possible to argue that consciousness has not been proven to exist, or that at any rate it is not a useful concept (e.g., Priest 1992). It seems to me, however, that a property of self-awareness can be inferred reasonably well from observable behavior; that it justifies the belief that self-aware species attach meaning to their behavior; and that this in turn is what many people would refer to either as consciousness itself, or at least as a sort of quantum leap in level of consciousness.

It could be argued, however, that language is prerequisite to consciousness, to ritual, or to both. This would be similar to making language prerequisite to culture itself, a position that always strikes me as a form of special pleading aimed at distancing ourselves qualitatively from all other life. What I want to stress here, however, is simply this: to regard ritual as inherently dependent on language would make it inconceivable for ritual to have preceded belief in the evolution of religion. This is to resolve the issue by resort to fiat rather than by reference to fact. If, however, the temporal relationship of ritual and belief is treated as an empirical one, the possible priority of ritual must not be ruled out a priori; and once we give evidence a chance to speak, its answer is clear: ritual preceded belief. Indeed, ritual probably originated before the emergence of hominids, making it quite possibly millions of years older than belief.

THE ORIGIN OF RELIGIOUS BELIEF

Jane Goodall also observed, of course, many behaviors in which there is a highly contingent relationship between performance and reinforcer. Especially noteworthy is the manufacture and use of simple tools, reinforced nonaccidentally by virtue of reliably producing a reward. Examples include "fishing" for termites with specially-prepared twigs, and sponging water from deep tree crooks using crumpled leaves.

A highly plausible assumption is that the earliest, prelinguistic hominids (humans) possessed inventories of both accidentally- and contingently-reinforced behaviors at least as complex as those of modern chimpanzees. When language evolved, humans would have found themselves confronting, symbolically, these two classes of their own behavior. It would have been easy enough to explain, at least superficially, why their simple tools worked; but what about a behavior analogous to the chimpanzee rain dance? When it succeeded, perhaps they had frightened someone or something? When it failed, perhaps they had done it incorrectly, or with insufficient fervor? The first religious beliefs may well have been just such rationalizations, born of the primordial strange meeting between nascent symbolic thought and the ancient, accidentally-reinforced precipitates of symbolism's prehistory.

THE SUBSEQUENT EVOLUTION OF RELIGION

As the rationalizations evolved in complexity, they reacted on the rituals from which they had arisen, making subsequent religious evolution an ongoing reciprocal interaction between ritual and belief. This process reveals both divergent and convergent trends.

The divergent forms religion is known to have taken clearly show the importance of ecological factors. Among the Pueblo Indians, e.g., subsisting by growing corn in the desert, we find a ritual not to stop rain but to start it. This too would have been controlled by accidental reinforcement, though the ritual clearly is of relatively recent origin, and as such has from its beginnings been associated with symbolic rationalizations.

General cultural evolution (Sahlins 1960) also pushed religion, both ritual and belief, in new directions. Especially notable, as some societies grew larger, was religion's role in rationalizing and maintaining increasingly unequal distributions of wealth and power (e.g., Harris 1988:469–70; Lenski and Lenski 1987:166–168). Though industrial societies include significant numbers of "true believers," they seem to be witnessing a decline in religion's hold over the human mind, accompanied by a rise in what might be termed "secular ideologies" (Lenski and Lenski 1987:260–269).

Added to these ecological and evolutionary causes for religious differentiation, however, is a differentiating tendency inherent in the mechanism of accidental reinforcement. Nature, after all, does not wait for us to perform a given act, the way a behaviorist's experimental apparatus typically does (Skinner 1948 being the brilliant exception); rather, nature "rewards" whatever behavior we happen to be performing when, or just before, it gives us what we want. In this the spectacular panoply of human magico-religious practices is reminiscent of the behavioral differentiation of Skinner's pigeons under accidental reinforcement.

These divergent trends have been accompanied, however, by convergent trends. Despite their variability, for example, human religions generally reveal a common wish to reestablish, for adults, the status of infants relative to parents. Even

when absent from a formal system, such as high Buddhism, this trend remains clear in the actual practices of most adherents (Spiro 1978:346–350). This is probably rooted firmly in a major trend of hominization: increasing immaturity at birth, and the prolonged dependency on adults this entailed (e.g., La Barre 1972:93–120). Accompanying this is a tendency—admittedly, by no means universal (e.g., Harris 1988:453)—no longer to intimidate but rather to supplicate the superhuman beings, as the child must its parents. This illuminates the striking contrast between the rain dance, chimpanzee style, and a human ritual having an identical aim. The Semang, who hunt and gather in the forests of the Malay Peninsula, have as their highest deity Karei, god of thunder. Living in frail, temporary shelters, they too dislike thunderstorms:

> The sound of thunder, the sign of Karei's anger, gives warning that someone has sinned. All who are conscious of guilt, or at least one person representing the band, must hasten to render atonement by a blood sacrifice. The performers gash their shins, mix the blood with water in a bamboo vessel, and toss it to the angry elements with prayers of "Stop! Stop!" This is by far the most prominent ceremony in Semang mythology. (Murdock 1934:104)

CONCLUSION: ACCIDENTAL REINFORCEMENT REVISITED

When there is no real dependence of the reinforcer on an organism's performance, the performance often goes unrewarded; hence, accidental reinforcement is a particular form of what psychologists call "partial reinforcement." Laboratory experiments have established that partially reinforced behavior is marked by (1) low rates of occurrence, but (2) high resistance to extinction (Jenkins and Stanley 1950). If we add to these a trait—already discussed—of accidentally reinforced behavior, namely, its great variability, we have a trio of features strikingly reminiscent of magico-religious activity in humans.

Though societies vary a good deal, it must be admitted that most human behavior is not magico-religious in nature. (Durkheim [1961] was particularly impressed by the extent to which the sacred realm was "set apart" and "extraordinary"—phrases in which a relatively low rate of occurrence seems implicit.) Probably the pressures of reality itself dictate that most of any species' behavior be contingently related to reinforcers.

Magico-religious beliefs and practices often seem to outlast other cultural forms. This may be in part because they have come under the control of accidental reinforcement. Critical rites, because they occur at times of crisis, are especially amenable to accidental reinforcement; and while other factors no doubt are involved, this may contribute to their longevity compared with calendrical rites (Titiev 1960). From this perspective, it is failure itself which equips practices such as personal prayer to survive prolonged periods of apparent failure. Language allows people to reinterpret apparently unanswered prayers as having been answered, but in unanticipated ways; from a strict behaviorist position, however, such reinterpretations are mere rationalizations of the resistance to extinction bred by accidental reinforcement.

The sheer variability of magico-religious performances finds partial explanation in their freedom from the stringent constraints reality imposes on truly reliable means of securing results. It should be remembered, however, that magico-religious phenomena are by no means entirely unconstrained: they must perform psychological and social functions, and they are subject to the standardizing effects of enculturation.

I would like to suggest, in conclusion, that the enduring inability of scholars to distinguish clearly between magic and religion finds explanation in the fact that both "kinds" of phenomena, try as we might to differentiate them, are crucially alike. Controlled by accidental rather than contingent reinforcement, they fall on the same side of a conceptual divide far more fundamental than any that might distinguish them. Such phenomena will persist, with their odd mix of colorful variety and cryptic exceptionality, for a very long time to come; for variety, infrequency, and persistence are their very nature.

NOTE

1. Tylor, as is well known, placed an intellect—an "ancient savage philosopher"—at religion's origin; belief preceded ritual. The first religious belief, for Tylor, was belief in the human soul. Freud also thought belief preceded ritual, but he imagined the first beliefs to have been beliefs in nature spirits. This humanization of nature he saw as motivated not by intellectual curiosity, but by anxiety—anxiety due to our apparent helplessness in the face of nature, rooted in our infantile experience of actual helplessness (Freud 1961:15–20). People anthropomorphized nature in order to gain ritual "control" over it. It seems to me, however, that the newer evidence favors neither the Tylorian sequence *belief—ritual,* nor the Freudian sequence *anxiety—belief—ritual,* but rather the sequence *anxiety—ritual—belief.*

REFERENCES CITED

Breslin, M.
    1992   Faculty Profile: Jonathan Schull. Haverford: The
        Alumni Magazine of Haverford College (Spring):8–9.
Durkheim, E.
    1961   The Elementary Forms of the Religious Life. J. W.
        Swain, trans. New York: Collier.
de Waal, F. B. M.
    1992   Intentional Deception in Primates. Evolutionary
        Anthropology 1:86–92.
Ferster, C. B., and S. A. Culbertson
    1982   Behavior Principles. 3rd ed. Englewood Cliffs:
        Prentice-Hall.
Ferster, C. B., and B. F. Skinner
    1957   Schedules of Reinforcement. Englewood Cliffs:
        Prentice-Hall.
Freud, S.
    1958   Totem and Taboo: Some Points of Agreement
        between the Mental Lives of Savages and Neurotics. *In*
        The Standard Edition of the Complete Psychological
        Works of Sigmund Freud, vol. 13. J. Strachey, ed. Pp.
        1–162. London: Hogarth.
    1961   The Future of an Illusion. *In* The Standard Edition of
        the Complete Psychological Works of Sigmund Freud,
        vol. 21. James Strachey, ed. Pp. 1–56. London: Hogarth.
Goodall, J.
    1967   My Friends the Wild Chimpanzees. Washington,
        D.C.: National Geographic Society.
    1968   The Behaviour of Free-Living Chimpanzees in the
        Gombe Stream Area. Animal Behaviour Monographs
        1:161–311.
    1986   The Chimpanzees of Gombe: Patterns of Behavior.
        Cambridge: Harvard University Press.
    1988   In the Shadow of Man. Revised Edition. Boston:
        Houghton Mifflin.
Harris, M.
    1988   Culture, People, Nature: An Introduction to General
        Anthropology. 5th ed. New York: Harper and Row.
Homans, G. C.
    1941   Anxiety and Ritual: The Theories of Malinowski and
        Radcliffe-Brown. American Anthropologist 43:164–172.
Jenkins, W. O., and J. C. Stanley, Jr.
    1950   Partial Reinforcement: A Review and Critique.
        Psychological Bulletin 47:193–234.
La Barre, W.
    1972   The Ghost Dance: Origins of Religion. London:
        Allen and Unwin.
Lenski, G., and J. Lenski
    1987   Human Societies: An Introduction to
        Macrosociology. 5th ed. New York: McGraw-Hill.
Murdock, G. P.
    1934   Our Primitive Contemporaries. New York:
        Macmillan.
Priest, S.
    1992   Theories of Mind. Boston: Houghton Mifflin.
Sahlins, M. D.
    1960   Evolution: Specific and General. *In* Evolution and
        Culture. M. D. Sahlins and E. R. Service, eds. Pp. 12–44.
        Ann Arbor: University of Michigan.
Skinner, B. F.
    1948   "Superstition" in the Pigeon. Journal of Experimental
        Psychology 38:168–172.
Spiro, M. E.
    1978   Culture and Human Nature. *In* The Making of
        Psychological Anthropology. G. D. Spindler, ed. Pp.
        330–360. Berkeley: University of California Press.
Titiev, M.
    1960   A Fresh Approach to the Problem of Magic and
        Religion. Southwestern Journal of Anthropology
        16:292–298.
Tylor, E. B.
    1871   Primitive Culture. London: Murray.

Rational Mastery by Man of His Surroundings

Bronislaw Malinowski

Bronislaw Malinowski (1884–1942) was one of the greatest anthropologists of the early twentieth century. He lived and wrote at a time when "savages" were widely considered to be inferior intellectually, morally, and developmentally to Northern Europeans and Americans. Scholars such as Lévy-Bruhl, argued that "savages" were incapable of rational, logical thought, and were beset by primitive superstitions rather than enlightened religion. One of Malinowski's goals was to prove these ideas incorrect.

In this essay (which is a section from his longer 1925 essay "Magic, Science, and Religion") Malinowski sets out to show that primitive people are, in fact, rational and logical. They have highly sophisticated systems of empirical knowledge that concern important aspects of their lives such as gardening and fishing. However, empirical knowledge has limits. Factors such as the weather, disease, and luck cannot be controlled using the technological means at the disposal of a preindustrial society (and in many ways remain out of control for us as well). According to Malinowski, primitive people use magic to attempt to gain control over factors like these.

In the second part of the essay, Malinowski's goal is to show the rationality of primitive religious forms. He argues, for instance, that initiation ceremonies perform at least two critical functions: they are "the dramatic expression of the supreme power and value of tradition" and they are an "effective means of transmitting tribal lore."

As you read, consider these questions:

1. Under what circumstances do the groups in this essay employ magic?
2. Why is magic used in some instances and not in others?
3. Do the native peoples of Melanesia use science? Explain.
4. How do Melanesians mix rational/empirical knowledge with magic in activities such as boatbuilding and navigation?

The problem of primitive knowledge has been singularly neglected by anthropology. Studies on savage psychology were exclusively confined to early religion, magic and mythology. Only recently the work of several English, German, and French writers, notably the daring and brilliant speculations of Professor Lévy-Bruhl, gave an impetus to the student's interest in what the savage does in his more sober moods. The results were startling indeed: Professor Lévy-Bruhl tells us, to put it in a nutshell, that primitive man has no sober moods at all, that he is hopelessly and completely immersed in a mystical frame of mind. Incapable of dispassionate and consistent observation, devoid of the power of abstraction, hampered by "a decided aversion towards reasoning," he is unable to draw any benefit from experience, to construct or comprehend even the most elementary laws of nature. "For minds thus orientated there is no fact purely physical." Nor can there exist for them any clear idea of substance and attribute, cause and effect, identity and contradiction. Their outlook is that of confused superstition, "prelogical," made of mystic "participations" and "exclusions." I have here summarized a body of opinion, of which the brilliant French sociologist is the most decided and competent spokesman, but which numbers beside, many anthropologists and philosophers of renown.

But there are also dissenting voices. When a scholar and anthropologist of the measure of Professor J. L. Myres entitles an article in *Notes and Queries* "Natural Science," and when we read there that the savage's "knowledge based on observation is distinct and accurate," we must surely pause before accepting primitive man's irrationality as a dogma. Another highly competent writer, Dr. A. A. Goldenweiser, speaking about primitive "discoveries, inventions and improvements"—which could hardly be attributed to any pre-empirical or prelogical mind—affirms that "it would be unwise to ascribe to the primitive mechanic merely a passive part in the origination of inventions. Many a happy thought must have crossed his mind, nor was he wholly unfamiliar with the thrill that comes from an idea effective in action." Here we see the savage endowed with an attitude of mind wholly akin to that of a modern man of science!

To bridge over the wide gap between the two extreme opinions current on the subject of primitive man's reason, it will be best to resolve the problem into two questions.

First, has the savage any rational outlook, any rational mastery of his surroundings, or is he, as M. Lévy-Bruhl and his school maintain, entirely "mystical"? The answer will be that every primitive community is in possession of a considerable store of knowledge, based on experience and fashioned by reason.

The second question then opens: Can this primitive knowledge be regarded as a rudimentary form of science or is it, on the contrary, radically different, a crude empiry, a body of practical and technical abilities, rules of thumb and

Bronislav Malinowski, "Rational Mastery by Man of His Surroundings."Reprinted in *Magic, Science and Religion and Other Essays*. Copyright © 1954 [1948].

rules of art having no theoretical value? This second question, epistemological rather than belonging to the study of man, will be barely touched upon at the end of this section and a tentative answer only will be given.

In dealing with the first question, we shall have to examine the "profane" side of life, the arts, crafts and economic pursuits, and we shall attempt to disentangle in it a type of behavior, clearly marked off from magic and religion, based on empirical knowledge and on the confidence in logic. We shall try to find whether the lines of such behavior are defined by traditional rules, known, perhaps even discussed sometimes, and tested. We shall have to inquire whether the sociological setting of the rational and empirical behavior differs from that of ritual and cult. Above all we shall ask, do the natives distinguish the two domains and keep them apart, or is the field of knowledge constantly swamped by superstition, ritualism, magic or religion?

Since in the matter under discussion there is an appalling lack of relevant and reliable observations, I shall have largely to draw upon my own material, mostly unpublished, collected during a few years' field work among the Melanesian and Papuo-Melanesian tribes of Eastern New Guinea and the surrounding archipelagoes. As the Melanesians are reputed, however, to be specially magic-ridden, they will furnish an acid test of the existence of empirical and rational knowledge among savages living in the age of polished stone.

These natives, and I am speaking mainly of the Melanesians who inhabit the coral atolls to the N.E. of the main island, the Trobriand Archipelago and the adjoining groups, are expert fishermen, industrious manufacturers and traders, but they rely mainly on gardening for their subsistence. With the most rudimentary implements, a pointed digging-stick and a small axe, they are able to raise crops sufficient to maintain a dense population and even yielding a surplus, which in olden days was allowed to rot unconsumed, and which at present is exported to feed plantation hands. The success in their agriculture depends—besides the excellent natural conditions with which they are favored—upon their extensive knowledge of the classes of the soil, of the various cultivated plants, of the mutual adaptation of these two factors, and, last not least, upon their knowledge of the importance of accurate and hard work. They have to select the soil and the seedlings, they have appropriately to fix the times for clearing and burning the scrub, for planting and weeding, for training the vines of the yam plants. In all this they are guided by a clear knowledge of weather and seasons, plants and pests, soil and tubers, and by a conviction that this knowledge is true and reliable, that it can be counted upon and must be scrupulously obeyed.

Yet mixed with all their activities there is to be found magic, a series of rites performed every year over the gardens in rigorous sequence and order. Since the leadership in garden work is in the hands of the magician, and since ritual and practical work are intimately associated, a superficial observer might be led to assume that the mystic and the rational behavior are mixed up, that their effects are not distinguished by the natives and not distinguishable in scientific analysis. Is this so really?

Magic is undoubtedly regarded by the natives as absolutely indispensable to the welfare of the gardens. What would happen without it no one can exactly tell, for no native garden has ever been made without its ritual, in spite of some thirty years of European rule and missionary influence and well over a century's contact with white traders. But certainly various kinds of disaster, blight, unseasonable droughts, rains, bush-pigs and locusts, would destroy the unhallowed garden made without magic.

Does this mean, however, that the natives attribute all the good results to magic? Certainly not. If you were to suggest to a native that he should make his garden mainly by magic and scamp his work, he would simply smile on your simplicity. He knows as well as you do that there are natural conditions and causes, and by his observations he knows also that he is able to control these natural forces by mental and physical effort. His knowledge is limited, no doubt, but as far as it goes it is sound and proof against mysticism. If the fences are broken down, if the seed is destroyed or has been dried or washed away, he will have recourse not to magic, but to work, guided by knowledge and reason. His experience has taught him also, on the other hand, that in spite of all his forethought and beyond all his efforts there are agencies and forces which one year bestow unwonted and unearned benefits of fertility, making everything run smooth and well, rain and sun appear at the right moment, noxious insects remain in abeyance, the harvest yields a superabundant crop; and another year again the same agencies bring ill luck and bad chance, pursue him from beginning till end and thwart all his most strenuous efforts and his best-founded knowledge. To control these influences and these only he employs magic.

Thus there is a clear-cut division: there is first the well-known set of conditions, the natural course of growth, as well as the ordinary pests and dangers to be warded off by fencing and weeding. On the other hand there is the domain of the unaccountable and adverse influences, as well as the great unearned increment of fortunate coincidence. The first conditions are coped with by knowledge and work, the second by magic.

This line of division can also be traced in the social setting of work and ritual respectively. Though the garden magician is, as a rule, also the leader in practical activities, these two functions are kept strictly apart. Every magical ceremony has its distinctive name, its appropriate time and its place in the scheme of work, and it stands out of the ordinary course of activities completely. Some of them are ceremonial and have to be attended by the whole community, all are public in that it is known when they are going to happen and anyone can attend them. They are performed on selected plots within the gardens and on a special corner of this plot. Work is always tabooed on such occasions, sometimes only while the ceremony lasts, sometimes for a day or two. In his lay character the leader and magician directs the work, fixes the dates for starting, harangues and exhorts slack or careless gardeners. But the two roles never overlap or interfere: they are always clear, and any native will inform you without hesitation whether the man acts as magician or as leader in garden work.

What has been said about gardens can be paralleled from any one of the many other activities in which work and magic run side by side without ever mixing. Thus in canoe building empirical knowledge of material, of technology, and of certain principles of stability and hydrodynamics, function in company and close association with magic, each yet uncontaminated by the other.

For example, they understand perfectly well that the wider the span of the outrigger the greater the stability yet the smaller the resistance against strain. They can clearly explain why they have to give this span a certain traditional width, measured in fractions of the length of the dugout. They can also explain, in rudimentary but clearly mechanical terms, how they have to behave in a sudden gale, why the outrigger must be always on the weather side, why the one type of canoe can and the other cannot beat. They have, in fact, a whole system of principles of sailing, embodied in a complex and rich terminology, traditionally handed on and obeyed as rationally and consistently as is modern science by modern sailors. How could they sail otherwise under eminently dangerous conditions in their frail primitive craft?

But even with all their systematic knowledge, methodically applied, they are still at the mercy of powerful and incalculable tides, sudden gales during the monsoon season and unknown reefs. And here comes in their magic, performed over the canoe during its construction, carried out at the beginning and in the course of expeditions and resorted to in moments of real danger. If the modern seaman, entrenched in science and reason, provided with all sorts of safety appliances, sailing on steel-built steamers, if even he has a singular tendency to superstition—which does not rob him of his knowledge or reason, nor make him altogether prelogical—can we wonder that his savage colleague, under much more precarious conditions, holds fast to the safety and comfort of magic?

An interesting and crucial test is provided by fishing in the Trobriand Islands and its magic. While in the villages on the inner lagoon fishing is done in an easy and absolutely reliable manner by the method of poisoning, yielding abundant results without danger and uncertainty, there are on the shores of the open sea dangerous modes of fishing and also certain types in which the yield greatly varies according to whether shoals of fish appear beforehand or not. It is most significant that in the lagoon fishing, where man can rely completely upon his knowledge and skill, magic does not exist, while in the open-sea fishing, full of danger and uncertainty, there is extensive magical ritual to secure safety and good results.

Again, in warfare the natives know that strength, courage, and agility play a decisive part. Yet here also they practice magic to master the elements of chance and luck.

Nowhere is the duality of natural and supernatural causes divided by a line so thin and intricate, yet, if carefully followed up, so well marked, decisive, and instructive, as in the two most fateful forces of human destiny: health and death. Health to the Melanesians is a natural state of affairs and, unless tampered with, the human body will remain in perfect order. But the natives know perfectly well that there are natural means which can affect health and even destroy the body. Poisons, wounds, burns, falls, are known to cause disablement or death in a natural way. And this is not a matter of private opinion of this or that individual, but it is laid down in traditional lore and even in belief, for there are considered to be different ways to the nether world for those who died by sorcery and those who met "natural" death. Again, it is recognized that cold, heat, overstrain, too much sun, overeating, can all cause minor ailments, which are treated by natural remedies such as massage, steaming, warming at a fire and certain potions. Old age is known to lead to bodily decay and the explanation is given by the natives that very old people grow weak, their oesophagus closes up, and therefore they must die.

But besides these natural causes there is the enormous domain of sorcery and by far the most cases of illness and death are ascribed to this. The line of distinction between sorcery and the other causes is clear in theory and in most cases of practice, but it must be realized that it is subject to what could be called the personal perspective. That is, the more closely a case has to do with the person who considers it, the less will it be "natural," the more "magical." Thus a very old man, whose pending death will be considered natural by the other members of the community, will be afraid only of sorcery and never think of his natural fate. A fairly sick person will diagnose sorcery in his own case, while all the others might speak of too much betel nut or overeating or some other indulgence.

But who of us really believes that his own bodily infirmities and the approaching death is a purely natural occurrence, just an insignificant event in the infinite chain of causes? To the most rational of civilized men health, disease, the threat of death, float in a hazy emotional mist, which seems to become denser and more impenetrable as the fateful forms approach. It is indeed astonishing that "savages" can achieve such a sober, dispassionate outlook in these matters as they actually do.

Thus in his relation to nature and destiny, whether he tries to exploit the first or to dodge the second, primitive man recognizes both the natural and the supernatural forces and agencies, and he tries to use them both for his benefit. Whenever he has been taught by experience that effort guided by knowledge is of some avail, he never spares the one or ignores the other. He knows that a plant cannot grow by magic alone, or a canoe sail or float without being properly constructed and managed, or a fight be won without skill and daring. He never relies on magic alone, while, on the contrary, he sometimes dispenses with it completely, as in fire-making and in a number of crafts and pursuits. But he clings to it, whenever he has to recognize the impotence of his knowledge and of his rational technique.

I have given my reasons why in this argument I had to rely principally on the material collected in the classical land of magic, Melanesia. But the facts discussed are so fundamental, the conclusions drawn of such a general nature, that it will be easy to check them on any modern detailed ethnographic record. Comparing agricultural work and magic, the building of canoes, the art of healing by magic and by natural remedies, the ideas about the causes of death in other regions, the universal validity of what has been established here could easily be proved. Only, since no observations have methodically been made with reference to the problem of primitive knowledge, the data from other writers could be gleaned only piecemeal and their testimony though clear would be indirect.

I have chosen to face the question of primitive man's rational knowledge directly: watching him at his principal occupations, seeing him pass from work to magic and back again, entering into his mind, listening to his opinions. The whole problem might have been approached through the avenue of language, but this would have led us too far into questions of logic, semasiology, and theory of primitive languages. Words which serve to express general ideas such as *existence, substance,* and *attribute, cause* and *effect,* the *fundamental* and the *secondary;* words and expressions used in complicated pursuits like sailing, construction, measuring and checking; numerals and quantitative descriptions, correct and detailed classifications of natural phenomena, plants and animals—all this would lead us exactly to the same conclusion: that primitive man can observe and think, and that he possesses, embodied in his language, systems of methodical though rudimentary knowledge.

Similar conclusions could be drawn from an examination of those mental schemes and physical contrivances which could be described as diagrams or formulas. Methods of indicating the main points of the compass, arrangements of stars into constellations, co-ordination of these with the seasons, naming of moons in the year, of quarters in the moon—all these accomplishments are known to the simplest savages. Also they are all able to draw diagrammatic maps in the sand or dust, indicate arrangements by placing small stones, shells, or sticks on the ground, plan expeditions or raids on such rudimentary charts. By co-ordinating space and time they are able to arrange big tribal gatherings and to combine vast tribal movements over extensive areas.[1] The use of leaves, notched sticks, and similar aids to memory is well known and seems to be almost universal. All such "diagrams" are means of reducing a complex and unwieldy bit of reality to a simple and handy form. They give man a relatively easy mental control over it. As such are they not—in a very rudimentary form no doubt—fundamentally akin to developed scientific formulas and "models," which are also simple and handy paraphrases of a complex or abstract reality, giving the civilized physicist mental control over it?

This brings us to the second question: Can we regard primitive knowledge, which, as we found, is both empirical and rational, as a rudimentary stage of science, or is it not at all related to it? If by science be understood a body of rules and conceptions, based on experience and derived from it by logical inference, embodied in material achievements and in a fixed form of tradition and carried on by some sort of social organization—then there is no doubt that even the lowest savage communities have the beginnings of science, however rudimentary.

Most epistemologists would not, however, be satisfied with such a "minimum definition" of science, for it might apply to the rules of an art or craft as well. They would maintain that the rules of science must be laid down explicitly, open to control by experiment and critique by reason. They must not only be rules of practical behavior, but theoretical laws of knowledge. Even accepting this stricture, however, there is hardly any doubt that many of the principles of savage knowledge are scientific in this sense. The native shipwright knows not only practically of buoyancy, leverage, equilibrium, he has to obey these laws not only on water, but while making the canoe he must have the principles in his mind. He instructs his helpers in them. He gives them the traditional rules, and in a crude and simple manner, using his hands, pieces of wood, and a limited technical vocabulary, he explains some general laws of hydrodynamics and equilibrium. Science is not detached from the craft, that is certainly true, it is only a means to an end, it is crude, rudimentary, and inchoate, but with all that it is the matrix from which the higher developments must have sprung.

If we applied another criterion yet, that of the really scientific attitude, the disinterested search for knowledge and for the understanding of causes and reasons, the answer would certainly not be in a direct negative. There is, of course, no widespread thirst for knowledge in a savage community, new things such as European topics bore them frankly and their whole interest is largely encompassed by the traditional world of their culture. But within this there is both the antiquarian mind passionately interested in myths, stories, details of customs, pedigrees, and ancient happenings, and there is also to be found the naturalist, patient and painstaking in his observations, capable of generalization and of connecting long chains of events in the life of animals, and in the marine world or in the jungle. It is enough to realize how much European naturalists have often learned from their savage colleagues to appreciate this interest found in the native for nature. There is finally among the primitives, as every fieldworker well knows, the sociologist, the ideal informant, capable with marvelous accuracy and insight to give the *raison d'être,* the function, and the organization of many a simpler institution in his tribe.

Science, of course, does not exist in any uncivilized community as a driving power, criticizing, renewing, constructing. Science is never consciously made. But on this criterion, neither is there law, nor religion, nor government among savages.

The question, however, whether we should call it *science* or only *empirical and rational knowledge* is not of primary importance in this context. We have tried to gain a clear idea as to whether the savage has only one domain of reality or two, and we found that he has his profane world of practical activities and rational outlook besides the sacred region of cult and belief. We have been able to map out the two domains and to give a more detailed description of the one. We must now pass to the second.

NOTE

1. *Cf.* the writer's *Argonauts of the Western Pacific,* chap. xvi.

2

Religion and Society

The cross-cultural diversity of religious belief might lead one to believe that the world of religion is truly random. In cultures around the world, and in our own, people seem to have so wide a range of beliefs that one might truly say that people can and do believe anything. However, though the range of religious beliefs is truly astounding, religion is neither random nor chaotic. Beliefs are tightly woven into the fabric of the society of those who hold them. This can best be seen when society and beliefs change.

For some people, thinking about religion and change seems almost like an oxymoron. We sometimes think of our religions as part of our traditions. The very act of doing ritual seems at times to connect us with our forebearers or with earlier members of our religious group. Nevertheless, religions do change, and changes in them are tightly tied to changes in society. The essays in this section explore the nature of the relationship between society and religion with particular reference to social change. As you read the essays in this section, keep the following points in mind:

- At most times and in most places, religion supports the social and economic arrangements of society. It is fairly common to hear people claim that the United States is God's country. However, in a sense, every country is "God's country." That is to say, overwhelmingly people believe that the moral, political, and economic precepts of their society are those ordained by the supernatural, however they conceive it. In most large, state-level societies, religious ceremonies celebrate the power of the government. Kings often claim to rule by divine right; they are frequently held to be leaders of religion in addition to being political leaders. (For example, the Japanese Emperor traditionally claimed to be the living descendant of the Sun Goddess Amaterasu-O-Mi-Kami.) Even in the United States, where separation of religion and state is enshrined in the Constitution, political speeches in general (and the State of the Union Address in particular) generally end with "God Bless the United States" or some variation on it. A good example of the connection between the state and religion is painted on the dome of the U.S. Capitol building. *The Apotheosis of Washington,* an 1865 fresco by Constantino Brumidi, shows George Washington ascending to heaven with allegorical figures representing fame and liberty. The subject matter of the *Apotheosis* was not unusual. In an 1840 statue by Horatio Greenough commissioned by Congress to celebrate the centenary of Washington's birth, the president is shown as Zeus. Throughout the nineteenth and early twentieth centuries, images of Washington's divinity were common in American homes and businesses.[1]

- There are, of course, cases where the social and moral order say very different things. Under such circumstances new religions may form or religious practices may change. These changed practices and new religions may be strong catalysts for social and political change. This topic is dealt with more fully in Part Five.

- Societies and religions are intertwined in many ways. One is through the notion that violations of the moral or social order are sins and therefore incur supernatural punishment. For example, if a king rules by divine right, overthrowing the king is not only an act of political revolution but also a religious violation (or so the king's supporters will claim). A second frequent connection between society and religion is a very broad mirroring effect. Social relations among people on earth very often reflect our conceptions of social relations among supernaturals. For example, if on earth the king is the leader of society and he is surrounded by noblemen,

21

then in the corresponding view of the supernatural world God likely is a king surrounded by lesser deities. This mirroring provides confirmation that earthly social arrangements are just—after all, they are the same as those in the supernatural.

- Given that social and economic relations are broadly linked to religious beliefs, it is not surprising that when the former change, the latter do as well. In fact, the success or failure of religious messages seems tightly linked to the social and economic conditions under which they occur. When religious practices and beliefs fit well with society, religions are likely to gain adherents. When the fit is poor, they are likely to lose them. But these changes may also fundamentally affect the beliefs of the group and the way those beliefs are enacted. Lang and Ragvald's essay on Chinese spirit-writing follows a single religion through a century of history and shows periods of decline and success. In this case, the success of religion led to basic changes in beliefs and practices.

- Globalization and industrialization are major forces driving social change and provide outstanding opportunities to see the effects of social change on religious belief. But they also provide the background for discussing issues of power and weakness, of modern versus traditional worldviews. In Aihwa Ong's essay, "The Production of Possession," all of these forces are displayed and analyzed. The movement of women from rural villages to factories has led to a basic change in beliefs about possession. However, this religious change is the overt expression of an underlying conflict between poor Malaysian workers, who understand their problems in terms of spirit possession, and wealthy American and Japanese factory owners and managers, who understand problems in terms of factory efficiency and mental illness. In this situation, religion has the power to catalyze resistance against the wealthy and powerful.

- Long-held beliefs or rituals can be abandoned as they become irrelevant to current circumstances. Hikaru Suzuki argues that this is what has happened with Japanese funeral customs. Traditionally, Japanese funerals were religious affairs held in Buddhist temples. Funerals were an essential part of the maintenance of extended families and the inheritance of property. However, since the end of the Second World War, urbanization and changes in Japanese law have greatly diminished the importance of both extended families and the inheritance of ancestral property. Consequently, the Japanese are increasingly choosing to have nonreligious funerals that have little to do with their society's traditional devotion to ancestors.

NOTE

1. Much has been written about images of Washington. A good recent source is Barbara J. Mitnick, ed., *George Washington: American Symbol* (New York: Hudson Hills, 1999).

Spirit-Writing and the Development
of Chinese Cults

Graeme Lang

Lars Ragvald

The religious economy model suggests that religious movements expand or contract and vary their messages according to the social and political climates under which they operate. The authors of this essay use this model to discuss the development of a Chinese spirit-writing religion from the late nineteenth through the early twentieth century. They explore the ways in which its practitioners constitute and maintain their authority in the face of critics, doubters, and changing circumstances.

Chine spirit-writing, or *fuji*, is a system of divination in which a shaman, possessed by a god, holds a stick that inscribes Chinese characters on a table. These characters are copied to a notebook by a scribe and the resulting messages are understood by followers as coming directly from the spirit world.

Spirit-writing mediums sometimes publish books of their work. Leung Yan Ngam, one such medium, was the founder of a religion called Wong Tai Sin. Wong Tai Sin began in China in the 1890s, a time of great social upheaval, political disaster, and disease. Using the books he produced, Lang and Ragveld show how Leung responded to the conditions of his era.

In 1915, Wong Tai Sin moved to Hong Kong, where shamans continued to practice *fuji* after Leung's death in 1921. The Hong Kong temple began in the midst of a refugee community. As this community prospered, the temple prospered as well. By the 1970s it had a mass following. However, *fuji* is a difficult art, requiring training and the right temperament. *Fuji*-writers must be able to make their messages sound like they come from a god and because such messages are easy to fake, it is sometimes difficult for writers to earn the confidence of their clients. Therefore, despite its critical role in the temple's formation, *fuji* has been replaced by fortune telling in recent decades, which is easier to learn and does not require the teller to speak in the voice of a god. Additionally, *fuji*-writers, because they are possessed by gods, cannot show concern for money, whereas fortune tellers can charge whatever the market will bear.

"Spirit-Writing and the Development of Chinese Cults" by Graeme Lang and Lars Ragvald, *Sociology of Religion* 59:4 (1998), 309-328. Revised for this edition by author. Copyright © Association for the Sociology of Religion, Inc. All rights reserved.

As you read consider these questions:
1. What are the major features of shamanism?
2. How can shamanism help a society in times of cultural stress?
3. How do "spirit-writings" solve problems facing society?

> *"The [foreign] powers are watching [China] with a tiger's voracity."*
> General Li Ping-heng, 1895 (quoted in Seagrave 1992).
>
> *"The strong neighbors [foreign powers] . . . look on China like a tiger."*
> Wong Tai Sin, a Chinese god, in a spirit-writing session in 1897 (quoted in Lang and Ragvald 1993: 17).

In the late 1890s China was in crisis. The Qing Court tried to contain incursions by foreign powers into Chinese affairs, but failed. "Treaty ports" acquired through military force or the threat of force were ruled by foreigners. A modern naval fleet was purchased by the Chinese regime, staffed, and almost immediately sunk by the Japanese in 1895. Meanwhile, in southern China the bubonic plague struck Guangzhou and Hong Kong, devastating the population and causing panic every summer from 1894 until the end of the century.

Amid these catastrophes, Chinese deities hovered above small groups of anxious supplicants, calling on them to strengthen the country and to enlist the help of the gods through a return to virtue and filial piety. We have an excellent record of some of these interactions between gods and humans in the form of "spirit-writings" recorded and published by believers. In this form of divine revelation, the god writes Chinese characters on a table, using a wooden stylus held by a believer.

Most of the scholarly analysis of Chinese spirit-writing has been carried out by anthropologists and historians of Chinese religion, mainly through study of spirit-writing cults in Taiwan (e.g., Jordan and Overmyer 1986). In this paper, we show the value of material from a cult which originated in China in the 1890s, and which later migrated to Hong Kong, for the comparative sociological study of religious responses to social crisis. We also explain why "spirit-writing" was abandoned in the version of the cult which achieved mass popularity later in Hong Kong. First, we propose a theoretical framework for the phenomenon of "spirit-writing."

SPIRIT-WRITING AND SOCIAL THEORY

The religious economy model (Stark and Bainbridge 1987) includes the study of religious innovation in response to changing or unmet needs and problems within a population. One type of religious entrepreneurialism is that of the shaman. Some sociologists seem to use the concept of "shaman" only with reference to the more dramatic forms of spirit-possession used by healers in some of the folk-level societies studied by anthropologists.[1] However, Lewis (1989) has demonstrated that the concept provides a way of comparing a type of religious specialism present in many cultures.

The term "shaman" was originally derived from the Tungus culture of Siberia, but has been used by Lewis and others to refer to persons who regularly engage in spirit-possession or serve as vehicles for spirits in order to deliver oracles, messages, and remedies (Harris 1987:266–7; Lewis 1989:43–50).[2] Lewis characterizes the shaman as "an inspired prophet and healer, a charismatic religious figure with the power to control the spirits, usually by incarnating them" (Lewis 1996:116). The concept can be used in this generalized sense to identify such religious specialists in a wide range of societies, and to compare figures as diverse as the charismatic Spiritualist mediums of contemporary industrial societies discussed by Nelson (1969) and the Umbanda spirit-mediums of Brazil (Pressel 1977).[3]

Lewis (1989:57) defines the central feature of the shaman's performance as controlled spirit possession, thus distinguishing the shaman from other spirit-mediums who do not claim or demonstrate such control (such as the Japanese mediums described by Davis 1980). This control, however, is inferred from the ability of the shaman to call up the spirits at will. Some shamans would not admit to complete control over their spirits, much less, to controlling everything which the spirits have to say. Nevertheless, the hypothesis that they produce their performances with skill and imagination but according to local needs and beliefs, and within the local conventions for spirit-possession behavior, is the best way for the sociologist to understand these performances.[4] It is clear that shamans are also sensitive to public opinion, or at least, to the opinions of their patrons and clients, and that the gods usually express through the shamans those norms and values already held by their audience (Lewis 1989:123). The shaman may offer advice, counsel, diagnosis, and healing, and usually receives some compensation for these services. The most successful shamans in some cultures may become rich on the offerings of petitioners, but many other rewards have also been reported.[5]

Shamanism has also been used by individuals who want to become leaders. If people believe someone can transmit valuable messages from the supernatural realm, that individual can gain recognition and political influence.

Social Conditions and Shamanism

Opportunities for and thus the incidence of shamanism vary with ecological, cultural, and social conditions. In this paper, we will ignore ecological and cultural factors,[6] and concentrate on the sociological factors which affect the character and prevalence of shamanism.

The religious economy model can be used to explain a number of the observed variations in shamanism between and within societies. For example, population density may influence the scope of the shaman's activities by determining the degree of specialization possible in the marketplace (Smith 1991:225). Shamans in populated areas of China, for example, had to compete with other kinds of diviners such as geomancers and fortune-tellers, and tended to specialize in their use of divination methods, while in sparsely populated areas where numbers were not sufficient to support many specializations, shamans also performed other services such as geomancy and picking propitious times for important activities. Whether diviners were specialists or "general practitioners" thus depended in part on proximity to major population centers.

Features of the political system could also influence the leadership opportunities available to shamans. In societies where there are no formal political offices and courts of law, for example, the shaman's functions may be very wide (Lewis 1989:142), while in societies with an elaborate and well-legitimated political regime, the shaman's functions are likely to be confined to specific problems such as illness. A corollary is that when the legitimacy of a regime declines sharply as in late-Qing China, or when the political system is perceived to be in chaos, opportunities for shamanistic leadership and authority multiply.

Social inequality could also provide opportunities for shamans. In societies with oppressed or deprived subgroups whose needs are not adequately addressed by established religious leaders, shamans may arise to address these needs, and to offer succour, help, and the promise of material benefits (Lewis 1989). For example, shamanism and spirit-possession have allowed women to assert themselves in cultures where they have otherwise been deprived of position and influence or suffer from insecurity as a result of male control of resources (Lewis 1989:64–79; Kessler 1977).[7]

Shamanistic activity tends to decline when a religious system becomes institutionalized, as those holding formal roles in the system canonize previous revelations while suppressing new ones. Shamanism may survive only on the fringes of such a society.

Shamanistic cults tend to revive and become attractive, however, when an institutionalized religion fails to adapt adequately to a social crisis. Thus, shamanism may revive in societies suffering the shocks of rapid social change, invasion and conquest, or conflict with colonial powers (Lewis 1989:126–7; Lan 1985; Tai 1983). In such societies, shamans may attract attention and gain influence by offering their compatriots the advice of gods, ancestors, and culture heroes from the past on how to deal with the crisis.

Typically, the revelations enjoin a return to the traditional beliefs and virtues of the past, under the guidance of the traditional gods or great ancestors. Under such conditions, the shamans often promise that a return to traditional virtues and loyalties will inspire the gods and ancestors to help them restore their past glory and overcome present difficulties. Failure to do so may lead to further disasters. The shamans may thus become the spokespersons for resurgent cultural nativism or political nationalism. The shaman's revivalism can be directed against urban elites, to the extent that they are perceived to be violating traditional values and imposing alien or oppressive conditions on a resistant rural population who see themselves as carriers of traditional culture.

Thus the concept of shamanism provides a way of linking earlier work on "prophetic" roles (e.g., Berger 1963) and on "transformative" prophetic movements in modern societies (Bromley 1997) to many similar phenomena in other cultures. The analysis applies equally well to some historical cases of shamanism in Africa and the Middle East, and to the case to be examined in this paper: spirit-writing in China.

DIVINATION BY THE "FUJI" METHOD OF SPIRIT-WRITING

Some Chinese shamans possessed by a spirit communicated orally, modifying their voices, as in many cultures where shamanism is practiced, to increase the appearance of possession by a spirit (Smith 1991:224; see also Park 1997, on Korean shamans, and Nguyen 1995, on Vietnamese shamans). Not everyone was impressed by such performances, however. These spirit mediums reportedly had low prestige and were frequently suspected of fakery and of venal motives (Potter 1974). There was another divination method which commanded more respect among the educated classes in pre-modern China: the production of written rather than spoken oracles, by a process known as *fuji*.

Fuji divination produces messages from a god or spirit through a stick, held by one or two persons, which writes Chinese characters on a table or tray. As soon as a character has been written on the tray and identified, it is copied into a notebook by one of the participants so that the complete message can be studied later. The procedure requires a minimum of two persons: one to wield the stick, and one to write the characters in the notebook.[8] The god was evidently thought to control the stick, but the wielder of the stick had to be worthy to serve as the god's spirit-writer and to inscribe the god's messages. Spirit-writers do not show dramatic manifestations of spirit-possession, but a mild kind of "trance" behaviour is frequently observed.[9]

Fuji apparently evolved from an earlier form of divination, operated by rural women, in which a female spirit possessed an object held by the women, causing it to jump and dance, but the practice was eventually taken up by educated persons and developed into the writing of messages from illustrious persons and deified culture heroes, who composed poems, moral homilies, and answers to questions about the future (Chao 1942).[10] *Fuji*-writers offered consultations with spirits and deities on a wide range of problems, including illness, family troubles, and career decisions. They also occasionally expounded on contemporary social and political conditions and crises, passing along the gods' prescriptions for reforming society and their threats of disasters if their exhortations were ignored. They deliberately avoided dramatic manifestations of trance and spirit-possession to better appeal to their genteel patrons, and avoid comparison with what their patrons would take to be the vulgar and primitive performances of village shamans who impersonated the spirits with dramatic alterations of voice and gesture. But however genteel their performances, the *fuji*-writers nevertheless offered all or most of the services characteristic of the shaman.

Many of the literati were intrigued by this method of communicating with famous generals, men of letters, Taoist immortals, and other luminaries of Chinese culture, and *fuji* circles composed of literati evidently met regularly in many cities during the Qing dynasty to conduct seances. They shared with the common people an interest in petitioning gods and spirits for help with illnesses and family troubles, but they also asked the gods about their career prospects. Those who had not yet passed the examinations for entry into the imperial bureaucracy sometimes even requested the spirits to give them tips about the questions in upcoming exams (Jordan and Overmyer 1986:40), while those who already held official offices asked for help with difficult decisions.

Some *fuji*-writers aspired to positions of moral and social leadership, and tried to attract and hold patrons ready to help them establish new shrines and publish volumes containing their revelations. Thus, some of these circles of *fuji*-devotees evolved into sectarian groups, which bear some resemblance to similar spirit-medium cults which gathered around "charismatic mediums" in other cultures.[11] These *fuji*-groups have been well-studied in Taiwan, both ethnographically and through their published volumes of revelations (see especially Jordan and Overmyer 1986). Groups which developed in China have remained largely unstudied, except for those few which migrated to Hong Kong (e.g., Tsui 1991).

Recently, two compilations of *fuji*-revelations connected to the origins of the cult of the very popular Hong Kong god, Wong Tai Sin (Huang Daxian), were recovered in Hong Kong (Lang and Ragvald 1993: 164, n. 7). These revelations were evidently produced by one individual—Leung Yan Ngam (Liang Renan)—who started the cult of Wong Tai Sin in Guangzhou in 1897 and later brought the cult to Hong Kong in 1915 after conditions deteriorated in China following the 1911 revolution. The two major compilations produced by Leung were titled *Jing Mimeng* (in two volumes, hereafter, *JM*), which means "Awake [from] Illusory Dreams," and *Xing Shi Yaoyan,* or "Important Words to Awaken the World." The former included the revelations produced by Leung between 1897 and about 1901 in two shrines near Guangzhou. The latter was produced after he left Guangzhou to return to his home village where he established a second major temple to Wong Tai Sin.

While the compilations of such writings published by some spirit-writing sects are typically edited (Jordan and Overmyer 1986:179), especially to remove purely personal revelations which have no wider moral significance, these compilations nevertheless preserve material which is lost in the oral revelations of most other types of shamans. Hence, they provide a rich source of information on the way the shaman counsels and controls his followers, deals with hostile outsiders, and addresses the social crises of his time.

In our 1993 book, we had space for only a brief analysis and a few quotations from these writings (Lang and Ragvald 1993:14–17). The main purpose of the book was to explain the origins of the cult in the 1890s, its migration to Hong Kong early in the twentieth century, and the reasons for its later great success in Hong Kong between the 1950s and the 1990s. In what follows we return to this material for a more in-depth analysis of what it reveals about the uses of spirit-writing to exhort and control a group of followers, using previously unpublished passages from these writings.

Virtue, Deference, and Social Order

The fuji-writer of Awake [from] Illusory Dreams and Important Words to Awaken the World, a former official in the Chinese Maritime Customs bureau, was conservative in his social and political philosophy like other fuji-writers who were officials or military men (Overmyer 1985:230). He advocated filial piety and the basic Confucian virtues of loyalty and deference to superiors as the foundation of morality and social order. Many passages in Jing Mimeng contain such injunctions. The same basic rules required faithful service to the emperor (JM 1:15). Such messages appealed to officials and conservative intellectuals, who were among Leung's circle at the beginning of his career as a part-time fuji-writer. Study of these messages shows how the fuji-writer tried to control and hold the interest of his circle of patrons.

Personalized Messages

Some messages were intended for particular individuals in attendance at Leung's fuji sessions. Like the cosmopolitan urbanites who may engage in religious behavior in many different settings in the modern U.S. (Ammerman 1997), and like the modern "inner circle" of patrons of prominent temples in Hong Kong,[12] persons who attended Leung's sessions in the 1890s had visited other temples and no doubt had also attended fuji sessions with other spirit-writers. If Leung wished to hold their interest, and induce them to return for further sessions, personalized messages from the gods to persons in attendance could be especially effective. Such messages undoubtedly heightened the interest of the writer's patrons, but they also offered the greatest risks since

a serious error could lead to defections and loss of credibility. Such material is often edited out of published fuji-volumes, but a number of such items survive in Jing Mimeng.

For example, one message was directed toward a man with two wives. Each wife had a son, and the sons evidently resented each other. The man was directed by the god to improve his relations with the two wives and their sons, and to try to improve the relations between the two resentful sons (JM II:86). Other followers were variously praised for their kindness and charity, admonished to make greater efforts, or chided for stubbornness (JM II: 37). From these personal revelations, it is possible to see beyond the writer, to his audience. Revelations directed toward women and toward officials and generals, for example, suggest their presence on those occasions. The revelations directed toward women in Jing Mimeng are similar to those in other compilations of fuji-writings produced in the 19th century (Jordan and Overmyer 1986:56–7; Russell 1997), and bear similarities to conservative moralistic literature in other cultures, such as the book of Proverbs in the Hebrew Bible and the Old Testament.[13] Jing Mimeng reflects the Confucian conservatism common among the officials and literati who comprised most of the spirit-writers during this period.

In his voluminous fuji-writings, Leung also included a number of revelations which provided advice and comment on the behaviour of generals and military officials. In Jing Mimeng, the advice is conventional: show bravery and leadership, and be loyal to the emperor. In Xing Shi Yaoyan, compiled after Leung had returned to his native village, he was much more blunt and critical. For example, in one passage, the spirit of a famous general from the past visited the shrine and provided the following commentary.

> These general-officials boast of their power when there is no danger. But as soon as a dangerous situation arises, they are frightened and flee. . . . Even worse are those generals who secretly reduce the number of their soldiers, and keep the funds meant to pay for the soldiers. When an emergency occurs, they quickly recruit men to fill up the ranks, but these troops are untrained and have no discipline. They are not even able to fight against thieves, let alone external enemies. A general must have the trust and respect of his soldiers in order to be victorious, but now generals exploit the soldiers and steal their salary. These soldiers obviously will not fight with a will; it is surprising that they do not mutiny (Xing Shi Yaoyan: 74).

This was written about 1901, after the Chinese government had been humiliated by the foreign military forces which captured Beijing after the Boxer uprising. The gods also commented on the social conditions and social relations in Chinese society at the time.

Mistreatment of the Common People

The fuji-writings contain a number of admonitions directed toward the wealthy, advising against mistreatment of common people, and suggesting charitable acts. For example, the spirit of a long-deceased emperor attended one of the sessions, and his message included the following.

> Those people who are wealthy should not exploit the common people. Observe how nature changes, and see that all things change. Even though you are wealthy, you labor only for money and for your descendants [because you may die before you enjoy the benefits]. It is better to build up credit for yourself by publishing [i.e. paying for the publishing expenses of] books on good morals, and by donating clothes and food to the common people (JM I:15).

Some urban merchants also seem to be the target of some of the messages. For example:

> Those people who make money in the market always intend to cheat their customers. They are not honest with their scales, and give less than what you pay for. Their goods are fake. They deceive simple people. While they make money now through such practices, eventually they will lose everything, and will not even retain a piece of roof above their heads (JM I:15).

These passages are very similar to some of those found in the Yahwist "prophetic" writings dating from the pre-exilic period in ancient Israel and Judah (Lang 1989); in both the Israelite and Chinese material, a deity calls for charitable treatment of the common people, and condemns the cheating and deception of urban merchants. In both, the prophet himself had a rural base or background (as we know in the case of Leung, and infer for several Israelite prophets), and is reflecting conservative rural disdain and mistrust of the commercialized, materialistic, and free-wheeling ways of the cities.

Dealing with Doubters and Opponents

As in many other *fuji*-cults (Jordan and Overmyer 1986:126–7), the *fuji*-revelations were frequently used to control and manipulate the inner circle of devotees and followers, rewarding, praising, exhorting, admonishing, condemning, and occasionally expelling followers according to the extent of their loyalty and their adherence to his moral program. Leung, for example, occasionally felt the need to deal with backsliders within his own circle of devotees. During one *fuji* session, someone left during the session, and the revelation, from the spirit of a general, included a diatribe against this person.

> I have heard that there are good people at this altar [says the general]. Still, the holy emperor sent me down to the altar to send away any immoral persons. Anyone who leaves is such a person. [then the scribe records, in a smaller script, that one man left the building]. . . . See! [continues the general] I come here with mightiness and power, and still he left without even greeting me. He deserves punishment. He is unfilial and he is also unfaithful to friends. He has a rivalry with his mothers and brothers over property (JM II:83).

Some of those who observed this incident and heard the message must have resolved not to risk similar condemna-

tion from the immortals by leaving during future sessions. Of course, as Jordan and Overmyer point out, such condemnations are likely to reflect the public opinion of the group, and will not often be directed toward the group's luminaries or principal benefactors (Jordan and Overmyer 1986:127).

The *fuji*-master occasionally hectored his circle, collectively, when they disregarded his admonitions (e.g., JM I:65). He was also not above trying to impress and intimidate them with displays of the god's presence. For example, as the god Guangong scolded the group for lack of diligence, the god called their attention to the incense sticks in the urn, which had burned out but not yet toppled over. Perhaps because they were not sufficiently impressed, the god then flung the *fuji*-stick violently across the room, frightening the worshippers. The scribe recorded both these incidents—using a different size of script to distinguish his words from those of the god—intending that his record of the incidents should serve as evidence of the god's power and presence.

It is clear from his writings that the *fuji*-writer was also aware of doubters who had visited the shrine and observed the sessions or read the revelations, but who questioned the authenticity of the messages.[14] In several passages, the god deals with such persons in the simplest possible manner: "For those who believe, follow my words. For those who challenge, just leave this place" (JM II:14). But the *fuji*-writer sometimes felt compelled to give a more vigorous response to these doubters.

He used several different strategies. The preface of *Jing Mimeng,* for example, written after the revelations had been compiled and when they were about to be published, asserts that the messages from the different gods were all consistent with the known or legendary character of those gods: "you read the words and you feel that the god is really beside you" (JM I:7). The messages are god-like, and focus on what those particular gods could be expected to be concerned about. But obviously, fraud was still possible. So the writer continues: "Anyone who claims to be writing revelations from a god, but is doing so falsely, will be harshly punished by the heavenly authorities" (JM I:7). Unfortunately for the skeptic, only the heavenly authorities know for certain when fraud is being practiced. In addition, the "harsh punishment" which they promise for frauds may be postponed to the afterlife. Hence, ultimately there is no way to convince doubters that the gods will identify and punish frauds in any visible way. So the final recourse of the *fuji*-master in the face of such doubters is to threaten them with the same punishment reserved for fraudulent *fuji*-writers— the harsh punishment of the heavenly authorities.

Apart from these passages in the preface, there are other sections where the *fuji*-writer had to deal with skeptics during his writing-sessions. On one occasion, for example, a guest or observer had evidently queried the identity of the "spirit" writing the poetic oracles; while Wong Tai Sin had identified himself as a Jenn dynasty saint, his poems, as inscribed by the *fuji*-master, seemed much less refined and elegant than those of other poets from that period.[15] Wong Tai Sin responded by *fuji* that in order to make his messages more widely accessible to the public, he must write in a colloquial and common manner, understandable to everyone and not just to scholars. It must be blunt and forceful, not subtle and refined, to accomplish its purpose.

> This text is to shout at the deaf to make them hear again; show the text to the blind to make them see; paralyzed people hold the text and can stand up; the tired follow it and regain their spirit (JM II: preface).

(The references to the blind and deaf are allegorical, but also allude to the god's healing powers.) We cannot tell whether the *fuji*-master was making a virtue of necessity—of his inability to produce elegant poetry during *fuji* sessions—or whether he was deliberately writing colloquial material to hold the attention of some persons attending the sessions. Classical poems would have been nearly unintelligible to anyone who lacked a classical education. But it is interesting to see the spirit-writer struggling with such doubters during his *fuji* session.

Of course, regular attenders may also be potential doubters, and the *fuji*-master must continue to impress them with his messages. As Jordan and Overmyer (1986:274–5) point out, the *fuji* circle encompasses only a small part of the social relations of the attendees, and hence defection from the circle of devotees is much easier than with communal religious groups. Hence, the *fuji*-master must deal not only with skeptical visitors, but also with the occasional secret doubts of some of his regular patrons.

The most potentially dangerous skeptics, however, were outsiders hostile to the cult's existence. As long as the cult carried out its activities in an obscure shrine with little publicity, it was relatively safe. However, the plagues of the 1890s and the desperation of the population for cures led many to patronize such shrines to try to get medicines, prescriptions, or charms to cure or prevent the devastating illness. The *fuji* manuscript records a number of observations which indicate that the reputation of Leung's *fuji* shrine was spreading. The plague produced such desperation that the *fuji*-writer became alarmed by the crowds of people who came to the shrine (JM I:60, quoted in Lang and Ragvald 1993:15). These crowds annoyed and perhaps frightened some of the regular attendees at the *fuji* sessions.

They may have feared that the crowds would attract the attention of the police, and might lead to arrests or to their becoming associated with discreditable religious practices. Certainly the Qing government was aware that some sectarian groups had become vehicles for political opposition to the regime, and it was a long-standing requirement in the Qing period that officials must investigate and suppress such movements.[16] On one occasion, the *fuji* record indicates that several of these followers had shouted at the crowd, and then stayed away from the shrine in the following days. The god Wong Tai Sin scolded two of these followers.

You two followers would not come to the temple [today]. You prefer to stay at home rather than come here to do your work. I know it is because you are afraid that your reputation will be ruined, and you will be criticized by others. . . . But the most important lesson of our shrine is not to be disgusted with a great crowd. People come to ask things from me [says the god], and not from you. I don't feel disgusted. Why do you two feel this way. People come to ask for medicine, and you are angry with them. You have lost charitable feeling in your hearts. . . . Now that you know what wrong you have committed, you must repent, otherwise I will not forgive you. [In future] anyone who acts like you have done will be expelled by me from this shrine (JM I:66).

It is likely that these two were among Leung's circle of relatively well-educated men who patronized his shrine to hear the discourses of the gods, and who were not accustomed to being beseiged by outsiders. We know that in some *fuji*-cults there is some tension even at the best of times between the ministry of the *fuji*-master to his immediate following, who prefer to have his exclusive attention, and his inclination to accept petitions to the gods from outsiders and newcomers, some of whom may thus be drawn into the group and so enlarge his following and his networks of patronage (Jordan and Overmyer 1986:125). This tension must have been even greater during the time of the plagues in Guangzhou. The tension was no doubt enhanced by the danger of attracting the hostile attentions of the local government authorities.

The increasing crowds and the shouting between the crowds of newcomers and his regular attendees made the *fuji*-master fear that the police might become involved. He had a great deal to lose if the authorities decided to investigate his operation, and to prosecute him for disturbing public order or for carrying out unauthorized religious ceremonies. So one of the gods visiting the shrine advised the group that the sessions must be temporarily halted (JM I:65). Wong Tai Sin also specified that in the future, outsiders could come to the shrine only on the third and eighth day of each ten day period, thus perhaps mollifying his inner circle while still allowing opportunities to expand his mission to a wider population.

Controlling the Revelations

In the *fuji* procedure, the stick itself writes the messages. The *fuji*-master must be deemed worthy by the god to wield the stick, but the revelations come from the moving stick, not (according to some believers) from the mind of the *fuji*-master. Hence, there is always a possibility that others who feel worthy and feel inspired to serve as the god's vehicle will want to try wielding the stick. This is obviously a great threat to the *fuji*-master's control over the group. *Jing Mimeng* records that on at least one occasion, some followers asked to have a turn holding the stick. The scribe recorded the question as follows: "The followers ask [Wong] Tai Sin to appoint an additional person to do the *fuji* so that they can share the responsibility" (JM I:14). The god responded as follows:

> Such a person is difficult to find. I know all of you have the heart to save people, and I also want to save more people. But the one who is responsible for *fuji* is a special person. His 'date and time of birth' [which determine his character] were very compatible with the erection of this shrine, so he can receive these messages; he has a unique and special spirit, which is joined with the temple. It is a matter of providence, so it is difficult for me to explain to you, but there is no need for you to worry about it (JM I:14).

The followers subsequently tried another approach: they asked if they could use a "hanging stick" suspended by a string, which was thought to be capable of writing characters from the gods if the gods agreed to control it. Again they were rebuffed by the god.

But perhaps Leung's control of the group was slipping. We know that eventually a powerful patron intruded into the group and organized the building of a new shrine (Lang and Ragvald 1993:19). We also know that Leung, sometime during this period, began to produce revelations indicating that the god Wong Tai Sin was being recalled to heaven after spending several years with the group giving his advice and counsel. Shortly after the return of the god to heaven, Leung himself left Guangzhou and returned to his native village, where he built another temple to the god and produced a new volume of revelations.

Leung, as noted, eventually moved to Hong Kong, found a group of new patrons, and set up a shrine in Kowloon, modelled on the one which he had started near Guangzhou. He died in 1921, but the organization which managed the temple after his death continued, and used the *fuji* method to seek further instructions and advice from the god. None of these subsequent revelations were published however.

Meanwhile, the temple and its god had begun to become famous in Hong Kong. Thousands of refugees had moved into the once vacant area around the temple in the late 1940s and early 1950s. They began to patronize the temple, begging the god for help in their desperate quest for success and security. As their standard of living rose throughout the 1960s and 1970s, the god got some of the credit, and the temple prospered. (Meanwhile, the remaining temples in China had been destroyed.)

When the elderly *fuji*-master finally died in the early 1970s, the new chairman of the organization forbade further *fuji* activity in the temple. In the time honoured fashion of non-ecstatic religious bureaucrats, he wished to avoid challenges from the conservative members of the organization while he continued with his mission of diverting the rapidly growing revenues of the temple into the sponsoring of schools, kindergartens, and homes for the elderly (Lang and Ragvald 1993: ch. 4). The *fuji*-revelations from the 1890s had by that time been lost (and were recovered only during renovations of the temple).

The great success of the temple in Hong Kong was not due to the god's *fuji*-revelations, but to the location of the temple in a sea of refugees, the gradual improvements in the living standard of those refugees (Lang and Ragvald 1993: ch. 3), and to the religio-entrepreneurial cunning of the temple keepers in allowing a major change in the manner in which the god began to deal with his worshippers.

From the 1890s to the 1970s—with a few interruptions occasioned by wars, revolutions, and migrations—Wong Tai Sin addressed his disciples and followers by *fuji*. This method produced several published volumes of divine pronouncements, along with hundreds of unpublished diagnoses and remedies for the problems and ills of his disciples. In the hands of a succession of skillful practitioners, the *fuji*-writings were able to hold the attention and interest of the faithful for years. But it is difficult to serve the needs of followers using the *fuji* method when the number of followers grows very large.

THE RISE OF THE FORTUNE-TELLERS

As a cult moves out of its sectarian phase and begins to attract a large number of outsiders, new methods of divination must be used. In the process, a different kind of diviner appears on the scene: the fortune-teller. The pressure for such a development during the earliest stages of the cult has left a trace in the *fuji*-writings from the late 1890s, which record that a god attending the sessions called on the disciples to bring a container of fortune-sticks to the shrine so petitioners could ask about their fate (JM II:13).

The fortune-stick method involves shaking a container of numbered sticks until one of them falls to the ground. The number refers to the number of a fortune-poem, from the set of numbered poems compiled for this purpose, which contains the god's answer to the worshipper's question (see Lang and Ragvald 1993: ch. 6). This method has parallels in some other cultures (e.g., If a divination among the Yoruba: see Bascom 1969).[17]

The poems typically deal with incidents from Chinese history and legend. However, they seldom provide any clear answer to the worshipper's question, and hence it is necessary to resort to a "fortune-teller" (a professional interpreter of the meanings of the poems) to explain how the poem encodes the god's meaning for the worshipper.

Fortune-Tellers and *Fuji*-Writers

In principle, a vast increase in the number of followers might be accommodated by a corresponding increase in the number of *fuji*-masters, so that the god could still communicate with his followers in his accustomed fashion. However, the *fuji* is a difficult art, and few people have had the ability, the temperament, and the opportunity to learn and to practice it.

One of the difficulties with *fuji* is that the *fuji*-writer may easily be suspected of manipulating the messages. Even believers in *fuji* admit this possibility. The messages must be carefully crafted to sound god-like, and to repeat the kinds of teachings which one expects from a god, while occasionally producing personalized messages capable of impressing at least some of the believing or half-believing followers.

The role of fortune-teller is much easier. It requires no dramatic performances or simulations of supernatural presence, and there is no written record, except the fortune-poem itself, to embarrass the fortune-teller later. The *fuji*-master is under continual pressure: to be somewhat original in each message, and yet to stay within the religious and moral expectations of the observers; to produce some individualized messages addressed to particular followers, yet without making any errors. Once the *fuji* messages are recorded in the written record, they cannot be recalled.

In contrast, the fortune-poems, which make reference only to historical or legendary stories, are already available on printed slips of paper at the temple, and the fortune-teller is only required to "interpret" each poem. The fortune-teller can shift his diagnosis and advice in response to cues from the client (Greenblatt 1979), while the *fuji*-master must produce complete messages with little or no chance to adjust them in the face of the client's reactions. The fortune-teller can make a living as a kind of "white-collar professional" whose knowledge of classical stories and poetic allusions, combined with perceptiveness and experience, are sufficient, while the *fuji*-master is a kind of shaman who must write like the gods. The fortune-teller can charge as much as the market will bear (and fortune-tellers are widely seen as mercenary for this reason), while the *fuji*-master must display a humility and relative unconcern for money which are in keeping with his/her worthiness to be used by the god to write messages to the world. The difficulty of successfully performing *fuji* are much greater than the difficulties faced by the fortune-teller. Hence, few are "called."

In the transition from a *fuji*-cult to a mass-worship cult, such as in the history of worship of Wong Tai Sin in South China and Hong Kong between 1897 and the 1990s, the method of revelation must change. The god's personalized messages to followers, produced by *fuji* when the cult is small, can accommodate mass worship only through the introduction of new procedures to handle questions and petitions, such as the method of fortune-sticks and fortune-poems. It might also be noted that in addition to offering the god's direct advice to a much larger number of worshippers than is possible with *fuji*, the fortune-stick method has the following additional advantages: (1) it produces direct and immediate answers from the god to personal questions, which is highly valued by the anxious urbanites who comprise, at present, the god's main constituency; (2) it allows worshippers to interact with a "counsellor" who, in the guise of interpreting the fortune-poems, supplies personalized advice and attention to worshippers; and (3) it generates substantially more revenue for the temple organization than could be accomplished by the publication of scriptures, and hence helps to aggrandize the temple and its associated charitable activities.

While the *fuji* method continued to be used at the Wong Tai Sin temple until the early 1970s, the increasing crowds at the temple in the 1950s attracted an increasing number of fortune-tellers, and these soon became one of the features of the temple which attracted more worshippers. There are now more than 150 stalls for fortune-tellers on the perimeter of the temple courtyard, and during Chinese New Year, most of these stalls are occupied by these professional "explainers,"[18] some of whom earn incomes comparable to those of shopkeepers during this period. The Wong Tai Sin temple is now unique in East Asia for the large number of fortune-tellers who work there, and it seems that there is no precedent in the history of Chinese religion for so many of these religious paraprofessionals to operate at a single shrine.

CONCLUSIONS

The religious economy model is useful in understanding shamanism in non-Western societies, particularly in regard to the services offered by shamans, and the exchange of benefits such as healing and messages from spirits for rewards such as wealth and status. The role of shaman, however, is more open-ended and complex, and on occasion more politically potent, than such simple types of exchanges suggest, as has been demonstrated in ethnographic studies by anthropologists and in the brilliant comparative synthesis of I. M. Lewis (1989). The roles of the shaman and the spirit-medium deserve more attention within the religious economy model as we expand its applications into non-Western cultures.

While the shaman's activities in dealing with illness or social problems are usually preserved only in the memory of witnesses, the Chinese *fuji*-writings provide a rich record of the shaman's arts in a particular cultural and historical setting. Analysis of this material reveals similarities with some "prophetic" writings which survived, perhaps for similar reasons, in other cultural settings. In addition, the material also preserves the shaman's responses to problems of doubt and backsliding within the group, the advent of outsiders and the danger of suppression, and crises and problems in the surrounding society. Analysis of shamanism can be expanded and enriched by extending the concept to include the Chinese spirit-writers.

Spirit-writing, however, has limits as a method of providing services to worshippers and controlling them. In the transition to mass worship, for example, the *fuji* method has been abandoned in the main Wong Tai Sin temple as a vehicle of revelation from the deity. It has been replaced with the fortune-stick method of selecting fortune-poems, supplemented by interpretive assistance from fortune-tellers, a method more amenable to the demands of the urban religious marketplace, and to the everyday problems and needs of urbanites. Personal problems with work, business, and family have generated a steady stream of petitioners to the temple long after the crises which led to the founding of the cult ended. This change in divination methods, in response to the changing market for supernatural aid and advice in the metropolis, must have many parallels in other cultures but has not previously been described (to our knowledge) in studies of the growth of cults.

Collective troubles such as the recent financial crisis in East Asia produce additional business for the fortune-tellers (Gargan 1998). However, the fortune-stick method is designed to give predictions about personal problems or decisions. The fortune-poems do not directly address the general conditions or future prospects of a society, nor do they explain general calamities.

Thus, a final observation may be made: if a severe social or political crisis occurred again in the region, comparable to the political crises and plagues in China during the late 19th century, it is likely that there would be a revival of interest in *fuji* revelations, which can be used for more impressive expositions on such matters than the fortune poems.[19] This could also lead to renewed interest in the *fuji*-writings analyzed above, which preserve the god's original revelations to his anxious supplicants a hundred years ago. Indeed, they contain the raw material for a sacred canon, and await only a religious revival and a charismatic exponent. If social or political distress afflicts large numbers of local believers in the future, we would predict such a revival and such exponents. We would also predict that some persons would once again begin to propagate messages from the gods through the mysteriously moving stick.

NOTES

1. See, for instance, references to shamanism in sociology of religion texts such as those by Johnstone (1983:38) and Roberts (1990:140).

2. We accept the critique by Lewis (1989:44–5, 1996:107–121) of the conceptualizations of shamanism proposed by Eliade (1951) and others, and follow Lewis's model in this paper.

3. After an extensive analysis of the concept, Lewis (1996:121) writes: "This exercise in unpacking an ethnically specific term for what is actually the very epitome of charismatic authority may, it is hoped, contribute to a more informed understanding of universal religious roles, which for too long have been treated as though they represented different species beyond the reach of effective comparative analysis."

4. The same point applies to glossolalia and other kinds of spirit-possession behavior associated with the charismatic movement in Christian churches. Spirit-possession behavior is often preceded or accompanied by strong emotion, but variations between settings and between cultures in the patterns of spirit-possession behavior can best be attributed to social learning.

5. For example, a leading male shaman may have privileged access to women, as among the Kaffa of Ethiopia (Lewis 1989:131), while female shamans may gain greater freedom

as among Umbanda spirit-mediums in Brazil (Pressler 1977:353).

6. One ecological factor which could affect the prevalence of shamanism was the availability of hallucinogenic substances. For example, among the Jivaro of Ecuador, local hallucinogenic vines were widely used by males to produce trance states, with the result that as many as one in four males eventually engaged in shamanistic activities (Harris 1983:266, citing Harner 1972:154; see also Vitebsky 1995:46–8). A cultural factor which facilitates shamanism is polytheism. For example, Chinese culture is more amenable to shamanistic activity than monotheistic cultures, since the former admits a multitude of deities and immortal humans holding a variety of statuses in the afterlife, and thus many voices can speak simultaneously to many persons.

7. Often the spirits by which most women in such societies are possessed are not those addressed in the male-controlled religious activities of the society, but amoral or marginal spirits outside the mainstream of orthodox worship. In one case, however, women adopted deities which had fallen out of fashion as the males assimilated Western religious culture, and were the principal shamans of these deities when the men returned to them during a nativistic reaction against Western culture during an anti-colonial revolt (Lewis 1989:127). Female shamans have lost ground to male religious leaders, however, during the institutionalization of some shamanistic movements (e.g., Baer 1993).

8. The first author has observed four variations of the *fuji* procedure (three in Hong Kong and one in a private apartment-shrine in New York City). The main differences include whether sand is used (thus preserving the character for a few moments before the tray is scraped to prepare for the next character), whether the wielder of the *fuji*-stick also calls out the characters or whether another person performs this function, and whether one or two persons hold the *fuji*-stick. A brush could also be attached to the stick, and the characters inscribed on paper. Rarely, *fuji* might also be used to produce a picture, such as the "self-portrait" of the god Wong Tai Sin which hangs in a private shrine to this god in Hong Kong (Lang and Ragvald 1993:133).

9. Some followers believe that the deity expresses his/her ideas by direct control of the stick, but *fuji*-writers sometimes describe or claim a kind of spirit-possession. A *fuji*-writer in Hong Kong, for instance, related to Lang's research assistant that she "heard the words in her mind." A spirit-writer in Taiwan expressed the view (i.e., the deity stated) that a deity enters into and controls the consciousness of the writer, but that sometimes this control is only partial, which would not, however, invalidate the revelations, according to the deity (Thompson 1982). Thompson suggests that such a message is intended to support the authority of the messages even when observers can clearly see that the spirit-writer is not fully or notably entranced.

10. The origin of this practice may be similar to that of so-called "automatic writing" in other cultures. A friend of the first author in Canada, after the death of her father, began to write messages which she felt were somehow from her father and not from her

own mind. The prophet "inspired" to write a deity's words to the world may experience a similar phenomenon.

11. See, for example, Nelson (1969, 1987:58) on the disciples who gathered around what he calls "charismatic mediums" in the Spiritualist movement. Some of these groups, like the Sik Sik Yuen devoted to worship of Wong Tai Sin in Hong Kong, formed centralized organizations after the death of the original charismatic medium.

12. For example, among the directors of the Sik Sik Yuen, the organization which manages the main Wong Tai Sin temple in Hong Kong, several also belong to other Taoist organizations in Hong Kong, dividing their time among these and other religious activities according to their current interests. The late Chairman of the Sik Sik Yuen was also an official in the Hong Kong Buddhist Association.

13. Proverbs, some of which appears to represent the "class ethic" of the senior administrative elite in pre-exilic Judea (Kovacs 1974:187), was evidently directed primarily toward younger males. However, passages such as that on the "good wife" (Proverbs 31:10–31) indicate that women were addressed in some of the sayings, if only indirectly.

14. Such doubts are mentioned in other *fuji* texts (Jordan and Overmyer 1986:55). Suspicions about the authenticity of spirit-utterances are reported in studies of spirit-mediums in many other cultures (e.g., among the Amhara of Ethiopia: Morton 1977:204), particularly when a "spirit" makes a demand which is obviously to the benefit of the spirit-medium, such as the case reported by Pressel (1977) of a spirit who demanded, through a Brazilian medium, that someone should repay a loan owed to the medium. In general, shamans and spirit-mediums are most suspected of fraud (even by people who generally believe in spirit-possession) when the spirit-medium's messages seem too obviously self-serving.

15. Jordan and Overmyer (1986:212) report a case in which a copyist complained about the poor quality of the *fuji*-poetry which he was copying, which led to the following result: "within a few days the oracle began delivering up obscure archaic characters that . . . [the copyist] was embarrassed to be unable to read. Humbled, he stopped deriding the revelations, and they returned to ordinary language."

16. Investigation and occasional suppression of heterodox movements, including *fuji*-cults, was carried out also in the Republican period, and continued after the establishment of the Nationalist government in Taiwan (Weller 1982; Jordan and Overmyer 1986:241–2). Some conservative *fuji*-groups produced and published revelations which called on believers to be loyal to the government (see Thompson 1982:117).

17. There are similarities between Ifa divination among the Yoruba and the Chinese system. In both procedures the god's answer to a worshipper's question or petition was provided through a poem or verse, which was selected from a large set of pre-existing numbered verses. The method for selecting the number, in both systems, was mechanical (with the god supposedly manipulating the outcome). The main difference is that printed copies of Ifa divination verses were not available to worshippers. (Verses were produced by the diviners from memory.) Greater literacy and familiarity with printed poems in China may account for this difference between these otherwise similar divination systems.

18. The colloquial Cantonese term for these persons (using the Yale pinyin system) is "gaai chim louh," which means "persons who explain fortune-poems." Thus, "professional explainers of fortune-poems" is more accurate, if less concise, than "fortune-tellers."

19. One possible source of future *fuji*-revelations is a private shrine to Wong Tai Sin, built in the hills west of the main temple in the 1950s by wealthy Chaozhou migrants to Hong Kong who wished to have their own exclusive private place of worship. Spirit-writings from Wong Tai Sin have continued in the shrine since the 1950s, uninterrupted by the rationalizing management policies at the main temple. This private shrine is unknown and inaccessible to most worshippers, but has produced several revelations for members of the private shrine in response to political crises such as the events of 4 June 1989 (Lang and Ragvald 1993:158). Thus, a minor offshoot of the cult has preserved elements of the original cult which were abandoned at the main temple, and could "re-seed" such practices into the mainstream of the cult at some future time.

REFERENCES

Ammerman, N. T. 1997. Organized religion in a voluntaristic society. *Sociology of Religion* 58:203–215.

Baer, H. A. 1993. The limited empowerment of women in Black Spiritual churches: An alternative vehicle to religious leadership. *Sociology of Religion* 54:65–82.

Bascom, W. 1969. *Ira divination: Communication between gods and men in West Africa.* Bloomington: Indiana University Press.

Berger, P. L. 1963. Charisma and religious innovation: The social location of Israelite prophecy. *American Sociological Review* 28:940–9.

Bromley, D. G. 1997. Remembering the future: A sociological narrative of crisis episodes, collective action, culture workers, and countermovements. *Sociology of Religion* 58:105–140.

Chao, W. P. 1942. The origin and growth of Fu Chi. *Folklore studies* [The Museum of Oriental Ethnology, The Catholic University of Peking] 1:9–27.

Crapanzano, V., and V. Garrison, eds. 1977. *Case studies in spirit possession.* New York: John Wiley and Sons.

Davis, W. 1980. *Dojo: Magic and exorcism in modern Japan.* Stanford, CA: Stanford University Press.

De Groot, J. J. M. 1964 [1892–1910]. *The religious system of China.* Taipei: Literature House (reprint of original edition).

Eliade, M. 1951. *Le Chamanisme et les techniques archaiques d l' extase.* Paris: Payot.

Gargan, E. 1998. Soothsayers' stocks surge in a market of ill-fortune. *Sydney Morning Herald,* 29 January.

Greenblatt, S. L. 1979. Individual values and attitudes in Chinese society: An ethnomethodological approach. In *Value change in Chinese society,* edited by R. Wilson, A. A. Wilson, and S. L. Greenblatt, 65–97. New York: Praeger.

Harner, M. 1972. *The Jivaro: People of the sacred.* Garden City, NY: Natural History Press.

Harris, M. 1987. *Cultural anthropology.* 2nd ed. New York: Harper and Row.

Johnstone, R. L. 1983. *Religion in society: A sociology of religion.* Englewood Cliffs, NJ: Prentice-Hall.

Jordan, D., and D. Overmyer. 1986. *The flying phoenix: Aspects of Chinese sectarianism in Taiwan.* Princeton, NJ: Princeton University Press.

Kessler, C. S. 1977. Conflict and sovereignty in Kelantanese Malay spirit seances. In *Case studies in spirit possession,* edited by V. Crapanzano and Garrison, 295–331. New York: John Wiley and Sons.

Kovacs, B. W. 1974. Is there a class ethic in Proverbs? In *Essays in Old Testament ethics,* edited by J. L. Crenshaw and J. T. Willis, 174–189. New York: KTAV Publishing House.

Lan, D. 1985. *Guns and rain: Guerrillas and spirit mediums in Zimbabwe.* Berkeley: University of California Press.

Lang, G. 1989. Oppression and revolt in ancient Palestine: The evidence in Jewish literature from the prophets to Josephus. *Sociological Analysis* 49:325–342.

Lang, G., and L. Ragvald. 1993. *The rise of a refugee god: Hong Kong's Wong Tai Sin.* Hong Kong: Oxford University Press.

Lewis, I. M. 1989. *Ecstatic religion,* 2nd ed. London: Routledge.

———. 1996. *Religion in context: Cults and charisma,* 2nd ed. Cambridge: Cambridge University Press.

Macklin, J. 1997. A Connecticut yankee in summer land. In *Case studies in spirit possession,* edited by Crapanzano and Garrison, 41–85. New York: John Wiley and Sons.

Morton, A. 1977. *Dawit:* Competition and integration in an Ethiopian Wuqabi cult group, in *Case studies in spirit possession,* edited by Crapanzano and Garrison, 193–233. New York: John Wiley and Sons.

Nelson, G. K. 1969. *Spiritualism and society.* London: Routledge and Kegan Paul.

———. 1987. *Cults, new religions, and religious creativity.* London: Routledge and Kegan Paul.

Nguyen, H. V. 1995. The particularity of popular beliefs among ethnic communities of the Hanhi-Lolo linguistic group. *Social Compass* 42:301–315.

Overmyer, D. 1985. Values in Chinese sectarian literature: Ming and Ch'ing Pao-chuan. In *Popular culture in late Imperial China,* edited by D. Johnson, A. Nathan, and E. Rawski, 219–254. Berkeley: University of California Press.

Park, S. H. 1997. An empirical study of the physical changes exhibited in Korean shamans during spirit-possession. *Korea Journal* 37:5–34.

Pressel, E. 1977. Negative spirit possession in experienced Brazilian Umbanda spirit mediums. In *Case studies in spirit possession,* edited by Crapanzano and Garrison, 333–364. New York: John Wiley and Sons.

Potter, J. M. 1974. Cantonese shamanism. In *Religion and ritual in Chinese society,* edited by A. P. Wolf, 207–231. Stanford: Stanford University Press.

Roberts, K. A. 1990. *Religion in sociological perspective.* Belmont, CA: Wadsworth.

Russell, T. C. 1997. The spiritualization of feminine virtue: Religion and social conservatism in the late Qing. In *East Asian cultural and historical perspectives,* edited by S. T. de Zepetnek and J. W. Jay, 135–151. Edmonton: Research Institute for Comparative Literature and Cross-Cultural Studies, University of Alberta.

Seagrave, S. 1992. *Dragon lady: The life and legend of the last empress of China.* New York: Vintage Books.

Smith, R. J. 1991. *Fortune-tellers and philosophers: Divination in traditional Chinese society.* San Francisco, CA: Westview Press.

Stark, R., and W. S. Bainbridge. 1987. *A theory of religion.* New York: Peter Lang.

Tai, H. T. H. 1983. *Millenarianism and peasant politics in Vietnam.* Cambridge, MA: Harvard University Press.

Thompson, L. G. 1982. The moving finger writes: A note on revelation and renewal in Chinese religion. *Journal of Chinese Religions* 10:95–147.

Tsui, B. P. M. 1991. *Taoist tradition and change: The story of the complete perfection sect in Hong Kong.* Hong Kong: Christian Study Centre on Chinese Religion and Culture.

Vitebsky, P. 1995. *The shaman.* Boston: Little, Brown, and Co.

Wallace, A. F. C. 1966. *Religion: An anthropological view.* New York: Random House.

Weller, R. P. 1982. Sectarian religion and political action in China. *Modern China* 8:463–483.

The Production of Possession:
Spirits and the Multinational Corporation
in Malaysia

Aihwa Ong

Religious experiences are often very closely tied to changes in social structure and other aspects of living conditions. In this well-known essay, Aihwa Ong explores a series of incidents of demon possession among young female factory workers in Malaysia. The women, sometimes as many as 120 at a time, are possessed by spirits that frequently inhabit the water tanks of Western-style toilets in the factories where they work. While possessed, the women claim to see spirits, rage against factory supervisors, and engage in violent behavior.

Ong analyzes possession incidents through a comparison with possession in traditional Malay villages. There, it is usually new mothers or women in middle age who become

Reproduced by permission of the American Anthropological Association from *American Ethnologist* 15:1. Not for sale or further reproduction.

possessed. Possession probably occurs at these times because it is then that women experience stress in the traditional village social structure. In factories, however, it is young women who are subject to stress. They are dominated by male managers and foremen. They are in unaccustomed roles and an unfamiliar setting. They often work under harsh, unremitting conditions and have frequent exposure to hazardous materials. Many aspects of their new lives violate the moral order of traditional Malay society.

The young women respond to conditions in the factory through possession. Factory managers, often Americans or Japanese, reject the moral claims of their Malay hosts. They interpret possession in purely medical and psychological terms and attempt to solve it through the administration of drugs and the firing of women who experience multiple episodes of possession.

The essay thus shows the relationship between a social change and changes in religious structures. It also shows one way in which possession, a religious phenomenon, can be a form of political and economic protest.

As you read, consider these questions:

1. How do spirit possession and spirit attacks relate to changes in social structure and economics?
2. Why are some places, such as factory toilets or locker rooms, more likely to be places of spirit attack?
3. How are changing male/female roles relevant to incidents of spirit possession?

The sanitized environments maintained by multinational corporations in Malaysian "free trade zones"[1] are not immune to sudden spirit attacks on young female workers. Ordinarily quiescent, Malay factory women who are seized by vengeful spirits explode into demonic screaming and rage on the shop floor. Management responses to such unnerving episodes include isolating the possessed workers, pumping them with Valium, and sending them home. Yet a Singapore[2] doctor notes that "a local medicine man can do more good than tranquilizers" (Chew 1978:51). Whatever healing technique used, the cure is never certain, for the Malays consider spirit possession an illness that afflicts the soul (jiwa). This paper will explore how the reconstitution of illness, bodies, and consciousness is involved in the deployment of healing practices in multinational factories.

Anthropologists studying spirit possession phenomena have generally linked them to culturally specific forms of conflict management that disguise and yet resolve social tensions within indigenous societies (Firth 1967; Lewis 1971; Crapanzano and Garrison 1977). In contrast, policymakers and professionals see spirit possession episodes as an intrusion of archaic beliefs into the modern setting (Teoh, Soewondo, and Sidharta 1975; Chew 1978; Phoon 1982). These views will be evaluated in the light of spirit posses-

sion incidents and the reactions of factory managers and policymakers in Malaysia.

Different forms of spirit possession have been reported in Malay society, and their cultural significance varies with the regional and historical circumstances in which they occurred (see Maxwell 1977; Skeat 1965 [1900]; Winstedt 1961; Firth 1967; Endicott 1970; Kessler 1977). In the current changing political economy, new social conditions have brought about spirit possession incidents in modern institutional settings. I believe that the most appropriate way to deal with spirit visitations in multinational factories is to consider them as part of a "complex negotiation of reality" (Crapanzano 1977:16) by an emergent female industrial workforce. Hailing from peasant villages, these workers can be viewed as neophytes in a double sense: as young female adults and as members of a nascent proletariat. Mary Douglas' ideas about the breaking of taboos and social boundaries (1966) are useful for interpreting spirit possession in terms of what it reveals about the workers' profound sense of status ambiguity and dislocation. Second, their spirit idiom will be contrasted with the biomedical model to reveal alternative constructions of illness and of social reality in the corporate world. I will then consider the implications of the scientific medical model that converts workers into patients, and the consequences this therapeutic approach holds for mending the souls of the afflicted.

ECONOMIC DEVELOPMENT AND A MEDICAL MONOLOGUE ON MADNESS

As recently as the 1960s, most Malays in Peninsular Malaysia[3] lived in rural kampung (villages), engaged in cash cropping or fishing. In 1969, spontaneous outbreaks of racial rioting gave expression to deep-seated resentment over the distribution of power and wealth in this multiethnic society. The Malay-dominated government responded to this crisis by introducing a New Economic Policy intended to "restructure" the political economy. From the early 1970s onward, agricultural and industrialization programs induced the large-scale influx of young rural Malay men and women to enter urban schools and manufacturing plants set up by multinational corporations.

Before the current wave of industrial employment for young single women, spirit possession was mainly manifested by married women, given the particular stresses of being wives, mothers, widows, and divorcées (see, for example, Maxwell 1977, and Kessler 1977). With urbanization and industrialization, spirit possession became overnight the affliction of young, unmarried women placed in modern organizations, drawing the attention of the press and the scholarly community (see Teoh, Soewondo, and Sidharta 1975; Chew 1978; Lim 1978; Jamilah Ariffin 1980; Ackerman and Lee 1981; Phoon 1982; Ong 1987).

In 1971, 17 cases of "epidemic hysteria" among schoolgirls were reported, coinciding with the implementation of government policy (Teoh, Soewondo, and Sidharta 1971: 259). This dramatic increase, from 12 cases reported for the entire decade of the 1960s, required an official response. Teoh, a professor of psychology, declared that "epidemic hysteria was not caused by offended spirits but by interpersonal tensions within the school or hostel" (1975:260). Teoh and his colleagues investigated a series of spirit incidents in a rural Selangor school, which they attributed to conflicts between the headmaster and female students. The investigators charged that in interpreting the events as "spirit possession" rather than the symptoms of local conflict, the *bomoh* (spirit healer) by "this devious path . . . avoided infringing on the taboos and sensitivities of the local community" (p. 267). Teoh had found it necessary to intervene by giving the headmaster psychotherapeutic counseling. Thus, spirit incidents in schools occasioned the introduction of a cosmopolitan therapeutic approach whereby rural Malays were "told to accept the . . . change from their old superstitious beliefs to contemporary scientific knowledge" (p. 268).

This dismissal of Malay interpretation of spirit events by Western-trained professionals became routine with the large-scale participation of Malays in capitalist industries. Throughout the 1970s, free-trade zones were established to encourage investments by Japanese, American, and European corporations for setting up plants for offshore production. In seeking to cut costs further, these corporations sought young, unmarried women[4] as a source of cheap and easily controlled labor. This selective labor demand, largely met by *kampung* society, produced in a single decade a Malay female industrial labor force of over 47,000 (Jamilah Ariffin 1980:47). Malay female migrants also crossed the Causeway in the thousands to work in multinational factories based in Singapore.

In a 1978 paper entitled "How to Handle Hysterical Factory Workers" in Singapore, Dr. P. K. Chew complained that "this psychological aberration interrupts production, and can create hazards due to inattention to machinery and careless behaviour" (1978:50). He classified "mass hysteria" incidents according to "frightened" and "seizure" categories, and recommended that incidents of either type should be handled "like an epidemic disease of bacteriological origin" (pp. 50, 53). In a Ministry of Labour survey of "epidemic hysteria" incidents in Singapore-based factories between 1973 and 1978, W. H. Phoon also focused on symptoms ranging from "hysterical seizures" and "trance states" to "frightened spells" (1982:22–23). The biomedical approach called for the use of sedatives, "isolation" of "infectious" cases, "immunization" of those susceptible to the "disease," and keeping the public informed about the measures taken (Chew 1978:53). Both writers, in looking for an explanation for the outbreak of "epidemic/mass hysteria" among Malay women workers, maintained that "the preference of belief in spirits and low educational level of the workers are obviously key factors" (Chew 1978:53; Phoon 1982:30). An anthropological study of spirit incidents in a Malacca shoe fac-

tory revealed that managers perceived the "real" causes of possession outbreaks to be physical (undernourishment) and psychological (superstitious beliefs) (Ackerman and Lee 1981:796).

These papers on spirit possession episodes in modern organizations adopt the assumptions of medical science which describe illnesses independent of their local meanings and values. "Mass hysteria" is attributed to the personal failings of the afflicted, and native explanations are denigrated as "superstitious beliefs" from a worldview out of keeping with the modern setting and pace of social change. "A monologue of reason about madness" (Foucault 1965:xi) was thereby introduced into Malaysian society, coinciding with a shift of focus from the afflicted to their chaotic effects on modern institutions. We will need to recover the Malays' worldview in order to understand their responses to social situations produced by industrialization.

SPIRIT BELIEFS AND WOMEN IN MALAY CULTURE

Spirit beliefs in rural Malay society, overlaid but existing within Islam, are part of the indigenous worldview woven from strands of animistic cosmology and Javanese, Hindu, and Muslim cultures (Mohd. Taib bin Osman 1972). In Peninsular Malaysia, the supernatural belief system varies according to the historical and local interactions between folk beliefs and Islamic teachings. Local traditions provide conceptual coherence about causation and well-being to village Malays. Through the centuries, the office of the *bomoh,* or practitioner of folk medicine, has been the major means by which these old traditions of causation, illness, and health have been transmitted. In fulfilling the pragmatic and immediate needs of everyday life, the beliefs and practices are often recast in "Islamic" terms (Mohd. Taib bin Osman 1972:221–222; Endicott 1970).

I am mainly concerned here with the folk model in Sungai Jawa (a pseudonym), a village based in Kuala Langat district, rural Selangor, where I conducted fieldwork in 1979–80. Since the 1960s, the widespread introduction of Western medical practices and an intensified revitalization of Islam have made spirit beliefs publicly inadmissable. Nevertheless, spirit beliefs and practices are still very much in evidence. Villagers believe that all beings have spiritual essence *(semangat)* but, unlike humans, spirits *(hantu)* are disembodied beings capable of violating the boundaries between the material and supernatural worlds: invisible beings unbounded by human rules, spirits come to represent transgressions of moral boundaries, which are socially defined in the concentric spaces of homestead, village, and jungle. This scheme roughly coincides with Malay concepts of emotional proximity and distance, and the related dimensions of reduced moral responsibility as one moves from the interior space of household, to the intermediate zone of relatives, and on to the external world of strangers (Banks 1983:170–174).

The two main classes of spirits recognized by Malays reflect this interior-exterior social/spatial divide: spirits associated with human beings, and the "free" disembodied forms. In Sungai Jawa, *toyol* are the most common familiar spirits, who steal in order to enrich their masters. Accusations of breeding *toyol* provide the occasion for expressing resentment against economically successful villagers. Birth demons are former human females who died in childbirth and, as *pontianak,* threaten newly born infants and their mothers. Thus, spirit beliefs reflect everyday anxieties about the management of social relations in village society.

It is free spirits that are responsible for attacking people who unknowingly step out of the Malay social order. Free spirits are usually associated with special objects or sites *(keramat)* marking the boundary between human and natural spaces. These include (1) the burial grounds of aboriginal and animal spirits, (2) strangely shaped rocks, hills, or trees associated with highly revered ancestral figures *(datuk),* and (3) animals like were-tigers (Endicott 1970: 90–91). As the gatekeepers of social boundaries, spirits guard against human transgressions into amoral spaces. Such accidents require the mystical qualities of the *bomoh* to readjust spirit relations with the human world.

From Islam, Malays have inherited the belief that men are more endowed with *akal* (reason) than women, who are overly influenced by *hawa nafsu* (human lust). A susceptibility to imbalances in the four humoral elements renders women spiritually weaker than men. Women's *hawa nafsu* nature is believed to make them especially vulnerable to *latah* (episodes during which the victim breaks out into obscene language and compulsive, imitative behavior) and to spirit attacks (spontaneous episodes in which the afflicted one screams, hyperventilates, or falls down in a trance or a raging fit). However, it is Malay spirit beliefs that explain the transgressions whereby women (more likely than men) become possessed by spirits *(kena hantu).* Their spiritual frailty, polluting bodies, and erotic nature make them especially likely to transgress moral space, and therefore permeable by spirits.

Mary Douglas (1966) has noted that taboos operate to control threats to social boundaries. In Malay society, women are hedged in by conventions that keep them out of social roles and spaces dominated by men. Although men are also vulnerable to spirit attacks, women's spiritual, bodily, and social selves are especially offensive to sacred spaces, which they trespass at the risk of inviting spirit attacks.

Spirit victims have traditionally been married women who sometimes become possessed after giving birth for the first time. Childbirth is a dangerous occasion, when rituals are performed in order to keep off evil spirits (see Laderman 1983:125–126). As a rite of passage, childbirth is the first traumatic event in the ordinary village woman's life. I visited a young mother who had been possessed by a *hantu,* which the ministrations of two *bomoh* failed to dislodge.

She lay on her mat for two months after delivering her first child, uninterested in nursing the baby. Her mother-in-law whispered that she had been "penetrated by the devil." Perhaps, through some unintended action, she had attracted spirit attack and been rendered ritually and sexually impure.

The next critical phase in a woman's life cycle comes at middle age. Kessler (1977) observes that among Kelantanese fisherfolk, possessed women were often those threatened with widowhood, divorce, or their husbands' plan to take a second wife. Laderman (1983:127) claims that Trengganu village women who resist their assigned roles as mothers and wives are said to become vulnerable to spirit attacks and may be transformed into demons. These ethnographic observations from different Malay communities demonstrate that in village life, spirit attacks are most likely to occur when women are in transition from one phase of life to another. On such occasions, they are perceived to be the greatest threat to social norms, and taboos enforce some degree of self-control in order to contain that threat.

In everyday life, village women are also bound by customs regarding bodily comportment and spatial movements, which operate to keep them within the Malay social order. When they blur the bodily boundaries through the careless disposal of bodily exuviae and effluvia, they put themselves in an ambiguous situation, becoming most vulnerable to spirit penetration.

Until recently, unmarried daughters, most hedged in by village conventions, seem to have been well protected from spirit attack. Nubile girls take special care over the disposal of their cut nails, fallen hair, and menstrual rags, since such materials may fall into ill-wishers' hands and be used for black magic. Menstrual blood is considered dirty and polluting (cf. Laderman 1983:74), and the substance most likely to offend *keramat* spirits. This concern over bodily boundaries is linked to notions about the vulnerable identity and status of young unmarried women. It also operates to keep pubescent girls close to the homestead and on well-marked village paths. In Sungai Jawa, a schoolgirl who urinated on an ant-hill off the beaten track became possessed by a "male" spirit. Scheper-Hughes and Lock remark that when the social norms of small, conservative peasant communities are breached, we would expect to see a "concern with the penetration and violation of bodily exits, entrances and boundaries" (1987:19). Thus, one suspects that when young Malay women break with village traditions, they may come under increased spirit attacks as well as experience an intensified social and bodily vigilance.

Since the early 1970s, when young peasant women began to leave the *kampung* and enter the unknown worlds of urban boarding schools and foreign factories, the incidence of spirit possession seems to have become more common among them than among married women. I maintain that like other cultural forms, spirit possession incidents may acquire new meanings and speak to new experiences in changing arenas of social relations and boundary definitions. In *kampung* society, spirit attacks on married women seem to be associated with their containment in prescribed domestic roles, whereas in modern organizations, spirit victims are young, unmarried women engaged in hitherto alien and male activities. This transition from *kampung* to urban-industrial contexts has cast village girls into an intermediate status that they find unsettling and fraught with danger to themselves and to Malay culture.

SPIRIT VISITATIONS IN MODERN FACTORIES

In the 1970s, newspaper reports on the sudden spate of "mass hysteria" among young Malay women in schools and factories interpreted the causes in terms of "superstitious beliefs," "examination tension," "the stresses of urban living," and less frequently, "mounting pressures" which induced "worries" among female operators in multinational factories.

Multinational factories based in free-trade zones were the favored sites of spirit visitations. An American factory in Sungai Way experienced a large-scale incident in 1978, which involved some 120 operators engaged in assembly work requiring the use of microscopes. The factory had to be shut down for three days, and a *bomoh* was hired to slaughter a goat on the premises. The American director wondered how he was to explain to corporate headquarters that "8,000 hours of production were lost because someone saw a ghost" (Lim 1978:33). A Japanese factory based in Pontian, Kelantan, also experienced a spirit attack on 21 workers in 1980. As they were being taken to ambulances, some victims screamed, "I will kill you! Let me go!" (*New Straits Times*, 26 September 1980). In Penang, another American factory was disrupted for three consecutive days after 15 women became afflicted by spirit possession. The victims screamed in fury and put up a terrific struggle against restraining male supervisors, shouting "Go away!" (*Sunday Echo*, 27 November 1978). The afflicted were snatched off the shop floor and given injections of sedatives. Hundreds of frightened female workers were also sent home. A factory personnel officer told reporters:

> "Some girls started sobbing and screaming hysterically and when it seemed like spreading, the other workers in the production line were immediately ushered out. . . . It is a common belief among workers that the factory is "dirty" and supposed to be haunted by a *datuk*" [*Sunday Echo*].

Though brief, these reports reveal that spirit possession, believed to be caused by defilement, held the victims in a grip of rage against factory supervisors. Furthermore, the disruptions caused by spirit incidents seem a form of retaliation against the factory supervisors. In what follows, I will draw upon my field research to discuss the complex issues involved in possession imagery and management discourse on spirit incidents in Japanese-owned factories based in Kuala Langat.

THE CRYPTIC LANGUAGE OF POSSESSION

The political economy of Islam is set up and orchestrated around the silence of inferiors.

Fatna A. Sabbah, *Woman in the Muslim Unconscious*

Young, unmarried women in Malay society are expected to be shy, obedient, and deferential, to be observed and not heard. In spirit possession episodes, they speak in other voices that refuse to be silenced. Since the afflicted claim amnesia once they have recovered, we are presented with the task of deciphering covert messages embedded in possession incidents.

Spirit visitations in modern factories with sizable numbers of young Malay female workers engender devil images, which dramatically reveal the contradictions between Malay and scientific ways of apprehending the human condition. I. M. Lewis has suggested that in traditionally gender-stratified societies, women's spirit possession episodes are a "thinly disguised protest against the dominant sex" (1971:31). In Malay society, what is being negotiated in possession incidents and their aftermath are complex issues dealing with the violation of different moral boundaries, of which gender oppression is but one dimension. What seems clear is that spirit possession provides a traditional way of rebelling against authority without punishment, since victims are not blamed for their predicament. However, the imagery of spirit possession in modern settings is a rebellion against transgressions of indigenous boundaries governing proper human relations and moral justice.

For Malays, the places occupied by evil spirits are non-human territories like swamps, jungles, and bodies of water. These amoral domains were kept distant from women's bodies by ideological and physical spatial regulations. The construction of modern buildings, often without regard for Malay concern about moral space, displaces spirits, which take up residence in the toilet tank. Thus, most village women express a horror of the Western-style toilet, which they would avoid if they could. It is the place where their usually discreet disposal of bodily waste is disturbed. Besides their fear of spirits residing in the water tank, an unaccustomed body posture is required to use the toilet. In their hurry to depart, unflushed toilets and soiled sanitary napkins, thrown helter-skelter, offend spirits who may attack them.

A few days after the spirit attacks in the Penang-based American factory, I interviewed some of the workers. Without prompting, factory women pointed out that the production floor and canteen areas were "very clean" but factory toilets were "filthy" *(kotor)*. A *datuk* haunted the toilet, and workers, in their haste to leave, dropped their soiled pads anywhere. In Ackerman and Lee's case study, Malay factory workers believed that they had disturbed the spirits dwelling in a water tank and on factory grounds. Furthermore, the spirits were believed to possess women who had violated moral codes, thereby becoming "unclean" (1981:794, 796–797). This connection between disturbing spirits and lack of sexual purity is also hinted at in Teoh and his colleagues' account of the school incidents mentioned above. The headmaster had given students instructions in how to wear sanitary napkins (1978:262),[5] an incident which helped precipitate a series of spirit attacks said to be caused by the "filthy" school toilets and the girls' disposal of soiled pads in a swamp adjacent to the school grounds (1978:264).

In the Penang factory incident, a worker remembered that a piercing scream from one corner of the shop floor was quickly followed by cries from other benches as women fought against spirits trying to possess them. The incidents had been sparked by *datuk* visions, sometimes headless, gesticulating angrily at the operators. Even after the *bomoh* had been sent for, workers had to be accompanied to the toilet by foremen for fear of being attacked by spirits in the stalls.

In Kuala Langat, my fieldwork elicited similar imagery from the workers[6] in two Japanese factories (code-named ENI and EJI) based in the local free-trade zone. In their drive for attaining high production targets, foremen (both Malay and non-Malay) were very zealous in enforcing regulations that confined workers to the work bench. Operators had to ask for permission to go to the toilet, and were sometimes questioned intrusively about their "female problems." Menstruation was seen by management as deserving no consideration even in a workplace where 85–90 percent of the work force was female.[7] In the EJI plant, foremen sometimes followed workers to the locker room, terrorizing them with their spying. One operator became possessed after screaming that she saw a "hairy leg" when she went to the toilet. A worker from another factory reported:

> Workers saw "things" appear when they went to the toilet. Once, when a woman entered the toilet she saw a tall figure licking sanitary napkins ["Modess" supplied in the cabinet]. It had a long tongue, and those sanitary pads . . . cannot be used anymore.

As Taussig remarks, the "language" emanating from our bodies expresses the significance of social dis-ease (1980). The above lurid imagery speaks of the women's loss of control over their bodies as well as their lack of control over social relations in the factory. Furthermore, the image of body alienation also reveals intense guilt (and repressed desire), and the felt need to be on guard against violation by the male management staff who, in the form of fearsome predators, may suddenly materialize anywhere in the factory.

Even the prayer room *(surau)*, provided on factory premises for the Muslim work force, was not safe from spirit harassment. A woman told me of her aunt's fright in the *surau* at the EJI factory.

> "She was in the middle of praying when she fainted because she said . . . her head suddenly spun and something pounced on her from behind."

As mentioned above, spirit attacks also occurred when women were at the work bench, usually during the "graveyard" shift. An ENI factory operator described one incident which took place in May 1979.

> "It was the afternoon shift, at about nine o'clock. All was quiet. Suddenly, [the victim] started sobbing, laughed and then shrieked. She flailed at the machine . . . she was violent, she fought as the foreman and technician pulled her away. Altogether, three operators were afflicted. . . . The supervisor and foremen took them to the clinic and told the driver to take them home. . . .
>
> She did not know what had happened . . . she saw a *hantu,* a were-tiger. Only she saw it, and she started screaming. . . . The foremen would not let us talk with her for fear of recurrence. . . . People say that the workplace is haunted by the *hantu* who dwells below. . . . Well, this used to be all jungle, it was a burial ground before the factory was built. The devil disturbs those who have a weak constitution."

Spirit possession episodes then were triggered by black apparitions, which materialized in "liminal" spaces such as toilets (see also Teoh, Soewondo, and Sidharta 1975:259, 262, and Chew 1978:52), the locker room and the prayer room, places where workers sought refuge from harsh work discipline. These were also rooms periodically checked by male supervisors determined to bring workers back to the work bench. The microscope, which after hours of use becomes an instrument of torture, sometimes disclosed spirits luring within. Other workers pointed to the effect of the steady hum and the factory pollutants, which permanently disturbed graveyard spirits. Unleashed, these vengeful beings were seen to threaten women for transgressing into the zone between the human and nonhuman world, as well as modern spaces formerly the domain of men. By intruding into hitherto forbidden spaces, Malay women workers experienced anxieties about inviting punishment.

Fatna Sabbah observes that "(t)he invasion by women of economic spaces such as factories and offices . . . is often experienced as erotic aggression in the Muslim context" (1984:17). In Malay culture, men and women in public contact must define the situation in nonsexual terms (cf. Banks 1983:88). It is particularly incumbent upon young women to conduct themselves with circumspection and to diffuse sexual tension. However, the modern factory is an arena constituted by a sexual division of labor and constant male surveillance of nubile women in a close, daily context. In Kuala Langat, young factory women felt themselves placed in a situation in which they unintentionally violated taboos defining social and bodily boundaries. The shop floor culture was also charged with the dangers of sexual harassment by male management staff as part of workaday relations.[8] To combat spirit attacks, the Malay factory women felt a greater need for spiritual vigilance in the factory surroundings. Thus the victim in the ENI factory incident was said to be:

> possessed, maybe because she was spiritually weak. She was not spiritually vigilant, so that when she saw the *hantu* she

was instantly afraid and screamed. Usually, the *hantu* likes people who are spiritually weak, yes. . . . one should guard against being easily startled, afraid.

As Foucault observes, people subjected to the "microtechniques" of power are induced to regulate themselves (1979). The fear of spirit possession thus created self-regulation on the part of workers, thereby contributing to the intensification of corporate and self-control on the shop floor. Thus, as factory workers, Malay women became alienated not only from the products of their labor but also experienced new forms of psychic alienation. Their intrusion into economic spaces outside the home and village was experienced as moral disorder, symbolized by filth and dangerous sexuality. Some workers called for increased "discipline," others for Islamic classes on factory premises to regulate interactions (including dating) between male and female workers. Thus, spirit imagery gave symbolic configuration to the workers' fear and protest over social conditions in the factories. However, these inchoate signs of moral and social chaos were routinely recast by management into an idiom of sickness.

THE WORKER AS PATIENT

Studies of work experiences in modern industrial systems have tended to focus on the ways time and motion techniques (Taylorism) have facilitated the progressive adaptation of the human body to machines, bringing about the divorce of mental and manual labor (Braverman 1974). Others have maintained that control over the exact movements of the workers allowed by Taylorism has banished fantasy and thoroughly depersonalized work relations in the modern factory (Gramsci 1971:303; Ellul 1964:387–410). Indeed, Taylorist forms of work discipline are taken to an extreme in the computer-chip manufacturing industries set up by multinational corporations in Malaysia (see Ong 1987). However, contrary to the above claims, I would argue that the recoding of the human body-work relation is a critical and contested dimension of daily conduct in the modern factory.

I have elsewhere described the everyday effects of the sexual division of labor and Taylorist techniques on Malay factory women (1987). Here, I wish to discuss how struggles over the meanings of health are part of workers' social critique of work discipline, and of managers' attempts to extend control over the work force. The management use of workers as "instruments of labor" is paralleled by another set of ideologies, which regards women's bodies as the site of control where gender politics, health, and educational practices intersect (cf. Foucault 1980).

In the Japanese factories based in Malaysia, management ideology constructs the female body in terms of its biological functionality for, and its anarchic disruption of, production. These ideologies operate to fix women workers in subordinate positions in systems of domination that proliferate

in high-tech industries. A Malaysian investment brochure advertises "the oriental girl," for example, as "qualified *by nature and inheritance* to contribute to the efficiency of a bench assembly production line" (FIDA 1975, emphasis added). This biological rationale for the commodification of women's bodies is a part of a pervasive discourse reconceptualizing women for high-tech production requirements. Japanese managers in the free-trade zone talk about the "eyesight," "manual dexterity," and "patience" of young women to perform tedious micro-assembly jobs. An engineer put the female nature-technology relationship in a new light: "Our work is designed for females." Within international capitalism,[9] this notion of women's bodies renders them analogous to the status of the computer chips they make. Computer chips, like "oriental girls," are identical, whether produced in Malaysia, Taiwan, or Sri Lanka. For multinational corporations, women are units of much cheap labor power repackaged under the "nimble fingers" label.

The abstract mode of scientific discourse also separates "normal" from "abnormal" workers, that is, those who do not perform according to factory requirements. In the EJI factory, the Malay personnel manager using the biomedical model to locate the sources of spirit possession among workers noted that the first spirit attack occurred five months after the factory began operation in 1976. Thereafter,

> "we had our counter-measure. I think this is a method of how you give initial education to the workers, how you take care of the medical welfare of the workers. The worker who is weak, comes in without breakfast, lacking sleep, then she will see ghosts!"

In the factory environment, "spirit attacks" *(kena hantu)* was often used interchangeably with "mass hysteria," a term adopted from English language press reports on such incidents. In the manager's view, "hysteria" was a symptom of physical adjustment as the women workers "move from home idleness to factory discipline." This explanation also found favor with some members of the work force. Scientific terms like *"penyakit histeria"* (hysteria sickness), and physiological preconditions formulated by the management, became more acceptable to some workers. One woman remarked,

> "They say they say *hantu,* but I don't know. . . . I believe that maybe they . . . when they come to work, they did not fill their stomachs, they were not full so that they felt hungry. But they were not brave enough to say so."

A male technician used more complex concepts, but remained doubtful.

> "I think that this [is caused by] a feeling of 'complex'—that maybe 'inferiority complex' is pressing them down—their spirit, so that this can be called an illness of the spirit, 'conflict *jiwa*,' 'emotional conflict.' Sometimes they see an old man, in black shrouds, they say, in their microscopes, they say. . . . I myself don't know how. They see *hantu* in different

places. . . . Some time ago an 'emergency' incident like this occurred in a boarding school. The victim fainted. Then she became very strong. . . . It required ten or twenty persons to handle her."

In corporate discourse, physical "facts" that contributed to spirit possession were isolated, while psychological notions were used as explanation and as a technique of manipulation. In the ENI factory, a *bomoh* was hired to produce the illusion of exorcism, lulling the workers into a false sense of security. The personnel manager claimed that unlike managers in other Japanese firms who operated on the "basis of feelings," his "psychological approach" helped to prevent recurrent spirit visitations.

> "You cannot dispel *kampung* beliefs. Now and then we call the *bomoh* to come, every six months or so, to pray, walk around. Then we take pictures of the *bomoh* in the factory and hang up the pictures. Somehow, the workers seeing these pictures feel safe, [seeing] that the place has been exorcised."

Similarly, whenever a new section of the factory was constructed, the *bomoh* was sent for to sprinkle holy water, thereby assuring workers that the place was rid of ghosts. Regular *bomoh* visits and their photographic images were different ways of defining a social reality, which simultaneously acknowledged and manipulated the workers' fear of spirits.

Medical personnel were also involved in the narrow definition of the causes of spirit incidents on the shop floor. A factory nurse periodically toured the shop floor to offer coffee to tired or drowsy workers. Workers had to work eight-hour shifts six days a week—morning, 6:30 A.M. to 2:30 P.M.; afternoon, 2:30 P.M. to 10:30 P.M.; or night, 10:30 P.M. to 6:30 A.M.—which divided up the 24-hour daily operation of the factories. They were permitted two ten-minute breaks and a half-hour for a meal. Most workers had to change to a different shift every two weeks. This regime allowed little time for workers to recover from their exhaustion between shifts. In addition, overtime was frequently imposed. The shifts also worked against the human, and especially, female cycle; many freshly recruited workers regularly missed their sleep, meals, and menstrual cycles.

Thus, although management pointed to physiological problems as causing spirit attacks, they seldom acknowledged deeper scientific evidence of health hazards in microchip assembly plants. These include the rapid deterioration of eyesight caused by the prolonged use of microscopes in bonding processes. General exposure to strong solvents, acids, and fumes induced headaches, nausea, dizziness, and skin irritation in workers. More toxic substances used for cleaning purposes exposed workers to lead poisoning, kidney failure, and breast cancer (Federation of Women Lawyers 1983:16). Other materials used in the fabrication of computer chips have been linked to female workers' painful menstruation, their inability to conceive, and repeated miscarriages (*Business Times* [*Asia*], 9 October 1982:19; *San*

Francisco Chronicle, 14 January 1987:23, 27). Within the plants, unhappy-looking workers were urged to talk over their problems with the "industrial relations assistant." Complaints of "pain in the chest" were interpreted to mean emotional distress, and the worker was ushered into the clinic for medication in order to maintain discipline and a relentless work schedule.

In the EJI factory, the shop floor supervisor admitted, "I think that hysteria is related to the job in some cases." He explained that workers in the microscope sections were usually the ones to *kena hantu,* and thought that perhaps they should not begin work doing those tasks. However, he quickly offered other interpretations that had little to do with work conditions: There was one victim whose broken engagement had incurred her mother's wrath; at work she cried and talked to herself, saying, "I am not to be blamed, not me!" Another worker, seized by possession, screamed, "Send me home, send me home!" Apparently, she indicated, her mother had taken all her earnings. Again, through such psychological readings, the causes of spirit attacks produced in the factories were displaced onto workers and their families.

In corporate discourse, both the biomedical and psychological interpretations of spirit possession defined the affliction as an attribute of individuals rather than stemming from the general social situation. Scientific concepts, pharmaceutical treatment, and behavioral intervention all identified and separated recalcitrant workers from "normal" ones; disruptive workers became patients. According to Parsons, the cosmopolitan medical approach tolerates illness as sanctioned social deviance; however, patients have the duty to get well (1985:146, 149). This attitude implies that those who do not get well cannot be rewarded with "the privileges of being sick" (1985:149). In the ENI factory, the playing out of this logic provided the rationale for dismissing workers who had had two previous experiences of spirit attacks, on the grounds of "security." This policy drew protests from village elders, for whom spirits in the factory were the cause of their daughters' insecurity. The manager agreed verbally with them, but pointed out that these "hysterical, mental types" might hurt themselves when they flailed against the machines, risking electrocution. By appearing to agree with native theory, the management reinterpreted spirit possession as a symbol of flawed character and culture.[10] The sick role was reconceptualized as internally produced by outmoded thought and behavior not adequately adjusted to the demands of factory discipline. The worker-patient could have no claim on management sympathy but would have to bear responsibility for her own cultural deficiency. A woman in ENI talked sadly about her friend, the victim of spirits and corporate policy.

> "At the time the management wanted to throw her out, to end her work, she cried. She did ask to be reinstated, but she has had three [episodes] already. . . . I think that whether it was right or not [to expel her] depends [on the circumstances], because she has already worked here for a long time; now that

she has been thrown out she does not know what she can do, you know."

The nonrecognition of social obligations to workers lies at the center of differences in worldview between Malay workers and the foreign management. By treating the signs and symptoms of disease as "things-in-themselves" (Taussig 1980:1), the biomedical model freed managers from any moral debt owed the workers. Furthermore, corporate adoption of spirit idiom stigmatized spirit victims, thereby ruling out any serious consideration of their needs. Afflicted and "normal" workers alike were made to see that spirit possession was nothing but confusion and delusion, which should be abandoned in a rational worldview.

THE WORK OF CULTURE: HYGIENE AND DISPOSSESSION

Modern factories transplanted to the Third World are involved in the work of producing exchange as well as symbolic values. Medicine, as a branch of cosmopolitan science, has attained a place in schemes for effecting desired social change in indigenous cultures. While native statements about bizarre events are rejected as irrational, the conceptions of positivist science acquire a quasi-religious flavor (Karnoouh 1984). In the process, the native "work of culture," which transforms motives and affects into "publicly accepted sets of meanings and symbols" (Obeyesekere 1985:147), is being undermined by an authoritative discourse that suppresses lived experiences apprehended through the worldview of indigenous peoples.

To what extent can the *bomoh*'s work of culture convert the rage and distress of possessed women in Malaysia into socially shared meanings? As discussed above, the spirit imagery speaks of danger and violation as young Malay women intrude into hitherto forbidden spirit or male domains. Their participation as an industrial force is subconsciously perceived by themselves and their families as a threat to the ordering of Malay culture. Second, their employment as production workers places them directly in the control of male strangers who monitor their every move. These social relations, brought about in the process of industrial capitalism, are experienced as a moral disorder in which workers are alienated from their bodies, the products of their work, and their own culture. The spirit idiom is therefore a language of protest against these changing social circumstances. A male technician evaluated the stresses they were under.

> "There is a lot of discipline. . . . but when there is too much discipline . . . it is not good. Because of this the operators, with their small wages, will always contest. They often break the machines in ways that are not apparent. . . . Sometimes, they damage the products."

Such Luddite actions in stalling production reverse momentarily the arrangement whereby work regimentation controls the human body. However, the workers' resistance[11] is not limited to the technical problem of work organization, but addresses the violation of moral codes. A young woman explained her sense of having been "tricked" into an intolerable work arrangement.

> "For instance, . . . sometimes . . . they want us to raise production. This is what we sometimes challenge. The workers want fair treatment, as for instance, in relation to wages and other matters. We feel that in this situation there are many [issues] to dispute over with the management. . . . with our wages so low we feel as though we have been tricked or forced."

She demands "justice, because sometimes they exhaust us very much as if they do not think that we too are human beings!"

Spirit possession episodes may be taken as expressions both of fear and of resistance against the multiple violations of moral boundaries in the modern factory. They are acts of rebellion, symbolizing what cannot be spoken directly, calling for a renegotiation of obligations between the management and workers. However, technocrats have turned a deaf ear to such protests, to this moral indictment of their woeful cultural judgments about the dispossessed. By choosing to view possession episodes narrowly as sickness caused by physiological and psychological maladjustment, the management also manipulates the *bomoh* to serve the interests of the factory rather than express the needs of the workers.

Both Japanese factories in Kuala Langat have commenced operations in a spate of spirit possession incidents. A year after operations began in the EJI factory, a well-known *bomoh* and his retinue were invited to the factory *surau*, where they read prayers over a basin of "pure water." Those who had been visited by the devil drank from it and washed their faces, a ritual which made them immune to future spirit attacks. The *bomoh* pronounced the *hantu* controlling the factory site "very kind"; he merely showed himself but did not disturb people. A month after the ritual, the spirit attacks resumed, but involving smaller numbers of women (one or two) in each incident. The manager claimed that after the exorcist rites, spirit attacks occurred only once a month.

In an interview, an eye witness reported what happened after a spirit incident erupted.

> "The work section was not shut down, we had to continue working. Whenever it happened, the other workers felt frightened. They were not allowed to look because [the management] feared contagion. They would not permit us to leave. When an incident broke out, we had to move away. . . . At ten o'clock they called the *bomoh* to come . . . because he knew that the *hantu* had already entered the woman's body. He came in and scattered rice flour water all over the area where the incident broke out. He recited prayers over holy water. He sprinkled rice flour water on places touched by the *hantu*. . . . The *bomoh* chanted incantations [*jampi jampi*] chasing the *hantu* away. He then gave some medicine to the afflicted. . . . He also entered the clinic [to pronounce] *jampi jampi*."

The primary role of the *bomoh* hired by corporate management was to ritually cleanse the prayer room, shop floor, and even the factory clinic. After appeasing the spirits, he ritually healed the victims, who were viewed as not responsible for their affliction. However, his work did not extend to curing them after they had been given sedatives and sent home. Instead, through his exorcism and incantations, the *bomoh* expressed the Malay understanding of these disturbing events, perhaps impressing the other workers that the factory had been purged of spirits. However, he failed to convince the management about the need to create a moral space, in Malay terms, on factory premises. Management did not respond to spirit incidents by reconsidering social relationships on the shop floor; instead, they sought to eliminate the afflicted from the work scene. As the ENI factory nurse, an Indian woman, remarked, "It is an experience working with the Japanese. They do not consult women. To tell you the truth, they don't care about the problem except that it goes away."

This avoidance of the moral challenge was noted by workers in the way management handled the *kenduri*, the ritual feast that resolved a dispute by bringing the opposing sides together in an agreement over future cooperation. In the American factory incident in Penang, a *bomoh* was sent for, but worker demands for a feast were ignored. At the EJI factory, cleansing rituals were brought to a close by a feast of saffron rice and chicken curry. This was served to factory managers and officers, but not a single worker (or victim) was invited. This distortion of the Malay rite of commensality did not fail to impress on workers the management rejection of moral responsibility to personal needs—*muafakat* (see Banks 1983:123–124). Women workers remained haunted by their fear of negotiating the liminal spaces between female and male worlds, old and new morality, when mutual obligations between the afflicted and the *bomoh*, workers and the management, had not been fulfilled.

The work of the *bomoh* was further thwarted by the medicalization of the afflicted. Spirit possession incidents in factories made visible the conflicted women who did not fit the corporate image of "normal" workers. By standing apart from the workaday routine, possessed workers inadvertently exposed themselves to the cold ministrations of modern medicine, rather than the increased social support they sought. Other workers, terrified of being attacked and by the threat of expulsion, kept up a watchful vigilance. This induced self-regulation was reinforced by the scientific gaze of supervisors and nurses, which further enervated the recalcitrant and frustrated those who resisted. A worker observed,

> "[The possessed] don't remember their experiences. Maybe the *hantu* is still working on their madness, maybe because their experiences have not been stilled, or maybe their souls are not really disturbed. They say there are evil spirits in that place [that is, factory]."

In fact, spirit victims maintained a disturbed silence after their "recovery." Neither their families, friends, the *bomoh*, nor I could get them to talk about their experiences.

Spirit possession episodes in different societies have been labeled "mass psychogenic illness" or "epidemic hysteria" in psychological discourse (Colligan, Pennebaker, and Murphy 1982). Different altered states of consciousness, which variously spring from indigenous understanding of social situations, are reinterpreted in cosmopolitan terms considered universally applicable. In multinational factories located overseas, this ethnotherapeutic model (Lutz 1985) is widely applied and made to seem objective and rational. However, we have seen that such scientific knowledge and practices can display a definite prejudice against the people they are intended to restore to well-being in particular cultural contexts. The reinterpretation of spirit possession may therefore be seen as a shift of locus of patriarchal authority from the *bomoh,* sanctioned by indigenous religious beliefs, toward professionals sanctioned by scientific training.

In Third World contexts, cosmopolitan medical concepts and drugs often have an anesthetizing effect, which erases the authentic experiences of the sick. More frequently, the proliferation of positivist scientific meanings also produces a fragmentation of the body, a shattering of social obligations, and a separation of individuals from their own culture. Gramsci (1971) has defined hegemony as a form of ideological domination based on the consent of the dominated, a consent that is secured through the diffusion of the worldview of the dominant class. In Malaysia, medicine has become part of hegemonic discourse, constructing a "modern" outlook by clearing away the nightmarish visions of Malay workers. However, as a technique of both concealment and control, it operates in a more sinister way than native beliefs in demons. Malay factory women may gradually become dispossessed of spirits and their own culture, but they remain profoundly dis-eased in the "brave new workplace."[12]

NOTES

Acknowledgments. I am grateful to the National Science Foundation (grant no. BNS-787639), and the International Development Research Centre, Ottawa, for funding the fieldwork and writing of the project. Some of the material contained in this paper has been published in my book, *Spirits of Resistance and Capitalist Discipline: Factory Women in Malaysia* (1987).

1. "Free-trade zones" are fenced-off areas in which multinational corporations are permitted to locate export-processing industries in the host country. These zones are exempt from many taxation and labor regulations that may apply elsewhere in the economy.

2. Singapore is an island state situated south of Peninsular Malaysia. Although separate countries, they share historical roots and many cultural similarities and interests.

3. That is, West Malaysia. East Malaysia is constituted by the states of Sabah and Sarawak in northern Borneo. In Peninsular Malaysia, more than half the population (approximately 13 million) is made up of Malays. Ethnic Chinese form the main minority group, followed by Indians.

4. Mainly between the ages of 16 and 26 years. Many dropped out after six or seven years because they saw no improvement in their jobs as production workers and because of marriage. In the cities, the women lived in rooming houses or dormitories or with relatives.

5. Most village girls began buying and wearing sanitary pads after they enrolled in secular schools or began work in factories. In some cases, schools and factories supplied these market items to encourage the girls to wear them, often against their will. Village girls had previously worn homemade girdles lined with kapok.

6. Most of the factory women in the Kuala Langat free-trade zone lived with their families in the nearby villages, commuting to work every day. Although parents were eager for their daughters to earn wages, they were also anxious about the social effects of their participation in the wider, culturally alien world (see Ong 1987: Parts II and III).

7. Government regulations required multinational factories to provide female workers with maternity leave of 60 consecutive days. This right has had the unintended effect of discouraging multinational factories from recruiting married women. Those who got married on the job were offered family planning classes and free contraceptives.

8. In a survey, the Malaysian Federation of Women Lawyers found that some managerial staff in multinational factories were guilty of demanding sexual favors in return for promises of work benefits, bonuses, and promotion. However, their victims "ignorant of their rights [had] nobody to turn to to voice their woes" (Federation of Women Lawyers 1983:18).

9. Such talk is not confined to Japanese corporations. In the world of semiconductor production, American and European firms also perpetuate such views.

10. I therefore see a more complex process at work than Ackerman and Lee who note that by reifying spirit possession as the cause of these bizarre incidents, the management of a shoe factory served "to reinforce the belief in the reality of spirit possession" (1981:797).

11. The vast majority of electronics workers in Malaysian free-trade zones are not unionized, even though government policy does not formally forbid union organization. However, the Ministry of Labour has repeatedly frustrated the efforts of electronics workers to unionize.

12. This phrase is borrowed from Howard's (1985) study of changing work relations occasioned by the introduction of computer technology into offices and industries.

REFERENCES CITED

Ackerman, Susan, and Raymond Lee
    1981   Communication and Cognitive Pluralism in a Spirit Possession Event in Malaysia. American Ethnologist 8(4):789–799.
Banks, David J.
    1983   Malay Kinship. Philadelphia, PA: ISHI.
Braverman, Harry
    1974   Labor and Monopoly Capital: The Degradation of Work in the Twentieth Century. New York: Monthly Review Press.
Chew, P. K.
    1978   How to Handle Hysterical Factory Workers. Occupational Health and Safety 47(2):50–53.
Colligan, Michael, James Pennebaker, and Lawrence Murphy, eds.
    1982   Mass Psychogenic Illness: A Social Psychological Analysis. Hillsdale, NJ: Lawrence Erlbaum Associates.
Crapanzano, Vincent
    1977   Introduction. In Case Studies in Spirit Possession. Vincent Crapanzano and Vivian Garrison, eds. pp. 1–40. New York: John Wiley.
Crapanzano, Vincent, and Vivian Garrison, eds.
    1977   Case Studies in Spirit Possession. New York: John Wiley.
Douglas, Mary
    1966   Purity and Danger: An Analysis of Pollution and Taboo. Harmondsworth, England: Penguin.
Ellul, Jacques
    1964   The Technological Society. John Wilkinson, trans. New York: Vintage.
Endicott, Kirk M.
    1970   Analysis of Malay Magic. Oxford, England: Clarendon Press.
Federation of Women Lawyers (Malaysia)
    1983   Women and Employment in Malaysia. Presented at the Seminar on Women and the Law, 29 April–1 May, 1983. Kuala Lumpur. Unpublished manuscript.
FIDA (Federal Industrial Development Authority), Malaysia
    1975   Malaysia: The Solid State for Electronics. Kuala Lumpur.
Firth, Raymond
    1967   Ritual and Drama in Malay Spirit Mediumship. Comparative Studies in Society and History 9:190–207.
Foucault, Michel
    1965   Madness and Civilization: A History of Insanity in the Age of Reason. R. Howard, trans. New York: Pantheon.
    1979   Discipline and Punish: The Birth of the Prison. Alan Sheridan, trans. New York: Vintage.
    1980   An Introduction. History of Sexuality, Vol. 1. Robert Hurley, trans. New York: Vintage.
Gramsci, Antonio
    1971   Selections for the Prison Notebooks. Quentin Hoare and Geoffrey Nowell Smith, trans. New York: International Publishing.
Howard, Robert
    1985   Brave New Workplace. New York: Viking Books.
Jamilah Ariffin
    1980   Industrial Development in Peninsular Malaysia and Rural-Urban Migration of Women Workers: Impact and Implications. Jurnal Ekonomi Malaysia 1:41–59.
Karnoouh, Claude
    1984   Culture and Development. Telos 61:71–82.
Kessler, Clive S.
    1977   Conflict and Sovereignty in Kelantan Malay Spirit Seances. In Case Studies in Spirit Possession. Vincent Crapanzano and Vivian Garrison, eds. pp. 295–331. New York: John Wiley.

Laderman, Carol
    1983   Wives and Midwives: Childbirth and Nutrition in
        Rural Malaysia. Berkeley: University of California
        Press.
Lewis, Joan M.
    1971   Ecstatic Religion: An Anthropological Study of Spirit
        Possession and Shamanism. Harmondsworth, England:
        Penguin.
Lim, Linda
    1978   Women Workers in Multinational Corporations: The
        Case of the Electronics Industry in Malaysia and
        Singapore. Ann Arbor: Michigan Occasional Papers in
        Women's Studies, No. 9.
Lutz, Catherine
    1985   Depression and the Translation of Emotional Worlds.
        In Culture and Depression. Arthur Kleinman and Byron
        Good, eds. pp. 63–100. Berkeley: University of
        California Press.
Maxwell, W. E.
    1977   Shamanism in Perak. In The Centenary Volume,
        1877–1977, pp. 222–232. Singapore: The Council,
        Malaysian Branch of the Royal Asiatic Society,
        1977–1978. [Originally published 1883]
Mohd. Taib bin Osman
    1972   Patterns of Supernatural Premises Underlying the
        Institution of the Bomoh in Malay Culture. Bijdragen tot
        de Taal-Land-en Volkekunde 128:219–234.
Obeyesekere, Gananath
    1985   Depression, Buddhism, and the Work of Culture in
        Sri Lanka. In Culture and Depression. Arthur Kleinman
        and Byron Good, eds. pp. 134–152. Berkeley: University
        of California Press.

Ong, Aihwa
    1987   Spirits of Resistance and Capitalist Discipline:
        Factory Women in Malaysia. Albany: State University of
        New York Press.
Parsons, Talcott
    1985   Illness and the Role of the Physician: A Sociological
        Perspective. In Readings from Talcott Parsons. Peter
        Hamilton, ed. pp. 145–155. New York: Tavistock.
Phoon, W. H.
    1982   Outbreaks of Mass Hysteria at Workplaces in Singapore:
        Some Patterns and Modes of Presentation. In Mass
        Psychogenic Illness: A Social Psychological Analysis.
        Michael Colligan, James Pennebaker, and Lawrence Murphy,
        eds. pp. 21–31. Hillsdale, NJ: Lawrence Erlbaum Associates.
Sabbah, Fatna A.
    1984   Woman in the Muslim Unconscious. Mary Jo
        Lakeland, trans. New York: Pergamon Press.
Scheper-Hughes, Nancy, and Margaret Lock
    1987   The Mindful Body: A Prolegomenon to Future Work
        in Medical Anthropology. Medical Anthropology
        Quarterly 1(1):1–36.
Skeat, Walter W.
    1965[1900]   Malay Magic. London: Frank Cass.
Taussig, Michael
    1980   Reification and the Consciousness of the Patient.
        Social Science and Medicine 148:3–13.
Teoh, Jin-Inn, Saesmalijah Soewondo, and Myra Sidharta
    1975   Epidemic Hysteria in Malaysian Schools: An
        Illustrative Episode. Psychiatry 38:258–268.
Winstedt, Richard O.
    1961   The Malays: A Cultural History. London: Routledge
        and Kegan Paul.

Japanese Death Rituals in Transit: From Household Ancestors to Beloved Antecedents[1]

Hikaru Suzuki

In this essay, Hikaru Suzuki explores modern death practices in Japan that might seem unusual to Americans. These include the living funeral, a funeral and party people who are still alive hold for themselves; the musical funeral; and the scattering of ashes. Suzuki notes that all of these are very modern ideas and

"Japanese Death Rituals in Transit: From Household Ancestors to Beloved Antecedents" by H. Suzuki (1998) *Journal of Contemporary Religion* 13:2, 171-188. Reprinted by permission of the author and Taylor & Francis Ltd., http://www.tandf.co.uk/journals.

are not only different from traditional Japanese notions of the right way to perform a funeral, but actively oppose them.

Suzuki argues that the change in funeral customs is directly related to changing social conditions in Japan. Before World War II, Japanese society was largely organized by extended households. Maintaining an extended family and the inheritance of wealth within that family was of primary importance both in the structuring of society and in people's understanding of themselves. Households were anchored by ancestors, and prayers and devotions to these were considered fundamental in assuring prosperity. Since World War II, social and legal changes have severed the relationship between people and their ancestors. Increasingly, people moved from the countryside to the city and from extended families to nuclear families. Both economic and social worth came to be understood as the result of individual effort rather than family ancestry. These changes have created basic changes in people's religious lives. Because ancestors are no longer very important, religious funerals aimed at creating and praying to them are not important either. Instead, funerals celebrate individual achievement and memory.

This essay is a fine example of the ways in which changes in social and economic conditions may change people's religious lives and their beliefs. Though American and Japanese religious beliefs vary widely, it is interesting to note that social changes have also caused a transformation in American death practices. As we note in section 9, the grand funerals and decorative cemeteries of late-nineteenth and early-twentieth-century America have increasingly been replaced by simple funerals, cremation, and low-cast, low-maintenance burial.

As you read, consider these questions:

1. Why are Japanese funeral customs changing?
2. What do "living funerals" tell us about the meaning of death in Japan?
3. Nonreligious funerals reflect changes in attitudes about ancestors and the afterlife. What are these changes, and why have they occurred?

INTRODUCTION

When I was conducting fieldwork at one of the funeral companies in Japan,[2] I observed many instances where Japanese people expressed their dissatisfaction with the commercialized funeral services offered by the industry. One warm autumn day I accompanied the company sales staff, who were marketing funeral discounts to Elder's Clubs (rôjinkai), to the home of Mr H., the head of Takano Elder's Club. As my colleagues began to explain the discount offer to Mr H., he looked at us with distaste and said, "Discount on funerals? Forget about funerals-after-death, we need discounts on funerals-while-alive!" Then he began to tell us about his plans for his living-funeral. "I am going to have my living-funeral on December 1, 1997, the year I turn 77."[3] Mr H. said with determination, "I am going to carry it out because I want to enjoy my own funeral when I am alive and not when I am dead!" I asked him why he wanted to have a living-funeral. Mr H. answered that he did not believe in an afterlife nor did he care too much about it. "Who knows exactly what will become of me after I am dead? Maybe the afterlife is heaven and our life now is hell. But the important

point is that I can only feel now." He said that he would reserve an auditorium in a hotel, inviting 200 to 300 people: relatives, colleagues and friends. He would borrow an altar from a funeral company and decorate the auditorium with many colorful western flowers, such as carnations, lilies and roses. "No chrysanthemums," he said.[4]

According to his plan, when the ceremony begins, the lights will be dimmed to simulate a real funeral, and his colleagues and friends will read memorial addresses about him. After the memorial addresses, he will have a birthday party. The altar and other funeral objects will be removed, the lights become bright, and cheerful music will be played. He said that he would not ask for any incense-money; instead, he would send invitation cards just as if he was having a birthday party. A new idea in Mr H.'s living-funeral is the return-gift[5] he will prepare for his attendants. "I will order my favorite apple pies from the best bakery. I've already told the baker that I will need 300 pies on that day!" While he explained this to me, his eyes were shining, as if he could hardly wait.

At the end of the interview,[6] he criticized contemporary funeral ceremonies, saying: "Funerals that cost so much are meaningless unless the deceased can see and enjoy them. The funeral should be for me, not for family members or others. Why do I need lots of flowers, food, and letters after I am dead and senseless?" I asked, "Then what should your family do when you really pass away? Would you mind if your family conducted another funeral for you?" "Of course not," was his answer. "I have already told my family to cremate me and just put me into a grave or something. After I am dead, well, I am dead! I don't ask for anything. Have you ever heard of a dead man asking for something?" *(Shindara, shindamadeno kotodesu, bokuwa nanimo yôkyû shimasen. Shindemademo monowo nedattanantekoto kiitakotoga arimasuka!?)* And this was said by someone who would be considered a paragon of Japanese tradition, namely a retired instructor of protocol for the Emperor.

Since the beginning of the 1990s new funerary practices, such as the 'living-funeral' *(seizensô)*, the musical-funeral *(ongakusô)* or non-religious funeral, and the scattering of ashes *(shizensô)*, have emerged not as deviant practices, but as a new trend. I consider it as a 'trend' because they are not only introduced by TV shows,[7] journals, magazines[8] and newspapers,[9] but are also promoted by the mass media. A wife who had conducted her husband's funeral by herself published her experience in a book entitled *Home-Made-Funeral (Tezukuri-sôshiki)* which became an instant best-seller (see Nakajô, 1991).

These new funerary practices are not limited to the elite and the professional class, and they have a considerable effect on the marketing of commercialized services.[10] The new trend reflects dissatisfaction with the commercialized funerals offered by funeral companies. In the post-war era, funeral companies greatly expanded, taking over community funeral co-operatives *(sôshiki-gumi)* and extending their services to handle everything from the deceased's physical remains to the ceremonial procedures, transportation and food. The proliferation of funeral services marketed by the industry, however, resulted in funerals that became highly standardized. According to one observer, "[commercialized] funeral ceremonies became a place where one's feelings are locked inside, instead of a location where one could naturally release one's emotions to the deceased" (*Sôgi*, March 1992: i).

What is happening in contemporary Japan is a search for new funeral and mortuary practices that mirror the deceased's life. "The meaning of contemporary funerals is being questioned as an opportunity to evaluate the death of the deceased as an individual person" (Shimada, 1992: 31). The changes in contemporary funerary practice reflect the quest for ceremonies that emphasise the deceased as an individual, not as a member of a household or as a 'household ancestor-to-be.' Thus, the contemporary trends in funerary practices can be understood as a challenge, not just to commercialized funerals, but to the notion that the purpose of a funeral is to create household ancestors.

This essay demonstrates how new funerary and mortuary practices commemorate the individual's death in the form of 'memorialism' (see Smith, 1974: 145–146)[11] and have shifted away from death ceremonies that are part of the collective rite of the kinship group and its continuation. To this end, I will introduce the emerging funerary customs—the living-funeral, the musical or non-religious funeral, and the scattering of ashes—and examine why and how such new trends have arisen. I argue that these contemporary funerary customs reflect the decline of ancestor worship, on the one hand, and the growing desire in Japan to be remembered as a unique individual person upon one's death, on the other hand.

THE LIVING-FUNERAL (SEIZENSÔ): WHO NEEDS A FUNERAL-AFTER-DEATH?

The Living-Funeral

Seizen-sô, which literally means a 'funeral-while-alive,' is a funeral conducted by oneself while one is still alive and healthy. When a TV station broadcast the first such funeral for the singer Mizunoe Takiko, the coverage by the mass media was widespread and intense. The deceased-to-be Mizunoe described her funeral by saying, "I wanted to express my appreciation to all those who have been dear to me while I am still alive" (Ei, 1994: 104). Her living-funeral took place at the Tokyû Hotel on February 19, 1992. The chairman of the ceremony, Ei Rokusuke, describes its success in his book *Happy Ending (Dai-ôjô)*. "Mizunoe's living-funeral was a parody of a common funeral ceremony," he wrote. "It followed the same practices as in typical funerals, such as the burning of incense to the deceased and the reading of memorial addresses" (ibid). What was different, however, was the way in which the *sutra* chanting and music

were presented. Ei edited and composed a tape which was a mixture of *sutra* chanting and music from various *genres*. He included, among others, Buddhist *sutra*, Koran prayers, Chopin's 'Funeral Procession,' Tibetan *sutra*, carols and Mozart's 'Requiem.' The musical selections were edited and cut into 1 or 2 minutes in sequence to make a 20-minute tape. While the tape was played, the deceased-to-be's friends and colleagues presented memorial addresses. At the last song on the tape, the piquant selection 'Santa Claus is Coming to Town,' the participants began to clap their hands and the funeral turned into a cheerful party (see Ei, 1994: 106).

Another example of a living-funeral was carried out for and by Mr Kaneda, a man of 53 who had retired from Mainichi Newspapers and established a publishing company called Tôyô-Media (see *Sôgi*, July 1993: 17). On April 26, 1993, Mr Kaneda, wearing an angel's halo above his head, wings on his back and a banner (displaying the epitaph 'today's hero'), welcomed 140 guests at the entrance to a hall in Tokyo. The first half of the ceremony imitated a traditional funeral; the chairman announced the beginning of the ceremony and memorial addresses were presented by his colleagues. One read:

> Mr Kaneda was a man who surmounted his hard times with his easy-going nature. He has been a successful journalist and I have heard that he will be reincarnated for the development of Tôyô-Media and return from the universe full of satellites flying around. At this solemn ceremony, I wish for his new life that he continues to expand his experiences, knowledge, and the relationships which were nurtured during his journalist years. (*Sôgi*, July 1993: 18)

The telegrams sent to him were as humorous as the memorial addresses. While both were being read, Mr Kaneda sat in the front of the audience as if he were listening from the 'Other World.' However, as soon as the chairman finished reading the telegrams, he took off his halo and wings, stood in front of the audience, and announced: "I have just come back from the world of the dead!" (ibid) At this statement, the funeral was transformed into a party, with champagne and games, which lasted late into the night.

The Changing Value of Death: The Implications of the 'Living-Funeral'

Why would someone wish to have a funeral, while s/he is still alive? In spite of the joyous images of living-funerals, the reasons behind them underscore serious problems in the dying process in present-day Japan. The meaning of the living-funeral is two-fold. It expresses the fear and uncertainty about what happens after death; it also demonstrates the isolation of the elderly, of those who are in the process of dying.

A living-funeral is the celebration of one's life. Like birthdays, living-funerals provide an occasion for gathering old friends and colleagues, and enjoying their friendship. Moreover, it is a time when one's deeds are commemorated.

Such a celebration gives the organizer the opportunity to reflect upon and appreciate the value of his/her own life. The desire to celebrate one's life goes hand in hand with the contemporary fear that one's death might not have any real meaning for the bereaved.

In the past, death explicitly meant becoming an ancestor of one's household. The son's sense of obligation to venerate the ancestors, to care for his elders, and to provide a funeral was firmly rooted, based on the succession of the household and its ancestors, which in turn assured one's own continuance into the future. This idea, however, was affected by the post-war Civil Code in which property inheritance and ancestral worship were divided into two separate categories, thus severing the link between succession and ancestral rites.[12]

The importance attached to the role of ancestors was also attenuated by the devaluation of the continuation of the household, which occurred in connection with the general reduction of inheritance, the large-scale migration to the cities, and the descendants' abilities to secure economic independence without depending on the ancestral land. Once the balanced relationship between the living and the ancestors of the household, which had been sustained by economic succession, as well as spiritual exchanges, was upset by social changes, the funeral ceremonies began to reflect the fact that the household succession was undermined. Although it is still considered the children's responsibility to provide a funeral for their parents (siblings and relatives take over in the cases where the deceased is without spouse or children), this relies more and more on the children's willingness and less on a sense of household obligation. Consequently, the present-day meaning of one's death depends on how the living value the deceased's life. With little inheritance to bequeath, and without the veneration of household ancestors, the ritual surrounding a person's death relies on the attachment and esteem of others. A living-funeral reflects a wish to be judged, while one is still healthy, when one's deeds have not been forgotten, and while one's friends and colleagues are still alive. In this sense, a living-funeral is a way to combat the uncertainty about the meaning of death by reasserting one's own feeling of worth.

The living-funeral is a response to the isolation that many of the elderly now face in the process of dying. The life-span of the Japanese has been significantly extended in the post-war era. The average life expectancy in 1992 was 76 years for men and 82 years for women, while in 1955, it was 63 for men and 67 for women (Keizai-Kikaku-chô, 1994: 43). While a longer life expectancy demonstrates medical advances, it also implies a growing problem in Japanese society. There are only 8,000 nursing homes and they serve only about 264,000 people (Asahi Shimbun Chôsabu, 1994: 639). Since there are about 11,000,000 Japanese over the age of 70 (Keizai Kikakuchô Chôsakyoku, 1994: 42), the current institutions can only handle 2.5% of the elderly population. Due to the shortage of nursing homes, 61.8% of the elderly

were living with their children as of 1985 (Sômuchô-Tôkeikyoku, 1990: 66). Many elderly people choose to live with their spouse or alone until they desperately need help. During interviews, the elderly have expressed feelings of guilt for burdening their children when they become feeble.

One of the results of longevity is that the funeral ceremony will be marred by the memories of a long-bedridden deceased. If all of the deceased's peers have died, no one will clearly recollect the person or what was good about their life. Moreover, a substantial portion of the inheritance might have been drained away by medical expenses. In a recent survey, 45.6% of the respondents thought that property succession should be accorded to those who cared for their parents and only 11.3% thought that property should be inherited by the eldest son (NLI Research Institute, 1994: 271–272; see also Table 1). As a result, more daughters are receiving property inheritance than before, because they are often responsible for taking care of their parents in old age.[13] "Property inheritance here is seen as the reward for taking care of their parents" (NLI Research Institute, 1994: 271–272) and demonstrates that most people see this as a heavy burden.

This condition disrupts one of the important functions of a funeral ceremony, namely to celebrate the deceased's life. "Funerals are inevitably occasions for summing up an individual's social personality, by a restatement not only of the roles he has filled, but also of the general way in which he has conducted himself during his lifetime" (Goody, 1962: 29). Through the transmission of inheritance and succession to a rightful heir the deceased's life is socially recognized and valued upon his death. Of course this still occurs in funeral ceremonies today, but not when the deceased has little inheritance, few surviving colleagues, and underwent a long period of senescence. The tension and fatigue that result when family members who are themselves entering old age must care for the elderly, is reflected in this excerpt from the magazine *Sôgi*:

> "I hate my mother." The words came out of my mouth during my mother's wake. My sister-in-law looked at me with distaste. My mother took care of me for twenty years [when I was growing up], but I took care of her for thirty years, ever since she collapsed of poor health. The last ten years of her life she spent in bed, responding little to the outside world. . . . Her body became smaller and smaller but cleaning her remained a troublesome task, for I myself was no longer young. . . . When the doctor, who came to write a death certificate for her, said to me, "you have done a good job," my eyes filled with tears. The tears were not for my mother's [death] but for myself. (*Sôgi*, January 1995: i)

A funeral mirrors the conditions of a person's dying process. Funerals for elders who have long been bedridden have an atmosphere of detachment, formality and aimlessness, created by the attitude of the participants. A long, drawn-out death which has burdened the living is a bad death. In such deaths, the bereaved express relief rather than

TABLE 1   Consideration Towards Inheritance (Multiple Choice)

Parent's generation	Percentage	Children's generation	Percentage
Majority to the eldest son	30.9%	To the child who takes care of parents	45.6%
No property bequeathed	24.0%	The child who will continue the household [this person probably takes care of parents]	37.3%
Equal amount to all children	23.8%	Equal amount to all children	26.6%
The child who takes care of parents	14.3%	Majority to the eldest son	11.3%
Not thinking of inheritance	11.4%	No inheritance needed	10.0%
The child who will continue the household	4.3%	The child who has the need	3.6%
To the eldest daughter [couples without sons]	4.1%	Division among sons	2.9%
Others	4.1%	Others	1.4%
Division among sons rather than daughters	1.2%	No answer	3.5%
Donation	1.2%		
The child who has the need	0.9%		
No answer	0.6%		

Source: NLI Research Institute, in *Nihon no kazoku wa dou kawattanoka (How the Japanese Family Changed),* 1994: 271.

appreciation for the deceased. This is a real problem for a 70-year-old who states, "I want to have a beautiful ending, leaving a good influence and beautiful memories of myself. For that reason, I want to avoid, by all means, becoming bedridden and demented, thus exposing the ugliness of old age" (*Sôgi*, January 1994: 29). However, a person can only leave 'beautiful memories' upon his/her death, if there are family, friends or colleagues who are willing to celebrate the deceased's life. The recent movement among the elderly to conduct a living-funeral is due to their sense of isolation and the very real possibility of a lonely death. Through organizing a living-funeral, they want to convince themselves and others that their life was meaningful.

NON-RELIGIOUS FUNERALS (*MUSHÛKYÔSÔ*): WHO NEEDS A PRIEST?

Non-Religious Funerals and Musical Funerals

The so-called 'non-religious funeral' (*mu-shûkyô-sô*) is a funeral conducted without priests or religious practices. Often these ceremonies use music to replace religious elements, which is why they are sometimes called 'musical-funerals' (*ongaku-sô*). In most cases, the non-religious funeral ceremony is arranged at the deceased's request, because the person did not belong to any religious sects or believed in a specific religion.

The non-religious funeral ceremony differs in a number of ways from the usual funeral. In his book, *The Funeral (Za Sôshiki)*, Kosugi Teppei, a funeral chairman, describes the non-religious funeral of a university president (Kosugi, 1992: 156–158). The president's ceremony, which was held in the university auditorium, opened with a symphony. Then the hall became dark and a slide show gave a visual account

of the personal history of the deceased, with explanations given by a professional narrator. Following the slides, a film illustrated the most recent phase in the president's life. The auditorium was full of memories of the president, further enhanced by his visualized face and reproduced voice. After the slides and the film, the deceased's enlarged photograph was exhibited at the front of the auditorium. As a chorus sang one of Bach's arias, participants lined up to present flowers to the deceased as a substitute for the incense burning that is traditional at Buddhist ceremonies. Singing gave way to a tape recording of the deceased speaking of his educational concerns and principles. The author Kosugi admired the funeral: "This is a real funeral, I thought. Throughout the event, participants' feeling towards the deceased enveloped the ceremony." (ibid)

Another noteworthy non-religious funeral ceremony was praised by a poet, Matsunaga Goichi, who attended the writer Nakano Shigeharu's funeral. Matsunaga writes:

> The deceased's funeral was simple. We each sent him off merely by presenting a carnation flower in front of his photo. However, we were touched by the beautiful tone of a bamboo flute playing a Romanian melody which summed up and expressed the deceased's personality and life. . . . There was no chanting of sutra, nor were there any Buddhist priests accompanying the funeral. But it was one of the rare funerals in which I was moved beyond expression. The music was not played by the deceased, but the piece had the power of identifying and speaking about the deceased as effectively as the deceased himself could have done. I myself hope to have such a funeral. (Matsunaga, March 1995: 98–99)

In typical Buddhist funerals, participants often fall asleep during the priests' *Sutra* chanting which comprises half of the ceremony. It is not surprising then that a non-religious, musical funeral is admired for its power to celebrate the deceased's life.

Complaints about Buddhist Funerals

The majority of Japanese funerals are Buddhist;[14] this means that Buddhist priests (generally called 'obô-san') are present to chant the *sutras*. What is expressed in the choice of a non-religious funeral ceremony is the wish to avoid these officiants. People find the roles of the priests in funerals meaningless; they also object to the high cost of services (including *sutra* chanting and posthumous titles). Clarifying the problem concerning service fees for priests will illuminate one of the central reasons for choosing non-religious funerals, which in turn will demonstrate the changing meaning of death among contemporary Japanese people.

The cost of the priests' services is openly criticised by the Japanese today. Why did priests raise the fee for the services? Why have the Japanese come to feel that it was too expensive? Are all Buddhist temples making an outrageous profit, as people generally believe? According to a study, carried out in 1990 by a mutual-aid group (*Gojokai*) called 'Living Friend' (*Kurashi no Tomo*), 48.5% of 400 families living in Tokyo, Kanagawa, Chiba, and Saitama believed that the priests' fees were exorbitant (Murakami, 1992: 104). The same study reveals that the cost of services (*o-fuse*) and posthumous names (*kaimyô*) rose by 36% in 3 years, with an average increase of $7,500. Considering that the average cost of funerals (including the outlay for the funeral company, food, gifts, and the priests' fees) is roughly $20,000 (Ôhashi, 1993: 100[15]), the fee paid to priests comprises more than 37% of the funeral expenses. Furthermore, the survey showed that 55.3% of the priests determined and requested the price of their services, rather than depending on what the family decided to pay (Murakami, 1992: 104). The data demonstrate the growing conflict between consumers and Buddhist temples. The question is whether Buddhist priests are really squeezing consumers? A statistical study which appeared in the *Buddhist Priests Monthly Magazine* (*Gekkan Jûshoku*, March 1988) reached a contrary conclusion. The study analysed the annual income of Sôtô-shû sect temples, taken from their total number of 14,007. The income variations are shown in Table 2.

According the these data, only 1,815 temples out of 14,007 have an annual income of more than $50,000. This shows that the gap between the wealthy city temples and the poor temples of the countryside is wide. Thus, the consumers' opinions about expensive service fees seem to be derived from their experiences with city temples.

Why do city temples demand such high fees and why do they continue to do so in spite of heavy criticism? Murakami states that "people who ask Buddhist priests for funeral services in cities are often the first ancestor of the 'household.' They are uncertain about their long-term residence and they have no interest in supporting the temple whose services they have requested" (Murakami, 1992: 105). As city people are not concerned about their relationship with the temples in the long term and merely interested in acquiring funeral services from the priest for that one occasion, priests naturally feel that they should ask for an amount which covers the other fees (subsequent memorial services) that they would have received in community funerals. Thus, the high charges are the result of changes on both sides: the priests are no longer committed to the deceased's families and the bereaved families are no longer committed to their temples.

What has occurred is that Buddhist services have become commodified as the relationship between people and temples changed. Regarding community funeral rituals in the past, Buddhist temples did not have to ask for, nor did they demand, a set price for their services, since their existence was assured by the communities. However, in commercialized funeral ceremonies the ties between temple and community are no longer based on co-operation and balanced exchanges.

It is most important to note that the consumers' perception of 'expensive Buddhist services' is linked to the weakened relationships between household members and Buddhist priests. The blending of ancestor worship and systematic Buddhist rituals occurred gradually, as more people chose to have Buddhist priests officiate at funerals (Nakamura, 1964: 585). In 1640, when the Tokugawa government (1600–1867) forced all commoners to declare their affiliation to Buddhist temples (with the aim of prohibiting Christianity), the ties between Buddhist temples and each household were further solidified. The registration

TABLE 2   Variations of Annual Income Among *Sôtô-shu* Sect Temples (14,007 Temples)

Amount of annual income (in yen)	Number of temples	Percentage of temples
>¥1,000,000 ($10,000)	5,601	40%
¥1,000,000–¥3,000,000	3,809	27.2%
¥3,000,000–¥5,000,000	1,615	11.5%
<¥5,000,000	1,815	13%
No answer	1,167	8.3%

Source: *Buddhist Priests' Monthly Magazine* (*Gekkan Jûshoku* 1988 March) taken from Murakami Kyôkô's "How to analyze the act of funeral ceremony" (*Sôgi to in kôi wo dô yomi tokuka*), *Sôgi* 2(5), 1992: 104.

TABLE 3   Variations of Total Funeral Expenses (461 families)

Funeral expenditures (in yen)	Differences in funeral expenses (per cent)
> ¥300,000 ($3000)	0.9
¥300,000–500,000	2.6
¥500,000–1,000,000	7.4
¥1,000,000–1,500,000	11.3
¥1,500,000–2,000,000	16.7
¥2,000,000–3,000,000	27.8
< ¥3,000,000	26.0

Source: Ôhashi Keiko, "Sôgi no jittai to sezen-keiyaku ni kansuru ishikichôsa" (The Condition of Funeral Ceremonies and Perception towards Living Contract), *Sôgi* 3(4), 1993: 98–100.

of households with Buddhist temples, called the 'parochial system' (*danka-seido*), also reinforced the conceptual link between households, ancestors, and Buddhism. In spite of the rise of State Shinto during the Meiji period (1868–1911), the state had little influence on the domination of Buddhist temples over funerals.[16] Buddhist prayers were pivotal, because they were the sole means by which the deceased could be safely transformed into ancestors. This was vital not only for the continuation of the household, but also for the living, who believed that the deceased would become malevolent spirits (*goryô* or *gaki*), if not properly venerated by their descendants (see Hori, 1968; Smith, 1974).

However, as nuclear families have become the predominant form of family structure over the years, contemporary Japanese people seem to be less concerned with the continuation of the household or the ancestral line (see Tables 4 and 5). Ultimately, what is at stake is the concept of the dead becoming the ancestors of the household. A non-religious funeral undermines the fundamental belief system revolving around the production of household ancestors. A non-religious funeral also devalues the role of Buddhist priests in the transitional process of the spirits and denies the existence of malevolent spirits. The music and slides in non-religious funerals are often used as substitutes for Buddhist prayers; they are the means by which the bereaved hope to keep alive the memory of the deceased as an individual person. Thus, non-religious funeral ceremonies reflect a de-emphasis on the significance of household ancestors on the one hand, and are a sign of the increasing importance of creating personalized memories of the deceased, on the other hand.

It is also clear that the change in the relationship between consumers and Buddhist temples has resulted in a lack of support and after-care for the deceased's families. Bereaved families view religious services as a meaningless expense, because the act of pacifying the spirits of the dead has lost its meaning. Buddhist services were important for the purification of the deceased's spirit and for the mental consolation of the family. Thus, one of the implications of the non-religious funeral is that death has become an isolated event for the bereaved.

Death generates anxiety and grief; Hertz stated that "death as a social phenomenon consists in a dual and painful process of mental disintegration and synthesis" (Hertz, 1960: 86). For this reason, one of the important functions of funerals is to assist the psychological recovery of the living. "A funeral should provide a set of psychologically healthy mourning practices for the bereaved, allowing mourners to act out their grief in the presence of a strong support group" (Dredge, 1987: 72). Buddhist priests traditionally visited the deceased's house, on the 7th, 49th and 100th day after death, and on the death date of each year; memorial services were held after the 1st, 3rd, 7th, 13th, 17th, 23rd and 33rd year. Priests' visits to the deceased's family not only provided a safe ushering of the deceased into ancestorhood, but also provided the bereaved with a sort of 'grief-recovery' period. Their close relationship with the priest had an effect on the family's psychological recovery from their loss. In today's funerals, such close relationships are practically absent in cities. The 7th day memorial of death, for example, is often carried out immediately after the funeral ceremony (after the deceased is cremated and the ashes are brought back). Priests' visits are decreasing in number and the kind of psychological support a family once received from Buddhist priests is further weakened by commercialized funeral ceremonies. In urban areas, priests and the bereaved often meet

TABLE 4   The Number of Family Members

Fiscal year	Members per household
1955	4.97
1965	4.05
1975	3.28
1985	3.14
1990	2.99

Source: Keizai-Kikakuchô, ed. (Office of General Affairs, Census Bureau), *Keizai-Yôran* (Economic Survey), 1994: 42.

TABLE 5   The Changing Family Structures (1955–1985)

Year	Households	Total nuclear families (mil.)	Single (mil.)	Three generation family (mil.)	Non-kin family (mil.)	% of nuclear family*
1955	17,383	59.6	3.4	36.5	0.5	63.0%
1960	19,678	60.2	4.7	34.7	0.4	64.9%
1965	23,085	62.6	7.8	29.2	0.4	70.4%
1970	26,856	63.5	10.8	25.4	0.4	74.3%
1975	31,271	64.0	13.7	22.2	0.2	77.7%
1980	34,106	63.4	15.8	20.7	0.2	79.2%
1985	36,478	62.6	17.5	19.7	0.2	80.1%

Source: Sômukyoku-tôkeikyoku (Office of General Affairs, Census Bureau), *Nihon jinkô no kôreika to kazoku kôzô no henbô (The Increasing Age of Japanese Population and Changing Family Structure),* Monograph Series No. 8, 1990: 61.

*Percentage of nuclear family here refers to the addition of both the nuclear family and the single family.

for the first time at the deceased's funeral and may never meet again, unless the family decides to keep the deceased's ashes in a charnel house of the Buddhist temple.

THE SCATTERING OF ASHES *(SHIZENSÔ)*: WHO NEEDS A GRAVE?

The Scattering of Ashes

My last example of the changing attitudes to death rituals concerns a new mortuary rite. The contemporary movement of scattering the ashes of the dead, as espoused by the Association for Promoting a Free Death Ceremony [my trans.] *(Sôsô no jiyû wo susumeru kai),* was devised in February 1991 by Yasuda Mutsuhiko, a former editor of Asahi Newspapers. This practice was initially considered somewhat radical and received support mainly from the intelligentsia. The Association for Promoting a Free Death Ceremony conducted its first scattering in October 1991, off the shore of Sagami Bay on the Miura Peninsula. This event was received with much interest and positive response from the public. The State, which until then had shown an ambiguous attitude toward the scattering of ashes, publicly announced that the practice was legal (Yasuda, 1992: 123[17]).

Since 1991, the Association has grown, gaining more than 700 members in a single year. By 1994, the Association could no longer handle the increasing demand for ceremonies, so a private funeral industry in Hiratsuka city, Kanagawa prefecture, was contracted to plan and carry out ceremonies for the scattering of the ashes of the dead (Asahi Newspapers, 2 March, 1994). This new mortuary rite has become popular throughout Japan.[18] In December 1991, another association promoting the scattering of ashes called The Association for Thinking about Scattering Bones[19] *(Sankotsu-wo-kangaeru-kai)* was established by Professor Itô Takamasa, a former President of the University of Buddhism (Bukkyô Daigaku) in Kyoto. This association has practised scattering on the Tsuruga Peninsula in October 1992 (Inoue, 1993: 60).

The dispersing of ashes presents the purest form of remembering loved ones. For example, Dr Baba Seiji,[20] a physician who spent his life working toward a cure for Hansen's disease (leprosy), privately scattered his wife's ashes into the sea around Miyako Island in 1975. The story of the doctor appears in the first pages of Yasuda Mutsuhiko's book, *Who Needs a Grave: Natural Burial for Your Loved Ones (Haka nanka iranai: Aisureba koso shizensô;* Yasuda, 1991). Dr Baba lost his wife in 1975 while he was working at the Nanseien clinic on the Island. The couple had been separated for 8 years while Dr Baba worked there. Upon the sudden death of his wife, Dr Baba remembered that she had mentioned that if she should die, she wanted to merge into the waters off Nanseien that he loved so much. Dr Baba scattered her bones into the Bay of Irimaza early one morning. He writes, "it was a beautiful morning with the sunrise [reflecting] on an ocean colored with burning gold and rosy red" (Yasuda, 1991: 12). For Dr Baba, the Bay of Irimaza became the grave site for his wife and he wished for his own bones to be dispersed there after his death (Yasuda, 1991: 9).

The ceremony of scattering ashes not only provides a memory of the deceased, it also continues to create and provide occasions to share memories with the deceased. Mrs Kusuda, after losing her husband who had loved traveling to exotic places, decided to scatter his ashes at different sites that he had not yet visited (Yasuda, 1991: 116–117). Mrs Kusuda scattered his ashes by making trips to mountains, waterfalls and hills, remembering the times when they traveled together. In this way, the places where the deceased's ashes were dispersed became intimate places where the bereaved could commune with their departed.

Beloved Antecedents: Beyond Ancestors

The scattering of ashes goes further than a living-funeral or a non-religious funeral. Not only does it express the devaluation of household ancestors, it indicates the denial of ancestors *per se.* The performance extends the production of pure individual memories to the point of embracing the deceased as an 'antecedent,' and not as an ancestor of a specific family or a household.

What went hand in hand with the creation of household ancestors was the notion of the impurity of death (*fu-jô*) and the household's obligation to worship ancestors so as to receive tutelary effects. Until the end of World War II, burial dominated over cremation (see Table 6) and the sense of impurity was present at most funerals. Like the Cantonese cases observed in the Hong Kong New Territories, the Japanese fear of death impurities was also based on the disintegration of the corpse/flesh (Watson, 1982: 180). Although customs surrounding Japanese death rituals were systematized by Buddhist traditions, the significant value placed on the bones of the dead in death rituals was structured by Confucianism (Kaji, 1990: 8). Buddhism focused on the purification of the soul and placed little importance on the preservation of the physical remains. Kaji Nobuyuki argues that the Japanese attachment to bones, as the containment of ancestral spirit, is based on the Confucian thought that views bones as the source of '*kô,*' ('*xiao*' in Chinese), the regeneration and continuation of ancestors (Kaji, 1990: 9–21).

Burial as a mortuary rite necessitated a series of prayers by priests and household members so as to transfer the deceased to the state of a purified ancestor as soon as possible. Because the notion of death impurity has been tied up with the decomposition of the physical body, eliminating the impurity was a gradual process that required much assistance in the way of memorial services. Mourning services were performed every seventh day until the forty-ninth day after death. On the seventh day (*shonanoka*), the bereaved dined on a vegetarian meal, praying for the rapid entry of the deceased's spirit into the other world. On the forty-ninth day (*chûin*) the bereaved gathered again to dine, but this time on a meat-based meal, for it was believed that by this time the deceased's spirit had departed for the other world.

What is of most importance in cremation was the rapid production of flesh-free bones and the resulting tendency to shorten the mourning periods. During my fieldwork in Kita-Kyushu, I observed that the majority of bereaved families squeezed the celebration of the mourning period (*shôjinage*) into the same day as the funeral. Immediately after coming back from the crematorium with the deceased's ashes, the bereaved devoted themselves to the commensality of a meat-based dinner with rice wine. Although the rite is still called the seventh day rite, its meat-based dinner coincides with the performance of the forty-ninth day (at the termination of mourning period) and indicates the insignificance of the impurity concept in contemporary funerals.

In the scattering of ashes, however, both the concept of impurity and the notion of ancestors are completely absent. The gradual lifting of the mourning period and the conventional memorial services are also irrelevant. This is because the act of scattering implies disposing of the bones and eliminating the graves that were the focal point for ancestor veneration. The denial of the importance of the actual bones of the dead is the denial of the value of household continuation and of descendants. Thus, the scattering of ashes appears as the creation of a non-specific 'antecedent,' rather than an ancestor. By the very act of dispersing the bones, the continuation of household ancestors is rendered impossible. Moreover, the concept of ancestors is cancelled by denying the vertical relationship with descendants and highlighting the emotions based on love.

What is at the heart of the performance of dispersing is the creation and preservation of memories of the deceased by those who loved them. The act of scattering ashes in the ocean or hills regenerates the feelings shared between the bereaved and the deceased, while nurturing the life-story of the dead. Lu Xun once wrote that "if a deceased cannot be buried inside the mind of the living, then the deceased is truly forgotten" (Lu, 1957: 204). In this sense, the scattering of ashes provides a suitable means for keeping the deceased's memory alive in one's own mind. Yet, these personal memories survive insofar as the living, who hold the deceased's memory, remain alive.

CONCLUSIONS

The ritual transformations described in this paper obviously have direct implications for the future development of Japanese family life and religious affiliations. On the one hand, the living-funerals, the non-religious funerals and the scattering of ashes all express the asymmetric relationship between the living and the deceased and "an increasing tendency to demonstrate an affection for recently deceased kinsmen only in the form of simplified memorialism"

TABLE 6   Changes in the Percentages of Cremation in Japan

Year	Percentage
1896 (Meiji 29)	26.8%
1909 (Meiji 42)	34.8%
1940 (Shôwa 15)	55.7%
1950 (Shôwa 25)	54.0%
1957 (Shôwa 32)	58.6%
1960 (Shôwa 35)	63.1%
1965 (Shôwa 40)	71.8%
1970 (Shôwa 45)	79.2%
1975 (Shôwa 50)	86.5%
1980 (Shôwa 55)	91.1%
1985 (Shôwa 60)	94.5%
1990 (Heisei 2)	97.1%

Source: Asaka Katsusuke, *Sôgi* 1(6), 1991: 43.

(Smith, 1974: 223). On the other hand, the movement toward scattering ashes demonstrates a further tendency to celebrate the deceased as separate from the line of ancestors.

The value of the household guaranteed that the deceased would become the household ancestor; this used to provide comfort to the living who "will someday become ancestors and they will live on in the rites throughout the ensuing generation" (Ooms, 1976: 79). The succession of the household, the inheritance of property, including the ownership of graves and other objects for ancestral rites, and the veneration of ancestors were all connected to the aim of household perpetuation. What was important in this continuation was the balanced relationship between the living and the dead: "just as the living would not exist without the ancestors, the ancestors exist only because the living remember and memorialize them" (Smith, 1992: 3). However, the relationship between the living and the ancestors of the household which had been sustained by economic succession as well as spiritual exchanges, became asymmetrical as a result of social changes in contemporary Japan.[21] Although providing a funeral for one's parents is still considered a duty, descendants have come to see it not as an obligation to household ancestors as such, but as returning a favor to their parents. Consequently, the meaning of one's death has come to depend upon how the living evaluated the deceased's personality, merit, and his or her good deeds. I believe that it is this asymmetric relationship between the living and the dead that has generated living-funerals and non-religious ceremonies.

A living-funeral is the celebration of one's life, an occasion on which an individual can be appreciated by others for his/her generosity. This kind of celebration of one's life became important when the elderly began to feel uncertain about how their children would think of them after they had passed away. One of the results of longevity is a funeral ceremony where family members can only recall a bedridden person, since few of them recollect the deceased in their prime. Thus, living-funerals are intended to assert one's own importance as an individual in a context where the value of the dead as ancestors has declined.

Non-religious funerals demonstrate the diminishing concern with the passage to the afterlife of the deceased's spirit, the deceased's state of impurity or the transition of the deceased to the status of ancestorhood. What concerns the bereaved in a non-religious funeral is the crystallization of positive memories of the deceased. Non-religious ceremonies also reflect the deceased's dependency on the living rather than the other way around. A non-religious funeral can be carried out when the deceased-to-be wish their families to remember them, not as household ancestors, but for the way they lived. In this relationship, the bereaved may or may not follow the wishes of the deceased. In other words, the decision to provide a non-religious funeral for the deceased depends on the survivors' willingness to do so. Rather than an obligation, the non-religious funeral is another opportunity for the living to express their sense of appreciation, sympathy, gratitude or even guilt toward the deceased. In other words, if the living think that the deceased does not deserve such treatment, the ceremony will not take place.

If we follow the distinction between 'pray to' and 'pray for' made by Robert J. Smith (1974), both the non-religious funeral and the living-funeral demonstrate that those who 'pray to' their deceased has declined. 'Praying to' the ancestor implies the belief that the deceased's spirits "both exercise direct tutelary functions by virtue of positions held in life and have a claim on their descendants for comfort and support" (Smith, 1974: 145). Thus, the act of 'praying to' is performed on the basis of a balanced exchange between the living and the dead, whereas, in the act of 'praying for,' the deceased's spirit is dependent on the living. The increasing emphasis on memories of the deceased rather than the role of ancestors derives from this asymmetric relationship between the living and the dead. Moreover, the scattering of ashes indicates a further shift from both the *sosen-sûhai*, the veneration of household ancestors, and *senzo-kuyô*, offerings and memorialism of the ancestors.[22] Instead of being prayed to or prayed for, scattering ashes is another step in the direction of the personal celebration of the deceased's life as a non-specific 'antecedent,' separate from the household ancestors, the continuation of the household or becoming an ancestor for the descendants. The ties between the living and the dead become increasingly horizontal, as opposed to vertical.

I conclude this paper with Mr H.'s comments about his living-funeral. "I will not have any Buddhist priests in my living-funeral nor shall I allow my family to call priests in when I am dead. What good does any sutra do to a dead man's ears? The point is, I want to be remembered just the way I am."

NOTES

1. An earlier version of this article was presented to the 95th annual meeting of American Anthropological Association, which was held in San Francisco, November 1996.

2. From October 1994 to May 1995, I conducted fieldwork in SunRay Co., one of the largest funeral companies in Kita-Kyushu, where I worked as an employee. During my stay, I worked in turn with all the funeral employees moving from one task to another so as to understand the whole process of marketing and producing funeral services.

3. In Japan, 77 years is called *'kiju,'* a lucky year to celebrate.

4. In Japan, chrysanthemums are traditionally used for funerals and ancestor worship.

5. A common return-gift at a Japanese funeral is sugar, seaweed (*nori*), dried mushrooms (*shiitake*), or other light food.

6. I met Mr H. for the first time in November 1994. The interview took place on 17 April, 1995.

7. See for example, "Jibunno sôgi ni nozomukoto" (What I desire in my funeral), Daiichi Terebi, September 26, 1994 and

"Osôshiki no kokoroe" (Preparing oneself for a funeral), NHK, October 18, 1994.

8. See for example, "Tokushû: sôshikiwo kangaeru" (Specials: Considering Funerals), *Bukkyô,* 7 (20), 1992: "Tokushû: kuinonai sôgi, ohaka no tameni" (Specials: In Order Not to Regret on Funerals and Graves), *Daihôrin* 65 (3, March), 1995, "Tokushû: yokuiki yokushinu tameno junbi" (Specials: The Preparation to Live Well and Die Well), *Fujinkôron* 79 (11, November), 1994.

9. See for example, "Tomuraino bade: osôshikino saidanura," Parts 1–5 (At the Place for Mourning: Behind Funeral Altars), *Asahi Shimbun,* 19–26 October, 1994, "Kojinrashisaka, sekenteika" ([Funeral Expressing] the Personality of the Deceased or for the Public Acceptance), *Asahi Shimbun,* 30 October, 1994, "Sôgishaeno omoi samazama" (Various Feelings toward Funeral Companies), *Asahi Shimbun,* 31 October, 1994.

10. While I was working at the funeral company there were many discussions among the executives about how to produce a 'more personalized' funeral service. One of the decisions was to encourage the deceased's friends and colleagues to read memorial addresses.

11. Smith used the term 'memorialism' (to separate it from ancestor worship) in which the ritual acts were centered on memories of the recently dead.

12. In the Meiji Civil Code, the maintenance of household succession was the central issue. Article 987 of the Meiji Civil Code stipulated that the rights to the ownership of graves as well as objects for ancestral rites were to be given to the household successor, namely the eldest son. Ancestral worship and graves were the representation of household succession. In the post-war Civil Code, however, the ownership of tombs, graves, and genealogical records was not a special right of the successor of the household; the Civil Code separated the rights of ancestor veneration and the rights of property succession. (see Idota, 1993: 183–208)

13. Robert J. Smith noted in the 1980s that there is a "developing trend for the prospective heirs to assign inheritance rights to the married daughter who took on the care of aged parents" (Personal communication, 03/11/97). "In some cases all the children but one and the widow will renounce their claims after it has been agreed that one of the children will accept both the assets and the responsibility for the care of the mother in her old age." (Smith, 1987: 13)

14. In Kita-Kyshu city where I conducted my fieldwork, 98% of the funerals were Buddhist, 1% were Shinto and 1% were Christian.

15. The data were taken from research conducted by Professor Ôhashi Keiko at Chûkyô College. The study was based on questionnaires answered by 461 families from 14 locations in Tokyo, Ohita City, Beppu City, and Kyushu. The study also showed that the average cost of funerals in Tokyo was $32,400. According to the study, the variation of overall funeral expenses was as shown in Table 3.

16. "By and large, the efforts to establish non-Buddhist funeral rites had little lasting effect, so great was the hold of Buddhist practice on the people." (Smith, 1974: 29)

17. Article 190 in the Penal Code states: "A person who damages, destroys, abandons or unlawfully takes possession of a corpse, the ashes or a lock of hair of a dead person, or of an object placed in a coffin shall be punished with imprisonment at forced labor for not more than three years." (Ministry of Justice Japan, 1960:62) The earlier debates with regard to scattering had centered around the question of whether scattering the bones of the dead could be construed as 'abandoning' or 'disposing' of the body, as described in the code. The Ministry of Justice, however, decided that the scattering of bones does not violate Article 190, since the aim of the law is to protect the religious feelings of the people.

18. The City Government of Kawasaki has produced a general plan for preparing a space for bones to be scattered in the city grave site which is now under construction (*Sankei Shimbun* (Sankei Newspapers) 5 June, 1994). It should be noted that the space for scattering ashes will be commonly shared by different people, just as the ocean or the hills are shared. This implies that there will be non-specific graves.

19. When a body is cremated, pieces of bone remain among the ashes, hence the terms 'bones' and 'ashes' are used interchangeably.

20. He received the Yoshikawa Eiji Prize in 1979 for his efforts in curing Hansen's disease. He retired from the Nanseien Clinic at Miyako Island in 1975, but has continued on as the director of Emergency Center there. (see Yasuda, 1991:9)

21. Social changes brought about by modernization, such as the division of labor, urban migration, the increasing number of elderly people left behind in the countryside, the low birth rate, and medical advances.

22. The distinction between *sosen-sûhai* and *senzo-kuyô* "can be understood in terms of their closeness to the direct descent line and in terms of the amount of time that has elapsed since their death. The axis of differentiation may well turn out to be sosen sûhai [worship of/reverence for ancestors] on the one hand, and sosen-kuyô [consolation/comforting of the "ancestors"] on the other" (Smith, 1976: 61).

REFERENCES

Asahi Newspapers. "Sankotsu, gyôsha ni itaku e" (Scattering Consigned to Funeral Industry). *Asahi Shimbun* March 2, 1994.

Asahi Shimbun Chôsabu ed. *Asahi-nenkan 1994: Asahi Data Book (Asahi Year Book 1994).* Tokyo: Asahi Shimbunsha, 1994.

Asaka, Katsusuke. "Kasôba towa? Hensen wo tadori kangaeru" (What is Crematory? A Consideration through its History). *Sôgi* 1 (6), 1991: 40–43.

Dredge, Paul C. "Korean Funerals: Ritual as Process." In Kendall, J. & Dix, G., eds. *Religion and Ritual in Korean Society.* Korea Research Monograph No. 12. Berkeley: University of California, Center for Korean Studies, 1987: 71–92.

Ei, Rokusuke. *Dai-ôjô (Happy Ending).* Tokyo: Iwanami Shoten, 1994.

Goody, Jack. *Death, Property, and the Ancestors.* Stanford: Stanford University Press, 1962.

Gubbins, John H. *The Civil Code of Japan* (Translation), Vol. II. Tokyo: Maruya & Co., 1899.

Hertz, Robert. *Death and the Right Hand*. Trans. Rodney & Claudia Needham. Glencoe: The Free Press, 1960 [1907].

Hori, Ichiro. *Folk Religion in Japan: Continuity and Change*. Chicago: The University of Chicago Press, 1968.

Idota, Hirofumi. "Saishi jôkô no kaisei to hôkôzô" (The Amendment on the Articles on Worship and the Legal Structure). In Idota, H., ed. *Kazoku no hô to rekishi (The History and the Family Law)*. Kyoto: Sekai Shisôsha, 1993: 183–213.

Inoue, Haruyo. "Sôsô shimin undô no genjô to kongo" (Present and Future Conditions of Civilian Movement on Funerals). *Sôgi* 3 (5), 1993: 59–63.

Kaji, Nobuyuki. *Jukyô towa nanika (What is Confucianism)*. Tokyo: Chûôkôronsha, 1990.

Keizai Kikakucho Chôsakyoku ed. (Office of General Affairs, Census Bureau) *Keizai-youlan (Economic Survey)*. Tokyo: Ohkurashô Insatukyoku, 1994.

Kosugi, Teppei. *The sôshiki (The Funeral)*. Tokyo: Asahishinbunsha, 1992.

Lu, Xun. "Kong-tan" (Idle Talk). In *Lu Xun Quanji*, Vol. 3. Hong Kong: Wenxue Yanjiusha, 1957 [1926]: 202–204.

Matsunaga, Goichi. "Kenka to takebue no ne to" (The Flower Offering and the Tune of the Bamboo Flute). *Daihôrin* 65(3), 1995: 98–99.

Ministry of Justice Japan. *The Constitution and Criminal Statues of Japan* (Translation): Tokyo: Ministry of Justice, 1960.

Ministry of Justice Japan. *The Civil Code of Japan* (Translation). Tokyo: Ministry of Justice, 1962.

Murakami, Kyôkô. "Sôgi to iu kôi wo dô yomi tokuka" (How to Analyze the Act of Funeral Ceremony). *Sôgi* 2(5), 1992: 101–105.

Nakajô, Takako. *Tezukuri-sôshiki (Home-Made-Funeral)*. Osaka: Kansaishoin, 1991.

Nakamura, Hajime. *Ways of Thinking of Eastern Peoples: India-China-Tibet-Japan*. Honolulu: University of Hawaii Press, 1964.

NLI Research Institute. *Nihon no kazoku wa dou kawattanoka (How the Japanese Family Changed)*. Tokyo: NHK Shuppan, 1994.

Ôhashi, Keiko. "Sôgi no jittai to seizen keiyaku ni kansuru ishiki chôsa" (The Condition of Funeral Ceremonies and Perception towards Living Contract). *Sôgi* 3 (4), 1993: 98–100.

Ooms, Herman. "A Structural Analysis of Japanese Ancestral Rites and Beliefs." In Newell, W. H., ed. *Ancestors*. Hague: Mouton, 1976: 61–90.

Shimada, Hiromi. "Gendaini Okeru Sôgiwa Ikaniarubekika" (How Should a Contemporary Funeral Be). *Bukkyô* 20, 1992: 10–31.

Smith, Robert J. *Ancestor Worship in Contemporary Japan*. Stanford: Stanford University Press, 1974.

Smith, Robert J. "Who are the 'Ancestors' in Japan? A 1963 Census of Memorial Tablets." In Newell, W. H., ed. *Ancestors*. Hague: Mouton Publishers, 1976: 33–60.

Smith, Robert J. "Gender Inequality in Contemporary Japan." *Journal of Japanese Studies* 13 (1), 1987: 1–25.

Smith, Robert J. "The Living and the Dead in Japanese Popular Religion." Unpublished paper. Presented at the Columbia University Modern Japan Seminar, May 8, 1992.

SÔGI. "Prelude." *Sôgi* 2 (2), 1992: i.

SÔGI. "Mou hitotsu no seizensô" (Another Living-Funeral). *Sôgi* 3 (4), 1993: 17–18.

SÔGI. "My Ending: watashiga kibô suru sôsô no arikata" (My Ending: The Way I Want My Funeral to Be). *Sôgi* 4 (1), 1994: 21–29.

SÔGI. "Prelude." *Sôgi* 5 (1), 1995: i.

Sômuchô-tôkeikyoku (Office of General Affairs, Census Bureau). *Nihon jinkô no kôreika to kazoku kôzô no henbô (The Aging in the Japanese Population and the Transformation of Family Structures)*. In *Shôwa 60, Kokusei-chôsa*, Monograph Series, No. 8. Tokyo: Nihon Tôkei Kyôkai, 1990.

Watson, J. L. "Of Flesh and Bones: The Management of Death Pollution in Cantonese Society." In Bloch, M. & Parry, J., eds. *Death & the Regeneration of Life*. Cambridge: Cambridge University Press, 1982: 155–186.

Yasuda, Mutsuhiko. *Hakananka iranai: Aisureba koso shizensô (Who Needs a Grave: Natural Burial for Your Loved Ones)*. Tokyo: Yûhisha, 1991.

Yasuda, Mutsuhiko. "Shizensô no susume" (Advocating Natural Burial). *Bukkyô* 20, 1992: 122–129.

3

Religion and the Environment

Religion articulates with the environment in a wide variety of ways. Most religions include some sort of statement about the relationship of humans to the environment. Sometimes, religious ideas seem to control people's relationship with their environment. Beyond this, religious traditions often imbue particular aspects of the environment with sacred meaning. As you read the essays in this section, keep the following points in mind:

- In a great many cultures, people have associated supernatural forces with environmental features such as mountains, lakes, and other aspects of the natural environment. Nineteenth-century anthropologists argued that the worship of awe-inspiring aspects of the environment was one of the earliest forms of religion. Most current-day anthropologists would dismiss the notion that religion has somehow progressed from a primitive form, but there is broad evidence that people have frequently associated both positive and negative aspects of the supernatural with large-scale features of the natural world. Native American groups living in the Black Hills of the Dakotas are a good example.[1] Successive Native American groups that occupied the Black Hills associated specific aspects of this environment with symbolic and mythological values. Living in a sacred environment, they were constantly put in mind of the central stories of their history and religion.

- Anthropologists have often argued that religious belief systems form some sort of homoeostatic mechanism that keeps human populations in balance with their environment. One of the most famous examples of this is Roy Rappaport's 1967 book *Pigs for the Ancestors*. There, Rappaport argues that among the Tsambega Maring, a group in New Guinea, religious ritual, warfare, pig husbandry, and population are bound together in a self-regulating system. Stephen Lansing's essay in this section makes a broadly similar case for Balinese water temples. He argues that the Balinese ritual calendar is related to the growth cycle of rice. Rituals regulate Balinese agriculture and order the relationships between communities.

- Religious practices might sometimes seem illogical or even counterproductive to outsiders. But when these same practices are considered within the context of their economic and ecological settings, they might make perfect sense. A classic example of this is Hindu beliefs about cattle. Throughout the colonial era in India, outsiders, particularly the British and the Americans, considered the Hindu taboo on the killing of cattle to be an example of an irrational religious belief. People in India are starving, they argued, yet because of their religious beliefs these same people refuse to eat the millions of head of cattle roaming the countryside. They literally starve for their beliefs. In a very famous 1966 essay, Marvin Harris argues that this is a misunderstanding of the economic and ecological role of cattle in India. He proposes that killing and eating cattle would result in short-term benefit but long-term disaster. In subtle but important ways, the Hindu ban on cattle killing lessens the effects of famine. Eating cattle would result in even more devastating famine than has historically been the case.

- It seems logical that many elements of religion were integrated into the subsistence systems of people living in traditional agricultural societies. For example, some elements of Maya Indian mythology reflect the cycle of slash-and-burn horticulture upon which they based their livelihoods.[2] In industrialized societies today, however, religion, the environment, and subsistence have only a tenuous link at best. For example, it is hard to see how working in an office or on an assembly line is affected by religious beliefs about the change of seasons or movement of constellations.

- As with many other aspects of religion, sacred places are also basic elements in political debate both within and between religious communities. Almost everyone, for example, has some familiarity with the political battles over the control of Jerusalem. Specific locations in that city have profound meaning for Jews, Muslims, and Christians. These groups have different understandings of the meaning of Jerusalem and different stories concerning particular locations within it such as the Temple Wall and the Dome of the Rock Mosque. Control of Jerusalem and its holy sites is a major stumbling block to peace in the Middle East

- In her essay on Anloga, a sacred site in Ghana, Sandra Greene exposes a sacred history that will be less familiar than Jerusalem. The principal religious site in Anloga, an area called Gbakute, has played an important role in the history of the community for more than two centuries. It has been a locus of conflict between traditional religious groups, British colonial authorities, and Pentecostal Christians.

NOTES

1. Linea Sundstrom, "Mirror of Heaven: Cross-Cultural Transference of the Sacred Geography of the Black Hills," *World Archaeology* 28, no. 2 (1996): 117–189.

2. R. Jon McGee, "Natural Modeling in Lacandon Maya Mythology," in *Explorations in Anthropology and Theology,* edited by Walter Adams and Frank Salamone, pp. 175–190 Lanham (MD): University Press of America.

Balinese "Water Temples" and the Management of Irrigation

J. Stephen Lansing

The purpose of Lansing's article is to further discussion on a theoretical question concerning the role of irrigation and state formation. However, more specifically to our purpose, he discusses the relationship between wet rice irrigation, water temple rituals, and the regulation of the rice terrace ecosystems. His essay provides a detailed example of the integration of religious rituals, farming, and the regional ecology of wet rice farmlands in Bali.

Lansing begins his discussion by describing the two calendars that are followed by the Balinese. The *uku* calendar is a 210-day calendar of thirty 7-day weeks that repeats itself indefinitely and is approximately the length of the rice-growing season. This calendar is a critical component in the water temple/rice-growing system. The *Icaka,* or lunar/solar calendar, is much more complex, fluctuates between the seasons, and is calculated by specialized Brahmin priests. Thus when the priests of the principal water temple send out invitations to celebrate the Temple Festival of the Tenth Month in the Icaka calendar, they also specify that the festival will start on a specific day in the uku calendar. The temple priests time the festival to the end of the rainy season, and the 210-day uku calendar helps farmers coordinate their planting and harvest schedules, water turns, and the fallow period before the planting of the second crop, which is critical to fighting pests that may infest rice fields. Lansing concludes that Balinese water temples play a crucial role in regulating the environmental factors necessary for successful rice harvests, and that, in the Balinese case, water temples and the irrigation networks they control are more stable and long-lasting than any government that has ruled Bali.

As you read, consider these questions:
1. How does the Balinese system of water temples regulate and stabilize agricultural production?
2. How does the water temple system manage the region as a whole, and what impact does it have on plant disease and insects?
3. How does the water temple system define the ecosystem as a whole?

If one tries to erect a theory of power one will always be obliged to view it as emerging at a given place and time and hence to deduce it, to reconstruct its genesis. But if power is in reality an open, more-or-less coordinated (in the event, no doubt, ill-coordinated) cluster of relations, then the only problem is to provide oneself with a grid of analysis which makes possible an analytic of the relations of power.
—Michel Foucault, *Power/Knowledge*

One of the most enduring theories of the state links the management of hydraulic irrigation to the centralization of power. For Marx, "the prime necessity of an economical and common use of water . . . necessitated in the Orient . . . the centralizing power of Government" (Avinieri 1969:7). But Marx was faced with the difficulty (pointed out to him by Engels) that his model of an "Asiatic mode of production" could not apply to existing states, then under European colonial rule. Marx replied that an "intact example" could still be found on the Indonesian island of Bali (Avinieri 1969:456). A century later, Karl Wittfogel found himself in a similar bind: his model of "Oriental Despotism" described early states, not those of the 20th century. Like Marx, he suggested that a still-functioning example could be found on Bali (Wittfogel 1957:53–54).

But despite a century of study, there is still no consensus as to whether irrigation is really centrally organized in Bali. Indeed, most scholars have argued the reverse: that Balinese irrigation is entirely in the hands of local-level farmer's associations called *subaks*.[1] In a recent cross-cultural comparison of irrigation systems, Hunt and Hunt concluded that the evidence from Bali remains ambiguous (1976:394; see also Happe 1919; van der Heijden 1924–25; Wirz 1927; Kron 1932; Millon 1962; Geertz 1972, 1980; Birkelbach 1973; Hobart 1982).

To put some flesh on the question, consider the irrigation systems of the Balinese district of Badung. Badung is 115 km long and up to 40 km across at the widest point. Several small rivers provide water for intricate networks of canals which irrigate 19,238 hectares (ha) of rice terraces. The largest *subak* in Badung, however, controls only 328 ha of terraces. Altogether there are presently 151 *subaks* in Badung, ranging in size from 328 down to 10.5 ha.

The question of whether these 151 *subaks* could function as completely autonomous units brings us to the question of the role of water management in wet-rice agriculture. For most crops, irrigation simply provides water for absorption by the plant's roots. But in a Balinese rice terrace, water is used to create an artificial ecosystem. The precise alternation of wet and dry phases achieved through controlled irrigation governs the basic biochemical processes of the terrace ecosystem. Water alters soil pH, induces a cycle of aerobic and anaerobic conditions in the soil which determines the activity of microorganisms, provides a range of mineral nutrients, fosters the growth of nitrogen-fixing algaes, excludes weeds, stabilizes soil temperature, and over the long term governs the formation of the plough pan and the maintenance of soil fertility (DeDatta 1981:297–298; Yoshida 1981). Phosphorus, for example, is increased from less than 0.05 ppm to about 0.6 ppm by submergence (Yoshida 1981:147–151), while potassium depends largely on drainage. Furthermore, the Balinese do not use storage devices, so that the success of irrigation depends on accurate judgment of the (seasonal) flow of rivers and springs. Altogether, a difference of a few centimeters in water depth, or a change of a few weeks in timing the alternation of wet and dry cycles, can have a major effect on the terrace ecosystem, directly affecting crop yields.

The most recent controversy over Balinese irrigation centers on the possible role of agricultural rituals as a scheduling mechanism. The points at issue in this dispute lead directly into the results of my own research, concerning the role of regional networks of "water temples" as managers of the terrace ecosystems.

HOBART'S CRITIQUE OF GEERTZ

Over the past two decades, Clifford Geertz has developed the hypothesis that irrigation is organized at the *subak* level by the timing of the rituals connected with the rice cult, which "are symbolically linked to cultivation in a way that locks the pace of that cultivation into a firm, explicit rhythm." Thus, according to Geertz, "a complex ecological order was both reflected in and shaped by an equally complex ritual order, which at once grew out of it and was imposed upon it" (1980:82). This argument was recently challenged by Mark Hobart, on the basis of Hobart's study of a single *subak* in the district of Gianyar, comprising less than 85 ha of terraces. Hobart's critique was based on a comparison of the rituals of the rice cult to the physiological growth of the plant in the fields, and the timing of agricultural labor. Hobart found that the intervals marked by the rice rituals did not match the phases of agricultural labor, and perhaps more importantly, that the rituals were very often quite out of phase with the stages of growth of the plants (1982:73). Hobart concluded that ritual was therefore not a "master plan for cultivation."

According to Hobart, the reason for the poor match between rituals, labor, and the growth of the plants was that the rituals do not really follow the natural rhythm of plant growth, but are instead pegged to the Balinese calendars. He observes that different phases of the "rice cult" make use of both of the Balinese calendars, the "Hindu system of 12 solar-lunar months . . . and the so-called Javanese-Balinese uku calendar," which is permutational and therefore "completely divorced from the flow of observable natural events" (1982:57). In the *subak* studied by Hobart,

> both calendrical systems intersect in the organization of the rice-cycle rites. So, for example, the main temple festival (pi)odalan agung occurs in Purnama kedasa, or every full moon of the tenth solar-lunar month . . . Although Geertz has argued that the ceremonies are synchronized with the stages of cultivation, in Tengah Padang at least, there is no simple correspondence, for the rites follow a largely predetermined pattern. [1982:57]

As an example of the bewildering ritual complexity generated by following two calendars at once, Hobart points to a particular ritual, *nyungsung,* "supposedly co-ordinated with the 'pregnancy' of the rice, when the growing panicle causes the rice to swell." To "confuse neat theories of timing still further," observes Hobart, "this ritual is supposed to follow the solar-lunar calendar for the first planting, and the permutational uku calendar for the second!" (1982:57).

By an odd coincidence, this particular piece of evidence (which Hobart uses to illustrate the detachment of Balinese rice ritual from cultivation practices) happens to be the most critical piece of planning in the regional management of irrigation. The timing of the *nyungsung* ceremony is one of the key pieces in the irrigation puzzle. But the significance of this timing appears only at the regional level, as one of the instruments of terrace management utilized by a regional network of water temples.

Thus Hobart notes elsewhere that the *nyungsung* ceremony for the first rice crop is timed for the full moon of the tenth solar-lunar month, which coincides with the major *subak* temple festival (1982:70). To understand the significance of this timing, we need to consider the physiology of the rice plant, the climate of Bali, the Balinese calendrical system, and the role of temples. Let us take them in order.

As Hobart notes, *nyungsung* is "supposedly co-ordinated with the 'pregnancy' of the rice, when the growing panicle causes the rice to swell" (1982:57). The appearance of the panicle primordia marks the beginning of the reproductive growth phase, a turning point in the need of the plant for two crucial requirements: water and sunlight. The plant's need for water is critical through the development of the panicle, but declines thereafter (DeDatta 1981:314). In contrast, the plant's need for sunlight increases at this stage:

> The solar radiation requirements of a rice crop differ from one growth stage to another. Shading during the vegetative stage only slightly affects yield and yield components. Shading during the reproductive stage, however, has a pronounced effect on spikelet number. . . . Solar radiation at the reproductive stage has the greatest effect on grain yield; that at the ripening stage, the next highest yield; and that at the vegetative stage, an extremely small overall effect. [Yoshida 1981:87]

Hobart noted that the ceremony marking the onset of the reproductive phase is timed for the full moon of the tenth lunar-solar month. This date falls somewhere between the end of February and the beginning of May on our Gregorian calendar. . . . [R]ainfall patterns for the different regions of Bali . . . differ markedly, with the greatest amounts of rain falling in the mountains of south-central Bali. Table 1 indicates the monthly mean annual rainfall by region.

Despite regional differences, it is clear that the rainy season tapers off abruptly in March and April. The *subak* studied by Hobart is located in Zone 2 High Rainfall. Data on sunshine for rice-growing areas are summarized in Table 2.

All other things being equal, the sunshine and water needs of the rice plant will obviously be best satisfied if the reproductive phase begins just at the end of the rainy season, around the month of March on our calendar. The choice of the full moon of the tenth Icaka month for the festival marking the appearance of the panicle, along with the major local water temple festival, optimizes these factors. But in fact this is only the beginning of the story. Not only Hobart's *subak* but all of the *subaks* in the district of Gianyar, traditionally held the panicle-appearance ceremony on the full moon of the tenth Icaka month. This meant that the whole district planted their first rice crop at the same time. If they all planted the same variety of rice, they would therefore also harvest at the same time: in mid-summer, when the danger of rainfall is minimal, and sunlight is assured for ripening. The fields would be dry, facilitating harvest and drying. More importantly, a regional fallow period would follow the harvest extending over approximately 15,000 contiguous ha,

thus effectively interrupting the food supply and/or life cycle of all the major rice pests (insects, rodents, bacterial and viral diseases) (Oka 1979). Specifically, then, timing the *nyungsung* ceremony for the full moon of the tenth month for an entire region has the following effects: (1) the plant's needs for rainfall and sunshine are optimized; (2) harvest is timed for the dry season; (3) pest populations are minimized.

But most Balinese farmers aim to get two rice harvests, not one. Traditionally, the first crop is a particularly long-maturing variety, which allegedly compensates the farmers for the extra time it takes to grow by being especially nutritious—good-tasting and life-sustaining. This rice, called *padi tahun* or *padi del,* matures in about 200 days, but the Balinese allow 210 days (six 35-day Balinese months) for the complete cycle. The second planting depends, not on rainfall, but on organized irrigation in the dry season. Each *subak* may select the variety of rice to be planted. These rices are generally termed *cicih,* and have an average duration of about 120 days. *Cicih* are nonphotosensitive varieties, and so may be planted at any time of year. But if two rice crops are to be harvested in one year, this leaves no more than a month of leeway for a fallow period between plantings. It is critical for pest control that this brief fallow period extend over a wide region, since otherwise pests will simply migrate from field to field. Obtaining two crops of rice every year thus requires very nice timing, particularly if dry-season irrigation requires a rotation of water turns.

In summary, all three factors—optimization of water and sunlight for the crucial first crop, provision for a brief but ef-

TABLE 1   Monthly Mean Rainfall by Region (mm)

Zone	Sep	Oct	Nov	Dec	Jan	Feb	Mar	Apr	May	Jun	Jul	Aug
I												
Low rain	72	178	200	252	230	232	187	113	99	77	95	65
High rain	65	145	253	378	365	343	315	190	190	85	98	73
II												
Low rain	23	56	149	247	350	303	296	137	77	47	42	23
High rain	110	156	168	234	254	252	162	116	116	140	188	104
IV												
Low rain	8	28	74	176	275	282	233	110	77	38	31	18
High rain	43	98	213	252	296	265	248	172	115	74	41	33

No irrigation in Zone III.

TABLE 2   Seasonal Sunshine by Region

	Zone I	Zone II	Zone IV
Mean sunshine	60%	76%	50%
Minimum	Jan (45%)	Feb (58%)	Jan (40%)
Maximum	Apr (67%)	Apr (89%)	Aug (75%)

fective regional fallow period between crops, and coordination to permit a possible second crop of fast-maturing rice—depend on timing the first planting so that the reproductive phase (panicle appearance, marked by the *nyungsung* ceremony) occurs at the end of the rainy season, at the full moon of the tenth month. However, it is clear from Tables 1 and 2 that there is at least a month's leeway as to when the rainy season actually ends. The reader is asked to bear this in mind, as we consider the role of the "master water temple" Pura Ulun Danu Batur in setting the calendar each year.

THE "MASTER WATER TEMPLE" PURA ULUN DANU BATUR

Along the rim of the crater of Lake Batur . . . , well above the elevation where rice can be grown, there is a temple called Pura Ulun Danu Batur, which is generally recognized as the supreme water temple (or *subak* temple) of Bali. The Balinese name for their religion is *agama tirtha,* the religion of holy water. Water is revered for its power to make things grow, and to wash away impurities both physical and spiritual. Pura Ulun Danu Batur includes shrines to 147 deities, foremost among them the supreme goddess associated with the life-giving properties of water, Dewi Danu. Temple scribes keep a list of the 204 *subaks* that constitute the primary congregation of the temple. Once a year, around the end of the rainy season, the scribes write formal messages to each of these 204 *subaks,* inviting them to attend the major annual festival of the temple. These invitations, written on palm-leaf lontar manuscripts in Balinese script, are then hand-carried to the *subaks* by the temple messengers. No other temple in Bali regularly sends such invitations.

The 204 *subaks* which receive the invitations (about half of all Balinese *subaks*) are located between the boundaries of four rivers, and are members of the temple's congregation because the goddess of Lake Batur is believed to be responsible for the gift of the waters that irrigate their fields. But the question is, why send formal written invitations to a festival that has been held on the same date for centuries—especially since no other Balinese temple issues such invitations? The text of the invitation itself provides a clue:

> May there be peace.

> Letter of invitation, to the head of village or *subak* X. My purpose is to inform you that we shall hold the "Temple Festival of the Tenth Month" on the following date [date specified on the 210-day *uku* calendar]. You are requested to bring ten coconuts, 1100 Chinese coins, ten measures of rice, one duck and one pig.

> Myself, the High Priest of Batur Temple

The request for offerings is formulaic, and nearly every *subak* brings more than is demanded. But the specification of the date provides real information, and (in my opinion) is the real reason for the use of these invitations. An explanation requires a brief digression into the workings of the Balinese calendar.

As noted by Hobart, the Balinese actually use two calendars. The first, called *uku,* is a 210-day calendar consisting of 30 7-day weeks. This calendar is independent of natural or astronomical events, and simply repeats itself indefinitely in 210-day cycles. As we shall see presently, the choice of a basic interval of 210 days seems related to the 210-day growth cycle of first-crop Balinese rice.

The Balinese also keep track of lunar months and solar years. The lunar calendar is accurate enough to stay in agreement with the actual phases of the moon, and so to check the date according to this calendar, in principle one need only look at the sky. But calculation of the solar year is much less straightforward. The Balinese use a version of the Indian Icaka luni-solar calendar, which adds an intercalary month every two or three years, so that while over 10 or 100 years, the passage of solar years is quite accurately counted, in any given year the marked "year" is either too short by 10 or 11 days, or too long by about 19 or 20 days. Moreover, the relationship of luni-solar (Icaka) months to the observed seasons fluctuates markedly. Thus, for example, the date called "Full Moon of the Tenth Month" may fall anywhere between the end of February and the beginning of May, and will change each year. One of the effects of this calendrical complexity is that the man in the rice fields is seldom sure exactly which month it is (on the luni-solar Icaka calendar), although he knows very well what day it is on the lunar month, and on the 210-day calendar. Keeping track of the insertion of intercalary months so as to get the year right is the province of Brahmanical specialists. Moreover, in the days of the rajahs each court had its own calendrical experts, whose systems often disagreed so that dates often varied by as much as a month, from one principality to the next.

To be precise, the point of uncertainty is the question of which month (marked by the phases of the moon) corresponds to which month (on the numbered, luni-solar Icaka calendar). The Sanskrit word for "Ten" *(dasa),* as in "Tenth Month," is close to the Balinese word *dasdas,* which means "to break off, to end or finish." Moreover, the "Tenth Month" in the (originally Indian) luni-solar calendar falls around March-April, approximately the end of the rainy season in Bali. So in each locality, the question of which month is the tenth month is resolved by estimating when the rainy season is actually about to end, as evidenced by natural signs. In one locality, the "tenth month" is marked by the appearance of a particular moss on a venerable and authoritative old tree; in another, by the appearance of "Dasa grass"; in another, by a change in the color of the sea. Even today, despite the widespread use of a printed, standardized calendar all over the island, it is still possible to hear someone say, "Well, it may be the tenth month down there, but around here it's still the ninth month!"

This does not mean that the Brahmancial experts lose track of the actual passage of Icaka months. The passage of luni-solar years is accurately recorded, and anyone wishing to know the "correct" date may consult the printed calendar (or get a second opinion from a calendrical specialist). However, the printed calendar has only become widely used in the last two decades, so that formerly each locality had its own view as to what time it was.

This clearly posed problems for the coordination of irrigation over river systems that encompassed several principalities, each engrossed in its own calendrical system. Hence the need for the annual "invitations" from the master water temple to its member *subaks,* which by pegging the "Full Moon of the Tenth Month" to a particular date (on the invariant *uku* calendar), established a sort of "Irrigation Year"—a common calendrical framework for farmers, essential for scheduling water turns, cropping patterns, and especially for ensuring uniform fallow periods. As the priests of the temple explained to me, this also enables the temple to bring the "Tenth Month" into conjunction with their estimate of the end of the rainy season *(musim mokoh).* Temple priests decide each year on the likely duration of the rainy season and fix the date of the temple festival accordingly.

It is at this point that the second calendar—the 210-day *uku* permutational calendar—reveals its uses. Since this calendar is independent of the seasons, it has no particular starting or stopping date.[2] Start on any given date, and the calendar helps mark out intervals (useful for regulating water turns, phases of rice growth, etc.) for the next 210 days. As far as the farmers I've talked to are concerned, the reason for the 210-day length of this calendar is obvious: it marks the passage of six 35-day "Balinese months," the growing cycle of first-crop rice. At the end of this 210-day cycle, the *uku* calendar is used again, to mark the duration of the regional fallow period, and then to establish planting dates and water rotations for the second crop. This explains Hobart's second point: that the panicle-appearance *nyungsung* ceremony is held on full moon of the tenth month for the first planting, and fixed according to the *uku* calendar for the second planting.

So the *uku* calendar is annually pegged to the luni-solar calendar at the end of the rainy season, and thenceforth enables the farmers to coordinate their labors, water turns, and rice-cult rituals. The date of the second planting (called *Gegadon* or "open cycle") is fixed by the *uku* calendar, generally soon after the first harvest. If plantings are to be staggered, this is arranged beforehand by meetings in the water temples, the dates of each water turn specified on the *uku* calendar. Because the second crop is considered optional, the rituals of the rice cult are generally reduced and abbreviated for the second planting. Major water temple festivals are almost always held only once a year.

REGIONAL WATER TEMPLE NETWORKS

The titles and precise functions of regional water temples vary from district to district, but the overall logic is reasonably clear. Looking at the system from the bottom up, each farmer has a small shrine *(bedugul)* located at the spot where irrigation water first enters his fields. Here, at the "upstream" end of his fields, he carries out the rituals of the "rice cult," from field preparation to harvest (Wirz 1927). Next, most (but not all) *subaks* possess temples called "Ulun Carik" (Head of the Fields), where they perform collective rites during the first crop *(kerta masa),* and hold *subak* meetings. Next, at the place where a major canal first enters a set of terraces there are temples called "Ulun Swi" (Head of the Terraces), which usually coordinate irrigation for a collection of *subaks.* There may also be temples called "Masceti," which are regional water temples, sometimes equivalent to "Ulun Swi," sometimes superior or subordinate. Finally, each weir, spring, lake, and the headwaters of each river have shrines or temples. Downstream, at the place where important rivers reach the sea, there are major temples associated with defense against pests and other malign influences believed to originate in the sea. Overall, then, the water temples exemplify the basic Balinese cosmo-logic, whereby "upstream" is associated with purity and the uranic, while "downstream" is linked to chthonic dangers. This logic, implicit in the physical layout of every temple, is imposed on every river system and indeed on the whole island by the regional systems of water temples, which mark out the paths traced by the waters of the goddess as they simultaneously cause growth and bear away pollution.

To see how the system works in practice, let us consider a couple of regional temple systems, and then return to the question of how the master water temple coordinates whole river systems.

Sukawati

The village of Sukawati . . . lies alongside the seacoast in the district of Gianyar. . . . It is downstream from Hobart's *subak* but in the same district, in which panicle appearance is timed for the full moon of the "tenth month," according to the "irrigation year" set by the master water temple at Lake Batur. There are 13 *subaks* in the system, with a total of 402.86 ha of rice terraces. Water is obtained from weirs on two rivers, the Wos and the Petanu. The *subaks* are divided into three groups, as follows:

> Group 1: *Subaks* Palak, Sango, Sungguhan, and Bubun (subdivided into two *tempeks*)
> Source of water: Petanu River
>
> Group 2: *Subaks* Laud, Landep, Somi, Juwuk
> Source of water: Wos River
>
> Group 3: *Subaks* Lango, Babakan, Cau Duur, Cau Beten, Lebo
> Source of water: Wos River

Traditionally, all *subaks* plant twice, in the first and seventh Icaka months (Sasih kasa and kapitu). Group 1 has sufficient water to plant rice both times. Groups 2 and 3 have less water, and so alternate rice with vegetables for their second crop. That is, in a given year Group 2 plants a second crop of rice in August, while Group 3 plants vegetables (and obtains water every fifth day). The following year, Group 3 plants rice and Group 2 plants vegetables. The fallow period extends for only 15 days, between the first and second plantings, to maximize water use.

. . . [There are] two types of local water temples: Ulun Carik and Masceti. There are four Ulun Carik (Head of the Fields) temples, where *subak* members perform the rites of the rice cult (Wirz 1927). Above these four temples is the higher-level "Masceti" temple, Pura Air Jeruk. The practical functioning of the temple system is explained by the village head in this interview, transcribed unedited from a tape:

Village Head: The Pura Air Jeruk is the largest temple hereabouts, that is, the temple whose congregation includes all the farmers of the village of Sukawati. Now below this temple there are also smaller temples, which are special places of worship for the *subaks*—each *subak* has its own. There are 14 of these temples, 14 *subaks*, all of which meet together as one here. They meet at the Temple Pura Air Jeruk. Every decision, every rule concerning planting seasons and so forth, is always discussed here. Then, after the meeting here, decisions are carried down to each *subak*. The *subaks* each call all their members together: "In accord with the meetings we held at the Temple Pura Air Jeruk, we must fix our planting dates, beginning on day one through day ten." For example, first *subak* Sango plants, then *subak* Somi, beginning from day 10 through day 20. Thus it is arranged, in accordance with water and "Padewasan"—that is, the best times to plant. Because here time controls everything. If there are many rodents and we go ahead and plant rice,

obviously we'll get a miserable harvest. So we organize things like this: when the rodent population is large, we see to it that we don't plant things they can eat, so that they will all die—I mean, actually, that their numbers will be greatly reduced, pretty quickly.

Lansing: And this is all organized by meetings . . . ?

Village Head: Here! [points at the temple Pura Air Jeruk]. The meetings held here, with the leaders of each *subak*.

Lansing: Is there a fixed schedule of meetings?

Village Head: Once a "year." Each new planting season, there is a meeting. If the planting schedule is not to be changed, there is no meeting. Of course, the ceremonies held here go on regardless—there are two temple festivals here, a one-day festival every six months, and a three-day festival every year. . . . This place is the home of the spirits of those who have preceded us, who built this temple—I would call this temple the fortress of the farmers hereabouts.

Kedewatan

Here, seven *subaks* share water from a single large canal originating from a major weir about 4 km upstream, in central Gianyar. . . . Where the water first enters the terrace complex, there is a major temple called "Ulun Swi" (Head of the Terraces). About 100 m downstream from this temple, the main canal splits in two, and there is a "Masceti" temple alongside the upstream branch canal. A second Masceti temple is located about a half kilometer downstream, where the second branch canal enters the second set of terraces. The two Masceti temples form the congregation of the Ulun Swi temple. Each *subak* thus belongs to the congregation of the Ulun Swi, and to one or the other of the Masceti temples (see Table 3).

The congregation of the Ulun Swi temple thus includes seven *subaks* with a total of 1,775 members, farming 558.04

TABLE 3   Ulun Swi Temple

Masceti Temple 1			Masceti Temple 2		
Subak	Hectares	Members	*Subak*	Hectares	Members
Lungsiakan	54.82	190	Mas	38.74	130
Kibul Bebek	28.37	108	Sindhu jiwa (includes two "tempeks")	94.59	317
Pacekan (includes four "tempeks")	133.41	446	Mandi	126.26	367
			Tebungkan	81.85	217
Subtotals	216.60	744		341.44	1,031

ha of rice fields. All *subaks* members share equally in the responsibility to maintain the main canal and weir. During the rainy season, the whole Ulun Swi unit plants the same variety of rice at the same time, ensuring a uniform fallow period after harvest to control pests. Traditionally, this planting is timed so that panicle development occurs at "full moon of the tenth month." For the second planting, each Masceti acts as a unit, choosing the crops to be planted, and assigning rotational irrigation if needed. Each *subak* (or in the case of large *subaks* like Pacekan, each *tempek* unit) takes turns in both maintenance of the irrigation works, and annual rituals at the Masceti and Ulun Swi temples. Moreover, each Masceti (rather than each *subak*) sends a delegation with offerings to the annual festival of the "master water temple" at the crater lake, Pura Ulun Danu Batur.

IRRIGATION FUNCTIONS OF THE "MASTER TEMPLE" ULUN DANU BATUR

Since space is limited, I will refrain from further exploration of variant regional water temple systems, and proceed on to the question of whether some centralized authority exists. We have already seen that the "master water temple" Pura Ulun Danu Batur plays a significant organizational role by setting the "irrigation year" calendar for its 204 *subaks*. But does the temple play an active role in irrigation management, or is it primarily a religious institution?

To answer this question, I wish to briefly recount three occasions in which I observed the activities of the temple priests in irrigation management.

Creation of a New *Subak*

In April 1983 I was summoned to the master water temple by the two high priests in order to film an unusual event: the creation of a new *subak*.[3] A group of dry farmers from a hamlet in the district of Gianyar had organized themselves into a work group, with the intention of forming a *subak*.[4] They terraced approximately 40 ha of hillsides (on two adjacent slopes), and hired a traditional irrigation tunnel engineer to guide them in the construction of tunnels and canals originating at a small spring about 4 km upstream. Before beginning work on the first tunnel, a delegation consisting of the newly elected head of the *subak* and half a dozen assistants made a pilgrimage to the master temple, to obtain blessings and practical advice on what is required to create a *subak*. A temple priest inspected the proposed tunnel and terrace sites.

On the morning I arrived at the temple, two large trucks carrying the entire membership of the *subak* arrived at the temple and made offerings to the deities concerned with irrigation, of whom the foremost is Dewi Danu (Goddess of the Lake). Afterwards, I accompanied eight priests from the temple and the *subak* on a journey by truck to the spring from which they hoped to obtain water for irrigation. The head priest selected a site for a small shrine, the "water-origin shrine" for offerings to the Goddess of the Lake,

about 10 m from the spring itself. Ground-purifying offerings were made by the whole *subak*, followed by a water-augmenting ceremony climaxed by the coaxing of a live duck to swim away downstream, in the direction of the terraces.

The duck was soon followed downstream by a procession consisting of the *subak*, the temple priests, anthropologist, and film crew, to the site of the new terraces. The high priest, who is regarded as an irrigation expert, began by surveying the terraces and the unfinished small tunnel which represented the last piece of the irrigation works. He criticized the placement of the tunnel, on grounds that it was too far down the slope, and the *subak* head agreed to change it. Next, he selected the site for the Ulum Swi (Head of the Terraces) temple, and other priests actually measured out and marked off its dimensions and explained the placement of shrines. These shrines included not only the Lake Goddess of the master temple, but also a shrine to the principal deities of the local Masceti (regional water temple).

Creation of a New Irrigation Tunnel

Balinese irrigation tunnels often extend for hundreds of meters, and in some cases apparently over a kilometer, through the volcanic rock. There are several teams of traditional engineers who are expert in the construction of these tunnels. I accompanied teams of tunnel builders to the master temple for blessings, and observed the construction of several new tunnels. According to the tunnel engineers and the priests, any new tunnels require the sanction of the master water temple, since all water is considered a gift from the goddess, and temple priests are responsible for mediating water rights of *subaks* sharing the same rivers.

Pest Control

In 1979 the priests of the temple came to the conclusion that a plague of rodents threatened to become widespread. Instructions were sent down to all member *subaks* to build a special temporary shrine at all water inlets in every field, and perform a brief prayer and offering every third day for 15 days. A widespread fallow period was also suggested, but due to confusion resulting from the adoption of new high-yielding varieties of rice and fertilizer, the fallow period was not uniformly observed. The small shrines duly appeared— on time—by the thousand.

In order to provide a succinct impression of the role of the master temple in irrigation, I have translated excerpts from an interview with the Jero Gde Alitan, one of the two high priests of the temple, the acknowledged expert on irrigation mentioned above. Also present were the chief Temple Scribe, a *subak* head who happened to be visiting, and a couple of other temple priests.

On establishing a new weir:

> *High Priest:* If someone wants to build a new weir, first he must come here to request a black

stone, to place underneath, as a symbol. The black stone is used as the foundation, and is positioned in a small ceremony. Then construction can begin—they can break ground.

Lansing: Where is the ceremony held?

High Priest: There are two—here at the temple, and also at the weir. The ceremony is called *pemunghkah empelan*—opening the weir. Afterwards, we build a shrine *(Asaghan)* at the weir, to worship the Deity who resides here at Ulun Danu, and also at Gunung Agung, and also at Masceti temples. Every day before working on such a project, the builders must offer prayers . . .

On tunnel building:

High Priest: This was about two years ago. Here was the problem: about 12 km from here, in the district of Bunutin (Bangli), there were two rivers. East of Bunutin there is a river, and also one to the west. The people wanted to use the larger river. But when they invited me for the first inspection, I saw that it wasn't feasible—using the larger river would be more difficult, and cost a lot more. I figured out a way to use the smaller river, and they agreed to try it. And it worked—they're getting harvests already. Later we added another weir to the west of the first one. And now water shortage is not a problem in Bunutin any more.

On settling a dispute over water rights:

High Priest: This was just downstream from Sekaan. There is a big spring there, called "Bulan." This spring had been used by local subaks, like Pejeng Aji. It wasn't producing a lot of water—about 100 liters per minute, I think. Now, downstream and off to one side there are a lot of villages—Lukan, Jasan, Tegal Suci, Jati, Belong, Pisan . . .

Temple Scribe: Batas, Tebuana . . .

High Priest: And they asked if some of the unused water could be brought up to them, like this (refers to sketch). But the *subaks* that were already using the water didn't want to permit this, because it was their water. They were worried that they would get less. So they wouldn't give permission. This was debated until it reached the Governor. So finally I went. I said to

them, "Who created this water? Who decides if this spring is full, or dries up?" And they had to answer! I said, "Do you understand that if we fight over this gift from the goddess, her spring might just dry up? Completely vanish?" I brought them all up to the temple here, and when we had it settled, work began. The new canal ran off below the spring, and took off quite a lot of water. But—now this is the point—not 200 m further downstream, the flow was back to normal. In fact, it actually increased after everything was finished! I tell you, that made quite an impression. The head of that *subak*—what's his name—he was here just two days ago . . .

Temple Scribe: That was around 1968. But they all come—if we have to repair part of the temple, or if we have a big ritual, they don't fail to send a big delegation to help.

High Priest: They're still afraid that the spring might dry up!

On the plague of rodents in 1979 (see above):

Subak Head: It was all over [the region of] Gianyar! In my *subak,* for a long time the numbers of rats had been growing . . .

Another priest: Around Kemenuh, and all the downstream *subaks* . . .

Another priest: Actually, from Payangan all the way to the sea!

Subak Head (speaking to the High Priest): And the Government helped out, right?

High Priest: No, it wasn't a government matter—it was a *subak* problem. We sent instructions to every *subak*. In truth, the government helped *cause* the problem, upsetting the fallow periods . . .

CONCLUSION

> *. . . dening ida amedalang ring tirtha iki sapunika ne kagaduh gaman ida, yan sira apreduha ring gaman sira, nora wnang malih dwen ida carike*
>
> *. . . because the goddess makes the waters flow, those who do not follow her laws may not possess her rice terraces*
>
> —Rajapurana Ulun Danu Batur, Vol. II:24 28.b.1

Hitherto the debate on Balinese irrigation has focused on two alternatives: the "centralized" model, in which irrigation is managed by a state bureaucracy (Marx, Wittfogel), and the "decentralized" model, in which each *subak* is an autonomous unit (Geertz, Hobart). The evidence I have submitted suggests a third alternative: irrigation is centrally organized by a system of water temples, separate from the state. The first question a skeptic might ask is why the existence of the water temple system had not been reported earlier. Part of the answer doubtless lies in the fact that previous studies concentrated on individual villages rather the regional patterns of irrigation—a problem that Hunt (1976:398) and Coward (1980:8) suggest is common for anthropological studies of irrigation. But more fundamentally, the attempt to identify a discrete system of irrigation management may have misconceived the problem. "Irrigation management" simply means providing water for crops. But as we have seen, Balinese water temples do a great deal more than this. Viewed from the standpoint of systems ecology, a rice terrace is a complex artificial ecosystem. The water temples make decisions which manipulate the states of the system, at ascending levels in regional hierarchies. For example, when the regional water temple Masceti Air Jeruk institutes a 15-day fallow period over 500 ha to control a pest outbreak, it is managing the regional terrace ecosystem, not just irrigation.

There are other reasons why the water temple networks should have remained nearly invisible to outsiders. Consider the temples called "Sea Temples" *(pura segara)*, usually located on a beach or islet near a river outlet. Superficially, there is nothing to connect these temples with irrigation, for they play no direct role in agricultural management. But by marking the downstream terminus of a water temple network, they play an important part in the internal logic of the water temple system. The ability of water temple networks to function as ecosystem regulators is predicated on fulfilling a role in Balinese cosmology which places the instrumental logic of agricultural decisions in a wider religious context.

But is the system really separate from the state? In response to this question, the priest of the temple Masceti Pamos Apuh told the following story:

> Around the year 1870, the neighboring princedoms of Bangli and Gianyar were at war with one another. The irrigation systems which provide water for Gianyar originate in Bangli, and Bangli is also the home of the "master temple" Ulun Danu Batur. Hostilities continued through the rainy season, so farmers from Gianyar were afraid to pass through Bangli on their way to the tenth-month festival at Ulun Danu Batur. Near the border of the two princedoms, where the Oos river leaves Bangli and enters Gianyar, there is a regional water temple, Pura Masceti Pamos Apuh. The farmers of Gianyar held special ceremonies at this, the most "upstream" of their water temples, to transform it into a temporary "way-station" *(penyawangan)* temple for the Goddess of the Lake and her retinue. For as long as hostilities continued between Bangli and Gianyar, the temple functioned as a substitute "master temple" for the *subaks* of Gianyar.

The very detachment of the water temple system from the political order has undoubtedly helped to preserve it, even after the demise of the traditional Balinese states (Lansing 1983). But recently, the "invisibility" of the system has worked to its disadvantage. Beginning in the 1970s, the Balinese were encouraged to increase rice production by adopting new high-yielding varieties of rice, along with new cropping patterns based on use of commercial fertilizers and pesticides. Most recently, a series of studies by foreign consultants have recommended changes in irrigation management. For these consultants, the water temple system is indeed invisible. Irrigation development plans invariably assume that the individual *subaks* are the highest-level "traditional" Balinese institutions concerned with irrigation. Major changes in irrigation are under consideration:

> The Bali Irrigation Project (B.I.P.) is the first large scale attempt in Bali island to improve the irrigation systems. Past interventions by the Department of Public Works have been limited to isolated improvements, with negligible external consequences. In contrast, the B.I.P. will intervene in 130 subaks (about 10 percent of the total Bali subaks), many sharing the water from the same river. The impact of the main improvements will concern:
> - River water sharing and Subak coordination;
> - New O & M rules;
> - Programmed cropping patterns;
> - Use of measurement systems;
> - Changes in cropping techniques;
> - Yield monitoring systems;
> - Taxes and water charges.
>
> In consequence the Subak may lose some of its traditional facets, especially part of its autonomy.
>
> Feasibility Study, Part Two (1981)
> Bali Irrigation Project

Some changes have already begun. Ten years ago, in the first flush of the "Green Revolution," Balinese farmers were instructed to ignore the temple-scheduling system, and plant as often as possible so as to increase yields. Religious ceremonies continued in the temples, but the system of region-wide fallow periods broke down. As a consequence, the incidence of bacterial and viral diseases, together with insect and rat populations, began to increase rapidly. Imported organochloride pesticides made some dents in the rising pest populations, but also killed off eels, fish, and in some cases farmers in the rice fields.[5] By the early 1980s, most *subaks* were hotly debating a return to the regional water-temple scheduling system in order to control pests, and reduce the need for pesticides.[6]

Today, two irrigation-management institutions coexist on the island, institutions so fundamentally dissimilar that they are all but invisible to each other. Downstream, foreign consultants dispatch airplanes to photograph Bali's rivers from above, and draw topographic maps of new irrigation systems. Upstream, a group of farmers drop frangipani flowers in their canals before beginning a new ploughing. The new *subak* prepares for the dedication of its Ulun Swi temples, two *subaks* arrive at the master water temple for advice on dealing with the brown plant-hoppers which have destroyed half their crop, and half a dozen men with picks and shovels shore up the sides of a field that has produced two crops of rice each year for the past eight centuries.

NOTES

Acknowledgments. This research was supported by a grant from the National Science Foundation, #BNS-8210124. I wish to thank Gusti Ngurah Bagus, Harold Conklin, Janet Hoskins, Robert Hunt, Kristina Melcher, Alexander Moore, Gary Seaman, and especially Therese de Vet.

1. For descriptions of the *subak* system, see Birkelbach (1973); Geertz (1972, 1980); Grader (1960[1938]); Korn (1932); Wirz (1927).

2. Various writers (e.g., Covarrubias 1937:284) have described the festival of Galungan, which occurs on the fourth day of the 11th week (Dungulan) of the *uku* calendar as a "New Year's Day," but in fact it is not. The New Year actually begins on the first day of the tenth month, e.g., the day after the new moon of Kasanga, following the new moon closest to the spring equinox.

3. The film, *The Temple of the Crater Lake,* is available from Documentary Educational Resources, 5 Bridge St., Watertown, MA 02172.

4. C. J. Grader briefly mentions the creation of two new *subaks* in North Bali in 1914 and 1931, but describes only matters relating to taxation (Grader 1960[1938]:284–285).

5. Hospital officials at R.S.U.P. Denpasar report several cases of apparent fatalities due to pesticide poisoning.

6. Three factors seem particularly salient: the fact that pesticides destroy the natural enemies of pests, as well as the pests themselves; the appearance of new resistant biotypes of pests such as the brown plant-hopper and tungro virus; and the environmental degradation caused by pesticides. Altogether, it would appear that there is a strong economic/ecological case to be made for reducing pesticide use in favor of the tried-and-true Balinese water temple system of region-wide fallow periods (see Conway 1983 and Oka 1979).

REFERENCES CITED

Avinieri, Shlomo, ed.
  1969 Karl Marx on Colonialism and Modernization. New York: Anchor Books.
Bali Irrigation Project
  1981 Bali Irrigation Project Feasibility Study. Jakarta: Ministry of Public Works, Directorate General of Water Resources Development, Republic of Indonesia.
Birkelbach, Aubrey
  1973 The Subak Association. Indonesia 16:153–169.
Conway, Gordon R., and D. S. McCauley
  1983 Intensifying Tropical Agriculture: The Indonesian Experience. Nature 302:288–289.
Covarrubias, Miguel
  1937 Island of Bali. New York: Alfred Knopf.
Coward, E. Walter, ed.
  1980 Irrigation and Agricultural Development in Asia. Ithaca, NY: Cornell University Press.
DeDatta, Surajit K.
  1981 Principles and Practices of Rice Production. New York: John Wiley & Sons.
Foucault, Michel
  1980 Michel Foucault: Power/Knowledge, Selected Interviews and Other Writings. Colin Gordon, ed. New York: Pantheon Books.
Geertz, Clifford
  1972 The Wet and the Dry: Traditional Irrigation in Bali and Morocco. Human Ecology 1:23–39.
  1980 Negara: The Balinese Theater State in the Nineteenth Century. Princeton, NJ: Princeton University Press.
Grader, C. J.
  1960[1938] The Irrigation System in the Region of Jembrana. *In* Bali: Life, Thought, Ritual. J. L. Swellengrebel, ed. Pp. 270–288. The Hague: W. van Hoeve.
Happé, P. L. E.
  1919 Een Beschouwing over het Zuid-Balische Soebakwezen en zijn Verwording in Verband met de Voorgenomen Vorming van Waterschappen in N.I. Indische Gids 41:183–200.
Hobart, Mark
  1982 Padi, Puns and the Attribution of Responsibility. *In* Natural Symbols in Southeast Asia. G. B. Milner, ed. Pp. 55–88. London: School of Oriental and African Studies.
Hunt, Robert
  1984 Measurement of Organization of Authority and Scale in Canal Irrigation Associations. Unpublished ms.
Hunt, Robert, and Eva Hunt
  1976 Canal Irrigation and Local Social Organization. Current Anthropology 17:389–411.
Korn, V. E.
  1932 Het Adatrecht van Bali. 2nd edition. The Hague: G. Naeff.
Lansing, J. S.
  1983 The Three Worlds of Bali. New York: Praeger.
Millon, Rene
  1962 Variations in Social Responses to the Practice of Irrigation Culture. *In* Civilizations in Desert Lands. Anthropology Paper #62. R. Woodbury, ed. Pp. 56–88. Salt Lake City: University of Utah.
Oka, Ida Nyoman
  1979 Cultural Control of the Brown Planthopper. *In* Brown Planthopper: Threat to Rice Production in Asia. Pp. 357–369. Manila: The International Rice Research Institute.
van der Heijden, A. J.
  1924–25 Het Waterschaps Wezen in het Voormalige Zuid-Balische Rijks. . . . Koloniale Studien 8:266–275; 9:425–438.
Wirz, Paul
  1927 Der Reisbau und die Reisbaukulte auf Bali und Lombok. Tijdschrift voor Indische Taal-, Land-, en Volkenkunde (Batavia) 67:217–345.
Wittfogel, Karl A.
  1957 Oriental Despotism: A Comparative Study of Total Power. New Haven, CT: Yale University Press.
Yoshida, Shouichi
  1981 Fundamentals of Rice Crop Science. Manila: The International Rice Research Institute.

Mother Cow

Marvin Harris

In "Mother Cow," a revision of his 1966 article "The Cultural Ecology of India's Sacred Cattle," Harris discusses the practical reasons behind the Hindu veneration of cows in India. Harris points out that the primary purpose of a cow in India is for traction, not milk production. Thus a cow's value is not measured in how much milk she produces, but how many plow-pulling calves she can bear. Harris also points out that the 700 million tons of manure produced by cows each year are rural India's primary source of fertilizer and cooking fuel. Indians consider cow dung to be a superior cooking fuel because it burns with a slow, long-lasting heat, sort of the Indian equivalent of crock-pot cooking. Also, contrary to popular belief that cows compete with humans for crops, Harris shows that cows generally graze on the stubble of harvested fields. Harris demonstrates that, in the long run, the prohibition against slaughtering cattle ultimately helps protect rural Indian farm production. In times of drought and famine, farmers might be tempted to slaughter cattle, but this is a solution only in the short term. Once their cattle were gone, farmers would surely starve because they would have no way to prepare their fields in the next season. Finally, Harris shows that Indians' use of cattle is far more efficient than our use of energy in the United States. He concludes that if you really want to see a sacred cow that is a wasteful use of resources, look at the American automobile.

As you read, consider these questions:
1. What are the economic implications and advantages of keeping cattle alive in India?
2. What happens to dead cows in India?
3. What does the author mean when he says that an Indian farmer will starve when he eats his cow?

Whenever I get into discussions about the influence of practical and mundane factors on lifestyles, someone is sure to say, "But what about all those cows the hungry peasants in India refuse to eat?" The picture of a ragged farmer starving to death alongside a big fat cow conveys a reassuring sense of mystery to Western observers. In countless learned and popular allusions, it confirms our deepest conviction about how people with inscrutable Oriental minds ought to act. It is comforting to know—somewhat like "there will always be an England"—that in India spiritual values are more pre-

cious than life itself. And at the same time it makes us feel sad. How can we ever hope to understand people so different from ourselves? Westerners find the idea that there might be a practical explanation for Hindu love of cow more upsetting than Hindus do. The sacred cow—how else can I say it?—is one of our favorite sacred cows.

Hindus venerate cows because cows are the symbol of everything that is alive. As Mary is to Christians the mother of God, the cow to Hindus is the mother of life. So there is no greater sacrilege for a Hindu than killing a cow. Even the taking of human life lacks the symbolic meaning, the unutterable defilement, that is evoked by cow slaughter.

According to many experts, cow worship is the number one cause of India's hunger and poverty. Some Western-trained agronomists say that the taboo against cow slaughter is keeping one hundred million "useless" animals alive. They claim that cow worship lowers the efficiency of agriculture because the useless animals contribute neither milk nor meat while competing for croplands and foodstuff with useful animals and hungry human beings. A study sponsored by the Ford Foundation in 1959 concluded that possibly half of India's cattle could be regarded as surplus in relation to feed supply. And an economist from the University of Pennsylvania stated in 1971 that India has thirty million unproductive cows.

It does seem that there are enormous numbers of surplus, useless, and uneconomic animals, and that this situation is a direct result of irrational Hindu doctrines. Tourists on their way through Delhi, Calcutta, Madras, Bombay, and other Indian cities are astonished at the liberties enjoyed by stray cattle. The animals wander through the streets, browse off the stalls in the market place, break into private gardens, defecate all over the sidewalks, and snarl traffic by pausing to chew their cuds in the middle of busy intersections. In the countryside, the cattle congregate on the shoulders of every highway and spend much of their time taking leisurely walks down the railroad tracks.

Love of cow affects life in many ways. Government agencies maintain old age homes for cows at which owners may board their dry and decrepit animals free of charge. In Madras, the police round up stray cattle that have fallen ill and nurse them back to health by letting them graze on small fields adjacent to the station house. Farmers regard their cows as members of the family, adorn them with garlands and tassels, pray for them when they get sick, and call in their neighbors and a priest to celebrate the birth of a new calf. Throughout India, Hindus hang on their walls calendars that portray beautiful, bejeweled young women who have the bodies of big fat white cows. Milk is shown jetting out of each teat of these half-women, half-zebu goddesses.

Starting with their beautiful human faces, cow pinups bear little resemblance to the typical cow one sees in the flesh. For most of the year their bones are their most prominent feature. Far from having milk gushing from every teat, the gaunt beasts barely manage to nurse a single calf to maturity. The average yield of whole milk from the typical hump-backed breed of zebu cow in India amounts to less than 500 pounds a year. Ordinary American dairy cattle produce over 5,000 pounds, while for champion milkers, 20,000 pounds is not unusual. But this comparison doesn't tell the whole story. In any given year about half of India's zebu cows give no milk at all—not a drop.

To make matters worse, love of cow does not stimulate love of man. Since Moslems spurn pork but eat beef, many Hindus consider them to be cow killers. Before the partition of the Indian subcontinent into India and Pakistan, bloody communal riots aimed at preventing the Moslems from killing cows became annual occurrences. Memories of old cow riots—as, for example, the one in Bihar in 1917 when thirty people died and 170 Moslem villages were looted down to the last doorpost—continue to embitter relations between India and Pakistan.

Although he deplored the rioting, Mohandas K. Gandhi was an ardent advocate of cow love and wanted a total ban on cow slaughter. When the Indian constitution was drawn up, it included a bill of rights for cows which stopped just short of outlawing every form of cow killing. Some states have since banned cow slaughter altogether, but others still permit exceptions. The cow question remains a major cause of rioting and disorders, not only between Hindus and the remnants of the Moslem community, but between the ruling Congress Party and extremist Hindu factions of cow lovers. On November 7, 1966, a mob of 120,000 people, led by a band of chanting, naked holy men draped with garlands of marigolds and smeared with white cow-dung ash, demonstrated against cow slaughter in front of the Indian House of Parliament. Eight persons were killed and forty-eight injured during the ensuing riot. This was followed by a nationwide wave of fasts among holy men, led by Muni Shustril Kumar, president of the All-Party Cow Protection Campaign Committee.

To Western observers familiar with modern industrial techniques of agriculture and stock raising, cow love seems senseless, even suicidal. The efficiency expert yearns to get his hands on all those useless animals and ship them off to a proper fate. And yet one finds certain inconsistencies in the condemnation of cow love. When I began to wonder if there might be a practical explanation for the sacred cow, I came across an intriguing government report. It said that India had too many cows but too few oxen. With so many cows around, how could there be a shortage of oxen? Oxen and male water buffalo are the principal source of traction for plowing India's fields. For each farm of ten acres or less, one pair of oxen or water buffalo is considered adequate. A little arithmetic shows that as far as plowing is concerned, there is indeed a shortage rather than a surplus of animals. India has 60 million farms, but only 80 million traction animals. If each farm had its quota of two oxen or two water buffalo, there ought to be 120 million traction animals—that is, 40 million more than are actually available.

The shortage may not be quite so bad since some farmers rent or borrow oxen from their neighbors. But the sharing of plow animals often proves impractical. Plowing must be coordinated with the monsoon rains, and by the time one farm has been plowed, the optimum moment for plowing another may already have passed. Also, after plowing is over, a farmer still needs his own pair of oxen to pull his oxcart, the mainstay of bulk transport throughout rural India. Quite possibly private ownership of farms, livestock, plows, and oxcarts lowers the efficiency of Indian agriculture, but this, I soon realized, was not caused by cow love.

The shortage of draft animals is a terrible threat that hangs over most of India's peasant families. When an ox falls sick a poor farmer is in danger of losing his farm. If he has no replacement for it, he will have to borrow money at usurious rates. Millions of rural households have in fact lost all or part of their holdings and have gone into sharecropping or day labor as a result of such debts. Every year hundreds of thousands of destitute farmers end up migrating to the cities, which already teem with unemployed and homeless persons.

The Indian farmer who can't replace his sick or deceased ox is in much the same situation as an American farmer who can neither replace nor repair his broken tractor. But there is an important difference: tractors are made by factories, but oxen are made by cows. A farmer who owns a cow owns a factory for making oxen. With or without cow love, this is a good reason for him not to be too anxious to sell his cow to the slaughterhouse. One also begins to see why Indian farmers might be willing to tolerate cows that give only 500 pounds of milk per year. If the main economic function of the zebu cow is to breed male traction animals, then there's no point in comparing her with specialized American dairy animals, whose main function is to produce milk. Still, the milk produced by zebu cows plays an important role in meeting the nutritional needs of many poor families. Even small amounts of milk products can improve the health of people who are forced to subsist on the edge of starvation.

When Indian farmers want an animal primarily for milking purposes they turn to the female water buffalo, which has longer lactation periods and higher butterfat yields than zebu cattle. Male water buffalo are also superior animals for plowing in flooded rice paddies. But oxen are more versatile and are preferred for dry-field farming and road transport. Above all, zebu breeds are remarkably rugged, and can survive the long droughts that periodically afflict different parts of India.

Agriculture is part of a vast system of human and natural relationships. To judge isolated portions of this "ecosystem" in terms that are relevant to the conduct of American agribusiness leads to some very strange impressions. Cattle figure in the Indian ecosystem in ways that are easily overlooked or demeaned by observers from industrialized high-energy societies. In the United States, chemicals have almost completely replaced animal manure as the principal source of farm fertilizer. American farmers stopped using manure when they began to plow with tractors rather than mules or horses. Since tractors excrete poisons rather than fertilizers, a commitment to large-scale machine farming is almost of necessity a commitment to the use of chemical fertilizers. And around the world today there has in fact grown up a vast integrated petrochemical-tractor-truck industrial complex that produces farm machinery, motorized transport, oil and gasoline, and chemical fertilizers and pesticides upon which new high-yield production techniques depend.

For better or worse, most of India's farmers cannot participate in this complex, not because they worship their cows, but because they can't afford to buy tractors. Like other underdeveloped nations, India can't build factories that are competitive with the facilities of the industrialized nations nor pay for large quantities of imported industrial products. To convert from animals and manure to tractors and petrochemicals would require the investment of incredible amounts of capital. Moreover, the inevitable effect of substituting costly machines for cheap animals is to reduce the number of people who can earn their living from agriculture and to force a corresponding increase in the size of the average farm. We know that the development of large-scale agribusiness in the United States has meant the virtual destruction of the small family farm. Less than 5 percent of U.S. families now live on farms, as compared with 60 percent about a hundred years ago. If agribusiness were to develop along similar lines in India, jobs and housing would soon have to be found for a quarter of a billion displaced peasants.

Since the suffering caused by unemployment and homelessness in India's cities is already intolerable, an additional massive build-up of the urban population can only lead to unprecedented upheavals and catastrophes.

With this alternative in view, it becomes easier to understand low-energy, small-scale, animal-based systems. As I have already pointed out, cows and oxen provide low-energy substitutes for tractors and tractor factories. They also should be credited with carrying out the functions of a petrochemical industry. India's cattle annually excrete about 700 million tons of recoverable manure. Approximately half of this is used as fertilizer, while most of the remainder is burned to provide heat for cooking. The annual quantity of heat liberated by this dung, the Indian housewife's main cooking fuel, is the thermal equivalent of 27 million tons of kerosene, 35 million tons of coal, or 68 million tons of wood. Since India has only small reserves of oil and coal and is already the victim of extensive deforestation, none of these fuels can be considered practical substitutes for cow dung. The thought of

dung in the kitchen may not appeal to the average American, but Indian women regard it as a superior cooking fuel because it is finely adjusted to their domestic routines. Most Indian dishes are prepared with clarified butter known as *ghee,* for which cow dung is the preferred source of heat since it burns with a clean, slow, long-lasting flame that doesn't scorch the food. This enables the Indian housewife to start cooking her meals and to leave them unattended for several hours while she takes care of the children, helps out in the fields, or performs other chores. American housewives achieve a similar effect through a complex set of electronic controls that come as expensive options on late-model stoves.

Cow dung has at least one other major function. Mixed with water and made into a paste, it is used as a household flooring material. Smeared over a dirt floor and left to harden into a smooth surface, it keeps the dust down and can be swept clean with a broom.

Because cattle droppings have so many useful properties, every bit of dung is carefully collected. Village small fry are given the task of following the family cow around and of bringing home its daily petrochemical output. In the cities, sweeper castes enjoy a monopoly on the dung deposited by strays and earn their living by selling it to housewives.

From an agribusiness point of view, a dry and barren cow is an economic abomination. But from the viewpoint of the peasant farmer, the same dry and barren cow may be a last desperate defense against the moneylenders. There is always the chance that a favorable monsoon may restore the vigor of even the most decrepit specimen and that she will fatten up, calve, and start giving milk again. This is what the farmer prays for; sometimes his prayers are answered. In the meantime, dung-making goes on. And so one gradually begins to understand why a skinny old hag of a cow still looks beautiful in the eyes of her owner.

Zebu cattle have small bodies, energy-storing humps on their back, and great powers of recuperation. These features are adapted to the specific conditions of Indian agriculture. The native breeds are capable of surviving for long periods with little food or water and are highly resistant to diseases that afflict other breeds in tropical climates. Zebu oxen are worked as long as they continue to breathe. Stuart Odend'hal, a veterinarian formerly associated with Johns Hopkins University, performed field autopsies on Indian cattle which had been working normally a few hours before their deaths but whose vital organs were damaged by massive lesions. Given their enormous recuperative powers, these beasts are never easily written off as completely "useless" while they are still alive.

But sooner or later there must come a time when all hope of an animal's recovery is lost and even dung-making ceases. And still the Hindu farmer refuses to kill it for food or sell it to the slaughterhouse. Isn't this incontrovertible evidence of a harmful economic practice that has no explanation apart from the religious taboos on cow slaughter and beef consumption?

No one can deny that cow love mobilizes people to resist cow slaughter and beef eating. But I don't agree that the anti-slaughter and beef-eating taboos necessarily have an adverse effect on human survival and well-being. By slaughtering or selling his aged and decrepit animals, a farmer might earn a few more rupees or temporarily improve his family's diet. But in the long run, his refusal to sell to the slaughterhouse or kill for his own table may have beneficial consequences. An established principle of ecological analysis states that communities of organisms are adapted not to average but to extreme conditions. The relevant situation in India is the recurrent failure of the monsoon rains. To evaluate the economic significance of the anti-slaughter and anti-beef-eating taboos, we have to consider what these taboos mean in the context of periodic droughts and famine.

The taboo on slaughter and beef eating may be as much a product of natural selection as the small bodies and fantastic recuperative powers of the zebu breeds. During droughts and famines, farmers are severely tempted to kill or sell their livestock. Those who succumb to this temptation seal their doom, even if they survive the drought, for when the rains come, they will be unable to plow their fields. I want to be even more emphatic: Massive slaughter of cattle under the duress of famine constitutes a much greater threat to aggregate welfare than any likely miscalculation by particular farmers concerning the usefulness of their animals during normal times. It seems probable that the sense of unutterable profanity elicited by cow slaughter has its roots in the excruciating contradiction between immediate needs and long-run conditions of survival. Cow love with its sacred symbols and holy doctrines protects the farmer against calculations that are "rational" only in the short term. To Western experts it looks as if "the Indian farmer would rather starve to death than eat his cow." The same kinds of experts like to talk about the "inscrutable Oriental mind" and think that "life is not so dear to the Asian masses." They don't realize that the farmer would rather eat his cow than starve, but that he will starve if he does eat it.

Even with the assistance of the holy laws and cow love, the temptation to eat beef under the duress of famine sometimes proves irresistible. During World War II, there was a great famine in Bengal caused by droughts and the Japanese occupation of Burma. Slaughter of cows and draft animals reached such alarming levels in the summer of 1944 that the British had to use troops to enforce the cow-protection laws. In 1967 *The New York Times* reported:

> Hindus facing starvation in the drought-stricken area of Bihar are slaughtering cows and eating the meat even though the animals are sacred to the Hindu religion.

Observers noted that "the misery of the people was beyond imagination."

The survival into old age of a certain number of absolutely useless animals during good times is part of the price that must be paid for protecting useful animals against slaughter during bad times. But I wonder how much is actually lost because of the prohibition on slaughter and the taboo on beef. From a Western agribusiness viewpoint, it seems irrational for India not to have a meat-packing industry. But the actual potential for such an industry in a country like India is very limited. A substantial rise in beef production would strain the entire ecosystem, not because of cow love but because of the laws of thermodynamics. In any food chain, the interposition of additional animal links result in a sharp decrease in the efficiency of food production. The caloric value of what an animal has eaten is always much greater than the caloric value of its body. This means that more calories are available per capita when plant food is eaten directly by a human population than when it is used to feed domesticated animals.

Because of the high level of beef consumption in the United States, three-quarters of all our croplands are used for feeding cattle rather than people. Since the per capita calorie intake in India is already below minimum daily requirements, switching croplands to meat production could only result in higher food prices and a further deterioration in the living standards for poor families. I doubt if more than 10 percent of the Indian people will ever be able to make beef an important part of their diet, regardless of whether they believe in cow love or not.

I also doubt that sending more aged and decrepit animals to existing slaughterhouses would result in nutritional gains for the people who need it most. Most of these animals get eaten anyway, even if they aren't sent to the slaughterhouse, because throughout India there are low-ranking castes whose members have the right to dispose of the bodies of dead cattle. In one way or another, twenty million cattle die every year, and a large portion of their meat is eaten by these carrion-eating "untouchables."

My friend Dr. Joan Mencher, an anthropologist who has worked in India for many years, points out that the existing slaughterhouses cater to urban middle-class non-Hindus. She notes that "the untouchables get their food in other ways. It is good for the untouchable if a cow dies of starvation in a village, but not if it gets sent to an urban slaughterhouse to be sold to Muslims or Christians." Dr. Mencher's informants at first denied that any Hindu would eat beef, but when they learned that "upper-caste" Americans liked steak, they readily confessed their taste for beef curry.

Like everything else I have been discussing, meat eating by untouchables is finely adjusted to practical conditions. The meat-eating castes also tend to be the leather-working castes, since they have the right to dispose of the skin of the fallen cattle. So despite cow love, India manages to have a huge leathercraft industry. Even in death, apparently useless animals continue to be exploited for human purposes.

I could be right about cattle being useful for traction, fuel, fertilizer, milk, floor covering, meat, and leather, and still misjudge the ecological and economic significance of the whole complex. Everything depends on how much all of this costs in natural resources and human labor relative to alternative modes of satisfying the needs of India's huge population. These costs are determined largely by what the cattle eat. Many experts assume that man and cow are locked in a deadly competition for land and food crops. This might be true if Indian farmers followed the American agribusiness model and fed their animals on food crops. But the shameless truth about the sacred cow is that she is an indefatigable scavenger. Only an insignificant portion of the food consumed by the average cow comes from pastures and food crops set aside for their use.

This ought to have been obvious from all those persistent reports about cows wandering about and snarling traffic. What are those animals doing in the markets, on the lawns, along the highways and railroad tracks, and up on the barren hillsides? What are they doing if not eating every morsel of grass, stubble, and garbage that cannot be directly consumed by human beings and converting it into milk and other useful products. In his study of cattle in West Bengal, Dr. Odend'hal discovered that the major constituent in the cattle's diet is inedible by-products of human food crops, principally rice straw, wheat bran, and rice husks. When the Ford Foundation estimated that half of the cattle were surplus in relation to feed supply, they meant to say that half of the cattle manage to survive even without access to fodder crops. But this is an understatement. Probably less than 20 percent of what the cattle eat consists of humanly edible substances; most of this is fed to working oxen and water buffalo rather than to dry and barren cows. Odend'hal found that in his study area there was no competition between cattle and humans for land or the food supply: "Basically, the cattle convert items of little direct human value into products of immediate utility."

One reason why cow love is so often misunderstood is that it has different implications for the rich and the poor. Poor farmers use it as a license to scavenge while the wealthy farmers resist it as a rip-off. To the poor farmer, the cow is a holy beggar; to the rich farmer, it's a thief. Occasionally the cows invade someone's pastures or planted fields. The landlords complain, but the poor peasants plead ignorance and depend on cow love to get their animals back. If there is competition, it is between man and man or caste and caste, not between man and beast.

City cows also have owners who let them scrounge by day and call them back at night to be milked. Dr. Mencher recounts that while she lived for a while in a middle-class neighborhood in Madras her neighbors were constantly complaining about "stray" cows breaking into the family compounds. The strays were actually owned by people who lived in a room above a shop and who sold milk door to door in the neighborhood. As for the old age homes and police cowpounds, they serve very nicely to reduce the risk of maintaining cows in a city environment. If a cow stops producing milk, the owner may decide to let it wander around until the police pick it up and bring it to the precinct house.

When the cow has recovered, the owner pays a small fine and returns it to its usual haunts. The old age homes operate on a similar principle, providing cheap government-subsidized pasture that would otherwise not be available to city cows.

Incidentally, the preferred form of purchasing milk in the cities is to have the cow brought to the house and milked on the spot. This is often the only way that the householder can be sure that he is buying pure milk rather than milk mixed with water or urine.

What seems most incredible about these arrangements is that they have been interpreted as evidence of wasteful, anti-economic Hindu practices, while in fact they reflect a degree of economizing that goes far beyond Western, "Protestant" standards of savings and husbandry. Cow love is perfectly compatible with a merciless determination to get the literal last drop of milk out of the cow. The man who takes the cow door to door brings along a dummy calf made out of stuffed calfskin which he sets down beside the cow to trick it into performing. When this doesn't work, the owner may resort to *phooka,* blowing air into the cow's uterus through a hollow pipe, or *doom dev,* stuffing its tail into the vaginal orifice. Gandhi believed that cows were treated more cruelly in India than anywhere else in the world. "How we bleed her to take the last drop of milk from her," he lamented. "How we starve her to emaciation, how we ill-treat the calves, how we deprive them of their portion of milk, how cruelly we treat the oxen, how we castrate them, how we beat them, how we overload them."

No one understood better than Gandhi that cow love had different implications for rich and poor. For him the cow was a central focus of the struggle to rouse India to authentic nationhood. Cow love went along with small-scale farming, making cotton thread on a hand spinning wheel, sitting cross-legged on the floor, dressing in a loincloth, vegetarianism, reverence for life, and strict nonviolence. To these themes Gandhi owed his vast popular following among the peasant masses, urban poor, and untouchables. It was his way of protecting them against the ravages of industrialization.

The asymmetrical implications of *ahimsa* for rich and poor are ignored by economists who want to make Indian agriculture more efficient by slaughtering "surplus" animals. Professor Alan Heston, for example, accepts the fact that the cattle perform vital functions for which substitutes are not readily available. But he proposes that the same functions could be carried out more efficiently if there were 30 million fewer cows. This figure is based on the assumption that with adequate care only 40 cows per 100 male animals would be needed to replace the present number of oxen. Since there are 72 million adult male cattle, by this formula, 24 million breeding females ought to be sufficient. Actually, there are 54 million cows. Subtracting 24 million from 54 million, Heston arrives at the estimate of 30 million "useless" animals to be slaughtered. The fodder and feed that these "useless" animals have been consuming are to be distributed among the remaining animals, who will become healthier and therefore will be able to keep total milk and dung production at or above previous levels. But whose cows are to be sacrificed? About 43 percent of the total cattle population is found on the poorest 62 percent of the farms. These farms, consisting of five acres or less, have only 5 percent of the pasture and grazing land. In other words, most of the animals that are temporarily dry, barren, and feeble are owned by the people who live on the smallest and poorest farms. So that when the economists talk about getting rid of 30 million cows, they are really talking about getting rid of 30 million cows that belong to poor families, not rich ones. But most poor farmers own only one cow, so what this economizing boils down to is not so much getting rid of 30 million cows as getting rid of 150 million people—forcing them off the land and into the cities.

Cow-slaughter enthusiasts base their recommendation on an understandable error. They reason that since the farmers refuse to kill their animals, and since there is a religious taboo against doing so, therefore it is the taboo that is mainly responsible for the high ratio of cows to oxen. Their error is hidden in the observed ratio itself: 70 cows to 100 oxen. If cow love prevents farmers from killing cows that are economically useless, how is it there are 30 percent fewer cows than oxen? Since approximately as many female as male animals are born, something must be causing the death of more females than males. The solution to this puzzle is that while no Hindu farmer deliberately slaughters a female calf or decrepit cow with a club or a knife, he can and does get rid of them when they become truly useless from his point of view. Various methods short of direct slaughter are employed. To "kill" unwanted calves, for example, a triangular wooden yoke is placed about their necks so that when they try to nurse they jab the cow's udder and get kicked to death. Older animals are simply tethered on short ropes and allowed to starve—a process that does not take too long if the animal is already weak and diseased. Finally, unknown numbers of decrepit cows are surreptitiously sold through a chain of Moslem and Christian middlemen and end up in the urban slaughterhouses.

If we want to account for the observed proportions of cows to oxen, we must study rain, wind, water, and land-tenure patterns, not cow love. The proof of this is that the proportion of cows to oxen varies with the relative importance of different components of the agricultural system in different regions of India. The most important variable is the amount of irrigation water available for the cultivation of rice. Wherever there are extensive wet rice paddies, the water buffalo tends to be the preferred traction animal, and the female water buffalo is then substituted for the zebu cow as a source of milk. That is why in the vast plains of northern India, where the melting Himalayan snows and monsoons create the Holy River Ganges, the proportion of cows to oxen drops down to 47 to 100. As the distinguished Indian

economist K. N. Raj has pointed out, districts in the Ganges Valley where continuous year-round rice-paddy cultivation is practiced, have cow-to-oxen ratios that approach the theoretical optimum. This is all the more remarkable since the region in question—the Gangetic plain—is the heartland of the Hindu religion and contains its most holy shrines.

The theory that religion is primarily responsible for the high proportion of cows to oxen is also refuted by a comparison between Hindu India and Moslem West Pakistan. Despite the rejection of cow love and the beef-slaughter and beef-eating taboos, West Pakistan as a whole has 60 cows for every 100 male animals, which is considerably higher than the average for the intensely Hindu Indian state of Uttar Pradesh. When districts in Uttar Pradesh are selected for the importance of water buffalo and canal irrigation and compared with ecologically similar districts in West Pakistan, ratios of female to male turn out to be virtually the same.

Do I mean to say that cow love has no effect whatsoever on the cattle sex ratio or on other aspects of the agricultural system? No. What I am saying is that cow love is an active element in a complex, finely articulated material and cultural order. Cow love mobilizes the latent capacity of human beings to persevere in a low-energy ecosystem in which there is little room for waste or indolence. Cow love contributes to the adaptive resilience of the human population by preserving temporarily dry or barren but still useful animals; by discouraging the growth of an energy-expensive beef industry; by protecting cattle that fatten in the public domain or at landlord's expense; and by preserving the recovery potential of the cattle population during droughts and famines. As in any natural or artificial system, there is some slippage, friction, or waste associated with these complex interactions. Half a billion people, animals, land, labor, political economy, soil, and climate are all involved. The slaughter enthusiasts claim that the practice of letting cows breed indiscriminately and then thinning their numbers through neglect and starvation is wasteful and inefficient. I do not doubt that this is correct, but only in a narrow and relatively insignificant sense. The savings that an agricultural engineer might achieve by getting rid of an unknown number of absolutely useless animals must be balanced against catastrophic losses for the marginal peasants, especially during droughts and famines, if cow love ceases to be a holy duty.

Since the effective mobilization of all human action depends upon the acceptance of psychologically compelling creeds and doctrines, we have to expect that economic systems will always oscillate under and over their points of optimum efficiency. But the assumption that the whole system can be made to work better simply by attacking its consciousness is naïve and dangerous. Major improvements in the present system can be achieved by stabilizing India's human population, and by making more land, water, oxen, and water buffalo available to more people on a more equitable basis. The alternative is to destroy the present system graphic, technological, politico-economic, and ideological relationships—a whole new ecosystem. Hinduism is undoubtedly a conservative force, one that makes it more difficult for the "development" experts and "modernizing" agents to destroy the old system and to replace it with a high-energy industrial and agribusiness complex. But if you think that a high-energy industrial and agribusiness complex will necessarily be more "rational" or "efficient" than the system that now exists, forget it.

Contrary to expectations, studies of energy costs and energy yields show that India makes more efficient use of its cattle than the United States does. In Singur district in West Bengal, Dr. Odend'hal discovered that the cattle's gross energetic efficiency, defined as the total of useful calories produced per year divided by the total calories consumed during the same period, was 17 percent. This compares with a gross energetic efficiency of less than 4 percent for American beef cattle raised on Western range land. As Odend'hal says, the relatively high efficiency of the Indian cattle complex comes about not because the animals are particularly productive, but because of scrupulous product utilization by humans: "The villagers are extremely utilitarian and nothing is wasted."

Wastefulness is more a characteristic of modern agribusiness than of traditional peasant economies. Under the new system of automated feed-lot beef production in the United States, for example, cattle manure not only goes unused, but it is allowed to contaminate ground water over wide areas and contributes to the pollution of nearby lakes and streams.

The higher standard of living enjoyed by the industrial nations is not the result of greater productive efficiency, but of an enormously expanded increase in the amount of energy available per person. In 1970 the United States used up the energy equivalent of twelve tons of coal per inhabitant, while the corresponding figure for India was one-fifth ton per inhabitant. The way this energy was expended involved far more energy being wasted per person in the United States than in India. Automobiles and airplanes are faster than oxcarts, but they do not use energy more efficiently. In fact, more calories go up in useless heat and smoke during a single day of traffic jams in the United States than is wasted by all the cows of India during an entire year. The comparison is even less favorable when we consider the fact that the stalled vehicles are burning up irreplaceable reserves of petroleum that it took the earth tens of millions of years to accumulate. If you want to see a real sacred cow, go out and look at the family car.

Sacred Terrain:
Religion, Politics, and Place in the
History of Anloga (Ghana)

Sandra E. Greene

In this essay, Sandra Greene looks at religious conflict in a community in Ghana called Anloga and investigates why an area called Gbakute, a place of execution and the location of a shrine of a powerful war god, has been the focus of religious conflict for more than two hundred years. In particular, Greene examines the spiritual meanings that were attached to Gbakute, the way these meanings have been used to contest power in the precolonial, colonial, and postcolonial periods, and whether these old meanings, associated with a sacred grove of trees at Gbakute had an impact on the 1987 conflict described at the start of the essay.

In the main part of the essay Greene discusses how Gbakute became the spiritual center of Anlo society and how the religious order that controlled the sacred grove at

Gbakute resisted Christianity and continued to influence political affairs in Anlo. When British colonial authorities destroyed the grove, they replaced it with a police station to indicate their political authority. Later the Church of Pentecost purchased a lot in the area of Gbakute and built a church as a symbol of the spiritual power of their beliefs. All this is possible, and has political meaning, because the old religious associations associated with the Gbakute and its former grove of trees continue to survive.

In this essay we can see how elements of the environment can be incorporated into religious beliefs, and Greene demonstrates how symbolic meanings and geography can be central to understanding the political and religious history of an area.

As you read, consider these questions:

1. How are sacred locations used to manipulate politics and power in Anloga?

"Sacred Terrain: Religion, Politics and Place in the History of Angola (Ghana)" by Sandra E. Greene frrom *International Journal of African Historical Studies* 30:1 (1997) 1-22. Reprinted with permission.

2. How did the meaning of the sacred location discussed in this chapter change through time?
3. In what ways do religious practices influence power and authority in Anloga society?

In May 1987, members of the Church of Pentecost in the town of Anloga found themselves under attack. Within a period of twenty days, a number of town residents unaffiliated with the church broke into one of two Pentecostal chapels used in the town and seized the drums that church members used in their worship and prayer services. The vandalized building was then set ablaze and burnt to the ground. Several days after this first fire, flames engulfed and destroyed the second chapel. Church members were swift in identifying the culprits. Earlier in the year, priests associated with the most powerful gods worshipped by traditional religious believers in Anloga had declared a ban on drumming for the period between April 26th and May 26th. The ban was imposed as part of the customary rites that community leaders had held for over one hundred years to renew the town's association with those deities that were believed to have the greatest influence over the well-being of the community and all its citizens. The Church of Pentecost—introduced into the town in 1948—had never recognized or acknowledged the importance of this ritual; in fact, from the first days of their existence in Anloga they defied the ban by refusing to silence their drums during the proscribed period. Why in 1987, after thirty five years, did their practices suddenly become so offensive that others within the community felt the need to take action against them?

Perhaps the most compelling explanation for this sudden upsurge in conflicts between traditional religious believers and the Pentecostal community has to do with the changes that occurred within the community and in the larger society after the death in 1984 of one of the most esteemed elders of the town, T. S. A. Togobo. Prominent in Anlo politics since the late 1940's, Togobo had positioned himself to serve as a bridge between the Christian and the traditional religious community in Anloga. As an advisor to the then paramount chief of Anlo, Fia Sri II, he strongly supported efforts by the so-called traditionalists within Sri's advisory council to maintain the seat of the Anlo local governance in Anloga (the center of Anlo political and religious authority since at least the 17th century) rather than relocate it to Keta (the commercial center of the area and site of the office of the British colonial district commissioner).[1] He very consciously respected the customs and rites associated with the traditional religious orders in Anloga. But he was also a prominent member of the Evangelical Presbyterian Church and a strong advocate for the "untraditional" levying of taxes to support both local government structures and educational initiatives. According to some, it was Togobo—in his position as advisor to both Togbui Sri II, and his successor Togbui Adeladza

II—who used his influence within the paramount chief's council to urge others to tolerate the activities of the Church of Pentecost despite their willful defiance of local customs.[2] On his death, the balance within the Council shifted in favor of taking a more uniform approach to violations of the ban. In 1984, the year in which Togobo became quite ill and died, the Church of Pentecost again ignored the ban on drumming imposed by the traditional religious authorities. Backed by the paramount chief and his council, the drums were seized, but then released to them after a warning was issued. The following year, in 1985, Pentecost members again defied the ban. This time their drums were seized and retained and Pentecost members were prohibited from worshipping outside their own homes. By 1987, the church had collected enough funds to purchase another set of drums and they again defied the ban. It was at this time that a number of individuals within the community—without the approval or knowledge of the paramount chief and his council—took it upon themselves to torch the Church of Pentecost chapels.

These clashes were not the first religious conflicts in Anlo's history. In 1769, the political and religious leaders of the polity felt their authority seriously threatened by the then newly established and quite popular Nyigbla religious order.[3] The leaders of Anlo responded by requiring the Nyigbla shrine to be situated in the grove later known as Gbakute. They did this to undermine the popularity of the Nyigbla order since the grove at that time was associated with the angry and dangerous ghosts of those whose lives had been terminated because of their criminal behavior. In the late nineteenth and early twentieth centuries, another set of religious conflicts developed between the Anlo traditional authorities and Protestant missionaries affiliated with the North German Missionary Society when the latter sought to establish their religion in Anloga. In 1953, clashes involving British government efforts to impose a new set of taxes on the Anlo also took on a religious tone when those opposed to the British initiative used Gbakute (as former execution ground and still home of the Nyigbla order) to conduct anti-government activities. The British responded by imposing their own belief system on the grove. They razed the forest to the ground and erected in its place a government-run police station. By the mid-twentieth centuries, religious conflicts in Anloga shifted to involve primarily the Christian community as Catholics, indigenous Christian movements and Pentecostals all competed amongst themselves for followers.[4]

Of particular interest in this essay is the fact that so many of these religious clashes involved the area known variously as Esreme, Nyikowe or Nyiblawe but whose other name, Gbakute, I will use exclusively in this essay. As noted above, Gbakute figured prominently in the clashes that occurred in Anloga throughout the last two hundred years. In 1769, the religious and political leaders in the town attempted to use the grove situated at Gbakute to undermine the prestige of those who challenged their authority. In 1953, opponents of a British colonial government taxation scheme situated their opposition in the grove that still housed the deity, Togbui Nyigbla, the national war god of the Anlos. In 1987, resistance to the Church of Pentecost's refusal to respect traditional customs began at Gbakute. In May of 1996, Gbakute again figured prominently in the religious conflicts in the town when Nyigbla adherents attacked two Christian groups that were using as a temporary worship site the classrooms of the Avete Primary School that were located on the site of the former Gbakute grove. These facts raise a number of important questions about the role Gbakute has played in Anlo history. What meanings did the Anlo attach to this area in the past? To what extent have these meanings continued to play a central role in the way power and influence were contested in Anlo throughout the precolonial, colonial and post-colonial periods? What impact did the 1957 razing of the grove by British colonialists have of these meanings? Did the old meanings associated with the grove play a role in making it a center of the conflict between the Church of Pentecost and those who opposed its practices? Or did the conflicts only conjure up memories of the grove, memories that could then be manipulated and used to guide current understandings and behaviors in the context of the contemporary conflicts?

In addressing these questions, I hope to illustrate the extent to which the symbolic and the geographic are central to an understanding of the political and the religious in Anlo history, and perhaps in African history generally. Numerous studies address one or another of these areas of inquiry, but rarely are they combined within a single study.[5] T. McCaskie and Benjamin Ray, for example, analyze the symbolic meanings of specific locations in 19th century Asante and Bugandan religious and political culture, but their discussions are largely ahistorical, in the sense that they do not document changes or continuities over time.[6] Matthew Schoffeleers and D. Maier discuss historic developments in the belief systems of the Mbona and Dente shrines in Malawi and Ghana, respectively, but they give very little attention to the symbolic meanings attached to the geographic sites where the shrines were situated.[7] In this essay, I combine an emphasis on the political, the religious, the symbolic and the geographic in order to demonstrate the extent to which the environment has been a critical element in the competition for power and influence within the polity of Anlo.

A second concern in this essay has to do with memory, an area that has been quite central to the study of African history. Studies on oral traditions by Jan Vansina, Joseph Miller, David Henige, Paul Irwin, David W. Cohen and others have established this genre as critical to historians' efforts to reconstruct an "objective," verifiable African past.[8] At the same time, recognition that memories are very much influenced by the concerns of those who retain (and reconstruct) them, has become the subject of yet another set of studies. In Terence Ranger and Eric Hobsbawm's *The Invention of Tradition* and in Isabel Hofmeyr's *"We Spend our Years as a Tale Told"* the authors are concerned not so much with [using] memory to recover the past. Rather they analyze the way memory is constructed, reconstructed and deployed for particular political purposes. My analysis of memory in this essay draws on both of these approaches. I use (in combination with documentary sources) the memories of the past that the Anlo maintain in the form of oral traditions to reconstruct the political, religious and symbolic uses of the Gbakute grove during the precolonial and colonial past. I also analyze the circumstances under which various individuals and groups in contemporary Anlo have invoked or denied the significance of the different memories associated with the grove as they attempt in these last years of the twentieth century to make sense of the political and religious difficulties that the town is currently facing.

In this essay, then, I combine an emphasis on the symbolic with an analysis of political and religious change in Anlo to examine the history and memories associated with a particular location. I discuss the ways in which meanings and memories have influenced the actions of people in Anlo, but I also indicate that these same phenomena have been subject to manipulation and alteration as various groups in Anlo have used them over a period of more than two hundred years to maintain, contest or undermine those in positions of authority in Anlo.

THE HISTORY AND SYMBOLIC SIGNIFICANCE OF GBAKUTE

According to Anlo oral traditions, the area in Anloga town that came to be known as Gbakute, was first known as Nyikowe, the Nyiko forest. It acquired this name because it was originally a grove (awe) that housed two barrel-shaped drums that were used in a ritual known as Nyiko.[9] The grove was also the site where the Nyiko ritual was performed. This association with Nyiko imbued the forested area with tremendous symbolic meaning within the Anlo traditional religious system, for it was in this location that those who were thought to be a menace to Anlo society were executed. The earliest written information about the grove and its use as a site for executions comes from the late nineteenth century. In a diary entry written in 1879, Christian Jacobson noted that in that year, a man by the name of Gadese was executed in Anloga by Nyiko.[10] This, however, was not the first time that the Nyiko custom was used. Oral traditions about Nyiko, dated with the assistance of European documentary sources, indicate that the custom became a part of the Anlo judicial system between 1730 and 1750 during the reign of Awoamefia Nditsi, the political and religious leader of Anlo.[11] During that period, the Anlo area is said to have suffered from increased levels of "rape, burglary and foul deeds." The custom is said to have been introduced to supplement the customary rules of social conduct that had previously been enforced through lineage control over their members. It was used primarily against those who repeatedly ignored the laws of the polity.[12] The custom as it was remembered in the 1920's is described below.

Some sixty years ago, virtue was the ideal of all boys and girls born in Anlo land. In order to preserve it, there existed two . . . customs for the punishment of wrong-doers: (a) Banishment by slavery and (b) the Nyiko custom. The chief evils of those days were (in order of gravity):

(1) Taking away any one's life through witchcraft or the practice of the native black-magic art.

(2) Stealing.

(3) Meddling with another's wife.

(4) Incurring debts.

(5) Disobedience to parents.

(6) Untruthfulness.

Of these evils, the first was always punished at the offense by the Nyiko custom (now to be explained), the second and third by the said custom, but only at the third offense; and the fourth, fifth and sixth were punished either by banishment in slavery or by the Nyiko custom, and that also at the third offense.

A young man, say, twenty-five had, for instance seduced another's wife for the third time. This meant that he had passed the limit considered proper, for his conduct in that line had, on each of two previous occasions, cost the family thirty-six shillings which debt had, perhaps, been paid by depriving two younger members of the family of necessaries. "This is more than is bearable in Anlo land"; "This son of ours will be the ruin of the family," muttered the elders who, forthwith, in secret consultation among themselves decided upon the punishment mentioned above.

One of the elders who had sat in the council was then dispatched next day to Anloga, the capital, to acquaint the elders of the relations there that Mr. So-and-So had been doomed by them for death by Nyiko. These latter in their turn would inform the Field Marshall [or the military commander of the Anlo army, the *awadada*]. . . . He would then appoint a day for the execution. The elder sent to Anloga then returned to his people with a message respecting the appointed day. Meanwhile, all was made ready in Anloga for the execution; to wit: the executioners were informed, and forthwith restored the two Nyiko drums . . . the beating of which announced the fact that someone had just been subjected to punishment by Nyiko.

Now all this preliminary business of consultation, et cetera, as just described was transacted with the most astonishing secrecy that the victim could not suspect the least evil.

In the early morning of the appointed day, however, the maternal uncle—if any—of the doomed person, or one of the elders, would say to the criminal, "I want you to go to our kinsman, Mr. So-and-So at Anloga to fetch me [something]. . . . The young man obeyed and at once set out. On arriving at Anloga at about 9 a.m. he was received by the head of his relatives, who would presently indulge in a flood of expressions, communicative partly of his pleasure to do his kinsman such a good turn, and partly of his regret that the required thing was not just ready at hand, and finally round off with the request that the messenger would kindly stay overnight to enable him to get back the required thing from Mr. So-and-So, who lived some miles off. . . .

At about 10 p.m., that is after the house had retired, the head or elder of the family would wake the doomed messenger from his sleep, and request him and another elderly person (also of the house) kindly to lead him with a lamp to the latrines, which were usually outside the town. The young man, having waked, would sleepily obey, and, with the lantern in his hand, join in the solemn procession of three, led by the first elder, and the rear of which was brought up by the second elder. This order was strictly kept, for the man in the middle was, according to a pre-conceived plan, the person to be assailed. Thus the three persons would wend their way through the lanes of the town and then through a winding path through the thick bush outside the town; and once come to a place called Agbakute—about half a mile from the town, the front man would pretend going to attend to his minor needs in the bush, while the rear man stopped. All at once there came out of the bush, a band of three or four persons who, armed with iron bars, beat the victim on the head and neck till he died. His body was then carried and buried in a shallow grave so that the hyenas could dig it up and eat it. His clothes and dresses, which had been sent secretly to Anloga a day previous by his maternal uncle or other responsible person . . . were spread on shrubs or cactus plants about the place. A messenger then ran to inform the drummers that the deed was done, upon which the drum at the south end would play: *Miede zã, miegbo zã; Miede zã, miegbo zã* (We went at night and came back at night).

Next day a messenger left Anloga to inform the uncles and elders that the deed was done. . . . No one spoke any more of him in the house. His absences was never remarked upon. But should any one be so incautious as openly to ask where he was, the intimation: *Eyi toko atolia* (he is gone to the fifth river side) was enough to satisfy him of his fate.[13]

This description of the Nyiko custom as it was carried out in the Nyiko grove in Anloga provides a number of clues about the symbolic significance that Anloga citizens attached to this particular geographical area for the more than one hundred years that the custom was practiced. Normally when a person died, the family performed a set of rituals specifically designed to facilitate the deceased's transition into Tsiefe, the land of the dead. One of the most important of these rituals was known as the *yofofo*, during which the family buried the fingernails and hair of the deceased in the lineage ancestral home so that his or her *luwo* (that part of a person's soul that was believed to define an individual's personality) could be formally commended to the care of the family ancestors. A second ritual, known as the *yofewowo*, was performed sometime later to ensure that the deceased had, indeed, made a complete transition into the land of the dead. Families maintained communication with an ancestor—particularly one whose life was memorable—by invoking that person's name, requesting that the person's *gbogbo* (that part of a person's soul that was said to be bequeathed to an individual on his or her birth by Mawu, the supreme being, and which returned to the latter on that individual's death) enter temporarily a physical object such as a stool that once belonged to the person. They then offered drink and/or food to the individual's spirit. It was believed that failure to perform these rituals could leave the deceased person's soul to wander about aimlessly as a ghost, *noali*. It could also bring disaster to the family, since the Anlo believed that the spirit of a deceased person could harm the living.[14]

None of these rituals, however, were performed for an individual consigned by his family to death by Nyiko. Instead, the person's body was left to be unearthed by wild animals. His[15] *luwo* wandered about, unable to join with those of his ancestors in the lineage home. The person's spirit was confined to the Nyiko grove since his most prized possessions, often his clothing, had been sent to the grove. No one was to invoke the person's name in any way. This was designed to prevent the executed person's spirit from being drawn away from the grove. Placing the person's clothing on shrubs and cacti in the grove even made these items an unwelcome vehicle for the spirit to manifest itself, although this did not prevent such spirits from showing themselves. As a result, the Anlos associated the Nyiko grove with unhappy and potentially vengeful spirits who like other ancestors had the power to cause illness, terrible suffering and death. Only those fortified spiritually against such forces were believed capable of entering the grove and leaving unharmed.

During the eighteenth century, the Anlo association of Gbakute with powerful spiritual forces took on even greater meaning as the Anlo attempted to cope with a series of military disasters. In 1702, the polity was conquered by the Akwamu and forcibly incorporated in the latter's empire until 1730. In 1741, it was defeated again by Anexo and administered by the same until 1750. During that period, Anlo was forced by Anexo to accept a Danish monopoly over trade in the area, which established a ceiling for the rates at which the Anlo were able to sell slaves to the Danes. In 1750, after gaining its independence from Anexo, Anlo engaged in a conflict known as the Nonobe war in which an initial victory over the Agave (then located immediately north of the Anlo littoral in the marshlands west of the Keta Lagoon) was reversed when the latter and their Ada allies received assistance from the Danes in the form of firearms and the paid cooperation of the Krobo and a Larte contingent from Akuapem. With these additions to their forces, the Agaves and their allies were able to cross the Volta, rout the Anlo from their towns on the littoral and capture at least 64 people whom they sold to the Danes.[16]

This stream of defeats had a devastating impact on the Anlo population's confidence in their leaders to militarily and spiritually deliver the battlefield victories that were so necessary if they were going to maintain control over the trade routes and fish production areas that were important for their economic prosperity. By the end of the first half of the eighteenth century, the Anlo were ready for new approaches and tactics.

FROM GBAKUTE TO NYIGBLAWE

In 1769 when the Anlos successfully defeated the Adas and gained control over the lower Volta, they attributed the victory not to the gods of those who held the most important

political, religious and military roles in the society, but rather to a stranger god called Nyigbla that originated from the Whydah area east of Anlo. Their support for this new god so threatened the political and religious establishment in Anlo that the latter attempted to force the god and its priest out of Anlo, but the popularity of the god among the general population prevented this. Eventually the political and religious leadership in Anlo accepted the Nyigbla priest as a member of the governing council, and they allocated land to the priest on which he could erect a shrine to Nyigbla.

Significantly, the land given to this new religious order was the same area in which the political authorities executed those who had committed particularly heinous crimes or who were repeat offenders. Why the authorities allocated this particular location to the Dzevi for their god is not mentioned in the oral traditions; similarly no information exists as to why the Dzevi—knowing that the particular area given to them was used for the mentioned purposes—chose to accept this location. It is likely, however, that by inviting the Nyigbla priest to establish the shrine to Nyigbla in a location that was also associated with powerful and potentially quite dangerous spiritual forces, the authorities hoped to decrease the order's appeal to existing and potential followers. If the order was not as powerful as the Anlo populace thought it was, this would become apparent if the Nyigbla priest and the god's followers began to suffer from any manner of illnesses. Nyigbla would be proven to be less able to protect its followers from disaster than it claimed. The Nyigbla order's acceptance of the offer demonstrated their confidence in the power of their god to overcome those forces that were associated with this particular geographical location. The fact that Nyigbla order not only survived, but thrived in this particular area, added even more to the symbolic significance of the area.

With Nyigbla's rise to power within the political and religious hierarchy of Anlo and the establishment of its shrine in the Nyiko forest, the grove became known not only as the location where the spirits of executed criminals roamed, it also became known as Nyigblawe, the site which housed the shrine to the most powerful war god in Anlo, a god that brought victory to the Anlos and defeat to its enemies, a god whose influence extended well beyond the confines of the forest to include the entire Anlo polity. In essence, Nyigbla and the Nyigbla forest came to represent the spiritual heart of Anlo society as indicated in the following 1858 discussion of Nyigbla's influence in Anlo.

> Nyigbla is . . . a personified revelation of Mawu [the supreme deity]. He is the most intimate servant of Mawu, charged with the most important mission. He procures the fertile rain for the earth, the blessing of fertility for the country. He especially rules over the fate of human beings, the wars on earth and supervises them. . . . They imagine him riding on a horse . . . the horse appears as a symbol of war. If the "shooting-star" appears, it is Nyigbla who has sat down on a horse in order to carry out important business or to amuse himself in the vast universe. If it is raining, they say . . . "Nyigbla is walking

about." . . . If there is a continuous lack of rain, which is a frequent plague of all African regions, they have to regain Nyigbla's goodwill. If he refuses rain for too long a time, they believe they must have committed a great sin and his disgust must be resting upon them. Then, his priests and the King of Anlo send messengers to Notsie to get advice from the "god's place." . . . Medicinal herbs are brought and put in water, with which the whole people have to bathe so as to rid themselves of their sins in order to appease Nyigbla. . . . This is the oldest, greatest and formerly the only intermediary god of the Anlo. He is still their principal god and only he is worshipped as a national god. The Anlo insist that they have seen him commanding them, and they insist that no enemy can stand in front on him. . . . Once a year, they celebrate him with a feast. Everyone in the entire Anlo nation smears themselves with a certain pollen, and the general procession marches through and around the towns and villages of the whole country singing, dancing and drumming.[17]

Even as the expansion of Christianity and colonialism during the late nineteenth and the first half of the twentieth centuries challenged Anlo belief in their war god and the other forces that gave the Nyigbla grove its symbolic power, the Nyigbla religious order and the importance that the people of Anloga accorded the Nyigbla grove (as the spiritual center of political and religious life in Anlo) continued to exert a major influence on religious and political affairs in Anlo. This is most apparent from the events that occurred in Anloga between 1949 and 1953.

GBAKUTE AND COLONIALISM

In 1949, a commission appointed by the colonial government and chaired by Sir J. H. Coussey, recommended that the governance structures that then operated in the Gold Coast Colony be reorganized to encourage greater local self-governance. Attempts to implement the recommendations in Anlo immediately brought into the open a number of internal conflicts and divisions within the area. Of particular concern here are those that involved the citizens of Anloga. Many in the town felt that Anloga had become increasingly marginalized within the polity despite the fact that it had traditionally served as the political and religious center of the polity. The majority of the local council meetings, chaired by the Anlo *awoamefia*, Togbui Sri II, took place in Keta. This latter town was also the local headquarters of the British colonial government. It was in Keta that decisions were made as to the kinds of taxes that were to be imposed on the local population. These moneys were supposed to be used for the development of the entire district, but many in Anloga felt that the town had been greatly neglected in terms of public works projects. Much of the revenues collected, it was thought, had gone into the pockets of particular individuals and/or were spent only on projects in Keta. Anloga resistance to their loss in status took the form of resistance to efforts by the local governance structure in Keta to levy a head tax of two shillings on all Anlos. Opposition, as the Acting District

Commissioner of the Anlo District, J. M. L. Peake, indicated in 1950, "comes from both literate and illiterates."[18] By 1951, hostility to the tax had become so strong, despite the support for it by the *awoamefia* and a number of chiefs who were based outside the Anloga area, that the citizens of Anloga resorted to the use of the Nyiko drums.[19] To those who opposed the tax, the beating of the Nyiko drums meant that the new proposed tax was banned. As an issue, no one was to discuss it again, unless they were prepared to court the power of the particular gods that were believed to manifest themselves in the drums.[20] Thereafter, the taxation issue no longer figured in the deliberations of the Anlo Council, but it wasn't long before it re-emerged again in a way that illustrated the extent to which the citizens of Anlo continued to imbue the Nyiko grove with deep symbolic meaning.

In December 1952, the colonial government subdivided the Anlo District into local councils as recommended by the Coussey Commission. These included the Keta Urban Council and the South Anlo Council. The latter was established as a separate body from the Keta Council in response to the citizens of Anloga who had insisted that the town be designated as the headquarters of its own local authority district so that it could avoid being dictated to and taxed by officials based in Keta. The elected members of this council included many of the literate individuals among the population who had worked together with others in the town to ban the two shilling head tax. But once they assumed office, they quickly came to realize that they were unable to pursue the particular projects they deemed important for the district, the same projects that had been ignored under the former Native Authority Council. As Sophia Amable indicated in her study of this particular period in Anlo history:

> each local council had to cater for itself, including paying its staff and financing its projects. The new councilors realized that the council could no longer depend on market tolls, court fines and fees as sources of revenue. [But] the councilors attempts to renew the suggestion on payment of a direct tax or levy [caused] unrest and a split within the Anlo Youth Association [A. Y. A., the group that had spearheaded the Anloga opposition to the head tax]. . . . Payment of the levy was to some an attempt at exploitation and economic coercion. To others it was a civic duty which patriotic citizens were obliged to render. Those who accepted payment of the levy were branded as Dzoemiduawo: "collect-and-let-us-squander." . . .[21]

The taxation issue came to a head on January 1953 when the town exploded in a riot that resulted in the death of two men, the destruction of the recently founded Zion Secondary School and the razing by fire of approximately 26 houses in the town. Of significance to this study is the way in which the events unfolded. According to Amable's reconstruction, the riot erupted when:

> . . . The local councils . . . asked all headteachers of primary schools to ensure that the parents of pupils seeking admission for the new term should prove they had paid their levy by

bringing their receipt. Immediately, this was known, the A. Y. A. replied by beating gong-gong to the effect that all the schools should be closed down. They said they preferred their children being uneducated than paying six shillings [the tax rate imposed by the local councils] to a fraudulent set up. That same day, the Assistant District Commissioner received news that Chief Famous Adjorlolo of Atokor, a town west of Anloga, was missing. He had previously declared his intention to pay the levy. His dead body was later discovered. . . . Simultaneously, two men . . . from Tsiame (one of the towns in Anlo) were brought in chains to Anloga and incarcerated in the Nyiko grove at Gbakute. Their charge was that they had reported one A. Y. A. member who had refused to pay the levy. That these two Tsiame men would be killed looked certain.

A call went out to A. Y. A. members in the surrounding towns and villages to converge on Anloga . . . [and] councilors of the local council . . . were chased out of town . . . as all . . . started looting and burning houses.[22]

From this description, it is clear that the Nyiko grove in Gbakute continued to function as a symbolically significant location for Anloga as well as other Anlo citizens. Those who were kidnapped because of their support for the tax were taken to the Nyiko grove. One of the first actions taken by the colonial government after troops entered the town to quell the riot, was to issue an order to destroy the grove. After this was completed, the government erected a police station where the grove was once situated to symbolize the triumph of the European colonial order over the traditional practices and beliefs of the Anlo people.

With the destruction of the grove, much changed in Anloga. The annual ritual for Nyigbla—in which all the priests and the *awoamefia* participated, and which previously had been shielded from public view by the thick forest cover of the grove—could no longer be performed in the old location. The Nyigbla order moved its shrine further out of town to another grove, but even this was subsequently razed in the early 1960's with the establishment of the Anlo Secondary School. After 1959, when Togbui Adeladza II was installed as the successor to Awoamefia Sri II, he confined his participation in the rituals for Nyigbla to those who took place during the national festival, Hogbeza, when all within the Anlo polity were expected to renew their associations with the gods with which they were associated, not just Nyigbla.[23] In the mid-1980's, the Church of Pentecost established its first chapel in Gbakute and refused to abide by a prohibition on drumming declared by the adherents on Nyigbla. In refusing to silence their instruments, the Church publicly defied the one remaining Nyigbla ritual that the citizens of Anloga were expected to respect. What was the significance of these developments? Did the Gbakute area continue to have symbolic significance for the people of Anloga?

GBAKUTE IN THE POST-COLONIAL PERIOD

In 1996, when I interviewed some of the oldest men and women (both Christian and non-Christian) in the commu-

nity, it was clear from their accounts that even though it no longer existed, thoughts about the grove and the area on which it stood still evoked vivid memories about the Nyiko custom and the god, Nyigbla.

The darkness and tranquillity in the grove created an atmosphere of sacredness. Therefore anytime we approached the grove we would stop our conversation. Sometimes you got that funny feeling that ritual murderers, wild beasts or an invisible power in the grove were watching or following you.[24]

the inside of the grove always looked so dark . . .[25]

it was always dark even on moonlit nights . . .[26]

People were executed at a place beside the Nyigbla grove called "Esreme." The land on which the Avete Primary school was built [just behind the police station] was the resting place of people executed by the Nyiko custom.[27]

Some people were afraid of meeting the executionist when passing the grove . . . most people didn't pass the place at night.[28]

Others were afraid they would see the ghosts of people who had been executed by the Nyiko custom.[29]

The continued significance of Gbakute as a symbolically powerful site is also suggested by the events of 1987 and 1996. In 1987, when conflicts erupted between the Church of Pentecost and the traditional authorities of Anloga, the Gbakute area figured prominently in the clashes. In 1996, conflicts developed again between the Pentecostalists (with a number of new Protestant and Catholic allies) and the traditional leadership in Anloga, and again one of the major confrontations between these groups took place at Gbakute.[30]

But what was the nature of this connection? Why did the Church of Pentecost decide to erect their first chapel in Gbakute in the first place? Like a number of religious organizations in Anlo, the Church of Pentecost began as a missionary church with origins in Britain.[31] Over time, however, it assumed the characteristics of syncretic churches. Members combine an emphasis on a literal reading of the Bible and belief in the healing power of prayer with a number of African traditional religious beliefs. This combination is particularly apparent in the doctrines espoused by the Church of Pentecost. Leaders of the Church, for example, emphasize the idea—as do other mainline Christian denominations—that God is the Supreme Deity. He is omniscient, omnipresent and omnipotent. But church members also recognize the existence of the gods and spiritual forces that stand at the center of the Anlo traditional religious belief system. According to the founding member of the Church of Pentecost in Anloga, Togbui Alex Afatsao Awadzi, God is preeminent *not* because he is the only god, but because He was here on this earth *before* the other spiritual entities; he is more powerful. This same belief in the existence of spiritual forces other than those associated with God is also evident in the way in which the Church members describe how particular individuals became Pentecostalists. The account included here describes the conversion of a woman who joined the Church after it was introduced into Anloga in 1953.

> One of the people brought into the church [in Anloga] was Afiwo. This Afiwo came to watch the church service and afterward, she went home. Less than thirty minutes later, the mother came to Awadzi to find out about this new church Afiwo visited. Awadzi went to their house and he heard the daughter shouting, I will worship you; I will worship you. The mother was alarmed but Awadzi said it was just Christ who was with her. They heard Afiwo throwing things out the window. She removed something from under Awadzi's chair and threw it away. The talismans on her door she threw away; a pot containing [traditional medicinal] materials for her healing were thrown out.
>
> The mother said those who prepared them would be annoyed but Awadzi said she was not herself and that she was only doing Christ's bidding. So they should collect the things the next morning and bury them. The mother was still afraid of offending the priests, but Awadzi assured her *Christ was more powerful* than that.
>
> The following day, Awadzi went to find out what happened and he questioned the daughter. She said as soon as she returned from the church, she saw Christ in her room and Christ asked her, "Look at me; it is because of you that I am suffering." Blood was oozing from the whole body of Christ. This is why she was shouting, "I will worship you." Awadzi told the mother that what he had said earlier was true then, and that Christ was with her. The mother, Aveyigbe, and the daughter joined the church. Six days later, Awadzi saw Afiwo who said that her illness was gone. Before this she couldn't move her left arm and leg and couldn't cook, couldn't do her washing, et cetera, but now she was able to do all this.[32]

This particular account, and others like it, are cited frequently by members of the Church of Pentecost in Anloga to describe those beliefs that are central to their faith. They are significant because they reveal the extent to which members combine aspects of Christianity with traditional beliefs. God is omnipotent, he has the power to heal when his believers pray, Christ suffered for the sins of his people, but other spiritual forces also exist. God is simply more powerful than these forces and is therefore in a position to protect believers from the actions of others who would use those spiritual forces for harmful purposes.[33]

Syncretism in the Church of Pentecost in Anloga exists not only in its doctrines, it may have also shaped the way in which the Church has chosen to relate to the physical world. Some years after the founding of the Church in Anloga, the congregation bought land on which to erect a building for their worship services. One of the plots acquired was located in the area of Gbakute. The decision to acquire property in this particular area no doubt had to do in part with its current usage, availability and price. Much of the area was already being used for public buildings. As we have seen, in 1952 the colonial government of the Gold Coast Colony erected a police station in Gbakute and in the 1970's the Ghana government established the Avete Primary School. The establishment of a church in this same district was

therefore consistent with its current usage. In addition, the area had limited value as agricultural or commercial land. The soils in the area consisted primarily of sand, while most people in the town preferred to erect their homes in the newer districts on the south side of town that stretched to the east and west of Anloga. Yet we also have seen that Gbakute represented more than an inexpensive plot of land available for purchase. It was also the former location of a thickly wooded grove where the spirits associated with the Nyiko custom existed, and where Nyigbla, the most powerful god in the Anlo traditional religious system, had its shrine. Did this matter to the elders of the Church of Pentecost?

Current members of the church deny any connection between the location of the church and the fact that the land once supported the Nyigbla grove. But to acknowledge that there was, indeed, a connection would also open them to accusations of provocation. In their most recent conflict in 1996 with the traditional authorities in Anloga, for example, Church of Pentecost pastor, P. K. Larbi took great pains to indicate that his church and those that stood with them in their defiance of the ban of drumming should be understood as the victims rather than instigators of the clashes that occurred.

> Recently we received a letter from the traditional council informing us of the ban on drumming from the 4th of April to the 24th of May. As we did not want history to repeat itself, members of the local Council of Churches which consisted of a pastor and three elders from each of the Roman Catholic Church, the Evangelical Presbyterian Church, the Church of Pentecost, the Church of the Lord Brotherhood, Zion Church, the Apostolic Church, the Christian Fellowship Center, the Assemblies of God, Calvary Ministry, Salvation Army, the New Apostolic Church and the Apostles Revelation Society called on the paramount chief on the 16th of April . . . he told us that he did not give the order for a ban on drumming. . . .
>
> [Until he clarified the questions] we explained that we would confine our drumming to our various church premises.
>
> Just recently, the congregations at the Christian Fellowship Centre and the Assemblies of God Church who were in fellowship in some of the classrooms of the Avete E. P. Primary School [located at Gbakute] were attacked by the advocates of Nyigbla.[34]

Given this testimony and the context in which it was given, it may never be known whether the Church of Pentecost consciously or unconsciously built in Gbakute because of their desire to use the place as a means to position itself symbolically to contest the traditional political and religious culture of Anlo.

What we do know, however, is that for many in Anloga (young and old, Christian and non-Christian alike), Gbakute's association with the Nyiko custom and Nyigbla forest is now only a memory. It no longer seems to have any intrinsic meaning based on its historic role that impinges on their daily lives of contemporary citizens of Anloga. The grove has been cleared for some forty years. The Nyigbla shrine has been displaced to a different location in the town not once but twice during this period. The number of Nyigbla adherents has dwindled considerably. Christianity has become the dominant faith in the town. Most residents of Anloga refer more often to the Gbakute site as the Avete Primary School area rather than by those names which conjure memories of the Nyiko custom and the Nyigbla religious order. Far more important for the residents of Anloga is the fact that memories about the symbolic significance of the Gbakute area continue to influence how the various individuals and groups within Anloga have chosen to use the site in their conflicts with others. Most are aware that the area was once the site for the Nyiko custom and the Nyigbla forest. Most are also knowledgeable about the fact that the site has also been a place that different groups have used symbolically during the precolonial and colonial period to position themselves within the political and religious culture of Anlo. Just as significantly, these memories periodically receive concrete reinforcement when once-buried bones—whether human or animal—work their way to the surface and are discovered by the school children, construction workers or policemen working in the area. But it is only in the context of the recent political and religious conflicts between the traditional political authorities and the Nyigbla adherents on the one hand, and the Christian churches, especially the Church of Pentecost, on the other, that the Anloga community has reinvested symbolic meaning into the Gbakute area, memories that all concerned have reconstructed and amended or denied as significant for their own purposes.

Leading elders in the town, for example, have stated that those who attacked the Christians at Gbakute did so (without their permission or approval) because of what they saw as the need to maintain the cultural heritage of Anlo in the face of an increasingly insistent evangelical Christian movement. The attacks themselves began at Gbakute for two reasons. It symbolized formerly revered practices and resistance to the intrusion of European colonialism, but perhaps more importantly Gbakute is now (with the tremendous demographic growth in the community since the 1950's) in the very center of Anloga, a town that has traditionally been the capital of Anlo political and religious culture. It is this memory of Anloga as the center of Anlo culture and the memory of Gbakute as a site of former revered practices and resistance, that opponents of the Church of Pentecost have conflated in their efforts to retain what they see as respect for the traditional customs and beliefs of Anlo. From their perspective, if Nyigbla adherents could not demand respect for their rites in Anloga, then where? As Klobotua Efia Nunyanu, linguist and elder of the Adzovia clan stated:

> . . . within every society there are rules and regulations that bind all together for a future purpose. . . . It is customary in this town that at certain seasons, particular actions are not permitted. . . . When we [the traditional authorities] started our celebrations, they refused to stop their drumming. . . . The church was ridiculing [the Nyigbla] customs and ridiculing [the Nyigbla adherents] because they were fetish people . . .

our celebrations will make the town good even for themselves, but they refused, so we said they should take their religion out of town.[35]

This concern with respect being shown for traditional cultural and religious practices, especially by those who live, work and worship in central Anloga, is also evident in the recent efforts to keep the Church of Pentecost from rebuilding their chapel at another location in town that is also in the center of town. After the Gbakute chapel had been destroyed by fire, a member of the affected church, D. D. Deku, donated some of his own land that was in the center of town to the Church. They have yet to complete the building, however, because the traditional council has indicated that they wish to use the site for a new post office.[36] From the perspective of the Church of Pentecost, of course, the traditional council's interest in the land as a possible site for a post office is just another effort to drive them out of town, an effort that has little to do with their actions in building their chapel and defying the ban on drumming instituted by the Nyigbla religious order and sanctioned by the traditional authorities in the town. According to the Pentecostalists, the symbolic significance of the former location of the Gbakute grove has never influenced their activities and has nothing to do with the current conflict. This is an opinion they claim to hold despite the widespread knowledge about the history and symbolic significance of the site. It is an opinion that stands in curious contrast to their own religious beliefs which hold that members need to recognize, and both abhor and respect the spiritual powers that have been associated with the Gbakute site. It also challenges a view held commonly by the residents of Anloga unaffiliated with either side of the dispute who, in viewing the clash from afar, invoke the memory of Gbakute to explain why the Church established its first chapel there and why it was the first to be attacked.[37]

In this regard, the actions and opinions of both the Church of Pentecost, the traditional elders and the Nyigbla adherents, and the residents of Anloga illustrate the extent to which Gbakute as a site and a symbol have continued to influence religious and political affairs in Anlo even as its meaning has shifted and changed under the influence of the British colonial destruction of the grove that once existed on the site and its incorporation into what is now considered the center of Anloga town.

CONCLUSION

The significance of place as symbol in the political and religious history of Africa is the primary concern of this article. By focusing on the history of an area in the town of Anloga known by many different names but called Gbakute here, I have traced the way in which this location became associated with specific meanings over a period of more than two hundred years. During the early eighteenth century, it was believed to be the place where the spirits of executed criminals roamed. By the late eighteenth century, it also served as the site for the worship of Anlo's most powerful god, Togbui Nyigbla, and contributed to the image of Anloga as the political and religious center of the Anlo polity. During the colonial period, the citizens of Anloga used the grove that stood on the site as a place to resist British colonial rule, and in so doing defined the grove as a symbol of Anloga political and religious culture in opposition to British colonialism. The British responded by attempting to impose their own meaning on the site. They razed the grove and erected a police station in its place. This destruction did, indeed, alter the material characteristics of Gbakute. It became thereafter a site that was more often associated with both the police station and later the primary school that was built in the area than with the Nyiko custom and the Nyigbla religious order. It no longer evokes as it did in the past immediate and tangible feelings of fear, dread and awe. Memories of its past still exist, however, and it is these memories— given new life primarily by the recent conflicts that have erupted between the traditional political authorities, the Nyigbla religious order, and the Church of Pentecost—that link this site to its past. Even with its alteration and transformation from precolonial grove to colonial and postcolonial public space, from a site associated with the beliefs attached to Nyiko and Nyigbla, to one in which only the memories of those meanings exist, Gbakute continues to figure prominently in the political and religious history of Anloga as a symbol to be revered, contested or intentionally forgotten.

NOTES

Acknowledgment. I would like to thank the anonymous reviewers of this article, whose comments encouraged me to revise this article in ways that more closely reflect my current research interests.

1. See Administrative Papers (hereafter cited as ADM) 39/1/120, Anlo State Native Affairs.

2. See for example, Greene, Field Note 62: Interview with Mr. K. A. Mensah, 5 January 1987, Anloga.

3. For a discussion of this history, see Sandra E. Greene, *Gender, Ethnicity and Social Change on the Upper Slave Coast: A History of the Anlo-Ewe* (Portsmouth, N.H., 1996).

4. Conflicts between different Christian denominations are discussed in Greene, Field Note No. 193: Interview with Mr. V. Y. Dotsey, Anloga.

5. An exception to this is Wyatt MacGaffey's *Religion and Society in Central Africa: The Bakongo of Lower Zaire* (Chicago, 1986). The anthropological literature on this subject is even more extensive. These studies combine the symbolic with an analysis of the geographical, but they also tend to be either apolitical or ahistorical. See, for example, Eugenia Herbert, *Iron, Gender and Power: Rituals of Transformation in African Societies* (Bloomington, 1993), 108 and 116; *Andrew Apter,*

Black Critics and Kings: The Hermeneutics of Power in Yoruba Society (Chicago, 1992), passim; Henrietta L. Moore, *Space, Text and Gender: An Anthropological Study of the Marakwet of Kenya* (Cambridge, 1986), passim; Marcel Griaule, *Conversations with Ogotemmeli* (London, 1965), Fourteenth Day; John William Johnson, *The Epic of Son-Jara: A West African Tradition* (Bloomington, 1986), 10–17.

6. T. C. McCaskie, *State and Society in Precolonial Asante* (New York, 1995); Benjamin C. Ray, *Myth, Ritual and Kingship in Buganda* (New York, 1991).

7. D. J. E. Maier, *Priests and Power: The Case of the Dente Shrine in Nineteenth Century Ghana* (Bloomington, 1983), 45–46, 169–172; Matthew Schoffeleers, "The History and Political Role of the M'Bona Cult among the Mang'anja," in *The Historical Study of African Religion,* ed. T. O. Ranger and I. N. Kimambo (Berkeley and Los Angeles, 1972), 73–94; Schoffeleers, "The Interaction of the M'Bona Cult and Christianity, 1859–1963," in *Themes in the Christian History of Central Africa,* ed. T. O. Ranger and John Weller (Berkeley and Los Angeles, 1975), 14–29. See also Schoffeleers, *River of Blood: the Genesis of a Martyr Cult in Southern Malawi c. a.d. 1600* (Madison, 1992).

8. Jan Vansina, *Oral Tradition as History* (Madison, 1985); Joseph Miller, *The African Past Speaks: Essays on Oral Tradition and History* (Folkstone, Kent, 1980); David Henige, *The Chronology of Oral Tradition: Quest for a Chimera* (Westport, Ct., 1987); Paul Irwin, *Liptako Speaks* (Princeton, NJ, 1981); David W. Cohen, *Womunafu's Bunafu: A Study of Authority in a Nineteenth Century Community* (Princeton, 1977).

9. C. R. Gaba, "Anlo Traditional Religion: A Study of the Anlo Traditional Believer's Conception of and Communion with the "Holy" (Ph.D. diss., University of London, 1965), 37–38; Conversation with D. Avorgbedor, 4 November 1991; Anlo Traditional Council Minute Book, Keta, 1 July 1938, 267.

10. S. C. 14/1: "The Old Diary—Remarkable Occurrences of the Gold Coast and Ashanti, started in 1879, by Mr. Christian Jacobson," 81.

11. R. S. Rattray, "History of the Ewe People," *Études Togolais* tome II, vol. 1 (1967), 92–96; ADM 11/1/1246, H. S. Newlands, "History of the Awunas, Some Dates," 18 January 1922.

12. Sandra E. Greene, Field Note 37: Interview with Boko Seke Axovi, 4 October 1978, Anloga; D. Westermann, *The Study of the Ewe Language* (London, 1930), 243.

13. Westermann, *Study of Ewe,* 242–245; see also G. Binetsch's 1906 description of Nyiko, which conforms quite closely with that of Westermann's, in "Berichte der Missionare G. Binetsch und G. Härtter fiber die Eweer bezw. Anglo-Eweer," *Zeitschrift für Ethnologie* 38 (1906), 50.

14. See G. K. Nukunya, "Some Underlying Beliefs in Ancestor Worship and Mortuary Rites among the Ewe," in *La Notion de Personne en Afrique Noire,* Colloques Internationaux du

Centre National de la Recherche Scientifique, no. 544, org. Germaine Dieterlen (Paris, 1973), 119–130. For more historical accounts of Anlo funeral customs and associated religious beliefs (all of which conform to Nukunya's more contemporary description) see J. Bernhard Schlegel, "Beitrag zur Geschichte, Welt- und Religionsanchauung des Westafrikaners, nametlich des Eweer," *Monatsblatt der Norddeutsche Missionsgesellschaft,* 7 (1858), 398; Binetsch, "Berichte," 35–36; A. B. Ellis, *The Ewe-Speaking Peoples of the Slave Coast of West Africa* (London, 1890, reprinted Chicago, 1965), 157–159.

15. I use "his" in this context rather than "his or her" because the Anlo state that women rarely, if ever, were subjected to the Nyiko custom. The norm was to sell them into the Atlantic slave trade.

16. For additional information on these battles, see Sandra E. Greene, "The Anlo Ewe: Their Economy, Society and External Relations in the Eighteenth Century" (Ph.D. diss., Northwestern University, 1981).

17. Greene, Field Notes 20 and 53, Interviews with Togbui Alex Afatsao Awadzi, 30 August 1978 and 16 December 1987, respectively.

18. Traditional Council Minute Book, March 1947–April 1952, "Minutes of the Meeting of the Anlo Native Authority Council, Anloga, 21 March 1950—Address by the Acting District Commissioner, Mr. J. M. L. Peake at 11:00am," 176.

19. Togbui Sri II's response to the Nyiko banning included an effort—that ultimately proved unsuccessful—to convince others on the council that the Nyiko ban could not apply to the tax because Anlo religious beliefs did not permit the tabooing of something that was financially beneficial to the state. He also argued that the banning did not mean that the tax issue was irrevocably dead. In his words, "Have you never heard that a person who had been tabooed 'in absentia' returned and later enjoyed life fully among ourselves?" See Traditional Council Minute Book, March 1947–April 1952, 178–179.

20. D. E. K. Fiawoo, "The Influence of Contemporary Social Changes on the Magico-Religious Concepts and Organization of the southern Ewe-speaking Peoples of Ghana" (Ph.D. diss., Edinburgh University, 1959), 106–108.

21. Sophia Amable, "The 1953 Riot in Anloga and its Aftermath" (B. A. Long Essay, History Department, University of Ghana, Legon), 20.

22. Amable, "The 1953 Riot," 24–25.

23. Greene, Field Note 67, Interview with Togbui Efia Nunyanu, 6 January 1988, Anloga.

24. Greene, Field Note 171, Interview with Togbui Awuku Dzrekey, 18 April 1996, Whuti.

25. Greene, Field Note 172, Interview with Tekpor Sedzorme, 15 April 1996, Anloga.

26. Greene, Field Note 171, Interview with Togbui Awuku Dzrekey, 18 April 1996, Whuti.

27. Greene, Field Note 202, Interview with Togbui Tudzi, 15 May 1996, Anloga.

28. Greene, Field Note 177, Interview with Togbui Akpate I, 22 April 1996, Srogbe.

29. Greene, Field Note 181, Interview with Hianvedzu Nyamadi, 23 April 1996, Anloga.

30. Greene, Field Note 196, Interview with Pastor P. K. Larbi and Elders, 7 May 1996, Anloga.

31. Fiawoo, "The Influence of Contemporary Social Changes," 175.

32. Greene, Field Note 68, Interview with Togbui Alex Afatsao Awadzi, 7 January 1988, Anloga.

33. For an excellent discussion of the transformation of spiritual concepts within Ewe religious thought into notions about the Devil in Ewe Christian thought, see Birgit Meyer, "Translating the Devil: An African Appropriation of Pietist Protestantism—The Case of the Peki Ewe in Southeastern Ghana, 1847–1992" (Ph.D. diss., University of Amsterdam, 1995).

34. Greene, Field Note 196, Interview with Pastor P. K. Larbi and Elders, 7 May 1996, Anloga.

35. Greene, Field Notes 64 and 67, Interviews with J. N. K. Dogbatse, 5 January 1988, Anloga and Togbui Klobotua Efia Nunyanu, 6 January 1988, Anloga.

36. Greene, Field Note 195, Interview with Mr. D. D. Deku, 6 May 1996, Anloga.

37. Greene, Field Note 62, Discussion with Mr. K. A. Mensah, 5 January 1988, Anloga.

4

Religion and Mythology

Essays in This Section:

Karl Kroeber   Unaesthetic Imaginings: Native American Myth as Speech Genre (1996)

Jayant Bhalchandra Bapat   A Jātipurāṇa (Clan-History Myth) of the Gurav Temple Priests of Maharashtra (1998)

Ithamar Gruenwald   God the "Stone/Rock": Myth, Idolatry, and Cultic Fetishism in Ancient Israel (1996)

G. S. Kirk argued that myths are stories of unusual narrative force, power, or character that explain an important phenomenon or custom, record or establish a useful institution, express an emotion in some way that satisfies some need in the individual, reinforce a religious feeling or act as a powerful support or precedent for an established ritual.[1] Thus, myths are sacred stories that can cover a wide variety of topics. Myths may describe human origins, the origins of society, deities, and the cosmos. They may describe what happens after death, and what the afterlife is like. Myths are sometimes used to justify the current state of society, and they can act models of behavior for the members of a society. They are typically perceived as happening in some remote past, but at the same time they are often reenacted in contemporary rituals to ensure the practitioners' continued well-being. The essays in this section look at different aspects of myth and the impact that myths can have in a culture. As you read the essays in this section, keep the following points in mind:

- Myths are found in sacred literature in all cultures that have writing. However, almost all myths started as oral traditions. They were spoken stories, not written ones. But the spoken word is in many ways different from the written word. Readers may interpret written words in their own way. Storytellers, however, emphasize different aspects of their tales according to what is relevant to their audience. In his essay on Native American myth, Karl Kroeber argues that these retellings allow cultural adaptation to changing circumstances and keep cultural traditions relevant.

- The telling and retelling of sacred stories occurs in different social and political contexts. Such stories

might hint at eternal truths, but they might also have immediate or short-term political ramifications. Thus the recounting of religious stories can be used to rally the troops, get out the voters, encourage resistance, build constituencies, and promote many other political and social purposes. Jayant Bapat's essay on a Hindu clan-history myth explores how leaders of the Gurav, a Indian caste, tried to use these stories to support their claim for higher caste status and increased temple privileges.

- Myths frequently express complex stories and only rarely have a single point or moral on which all can agree. Further, though the stories themselves may persist relatively unchanged for thousands of years, their meanings, the basic ways in which they are interpreted, may change as society changes. The myths of the Hebrew and Christian Bibles are excellent examples of this; their meanings have been discussed and debated for thousands of years. The essay by Ithamar Gruenwald is an outstanding contribution to this debate. Gruenwald focuses on passages in the Hebrew Bible that describe God as a rock or stone. It seems common sense to us to understand these passages as saying that God is *like* a rock or stone. But what if God was literally a rock or stone? Gruenwald argues that that is exactly what the Ancient Israelites had in mind.

NOTE

1. Geoffrey Steven Kirk, *Myth: Its Meaning and Function in Ancient and Other Cultures* (Berkeley: University of California Press, 1970).

Unaesthetic Imaginings:
Native American Myth as Speech Genre

Karl Kroeber

In this essay, Kroeber asks us to recognize that Native American Indian myth is a specialized form of oral performance. Kroeber first points out that myths in preliterate societies are performances enacted in front of an audience. Myths are not literature, and these performances are embedded within certain cultural and social contexts that give them meaning. Myths lose meaning when studied outside the context in which they are enacted—in particular, when written down as a story. Kroeber argues that the importance of myth in preliterate Native American societies was that it allowed people to reimagine, and thus sustain and preserve, their culture. For example, Kroeber contrasts a Western story about death with a myth told by Blackfoot Indians. The Western story has an ironic conclusion focusing on the inevitability of death; the Blackfoot story has a variety of possible interpretations. Kroeber concludes that an essential feature of myths is that they are variable, and that multiple versions of a myth are normal. He argues that myths are told to be repeated and that storytellers may emphasize different aspects of the same story according to what is relevant to their audience. It is these retellings, Kroeber claims, that keep alive particular features of culture in these societies. The storyteller's imagination creates the different tellings of a story. These variations are part of what allows a culture to adapt to changing circumstances and keeps cultural traditions relevant.

As you read, consider these questions:
1. What are the functions of myth?
2. What is the purpose of different versions of a single myth?
3. What is a "speech genre," and how can this affect the meaning of a particular myth?

Since the largest body of traditional Native American discourse that has been preserved consists of myths, it is unfortunate that nobody agrees on what myths are or on what their functions may be. For nearly one hundred and fifty years, since Max Müller began promulgating his "solar myth" theory, polemical debates about what myth is and

what it does have been as unremitting as indecisive. The fiercest combats, involving folklorists, anthropologists, philosophers, psychologists, linguists, literary critics, and a wide spectrum of eccentrics (the categories frequently overlapping), have centered on claims—a new one about every twenty years—for a "science" of mythology. Surveying this darkling plain where corpses of theories are piled high, one perceives the compulsion to fabricate "scientific" validity for a mode of discourse obsolete in modern culture as revelatory of the fantasies on which depend much contemporary criticism. "Sciences" of myth seem analogous to what, after the Civil War, was called the experience of "the phantom limb," a feeling by mutilated veterans of sensations in arms or legs that had long before been amputated.

Frightened by such hallucinations, I will propose a hypothesis not as to what myth is but as to what may be a central feature of mythic imagining. A major implication of my hypothesis is that analyses of mythologies can be productive to the degree that they rely on methods of humanistic interpretation. I illustrate the kind of insights my approach offers by reference to a few traditional North American Indian myths. Many more Native American myths are discussed in a book to which this essay serves as what movie folk call a trailer—a genre attractive because inaccuracy in its representativeness is expectable.[1]

An overview of the past one hundred fifty years' controversies about myth suggests one positive tendency: an increasing inclination to emphasize that all myths are stories. Standard dictionaries today, for example, almost universally define myth as a form of narrative. Understanding what *narrative* is and how it functions, therefore, is indispensable to understanding myths. Myth narrative, however, possesses its own attributes, which distinguish it, for instance, from novelistic narrative. Primary among these is the feature dramatized by Bronislaw Malinowski's thunderous insistence that mythic story is also always more than story. Malinowski's linkage of mythic narrative to "ritual" should not distract us (as it is all too likely to do) from the essence of his argument, which is that myths are mutilated if torn away from their sociocultural context, their embeddedness in the physical, ongoing practices of a particular way of life. Malinowski rightly warns that we should never allow fascination with mythic story in itself to distract us from the manner in which it is integral to the ongoing experience of its tellers and listeners.[2]

Ethnographic evidence overwhelmingly supports the soundness of Malinowski's contention, which explains why all attempts to treat mythic narratives as "literature" are finally unsatisfactory. What *we* refer to as literature is "aesthetic" discourse, that is to say, discourse distinguishable from other, nonaesthetic, "practical" discourses. Our aesthetic discourse may have some practical effects, but it is by definition differentiated from "nonaesthetic" practices of our sociocultural life—special and valuable to us *because* thus distinct. Genuine myths cannot be so detached. Myth arises out of, and remains totally enmeshed in, practical aspects of the life of myth tellers and myth listeners. Myth is practice—one reason why I prefer to speak of myth tellings as enactments.[3]

Although we flounder into difficulties when we refer to myths as "literature," they indubitably can be shaped with remarkable artistry. Like every other kind of practice, they can be carried out with economic grace, elegant elaboration, cogency, vividness; their pleasing formal relations can be intensely evocative. All stories can be well told or badly told, and the excellence of their telling, the skill of their making, is a feature of myths that should not be ignored. For peoples active in creating myths, such as American Indians, skillful telling is always esteemed—just as skill is admired by these peoples in the practice of making arrows, tanning hides, or speaking in council.

Recognition that Indian myth enactments (however skillfully or unskillfully wrought) are solidly embedded within the web of other interactions of social life allows us to distinguish productively between the "artistry" of myth and the "artistry" of our literature. The distinction offers our best access to appreciating the determinative oral character of Native American myths. Failure to address the simple fact that these myths originated in preliterate societies has vitiated most analyses of their narrative forms. We must begin by acknowledging that any commentator from a print-dominated society is almost certain to misrepresent essential features of traditional myths. We read traditional American Indian myths in profoundly distorting translations, not merely of the original language but also of transient oral events transposed into printed objects. Yet, to my knowledge, there still are no systematically detailed examinations of how and why oral narratives differ from written ones.

Admitting how deaf we print-oriented readers are to the constraints and potentialities of oral artistry should focus our attention on the contrast of audiences. As Father Ong has demonstrated, the audience of any written work is necessarily fictional: writers must imagine their audiences.[4] The audience of oral discourse is visibly and audibly present, *here* imagining, rather than somewhere else, *imagined.* Myth audience's shaping physical presence makes this discourse always a practical social transaction. Each oral myth enactment, nevertheless, is an act of a human imagination. That permits us, who are in time and by orientation of cultural perception estranged from such transactions, to be intellectually stimulated and emotionally moved even by distorting transcripts of powerful myths. We should not, however, mistake the cause of our response by identifying mythic "artistry" with that which makes our own written literature analogously evocative. The excellences are related, of course: Indian myths and our literature are both artifacts created by human beings. But the functioning of individual imagination in traditional American Indian societies and in our society differs radically.

The core of my hypothesis, then, is that myths are imaginative acts of a kind with which we have become unfamiliar. My hypothesis assumes (to eliminate at once a bugaboo of some mythographers) an individual as the immediate source of every myth enactment, because only individuals imagine. To speak of "communal imagination" is to invoke a metaphor of dubious value. Yet, every individual mind exists within, and is constituted by (influenced, yet reciprocally influencing), its specific sociocultural circumstances—which, in an oral society, are significantly determined by repeated mind-shaping recitations of myths. This obvious point needs to be emphasized, because empirical evidence is overwhelming that myths are most often, perhaps always, focally expressive of interactions between individualistic and communal forces. These relations in most nonliterate communities, however, are imagined in fashions surprising, even baffling, to us.

I find the most useful definitions of *imagination* to be those of common usage, in which "to imagine" ordinarily means two different, but closely related, things linked by a conception of "fantasy." When someone says, "Ah, you're just imagining that," you are being accused of "fantasizing" in its most usual sense, inventing mentally what has never existed and presumably never can, of willfully ignoring physical actualities for psychically engendered "unrealities." When, however, you are urged to "use your imagination, stupid," there is a positive appeal to fantasy, a demand that you employ your psychic capacities to go beyond what is immediately present here and now, and beyond routinized rational patterns, to reach toward some novel possibility. The injunction to "use your imagination" urges you to allow your mind to move toward something not yet realized but practically, probably valuably, *realizable*. Imagination, in this sense, is regarded as an admirable quality, the quality that underlies every kind of human planning, every purposeful human accomplishment, that, in fact, is the primary force in *constituting* cultures.

Contemporary psychologists and philosophers seem fearful of talking about imagination (a phobia perhaps related to compulsions to rationalize mythology), so I shall turn back to the English romantic poet Percy Bysshe Shelley for a cogent cultural analysis of imagination. Shelley defined the services imagination rendered human beings through a counterattack on an essay by his friend Thomas Love Peacock. Peacock argued with astringent humor that the imagining that produces poetry (poetry for him, as for Shelley, being representative of all aesthetic accomplishment) had become useless in contemporary, rationalized, technologically sophisticated cultures. Shelley perceived that Peacock's view would become a dominant presupposition in Western society—as indeed it has—unless it could be refuted by a demonstration that imagination is the *generative* force of *all* cultural accomplishments. Shelley, therefore, carefully distinguished imagination from reason. He identified the latter as the capacity of the human psyche to organize already existent ideas and perceptions, and the former as the power to achieve new perceptions and novel thoughts, to arouse consciousness of hitherto "unapprehended relations."

The power to go beyond, to improve upon, what already exists, what has been given to us, undergirds humankind's manipulations of natural phenomena to create cultures. As important as this observation is Shelley's conception that culturally formed practices, thinking patterns and modes of perceiving, grow old, wear out, and become worse than useless. Shelley, that is, understands successful culture as necessarily always self-reconstituting, self-renewing. This is why he emphasizes defamiliarization, the concept later developed by Russian formalist literary theorists. They identified defamiliarization as a major function of Western art, which strips away the veiling film of familiarity that blinds us to the vibrant, ever changing reality of things and relations to which we have become too accustomed—such as the painting we so carefully place on a living room wall and within months never notice.

Shelley differed from the Russian formalists, however, in concentrating on defamiliarization not as a feature of personal psychology but as a cultural phenomenon. He was especially concerned with the renewal of communal constructs and social systematizations, which he called "forms of opinion."[5] Unless these are consistently reconstituted, they become mere mechanistic routines, burdens and hindrances to further development of both individuals and communities. Unless a people's imagination actively reworks these received systems, they rigidify, constricting and deforming the life their organizations had originally enhanced. Probably because he was a poet, Shelley saw a deadly symptom of this reification in the routinization of language. The appearance of clichés is primary evidence, a disregarded danger signal, that we are no longer vitally imagining what we talk or write about.

Cliché is the exact opposite of formalized language, wherein a word or phrase is deliberately repeated, even though (or because) it is recognized as archaic, perhaps even so archaic that its meaning is no longer understood. Such formally archaic language compels listeners to contemplate the strange power of language (as well as its historical character). Such formalized language is, in fact, a technique of defamiliarization, because it disables us from taking our language for granted. Myths frequently play an analogous role in refreshing our self-consciousness of social systems and "forms of opinion" by using archaic language, archaic stories, and archaic modes of enactment.

Shelley's idea that culture persists vitally *only* through continual self-renovations, although unusual in our intellectual tradition, is analogous to an enormous number of Indian beliefs and practices that ethnologists commonly refer to under the rubric of *world renewal.* The term normally points to ceremonies combining speech and behavior intended to assure revitalization of a sustaining interplay between a particular culture and its natural environment. Shelley was a progressive, even a revolutionary, trying to break free of the feudal mind-sets epitomized by the term *ancien régime,* so he regularly emphasizes how imagination enables what is "new" and "novel" to break through reified conventions. But his emphasis on defamiliarization displays his belief in the social healthiness of continuously reawakened awareness of the conditions of our existence, both natural and cultural. Inversely, American Indian ideas of "renewal" as restoration of traditional ways are misunderstood when treated as mere exercises in repetition. Indian imaginings that revitalize their culture and their world never exclude the possibility (even the desirability) of transformation through reassessment of tradition.

The foundation of my hypothesis about mythmaking, then, is that by continually reimagining their cultures through myths, human beings sustain, preserve, and enhance their cultures. Myths help to affirm a special way of life by "defamiliarizing" it. A central function of myths is to enable a people to revitalize their imagining of their culture, which is, after all, their imaginative creation. Shelley is the first of a small group of modern thinkers, among whom most notable, perhaps, is Ortega y Gasset, who perceive a profound danger in modern, technological, print-based culture's encouraging people to take it for granted. Most people in our culture do not actively, participatively, continuously reimagine it; so they become—unwittingly—alienated from their culture, even while they think they support it fervently. But one does not truly "support" a given way of life when one takes it for granted, thinking and speaking of it only in clichés.

Among American Indians, whose traditional societies were without writing, continuous reimagining of culture was an absolute imperative. Their cultures continued to exist only through being acted out, conversed about, realized in speech and behavior. If a preliterate people stops talking self-consciously about its culture, that culture vanishes. I suspect this fact helps to explain the importance of dreams to numbers of Native American peoples; many Indians felt that if they were to stop "dreaming" their culture, it would disappear.

Contrarily, the reward for constantly reimagining one's culture both when dreaming and when awake is immediate and powerful, the satisfaction of participating in the renovating of one's cherished and nurturing way of life. The force of social interdependence is thus experienced directly and positively by each imagining individual. In this mode of cultural existence, everything, every least thing, becomes intensely charged with social meaning and is, one might say, culturally overdetermined. Not surprisingly, individual behavior in such societies tends toward the ceremonious rather than, as with us, tending toward the casual and spontaneous. Indian decorations illustrate the point. The tiny caret on a moccasin is simultaneously a bead decoration and "symbolic" (meaning imaginatively stimulating) of how its wearer can race over mountains. The jagged streak of white painted on a pony's side evokes imagination of the brilliant swiftness of the lightning flash with which the rider has been blessed in his dream of grandfathers bestowing on him the power to be a powerful warrior. The Indian's culture exists through the fashion in which every part of his world is both the object and the inspiration of continual imagining and reimagining.

• • • •

If we think of myths as imaginative reenactments of the kind I have sketched, we may hope to study them without converting them into "oral literature," deforming them to fit our conception of the "aesthetic." Study of specific tellings might permit us to recognize something like "mythic styles" of narration, although these will not lead to definitions of any universal mythic form, at best only to what Clifford Geertz calls "local knowledge," and more specifically to something akin to what Wittgenstein called "family resemblances." One can rather crudely illustrate the "nonliterary" form of mythic narrative by contrasting a famous parable about Death from our tradition to a Blackfoot myth treating a death.

> A man who was walking in the market of Damascus came face to face with Death. He noticed an expression of surprise on the spectre's horrid countenance, but they passed one another without speaking. The fellow was frightened, and went to a wise man to ask what should be done. The wise man told him that Death had probably come to Damascus to fetch him away next morning. The poor man was terrified at this, and asked how he could escape. The only way they could think of between them was that the victim should ride all night to Aleppo. So the man did ride to Aleppo—it was a terrible ride which had never been done before—and when he was there he walked in the market place, congratulating himself on having eluded Death. Just then Death came up to him and tapped him on the shoulder. "Excuse me," he said, "but I have come for you." "Why," exclaimed the terrified man, "I thought I met you in Damascus yesterday!" "Exactly," said Death. "That was why I looked surprised—for I had been told to meet you today, in Aleppo."[6]

This famous story has been ceaselessly repeated throughout the West since its appearance in the Middle East twenty-five hundred years ago in the version of T. H. White's popular reworking of Malory's *Morte d'Arthur* as *The Once and Future King*. White identifies the tale not inaptly as a "gruesome chestnut." Like John O'Hara in his contemporaneous reference to the tale in *Appointment in Samarra*, White represents the story as epitomizing belief in an inescapable destiny. Commentators have suggested that the irony structuring the parable parallels that which is characteristic of Greek tragedy, as when Oedipus blindly brings destruction on himself. It is the *absence* of such dramatic clarity, I suggest, that

for us distinguishes the following representative Blackfoot myth.

> Once a man was hunting buffalo near the Sand Hills. That is where the dead go. He killed a buffalo, and when he went up to butcher it, he saw a man come towards him, whom he knew to be a dead man. He was very much afraid, so he said to the dead man, "Now I will divide up this buffalo with you, but first I must go back there and bring up my pack-horses. You can go on with the butchering." The man lied, for as soon as he reached his horse he mounted and galloped away. A long time after this, the man was back in the same part of the country, and thought to himself, "I will go to get the arrow-points I left at the place where I killed the buffalo." When he came to the place, he found the skeleton of the buffalo and also his arrow-points. As he looked up he saw the same man he had seen before. The man spoke to him and said, "My friend, where have you been? I have been waiting for you all this time." This frightened the man so much that he sprang upon his horse and galloped away at great speed. Shortly after he returned to his camp, he took sick and died.[7]

Against the Western tale ordered by fated inevitability, the Blackfoot myth exploits a mode of uncertainty that diffuses, rather than focuses, irony. The myth definitively concludes, but without absolute self-closure. The hunter dies, but for causes not certain; death's inevitability in this story becomes background, not dramatized figure. We are left with diverse possibilities about which to wonder. Why did the hunter take sick and die? Because he lied to the dead man? By chance (as he had chanced on the buffalo), without any influence from his meeting the dead man? Or was what killed him primarily his fear of death? Some orientation might be given if we could hear the tone in which the dead man addresses him—plaintively or threateningly. Thus, to seek answers in the *manner* of oral enactment, however, is to perceive that the Blackfoot narrative is constructed to allow, even to encourage, variability of interpretation, not finality of meaning. We recognize that two tellers might justifiably differ radically in the intonation they bestow on the dead man's speech. After all, we here deal not with the absoluteness of death but with the contingencies of a dead buffalo and a dead man. Blackfoot narrative logic here opens out rather than focuses in, because it speaks to the complex contingentness of death's relation to life—the man returns for arrow-points needed to kill so he can live. The listener is thus oriented toward speculations precluding the definitive closure, which in our tradition is a major formal manifestation of "aesthetic" order.

Without claiming much representativeness for this necessarily arbitrary contrast, I do propose that it alerts us to the circumstance that very often Native American traditional myths conclude in a manner preventing the kind of formal completeness that we tend to associate with aesthetic artistry. One cause for the difference is obvious: myths in a preliterate society are told in order to be *re*told, retellings being what keep a particular culture alive. Oral myths are structured as transmissive enactments that foster reinterpretations. The ironic finality of the "Death in Aleppo" story allows it, one might say, to be repeated but not retold, because it has already achieved an "essential" form.[8] The Blackfoot myth, to the contrary, is arranged to facilitate the transformativeness implicit in interpretive retellings. Each new teller offers a "version" (deriving from what he or she made of the story when listening to it being told, whether once or many times) and expects listeners to make their own reinterpretations of what they hear.

Mythographers' reluctance to admit that myths may thus be *essentially* variable arises from a misconception (nurtured by our submergence in print culture) about the primary functions of myth. Myths in preliterate societies are major means by which culture is kept alive—and what never changes is dead. Myths permit cultures to adapt to changing circumstances, physical or historical, external or internal, by sustaining continuity even while undergoing modification. The perfected ideals of Western literary artistry foster aspiration for the creation of absolutely unique, fully "original," that is, unrepeatable, works of art that therefore exist, as it were, distinct from their culture, like boulders in a stream. Mythic artistry in preliterate societies tends toward fabrication of endlessly reinterpretable forms, differentiations not aimed at uniqueness nor the creation of aesthetic, that is, autonomous, artifacts but instead that seek to assure the continuing survival of the cultural practices on which depend the production of any artifacts.

Oral myths are transmissive. Most frequently, transmissiveness is facilitated by reinterpretive variations in tellings. There are, however, examples of oral enactments separated by many years that are almost verbatim verbal repetitions. "Oral memory," on occasion, can be incredibly precise. Such extraordinary repetitions occur, I suggest, because a teller has decided that an occasion of reenactment calls for as exact a repetition as possible. Deliberate variations or attempts at nonvariation are equally purposeful.[9] Native American mythic retellings, however, normally do not strive to be identical with earlier tellings, not simply because, in oral enactments, no two tellings *can* be identical but also because the ongoing vitality of preliterate cultures depends on processes of continuous self-renewal. Writing, and, above all, print, seems to release culture from the imperative awareness of the need for continuous self-reconstituting. However, all life forms, especially complex ones such as cultures, survive only by adapting, being capable of change and adjustment to new circumstances. Myths are means for cultural adaptations. Contrary to popular misconceptions of them as mere preservatives of tradition, these narratives are, in fact, an essential discourse technique by which preliterate societies modify, as well as reaffirm, their cultural systems. Myths so function because they articulate (thereby offering to renewed scrutiny and possible reassessment) the shifting forces that *generate* specific cultural practices. This crucial feature is difficult to illustrate briefly, but I will attempt to do

so by juxtaposing four "versions," four different tellings, of a Yurok blood-money myth. Even this mode of illustration is problematic, because contemporary critical discourse infrequently addresses issues posed by versions, except, significantly, when editorial issues are at stake. Since for us "artistry" is oriented toward the attainment of uniqueness, we seek to regularize in one way or another different "versions," which usually appear to us as inadvertent obstacles or difficulties. We have developed no sophisticated critical methods for evaluating deliberate variations, and, indeed, the predominant methods of myth study, still usually a form of Lévi-Straussian structuralism, are principally directed to explaining away differences in myth tellings by describing them as manifestations of concealed, yet determinative, regularities.

The four Yurok blood-money myths were all told to my father on an early visit to the Yurok nearly a century ago. He made some comments on the characteristics of each of the four tellers, all of whom were in the same telling situation, speaking to an inquiring young anthropologist. There are many other Yurok stories about their "money," dentalium, which was an imported seashell. We might better call the dentalium shells "treasure," since the Yurok saved up dentalia strings more often than they used them for everyday exchanges. It would be difficult, however, to find a society that was more concerned with its "money" than the Yurok, and many of their myths focus intensely on dentalia and other forms of wealth, such as woodpecker crests. Dentalium, as we learn from the third of these stories, belongs among the *woge,* supernatural "people" who lived along the Klamath River before the coming of the Yurok there. The chief Yurok culture hero, who kills dangerous monsters and puts the world to rights, was Pulekekwerek, the protagonist of the first and fourth versions. Wohpekumeu, another culture "hero," usually appears as more shifty and sensually distractable than the morally austere Pulekekwerek.[10]

The teller of the first version of the institution of the Yurok custom of blood money in compensation for killing was Kate of Wahsek, a middle-aged woman with a well-educated daughter who was fluent in English. Kate was married to another full-blooded Yurok totally uncontaminated by White influences. Kate's stories, my father judged, were of the kind Yurok would customarily tell to younger children and strangers; they provide a rapid, but accurate, summary of basic Yurok philosophy and cosmology and the role of the central figures in Yurok mythology. One notices in Kate's telling how directly the origin of blood money is linked to the physical condition of the present earth and sky, for example, and that the tradition of payment for killing is founded in actions by the Thunders, great natural/supernatural powers that can be confronted only by a hero as potent as Pulekekwerek.

There was a flood. Before this the world had been smooth and level; afterwards it was rough. This is how it happened. A young Thunder went out and was killed. The Thunders did not know what had killed him; they had thought that no one was left. They were angry. It began to storm constantly. There was a great wind, the sky was torn, and rocks were flying about.

Then Pulekekwerek went south to Humboldt Bay. Here the man lived who had killed the Thunder. Pulekekwerek wanted to make him pay (blood money). He found him, his house all blown away, lying with one board to cover him. Pulekekwerek told him that he should offer to settle for the Thunder. Then Pulekekwerek went up to the sky to tender the payment. The Thunders saw him coming, thought he was the murderer, and prepared to kill him. He said, "I know what you want to do. But if you try to hurt me, I will swallow the place where you are. Take this pay for the dead one or you will all be killed." Then they accepted his settlement, and the storm stopped. That is why people pay when they have killed. If the Thunders had not accepted there would be no settlement now. Then Pulekekwerek also repaired the rents in the sky.

The second telling is by Jack of Murek, a wealthy man who belonged to a family of consequence, particularly notable for its doctors (who, among the Yurok, are always women). Although clearly a traditionalist, Jack's version of the institution of blood money concentrates on the psychology of the custom: in Kate's version, the originating acts by Jack are summarized in two sentences. Thunder's instructions explain why the custom works, because, for the Yurok, money is emotionally equivalent to kin-feeling. One notices that it is when the survivor looks at his hidden treasure, like our stereotypical miser examining his hoard, that he will remember and feel sorry for his kinsman—not the other way around. This is unsentimental, yet Jack's psychology seems sound: unless wealth is very highly valued, the blood-money system could not function.

> Thunder's boy was killed. That is how it came about that those who are killed get paid for. When his son was killed, Thunder took settlement. He said, "I want you all, when your relative is killed, and they come to pay for him, to take those dentalia. That is why I am going to accept it now: I want it to be offered to all of you. When they have paid you, hide the money somewhere. Sometimes, when you want to see your dentalia, and go to look at them, you will feel sorry because you will remember your poor kinsman who was killed."

The third telling is by William Johnson, who came from a good family but had been crippled so that his legs were useless. He had become a skilled craftsman with his hands, however, especially at making woodpecker headbands, highly prized by the Yurok, selling in 1900 for as much as twenty-five dollars. This is the only myth told by Johnson that my father recorded, which is unfortunate, since it is a small masterpiece—even having amusing overtones of something like locker-room boasting. But the insight into why money is so valued by the Yurok is brilliant—and considerably more attractive than Freudian explanations. Dentalium is the only one of the *woge* that has remained with the Yurok. Money may be small, but it is powerful because it is the sole divin-

ity that remains with humans, on their person, in their purses. It is interesting that William Johnson, in a sense, reverses the causality of the other tellings: Dentalium remains *so* that there can be a blood-money system. Johnson (like Jack of Murek) uses his story to explore how, and why, the custom functions as it does, though his focus (unlike Jack's) is the psychology of money rather than of compensation.

> Once all things were alive. Baskets were people, dentalia were people, and all other things were people. Now the *woge* knew that they must all leave: they were already in the sweathouse talking about it. Some said they were going to the sky. Others said that they would go off to the mountains.
>
> But Dentalium said, "I will not go. I wish to live where I am. I shall stay." Now he who had said they must go asked, "What shall you be able to do? You are very small." Dentalium said, "I know it. I am small, but it would be a bad thing if I went off. People would not live well. They would kill one another, and they would have no way of settling the feud. So I shall remain here." The he began to suck in and swallow the sky (to show his power) and ate most of it. Then that one said, "Stop!" So Dentalium remained, and is kept in purses by human beings.

The last telling is by Lame Billy of Weitspus, also from a good Yurok family, but crippled, although before his disability, he had been an active hunter, fisherman, and boatman—the last especially significant because all Yurok life is centered on the Klamath River. Their principal directions, for example, are upriver and downriver—and a good boatman probably would have experienced most aspects of traditional Yurok life. My father thought Lame Billy was the best teller of his many informants, characterizing him as "equally at ease in narrating a story of the folktale type, of the hero order, a myth of the origin of institutions, or one of the conventional Yurok creator-rectifier-trickster traditions. The subject mattered very little, provided it allowed treatment in his concrete and expansive manner. A bald incident he developed into a definite plot. . . . His personages command sympathy because they are quickly worked into people. . . . Billy's heroes and their friends and opponents maintain an invariable dignity of character."

> Wohpekumeu was going downstream. Looking back, he saw a man following. That one carried a quiver, drew out arrows, held them in his teeth, took his bow in his hand, and looked about him. Wohpekumeu thought, "He looks like Pulekekwerek." He watched him. He saw him approach a man and shoot. The man fell. Then that one went on.
>
> Wohpekumeu followed his tracks. He came to a large tree and the tracks stopped. Wohpekumeu looked on this side and on that side of the tree but could find no more tracks. Then he heard someone above him. "Here I am." Pulekekwerek was in the tree. "Why did you do that?" asked Wohpekumeu. "I did it in order that they may not kill each other too much, that they may not kill all the time," said Pulekekwerek. "Take this and go and tell them to accept it in settlement." He gave him dentalium money.
>
> Then Wohpekumeu went where they were mourning for the dead man. He said, "Accept a settlement. He will give you

woodpecker crests and boats and money, whatever you like. Ask for what you want and he will pay you." Then they were persuaded and said, "I want this and that," and received it.

Now Pulekekwerek said, "I have made it that it is good. Now they will not kill often. When they do kill one another, they will settle for it and that will be the end. If anyone does not pay he will die in ten days. Even while they were crying I nearly fell off the tree. I was so weak that I could hardly hold my place."

Billy's skills as a storyteller are vivid even in this brief myth, one of the shortest of Billy's narratives recorded by my father, especially his capacity swiftly to create an intriguing plot, here by having us first observe *with* Wohpekumeu: that looks like Pulekekwerek, but why would he kill a man? This is not mere plot for the sake of plot. Notably absent from Billy's version is any reference to Thunder or the *woge*. What Billy's telling dramatizes is how a "reasonable" system of justice is established by a random killing—and it is difficult not to think he thus illuminates something crucial about all cultural creations, their originative arbitrariness.

The final paragraph raises other interesting issues, besides being the first to describe sanctions if the custom is violated. Perhaps a modern Western reader would go too far in seeing Pulekekwerek's nearly falling off the tree as symbolic—the moral/emotional price of instituting the blood-money practice is high, and even a hero almost loses his power in establishing the necessary institution. But there can be no doubt that Billy's story evokes some of the anguish and pain that results from the harsh reality that makes necessary a blood-money custom. Yurok life is violent; Pulekekwerek claims no more than, "Now they will not kill often."

Each of these versions tells of the origin of an important Yurok institution, not merely from a different perspective but also unfolding an individual imagining of how this particular cultural formation might have taken shape so as to accommodate common personal feelings and recognized social imperatives. These tellings dramatize root social and psychological pressures to which the institution of blood money must appeal for its communal efficacy. The tellings, therefore, may fairly be described as exploratory in character rather than simply doctrinal. Each offers the listener an opportunity to think about a different aspect of what gives rise to an accepted custom, rather than abstractly describing or affirming the custom's appropriateness. All these versions "confirm" the custom only by individualistically imagining the psychosocial tensions that the blood-money system aims to (but does not always entirely) resolve: "if they don't pay . . ." These tellings, therefore, suggest how myths can be used in oral societies to test and even modify the social systems and customary attitudes they simultaneously justify.

It is all too easy for us to forget that myths in oral societies were always told by particular individuals to particular audiences and were, therefore, always potential vehicles for imaginings that did not conform perfectly to "standard" or traditional attitudes. Perhaps among these Yurok enactments a personal "style" is fully visible for a contemporary reader only in Lame Billy's telling, through his skill in constructing a gripping narrative, although it seems to me that a distinctively wry thoughtfulness distinguishes William Johnson's tale. My point, however, is not that we should try to deduce particular personalities of the tellers from their tellings but that we should recognize how oral myths always come into being through individual imaginings of the cultural conditions of the imaginers, and that frequently myths serve as the means to investigate and bring into view pressures that have produced practices articulated in a received mythic narrative. Careful examination of the artistry of myths, if we can free ourselves from disabling preconceptions induced by our criticism's total dependence on written texts and print culture, regularly supports this view that Native American myths often could, and did, function in such consciously evaluative fashions. . . .

[We have omitted a multipage segment with which Kroeber ends his essay. In it Kroeber critiques Lévi-Strauss's view of myth, and discusses the ideas of Mikhail Bakhtin (1895–1975), a Russian theorist on language and discourse. Much of this section is devoted to a discussion of Bakhtin's notion of language as a form of social interaction and the performance of myth in Native American society. In Kroeber's view, myth constitutes a form of what Bahktin called a "complex speech genre."—Editors]

NOTES

1. A major omission from this "trailer" is reference to ethnographic particularities, since my purpose here is to focus attention on the oral character of all Indian mythic enactments. Another omission is analysis of the foundations of current ethnological theory. It is worth mentioning, however, that Pierre Bordieu, for example, in *Outline of a Theory of Practice,* trans. Richard Nice (Cambridge: Cambridge University Press, 1988), offers thoughtful descriptions from a Western European perspective of how confronting an unfamiliar culture facilitates testing of unexamined assumptions about the "scientificness" of particular anthropological methods. As will become clear even in this brief essay, that perspective, in my opinion, requires significant revision through the application of Bakhtinian and Boasian approaches.

2. See Bronislaw Malinowski, *Magic, Science and Religion and Other Essays* (Garden City, N.Y.: Doubleday, 1954). The key essay in this volume is "Myth in Primitive Psychology," a reworking of Malinowski's first articulation of his view of myth originally enunciated in a lecture honoring Sir James Frazer in 1925.

3. I employ the term *enactment* rather than *performance* in order to emphasize that myth tellings are social events of intensity and complexity, as is admirably described by Roger D. Abrahams in his essay "Toward Enactment-Centered Theory of Folklore," in *Frontiers of Folklore,* ed. William R. Bascom,

American Association for the Advancement of Science, Selected Symposia Series 5 (Boulder: Westview, 1977), 79–120.

4. See Walter J. Ong, *Interfaces of the Word: Studies in the Evolution of Consciousness and Culture* (Ithaca: Cornell University Press, 1977). Notable among Father Ong's other associated works (whose importance to discourse theory and cultural studies is still undervalued) is his *Orality and Literacy* (London: Methuen, 1982). Stephen A. Tyler, in "The Vision Quest in the West, or What the Mind's Eye Sees," *Journal of Anthropological Research* 40 (1984): 23–40, acutely analyzes (in a fashion complementing some of Ong's philological researches) the "hegemony of the visual" in Western critical thinking from antiquity through Derrida, defining a profound bias in our culture toward conceiving of thought processes in visual terms—which renders oral forms of structuring difficult for us to comprehend.

5. A well-edited text of "The Defence of Poetry" can be found in *Shelley's Poetry and Prose,* ed. Donald H. Reiman and Sharon B. Powers (New York: Norton, 1977), 480–508, from which my citations are drawn.

6. T. H. White, *The Once and Future King* (London: Collins, 1939), 295.

7. Clark Wissler and D. C. Duvall, *Mythology of the Blackfoot Indians,* Anthropological Papers of the American Museum of Natural History, vol. 2, part 1 (New York: American Museum of Natural History, 1908), 163.

8. John O'Hara exploits this certainty of essential reference by employing it as his novel's title. This might remind us that oral stories do not possess, in our sense, "titles." They are, however, very often "framed," that is, introduced formally, or recited in ritualized circumstances, the significance of such "oral framings" (or their absence) being of some concern to me in my longer study. On retelling as reinterpretation, even of fundamental religious myths, see Dennis Tedlock, "The Spoken Word and the Work of Interpretation in American Indian Religion," in *Traditional American Indian Literatures,* ed. Karl Kroeber (Lincoln: University of Nebraska Press, 1982), 45–59.

9. In "Religion, Literary Art, and the Retelling of Myth," *Religion and Literature* 26, no. 1 (1994): 9–30, I discuss a spectacular revision of the Stone Boy myth, one of the most fundamental in Lakota mythology.

10. The four versions can be found in A. L. Kroeber, *Yurok Myths* (Berkeley: University of California Press, 1976), the texts appearing, respectively, on 321, 364, 438, and 140, with comments about the narrators found on 315–17, 359, 437, and 15–17. My father first visited the Yurok on the Klamath River in the spring of 1900, and he continued to work with them for more than fifty years.

A Jātipurāṇa (Clan-History Myth) of the Gurav Temple Priests of Maharashtra

Jayant Bhalchandra Bapat

The primary religion in India is Hinduism, and a major feature of Indian society is the caste system, or *jati,* which provides for the religious and social ranking of all Hindus. As described in the essay "Hinduism" in Part Six, there are five major caste divisions: the brahmins, kshatriya, vaishya, shudra, and untouchables. Within these five divisions there are hundreds of subcastes, each of which traces its origin to a mythical ancestor. The *Jātipurāṇas,* or caste puranas, are stories that chronicle the history of each subcaste. The essay by Bapat is especially interesting because it shows how myth, history, politics, and religion interact and can be manipulated for different purposes.

The *Jātipurāṇas* were composed to legitimize the ranking of each caste within the Hindu social and religious hierarchy. However, the caste hierarchy is not rigid—it allows some measure of caste mobility. A person may not change their caste, but the position of the caste within the hierarchy can be changed, resulting in a shift of the duties and privileges of the caste members. When caste leaders sense an opportunity, they often make a move to raise their caste's status. They typically do this by hiring a brahmin priest or scholar to investigate the matter and look for scriptural justification. They might even pay a brahmin to compose a *Jātipurāṇa* to find scriptural justification for their claim for higher status or more privileges.

This essay discusses how caste leaders for the S'aiva-Gurav caste, temple priests who claim brahmin status, have commissioned three *jātipurāṇas* to support this claim and how their claim has been received by their rival castes. Thus Bapat's essay provides us with an example of how myth can be manipulated for a group's political and social ends.

"A Jātipurāṇa (Clan-History Myth) of the Gurav Temple Priests of Maharashtra" by Jayant Bhalchandra Bapat, *Asian Studies Review* 22:1 (March 1998), 63-78. Copyright © Blackwell Publishing. Reprinted with permission.

As you read, consider these questions:
1. What are the functions of clan-history myths in India?
2. How is myth used to elevate social status?
3. What techniques are used to "legitimize" myth?

THE GURAV JĀTIPURĀṆAS

Purāṇic scholarship usually deals with the eighteen Mahāpurāṇas, the same number of secondary or Upa-Purāṇas and occasionally the Sthala or Kshetra-Purāṇas. This last category deals primarily with the religious history and celebration [Mahātmya] of holy places. However, I agree with Bailey who points out (Bailey 1995) that a purāṇic text, in addition to being a literary object, must also be considered as a cultural object that appears at a certain time to fulfil a cultural need during the historical development of Indian culture. Thus, from a sociological and cultural standpoint, one must add to this list an important fourth class, the *Jātipurāṇas* (Caste Purāṇas), which expressly trace the origin of a caste group from a mythological ancestor. These Purāṇas constitute a large body of literature relevant to particular caste groups. Typically in their accounts they span several centuries of narrated time, and although often of dubious historical merit as a record of the actual development of the caste, they can shed important light on the pressures within Hindu society to justify particular positions within the caste system. This aspect of the sociological significance of the *Jātipurāṇas* has largely been ignored in the literature, and as Rocher aptly points out, "they are far more important than our present knowledge of them" (Rocher 1986, 72). In spite of this statement, however, he devotes only one paragraph to *Jātipurāṇas* in his work on Purāṇas.

The *Jātipurāṇas* were composed primarily with a twofold purpose: to establish and to legitimate the placement of a caste group within a caste hierarchy (usually higher than their existing placement in the eyes of the significant others) and, secondly, to detail the exalted or even divine origin of their group.[1] They are thus cast in the traditional style of purāṇic composition. Almost all of them are composed in verse, and, in the Agama style, they are revealed by either a God or a Ṛṣi in the form of a dialogue between a seeker of knowledge and an expounder. In this paper, I wish to explore one such *Jātipurāṇa* written on behalf of a priestly community from Maharashtra who call themselves S'aiva-Brahmins or S'aiva-Gurav.

BACKGROUND TO JĀTIPURĀṆAS

The attempt to bring the social reality of *jātis* in line with the ideological notion of their creation from the four fold *varṇa* system through miscegenation is at least as old as the *Manusmṛti*. This reality was characterised by the existence of innumerable closed social groups defined by heredity,

pursuit of profession, division of labour, ritual evaluation of lifestyle and occupation, access or denial of the *jāti* to the Vedas and so on. Manu utilised the concepts of miscegenation and hierarchy, i.e., *anuloma* (hypergamy) and *pratiloma* (hypogamy) to explain the diversities of his time. Ever since, hypogamy, which implies sexual transgression on the part of the female, and other types of sexual deviations from the norm, such as adultery or violation of the ritual rules of intercourse, have been used in Hindu social thought to explain the fall of a caste from a higher status. The thousands of resulting *jātis* and *upa-jātis* were termed castes and sub-castes by the Portuguese and the British [Portuguese: *casta*]. It must however be remembered that the separation and divide between the *jātis* quite often remained very vague and difficult; and, as Cohn points out (Cohn 1968), the *jāti*, like the *varṇa*, is "essentially a theoretical level of the Indian social system, of itself possessing no social reality." Cohn's assertion is supported by Silverberg who found that "much social interaction in the Indian peasant community is not merely, not even principally intercaste behaviour" (Silverberg 1959, 150). It is a well established fact that the caste hierarchy was far from being a rigid, die-cast entity. It could be said to be then (and now) in a state of dynamic equilibrium. The system did allow individual castes a measure of mobility. However, as Srinivas correctly notes, "there were only positional changes and the fundamental structure itself remained intact" (Srinivas 1967, 7).

These positional changes were precipitated by one or the other caste, for a variety of reasons. The Weberian equation of the interplay of politics, power and status played a dominant part. For example, the ruling classes, superior in political might, vied with the brahmins for higher social, if not ritual, status. Thus, as early as the reign of the *Rashtrakutas* in Maharashtra, the royalty formed a sub-caste for themselves amongst ks'atriyas called *"Sat Ks'atriyas,"* claimed—and apparently were held in—a status even higher than the brahmins (Altekar 1960, 309). Such caste mobility was of course politically determined between the brahmins and ks'atriyas; the literature abounds with such examples. Among the vais'yas and s'udra *varṇa* however, upward mobility vis-à-vis each other was an uphill battle. As soon as a caste saw an opportunity, it would make an effort to raise itself. The methods adopted by caste leaders were almost always the same. They would employ a learned and well-respected brahmin to look into their case and come up with a justification for raising their position in the caste hierarchy. To give authenticity to their claim, a powerful and well-to-do caste would go even further: it would commission the brahmin to compose a *Jātipurāṇa* for them. A brahmin could usually be found to undertake such a task, most often for a reward. Occasionally a king, on being approached by a caste, would commission brahmins to study the caste's claim. He would then give a ruling according to the advice received (Das 1968, 141; Hutton 1961, 94; Srinivas 1967, 95). There is no doubt that kings wielded substantial authority in the legitimisation of caste status. Quoting several examples, O'Malley notes that "The king issued marriage regulations for castes, he fixed the social rank of different sub-castes, he promoted members of one caste to another level and he degraded them to a lower" (O'Malley 1974, 56).

The eighteenth century saw the rule of the Peshwas in Maharashtra and Mughal rule in most other parts of India. There is evidence to suggest that both the Peshwas and the Moslem rulers maintained control over caste matters, the latter albeit indirectly (O'Malley 1974, 59). With the takeover by the British, and the consolidation of their legislative power, these functions were inherited by the British rulers. The British were reluctant, especially after the 1857 revolt, to interfere with the socio-religious matters of the Hindu population, but were often forced to do so. O'Malley (1974, 63) noted in 1932 that:

> There is no official control of caste and no state interference with caste customs in British India. The Government follows a policy of non-intervention, for it is a fixed principle that it should not interfere with social laws and personal customs unless there is a general and unequivocal demand for reform on the part of the people themselves. Yet such is the force of the immemorial tradition that the castes expect the British Government to exercise the prerogative of the ancient Hindu kings by prescribing the social status of the castes. At each recurring census, the census authorities are inundated by memorials from different castes petitioning the Government to recognise their claim to a higher rank than they are actually accorded by the Hindu Community at large.

For the ease of administration, for introducing a fair and logical system of justice, and to fulfil their orientalist pursuit, the Imperial government in India embarked upon several courses of action. Their major initiatives were:

1. establishment of a central bureaucratic information gathering machine;

2. research into the origin, functioning and structure of the caste system with a view to simplifying the administration of the law of the land. Having noted that the law of the land was markedly different for different caste groups, this was a logical course for the British to embark upon;

3. undertaking of ethnographic research resulting in the production of caste histories;

4. introduction of a "Social Preference Scale" classification in the 1901 census which ranked the castes according to their social precedence.

The Imperial Government was of course expanding upon some of the measures already taken earlier by the East India Company. The ethnographers employed by the British attempted to simplify and rationalise the complexities of Indian society and in doing so, gave a disproportionate importance to caste-cluster as a level of the society. As Carroll puts it:

> The ethnological monographs produced by the colonial rulers stimulated similar inquiries by the Indians. The Indian informants . . . went beyond their subsidiary role to compile their own monographs. The Western authorities drew upon these researches by the Indians, who in turn drew upon the Western authorities; the result was the production of a highly interrelated series of "Caste-histories" (Carroll 1978, 233).[2]

This course of action proved to be a threat to the delicate equilibrium of the caste system, albeit inadvertently. The fact that the British were now engaged in a continuous attempt to describe, define, interpret and categorise the social complexity of Indian society enhanced caste consciousness amongst all castes. This was the first time ever that the details of the castes and sub-castes within the population were being reduced to writing by an authority. Also, many caste groups saw, in this Manu-like attempt at defining caste hierarchy, an opportunity to elevate their own caste in the total system. To achieve this goal, *Caste-Sabhas* (Organisations) were rapidly formed which sometimes mounted legal challenges in secular courts against their particular placements in the caste structure. The newly educated amongst the middle and the low castes also researched mythology and caste histories, and wrote about their group or commissioned a brahmin to write *Jātipurāṇas* to support their claims. The *Jātipurāṇas* were by far the best means of mounting a challenge in the colonial period. They were written in the language of the S'astras and were written mostly by brahmins. Both these facts tended to give authenticity to a claim, because both the British and members of the indigenous population held the brahmins in high esteem. In the early period of the British Raj, they were often the only link between the British and the local population.

It can thus be seen that challenges to caste status in the form of petitions to authority (made preferably with the help of *Jātipurāṇas*) were concerted attempts, albeit from diverse and often opposing quarters, to recast the balance of the regional caste hierarchy. Many *Jātipurāṇas* appeared around AD 1900 in anticipation of the second census to be held a year later. The plots of all *Jātipurāṇas* almost invariably contain common structural elements. In the style of a Purāṇic narrative, a *Jātipurāṇa* describes:

1. the committing of a sin by the caste's distant forebears or the performance of any other behaviour deviating substantially from the norm to which the caste aspires;

2. incurring of the wrath of God or a Seer [Ṛṣi]

3. a resultant curse in the form of a downgrading to a lower (mostly to the s'udra) *varṇa;*

4. expiation of the sin;

5. the rehabilitation at a level lower than original but higher than its erstwhile status.

Employment of this plot structuring device in literature enabled many a caste to lay claim to an original high status and, although immediate success was not always achieved, the device enabled the caste to keep its claim alive so that it could be reactivated at a later date. The laying of a claim in this manner was itself a mark of both modernity and education and hence of status higher than that of other similar castes who had not yet done so. While many of these claims were fanciful, it appears that those of other castes, such as for example those of the S'aiva-Gurav, had a prima facie validity for having a high status in the distant past as suggested by the evidence they put forward in support of their claim.

The Gurav *Jātipurāṇas*, therefore, perhaps not surprisingly, tell us of the Gurav's erstwhile brahmin origin from Sudars'ana, son of the great sage Dadhici. Sudars'ana commits a sin and is cursed by S'iva. As a result of the curse, he loses his right to perform Vedic rituals. Dadhici worships S'iva on behalf of his sons and seeks redress. Pleased with Dadhici's devotion, S'iva appears before him and even though he is unable to take back the curse, gives Sudars'ana and his progeny exclusive rights to S'iva's *pūjā*. The S'aiva-Gurav claim to be the descendants of Sudars'ana.

THE S'AIVA-GURAV AND THEIR JĀTIPURĀṆAS

The Gurav act as temple priests mostly in the S'iva, Devi and Hanuman temples of Maharashtra. As I have explained elsewhere (Bapat 1993, 79), there are many different endogamous groups among the Gurav. Those who call themselves S'aiva-Gurav are considered by all Gurav and other castes to be the highest among themselves. It is the S'aiva-Gurav who have laid a claim to brahminhood and there are three *Jātipurāṇas* that support their claim. The first, *Devalaka Kathāmṛt* was published in 1905, the second, *Sthūla-S'aivāgama*, in 1909 and finally the *Laghu-S'aivāgama* in 1907. The two latter works are mere compilations of chapters from various S'aivite texts compiled by the Gurav for their own communities. In this article I will therefore examine only the *Devalaka Kathāmṛt*.

The Devalaka Kathāmṛt

This *Jātipurāṇa* is written in Marathi verse. The printed text measures 13 cms × 9 cms and consists of five chapters comprising forty-three pages. The Purāṇa was published at the Jagaditecchu Press in Pune in 1905 and the title page states that it was "written by Balshastri Upasani, a brahmin well versed in the Vedas and S'astras[3] according to the wishes of the late Martand Ramji Gurav Punekar and published by his son Nagesh Martand Gurav." The next page contains an invitation to all Gurav to advertise the book among Gurav brethren and to sell it to them. It advertises that the publishers also wish to put in print information about their daily rituals [*Nityavidhi*] and invites them to send details of such information. This invitation is dated 25 July 1905. Its oblique purpose was to obtain one more proof for the Gurav's brah-

minic identity. Daily rituals identical to those practised by the brahmins would add weight to the Gurav's claim to brahminhood. I have found no evidence of such work being published.

In the typical traditional style of evocation such a work demands, Upasanishastri devotes the first few pages of chapter one to invoking Ganes'a, the auspicious god, Sarasvati, the goddess of knowledge, and Vālmiki, the first poet-author [*ādikavi*] of the *Rāmāyaṇa*. He then goes on to say that the three of them appeared before him and blessed his work, thus adding one more proof to the authenticity of its content. On page six begins the replication of the typical Purāṇic scene: Vyasa and other sages are engaged in discourse in the Naimiś'a Forest when the sages plead with Vyasa to expound to them the greatness of a deity or to solve a difficult theological problem. Thus, the gathered devotees tell Upansanishastri that he is none other than their Suta[4] and beg him to narrate to them tales of the greatness of S'iva. They then say to him:

> When we visit a S'iva temple, we always see abnormal [*viparita*] practices there. Thus the first *pūjā* is always performed by the Gurav and S'iva and Gauri accept this *pūjā*. Can you therefore explain to us the reasons behind this mystery and also explain to us the genealogy of the Gurav?

Upasani replies that the great sage Vyasa[5] himself explained the origin of the Gurav in the S'ivapurana. He further adds that, according to him, the person described in Sanskrit by Vyasa as a *Devalaka* is none other than the present day Gurav. Here ends chapter one.

Chapter two starts with the formulaic description of the Naimiś'a Forest as an idyllic place, the abode of the great sages. The forest is full of fruit laden trees and countless shrubs with fragrant flowers. Thick smoke rising from the "Homa" sacrificial fires of the Ṛsis has blackened the leaves of some of the trees. The Ṛsis are sitting together with their disciples in the afternoon, some discussing S'astras and Nyāya, others giving lessons in grammar and in music. The Suta enters the scene and the Ṛsis and brahmins, overwhelmed with joy, ask him to narrate the story of the *devalaka*. He replies that the story of the *devalaka* is sacred and the audience should therefore listen to it carefully. In chapters three and four he then narrates this story:

> There was a great brahmin called Dadhici who knew all the four Vedas, six S'astras and eighteen Purāṇas. He was a great devotee of S'iva whom he worshipped day and night. Dadhici had a son called Sudars'ana and Sudars'ana's wife was called Dus'kūla.[6] She was so named because she was born into a sinful family. One day Dadhici had to go to another town for a meeting with caste members. He therefore instructed Sudars'ana to perform the daily *pūjā* of S'iva in his absence. Sudars'ana naturally obeyed his father. Then the day of Sivarātri came and all S'iva devotees fasted on that day. However, due to his association with his wife and her evil influence, Sudars'ana had become polluted and he was therefore not scared of committing a sin.[7] Thus, he performed

the *pūjā* of S'iva on this auspicious day and went home. However, instead of fasting, he had dinner with his wife at night and then had intercourse with her as well. Next morning, he got up in a hurry and went to S'iva's temple without taking a bath. In that impure state, he performed S'iva's *pūjā*. S'iva was infuriated and appeared before Sudars'ana in his terrible form with five heads, and ten hands all holding shining armour. The fire of the destruction of the world poured out of his eyes. He kicked Sudars'ana and told him that there was no sinner greater than him. The god said that Sudars'ana had committed three unpardonable sins: consuming food on a sacred day instead of fasting, engaging in intercourse on such a day and finally, performing his *pūjā* without first taking the purificatory bath. For these sins, S'iva cursed Sudars'ana and turned him into a stone. The curse took immediate effect; Sudars'ana turned into a stone while Dus'kula died instantly from grief. Sudars'ana was denied entry into heaven and returned to earth. Grief-stricken by his wife's death, he cremated her and cursed himself for being the one responsible for all the terrible happenings and that he was paying for his sins in his previous births.

Chapter four continues the story:

Having heard this terrible news, Dadhici returned home in a hurry and blamed Sudars'ana for inviting the wrath of S'iva. He then invoked S'iva and his consort Pārvati. He pleaded with them and said that since Sudars'ana was their son, they should therefore forgive him. Pleased with Dadhici's penance, Pārvati appeared before Dadhici and begged S'iva to forgive Sudars'ana. S'iva appeared before Sudars'ana and holding his hand, made Sudars'ana sit next to him.

S'iva then gave Sudars'ana the sacred thread with three strands and also initiated him in the very sacred S'iva-Gāyatri Mantra.[8] He advised Sudars'ana to worship Gauri (Bhavāni, Pārvati) first and then perform the detailed sixteen part *pūjā* of S'iva.[9] The god then gave Sudars'ana many boons and gave him the prime place among his devotees. He advised that the first worship of the day would be performed from then on by Sudars'ana (and his descendants) and by no one else. He also allowed Sudars'ana to appropriate for his own use the offerings of grain, cloth, ghee, etc. brought to the temple by other devotees. The god further stressed that no *pūjā* would be complete unless Sudars'ana said, "Let it be so." S'iva also insisted that on auspicious occasions there should be at least one Gurav[10] among the brahmins who are fed, otherwise the deed would not be meritorious. S'iva then appointed Sudars'ana's four sons as religious mentors to the four corners of earth. He then explained the Dharma (of the *Devalaka*) to Sudars'ana. This consisted of 1) a ritual daily bath in a sacred river; 2) rigorous performance of the rituals; 3) putting a round sandalwood mark [*tilaka*] on the forehead;[11] and 4) performance of the S'ivasandhyā. S'iva said that Sudars'ana should perform the S'ivasandhyā three times a day, recite the S'iva-Gāyatri all the time and worship Pārvati before the worship of any other god. He also decreed that Sudars'ana must not recite mantras from the Vedas, and that he should respect brahmins and eat only vegetarian food.

The bar on reciting the Vedic Mantras was extended to Sudars'ana progeny as well. S'iva said that, although the progeny of Sudars'ana had lost their vedic rites, they should worship him constantly and that he was giving a special name "*Devalaka*" (temple priest) to them. The god said that no one ought to perform his *pūjā* before a *Devalaka* did it. He decreed that a *Devalaka* must be respected whether he be pure or sinful. Those who fed brahmins in order to please S'iva or Pārvati ought to include at least one *Devalaka* amongst the invitees. When the *Devalaka* was satiated by the meal, then S'iva himself would be equally happy. Here ends chapter four.[12]

In the fifth and final chapter, the story of the great king Bhadrasen is told which affirms the new status of the *Devalaka* objectively:

Bhadrasen conquered the whole world. He remained, however, extremely kind to all his people and he was also a great devotee of S'iva. Pleased with his singular devotion, S'iva appeared before him and offered him whatever he wanted, including Indra's throne. Bhadrasen refused to ask for any material reward. However, he asked S'iva to grant him some means that would act as an indicator to show if Bhadrasen had fulfilled his daily rituals and duties. S'iva therefore gave Bhadrasen a special pennant and asked him to raise it every morning. If Bhadrasen performed his daily duties properly, then the pennant would fall to the ground. However, in spite of all his good deeds including feeding thousands of brahmins daily, the pennant remained upstanding. The saddened king did not know what to do. One day a *Devalaka* visited the king and was fed along with the brahmins. The pennant fell to the ground instantly. The brahmins then explained to the king that it was due to the very special meritorious deed of feeding a *Devalaka* that the pennant fell. They also explained to him that feeding even a *crore* (ten million) of brahmins was not much good unless a *Devalaka* was fed as well. They also stated that the right to his first *pūjā* of th day was given by S'iva himself to the *Devalaka*. After that event, Bhadrasen made sure that a *Devalaka* was properly fed and clothed every day.

To end the chapter and the Purana, Upasanishastri says that this historical account of the *Devalaka* was narrated by the Suta to S'aunaka and other Ṛṣis, and that he, Upasanishastri, is now telling it to the gathered devotees. He says that just as S'iva and S'ankara are the two names of the same god, *Ghata* and *Ghāgara* are the two names for the same pot, S'arkarā and Sākhar are the two names for the same sugar, similarly, *Devalaka* and Gurav are the two names for the same people.

Upasani finally declares that those Gurav who read this Purāṇa everyday[13] will be looked after by S'iva and will acquire a good family, wealth and happiness. The Purāṇa ends here.

THE DEVALAKA KATHĀMṚT: AN ANALYSIS

As Veena Das argues (Das 1967–68, 141), it is very rewarding to treat a *Jātipurāṇa* as a sociological resource. The best way to approach this problem in the case of the *Devalaka Kathāmṛt* is to pose a series of questions as follows:

1. What prompted the Gurav to write/commission this *Purāna*?

2. Is this *Purāna* authentic in terms of the accepted fictional social history of the Gurav? In what sense are "the facts" provided in them acceptable?

3. What is the logic of validation of this *Purāna* used by the Gurav?

4. Has the acquisition of this *Purāna* by the Gurav had the desired effect in raising the status of the Gurav community?

5. Do other castes accept the Gurav claim?

I shall attempt to answer these questions in light of the available background information about the status of the S'aiva-Gurav in Marathi society. I will begin with the second question, as it relates directly to the subject of the legitimisation of the Gurav as a caste and also throws light on the logic of validation of this *Purāna*.

Although a *Jātipurāna* is a sacred text, it is designed to fulfil the cultural aspirations and needs of the group of people who are its subject. These people would then take the myths conveyed in this *Purāna* as evidence of their caste status so as to submit their claims of belonging to a particular earlier caste, invariably higher in status than their erstwhile position. In other words, the *Jātipurāna* serves as a strong statement of intention to lodge such a claim on the part of the community involved. For it to attain such a position, one of the major criteria the *Jātipurāna* must fulfil is that it must appear authentic in terms of convergence with the traditionally sanctioned yet fictional social history found in the *Purāna*, and it must be taken as part of the caste *Parampara*.

The *Devalaka Kathāmṛt* was authored by a brahmin, Upasanishastri. His work shows all the hallmarks of a classical *Purāna*. As tradition demanded, Upasani sought to prove, first of all, that the *Purāna* was authentic in terms of the *Purānic* tradition. In order to do so, he linked his work directly to an ancient text like the *S'ivapurāna*, thus bringing sanction through tradition [*parampara*] to his work. It also made his work as authentic as the *S'ivapurāna*. He was also able to model his work stylistically on the *S'ivapurāna* story, claiming that whatever he had to say was not at all new since it had appeared in the S'astras before and that he was thus a mere mortal who was ordered by god to produce the work. Hence his claim that Ganes'a, Sarasvati, the goddess of knowledge, and Vālmiki, the author of the *Rāmāyana*, appeared before him and sanctioned his work. As the formula demanded humility of all mortal authors, Upasani said that, "he knew that as an author he was most inferior but he was also convinced that god would forgive him for his transgression." This tendency is to be understood in terms of "Canons of legitimisation in traditional Sanskritic learning" (Das 1967–68, 152). Later authors try to graft their work onto celebrated older authors in order to make their own words appear authentic.

Replication of archaic forms of literature is another important device that Upasani uses in the process of legitimisation. He thus opens up with salutations to Ganes'a, Sarasvati and Vālmiki.[14] The narrative then proceeds in the classical *purānic* style. As the third device in the legitimisation process, the *Devalaka* appears as the ancient temple priest and the story is woven around the *Devalaka* myth in the *S'ivapurāna*. The myth must now explain, why, in spite of his s'udra ways, the Gurav is a brahmin. Hence the story of Sudars'ana and S'iva's curse. The restoration of Sudars'ana as S'iva's premier devotee comes at the expense of the loss of the right to Vedic *mantras*, an expiation for the sin. Being a select devotee, Sudars'ana (and hence the Gurav) is allowed to keep for his own use the offerings made by other devotees to S'iva. Thus a justification is created for the Gurav to accept money and other gifts for his services. This introduces a different form of legitimisation than the two discussed above. The legitimisation is attempted here through arguments made in a myth, whereas the previous devices sought to legitimise the Gurav through broad appeal to tradition. As Das would put it (Das 1967–68, 151), the myth that the Gurav wish to contend may be syllogistically summarised as follows:

1. All brahmins have a particular style of sacred life;

2. the Gurav do not have this style;

3. therefore they are not brahmins;

4. the Gurav fell into non-brahmin ways due to a sin committed by their ancestor Sudars'ana;

5. expiation followed and the Gurav were given exclusive rights to S'iva's *pūjā* and were also allowed to keep for their own use the offerings to S'iva made by other devotees;

6. therefore, although the right to Vedic rites has been taken away, the Gurav are really brahmins.

This brings me to the fourth question of whether the acquisition of the *Purāna* had the desired effect for the Gurav? In other words, has it arguably raised the status of the Gurav? There is some evidence to believe that the argument is accepted by both parties as an interim measure, a contention. The outcome is thus a compromise, not a solution. The Gurav remains a "select devotee" but does not rise in caste status. The brahmin dare not enter the *sanctum sanctorum* until the Gurav has done his first *pūjā* in the morning. And although he is clearly unhappy and jealous of the Gurav's daily income, he has never challenged it. The brahmin on the other hand refuses to entertain the Gurav's claim to brahmin *varna*.[15] One thus deals with two separate categories and the conflict is dissolved but not resolved. The Gurav accept the status quo not only because they have obtained official sanction for the use of the offerings made to being the exclusive *Pujāris* in S'iva temples. Furthermore, they have kept their claim to brahminhood alive. The brahmins accept it, albeit grudgingly, because they have succeeded in keeping the Gurav out of the elite brahmin class. And although the partial success of the Gurav in achieving his goal must be attributed to several factors, the *Jātipurāṇas* must account for a substantial proportion of it.

On formal bureaucratic and religious levels, the S'aiva-Gurav have been far more successful and they have been able to appropriate the nomenclature of S'aiva brahmins. This can be seen from the fact that when the S'ankarācārya of S'ringeri Math came to the town of Wai in Maharashtra in 1811 he accepted their claim to brahminhood after discussion with the Gurav community there (Upadhye 1913). However, it is difficult to ascertain what precise role the above *Purāṇa* played in raising their status. I have little doubt that at the very least, it would have united the S'aiva-Gurav together in their disputes over status with the colonial bureaucracy and the brahmins. Thus in 1911, in a dispute before the collector of Solapur district, the Gurav were allowed to write their caste as "S'aiva brahmins," albeit as a compromise.[16] Also, in a law suit in 1938, the Gurav were able to get Nyayaratna Vinod, a well known Marathi brahmin pandit and scholar to give evidence in court on their behalf that the S'aiva-Gurav were in fact brahmin. Vinod is said to have spent several weeks studying S'astras and *Purāṇas* before he came to this conclusion (Vinod 1984, 154).

It must however be remembered that the brahmins of Maharashtra have never taken the Gurav's claim to brahminhood seriously and such determination on the official level has made no difference to the treatment meted out to the Gurav by the brahmins at the societal level. While in other parts of India where S'aivite temple priests are considered to be lower-class brahmins, the Marathi brahmins have always considered the Gurav to be a s'udra. This is because the former generally quote a Vedic reference (Israel 1987, 145) whenever their exclusivity and status are challenged, and declare that in the Kali age, the ks'atriyas and vais'yas ceased to exist and thus only two *varṇas* remained: the brahmins and the s'udras. Not being accepted as brahmins, the Gurav are regarded as s'udras. Therefore, when the British sought to formalise the *varṇa* and *jāti* identity for each group within Hinduism through the 1901 census, the Gurav, like many other castes, saw it as an opportunity to raise themselves in the *varṇa* hierarchy. The fact that they firmly believed that they were brahmins—and also that they had a number of historical facts on their side—added weight to their claim. Part of the answer to question one regarding what prompted the Gurav to produce these *Jātipurāṇas* is now patently obvious: the desire of the Gurav to challenge their placement into the s'udra *varṇa* and to lay claim to belonging to the brahmin *varṇa*. However, it appears that the S'aiva Gurav had two other major concerns. These were: firstly, the need to justify their lack of education in general and lack of knowledge of Sanskrit and the S'astras in particular; and secondly, the need to show their superiority over the Lingāyats [Viras'aivas] who had taken over the priestly functions in many important S'iva shrines in Maharashtra. The modern day Gurav are painfully aware of their lack of education and lack of knowledge of S'astras. They are,

therefore, at pains to point out that their forebears were generally well read and educated. What better examples of this can one find than the two *Jātipurāṇas*, *Sthūls'aivāgama*, and *Laghus'aivāgama*, produced by two members of their own community? That both authors were able to peruse Sanskrit literature at length, interpret it and provide a detailed commentary, would in itself have proven the truth of their claims. Once again, no s'udras could have done this as they were prohibited from learning the divine language.[17] Also, the father of the author of the *Sthūls'aivāgama*, Bhagawanstswami Jahurkar held the title of "Vedamurti" (one who is the image of Vedas), a title used to refer to one with a deep knowledge of the Vedas. His title of "Swami" suggests that he was a Sanyasin and that he also stayed in a Math. Similarly, a present day Gurav from Madhya Pradesh by the name of Omdatta Arya has written a book entitled *Gaurav* in Hindi (Arya 1981). This book also deals with the Sudars'ana myth. Omdatta's guru and father was a well-respected Gurav who became a Sanyasin in his old age.

EPILOGUE

Although acting as temple priests may be their "right" as far as the Gurav are concerned, to the other brahmins it has always been paid temple service. The *Devalaka* brahmin, claimed by the Gurav as their ancestor, appears even at the time of the *Manusmṛti* (Jha 1939) as a brahmin of lower standing because he performs temple service for money. To the brahmins this is against the brahmin "Dharma" of avoiding contractual payment of any kind for religious services performed. Brahmins have always differentiated between the *Daks'inā* they receive for performing rituals and the regular income of the temple priest. The *Daks'inā* is an honorarium which also imparts merit [*puṇya*] to the host. The amount of *Daks'inā* can vary considerably depending on the financial position and wishes of the donor. As against this, the temple priest receives a regular income and orthodox brahmins have frowned upon this. Since the Gurav as temple priests do not observe this brahmin "Dharma," they are non-brahmins and hence s'udras to the Marathi brahmins. All over India, the lower status of the temple priest has been a point of great debate and as stated earlier, Indologists such as Kane, Stietenkron, Fuller and Appadori have suggested various explanations for the phenomenon. The above differentiation based on the Dharma of the brahmin and that of the s'udra is one such explanation.

It is significant to note that the Gurav are not jockeying for a superior position vis-à-vis any other caste. They are simply ascertaining their priestly brahmin status. And while many Gurav claims to brahminhood arose just prior to the time of the 1911 Indian census, the Gurav attempts to establish their brahmin status, such as their claim before the S'ankarācārya in 1811, predate the census by at least a hundred years. The ritual awareness and assertiveness of the Gurav is certainly pre-British. Another point worth noting about the Gurav claim of 1811 before the S'ankaracārya is that they chose to go to him rather than the state, in this instance, the Peshwa. The Peshwas were brahmins and it would therefore have been difficult to approach them. It is unlikely that they would have entertained the Gurav claim.

NOTES

1. I use the words *jāti* and *caste* interchangeably in this paper.

2. In a scathing attack on Herbert Risley, the well known British ethnographer who published such complete caste histories in his "People of India," Ronald Inden remarks, "previous accounts of castes had been drawn from texts composed by the self-serving Brahmans or had been anecdotal, penned by Western travellers, missionaries or revenue-collectors. Now we were to have fully systemic and scientific, that is, quantitative knowledge of India's essence" (Inden 1990, 58–59).

3. *Vedas'āstrasampanna* is a title bestowed upon a brahmin who has learned the four Vedas and six S'astras rigorously.

4. As early as Vedic times, sutas represent a class of people who are brahmins born out of *Pratiloma* (hypogamaous) unions (*Manusmṛti* 10:17). The *Padmapurāṇa* says that the main duty of sutas is to sing praises of great kings and construct genealogies of gods, Ṛṣis and great kings (*Padmapurāṇa*: 1:1:28).

5. The great mythical sage Vyasa is claimed to be the originator of all the eighteen main *Purāṇas*. See *Mahāpurāṇas*.

6. In the *Devalaka* myth in the *S'ivapurāṇa* and in all three Gurav *Jātipurāṇas*, Dus'kulā has been portrayed as the instigator of the sin of having intercourse on a holy day. Dus'kulā is not a name that any parents would choose for their daughter. Her name therefore is generic and signifies a sinful woman. Laying the blame on her is a device by which the authors keep the blame away from Sudars'ana. It also reflects on the society of the time when women were considered inferior, polluting and inauspicious. (*Dus'kulā* mean "one of an evil family.")

7. Upasani comments here that, "As it is, women are inauspicious and polluted. On top of this, Dus'kulā came from a sinful family. It was therefore hardly surprising that Dus'kulā's husband Sudars'ana would entertain sinful thoughts as well." *Devalaka Kathāmṛt.*

8. The S'iva-Gāyatri Mantra is *Om Namah S'ivāya.* The Vedic Mantra given to the Brahmins at the Sacred Thread Ceremony, the *Upanayana*, is the Gāyatri Mantra addressed to Savitṛ, the sun god. Neither the *S'ivapurāṇa* nor the Gurav *Jātipurāṇas* explain why Sudars'ana, the son of the brahmin Ṛṣi Dadhici, got the *S'iva-Gāyatri Mantra.* The Vedic Gāyatri is also a metre. S'iva-Gāyatri is chantable but is not in the Vedic metre.

9. *Sodas'opacāra Pūjā* is the complete sixteen-part worship that can be offered to any god. See Gudrun Bmhemann 1988.

10. It is significant to see that the word "Gurav" appears only in the Gurav *Jātipurāṇas*; the *S'ivapurāṇa* mentions only the *Devalaka* (temple priest). As the Gurav are the present temple priests, they claim to be descendants of Sudars'ana, and that they made the change from *Devalaka* to Gurav. The point is that the Maharashtrian Gurav do need to bridge the gap between themselves and the *Purāṇic Devalaka.*

11. The brahmins who worship Visnu put three vertical lines on their foreheads, the S'aivites put the *tripundra* mark (three horizontal lines) on their foreheads, whereas the Gurav put a *tilaka,* a circular dot, on their foreheads. Neither the *S'ivapurāṇa* nor the Gurav *Jātipurāṇas* explain why the S'iva temple priest has to be different from the other brahmins in this diacritical mark.

12. Each chapter of this *Jātipurāṇa* ends as follows: "Those who are known as *Devalakas* in the Sanskrit language are without doubt the Gurav (of the present day). Let everyone hear this biography of them. It is dedicated to S'iva, Sāmbasadās'iva." *Devalaka Kathāmṛt,* ch. 1, p. 8, verse 41; ch. 2, p. 14, verse 26; ch. 3, p. 20, verse 28; ch. 4, p. 29, verse 45 and ch. 5, p. 43, verse 66.

13. Few modern day Gurav seem even to know about the existence of this *Purāṇa,* let alone read it daily.

14. The choice of Vālmiki instead of Vyasa is interesting. Vālmiki, the author of the *Rāmayāṇa,* came from a low caste. There is a caste that claims to be Vālmiki-Brahmins who perform the rites of the untouchables.

15. I attended a religious festival at a S'iva temple in Satara, Maharashtra State, in January 1992. At the conclusion of the festival there was a feast at which the Gurav and his family were not allowed to eat alongside the brahmins. As the custom dictated, they were asked to bring their own utensils and food was transferred into these from above, without contact by the brahmin cooks. The brahmins would not even touch the utensils. The Gurav and his family then helped themselves and had to sit together in one corner, well away from the brahmins.

16. The census officials had included the Gurav as s'udras. The Gurav challenged this classification and the matter went before the collector. Upon hearing the Gurav claim, the collector made the above determination.

17. Except for the brahmin and ks'atriya men, women and the lower castes were not allowed to learn and speak Sanskrit. They could only use Prakṛt. This practice is evident in Sanskrit literature, in the plays of Kalidasa, for example, where even the queen can speak only in Prakṛt.

18. I have discussed this aspect of the Gurav-Lingayat interaction at some length in an extensive treatment of Gurav Jātipurāṇas soon to be published in the *International Journal of Hindu Studies.*

REFERENCES

Altekar, A. S. [1960] 1982. The Rashtrakutas. In *The Early History of the Deccan,* vol. 1, ed. G. Yazdani. Reprint, New Delhi: Oriental Book Reprint Corporation.

Appadorai, Arjuna. 1983. The puzzling status of the Brahmin temple priest in Hindu India. *South Asian Anthropologist* 4:43–52.

Arya, Omdatta. 1981. *Gaurav* (in Hindi). Ujjain: Kirti Printing Press.

Bailey, G. M. 1995. *Ganes'purāṇa,* vol. 1 of *Upāsanākhanda.* Wiesbaden: Otto Harrassowitz.

Bapat, J. B. 1993. The Gurav temple priests of Maharashtra. *South Asia* 16 (special issue): 79–100.

Carroll, Lucy, 1978. Colonial perception of Hindu society and the emergence of caste associations. *Journal of Asian Studies* 37:233–50.

Cohn, B. S. 1968. Notes on the history of the study of Indian society and culture. *Structure and Change in Indian Society*, ed. M. Singer and B. S. Cohn: 3–28. Chicago: Aldin.

Das, Veena. 1967–68. A sociological approach to the caste Purāṇas: a case study. *Sociological Bulletin* 16–17:141–64.

Fuller, C. J. 1984. *Servants of the Goddess.* Cambridge: Cambridge University Press.

Gudrun Bmhemann. 1988. *Pūjā, A Study in Smarta Ritual.* Leiden: E. J. Brill; Vienna: Gerold & Co.

Hutton, J. H. 1963. *Caste in India.* London: Oxford University Press.

Inden, Ronald. 1990. *Imagining India.* Oxford: Basil Blackwell.

Jha, Ganganatha, ed. 1939. *Manu-smṛti.* Allahabad: Indian Press.

Kane, P. V. n.d. *History of Dharmas'astra,* vol. 2, parts 1–2. Poona: Bhandarkar Oriental Research Institute.

Milton, Israel, and N. K. Wagle. 1987. *Religion and Society in Maharashtra.* Toronto: Centre for South Asian Studies, University of Toronto.

O'Malley, L. S. S. [1932] 1974. *Indian Caste Customs.* Reprint. Delhi: Vikas Publishing.

Rocher, Ludo. 1986. *The Purāṇas.* Wiesbaden: Otto Harrassowitz.

Silverberg, J. 1959. Caste ascribed "status" versus caste irrelevant roles. *Man in India* 39:150.

Srinivas, M. N. 1967. *Social Change in Modern India.* Berkeley and Los Angeles: University of California Press.

S'ri S'udrakamalākara or *S'udradharmatatvaprakās'a.* 1910 3d edition. Translated by Vamanshastri Islampurkar. Bombay: Tukaram Javji.

Upadhye, Kashinath Bhagwant. 1913. *Mahiti Patrak.* Solapur: K. B. Upadhye. Brochure published for the Gurav Community.

Vinod, Maitreyi. 1984. *Aho Saubhāgyam.* Pune: Siddhashrama Prakashan.

Von Stietencron, Heinrich. 1977. Orthodox attitudes towards temple service and image worship in ancient India. *Central Asiatic Journal* 31:126–38.

God the "Stone/Rock":
Myth, Idolatry, and Cultic Fetishism
in Ancient Israel*

Ithamar Gruenwald

This is an essay about the interpretation of biblical texts and re-creating the ancient Israelites' conception of God. In this article Gruenwald argues that how biblical theology is established depends a great deal on the manner in which the texts are interpreted. He says that a metaphorical understanding of biblical language has become so imbedded in our culture that we miss other possible ways of interpreting Scripture. In particular, he outlines the Old Testament use of the words *rock, stone,* and *mountain* as synonyms for *God,* and discusses the various ways in which this choice of words may be interpreted. It seems natural to a modern audience to understand the references to God as a rock or stone as metaphors for God's strength and permanence. However, Gruenwald suggests that the original use of these terms in ancient Israel was literal.

In the first part of his essay, Gruenwald outlines how Jewish theologians popularized a metaphorical interpretation of passages that described God as a rock. He then discusses how in many parts of the world rocks or specially shaped stones are singled out as sacred spots or invested with supernatural energy or creative powers. Mountains often bear the names of deities and are often identified with the gods themselves, and Gruenwald provides numerous examples of Old Testament passages that refer to rocks and can be understood as referring to the rock as God, as containing some essence of God, or as being God's home. Gruenwald concludes by stating that he is not trying to contradict the weight of Jewish theological opinion on the metaphorical interpretation of Scripture, but to suggest that mythic forms of thinking are deeply embedded in scriptural literature.

As you read, consider these questions:

1. What is the role of allegory in myth?
2. How is metaphor important in the interpretation process?
3. How do references to stone/rock relate to concepts of deity?

Ithamar Gruenwald, "God the 'Stone/Rock': Myth, Idolatry, and Cultic Fetishism in Ancient Israel." *Journal of Religion* 76:3 (July 1996), 428–449. Reprinted by permission of the author and The University of Chicago Press.

✳

I

One of the peculiar features of the divine nomenclature in Scripture is that it occasionally engages the semantic field of Stone-Rock-Mountain-Place. Among these names, those of *tsur* (or *sel'a*), "rock," and *even,* "stone," occupy a unique position. Notable examples include "The Rock, his work is perfect; for all his ways are justice" (Deut. 32:4); "then he forsook God who made him, and scoffed at the Rock of his salvation" (Deut. 32:15); "How should one chase a thousand, and two put ten thousand to flight, unless their Rock had sold them, and the Lord had given them up? For their rock is not as our Rock" (Deut. 32:30–31); "For who is God, but the Lord? And who is a rock, except our God" (2 Sam. 22:32). In a more evocative context we find: "The Lord is my rock, and my fortress, and my deliverer, my God, my rock, in whom I take refuge" (2 Sam. 22:2–3; Ps. 18:2); "Yea, thou art my rock and my fortress" (Ps. 31:3; 71:3); "I say to God, my rock" (Ps. 42:10 [9]).[1]

Since in a number of these cases the word *tsur* is actually synonymous, or parallel, to that of Elohim and even the Tetragrammaton,[2] it is reasonable to argue that all these divine names can be treated on one and the same notional level. However, since in some of the cases the word "rock" is used synonymously with "fortress" and "deliverer," the reader may be induced to think that "rock" should be understood as a simile and not as one of the proper names of God. This article will discuss the various interpretive options that such nomenclature implies and their significance for the study of the history of religions, in general, and that of the religion of Ancient Israel, in particular.

Similarly, we find that God is referred to, though less frequently, as "stone": "by the name of the Shepherd, the Stone [Hebrew: *even*] of Israel" (Gen. 49:24): "The stone which the builders rejected has become the head of the corner" (Ps. 118:22).[3] The implied difference between "rock" and "stone" is of no substantial consequence: the two terms belong to the same semantic field. Thus, in whatever context and mode of interpretation they appear, they share a similar notional framework. Admittedly, as indicated above, if we view them from a frequently maintained interpretive perspective, the cases under discussion may indeed imply what may be referred to as metaphorical notions. Accordingly, a certain quality of the divine may be implied by those terms, but not God's actual name or his real essence or being.

In fact, a first reading of most of these verses is likely to take into consideration established reading habits. Accordingly, nothing could be more natural than maintaining in these cases the relevance of a metaphorical reading. Furthermore, a literal understanding of these names, according to which God really is a "rock" or "stone," is viewed as running counter to customarily maintained theological beliefs and assumptions. These hold fast to the basic concept according to which Scripture unambiguously maintains an-

timythic and antifetishist positions.[4] However, what in the eyes of many looks like an inevitable assumption, and for that matter the only possible interpretative option, constitutes in our eyes a hermeneutical problem deserving serious consideration.[5]

This article, then, deals with a number of key issues in the study of religious expression and language. More specifically, it deals with mythic language in Hebrew Scripture. As we shall see, mythic language constitutes a special type of language that uses ordinary language to refer to supernatural realms in intensely anthropomorphic terms. If we assume that it addresses issues relating a special, paranatural (or supernatural) nature, it actually constitutes "a language within a language."

In many ways, mythic language is the basic language of religion. However, it is often assumed that the "monotheistic religions" are diametrically opposed to anything that hints of myth or mythopoesis. We should make clear that we distinguish between mythological materials—remnants of which may be found in Scripture, Jewish and Christian alike—and mythic language and mythic forms of conceptualizing religious experience and perception. The latter are the subject of this article. As we shall see, this assumption about myth and "monotheistic religions" requires modification. Briefly stated, myth and mythopoesis occupy a central position at the heart of religion in general. In this respect, the "monotheistic religions" are no exception to the rule.[6] Thus, mythic modes of expression are paradigmatic: they set the quality, nature, and framework of religious language in general. They likewise make evident the most adequate forms for the study of religious language. It is commonly assumed that mythic forms of expression are fictional and cast in poetic form. When used in a poetic context, objects usually take on personified dimensions. On theological grounds, then, it is often assumed that such forms of expression require special hermeneutical decoding. However, since the borderlines of hermeneutical decoding are not set by the text itself, the question arises, What are the limits of such a decoding, and in whose hands should their setting be entrusted?

In the history of Jewish and Christian exegesis of Scripture we often find that allegory dominates the interpretative scene. Words and notions are relegated to other spheres of signification, mostly those that can be accounted for on rational, or rationalistic, grounds. However, allegory should not be viewed in the narrow context of a tactical solution. It often becomes an exegetical strategy that addresses matters of conceptual substance. Allegory often sets the contents of religious belief. In any event, it forces on the text something that comes from without, something that is not intrinsically implied by the text in question. It is not dictated by the objectively formulated needs of the text from "within." In the context of the present discussion, allegory will be viewed as tantamount to a metaphorical interpretation of Scripture. It is applied to help certain people read Scripture in a way that removes for them interpretative obstacles that, to the best of their theological perception, cannot be found in the text.

With the passage of time, certain modes of interpretation become so deeply embedded in the general reading experience and habits of the readers that these modes, and their underlying interpretative assumptions, are viewed as intrinsically implied by the text itself. What is even more interesting to note from our point of view is the fact that certain interpretative habits that have crystallized in a theological milieu are taken over by scholars for whom rationalism is the sine qua non of their interpretative stances. For instance, many people would still find it difficult to accept another interpretation of the word *bara*—"created," in Gen. 1:1—than the one suggesting the notion of creatio ex nihilo. It is indeed difficult, even for a modern reader of Scripture, to think of the verb *bara* in terms that are different from the usually accepted notion of a spiritual, rather than mythical, creation.

As we shall see, a similar problem exists with regard to those utterances in Scripture in which God is spoken of in terms such as "stone" and "rock." People would indeed find it difficult to read these words in terms different from their usually accepted metaphorical meaning. Hence, once again, an interpretative tradition has established itself in the context of which all utterances implying cultic fetishism and corporeal anthropomorphism are explained away as similes and metaphors.

On a general hermeneutic level, then, this article deals with the problems that arise when people assume that a certain type of biblical language necessarily requires a theological or rationalistic transposition. If the metaphorical interpretation of Scripture is not made the order of the day, new options are opened for a better understanding of the nature of biblical religion and language. In dealing with religious language and expression, one touches upon questions that do not necessarily belong to the area of literary criticism. They concern the very essence of religious language as such, and in this respect they require separate methodological attention.

II

Newly discovered materials, as well as improved editions of ones already known, are constantly being published in great quantities and make it clear that those sections in the Hebrew Scriptures that appear to propagate the purist's notion of religious monotheism and its consequent cultural separatism have to be read in a different light. Actually, our overall picture of the scriptural world has to be modified in a substantial manner. Parts of this modification, as well as some of its more important consequences, will be discussed here.

In this respect, questions relating to the very identification of what are assumed to be coded forms of expression and their respective deciphering occupy a central position.

The question is always an open one: how are we to identify religious codes? What is a code, and on what grounds are we entitled to assume that what seems to be the simple and plain language of Scripture potentially carries coded messages? When can we treat words as if they are dressed in a metaphorical garb, and when should we stick to reading them in their downright and unimpeded lexical immediacy? The answers to these questions are not as easy as one could wish. As we shall see, different views hold equal rights to interpretative validity. The act of interpretation easily reaches slippery ground. For it has long been recognized that the truth of any interpretation is more often than not configured as the self-projected identity of a personally engaged reader. If this is the case, subjective considerations always play a major role in the choice of the interpretative options.

However, I believe that scholars should be exempted from the task of having to upgrade seemingly ambiguous texts to the status of theological formulations that are dictated by rationalistic considerations. For scholars, metaphorical modes of interpretation should not be seen as the escape exit when the theological roof is in flames. There are no self-evident interpretative principles on the basis of which texts have to be read metaphorically. As a matter of common practice, texts should be allowed to address us in their unimpeded lexical immediacy. In any event, we should be alert to the fact that interpretation all too easily becomes hyperinterpretation.

In other words, when used as a maximizing rhetorical device, metaphoricism, as a hermeneutic principle, is very likely to do the opposite of what is expected. Instead of making us hear the voice of the text in all its clarity, it may critically distort the issues involved. The extensive discussion of theoretical issues, therefore, has one purpose: to make us aware of the fact that what we establish in biblical theology is very much dependent on the kind of hermeneutical activity we are engaged in. The answer to the question, How did the Ancient Israelites conceive of their God? depends on how we read the relevant scriptural texts. That is to say, what matters most in the framing of our conceptual world is the kind of interpretation we bring to the texts in question.

But there is more to our subject than just the formal question of interpretative metaphoricism. It has become a theological commonplace in Judaism (and also in some sectors of Islam and Christianity) that almost every name attributed to God is considered a metaphor. God's essence is above and beyond every form of human conceptualization, cognition, and expression. This, so the line of theological argumentation goes, turns every name or attribute of God into a metaphor. "Metaphor" here means any form of expression that is attributed to God without implying anything essential.

In discussing the framework in which these terms were interpreted in the past, attention should first be given to Maimonides. For it may well be argued that, at least in the framework of the Jewish tradition of interpreting Scripture,

Maimonides more than any other personality colored the hermeneutical scene and left there an indelible mark. Consequently, the metaphorical interpretation of Scripture has become almost the order of the day.[7]

This is what Maimonides says on some of the verses quoted above: "Rock [*zur (tsur)*] is an equivocal term.[8] . . . God, may He be exalted, is designated as the Rock, as He is the principle and the efficient cause of all things other than himself."[9] With this kind of statement, the metaphorical scene is clearly set. Maimonides goes on to say that what is implied in these verses is the notion that one should "rely upon, and be firm in considering God, may He be exalted, as the first principle. This is the entryway through which you shall come to Him, as we have made clear when speaking of His saying [to Moses]: *Behold, there is a place by Me* [where you shall stand upon the Rock]" (Exod. 33:21).[10] The last verse was not included in the list quoted above, nor was the verse, "Behold, I will stand before you there on the rock at Horeb" (Exod. 17:6), as these verses will receive special attention below.

In dealing with the interpretative oeuvre of Maimonides, one has to take into consideration the fact that for him the philosophical end justified the interpretative means and result. As we shall immediately realize, Maimonides, like many other philosophers and commentators, preferred interpretative metaphoricism to any other way of reading problematic religious texts. Problems arose for him when, because of their anthropomorphic or materially concrete language, texts spoke a philosophically redundant language. Originally, Maimonides explained, language had to be used to meet the needs of the uninformed audience of the time. In its original setting, that language indeed was mythical and anthropomorphic. However, philosophers and correctly informed readers have more sophisticated *agenda*. As a result, they apply hermeneutical tools in which problematic expressions are explained as metaphors. In other words, the philosophical layer of meaning is decoded in the language used by Scripture.

The hermeneutical presuppositions upon which Maimonides builds his interpretative oeuvre are defined in the first chapter of his magnum opus, *Mishneh Torah:* "The Torah speaks in the language of men. All these phrases[11] are metaphorical. . . . The term is used allegorically and all these phrases are to be understood in a similar sense."[12] There is no need to enter into a full-scale discussion of Maimonides' interpretative stance here. Suffice it to repeat that since certain expressions in Scripture imply anthropomorphism in relation to God, they all demand a metaphorical transposition. In the eyes of Maimonides, and many who adopted his line of thinking, anthropomorphism was likely to breed the worst kind of idolatry, which in his eyes was conceptual or theological idolatry. In short, Maimonides represents a classical example of what may be called "metaphorical reformatting," or interpretative metaphoricism.

III

To come back to the initial point, several of the scriptural quotes to which I referred at the beginning of this study occur in a poetic context. Thus, from a purely literary point of view they can easily be viewed as demanding metaphorical interpretations.[13] One does not have to heed philosophical concerns to indulge in metaphoricism. Metaphoricism indeed has enriching potential. It opens up hermeneutical possibilities and enriches the evocative potential of language, in general, and of the interpretation of texts, in particular. However, it should be made clear that, as a matter of interpretative principle, the metaphorical kind of interpretation is not a logical *conditio sine qua non*. Its alleged conclusiveness cannot pass unchallenged. In this respect, we follow the midrashic way of approaching scriptural texts. For, and this is the crucial point, we shall see that the rabbis did not always find it necessary to employ what may be called "metaphorical circumvention" in order to mitigate the rather bewildering effect that certain expressions in Scripture might have left on certain readers.

Although methodological observations take up much of the space here, my discussion is not taking issue with abstract questions alone. On the contrary, from a phenomenological point of view there is ample comparative material that should give rise to similar questions.[14] Stones and rocks are almost universally identified with cultic sites on which a great variety of rituals is enacted.[15] In some cases stones and rocks become the foundations of temples.[16] In any event, rocks and outstandingly shaped stones are universally singled out as sacred sites in many parts of the world, including the Near East.[17] Evidently, stone structures can inspire a sense of the "numinous."[18] The same holds true of rocky mountains, which are often described as sites upon which theophanies have taken place (e.g., Mount Sinai). Such mountains become the places on which temples are built (e.g., Mount Moriah), and in some cases they even bear the names of gods ("The Mountain of God": 2 Sam. 21:6, 9; Ps. 24:3).[19] The question that needs to be asked, then, is: Are these rocks, stones, and mountains only a dwelling place of the gods, or are they identical with them?

Mountains and rocky sites in many cases bear the names of deities. "Sinai" may be understood as a divine name (Judg. 5:4–5; Ps. 68:9), as well as "Moriah" in relation to Adonai Yir'eh (Gen. 22:14). Beth-El, which is the place of the stone consecrated as an altar by Jacob (Gen. 28:18–19; see the discussion below), is another case of the same kind. Of particular interest in this respect is the divine name Har ha-Gadol (the Great Mountain) mentioned along with the term *even ha-roshah* (apparently the "head stone") in Zach. 4:7. We know that the term the "Great Mountain" is also a standard name of Enlil, head of the Sumerian pantheon, who was equated with Assur.[20] Thus, it appears that one is justified in identifying these objects with the gods themselves.

I have already referred to the fact that stones found in cultic places are likely to be treated as the foundation of the world, the axis mundi, or the navel of the world.[21] In this connection, they may have a phallic—that is, sexually creative—function, too.[22] It may not be insignificant to notice that in Hebrew words for "rock" and "stone," respectively, belong to different genders: *zur* or *tsur* ("rock") is masculine, while *even* ("stone") is feminine. Stones are often considered as the birthplace of gods and special heroes: Mithraism is a notable example.[23] I should also mention that Abraham is called *tsur* in his capacity as the patriarchal forefather of the Israelites (Isa. 51:1–2). In this connection we should also be reminded of the words of John the Baptist: "God is able from these stones to raise up children to Abraham" (Matt. 3:9; Luke 3:8). God himself, called *tsur* ("rock") is mentioned as the forgotten "Father" of the Israelites (Deut. 32:18). In short, the comparative study of "stone/rock" imagery leads into semantic territories that substantially transform the way in which the corresponding material in Scripture should be read.

Interesting as this comparative material is in itself, it also shows that the metaphorical interpretation is not as inevitable and self-sustained as it often appears to be. Phenomenologically speaking, the exclusivity of this approach can no longer be sustained or justified. Contrary to what established itself as a rationalistic way of reading Scripture, we may now adapt a more open, that is, mythic way of reading it. Many people in the past did indeed feel that their concept of God was strengthened, rather than weakened, through its association with such a nomenclature as the "stone/rock." What it signaled to them came through the plain and immediate sense of the terms, not its alleged metaphorical explanation.

IV

If the foregoing discussion makes sense, its consequences are likely to achieve a breakthrough in our attempts to obtain a clearer, more nuanced, and hence also more accurate picture of biblical religiousness. In this respect, scriptural myth and mythopoesis will escape being swept under the carpet of prejudicial opinion. What is of crucial importance for this discussion is not only the realization that myth or mythic materials are found in Scripture but that myth itself and, what is even more important, *mythic forms of thinking* are a deeply rooted factor in scriptural literature.

One further observation has to be made at this point. In Ancient Israel there was no such term as "myth," or any other term, that implied what this one does in modern philosophy and scholarship.[24] Thus, no distinction was maintained, as is the case in phases of modern study, between mythic, nonmythic, and even antimythic materials. However, it should be noted that in the modern history of the term, a tinge of negative judgment is often implied.[25] In such cases, the term does not serve descriptive and phenomenological aims. In a wider sense, the term "myth" implies tendencies toward prejudicial refutation rather than sincere attempts at scholarly realization. Myth, we should notice, is a special way of approaching reality, both natural and supernatural. It involves cognitive modes and forms of expression that are different from the ones applied in, or as a result of, ordinary perception. When, however, myth is conceived as synonymous with pagan, hence primitive or idolatrous, forms of religiousness, it is likely to lose its usefulness as a term objectively designating a cognitive mode or, as Ernst Cassirer called it, a unique "symbolic form."[26]

Briefly stated, value judgments are frequently involved in how the term "myth" is used. Doing so implies the scaling and grading of higher and lower forms of religiousness. In my view of the matter, myth is a perceptive attitude rather than a descriptive or expressive performance. It presupposes, or actually enacts, certain modes of perception that substantially expand the borders of the realizable world, such that the commonly observed distinctions between various forms of reality are crossed. Consequently, modes of expression different from the ones applied to ordinary human experience, as established by sense perception and normal rules of logical perception, are allowed to prevail.

Generally speaking, the mythic aspects evolving in Scripture are mostly connected with theophanies and angelophanies. Among these, theophanies in the Sanctuary, or the Temple, occupy a special place.[27] However, in this discussion I will limit myself to theophanies that are in one way or another connected with rocks and stones. The first example comes from Exod. 17:6: "Behold, I will stand before you there on *the rock* at Horeb; and you shall strike *the rock,* and water shall come out of it" (my emphasis). The midrashic comment of the *Mekhilta de Rabbi Ishmael* suggests this: "God said to him [Moses]: In every place in which you find the imprint(s) of a man's legs, there I am before you."[28] What the *Mekhilta* appears to imply is that God's image can take a physical shape, and even leave a physical—humanlike—imprint in or on a rock.[29] Although, *strictu sensu,* what the *Mekhilta* says is that Moses could see vestiges of the divine presence in that particular rock, there is more to what the *Mekhilta* text implies than is usually conceded. We can safely say that, since the scriptural verse reads "there I am before you," the Midrash actually implies that God's imprints in the rock indicate his presence there.

There are good reasons to read this comment of the *Mekhilta* in light of the complementary notion, frequently referred to in other places in rabbinic literature, that physical representations of kings and gods actually indicate the virtual presence of the represented being in their engraved or painted images.[30] I would even argue that this notion comes as close as one can to what is generally referred to as a fetishist visualization, even conceptualization, of the represented essence, whether divine or human. Thus, for instance, Genesis 1 maintains that man was created in the image of God. This is often interpreted as indicating the consubstantial identity of God and man.[31] It is also said, once again in the *Mekhilta de Rabbi Ishmael,* that, if people break the sculpted images of emperors and other rulers displayed in public places, they actually "diminish the image of the King."[32] If this saying of the *Mekhilta* is to make any sense, we should read it in the context of rulers' cult and royal worship in late antiquity. In this respect, it cannot but convey the then prevailing notion of fetishist veneration of deities and rulers.[33] What is of even greater interest is the fact that this saying of the *Mekhilta* comes by way of illustrating the theurgically expressed notion that, in disobeying God's decrees, people not only affect but actually diminish his (spiritual) essence.[34]

What interests us most here is the fact that, according to the *Mekhilta* (and it is not unimportant to notice that there are quite a number of midrashic parallels to this saying), the spiritual essence of the divine may assume physicality of one kind or another. Otherwise, the rabbis of the Midrash would not have treated the breaking or the desecration of those royal images in terms of the "diminishing the image of the king" nor have associated it with the severe consequences of the actual desecration by diminution of God. The rabbis' aim was to make clear to their listeners the severe consequences of religious blasphemy. It amounted to inflicting physical offense on God and, hence, made the desecrating person liable to and deserving of death.

Those trained in rational theology may see in this an inherent contradiction in terms. How can one compromise between such conflicting notions as the physical presence of God in or on a rock, on the one hand, and the notion of the alleged incorporeality of God, on the other? Indeed, there is an implied ambiguity in Jewish religiousness in this respect. Among other things, this self-contradictory element derives from the fact that in some places it is explicitly stated that on the occasion of receiving the Law on Mount Sinai the People of Israel did not see any *temunah,* that is, physical image (Deut. 4:12, 15). This is often interpreted as maintaining the absolute incorporeality of God. Since, however, we know that Moses did in fact see the *temunat adonai* (Num. 12:8), we must assume that Scripture holds two conflicting—though somewhat complementary—views on the same subject. According to one view, there was in fact a *temunah* of God seen by the people, and according to the other, no human being except Moses actually saw it.[35]

In any event, contradictions should not be explained away through metaphorical interpretation. As I have pointed out above, if this is done, dialectical nuancing loses its effectiveness, and scholars are likely to be deprived of the comprehension of scriptural religiousness in all its rich diversity.[36] In short, metaphorization in our case is likely to flatten diversity into apologetic harmonizations.

Let me be more specific on this issue. The injunction that one should not make "a graven image [*pesel*] in the form [*temunah*] of anything which the Lord your God has forbidden you" (Deut. 4:23, 25) is very clear about its limited inclusiveness: it forbids only the *making* of such "*pesel* in the *temunah* of anything."[37] It does *not* preclude the existence of

a *temunah* altogether. Furthermore, it does not say anything about cultic objects and places that make no use of such a *temunah.* These are elsewhere forbidden in the form of the *asherah, matsevah,* and *bamah* (e.g., 1 Kings 14:23).

Initially, then, rocks and stones could be worshiped or served as cultic places. It made sense to worship such a rock only when it was believed actually to contain an aspect of divine essence or representation. The cult objects that were initially prohibited were handmade *reproductions* of certain divine images. Obviously, this does not exclude the possibility of a physical presence of God in or on a rocky place. When *spoken to* (Num. 20:7 ff.) or beaten with the magical staff of Moses (Exod. 17:7), a divine rock could even render drinking water, whatever that meant. When that rock was not properly handled, God himself was virtually desecrated, and the people involved—in this case, Moses and Aaron—were severely punished.

In short, the above-mentioned case of the *Mekhilta* (and its parallels) makes one thing clear: the rabbis in question would not have elaborated on the rock issue in the way they did if there had been anything in their very concept of *religion* or of God that in principle spoke against it. What I have in mind is this: the law prohibiting the making and worshiping of cultic images in all likelihood received its special status already in the various forms of Pentateuchal religion, and particularly in its Deuteronomistic sections. However, many people in the ancient world shared the opposite belief that, "theologically" speaking, there was nothing wrong with the presence of a divine essence in certain material objects. Notice how the People of Israel rejoiced at the golden calf, actually referring to it as "the God of Israel" (Exod. 32:4, 8). Moses saw the *temunat Adonai* and thus could make the proper distinctions of essence. The People of Israel, who had not seen such a *temunah*—that is, had no actual vision of a physical shape—were accused of confusing essence and appearance.

As we shall see, scriptural religion did not fight idol worship just because that kind of worship was nonsensical. Admittedly, there are in fact voices in Scripture, and later on in rabbinic writings, that actually ridicule idolatry. However, for most scriptural writers, the *agendum* was set at establishing a different kind of God, one that was conceived of as physically dwelling in the sanctuary or temple. Although God was not conceived as being in any *hand*made objects, he *was* conceived of as occupying a certain place. Here, "place" (in Hebrew, *maqom,* which later on became the actual name of God)[38] rather than a certain object was the key factor. At times, however, that "place" could still be identified with a cultic object, a stone[39] or a rock, as the case might be.

V

This brings us to a point in which a few words are due on idolatry in ancient Israel. Occasionally, idolatry became the target of theological ridicule. In principle, however, it could not, and should not, be taken as a cultic joke. It is one thing to treat idolatry as "cultic abomination" (Deut. 29:16) and another to ridicule it, as some of the prophets and psalmists did in their poetic enthusiasm.[40] Primarily, I maintain that any theophany in nature implied a physical presence of God in a specific location. Evidently, this led to the consecration of sacred places (e.g., the theophany in the burning bush in Exodus 3). Idol worship is often connected with such places, but it had other aspects, too. In the face of the archeological evidence, also reflected in the sharp criticism that the prophets leveled at it, idolatry must be viewed as a live issue in Ancient Israel. No legal rulings were effective in eliminating its existence from the cultic scene.

As a matter of theological principle, people were directed to believe that God could not be contained in a small place or object. As the prayer of King Solomon so clearly says on the occasion of the inauguration and consecration of the Jerusalem Temple, "But will God indeed dwell on the earth? Behold, heaven and the highest heaven cannot contain thee; how much less this house which I have built!" (1 Kings 8:27). However, the various occasions on which God or his glory were described as descending into, or on (as the case might be), the sanctuary (e.g., Exod. 40:34–35; Lev. 9:23–24), the Temple (1 Kings 8:10–11; 2 Chron. 5:13–14), and Mount Sinai (Exod. 19:18; Deut. 4:11; 5:19–21) make it clear that a different view was allowed to prevail in practice. Accordingly, something of the divine essence could be experienced spatially.

In light of the above, new explanations have to be offered for the prohibition of idol worship in Ancient Israel. It seems safe to say that the prohibition of worshiping idols came as a result of the fact that idolatry could all too easily lead to a desecration of the worshiped deity. Idols could be physically abused, mishandled, and damaged. The Israelite concept of God maintained his aloofness: God was above everything that could either harm or damage him, and this, first and foremost, in the physical sense of the term. Sacral profanation was always a real threat, even in the case of the God of the Israelites. God's aloofness protected him from physical damage.[41] However, in a considerable number of cases, different things happened: God was either seen or envisioned in some aspect of corporeality or physicality. One such form of corporeality was the rock or the stone.

Diagnosing, as we do, a theological conflict of interests is not something that should be interpreted as an open door for scholarly relativism. Quite to the contrary, in nuancing one's scholarly observations in face of conflicting evidence, one becomes better equipped to judge data in the reality of their phenomenal complexity. In this respect, certain pages in the history of religiousness in Ancient Israel have to be rewritten.

Moreover, it should be noticed that the rabbis of the Mishnah and Talmud were very serious in their handling of idolatry. Their halakhic opposition to participating in anything that was likely to tempt their Jewish coreligionists to commit idolatry was extremely well informed. In fact, it is amazing to note how seriously they took the practice of idolatry. Too much was at stake for them to engage in frivolity. In this respect, even when discussing the issue of the one who "sits in the seat of scoffers" (Ps. 1:1) in the context of idolatry, the talmudic sages (*Bav. 'Avodah Zarah* 18b–19a) did not fall into the trap of sarcastically condemning their opponents. The rabbis were well aware of what was at stake in such matters and cases. They were also fully aware of what was expected of them. After all, their non-Jewish neighbors were no literary fictions or social failures. They were friends, or real enemies, as the case might be, but not nonentities. If so, their idolatrous customs had to be treated seriously. Borderlines created by disinformation can be effective only where ignorance prevails. But this was not the case with the talmudic rabbis nor even with their medieval successors: they very well understood that sarcasm and mockery could make people laugh but not convince them of the need to engage all their mental resources in fighting idolatry.

VI

Two further examples of this rock/stone imagery will bring us to the end of this study. When Jacob fled from his parents' home in Be'er Sheb'a, he "came to *the Place,* and stayed there for the night. . . . He took from the *stones* of *the Place* and put [it/them] under his head. . . . And he was afraid, and said, 'How awesome is *this Place!* This is none other than the House of God, and this is the Gate of Heaven.' So Jacob rose early in the morning, and he took *the stone* which he had put under his head and set it up for an altar and poured oil on the top of it. He called the name of *that place* Bethel [= the House of God]" (Gen. 28:10 ff.).[42] It is interesting to notice that Midrash *Bereshit Rabbah* (par. 68) interprets the word *Makom* ("the Place") as one of the epithets of God.[43] Following this interpretation, the first verse in our passage would read: "And he came 'to God,'" *Maqom* being a metonym of God. In accordance with this translation, the verse "and he took from the stones of *the Place*" would read: "And he took from the stones of 'God.'"

This brings us to Philo and to his interpretation of some of the verses quoted above. It is interesting to note that Philo *ad locum* does not sound as allegorical as he does on many other occasions. When, for instance, Philo comments on the passage describing Jacob and the stone(s) at Bethel, he writes in almost mythical terms:

> Now "place" [*topos*] has a threefold meaning, first that of a space filled by a material form, secondly that of the Divine Word [*ho theios logos*], *which God Himself has completely filled throughout with incorporeal potencies* [italics added]; for "they saw," says Moses, "the place where the God of Israel stood" (Exod. 24:10). Only in this place did He permit them to sacrifice, forbidding them to do so elsewhere: for they were expressly bidden to go up "to the place which the Lord God shall choose" (Deut. 12:5), and there to sacrifice. . . . There is

a third signification, in keeping with which God Himself is called "a Place," by reason of his containing things, and being contained by nothing whatever, and being a place for all to flee into, and because He is Himself the space which holds Him; for He is that which He Himself has occupied, and naught encloses Him but Himself. "I, mark you, *am not a place, but in a place*" [italics added].[44]

Among other things, it is interesting to observe how Philo creates an interpretative link between "the stone[s] of the place," the name of God, and the cultic place of worship. In doing so, something of the mythical is allowed to shine through.

A similar passage of Philonian interpretation says this: "For, then, they shall behold the place[45] which in fact is the Word [*logos*], where stands God the never changing, never swerving, and also what lies under his feet like 'the work of a brick of sapphire, like the form of the firmament of the heaven' (Exod. 24:10)."[46] We need not enter here the ensuing discussion in Philo's text. It should, however, be clear to the reader that with the addition of the reference to Exod. 24:10, the circle is closed: the "brick of sapphire," alias a heavenly stone, cannot be accidental in this context of "place" and "God."

In this connection mention should be made of Exod. 33:21–23: "And the Lord said, Behold, there is *a place* by me where you shall stand upon *the rock,* and while my glory passes by I will put you in a cleft of *the rock,* and I will cover you with my hand until I have passed by . . . and you shall see my back." The italicized words, *a place* and *the rock,* fit very well into the picture that has been drawn so far. It is also interesting to notice that "seeing" here, as "seeing *the place*" in Gen. 22:4, is best taken as a technical term implying a theophany, or divine vision. It is said of Abraham: "On the third day, Abraham lifted up his eyes and saw *the place* afar off." Elsewhere, I have shown that the words "lifted up his eyes" indicate a supernatural vision (perhaps a prophetic clairvoyance). If this is the case, it is once again noteworthy that Abraham saw "the place." In the biblical narrative, that place was a (or on a) mountain. In line with our current interpretation, it is reasonable to argue that the verse in question gives expression to the view that Abraham actually had a divine vision of God dwelling in a mountainous location. In fact, *Midrash Rabbah,* treating the verse explicitly, says that Abraham saw a cloud (of the glory of God).[47] In other words, Abraham saw God.

It is reasonable, therefore, to argue that in this case, as also in many others, both Scripture and its midrashic interpretations use the same technical language with the same framework of significations in mind. This being the case, the intertextual relationship between Scripture and Midrash should be viewed, not as is usually the case in the framework of a hermeneutic stance only, but actually as manifesting an ongoing tradition of technical terminology.[48] In fact, the Midrash helps the scriptural verse to convey its mythic content or meaning.

Understandably, we cannot enter here a full-scale discussion of all the different aspects of the stone/rock symbolism, including for that matter the Qabbalah literature. However, in order to realize how far-reaching that symbolism is, we shall refer to one example taken from Joseph Gikatilla's *Sha'arei Orah* (Gates of light).[49] This book, most probably written around the time of the completion of the *Zohar,* often functions as a systematic compendium to the symbolism of the *Zohar.* However, it can well stand in its own right, independently stating important Qabbalistic positions and issues.

Sha'arei Orah has a rather long entry on *even* (stone). It starts with this statement: "Adonai is also referred to as EVEN, for it is the foundation of all the building in the world. All the world depends on it and its needs are fulfilled by it. It was called *Even ha-Ro'shah* [the first stone; Zech. 4:7], from here came forth the celestial and earthly multitudes of Creation."[50] The reference here is twofold. In the first place, mention should be made of the general Qabbalistic context. *Even* in the Qabbalah is a symbol[51] of the tenth, and hence lowest, Sephirah, *Malkhut* (kingdom). In a sense, it functions as a junction between the upper and the lower worlds: "and after it draws from these higher sources, it then sustains all that is found below it, each according to his need."[52] Through that Sephirah, the flow of the divine emanation into the lower world(s) becomes possible. In this sense, "the world [really] depends on it." Obviously, this marks a completely new turn of the stone/rock imagery. Still, it is noteworthy that one of the chief attributes of *Malkhut* (kingdom), especially in its creative capacity, is *Even.*

Briefly, then, the "kingdom" of god, technically viewed as the tenth Sephirah, is symbolically configured as "stone." That "stone" is viewed as a fountainhead of all the divine emanations that stream into the lower world. Qabbalah, then, transforms an old notion and adapts it for its own purposes. It is unlikely that this could have been done, unless an ancient tradition sustained it.

VII

Although there is much more to our subject than could be included in the present article, I hope that the materials discussed prove useful not only for the study of the language of Scripture, but also for a fuller realization of the mythic structures that are implied in that language. Over against a rationalistic, demythicized reading of Scripture, I have suggested a reading of certain sections of it in light of a more relaxed attitude toward myth and mythopoesis. In employing that kind of reading, I tried to expose both a mythic superstructure as well a mythopoetic infrastructure in the language used in Scripture. I have shown that myth in Scripture is not only a matter of casual borrowings from the pagan environment but actually a basic mode of cognition that characterized the Israelite perception of God. In other words, I have suggested that we realize the presence in scriptural language of a dimension, or layer, of mythic expression that for a long time has evaded readers and scholars alike.

Among other things, that reading can help us in understanding important issues in relation to the concept of idolatry in the various phases of Israelite religiousness in antiquity. I took issue with Maimonides over several principle issues because in my view his is a classic example of an approach that engages all of its intellectual resources for the sterilization of the mythic aspects of Scripture. From his own philosophical point of view, Maimonides may have had good reasons for doing so, but, as I have argued, that kind of rationalistic approach was not contained within its own medieval limits. It spilled over and later on, during the time of the Enlightenment, was reinforced by all kinds of philosophical considerations. Since then, it has also substantially colored the academic and scholarly scenes.

The point here is not to take issue with Maimonides, but to clarify some positions that used to, and sometimes still do, shape scholarly views. It may be argued that even when not directly reflecting theological interests, those positions and views have prevented people from approaching the phenomenological subject matter in an openminded and unbiased manner. For a long time now, scholars have found it convenient to concentrate mainly on textual and historical issues. The scholarly agenda have been set by the historical-critical approach, which relegates issues such as the ones raised here, to conditions that allegedly prevailed in a distant and primitive past. It has been argued that once religion made its first steps toward liberating itself from the ancient world, it turned everything upside down. Myth was converted by theology and for that matter could be declared "liquidated." Writing on myth in Judaism, G. Scholem made this comment: "In any case, *the tendency of classical Jewish tradition to liquidate myth as a central spiritual power* is not diminished by such quasi-mythical vestiges transformed into metaphors."[53] This article has tried to show that such a position can no longer be maintained in the scholarly study of Jewish religion. The question here is, what is "classical Jewish tradition"? If it is Scripture, then Scholem is wrong, because there *is* myth in Scripture. If, however, "classical Jewish tradition" stands for the Maimonidean type of interpretation, the question arises, is this indeed "classical Judaism"?

NOTES

*This article is part of a larger project in which the nature of Jewish religiousness in biblical and postbiblical times will be studied and extensively discussed. Special attention will be given in it to matters relating the assessment of mythic language. As will be made clear in the course of this article, these subjects belong to an area of studies in which the nature of religious language as "second language" or "a language within a language" is taken up. Previous versions of this article were read as lectures at New York University and the Divinity School at the University of Chicago. Many people offered their kind help in addressing questions and in making useful suggestions. Among them I

would like to single out Professors H. D. Betz and Michael Fishbane of the Divinity School at the University of Chicago. Two earlier versions of this paper were read by Professor Simo Parpola, the University of Helsinki, who encouraged me at a time when I most needed his critical observations. This is also the place to thank Professor W. Clark Gilpin, dean of the Divinity School, and Professor Frank E. Reynolds, program director of the Institute for the Advanced Study of Religion—both of the University of Chicago—for their kind hospitality. Professor Josef Stern, the Department of Philosophy, the University of Chicago, took great interest in this article in the final stages of its composition and provided a few helpful comments.

1. Unless indicated otherwise, all English quotes in this article are from the Revised Standard Version.

2. See, e.g., Deut. 32:15, 30–31.

3. The meaning of this particular verse from the Book of Psalms is not indisputable. However, the immediate context—the neighboring verses—speak about God. A messianic interpretation is suggested in a saying attributed to Jesus as quoted in Matt. 21:42.

4. See, e.g., Deut. 4:16–18, 5:7–8, 12:3. See, further, Moshe Weinfeld, *Deuteronomy 1–11* (the Anchor Bible) (New York: Doubleday, 1992), pp. 289 ff.

5. It is worth comparing the position taken here with that of Arthur Marmorstein, *The Old Rabbinic Doctrine of God* (London: Oxford University Press, 1927).

6. In this respect, the work of Y. Kaufmann played a most influential role, particularly on the Israeli scholarly scene. Kaufmann's contributions to modern biblical scholarship are still very much "in the air," but in recent years a growing amount of criticism is accumulating demanding a substantial revision of Kaufmann's positions. Eventually that criticism will change the scholarly scene, even where it has not yet succeeded in doing so. It should, however, be remarked that, in stating his positions, e.g., in questions relating to myth and the Ancient Israelite attitude toward Canaanite idolatry, Kaufmann was remarkably careful to use nuanced, and hence dialectical, formulations. Most of Kaufmann's studies were published in Hebrew.

7. This is also true of those Jewish interpreters of Scripture who tried to introduce Midrashic and Qabbalistic notions into their commentaries. Here the name of Ramban, Rabbi Moshe ben Nahman, comes to mind in the first place. Ramban was one of the chief voices on the Jewish scene reacting against many of the Maimonidean presuppositions in the interpretation of Scripture. Nevertheless, even in his work, a substantial degree of metaphoricism enters the interpretative scene.

8. That is, it belongs to the sphere of the "accidentals." For a good summary of the problems involved in this subject, see Majid Fakhry, *Islamic Occasionalism and Its Critique by Averroes and Aquinas* (London: George Allen & Unwin, 1958).

9. What Maimonides has in mind here is the Hebrew word for rock, *zur,* which is close to the root, *yzr,* to create or craft.

10. Maimonides, *The Guide of the Perplexed,* trans. Shlomo Pines (Chicago, 1963), pt. 1, chap. 16. p. 42.

11. That is, all the terms and scriptural utterances that speak of God in terms that allude to him as having human qualities.

12. Maimonides, *The Book of Knowledge,* trans. H. M. Russell and J. Weinberg (New York: Ktav, 1983), "Laws Concerning the Basic Principles of the Torah," chaps, 1, 9.

13. It is essential in this connection to distinguish between metaphors as conceived of in the mind of the original writer and metaphors that are the result, or actually the presupposition, of the interpretative act.

14. In this connection mention should be made of Mircea Eliade, *The Sacred and Profane: The Nature of Religion* (San Diego: Harcourt Brace & Co., 1959). Eliade refers to the concept of "hierophany," that is, "the manifestation of the sacred in some ordinary object, a stone or a tree" (p. 11). Eliade expresses the view that "a *sacred* stone remains a *stone;* apparently (or, more precisely, from the profane point of view) nothing distinguishes it from all other stones. But for those to whom a stone reveals itself as sacred, its immediate reality is transmuted into a supernatural reality" (p. 12). It should be noted, though, that I go one step further than Eliade. For Eliade speaks about a sacred manifestation *in* material objects, whereas I refer to the identification of deities with stones. The difference between these two positions may seem too insignificant to dwell upon, but in my eyes it is substantial.

15. Stones and rocky structures are part of the cultic life of many religions. The comparative materials will be discussed below; however, by way of introduction, I mention here that in Islam the Ka'ba still functions as the central cult place. It is a large black stone. As already noted by Maimonides in *Responsa* (ed. Joshua Blau, 2:725–27 [the Responsum to 'Ovadia the proselyte]), its history goes back to pre-Islamic days, so also its cult(s). In the Koran, Sura 106, the Ka'ba is only briefly mentioned as "the House"; but in a later text, Sura 2 (115), the Ka'ba is mentioned in relation to Abraham as "the [praying] Place" of the Patriarch. (The special meaning of the term "the place" will be discussed below.) Mention should also be made in this connection to the Dome of the Rock in Jerusalem, which in some cases was declared a substitute for the pilgrimage to Mecca. Mircea Eliade, *Myths, Rites, Symbols* (New York: Harper & Row, 1976), 2:377 ff., links sacred stones with the Omphalos, the Naval of the Earth, and sacred mountains in general. See, further, Robert Graves and Raphael Patai, *Hebrew Myths: The Book of Genesis* (New York: McGraw-Hill, 1966), pp. 207–8, who point to the location of temples on mountain tops as also to the Matsebah, the sacred pillar or altar, which had to be avoided in the cult of the Israelites, and even destroyed along with other Canaanite cult objects; see Exod. 34:13; Deut. 12:3. If Frank Moore Cross, *Canaanite Myth and Hebrew Epic* (Cambridge, Mass.: Harvard University Press, 1973), pp. 52 ff., is right, then the Hebrew epithet for God, Shadday, means "the mountain of [God]."

16. This is the case with the *even ha-shetiyah,* placed in the Holy of Holies of the Jerusalem Temple. I shall discuss this issue in a longer, forthcoming version of this article. On stones and temples, see also N. Na'aman, "Bethel and Bet-Aven: An Investigation into the Location of the Early Israelite Cult Places" (in Hebrew), *ZION* 50 (1985): 15–25 (this is the jubilee volume of the journal published by the Historical Society of Israel, Jerusalem, celebrating the years 1935–85). Na'aman collects interesting materials that are relevant to the discussion here, though his major purpose is to show that cult places "in Israel during the premonarchical and early-monarchical periods were built outside of their respective towns" (see the English summary, pp. viii–ix). Notice should be taken, too, of Na'aman's argument to the effect that *"Beth-aben* [mentioned seven times in Scripture] ('House of the Stone Pillar') was the original name of Bethel's early sanctuary. . . . The name *Beth-aven* ('House of Wickedness') was developed by the prophets of the eighth century B.C.E. as a pejorative substitute for Bethel and its sanctuary" (p. viii). A line of thinking that has still to be explored is connected with the Sanctuary-Temple topos in the Hebrew Scripture. It is very often argued that the scriptural narratives about the Sanctuary built by Moses in the desert should be viewed as a polemical statement against the Stone-Temple built by King Solomon.

17. In Eretz Yisrael such stones were found at Gezer. See M. D. Coogan, "10 Great Finds," *Biblical Archaeologist* 21 (1995): 40. Famous, too, are the "stones" at Stonehenge, Wiltshire, England, and the stone formations, called "Lord and Madam Mayor," in the Adrshpach Rock Hills in the Czech Republic. Those who travel in the state of Arizona cannot avoid noticing the endless and different stone formations there. Doubtlessly, all these formations originally served cultic purposes. See also the materials surveyed in Fredric Lehrman, *The Sacred Landscape* (Berkeley: Celestial Arts, 1988). In this connection, mention should be made of the name *"ha-Even ha-Gedolah"* (the Great Stone) given to the Bamah at Giv'on (2 Sam. 20:8).

18. Such a "numinous" feeling is certainly inspired on visiting, e.g., Temppeliaukio Church in Helsinki, Finland. This church is cut and built into a granite rock hill. Its walls actually are the roughly cut colored rocks of the place.

19. In the eyes of Nepalese Buddhism, the Himalayas are the abode *(alaya)* of the Snow-God Hima. On the whole, there is a vast scholarly literature on this subject as it appears in many cultures and religions.

20. This information was kindly passed on to me by Professor Simo Parpola. For recently published references, see James B. Pritchard, *Ancient Near Eastern Texts Relating to the Old Testament,* 3d ed. (Princeton, N.J.: Princeton University Press, 1969), p. 574, lines 35–40: "In the city, the holy seat of Enlil, / In Nippur, the beloved shrine of the Father, the Great Mountain . . ."; ". . . planted in it a pure place like a (high) rising mountain, / Its prince, the Great Mountain, Father Enlil . . ."; and p. 575, line 124: "Without Enlil, the Great Mountain. . . ." In a letter dated March 27, 1995, Parpola kindly informed me that he had "checked the Assyrian database for theophoric personal names containing the element of *shaddu,* 'mountain,' and found all of them to be of the type 'DIVINE NAME-is-my/our-mountain' *(DN-shaddua/ni),* with only four divine names attested as the theophoric element: Assur, Bel,

Marduk and Nabu. As you know, both Assur and Marduk were equated with Enlil; Nabu was equated with Ninurta, specifically in the aspect of the exalted saviour; and Bel was an appellative of both Marduk and Nabu/Ninurta as Victorious God. . . . This not only confirms that the God/Mountain imagery was current in Assyria too, but specifically suggests that it had as its mythological background the reunion of Ninurta and Enlil in *Lugale* and very probably was also used in the allegorical sense of Ps. 118:22/Matt. 21:42."

21. I shall discuss this particular issue later on in relation to the notion of the *Even ha-Shetiyah*. However, at this point we can already mention the *Even ha-R'oshah* (most probably, "the head stone" = "the Foundation Stone") in Zach. 4:7.

22. See the discussion below.

23. See Leroy A. Campbell, *Mithraic Iconography and Ideology* (Leiden: E. J. Brill, 1968), pp. 275–77.

24. For a comprehensive overview of major scholarly positions taken in relation to myth and Scripture, see Frederick H. Cryer, *Divination in Ancient Israel and Its Near Eastern Environment: A Socio-historical Investigation* (Sheffield: Journal for the Study of the Old Testament Press, 1994), pp. 42 ff.

25. In this respect, a considerable amount of rationalistic apologetics still enters the modern discussion of myth. See, e.g., K. Hübner, *Die Wahrheit des Mythos* (Muenchen: Verlag C. H. Beck, 1985); I owe this reference to Professor H. D. Betz.

26. I prefer here the term "cognitive mode" to "symbolic form," as it implies psychological aspects of which Cassirer was unaware.

27. It is interesting to notice, in this connection, that the "Sanctuary/Temple" symbolism in Qabbalah is "heavenly," too.

28. Horovitz and Rabin, *Mekhilta de Rabbi Ishmael,* p. 175. The English translation is mine. Notice should be taken of the fact that mentioning the footprints of God can here mean that the midrashist wanted to avoid the notion implied by the verse in the Book of Exodus to the effect that Moses actually hit the rock, that is, God, so as to bring water out of it. This is probably the sense in which the so-called Jerusalem Targum uses the suggestion that the "rock" here did not mean God but only his footprints.

29. It is interesting to compare here the information brought by Peter Harvey, *An Introduction to Buddhism* (Cambridge: Cambridge University Press, 1992), p. 191: "Pilgrims also visit Mount Siripada [in Sri Lanka], known in English as 'Adam Peak'. . . . On its summit is a 1.7 metre long depression in the rock, held to be a footprint of the Buddha when he used his meditative powers to fly to the island on a teaching trip. Such 'footprints' exist elsewhere in the Buddhist world, and are greatly valued as objects associated with Gotama." Notice should also be taken of the fact that the cultic symbol of the God Shiva is the Linga, that is, a phallic-like stone pillar.

30. The Mesopotamian background of this belief is discussed by Irene J. Winter, "Idols of the King: Royal Images as Recipients of Ritual Action in Ancient Mesopotamia," *Journal of Ritual Studies* 6 (1992): 13–42. I owe this reference to Professor Simo Parpola of Helsinki. For a wide-ranging discussion of icons and images in cult and art see Hans Belting, *Likeness and Presence* (Chicago: University of Chicago, 1994).

31. See, e.g., *Mishnah Sanhedrin in Mishnah,* trans. H. Danby (Oxford, 1933), 6:5: "Rabbi Meir said: When a man is sour troubled, what says the Shekhinah? My head is ill at ease, my arm is ill at ease!"

32. See the *Mekhilta,* p. 233. In another text that reflects Roman or Byzantine customs, it is said that, if a person throws a stone and even curses the "icon" of a king put up in the public square, he risks capital punishment. See Sh. A. Wertheimer, *Batei Midrashot,* 1:170.

33. It is interesting to notice that, in commenting on the halakhic discussions of ruler cults in late antiquity as we find them in the Talmud, some medieval commentators make a clear distinction between idols of gods and representational images of human beings. Prostration to the second class is not always considered *'Avodah Zarah.* See in the Talmud *"Tosafot"* to *Bav. 'Avodah Zarah 3/a,* s.v. *"She-l'o."* In biblical times it was not uncommon to bow down to distinguished people. However, Mordecai "did not bow down or do obeisance" to Haman (Esther 3:2). The three men of Jewish origin did not "fall down and worship the [golden] image" that Nebuchadnezzar had erected. The prevalent and official rabbinic view on these matters was formulated rather sweepingly in Mishnah *'Avodah Zarah* 3:1: "All images are forbidden [for any kind of utility] because they are worshipped once a year. So Rabbi Meir. But the sages say: Only that is forbidden which bears in its hand a staff or a bird or a sphere [symbols of lordship]. Rabban Simeon ben Gamliel says: That which bears aught in his hand" (*Mishnah,* trans. and comments by Danby).

34. See the extensive discussion in Moshe Idel, *Kabbalah: New Perspectives* (New Haven, Conn.: Yale University Press, 1988), pp. 156–99. I thank Professor Idel for several comments made on an early version of this article.

35. U. Cassuto, *La questione della Genesi* (Florence: University of Florence, 1934), tried to show that the view held in biblical criticism according to which these conflicting views can be attributed to two different "documental sources" has no evidential substance to it.

36. Whether this difference between Moses and the People of Israel reflects two contrasting points of view or only two accidental cases is an issue that need not be discussed here.

37. The word *temunah* is also used in the Decalogue (Exod. 20:3; Deut. 5:7), where idol worship is forbidden.

38. See Efraim Elimelech Urbach, *The Sages* (Cambridge, Mass.: Harvard University Press, 1987), pp. 66–79.

39. One should mention in this connection the cultic stones that the high priest was wearing in the temple and that were believed to be shining on special occasions; see Exod. 39:2–32.

40. A typical example of this ridicule is found in Isa. 44:9–20 and 46:6–7. In medieval times, it was Maimonides who mocked at idols and considered their manufacturing as expressive of

human vanity. A strong polemical strain runs through most of Maimonides' writings, from the early days of his *Commentary to the Mishnah* (e.g., Tractate *'Avodah Zarah*) to the late days of *The Guide of the Perplexed.* However, no ridicule but deep philosophical concern runs through most of Maimonides' polemics. In rabbinic writings of the talmudic period, we find the notion of *"leitsanuta de-'Avodah Zarah"* (ridiculing the idol). As Saul Lieberman has shown in *Hellenism in Jewish Palestine* (New York: Jewish Theological Seminary of America, 1962), pp. 115 ff., there is very little mockery and sarcasm in the way in which the rabbis gave expression to their resentment of idol worship. The rabbis very seldom ridiculed idol worship in a manner that is reminiscent of the church fathers of their times.

41. That kind of aloofness is quite commonly interpreted as indicating scriptural notions of transcendentalism. However, philosophical transcendentalism can hardly go together with the idea of a personal God. Thus, those who use the term actually do so by substantially misusing it, or using it out of its strict philosophical context.

42. To set the context of the ensuing discussion, see above note 11. The fact that the vision is a dream need not bother us here. A similar terminology would have been used had it been a "real vision."

43. A survey of various rabbinic sayings that relate to God in terms of "place" and "space" are discussed in Urbach, pp. 66–67. This discussion takes a completely different turn than the one taken by Urbach. For Urbach still considers the "place" terminology as applied to God to be on the conceptual, rather than the mythic, side.

44. Philo, *De Somniis* (On dreams) I, 61–64 [630], in the Loeb Classical Library, 5: 328–29.

45. Here Philo refers to the Septuagint, Exod. 24:10: "and they saw the God of Israel"—"And they saw the place where the God of Israel stood." This clearly reminds us of the comment made by the *Mekhilta de Rabbi Ishmael,* quoted above, to the effect that the vestiges of God's feet can be seen upon the rock.

46. Philo, *De confusione linguarum* (The confusion of tongues) 96 [419].

47. See *Midrash Rabbah to Gen.,* ed. Theodor-Abeck, p. 595. See also the legendary conversation Abraham conducts with his young attendants and son. The former had to admit that they did not see the cloud and were left behind, whereas Isaac saw the cloud.

48. The same would hold true in the case of certain materials incorporated in the pseudepigraphic literature of the so-called intertestamental period.

49. Unless otherwise indicated, I quote from the new translation, Joseph Gikatilla, *Gates of Light,* trans. A. Weinstein (San Francisco: Harper Collins, 1994).

50. Ibid., p. 21. Weinstein's translation here wrongly has *Ha-Rishonah* instead of *Ha-Ro'shah.*

51. The names of the Sephirot are commonly referred to in the scholarly jargon as "symbols." However, the term "symbol" as used in literary and philosophical research does not fully cover the semiotic complexity of the names of the Sephirot.

52. *Gates of Light,* p. 22.

53. Gershom Scholem, *On the Kabbala and Its Symbolism* (New York: Schocken, 1965), p. 88; the italics were added.

PART TWO

Ritual, Religion, and the Supernatural

Individuals and objects of great holiness and power are venerated by religions throughout the world. This image shows the Nghtatgyi (or five story) Buddha at the Asay Tawya monastery in Yangon, Myanmar. The Buddha was not a God; the name means simply "The Enlightened One," but Buddha images are common and are greatly revered.

5

Supernatural Beings and Powers

Essays in This Section:

A critical aspect of all religions is that they claim the existence of something that is nonempirical; that is, something that cannot be measured in any agreed-upon, scientific sense. As you read the essays in this section, keep the following points in mind:

- As we pointed out in the introduction, saying that something is supernatural is different from saying that it does not exist. There is no scientifically agreed-upon way to measure the existence of God or spirits, but neither is there a scientifically agreed-upon way to measure love, beauty, or goodness.

- Anthropologists have never agreed upon an exhaustive way to classify nonempirical beings. Despite this, most would probably agree that the same sorts of supernaturals are common to many of the world's religions. Some supernaturals present in many religions are gods, lesser spirits, spirits of human origin, and trickster spirits.

- The totality of gods, spirits, and other supernaturals found in a religion is generally referred to as that religion's pantheon. Pantheons are frequently hierarchical; that is, they are composed of a high god with lesser gods and spirits ranked below the supreme being.

- Gods are generally thought of as either creating or controlling substantial sectors of the world. The creator God of the Jewish, Christian, and Islamic traditions is one obvious example. The gods of Greek and Roman antiquity are another. The Bhils, described in the essay by Mahipal Bhuriya, have such a god as well, but unlike the Western gods just mentioned, their god, *Bholo Isvar,* is not very interested in human affairs.

- Lesser spirits are generally sprits of particular places or of particular events. While they may be quite important and powerful, their effect is limited to certain locations or fields of interest. Parke's essay on the Qawa incident, which describes spirits associated with sacred wells in Fiji, gives us an excellent example of such spirits.

- What about the devils, tricksters, and other spirits of passion? Most religions include spirits that celebrate the forces of destruction and chaos in the world. However, this category is very broad and extremely difficult to describe. Some religions, such as Christianity, have devil figures, representing evil. However, the nature of such figures usually is much more ambiguous. Spirits of this sort can also represent wisdom, cunning, sexuality, and greed. In many cultures, worship of destructive forces is as important as worship of benevolent forces. You will find a good example of this principle in Fernando Cervantes' essay, "The Devil and the Saints in the Conquest of Mexico."

- Spirits of human origin are spirits of people. In some cases, a person can be simultaneously alive and a spirit (for example, when an individual having a religious experience travels to a spiritual world). However, in most cases, spirits of human origin are the dead. These may be ancestor spirits, ghosts, or partially alive creatures such as zombies. They may be benevolent, malicious, or both. Interesting (and challenging) examples of the power of individuals to become spirits are found in John Frow's essay on Elvis as a god.

- In addition to beings, many religions also include the idea of *mana* an impersonal power. The term itself comes from the Pacific Ocean Islands (and has nothing to do with the *manna* of the Hebrew Bible, food that the Israelites ate during their wanderings). In Melanesia, *mana* was a power that could fill objects or people. In Polynesia, it was a power that filled kings, nobles, and priests. Possession of *mana* made individuals or objects powerful. In Polynesia, the fact that high-ranking members of society were filled with *mana* meant they were hedged about with taboos—rules that prevented commoners from coming in contact with them.

- The idea of *mana* is appealing because we so frequently believe that objects or individuals are filled with nonempirical power. Objects of religious symbolism, lucky or unlucky charms, stars (like Elvis), saints, and objects that came in contact with the pious, famous, or infamous seem to be filled with power, and we treat them in special ways as a result.

- Though this section deals with supernatural beings, keep in mind that not all religious presence is personified as a being or a power. The Jewish, Christian, and Islamic traditions tend to be "about" God; others are not. Buddhism is about enlightenment and the achievement of *nirvana,* a state in which one attains disinterested wisdom and compassion. The Society for Ethical Culture, an offshoot of Reform Judaism, is about, among other things, seeking a truth that is larger than ourselves and has a meaning that is ineffable—that is, a meaning that is beyond rational human comprehension.

Tribal Religion in India:
A Case Study of the Bhils

Mahipal Bhuriya

In this brief essay, Mahipal Bhuriya provides a description of the religion of the Bhils, a large tribal group located in central and northern India. Bhuriya's essay is important, not because it provides details of the religious life of the Bhils, but because it lays out categories and characteristics common to many religions. The particular names of major and minor gods in the article are particular to Bhil religion, but the idea of major and minor gods, and many of the characteristics associated with them, are common to a great many religions. The same is true of many of the other topics covered in the essay. The Bhils are not alone in their beliefs in witchcraft, ancestor worship, or the roles played by hereditary priests.

Some aspects of Bhil religion will probably strike most readers as unusual. This is particularly the case with the author's assertion that the Bhils create minor gods and goddesses whenever they need them.

As you read, consider these questions:
1. Bhil religion is clearly very different from the religious notions common in Judaism, Christianity, and Islam. Are there underlying similarities between these and Bhil religion?
2. The Bhils claim to make up gods and yet treat the worship of these made-up gods seriously. How is it possible to be consciously aware of creating a god and yet, at the same time to understand that god as real? Hint: reading the essay on Hinduism in Part Six might make it easier to answer this question.
3. In what ways does Bhil devotion to the major god differ from devotion to the minor gods? Are their parallels to this in the Jewish, Christian, and Islamic traditions?

INTRODUCTION

The Bhils are the third largest tribal group in India, numbering over five millions according to the Census of 1971. The concentration of their population is mostly in Madhya Pradesh, Rajasthan, Gujarat, Maharashtra, etc. The other states where the Bhils are found are Karnataka, Andhra Pradesh, Orissa, West Bengal, Tripura, Punjab and in Pakistan. But in these areas their population is negligible.

Inconclusive debate is still going on regarding their origin on the sub-continent of India. The findings of D. N. Majumdar (1942), Macfarlane (1942), Haddon (1924), Fuchs, present a confusing picture in resolving the origin of the Bhils through anthropomorphic measurements and seriological studies. Prehistorians and social anthropologists are of the opinion that the Bhils are the autochthons of the Indian sub-continent. In various other accounts such as the sacred books of the Hindus and in sanskritic literature, we get alluring indications that the Bhils had at one stage developed their culture which declined in the course of history. In the year 57 B.C. the Bhils had already attempted to raise themselves from the status of chiefdom to kingship but they were suppressed by the Sakas on the invitation of the Jainas (Kosambi 1977: 172). Somadeva's *Katha Sarit Sagar* (Penzer 1968) gives several accounts of the Bhils, where he speaks of two Bhil kings mounted on elephants waging war with one another. Similar accounts are also found in literature (Forbes 1924; Tod 1978; Malcom 1970; Abul Fazl 1965; Singh 1936; Haig 1958) which furnish us with proofs that the Bhils were powerful and ruled some parts of central and western India as chiefs and petty kings. During the supremacy of Maratha and British rule, the Bhils were submissive, retreated into the hilly gorges and infertile lands (Doshi 1969). The personalities of Eklavya, Shabari, King Guha, Valmiki in Mahabharata and Ramayana are depicted in the oral tradition of North India as Bhils or Proto-Bhils. Their social organisation, magico-religious systems, totems (Ferriera 1964), and adherence to traditional values help us to assume that the Bhils in the past had their own religious system. Their ancient traditional elements are still visible among the Bhils of Jhabua district of Madhya Pradesh.

Linguistically the Bhils speak Aryan languages. Their own original language is still spoken by the Nahal tribe (Kosambi 1977) in some of the ravines of the Satpura and Vindhya mountains. The Bhils do not possess any of the roots of their language though there may be some possibility of finding them. Hence the Bhils have lost a good deal of their oral tradition, which is a repertoire of the tribe.

This paper presents remnants of the Bhil religion from the sociological and anthropological context of the Bhils of Jhabua. The period of the collection of data on the Bhil religion stretches from 1970–1985, during which time I observed the phenomena of their religion, regarding rituals and myths in and contextual situations. The data collected relating to their religion, myths, rituals, festivals, shamanism, places of worship are from four tehsils of Jhabua district, namely, Jhabua, Petlawad, Thandla, and Meghnagar, which form a composite unit for their tribal culture, historical and political background. Earlier some authors have already studied Bhil culture and their religion in the past (Koppers 1940, 1942; Jungblut 1942; Ahuja 1965; Doshi 1971). But outside authors lack insight into penetrating into the depths of the phenomena in their contextual situation. The information that I gathered could provide sufficient material for a volume.

2. GEOGRAPHICAL AND SOCIAL SITUATION OF THE JHABUA DISTRICT

Jhabua district is one of the most backward districts in India. There are 1,366 villages in all six tehsils with a population of 667,811, according to the 1971 Census. Of the 85% of the total population the Bhils form the majority. Their district, being located in the western part of Madhya Pradesh, touches the borders of three states, namely Rajasthan, Gujarat and Maharastra. A railway route passes through the Jhabua district linking Bombay and Delhi. Though the district lacks natural resources still it attracts tourists from various parts of the country because of its rich folk festivals, such as Holi, *Gal, Gad, Bhagoria,* marriages, etc. The tribes are blessed with all aspects of folklore such as material, both oral and symbolic, which is a rich source for study. This section of the Bhil population has preserved the old traditional elements in their folkloric tradition which has harmoniously blended into the environment.

The district has all the religions of India: Buddhism, Jainism, Hinduism, Islam and Christianity. But the Census of 1971 does not provide correct figures on this matter. Most tribals have taken to the Hindu way of life and they identify themselves in many ways with the Hindus, even though Hindu society has not accepted them. Jainism and Buddhism do not have much influence on the Bhils. Islam has recently began the proselitisation of the Bhils. Christianity exists among them since about a century, yet it has contributed much to their development. For centuries a plethora of 'religious missionaries' of various castes and creeds such as Hindu Sadhus, Jain monks, Buddhist monks, *Pirs, Fakirs* and Christian missionaries are still at work. Today it is a difficult task to trace and identify the tribal elements of their culture. We will now touch on the various aspects of Bhil religions, beliefs and practices.

3. BHIL RELIGION

The phenomena of the Bhil religion are quite different from those of other tribal groups in the continents of the world. For this reason we are describing in the tribal context the total phenomena as it exists such as the concept of High God, functioning of the deities and spirits, ancestral worship, shamanism, witchcraft, religious rituals and festivals.

One final point is to be noted: as we analyse the elements of the Bhil religion there appear traces of Hinduism. A closer view will indicate that the tribal religion is different in axiom, assumptions, expectations and fears, from the rest of the major religions in the ecological setting. We need a different approach than those prescribed by Evans-Pritchard and Emile Durkheim.

3.1. High God

The High God of the Bhils is *Bholo Isvar, Dharmi Rajo* and *Bhagwan,* one and the same though under different names. The concept of High God is popular among various tribes of the world. But the characteristics of the High God as conceived by the Bhils differ considerably. In some parts of the world, the High God is a 'disinterested deity' who leaves the functioning of the world, and supplicatory rituals, to minor gods and goddesses. The High God of the Bhils is not fully beyond *Bhog* (sacrifice) and rituals that are offered to the deities. Since he is the supreme and omnipotent God, he demands the greatest *Bhog* of all consisting of one male buffalo, five rams, five cocks, and liquor. He is invoked during the rite of *Nortan,* a nine day celebration after the harvesting of the first crops, during the Hindu festival of Dasera. The *Badwo* (priest and medicine man) officiates the rituals daily in His honour, trains the disciples for the post of *Badwo.* The women folk from the surrounding villages invoke the *Dharmi Rajo* with songs, such as:

> Dharmi, Dharmi *O King,*
> *We have come to sing songs in your garden.*
> Dharmi, Dharmi, *O King,*
> *We have come to dance in your garden . . .*

The fundamental difference between *Dharmi* and other deities is that this God is not greedy of the rituals and *Bhog.* He does not need the rites to appease Him, nor has he any symbol of image for this worship and honour.

3.2. Minor Gods and Goddesses

Next to the *Dharmi Rajo,* the High God, are Gods *(devs, babos)* and goddesses *(mata),* who play a significant role in the lives of the people. Some of these may resemble in the names the deities of the Hindu pantheon. But they differ characteristically in attributes from the deities of Hindu pantheon. I once asked the Bhils of Bijyo Dungri as to where these gods and goddesses come from? Their leader spontaneously replied, 'Where do they come from . . .? We create them whenever we need them. Just last year only we invented two devs, Kankro Kundhlo and Harhel dev, when the time became difficult for us.' Thus in the course of time, I observed the people attributing to the tribal deities some qualities of the Hindu deities. Some of the popular devs (gods) and matas (goddesses) worshipped in the region are the following:

Sitla Mata: The deity is the most popular titulary protectress of the villages, called *Gam devi.* The place where her *thanu* (altar) is made is in the shadow of the trees of the sacred grove called *van,* literally meaning: a forest. The clay pots, clay horses, stones smeared with red powder, etc, are the symbols of the *mata* and other deities worshipped by the village community. She receives all the magico-religious rites during the year and she is also responsible for averting catastrophes and other dangers affecting human beings, cattle and crops in the village. She is believed to appear to human beings in the form of chicken pox. During this sickness the members of the clan take the patients in their midst and sing numerous devotional folksongs to appease the deity and respond positively to all the needs of the patient in the belief that it is the demand made by the *mata*. In such moments even their neighbours and members of the village community cooperate with them. She is also believed to bring the monsoon ram and prosperity in the village. Thus all the festivals of fertility are celebrated in her honour, such as *Nani Jatar* (the feast of greenery), *Moti Jatar* (feast of the arrival of first fruit), Garbo is danced, hens, *daru* (country liquour), and field fruits are offered to her.

Kalka Mata: Kalka mata has the image of being the most fierceful and consequently most dreaded deity among the people. Even the low-caste Hindus such as the Balahis of the Nimar, in the neighbouring area, have the same image of *Kalka* (Fuchs 1950: 261). She is the patron of robbers and, like *Sitla*, appears to individuals in the form of chicken pox. The *Bhog* that she wants consists of a black hen, *Daru*, offered to her at the distillery, and a coconut. Kalka too is worshipped in *van*. There is a song in her honour sung at the time when chicken-pox appears on children. The clan members sing it during the night while the head of the family takes the child on his lap (Bhuriya 1979: 121):

Kalka mata *has come from Pawagarh!*
please, come and play in our courtyards.
The goddess from Pawan has come
And stands at our door.
Mata, *please, play in our courtyard.*
Then mata took a piece of chalk,
And she took a clean sheet of paper,
And wrote on one side of it;
But we could read on the opposite side.
Mata, *my children are sick.*
Please come and play with them in the courtyard.
They scream and cry, O Mata.
Please, come and play with my children.
When they are well again,
I shall have them married happily,
If you are jealous and unjust,
We shall blame you, O Mata.
Your reputation will suffer . . .

Hoorvan Mata: She is an indigenous goddess responsible for causing sickness among human beings and cattle. During the ritual of relieving sickness called *Salavani* officiated by the *Badwo*, before a public and private audience, she is offered a virgin goat in appeasement.

Lohan dev: Among the male gods he gets the privilege of being a tutelary deity *(Gam dev)* of a village. In turn, for his service, he demands for *bhog* the same as for the tutelary deity the only difference being that a male goat is offered in place of a female goat. His *thanu* is in Navagam and Nahrpura villages in Meghnagar tehsil.

Galio Babo: Galio babo has a unique function to play among the Bhils and other tribes such as Bhilas, Patelias, and Rathias. He is also known under different names such as *Gal dev* and *Gal devrvo*. There is a folktale prevalent among the Bhils of Jhabua concerning the origin of the hook swinging festival, called *Gal*. It runs thus:

Once upon a time there was a Bhil called Khando Rawji who lived in one of the princely states. He was a notorious robber and had killed many people during his raids. The King got him arrested and sentenced him to be hanged. On the night before he was to be hanged, he invoked *Galio babo*, saying that if he would be freed from imprisonment he would erect a high altar and swing around it several times, and in place of his own head he would offer a coconut, and smear red powder at the foot of the altar, offer liquor, a he goat, and thus popularise his feast. *Galio babo* heard his pleading and freed him from imprisonment. Today people make solemn promises to this deity when faced with various problems, such as field disputes, family quarrels, court cases, police assaults and for the birth of a male child etc. During this festival the people try to avenge the enmity of the past. The altar of *Gal dev* which receives the *bhog* of human blood is considered to be the most venerated place. In the olden days there were some cases of this sort.

Gunan Babo: Like *Sitla*, and *Kalka mata*, the appearance of chicken pox are the symbols of *Gunan babo*. The patient is provided with all his needs. He is appeased during the sickness with songs and other rituals. One of the songs in his honour sung during the sickness is given below: (Bhuriya 1979: 120)

. . . God Gunan Babo will also join him (the child)
And play on the swing.

Akhadyo Dev: This God is responsible for human fertility and especially worshipped by barren women. *Akhadi* is the term used for the thread tied by the *Badwo* on the wrist of the barren woman who takes a vow. This thread is the symbol of her contract with the God. From the time she takes her vow till the untying of the thread after the child's safe delivery, a woman is supposed to strictly observe certain instructions. This period is called '*Akhadi Rakhi*' or *Korun* (dry).

Babo Vagajo: The *thanun* of *Babo Vagajo* is near Jhabua in Kardawad village, and in Navegan near Meghnagar.

He is the god of wonders and bullock carts. People appease him for successful journeys. In the village of Kardawad, I have observed people passing on the road place grass, bricks, firewood, sweets, coconuts at his shrine on their return from the market of Jhabua. At night he is offered a lamp of *ghee* (purified butter) by devotees in the village living in the vicinity of this *thanu*. A Bhil residing near Jhabua, named Somlo Damor falls into trance (bhar) in honour of *Babo Vagajo.*

Savan Mata: The most popular, the least harmful and most amicable of all the deities is *Savan mata.* She is supplicated during *Nani Jatar, Moti Jatar,* and during *Jhapa hedvun,* a ceremony in remembrance of the dead. Her *Bhog* is a virgin goat and a virgin hen, both symbols of purity and modesty among the domesticated animals. By name the mata belongs to the Hindu pantheon, but in fact, she is a Bhil deity.

Ganesh: This God is the symbol of fertility and power. He is worshipped during the monsoon and while agricultural pursuits are going on, activities such as ploughing, sowing, weeding, harvesting, thrashing of grain, etc. The elders of the village including the elderly women are found invoking his name during their manual labour. Before training a young bullock, the Bhils worship and offer a coconut to the deity.

Ghuntai Mata: One can hardly find a temple built of stone and mortar in the Bhil country. But the place of worship for the *Ghuntai mata* is found in a small hut, in Dundka village near Meghanagar. When questioned why he built a temple in honour of the *mata,* the owner could not answer, perhaps because it is not a known tradition of the tribe. Only flowers are offered to the goddess.

Kankaryo Kundlayo Dev: He is a god of sickness and death and in the issues relating to the village community, he is more powerful than the *Tadvi* (village headman). His thanus are in the villages of the Bhuriya clan called Bijya Dungri and Maslya Jhar near Jhabua.

Herbal Dev: A male deity worshipped for any general purpose by the village community whose *thanu* is in Padlva village near Ranapur in Jhabua tehsil. He accepts the *Bhog* of a ram.

Vagilo Dev: This deity derives its name from a tiger termed *vag* in Bhil dialect. This animal is the symbol of insecurity and fear. To avoid the fear-complex the people have created many myths and legends depicting the animal as shy and timid. But in the heart of hearts the fear that overwhelms them has compelled them to worship the animal as a deity. Today tigers are not as frequent as in the past. Then they were a real danger. A *thanu* where a male buffalo is sacrificed to *Vagillio dev* is near Ranapur. In the princely state of Jhabua the sacrifice of a male buffalo was prohibited though the tribes often did it clandestinely.

Pidyo Dev: Consulting omens in the uncertainty of life is considered beneficial. There are experts who predict the future of people and their art is called *Vadavo.* Persons skilled in divination and prophecy (*vadavo*) worship a god called *Pidyo dev* whose altar is in Mor dundyun village near Ranapur.

Bandya Sod Bapsi: The god who looses prisoners bonds and pregnant women. Bhils supplicate and appease the deity by offering a cock, coconut and pulses. He is supposed to be living in the fort of Dhar city, in the neighbouring district in Madhya Pradesh.

Other Deities: People according to their imagination and needs have created many more indigenous deities to give meaning to their lives. These deities are: *Bijyo dev, Vanjyo dev, Kheda dev, Goran mata, Parvati, Bhovani, Khedan mata, Godia mata, Lalbai mata, Foolbai mata, Usan mata, Rangan mata, Pagan mata, Kodri mata, Isan mata, Visan mata, Lalmadi mata, Godri mata, Bodhri mata, Ghumsi mata, Pangli mata, Balio babo,* etc.

4. SPIRITS AND WITCHCRAFT

The knowledge of the human anatomy and physical functioning of the human body are practically unknown to the Bhils. In such a situation the psycho-somatic diseases and unknown factors causing illnesses are attributed to the work of evil spirits *(Bhut)* and to witchcraft *(Dakan).* Persons, possessed by spirits who are mostly malevolent, are treated by the *Badwo* in a therapeutic and cathartic manner through magical means. The evil spirits who are commonly known as *Bhuts* are believed to be residing in haunted places, such as gorges, river sides, hollows of trees and water ponds.

Witchcraft is another powerful method of harming the individual. Any of the offences by witches to the village community or individuals are taken seriously and punished even to the extent of expulsion from the village or chopping off their nose, besides a sound flogging.

5. ANCESTRAL WORSHIP

The ancestors *(Khatris)* are the symbol of a clan or phratry unity both being a common progenitor symbolised in the form of animal, plant or tree. The ancestors' spirits are believed to visit the families of the clan on certain occasions. They are appeased by offerings of pulses, cocks, liquor and cereals to appease their malevolence on the feast of *Nani Jatar, moti Jatar* and *Jhapa hedvun* (memory of the dead). The ancestors unite the members of the phratry during the memorial ceremony of the dead called *nakto.* The elders of the clans abstain from eating the first fruit until they have offered them to the ancestors at the *gatla* (memorial) stones.

Some of the great *Khatris* among the Bhils who later became deified heroes are Kasumor Damor, Babo Halun and Somlo Bhuriyo and Tantia Bhil who helped the Bhils to survive during 'difficult days.'

6. PLACES AND SYMBOLS OF WORSHIP

The rituals and religious festivals, even though they attract a significant gathering in public and private places, attach no importance to the structured places of worship in the district of Jhabua and other places such as *van* where the symbols of the deities are placed are the nights. The ceremonies may continue until the morning, for the Bhils believe that the deities come to visit human beings in the dark hours in haunted places. The *Tadvi* (headman) is the ex-officio chairman of the religious and other social gatherings and the *Badwo* officiates at the religious rituals. The images of the deities are represented by clay pots, clay and bronze horses, stones placed under *sag* or *pipal* trees; all have religious importance for worshippers. These images lack sophistication and artistic embellishment. At the time of private rituals, members of the clan still worship totems called *ataks* or atkavanis. But the practice of totem worship and other observances are on the decline since the last two decades.

7. BADWO: THE BHIL PRIEST AND MEDICINE MAN

The duties of the *Badwo* are hereditary and formal. He is paid both in kind and cash by the village community for his services rendered to the villagers. His duties are mainly officiating of the rituals, healing the sick, haruspication, sorcery, herbal treatment, maintenance of the oral tradition, astrology and tribal epistemology. Outside the official duties, he is free to offer his services in neighbouring villages. The faithful consult him on various matters related to his profession and expertise. He is expected to stay away from the Christian churches and places which can defile his *veer* (power) and thus underestimate his powers.

8. IMPORTANT FESTIVALS

The Bhils of the district of Jhabua celebrate all the important festivals of the Hindus and Christians as well. Since a few decades they are: *Dipavali, Dasera, Nortan, Holi, Rakhi,* Christmas, *Bhagoria, Nani jatar, Moti jatar, Gal,* Marriage, *Gad,* etc. The celebration of these festivals and other fairs give more vigour and hope in their lives and help them to sustain themselves in difficult times. In no way, they minimise the value of the celebration to which they give primary importance. *Daru* is consumed in great quantity on such occasions.

9. CONCLUSION

1. The deities of the Bhils differ considerably in form and attributes from those of the Hindu pantheon. The recent observance of the phenomena indicates that there is an amalgamation in their forms of worship.

2. Their lack of sophistication, aesthetic touch, the difference in the place and symbols of worship, indicate many dissimilarities.

3. The *Badwo* is the repository of Bhil tradition and cultural heritage and perpetuates the traditions of the tribe.

4. Even though the great religions of South Asia and Europe are present in the tribal ecology, the Bhil tradition still persists in a potent manner. It appears from their religious world views that the tribal religion of the Bhils is older than even Hinduism. The proof of it lies in the cult of female deities, popular till today.

5. Devotion and faith in the deities are the main dogmas inherent in their religious belief. The adherence to the rituals indicates that the Bhils have religious fervour and strength to communicate not only with one another but also with the supernatural powers which are unique elements in their Psychological *energia* cultivated only by them so as to fight out any oppression through the centuries.

BIBLIOGRAPHY

Ahuja, R. 1965. Religion of the Bhils: A Sociological Analysis. Sociological Bulletin. 14: 21–23, Bombay.

Bhuriya, M. 1977. The Nature of the Religious Songs of the Bhils. Folklore. 18: 325–332. Calcutta.

— 1977. The Nature of the Bhil Folksongs. Folklore. 18: 219–227, Calcutta.

— 1979. Folksongs of the Bhils. Indore: Mahipal Publications.

— 1981. The Songs of the Bhil Women. Cahiers de Litterature Orale, NO 10, pp. 99–109, Paris.

Doshi, S. L. 1971. The Bhils: Between Societal Self-awareness and Cultural Synthesis. New Delhi: Sterling Publications.

Ferreira, J. V. 1964. Totemism in India. Bombay: Oxford.

Forbes, A. K. 1924. Ras Mala, Hindoo Annals of the Province of Goozerat in Western India. London: Oxford University Press.

Fuchs, S. 1950. The Children of Hari. Vienna: Verlag Herald.

— 1960. The Gonds and Bhumia of Eastern Mandla. Bombay: Asia Publishing House.

Haddon, A. C. 1924. The Races of Man and their Distribution. London: Cambridge University Press.

Hammond, B. 1967. Cultural and Social Anthropology. New York: Macmillan Company.

Jungblut, L. 1943. Magic Songs of the Bhils of Jhabua State. C. I. Leiden: International Archiv für Ethnographie.

Koppers, W. 1940. Bhagwan the Supreme Deity of the Bhils. Anthropos, 35–36: 265–325, Sank Augustin. Germany.

Macfarlane, E. W. E. 1941. Blood groups among Balahis Weavers, Bhils, Korkus and Mandas with a Note on Pardhi and Aboriginal Blood Types. Journal of Royal Asiatic Society of Bengal. 9: 15–26, Calcutta.

Majumdar, D. N. 1942. The Raciology of the Bhils. Journal of Gujarat Research Society, 6: 3, Bombay.

Momin, A. R. 1984. On the Study of One's Own Culture, in 'Anthropology as a Historical Science,' Essays in Honour of Stephen Fuchs, ed. by Mahipal Bhuriya and S. M. Michael. Indore: Satprakashan, India.

The Qawa Incident in 1968 and Other Cases of "Spirit Possession": Religious Syncretism in Fiji

Aubrey L. Parke

This essay recounts events that took place several decades ago in Fiji, where people of Hindu, Muslim, and Fijian religious traditions live together. In addition to their own religions, Fijians have been heavily exposed to Christianity brought by missionaries. Fijians believe that two pools near the town of Vanivau are the homes of spirits and that insults to the pools may result in sickness. One of these pools was destroyed by a Hindu in the process of leveling ground to build a school. Later, eighteen girls who were attending the school became ill. The girls manifested symptoms that Western-trained psychologists diagnosed as mass hysteria, but that local people understood as spirit possession. In their ultimately successful attempts to cure the girls, local people turned to Western medicine, but also first to a Muslim, then to a traditional Fijian healer, and finally to several Hindu holy people. The essay thus demonstrates how people of one tradition may use the religious practices of other traditions.

The description of the spirits in this essay is particularly germane to our interests in this section. In this essay, the supernatural beings are spirits tied to particular places. The actions of the Hindu man who damaged the Fijian holy place did not offend Fijian spirits in general, but only those specific to the sacred pool he damaged. The Fijian relationship to the spirits was two-way: the spirits received respect during ceremonial presentations, in return the people have received courage or strength. However, both Fijians and others clearly believed that offense to the spirits could affect Hindus, Muslims, and outsiders as well as Fijians.

As you read, consider these questions:
1. The spirits described in this reading are Fijian, yet many members of the Hindu, Muslim, and Christian community clearly believe in them. What does that suggest about religion on Fiji?
2. The author points out that this incident happened during colonial rule. What effects might colonization have had on the way the incident was handled by both the authorities and those directly involved?
3. Which was more effective at treating the afflicted girls, traditional medicine or modern medicine? Why?

4. The ceremonies done to cure the girls proceeded from private ceremonies to public ceremonies. What does this suggest about the nature of curing rituals?

This paper investigates a case of an outbreak of overbreathing (hyperventilation) and twitching involving a group of 18 adolescent Indian schoolgirls that occurred in November 1968 in the then British Crown Colony of Fiji.[1] At the time, the girls were day pupils at the Qawa Indian Primary School near the township of Labasa on the island of Vanua Levu. Other incidents leading up to and following the outbreak are also described, including the disturbance of a Fijian sacred pool known as Davuiyalayali located in the school grounds. A widely-held belief that the outbreak indicated a state of possession of the girls by aggrieved spirits of the pool, which were manifested by tiny prawns, is investigated. The paper illustrates how the various communities living in the area (i.e. Hindu and Muslim Indians, Fijians and Europeans) explained and individually or jointly attempted to deal with the situation, using a variety of beliefs and practices. . . .

Over the past two decades, the spread of urbanisation and cash crop agriculture has affected a number of traditional sacred places. For example, cane farmers (especially Indians) have disturbed or levelled several sites, especially those of *yavu* or mounds associated with deified Fijian ancestors. Local Fijian landowners spoke of the death of some of those involved in such disturbances. They regarded this as an expression of anger by the spirits at having been disturbed without request or apology. One such mound at Rakiraki had been totally destroyed as part of the development of the Vaileka urban centre. This site is closely associated with one of the local deified ancestors, Leka, and it was here that, following a hurricane in the early 1950s, a banyan tree sacred to Leka had been damaged. Some more branches had to be lopped. Leka expressed his anger by making an appearance at a nearby house. His descendants then performed ceremonies of apology by first presenting dried *yaqona* or kava and then pouring a libation made from it onto Leka's mound. When the site was destroyed in the 1980s, it is not clear whether any ceremonies of request or apology had been made, but his present descendants said that nothing untoward occurred. . . .

"The Qawa Incident in 1968 and Other Cases of 'Spirit Possession'" by A.L. Parke, (1995) *The Journal of Pacific History* Vol. 30 (2). Reprinted by permission of the author and Taylor & Francis Ltd., http://www.tandf.co.uk/journals.

SPIRIT POSSESSION

The incidents discussed here can be considered in the context of general observations about the nature of spirits, the circumstances under which benign spirits can become hostile, afflictions resulting from hostility, the discovery of the cause of affliction through divination, and the cure of affliction by therapeutic ritual. Although there is widespread agreement on the reality and importance of supernatural beings, different communities and cultures have different ideas about their nature; indeed any attempt to draw up a general taxonomy of spirits would be pointless because their attributes and powers would relate within the overall structure and characteristics of each particular culture; conversely such a taxonomy recognised by a particular culture can be useful.[2]

The same agency may on some occasions be benign and on others hostile. Possession affliction may be regarded by a community as having been imposed on a person by usually benign spirits who have become hostile because that person has neglected or insulted them. On the other hand, a person who has become afflicted may be seen by a community to be morally blameless. In this case, the affliction may be interpreted by the community as a malicious act against the afflicted person by another person who is familiar with a spirit and has accordingly invoked it to possess and afflict him.

Ritual concerned with possession affliction may be regarded from two points of view—therapeutic ritual which aims at bringing help to the afflicted person, and antitherapeutic ritual or witchcraft by which another person aims at bringing injury to a human target. If a person has been afflicted and members of his community believe that the affliction is caused either through possession by a spirit which has been insulted or by an evil spirit which has taken possession through witchcraft, then the origin of the affliction may be determined by divination, the art or practice of discovering hidden knowledge through supernatural means.[3] Once the origin of the affliction has been determined by divination, the normal means of combating the affliction and its cause is therapeutic ritual, which may be conducted under relatively private conditions, especially in the case of an individual, or in full public view, especially in the case of more widespread affliction.

Possession by spirits is a well-recognised phenomenon in Fiji; and the disturbance at Qawa and its associated incidents in 1968 are still as relevant to understanding the interrelationships between the mixed communities of Fiji as they were when they occurred 25 years ago.

The traditional realm of the Fijian supernatural is not easy to describe or analyse. The task is not made any easier given the introduction of Christian concepts and of general European concepts of ghosts and spirits. Further, Fijian beliefs come into everyday contact with local Indian beliefs. Hindu polytheism and recognition of *shaitan* (a Hindustani word for evil spirits) have introduced concepts that are easily understood by Fijians with their own beliefs in a multitude of spirits, including deified ancestral spirits, and the potential for trouble if the spirits are offended. Fijians are fully aware of the local Hindu temples, religious processions and gatherings, fire-walking and sacred places. Near Labasa is a great rock shaped like a snake which is the object of Hindu ceremonies and presentations. Both Fijians and Hindus associate the snake with supernatural powers. Indians, both Hindus and Muslims, are well aware of Fijian spirits and the importance of presenting *yaqona* when making requests to Fijians. In a community which inevitably brings together Indians and Fijians in a variety of social and economic situations, it is quite comprehensible that traditional beliefs about the supernatural and their interrelationship with the affairs of daily life should be mutually understood and accepted.

Traditional Fijian society is ideally based on a number of groups of people claiming usually patrilineal descent from a common ancestor (referred to as the *vu*), and every Fijian is a member of one of these groups (referred to as a *yavusa*). The common ancestor may be a mythological figure (referred to as the *kalou vu* or deified ancestor) who is associated with an object, usually a bird, animal, insect or fish, referred to as its *waqawaqa* or *ivakatakilakila*, 'the body assumed by a *kalou vu* for the purposes of self manifestation.'[4]

As well as deified ancestors, Fijians recognise a variety of other mythological spirits *(yalo)*, including the spirits of the dead *(yalo ni mate)*. Mythological spirits are usually associated with specific *vanua tabu* (sacred places) and may be benign or hostile, according to the situation. They may manifest themselves in the same way as deified ancestors, and, like the ancestors, may show their hostility (if they are insulted) through the sickness or death of the person who has caused the insult or of some other person associated with or related to that person. If people wish to seek help from the spirits or to apologise to them for an insult, they present kava *(sova yaqona)* to them, often at the sacred place with which they are associated. Only when offended spirits are appropriately appeased will they cease to be angry with the offender, his associates and relations. If the offender does not seek to appease the spirits, he may die. Then the anger of the spirits may well continue to be felt by surviving associates and relations, even by members of succeeding generations, until such time as the spirits are appeased. Spirits of the dead may manifest themselves as ghosts.

Communication with the deified ancestor is usually through a member of the Fijian descent group who holds the traditional office of *bete* (priest). In this case, the medium is the institutionalised or official priesthood.[5] With other spirits, communication is usually through a member of a group who is recognised as having the necessary supernatural powers.

The Qawa-i-ra *yavusa* now live in the Fijian village of Vunivau. Their original settlement *(yavu tu)* was in that part of the nearby area of Vatunibale known as Vitadra. They then moved to below the present Qawa school site and thence to the present site beside the Qawa river. They have two *vanua tabu,* each being a pool associated with supernatural spirits. One of the pools, known as Nadranutabu (the sacred fresh-water pool), is a pool of fresh water at Vunivau, surrounded by trees usually associated with salt water, such as *dogo* (mangrove: *Bruguiera gymnorhiza, Rhizophoraceae*) and mulomulo *(Thespesia populnea, Malvaceae).* The other pool, known as Davuiyaliyali, is in a round depression in a rock on Qawa hilltop, and is referred to by the Qawa-i-ra people as the *tanoa* (kava bowl). Before it was damaged by a bulldozer, the depression was about one metre across and round in shape. After being damaged, it has become more triangular in shape and was deeper at one end. Before the damage there used to be a small pool of fresh water even in times of drought. It was in this pool that tiny prawns used to be seen swimming about, regarded as the manifestations of the spirits of the pool.

The Qawa-i-ra people, when discussing these pools, described the supernatural spirits associated with each pool as the *itaukei* (owners) of the pool, just as they described themselves as the *itaukei* of the Qawa hilltop. The relationship between the *itaukei* of the hilltop (the Fijians) and the *itaukei* of the pools (the supernatural spirits) was two-way. In return for *yalo vakarokoroko* (respect) paid to the spirits, the Qawa-i-ra people could make requests to the spirits for *yaloqaqa* (courage) and *kaukauwa* (physical strength), especially when seeking strength or reassurance for some venture, such as the public performance of a *meke* (action song). Such a request would be made through the medium of *sova yaqona* (the ceremonial presentation of kava) to the spirits at one of the pools. The pool at Nadranutabu was more powerful than the one at Davuiyaliyali.

On the other hand, if any person who was either a member of the Qawa-i-ra group (an *itaukei* or traditional landowner of Qawa hill) or a *vulagi* (a person other than such an *itaukei,* who might be Fijian or non-Fijian) interfered with the pools or otherwise showed disrespect to the spirits of the pools, the spirits would punish them, usually by making him or her sick *(tauvimate).* On such an occasion, it would be necessary to determine why that person was sick. This study is concerned with damage to the pool at Davuiyaliyali, and events preceding and following the disturbance of this shrine.

Poe, the chief of the Qawa-i-ra Fijians at Vunivau, said that his grandfather had told him that people ceremoniously offered *yaqona* at the pool at Davuiyaliyali not only when they still held traditional ownership of the site but also later when it fell within land owned by the sugar company and became a horse-paddock. Poe said that the traditional landowners would know if the spirits of the *tanoa,* the kava bowl formed by the depression in the rock at Davuiyaliyali, were willing to assist in the success of a venture, because the *waqawaqa* or manifestation of the spirits would appear in the form of tiny fresh water prawns swimming in the water in the *tanoa.*

Indians from Vunivau Indian settlement were fully aware of the significance of the pool at Davuiyaliyali. Those who wished to collect firewood in the area would first of all present kava to my informant, Poe, or to his parents, and seek permission to do so, thereby appeasing the spirits of the rock pool. Both Fijians and Indians respected and were fright-

ened of the area, not only because of the pool but also because of two ghosts which appeared nearby, one of a white horse which used to appear on top of the hill, the other the ghost of a man which would disappear whenever people got very close to it. There was a grave nearby. Qawa hilltop was and still is a place of considerable supernatural significance to both the Fijian and Indian communities.

THE 1968 OUTBREAK

Qawa Indian Primary School lies about five kilometres east of Labasa in a mixed area of nuclear Fijian villages and dispersed Indian settlements on the island of Vanua Levu. It is located on Qawa hill near the Indian settlement of Vunivau and the Fijian village of the same name. At the time of the outbreak which is the subject of this study, the school consisted of eight classrooms for children aged five to 13, a house for the headmaster, and a playground. The pool and the rock at Davuiyaliyali were on the edge of the playground. All the pupils were Indian, as were all members of the staff. The school was managed by a local committee under the general auspices of the Government Education Department.

The majority of the Indians living near Qawa hill were Hindus of the Sanatan Dharm sect. Others were either Hindus of the Arya Samaj sect or Muslims. A few were Christians. These Indians formed the majority of the parents who sent their children to Qawa Indian Primary School. Most of the Fijians living in the Fijian village of Vunivau were members of the Qawa-i-ra descent group which included the traditional owners of Qawa hill before it became freehold in the 19th century. The Qawa-i-ra group recognised the traditional authority of the Tui Labasa, paramount chief of the Labasa polity based in the Fijian village of Nasekula. The villagers of Vunivau village were Methodists.

Although the Indians and Fijians lived separately, there was considerable opportunity for social mixing. They worked together in cane-cutting gangs and at the sugar mill. They gathered together around the *tanoa* (kava bowl) and drank *yaqona* (kava or *Piper methysticum*) on the verandahs of the Indian stores. A number of Fijians spoke the local form of Hindustani, known as Fiji *bat,* and Indians generally had some working knowledge of Fijian.[6]

In the early 1960s the local sugar company had agreed to make land available on Qawa hilltop for the establishment of a community primary school. At one stage the Indians had proposed that there should be a joint school for themselves and for the local Fijians, and this was agreed to by all. In the event, the Fijians did not take part, but it is not clear why this joint proposal failed. Nevertheless the Indian community living at Vunivau settlement and on the neighbouring cane-farms carried out the work by themselves with the support of the sugar company.

It was necessary first to level part of the top of the hill. Work began in 1963. The man behind this work was Munsami Sirdar, a South Indian living at Vunivau Indian settlement and working as the leading *sirdar* or foreman at the sugar-mill. Munsami was chairman of the school committee and took a leading part in the building and running of the school. When the hilltop was being levelled off by bulldozer, Fijians and Indians came from the neighbourhood to ask that the sacred pool and rock at Davuiyaliyali at the edge of the proposed playground should not be touched as they were afraid of the spirits associated with it. Munsami did not believe in such stories and tried himself to bulldoze away the rock. As a result the rock was cracked by him and the sacred pool was filled with loose stones. However the rock could not be moved.

After the school had been completed in 1965, Munsami came one day to cut the grass on the playground. Although he appeared to be in good health, the next day a foul skin disease broke out on his body, his general health deteriorated, and he died in October 1968. As soon as he fell ill, Fijians and Indians said that this was because he had offended the spirits of the sacred pool at Davuiyaliyali by trying to bulldoze away the rock.

Soon after Munsami's death, a number of schoolgirls started to experience a form of breathing irregularity, identified by medical officers as hyperventilation. Most of the girls affected were South Indians and all were Hindus, 17 being of the Sanatan Dharm sect and one an Arya Samaji.[7]

Dr G. R. Randall, a government medical officer at Labasa Hospital, recorded that on 13 November 1968 'a medical officer from Labasa Hospital was sent to Qawa Primary School, Vunivau, to investigate a report of a mysterious illness that was affecting a dozen or more of the Indian girl pupils there. When he arrived at the school he found 13 of the girls affected, all of them behaving in almost exactly the same manner. They were all over-breathing, taking deep inspirations and exhaling with a musical wheeze, at a rate of about 50 respirations per minute. Some were standing, some sitting, some tended to faint and quickly recover.'[8]

The medical officer arranged for five of the girls to be taken to the hospital, and for the remainder to be sent home. On arrival at the hospital the girls were fully conscious and fully co-operative, but still over-breathing at about the same rate, all in an identical manner, some continuously and some intermittently. Dr Randall recorded that 'all of them had a pyrexia of about 99F, but otherwise had no abnormal physical signs. They could be made to stop hyperventilating at any time by simply asking them questions. They would answer breathing normally, then return to over-breathing again. One girl, the youngest, could be made to stop easily by simple re-assurance, but one, aged twelve, continued to over-breathe even when answering questions, and she was showing a tendency to faint, needing to lie down. She was given Largactil [a tranquilising drug] intramuscularly. After a few hours all the girls settled down and all were sent home after a further short period of observation.'

He found that 'the trouble had been developing over a matter of weeks. One girl had been affected early in October, and had been seen by a private practitioner. Two differ-ent girls had then developed the same symptoms on November 8. On the 12th, 3 or 4 were affected and then on the 13th the situation really came to a head. Of the 18 girls affected, all except one were aged between 12 and 14 years, the exception being about 8 years old. They were thus all either nearing or at the menarche, and in addition term school examinations were due to begin on the 18th October. None of the boys was affected. The girls on questioning were unable to explain their behaviour, insisting that they were not unduly worried about the exams or about anything in particular.' He also found that the most severely affected 12 year old girl 'had a past history of unstable emotional behaviour going back for possibly as long as 3 years. She had seen repeatedly both doctors and others for so-called "black-outs," but the trouble had persisted . . . As well as the black-outs she had also had over-breathing episodes. So it seemed here we had the "trigger girl," whom all the other girls were copying, and the whole epidemic could be traced to her, with the impending exams, and the impending menarche, tipping the "hysterically inclined" girls in the class into hysteria. The only girl who really needed any treatment was the "trigger" girl herself.'

The following day, most of the girls affected were still having trouble and were taken by their parents to an Indian women 'healer' at Bulileka. These included all the girls who had been seen at the hospital.

In order to investigate a possibly deteriorating situation, the Consultant Psychiatrist, Dr D. N. Sell, was sent to Labasa by the Director of Medical Services. Dr Sell asked Dr Randall to arrange for as many of the affected girls as possible to attend the hospital on the afternoon of 15 November. On his arrival, only one girl presented at the hospital. The parents of the girls either could not be found or refused to bring their children to the hospital because they were being treated by the Indian woman at Bulileka. The girl who came was the one who was most severely affected and had been given Largactil two days before. She told Dr Sell that 'she felt dizzy and strange,' and he noted that she 'began to overbreath and twitch her hands and arms. This was sufficient confirmation of the original diagnosis and she was told to stop what she was doing. She stopped immediately, and on being asked to leave the room, she got up and left in a normal manner.'

Dr Sell went to the school, but he only encountered another one of the original 18. She began to hyperventilate and twitch, but this was stopped immediately and she left the classroom in a normal manner. Next day the parents of five of the girls were persuaded to bring them to the hospital from Bulileka, and Dr Sell 'saw all five sitting on a bench on the hospital verandah. Each was hyperventilating with hands and arms twitching and "moueing" sounds coming from their throats in perfect chorus and identical pitch. Each was sent off singly, their symptoms subsiding as they left.'

He reported to the Director of Medical Services about his investigations at Qawa, recording that by 25 November five more cases had occurred with the same symptoms, and confirming the outbreak as mass hysteria. He noted that mass hysteria had been frequently observed in schoolchildren. He himself had been obliged to temporarily close down two schools in South Africa after 'witnessing chaotic scenes of children and teachers screaming and whirling about like dervishes, with the local witch-doctors hovering like hyenas in the background, shrewdly observing the most suggestible, who would, in the future, provide regular and lucrative incomes.' He observed that 'Hysterical symptoms are commonest at the two ends of life, before the organisation of the central nervous system has yet achieved maturity, and after it has entered in its decline, and the menarchal girl exposed to emotional tension is particularly at risk.' He finally observed that 'although it is fashionable nowadays to deny the existence of hysteria, most doctors know exactly what they mean when they diagnose hysteria . . . The whole subject of hysteria is a little scruffy and topsy-turvy but it is recognisable; as Groucho Marx once said of a waiter in New York "He may not be an Adonis, but at least he's a Greek." '9

On Dr Sell's advice, the school was closed for the week following his visit. He advised that the parents should be reassured that the symptoms would gradually subside over a few days, and that the children should be taken home and kept quiet and separated from one another. He considered it essential that the afflicted girls should not stay together as a group. As far as Dr Randall and Dr Sell were concerned, the diagnosis of the phenomena at the school as mass hysteria and the psychiatric advice to parents and children were straightforward; but to get the parents to accept the advice and explanation was less so.

CULTURAL SOLUTIONS

The parents agreed that the school should be closed but could not accept the explanation. Their own explanations of the phenomena were far more acceptable to themselves, but they needed more positive action than mere reassurance.

Most of the parents believed that the hyperventilation and other phenomena were caused by the spirits of the sacred pool at Davuiyaliyali, which had been damaged by Munsami Sirdar when bulldozing the playground. It was noted by parents that the trouble started in the classroom closest to the desecrated pool. One of the parents had perceived the desecration and had gone to the school and cleared out the empty and dry rock pool. He reported that soon afterwards it mysteriously filled with water. Not only were the parents and children worried about the damage to the sacred pool but also by the fact that some schoolboys had thrown stones at an Indian grave near the playground, and the ghost of a man appeared. The boys had also thrown stones at a mango tree near the school compound. This tree was important because parents used to take leaves from it in connection with local Hindu religious ceremonies. To the parents, the girls were possessed by some supernatural power, and the only

problem was to determine which power or spirit (shaitan) had been aroused and how it should be exorcised. So they took them to various Hindu Indian 'healers' in the district. But none of them seemed able to help.

Eventually one of the fathers had been told of a Muslim woman, named Amina, living in the nearby Indian settlement of Bulileka, who had a reputation as a 'healer.' She said that she had acquired Fijian powers of healing while living on the island of Taveuni, renowned for its Fijian healers and witchdoctors. Although all the girls involved were Hindu, Amina agreed to heal them provided that they stayed in her compound.

Seven girls were taken to her and were treated as a group. She placed one hand on the back of their heads and rubbed their throats with coconut oil, telling them to be calm and not to worry. Immediately the hysteria left the girls and they calmed down. However, as soon as the parents of the girls took them out of the compound, they were once more afflicted. This happened before the visit by the Consultant Psychiatrist; and Dr Sell observed that 'It is of interest that the Indian woman "healer" at Bulileka rubbed oil over the girls' throats. Was she simply applying a salve over the area from which the odd sounds emanated or did she have some knowledge of Ayurvedic medicine and Tantric literature? In Kundalini Yoga the region of the throat is said to contain a plexus called Vishuddhi-Chakra which probably corresponds to the pharyngeal plexus of the sympathetic. This Chakra is traditionally associated with the purification of diseases and ailments and a Yogi or Yogini in command of this plexus is said to be able to exercise control over both valediction and malediction.'

Although Amina had never been to Qawa hilltop, she knew from her own powers that there was a sacred rock pool there which had been tampered with, and that the spirits of the pool were angry and were troubling the girls. She said that she 'saw' figures like tiny children around the damaged pool. So she and another friend from Taveuni went to Malla Rao, the chairman of the school committee, and told him what she had 'seen' and knew about the sacred pool. She suggested that members of the school committee should go and ask the Fijian landowners to present yaqona to the spirits of the pool in order to appease them.

Malla Rao and some other members of the school committee went with yaqona to seek the assistance of Poe, the chief of the Qawa-i-ra Fijian traditional landowners of the hilltop and the pool. He accepted the yaqona and agreed to help. In the presence of many of the parents, he performed the Fijian traditional ceremony of sova yaqona, presenting yaqona to the spirits of the pool. He addressed the spirits saying that the damage to the pool had been done in ignorance, and asked that the people involved be excused. After the presentation, Poe suggested that the girls in Amina's compound should return to their parents. However as soon as the girls left the compound they once more became afflicted.

All the parents became disheartened but decided to seek alternative powers and called on Mara Sirdar, the leading *pujari* or prayer man of the Vunivau Hindu fire-walking temple, to come and perform a *puja* at the school. Mara Sirdar also had the power of healing. He prayed mainly to Ganesh, the Hindu elephant god, as his parents had done before him, and claimed that he could heal anyone of any religious sect who was suffering from fear, worry or insomnia, provided that the sufferer had complete faith in him.

Mara Sirdar agreed to help. First he prepared at home temporary talismans made of white cloth filled with *bhabut* (sacred ash) and chopped up *nim (margosa* tree) leaves—these he tied up with yellow cotton. He then went to the school and prayed to Ganesh, asking him to come and help and look after the school. He walked all round the school compound to see if any feeling of the presence of *shaitan* or evil Hindu spirits came to him. None did, and he determined that the place was clean and good. Two of his disciples were sent to bring the girls from Bulileka. Amina raised no objection to them leaving her. However, as soon as they left Amina's compound, the girls once more became afflicted until they were calmed down by Malla Rao's disciples who placed a *tilak* or spot of *bhabut* on their foreheads.

When they arrived at the school, the *puja* began. Mara Sirdar called again on Ganesh to come and help, and assured the girls that there was nothing for them to be frightened of and told them to stop worrying. He hung a temporary talisman around the neck of each girl. He took the girls to the sacred pool, and there, following Hindu custom, he burnt camphor around the pool into which he poured milk. Then, in accordance with Fijian custom, he poured *yaqona* around the sides of the pool. He addressed the spirits of the pool, begging their forgiveness if in any way they had been offended.

The girls waited with Mara Sirdar beside the pool to see if any evil would come upon them from the spirits of the pool. Mara Sirdar said that if there had been a spirit there who was angry, that spirit would have entered into one of the girls and he himself would have got a bad feeling in his heart. He got no such feeling, and he told the girls that this proved that there was nothing evil still there. He considered that the spirits of the pool had produced the affliction in the first place because Munsami Sirdar had offended the spirits by bulldozing the rock and their pool. He said that after these rites had been performed, the spirits had been appeased. There was therefore no reason why the girls' affliction should continue and so they had nothing further to fear from the spirits.

After this *puja* was over it was agreed to hold a great *puja* on the following Sunday and to invite a *pandit* or Hindu priest to pray to the nine great Hindu gods of the planets in order to urge the parents to take heart. Nevertheless several of the parents were still considering taking their children away from the school. For the great *puja* the women collected ghee, rice, flour and money which they took to the headmaster's house. They also sold rice and flour so that they could buy semolina for the *prasad* (sacred food) to be used in the ceremony. On the day, the men came early to the school to make a large quantity of *prasad*. They prepared a sacred area in the playground for the *puja*, cutting away the grass and spreading cow dung. In the middle of it they made a pit in which dried mango twigs for the *hawar* or sacred fire were placed. The *pandit* arrived at 10 a.m. He sat down facing northwards with his right-hand side towards the sun, because it was the planet for that day of the week. The girls sat facing the sun. The ceremony of Om Shanti took place and the *pandit* prayed to the nine gods of the planets to exorcise the evil spirits. The girls poured ghee onto the fire. The *prasad* was distributed to the assembled crowd, and presents given to the *pandit*. Finally the sacred remains of the *puja* were collected and placed under the sacred mango tree.

Meanwhile Mara Sirdar, who had taken no active part in the great *puja*, prepared a permanent talisman for each of the girls. These were little copper cylinders filled with *bhabut* and with *nim (margosa)* leaves, with the sacred Hindu word Om written on the outside. Each was threaded on a piece of cotton. He placed one around the neck of each girl and told her to look after it carefully. The great *puja* ended and the parents returned home.

The first sign of the abatement of the affliction appeared to the parents to result from the soothing touches of the Muslim woman 'healer.' She had wanted to make sure of success by not only using her own Fijian-derived powers but also by enlisting the services of the local Fijian chief who carried out the initial ceremonial presentation of *yaqona* to appease the spirits of the pool. However, final success was achieved, as far as the community was concerned, firstly by the Hindu prayer man who included in his Hindu rituals the traditional Fijian way of appeasing spirits by the presentation of *yaqona*, and then by a Hindu priest who invoked the aid of the Hindu gods of the nine planets in the Om Shanti ceremony.

All those girls who participated in these ceremonies apparently recovered. The only girl who was treated exclusively with Western medicine apparently did not. The parents therefore argued that it was the ceremonies of appeasement of the angry spirits that brought about the girls' recovery. They concluded that the epidemic had been related to the anger of the Fijian spirits, which had arisen from the desecration of the sacred pool of the spirits by a member of the Indian community.

School began the Monday following the Om Shanti ceremony, by which time most of the girls had settled down. However on the first day back, five of the 18 affected girls had further over-breathing attacks. The Consultant Psychiatrist, on being told of this recurrence, noted that the ceremony had been held to exorcise the evil spirits affecting the girls and that ceremony was, of course, just about the most effective method possible to start the whole business over again. Of the five girls affected, two were sent home for the day. It was feared at one stage that the matter would flair up again, but, as Dr Randall noted, 'the girls settled down from then on and no more has been heard of the epidemic since.'

Only one girl of the 18 affected did not return to the school at all—the 'trigger' girl who was being treated with Largactil and had been advised to stay away. At the time of the investigations, the headmaster and other Indians claimed that this girl had not yet recovered. People in the Vunivau settlement were quick to point out that she had only been to the hospital and had not been to the *puja* of Mara Sirdar or to the great *puja*. However Dr Randall said that 'She was in fact doing well without drugs when last seen in February 1969.'[10]

The resolutions of the Qawa incident were sought and accomplished within a colonial context in which it might be said that harmony and a spirit of co-operation between the different racial and religious communities were fostered as a matter of policy by an external and unbiased colonial power. It might further be said that Labasa was fortunate at the time of the incident in having available the services of doctors of the standing and understanding of Drs Randall and Sell. Both appreciated that elements other than Western medicine were important in dealing with the situation within the broad context of the beliefs and practices of the various religious and ethnic groups in the community.

It could be asked how this situation would be expressed and dealt with in the modern context of Fiji as an independent republic. The same beliefs and practices both traditional and modern appear today to be as strong and significant as in 1968, as is the understanding of, and appreciation of the values of other people's beliefs and practices. It is likely that the recurrence of a situation such as occurred at Qawa would be dealt with now in very much the same spirit of co-operation and mutual understanding by government officials and neighbours irrespective of race or religion, practice or belief, especially in areas where there has been a long-time mutual understanding between the communities.

Apart from the efficacy (or otherwise) of Western medical treatment and advice by Western-trained medical officers, the situation at Qawa also involved a Muslim healer, a traditional Fijian appeasement ceremony, and Hindu ceremonies, including prayers and a *pujari* and finally a full Om Shanti ceremony with a *pandit*. These attempted resolutions acted at three levels. The Muslim healer attempted to heal the girls in a private situation within the bounds of her own home. The Fijian ceremony was held with limited publicity and with an atmosphere of seriousness which occurs at such ceremonies. Both the Fijian and the Indian communities were aware of what was happening although only a limited number of each community actually participated in the ceremony aimed at appeasing the spirits of the desecrated pool. The Hindu ceremonies, especially the impressive and elaborate Om Shanti, were conducted in full public view, aimed at restoring the confidence of the girls, the parents and the community generally as well as appeasing the disturbed Fijian spirits.

Two other comparable incidents involving desecration and sickness occurred at Labasa in 1968 and 1969, of which the Fijians were fully aware. As in the Qawa incident, non-Fijians had disturbed a Fijian *vanua tabu* (sacred place). In each case the offending parties had suffered some physical disadvantage, and the Fijians had their own explanations for the eventual recovery or continuing affliction of the sufferer. In each case medical or other authorities were also concerned.

In both of these cases, the sacred place disturbed was a *qara ni bulubulu* (burial cave) on the rocky slopes of Uluibau (also known as The Three Sisters), a triple mountain peak behind Labasa and not far from Qawa. In each case, the person who interfered with the sacred place was a European—in the first case a male English police officer; in the other case a female school teacher from New Zealand.

The traditional Fijian landowners of the Uluibau site were the Labasa people, living in the village of Nasekula, between the township and the sea. Their leader was the Tui Labasa, a member of the Wasavulu *yavusa*. Normally they would have had no objection to a European visiting the burial cave, provided that the visitor had first presented *yaqona* to them. This presentation through the ceremony of *sevusevu* would have the double object of seeking permission from the landowners to visit the sacred place, and of appeasing the *yalo ni mate*, the spirits of the dead whose bones were in the cave.

The English police officer said that he had been given permission by the Nasekula Fijians to visit the cave but was told that he must not take away any of the bones. However, he unobtrusively pocketed some human teeth. Soon afterwards he became deaf but Western medical treatment was unavailing. His condition deteriorated so that he had to be invalided out of the police force. The teeth were never returned to the cave.

The school teacher from New Zealand, who was a member of the staff of the Labasa Anglican High School, was also given permission by the Nasekula Fijians to visit the same cave. She was told not to remove any bones. However she did so. In due course she became very ill, developing long body hair and a deepening of the voice. The multi-racial Anglican church congregation prayed for her recovery. The medical officers at Labasa hospital treated her as best they could. Neither approach resulted in any improvement, and she was sent back to New Zealand. On the advice of a Fijian woman of Nasekula who wrote to her, she returned the bone to the Labasa people, and the bone was replaced in the cave. The vicar later said that news had been received from New Zealand that the school teacher had recovered.

A similar incident involved a New Zealand dentist who removed a skull from a burial cave near Sigatoka and took it back to New Zealand. A Fijian dentist friend of his related how the New Zealand dentist was disturbed by the sound of teeth chattering at night. This continued until, on the advice of the Fijian dentist, the skull was returned to Sigatoka.

In both of the Uluibau cases, the Fijians attributed the sufferer's affliction to the offended spirits of the dead in the cave at Uluibau. They could fully understand why the police officer who failed to return the teeth did not recover his hearing. They could equally easily understand that the eventual recovery of the school teacher was due to the appeasement of the spirits by the return of the bone, which was replaced with proper Fijian ceremony. In the case of the recovery of the school teacher, the Anglican church at Labasa was able to point to the efficacy of prayer; whereas the doctors attributed the eventual recovery to a long period of treatment through Western medicine.

This paper has been concerned with the sacredness of place, the respect for shrines and consultation with deities in a multi-ethnic and multi-religious landscape where indeed the same geographical feature may be a shrine for two quite different centres of religious belief. Such places include mounds, pools and burial caves. The case studies have concerned the animation of shrines and the ritualistic practices that must be entered into if a disturbance, however minor, planned or unplanned, is allowed to occur.

Whatever spirit is disturbed, it appears to strike believers of one or other faith or indeed cross-faith. The main case is viewed in a variety of ways, from a case of 'mass-hysteria' by Western-trained doctors and treated as such, to one of spirit possession—a phenomenon well-understood in both the Fijian and Indian worlds. Such an understanding enabled the Western-trained doctors to come to terms with a complex medical and psychological situation, and to treat it accordingly.

In the case of the Qawa schoolgirls both the Fijian and the Indian communities were anxious to appease the spirits—the Fijians, lest further troubles should occur; the Indians, in order to cure the affected girls and to remove the troubles from the school. Once the cause of the affliction became known, help was brought to the afflicted girls by therapeutic rituals of exorcism conducted both relatively privately in the Fijian ceremony and in full public view in the final Om Shanti ceremony.

The incidents illustrate the interplay of ancient and modern beliefs (both medical and religious) of people of widely different cultural backgrounds living closely as neighbours.[11] The lesson to be learned from the study is that what would appear to be incompatible can be made compatible, to the general satisfaction and understanding of all those involved.

NOTES

1. At the time of the epidemic at Qawa I was Commissioner of the Northern Division of which the island of Vanua Levu formed a part. In this role, I carried out investigations into the circumstances surrounding the epidemic which had become a matter of considerable interest to the local community as well as to officers of the District Administration, Dept of Education and the Medical Dept. At the time of the events described the Commissioner Northern Division was responsible to the Governor of Fiji, through the Chief Secretary, for the administration of the Division and for co-ordinating the affairs of the local officers of central government departments.

    I would like to express gratitude to Dr Don Gardner, Dr Margot Lyon, Mr Ian Farrington, Mr Peter Dowling and Dr George Boeck, all at some time of the Dept of Archaeology and Anthropology, The Faculties, at the Australian National University, for invaluable advice on the preparation of the paper; also to Mrs Jan Mattiazzi for typing early drafts and to my son John who gave much time to preparing final drafts.

2. For discussions of spirit possession see V. Caprazano and V. Garrison, *Case Studies in Spirit Possession* (New York 1977); I. M. Lewis, *Ecstatic Religion—An Anthropological Study of Spirit Possession and Shamanism* (Harmondsworth 1975); R. C. Zaener, *Mysticism, Sacred and Profane* (Oxford 1961); A. F. C. Wallace, *Religion—An Anthropological View* (New York 1966); B. Kapferer, *A Celebration of Demons* (Bloomington 1983); J. Boddy, 'Spirit possession revisited: Beyond instrumentality,' *Annual Review of Anthropology,* 23 (1994), 407–34.

3. Claimed by Lessa and Vogt to be a cultural universal. W. A. Lessa and E. Z. Vogt, *Reader in Comparative Religion—An Anthropological Approach,* 2nd ed. (New York 1966), 299.

4. A. Capell, *A New Fijian Dictionary,* 3rd ed. (Sydney 1990), 280.

5. N. Thomas and C. Humphrey, *Shamanism, History and the State* (Ann Arbor 1994), 5.

6. Cf A. W. McMillan, *Hindustani Handbook* (Suva 1931), vi; and J. Seigel, 'Pidgin Hindustani in Fiji,' in Jeremy H. S. C. Davidson (ed.), *Pacific Islands Languages, essays in honours of G. B. Milner* (London 1990), 173.

7. This study is based on first-hand accounts of incidents at Qawa given to me by many of those who played major parts in it. Interviews were held with the school headmaster, the chief of the local Fijian polity, the chairman of the school committee, healers, holy men including the *pujari* or prayer man at the local Hindu temple, Hindu priests, parents, medical officers at the Labasa Government Hospital, especially Dr G. R. Randall and the Government Consultant Psychiatrist Dr D. N. Sell. All these people seemed ready to talk freely about their experiences except for the *pujari,* a little old bent man, who was afraid to talk too much lest he lose his powers as a fire-walker. The headmaster said that he believed in 'none of this rubbish,' but his family had left home in a fright and he himself was obviously very ambivalent. Members of the school staff were hesitant to go to work. Indeed even before the outbreak, some had asked for transfers from the school, because they were afraid of evil spirits in the compound. Qawa hilltop, the school and the pool were visited on several occasions. On one occasion, movements were noticed in the murky water in the pool and every few minutes tiny prawns came to the surface and were swimming about, the first time that the prawns had been seen since the pool had been damaged several years previously.

8. *Fiji School of Medicine Journal*, 4:12 (Dec. 1969), 4.

9. Dr D. N. Sell to Director of Medical Services, Memorandum 22464, 1/5 of 25 Nov. 1968, Suva, Fiji Government Archives (copy with author).

10. Ibid.

11. The situation at Qawa has some parallels with the religious situation in Java as described by Geertz, where underlying animistic traditions had become fused first with Hindu-Buddhist culture patterns and later with Islamic patterns. 'The result was a balanced syncretism of myth and ritual in which Hindu gods and goddesses, Moslem prophets and saints, and local place spirits and demons all found a proper place' (C. Geertz, *The Religion of Java* (Glencoe 1960), 550). However at Qawa (as in other parts of Fiji) different religious and ethnic groups continued to pursue their own beliefs and practices. However, on the occasion of the epidemic at Qawa there was a deliberate syncretism of belief and ritual, when the different groups in the community co-operated in an attempt to deal with the situation.

The Devil and the Saints in the Conquest of Mexico

Fernando Cervantes

In this essay, historian Fernando Cervantes examines the beginnings of Christianity in Mexico. In doing so, he throws light not only on the ways in which Mexican Christianity developed but also on the nature of both pre-Christian Mexican gods and Christianity as it was practiced in Spain five centuries ago.

Christian monks and missionaries were dualists, understanding Jesus as entirely good and the devil as evil. They equated pre-Christian Mexican gods with the devil and declared that sacrifices to such gods were sacrifices to the devil. Mexican Indians, on the other hand, were monists and believed that gods had both creative and destructive aspects—that the gods were both good and evil. They viewed sacrifice as humanity's role in maintaining the balance between creation and destruction. Jesus and the devil were easily incorporated into their understandings, and sacrifices to the devil were understood as essential. In trying to condemn sacrifice to both the devil and pre-Christian gods, missionaries were actually promoting it.

Cervantes points out that although the intellectual Christianity of the monks was quite different from the understandings of the Indians, Indian and Spanish peasant understandings were not as far apart. Like the Indians, European peasants often understood saints as being both good and bad. While honoring them might benefit a town, ignoring or insulting them might cause disease and evil.

As you read, consider these questions:

1. How were Mexican Indian understandings of gods different from Christian understandings? Was the difference absolute, or rather one of degree?

2. What role did power (in particular the power of the colonizing Spanish) play in the native acceptance of Christianity?

3. In altering Christianity to fit their understandings of the nature of God, were the Mexican Indians rebelling against the authority of Spaniards and the Church?

A recurring problem in the study of pre-Hispanic Mesoamerica is that most of what we know about it we owe to the efforts of the early friars who, naturally, studied the subject with very particular aims in mind. As the great Franciscan ethnographer, Bernardino de Sahagun, put it, native cultures were to be studied as a doctor studies an ailment in order better to diagnose it and prescribe a remedy.

The distortions that ensue from this are well known to anyone who has attempted to study pre-Hispanic religion, but they become especially evident when dealing with the concepts of good and evil; for in Mesoamerica, as in most non-Western traditions, the gods represented both benevolence and malevolence. The very word *teotl* has an ambivalence in Nahuatl that its common translation as 'god' fails to capture. Its glyph is the figure of a sun, which conveys a sense of awesomeness, but also one of danger. Thus the friars can hardly be accused of inconsistency for comparing the great Mesoamerican deities with both classical gods and Lucifer, for there is an equal dose of the divine and of the demonic in them. By contrast, our notions of good and evil imply degrees of benevolence and malevolence that would have been quite alien to the Mesoamerican mind. A good

"Devil and saints in the conquest of Mexico" by Fernando Cervantes, *History Today* 44:4 (1994) 38-46. Copyright © History Today. Reprinted with permission.

god, for instance, would have lacked the power to disrupt which was considered essential to the act of creation.

If such was the case it seems difficult to make sense of the apparent success of the early friars, and especially of the euphoric millenarianism so vividly described by the first Franciscans who arrived in Mexico in 1524. It seems safer to suggest that the initial enthusiasm of the Indians to accept Christianity had more to do with the Mesoamerican tradition of incorporating alien elements into their religion than with any deep conviction about the truth of the Christian faith. A people whose glyph for conquest was a burning temple was likely to see victory as sufficient evidence of the strength of the victor's god. The incorporation of the Christian god was thus not merely a matter of prudence but a welcome addition into a supernatural pantheon already heavily populated by foreign deities. What soon emerged, however, was that the Christian god posed a fundamental challenge to the existing system by his claim to total goodness and absolute sovereignty. More alarming were the bans imposed by the friars on native sacrifices, for if obeyed they would threaten to destroy the Mesoamerican corporate relationship with the supernatural and to bring about an end to the present cosmos and a return to the original chaos.

The insistence on the need for sacrifice is difficult for us to grasp and even more difficult to reconstruct. The notion of 'propitiation' which sees in sacrifice an offering that provides 'nourishment' for the gods is too functional and it fails to convey the full sense of the action. A more adequate understanding may be gained by considering the Mesoamerican belief that human flesh and maize were the same matter in different transformations; and since the transformations were cyclic and the cycles constantly in jeopardy, men's actions, and human sacrifice in particular, played a crucial part in maintaining the balance.

But the need for sacrifice could have resided at an even deeper level. As the French scholar Rene Girard has explained, in societies that have no judicial system the risk of violence is so great and the cure so problematic that the emphasis tends to fall on prevention. Sacrifice in such cases may operate by appropriating certain aspects of violence and hiding them from sight by the machinery of ritual. A ban on sacrifice would thus be tantamount to a ban on social coexistence, since it is only through sacrifice that the destructive vicious circle of reciprocal violence can be replaced by the protective and creative circle of ritual violence.

In Mesoamerica, therefore, sacrifice may have played a central role in the protection of the entire community from violence among its members, and the ban on sacrifices may well have posed a challenge to those very principles upon which its social harmony and equilibrium depended. Moreover, such a danger became especially evident when the bans were seen to coincide with a marked increase in Indian suffering and mortality, a coincidence that led many Indian leaders into positions that the friars could only interpret as open apostasy.

If the spread of such early anti-Christian reactions points to a conscious native opposition to the new religion, in practice the process was much more flexible. As early as the 1540s, for instance, many Indians who were found to oppose Christianity would readily explain that they had been deceived by the devil. It is true that such an early assimilation of a Western concept could be interpreted as the result of a mistranslation, or of the mendicant attempts to impose their own views upon the natives. Yet too much stress on this assumption can also lead to an anachronistic reading of the process which hides the possibility that Christianity might have made some sense to the Indians.

Three crucial considerations should preclude this danger: firstly, the importance of sacrifice and the need the Indians felt to preserve it; secondly, the insistence of the friars that sacrifices were the work of the devil; and finally, the Mesoamerican understanding of deity as a compound of both good and evil. When these three points are considered together, the suggestion that the Indians did not see any inconsistency in agreeing with the friars that their sacrifices were addressed to the devil should not appear far-fetched. For despite the friars' efforts to make the Indians see in the devil an enemy to be feared and avoided, often what the Indians saw was simply a further deity that they could incorporate into their existing pantheon. Indeed if, as the friars insisted, it was the devil to whom the sacrifices were addressed, then it is likely that the Indians would have come to see the devil as crucially important in the effort to protect and continue the sacrifices. By insisting that the devil was the central object of the sacrifices, the friars were in fact making it difficult for the neophytes to conceive of him as an enemy.

This process can be seen at work in some of the early codices, where the devil was associated with some of the more malevolent of Mesoamerican deities and depicted as a clawed monster inciting Indians to eat hallucinogenic mushrooms. The aim of the friars was to encourage an identification of the devil with evil through the mushrooms; but since the Indians traditionally attributed divinity to the mushrooms, many would have been persuaded of the importance of the devil precisely because of his association with the mushrooms. It was such confusions that gave rise to the paradoxical development of a demonic ethos among the Indians which to some extent persisted, as inquisitorial records show, throughout the colonial period and beyond.

Interestingly, the recurrence of the concept of the devil indicates that an effective affirmation of the Indian identity required the use and manipulation of Christian concepts. Just as modern non-Western nationalisms use an unmistakably Western ideology in order to oppose the West, some Indians appear to have used a conspicuously Christian concept when they needed to oppose Christianity. Indeed, the way in which they assimilated the concept of the devil seems to have gone hand in hand with their acceptance of and participation in the Christian ritual. As a rule it was precisely those Indians most actively involved in the Christian liturgy who were most often found to participate in proscribed pre-Hispanic practices. Perhaps the best example of this process received the attention of the Mexican Inquisition in the 1680s. It involved the Indian Mateo Perez, who was found guilty of devil-worship in the southern region of Oaxaca. According to an Indian witness, Perez always insisted that the sacrifices should be performed in the church and especially on the feast of the town's patron saint. When Perez himself was questioned about this he explained that he had been persuaded of the need for such sacrifices by the devil himself in a dream.

This example points to a clear indigenous effort to incorporate pre-Hispanic elements into the Christian liturgy, an effort where the use of the church and of the patron saints in the performance of the sacrifices seemed perfectly logical. It was the insistence of the friars that such sacrifices were the work of the devil that led to the paradoxical identification of the devil with the saints, especially those saints who had taken over the role of some previous tutelary deity. But the identification was in no way part of an effort to oppose Christianity. Mateo Perez was known as an exemplary Christian who 'encouraged the divine cult, the rosary and taught the Christian doctrine' and who, as sacristan of the town church, was willingly engaged in the Christian liturgy and ritual. Far from opposing Christianity, Perez was engaged in an effort to reconstitute a pagan past through the reinterpretation of Christian elements.

All this sheds some light upon the insistent association of Indians with demonic activity that can be detected in inquisitorial records throughout the colonial period. But it would be dangerous to forget that cases like Mateo Perez's are peculiar to remote and relatively unacculturated regions. Such examples are scattered and they contrast sharply with developments in central Mexico, especially those areas where the early Franciscans left their mark and where Indian testimonies are full of romantic evocations of the sanctity, humility and chastity of the friars, remembering the first years of conversion as a golden age when the message of the gospel finally liberated them from the yoke of idolatry.

This evidence points to a process of conversion where, underneath the growing distrust of native beliefs among the friars, the identification of Christian saints with native deities was often tolerated and even encouraged. The early development of cults such as those of the Virgins of Guadalupe and Ocotlan on the sites of the native goddesses Tonantzin and Xochiquetzalli would be inexplicable otherwise, and they point to the existence of a strong unofficial tradition that tolerated the persistence of pre-Hispanic elements and their incorporation into the ceremonies and rituals of Christianity. The trend is especially evident in the recurrence of themes such as the story of the Magi in Nahuatl songs and plays throughout the colonial period, as well as of stories that stress the essential goodness of pagan traditions. Perhaps the best example is the Nahuatl play about St. He-

lena and the Holy Cross, preserved for posterity by Manuel de los Santos y Salazar, the Tlaxcalan collector and editor of the late Nahuatl annals, who copied or revised the text in 1714. In a revealing passage Constantine's conversion to Christianity is strategically placed after a eulogy of the emperor for honouring the ancient Roman gods, who are acknowledged as great and powerful, 'for they have put at his feet his various enemies, who greatly feared him.'

These and similar examples call into question the view—still widespread among scholars—that denies the existence of a common ground between the sacrifice-orientated monism of Mesoamerican religions and the salvation orientated matter/spirit dualism of Christianity. For it should be clear that such an interpretation reads too much into the contemporary intellectual assumption that Christianity and paganism were mutually exclusive alternatives from which the Indians had to choose and between which they might switch back and forth. At the practical level, the kind of Christianity that the Indians encountered was not so much the Christianity of the intellectuals, but the more traditional or 'local' religion characteristic of early modern Castile, whose points of contact with the Mesoamerican world were innumerable.

As William Christian has shown, the saints in sixteenth-century Castile were widely regarded as the resident patrons of their communities, very much in the same way as the tutelary deities were perceived by Mesoamericans. Most vows were made in response to some natural disaster, and, although men and women approached the saints as advocates of the community, some reports point to a belief that the saints were capable of inflicting harm on communities if the latter did not observe their sacred contracts. Each Castilian village had its own calendar of sacred times, marked on the village memory by natural disasters or other supernatural signs which had become solemn contracts with the saints. Everyone thus knew that it was a collective responsibility to observe these sacred contracts and that dire consequences could follow lapses. As much as in Mesoamerica, therefore, religion in sixteenth-century Castile was a corporate affair involving the propitiation of a host of supernatural beings who displayed benevolent and malevolent attributes.

Thus the view that Christianity sat in its purity like a layer of oil over Mesoamerican magic, is a highly misleading one. For the Christian religion was itself intermingled with a great deal of magic. Necromancers, enpsalmers and conjurers of clouds often competed directly with parish priests in early modern Castile. Inquisition records show that many of them were themselves clergy or religious, sometimes involved in such practices as dealing with locusts by holding them up for trial and excommunicating them, or holding matches with wizards to see who was best at chasing clouds. It is true that they were widely regarded with suspicion and often accused of having sided with the cause of Satan; but even so, it could not be denied that the church itself had its own arsenal of orthodox and legal prayers and exorcisms to be used on similar occasions. There thus existed a symbiotic relationship between the official orthodox remedies and the apparently superstitious practices that became the most common objects of concern and criticism among the educated.

If by the middle of the sixteenth century such practices had come under deep suspicion, the line between 'magical' and 'orthodox' remedies remained thin. In seventeenth-century Mexico, for instance, it is interesting to observe that those very people who were especially suspicious of Indian magical practices often found themselves working almost on identical assumptions to those they were so keen to condemn. The well known 'extirpator of idolatry,' Jacinto de la Serna, had no qualms about attributing the healing powers of an Indian to a demonic compact; yet, in the very same passage, he describes how he himself performed a similar healing rite on his Indian servant with the bone of a saintly man he had in his possession.

If such attitudes characterised the likes of Serna, they were far more common among the average immigrants to the new continent. Indian healing rites soon came to be accompanied by Christian prayers and invocations, and hallucinogens are known to have been associated with Christ, the angels, Mary, the Child Jesus, the Trinity, St Nicholas and St Peter. In an illustrative example recorded by Serna, an Indian healer claimed that she had not been taught the art of healing by any human person but directly by God. An angel, she claimed, had appeared to her telling her not to be afraid and teaching her the art of healing while he nailed her to a cross.

Despite widespread fears that such examples were further proofs of the perfidious ways of Satan to keep the Indians under his grip, there are no signs here of any clandestine persistence of idolatry or of any sort of opposition to the Christian faith. Such examples point more in the direction of a process where the Indians were piecing their cosmos together in the new Christian configuration. It was inevitable that in this nascent form of Christianity, many of the Christian friars should have adopted features formerly associated with the native shamans and demigods. That their rising prestige should have depended upon their power as wonder-workers, or that men and women should have sought them in the same way as they had formerly resorted to pagan shrines or healers, is often seen as evidence of the limitations of the missionary enterprise or even of the non-Christian character of Spanish American religion. Yet the climate of these years is no less genuinely Christian than that of the early centuries of the Middle Ages, which saw the rise of the cult of the saints.

Behind its syncretic mixtures, it was in this twilight world that the Indians came face to face with a transcendent power in which the harsh realities of existence no longer dominated their lives and where human suffering and misfortune could find a remedy. Indeed, it was precisely in this world of mythology—of the cult of the saints and their relics and their miracles—that the vital transfusion of Christianity with Mesoamerican tradition was most successfully achieved. It would have been very difficult for a people without a tradition of written literature or philosophy to assimilate the metaphysical distinctions of Christian doctrine or the subtleties of medieval scholasticism. But when the new religion was manifested visibly in the lives and example of men seemingly endowed with supernatural powers, it became incomparably more accessible.

Thus the process of conversion in Mesoamerica was carried out not so much by the teaching of a new doctrine as by the manifestation of a new power. Just as in the European 'Dark Ages' the monks had been the apostles of the new faith among the pagans of Europe, so now the ascetic friars became the principal channels of Christian culture among the Indians.

The process was not so much one of assimilation or even of acculturation, but rather one of contradiction and contrast. The friars impressed the Indians because they represented a way of life and a scale of values that opposed virtually everything they had hitherto known. But the contrast was not one of 'civilisation' against 'barbarism,' for at the practical level the Christian religion did not try to impose a civilising mission or to instill any conscious hope of material well-being or social advancement. Its message was primarily one of divine judgment and salvation, and it sought expression in the eschatological distinction of the present world and the world to come set in the dramatic context of the belief that the human race, through original sin, was enslaved to the powers of evil and was sinking deeper under the weight of its own guilt.

This stern doctrine was presented with deep conviction by the early Franciscan missionaries, and it came with peculiar force to the declining world of Mesoamerican civilisation, a world in which poverty and exploitation, illness and death had become the unavoidable facts of daily experience. It was natural that if the present world was visibly falling to pieces the newly converted Indians should have turned their eyes in hope to the world to come.

Consequently, the intense asceticism of Mesoamerican Christianity is not to be explained as a mere imposition of the Franciscan way of life; for at a deeper level it responded to an urgent and essential psychological need. Its marked other-worldliness, moreover, differed emphatically from much that we have come to associate with the word in its modern pietist sense, with its individualist, subjective and idealist connotations. Nothing could be further from the otherworldliness of Mesoamerican Christianity, which was collective, objective and realist. Although the world to which it aspired was outside history and beyond time, it was, nonetheless, the ultimate end towards which time and history were moving.

Furthermore, the church could claim to possess a corporate experience and communion with the eternal world in the sacred mysteries. Just as the Mesoamerican world had found its centre in the ritual order of sacrifice around which the whole life of the community revolved, so now the Christian liturgy came to hold a similar position. And just as in the European 'Dark Ages' the impoverishment of material culture did not prevent an enormous creativity in the field of liturgy, so now indigenous art came to the service of the Christian liturgy in a way that was as spontaneous as it was genuinely Christian in spirit.

Whatever else might be lost and however dark might be the prospects of indigenous societies, the Christian liturgy came to provide a new principle of unity as well as a means by which the mind of the Indians could be attuned to a new view of life and a new concept of history. For although the new liturgy came to hold the same key significance as the sacrificial rituals of the Mesoamerican world, its spiritual content was very different. Where the Mesoamerican ritual order was conceived as the pattern of the cosmic order and its central mysteries were the mysteries of nature itself, the Christian mysteries were essentially related to the mystery of eternal life, and although they were tuned into the cyclical life of nature in the liturgy, their central object of concern was the redemption of humanity brought about by the death and resurrection of Christ. Additionally, since all the articles of the Christian faith were historically situated, the Christian mystery was also a historical mystery. Instead of the nature myths that were at the centre of the Mesoamerican ritual order, the Christian mystery was based on a sacred history, and the Christian liturgy itself developed into a historical cycle where the progress of humanity, from creation to redemption, was seen to unfold.

It is in this climate of ascetic otherworldliness and corporate liturgical expression that the best sense can be made of what has misleadingly come to be known as the 'spiritual conquest.' What we see at work is not so much an imposi-

tion of a new way of life but a manifestation of a new spiritual power that the Indians came to find virtually inescapable. No matter how many similarities there might have been between the cult of the saints and the sacrificial propitiation of the old tutelary deities, in practice the cult of the saints became inseparable from the Christian liturgy and the commemoration of the feasts of the saints provided an element of corporate identity and social continuity by which every community and every town found its liturgical representative and patron.

It is hardly an exaggeration to suggest that for the Indians of central Mexico the Christian liturgy had become the only context in which the passing of the old ritual order could be explained and raised on to a plane where eternity had invaded the world of time and where creation had been brought back to the spiritual source that kept it in being.

FOR FURTHER READING

Robert Ricard, The Spiritual Conquest of Mexico, trans. L. B. Simpson (University of California Press, 1966); Inga Clendinnen, Aztecs: An Interpretation (Cambridge University Press, 1991); Serge Gruzinski, The Conquest of Mexico: The Incorporation of Indian Societies Into the Western World (Polity Press, 1993); James Lockhart, The Nahuas After the Conquest: A Social and Cultural History of the Indians of Central Mexico (Stanford University Press, California, 1992); Louise M. Burkhart, The Slippery Earth: Nahua-Christian Moral Dialogue in Sixteenth Century Mexico (University of Arizona Press, 1989); Nancy M. Farriss, Maya Society under Colonial Rule: The Collective Enterprise of Survival (Princeton University Press, 1984).

Is Elvis a God?
Cult, Culture, Questions of Method

John Frow

We often hear celebrities spoken of as if they were gods, but generally we don't take this too seriously. It is only an analogy. In this essay, John Frow tries to ask to what extent devotion to celebrities is truly a form of religion. Does Elvis indeed have the characteristics of divinity?

Frow does not come to a fully satisfactory answer, but he does approach the question using concepts that are im-

portant to the anthropological study of religion. He explores Emile Durkheim's notion that all people divide the world into sacred and profane spheres. He examines Rudolf Otto's formulation of religious experience as *numinous*—that is, mysterious, awe-inspiring, and exercising a powerful attraction. In each case Frow asks if fans do indeed understand celebrity as having these characteristics.

Frow also focuses on the relationships between celebrity, divinity, and technology. He argues, in the case of recording stars, that the copy is ultimately more real than the original. That is, Elvis's fans (and those of other celebrities) understand these individuals primarily through their recordings, which are enduring and unchanging. The

"Is Elvis a God?: Cult, culture, questions of method" from *International Journal of Cultural Studies* 1:2 (1998) 197-210, copyright (c) 1998 International Journal of Cultural Studies. Reprinted by permission of Sage Publications Ltd.

actual person is thought of as the manifestation of the recording, rather than the recording being thought of as simply produced by the person.

Regardless of whether or not you end up believing that Elvis is indeed divine, Frow raises important challenges to us: First, to take people's search for the numinous seriously, even though it may occur in forms that seem comedic; and second, to understand the roles technology plays in creating and reinforcing the experience of the sacred.

As you read, consider these questions:

1. What do you believe the general characteristics of a God are? Do you think Elvis has any of them?
2. Some of Elvis's followers clearly see religious aspects to being a fan. Yet, at the same time they acknowledge that much about devotion to Elvis is comic. How is this possible?
3. The notion of Elvis as a god will strike non-fans as humorous. What do Elvis and other celebrities have that would prevent us understanding them as gods?
4. What is the relationship between technology and the spread of religion? How does the development of new technologies affect our understanding of religion?

There are two texts. The first is from 'A Love Letter to Elvis on the Anniversary of his Death, August 16, 1977, by Joni Mabe'; the letter is a collage of text and images of a woman, presumably Joni Mabe herself, photographed in various loving and at times explicitly sexual postures with a life-size plastic Elvis doll, and it serves as a frontispiece to Marcus (1991). The text reads:

Dear Elvis,

You don't know how many times I've dreamt and wished that you were my lover—or father. But you died without a trace of myself ever touching your life. I could have saved you Elvis. We could have found happiness together at Graceland. I know that I could have put your broken self back together. It's as if you could have discovered that sex and religion could be brought together in your feelings for me.

The hurt you carried every day, the passion that dried up with the years, I could have restored. All of those women sapped your spirit and gave you nothing but the simulation of passion. I know the secrets of the Southern night.

I worship you. My sleep is filled with longing for you. I try to make a go of daily life but all else fades before this consuming image of yourself always present in my mind. This image guides me to the places I want to be. I lay here now thinking, agonizing—in other words—masturbating over the impossibility of ever being your slave. Sometimes I feel I've been hypnotized, that I can no longer bear existence without you. Other men in their fleshly selves could never measure up to your perfection. When making love to you in the later years, I still could sense your throbbing manliness. You really touched the woman in me. I no longer know the difference

between fact and fantasy. My poisoned spirit cries out for relief, for just one caress to remind me that you really were a man and not a god. If God listened to my prayers you'd be lying beside me now.

No matter who I'm with it's always you. Elvis I have a confession to make. I'm carrying your child. The last Elvis imitator I fucked was carrying your sacred seed. Please send money. Enclosed are the photographs of myself and the earthly messenger you sent.

Love sick for you, baby . . .
Joni Mabe

The second text is a story from the *National Examiner,* cited in Fiske (1993), in which Elvis appears to a group of US marines on duty in Saudi Arabia and says to them: 'Don't worry, I'll be watching over you and all your fellow servicemen. I'll act as your guardian angel and be alongside you during the battles to come.'

Let me make two brief points about these texts before I open out to some more general considerations. The first is that their truth status—the utter ambivalence of Joni Mabe's text, where the possibility of irony and parodic mockery in no way affects the emotional intensity of the message, and the irrelevance of the protocols of journalistic verification to supermarket tabloids like the *National Examiner*—is beside the point; they develop fantasies which are carried with equal force in parodies, in pastiches, in fictional narratives, and in the most intimate and personal testimonies of fans. The second point is that these fantasies form part of a thematically coherent and widely diffused corpus of recurrent narratives. Hinerman (1992), for example, reports similar stories of the visitation of those who are troubled or dying by an Elvis who tells them 'I'll be with you,' and Marcus (1991: 121–2) indeed argues that 'the identification of Elvis with Jesus has been a secret theme of the Elvis story since 1956.' And what's perhaps most striking about this identification is the ease with which it fits into Christian orthodoxy, even and perhaps especially in the heartland of Southern Baptism.

With these two texts I adumbrate both the concern of this article with the religious dimensions of celebrity, and a set of full-blown cliches about the role of apotheosis and the cult of the dead and immortal god in popular culture. For there is nothing that has not already been said a thousand times about the cultic aspects of stardom. In the case of Presley, the central focus has been on the status of Graceland and the Elvis Presley Birthplace in Tupelo as cult centres. Graceland is the object both of everyday pilgrimage and of especially intense commemoration during the vigils of Tribute week, culminating in the candle-lit procession around Presley's grave on the eve of the anniversary of his death—a ceremony, writes the archaeologist Neil Silberman (1990: 80), directly parallel to the fire rituals associated with ancient solar heroes. Gary Vikan's and Gilbert Rodman's analyses of Graceland as *locus sanctus* similarly point to the votive graffiti and offerings, including elaborate hand-crafted homages such as posterboard collages and box dioramas depicting scenes from Elvis's life (Rodman, 1996: 117; Vikan, 1994); this central site is then repeated in local sites of commemoration—the 'handmade Elvis shrines that can be found on front porches, yards, and roadsides scattered across the rural South' (Rodman, 1996: 175). Other commentators invoke the Aztec sacrificial Sun King whose insignia Elvis wore on his Las Vegas costumes (Kroker et al., n.d.), or point to the communion-like performances by Elvis impersonators in which the white scarves ritually thrown to female fans pass on the bodily traces of the communicant (Fiske, 1993: 116; Spigel, 1990: 181). And Harrison (1992) exhaustively documents every aspect of the Elvis cult in a sustained transposition of a religious vocabulary on to the phenomena of stardom—without, however, ever managing to notice the constitutive role of joking and irony in the reverence paid to Elvis.

A small handful of stars and public figures experiences this adoration that raises them beyond the human plane: in our century, perhaps, in addition to Elvis, Rudolph Valentino, Lenin, Stalin, Hitler, Mao, James Dean, Kurt Cobain, Bruce Lee, Che Guevara, Evita Peron, and that other dead princess whose ghost is now haunting cultural studies. Even the most extreme fame, as in the case of Marilyn Monroe or John Lennon or Pele, falls short of this transsubstantiation that is apotheosis. And yet—and this is my argument—we lack almost completely the intellectual tools to make sense of this process. At best, in what is still in many ways the most interesting analysis of stardom, Edgar Morin elaborates the banal vocabulary of the idol, the pantheon, the cult into an account of the imaginary processes of identification and projection by which the systems of religious worship and fan culture both bring to bear that 'immense affective surge which constitutes the participation of the spectator' (Mori, 1960: 40). But Morin is never sure whether to take the analogy between stars and gods seriously; his ambivalence is nicely summed up in his quotation of Parker Tyler to the effect that the term ' "Anthropomorphic gods . . . must not be taken literally, but it is not merely a manner of speaking" ' (quoted without further attribution in Morin, 1960: 105). Neither a figure nor not a figure, the religious relation exists midway between dead metaphor and a theory which has yet to find itself.

No such caution and no such subtlety afflict the tradition of analysis that, for convenience, I shall call Jungian, and whose noisiest proponent in the field of popular culture is perhaps Camille Paglia. The emphasis here is all on the continuities of a changeless human nature which allow the 'modern cult of celebrity' to reawaken in its audience 'atavistic religious emotions'; the image of Princess Diana thus 'taps into certain deep and powerful strains in our culture, strains that suggest that the ancient archetypes of conventional womanhood are not obsolete but stronger and deeper than ever' (Paglia, 1995: 164), and Elvis becomes the direct inheritor of the 'youth cult' created—single-handedly,

it would seem—by Byron (Paglia, 1990: 364). For Greil Marcus, coming from a quite different angle, Elvis is at once an exemplary culture hero, one of those 'pure products of America' who 'go crazy,' 'a man who lived with nearly complete access to disaster, all the time' (Marcus, 1991: 6–7), and the bearer thereby of a mystical national theodicy. In him we find 'a presentation, an acting out, a fantasy of what the deepest and most extreme possibilities and dangers of our national identity are'; a mystery is revealed to us, so that 'we gasp. We get it. We feel ennobled and a little scared, or very scared, because we are being shown what we could be, because we realize what we are, and what we are not. We pull back' (Marcus, 1991: 31). Our understanding of him is too small, too human: this is a person who 'appeared on the *Ed Sullivan Show* not as a country boy eager for his big chance but as a man ready to disorder and dismember the culture that from his first moment had tried to dismember him, and that *had failed'*; he was, writes Marcus in a sentence that only an American could have written, 'the first public figure since Jesus that couldn't be ignored by any segment of his civilization, yet that foretold and embodied a new mode of being that would eventually dismantle the very society that was so fascinated by his presence' (Marcus, 1991: 95).

In none of these analyses (and the countless others like them) is there a clear sense of how seriously the concept of the sacred should be taken, and of how the sacred might have come to be caught up with, and indeed produced as a central auratic effect by, the mass-representational systems of film, of rock, and of the theatre of mass politics. More problematically still, these analyses tend to partake of the very religious ethos that they describe: the notion of the charismatic genius and of the atavistic reincarnation each in its own way inscribes itself within an imaginary of ineffable presence. Against this imaginary, let me invoke the dry caution of William James, running a thread between Kant and the epistemologies of Bachelard and Althusser: 'Knowledge about a thing is not the thing itself,' says James (1961: 379) to his Scottish audience. 'You remember what Al-Ghazzali told us in the Lecture on Mysticism—that to understand the causes of drunkenness, as a physician understands them, is not to be drunk.'

I propose that the form of apotheosis associated with the modern star system is a phenomenon of a strictly religious order; and in what follows I seek to trace out, very schematically, some of the implications of this proposition for the study both of contemporary religious experience and of systems of mass representation. My aim here is not to undertake such a study; it is to ask what its methodological and disciplinary conditions might be, and in particular to ask whether cultural studies has an appropriate take on these questions.

It is conventional to distinguish between the institutional and doctrinal dimensions of religion and what we might call its *ethos*. Religious affect never floats freely, but the structure to which it is tied need not be that of systematically orga-nized religion. The 20th-century philosophy of religion, largely accepting this distinction, has sought to apprehend the nature of the experience of the sacred through the concept of the *numinous.* In Rudolf Otto's (1958) formulation there are three aspects to that intense experience of presence that he calls the numinous: first, it is understood as a *mysterium:* it is completely other than ourselves, and cannot be translated into the ordinary categories of human thought; nor can this experience be conveyed to someone who has not undergone it. Second, this *mysterium* is *tremendum:* it inspires awe, even terror at the overwhelming power which is revealed in religious experience, and which threatens to annihilate indi-vidual consciousness. Third, it is *fascinans:* it exercises an uncanny attraction, and inspires an emotion which is at once like love and like fear or even revulsion.

Otto's influential analysis operates at the highest level of abstraction to isolate an essence of the religious experience, understood as being the shared foundation of all religions. At a lower level of abstraction, a certain tradition of com-parative anthropology seeks to understand the sacred not as an experience in itself but as a taxonomic operation which plays a central role in the formation of a religious cosmos. Finally, there are numerous accounts of socially and cultur-ally specific religious formations, describing an enormous range of variations in the techniques and the cognitive frameworks from which particular experiences of the numi-nous arise—and indeed, that experience is not necessarily a component of all religions. For my purposes it is not neces-sary to descend to this level of concreteness, although any more detailed analysis of the cult of Elvis would certainly have to take into account, for example, the institutional par-ticularities of Southern Baptism in relation to which it has flourished, its white southern working-class basis, its gener-ational structure, as well as the ways in which it is *not* re-stricted to or defined by these structures.

For now, let me focus on that intermediate level of ab-straction at which, in the classic Durkheimian formulation, the sacred is understood as an empty category defined struc-turally by nothing but its opposition to the profane (Durkheim, 1915: 38). This opposition then comes to gov-ern a series of further structural relations within the cosmos. Against the homogeneous, amorphous, undifferentiated space of the profane world is set the radical heterogeneity of sacred space, which—'saturated with being' and with sig-nificance (Eliade, 1961: 12)—interrupts it, breaks its flow, opens out on to absolute otherness. Time is similarly hetero-geneous: unlike profane time, sacred time is reversible, be-cause 'every religious festival, any liturgical time, represents the actualization of a sacred event that took place in a myth-ical past, "in the beginning"' (Eliade, 1961: 68–9). But this sheer otherness of the sacred is itself a kind of content; and already in Durkheim it is possible to see the emergence of a positive characterization of the sacred as it divides internally to produce a distinctive ambivalence, an oscillation between

repulsion and fascination, dread and desire, the *tremendum* and the *fascinans.* For Durkheim (1915: 411) this takes the form of a division between the pure and the impure, and be-tween beneficence and malevolence, both of which are the object of interdiction: thus 'the pure and the impure are not two separate classes, but two varieties of the same class, which includes all sacred things.' The sacred, as evidenced in its ambiguous Latin root *sacer,* designates at once the ac-cursed, the outcast, and the holy, a force which is above all dangerous, contagious, and compelling; it is, in Roger Cail-lois's words (1959: 21), 'what one cannot approach without dying.'

The sacred is thus a force or a presence, whether anthro-pomorphized or not, which is conceived non-naturalistically as a suspension or rupture of normal time and space by the uncontrollable outbreak of 'spots' of transcendence. Gods are positioned directly in relation to this force, as the force itself or as emanations of it. Demi-gods and their Christian variant, saints—and we must not be misled by centuries of humanism into believing that the categories of 'god' and of 'human being' are incomparable—mediate between the pro-fane world and its transcendental other.

Demi-gods of the type of Elvis and Diana are interces-sionary figures, gods in human form whose presence spans and translates between two worlds. This positioning is clearly apparent in Lynn Spigel's analysis of Elvis imper-sonators. She writes: 'Religious worship is not just a handy metaphor; . . . the impersonator is often considered a medium who channels the spirit of Elvis, which in turn channels the will of God' (1990: 191). At once a virtuoso performance of resurrection and a ruse, a trick, a game, these half-parodic simulations are, in their odd way, a form of worship. A female Elvis impersonator tells Spigel (1990: 191) that Elvis '"showed a great love for his fans. That's what bonds us all together: the love that he showed for hu-manity."' For another fan she interviews, Mae Gutter, Elvis is 'a Christ figure—someone who Gutter believes mediates between heaven and earth and fills his followers with love' (Spigel, 1990: 192). And at the convention of Elvis imper-sonators that Spigel attends a Hawaiian/Swiss impersonator, after singing his song 'He's living' ('He's living in my heart, he's living in my soul'), then invites the audience 'to pray with him for the dead Elvis, imploring us in prayer to thank God "for giving us Elvis and the one true King, Our Lord Jesus Christ."' The impersonator, says Spigel (1990: 193), has a special relation to the redemptive logic of the Christian sacrament, 'for he or she works as a medium who channels the spirit of a saviour, all the while opening up a public space where people can express their mutual faith in an ab-stract principle that no one can name.'

Yet this performative evocation of the living presence of the dead King is always just that, an evocation, a repetition, a re-presentation. This is the gist of the argument that McKenzie Wark makes in an attempt to shift the reading of Elvis away from that myth of presence in which both fan culture and most rock criticism are entrapped, and to pose instead the question of the economy of representation within which stardom is constituted. That 'pure moment of original presence in Elvis's music and image,' writes Wark (1989: 25–6), does not precede the moment of recording but rather follows it; it is 'an echo, a recording, a remix and edit from the vast palette of reproducible art.' One figure of this causal reversal operated by the mass mediation of sound and image might be the echo effect created for Elvis's voice by Sam Philips by cutting a master tape from two vocal tracks mixed a split-second apart, producing thereby 'a weird, non-architectural, electric space' which is, says Wark (1989: 26),

> the doubled space of recording, sound shadowed by its twin, its echo, the trace of its passage into recording. From the beginning Elvis was lost to this other space of recording totally. His 'live' performances are merely a dissimulation of the real Elvis, the recorded Elvis.

The power that Elvis wielded, and that he himself sought to explain by means of astrology, numerology, and Christian revivalist lore, had a much more mundane origin in a technology of repetition: at once the withdrawal of sound and image from the linear flow of time, and their dissemination in an endless series of copies. The real person of Elvis is always and from the beginning a copied person, the authenticity of which derives from the fact and the extent of copying, of representation, rather than from anything that precedes it. His charismatic force is an effect of

> the modern power of recording, piling up rhythms and images and sounds and stories like so many bones of the body of Elvis, laying them up until they piled up high into the air. . . . Till the time came when Elvis himself became a mere corporeal appendage to so great a body of recording. (Wark, 1989: 27)

To relate the apotheosis of Elvis to an economy of representation seems to me a crucial move. At the same time, Wark sidesteps a number of important questions by setting recording and religion in opposition to each other (this move, I will suggest later, is an almost inevitable one for the modernizing intellectuals who work in cultural studies). The question that I pose instead is this: how is it that a form of religious experience can, under certain circumstances, be so central to the secular culture of mass-recording? But before I broach this question, let me pose three preliminary questions which I hope will take me to the heart of the matter. Why does so much of the cult of Elvis take the form of parody? Why is the Elvis mythology so insistent on his doubleness? And why was his death such a good career move?

Even a quick look at some of the hundreds of Elvis-related websites is enough to convey a sense of his cultural ambivalence. The various lists of Elvis sightings, the speculations on whether and where he is still alive, the conspiracy theories concerning his death, the First Presbyterian Church of Elvis the Divine, the 24-Hour Church of Elvis, the vari-

ous web-shrines, the list of parallels with the life and teachings of Jesus, the petitions for a national Elvis holiday in the US and for the creation of an Elvis clone, the endless tributes, the 'scientific evidence (in the form of a Masters thesis) that the woman Michael Jackson wed is in fact not Elvis Presley's daughter' (Elvis fans hate Michael Jackson)—all these are either directly parodic or, more usually, an extraordinary mix of mockery and reverence. The King is a joke, an object of ridicule, as much as and indeed precisely to the extent that he is an object of worship and one of the central figures through which American popular culture imagines the relation between the living and the dead. This is to say that the categories of the sacred and the comic are not necessarily antagonistic, and certainly within contemporary popular culture they are inextricably fused. Marcus (1991) gets it precisely right when speaking of the emergence within popular culture of strange new Elvis hybrids: 'Elvis Christ, Elvis Nixon, Elvis Hitler, Elvis *Mishima,* Elvis as godhead, Elvis inhabiting the bodies of serial killers, of saints, fiends. Each was a joke, of course; beneath each joke was bedrock, obsession, delight, fear.'

Nowhere is this ambivalence clearer than in the case of those multipliers of Elvis, the impersonators, estimated at some 3000 in the US alone in 1992, whose performance is at once a take-off, a camp parody of a piece of cultural kitsch (this is why almost all impersonators mime the overweight, white-jumpsuited Elvis of the Las Vegas years rather than the young Elvis) and at the same time a reverential reproduction of that presence that cannot be copied but that can be evoked, alluded to, signified through the very imperfection of the impersonator, where the word 'impersonator' has the sense both of impostor and of one who enters into the person of the dead and resurrected singer.

Impersonation is one aspect of the theme of doubleness that runs through the Elvis narrative. There is the fact that already in 1956 the warm-up act for Elvis's show at the Louisiana Fair Grounds was done by exact replicas who dressed like him and sang his songs (Garber, 1993: 370); and that Elvis is said to have selected the material he would record by listening to impersonators who would give him a sense of how the songs would sound (Goldman, cited in Joyrich, 1993: 88). There are the stories of the faked death, in which the body displayed in the casket is said either to have been a wax dummy, or 'the body of an English look-alike fan who had been invited to Graceland because he was dying of cancer' (Fiske, 1993: 112). And there are the various forms in which Elvis takes on the role of *revenant*—as comeback artist, as phantom hitchhiker, as the man who haunted the rock revolution which he initiated and then sat out. The essence of superstardom, says Garber (1993: 373), may be 'to be simultaneously belated and replicated; not to be there, and to cover up that absence with representations.' For Edgar Morin, speaking of the process of projection in which the star acquires a superhuman status, the double is 'the repository of latent magical powers: every double is a virtual god' (Morin, 1960: 98). But doubling is also the structure of iteration by which the effect of presence is produced in representation, and by which, in the case of mass-recording, an infinite number of identical representations produces a correspondingly magnified effect of presence, the superhuman presence of the star who is at once absent and immortal.

This absence of the recorded star, their presence as recording, is the reason why the worship of stars is a cult of the dead.[1] The image and the recorded sound of Elvis precede his person in the circuit of recognition in which they have their life; he is remembered before he is known, recognized as an ideality in ways that his actual bodily being could never match. The star competes with his ghostly rival, the double that is more real, more authentic, and unchanging for all time. The effect of his death is only that he can now become himself, *tel qu'en lui-même enfin l'éternité le change:* eternity changes him at last into the person he really was.

It is for this reason, as John Castles argues in a remarkable thesis to which this paper is heavily indebted, that the star's biography is always tragic in form: like the hagiography from which it derives,[2] it is structured by premonition—'James Dean Knew He Had a Date With Death' (Castles, 1993: 152): by a subordination of profane, linear, irreversible time to a temporality in which the moment of death is always given in advance, and in which every gesture, every choice, every session in the Beale St bars, every step towards Sun Studios, is laden with significance. The star is always already dead; by the same token, however, the star lives forever. 'James Dean dies; it is the beginning of his victory over death' (Morin, 1960: 123). Morin thus lists the four phenomena that accompany the star's apotheosis: first, a spontaneous refusal to believe that the star is actually dead; second, legends of their survival and of the fabrication of evidence of death; third, spiritualist notions of the continued existence of the dead among the living—the phantom hitchhiker; and fourth, the development of a cult establishing connections between the living and the immortal dead (Morin, 1960: 132). The final corollary to this argument is that 'living stars . . . are a subset of dead ones' (Castles, 1993: 170). The life of the recording artist and the movie star is realized in reversible and repeatable time; their fullest being is lived here, in what we can recognize as sacred time, time outside of time, the time of circulated representations which transcends and transfigures whatever it is we think of as ordinary life.

The first thing to say about this mechanism, I think, is that it involves a quantitative effect: the 'passages of recorded time' in which stars are constituted are multiplied in time as repetition and in space as replication (Castles, 1993: 47). The star is thus not just a recorded but a disseminated person, not just widely known but widely known to be widely known. 'Every star image is composed of the fact that stars contain in their singular body the gaze of a collec-

tivity' (Castles, 1993: 109), and this is in the first place an arithmetical fact.

But how does this fact of being known to many people then undergo a qualitative change to transform the star from a human being into a nonhuman, a more-than-human being? Let me suggest an answer by way of analogy. Jaynes (1976: 167–72) argues that neolithic representations of the gods always have a greater ratio of eye size to overall facial size (up to 20%) than is found in human beings (about 10%): the gaze of the god is of greater intensity than that of humans. We might remember that one of the things that was held against the young Elvis was his use of eye shadow, artificially enlarging the size of his eyes (Garber, 1993: 367). What this suggests is that the gaze of the god is an intensifier, a manifold which condenses a multiplicity of looks and returns them with increased force to the single fan. That is what is overwhelming—*tremendum* and *fascinans*—about the look of the star, the gaze of the god: this concentration of the energy of the many into a spell-binding focus on the one. My recognition of this look which reflects and magnifies my own is a kind of love, a kind of adoration; Morin (1960: 18) speaks of it as a 'phenomenon of the soul which mingles most intimately our imaginary projection-identifications and our real life,' and he points to its ambivalence, the desire of the worshipper to consume his god. Marcus (1991: 202) too notes 'the complex of worship and resentment all fans carry,' and the Vermorels' (1992) research into fan cultures reveals the same oscillation, often within the one letter or testimony, between adoration and hatred.

John Castle's metaphor for the construction of the divinity of the star in the returned and intensified gaze is the relation of the performer to the crowd in the ritualized structure of the rock concert. What takes place in this ritual is a mutual constitution of the audience and the star in ecstatic identification: 'When the crowd screams at the appearance of the star they are performing the essential task of making themselves into a crowd which then tumbles down into the star figure who absorbs it and can then give it back or withhold it' (Castles, 1993: 135). This mirror-recognition, in which the crowd alternately loses itself and recomposes itself, then gives way to a third moment in which 'each member of the crowd can then copy the star's embodiment of all of them. The "super-self" made by the crowd is then imaginarily reappropriated, repossessed by each of its moments' (Castles, 1993: 137); each spectator is swollen with the energy and presence they absorb from the star made big by the crowd.

Underlying and enabling this directly specular relation to the crowd, however, is the prior relation of the star to an inchoate 'mass' by way of the recordings which constitute in advance his or her recognizable presence. As Connor (1989: 153) notes, the live concert builds upon an 'inversion of the structural dependence of copies upon originals,' by means of technologies of amplification, magnification, and repetition—sound equipment, huge video screens, and the playing of material that is already familiar from recordings. The core of stardom is thus of a semiotic order. The star belongs to a domain constructed by recording and the modes of repetition specific to it which exists outside or beyond ordinary life, profane time; this is the basis for the promise that, in identifying with the star, we too will overcome death. . . .

[Frow ends his essay with an 800 word conclusion where he discusses the failure of the field of culture studies to propose adequate theories for the study of religion. In this conclusion he makes three observations: first, that students in cultural studies need to receive a background in the history and sociology of religion. Second, that scholars in cultural studies need to take religion seriously because of its centrality in the modern world. Finally, Frow observes that for many Australians these lessons have been based in an increased awareness of Australian Aboriginal spirituality and by the tensions that exist between a religious view of the world and one based on the philosophy of the Enlightenment.—Editors]

NOTES

1. Cf. Wark (1989: 28): by his death Elvis became 'the King of the passage into the better world of recording,' into 'recorded culture . . . the cult of the dead.'

2. Vikan (1994: 150) writes of the Elvis *vitae* as speaking 'of a dirt-poor southern boy who rose to fame and glory, of the love of a son for his mother, of humility and generosity, and of superhuman achievement in the face of adversity,' as well as of a death which is a martyrdom to and for his fans.

REFERENCES

Caillois, Roger (1959) *Man and the Sacred,* trans. Meyer Barash. Glencoe, IL: The Free Press.

Castles, John (1993) 'The Individual and Stardom,' PhD Thesis, University of Technology, Sydney.

Connor, Steven (1989) *Postmodernist Culture: An Introduction to Theories of the Contemporary.* Oxford: Basil Blackwell.

Durkheim, Emile (1915) *The Elementary Forms of the Religious Life,* trans. Joseph Ward Swain. London: George Allen & Unwin.

Eliade, Mircea (1961) *The Sacred and the Profane* (1959), trans. Willard R. Trask. New York: Harper & Row.

Fiske, John (1993) *Power Plays, Power Works.* London: Verso.

Garber, Marjorie (1993) *Vested Interests: Cross-Dressing and Cultural Anxiety.* New York: Harper Perennial.

Goldman, Albert (1981) *Elvis.* New York: McGraw.

Harrison, Ted (1992) *Elvis People: The Cult of the King.* London: Fount.

Hinerman, Stephen (1992) ' "I'll Be Here With You": Fans, Fantasy and the Figure of Elvis,' in Lisa A. Lewis (ed.) *The Adoring Audience: Fan Culture and Popular Media,* pp. 107–34. London: Routledge.

James, William (1961) [1902]) *The Varieties of Religious Experience.* New York: Collier.

Jaynes, Julian (1976) *The Origin of Consciousness in the Breakdown of the Bicameral Mind.* Boston: Houghton Mifflin.

Joyrich, Lynne (1993) 'Elvisophilia: Knowledge, Pleasure, and the Cult of Elvis,' *Differences* 5(1): 73–91.

Kroker, Arthur, Marilouise Kroker and David Cook (n.d.) *Panic Encyclopaedia: The Definitive Guide to the Postmodern Scene.* http://ctech.concordia.ca/krokers/panic.html

Marcus, Griel (1991) *Dead Elvis: A Chronicle of a Cultural Obsession.* New York: Doubleday.

Morin, Edgar (1960) *The Stars,* trans. *Richard Howard.* New York and London: Grove Press and John Calder.

Otto, Rudolph (1958) *The Idea of the Holy* (1923), trans. John W. Harvey. Oxford: Oxford University Press.

Paglia, Camille (1990) *Sexual Personae: Art and Decadence from Nefertiti to Emily Dickinson.* New Haven: Yale University Press.

Paglia, Camille (1995) *Vamps and Tramps: New Essays.* London: Viking.

Rodman, Gilbert (1996) *Elvis After Elvis: The Posthumous Career of a Living Legend.* London: Routledge.

Silberman, Neil Asher (1990) 'Elvis: The Myth Lives On,' *Archaeology* 43(4): 80.

Spigel, Lynn (1990) 'Communicating With the Dead: Elvis as Medium,' *Camera Obscura* 23: 176–205.

Vermorel, Fred and July (1992) 'A Glimpse of the Fan Factory,' in Lisa A. Lewis (ed.) *The Adoring Audience: Fan Culture and Popular Media,* pp. 191–207. London: Routledge.

Vikan, Gary (1994) 'Graceland as *Locus Sanctus,*' in Geri DePaoli (ed.) *Elvis + Marilyn: 2 × Immortal,* pp. 150–66. New York: Rizzoli.

Wark, McKenzie (1989) 'Elvis: Listen to the Loss,' *Art & Text* 31: 24–8.

6

Religious Specialists
Shamans, Prophets, and Priests

Essays in This Section:

Laurel Kendall   Korean Shamans and the Spirits of Capitalism (1996)

Julie Cruikshank   Claiming Legitimacy: Prophecy Narratives from Northern Aboriginal Women (1994)

Peter Gose   Oracles, Divine Kingship, and Political Representation in the Inka State (1996)

There is no religious community in which everyone truly participates equally. That is to say, in all cultures there are people who play special roles in religion. Anthropologists have generally referred to such people as shamans and priests. As you read the essays in this section, keep the following points in mind:

- Shamans are found in all societies. In small-scale societies such as foraging bands, they are the only religious specialists. Priests are found in large-scale societies. They are full-time specialists, and priesthoods are often linked with political institutions.

- There is no agreed-upon, precise definition of *shaman*. In fact, there is considerable controversy over the use of the word. Some anthropologists argue that the use of the word should be strictly limited, applying only to cultures of Siberia and parts of Asia where the term was originally found. Others, including the editors of this volume, believe that it is more valuable to identify shamans as a type of practitioner common in cultures throughout the world, including our own.

- While we do not believe there is a set of characteristics that will identify shamans in every possible circumstance, the following should help. First, most shamans are part-time practitioners. That is, in addition to being shamans, they have other sources of livelihood. In small-scale societies, they participate fully in the production system of the society (they garden, forage, or herd). In larger-scale societies they may have full- or part-time jobs. Priests, on the other hand, are generally full-time employees of an institution. Second, shamanic authority derives from the shaman's stated ability to travel between the material and spiritual worlds and act as a mediator between humans and intangible

beings. Shamans do much of their work in trance, and use a variety of techniques to enter into these altered states of consciousness. In these states, they have direct contact with God, ancestors, spirits, or whatever the members of the group understand as inhabiting the nonempirical realm. Priests may also use many different techniques to have ecstatic religious experiences. However, their right to do this and the credibility of the experiences, however achieved, derives from their position within their religious hierarchy.

- Though shamans do many different things, one of the most important aspects of shamanic practice is health and healing. Shamans travel into the spirit world to diagnose sickness and find cures for their patients. Shamanic healing may sound very exotic to modern Western readers. However, as you read about it, please remember that truly effective medicine in the West is really a very recent phenomenon. As we discuss more fully in the introduction to Part Four, "Sickness and Health," before the twentieth century many Western healing practices were quite magical.

- In the West, shamanism is often associated with small-scale, traditional societies or with activities like astrology, tarot card reading, and fortune telling. Though many people engage in these occult practices, they are not taken terribly seriously by most in wealthy, industrialized nations. However, as Laurel Kendall's essay on the spirits of capitalism in Korea shows, shamanism can be an important and vibrant part of modern, capitalist society. Kendall reports that shamanism has adapted to the changing social and economic situation in Korea. Whereas spirits used to speak primarily about issues of health and disease, today they speak about the success or failure of business enterprises. However, there is an important element of continuity between past and present practices: in the past, shamans were consulted about physical health, which was vitally important to the small-scale agricultural enterprises of that era. Today, they are consulted about economic health, vital to the business concerns of the present.

- Prophets are another type of religious practitioner. Prophets do sometimes hold priestly offices, but in a sense all prophets are ultimately shamanic. That is, though they might hold offices, their power and their ability to influence those around them stem from the fact that they are understood as inspired by or in contact with the supernatural world.

- Most anthropological accounts of prophets argue that prophets are most evident in times of rapid social change, when people's religion no longer accurately reflects their world. Prophets announce a prophetic code, which generally identifies something wrong with society, instructs followers on how to overcome this problem, and paints a vivid picture of the world to come after the identified evil is removed. Prophecies are sometimes judged to be successes or failures depending on whether the prophet's

followers succeed in changing their society. This is discussed further in Anthony F. C. Wallace's essay in section 12.

- While the account above is a powerful way of understanding prophets, it is probably too tied to Western society and the histories of Judaism, Christianity, and Islam. As Julie Cruikshank shows in "Claiming Legitimacy: Prophecy Narratives from Northern Aboriginal Women," prophecy might be a regular feature of some societies. Prophets do not emerge to change society; rather, people invoke their words, long after their deaths, as after-the-fact explanations of the ways in which their society has changed. Cruikshank argues that in so doing, those who tell these stories claim legitimacy both for themselves and for their traditional culture.

- Priests are found in larger-scale societies. Often, as described in Peter Gose's essay on Inca priesthood, they are linked with the power of state governments. Gose's essay shows how Inka priests legitimized and supported the leading role of the Inca ruler and his delegates while at the same time providing a way for the concerns of subordinate groups to be heard.

Korean Shamans and the Spirits of Capitalism

Laurel Kendall

In this essay, Laurel Kendall examines the role of shamanic beliefs in modern-day Korea. Far from being part of a preindustrial traditional past, shamanism is a thriving part of current Korean society. Shamans say that in the past, their clients asked them to contact spirits to cure illness and relieve misfortune, but that today, clients are increasingly concerned with having shamans contact spirits in order to ensure wealth, particularly through success in business.

The clients of the shamans are largely drawn from the ranks of middle-class entrepreneurs. In Korea, which has placed enormous emphasis on the development of very large corporations, this is a marginal group. Its members frequently experience substantial business success, but also live through quick reversals of fortune and periods of poverty. In these circumstances, they turn to the shamans to help ensure prosperity. Though Kendall doesn't mention it, their use of shamanism echoes Malinowski's insight that people are most likely to use supernatural means of control when outcomes are unpredictable.

Kendall also notes that there is really a great deal of continuity between old and new shamanic beliefs. A generation ago, when shamans were mainly concerned with health and illness, may people were small-scale farmers. Accidents and disease were common, and these could destroy a family's ability to bring a profitable crop from the ground. Thus, prosperity and health were directly linked. Today, people are shopkeepers and small-scale entrepreneurs. Their prosperity now depends more on the success of business ventures than on health, and shamanic practices have shifted accordingly.

As you read, consider these questions:
1. When are Koreans most likely to consult shamans?
2. What sorts of spirits are shamans able to contact for their clients? Why do you think these spirits take the forms that they do?
3. How do shamans and their clients understand each other?
4. Is the role that shamans play in modern Korean society different from the role they played a generation or two ago?
5. Korean use of shamans to ensure that cars and engines run well might strike some readers as unusual. Do Americans have similar practices?

I AM OFTEN TOLD that I am lucky to have worked with Korean shamans in the mid-1970s, for certainly by now such practices as I described in my dissertation and subsequent book must all have died out (Kendall 1985b).[1] I smile, for even when I began, I was told that I must seek my informants among hoary crones in the deep countryside. Then, as now, I found a vital practice in the immediate environs of Seoul, invigorated by young and dynamic practitioners. . . . This is not to deny that the shamans of my acquaintance, along with most Koreans who have lived through recent decades, perceive dizzying changes. I am interested in how shamans, clients, and spirits continue to make sense of the ground that moves beneath their feet.

The shamans I know often remark upon their clients' preoccupations with wealth and advancement. Some shamans are inclined to boast of the financial rewards their clients have gained through ritual observances. Others are more cynical. One young shaman spoke with great heat and humor about profit-driven clients who will invest in repeated shamanic rituals, or *kut,* for good fortune, even within the space of a single year, and clients who will promptly sever their relationship with a shaman if the ceremony they have sponsored does not bear fruit in immediate financial gain. The shaman Kim Pongsun offers the acerbic view that the rituals for good fortune, *chesu kut,* are very popular because "if this house has so much money, then that house will sponsor a kut to get yet more money," a Korean version of keeping up with the Joneses. She claims that in the past such rituals for good fortune were rare since "Who had money for that sort of thing? If someone was sick, then you would hold a healing ritual, or *uhwan kut.* Even if you went into debt for it, you had to do it. It was a matter of life and death." Rituals held to send the ancestors to paradise, known as *chinogi kut,* were also more common 20 years ago. "Nowadays, do they concern themselves with the ancestors? People only care about themselves. No one bothers to send the ancestors off properly. They just add a small send-off at the end of a kut held for their own benefit."[2]

The researcher is tempted to join the shamans in a disgruntled discourse upon the mercurial preoccupations of the contemporary Korean moment. I shall, however, resist making a simple comparison between the materialistic present and a more innocent time when all of us were younger, the ethnographic present of nearly 20 years past. Rather, I would use these different observations, theirs and mine, distant and more recent, as still shots recording serendipitous events in an unfolding historical process. To pursue the analogy, my first book was, in the manner of structuralist ethnography, an immobile formal portrait (Kendall 1985b).

These more recent observations are slightly blurred snapshots, imperfect attempts within a frozen frame to record subjects in motion. . . .

GETTING AND SPENDING

The flavor of the new Korea burst upon me one autumn day in 1989 with the arrival at a kut of the apprentice shaman, Kwan Myŏngnyŏ, in a state of great laughter and excitement.[3] Kwan's sister, who runs a clothing shop in the South Gate Market, had been told at one of Kwan's rituals that her supernatural Official (Taegam) wanted a drink of wine.

> She had intended to pour the wine and set it down right there [in front of her shop] but she may as well have done it in broad daylight [the South Gate Market is always filled with people]. She had bought the tiniest little plastic cup, but even if she had tried to offer the wine in that, the people passing by would have thought that she was crazy. My sister couldn't bring herself to pour the wine. So he said, "Official mine, let's go to South Mountain." [Kwan laughs.] Oh, that kid! She said, "It's very congested here so let's go to some breezy place where you can carouse in private." And then she said, "Please get in the car so we can go." She did all that, it was so funny to hear her tell it.
>
> She says she drove up South Mountain, there are spirits up there after all. She drove up and then she got out of her car and looked around. It was absolutely perfect. So then she said, "Dear Official, aren't you pleased? Why don't you get out of the car and look around." She didn't leave anything out. ["She did well," an older, more experienced shaman interjects.] She poured out a serving of rice wine [tongdongju] and said, "Please have a drink." And then, she says, she kowtowed. In a little while, she poured out the wine in a line meaning "Drink your fill," and came back down. The very next day, right then in the morning, she got the proceeds from an eight-million-wŏn order [approximately U.S. $11,430]. ["That's great," the other shaman interjects.] . . . And the shop right next to hers, a big enterprise that had been in the business for ten years, she says that this year their business failed. In the South Gate Market there are some 500 shops and they say that only four of them are doing well, just four. What can it mean that only four of them are doing well this year?

A third shaman caps the discussion, "Yep, all you have to do is treat the Official well and then things will work out for you. That's what it takes."

Later that same day, Kwan again returned to the subject of her sister's business, this time to affirm that when their father died, he had entered Kwan's pantheon as a spirit, and thereafter the sister's business flourished:

> Within a year of our father's death, my sister began to make money like wildfire. In the space of two years she'd taken in a billion wŏn [by this inflated claim, over a million dollars]. Our father died in the eighth month, and from the tenth month she began to make money. Since my father's death, all of my siblings are doing well. . . . [More generally she attributes her family's prosperity to her own acceptance of the shaman's

profession, a decision her kin opposed because they claimed to be members of a noble (yangban) lineage.] In the past, I was poor and my brothers and sisters didn't have anything either. Now it's so much better, they're driving their own cars, they've all bought houses. Now that I've become a shaman they take me here and there to treat me and buy me presents.

This wins a cynical affirmation from her client's mother: "You have to have money, and then they call you 'noble,' [toni issŏya yangban irago]." "So what else is new? Money is nobility [toni yangban iranikka muŏlkŭrae]," a cynical shaman observes.

I was surprised. The assertion that money is nobility, that the rich are considered noble, was not new to me. The old men of Enduring Pine Village used similar words to describe the local gentry of their remembered past. I would hear these sentiments again in the utterances of spirits during rituals performed by these and other shamans: "In our country, if you just have money, then they call you 'noble.'" But never before had I heard a shaman make such an immediate connection between honoring the spirits and quantified material success.

I knew secondhand of such grand claims, knew that mainline Protestant theologians sometimes blame "shamanism" for predisposing Koreans to pentecostal religions in which prayer is a magical means to a materialist end.[4] The underlying logic of Kwan Myŏngnyŏ's story was familiar: treat the spirits well and they will do well by you, as when the gods and ancestors in Yongsu's Mother's shrine promised to give her the rent money, a pledge to help her earn her living as a shaman (Kendall 1985b:56).[5] In the past, the claims made for successful rituals had been modest and vague: "and now they're living well" or "things have gotten a bit better for them." I mused that the young shaman's bald assertions of wealth reflected the worldview of a newly prosperous urbanite. By the late 1980s, brash new patterns of consumption in Korean cities incited official alarm and even piqued the curiosity of the foreign press.[6] I mused that perhaps Kwan Myŏngnyŏ's understanding of the relationship between wealth and spirits, far from reflecting an innate "shamanic" worldview, funneled new sentiments and experiences into religious practice.

THEN AND NOW

In 1977 and 1978, when I first lived in Enduring Pine Village on the periphery of Seoul, harbingers of what would soon be regarded as the "Korean economic miracle" were evident in the prevalence of new television sets and the absence of village daughters, gone to work in urban factories. More than half of the village households described themselves as primarily "nonagricultural," their income derived from taxicabs, cottage industries, or hired labor in the nearby town (Kendall 1985b:45). The Republic of Korea was then in the middle of three decades of rapid industrialization that would transform an essentially agricultural society into a highly urbanized, newly industrialized country in the space of one generation (Koo 1990).[7] The story of an interventionist Korean state favoring large corporations and stifling labor unrest among an educated and highly motivated new proletariat has been told and debated.[8] The social consequences of this transformation have only just begun to be digested. The rural population is now half of what it was in 1960.[9] In its place, one finds a large working class, a class of white-collar technocrats, professionals, and managers, and an increase in the ranks of the petite bourgeoisie (Koo 1987). Very few of the men and women who were teenagers in 1977 can still be found in Enduring Pine Village, and some of those who remain now commute to work in their new private cars. People talk constantly about how their lives have improved, then measure themselves against their neighbors and measure their achievements against their aspirations for their children.

By the late 1970s, when I began my first fieldwork, a majority of the Korean population already lived in cities. Even so, I assumed that the proper subjects for an anthropology of Korea were village people ("peasants" we called them then). Following anthropological custom, I took up residence in a village, albeit not an isolated village, and wrote about household-centered religious practices in the context of rural lives.

The household of my ethnographic imagination was a small family farm, a kin-based agrarian unit of production and consumption embedded in a larger market economy (Wolf 1966). Such people as the Rice Shop Auntie and Yangja's Mother, whose husband drove a taxicab, appeared in my ethnography, brushing elbows in the shaman's shrine with women who still lived in villages. The religious practices of farm wives had followed their daughters into the brave new world of first-generation urban entrepreneurs, but as dynamic practice, not frozen custom.

In the shaman shrines of Seoul and its immediate environs, I have encountered wage workers and farmers, and occasionally white-collar workers, but the core adherents are the members of a new urban class of shop owners, restaurateurs, and proprietors of small companies. Small entrepreneurs, an ill-defined group rarely mentioned in the scholarly literature, constitute a significant segment of the Korean population (Koo 1987:379–380). Slightly less than one-third of all non-farm workers are self-employed or work for family businesses (*Korea Statistical Yearbook* 1990:75). While the government's developmental strategies have consistently favored large monopolies at the expense of small businesses, most petty entrepreneurs would describe themselves as middle class and see themselves as capable of advancing through the system, an optimism manifest in the rituals they perform.[10]

CAPRICIOUS FORTUNES

One summer evening in 1991 I accompanied the shaman Yongsu's Mother when she went to a client's house to perform a small ritual honoring the spirits of a newly purchased family car (*ch'a kosa*). This was my first opportunity to observe such a ritual, although Yongsu's Mother claimed that she and her colleagues routinely performed it as private car ownership proliferated among their clients. In this instance, the sponsors were the son and daughter-in-law of one of her longstanding clients. The man—let us call him Mr. Kim—had purchased his car without having Yongsu's Mother check his horoscope. . . . Had he taken this precaution, he would have learned that this was not an auspicious year for him to bring a new vehicle into his household. A precautionary placation was in order.

I could appreciate the Kim family's concern, having heard tales of the huge sums of compensation money exacted after traffic accidents, to say nothing of Korea's having one of the world's highest rates of traffic fatalities. The logic of the ritual was also familiar to me: grain or goods brought into or removed from the household without a bribe to the supernatural Officials piques their ire and brings misfortune. In the 1970s, new consumer goods such as televisions and stereos were cited in shamans' divinations as "shiny things" that had unleashed misfortune when brought into the house without due precaution (Kendall 1985b: ch. 5).

In Yongsu's Mother's view, there were particular reasons why the spirits might be vexed with this family. As the son of a regular client, Mr. Kim had grown up under the spirits' protection. After establishing a household of his own, he and his wife had dedicated a prayer cushion to the Buddhas in Yongsu's Mother's shrine. Nevertheless, his wife was swayed by a Christian neighbor, and the couple abandoned their obligations to the spirits (and Yongsu's Mother) by attending the Christian church. The results were disastrous. Suffering all manner of financial reverses, the husband lost his own small factory and the couple was forced to sell their house. They returned to Yongsu's Mother and sponsored a kut. This had all happened a year before the ill-advised purchase of the new car.

When I met them, the husband was working for another company and the family lived in a modest but well-appointed apartment. Some of the family's dialogue with the spirits would include a discussion of their prospects for building a new house. Later that night, when he drove me to the subway in his new car, Mr. Kim would express profound relief at having completed the ritual. He told me that he respected Yongsu's Mother's skills as a shaman, volunteering the information that he had known her for 20 years and considered her his "foster mother" (*suyang ŏmma*).[11]

Beyond the curiosity value of placating a Car Official (Ch'a Taegam) and Engine Official (Enjin Taegam), of a middle-class couple kowtowing in the street to the spirits that inhabited their shiny black vehicle, I was intrigued by Mr. Kim's history of sudden and dire financial reverses. The precipitous failure of his small factory would seem well-matched to perceptions of terrible supernatural wrath even as a successful gamble—the shop in South Gate market—implied tremendous blessing. This theme appeared again in the two rituals I observed in the spring of 1992. This was a period of record bankruptcies among small and medium-sized businesses as a consequence of a slump in the Korean stock market and the reluctance of banks to guarantee credit.[12] These kut were for the clients of Sim Myŏnghŭi, an apprentice shaman active in the satellite town of Ansan. Both client profiles matched that of the shaman herself as migrants from further south, now in their thirties, attempting to establish themselves through small-scale enterprises.

The Pak family seemed fairly successful. They and their small daughter were nicely dressed and drove to the public shrine in the family car. The expressed purpose of their shamanic ritual was to tend the ancestors of Mr. Pak's family, but their overriding concern, as explained to me by the wife and as addressed by nearly every spirit manifested by the shamans, was the family's desire for a business of their own. Mr. Pak works for a major corporation and his wife runs a small clothing shop. Should Mr. Pak quit his job and combine forces with his wife to run an expanded family business? The spirits, through the agency of three shamans, urged caution, suggesting a delay of two or three years but promising the couple eventual success.[13] (In my experience, the spirits tend to be fiscally conservative.)

Mrs. Yi's circumstances were far more serious. Her husband was a contractor, but when his business failed, he had given up, stayed at home, and worked himself deeper into debt. Attempting to sustain the family, Mrs. Yi worked as a daytime housekeeper, but now she was thin and pale and ached all over. Most immediately, the kut was for her health, but her household's financial situation was an overriding concern. The shaman Yongsu's Mother made an explicit connection between body and circumstance, noting that when people have such acute financial troubles they understandably worry and brood until it makes them ill.[14] Mrs. Yi seemed shy and forlorn going off in a van to a distant mountain in the company of three flamboyant shamans and, on this particular occasion, with two Americans toting a video camera as well. The shamans coached her through the ritual, while the spirits, speaking through the shamans, affirmed her pain, stroking her gently as they expressed pity. When it was done, she would comment that the ancestors' sympathetic understanding of her plight had given her comfort. Like the Pak family, Mrs. Yi was given hope for the future. Like the Pak family and probably many others as well, she was told, "You don't get rich in a single morning. You have to make a great effort and also honor the spirits."

The stories told here suggest that their subjects are motivated by something more than the simple greed imputed to clients by cynical shamans. Like Kwan Myŏngnyŏ's sister, who took her supernatural Official to South Mountain, the Kim, Pak, and Yi families, are (or were) engaged in high-risk enterprises at the margins of the Korean economic miracle. The consequences of good and bad fortune have a crushing immediacy for them. Because access to capital is restricted in Korea, small businesses have difficulty securing bank credit (Janelli 1993:64). Consequently, they have been drawn into the informal curb market for high interest and more precarious loans.[15] In the first five months of 1992, 3,646 companies—mostly small and medium-sized businesses—went bankrupt (*Korea Newsreview* 1992a).

By the late 1980s, I realized that a great many of the kut that Yongsu's Mother and her colleagues performed concerned business. Many were held not merely for "good fortune," "wealth," or "so the business will go well," the bland summations that are offered in passing to curious anthropologists, but in response to disastrous financial reversals and failed enterprises. The volatility of the market, the seeming arbitrariness of success or failure, is consistent with perceptions of how the spirits behave: do well by them and they grant you good fortune; offend them and they harass you (Kendall 1977, 1985b: ch. 6).

Consider, for example, Mrs. Pok's story. She is the child of a shaman and has honored the spirits throughout her adult life. Her husband had worked for a major electronics firm but was forced into early retirement in his forties.[16] Now it was Mrs. Pok who went into business. In 1994 she opened a florist shop in a neighborhood where there were several other similar shops.[17] She had been in business for only a short while when someone placed an order with her for 1,400,000 wŏn (U.S. $1,750). The shopkeepers in the neighborhood said that this was an unprecedented windfall for a new business. She began to dream of securing a major account from her husband's former company. Mrs. Pok, her shaman mother, and just possibly her neighbors attributed her early good fortune to the benevolence of the spirits that the shaman mother had zealously invoked and propitiated on Mrs. Pok's behalf.

But then, only a few months later, business was off. For three weeks, barely a customer a day visited her shop. Now the neighboring florists confirmed her dismay, telling her that this was not normal. This sudden falling off of business was ominous, suggestive of divine displeasure. Mrs. Pok began to suffer pains in her legs, a further confirmation that a kut was in order. The spirits who appeared at her ceremony affirmed that yes, a ritual lapse had left her vulnerable to misfortune. They also suggested that her shopkeeping neighbors had taken ritual measures to shore up their own good fortune at her expense.[18] She was told to perform ritual countermeasures, avoid any food bestowed by her neighbors, and cast salt in the wake of any rival shopkeeper who might drop by for a visit.

If kut such as these articulate the worldview of petty capitalist entrepreneurs who inhabit a new and precarious economic terrain, how representative are these people among the shamans' clients? I gained my initial impression from rituals performed by shamans with whom I have enjoyed long and close ties and who are used to my working among them. I am aware that certain shamans are renowned for particular specialties: astute divinations, curing, or successful initiations. I wanted to be certain that this new emphasis on business success and failure was not simply an artifact of specialization among the network of shamans I knew or, in their terms, of the particular spirits that "play well" with them.

THE SMALL RANDOM SAMPLE

In the summer of 1994 I made random observations of 18 kut and minor offerings *(ch'isŏng).* Two of these I attended in the company of Yongsu's Mother. For the rest, I bumbled into commercial shaman shrines in the mountains surrounding Seoul and, with the aid of a smooth-talking research assistant, gained permission to observe and ask questions.[19]

Although commercial shrines were known in Korea from dynastic times (Korean Mudang and Pansu 1903:204), they have flourished in recent years in response to the constraints of apartment living and antinoise ordinances designed specifically to suppress the shamans' activities (Hwang 1988:18; Sun 1991:163). Here, room by room, different regional styles are performed simultaneously, their distinctive rhythms and stories spilling into the common courtyard in a montage of action and sound, a postmodern ritual happening. . . .[20] But the summer is a slow season, and the record-breaking heat of the summer of 1994 was particularly daunting.[21] On those sweltering July days when even popular shrines were silent, we could usually find some shaman at work with her clients on the hillside behind one particular shrine in an area sacred to the mountain god *(sansin'gak).*[22]

Shamans and clients were necessarily suspicious of a foreign observer with a notebook and a camera, sometimes confusing the role of scholar with that of the journalist who would splash the intimate details of their kut onto the pages of the popular press. A few had suffered unpleasant exposure in the past. Some of the clients were performing covert rituals and were anxious lest their husbands discover what they had been up to. Because many Seoul shamans were now aware and proud of international scholarly interest in their work, my academic credentials were helpful, up to a point. But I was more effective in establishing rapport when I described my own involvement in the shaman world as a client who had sponsored rituals, had prayed on sacred mountains, and was familiar with the ritual vocabulary.

In each instance, I combined a brief interview with hours spent observing the interactions between clients, gods, and ancestors. The advice and recriminations put forth by the spirits revealed the client's motivation for sponsoring a kut and allowed me to retrieve a more full-blooded story than could be garnered, out of context, by simply asking "Why are you doing this?" Questions posed of clients before the start of a ritual usually prompted cursory summations: "I'm doing this for my business," "My husband is ill," "Things aren't going so well." Such pro forma remarks, precisely because they are pro forma, lend themselves to tabulation, and had I chosen to rush from ritual to ritual and shrine to shrine, firing questions on the way, I might have garnered a satisfactory universe of quantifiable data. I would not, however, have gained a textured sense of what these rituals were all about and would never have retrieved Mrs. Pok's story, as recounted above. Before her kut, she had told me that she was holding the ritual because of the pain in her legs. After we had watched for a while, she went on at great length about her suspicions regarding her neighbors. "People are greedy," she said. "They might even take ritual measures" (as she, herself, was taking ritual measures).

My initial hunch was correct. Fully 15 of the 18 sponsors of kut were engaged in some form of small business, although they ranged across a spectrum of wealth and opportunity from the proprietors of small factories, a mushroom-importing business, restaurants, and shops, to a freelance furniture mover, the proprietress of a hole-in-the-wall bar, and an electrician. Divinations revealed that in addition to these enterprises, several of the female sponsors were also involved in various real estate ventures.[23]

Although dissident intellectuals within the Korean Popular Culture Movement (Minjung Munhwa Undong) romanticize shaman practices as expressing the concerns of the most victimized segments of Korean society (K. Kim 1994)—and some kut do (see Kendall 1977; S. N. Kim 1989a, 1989b)—only three of the sponsors in my sample would in any sense fit the profile of marginalized proletarians: a retired laborer who now worked in his brother's factory and had incurred a huge debt through a fraud perpetrated by his own son-in-law, a domestic worker married to a laborer whose daughter had gone mad, and a floating bar hostess who aspired to a bar of her own. Conspicuously absent from my sample were the households of salaried corporate workers and civil servants, those who inhabit the more secure and respectable rungs of the Korean middle class. I did hear in shrines, and in conversations with shamans, how the wives of these men would sponsor kut to secure their husbands' promotions, and that high monopolists would themselves sponsor kut.[24] But on my random visits to the shrines, I did not encounter them.

I suspect that members of the upper middle class hold their rituals in more discreet settings and that these events are more likely to enter the field notes of scholars who work closely with "superstar shamans" (Chungmoo Choi's [1991] term). It is also logical that households whose futures rest upon the relative stability and predictability of corporate life or civil service would be far less inclined to sponsor rituals than would those imbued with the "adventurous, aggressive, risk-taking, high-roller element" that has had as much or more to do with capitalism than has Calvin's or Max Weber's Protestant ethic (Taussig 1995:394). Despite great variation in the circumstances of the petty capitalist entrepreneurs who are the majority of my sample, they have in common a need for gambler's luck. The internal dramas of their kut turn on risk, uncertainty, and the potential for sudden and severe loss.[25]

In all but five of the rituals in my sample, business success was a salient concern, while prognostications of wealth or good business were routinely promised by the spirits in every single ritual.[26] Several kut were held in response to loss or the threat of loss—two failing restaurants, a fraudulent claim on an order of mushrooms, responsibility for a debt fraudulently incurred by another, and Mrs. Pok's flower shop. Business concerns sometimes came bundled with other issues, like the pain in Mrs. Pok's legs or Mrs. Yi's aches and pains, or when financial anxieties caused husbands to drink to excess, undermine their health, and abuse their wives.

MATERIALIST SPIRITS

The spirits that shamans manifest solidly inhabit the world of family enterprise.[27] Their songs and divinations package auspicious prognostications in the imagery of client enterprises. For Mrs. Pok, "Bunches of flowers are going in [to fill a large order]; whether sitting or standing you will hear the sound of the door [opening constantly for clients] . . . . Those who come in will not leave empty-handed. The luck of the XX Flower Shop will open wide." For the electrician, "Though my client goes east, west, south, and north . . . I will help so that there will be no power failure." For a family that runs a travel agency, the spirit Official of the vehicle (Ch'a Taegam) will "seize the front tire and seize the back tire and move the vehicle to an auspicious place."

The apprentice shaman Sim Myŏnghŭi claimed the active presence of a particular spirit, Grandfather Sage (Tosa Harabŏji), whom her colleagues described as "an ancestral grandfather who studied a great deal—honor him and you will get lots of money." I was not familiar with this spirit. He had not been a significant presence in the rituals I observed in the 1970s, although the shamans assured me that he had a venerable pedigree. He seems to be enjoying a great surge of popularity, for in addition to the Yi and Pak family kut, a Grandfather Sage was also found among the Protestant American ancestors of my husband's family. Grandfather Sage appears in kut wearing the long, broad-sleeved robe and crownlike hat of a man of letters, the very costume worn by a mannequin in scholarly pose in the American Museum of Natural History's Korea exhibit. But when Sim Myŏnghŭi manifests Grandfather Sage, she gives him the full-bellied waddle of a rich man, rather than the decorous gait of a literatus.[28] This conflated imagery is well-suited to Grandfather Sage's message. Like Kwan Myŏngnyŏ's father, who entered her shrine as a Spirit Warrior and subsequently helped his children gain wealth, the Grandfather Sage is among those potent ancestors who, if recognized and honored, benefit the family, but who, if neglected, bring hardship and strife. Grandfather Sage's ancestral wisdom and virtue, his cultural capital (Bourdieu 1977:188–189), are overliterally transformed into economic capital. (Grandfather Sage is definitely not what those commentators had in mind who maintain that a "Confucian" heritage predisposes Koreans for capitalism.)

Good clothes, comfortable housing, and private cars give the shamans' clients visible evidence of new identities constructed upon material success. The shamans themselves flourish jewelry and clothing as signs of a successful practice, advertisements of the efficacy of their spirits. The simple robes of synthetic gauze they wore during rituals back in the 1970s are now often made of heavy satin and fairly blossom with embroidery and spangles. . . . Even the spirits' tastes are changing, as bottles of whisky, imported fruit, and American brand-name candy appear among the offerings in the shrines. . . . For shaman and client alike, the assertion that money makes nobility is a counterhegemonic validation of their own experience, at once a wry comment upon and a celebration of contemporary materialism. Korean elites claim just the opposite, that social standing is not merely a function of money, but of education, breeding, and family background, attributes that are commonly invoked in discussions of Korean values and have a practical validity in elite and middle-class matchmaking (Kendall 1996a).[29] Families like the Kims, the Paks, and the Yis claim to value these same qualities, and yet they also know that such significant social capital will not be theirs within the present generation.

The Korean elite—a constellation of capitalist, military, and political interests—has flowered in the late 20th century from roots struck in the colonial period. This group is an awkward replacement for the landed Confucian nobility who were politically dispossessed under Japanese rule, then saw the land reform that followed liberation complete the erosion of their economic dominance in the countryside.[30] Eckert describes how early Korean capitalists of the colonial period found it necessary to construct an image of the businessman as a moral paragon to circumvent the old neo-Confucian contempt for commerce (Eckert 1991:225). The absence of a self-justifying ideology for the new capitalist class is resolved, in part, by traditionalist assertions of familism and education, a claiming of the moral high ground to which the newly minted middle class might also aspire. At the same time, old school ties and family connections are mustered as an instrumental means of advancing elite interests while preserving a monopoly of privileged access to information and power (O. Cho 1987; D. Kim 1990).[31] But the new elite has not successfully appropriated the respect once accorded scholar-officials and learned gentry, nor are they likely to in the wake of the corruption scandals that exploded at the end of 1995. Portrayals of the lifestyles of monopolist families in the popular press and in television soap operas convey a double-edged image of wealth and power, at once celebratory and critical. A similar ambivalence may be found in shaman rituals where families like the Yis and the Paks recognize the worth of family background, education, and breeding but also know that they cannot call these things their own. Instead, Sim Myŏnghŭi manifests for them a noble ancestor in a waddling comic portrayal whose very existence is evidenced in their own financial gain.

The portrayal of greedy spirits in kut becomes a fun-house mirror of client (and also shaman) aspirations as the spirits proclaim, "Your greed is even greater than my own." . . . [32] The supernatural Official who figures so prominently in rituals for good fortune, promising wealth in exchange for cash but always with the threat of ruin, becomes a ready parody of investment particularly well suited to the current zeitgeist. Chungmoo Choi suggests that in Korean shaman ritual, the constant boundary crossings between real and unreal, between obvious performance and claims for the literal presence of the spirits, engage the participants in a manner akin to Brechtian theater, causing them to reflect upon their own immediate condition (Choi 1989). If, as the shaman Yongsu's Mother sees it, anxiety over money ultimately makes people ill, then the antics of the spirits are therapeutic insofar as they parody the very ambitions they extol, injecting a capacity for laughter into the serious business of finance. Yongsu's Mother tells a droll story about a ritual held for the proprietress of a small bar, the sort of place where men are extravagantly overcharged for small amounts of liquor and titillation; indeed, the bar is almost its own parody of conspicuous consumption. The proprietress had boasted that although her rent is high, clients run huge tabs and she can easily take in a million wŏn (U.S. $1,250) in an evening. On one occasion, a sodden company president, drinking alone, produced a million-wŏn money order to cover his tab, and when the proprietress claimed to have no change, he staggered off into the night leaving the ridiculously large sum in her hands.[33] Sober the next day, he returned to ask if he hadn't mistakenly given her a million-wŏn money order. She callously told him that it was too late, the deed was done. When the supernatural Official played at her ritual, he/Yongsu's Mother stretched out his/her hand and demanded, "Give me a million-wŏn money order."

"Auntie, how ever did you know?"

"This isn't my auntie, this is the Official."

"I don't have it anymore. I spent it all on the business."

The transactions between supernatural Official and bar proprietress, proprietress and patron, shaman and client blur like the whirling riders on a carousel, spun round to the predictable rhythm of the contraption.

CONCLUSION

The gamble of the marketplace assumes the possibility of luck, nurtured in the Korean shaman shrines in abiding relationships with the spirits. The shamans who perform into being the Spirit Warrior of Commerce or the Supernatural Official of the Florist Shop offer connections with a spirit world that matches their clients' own. Relationships with the spirits are conducted in the idiom of a bargain and rituals function as investments conducted with a touch of self-satire, a bubble of wry humor. Despite the wicked impulse to pun in my title, it should be obvious by now that I do not see shamanic practices as fueling a particularly Korean "spirit" of high-risk capitalism. Max Weber, who held that advanced capitalism moved to the drumbeat of "rationalization" and had no place for spirits and magic, who explicitly distinguished his "spirit of capitalism" from "the impulse to acquisition, pursuit of gain, of money" (Weber 1958:14, 17), would undoubtedly turn over in his grave at the things described here. These stories from the Korean shaman world are more in sympathy with R. H. Tawney's remarks in his foreword to the English translation of Weber's *The Protestant Ethic and the Spirit of Capitalism,* suggesting that while much can be learned by tracing the influence of religious

ideas on economic development, "It is no less instructive to grasp the effect of the economic arrangements accepted by an age on the opinion which it holds of the province of religion" (Tawney 1958:11).

We have learned from the work of Jean Comaroff (1985), David Lan (1985), June Nash (1979), Aihwa Ong (1987), Lesley Sharp (1993), Michael Taussig (1980), and others that religion is neither a dead nor a fixed category, but an instrument of popular consciousness. If, however, we consider only the religions of the oppressed, the consciousness of disadvantaged and marginalized peoples, we risk replicating older dichotomies: the oppressed practice an inarticulate and natural-seeming popular religion (Bourdieu's *doxa*), while the dominant class espouses rationality or at least rational-seeming orthodoxies (Bourdieu 1977:169; Thomas 1971:666). Jean Comaroff (1994) has recently cautioned against stereotypic dualisms that make the cosmic chaos of modernity the flip side of traditional order and that spatialize this contrast as "the West and the rest." I am concerned lest an otherwise fruitful interest in the religious consciousness of the oppressed lead us to ignore the rest. As we have seen, the religious practices of Korean petite bourgeoisie, no less than those of the peasants, miners, and proletarians described in other places, are a means of apprehending, of attempting to exert some control over the seemingly arbitrary motions of the political economy.

While this study owes much to Michael Taussig's insight that capitalism breeds its own wily magic, the clients one meets in the shaman shrines of Seoul are worlds apart from the Colombian cane-cutters of his account, the recently proletarianized peasants who do not yet accept a moral order in which capitalist commodities define human relationships (Taussig 1980). Mrs. Pok, Kwan Myŏngnyŏ's sister, and the Kims, Paks, and Yis have journeyed not between two distinct modes of thought but, at most, from market-oriented family farms to more expansive family-centered urban enterprises. They are a petite bourgeoisie in the classic Marxist sense; they control their own elementary means of production, be it a small shop, an electrician's tool kit, a furniture-mover's truck, or a stock of imported mushrooms. Albeit they do not in any sense control the market forces that govern their enterprises. They accept the terms of the marketplace, but like many in similar circumstances, they regard the market as animate, arbitrary, and risk-ridden. In Taussig's reading of Marx, they are, with the rest of the capitalized world, within the domain of the commodity fetish (Taussig 1980:31).

The lost world of their youth was not a place of precapitalist innocence.[34] Korean farmers have long been engaged in grain production for the market and have measured their gains against rent and taxes.[35] The metaphoric linkage of house and household in the beliefs and practices I observed in the 1970s, a system that acknowledged the danger of wealth carried in and out of the house walls, was an appropriate reflection of the small family farm within an increasingly commercialized economy. A few decades ago, sudden and often inexplicable illness posed the most dire threat to the integrity and continuity of the rural family. Today, entrepreneurs' households are vulnerable to human fallibility, to bad debts, thieving employees, and fraud, and to the fluctuations of the overheated market. A system of religious practices oriented toward the health, harmony, and prosperity of the small family farm has been adapted to a world in which these concerns still apply but where the fate of the family, for good and ill, is seen as dangling on volatile external forces in a moment of intense opportunity and danger. The shaman's perception that in the past, shamanic rituals were usually held in response to life-threatening illness whereas now most kut are held in the hope of riches makes perfect sense in light of the medical options and economic possibilities of the 1990s. This is a matter of calibration, not a radical transformation.[36]

In a similar fashion, the popular religion of China's recommercialized Canton delta and of thoroughly industrialized Taiwan offers exaggerated promises of wealth and commercial success through an extant ritual language of blessings and good fortune, a language developed by family farmers engaged in a market economy.[37] The study of popular religion in the booming economies of eastern Asia does not yield a facile contrast between capitalist and precapitalist modes of production and consciousness. Instead, one finds yet another instance of how "lived realities defy easy dualisms, . . . worlds everywhere are complex fusions of what *we* like to call modernity and magicality, rationality and ritual, history and the here and now" (Comaroff and Comaroff 1986:5).[38]

A client who drives her supernatural Official to South Mountain for a drink of wine and the spirit who requests the company president's million-wŏn money order may provoke a smile. These developments are not without humor to shaman and client as they reflect upon what their world has become. In humor, they remind us to take popular religion seriously as one means by which some "modern" and "middle-class" people both play and reflect upon a game whose odds are most likely stacked against them.

NOTES

Acknowledgments. Research for this paper was supported by the Korea Research Foundation and the American Museum of Natural History Belo-Tanenbaum Fund. I am grateful to the shamans and clients who have allowed me to observe their rituals. Diana Lee's videotapes and our transcripts made it possible to retrieve Kwan Myŏngnyŏ's story in her own words. Ms. Seong-ja Kim served as my research assistant in the summer of 1994 with great skill and fortitude. This paper owes its inspiration to Robert Weller's (1994) imaginative study of ghost cults in Taiwan. Eun Mee Kim shared her valuable knowledge of Korean businesses and Homer Williams provided statistical information. I am grateful for comments from Chungmoo Choi, Roberte Hamayon, Seong-Nae Kim, Robert Weller, and Homer Williams. Marjorie Mandelstam Balzer, Clark Sorensen, and Edith Turner had many helpful things to say when they reviewed this manuscript for the *American Anthropologist.* I alone am responsible for the shortcomings of this effort.

1. In Seoul and its environs, shamans are called *mudang, mansin,* and, more recently, *posal.*

2. The inflated costs of kut, now figured in millions of wŏn (or thousands of U.S. dollars) have undoubtedly also discouraged the performance of double-length rituals.

3. In my previous work, I have used pseudonyms that approximate terms of address (Yongsu's Mother) or professional nicknames (Chatterbox Mansin) to protect the confidentiality of my informants. When Diana Lee and I began to film shamans, we asked our subjects how they wished to be credited for their work and raised the possibility of using pseudonyms. They desired recognition and requested that they be credited with their legal names (such as Kwan Myŏngnyŏ), although these names are almost never used in social contexts. Where I use quotations and incidents derived from videotapes of these shamans, I follow the later style for consistency and so as not to link a confidential alias with a visual image.

4. See Harvey 1987:156; Y. Kim 1977:208; and Lee 1977.

5. In writing about the Korean shaman world I use the term *god* for spirits in a shaman's or a household's pantheon who have powers above and beyond those of ordinary ancestors, although they may once have been ancestors. I use *spirits* as a broad general term for all of the entities evoked and tended by shamans, including both gods and ancestors. (The shamans seem to use *sin* to refer to gods but sometimes in a more general sense as well.) Some scholars of religion are uncomfortable with the *god* designation since the shaman's spirits do not evidence an ontologically transcendent position—indeed they enter into bargains with the living (Roberte Hamayon, personal communication, March 1993). Terminology is a fundamental obstacle in the study of comparative religions. Tambiah suggests that distinctions between "sovereign deity and manipulable divine being were the product of a specific historical epoch in European history and its particular preoccupations stemming from Judaeo-Christian concepts and concerns" (Tambiah 1990:20–21). I write of a non-monotheistic religious tradition and am wary of applying hierarchical standards derived from an utterly different context. It will be recognized that terms such as *god, spirit,* and *shaman* are, at best, approximations of local concepts.

6. See Darlin 1990 and Emerson and Martin 1991:12–17.

7. Sociologist Hagen Koo writes that "In the late 1950s, four out of five working people were farmers but in less than thirty years only one in five remained on the farm. . . . The magnitude of change South Korea has experienced in the past three decades was greater than that experienced by European countries over a century" (Koo 1990:672). Perhaps Koo overstates the case, insofar as the rural population of the 1950s was swollen with war refugees and with return migrants from Manchuria, northern Korea, and Japan after the liberation in

1945 (Cumings 1981: ch. 2), but there can be no doubt that a major transformation took place.

8. See Amsden 1989; Eckert et al. 1990: ch. 20; Haggard et al. 1991; Koo and Kim 1992; and Moskowitz 1982.

9. See *Agricultural Census* 1960:80–81; *Korea Statistical Yearbook* 1990:99; and H. Williams 1982: tables.

10. See Eun Mee Kim 1991:280–281 for a discussion of Korean economic policy. See Seung-Kuk Kim 1987 and Hagen Koo 1987 for discussions of class and perceptions of class.

11. His mother had probably dedicated him to the Seven Stars in Yongsu's Mother's shrine, ensuring their protection and also establishing a fictive kinship of "mother" and "son" (Kendall 1985b:80–81).

12. *Korea Newsreview* 1992a, 1992c, 1992d.

13. As in all other kut, other family issues were also addressed. On this occasion, the spirits expressed concern for the husband's lack of diligence, for the (absent) mother-in-law's health, for the wife's prospects of reversing a tubal ligation, and for the daughter's minor medical problems.

14. As a parallel explanation she attributed the immediate source of the woman's pain to a bungled ritual. Mrs. Yi had ill-advisedly paid a large sum of money to an incompetent shaman who, midway into her initial chant, had shouted "The spirits are stirred up, get out of here!" This, of course, had merely made the spirits angry since they had been led to anticipate a full ceremony. Predictably, the telling of this story led Yongsu's Mother into a tirade against the numerous incompetent, irresponsible, and immoral shamans practicing today.

15. In 1979 the government extended protection to small enterprises in certain areas of manufacture and in 1985 simplified procedures for licensing businesses. In 1992 protection extended to small businesses in certain areas of manufacture was lifted (Eun Mee Kim, personal communication, June 24, 1992, and *Korea Newsreview* 1992d).

16. Roger Janelli and Dawnhee Yim, writing of the salaried elite within a major South Korean conglomerate in the late 1980s, describe a relatively stable pattern of employment, with most resignations occurring among more recent hires. Resignations were possible after an unfavorable transfer or when given pointed indications that one's performance was unsatisfactory (Janelli 1993:152–155). Writing more generally, and in the troubled economy of the early 1990s, Denise Lett gained the impression that many white-collar workers were either terminated at midcareer or given the incentive to resign through lack of promotion (Lett 1994:109, 150–151). My field assistant readily recognized the early retirement of Mrs. Pok's husband as part of a current trend.

17. Although she denied any prior business experience, we may assume that Mrs. Pok, like many Korean housewives, had at the very least invested money in informal credit associations.

18. The term *yebang* means "prevention" or "prophylaxis." I had encountered it previously in ritual contexts as an exorcistic measure to prevent future misfortune, but here it was described in a manner suggestive of sorcery.

19. On a few occasions, we were refused access and I chose not to press the matter.

20. The public shrines offer a number of services in addition to renting rooms. They provide vessels for the offering food, cook the offering rice and steam the rice cake that the shamans or the clients provide, cater meals on request, and vend cigarettes, drinks, and tonics. Some shrines also maintain grottos for a streamlined version of the mountain pilgrimage (described in Kendall 1985b:128–131). I made a point of visiting both "up-market" and "down-market" shrines, those that seemed to draw renowned shamans and wealthy clients, and those that seemed to draw marginal people for abbreviated rituals, some performed by what were, to my subjective gaze, incompetent shamans. They did not manifest a full pantheon of deities and provided only the most stereotypic ancestral wailing and reproaches. Yongsu's Mother considers ancestral manifestations the easiest segment of a kut and is highly judgmental of shaman competence. See note 14 above.

21. One of the shrines that I visited had air-conditioned its small chambers, but the others relied upon cross-drafts and electric fans.

22. These rituals (ch'isŏng), although not as elaborate as full-dress kut, included manifestations of the gods and ancestors in tragicomic portrayals and the giving of divinations (kongsu). Four ch'isŏng have been included in my sample of 18 rituals.

23. In some cases, the businesses were run by the women who themselves sponsored the kut. In others, the business was a family enterprise—two of the restaurants and the mushroom-importing business—or more exclusively the husband's domain—the two small factories, the electrician, and the mover.

24. In his study of the Poongsan Corporation, Choong Soon Kim describes a steel plant manager who makes offerings to the spirits (kosa) for the prosperity and safety of the plant (C. S. Kim 1992:101–104).

25. These kut resonate with the observations of other scholars working in industrialized societies who find that rituals crop up with great intensity and elaboration in those times and places where uncertainty and chance play the greatest role (Bocock 1974; Gillis 1985:260–261). Resonant, too, is the observation of the 17th-century folklorist, Sir Thomas Browne: "'Tis not ridiculous devotion to say a prayer before a game at tables" (quoted in Thomas 1971:115).

26. Three of these kut were intended to satisfy the troubled souls of the dead (chinogi kut), including one "ghost wedding" so that a dead bachelor would stop hampering the marital prospects of his nieces and nephews. One ritual was held on behalf of an insane daughter, and one small ritual was held to counter the inauspicious potential of a bad horoscope year (although the sponsor also seemed to be having difficulties with her stepchildren).

27. Korean shamans do not claim a one-on-one possession so much as an experience of visions and inspiration sufficient to sense the spirits' will and perform it into being (Kendall 1996b).

When manifesting spirits that inhabit the world of family enterprise, a shaman might proclaim: "I am the Spirit Warrior of Business, the Spirit Warrior of Commerce, the Electrician's Spirit Warrior (Changsa Sinjang, Yŏngŏp Sinjang, Chŏnŏpkisul Sinjang)." "I am the Official of Commerce, the Official of the Automobile, the Commerce Official of the XX Flower Shop (Sangŏp Taegam, Chagayong Taegam, XX Hwawŏn Sangŏp Taegam)." For the proprietors of a faltering rib restaurant (*kalbijip*): "I am the Official of the Kitchen, the Official of the Kitchen Knife [particularly important in a rib house], the Official of the Restaurant Counter (Chubang Taegam, Chubang K'al Taegam, K'aunt'ŏ Taegam)."

In one kut, a male shaman (*paksu mudang*), speaking for the spirit Officials, claimed that the Officials of Business and Commerce appear only when the female shamans perform, that *his* Officials play on a high mountain, that they are more elevated than those that succor business pursuits. His remark not only echoes the old Confucian bias against commerce but also affirms the stereotype of Korean women as being temperamentally suited to business schemes and haggling.

28. For example, the scholar's gait is parodied in the Yangju Pyŏl Sandae Nori masked play.

29. *Kamun* (family background) and *hakpŏl* (educational background) are, with age, the most frequently mentioned concerns of matchmakers who attempt to join like with like. The expressed purpose of having relatives of both sides attend an arranged first meeting (*massŏn*) is to observe the two marriage candidates' deportment and table manners, as an indication of their breeding, and to gain some sense of family deportment (Kendall 1996a: ch. 4).

30. See O. Cho 1987; Eckert 1991; and Koo 1987.

31. Matrimonial links among monopolist families, and between monopolist and well-placed political families, have so intrigued the popular imagination that they have been described in women's magazines (Pae 1984; Yi 1983), elaborated in a book-length monograph (reviewed in *Korea Newsreview* 1992b), and even prompted the *Wall Street Journal* to publish an elaborate kinship diagram (Darlin 1992). In the recent scandal regarding the finances of former president No, a great deal was made of his family's marriage alliance with a monopolist family.

32. The notion of greedy gods seems intrinsic to the humor of the kut I have observed, both past and present, an expression of the power of the spirits that borrows upon an imagery of corrupt officialdom dating from dynastic times (Kendall 1985b: ch. 1, 1985a; cf. Rutt and Kim 1974:293–333, et passim). Some authorities insist that the spirits' repeated demands for cash are a very recent and embarrassing addition to shaman practice (H. Cho 1985), but in very recent kut, this playful bantering seems to have been much reduced, in the interest of time, because shrine kut no longer draw the crowd of neighbors and kin who entered into these exchanges, and because many young clients are so inexperienced that they must be constantly coached. I noted that in the two rituals I observed in 1992 and in the one I sponsored that same spring, only a small number of bills from the initial fee were returned to the client for distribution during the kut. Sequences once marked by extensive banter were abbreviated to one or two exchanges.

33. Money orders are now commonly used in Korea in the absence of large-denomination currency.

34. Robert Weller (1994) makes a similar point in discussing the inapplicability of Taussig's formulation to cult activity in Taiwan.

35. Some would even claim that the commercialization of customary relationships in land and labor was already underway in some parts of Korea by the 18th century, while others would chart significant developments from the closing decades of the last century. (The debate is summarized in Eckert 1991: ch. 1.) The story of Korean agriculture under colonial rule (1910–45) is a tale of expanding markets, intense population pressure, increasing tenancy, and out-migration (Williams 1982). More recent decades saw intensive capitalization and mechanization as the rural population shrank (Sorensen 1988).

36. The oscillating emphasis on health or wealth is, in all kut, a matter of degree; prayers for wealth (chesu) have long been intertwined with wishes for health, harmony, and blessings, as noted in the healing (uhwan) kut for Grandfather Chŏn described in my first ethnography (Kendall 1985b: ch. 1) and in some of the cases described in this essay.

37. Myron Cohen, personal communication, 1992; Siu 1989; and Weller 1994.

38. Tambiah (1990) has illuminated how the commonsensical distinctions between "magic" and "rationality" that have been deployed in the study of non-Western religions are themselves anchored in the specificities of Judeo-Christian thinking and the particular history of the Enlightenment.

REFERENCES CITED

Agricultural Census
    1960   Seoul: Republic of Korea, Ministry of Agriculture and Forestry.
Amsden, Alice H.
    1989   Asia's Next Giant: South Korea and Late Industrialization. New York: Oxford University Press.
Bocock, Robert
    1974   Ritual in Industrial Society: A Sociological Analysis of Ritualism in Modern England. London: Allen and Unwin.
Bourdieu, Pierre
    1977   Outline of a Theory of Practice. Cambridge: Cambridge University Press.
Cho, Hung-youn
    1985   *Review of* Shamans, Housewives, and Other Restless Spirits: Women in Korean Ritual Life, by Laurel Kendall. Korea Journal 25(10):54–57.
Cho, Oakla
    1987   Social Resilience: In the Korean Context. Korea Journal 27(10):28–34.
Choi, Chungmoo
    1989   The Artistry and Ritual Aesthetics of Urban Korean Shamans. Journal of Ritual Studies 3(2):235–249.
    1991   Nami, Ch'ae, and Oksun: Superstar Shamans in Korea. *In* Shamans of the 20th Century. Ruth Inge-Heinze, ed. Pp. 51–61. New York: Irvington Publishers.

Comaroff, Jean
    1985   Body of Power, Spirit of Resistance: The Culture and History of a South African People. Chicago: University of Chicago Press.
    1994   Defying Disenchantment: Reflections on Ritual, Power, and History. *In* Asian Visions of Authority: Religion and the Modern States of East and Southeast Asia. Charles F. Keyes, Laurel Kendall, and Helen Hardacre, eds. Pp. 301–314. Honolulu: University of Hawaii Press.
Comaroff, John, and Jean Comaroff
    1986   Ethnography and the Historical Imagination. Boulder: Westview Press.
Cumings, Bruce
    1981   The Origins of the Korean War: Liberation and the Emergence of Separate Regimes. Princeton: Princeton University Press.
Darlin, Damon
    1990   Affluent Koreans Go on a Shopping Binge That Worries Officials. Wall Street Journal, February 9: 1, 6.
    1992   South Korea Contract Award Spotlights Marriage of the Nation's Political and Business Families. Wall Street Journal, August 21: A8.
Eckert, Carter J.
    1991   Offspring of Empire: The Koch'ang Kims and the Colonial Origins of Korean Capitalism 1876–1945. Seattle: University of Washington Press.
Eckert, Carter J., Ki-baik Lee, Young Ick Lew, Michael Robinson, and Edward W. Wagner
    1990   Korea Old and New: A History. Cambridge, MA: Ilchokak (Seoul), Publishers for the Korea Institute, Harvard University.
Emerson, Tony, with Bradley Martin
    1991   Too Rich, Too Soon. Newsweek, November 11: 12–17.
Gillis, John R.
    1985   For Better, for Worse: British Marriages, 1600 to the Present. Oxford: Oxford University Press.
Haggard, Stephan, Byung-kook Kim, and Chung-in Moon
    1991   The Transition to Export-Led Growth in South Korea: 1954–1966. Journal of Asian Studies 50:850–869.
Harvey, Youngsook Kim
    1987   The Korean Shaman and the Deaconess: Sisters in Different Guises. *In* Religion and Ritual in Korean Society. Korea Research Monograph, 12. Laurel Kendall and Griffin M. Dix, eds. Pp. 149–170. Berkeley: Center for Korean Studies, Institute of East Asian Studies, University of California.
Hwang, Rusi
    1988   Han'guginǔi kut kwa mudang (Shamans and *kut* of the Korean people). Seoul: Munǒnsa.
Janelli, Roger L., with Dawnhee Yim
    1993   Making Capitalism: The Social and Cultural Construction of a South Korean Conglomerate. Stanford: Stanford University Press.
Kendall, Laurel
    1977   Caught between Ancestors and Spirits: A Field Report of a Korean *Mansin*'s Healing *Kut*. Korea Journal 17(8):8–23.
    1985a   Death and Taxes: A Korean Approach to Hell. Transactions of the Royal Asiatic Society, Korea Branch (Seoul) 60:1–14.
    1985b   Shamans, Housewives, and Other Restless Spirits: Women in Korean Ritual Life. Honolulu: University of Hawaii Press.
    1996a   Getting Married in Korea: Of Gender, Morality, and Modernity. Berkeley: University of California Press.
    1996b   Initiating Performance: The Story of Chini, a Korean Shaman. *In* The Performance of Healing. Carol Laderman and Marina Roseman, eds. Pp. 17–58. New York: Routledge.
Kim, Choong Soon
    1992   The Culture of Korean Industry: An Ethnography. Tucson: University of Arizona Press.
Kim, Dongno
    1990   The Transformation of Familism in Modern Korean Society: From Cooperation to Competition. International Sociology 5:409–425.
Kim Eun Mee
    1991   The Industrial Organization and Growth of the Korean *Chaebǒl:* Integrating Development and Organizational Theories. *In* Business Networks and Economic Development in East and Southeast Asia. Gary Hamilton, ed. Pp. 272–299. Hong Kong: University of Hong Kong Press.
Kim, Kwang-ok
    1994   Rituals of Resistance: The Manipulation of Shamanism in Contemporary Korea. *In* Asian Visions of Authority: Religion and the Modern States of East and Southeast Asia. Charles F. Keyes, Laurel Kendall, and Helen Hardacre, eds. Pp. 195–219. Honolulu: University of Hawaii Press.
Kim, Seong-Nae
    1989a   Chronicle of Violence, Ritual of Mourning: Cheju Shamanism in Korea. Ph.D. dissertation, Anthropology Department, University of Michigan.
    1989b   Lamentations of the Dead: The Historical Imagery of Violence on Cheju Island, South Korea. Journal of Ritual Studies 3(2):251–285.
Kim, Seung-Kuk
    1987   Class Formation and Labor Process in Korea: With Special Reference to Working Class Consciousness. *In* Dependency Issues in Korean Development: Comparative Perspectives. K. Kim, ed. Pp. 398–415. Seoul: Seoul National University Press.
Kim, Yung-Chung, ed. and trans.
    1977   Women of Korea: A History from Ancient Times to 1945. Seoul: Ewha Womans University Press.
Koo, Hagen
    1987   Dependency Issue, Class Inequality, and Social Conflict in Korean Development. *In* Dependency Issues in Korean Development: Comparative Perspectives. K. Kim, ed. Pp. 375–397. Seoul: Seoul National University Press.
    1990   From Farm to Factory: Proletarianization in Korea. American Sociological Review 55 (October): 669–681.
Koo, Hagen, and Eun Mee Kim
    1992   The Developmental State and Capital Accumulation in South Korea. *In* States and Development in the Asian Pacific Rim. R. P. Applebaum and J. Henderson, eds. Pp. 121–149. Newbury Park: Sage Publications.
Korea Newsreview
    1992a   Bankruptcies Highest Since '87. August 1: 15.
    1992b   Rich Marry Rich and Powerful. March 14: 32.

1992c   Small Firms in Trouble. March 14: 25.
1992d   Will the Doomsday of Small Businesses Come?
            August 1: 14.
Korea Statistical Yearbook
    1990   Seoul: Republic of Korea, Economic Planning Board,
            Bureau of Statistics.
Korean Mudang and Pansu
    1903   Korea Review (Seoul) 3:145–149, 203–208,
            257–260, 301–305, 342–346, 383–389.
Lan, David
    1985   Guns and Rain: Guerrillas and Spirit Mediums in
            Zimbabwe. Berkeley: University of California Press.
Lee, Hyo-chae [Yi Hyojae]
    1977   Protestant Missionary Work and Enlightenment of
            Korean Women. Korea Journal (Seoul) 17(11):33–50.
Lett, Denise Potrzeba
    1994   Family, Status, and Korea's New Urban Middle
            Class. Ph.D. dissertation, Department of Anthropology,
            University of Washington.
Moskowitz, Carl
    1982   Korean Development and Korean Studies—A Review
            Article. Journal of Asian Studies 42:63–90.
Nash, June
    1979   We Eat the Mines and the Mines Eat Us:
            Dependency and Exploitation in Bolivian Tin Mines.
            New York: Columbia University Press.
Ong, Aihwa
    1987   Spirits of Resistance and Capitalist Discipline:
            Factory Women in Malaysia. Albany: State University of
            New York Press.
Pae, Pyŏnghyu
    1984   Chaebŏlgaŭi hugyeja, sawi myŏnŭri (Monopolist
            families' heirs, son-in-law daughter-in-law). Yŏng Redi
            (Seoul) 8 (August): 124–129.
Rutt, Richard, and Kim Chong-Un, trans.
    1974   Virtuous Women: Three Classic Korean Novels.
            Seoul: Royal Asiatic Society, Korea Branch, for
            UNESCO.
Sharp, Lesley A.
    1993   The Possessed and the Dispossessed. Berkeley:
            University of California Press.
Siu, Helen F.
    1989   Agents and Victims in South China: Accomplices in
            Rural Revolution. New Haven: Yale University Press.
Sorensen, Clark
    1988   Over the Mountains are Mountains: Korean Peasant
            Households and Their Adaptations to Rapid
            Industrialization. Seattle: University of Washington Press.

Sun, Soon-Hwa
    1991   Women, Religion, and Power: A Comparative Study
            of Korean Shamans and Women Ministers. Ph.D.
            dissertation, Department of Religious Studies, Drew
            University.
Tambiah, Stanley Jeyaraja
    1990   Magic, Science, Religion, and the Scope of
            Rationality. Cambridge: Cambridge University Press.
Taussig, Michael
    1980   The Devil and Commodity Fetishism in South
            America. Chapel Hill: University of North Carolina
            Press.
    1995   The Sun Gives without Receiving: An Old Story.
            Comparative Studies in Society and History 37:368–398.
Tawney, R. H.
    1958   Foreword. In The Protestant Ethic and the Spirit of
            Capitalism, by Max Weber. New York: Charles Scribner's
            Sons.
Thomas, Keith
    1971   Religion and the Decline of Magic. New York:
            Scribner.
Weber, Max
    1958   The Protestant Ethic and the Spirit of Capitalism.
            Talcott Parsons, trans. New York: Charles Scribner's
            Sons.
Weller, Robert P.
    1994   Capitalism, Community, and the Rise of Amoral
            Cults in Taiwan. In Asian Visions of Authority: Religion
            and the Modern States of East and Southeast Asia.
            Charles F. Keyes, Laurel Kendall, and Helen Hardacre,
            eds. Pp. 141–164. Honolulu: University of Hawaii Press.
Williams, Homer Farrand
    1982   Rationalization and Impoverishment: Trends
            Affecting the Korean Peasant under Japanese Colonial
            Rule, 1918–1942. M.A. thesis, Department of History,
            University of Hawaii.
Wolf, Eric R.
    1966   Peasants. Englewood Cliffs, NJ: Prentice Hall.
Yi Kyŏngnam
    1983   Han'gugŭi honbŏl (Korea's marriage cliques). Chubu
            Saenghwal (Seoul) 4 (April): 261–267.

Claiming Legitimacy
Prophecy Narratives from Northern
Aboriginal Women

Julie Cruikshank

Anthropologists have often argued that prophets arise in times of radical social change. Prophets announce a vision of a society to come, and then, through their followers, either succeed in changing society or fail. In this essay, Julie Cruikshank claims that, at least for Athapaskan women in the Yukon, this understanding misses the point. Rather than being an exceptional event, prophecy was probably a regular part of aboriginal life. Further, prophets are not understood as emerging to change society. Instead, people invoke their words, long after their deaths, as after-the-fact explanations of the ways in which their society has changed. In so doing, those who tell these stories claim legitimacy both for themselves and for their traditional culture. The repetition of prophecy thus reinforces the ethnic identity of its tellers, even as they join Christian or Baha'i religious movements.

Cruikshank presents narratives from four different types of prophecy present among the Athapaskans: prophecies in which the prophet journeys to a world where whiteness is a significant feature, prophecies predicting a changed world, prophecies in which the prophet is transported to heaven, and prophecies that center on the use of new religious symbols. In each case, she presents examples that give us insight into the ways, styles, textures, and patterns of Athapaskan prophecy.

This essay is powerful in its presentation of prophecy narratives, and important as well. It demonstrates the role of religion and prophecy in giving meaning to the lives of members of a community. It reminds us that religious understandings are extremely complex. Religions do not simply succeed or fail. Rather, they are molded by political, economic, and environmental factors and in turn help form the models through which people understand and negotiate their worlds and their identities.

As you read, consider these questions:
1. Why do Athapaskans consider it so important to tell prophecy narratives to children?
2. Four types of prophecy narratives are described in this essay. What elements do all four have in common?
3. How do the prophets described in this essay differ from the shamans described in earlier essays?

4. How are Athapaskan understandings of prophecy similar to and different from prophecy as it is generally understood in the Jewish, Christian, and Islamic traditions?

During 1992, compelling questions were raised—in the mass media, in museum exhibits, and in popular and academic writings—about the construction of history. The Columbus Quincentenary framed these issues on an international level. In Canada, debates were phrased with reference to local anniversaries. In British Columbia, for example, we heard a great deal about the bicentenary of Captain George Vancouver's visit to the West Coast of North America. In the Yukon Territory, where the 50th anniversary of the Alaska Highway construction was celebrated, some Aboriginal people questioned the appropriateness of eulogizing an event which had such farreaching implications for their lives. The year 1992 has become a metaphor for transition from a neo-colonial world to a post-colonial world (Hill 1992).

All of these anniversaries have highlighted concerns about *voice* in human history—whose voices are included and whose voices left out. Contesting the legitimacy of the dominant discourse is not new, of course. Certainly, a concern that many voices are systematically erased from written history has been recognized for a long time in northern Aboriginal communities. It is fundamental to the collaborative work which has engaged me in the Yukon where I lived for many years and where I continue to work. As feminists have pointed out, enlarging discourse involves much more than adding and stirring additional voices; there are fundamental methodological problems involved in rethinking familiar genres of historical narrative.

This paper examines prophecy narratives told by Aboriginal women from the Yukon Territory in the course of recording their life stories. When I first heard these narratives, I set them aside because I didn't understand how they fit into the larger autobiographical project. Yet the persistence with which prophecy narratives are told is compelling, and they provide an opportunity to frame some questions about how people use oral tradition to make connections between past and present.

One of the reasons I set these narratives aside is because of the scholarly literature about prophecy—in ethnohistory, in anthropology, in sociology—and, following academic convention, I wanted to spend some time reading that literature to locate narratives I was hearing in terms of a larger debate. The convention is not frivolous: we consult what has already been written to avoid the conceit that our interpretations are somehow original. Reading that literature, though, I was struck by how clearly our academic narratives can be seen as only one set among many. When we listen to contemporary Aboriginal people draw on oral narratives to explain the ways past connects with present, we encounter other narratives that compete with academic narratives for legitimacy.

The ongoing academic debate about prophecy seems to focus on the behavior, activities and predictions of particular prophets and to turn on two axes. In North American ethnohistory by historians and anthropologists, the central question seems to be whether prophetic movements were indigenous, or a response to European contact (Spier 1935; Wallace 1956; Suttles 1957; Aberle 1959; Walker 1969; Ridington 1978; Miller 1985; Abel 1986; Peterson 1988). In the more generalized sociological literature, shaped by Max Weber, the discourse concerns the success or failure of specific prophets, judged in terms of their ability to transform the social and political order.

I propose to shift the emphasis to analysis of narrative discourse (which I will argue is deeply embedded in social organization), from the activities of individual prophets to oral traditions—the narratives about prophets—that continue in contemporary communities, specifically in the western Subarctic near the upper Yukon River. While much of the scholarly literature treats prophecy as exceptional behavior needing analysis and interpretation, indigenous traditions in the southern Yukon Territory discuss prophecy as consistent with the routine behavior of shamans, well within the bounds of what these specialists were expected to do. It is the retrospective discussion of prophecy stories as routine explanations for contemporary events that is of particular interest. My broader question would be this: If these narratives are still told and understood in the 1990s as common sense explanations, what can this contribute to our understanding of indigenous discourse about connections between past and present, particularly when local explanation heads in a direction very different from the western scholarly debate?

The narratives I will discuss are all told by elderly Yukon Athapaskan women who are or were involved in long term work with the Yukon Native Language Centre.[1] The context in which they were told to me may be relevant and later we will turn to the more interesting question of how they are invoked in everyday conversation. Individuals who told these narratives were all selecting accounts they considered important to record and pass on to younger people. Some of the accounts they chose to tell concern late nineteenth century and early twentieth century prophecies, and it was clear from narrators' performances that they continue to take these narratives very seriously. The recurring theme is that particular shamans predicted social transformations that would accompany the arrival of Europeans, in some cases before they met the first whites. The inevitable point of these stories is that events that have subsequently come to pass were foretold long ago.

Two striking features about the process of narration are:

- That prophecy accounts are singled out from a much larger body of narratives as important stories to pass on to younger listeners, and
- That they are told as though they provide a kind of self-evident explanation, one that tellers consider routinely accessible to any listener.

It is precisely at the level of explanation that the accounts clash with scholarly discourse, where their meaning is taken to be far from self-evident. I would suggest that this makes them an ideal focus for ethnohistorical analysis by raising the question: What are the contexts in which these narratives continue to have meaning?

PROPHECY AND EXPLANATION: ACADEMIC NARRATIVES

The theoretical framework surrounding interpretation of prophecy has remained grounded in Max Weber's analysis of Old Testament prophets. Sociological explanation stems from Weber's classic definition which portrays prophets as emerging outside routine institutional order to contest the social and political authority of established leaders. The implication is that prophets are outsiders: charismatic but marginal individuals who challenge authority yet fail to transform the political and social order. Transferred to a Native American setting, such explanations may privilege an interpretation emphasizing early Euroamerican contact history, or resistance to external events such as disease, population decimation or natural disaster (e.g., Walker 1969).

This definition of prophecy as a response to external events transfers easily enough from sociological analysis to narrative analysis. Percy Cohen, for example, in an article reviewing theories of myth, proposed that prophecy is a kind of inversion of myth that develops when social organization breaks down and is no longer capable of explaining events, causing people to turn away from the past and toward the future (Cohen 1969:351–52).[2] Given the pervasiveness of this sociological framework, the "failure" of nineteenth century prophets seems inevitable.

Such explanations contrast sharply with those of Subarctic Aboriginal narrators who regard stories about prophecy as evidence not of failure but of successful engagement with change and detailed foreknowledge of events. These explanations speak directly to the issue of how one claims a legitimate voice in contemporary discussions about historical reconstruction (Kan 1991; Friedman 1992). Despite growing scholarly interest in indigenous ethnohistory, Native Americans' views of their own history remain rare in scholarly literature. As Sergei Kan has pointed out, those that do enter this literature demonstrate that (a) the past is regularly used to make sense of the present and to explain the current predicament of indigenous peoples in North America, and that (b) this discourse does not develop hermetically but in a dialogue with other ideologies. Subarctic prophecy narratives, for example, include elements of both the distant Plateau Prophet Dance[3] and Christianity. Elements of such different ideologies are carefully synthesized and incorporated into an existing narrative framework by indigenous peoples in their attempts to defend their past against Western-imposed discourses, incorporating new ideas rather than being colonized by them (see Kan for a detailed discussion of this).

In her thoughtful discussion of narratives told by Yukon elders about the coming of the first whites to Northwestern North America, Catharine McClellan has reminded us that aboriginal oral traditions are not simply one more set of data to be sifted for historical veracity, and that they "can be fully understood only in relation to the total bodies of literature in which they appear" (1970:128). For that reason, I attempt to discuss the broader indigenous narrative traditions within which prophecy stories fit on the upper Yukon River.

I would like to investigate the hypothesis that if prophecy narratives provide a conventional way of making sense of dislocating change, then the relevant framework for interpreting them may be with reference to prophecy's long-term cultural consequences rather than (as Weber would direct us) its short-term political effects (see Long 1986). This approach builds on the work of anthropologists who suggest that:

- Prophecy may have been more widespread in early times than Spier recognized (McClellan 1956, 1975:577; Suttles 1957; Ridington 1978);
- In the western Subarctic it has long provided a routine, conventional kind of explanation that makes sense of complex changes in familiar ways (McClellan 1963; Moore and Wheelock 1990:59–60);
- Indigenous narrative frameworks continue to have a capacity to make sense of anomalous events (McClellan 1970; Cruikshank 1990, 1992); and
- Prophecy narratives provide a striking example of how southern Yukon women, at least, draw on traditional narrative as an authoritative explanation of contemporary events, an explanation which competes with western discourse for legitimacy.

PROPHECY NARRATIVES FROM THE UPPER YUKON RIVER

From the mid 1970s to the mid 1980s I lived in the southern Yukon Territory documenting oral traditions, life stories, traditional narratives, place names, and songs. Initially I focused on a seemingly straightforward project of trying to

help balance a documentary record about Yukon Aboriginal history which relies disproportionately on the writings of traders, missionaries and government agents who were often lamentably uninformed about what they were describing. The ethnographic record was growing by the mid 1970s, with works by Catharine McClellan, Richard Slobodin, John Honigmann, and Asen Balikci. McClellan's two-volume ethnography (1975) had just appeared and fieldwork by Roger McDonnell (1975), Robin Ridington (1978), and Dominique Legros (1985) was only recently under way. Much of my work was done with elderly Athapaskan men and women with support from the Council for Yukon Indians, which provided honoraria for elders willing to record such accounts.

Frequently, elders chose to respond to questions about the past with a complex story, and only gradually did I come to recognize that many of these narratives shared a common scaffolding. My initial failure to recognize the patterns undoubtedly came from the scaffolding I brought to the project—a sense that these accounts could be viewed as archival documents rather than as fully developed narrative constructions of the past. What I am suggesting here is that a similar problem—an interpretive framework which predisposes us to interpret unfamiliar narratives in terms of familiar theoretical frameworks—may color our attempts to understand prophecy narratives as serious representations of the world.

The narrative structures shaping academic discourse about prophecy should also be kept in mind. Anthropologists writing about prophecy pay particular attention to the form and process of religious revitalization (Wallace 1956; Aberle 1972); historians show a preference for a discussion of the specific circumstances in which prophets arise (Miller 1985). Ethnohistorians, drawing on both frameworks, have described their project as incorporating Native American perspectives (Axtell 1981; Jennings 1982; Trigger 1982). Such a partnership surely should turn critical attention to the symbolic and structural nature of scholarly accounts as well as indigenous accounts and to closer investigation of social processes in which all our narrative accounts are embedded.

The documentary record from northwestern North America provides us with ample evidence of early missionaries' narratives about prophecy. Most missionaries described prophets as self-interested charlatans whose primary motive was to dupe unwitting members of their own community. For instance, one of the first Anglican missionaries in the northern Yukon in the 1860s, the Rev. Robert McDonald, included in his diaries regular reports of "pretensions to prophecy" with accounts of his injunctions advising Native people to stop "conjuring."[4] On June 23, 1863, McDonald reported:

> [S]ome (Indians) at Peel River have pretended to divine communications in which, among other things, they say they were told it is wrong to kill foxes and martens. But I need not specify more of their delusions.

Writing from down the Yukon River at Fort Yukon a few months later on September 9, 1863, he reported:

> An Indian who makes pretensions to prophetic authority was present. His pretensions are as follows: that he has supernatural communication with heaven, has received a command to teach his fellow man, that those who do not receive his instructions will be punished by God, that the end of the world will be ten years hence. . . . (He) also recommended that people not set fire to the woods because visiting angels do not like the smell of smoke (McDonald 1985).

A few days later, he claims to have encountered this same prophet, whom he identifies as Shahoo and reported he "had a talk with him about making pretensions to prophecy." He notes that he was "[g]lad to find him acknowledge that he felt he was in error, and he said he would endeavour to follow what he learnt out of the Bible." From then on, McDonald refers regularly to prophecy as "conjuring" (e.g., October 18, 1863: June 6, 1866).[5]

While Shahoo may have responded politely to accommodate the missionary, he must surely have found the injunction odd. The ethnographic record suggests that shamans in northwestern North America were routinely expected to locate and control game, to cure the sick, to ensure success in disputes with neighboring peoples, to foretell the future, to provide dietary rules and amulets to protect their clients—all duties enmeshed in behaviors that missionaries associated with what they called prophecy. Undoubtedly, some shamans in contact with missionaries also responded by incorporating Christian concepts and making them part of their own indigenous narratives as a way of strengthening their own influence (McClellan 1956:136–37). From the earliest stages of contact, then, discourse surrounding prophecy was contested.

Before introducing Aboriginal narratives, it is important to locate them—as McClellan (1970) advises—within the total body of literature in which they appear. Recent discussions about the nature of discourse in Subarctic hunting societies center on ways in which knowledge is accumulated, maintained and passed on, but also on ways in which legitimacy is claimed for particular kinds of explanations in opposition to other kinds of explanation (see especially Rushforth 1992, 1994). Attention has also turned to narrative frameworks shared by a narrator and his or her listeners and the ways in which shared metaphors are mutually understood and reproduced through oral tradition (Ridington 1990). Even when prophecy does not lead to short-term political and social transformations, it nevertheless may reproduce shared cultural meanings and underscore the importance of using familiar narrative frameworks to explain the present, particularly as it now is invoked by indigenous people to claim authoritative interpretations of their past.[6]

Prophecy narratives in the southern Yukon seem to fit within a constellation of narratives that address a longstand-

ing intellectual concern for northern hunters; that is, how humans and animals with their overlapping and often conflicting powers and needs can share the world (discussed in detail by McClellan 1975; McDonnell 1975). A recurring metaphor presents the world as incorporating two parallel realities—one, the dimension which underlies the secular, material, temporal world of everyday life; the other, a domain which could more aptly be called superhuman and timeless. At the beginning of time, the narratives state and restate, a physical boundary, the horizon, separated these dimensions. On one side of the horizon was a snow-covered winter world where everything was white.[7] On the other side, was the summer world full of color and warmth. Eventually, the animals trapped on the winter side conspired to puncture the boundary so that the world could be brought into balance through its alternating seasons. In narrative, however, these dimensions remain distinct and must be negotiated by all thinking beings, particularly the shamans who are more likely to travel between dimensions. Everyone has access to such journeys, the difference between the powers of a layman and a shaman are one of degree rather than kind (McClellan 1956).

In such narratives, a protagonist meets a superhuman being who takes him or her on a journey from the secular, material temporal world of everyday life to a supernatural, timeless domain. The two domains are marked off in some physical way. The protagonist may pass under a log, into a cave, or beyond the horizon to enter a world whose characteristics are usually the reverse of those found in the familiar world. One of the usual characteristics of this world, for example, is that everything, including humans and animals, is white. In such a world, the protagonist acquires new knowledge about proper behavior and, with great difficulty, brings that knowledge to the human world where it can benefit the community. Usually this knowledge includes instructions about how people should behave to ensure proper relations with game and with other humans, as well as the injunction that if certain guidelines are followed the world will be a better place. As a consequence of this experience, the protagonist usually returns as a shaman, often with a special song learned on the journey.[8] One of the points of such narratives is to dramatize the role of powerful beings in ushering in world transformations, specifically concerning relations between the human and natural worlds.

Southern Yukon elders tell a range of narratives in which prophets figure significantly and these stories seem to circle around related themes. Most of the prophecy narratives I have heard take the juxtaposition of these parallel worlds as a central metaphor and follow one of four distinct patterns. First, there are narratives which involve a protagonist's journey to a world where whiteness is a significant feature and s/he is able to return with predictions about the coming of white people. Second, there are narratives predicting world transformation in which the other dimension often described in terms of its whiteness becomes the world of ordinary experience. Third, are narrative journeys where the protagonist travels to heaven and returns as a shaman. Fourth, are the stories commemorating shamans who foresaw and incorporated symbols and ideas from other religious cosmologies. As the twentieth century draws to a close, these narratives are retrospectively presented as ushering in the transformations which have become part of the routine experience of contemporary Aboriginal peoples. Each of these four kinds of prophecy narrative is summarized below with examples of how and where they are used in public discussion.

CONTEMPORARY ACCOUNTS OF PAST PROPHETS

The first kind of prophecy narrative involves a protagonist's journey to a world where "whiteness" is a significant feature and where he or she acquires foreknowledge of the impending arrival of strangers.

A protagonist travels to a world where s/he learns about the eventual coming of white people and returns with talismans as proof, both of the journey taken and of the knowledge acquired. Kitty Smith, a Southern Tutchone woman in her nineties, tells a story which she calls "The First Time People Knew *K'och'en.*" The term *K'och'en* is the word in Tutchone and Southern Tutchone for "white people," *K'o* comes from the Tutchone word for "cloud," and *ch'en* from the word for "people," their fair skins implying they came from the "white" world removed from ordinary reality. In Mrs. Smith's narrative (Cruikshank et al., 1990:254–58) a young boy undertakes a journey with an invisible helper who guides him. He enters the unfamiliar dimension by walking under a rainbow, and receives instruction about what to eat, a bag of special (whiteman's) food, and a special song, all of which he is able to bring back with him. He returns to teach people about the habits of these strangers before white people arrive. He predicts that eventually "everyone will become whitemen."

A similar narrative is told by Rachel Dawson, a Tutchone-speaking woman who grew up at Fort Selkirk on the upper Yukon River. A protagonist whose journey takes him to the dimension inhabited by white animals and people returns as a shaman with a special song no one had ever heard. He uses his new powers to escort people to see these strangers, though he is the only one who can communicate with them. When his companions arrive, they see domestic (white) sheep wearing bells and pale people wearing "Japanese scarfs." He instructs his followers that if they try to communicate with the strangers, they will be responsible for his (the shaman's) death. Each of the white strangers ties a scarf around the neck of a Native man or woman and then the strangers disappear. One sheep is left as evidence of the meeting and the people return home with it, wearing their new item of clothing as further proof of the encounter. From that time on, the shaman or "doctor" is able to see and communicate with white people whenever he chooses. Part of the power he acquires includes (white) swan power, conventionally a symbol of a particularly powerful transformation (Dawson 1975; see also Ridington 1978, on the special characteristics of swan power among Dunne-Za).

A second kind of narrative is centered around a shaman's prediction of world transformation in which, with the coming of Europeans, the "other" unfamiliar world will engulf the world of ordinary reality.

Angela Sidney, a woman of Tagish and Inland Tlingit ancestry, tells a story about a shaman named Matal, who told people in 1912, "This ground is going to burn all over." She reported seventy years later about a time when she was ten years old:

I saw this old man, too: he was Indian doctor. One night he was singing: he made Indian doctor. In the morning, he told people: "This place is on fire all over." And people thought it was the flu. That flu was going to come in 1918, or whenever, when lots of people died. That's the one he talked about. That's just like fire, all. "Lots of people are going to die. But if you pray to God all the time, you are going to pass through this fire." In 1918, –19, –20, there was flu. Lots of people died (ibid.:155).

She goes on to describe the impact that epidemic had on her own family. She lost her father, her aunt, and several cousins. She, her mother, and her own children became ill. Everyone was relocated to the missionary's house where they could be fed and looked after. She continues with her account, and the entire point of her story is to indicate the clarity of Matal's vision:

That was the old man who said, "This world is on fire." That's the sickness. He sees it like fire. And when he died, before he died, he says he is going to come back again. "Tie your dogs a long way from the camp" he tells people. But you know nowadays people don't listen to each other—he was sick, badly sick, and they thought he was crazy, I guess. "In four days I'm going to come back," he said. Here on the fourth day, those dogs started to bark all over. They heard just like somebody's singing or something. That's what the dogs were barking at—the dogs chased that spirit away again. That's what they say. That's what I heard about him, that old man. Matal, they call him (ibid.: 156).

Elders are not the only members of the community who take prophecy seriously. At public hearings in 1975 on a proposed pipeline across the Yukon Territory, Joe Jack, a young Southern Tutchone man, spoke publicly about a Pelly River shaman[9] who had foreseen the coming of tremendous changes:

[H]e said that he saw many white people coming to this land and that they will build trails to travel on. He said they will block off waterways and they will tear up the land to take out rocks . . . lastly he said they will build an iron road that will not be driven on. And, he said, when this happens . . . it will be the end of the Indian people.[10]

Mr. Jack's point in invoking this prophecy at a public hearing underscored the vision embodied in the prediction, a vision whose meaning is understood to be ambiguous until after the event occurs. The fact that he chose to make that part of his formal testimony suggests that he considers it an example which speaks for itself—one which legitimizes local knowledge in the face of the scientific and bureaucratic discourse dominating these hearings.

Similarly, a younger Tutchone woman told me about a story passed on to her by her grandmother, reporting how an early prophet predicted that strangers from the "white snow-bound world" would bring white material culture which would do grave danger to indigenous people: she interprets that as foreknowledge of flour, salt, and sugar, all sources of health problems, all white. Her comments reformulate the claims made by health-care professionals about the dangers of excessive carbohydrates, salt, and starch but they do so in a locally meaningful idiom.

The contested nature of explanation is very much at issue here. Each of these accounts is told as a way of making intellectually consistent sense of disruptive changes—some past, some contemporary, some anticipated—with reference to an authoritative narrative framework.[11] Each is offered as evidence for the legitimacy of local knowledge and discourse.

A third kind of narrative involves a journey to heaven with the protagonist returning as a prophet or shaman.

Even before direct contact with Europeans, shamans visited heaven and returned with instructions about behavioral codes. In these stories, heaven often assumes the same dimensions as the "winter world" being bright, or white, and providing the protagonist with a new way of seeing.

A recurring theme in accounts of Yukon shamanism dramatizes how a particular shaman "died," visited an upper world and returned with new songs, new amulets and new guidelines. Such visits, McClellan suggests, were part of an old well-established pattern of shamanism (1975:556. See also Brown 1982, 1988 for parallel experiences in the eastern Subarctic).

Narratives about journeys to heaven follow this familiar framework. Southern Yukon elders, for example, report that they first learned about Christianity from a coastal shaman named Nasq'a who travelled to heaven. An old blind man, mistreated by his young wife, wandered off by himself in great distress. He was summoned by a stranger who restored his sight and led him on a journey from the world of ordinary reality (which is portrayed as appearing "blue") up a long ladder to a bright and shining place, heaven:

> Half of the Earth was dark, and Heaven was shining everywhere. There was no dark anywhere there. All the time there was sunshine and there were green leaves (McClellan 1975:554).

There, he met Jesus, learned powerful songs, mastered new behavioral codes and brought back physical evidence of his journey—a magical gunnysack. From then on, according to

John Joe, an elderly Southern Tutchone man who told me this story in the mid-1970s, he was able to tell his story by preaching like Christian missionaries.

A more detailed account of such a journey comes from Annie Ned, a Southern Tutchone woman who is now almost 100 years old. We are able to compare the narrative structure of her version with a brief account left by a missionary and echoing the conviction expressed by the Rev. McDonald fifty years earlier, that prophecy must be eradicated. Mrs. Ned's husband, Johnny, is remembered by many elders as a powerful shaman who was widely known as a prophet. Reportedly, he made a journey to heaven where he met with God and returned with the ability to speak and preach in English, and with a song sounding very much like a Christian hymn:

> I can't talk about Johnny: it might be we'd make a mistake. I can't speak for other people. I can't show my husband's song.[12] I can tell you what *happened,* though. To start with, he got [an] Indian song. That man doesn't know anything, doesn't talk [English]. How come he talked [English] that time? He started to talk. I thought he's gone crazy! So I got Mr. Young [the missionary], and he said, "Don't bother Annie. I think he's going to go somewhere [to heaven?]. He's believing [i.e., he's experiencing conversion]." My husband took control all over: Carmacks, Dawson, all over. He took it around, that control. . . . After he got power, he can heal people (Cruikshank et al., 1991:326).

In fact, the missionary, possibly the same "Mr. Young," left his own impressions about Johnny Ned's prophesies in an unsigned letter on file in the Anglican Church records, advising an incoming missionary about the delicacy of the situation. His frame of understanding is quite different from that provided by Mrs. Ned, and if he understood her interpretation of those events, that interpretation has certainly been marginalized in his competing narrative:

> There is a cult in existence in the Champagne district under the leadership of Johnny Ned. For the most part, his teaching is alright. However, he has some fantastic ideas and has mixed on [*sic*] some native superstition to Christianity. I think that it is better to recognize everything that is good in his teaching than to attempt to antagonize him. After a while, when you get to know him you may be able to steer him along the right lines. A great many Indians throughout the country have been more or less worked up over his teachings and some of them believe his story regarding visions that he has had. Mr. Swanson [another missionary] and I talked over the subject and agreed that it was better to approve of his teachings as far as they agreed with Christian and to emphasize the fact that what he is teaching is the religion of Christ as practised and taught for hundreds of years.[13]

Mrs. Ned and I have discussed this letter and she explicitly rejects this interpretation of her husband's powers, situating him firmly in Aboriginal shamanic understanding: "It didn't come from God! He got it himself!" Her claim to authority comes from a framework she considers more encompassing than that provided by an Anglican missionary, whom she remembers as a short-term visitor at best. Once again, these accounts underscore the contested nature of prophecy narratives. On one hand, Johnny Ned seems to be incorporating Christian concepts to his own advantage. On the other, missionaries are adopting a kind of bureaucratic pragmatism in their attempts to incorporate and subsume local knowledge as a way of extending their influence.

A final set of prophecy narratives centers on the issue of how prophets incorporated unfamiliar religious symbols in ways subsequently interpreted as transformative. Shamanic prophets are now said to have foretold the coming of new religious ideas, specifically Christianity and Baha'i.

Angela Sidney, a Tagish elder who passed away in 1991 at the age of eighty-nine, engaged in a continuing intellectual struggle to integrate traditional understandings with modern ideas. As a young woman, she became extremely involved with the Anglican Church, and during the final years of her life she became very active in the Baha'i faith. She devoted a great deal of attention to reconciling her present beliefs with the shamanistic ideas she learned from her parents, uncles, and aunts, and provided a splendidly coherent account of the connections between past ideas and present understandings. She took the ability of prophets to communicate with a higher being as a given. In the course of recording her life history, she asked:

> What about Oral Roberts? He got messages from God. What about Father Divine? Well, that's why I think Indians are like that . . . [able to communicate directly with superhuman beings]. But we call it Indian doctor" (Cruikshank et al. 1991:154).

In her narratives about the shaman Malal and the Pelly River shaman remembered as Major, she demonstrates that she, like the younger people cited above, continues to struggle with the issue of how traditional paradigms inform contemporary understanding. Her vehicle for linking these ideas centers on prophecy, as demonstrated in two stories she tells about the Pelly River shaman Major. One story links his predictions to Christianity; the other links them to Baha'i. For some years, the question of conflicting loyalties to such different institutional religions troubled her, but near the end of her life she reconciled any conflict between these two religious frameworks by showing how Major demonstrated foreknowledge of both of them.

When Angela Sidney was nine years old, she says, she learned about Major from her mother. She claims her own authority to tell about this prophet with reference to her mother's words. Major reportedly named a particular day *Linday* or "Sunday" before anyone knew that days might have special names, and designated the day prior to Sunday as *Linday K'esku* or "little Sunday."

> They tell about that old man—his name was Major—there were no English people in this country, that time. My mother saw him when she went to Pelly, a long time ago. And she said nobody knows about Sunday, Saturday, or anything like that. But he used to call it Linday, that means "Sunday." Linday K'esku means "little Sunday." That means "Saturday." But I guess he can't say it very good and he said Sunday as "Linday," Linday Tlein, that means "Big Sunday." I guess that was a white man name, but he can't say it (Cruikshank et al. 1990:154).

He encouraged his followers to make crosses out of Golden Eye Eagle feathers, and to wear them when they went hunting.

> Year 1910, I see everybody's got crosses made out of Golden Eye Eagle feathers. They made crosses, and everybody wore them if they were going out hunting, anything like that. And they say that's what Major told them to do. I was about nine years old and I asked my mother "What's that for?"
> And she said that's what Old Major told them to wear, to use when they go out hunting so they would get their game easily and things like that. Nothing would bother them. That's what she told me at that time. I just thought of that now! I guess it was a cross. I guess that's what it was. At that time I never thought of it, see?
> . . . That's why I go to anybody that's praying. Don't care what kind of people they are. I was a good Anglican. I used to go to W.A.,[14] go to Easter Sunday, go to World Day of Prayer (ibid.:158).

Catharine McClellan, who heard similar accounts from Mrs. Sidney's mother, Maria, and her contemporaries in the 1940s and 1950s wrote about the use of crosses by shamans but pointed out that this same shaman, Major, also urged people to put the sign of the cross in charcoal on their legs and arms. The symbol, she points out, may be borrowed but the emphasis on the four limbs and on the ceremonial use of charcoal are Aboriginal (1956:135). She also points out the utility of designating a special day when people would be called together for meetings. The missionaries' "Sunday" worked to the advantage of shamans whose efficacy was enhanced by the participation of an audience. The idea of Sunday was fortuitous because it brought people together for regular meetings. According to McClellan, these sessions were usually described as "prayer meetings" and attendance was heavy. The head shaman laid his hands on people's heads foretelling sickness or death, expelling menstruants from the group, singing songs which were then remembered as "hymns." She concludes that, "in brief, holding the seance on Sunday did little to change its essentially aboriginal nature" (1956:135). Shamans, then, were able to incorporate Christian symbolism and to use Christian narrative in ways that enhanced their own authority.

In the late 1980s, as her own ideas continued to change, Mrs. Sidney had given more thought to the role of Major's prophesies in foreshadowing new ideas. Rethinking them, she found his words prophetic with reference to the coming of Baha'i to the Yukon. Major, she says,

> [T]ells about how it's going to be the last day, someday. So he said, "It's not going to happen right away. It's going to be long time yet," he said. "And," he said, "that animal is going to have nine legs. A nine-legged animal is going to be our food," he said.

And that's the one us Indians think maybe that's Baha'i. That Baha'i assembly has nine points. That's what we think. That's what it is. And he said, "If the people believe and live my way, I'm going to be very, very old. But if people don't accept me, God will take me away . . .

Well, nothing like that happened until Baha'i people started coming here, telling about things like that. That's why we think—my family—we think that's what he meant. Because there's no animal got nine legs. And he said, "That's going to be your food, isn't it?" It's just like food. So there's lots of us joined in. I think I was the last one joined in because I'm Anglican. All of my kids joined the Baha'i. That's why I joined in, me too" (ibid.:154–55).

By juxtaposing these two prophecy narratives, Mrs. Sidney establishes that intellectually there is no necessary conflict between Anglicanism, Baha'i, and indigenous shamanism. She is able to use this framework to provide a satisfactory explanation of her ability to integrate ideas which others might find contradictory. Pleased with this reconciliation, she asked that the (much longer) recorded tape from our interview be duplicated as her "teaching tape." She then requested that her daughter take it to Baha'i meetings to play for other members of the Baha'i faith so they could understand the linkages between the activities of the Baha'i prophet and indigenous prophets.

The prophecy narratives summarized above work within a familiar narrative framework where teller and listener share an understanding of the relationship between parallel dimensions of reality. Knowledge from one dimension can be brought to the other by a shaman, who can then draw on his/her experience to dispense prophetic advice. These prophesies are evaluated by contemporary narrators not in terms of whether they altered social circumstances. Rather, they are evaluated in terms of their ability to forge legitimate links between knowledge experienced by past prophets and events experienced by present tellers.

Underscoring all of the narrators' accounts is the view that this is a conventional, routine, self-evident way of explaining the linkages between past and present. As has been suggested for neighboring Dene Dhaa prophets, prophecy long has been a normal part of experience. "Stories provided the landscape in which visions could occur, and songs provided the trail through the landscape" (Moore and Wheelock 1990:59). Competing with this, we have the scholarly analysis of prophecy and prophetic movements which interprets such accounts as unusual, extraordinary, problematic, and in need of a different foundational explanation.

DISCUSSION

In conclusion, it is worth returning to questions raised at the outset of the paper. Elderly Athapaskan women tell prophecy narratives in the 1980s and 1990s as though these narratives speak for themselves—as though their message is a self-evident, common-sense explanation. What can this contribute to understandings about how connections between past and present are formulated and publicly presented? What do these narratives tell us about the construction, performance and communication of knowledge? Why do elders specifically select these narratives to pass on to younger people in the 1990s?

Much of the academic debate surrounding prophecy concerns the issue of historical reconstruction of past events. Historians may treat oral traditions as one of many kinds of sources and approach them as "evidence" of "what really happened." Tellings by contemporary Athapaskan elders raise different questions. Oral traditions are presented not as evidence but as fully developed narrative constructions. Their tellings may cause us to re-examine the scholarly debate about prophecy.

To review that debate briefly again: ethnohistorians pose the question of whether prophetic movements were indigenous, or a response to external crises. Certainly the archaeological and documentary record for the upper Yukon River shows no shortage of disruptive events.[15] Prophecy narratives, at least in the western Subarctic, may have provided a way to explain changing circumstances, by embedding unfamiliar events with reference to a familiar narrative framework. If this is the case, the relevance of "indigenous" vs. "contact" distinctions may blur, and prophecy narratives may direct us to the issue of legitimacy of explanation rather than causality.

The sociological literature emphasizes the short-term success or failure of prophets in their attempts to transform social and political order. Yet the narrators seem to pay more attention to the explanatory powers of words than to when individual prophets arose or what they achieved. Shamans like Major, Malal or Johnny Ned can foretell Christianity, Baha'i, or apocalypse and their prophecies are reinvoked years later not with reference to their short-term efficacy but to give meaning to events. In other words, following Renato Rosaldo's insight that narratives *shape* rather than *reflect* human conduct (1989:129), telling a prophetic narrative may give a storied form to proper relations. Such narratives may provide listeners with ways to think about how they should respond to external events.

Told now, prophecy narratives seem to establish meaning for events that have come to pass during narrators' own lifetimes—events as diverse as the arrival of newcomers, cataclysmic epidemics, the expansion of state control, and the introduction of religious orthodoxies. Meanings of oral narratives are not fixed: they have to be understood in terms of how they are used. By explaining events in ways intellectually consistent with the framework oral tradition has long provided, prophecy narratives establish a complex relationship between words and events. Words are not merely evidence for events (as they might be in a formulation where written documents are analysed): events legitimize the words. Words have power to foretell events, and in this way, as Southern Tutchone elder, Annie Ned, puts it: "Old time words are just like school." The words provide food for thought, but their meaning becomes clear only after the event has come to pass.

Scott Rushforth has recently written two thoughtful papers about knowledge, authority and legitimation of beliefs among Dene hunters at Bear Lake, Northwest Territories (Rushforth 1992, 1994). Based on lengthy conversations with Dene men in the Mackenzie Valley, Rushforth discusses how, in Dene society, knowledge comes to be seen as legitimate when it is based on what he calls primary experience. He provides examples of Dene men who spoke to the Mackenzie Valley Pipeline Inquiry from their own experience about land-based activity and how they place far greater value on that knowledge than on that provided by "expert witnesses" several steps removed from direct experience. He proposes that for Dene hunters, primary experience is the epistomological foundation of knowledge and is given far greater weight than secondary experience. Using the Mackenzie Valley Pipeline Inquiry as a case in point, he shows how expert systems invoked in hearings are resisted precisely because they threaten local authority. Indigenous people repeatedly assert the authority of their own local knowledge and reject the validity of those expert systems, which they see as derived from second-hand knowledge rather than from direct experience.

Accounts about prophecy told by Yukon women add an additional dimension to Rushforth's thesis, one which I suspect is related to gender. These narratives suggest that a woman's knowledge and her right to speak come not only from her own experience but also from experiences conveyed to her by her mother, grandmother, or other elders. Until recently, Aboriginal people in the Subarctic acquired knowledge in two ways: one of those ways was by direct experience and observation; the other was through oral tradition—the narratives and instruction passed from one generation to the next. A woman's own knowledge and her right to speak derives from her connection with those words and with the experience of hearing those words from grandmothers, grandfathers, mothers, and aunts (see also Binney 1987 for parallel observations from New Zealand). The purpose of these narratives is evaluated not in terms of whether shamans effected changes, but in terms of how words give meaning to events and how events, in turn, legitimize the words.

Increasingly, we understand that histories are interpretations that change in relation to changing circumstances. However, this ideology coexists with a competing ideology of history as "just the facts" (see Gable, Handler, and Lawson 1992). Ironically, historical relativism gets invoked more frequently for indigenous history than for mainstream history: in the Yukon Territory, for example, the goldrush and the Alaska Highway are taken for granted as reference points for local history and juxtaposed with Aboriginal narratives "about" the goldrush or the highway. Thus consti-

tuted, relativism reinforces the legitimacy of mainstream history by making it seem more "real" or more "truthful."

At an obvious level, indigenous prophecy narratives have always been contested by the dominant ideology. But the context is less about facts or causality than it is about legitimacy. If they are taken to be fully developed narratives, they can be understood not just as evidence, or as one interpretation among many, but as an explanation competing for legitimacy, performed in a way that invokes ethnographic authority.

The enduring tradition of storytelling in the southern Yukon Territory suggests that narratives continue to address important questions during periods of social upheaval. Rather than viewing them as evidence of failure to cope, or social breakdown, prophecy narratives may be viewed as successful engagement with changing ideas. Social sciences conventionally make a distinction between behaviors that might be characterized as "adaptive strategies" and those identified as "expressive forms." The former are usually located with reference to the business of making a living and the latter to literary and artistic activities. Such a distinction, I would suggest, is inappropriate in situations where people see storytelling as central to the ongoing reproduction of their culture. Yukon storytellers demonstrate the critical intelligence embedded in oral narrative by showing how contemporary events are discussed with reference to traditional narrative, how an understanding of the past informs our comprehension of the present. Prophecy narratives provide one more instance of the continuing use of tradition to frame explanations about the contemporary world. They offer a competing form of historical consciousness that deserves to be taken seriously.

NOTES

1. I recorded these narratives between 1974 and 1984 as part of my work with the Yukon Native Language Centre, based in Whitehorse, Yukon Territory.

2. Spier's monograph on the Plateau Prophet Dance originally posed the question of whether this was an Aboriginal or contact phenomenon. It is worth noting that subsequent analyses focusing on the Plateau seem to favor a contact thesis (Aberle 1959; Walker 1969; Miller 1985) while studies with a more northerly geographical focus favored Aboriginal origins (McClellan 1956; Suttles 1957; Ridington 1978; Moore and Wheelock 1990). It may also be significant that publications emphasizing Aboriginal origins seem to rely on indigenous concepts whereas those elaborating a contact hypothesis emphasize the broad historical and ecological context in which those ideas emerged.

3. Spier documented the spread of the Prophet Dance from the Columbia Plateau as far as southern Alaska and the Mackenzie River by the early 1800s. While certain diagnostic features of the Prophet Dance (world renewal, a special dance, structured community ritual) were not incorporated into Yukon prophecy narratives, news of the Prophet Dance undoubtedly

reached the Yukon River and contributed to the activities of early prophets in this region (McClellan 1956:136).

4. Born near the Red River to an Ojibwa mother and a Scottish trader, McDonald came to the northern Yukon in the early 1860s. While he shared the Church's enthusiasm for collecting converts, he was less zealous than his contemporaries in the Church Missionary Society about trying to modify the local indigenous cultures. Prophecy, though, seemed to trouble him, perhaps because he interpreted its manifestations as competing with Christian teachings.

5. As an indication of how prevalent prophecy was on the upper Peel and upper Yukon Rivers at this time, the following notes can be gleaned from McDonald's diaries. On January 3, 1864, he refers to "an Indian pretending to prophesy at Peel River but Mr. A. Flett (the trader) has prevented him from going too far with it." More references appear in 1865: on January 11, he refers to a man who "pretends to receive divine revelations" and the next day (January 12) names "Tiujito, a Mackenzie River Tukudh who has been making extravagant pretensions to prophesy, and to being favoured with divine revelations." On February 5, he spoke with people on the Bonnet Plume River about their Peel River neighbors, noting that "there is still one among them pretending to divine authority to teach the Indians in religion, but he is not attended to." On May 25, he spoke against "delusions of the Indians led astray by those making pretensions to prophesy." On June 25, he spoke directly to one of the nuk-kut [sic] "who makes pretensions to prophesy." Several years later on July 27, 1874, he referred by name to the prophet Larion and his wife who told their followers that they would die if baptized. Larion's wife, especially, claimed direct communication with and advice from supreme beings. The general tone of McDonald's notes suggests that it was missionaries who saw themselves competing with shamans, rather than the reverse.

6. There is, of course, a difference between *explaining* the local meaning of events and publicly *legitimizing* local discourse or knowledge. One dilemma faced by indigenous people trying to convince outsiders of the legitimacy of their perspective may be that within any one community, interpretations based on oral tradition are inevitably contested, debated, discussed in daily conversation. However in publicly presenting an authoritative stance to outsiders, in arguing for the legitimacy of oral tradition as a valid historical perspective, claimants sometimes feel compelled to present oral tradition as though it were uncontested "truth."

7. Yukon narratives tell how, at the beginning of time, the Trickster Crow was white "like a seagull" before he was blackened trying to escape through a smokehole in one of his escapades (Cruikshank et al. 1990:274, 313). Ridington (1978) suggested that for Prophet River Dunne-za, prophets were specifically the people with swan power, swans belonging to that separate dimension of whiteness. Moore and Wheelock note that this separate dimension is the home for seagulls and snow geese, also white (1990:60).

8. Classic examples include "Moldy Head," and "The Man Who Stayed with Groundhog Woman" (see Cruikshank et al. 1990, 75–8; 208–13).

9. This Pelly River shaman was one of the most widely remembered in narrative (see also McClellan 1956; Cruikshank et al. 1990:154, 158).

10. Alaska Highway Pipeline Inquiry, Carcross, J. Jack, vol. 44, p. 5,967.

11. Similarly, the story of Skookum Jim or Keish the Tagish man associated with the discovery of Klondike gold that triggered the 1898 gold rush attributes his success and his foreknowledge of that success to his relationship with a Frog Helper who urged him to travel downriver where he would "find his fortune" (McClellan 1963; Cruikshank 1992).

12. By saying this, she is indicating her understanding of the power of spoken words, that if used inappropriately they might bring harm to speaker and listener. An essential component of a shaman's power was his song, which came to him as a result of his contact with an animal spirit helper. Earlier, Mrs. Ned made a similar statement about her father's power. She has sung her husband's song for me several times, but it would be inappropriate to make a recording of it because once recorded, it could be used out of context.

13. This letter is on file in the Anglican Church records, Yukon Territorial Archives, and is dated April 25, 1917.

14. She refers here to the Women's Auxiliary of the Anglican Church.

15. An enormous volcanic eruption on the Alaska-Yukon border more than 800 years ago undoubtedly displaced human populations on the upper Yukon. The so-called Little Ice Age between 1600–1800 had a dramatic effect on people living in the southern Yukon not only because of deteriorating climatic conditions but also because of the building and draining of glacier-dammed lakes and the shifting drainages caused by surging glaciers in southwest Yukon. The arrival of fur traders first from the Northwest Coast and then from the eastern Subarctic in the nineteenth century was closely followed by arrival of competing Roman Catholic and Anglican missionaries. The Klondike goldrush at the beginning of the twentieth century brought some 40,000 would-be prospectors to the upper Yukon. The expansion of the Canadian state into northwestern North America imported governing and legal infrastructures with serious, long-term consequences for Aboriginal people. The imposition of residential schools, the growing pressures on wildlife, the economic dislocations after the introduction of gold, silver, lead, and zinc mines, the construction of the Alaska Highway in the 1940s, projected pipeline developments in the 1970s, the ongoing disruptions associated with the negotiation of a land claims agreement in the Yukon—certainly all these changes could support the hypothesis that prophets could have arisen in response to externally induced stresses.

REFERENCES

Abel, Kerry. 1986. "Prophets, Priests and Preachers: Dene Shamans and Christian Missions in the Nineteenth Century." In *Report of the Canadian Historical Association Annual Meeting: Historical Papers* 1986:211–14.

Aberle, David. 1959. "The Prophet Dance and Reactions to White Contact." *Southwestern Journal of Anthropology* 15(1):74–83. 1972 "A Note on Relative Deprivation Theory as Applied to Millenarian and Other Cult Movements." In *Reader in Comparative Religion: Anthropological Approaches,* edited by William Lessa and Evon Z. Vogt. Third Ed. New York: Harper and Row.

Axtell, James. 1981. "Ethnohistory: An Historian's Viewpoint." In *The European and the Indian: Essays in the Ethnohistory of Colonial North America,* edited by James Axtell. New York: Oxford University Press.

Binney, Judith. 1987. "Maori Oral Narratives, Pakeha Written Texts: Two Forms of Telling History." *The New Zealand Journal of History* 21(1):16–28.

Brown, Jennifer. 1982. "The Track to Heaven: The Hudson Bay Cree Religious Movement of 1842–1843." *Papers of the Thirteenth Algonquian Conference* ed. by William Cowan. Ottawa: Carleton University Press. pp. 53–63. 1988 "Abishabis." In Dictionary of Canadian Biography Vol. 7, Toronto: University of Toronto Press. pp. 3–4.

Brown, Jennifer and Robert Brightman. 1988. *"The Orders of the Dreamed: George Nelson on Northern Ojibwa"* Religion and Myth, 1823. Winnipeg: University of Manitoba Press.

Cohen, Percy. 1969. "Theories of Myth." *Man* 4(3):337–53.

Cruikshank, Julie. 1992. "Images of Society in Klondike Gold Rush Narratives: Skookum Jim and the Discovery of Gold." *Ethnohistory* 39(1):20–41.

Cruikshank, Julie in collaboration with Angela Sidney, Kitty Smith and Annie Ned. 1990. *Life Lived Like a Story: Life Stories of Three Yukon Elders.* Lincoln: University of Nebraska Press.

Dawson, Rachel. 1975. Life story, recorded by Julie Cruikshank. Manuscript with Curriculum Development Branch, Council for Yukon Indians, Whitehorse.

Gable, Eric, Richard Handler and Anna Lawson. 1992. "On the Uses of Relativism: Fact, Conjecture and Black and White Histories at Colonial Williamsburg." *American Ethnologist* 19(4):791–805.

Hill, Jonathan. 1992. "Contested Pasts and the Practice of Anthropology." *American Anthropologist* 94(4):809–15.

Jennings, Francis. 1982. "A Growing Partnership: Historians, Anthropologists and American Indian History." *Ethnohistory* 29(1):21–34.

Kan, Sergei. 1991. "Shamanism and Christianity: Modern Day Tlingit Elders Look at the Past." *Ethnohistory* 38(4):363–87.

Legros, Dominique. 1985. "Wealth, Poverty and Slavery among the 19th Century Tutchone Athapaskans." Research in *Economic Anthropology* 7:37–64.

Long, Theodore E. 1986. "Prophecy, Charisma and Politics: Reinterpreting the Weberian Thesis." In *Prophetic Religions and Politics,* edited by Jeffrey K. Haddon and Anson Shupe. New York: Paragon House.

McClellan, Catharine. 1956. "Shamanistic Syncretism in Southern Yukon." *Transactions of the New York Academic of Sciences,* series 2, 19(2):130–73.

—1963. "Wealth Woman and Frog Among the Tagish Indians." *Anthropos* 58:121–28.

—1970. "Indian Stories About the First Whites in Northwestern North America." In *Ethnohistory in Southwestern Alaska and the Yukon,* edited by Margaret Lantis. Lexington: University Press of Kentucky.

—1975. "My Old People Say: An Ethnographic Survey of Southern Yukon Territory. 2 vols. *Publications in Ethnology* 6 (1 & 2). Ottawa: National Museums of Canada.

McDonald, Robert. 1985. Journals of Rev. Robert McDonald, 1862–1913. Manuscript in Yukon Archives with index by Linda Johnson. Whitehorse: Yukon Native Language Centre.

McDonnell, Roger. 1975. Kasini Society: Some Aspects of the Organization of an Athapaskan Culture Between 1900–1950. Doctoral dissertation, University of British Columbia.

Miller, Christopher. 1985. *Prophetic Worlds: Indians and Whites on the Columbia Plateau.* New Brunswick: Rutgers.

Moore, Patrick and Angela Wheelock. 1990. *Wolverine Myths and Visions: Dene Traditions from Northern Alberta.* Lincoln: University of Nebraska Press.

Neylan, Susan. 1992. Revitalization Movements Among the Central Subarctic Indians. Unpublished paper, Department of History, University of British Columbia.

Peterson, Jacqueline. 1988. "Review of 'Prophetic Worlds': Indians and Whites on the Columbia Plateau." *Ethnohistory* 3(2): 191–96.

Ridington, Robin. 1978. "Swan People: A Study of the Dunne-za Prophet Dance." Canadian Ethnology Service, Paper 38, *National Museum of Man Mercury Series.* National Museums of Canada.

—1990. Little Bit Know Something: Stories in a Language of Anthropology. Iowa City: University of Iowa Press.

Rosaldo, Renato. 1989. *Culture and Truth.* Boston: Beacon Press.

Rushforth, Scott. 1992. "The Legitimation of Beliefs in a Hunter-Gatherer Society: Bearlake Athapaskan Knowledge and Authority." *American Ethnologist* 19(3):483–500.

—1994. "Political Resistance in a Contemporary Hunter-Gatherer Society: More About Bearlake Athapaskan Knowledge and Authority." *American Ethnologist* 21(2):335–52.

Sidney, Angela, Kitty Smith and Rachel Dawson. 1975. *My Stories Are My Wealth.* Recorded by Julie Cruikshank. Whitehorse: Council for Yukon Indians.

Slobodin, Richard. 1970. "Kutchin Concepts of Reincarnation." *Western Canadian Journal of Anthropology* (special issue: Athapaskan studies) 2(2):67–79.

Spier, Leslie. 1935. *The Prophet Dance of the Northwest and Its Derivative: The Source of the Ghost Dance.* Menasha, Wisconsin: George Banta Publishing Company.

Suttles, Wayne. 1957. "The Plateau Prophet Dance Among the Coast Salish." *Southwestern Journal of Anthropology* 13: 352–398.

Trigger, Bruce. 1982. "Ethnohistory: Problems and Prospects." *Ethnohistory* 29(1):1–19.

Walker, Deward E. Jr. 1969. "New Light on the Prophet Dance." *Ethnohistory* 16:245–55.

Wallace, Anthony. 1956. *"Revitalization Movements."* American Anthropologist 58(2):264–81.

Oracles, Divine Kingship, and Political Representation in the Inka State

Peter Gose

This insightful essay draws us into the world of pre-Columbian Inca kings, where religion and the state intertwined in forms that are unfamiliar to most Americans. The Inca was the supreme ruler, understood to be divine both in life and after death. In theory, all decisions concerning the empire were taken by the Inca, but because this was impossible in practice, the Inca appointed other rulers and had statues made of himself that could rule in his stead. These doubles of the Inca were operated by a hierarchy of priests, the greatest of whom, the High Priest of the Sun, was second in power only to the Inca himself.

In addition to the Inca's double, there were many other deities. Many of these were the mummified remains and statues of earlier Inca rulers. Others were deities of people who had been conquered by the Inca. Each of these deities spoke through a priest who, using alcohol as well as hallucinogenic drugs, would fall into a religious trance and speak for the deity. Deities and their oracles were ranked by the accuracy of their predictions.

Inca priests and oracles did not simply mediate between the people and the nonempirical world. They formed a highly active part of the Inca state. Because the Inca himself was divine, he was unable to accept contradiction or advice from any human. However, through the priests and their oracles, the Inca could consult with other divinities. Because these divinities represented Inca royal families and other groups within the empire, something like a political consensus could emerge.

As you read, consider these questions:

1. What are the characteristics of Inca divine kings?
2. In much of the anthropological literature, ecstatic trance is associated with shamans. Here it is associated with priests. What elements make these religious practitioners priests rather than shamans?
3. What techniques do priests use to establish and reinforce their power?
4. How did Inca rulers use religion to maintain control of their empire?
5. In this essay, Gose argues that a divine king is an attribute of a relatively weak state. Why should this be the case?

INTRODUCTION

From the perspective of Western individualism, oracular possession is doomed to appear as either pathological or exotic (see Lambek 1981; Boddy 1989). We find it difficult to see oracular possession as a practical way to get things done because it undermines our very notion of human agency as something personal, bounded, and coherent. Under the Inkas, however, Andean people had different working assumptions about the expansive agency of divine kings, which made oracular possession not only "believable" but a uniquely "realistic" method of everyday political decision making and maneuver. This essay explains how oracles and their priests came to play a central role in Inka court politics and explores the distinctive genre of political representation that they created in Andean society.

Until the recent studies of Patterson (1985), Rostworowski (1988), and MacCormack (1991), the role of oracles in the Inka court was virtually ignored. I join these authors in thinking that Inka oracles were politically important, but differ from them in asking why Inka politics took an oracular form. The answer may lie in the broader institutional and ideological realities of Andean divine kingship, in which the subjectivity of the sovereign tended to engulf and obliterate that of his subjects. Under such conditions, those outside the current ruling clique found an effective way to represent their sectional interests by attaching themselves to the oracular cult of a previous divine king. The voices that spoke through oracular shrines and priests were held to be those of dead ruler-ancestors, particularly those who founded or expanded political units. Oracular performances centered on the mummified body or a statue of this ruler-ancestor. As illustrious and unimpeachable ex-rulers, oracular deities spoke with an authority that might constrain, decenter, and fragment the power of the living sovereign, whose relation to his predecessors was always at least potentially ambivalent. Mummified sovereigns also spoke as representatives of the living descent groups or corporations (*ayllus, panaqas*) that each founded during his reign. Oracles thus became an important channel for these groups to influence and even challenge the living ruler's agenda. As a first approximation, then, oracles allowed the political representation of subaltern peoples in a regime excessively oriented toward divine kings. The oracular mode was prominent in Inka politics because it allowed the dissemination of information, advice, and dissident opinions without challenging the ruler's supreme authority. Thus oracles were one of the few aspects of Andean divine kingship that actually facilitated the task of government, in which consultation and compromise were ultimately inevitable.

Oracular mediums also established possession as an important cultural idiom of delegated power, one that orchestrated several bureaucratic developments within the Inka state. For the Inkas, the living ruler was an umbrella figure who was in theory expected to conduct imperialist warfare, to run an administration, and to perform important priestly activities, all more or less simultaneously. Since he could not do all these things at once, the reigning Inka appointed a living "substitute" and had a statue of himself made (known as his "brother"), both of whom were expected to speak and receive reverence on his behalf. Oracular possession provided the cultural model for this delegation of power and thus became one of the few quasi-bureaucratic idioms available in an otherwise weakly institutionalized and excessively personalistic political regime.

[In a 2,100-word section entitled "Oracles and Politics: Background," Gose notes that Spanish sources of the sixteenth and seventeenth centuries say oracles were present throughout Inca lands. The deities (waka) who spoke through the oracles were the founders of descent groups and often mythical heroes. For Andean peoples, all gods were oracles and had to prophesy. Such speech was considered a sign of the continued vitality of divine rulers. The Inca expected that all rulers who had made conquests during their lives would become gods, and thus oracles.

Dead rulers were mummified and taken to their country estates. Their wives and children formed a panaqa and lived on the profits from the estate but often stayed in Cuzco. The son who inherited the position of high king did not join the panaqa but went on to form his own. The mummy of a former ruler (and often that of his wife) spoke as oracles through a pair of mediums, advising on marriages, alliances, and political interests of the panaqa.

Because the Sun was considered the founder of the Inca elite, its oracle was the most important and its priests spoke for the interests of the entire Inca elite. Pronouncements by the high priest of the Sun were particularly important in affirming the selection of a new highest Inca ruler, but such a selection ultimately had to be affirmed by the oracles of the ancestral mummies of each panaqa. Once installed, Inca rulers consulted oracles before making even trivial decisions.

In addition to frequent consultations with royal oracles, the Inca high king also participated in the yearly capacocha ritual. In the capacocha, provincial people brought their most important deities to Cuzco where they paid homage to the Sun. Then the high king or priest of the sun consulted each deity through its oracle. In this way, the king received consultation from the provinces. Records of these consultations were kept, and those oracles whose prophesies proved false lost status or were weeded out.

The war between Huascar and Atahuallpa shows that the king clearly expected the oracle to accurately predict the activities of its people. When oracles at Pachacamac incorrectly predicted Atahuallpa's actions to Huascar, he vowed to become their greatest enemy. Atahuallpa also lost faith in Pachacamac and ultimately encouraged the Spanish to sack the shrine.

One effect of the use of oracles was to bypass living political leaders of subordinate groups while paying exaggerated respect to their social groups. Thus oracles could give voice to both conquered provincial peoples and the descent groups of previous Inca kings without threatening the current king.

Oracles continued to be important after the Spanish conquest. In one instance oracles revealed a plot to assassinate the Conquistador Pizarro. In another, oracles were involved in an attempt to overthrow Spanish rule.

Having shown the importance of oracles in political representation under the Incas, Gose now turns to an examination of oracles as a cultural form.—Editors]

THE ORACULAR FORM: IDEOLOGY AND PERFORMANCE

Oracles enjoyed considerable material backing from Inka and provincial elites, who built temples and plazas for them, offered sacrifices, and brewed endless quantities of corn beer in their name. It was during daily bouts of festive drinking in the plaza of Cuzco that mummified Inka rulers gave oracles to their descendants and established ongoing relations with them:

> And the body always had a captain who was in charge of all of those people [the mummy's descent group] since he died. . . . this captain sat in the plaza with him, and in his name sent women with glasses of corn beer to the living Inca, to the Sun and to the other bodies, by way of a toast, and they received them . . . and those glasses which the Sun and the Inca sent with their women to the bodies were drunk in their name: when the captain of the body went to urinate, he took the body on his back. (Polo de Ordegardo 1916 [1585]: 124; see also P. Pizarro 1978 [1571]: 89–90)

This surrogate drinking heightened the mutual identification of mummy and "captain" into an oracular trance, just as the rest of the kin group and the mummy were united in the communion of drink. According to Estete (1924 [1535]: 55), the plaza of Cuzco was equipped with drains to get rid of the incredible quantities of urine generated during these oracular festivities. It was through such routine public festivities that the enduring influence of dead kings became manifest and acquired a populist tone. Although the experience of drunkenness was undoubtedly shaped and subsumed by ideologies of divine kingship, it also must have made its own irreducible contribution to these events and the "collective representations" they produced. To properly appreciate the performative dimension of oracular possession, then, we must first ground it in popular festivity.

Cieza de León notes that during festivities in the plaza of Cuzco, mediums spoke "glad words" to the assembled multitudes on behalf of the mummified ex-rulers (1984 [1553], 2: chap. 11; see also Romero 1918: 187). He also records that Huayna Capac's military victories were celebrated in the plaza of Cuzco with sacrifices, dancing, and oracular performances (Cieza de León 1984 [1553], 2: chap. 60; see also Betanzos 1987 [1551], 1: chap. 19). Thus the speech of dead rulers was valued for its own sake, as a sign of cultural well-being, and not simply for the guidance it could give in specific matters. Conversely, when oracles refused to talk to the Inka, as was reported to have happened to Huayna Capac, it was a sign of the impending disaster of the Spanish conquest and loss of native sovereignty (Guaman Poma de Ayala 1936 [1615]: 252; see also Romero 1918: 187).

Oracular speech was an unqualified good because it signified a particularly intense form of the desired life-giving relation between a dead sovereign and his people. Thus oracular speech, along with the entire complex of Andean divine kingship, was semantically inscribed in the Quechua root *kama* (existence), which Taylor rightly regards as a fundamental Andean spiritual concept (1974–76: 232). First, the ruler-ancestor was often described as a "source of life" (*camaquen* or *camac*[1]), while the people whose lives he sustained were spoken of as "animated," or "infused" (*camasca;* see ibid.: 234). This animation should not be understood simply as a spiritual relation, however, since it clearly involved notions of material sustenance that tied particular groups of people to specific localities.[2] Oracular mediums and other religious specialists were also described as camasca (see Polo de Ondegardo 1916 [1585]: 27; Guaman Poma de Ayala 1936 [1615]: 72, 330), so we may suppose that their meditations and trance states were an intensified form of the same animating influence that a camaquen exercised on ordinary mortals. This idea is further suggested by the use of *camachinacuy* and similar forms to refer to prayer, reasoning, counsel, and consultation, all of which were applicable to oracular communication (Santo Tomás 1951 [1560]: 114; González Holguín 1952 [1608]: 47–48; Guaman Poma de Ayala 1936 [1615]: 329). Finally, there are several derivations of *kamachi* that denote power and command (see Santo Tomás 1951 [1560]: 114; González Holguín 1952 [1608]: 46–47; Guaman Poma de Ayala 1936 [1615]: 321, 328). They are particularly interesting because on strictly analytical grounds, *kamachiy* ought to mean "to cause to exist," yet in actual usage it seems to have denoted communications shaped by power and command. We do not have to choose between these meanings, however, since the entire semantic field of kama, and the complex of ritual and theology that backed it up, constantly linked existence, animation, and material prosperity with notions of hierarchy, command, and oracular communication.

Additional details confirm that Andean people saw trance as an intensified "infusion" of ancestral vitality, often ingested into the body of the medium in a liquid form. Sometimes oracles prepared for their work simply by keeping their own company and meditating on the deity for whom they spoke (Anonymous Jesuit 1968 [ca. 1590]: 161). How-

ever, we have already seen that oracles drank large quantities of corn beer on behalf of the royal mummies, and it is likely that drunkenness may have further promoted their mutual identification into something like an oracular trance (see Arriaga 1968 [1621]: 207). Pedro Pizarro gives a vivid account of the Inca Atahuallpa's subjects falling down on the ground before him as if drunk (1978 [1571]: 65), which suggests that intoxication was an appropriate way to experience the animating influence of Inka royalty. Polo de Ondegardo mentions that some mediums added a hallucinogenic herb called *willka* to the corn beer that they drank (1916 [1585]: 30). We also know that during the Taki Onqoy, when Andean people attempted to stage a congress of regional deities similar to the ones that used to take place in imperial Cuzco, their mediums took a hallucinogen called *maka* in an attempt to embody and speak for various important regional deities (Duviols 1974–76: 291). According to Guaman Poma de Ayala, both willka and maka were ground and mixed to make a purgative liquid, half of which was drunk, and the other half injected as an enema with a syringe called a *willkachina* (1936 [1615]: 71, 119; see also Santo Tomás 1951 [1560]: 177; González Holguín 1952 [1608]: 352). Guaman Poma de Ayala describes these purges as a way to extend life, to improve health and strength, and to prepare for war. Santacruz Pachacuti adds that willka expelled all bad humors and choleras from the body (1927 [1613]: 180). In so doing, it prepared the way for an influx of ancestral health and vitality into the body. Significantly, willka also referred to "ancestral deity" and, in this regard, was a synonym for waka (Cobo 1956 [1653]: 149). There is therefore good reason to believe that the hallucinations it induced in the medium would be taken as a particularly strong dose of the ancestral essence that sustained all life.

Ritualized homosexuality also may have been a means by which oracular mediums were "infused" with the vitality of rulers. Cieza de León (1984 [1553], 1: chap. 64) notes that on the northern coast, boys were kept in oracular temples so that they could be sodomized by the local rulers when sacrifices were offered (see also Romero 1918: 189). Quoting a letter from Santo Tomás, Cieza de León goes on to write that "the devil has introduced this vice as a kind of holiness, and so in every temple or principal shrine he has a man or two or more, according to the idol, who go about dressed as women. . . . With these, almost by way of holiness or religion, they have their vile and carnal unions on celebrations and important days, especially the lords and notables" (1984 [1553] 1: chap. 64). In evaluating this passage, we must bear in mind that Spaniards considered sodomy to be the "unspeakable sin" and often attributed it to native cultures they wished to definitively stigmatize. If believable, however, this account suggests that sodomy formed a distinctive and significant backdrop to oracular possession. Just as the mediums were penetrated by hallucinogenic enema syringes representing dead rulers, so these boys and transvestites were penetrated by living rulers. Whether or not these transvestites were also mediums is less important than the orchestration of oracular possession itself around acts and images of lordly penetration.

Although oracular communication might take place openly amid public festivity, it was more often done in secret. Several sources confirm that even when oracular speech was featured in community-wide celebrations, it was not always public. Rather, a priest retreated with offerings and sacrifices to the inner recess of the shrine, and at some remove from the public eye, consulted the oracle and emerged with the reply: "And he said that the camaquen of the idol Guamancama Ratacura, that the soul of that mummy, came down into his heart and told him what he had to do in that matter about which it had been consulted, and that in the same manner that he was given a reply, the witness went down to the town and told all the aristocratic Indians and the rest of the commoners what his lord and creator had told him" (Duviols 1986: 143–44; cf. Arriaga 1968 [1621]: 205). Santillán states that the common people were never privy to the actual consultation of their deities but always heard of their pronouncements indirectly, through the priests, who approached the deities for them (1927 [1553]: 32–33). The verb *willay*—meaning to refer, recount, announce, advise, or send word—seems to have denoted what oracular priests did when they reported the speech of their deities to the people (e.g., *villampuni:* "to return with a reply"; González Holguín 1952 [1608]: 352).

It is tempting to speculate that the more important an oracular shrine was, the more this indirect and secretive pattern of consultation prevailed. All shrines were marked off by taboos, whose stringency typically increased with the rank of the deity they housed. To enter the precinct of Pachacamac, for example, one had to abstain (typically from salt, chile, dried meat, and sex) for twenty days; to proceed to the upper patio of the temple, one had to abstain for a year, but the deity was still concealed in a dark hut from those who reached this exclusive vantage point and was consulted privately by the priests (H. Pizarro 1920 [1533]: 176–77; Xerez 1987 [1534]: 137; Estete 1924 [1535]: 38–39). To enter Coricancha, the Temple of the Sun in Cuzco, people also had to abstain for a year, and even then they entered barefoot, carrying a burden (Trujillo 1987 [1571]: 206). These prohibitions often ensured that oracles performed to a select few, but even then, the medium spoke from behind an image of the deity in question, behind a partition in the room where it was housed, or in a darkened room.[3] In extreme cases the medium would not perform in front of any audience at all. According to the testimony of Tupac Amura I, the Inka sovereign was expected to commune privately with the golden image of Punchao (Mid-Day Sun) in the innermost recesses of Coricancha and to emerge with advice from this tutelary deity of the Inka ruling elite (Cobo 1956 [1653]: 106; see also Betanzos 1987 [1551]: 149–50). These oracular consultations were secretive by their very nature and would be divulged only in a second-hand, interpreted form, if they were divulged at all.

Nonetheless, Cieza de León describes how the oracle of Pachacamac, second in rank only to the Sun, was consulted and gave answers before very large crowds during important public rituals (1984 [1553], 1: chap. 72). His account contrasts remarkably with the pattern of seclusion described above and suggests that even the most elite oracles occasionally might be required to operate in a public, festive mode. Although Inka mummies regularly spoke platitudinous "glad words" to their descendants during rituals, Pachacamac actually seems to have made public predictions. Thus important oracles did not always do their work in secret, even if this was commonly the case. In fact, it was still possible to uphold the pattern of secretive consultation while engaging in spectacular and public forms of oracular possession: "When it came time to hear the oracle, that minister was overtaken by a diabolical furor which they call *utirayay,* and afterwards he declared to the people what the oracle had told him" (Anonymous Jesuit 1968 [ca. 1590]: 164). Here, the verb *utirayay* denotes becoming enraptured (González Holguín 1952 [1608]: 358), and it describes the medium's state while *hearing* the oracular message (see also Duviols 1986: 143). However, this message was not directly or immediately conveyed to the assembled multitudes but only reached them in a post hoc, interpreted form, once the possession was over. Similarly, Polo de Ondegardo (1916 [1585]: 29) and Murúa (1987 [1613]: 434) observe that oracular mediums got drunk and lost their senses and only gave their reply on the following day. During the actual performance, there seems to have been more emphasis on sound effects than on the actual message conveyed. The medium's thick, hoarse voice is emphasized in some accounts (e.g., Romero 1918: 187), whereas others describe oracular priests

> in front of the idols, hunching their shoulders, putting their chins on their chest and making great jowls, so that they themselves resemble fierce devils, and they begin to speak in a high, harmonious voice. A few times I, with my own eyes, certainly have heard the Indians talk with the Devil; and in the province of Cartagena, in a coastal town called Bahayre, I heard the Devil reply in a tenorous whistle, and in such tones as I cannot describe, except that a Christian who was in the same town as I [but] more than half a league away heard the same whistle, and was somewhat ill disposed from fright; and the Indians gave a huge shout another day, publicizing the Devil's reply. (Cieza de León 1984 [1553], 2: chap. 41)

Although these performances were at least partly verbal, apparently they were not readily decipherable (ibid., 1: 70). Their ostensible goal, making predictions in a propositional mode, was probably secondary. At least as important was the depiction of a nonordinary state in the medium that underwrote the authority of whatever message would ultimately be conveyed. Although the reality of oracular possession was primarily manifested through nonverbal performance, the opacity of any pronouncements made by the medium must also have contributed to this effect. The value of oracular communication as a scarce resource necessarily required that it be less accessible than ordinary speech and therefore dependent upon authoritative interpretation. The performance of a medium while possessed rarely, if ever, spoke for itself. Indeed, this passage suggests that an interval measured in days may have separated the performance from its interpretation, so that the immediacy of possession was seldom echoed in an immediacy of the communicated message.

What is most notable about Inka oracular practice, then, was its double nature. On the one hand, it was public and even carnivalesque in tenor, featuring intoxication and spectacle, but on the other hand, it was resolutely private and potentially subject to the crudest of manipulations. Neither of these aspects of oracular performance can be denied or reduced to the other, and both were integral to a larger pattern of divine kingship that was at once profoundly elitist and highly populist in character. The following section attempts to reconcile these apparently opposed dimensions of the oracular phenomenon.

ORACULAR REPRESENTATION

How did oracles represent the social groups to which they were connected? Previous answers to this question have argued either that oracles cynically appropriated the voice of the group or that they gave voice to genuine consensus. Neither answer on its own is adequate, since any system of political representation inevitably involves both. Like electoral democracy, Andean oracles were a form of political ventriloquism, in which a few people spoke for many more. By their very nature, these systems of political representation confound any hard distinction between appropriation and articulation of the group's voice. Yet precisely because this problem is endemic, each system also creates its own standards of adequacy. Inka standards turn out to be different from those of the West.

The chroniclers were highly cynical about oracles. According to Santillán, it was primarily the ethnic lords and Inkas who consulted the oracles, usually in private, which led him to feel that they used religion politically (1927 [1553]: 34). Certainly, the private consultations in which definitive interpretations of performance were negotiated could have been a foolproof way of getting the "right" answer to important questions. Thus many chroniclers could not help but portray the oracles as a political fraud,[4] even though they also subscribed to the official view that it was the Devil who spoke through them (see MacCormack 1991). Ironically, the diabolical view was much more compatible with Andean ideas because it at least recognized the reality of the supernatural agency behind the oracles. It is the materialist view of oracles that proves to be more pernicious, because it imputes the disbelief of the observer to the actors themselves. Empty conventional forms may exist in any cul-

ture, but they are rarely used to make the most important decisions. Following Evans-Pritchard (1937), one might note that the verdicts of the oracles sometimes went against the interests of those who consulted them, and that skepticism about particular oracles did not imply skepticism about their kind as a whole, points easily demonstrated with Inka material. The Inkas carefully remembered every oracle's predictions and kept an overall track record for each, constantly reevaluating its position in the imperial hierarchy of deities and its system of sacrificial rewards. These outlays in goods and services were considerable and would not have occurred if the motives behind oracular consultation were entirely cynical. In short, we must assume that the Inkas and their subjects believed in oracles and gave them a certain degree of political autonomy.

On closer examination, the chroniclers' skepticism about oracles also derives from Christianity. They generally imply that oracles had a greater moral authority than living rulers who, under the guise of consulting them, got oracles to articulate an agenda that the people otherwise would not accept. For Spanish Christians, who distinguished religion from worldly affairs and used the former as a transcendental standard to judge the latter (see Dumont 1986: chaps. 1–2), these assumptions were reasonable, but they ran entirely counter to the principles of Andean divine kingship. Here the goal of the ruler was to aggrandize himself in a manner that knew of no distinction between the spiritual and the worldly. He wanted to be commemorated for realizing the agenda that he brought before the oracles, not that they announce it on his behalf. Nor did he particularly care if this agenda was "legitimate" in the eyes of God or his subjects, since he was not morally dependent on them. Rather, his goal was to constitute his own divinity through an irresistible display of imperialist might. He wanted to know whether his plans would succeed, not whether they were right or wrong. Oracular advice was given privately to the elite because it concerned their plans, and they were the ones considered strong enough to speak directly to the deity. Oracles were treated as sources of wisdom and information, not as sources of a moral authority that the sovereign lacked. Oracular performance did not dramatize a transfer of moral authority from oracles to ruler, nor did it attempt to "convince" the drunken audience that the ruler's agenda was morally right. Thus the pious fraud view of Andean oracles is wrong because it smuggles inappropriate Christian assumptions about the moral degradation of worldly power into the Andean context and cannot ground them in the details of oracular performance.

Equally problematic, however, are those modern views that portray oracles as a kind of informal democracy. For example, MacCormack (1991: 59) writes that oracles worked by "establishing and then articulating consensus." Undoubtedly they did, but this view cannot explain the indirect and hierarchical nature of oracular communication. If the goal was to achieve consensus, then why was it advanced through private oracular consultation and not public discussion? Although oracles were supposed to represent their living descendants, the mistake is to assume that they did so on a democratic model. We misread the festive intimacy that oracular deities sometimes shared with their subjects when we take it as mundane familiarity and fail to connect it to the cloistered aloofness that they otherwise maintained. Oracles were supposed to know their subjects, but not in the manner of a public opinion poll. These detached, omniscient deities predicted the future because they were the creators and animators of their peoples; they knew the latter's destinies because they lay at the very source of their being.[5]

The notion of consensus is not entirely wrong, however. Without denying the hierarchical and frequently autocratic nature of Inka rule, the reality of Inka government was undoubtedly more complex and ridden with compromise than their myths of heroic divine kings indicate. As Hocart (1970 [1936]: 151) rightly observes, our own democratic myths also consistently characterize premodern states as despotic, when in fact they were far less powerful and centralized than our own. The lords of previously independent polities, whom the Inkas retained in their "decimal system," did most of the empire's local and regional administration. Such indirect rule indicates that the state is weak as a centralized governing institution, and following Weber (1978: 243–44), one could argue that charismatic authorities like divine kings emerge under precisely these conditions. Although the cult of the heroic sovereign can represent a preliminary step in the process of state building, it tends to be self-limiting in its personalistic form. This divine kingship commonly indicates an absence rather than an excess of despotically centralized executive power. There are obvious reasons why this absence is seldom openly proclaimed: either such power has yet to be invented, or the cult of the charismatic sovereign attempts to remake it where it no longer exists. Compared to many divine kings, the Inka's executive power was considerable: contrary to Hocart's (1970 [1936]: 135) formula, he not only reigned but governed. Yet neither was the Inka the tyrant that Andean and Western mythologies portrayed him to be.

As a form of political representation, oracles allow us to understand how the realities of consultation and negotiation in a weakly organized state were coordinated with the theoretical absolutism of Andean divine kingship. On the one hand, oracles simply followed the ideology of divine kingship to its logical conclusion: the king is a deity who continues to speak and dispense life even in death. On the other hand, the very perpetuity of divine kings ensured a plurality of authoritative voices, each one speaking for the corporate descent group it founded. Through the voice of their mummified ancestor, these groups could assert their own perspective and interests without questioning the nominally absolute power of the current sovereign. For in speaking through the voice of their founding ancestor, they ceased to be the authors of their own words. Any conflicts that arose

were no longer between the king and his subjects but between the king and his predecessors. Although oracles had an influence potentially equal to that of the living sovereign, the fact that they issued from his dead predecessors meant that they could not challenge his hold on power. Oracles made the king listen, without having to listen to a rival. Conversely, oracles gave those without power a voice, but not a voice of their own. It was only through a medium, penetrated by the voice of a more powerful animating and commanding being, that subaltern groups could make themselves heard. This form of empowerment implied and reproduced subordination, but it also allowed the current divine king to govern effectively without appearing to heed his conquered subjects.

With the death of every exemplary sovereign, another node was added to this oracular network. Inevitably, the sheer multiplicity of influential dead voices among successful groups like the Inka must have partially decentered and fragmented the authority of the incumbent ruler. Through its resolutely monolithic and elitist character, Andean divine kingship paradoxically sowed the seeds of diversity within itself. For if oracles were not a simple expression of popular will, neither was it possible to dispense with the heterogeneous perspectives they could offer. Oracular councils like the capacocha would not have been convened if the Inka was not somehow dependent on the diversity of information he could gather from them. In their own stilted manner, oracles restored communication where it otherwise would have been impossible because of the constraints of divine kingship. Without oracles, the Inka empire would have been even less governable than it already was. Thus, as Patterson (1985: 170) argues, the importance of provincial oracles disproves the official ideology of the Inka state, in which all power supposedly derived from the sovereign and ruling elite. Yet it is unlikely that oracles could have implemented a de facto sharing of power if they did not also support the ideology of divine kingship.

ORACLES AND THE BUREAUCRATIC DELEGATION OF POWER

The accumulation of illustrious predecessors was not the only reason the theoretically monolithic power of the Inka was in fact quite fragmented. Apart from any backseat driving by his dead predecessors, the ruler faced a tremendous task in governing the empire, one that absolutely required a bureaucratic delegation of powers. Although the Inka was theoretically in charge of war, administration, and religion, in practice he undertook each activity sequentially. He periodically delegated his military duties to various "generals," his religious duties to the high priest of the Sun, and his administrative duties to a figure called the *Inkap rantin*, or "Inka's substitute."[6] Descriptions of an Inka's exploits frequently included everything done by these delegates in the Inka's name. Thus the Inka became something of an umbrella figure or corporate persona who hierarchically subsumed under his identity an entire supporting cast of lesser individuals. The same process also characterized Andean deities, where segmentary identity was even more clearly developed.[7] The ability to work through multiple embodiments was a sign of the ruler's power, but it necessarily involved some risk. During life, the ruler usually held together as the center, but this only made for a greater crisis when he died, since he was supposed to personify the unity of the realm. Consequently, provincial revolts and wars of succession inevitably broke out upon the death of each sovereign. In this section I intend to explore this dissimulating delegation of administrative power and to show that it was at least partly modeled on oracular possession.

Only administrators of the very highest level received the title of "Inka's substitute." Typically they were half or full brothers of the Inka, and they never appeared to have occupied a position lower than governor of one of the four quarters of the empire, itself a kingly station (Santillán 1927 [1553]: 15). Governors who went by this title often traveled in a litter: a royal privilege that further underlined their identification with the Inka (see Sarmiento de Gamboa 1942 [1572]: 231; Guaman Poma de Ayala 1936 [1615]: 184).[8] Indeed, they often dressed like the Inka, the only difference being that instead of wearing the royal fringe over the forehead, they wore it to one side (Ramos Gavilán 1976 [1621]: 67). But as Santillán writes: "Besides these four [governors], the Inka had a secretary, who before any business came before the Inka, informed and acquainted himself with it, and then he let the Inka understand it through an account, and then each governor in his district, and after the Inka and the governor discussed it, that which they determined the secretary made known to the contenders before the Inka and before the governor" (1927 [1553]: 15–16). This "secretary" also counted as an "Inka's substitute," but he lived in Cuzco and worked closely with the Inka in administering and resolving disputes in the provinces: "The Inka did not hear cases from dealers sent from the provinces by their governors, but rather the rule was that the Inka had indicated and nominated a serious person from his lineage with whom he discussed and defined all matters, and he discussed it with the Inka and between them they agreed on what should be done and this second person had it put into operation and this second person of said Inka was elected on the day that he was invested as lord because his election fell to the priests of the Sun" (Molina 1925 [1582]: 280). Sarmiento further describes the role of this figure: "And for those who had some business with him [the Inka] he had appointed a lieutenant who was called *inga apo* which means the "Inka's lord," who stayed apart from the Inka, sitting down. With him negotiated those who had something to negotiate, and they entered with a burden on their back and their eyes to the ground, and they discussed their business with that *apo,* who got up and went to give an account of it to the Inka Atahuallpa, and he settled what should be done. And the *apo*

replied to the messenger or dealer, and by this order they transacted" (1942 [1572]: 258–59). Guaman Poma de Ayala describes this person as the Inka's "assessor" and gives his full title as "Inka's substitute speaker" (*yncap rantin rimac* [1936 (1615): III]), or "Inka's substitute speaker powerful lord" (*yncap rantin rimaric capac apo* [ibid.: 184]). This title further specifies the role of verbal intermediary that the "substitute" played between the sovereign and his people, a role also described in an offhand manner by H. Pizarro (1920 [1533]: 170) and Betanzos (1987 [1551]: 271).

The role of verbal intermediary casts a new light on the "substitute speaker." Rather than being a simple administrative deputy who took care of routine business to free the Inka for other tasks, he allowed the Inka to maintain a system of indirect communication with his subjects. To be sure, personal audiences with the Inka were sometimes granted to the nobility of Cuzco and ethnic lords, and they may well have spoken to each other directly. But these encounters were supervised by the substitute, who made everyone who appeared before the Inka carry a burden as a sign of humility (ibid.: 193). Whether or not he always acted as a verbal intermediary, the substitute speaker clearly enforced an appropriate degree of social distance between the divine king and his subjects. There were a whole series of prohibitions on having eye contact with the sovereign,[9] and touching him or even the vessels from which he ate and drank (MacCormack 1990: 4). Betanzos develops the same point: "You must know that while these lords were alive they were held in awe and reverenced as sons of the Sun and once dead their mummies were held in awe and reverenced like gods and thus they made sacrifices in front of them just as was done for the image of the Sun" (1987 [1551]: 166). Clearly, there were religious reasons for the existence of this "substitute" as mediating figure between the ruler and his people. As a living god, the Inka was simply too powerful to interact directly with his subjects.

There is every reason to suppose that the relation of a substitute to a living king was identified with that between a medium and a dead king. Both upheld the same pattern of indirect communication between a remote sovereign and his subjects, brokered by an intermediary who relayed requests and replies. In fact, the transition from "substitute" to medium was direct. After the death of an Inka sovereign, his statue and mummy continued to have a living human "substitute" (Ávila 1966 [1598]: 125; Polo de Ondegardo 1916 [1585]: 124), who necessarily had to act as a medium to carry out communication between the (dead) ruler and his people. Conversely, to be a medium, one would have to be appointed as the "substitute" of a dead ruler. The delegation of administrative power from sovereign to "substitute" evidently took place on an oracular model, and thus the governmental structure of the Inka empire was significantly shaped by the commemorative cult of divine kings.

Another kind of substitute also stood in for the living sovereign. During his lifetime, each ruler made a statue of gold, silver, wood, or stone and called it his "brother" (*wawqe*), which was treated with the same reverence as the sovereign himself (ibid.: 8–10; Cobo 1956 [1653]: 162). Betanzos describes how Inca Atahuallpa

> upon seeing himself king, had made an image with his own nails and hair which imitated his person and he ordered that this image be called Ynga Guaquin, which means brother of the Inka, and once this image was made, he ordered that it be placed in a litter, and he sent one of his dependents named Chima to serve this image and to be in charge of guarding it and looking after it, and giving this image many attendants and [a] service, he ordered that it then be taken in a litter to the post where his captains Chalcuchima and Quizquiz were, so that the provinces and peoples they subjected might give obeisance to that image instead of his person, and so the image was taken and given to the captains who received it and celebrated greatly with it, and made many and very large sacrifices to it, and thus they served and respected this image as if Atagualpa himself were there in person. (Betanzos 1987 [1551]: 220; see also Sarmiento de Gamboa 1942 [1572]: 265)

Clearly, this statue was a substitute and a stand-in for the sovereign. The fact that the statue was called the Inka's "brother" further underscores its similarity to the living "substitutes" of the Inka, since they were usually his brothers of flesh and blood.

Just as the Inka sought counsel from his living brothers, so he did from his statue. Certain Inka rulers were said to be accompanied by their "brothers" and other royal statues, which regularly pronounced oracles (Betanzos 1987 [1551]: 215; Sarmiento de Gamboa 1942 [1572]: 121, 134, 137–38). In these cases the statue clearly did not act as a proxy for the sovereign, since he was already present as its interlocutor. Nonetheless, the statue represented a similar fragmentation of his persona, albeit one to which he was party through oracular dialogue. The sovereign related to his own statue in much the same way as he did those of his predecessors, namely as the ancestral aspect of his own personality destined for deified immortality. According to Betanzos (1987 [1551]: 147–48, 166–67, 177, 209), more golden statues of the sovereign were made shortly after his death, and though his body might be mummified immediately, it was not "canonized" until the final mortuary ceremonies a year later. Thus a sovereign's statue(s) provided continuity during his transformation from a living ruler into an ancestral deity, particularly during the interregnum between his primary and secondary mortuary rituals. This imperishable "brother" most clearly reveals the concatenation of government and the cult of the dead under the Inkas, both of which aimed to extend the sovereign's presence and render it eternal.

There can be little doubt, then, that oracular possession was a significant idiom of delegated power for the Inkas. Like an "Inka's substitute," a medium did not (in theory) speak on his own behalf but rather for the ruler-deity that "infused" him. In acting as a vehicle for an external power, the words and actions of a medium became depersonalized and were not attributable to himself but to the separate and far more powerful agency of the ruler-deity. Although the idiom was not fully bureaucratic, the parallels are unmistakable. By working through the multiple embodiments of "substitutes," statues, and mediums, a ruler extended his influence in space and time and delegated enough power to govern effectively. At the same time, he demonstrated his divinity by "animating" these far-flung subdivisions of himself, thereby making an ideological virtue out of administrative necessity. This style of delegation reinforced the personal, patrimonial emphasis of Andean divine kingship, which discouraged strong governing institutions. Within the limits of the Inka framework, however, this oracular delegation of power was perhaps the most extensive possible.

In summary, the royal mummy cults and their oracular delegation of power provided the idiom by which governors and other "Inka's substitutes" operated in the most exclusive circles of the Inka court. The secularizing accounts of Moore (1958) and Murra (1958) generally ignore or misrepresent the workings of Inka government at this elite level, since they do not recognize how Inka administration was shaped by the oracular, protobureaucratic dynamics of substitution and delegation. Equally problematic is the notion of diarchy originally advanced by Zuidema (1964:127), which incorrectly limits this delegation of the sovereign's power to a single "substitute," when in fact there were many (for a more extensive critique of the diarchy thesis see Gose forthcoming). The concept of divine kingship, however, makes perfect sense of these peculiarities of Inka government. . . .

[In a 1,500-word section titled "The Recentralization of Oracular Power," Gose argues that oracles tended to fragment power and that this had to be countered. He provides several examples of how the high king and priest preserved the center against fragmentation. Conquered peoples' main idols were taken to Cuzco, where their presence both signified the subordinate status of the conquered and allowed the Inkas to co-opt their oracles. Eventually such deities were returned, but now they represented Inka interests. Additionally, the annual *capachocha* ritual gave the Inka a chance to evaluate the oracles, rewarding those who were accurate and demoting those who were not. This practice made the oracles dependent on a reward system controlled by the Inka.

The high priest of the Sun had the most power in the oracle system and could demote or even eliminate lower-level oracles. This gave him substantial control over what they said. High priests could accumulate power to rival the high king. As a result, high kings often replaced high priests on their accession, frequently assuming priestly duties themselves. This shows the extremely close relationship between kingly and priestly roles. The example of the oracle Catequil and the high king Atahuallpa shows where real power lay in the system. When the oracle predicted a bad end for Atahuallpa, Atahuallpa beheaded the priest and totally destroyed the oracle's shrine. The oracles of the royal *panaqas* of Cuzco had greater independence than provincial oracles, but even they could be destroyed if they were too vehement in their opposition to the king.

There were limits to the high king's power. For example, when the oracles refused to speak to him, the high king Huayna Capac (father of Atahuallpa) had all minor oracles destroyed. However, he could not destroy the major oracles—these played critical roles in the functioning of the government, and destroying them would have left the empire extremely difficult to govern.

Andean divine kings depended on their history and divine ancestry to legitimize their governance. Thus they became, in a sense, junior to the kings who came before them. It was only through conquest and the subsequent attainment of divine status that they cemented their own position. This kept the empire vital but created numerous contradictions.—Editors]

CONCLUSION

Until recently, the political influence of Andean oracles has been systematically underestimated, even though they pronounced on most of the Inka empire's important decisions and consumed a significant proportion of its material and human resources. However, this neglect of oracles is not entirely surprising, for they lacked the initiative of the living sovereign. Although they still had the power to possess and speak through mediums, oracular deities could never again presume to rule. Conversely, those whom the deities possessed might be momentarily empowered but were soon discarded as just another of their many embodiments. The possession state was vividly portrayed (both in performance and linguistic commentary) as the exercise of power upon the medium by an external source of life and authority. Oracular communication was a discourse in subordination: the heightening it brought about in the medium cannot be confused with the inherent power of the sovereign.

It was precisely because oracular performances dramatized and embodied major imbalances of power that they also could give voice to the concerns of subaltern groups. No matter what an oracle said, its message was always bracketed by the doubly nonthreatening form that it took in relation to the living sovereign, that of a dead ruler speaking through a subordinated human vehicle, neither of whom could challenge the incumbent ruler as a center of influence. Without this deferential mode of presentation, oracular communication might never have achieved the degree of frankness that living sovereigns so desired. As long as their power was not directly challenged in the process, they realized that their interest was in knowing the truth, even if it was not pleasant. Ironically, it was the profound indirectness of the oracular form that permitted and even institutionalized the Inka obsession with truth and frankness from their deities.

In this essay I have shown that oracular communication had many functions, one of the most important being political representation. All these functions could have been carried out through different and more direct cultural forms, but the institutional and ideological realities of Andean divine kingship funneled the political process in an oracular direction. Once the ruler becomes a center of divine authority, it is difficult for him to accept advice from lesser lords and apparatchiks without appearing to defer to them, something that no self-respecting Inka could contemplate. For the Inka, to have a living peer was to have a rival; therefore, he kept the company of the statues and mummies of his predecessors, who told him things that could not be said in the name of his subjects. In a cultural regime committed to the heroic ruler as a dominant form of subjectivity, oracular possession was neither pathological nor exotic but one of the few ways that more mundane social realities could assert themselves.

NOTES

1. See the excellent discussions of these terms in Taylor 1974–76 and Duviols 1978b.

2. Santo Tomás (1951 [1560]: 114) gives many kama derivatives that involve the notion of "supply" and "provision" (see also González Holguín 1952 [1608]: 47). The same meaning is present in the Inka and colonial practice of "camarico" (gifts, hospitality; see Guaman Poma de Ayala 1936 [1615]: 355). Finally, the separatist sermons attributed to the "ministers of idolatry" in the Cajatambo documents consistently dwell on the idea that the life and prosperity of the various local descent groups (ayllus) comes from their mummies and camaquenes, not the Christian god. In particular, food, clothing, water, fields, human health and fertility, and good advice were attributed to the camaquenes (see Duviols 1968: 69, 74, 76, 99, 100, 106, 145, 174, 282, 335, 343). By the same token, the camaquenes would send sickness to their ayllus, devour them, or at the very least withhold the bounty of the fields from them should they neglect their sacrificial obligations to the dead (ibid.: 76, 189, 196, 212, 221, 237, 275, 407).

3. See Sarmiento de Gamboa 1942 [1572]: 173; Cieza de León 1984 [1553], 1: chap. 72; Guaman Poma de Ayala 1936 [1615]: 263; Polo de Ondegardo 1916 [1585]: 30; Ramos Gavilán 1976 [1621]: 88; and Calancha 1972 [1639]: 156.

4. See H. Pizarro 1920 [1533]: 177; Cieza de León 1984 [1553], 2: chaps. 63–64, 66; Betanzos 1978 [1551]: 149–50; Sarmiento de Gamboa 1942 [1572]: 173, 260; and Cobo 1956 [1653]: 224.

5. There is interesting semantic evidence for the existence of a local concept of this specialized type of oracular knowledge. Oracular mediums were sometimes called "knowers" (yachac; see Archivo Arzobispal de Lima, Hechicerías e Idolatrías, Lagajo 11, Expediente 7, Checras 1724, folio 7v). Whereas the verb yachay means "to know" and could be extended as yachachiy to mean "to cause to know" or "to counsel," we often find that the term yachachi was synonymous with camaquen as "creator" or "source of life" (Santo Tomás 1951 [1560]: 114). Just as deities are sources of life for their people, so they are also sources of knowledge about them, and not just at the moment of consultation but also in the future.

6. *Ranti* also described the successor to an office (Betanzos 1987 [1551]: 131) and had a more abstract connotation of equivalence that was applied to monetary transactions. The standard Spanish translations of this word are "second person" (*segunda persona*) and "place-taker" (*lugarteniente*).

7. The coastal deities of Pachacamac, Pariacaca, and Chaupiñamca were all subject to five-part divisions, which were sometimes described as their children and other times as envoys or aspects of a unitary identity (see Santillán 1927 [1553]: 30–32; Ávila 1966 [1598]: chaps. 5, 8, 13). Descent was a common model for segmentary hierarchy among deities, but it did not imply discrete identities and usually meant that lower-level wakas could be subsumed by higher-level ones.

8. Guaman Poma de Ayala further confirms that these governors personified the Inka when he describes the official (*alcalde*) they communicated with in each province (*repartimiento*) as the "hearer of the Inka's word" (*yncap cimin oyaric* [1936 (1615): 184]).

9. See Xerez 1987 [1534]: 106, 125; Estete 1924 [1535]: 41; Sarmiento de Gamboa 1942 [1572]: 209; and Murúa 1987 [1613]: 69).

REFERENCES

Albornoz, Cristobal de
    1967   Instrucción para descubrir todas las Guacas del Piru y sus camayos y haziendas. Journal de la Société des Américanistes 56: 8–39.

Anonymous Jesuit
    1968 [ca. 1590]   Relación de las costumbres antiguas de los naturales del Pirú. *In* Biblioteca de Autores Españoles. Vol. 209, pp. 153–77. Madrid: Ediciones Atlas.

Arriaga, Pable José de
    1968 [1621]   Extirpación de la idolatría en el Perú. *In* Biblioteca de Autores Españoles. Vol. 209, pp. 191–277. Madrid: Ediciones Atlas.

Ávila, Francisco de
    1966 [1598]   Dioses y hombres de Huarochirí. Lima: Instituto de Estudios Peruanos.

Betanzos, Juan de
    1987 [1551]   Suma y narración de los Incas. Madrid: Ediciones Atlas.

Boddy, Janice P.
    1989   Wombs and Alien Spirits: Women, Men, and the Zar Cult in Northern Sudan. Madison: University of Wisconsin Press.

Cabello Valboa, Miguel
    1951 [1586]   Miscelánea antárctica. Lima: Universidad Nacional Mayor de San Marcos.

Calancha, Antonio de la
    1972 [1639]   Chronica moralizada del orden de San Augustin en el Peru, con sucesos egenplares en esta monarquia. Madrid: Consejo de Investigaciones Cientificas Instituto "Enrique Florez."

Cieza de León, Pedro de
    1984 [1553]   La crónica del Perú. Pts. 1, 2. *In* Obras Completas. Vol. 1. Madrid: Consejo Superior de Investigaciones Cientificas, Instituto "Gonzalo Fernández de Ovideo."

Cobo, Bernabe
    1956 [1653]   Historia del Nuevo Mundo. *In* Biblioteca de Autores Españoles. Vol. 92. Madrid: Ediciones Atlas.

Doyle, Mary Eileen
    1988   The Ancestor Cult and Burial Ritual in Seventeenth- and Eighteenth-Century Central Peru. Ann Arbor, MI: UMI Dissertation Services.

Dumont, Louis
    1986   Essays on Individualism: Modern Ideology in Anthropological Perspective. Chicago: University of Chicago Press.

Duviols, Pierre
    1973   Huari y Llacuaz: Agricultores y pastores. Un dualismo prehispánico de oposición y complementariedad. Revista del Museo Nacional 39: 153–91.
    1974–76   Une Petite Chronique Retrouvée: Errores, ritos, supersticiones y ceremonias de los yndios de la provincial de Chinchaycocha y otras del Piru. Journal de la Société des Américanistes 63: 275–97.
    1978a   Un Symbolisme Andin du double: La Lithomorphose de l'ancêtre. *In* Actes du XLIIe Congrès International des Américanistes. Vol. 4, pp. 359–64.
    1978b   Camaquen, Upani: Un Concept Animiste des anciens Peruviens. In Estudios Américanistas. R. Hartmann and U. Oberam, eds. Vol. 1, pp. 132–44. Bonn: Collectanea Instituti Anthropos, vol. 20.
    1979   Un Symbolisme de l'occupation, de l'aménagement et de l'exploitation de l'espace: Le Monolithe 'Huanca' et sa fonction dans les Andes préhispaniques. L'Homme 19 (2): 7–31.
    1986   Cultura andina y represión: Procesos y visitas de idolatrías y hechicerías Cajatambo, siglo XVII. Cuzco: Centro de estudios rurales andinos "Bartolomé de las Casas."

Estete, Miguel de
    1924 [1535]   Noticia del Perú. *In* Colección de libros y documentos referentes a la historia del Perú. H. Urteaga and C. Romero, eds. Vol. 8, pp. 3–56. Lima: Imprenta y Librería Sanmarti.

Evans-Pritchard, Edward E.
    1937   Witchcraft, Oracles, and Magic among the Azande. Oxford: Oxford University Press.

González Holguín, Diego
    1952 [1608]   Vocabulario de la lengua general de todo el Perú llamada lengua Qqichua o del Inca. Lima: Imprenta Santa Maria.

Gose, Peter
    forthcoming The Past Is a Lower Moiety: Diarchy, History, and Divine Kingship in the Inka Empire. History and Anthropology.

Guaman Poma de Ayala, Felipe
    1936 [1615]   Nueva Corónica y Buen Gobierno. Paris: Université de Paris.

Hocart, Arthur M.
    1970 [1936]   Kings and Councillors: An Essay in the Comparative Anatomy of Human Society. Chicago: University of Chicago Press.

Lambek, Michael
    1981   Human Spirits: A Cultural Account of Trance in Mayotte. Cambridge: Cambridge University Press.

MacCormack, Sabine

1990   Children of the Sun and Reasons of State: Myths, Ceremonies, and Conflicts in Inca Peru. 1992 Lecture Series, Working Papers No. 6. Department of Spanish and Portuguese, University of Maryland at College Park.

1991   Religion in the Andes: Vision and Imagination in Early Colonial Peru. Princeton, NJ: Princeton University Press.

Millones, Luis, comp.

1990   El Retorno de las Huacas: Estudios y documentos sobre el Taki Onqoy, siglo XVI. Lima: Instituto de Estudios Peruanos; Sociedad Peruana de Psicoanalisis.

Molina, Cristobal de

1925 [1582]   Información hecha en el Cuzco, por orden del Rey y encargo del Virrey Martín Enríquez acerca de las costumbres que tenían los Incas del Perú. *In* Gobernantes del Perú. R. Levillier, ed. Vol. 9, pp. 268–88. Madrid: Imprenta de Juan Pueyo.

Moore, Sally F.

1958   Power and Property in Inca Peru. New York: Columbia University Press.

Murra, John

1958   On Inca Political Structure. *In* Systems of Control and Bureaucracy in Human Societies. Verne Ray, ed. Pp. 30–39. Seattle, WA: American Ethnological Society.

Murúa, Martin de

1987 [1613]   Historia general del Perú. Madrid: Historia 16.

Patterson, Thomas C.

1985   Pachacamac—An Andean Oracle under Inca Rule. In Recent Studies in Andean Prehistory and Protohistory. D. P. Kvietok and D. H. Sandweiss, eds. Pp. 159–76. Ithaca, NY: Cornell University Press.

Pizarro, Hernando

1920 [1533]   A los señores oydores de la Audiencia Real de su Magestad. *In* Informacions sobre el antiguo Perú, Colección de libros y documentos referentes a la historia del Perú. Vol. 3, 2d ser. H. Urteaga, ed. Pp. 167–80. Lima: Imprenta y Librería y Ca.

Pizarro, Pedro

1978 [1571]   Relación del descubrimiento y conquista de los reinos del Perú. Lima: Pontificia Universidad Católica del Perú.

Polo de Ondegardo, Juan

1916 [1585]   De los errores y supersticiones de los indios, sacadas del tratado y averiguación que hizo el Licenciado Polo. *In* Informaciones acerca de la religión y gobierno de los Incas. H. Urteaga and C. Romero, eds. Vol. 1, pp. 3–43. Lima: Imprenta y Librería Sanmarti.

Primeros Agustinos

1918 [1560]   Relación de la religión y ritos del Perú hecha por los primeros religiosos Agustinos que allí pasaron para conversión de los naturales. *In* Collección de libros y documentos referentes a la historia del Perú. H. Urteaga and C. Romero, eds. Vol. 11, pp. 1–56. Lima: Imprenta y Librería Sanmarti.

Ramos Gavilán, Alonso

1976 [1621]   Historia de nuestra Señora de Copacabana. La Paz: Academia Boliviana de la Historia.

Romero, Carlos

1918   Idolatrías de los Indios Huachos y Yauyos. Revista Histórica 6:180–97.

Rostworowski de Diez Canseco, Maria

1983   Estructuras andinas del poder: Ideología religiosa y politica. Lima: Instituto de Estudios Peruanos.

1988   La historia del Tahuantinsuyo. Lima: Instituto de Estudios Peruanos.

Sancho de la Hoz, P.

1968 [1543]   Relación para SM de lo sucedido en la conquista y pacificación de estas provincias de Nueva Castilla y de la calidad de la tierra. *In* Biblioteca Peruana. Ser. 1, vol. 1, pp. 275–344. Lima: Editores Técnicos Asociados.

Santacruz Pachacuti, Joan de

1927 [1613]   Relación de Antiguedades deste Reyno del Piru. *In* Colección de libros y documentos referentes a la historia del Perú. H. Urteaga, ed. Vol. 9, pp. 125–235. Lima: Imprenta y Librería Sanmarti.

Santillán, Hernando de

1927 [1553]   Relación del origien, descendencia, politica y gobierno de los Incas. *In* Colección de libros y documentos referentes a la historia del Perú. H. Urteaga, ed. Vol. 9, pp. 1–124. Lima: Imprenta y Librería Sanmarti.

Santo Tomás, D. de

1951 [1560]   Lexicon o vocabulario de la lengua general del Peru. Lima: Universidad Nacional Mayor de San Marcos.

Sarmiento de Gamboa, Pedro

1942 [1572]   Historia de los Incas. Buenos Aires: Biblioteca Emecé.

Segovia, Bartolomé de (formerly attributed to Cristóbal de Molina [el Almagrista])

1968 [1553]   Relación de muchas cosas acaesidas en la Perú. *In* Biblioteca de Autores Españoles. Vol. 209, pp. 56–95. Madrid: Ediciones Atlas.

Taylor, Gerald

1974–76   *Camay, Camac* et *Camasca* dans le manuscrit Quechua de Huarochirí. Journal de la Société des Américanistes 63: 231–44.

Trujillo, Diego de

1987 [1571]   Relación del descubrimiento del reino del Perú que hizo Diego de Trujillo en compañía del gobernador don Francisco Pizarro y otros capitanes, desde que llegaron a Panama el año de 1530, en que refiere todas derrotas y sucesos, hasta 15 de abril de 1571. *In* Verdadera relación de la conquista del Perú. F. de Xerez, primary author. Pp. 191–206. Madrid: Historia 16.

Weber, Max

1978   Economy and Society: An Outline of Interpretive Sociology. Guenther Roth and Claus Wittich, eds. Ephraim Fischoff et al., trans. Vol. 1. Berkeley and Los Angeles: University of California Press.

Xerez, Francisco de

1987 [1534]   Verdadera relación de la conquista del Perú. Madrid: Historia 16.

Zuidema, R. Tom

1964   The Ceque System of Cuzco: The Social Organization of the Capital of the Incas. Leiden: Brill.

7

Ritual and Ceremony

Essays in This Section:

Religion is composed of two basic parts: an ideological component consisting of beliefs and a behavioral component consisting of practices based on those beliefs. This section deals with one aspect of the behavioral component—ritual. Rituals are prescribed, stylized, stereotyped ways of performing a religious action and are one of the basic characteristics shared by all religions. As you read the essays in this section, keep the following points in mind:

- In the general sense, ritual can refer to any repetitive action such as drinking a cup of coffee each morning or brushing one's teeth. Traditionally, anthropologists use the term *ritual* for specific actions that establish some connection with the nonempirical or supernatural realm.

- The terms *ritual, ceremony,* and *rite* are frequently used interchangeably, but occasionally the latter two are used to describe a set of religious actions that are composed of related rituals.

- Rituals are formulaic; that is, they are performed according to an established pattern. They can vary from simple to complex. Within a culture, some are widespread and performed by all or many members of a society, others are restricted to specific groups within a society, and others still are performed only by a specific individual. Within societies with well-defined centralized authority, certain rituals are performed only by individuals authorized to conduct them.

- Rituals may serve to structure society or social relationships, reinforce concepts of the spiritual through symbolic actions, or manipulate perceived immaterial beings or powers.

- Ritual can function to define groups or status within society. Several of the essays in this section directly address this issue. Consider why definitions of social

groups are important and what implications this might have for the political and economic systems of a particular society. Consider the social power of rituals and how they can establish status in society or membership within a particular group. These rituals also promote group solidarity among the participants.

- Rites of passage are rituals that mark the transition from one stage of life to the next. One characteristic of these rituals is the *liminal* state in which the participants' status and very existence as members of society is ambiguous and uncertain. Individuals in this state often reverse or violate their accustomed social roles. Turner's essay on liminality in rites of passage, Stevens's on play and liminality, and Leonard's on female circumcision in Southern Chad, examine this state. As these essays show, the analysis of liminality in ritual highlights and provides insight into social roles and practices.

- Religious ritual serves to forge a link between the everyday world and the nonempirical realm. Ritual can function to ease the anxieties associated with the uncertainties of the present. It does this by giving participants a partial sense of security. Having participated in a ritual, they have done something to affect the outcome in uncertain situations. This is particularly evident in George Gmelch's essay on baseball magic. You will find another example of the same idea in Laurel Kendall's essay on Korean shamans in section 6.

- Establishing a link with the supernatural can also play an important role in the maintenance of good health. Healing rituals are a cultural universal and illustrate the perceived relationship between the nonempirical (supernatural) and physical worlds. Miner's essay on the Nacirema discusses this association, which is also explored more fully in Part 4.

Betwixt and Between:
The Liminal Period in *Rites de Passage*

Victor W. Turner

Rites of passage mark the transition from one stage of life to the next. In this essay, Turner elaborates on a model of these rituals originally proposed by Arnold van Gennep, a French ethnographer who wrote a classic work on ritual in 1909. Van Gennep divided rites of passage into three stages: separation, margin, and aggregation. Turner follows and elaborates on Van Gennep's model, focusing particularly on the characteristics of the margin or transitional stage, particularly liminality. In this stage, the subjects of the ritual are somewhere in between; they have left their old status but have not yet attained their new one. In this liminal state, the behavioral rules of their old status no longer apply but neither do the rules of their future status. As a result, unusual ritual behavior is common.

Turner's analysis focuses on initiation rites, one form of rite of passage, because the liminal state is clearly evident and well marked in this form. Social position is an important organizing principle in many societies, and initiation rites are critical in clearly marking the transition from one status to another. In these rituals, participants are stripped of their old identities and given new ones. Symbolic elements of the life cycle characterize the liminal state and are frequently expressed in ritual components that emphasize death, decomposition, and loss of all identity. This is followed by the emergence of participants as embryos, newborns, or infants. Turner contends that analysis of the liminal state in rites of passage can reveal important clues to the cultural foundations of any particular society.

As you read, consider these questions:

1. Are rites of passage performed for the benefit of society, the people going through them, or both? Why?
2. Why are initiates in rites of passage sometimes treated as corpses or embryos, and why is this important?
3. Why are initiates hidden from society while in the liminal stage of the ritual?
4. What are some examples of liminal states in American rites of passage?

Reprinted from Victor W. Turner, "Betwixt and Between: The Liminal Period in *Rites de Passage*" from the Proceedings of the America Ethnological Society (1964) Symposium on *New Approaches to the Study of Religion*, pp. 4–20, by permission of the American Ethnological Society.

In this paper, I wish to consider some of the sociocultural properties of the "liminal period" in that class of rituals which Arnold van Gennep has definitively characterized as *"rites de passage."* If our basic model of society is that of a "structure of positions," we must regard the period of margin or "liminality" as an interstructural situation. I shall consider, notably in the case of initiation rites, some of the main features of instruction among the simpler societies. I shall also take note of certain symbolic themes that concretely express indigenous concepts about the nature of "interstructural" human beings.

Rites de passage are found in all societies but tend to reach their maximal expression in small-scale, relatively stable and cyclical societies, where change is bound up with biological and meteorological rhythms and recurrences rather than with technological innovations. Such rites indicate and constitute transitions between states. By "state" I mean here "a relatively fixed or stable condition" and would include in its meaning such social constancies as legal status, profession, office or calling, rank or degree. I hold it to designate also the condition of a person as determined by his culturally recognized degree of maturation as when one speaks of "the married or single state" or the "state of infancy." The term "state" may also be applied to ecological conditions, or to the physical, mental or emotional condition in which a person or group may be found at a particular time. A man may thus be in a state of good or bad health; a society in a state of war or peace or a state of famine or of plenty. State, in short, is a more inclusive concept than status or office and refers to any type of stable or recurrent condition that is culturally recognized. One may, I suppose, also talk about "a state of transition," since J. S. Mill has, after all, written of "a state of progressive movement," but I prefer to regard transition as a process, a becoming, and in the case of *rites de passage* even a transformation—here an apt analogy would be water in process of being heated to boiling point, or a pupa changing from grub to moth. In any case, a transition has different cultural properties from those of a state, as I hope to show presently.

Van Gennep himself defined *"rites de passage"* as "rites which accompany every change of place, state, social position and age." To point up the contrast between "state" and "transition," I employ "state" to include all his other terms. Van Gennep has shown that all rites of transition are marked by three phases: separation, margin (or *limen*), and aggregation. The first phase of separation comprises symbolic behavior signifying the detachment of the individual or group either from an earlier fixed point in the social structure or a set of cultural conditions (a "state"); during the intervening liminal period, the state of the ritual subject (the "passenger") is ambiguous; he passes through a realm that has few or none of the attributes of the past or coming state; in the third phase the passage is consummated. The ritual subject, individual or corporate, is in a stable state once more and, by virtue of this, has rights and obligations of a clearly defined and "structural" type, and is expected to behave in accordance with certain customary norms and ethical standards. The most prominent type of *rites de passage* tends to accompany what Lloyd Warner (1959, 303) has called "the movement of a man through his lifetime, from a fixed placental placement within his mother's womb to his death and ultimate fixed point of his tombstone and final containment in his grave as a dead organism—punctuated by a number of critical moments of transition which all societies ritualize and publicly mark with suitable observances to impress the significance of the individual and the group on living members of the community. These are the important times of birth, puberty, marriage, and death." However, as van Gennep, Henri Junod, and others have shown, *rites de passage* are not confined to culturally defined life-crises but may accompany any change from one state to another, as when a whole tribe goes to war, or when it attests to the passage from scarcity to plenty by performing a first-fruits or a harvest festival. *Rites de passage,* too, are not restricted, sociologically speaking, to movements between ascribed statuses. They also concern entry into a new achieved status, whether this be a political office or membership of an exclusive club or secret society. They may admit persons into membership of a religious group where such a group does not include the whole society, or qualify them for the official duties of the cult, sometimes in a graded series of rites.

Since the main problem of this study is the nature and characteristics of transition in relatively stable societies, I shall focus attention on *rites de passage* that tend to have well-developed liminal periods. On the whole, initiation rites, whether into social maturity or cult membership, best exemplify transition, since they have well-marked and protracted marginal or liminal phases. I shall pay only brief heed here to rites of separation and aggregation, since these are more closely implicated in social structure than rites of liminality. Liminality during initiation is, therefore, the primary datum of this study, though I will draw on other aspects of passage ritual where the argument demands this. I may state here, partly as an aside, that I consider the term "ritual" to be more fittingly applied to forms of religious behavior associated with social transitions, while the term "ceremony" has a closer bearing on religious behavior associated with social states, where politico-legal institutions also have greater importance. Ritual is transformative, ceremony confirmatory.

The subject of passage ritual is, in the liminal period, structurally, if not physically, "invisible." As members of society, most of us see only what we expect to see, and what we expect to see is what we are conditioned to see when we have learned the definitions and classifications of our cul-

ture. A society's secular definitions do not allow for the existence of a not-boy-not-man, which is what a novice in a male puberty rite is (if he can be said to be anything). A set of essentially religious definitions co-exist with these which do set out to define the structurally indefinable "transitional-being." The transitional-being or "liminal *persona*" is defined by a name and by a set of symbols. The same name is very frequently employed to designate those who are being initiated into very different states of life. For example, among the Ndembu of Zambia the name *mwadi* may mean various things: it may stand for "a boy novice in circumcision rites," or "a chief-designate undergoing his installation rites," or, yet again, "the first or ritual wife" who has important ritual duties in the domestic family. Our own terms "initiate" and "neophyte" have a similar breadth of reference. It would seem from this that emphasis tends to be laid on the transition itself, rather than on the particular states between which it is taking place.

The symbolism attached to and surrounding the liminal *persona* is complex and bizarre. Much of it is modeled on human biological processes, which are conceived to be what Levi-Strauss might call "isomorphic" with structural and cultural processes. They give an outward and visible form to an inward and conceptual process. The structural "invisibility" of liminal *personae* has a twofold character. They are at once no longer classified and not yet classified. In so far as they are no longer classified, the symbols that represent them are, in many societies, drawn from the biology of death, decomposition, catabolism, and other physical processes that have a negative tinge, such as menstruation (frequently regarded as the absence or loss of a fetus). Thus, in some boys' initiations, newly circumcised boys are explicitly likened to menstruating women. In so far as a neophyte is structurally "dead," he or she may be treated, for a long or short period, as a corpse is customarily treated in his or her society. (See Stobaeus' quotation, probably from a lost work of Plutarch, "initiation and death correspond word for word and thing for thing" [James 1961, 132]). The neophyte may be buried, forced to lie motionless in the posture and direction of customary burial, may be stained black, or may be forced to live for a while in the company of masked and monstrous mummers representing, *inter alia,* the dead, or worse still, the un-dead. The metaphor of dissolution is often applied to neophytes; they are allowed to go filthy and identified with the earth, the generalized matter into which every specific individual is rendered down. Particular form here becomes general matter; often their very names are taken from them and each is called solely by the generic term for "neophyte" or "initiand." (This useful neologism is employed by many modern anthropologists.)

The other aspect, that they are not yet classified, is often expressed in symbols modeled on processes of gestation and parturition. The neophytes are likened to or treated as embryos, newborn infants, or sucklings by symbolic means which vary from culture to culture. I shall return to this theme presently.

The essential feature of these symbolizations is that the neophytes are neither living nor dead from one aspect, and both living and dead from another. Their condition is one of ambiguity and paradox, a confusion of all the customary categories. Jakob Boehme, the German mystic whose obscure writings gave Hegel his celebrated dialectical "triad," liked to say that "In Yea and Nay all things consist." Liminality may perhaps be regarded as the Nay to all positive structural assertions, but as in some sense the source of them all, and, more than that, as a realm of pure possibility whence novel configurations of ideas and relations may arise. I will not pursue this point here but, after all, Plato, a speculative philosopher, if there ever was one, did acknowledge his philosophical debt to the teachings of the Eleusinian and Orphic initiations of Attica. We have no way of knowing whether primitive initiations merely conserved lore. Perhaps they also generated new thought and new custom.

Dr. Mary Douglas, of University College, London, has recently advanced (in a magnificent book *Purity and Danger* [1966]) the very interesting and illuminating view that the concept of pollution "is a reaction to protect cherished principles and categories from contradiction." She holds that, in effect, what is unclear and contradictory (from the perspective of social definition) tends to be regarded as (ritually) unclean. The unclear is the unclean: e.g., she examines the prohibitions on eating certain animals and crustaceans in Leviticus in the light of this hypothesis (these being creatures that cannot be unambiguously classified in terms of traditional criteria). From this standpoint, one would expect to find that transitional beings are particularly polluting, since they are neither one thing nor another; or may be both; or neither here nor there; or may even be nowhere (in terms of any recognized cultural topography), and are at the very least "betwixt and between" all the recognized fixed points in space-time of structural classification. In fact, in confirmation of Dr. Douglas's hypothesis, liminal *personae* nearly always and everywhere are regarded as polluting to those who have never been, so to speak, "inoculated" against them, through having been themselves initiated into the same state. I think that we may perhaps usefully discriminate here between the statics and dynamics of pollution situations. In other words, we may have to distinguish between pollution notions which concern states that have been ambiguously or contradictorily defined, and those which derive from ritualized transitions between states. In the first case, we are dealing with what has been defectively defined or ordered, in the second with what cannot be defined in static terms. We are not dealing with structural contradictions when we discuss liminality, but with the essentially unstructured (which is at once destructured and prestructured) and often the people themselves see this in terms of bringing neophytes into close connection with deity or with superhuman power, with what is, in fact, often regarded as the unbounded, the infinite, the limitless. Since neophytes are not only structurally "invisible" (though physically visible) and

ritually polluting, they are very commonly secluded, partially or completely, from the realm of culturally defined and ordered states and statuses. Often the indigenous term for the liminal period is, as among Ndembu, the locative form of a noun meaning "seclusion site" (*kunkunka, kung'ula*). The neophytes are sometimes said to "be in another place." They have physical but not social "reality," hence they have to be hidden, since it is a paradox, a scandal, to see what ought not to be there! Where they are not removed to a sacred place of concealment they are often disguised, in masks or grotesque costumes or striped with white, red, or black clay, and the like.

In societies dominantly structured by kinship institutions, sex distinctions have great structural importance. Patrilineal and matrilineal moieties and clans, rules of exogamy, and the like, rest and are built up on these distinctions. It is consistent with this to find that in liminal situations (in kinship-dominated societies) neophytes are sometimes treated or symbolically represented as being neither male nor female. Alternatively, they may be symbolically assigned characteristics of both sexes, irrespective of their biological sex. (Bruno Bettelheim [1954] has collected much illustrative material on this point from initiation rites.) They are symbolically either sexless or bisexual and may be regarded as a kind of human *prima materia*—as undifferentiated raw material. It was perhaps from the rites of the Hellenic mystery religions that Plato derived his notion expressed in his *Symposium* that the first humans were androgynes. If the liminal period is seen as an interstructural phase in social dynamics, the symbolism both of androgyny and sexlessness immediately becomes intelligible in sociological terms without the need to import psychological (and especially depth-psychological) explanations. Since sex distinctions are important components of structural status, in a structureless realm they do not apply.

A further structurally negative characteristic of transitional beings is that they *have* nothing. They have no status, property, insignia, secular clothing, rank, kinship position, nothing to demarcate them structurally from their fellows. Their condition is indeed the very prototype of sacred poverty. Rights over property, goods, and services inhere in positions in the politico-jural structure. Since they do not occupy such positions, neophytes exercise no such rights. In the words of King Lear they represent "naked unaccommodated man."

I have no time to analyze other symbolic themes that express these attributes of "structural invisibility," ambiguity and neutrality. I want now to draw attention to certain positive aspects of liminality. Already we have noted how certain liminal processes are regarded as analogous to those of gestation, parturition, and suckling. Undoing, dissolution, decomposition are accompanied by processes of growth, transformation, and the reformulation of old elements in new patterns. It is interesting to note how, by the principle of the economy (or parsimony) of symbolic reference, logically antithetical processes of death and growth may be represented by the same tokens, for example, by huts and tunnels that are at once tombs and wombs, by lunar symbolism (for the same moon waxes and wanes), by snake symbolism (for the snake appears to die, but only to shed its old skin and appear in a new one), by bear symbolism (for the bear "dies" in autumn and is "reborn" in spring), by nakedness (which is at once the mark of a newborn infant and a corpse prepared for burial), and by innumerable other symbolic formations and actions. This coincidence of opposite processes and notions in a single representation characterizes the peculiar unity of the liminal: that which is neither this nor that, and yet is both.

I have spoken of the interstructural character of the liminal. However, between neophytes and their instructors (where these exist), and in connecting neophytes with one another, there exists a set of relations that compose a "social structure" of highly specific type. It is a structure of a very simple kind: between instructors and neophytes there is often complete authority and complete submission; among neophytes there is often complete equality. Between incumbents of positions in secular politico-jural systems there exist intricate and situationally shifting networks of rights and duties proportioned to their rank, status, and corporate affiliation. There are many different kinds of privileges and obligations, many degrees of superordination and subordination. In the liminal period such distinctions and gradations tend to be eliminated. Nevertheless, it must be understood that the authority of the elders over the neophytes is not based on legal sanctions; it is in a sense the personification of the self-evident authority of tradition. The authority of the elders is absolute, because it represents the absolute, the axiomatic values of society in which are expressed the "common good" and the common interest. The essence of the complete obedience of the neophytes is to submit to the elders but only in so far as they are in charge, so to speak, of the common good and represent in their persons the total community. That the authority in question is really quintessential tradition emerges clearly in societies where initiations are not collective but individual and where there are no instructors or *gurus*. For example, Omaha boys, like other North American Indians, go alone into the wilderness to fast and pray (Hocart 1952, 160). This solitude is liminal between boyhood and manhood. If they dream that they receive a woman's burden-strap, they feel compelled to dress and live henceforth in every way as women. Such men are known as *mixuga*. The authority of such a dream in such a situation is absolute. Alice Cummingham Fletcher tells of one Omaha who had been forced in this way to live as a woman, but whose natural inclinations led him to rear a family and to go on the warpath. Here the *mixuga* was not an invert but a man bound by the authority of tribal beliefs and values. Among many Plains Indians, boys on their lonely Vision Quest inflicted ordeals and tests on themselves that amounted to tortures. These again were not basically self-

tortures inflicted by a masochistic temperament but due to obedience to the authority of tradition in the liminal situation—a type of situation in which there is no room for secular compromise, evasion, manipulation, casuistry, and maneuver in the field of custom, rule, and norm. Here again a cultural explanation seems preferable to a psychological one. A normal man acts abnormally because he is obedient to tribal tradition, not out of disobedience to it. He does not evade but fulfills his duties as a citizen.

If complete obedience characterizes the relationship of neophyte to elder, complete equality usually characterizes the relationship of neophyte to neophyte, where the rites are collective. This comradeship must be distinguished from brotherhood or sibling relationship, since in the latter there is always the inequality of older and younger, which often achieves linguistic representation and may be maintained by legal sanctions. The liminal group is a community or comity of comrades and not a structure of hierarchically arrayed positions. This comradeship transcends distinctions of rank, age, kinship position, and, in some kinds of cultic group, even of sex. Much of the behavior recorded by ethnographers in seclusion situations falls under the principle: "Each for all, and all for each." Among the Ndembu of Zambia, for example, all food brought for novices in circumcision seclusion by their mothers is shared out equally among them. No special favors are bestowed on the sons of chiefs or headmen. Any food acquired by novices in the bush is taken by the elders and apportioned among the group. Deep friendships between novices are encouraged, and they sleep around lodge fires in clusters of four or five particular comrades. However, all are supposed to be linked by special ties which persist after the rites are over, even into old age. This friendship, known as *wubwambu* (from a term meaning "breast") or *wulunda*, enables a man to claim privileges of hospitality of a far-reaching kind. I have no need here to dwell on the lifelong ties that are held to bind in close friendship those initiated into the same age-set in East African Nilo-Hamitic and Bantu societies, into the same fraternity or sorority on an American campus, or into the same class in a Naval or Military Academy in Western Europe.

This comradeship, with its familiarity, ease and, I would add, mutual outspokenness, is once more the product of interstructural liminality, with its scarcity of jurally sanctioned relationships and its emphasis on axiomatic values expressive of the common weal. People can "be themselves," it is frequently said, when they are not acting institutionalized roles. Roles, too, carry responsibilities and in the liminal situation the main burden of responsibility is borne by the elders, leaving the neophytes free to develop interpersonal relationships as they will. They confront one another, as it were, integrally and not in compartmentalized fashion as actors of roles.

The passivity of neophytes to their instructors, their malleability, which is increased by submission to ordeal, their reduction to a uniform condition, are signs of the process whereby they are ground down to be fashioned anew and endowed with additional powers to cope with their new station in life. Dr. Richards, in her superb study of Bemba girls' puberty rites, *Chisungu,* has told us that Bemba speak of "growing a girl" when they mean initiating her (1956, 121). This term "to grow" well expresses how many peoples think of transition rites. We are inclined, as sociologists, to reify our abstractions (as is indeed a device which helps us to understand many kinds of social interconnection) and to talk about persons "moving through structural positions in a hierarchical frame" and the like. Not so the Bemba and the Shilluk of the Sudan who see the status or condition embodied or incarnate, if you like, *in* the person. To "grow" a girl into a woman is to effect an ontological transformation; it is not merely to convey an unchanging substance from one position to another by a quasi-mechanical force. Howitt saw Kuringals in Australia and I have seen Ndembu in Africa drive away grown-up men before a circumcision ceremony because they had not been initiated. Among Ndembu, men were also chased off because they had only been circumcised at the Mission Hospital and had not undergone the full bush seclusion according to the orthodox Ndembu rite. These biologically mature men had not been "made men" by the proper ritual procedures. It is the ritual and the esoteric teaching which grows girls and makes men. It is the ritual, too, which among Shilluk makes a prince into a king, or, among Luvale, a cultivator into a hunter. The arcane knowledge or *"gnosis"* obtained in the liminal period is felt to change the inmost nature of the neophyte, impressing him, as a seal impresses wax, with the characteristics of his new state. It is not a mere acquisition of knowledge, but a change in being. His apparent passivity is revealed as an absorption of powers which will become active after his social status has been redefined in the aggregation rites.

The structural simplicity of the liminal situation in many initiations is offset by its cultural complexity. I can touch on only one aspect of this vast subject matter here and raise three problems in connection with it. This aspect is the vital one of the communication of the *sacra,* the heart of the liminal matter.

Jane Harrison has shown that in the Greek Eleusinian and Orphic mysteries this communication of the *sacra* has three main components (1903, 144–160). By and large, this threefold classification holds good for initiation rites all over the world. *Sacra* may be communicated as: (1) exhibitions, "what is shown"; (2) actions, "what is done"; and (3) instructions, "what is said."

"Exhibitions" would include evocatory instruments or sacred articles, such as relics of deities, heroes or ancestors, aboriginal *churingas,* sacred drums or other musical instruments, the contents of Amerindian medicine bundles, and the fan, cist and tympanum of Greek and Near Eastern mystery cults. In the Lesser Eleusinian Mysteries of Athens, *sacra* consisted of a bone, top, ball, tambourine, apples, mirror, fan, and woolly fleece. Other *sacra* include masks, images, figurines, and effigies; the pottery emblems (*mbusa*) of the Bemba would belong to this class. In some kinds of initiation, as for example the initiation into the shaman-diviner's profession among the Saora of Middle India, described by Verrier Elwyn (1955), pictures and icons representing the journeys of the dead or the adventures of supernatural beings may be shown to the initiands. A striking feature of such sacred articles is often their formal simplicity. It is their interpretation which is complex, not their outward form.

Among the "instructions" received by neophytes may be reckoned such matters as the revelation of the real, but secularly secret, names of the deities or spirits believed to preside over the rites—a very frequent procedure in African cultic or secret associations (Turner 1962a, 36). They are also taught the main outlines of the theogony, cosmogony, and mythical history of their societies or cults, usually with reference to the *sacra* exhibited. Great importance is attached to keeping secret the nature of the *sacra,* the formulas chanted and instructions given about them. These constitute the crux of liminality, for while instruction is also given in ethical and social obligations, in law and in kinship rules, and in technology to fit neophytes for the duties of future office, no interdiction is placed on knowledge thus imparted since it tends to be current among uninitiated persons also.

I want to take up three problems in considering the communication of *sacra.* The first concerns their frequent disproportion, the second their monstrousness, and the third their mystery.

When one examines the masks, costumes, figurines, and such displayed in initiation situations, one is often struck, as I have been when observing Ndembu masks in circumcision and funerary rites, by the way in which certain natural and cultural features are represented as disproportionately large or small. A head, nose, or phallus, a hoe, bow, or meal mortar are represented as huge or tiny by comparison with other features of their context which retain their normal size. (For a good example of this, see "The Man Without Arms" in *Chisungu* [Richards 1956, 211], a figurine of a lazy man with an enormous penis but no arms.) Sometimes things retain their customary shapes but are portrayed in unusual colors. What is the point of this exaggeration amounting sometimes to caricature? It seems to me that to enlarge or diminish or discolor in this way is a primordial mode of abstraction. The outstandingly exaggerated feature is made into an object of reflection. Usually it is not a univocal symbol that is thus represented but a multivocal one, a semantic molecule with many components. One example is the Bemba pottery emblem *Coshi wa ng'oma,* "The Nursing Mother," described by Audrey Richards in *Chisungu.* This is a clay figurine, nine inches high, of an exaggeratedly pregnant mother shown carrying four babies at the same time, one at her breast and three at her back. To this figure is attached a riddling song:

My mother deceived me!
Coshi wa ng'oma!
So you have deceived me;
I have become pregnant again.

Bemba women interpreted this to Richards as follows:

Coshi wa ng'oma was a midwife of legendary fame and is
merely addressed in this song. The girl complains because her
mother told her to wean her first child too soon so that it died;
or alternatively told her that she would take the first child if
her daughter had a second one. But she was tricking her and
now the girl has two babies to look after. The moral stressed is
the duty of refusing intercourse with the husband before the
baby is weaned, i.e., at the second or third year. This is a
common Bemba practice (1956, 209–210).

In the figurine the exaggerated features are the number of
children carried at once by the woman and her enormously
distended belly. Coupled with the song, it encourages the
novice to ponder upon two relationships vital to her, those
with her mother and her husband. Unless the novice observes the Bemba weaning custom, her mother's desire for
grandchildren to increase her matrilineage and her husband's desire for renewed sexual intercourse will between
them actually destroy and not increase her offspring. Underlying this is the deeper moral that to abide by tribal custom
and not to sin against it either by excess or defect is to live
satisfactorily. Even to please those one loves may be to invite calamity, if such compliance defies the immemorial
wisdom of the elders embodied in the *mbusa*. This wisdom
is vouched for by the mythical and archetypal midwife
Coshi wa ng'oma.

If the exaggeration of single features is not irrational but
thought-provoking, the same may also be said about the representation of monsters. Earlier writers—such as J. A.
McCulloch (1913) in his article on "Monsters" in *Hastings
Encyclopaedia of Religion and Ethics*—are inclined to regard bizarre and monstrous masks and figures, such as frequently appear in the liminal period of initiations, as the
product of "hallucinations, night-terrors and dreams."
McCulloch goes on to argue that "as man drew little distinction (in primitive society) between himself and animals, as he
thought that transformation from one to the other was possible, so he easily ran human and animal together. This in part
accounts for animal-headed gods or animal-gods with human
heads." My own view is the opposite one: that monsters are
manufactured precisely to teach neophytes to distinguish
clearly between the different factors of reality, as it is conceived in their culture. Here, I think, William James's so-
called "law of dissociation" may help us to clarify the problem of monsters. It may be stated as follows: when *a* and *b*
occurred together as parts of the same total object, without
being discriminated, the occurrence of one of these, *a*, in a
new combination *ax*, favors the discrimination of *a*, *b*, and *x*
from one another. As James himself put it, "What is associated now with one thing and now with another, tends to be-

come dissociated from either, and to grow into an object of abstract contemplation by the mind. One might call this the law
of dissociation by varying concomitants" (1918, 506).

From this standpoint, much of the grotesqueness and
monstrosity of liminal *sacra* may be seen to be aimed not so
much at terrorizing or bemusing neophytes into submission
or out of their wits as at making them vividly and rapidly
aware of what may be called the "factors" of their culture. I
have myself seen Ndembu and Luvale masks that combine
features of both sexes, have both animal and human attributes, and unite in a single representation human characteristics with those of the natural landscape. One *ikishi* mask is
partly human and partly represents a grassy plain. Elements
are withdrawn from their usual settings and combined with
one another in a totally unique configuration, the monster or
dragon. Monsters startle neophytes into thinking about objects, persons, relationships, and features of their environment they have hitherto taken for granted.

In discussing the structural aspect of liminality, I mentioned how neophytes are withdrawn from their structural
positions and consequently from the values, norms, sentiments, and techniques associated with those positions. They
are also divested of their previous habits of thought, feeling,
and action. During the liminal period, neophytes are alternately forced and encouraged to think about their society,
their cosmos, and the powers that generate and sustain them.
Liminality may be partly described as a stage of reflection.
In it those ideas, sentiments, and facts that had been hitherto
for the neophytes bound up in configurations and accepted
unthinkingly are, as it were, resolved into their constituents.
These constituents are isolated and made into objects of reflection for the neophytes by such processes as componential
exaggeration and dissociation by varying concomitants. The
communication of *sacra* and other forms of esoteric instruction really involves three processes, though these should not
be regarded as in series but as in parallel. The first is the reduction of culture into recognized components or factors;
the second is their recombination in fantastic or monstrous
patterns and shapes; and the third is their recombination in
ways that make sense with regard to the new state and status
that the neophytes will enter.

The second process, monster- or fantasy-making, focuses
attention on the components of the masks and effigies,
which are so radically ill-assorted that they stand out and
can be thought about. The monstrosity of the configuration
throws its elements into relief. Put a man's head on a lion's
body and you think about the human head in the abstract.
Perhaps it becomes for you, as a member of a given culture
and with the appropriate guidance, an emblem of chieftain-
ship; or it may be explained as representing the soul as
against the body; or intellect as contrasted with brute force,
or innumerable other things. There could be less encouragement to reflect on heads and headship if that same head were
firmly ensconced on its familiar, its all too familiar, human
body. The man-lion monster also encourages the observer to

think about lions, their habits, qualities, metaphorical properties, religious significance, and so on. More important than these, the relation between man and lion, empirical and metaphorical, may be speculated upon, and new ideas developed on this topic. Liminality here breaks, as it were, the cake of custom and enfranchises speculation. That is why I earlier mentioned Plato's self-confessed debt to the Greek mysteries. Liminality is the realm of primitive hypothesis, where there is a certain freedom to juggle with the factors of existence. As in the works of Rabelais, there is a promiscuous intermingling and juxtaposing of the categories of event, experience, and knowledge, with a pedagogic intention.

But this liberty has fairly narrow limits. The neophytes return to secular society with more alert faculties perhaps and enhanced knowledge of how things work, but they have to become once more subject to custom and law. Like the Bemba girl I mentioned earlier, they are shown that ways of acting and thinking alternative to those laid down by the deities or ancestors are ultimately unworkable and may have disastrous consequences.

Moreover, in initiation, there are usually held to be certain axiomatic principles of construction, and certain basic building blocks that make up the cosmos and into whose nature no neophyte may inquire. Certain *sacra,* usually exhibited in the most arcane episodes of the liminal period, represent or may be interpreted in terms of these axiomatic principles and primordial constituents. Perhaps we may call these *sacerrima,* "most sacred things." Sometimes they are interpreted by a myth about the world-making activities of supernatural beings "at the beginning of things." Myths may be completely absent, however, as in the case of the Ndembu "mystery of the three rivers." . . . This mystery (*mpang'u*) is exhibited at circumcision and funerary cult association rites. Three trenches are dug in a consecrated site and filled respectively with white, red, and black water. These "rivers" are said to "flow from Nzambi," the High God. The instructors tell the neophytes, partly in riddling songs and partly in direct terms, what each river signifies. Each "river" is a multivocal symbol with a fan of referents ranging from life values, ethical ideas, and social norms, to grossly physiological processes and phenomena. They seem to be regarded as powers which, in varying combination, underlie or even constitute what Ndembu conceive to be reality. In no other context is the interpretation of whiteness, redness, and blackness so full; and nowhere else is such a close analogy drawn, even identity made, between these rivers and bodily fluids and emissions: whiteness = semen, milk; redness = menstrual blood, the blood of birth, blood shed by a weapon, etc.; blackness = feces, certain products of bodily decay, etc. This use of an aspect of human physiology as a model for social, cosmic, and religious ideas and processes is a variant of a widely distributed initiation theme: that the human body is a microcosm of the universe. The body may be pictured as androgynous, as male or female, or in terms of one or other of its developmental stages, as child, mature adult, and elder. On the other hand, as in the Ndembu case, certain of its properties may be abstracted. Whatever the mode of representation, the body is regarded as a sort of symbolic template for the communication of *gnosis,* mystical knowledge about the nature of things and how they came to be what they are. The cosmos may in some cases be regarded as a vast human body; in other belief systems, visible parts of the body may be taken to portray invisible faculties such as reason, passion, wisdom and so on; in others again, the different parts of the social order are arrayed in terms of a human anatomical paradigm.

Whatever the precise mode of explaining reality by the body's attributes, *sacra* which illustrates this are always regarded as absolutely sacrosanct, as ultimate mysteries. We are here in the realm of what Warner (1959, 3–4) would call "nonrational or nonlogical symbols" which

> arise out of the basic individual and cultural assumptions, more often unconscious than not, from which most social action springs. They supply the solid core of mental and emotional life of each individual and group. This does not mean that they are irrational or maladaptive, or that man cannot often think in a reasonable way about them, but rather that they do not have their source in his rational processes. When they come into play, such factors as data, evidence, proof, and the facts and procedures of rational thought in action are apt to be secondary or unimportant.

The central cluster of nonlogical *sacra* is then the symbolic template of the whole system of beliefs and values in a given culture, its archetypal paradigm and ultimate measure. Neophytes shown these are often told that they are in the presence of forms established from the beginning of things. (See Cicero's comment [De Leg. II. 14] on the Eleusinian Mysteries: "They are rightly called initiations [beginnings] because we have thus learned the first principles of life.") I have used the metaphor of a seal or stamp in connection with the ontological character ascribed in many initiations to arcane knowledge. The term "archetype" denotes in Greek a master stamp or impress, and these *sacra,* presented with a numinous simplicity, stamp into the neophytes the basic assumptions of their culture. The neophytes are told also that they are being filled with mystical power by what they see and what they are told about it. According to the purpose of the initiation, this power confers on them capacities to undertake successfully the tasks of their new office, in this world or the next.

Thus, the communication of *sacra* both teaches the neophytes how to think with some degree of abstraction about their cultural milieu and gives them ultimate standards of reference. At the same time, it is believed to change their nature, transform them from one kind of human being into another. It intimately unites man and office. But for a variable while, there was an uncommitted man, an individual rather than a social *persona,* in a sacred community of individuals.

It is not only in the liminal period of initiations that the nakedness and vulnerability of the ritual subject receive symbolic stress. Let me quote from Hilda Kuper's description of the seclusion of the Swazi chief during the great *Incwala* ceremony (1961, 197–225). The *Incwala* is a national First-Fruits ritual, performed in the height of summer when the early crops ripen. The regiments of the Swazi nation assemble at the capital to celebrate its rites, "whereby the nation receives strength for the new year." The *Incwala* is at the same time "a play of kingship." The king's well-being is identified with that of the nation. Both require periodic ritual strengthening. Lunar symbolism is prominent in the rites, as we shall see, and the king, personifying the nation, during his seclusion represents the moon in transition between phases, neither waning nor waxing. Dr. Kuper, Professor Gluckman (1954), and Professor Wilson (1961) have discussed the structural aspects of the *Incwala* which are clearly present in its rites of separation and aggregation. What we are about to examine are the interstructural aspects.

During his night and day of seclusion, the king, painted black, remains, says Dr. Kuper, "painted in blackness" and "in darkness"; he is unapproachable, dangerous to himself and others. He must cohabit that night with his first ritual wife (in a kind of "mystical marriage"—this ritual wife is, as it were, consecrated for such liminal situations).

> The entire population is also temporarily in a state of taboo and seclusion. Ordinary activities and behavior are suspended; sexual intercourse is prohibited, no one may sleep late the following morning, and when they get up they are not allowed to touch each other, to wash the body, to sit on mats, to poke anything into the ground, or even to scratch their hair. The children are scolded if they play and make merry. The sound of songs that has stirred the capital for nearly a month is abruptly stilled; it is the day of *bacisa* (cause to *hide*). The king remains secluded; . . . all day he sits naked on a lion skin in the ritual hut of the harem or in the sacred enclosure in the royal cattle byre. Men of his inner circle see that he breaks none of the taboos . . . on this day the identification of the people with the king is very marked. The spies (who see to it that the people respect the taboos) do not say, "You are sleeping late" or "You are scratching," but "You cause the king to sleep," "You scratch him (the king)"; etc. (Kuper 1947, 219–220).

Other symbolic acts are performed which exemplify the "darkness" and "waxing and waning moon" themes, for example, the slaughtering of a black ox, the painting of the queen mother with a black mixture—she is compared again to a half-moon, while the king is a full moon, and both are in eclipse until the paint is washed off finally with doctored water, and the ritual subject "comes once again into lightness and normality."

In this short passage we have an embarrassment of symbolic riches. I will mention only a few themes that bear on the argument of this paper. Let us look at the king's position first. He is symbolically invisible, "black," a moon between phases. He is also under obedience to traditional rules, and "men of his inner circle" see that he keeps them. He is also "naked," divested of the trappings of his office. He remains apart from the scenes of his political action in a sanctuary or ritual hut. He is also, it

would seem, identified with the earth which the people are forbidden to stab, lest the king be affected. He is "hidden." The king, in short, has been divested of all the outward attributes, the "accidents," of his kingship and is reduced to its substance, the "earth" and "darkness" from which the normal, structured order of the Swazi kingdom will be regenerated "in lightness."

In this betwixt-and-between period, in this fruitful darkness, king and people are closely identified. There is a mystical solidarity between them, which contrasts sharply with the hierarchical rank-dominated structure of ordinary Swazi life. It is only in darkness, silence, celibacy, in the absence of merriment and movement that the king and people can thus be one. For every normal action is involved in the rights and obligations of a structure that defines status and establishes social distance between men. Only in their Trappist sabbath of transition may the Swazi regenerate the social tissues torn by conflicts arising from distinctions of status and discrepant structural norms.

I end this study with an invitation to investigators of ritual to focus their attention on the phenomena and processes of mid-transition. It is these, I hold, that paradoxically expose the basic building blocks of culture just when we pass out of and before we re-enter the structural realm. In *sacerrima* and their interpretations we have categories of data that may usefully be handled by the new sophisticated techniques of cross-cultural comparison.

BIBLIOGRAPHY

Bettelheim, B. 1954. *Symbolic Wounds.* Glencoe: Free Press.

Cicero, M. Tullius. 1959. *De Legibus.* Ed. by de Plinval. Paris: Les Belles Lettres.

Douglas, Mary. 1966. *Purity and Danger.* London: Routledge & Kegan Paul.

Elwin, Verrier. 1955. *The Religion of an Indian Tribe.* London: Geoffrey Cumberlege.

Gennep, A. van. 1960. *The Rites of Passage.* London: Routledge & Kegan Paul.

Gluckman, Max. 1954. *Rituals of Rebellion in South-East Africa.* Manchester University Press.

Harrison, Jane E. 1903. *Prolegomena to the Study of Greek Religion.* London: Cambridge University Press.

Hocart, A. M. 1952. *The Life-Giving Myth.* London: Methuen.

James, E. O. 1961. *Comparative Religion.* London: Methuen.

James, William. 1918. *Principles of Psychology.* Vol. 1. New York: H. Holt.

Kuper, Hilda. 1947. *An African Aristocracy.* London: Oxford University Press, for International African Institute.

McCulloch, J. A. 1913. "Monsters," in *Hastings Encyclopaedia of Religion and Ethics.* Edinburgh: T. & T. Clark.

Richards, A. I. 1956. *Chisungu.* London: Faber & Faber.

Turner, V. W. 1962. *Chihamba, the White Spirit* (Rhodes-Livingstone Paper 33). Manchester University Press.

Warner, W. L. 1959. *The Living and the Dead.* New Haven: Yale University Press.

Wilson, Monica. 1959. *Divine Kings and the Breath of Men.* London: Cambridge University Press.

Play and Liminality in Rites of Passage:
From Elder to Ancestor in West Africa

Phillips Stevens, Jr.

In this essay, Phillips Stevens Jr. documents a series of funeral practices among the Bachama that may seem shocking to Americans. We are accustomed to view funerals as occasions for decorum and proper behavior; dress should be dark, music somber, and reflections serious. The Bachama, on the other hand, greet some parts of their funerals with joking behavior: some of those invited wear torn and dirty clothing or dress in the clothes of the opposite sex. They mock the solemnity of the proceedings and in some cases may even take the corpse and hold it for ransom. How can these practices be explained?

Stevens argues that such practices can best be understood as examples of liminal behavior. He notes that for us it is perhaps natural to understand funerals in terms of the separation of the dead from the living. Victor Turner (see his essay earlier in this section) in particular understood them in that fashion. However, van Gennep's original work on rituals emphasized that such ceremonies often actually focused on transition: it is not simply that an individual is now dead, but that a person of elder status is moving to ancestor status, and for the Bachama, ancestors play an important and active role in daily life. The result is that the transitional, liminal phase of the funeral is emphasized in Bachama death ritual, and joking behavior is seen not as offensive but rather as easing the deceased's soul in its transition to ancestor status.

As you read, consider these questions:
1. What are the major stages of a Bachama funeral, and how do they compare to an American rite of passage such as graduation?
2. How do these stages define the rite of passage from elder to ancestor?
3. How do joking or play help to create a liminal state, and what functions do these behaviors serve in this context?

Recognition of liminal states in cultural conceptualization and expression has been an important focus in anthropology in recent decades and has special significance for students of

play in culture. Thanks to the late Victor Turner for elaborating on some early and pioneering insights of Arnold van Gennep, we have seen that the concept of liminality is especially salient in rites of passage and that institutionalized play behavior frequently characterizes the liminal state. But Turner's work has been so influential that it has nearly obscured van Gennep's. Indeed, some recent scholars credit only Turner for the liminality concept, losing sight of van Gennep's introduction of the idea; many tend to focus exclusively on initiation, as Turner did, ignoring rituals surrounding other critical passages, especially funerals, in which van Gennep showed liminality to be important.

In this paper I want to return to some of van Gennep's original insights. Through the exploration of a West African case, I want to show that, as celebrations of liminality, funerals may be occasions for richly expressive institutionalized play. I do this for two reasons: (a) to broaden our perspectives on play and culture, and (b) as a tribute to Brian Sutton-Smith, who by the example of his own original thinking constantly urged us to look at cultural behavior in new ways.

VAN GENNEP AND TURNER, LIMINALITY AND PLAY

In 1908 Arnold van Gennep published his great work *Les Rites de Passage*. For the next half century it was consulted only sporadically by British and American anthropologists (and not at all for the reasons we find him so insightful today). In his introduction to the 1960 translation by Monika Vizedom and Gabrielle Caffee, Solon Kimball indicated ways in which van Gennep's work did and did not mesh with theoretical trends and developments in anthropology and religious studies and, indeed, why an earlier translation of the work might not have been well received. But by the 1960s anthropology was interested in the *content* of culture, in both the form and *meaning* of symbolic expression, and was ready for *The Rites of Passage*. Within a short time at least a general idea of van Gennep's tripartite scheme was known throughout academia; "rite of passage" had become a standard English phrase.

Under this heading, van Gennep identified and analyzed a distinct set of ceremonies that mark the culturally recognized departure from one stage, status, phase, or season and entry into the next. He observed that such rituals invariably constitute a series of three more-or-less discrete emphases: separation, transition, and incorporation. His analogy was of

Reprinted by permission from P. Stevens, Jr. "Play and liminality in rites of passage: from elder to ancestor in West Africa," *Play & Culture* 4:3 (1991), 237–257.

spatial movement, the points of departure and entry separated as if by a doorway. Separation rituals are conducted on this side of the door, rituals of incorporation on the other. Rituals of transition take place in the doorway itself, right on the boundary (*marge,* his original term) or threshold. This is a conceptual space, not real in profane physical, geographical, or chronological terms. It has the quality of the sacred. He called it liminal, from the Latin *limen,* threshold. So important is this element in transition rites that van Gennep referred to the other two stages as preliminal and postliminal (1960, p. 21).

The concept of liminality today, however, is more immediately associated with Victor Turner, who seized on and elaborated this idea, focusing especially on its "betwixt and between" aspect (Turner, 1964, 1969, 1974a, 1974b). Ethnographic cases reported earlier took on new significance, as it quickly became clear that the liminal state is often culturally recognized as one in which things are turned around, inverted, or replaced by their opposites and that culturally institutionalized behavior associated with this state is often what we readily identify as *play.* Subsequently, various liminal states in cultural conception and expression have been identified and used by scholars from many disciplines as testing grounds for various propositions about the nature, forms, and functions of play. New insight was afforded into earlier interpretations.

Turner's ideas of "structure and antistructure" (1969), for example, provided a theoretical framework against which to answer some questions Max Gluckman posed when he identified "rituals of rebellion" (1954). Situations characterized by other institutionalized forms of "reversal"—social and sexual licentiousness, transvestism and role reversals, masking and mummery, ritual clowning, law or taboo violation, or any formally recognized, even obligatory, relaxation of norms of appropriate behavior (see e.g., Babcock, 1978)—could now be shown to occur during interstices between periods of intense or "serious" activity. Sutton-Smith (1977a, 1977b) noted that the apparent destruction represented in liminal rituals contains the seeds for construction: out of disorder there arises new order. The late Frank Manning (1983) observed,

> The ambiguity of celebration affects both its textual portrayal of society and its active role in the social process. As a communicative agent, celebration embraces two modes: play and ritual. Play inverts the social order and leans toward license, whereas ritual confirms the social order and is regulated. The two modes are complementary as well as contrastive, and the tension between them gives celebration much of its piquancy and power. (p. 7)

Recognition of the play element in liminal contexts has allowed the social sciences new insight into what Edward Bruner (1988) more recently referred to as "the ambiguous spaces in social life" (p. 15). A conclusion drawn from such studies and re-studies is now axiomatic: Structure and order are reaffirmed and strengthened by peoples' witness to and participation in antistructure and disorder. The periodic,

active observance of liminal states, then, is critical to the maintenance of social structure, sentiments, and expectations—indeed, to the integrity of culture itself.

Turner and subsequent scholars (e.g., Mahdi, Foster, & Little, 1987) have focused principally on the phenomenon of *initiation* as most clearly demonstrating the "betwixt and between" aspect of transition rites; initiation is most dominant in the passage between youth and adult. For many clear reasons, the general study of passage rites has focused on rituals of initiation into adulthood. Van Gennep himself devoted far more space to initiation rites than to others. He insisted that these not be called puberty rites, pointing out the lack of universal correlation between the initiation celebration and the biological condition (van Gennep, 1960, p. 66). It is, nevertheless, the state, or the expectation of the state, of physiological puberty—*readiness for parenthood*—around which the rites are constructed and by which they are justified.

Recognizing puberty as the justifying condition for these rites, then, we can note that this state is marked by the most profound physiological changes in both sexes, specifically in male genitals and female breasts, both universally symbolic of fertility. Psychologists, especially of Freudian persuasion, have "discovered" in this period the emergence of problems whose resolutions are critical not only to the emotional stability of the adult, but indeed to some fundamental bases of culture itself. The celebration of initiation to adulthood is of central interest to the social anthropologist, too, because it is often the pivot around which age grades and age sets are constructed, and in this period of transition the most durable interpersonal relationships may be formed. We should note, too, that initiation to adulthood is often marked by physical, especially genital, mutilations, which are sometimes severe and which are always remarkable to Western sensibilities. Whatever the analyst's focus, rituals of transition to adulthood are often the longest, the most dramatic, and the richest in symbolic expression of all passage rites.

I want to suggest another possible reason for the almost exclusive social science attention to initiation over other passage rites. It is an unfortunate fact that students tend to read *about* the old masters through secondary sources, rather than consulting the complete originals. This is understandable because the field has advanced, much of the early scholars' data may now be obsolete or erroneous, writing styles and preferences have changed so that reading the original may be tedious, and because there is simply too much current material for us to spend time on the original works of writers of an earlier era. The risk, of course, is that the secondary source may have misrepresented the original or selected from it for a specific purpose; the secondary source might not be trustworthy for our purposes. This may have been the fate of van Gennep's statements about the importance of transition, liminality, in passage rites.

In his introduction to the English translation, Kimball noted variability of thematic emphases among the three stages of a passage rite and quoted van Gennep:

Rites of separation are prominent in funeral ceremonies, rites of incorporation at marriages. Transition rites may play an important part, for instance, in pregnancy, betrothal, and initiation; or they may be reduced to a minimum in adoption, in the delivery of a second child, in remarriage, or in the passage from the second to the third age group. (Kimball, 1960, p. viii)

This statement appeared on page 11 of van Gennep's work. Kimball did not give the page reference with his quotation of it; perhaps the principles of proper scholarship did not require him to. But in his 1974 "Liminal to Liminoid" essay, and in the 1982 reprinting of it, Turner quoted just the first sentence and part of the second, ending at *initiation,* also without page reference (1974a, p. 57; 1982, p. 25). In this case, the omission is not only poor scholarship but it is inconsistent with the careful documentation he provided for all other quotations and references in that article. This essay by Turner is much used by play scholars.

These statements appear in van Gennep's first chapter. But then in his eighth chapter, "Funerals," the opening paragraph cannot be missed:

On first considering funeral ceremonies, one expects rites of separation to be their most prominent component, in contrast to rites of transition and rites of incorporation, which should be only slightly elaborated. A study of the data, however, reveals that the rites of separation are few in number and very simple, while the transition rites have a duration and complexity sometimes so great that they must be granted a sort of autonomy. Furthermore, those funeral rites which incorporate the deceased into the world of the dead are most extensively elaborated and assigned the greatest importance. (van Gennep, 1960, p. 146)

The entire chapter is a discussion of elements in funeral celebrations in different cultures, with strong emphasis on transition. The earlier statement is clearly contradictory to van Gennep's intent, but without going back to the original French, we can't try to explain it. How can we explain Kimball's and, especially, Turner's apparently selective quoting? It certainly justifies Turner's emphasis on initiation. And in spite of the detailed and insightful study of mortuary rituals by Huntington and Metcalf (1979), who gave due credit to van Gennep, the idea that the theme of separation dominates in funerary rituals has been accepted by later scholars, notably Barbara Myerhoff (1982) in her excellent discussion of the cultural meaning in passage rites (p. 116).

Much of van Gennep's discussion of culture customs reflected the ethnological scholarship of his time: (a) an interest in *things* selectively taken out of context and classified to "make possible the delineation of cultural sequences and the stages of civilization" (van Gennep, 1960, p. 191), and (b) a lack of interest in the relationships among things and in their cultural meanings. Often, too, his primary data were incomplete, or even wrong. Yet in his writings we can find a delightful freshness and insights into cultural behavior still useful for anthropology 83 years later. As Huntington and Metcalf (1979, p. 9) said, he is "strikingly modern." His discussion of funerals can provide some guidelines for the discussion I will present in the following sections. Van Gennep emphasized that the element of transition may be central. Remembering his equation of transition with liminality, and our recognition of the role of play in the liminal, the West African case that follows will suggest that in funerals there may be a wealth of data that anthropologists, and particularly students of play and culture, have missed.

FROM ELDER TO ANCESTOR IN WEST AFRICA

It is difficult for modern westerners to appreciate the position of the elderly in Africa. The term *elder* denotes that stage beyond productive parenthood, the last stage of earthly life. As van Gennep noted (1960, p. 145), there is no ritual marking passage into it (no counterpart to the unique and brutal American ceremony of retirement). But it is a special status for two broad sets of reasons.

African peoples recognize full well what a great success it has been for a person to reach old age. In some areas two to three of every five babies die in infancy; weaning is a problematic process, as the child is cut off from its mother's immunities; and throughout life the individual is subject to many debilitating and potentially fatal diseases. Other factors, normal hazards of life exacerbated by problematic nutrition and medical care, combine to present to the traditional African a continual series of trials.

The status of elder is enhanced, too, by the nature of African kinship. Seniority is respected. The older one becomes, the greater the experience of life one has had, the more wisdom one has accrued, and the closer one is to the source of all wisdom and certainty. The elderly are, simply, revered. They occupy a special place in the life cycle, an exclusive place, a place of great authority and respect.

As van Gennep correctly recognized, death is a transition. The next stage in the life cycle is *ancestor*. There is sufficient literature on the nature of African ancestors as distinct from other conceptual categories of the dead. A good summary is contained in the exchange between Kopytoff (1971) and Brain (1973). Sub-Saharan African peoples distinguish different categories of spirits of the departed, mainly designated by circumstances of death. There is another world, usually vaguely understood, where all departed souls should go. The category of ghosts, recognized elsewhere as souls who for some reason have not gained entry into the other world and linger about the fringes of this one, is not widely important in Africa; more commonly feared beings of the night and the bush are spirits of nonhuman origin and witches.

The category of ancestors is, however, very important. Spirits in this category are variously referred to by writers as ancestors, ancestral spirits, ancestral ghosts, or sometimes ghosts. Sometimes the label *ancestral gods* appears, but this refers not to lineal ancestors but to deified culture heroes, in a sense ancestral to all the people. These are elevated divinities, accessible through priests. The student must take care to understand exactly what is meant by whatever terms are used. In Africa, as generally elsewhere, ancestors are *souls of people in one's direct line of descent.* These periodically return from the other world: (a) collectively, to be honored in great calendrical festivals in which they may enter into masked dancers who become their vehicles for communication with the living, or (b) individually, to visit and counsel their descendents, at home, in dreams, or in visions. They may be specifically recognized as individuals; more often they are simply the ancestors, venerable spirits of one's lineal forebears.

Not all lineal kin become ancestors. Van Gennep noted (1960, pp. 152–153) that people who haven't passed through certain ritual stages in life might not be granted an honored status in death. Thus, the souls of children, unmarried youth, or even childless adults might pass directly to the other world, and the ceremonies marking their passage may be considerably less elaborate than those for elders who have lived full lives and are qualified to make the transition to ancestor.

The most important aspect to note about African ancestors is that *ancestor* is a *kinship category,* one step removed from *elder.* The reciprocal obligations and expectations that obtain between kin continue between the living and their ancestors. Each party recognizes the reciprocity of the relationship; if either side lapses in its care for the other, the relationship may weaken. The living know that they are under the watchful care of the ancestors who will protect them, guide them through crises, and intervene with the gods on their behalf. To ensure such care, they honor their ancestors, communicating with them through simple divination methods and periodically cleaning, decorating, and leaving food offerings on the family shrine, which is centrally located within the compound. Some societies make elaborate preparations for the ancestors' return at periodic festivals. It can easily be concluded that in many parts of Africa ancestors are the most important of all supernatural beings.

Therefore, ceremonies of transition to that status can be very grand indeed. The death of a young person who has been unable to fulfill his or her life's potential is marked by deep grief. The ceremony is short, the participants grim, and the events are mainly religious, conducted to ensure the safe and smooth passage of the soul to the other world. For the death of a child who has not passed puberty there may be no funeral at all. In the passing of an elder, expressions of grief and mourning are less intense and shorter lived, mainly exhibited by the closest relatives and friends who lament the loss of their kin and companion.

The burial ceremony, and other ceremonies marking stages in the transition of the soul, can be grand social affairs, dominated by celebration. Principal events in them demonstrate peoples' remembrance of aspects of that individual's life both to the living and to the soul, who is a witness to the people's behavior. In some societies, the celebration of the passage may be marked by comic, and even lewd, behavior that in any other context might be disrespectful at best, downright scandalous at worst. Its brazenness intensifies with public esteem for the deceased. To illustrate this aspect of African funeral processes, I will turn to the kingdom of Bachama in northeastern Nigeria, where I conducted field work in the 1970s.

Bachama Joking

The Bachama are a kingdom of farmers, fishers, and hunters whose territory extends along both sides of the Benue River, about 45 miles downstream from the confluence of the Gongola River with the Benue, from 3 to 16 miles inland. Their language belongs to the Chadic branch of the Afro-Asiatic family. Descent is patrilineal, although individuals recognize filiation with their mothers' lines. The most durable social unit, and the most common referent for individual social identity, is the clan. Many aspects of their culture are similar to those among the savannah dwellers throughout West Africa to their west and the Bantu peoples of central and southern Africa to their east, and some generalizations are justified.

At the time of my field work (in 1969–1971, 1974, and 1976), the Bachama had experienced over 60 years of continuous European presence in the form of missionaries and government personnel, and they were noted elsewhere in Nigeria for their modern aspirations. The traditional population was still substantial, but the elders, the custodians of traditional culture values, were grimly aware that the younger generations were "taking a different road." Since then, in their territory a road bridge has been built over the Benue, a huge sugar plantation and refinery have been operating, and the pace of modernization has accelerated. The Bachama are quite history conscious and proud of their traditions; they responded to the growing threats to their cultural integrity by declaring a cultural union with the western Bata, their immediate eastern neighbors. Several concerted efforts to record and preserve traditions have resulted. But my "ethnographic present" in the following discussion should be regarded as about 1970.

Within Bachama society, individuals and groups standing in well-defined relationships with others enjoy with those others special license of speech and behavior. They can "abuse," joke with, or "snatch from" their counterparts; indeed, in many contexts such behavior may be obligatory. They share in what anthropologists have called joking relationships, joking partnerships, or joking alliances. Every individual participates in a range of categories of joking with some others; the license permitted depends on the history and nature of the relationship. Thus, networks of institutionalized joking relationships operate throughout the entire society.

The joking relationship is called *gboune;* this term refers to the institution, to its behavioral attributes, and to the specific relationships within it. Participants can be referred to as *gbouna* with a personal pronoun for the singular; *gbounye*, plural. I have described the institution in detail elsewhere (Stevens, 1974, 1978). The dominant form of *gboune* is that shared between members of clans who recognize an old history of association, and these enjoy the most extreme license of behavior tolerated at any level of the institution. They can verbally insult each other and each other's patriline, to the ultimate sexual extreme of making reference to the genitals of the other's father or grandfather. They can indulge in various degrees of mockery, public horseplay, and snatching at loose items. Social contexts dictate the appropriateness of such behavior; close neighbors limit their snatching, for example.

The strictest rule governing such behavior is that one's license is severely tempered when addressing a person significantly senior to oneself, and to an elder one's behavior is always restrained, even in response to *gboune*-type abuses from that elder. Traditionally, children do not participate at all, though they constantly witness and thereby learn *gboune* behavior; but between children and elders, persons at both extremes of the life cycle, a light, frivolous banter is permissible. And when an elder dies, able-bodied men and women of the clans that share *gboune* with the clan of the deceased come at once to assist and to mount the most brazen of all public displays of their special privilege.

Death and Funerals

The land of the living is *Njiya Bwàrà,* the land of the Bachama people; the other world is *Njiya Kpalame,* commonly translated as "the Red Land." Some Bachama say this place is in the land of the Chamba people, old historic friends of the Bachama, about 150 miles to the south (see Stevens, 1976a). People could not explain the term, but we can note that *kpalame,* also "yellow," refers to the middle range of colors between the extremes of black and white. This is the color of a newborn infant before full pigmentation has developed, the color somewhere between that of a normal adult and an albino, or a European. Referring to the land of the dead, it surely refers not to color, but to this in-between condition. There is ambiguity in the people's understanding of the Red Land; it is the final destination of some souls (those whose life potential was unfulfilled) but more like a way-station for the ancestors, who presumably move about the cosmos and return occasionally to the land of the living.

A funeral is one of the most complex series of events in Bachama culture and a focus of cosmological, religious, and social meaning. Its specific details vary according to the age, sex, status, profession, personal interests, residence, and clan membership of the deceased, his or her religious focus and that of the family, the season of the death, and other factors. The passage of the soul is a lengthy process marked by several discrete events held in accordance with major seasonal events in the annual ritual calendar. Depending on the season of the death, observances from burial until incorporation of the soul in the status of ancestor may extend over several months, up to more than a year. The nature of the transition is manifested in three ways, all corresponding with each other: the behavior of the living, the disposition of the body, and the experiences of the soul itself. We can delincate five distinct stages in the transition that mark decreasing anguish and discomfort for the soul and decreasing expression of bereavement and grief by the living, to a state of new stability and comfort for both: (1) celebration and burial, (2) the end of formal mourning, (3) the "second burial," (4) dismissal of the soul by destruction/distribution of its property, and (5) the soul's final departure, with all other souls of the previous year, to the Red Land. The first and fourth are grand, widely attended events, occasions for the most brazen *gboune* behavior, and must be discussed here in some detail. The second and third stages are relatively small and quiet affairs, and the final stage is not marked by a specific ceremony but is presumed to occur in the context of the great end-of-year festival. I have given some analysis elsewhere (Stevens, 1974, pp. 196–237); here I will summarize the process and elaborate on those aspects that are relevant to our discussion of transition and play. I will first outline the principal events of each of these stages and will then discuss the clowning behavior of the *ghounye.*

Celebration and Burial

A corpse is normally buried within 24 hours of death. However, in the case of an elder, the body will be kept inside the compound for up to 3 days, time for beer to be brewed, distant visitors to arrive, and numerous tasks to be done. The first task is digging the grave, done by members of a priestly clan, *ji-njiya* ("people of the soil"), responsible for matters involving penetration of the earth. The grave is dug in the floor of the deceased's sleeping hut if he or she was a commoner, or in the princes' burying ground if he or she was a member of a royal clan. The grave is about 6 feet deep; the bottom and lower sides are lined with mats. The body, wrapped in cloths, is laid against one wall. Poles are placed on the floor against the opposite wall to extend diagonally up the wall above the body; mats are laid over the poles, creating a compartment in which the body is protected from contact with the earth, until the second burial.

At the news of a death, the *gbounye* respond immediately to help with many other tasks. A bier must be constructed of poles and reeds to carry the body in procession. Shelters must be erected outside the compound for visitors. Food must be provided, represented by two or three cows that are killed and left on display, to be butchered later. Special decorative and aromatic grasses must be gathered from the bush. Musicians and singers must be hired if there are none in the participating clans. A funeral of a distinguished elder can be an expensive affair. Contributions come from many sources in the family's social network, but most of the labor is provided by the *gbounye.*

The corpse is washed and wrapped in cloths by its closest female relatives, then is laid on the bier in a section of the inner compound. On the morning of the 3rd day, the many people assemble, all in their finest dress, and sit together by sex and by kin group. Their proximity to the body corresponds to the distance of their relationship to the deceased. Inside the compound are family and age-mates; others, including the *gbounye,* are outside. The women inside wail in mourning; the women outside sing the favorite songs of the deceased and songs associated with his or her interests in life. When all is ready, the bier is lifted by close male relatives and age-mates to the center of the compound. A close friend recites a prayer and a eulogy over the head of the corpse, then smashes a calabash drinking cup under his or her foot. The pallbearers lift the bier high and carry it outside the compound, as the din of wailing and singing increases.

A grand procession forms in front of the bier, comprised of any persons who were important to the deceased, who shared in his or her interests or profession. All carry appropriate items (e.g., weapons, fishing implements, tools), and, led by professional singers (see Stevens, 1976b), they sing the appropriate songs. The procession moves about the village and to various points outside it, "showing" the deceased places that were important to him or her during his or her lifetime. Musicians, drummers, and xylophonists move alongside the procession, playing variants on *tyebshi gubato ka we,* "music for marching with the dead." At the front, people perform little skits, enacting themes from the deceased's life; if the deceased was a hunter or warrior, they may "stalk" or "attack" each other, and from time to time they rush back toward the bier, arms and implements raised, and shout praises and keen in high-pitched voices. Behind, close to the bier, the mourners continue their wailing; however, they are all but drowned out by the sounds of joyous celebration. Occasionally the procession rests and singers lead the crowd in songs.

Finally, the body is brought to the grave. The pallbearers swing the bier back and forth several times over the carcass of a cow that had been provided by the deceased's clan. This is done, I was told, to show the deceased what the people have done for him or her; but there is a scapegoating element here as well, involving the symbolic transfer of evil or social shortcomings into the body of the animal. The bier rests near the grave during some final singing. Then the body is taken into the hut by siblings and close age-mates where they make a final selection of robes for burial, and the body is laid to rest. The *ji-njiya* fill it in later, after people have dispersed. If the grave is away from the compound, they construct a special hut over it and erect a three-pronged offering post, resembling an inverted tripod, in the ground next to it.

Mourning, Remembrance, and Second Burial

All expressive behavior at the funeral is clearly cathartic for the living, but a main purpose is to cheer the soul, to assure it of the support of the living, and to thereby strengthen it for its lonely passage through the next two stages of transition. The soul attends all these events. At the burial of the body, the soul enters into the most difficult stage of its transition. It is confused and afraid, isolated from lineage ancestors who will help it later but avoid it now because it "smells too human." Without such protection, the soul is especially vulnerable to evil or capricious spirits, so it stays near the grave, presumably inside the hut at night, while it loses some of its earthly taint. For its descendants, this is a period of formal mourning, which lasts from 10 days to 2 weeks. Close relatives and friends sit near the grave each day, receiving visitors; every day a calabash of fresh food or drink is placed on the offering post.

This period culminates in the small ceremony of *Su-padato* (literally, "affairs of loosening and rearranging"), with offerings and prayers for guidance at the shrine of the deceased's principle deity. Following this ceremony, the soul, now partially cleansed, moves off to a sacred grove near the village of Fare, home of Nzeanzo, the major deity. There, it and the souls of all others who died in that year are separated from one another and from the ancestors by fences of thorns (in the spiritual realm) for their final period of cleansing and preparation, supervised by Nzeanzo. Van Gennep saw strict mourning as a transitional state for the bereaved, and so it is for the Bachama. Following *Su-padato,* the people return to their daily routines, but their active obligation to their departed continues, and they care for the grave site and occasionally refresh the contents of the calabash on the offering post. The lonely soul still returns to its family compound from time to time.

Around the end of October, just after the end of the rains and shortly before the ritual closing of the agricultural cycle, the so-called second burial is performed. This is called *Folkpang* (literally, "break the calabash"). This, too, is a small affair, attended only by close relatives and friends (though the family ceremony corresponds with a societal observance of seasonal liminality, as I will indicate later), and it signifies the end of active remembrance. The offering post is removed, the calabash food container (*kpe*) is broken, and the hut over the grave is destroyed. The grave is dug up, and the poles and mats that had separated the body from the earth are broken in. It is presumed that by this time the flesh has separated from the bones of the corpse and most soft tissue has dried up, although the remains are not actually inspected. The grave is filled in again, and the crumbled remains of the hut are left over the top, to settle and be washed down by the next rains, just when the souls are led away by Nzeanzo to the Red Land. Gradually, all superficial traces of the burial site are erased. With this "second burial," the soul is informed that no more special accommodations will be available for it here, and the bereaved are assured that the soul is adjusting well to its spiritual existence.

"Breaking the Things"

The final ceremony to be conducted at home, marking the fourth state in the soul's transition, is held toward the end of the dry season, after the ceremonies that open the agricultural cycle, in late March or early April. This is called *Folshe* (literally, "breaking the things") and is the other great occasion for *gboune* foolishness, as we will see shortly.

In many ways, *Folshe* mirrors the funeral celebration. It lasts for 3 days. On the 1st day visitors gather to greet the bereaved. There is some wailing, but the whole atmosphere is far lighter than it was at the funeral. The deceased's favorite songs are sung and favorite dances performed. An empty bier is set outside the compound and is surrounded by breakable domestic items—pots, calabashes, utensils, all of the finest quality the family can afford. Next to the bier are the deceased's personal items: weapons, tools of trade, smoking materials, cosmetics, and toiletries.

Prior to this event, a pot maker was commissioned to make a pottery sculpture in the general form of a narrow-necked water pot—with the swelling of the pot resembling a belly, a head sculpted at the top, and arms incised over the belly or represented as small appendages at the base of the neck. This pottery sculpture is placed just inside the entrance to the compound, visible—and reachable—from outside.

The major event of this day is the smashing of domestic breakables at a spot outside the village, signifying the breaking of the deceased's final ties to its domestic life. Relatives and friends form a long procession. Those in front carry pots and calabashes. One, bearing the sculpture, follows behind in the approximate position of the bier in the funeral procession. Musicians move up and down, alongside the procession. The procession, comprising possibly several hundred people, moves single file out of the village to a preselected and cleared area. All the breakables except the sculpture are thrown down, smashed, and beaten into rubble with sticks. (Treatment of the sculpture varies; for an important person it may be kept in the compound for many years, vaguely regarded as a repository for the returning ancestor, but more often it is broken or discarded.) Then the people turn their backs on the pile and quickstep, nearly running, back to the village. The soul, thus rejected but now liberated from its isolation, joins the other souls under Nzeanzo at Fare, to await their journey to the Red Land.

On the evening of this day there is general celebration, with singing and dancing at the family compound. On the 2nd day, the deceased's debts and credits are discussed and settled, and property is distributed among the heirs. On the 3rd day, all the children of the deceased's clan are assembled and introduced to their distant relatives and to the friends and to the *gbounye* of their parents' clans. There are the grandchildren and possibly great-grandchildren of the deceased. The cycle of life and the continuity of the generations is recognized.

The fifth and final stage in the transition of the soul is assumed to take place at the end of the great 5-day festival of Vunon, held at Fare around the end of April and beginning of May, at the first rains. This festival, named for the mother of Nzeanzo, marks the end of one year and the beginning of the next. It is attended by thousands of people from Bachama and neighboring societies. The significance and symbology of its many events are exceedingly complex. The symbolism of rebirth and fertility are dominant. As the occasion for the final assemblage of the past year's departed, it can be seen to correspond to observances of All Saints' (or All Souls') Day in the Christian liturgical calendar, which takes place on the 1st of November, also a logical ending/beginning of a year (and is preceded by a well-known liminal event, the celebration of All Hallows' Eve).

Play in the Liminal State

At the funeral celebration and at *Folshe,* the first and last ceremonies of the transition to be conducted at home, the clan joking partners exercise their most extreme license of verbal and physical behavior. A *gboune* funeral is the ideal, hoped for by every person for himself or herself. Speaking of a distinguished elder, one man said to me, "When such a man dies, should people cry with tears? No, they should go and dance." Certainly all the interpretations of such reversals, indicated earlier in this paper, can be seen to apply here. All sociological and psychological explanations of the functions of *gboune*-type behavior for the living may be valid; but the Bachama insist that the primary beneficiary is the soul. *Gbounye* perform, they say, to alleviate grief, to entertain, and to give the soul of our dear friend and relative a truly grand send-off.

At the funeral, *gbounye* arrive early; they postpone their own domestic obligations and do much of the necessary preparatory labor. As guests arrive and seat themselves in and around the compound, the *gbounye* assemble nearby. Although the guests are well-dressed, many *gbounye* wear torn and dirty clothing. . . . Exaggerated transvestism is common: Women may dress and accoutre themselves as men, and men as women; women may construct phalluses of sticks or calabashes under their dresses; men display breasts made of brassieres stuffed with cloth. The hair of either sex may be combed straight and matted with mud or wet flour; the body may be smeared with dirt or flour; broken or rusty jewelry may be worn (or horse bridles, cow bells, ropes, and even strips of bark may be worn as jewelry). There is no prescribed mode; all variations are of individual whim. The aim is simply to look slovenly or just ridiculous. All manner of rubbish may be collected from about the village and displayed in large calabashes. *Gbounye* assemble their own musical instruments: gongs wrapped in cloth to flatten their sound, broken horns, drums with split heads, and xylophones with broken keys or resonators.

While the activities of the funeral are going on, the *gbounye* make mockery of nearly everything. As with dress, imagination and creativity are free: The antics of *gbounye* are never just the same at any two funerals. As the body is being prepared, and women wail, the *gbounye* perform

A *gbouna* mocks men. She has a calabash under her skirt to simulate oversized male genitalia; and she and a chorus of her friends sing a popular song of male courage.

loudly in their area: Their musicians bang and honk; they dance—improvisational steps with greatly exaggerated body movements but also grotesque parodies of the favorite and most dignified social dances. Songs of hunting, of war, of bravery, and of noble adult virtues are parodied loudly and raucously. Various professions and character types are mocked. Occasionally, unnecessarily, they sing, as if to remind people who they are:

Gboune a su-muruno (Gboune *is not a thing of annoyance*)
Gboune a su-mune (Gboune *is not a thing for anger*)
Gboune a su-kwa-dakato (Gboune *is not for complaining*)

There are acts of individual brashness and foolishness, all precisely contrary to established behavioral norms. . . . A man or woman may leave the group and go among the mourners, making grotesque sounds or lewd gestures, snatching personal items from people and playing with them. Sometimes a *gbouna* persists in such harassment until the victim hands over a few coins. Women strut and swagger, mocking male virtues. They may stage a hunt, stalking an "animal" with spears raised, then flee, shrieking, when it turns to confront them. They may swing their contrived phalluses, proclaiming something like, "Look! I'm a man! This is what I've got! This is *all* I've got!" and make lewd

Clan joking partners make off with the corpse.

thrusting motions with their hips. . . . Men adopt feminine manners, accenting the swing of their hips, struggling with their wrappers while trying to balance a head-load, occasionally identifying their actions: *"We meto!"* (the walking of a woman).

The deceased and the deceased's family are mocked. People grab items from the piles of rubbish and hold them up, proclaiming, "See the fine gift ___ gave me!" A broken weapon may be "___'s favorite spear!" Some rotting garbage is scattered: "Have some of ___'s favorite food!" And trash is identified as the deceased's worldly possessions, to be distributed at *Folshe*. . . . The *gbounye* dance around the cow that was killed for them—for their friendship and their valuable services—and loudly proclaim how small and scrawny it is and what stingy people the family are.

As the procession forms, they join it, carrying on their play as it moves along. At each place where the procession stops to show the deceased this or that activity area, the *gbounye* loudly mock the sort of activity that is conducted there. They disturb the singers as they try to perform, mocking their styles and their concentration. At some point in the procession and at some prearranged signal, the *gbounye* converge upon the bier, wrest it away from the pallbearers, and run away with the body. . . . At one funeral I attended, the corpse rolled off the bier and off the shoulder of the road during this scuffle. The *gbounye* declare that they will relinquish the corpse of their friend only on payment of a sum of money. The pallbearers make a show of indignation, but they finally agree to pay.

While the body is being swung over the killed cow, the *gbounye* return to their own animal, and now they proclaim what a fine cow it is compared to the pitiful one the family has provided for this ritual. It must be that they think more highly of their *gbounye* than they do of their own deceased. During the selection of burial robes, the *gbounye* come forward with strips of torn and dirty rags.

During the actual internment they are fairly quiet, as they are for the eulogies. They observe other limits throughout as well: As *gbounye,* they avoid vulgarisms and obscenities that might be truly offensive to family or guests, and they do not enter the compound of the deceased.

After the burial, a representative of the deceased's clan makes a speech thanking the *gbounye* for their participation but warning them with feigned seriousness that their behavior has been disgraceful and that they should behave themselves hereafter. They, seated together to one side, pretend to ignore the speaker and mutter loudly that they are thirsty and where is the beer, or has the host clan decided to keep it all for themselves? When requests are made for disclosure of the deceased's debts and credits to be settled at *Folshe,* the *gbounye* arise and make absurd claims of debts owed them. When the beer is served, they grumble that it is about time. Why is there so little of it? Why is it so poorly made? What's wrong with those women that they cannot make beer correctly?

As the guests disperse, the clowning of the *gbounye* subsides. Their men assist the other men in butchering the cows and distributing the meat; the women join the women of the deceased's compound, consoling them and helping to receive visitors. They will assist in similar ways over the next 2 weeks, up to *Su-padato.*

At *Folshe,* the final domestic ceremony of the transition that marks the dismissal of the soul, grief is considerably less intense and *gboune* behavior is consequently more brazen. Events at *Folshe* parallel those of the funeral, and the *gbounye* seize on similar opportunities. When the guests are assembling, *gbounye* clown and heckle. When the domestic and personal items are collected and displayed, the *gbounye* attempt to replace them with trash. As the procession forms, a *gbouna* snatches the pottery figure from the compound gate and keeps it throughout, dancing with it, appearing to handle it carelessly. . . . The serious business of debt resolution and inheritance conducted on the 2nd day is frequently interrupted by the *gbounye,* who claim their pieces of trash are the deceased's true possessions, entrusted to them before he or she died.

The same type of cross-sex mockery and belittling of professions, social dances, and clan affiliations take place throughout, with extremely bold language and freedom of physical license, but again limits are observed. The *gbounye* fall quiet when the procession reaches the clearing and throughout the breaking of the pots, and the extreme of *gbounye* language, genital references, is avoided. When the ceremony ends, they stay and help their friends with the considerable cleanup necessary after such a grand occasion. They know that when one of their own elders dies these people will come and perform similar services.

SOME FINAL THOUGHTS

Much of the foregoing discussion should have more explanation and elaboration. The fullest possible analysis would consider the conjunction of stages in the funeral with other societal observances, as I have indicated in the case of the final dismissal of all souls at the end of the year. *Folkpang,* the occasion for the second burial, is the name for the 5th day of a complex 6-day fall festival. On the last 2 days the character of the trickster deity, itself a liminal figure, is evoked by performers (see Stevens, 1980). During the evening of *Folkpang,* one area of *gboune* license, snatching, is extended to children, who may go about the village taking for themselves any item of unclear ownership, anything left outside compounds (perhaps intentionally), any untethered animal. The resemblance to American children's trick-or-treat activity at Halloween, held at roughly the same time—at the close of the agricultural cycle, midway between the autumnal equinox and the winter solstice, a point of seasonal liminality—is probably not coincidental. The possibil-

ities for exploration of incidents of cultural recognition of liminality, in Africa and elsewhere, are still vast.

The Bachama data invite many ethnological comparisons. Specific details in the funeral processes, and in the stages of transition of both the dead and the bereaved and associated modes of symbolic expression, have parallels all over the world. Death is a transition, and in funeral ceremonies the recognition of the transition—liminality—is often dominant. Specific studies and surveys, such as by Rosenblatt, Walsh, and Jackson (1976) and Huntington and Metcalf (1979), confirm this. It's too bad we have missed van Gennep for so long.

The antics of the *gbounye* seem, so far, to have few parallels elsewhere, but I think this is not because they are not there, but because earlier researchers were asking different sorts of questions. Let me make a brief elaboration on this thought.

Ethnographic description of specific African customs is today voluminous. There is a sizable literature, too, on institutionalized joking relationships in Africa, particularly of the sort that obtains between clans; descriptions of clan joking partnerships almost invariably say that they attend on each other's funerals to alleviate grief through their clowning. Jack Goody's (1962) is probably the most detailed of such studies, and his descriptions of funeral play among the LoDagaa and LoWiili of Ghana show strong similarities to Bachama customs. Many cultural similarities are evident throughout the entire savannah belt, which extends across West and central Africa, a cultural continuum, in fact, of which the Bachama are representative. It is logical to expect similarities in funeral observances as well. But where funeral play is discussed in the literature, most accounts mention it in the broader context of interclan joking, not in the context of the liminal state in the final rite of passage. Hence, the surveys, such as by Rosenblatt, Walsh, and Jackson (1976) and Huntington and Metcalf (1979), miss it, too.

There are some tantalizing suggestions that a re-search of the literature would be rewarding. Van Gennep (1960) himself said, almost in throw-away fashion,

> There are struggles for the corpse, widespread in Africa, which correspond to the bride's abduction. Their true meaning seems not to have been understood up to now; it is that the living do not want to lose one of their members unless forced to do so, for the loss is a diminution of their social power. These struggles increase in violence with the higher social position of the deceased. (p. 164)

The *gbounye* do struggle for and run away with the corpse, although van Gennep's explanations, if applicable at all, are not sufficient for the Bachama. But what about "widespread in Africa"? He cited Hertz (1907) "for references." Huntington and Metcalf also have admired this insightful, young French ethnologist who was interested in correlations between treatment of the body and beliefs in the progress of the soul but who died in World War I and did no field work himself.

There is surely much more out there. I hope that this paper will prompt a fresh look at van Gennep, a reformulation of research questions, and more reexamination of earlier studies that were stimulated by the concept of liminality itself when it caught on in the 1960s and 1970s.

REFERENCES

Babcock, B. A. (Ed.) (1978). *The reversible world.* Ithaca, NY: Cornell University Press.

Brain, J. L. (1973). Ancestors as elders in Africa—further thoughts. *Africa.* 43, 122–133.

Bruner, E. M. (Ed.) (1988). *Text, play, and story: The construction and reconstruction of self and society.* Prospect Heights, IL: Waveland Press.

Gluckman, M. (1954). *Rituals of rebellion in south-east Africa.* Manchester, England: Manchester University Press.

Goody, J. (1962). *Death, property and the ancestors: A study of the mortuary customs of the LoDagaa of West Africa.* Stanford, CA: Stanford University Press.

Hertz, R. (1907). Contribution à une étude sur la representation collective de la mort. *Année sociologique,* 10, 48–137.

Huntington, R., & Metcalf, P. (1979). *Celebrations of death: The anthropology of mortuary ritual.* Cambridge, England: Cambridge University Press.

Kimball, S. T. (1960). Introduction. In A. van Gennep, *The rites of passage* (pp. v–xviii; M. B. Vizedom & G. L. Caffee, Trans.). Chicago: University of Chicago Press.

Kopytoff, I. (1971). Ancestors as elders in Africa. *Africa,* 41, 129–142.

Mahdi, L. C., Foster, S., & Little, M. (Eds.) (1987). *Betwixt & between: Patterns of masculine and feminine initiation.* LaSalle, IL: Open Court.

Manning, F. E. (Ed.) (1983). *The celebration of society: Perspectives on contemporary culture performance.* Bowling Green, OH: Bowling Green University Popular Press.

Meyerhoff, B. (1982). Rites of passage: Process and paradox. In V. Turner (Ed.), *Celebration: Studies in festivity and ritual* (pp. 109–135). Washington, DC: Smithsonian Institution Press.

Rosenblatt, P. C., Walsh, R. P., & Jackson, D. A. (1976). *Grief and mourning in cross-cultural perspective.* New Haven, CT: HRAF Press.

Stevens, P., Jr. (1974). *The Bachama and their neighbors: Non-kin joking relationships in Adamawa, northeastern Nigeria* (Doctoral dissertation, Northwestern University). Ann Arbor, MI: University Microfilms International, No. 74–7828.

Stevens, P., Jr. (1976a). The Danubi ancestral shrine. *African Arts,* X, 30–37, 98–99.

Stevens, P., Jr. (1976b). Social and judicial functions of Bachama song contests. In D. F. Lancy & B. A. Tindall (Eds.). *The anthropological study of play: Problems and prospects* (pp. 237–249). West Point, NY: Leisure Press.

Stevens, P., Jr. (1978). Bachama joking categories: Toward new perspectives in the study of joking relationships. *Journal of Anthropological Research,* 34(1), 47–71.

Stevens, P., Jr. (1980). The Bachama trickster as model for clowning behavior. In C. M. S. Drake (Ed.), *The cultural context: Essays in honor of Edward Norbeck* (pp. 137–150). Houston: Rice University. [Studies, 66(1)]

Sutton-Smith, B. (1977a). Games of order and disorder. *The Association for the Anthropological Study of Play Newsletter,* 4(2), 19–26.

Sutton-Smith, B. (1977b). Towards an anthropology of play. In P. Stevens, Jr. (Ed.), *Studies in the anthropology of play: Papers in memory of B. Allan Tindall* (pp. 222–237). West Point, NY: Leisure Press.

Turner, V. W. (1964). Betwixt and between: The liminal period in *Rites de passage.* In J. Helm (Ed.), *Symposium on new approaches to the study of religion* (pp. 4–20). Seattle: American Ethnological Society.

Turner, V. W. (1969). *The ritual process: Structure and anti-structure.* Chicago: Aldine.

Turner, V. W. (1974a). Liminal to liminoid in play, flow, and ritual: An essay in comparative symbology. In E. Norbeck (Ed.), *The anthropological study of human play* (pp. 53–92). Houston: Rice University. [Studies, 60(3)]

Turner, V. W. (1974b). Metaphors of anti-structure in religious culture. In A. W. Eister (Ed.), *Changing perspectives in the scientific study of religion* (pp. 63–84). New York: Wiley.

Turner, V. W. (1982). *From ritual to theatre: The human seriousness of play.* New York: Performing Arts Journal Publications.

Van Gennep, A. (1960). *The rites of passage* (M. B. Vizedon & G. L. Caffee, Trans.). Chicago: University of Chicago Press. (Original work published 1909).

Female Circumcision in Southern Chad: Origins, Meaning, and Current Practice

Lori Leonard

Female circumcision—the partial cutting, removal, or mutilation of female genitals—has been documented among many groups in Africa. It is generally associated with rites of passage initiating children into adulthood. However, most studies of the practice have focused on Islamic groups. In this essay, Lori Leonard presents the results of her study on female circumcision among the Sara of southern Chad, many of whom are Christian. In this group, the cutting of the clitoris is a critical component of the transition from child to adult woman. The Sara believe that women are born with two souls, one a child and the other an adult. During the ritual the child spirit is expelled and the adult spirit is developed.

Female circumcision strikes many Western observers as horrific and barbaric. Some see it as a critical mechanism through which men in patriarchal societies control women's sexuality. However, Leonard shows that the situation among the Sara is extremely complex. For Sara women, circumcision performs important functions. The majority of Sara women interviewed want their girls circumcised, and many describe their own circumcision in favorable terms. Thus, this essay serves as an important reminder of the differences in mores and values among societies and the difficulties of criticizing practices that to us seem inhumane.

As you read, consider these questions:

1. Many organizations are opposed to female circumcision, seeing it as a violation of human rights. What are the ethical issues concerning intervention to eliminate this practice?
2. What is the function of female circumcision among the Sara, and why is the practice supported by males and females?
3. What similarities do you see between this rite of passage and others presented in this section of the book?

INTRODUCTION

The practice of female circumcision is widespread in Africa. It is estimated that over two hundred million African women

have been circumcised, and that an additional two million undergo the procedure each year [1, 2]. Currently, genital operations are performed on women in approximately 26 African countries, spanning the continent from Somalia to Senegal and extending as far south as northern Zaire and Tanzania [3].

The severity and extent of these genital operations vary; however, they generally fall into one of three distinct groupings. Sunna circumcision, the least severe, involves reducing the size of the clitoris by cutting the prepuce. A second, 'intermediate,' type of genital operation entails the removal of the clitoris and some or all of the labia minora and labia majora. In the most radical procedure, Pharaonic circumcision, the clitoris, labia minora and labia majora are removed and the sides of the wound are infibulated, or joined together, ensuring the almost complete closure of the vaginal opening.

Much of the current literature on female circumcision in Africa describes its practice in the Sudan, Egypt, and Somalia [4–9]. These studies generally focus on Islamic societies where Pharaonic circumcision is practiced. Comparatively few studies of female circumcision have been conducted in other parts of the continent, and notably absent are descriptions of female genital operations in non-Islamic, sub-Saharan populations.

This paper examines female circumcision as it is practiced by one such group in southern Chad. The Sara are one of Chad's largest ethnic groups and practice circumcision, called *baya* or *gaja* in the Sara language, as part of the female initiation ceremony. The initiation serves as a rite of passage from childhood to adulthood for Sara girls. In most cases, sunna circumcision is performed; however, in some cases, the labia minora are also reduced or removed [10, 11].

Data collected through household surveys in Sarh, an urban center in southern Chad, allow us to describe the attitudes and practices of urban Sara women with regard to circumcision. These reports, together with in-depth interviews with key informants and information garnered from unpublished manuscripts, provide a framework for understanding ritual circumcision in the much broader context of the group's traditions and culture. The data draw attention to the recent origins of female circumcision among the Sara, and provide clues to modifying the practice.

PREVIOUS RESEARCH ON CIRCUMCISION IN CHAD

Relatively little is known about female circumcision in Chad or, more specifically, among the Sara. A 1992 survey of the health of mothers and children in the Moyen-Chari, one of Chad's 14 administrative regions and home to the Sara, is the only source of current, population-based data on circumcision for this group [12]. The survey covers a wide range of health-related topics and was administered to a representative sample of 1270 mothers 45 years of age and younger. The sample includes Sara women as well as women from other ethnic groups.

The report indicates that 80.3% of 'young' women and 84.9% of 'older' women were circumcised [12] (p. 37). No substantial difference in prevalence was noted between literate and illiterate women (78% and 86%). Data on circumcision are stratified by region (i.e. urban or rural) and religion, with the highest rates reported among rural Catholics (96%) and the lowest among urban Protestants (53%). Women's age at circumcision ranged from 4 to 20; however, most women were circumcised between the ages of 8 and 12.

A non-representative study carried out by UNICEF in 1990 focuses on attitudes toward circumcision in three distinct areas of Chad—the south, the capital city, and the Islamic northeast [11] (p. 2). The sample is comprised primarily of students and educated professionals: health care providers, teachers, government employees and religious leaders. The ratio of male to female respondents is nearly two to one (1670 and 981), reflecting the under representation of women in these positions.

The UNICEF report describes, from the perspective of this select group of respondents, the conditions under which the operation takes place, the types of treatment girls receive, the profile of the women who perform the operation, and the reasons for the continuation of the practice. In the southern region, marked differences in attitudes toward circumcision were noted by sex. The majority of women (68.5%) surveyed supported the practice, while nearly the same proportion of men (63%) expressed an unfavorable opinion toward it.

METHODS

Survey research for the current study was conducted in Sarh, the capital of the Moyen-Chari region and Chad's third largest urban area. . . . The city has an estimated population of 70,000, and is located in the south-central portion of the country, approximately 125 km north of Chad's border with the Central African Republic.

The Sara, a sedentary, agricultural people, are the primary ethnic group in Sarh, and comprise 25–30% of Chad's total population [13]. Though they are often viewed as a homogeneous group, the Sara are an aggregate of over 15 smaller ethnic groups that share a cultural heritage and speak similar languages. Sara society is patrilineal, and is organized around the *gir ka* (the common ancestor) or the lineage [14]. Marriages are strictly exogamous, and polygamy is practiced, particularly in rural areas.

Data on female circumcision were gathered as part of a larger investigation of sub-fertility among the Sara. A cross-sectional population survey was carried out between December 1993 and June 1994. The survey sample was selected using maps drawn by the Census Bureau for the 1993 census and a clustered sampling design. Census tracts served as the primary sampling unit. To be included in the study, women had to be of Sara ethnicity and 15 years of age or older. Interviews were conducted in French or in Sara with the help of a female interviewer from the region and took place in the privacy of the respondent's concession or home.

The section of the questionnaire pertaining to female circumcision was semi-structured, with approximately equal proportions of open and closed-ended questions. Women were asked about their own circumcision status as well as that of their mother, their sisters and their daughters. They were also asked about their age at circumcision, the site of the operation, and their female caretakers. Queries relating to treatment received, complications experienced, and decisions about circumcision relative to their own daughters (or future daughters) were also made.

In-depth interviews were conducted with women, religious leaders, local historians, elders and chiefs from villages throughout the Moyen-Chari region. These conversations, along with secondary sources, helped to trace the origins of female circumcision, gain insight into its role and function for this group, and understand current trends in its practice. Few published ethnographies of the Sara are available; therefore, secondary sources consist primarily of unpublished student theses and manuscripts written by European missionaries.

THE ORIGINS OF FEMALE CIRCUMCISION AMONG THE SARA

To understand why the vast majority of Sara women are circumcised and many Sara, of both sexes, support the practice, this ritual must be viewed in its broader cultural and historical context. For contemporary Sara, ritual circumcision is an intrinsic part of the transition to adulthood. Its meaning and importance are definitively linked to the meaning and importance of the female initiation ceremony. Historically, however, this has not always been the case.

The history of female circumcision in southern Chad has not been documented. However, elderly members of the community and local historians contend that female circumcision is a fairly recent phenomenon among the Sara, and available evidence supports this view. While impossible to situate precisely, ritual circumcision likely began only about 150 years ago, in the middle of the 19th century.

Female initiation ceremonies antedate the introduction of circumcision, although there is less precision about their date of origin. According to Jaulin [15], male initiation ceremonies began at least two to three centuries ago (and perhaps as many as four or five), corresponding with the sedentarization of the Sara sub-groups. Female ceremonies likely began in the same era. In conversations with Jaulin [15] (p. 122), elders were unable to remember a past without initiation ceremonies; yet even today, elders clearly remember a time when female circumcision was unknown to the Sara.

According to these elders, the Sar, who are also called the Sara Madjingaye and are the largest of the Sara sub-groups, were the first to practice female circumcision. They migrated to their current homeland from northern Chad in the late 18th and early 19th centuries, arriving in the region after most other Sara sub-groups [16]. The evidence suggests that the Sar did not bring circumcision with them, but rather started the practice shortly after settling in the Moyen-Chari region.

Elders situate the onset of ritual circumcision prior to the arrival of westerners (i.e. 1890) and during the reign of Béso as chief of Koumra (dates unknown). According to local folklore, circumcision was originally practiced in Boy, a small village outside Koumra . . . and was performed by a single woman, who alone had knowledge of the operation. Sar girls from surrounding communities were brought to Boy to be circumcised, an event captured in the lyrics to songs still sung by older women.

The pattern of diffusion of ritual circumcision also supports the notion that the practice was adopted post-migration. Sar women living west of the Bahr Sara, a river dissecting the region from north to south, began practicing circumcision much earlier than Sar women living east of the river. . . . Indeed, the Daye, a smaller Sara sub-group who live south of the Sar and west of the river, were earlier converts than their Sar neighbors to the east. This latter group, referred to as the *Sar Gidiman* or, literally, 'the Sar behind the water,' adopted circumcision after the turn of the century. As a result, many older Sar women from villages east of the Bahr Sara are not circumcised.

Female circumcision has become increasingly common throughout this century, spreading not only to 'the Sar behind the water,' but further east to the other Sara sub-groups. Ngam women began to practice circumcision around 1937, according to an elderly informant whose sisters participated in the first ceremony. Today, the practice is widespread among this sub-group. By 1950, the Sara-Kaba, who inhabit the eastern-most portions of Sara territory, had begun to practice circumcision [17]. Several of the Sara-Kaba women we interviewed reported that they represent the first generation of women in their families to be circumcised. While circumcision has not been adopted in a handful of settings, it is now an integral part of the female initiation ceremony in the vast majority of Sara communities.

CIRCUMCISION AS AN INTEGRAL PART OF FEMALE INITIATION

Initiation, which typically occurs during adolescence, is the Sara's primary ritual event. The ceremony is designed to educate Sara youth to be responsible members of the adult community, to venerate their ancestors and to respect the group's traditions. During this period, character traits valued by the Sara—strength, bravery, endurance and industry—are inculcated through a series of rites; with few exceptions, ritual circumcision is the principle rite associated with the female ceremony.

At the core of the lengthy and multifaceted initiation ritual is the belief that individuals are born with two distinct souls or spirits. The undesirable, child-like spirit is called *koy*, and must be permanently expelled from the individual around adolescence. At the same time, the mature, adult spirit, called *ndil ke madji*, is drawn out and developed. In its most general sense then, ritual initiation involves shedding the koy and celebrating the emergence of the *ndil ke madji*.

The 'death' of the child and the development of the 'new,' adult person are accomplished through rites which teach initiates to endure pain and physical deprivation with the dignity, character and spirit of an adult. Successful passage through this difficult and painful set of tests signifies to potential marriage partners and to the society at large that the woman is now guided by her benevolent, responsible self. The principal stages of the initiation ceremony and the circumcision ritual are described in the following section.

A woman's shift in status from child to adult is demonstrated symbolically, as well as through her behavior and physical appearance. An independent hut is built within the family compound, and, upon returning from the ceremony, the initiate leaves her mother's hut for her own. Reminders of her past life are removed; her clothes and other possessions are discarded, and her name is changed. Once initiated, women observe a long list of prohibitions. They are not allowed to eat certain foods or to eat at all in certain places, to intervene in men's conversations or look men in the eye [18]. They are expected to forsake 'childish' activities—playing games, running, speaking or laughing loudly—and to adopt a modest, reserved manner. In addition to being circumcised, initiates receive facial scars which identify them as non-*koy* women, and, by the pattern in which they are applied, as members of a particular ethnic group.

Uninitiated, or *koy*, women retain the inferior status of children and uninitiated men. Considered uneducated, unreliable and immature, these women receive little respect from other Sara adults. This dichotomy, while real, is also relative. From the male perspective, all women are categorized as *koy*, though uninitiated women are viewed as more child-like than those who have participated in the ceremony.

THE INITIATION CEREMONY

The female initiation ceremony typically lasts one month, but can vary from several weeks to several months. It is usually conducted between February and May, after the harvest and prior to the onset of the rainy season. Adolescent girls whose ancestors were born or lived in the same village attend the ceremony together [10] (p. 7); the daughters of urban parents often return to their villages of origin to participate.

Preparation of the young woman for initiation is generally considered to be the responsibility of the paternal family, though women interviewed for this study reported that mothers and maternal relatives often take an active role in this process. The initiate's father and his relatives are expected to pay for her circumcision and for the foodstuffs and other necessary provisions. Their most important responsibility, however, is in the selection of the *kóondò,* or 'mother of the initiation.' The *kóondò* is typically a close relative, and must have been previously initiated. Sterile women or women whose husbands or children have died are not desirable as *kóondòs* as their propensity for bad luck is believed to be transferable to the initiate. The *kóondò* serves as primary caretaker and educator throughout the entire period of the initiation; in return, the initiate incurs lifelong obligations to her sponsor. When she marries, for example, the *kóondò* is entitled to a portion of her brideprice. In the absence of payment, the *kóondò,* who is widely believed to possess extraordinary powers, may place any of a variety of curses upon her, impeding her ability to marry, reproduce or find happiness in life.

Like other rites of passage, the female initiation ceremony for the Sara consists of three distinct phases [19]. The first involves the initiates' physical removal from society and symbolic disconnection from their former lives. This process of separation and depersonalization prepares initiates for the middle stage, the heart of the ceremony. Once outside the village, initiates are no longer children, but have entered a liminal or transitional state. To successfully complete the shift to adulthood, they must acquire the skills and knowledge that define what it means to be Sara, as well as the symbols of group membership. At the conclusion of this period of acculturation, initiates are gradually reincorporated into Sara society.

Separation

For the duration of the initiation period, initiates are isolated from the village and from virtually all contact with the outside world. They live in small, temporary huts, constructed specially for the event and located at some distance from the village [10] (p. 6). This physical separation is important for symbolic as well as practical reasons.

The Sara commonly view the village as the center of life, and the bush surrounding the village—the site of the initiation—as the domain of the ancestors. This space is believed to be inhabited by their spirits, the *ndil ka ge.* The appropriate setting for the loss or death of the *koy*—the goal of initiation—is therefore in the bush, the realm of the dead. The return to the village, the center of life, occurs only after the *koy* has been permanently cast off and the adult self, the *ndil ke madji,* has emerged. In this way, the clear separation of the living from the dead is maintained and reinforced.

Initiation is a secret and exclusively feminine event, and the physical distance between the initiation site and the village help to preserve this secrecy. Men and uninitiated women are excluded from participating in all aspects of the ceremony. Indeed, men's participation, even inadvertent, is believed to result in various misfortunes, including the loss of virility and blindness [10] (p. 6).

The Transition Period

Ritual circumcision is conducted on the first day of the initiation ceremony, and begins with a communal bath. Initiates, heads shaved and nude, lie on a bed of *rombé* leaves, known for their medicinal properties [20, 21]. The order in which initiates are circumcised is determined by the age of their fathers; descendants of the oldest living members of the lineage are circumcised first. Together, the *kóondòs* hold each girl's arms and legs in turn, while the clitoris is cut.

The woman responsible for excising initiates, the *kode,* is usually from a casted group of artisans called the *noy.* Members of this caste live on the margins of Sara society, physically and socially. The Sara are strictly prohibited from marrying into this group; indeed, in former times, sexual contact with a member of this caste led to permanent ostracism [22]. Paradoxically, the *noy* are responsible for many of the Sara's ritual functions, among them the circumcision of Sara girls. The role of the *kode* in the initiation ceremony consists of cutting the clitoris with a knife or razor blade and saying a benediction over the initiate while spitting water on the wound. Throughout this procedure, the *kóondò's* ululate to encourage the initiate to be brave and to prevent those waiting to be circumcised from growing fearful. Girls who exhibit little fear are painted with kaolin, a red clay-like substance that is a symbol of courage for the Sara [20] (p. 31).

The post-operative healing period is one of intensive education for the initiates, and much of the instruction occurs in the course of the twice daily treatment of the circumcision wound. Each morning and evening, the *kóondò* cleanses the wound with leaves steeped in hot water [23]. Any attempt to avoid these treatments or any expression of pain in connection with them is severely punished. It is on these occasions that initiates are reminded of their weaknesses, past wrongdoings and instances of unacceptable behavior and are 'corrected,' often through the use of corporal punishment [10] (p. 11), [20] (p. 32), [21] (p. 67).

Older, female relatives also visit the site regularly to school the initiate, in conjunction with her *kóondò,* in how to keep a household, raise children, and conduct herself, particularly in the presence of men [18] (p. 30), [20] (p. 33), [21] (p. 69). The time is used to better acquaint initiates with their heritage, clan and lineage; they learn about their genealogy and the feats of the ancestors [18] (p. 31). Their female mentors also stress the importance of upholding the traditions. Initiates spend many hours listening to the folk-tales and learning the songs and dances specific to their ethnic group [18] (p. 30). Several days after the circumcision they receive facial scars which identify them as members.

Reincorporation

At the close of the initiation period, which coincides with the healing of the circumcision wounds, initiates are renamed, usually by their mothers or *kóondòs*. The new name, the *ri ndo* or 'name of the initiation,' replaces the *ri koy*, the name given to a child at birth. Sara names are highly individualized and convey a great deal of meaning. They are 'composed' by an 'author' and reflect his or her thoughts or preoccupations of the moment. Many of the *ri ndo* given to women allude to the initiation event itself, and reveal a mother's fear in sending her daughter to the ceremony (*Notoàl*, 'I won't cry anymore'), trust in the *kóondò* (*Menikèmm*, 'I give you my heart'), or pride in her daughter's education (*Rèeáà*, 'Come and see!') [24].

Elaborate preparations are made for the initiates' return to the village and reintroduction to the community. As on the first day of the ceremony, initiates take a communal bath (their first since the ceremony began) and have their heads shaved [21] (p. 70). Their bodies are covered with kaolin and karité oil to give the skin a reddish sheen. Initiates are adorned with brightly-colored beads worn around the neck and torso, multiple belts made from pieces of iron, and heavy copper bracelets worn on the wrists and ankles. A mask, also made of colored beads, completely covers the initiate's face.

The group's return is followed by a period of celebration and gradual reintegration which may last for months. During this time, the newly initiated visit the homes of their relatives where they perform a series of dances meant to showcase their learning as well as their beauty and feminine charms [20] (p. 35). In the course of these visits, family members are expected to contribute to the initiate's education by remunerating the *kóondò* for her expert guidance and supervision. Over time, initiates remove their masks, allowing their relatives to see their new faces, make short visits to their parents' homes to help with the daily chores before rejoining their group, and gradually abandon the attire which identifies them as initiates. Permission to speak to members of the community, granted by the *kóondò*, signifies the successful completion of the rite and marks the initiates' total reintegration into Sara society.

Having placed ritual circumcision in its proper context with the aid of narrative accounts, we now turn to an examination of its actual practice among a sample of urban women. Women's attitudes and practices with regard to circumcision were recorded as part of a standardized household survey. While the questionnaire included some open-ended queries and opportunities for narration, most of the data which follow reflect the more structured format characteristic of survey research.

SURVEY RESEARCH FINDINGS

Of the 133 women in our survey sample, 4 declined to be interviewed or to finish the interview, resulting in a total sample size of 129 and a response rate of 97%. Women in the sample ranged in age from 15 to 74, with a mean age of 29. The largest proportion of women (48.8%) earn a living from small-scale trade, selling peanuts and peanut oil, sorghum beer and home-made whiskey, and an assortment of agricultural products, typically from their homes. An additional 24% of the respondents identified as housewives; most of these women also engage in small-scale trade, albeit less frequently. Approximately one-fifth (21.7%) of the respondents in our sample were students.

Most of the women surveyed (70.5%) had received some formal education; however, the level of formal schooling was low. On average, women had completed 4 years in the classroom. Fifty women in the sample (38.8%) had completed primary school, three had completed secondary school, and none had attended university.

Nearly three-quarters of the women (73.6%) had, at one time, been married or in a stable union, and most of those currently married were in monogamous unions (67.1%). Among the 25 women in polygamous unions, 7 reported having multiple co-wives. Over 75% of the sample described themselves as Christian, of these, 65% were Catholic and 35% were Protestant. Approximately 14% of respondents practiced an indigenous religion exclusively, and 7% had adopted Islam.

Prevalence of Female Circumcision

The vast majority of women surveyed (80.6%) had been circumcised. Similar proportions indicated that their mothers (79.8%) and all of their sisters (78.9%) had been circumcised. Among the 123 women with female siblings, an additional 18.7% reported that some, though not all, of their sisters had been circumcised. In most instances, the siblings who had not been circumcised were still children too young to participate in the ritual. Six women were unsure of their mother's circumcision status; in most of these cases the mother died when the respondent was young.

Age at Circumcision

Of the 104 women who had been circumcised, 18 were unsure of their age at the time of the operation. Most of these women described themselves as "very young" or "very small." The average age at circumcision for the remainder of the sample ($n = 86$) was 12.3 years. Although the majority of women (56.3%) were circumcised between the ages of 10 and 15, the range extended from 2 to 18 years of age.

The Circumcision Site

Most women (80.2%, $n = 101$) were circumcised on the outskirts of their natal village or the village in which they or their family members were living. The remainder of the sample (19.8%) had the operation performed at home.

The *Kóondò*

The *kóondò*, the sponsor or 'mother of the initiation', was most commonly (46.1% of the time, $n = 102$) the initiate's paternal aunt. Mothers (12.7%), older sisters (15.7%), and other family members (25.5%) also played this role.

Treatment and Complications

Ninety-five women talked to us about the type of care they received following their circumcision. Standard treatment, provided by the *kóondò*, involved washing the circumcision wound twice daily with leaves steeped in hot water. The wound was then dressed with a powder made from crushed bark, leaves or roots. Twelve women reported that their *kóondòs* used rubbing alcohol or mercurochrome in addition to these substances. Those treated with any type of 'modern' pharmaceutical product in addition to the local pharmacopeia outnumbered those receiving only the latter by a ratio of nearly two to one (62 to 33). The pharmaceutical products mentioned most frequently were antibiotics (20), "injections" (unspecified) (15), anti-tetanus serum (10) and anti-malarials (9).

Women were also asked about any complications or health problems related to their circumcision. Of 91 respondents, 12 (13%) reported hemorrhaging or bleeding excessively, and 7 (7.7%) reported an infection, high fever or complication other than hemorrhage which required some type of intervention. Included in this latter grouping are illnesses which may be directly or indirectly linked to the circumcision procedure (i.e. psychological disorders) or may not be linked at all (i.e. stomach ailments).

For the Sara, excessive bleeding following circumcision is believed to be a sign of disequilibrium within the family and is therefore treated differently than other health problems. Decisions regarding the initiation ceremony—who serves as the *kóondò* or the relative roles of the maternal and paternal families in the event—are often pointed to as the cause of dissension. The cessation of bleeding is believed to follow reconciliation; therefore, cases of hemorrhage are often treated by bringing family members together to resolve their differences.

Attitudes toward Circumcision

Seventy-four of the 129 women in the sample had daughters of their own. At the time of the interview, 10 of these women reported that all of their daughters had been circumcised. The majority of mothers (86%) had one or more daughters who had not yet undergone the operation.

A follow-up question was asked of these mothers and of the women who currently had no daughters to assess their future intentions regarding the circumcision of their children. Among the 119 mothers and potential mothers-to-be, 61 (51.3%) said they would have their daughters circumcised, 46 (38.7%) said they would not, and 12 (10.0%) were undecided.

Some women favoring circumcision for their daughters described their own experience as positive or useful

> When you're not circumcised you have the spirit of a child. Now you can't do things that you did as a child. [As a child] you don't work, you have a hard head, you refuse to do things that your mother asks you to do. . . . I received a good education. Everything they did to me I want done to my child.

> When you are circumcised you have to change your character. They make you change it in the bush. Before, you play with bottles, make small houses, babies. When you come back you make gumbo so people can eat. . . . My mother brought me. I was happy.

> I learned things that were useful to me. They taught me to change my behavior. They gave me advice. . . . You should leave your bad habits in the bush.

Others described their own experience less favorably, but desired to send their daughters nonetheless

> I received no treatment. It hurt a lot and I bled a lot. . . . I didn't know what was going to happen or I wouldn't have gone. I'm not going to tell my girls about this before they go. They won't hear about it—if you tell them they will be afraid. This is why we don't tell.

> If I knew what was going to happen I wouldn't have gone. It hurts, but you have to support it. If you cry people will make fun of you. . . . After circumcision you learn to sing and dance. . . . After, you feel like a big woman and people respect you.

Among women who had been circumcised but preferred not to circumcise their daughters, some saw little value in the practice

> My father didn't send me. I ran after my friends. My father worked, so he bought antibiotics. I had a hemorrhage. They sang to stop it. Although my father didn't want me to go—I was too young—he took care of me. My aunts made me cut the leaves to sit on to stop the bleeding all by myself. I had a little infection. I saw the others go and I wanted to go. It is just harassment. They hit you. They give you advice on how to keep a house. These are useless things.

Others, while opposed to sending their daughters, expressed no negative feelings about their own circumcision

> I ran away with my friends. No one in my family did it, but if I didn't my friends would insult me. If I had a daughter I wouldn't want her to go. I'm raising someone else's girl who wants to go, but I don't want her to. But I don't regret this for myself.

> I don't want to send my daughters, but I didn't have a bad experience.

Support for Circumcision

Among the 71 women whose daughters had been or likely would be circumcised, the most common reason for supporting the practice, reported by 80% of women, had to do with inter-generational continuity and the continued observance of tradition. None of the women were aware of the origins of female circumcision or had heard an explanation given as to why their ancestors had adopted it. Yet, many believed that circumcision had been practiced in their family for generations, and most firmly believed that it was a custom that should be perpetuated.

In addition, women described extraordinary social pressures, both to be circumcised and to have the operation performed on their daughters. Thirty-one percent of the approving sub-sample expressed concern that their uncircumcised daughters would be ridiculed by age-mates, future co-wives or husbands. Several women noted that such ostracism would be more pronounced in the village than in an urban setting like Sarh; however, since urban dwellers generally maintain close ties with relatives in the village and visit frequently, these pressures remain highly relevant.

Opposition to Circumcision

Forty-one percent of the 46 women opposed to having their daughters circumcised cited a religious injunction against the practice. Of these women, all but one were members of the local Protestant church. The Protestant women were unsure of the reasons for their church's opposition, but nevertheless felt strongly about respecting the policy. Local pastors explained the church's position, based on their literal interpretation of the bible, in terms of a larger plan to eradicate all 'traditional' religious practices. By contrast, Catholic clergy have been more tolerant of local practices, preferring to integrate them, where possible, into the life of the church, and generally taking a less combative stance [22].

Thirty-five percent of the 46 respondents who had decided against circumcision for their daughters were members of families or ethnic sub-groups that hadn't adopted the practice or were married to men from one of these groups. One-third were Sara-Kaba, the last sub-group to begin practicing circumcision. Health concerns were mentioned by 22% of women who had decided against sending their daughters to the ceremony. They worried about the immediate complications of the practice as well as long-term effects—closure of the vaginal opening or the need for an episiotomy—which might impede or complicate a daughter's fertility.

DISCUSSION

For most outsiders, and many insiders, female circumcision confounds understanding. A variety of individuals and interest groups have been vocal advocates of the need to alter, decrease, or eliminate the practice [1, 3, 4, 25–27]. The World Health Organization, along with other international bodies, has pledged its support to national efforts aimed at eradicating female circumcision [2] (p. 154). This stance reflects the belief that such efforts must incorporate an understanding of the role and function of the practice for a particular group.

For the Sara, ritual circumcision is part of an essential phase in a girl's education. It represents the culmination of a family's efforts to properly raise their daughter and fully integrate her into adult society. From this perspective, female circumcision is a sign of social superiority, of proper upbringing, and of belonging.

As practiced by the Sara, female circumcision is a vehicle, and of necessity a painful one, for the transmission of the group's most important lessons about life and morality. The relative focus on sexuality, whether on a conscious or symbolic level, during the initiation period and via the circumcision ritual remains unclear and merits further investigation. However, in this setting, circumcision is not solely about preserving women's chastity or regulating their sexual behavior. Indeed, in the context of the initiation ceremony, circumcision serves a much broader educational purpose. Within this system, circumcision has questionable intrinsic worth; its significance lies primarily in its ability to facilitate the communication of group values, and to function as a symbol of having acquired them.

An examination of the origins of the practice reveals that the Sara have not always used circumcision to accomplish these goals. Indeed, female circumcision is a recent acquisition, in some sub-groups dating back no further than the current generation. Yet, we know little about the process of acculturation for Sara girls in its absence. No descriptions of early initiation ceremonies exist, nor have contemporary rituals in the few Sara communities where circumcision is not practiced been documented. The study of these settings may provide valuable clues about alternatives to circumcision. Daughters of the Sara nobility, for whom circumcision has never been part of the initiation process [22] (p. 148), offer another opportunity for such study.

The Protestant church provides a second, and very different, model for change. Through the denigration of all 'traditional' practices, including initiation and female circumcision, the church is attempting to bring about a radical shift in perspective. Adherents are challenged to adopt an entirely different belief system and world view; yet it is apparent from our interviews that the opposing pressures of this western religion and Sara tradition are a frequent source of conflict. Protestant women in this study acknowledged and, in some cases, adopted church doctrine regarding female circumcision; however, the church's ability to effect change in this practice is limited to its membership.

Female circumcision serves a clear and essential function for most Sara. Efforts to reduce or eradicate the practice in southern Chad will be more likely to succeed if they acknowledge that function. The challenge, then, is to identify suitable alternatives to circumcision which facilitate the transmission of group values without compromising women's health and well-being.

NOTE

Acknowledgments—Funding for this research was provided by a J. William Fulbright Fellowship through the Institute for International Education and by a Frederick Sheldon Traveling Grant from Harvard University. I would like to thank the University of Chad, Dr. Zakaria Fadoul of the Institut National des Sciences Humaines, the Chadian Ministry of Health, and Rhemadj-Haroune Tatola, mayor of Sarh, for permission to carry out this study. I also thank Tadjinati Ridjiti and Isabelle Tatola for their energy and assistance with the household surveys, and the men and women in Sarh and throughout the Moyen-Chari region who kindly agreed to be interviewed. Particular thanks are due to Mr. Paul Rarikingar, chief of the canton of Balimba, and the Surveillant General of the Museum of Sarh who agreed to sit for several lengthy interviews. I am grateful to Carla Obermeyer, who suggested that I undertake this portion of the study, and to Shelah Bhatti, Allan Hill, Tamyam Massingar, Rima Rudd, Randall Sell, and Jonathon Simon for their thoughtful comments on earlier versions of this paper.

REFERENCES

1. Ruminjo J. Circumcision in women. *E. Afr. med. J.* 69, 477, 1992.
2. World Health Organization. Female circumcision. *Eur. J. Obstet. Gynecol. Reprod. Biol.* 45, 153, 1992.
3. Hosken F. Female genital mutilation in the world today: a global review. *Int. J. Hlth. Serv.* 11, 415, 1981.
4. Assaad M. Female circumcision in Egypt: social implications, current research, and prospects for change. *Stud. Fam. Plan.* 11, 3, 1980.
5. Boddy J. Womb as oasis: the symbolic context of Pharaonic circumcision in rural northern Sudan. *Am. Ethnol.* 19, 682, 1982.
6. Gallo P. and Viviani F. Female circumcision in Somalia. *Mankind Q.* 29, 165, 1988.
7. Gordon D. Female circumcision and genital operations in Egypt and the Sudan: a dilemma for medical anthropology. *Med. Anthrop. Q.* 5, 3, 1991.
8. Kheir H., Kumar S. and Cross A. Female circumcision: attitudes and practices in Sudan. In *Proc. Demogr. Hlth Surveys World Conf.* p. 1679. IRD, Columbia, Maryland, 1991.
9. Van der Kwaak A. Female circumcision and gender identity: a questionable alliance? *Soc. Sci. Med.* 35, 777, 1992.
10. Dagoma A. L'excision, cette mal-aimée du Tchad. Centre Droit et Cultures, Université de Paris X, Nanterre, 1990.
11. Nabia A. *L'excision Féminine.* UNICEF, N'Djaména, Chad, 1991.
12. Chaine J. P. and Saidel T. *The Chad Child Survival Baseline Survey.* Devres, Washington, DC, 1992.
13. Cabot J. and Bouquet C. *Le Tchad.* Presses Universitaire de France, Paris, 1982.
14. Magnant J. P. *La Terre Sara Terre Tchadienne.* Editions l'Harmattan, Paris, 1986.
15. Jaulin R. *La Mort Sara: L'ordre de la Vie, ou, la Pensée de la Mort au Tchad.* Plon, Paris, 1967.
16. Kokongar G. J. Introduction à la vie et à l'historie précoloniale des populations Sara du Tchad. Université de Paris I, Paris, 1971.
17. Ngoussou N. *Les Sara-Kaba de Ngague.* Centre d'Etudes Linguistiques, Sarh, Chad, 1984.
18. Koungar K. L'Education et la condition de la femme traditionelle en pays Sara. Université du Tchad, N'Djamena, Chad, 1991.
19. Gennep A. V. *The Rites of Passage.* The University of Chicago Press, Chicago, 1960.
20. Kaya S. L'education de l'enfant dans la société Sara Madjingaye de Koumogo. Ecole Normale Superieure, N'Djamena, Chad, 1989.
21. Doh N. Faits et traditions des Day. Université du Tchad, N'Djamena, Chad, 1984.
22. Fortier J. *Le Couteau de Jet Sacré.* Editions l'Harmattan, Paris, 1982.
23. Anonymous. Le Tchad: Essai de classification des tribus Sara, les superstitions locales, les coutumes, les pratiques de la médecine indigène dans la race Sara. Centre de Formation et de Developpement, N'Djamena, Chad, 1963.
24. Hallaire J. Des noms qui parlent: homes et femmes dans la société sar d'après les noms d'initiation. Collège Charles Lwanga, Sarh, Chad, 1977.
25. Gallo P. Female circumcision in Somalia: some psychosocial aspects. *Genus* 41, 133, 1985.
26. Kouba L. and Muasher J. Female circumcision in Africa: an overview. *Afr. Stud. Rev.* 28, 95, 1985.
27. Sochart E. Legislating against female circumcision: social reform or placebo politics. *Strathclyde Papers Govt Politics* 54, 1, 1987.

Baseball Magic

George Gmelch

Bronislaw Malinowski, one of the founders of modern anthropology, argued that "primitive" people are as rational as people living in industrialized societies. One cornerstone of his argument was concerned with the use of science and magic (see Malinowski's essay in Part One). Briefly, Malinowski argued that where primitive people had the techniques to understand and control results (for example, in the planning and making of gardens), they were as scientific and rational as anyone else. Where the results lay outside of their ability to understand and control (for example, in the prediction and control of the weather), they resorted to magic.

Most people living in wealthy, technologically advanced societies probably like to consider themselves more rational than "savages" living in "primitive" societies. We point with pride to our scientific achievements and only rarely describe ourselves as superstitious. However, as George Gmelch shows in this classic essay about baseball, we tend to behave in the same way as people in traditional societies. Gmelch shows that ballplayers frequently resort to magic, carrying a wide variety of charms and engaging in many rituals. Similar to people in other societies, the baseball players' use of magic is patterned: When the situation is predictable, under control, they use little or no magic; but when chance and luck play a large role, they resort to more magic.

Gmelch should know about ballplayers. He played minor league ball in the Detroit Tigers organization and Independent league ball in Canada before finishing his undergraduate degree. In addition to several books in anthropology, he is also the author of *Inside Pitch: Life in Professional Baseball* and, with J. J. Weiner, *In the Ballpark: The Working Lives of Baseball People.*

As you read, consider these questions:

1. Gmelch identifies three aspects of baseball: pitching, hitting, and fielding. Why is magic associated with only two of these?
2. The author writes about rituals, taboos, and fetishes. What are these, and how do they function?
3. What kinds of rituals, taboos, and fetishes are elements of your behavior? What are they, how do they function, and under what circumstances do you employ them?

On each pitching day for the first three months of a winning season, Dennis Grossini, a pitcher on a Detroit Tigers farm team, arose from bed at exactly 10:00 A.M. At 1:00 P.M. he went to the nearest restaurant for two glasses of iced tea and a tuna sandwich. Although the afternoon was free, he changed into the sweatshirt and supporter he wore during his last winning game, and, one hour before the game, he chewed a wad of Beech-Nut chewing tobacco. After each pitch during the game he touched the letters on his uniform and straightened his cap after each ball. Before the start of each inning he replaced the pitcher's resin bag next to the spot where it was the inning before. And after every inning in which he gave up a run, he washed his hands.

When asked which part of the ritual was most important, he said, "You can't really tell what's most important so it all

becomes important. I'd be afraid to change anything. As long as I'm winning, I do everything the same."

Trobriand Islanders, according to anthropologist Bronislaw Malinowski, felt the same way about their fishing magic. Among the Trobrianders, fishing took two forms: in the *inner lagoon* where fish were plentiful and there was little danger, and on the *open sea* where fishing was dangerous and yields varied widely. Malinowski found that magic was not used in lagoon fishing, where men could rely solely on their knowledge and skill. But when fishing on the open sea, Trobrianders used a great deal of magical ritual to ensure safety and increase their catch.

Baseball, America's national pastime, is an arena in which players behave remarkably like Malinowski's Trobriand fishermen. To professional ballplayers, baseball is more than just a game. It is an occupation. Since their livelihoods depend on how well they perform, many use magic to try to control the chance that is built into baseball. There are three essential activities of the game—pitching, hitting, and fielding. In the first two, chance can play a surprisingly important role. The pitcher is the player least able to control the outcome of his own efforts. He may feel great and have good stuff warming up in the bullpen and then get into the game and not have it. He may make a bad pitch and see the batter miss it for a strike out or see it hit hard but right into the hands of a fielder for an out. His best pitch may be blooped for a base hit. He may limit the opposing team to just a few hits yet lose the game, or he may give up a dozen hits but still win. And the good and bad luck don't always average out over the course of a season. Some pitchers end the season with poor won-loss records but good earned run averages, and vice versa. For instance, this past season Andy Benes gave up over one run per game more than his teammate Omar Daal but had a better won-loss record. Benes went 14–13, while Daal was only 8–12. Both pitched for the same team—the Arizona Diamondbacks—which meant they had the same fielders behind them. Regardless of how well a pitcher performs, on every outing he depends not only on his own skill, but also upon the proficiency of his teammates, the ineptitude of the opposition, and luck.

Hitting, which many observers call the single most difficult task in the world of sports, is also full of risk and uncertainty. Unless it's a home run, no matter how well the batter hits the ball, fate determines whether it will go into a waiting glove, whistle past a fielder's diving stab, or find a gap in the outfield. The uncertainty is compounded by the low success rate of hitting: the average hitter gets only one hit in every four trips to the plate, while the very best hitters average only one hit every three trips. Fielding, as we will return to later, is the one part of baseball where chance does not play much of a role.

How does the risk and uncertainty in pitching and hitting affect players? How do they try to exercise control over the outcomes of their performance? These are questions that I first became interested in many years ago as both a ballplayer and an anthropology student. I'd devoted much of my youth to baseball, and played professionally as first baseman in the Detroit Tigers organization in the 1960s. It was shortly after the end of one baseball season that I took an anthropology course called "Magic, Religion, and Witch-craft." As I listened to my professor describe the magical rituals of the Trobriand Islanders, it occurred to me that what these so-called "primitive" people did wasn't all that different from what my teammates and I did for luck and confidence at the ball park.

ROUTINES AND RITUALS

The most common way players attempt to reduce chance and their feelings of uncertainty is to develop and follow a daily routine, a course of action which is regularly followed. Talking about the routines ballplayers follow, Pirates coach Rich Donnelly said:

> They're like trained animals. They come out here [ballpark] and everything has to be the same, they don't like anything that knocks them off their routine. Just look at the dugout and you'll see every guy sitting in the same spot every night. It's amazing, everybody in the same spot. And don't you dare take someone's seat. If a guy comes up from the minors and sits here, they'll say, 'Hey, Jim sits here, find another seat.' You watch the pitcher warm up and he'll do the same thing every time. And when you go on the road it's the same way. You've got a routine and you adhere to it and you don't want anybody knocking you off it.

Routines are comforting, they bring order into a world in which players have little control. And sometimes practical elements in routines produce tangible benefits, such as helping the player concentrate. But what players often do goes beyond mere routine. Their actions become what anthropologists define as *ritual*—prescribed behaviors in which there is no empirical connection between the means (e.g., tapping home plate three times) and the desired end (e.g., getting a base hit). Because there is no real connection between the two, rituals are not rational, and sometimes they are actually irrational. Similar to rituals are the nonrational beliefs that form the basis of taboos and fetishes, which players also use to reduce chance and bring luck to their side. But first let's look more closely at rituals.

Most rituals are personal, that is, they're performed by individuals rather than by a team or group. Most are done in an unemotional manner, in much the same way players apply pine tar to their bats to improve the grip or dab eye black on their upper cheeks to reduce the sun's glare. Baseball rituals are infinitely varied. A ballplayer may ritualize any activity—eating, dressing, driving to the ballpark—that he considers important or somehow linked to good performance. For example, Yankee pitcher Denny Naegle goes to a movie on days he is scheduled to start. Pitcher Jason Bere listens to the same song on his Walkman on the days he is to pitch. Jim Ohms puts another penny in the pouch of his sup-

porter after each win. Clanging against the hard plastic genital cup, the pennies made a noise as he ran the bases toward the end of a winning season. Glenn Davis would chew the same gum every day during hitting streaks, saving it under his cap. Infielder Julio Gotay always played with a cheese sandwich in his back pocket (he had a big appetite, so there might also have been a measure of practicality here). Wade Boggs ate chicken before every game during his career, and that was just one of dozens of elements in his pre and post game routine, which also included leaving his house for the ballpark at precisely the same time each day (1:47 for a 7:05 game). Former Oriole pitcher Dennis Martinez would drink a small cup of water after each inning and then place it under the bench upside down, in a line. His teammates could always tell what inning it was by counting the cups.

Many hitters go through a series of preparatory rituals before stepping into the batter's box. These include tugging on their caps, touching their uniform letters or medallions, crossing themselves, tapping or bouncing the bat on the plate, or swinging the weighted warm-up bat a prescribed number of times. Consider Red Sox Nomar Garciaparra. After each pitch he steps out of the batters box, kicks the dirt with each toe, adjusts his right batting glove, adjusts his left batting glove, and touches his helmet before getting back into the box. Mike Hargrove, former Cleveland Indian first baseman, had so many time consuming elements in his batting ritual that he was known as "the human rain delay." Both players believe their batting rituals helped them regain their concentration after each pitch. But others wonder if they have become prisoners of their own superstitions. Also, players who have too many or particularly bizarre rituals risk being labeled as "flakes," and not just by teammates but by fans and media as well. For example, pitcher Turk Wendell's eccentric rituals, which included wearing a necklace of teeth from animals he had killed, made him a cover story in the *New York Times Sunday Magazine*.

Some players, especially Latin Americans, draw upon rituals from their Roman Catholic religion. Some make the sign of the cross or bless themselves before every at bat, and a few like the Rangers' Pudge Rodriquez do so before every pitch. Others, like the Detroit Tiger Juan Gonzalez, also visibly wear religious medallions around their necks, while some tuck them discretely inside their undershirts.

One ritual associated with hitting is tagging a base when leaving and returning to the dugout between innings. Some players don't "feel right" unless they tag a specific base on each trip between the dugout and the field. One of my teammates added some complexity to his ritual by tagging third base on his way to the dugout only after the third, sixth, and ninth innings. Asked if he ever purposely failed to step on the bag, he replied, "Never! I wouldn't dare. It would destroy my confidence to hit." Baseball fans observe a lot of this ritual behavior, such as fielders tagging bases, pitchers tugging on their caps or touching the resin bag after each bad pitch, or smoothing the dirt on the mound before each new batter or inning, never realizing the importance of these actions to the player. The one ritual many fans do recognize, largely because it's a favorite of TV cameramen, is the "rally cap"—players in the dugout folding their caps and wearing them bill up in hopes of sparking a rally.

Most rituals grow out of exceptionally good performances. When a player does well, he seldom attributes his success to skill alone. He knows that his skills were essentially the same the night before. He asks himself, "What was different about today which explains my three hits?" He decides to repeat what he did today in an attempt to bring more good luck. And so he attributes his success, in part, to an object, a food he ate, not having shaved, a new shirt he bought that day, or just about any behavior out of the ordinary. By repeating that behavior, he seeks to gain control over his performance. Outfielder John White explained how one of his rituals started:

> I was jogging out to centerfield after the national anthem when I picked up a scrap of paper. I got some good hits that night and I guess I decided that the paper had something to do with it. The next night I picked up a gum wrapper and had another good night at the plate . . . I've been picking up paper every night since.

Outfielder Ron Wright of the Calgary Cannons shaves his arms once a week and plans to continue doing so until he has a bad year. It all began two years before when after an injury he shaved his arm so it could be taped, and proceeded to hit three homers over the next few games. Now he not only has one of the smoothest swings in the minor leagues, but two of the smoothest forearms. Wade Boggs' routine of eating chicken before every game began when he was a rookie in 1982. He noticed a correlation between multiple hit games and poultry plates (his wife has over 40 chicken recipes). One of Montreal Expos farmhand Mike Saccocio's rituals also concerned food: "I got three hits one night after eating at Long John Silver's. After that when we'd pull into town, my first question would be, 'Do you have a Long John Silver's?'" Unlike Boggs, Saccocio abandoned his ritual and looked for a new one when he stopped hitting well.

When in a slump, most players make a deliberate effort to change their rituals and routines in an attempt to shake off their bad luck. One player tried taking different routes to the ballpark; several players reported trying different combinations of tagging and not tagging particular bases in an attempt to find a successful combination. I had one manager who would rattle the bat bin when the team was not hitting well, as if the bats were in a stupor and could be aroused by a good shaking. Similarly, I have seen hitters rub their hands along the handles of the bats protruding from the bin in hopes of picking up some power or luck from bats that are getting hits for their owners. Some players switch from wearing their contact lenses to glasses. Brett Mandel described his Pioneer League team, the Ogden Raptors, trying to break a losing streak by using a new formation for their pre-game stretching.[1]

TABOO

Taboos are the opposite of rituals. The word *taboo* comes from a Polynesian term meaning prohibition. Breaking a taboo, players believe, leads to undesirable consequences or bad luck. Most players observe at least a few taboos, such as never stepping on the white foul lines. A few, like the Mets Turk Wendell and Red Sox Nomar Garciaparra, leap over the entire basepath. One teammate of mine would never watch a movie on a game day, despite the fact that we played nearly every day from April to September. Another teammate refused to read anything before a game because he believed it weakened his batting eye.

Many taboos take place off the field, out of public view. On the day a pitcher is scheduled to start, he is likely to avoid activities he believes will sap his strength and detract from his effectiveness. Some pitchers avoid eating certain foods, others will not shave on the day of a game, refusing to shave again as long as they are winning. Early in the 1989 season Oakland's Dave Stewart had six consecutive victories and a beard by the time he lost.

Taboos usually grow out of exceptionally poor performances, which players, in search of a reason, attribute to a particular behavior. During my first season of pro ball I ate pancakes before a game in which I struck out three times. A few weeks later I had another terrible game, again after eating pancakes. The result was a pancake taboo: I never again ate pancakes during the season. Pitcher Jason Bere has a taboo that makes more sense in dietary terms: after eating a meatball sandwich and not pitching well, he swore off them for the rest of the season.

While most taboos are idiosyncratic, there are a few that all ball players hold and that do not develop out of individual experience or misfortune. These form part of the culture of baseball, and are sometimes learned as early as Little League. Mentioning a no-hitter while one is in progress is a well-known example. It is believed that if a pitcher hears the words "no-hitter," the spell accounting for this hard to achieve feat will be broken and the no-hitter lost. This taboo is also observed by many sports broadcasters, who use various linguistic subterfuges to inform their listeners that the pitcher has not given up a hit, never saying "no-hitter."

FETISHES

Fetishes or charms are material objects believed to embody "supernatural" power that can aid or protect the owner. Good luck charms are standard equipment for some ballplayers. These include a wide assortment of objects from coins, chains, and crucifixes to a favorite baseball hat. The fetishized object may be a new possession or something a player found that happens to coincide with the start of a streak and which he holds responsible for his good fortune. While playing in the Pacific Coast League, Alan Foster forgot his baseball shoes on a road trip and borrowed a pair from a teammate. That night he pitched a no-hitter, which he attributed to the shoes. Afterwards he bought them from his teammate and they became a fetish. Expo farmhand Mark LaRosa's rock has a different origin and use:

> I found it on the field in Elmira after I had gotten bombed. It's unusual, perfectly round, and it caught my attention. I keep it to remind me of how important it is to concentrate. When I am going well I look at the rock and remember to keep my focus, the rock reminds me of what can happen when I lose my concentration.

For one season Marge Schott, former owner of the Cincinnati Reds, insisted that her field manager rub her St. Bernard "Schotzie" for good luck before each game. When the Reds were on the road, Schott would sometimes send a bag of the dog's hair to the field manager's hotel room.

During World War II, American soldiers used fetishes in much the same way. Social psychologist Samuel Stouffer and his colleagues found that in the face of great danger and uncertainty, soldiers developed magical practices, particularly the use of protective amulets and good luck charms (crosses, Bibles, rabbits' feet, medals), and jealously guarded articles of clothing they associated with past experiences of escape from danger.[2] Stouffer also found that pre-battle preparations were carried out in fixed ritual-like order, similar to ballplayers preparing for a game.

Uniform numbers have special significance for some players who request their lucky number. Since the choice is usually limited, they try to at least get a uniform that contains their lucky number, such as 14, 24, 34, or 44 for the player whose lucky number is four. When Ricky Henderson came to the Blue Jays in 1993 he paid outfielder Turner Ward $25,000 for the right to wear number 24. Oddly enough, there is no consensus about the effect of wearing number 13. Some players will not wear it, others will, and a few request it. Number preferences emerge in different ways. A young player may request the number of a former star, hoping that—through what anthropologists call *imitative* magic—it will bring him the same success. Or he may request a number he associates with good luck. While with the Oakland A's Vida Blue changed his uniform number from 35 to 14, the number he wore as a high-school quarterback. When 14 did not produce better pitching performance, he switched back to 35. Former San Diego Padre first baseman Jack Clark changed his number from 25 to 00, hoping to break out of a slump. That day he got four hits in a double header, but also hurt his back. Then, three days later, he was hit in the cheekbone by a ball thrown in batting practice.

Colorado Rockies Larry Walker's fixation with the number three has become well known to baseball fans. Besides wearing 33, he takes three practice swings before stepping into the box, he showers from the third nozzle, sets his alarm for three minutes past the hour and he was wed on November 3 at 3:33 P.M.[3] Fans in ballparks all across America rise from their seats for the seventh inning stretch before the home club comes to bat because the number seven is lucky, although the origin of this tradition has been lost.[4]

Clothing, both the choice and the order in which they are put on, combine elements of both ritual and fetish. Some players put on their uniform in a ritualized order. Expos farmhand Jim Austin always puts on his left sleeve, left pants leg, and left shoe before the right. Most players, however, single out one or two lucky articles or quirks of dress for ritual elaboration. After hitting two home runs in a game, for example, ex-Giant infielder Jim Davenport discovered that he had missed a buttonhole while dressing for the game. For the remainder of his career he left the same button undone. For outfielder Brian Hunter the focus is shoes, "I have a pair of high tops and a pair of low tops. Whichever shoes don't get a hit that game, I switch to the other pair." At the time of our interview, he was struggling at the plate and switching shoes almost every day. For Birmingham Baron pitcher Bo Kennedy the arrangement of the different pairs of baseball shoes in his locker is critical:

> I tell the clubies [clubhouse boys] when you hang stuff in my locker don't touch my shoes. If you bump them move them back. I want the Pony's in front, the turfs to the right, and I want them nice and neat with each pair touching each other. . . . Everyone on the team knows not to mess with my shoes when I pitch.

During streaks—hitting or winning—players may wear the same clothes day after day. Once I changed sweatshirts midway through the game for seven consecutive nights to keep a hitting streak going. Clothing rituals, however, can become impractical. Catcher Matt Allen was wearing a long sleeve turtle neck shirt on a cool evening in the New York-Penn League when he had a three-hit game. "I kept wearing that shirt and had a good week," he explained. "Then the weather got hot as hell, 85 degrees and muggy, but I would not take that shirt off. I wore it for another ten days—catching—and people thought I was crazy." Also taking a ritual to the extreme, Leo Durocher, managing the Brooklyn Dodgers to a pennant in 1941, is said to have spent three and a half weeks in the same gray slacks, blue coat, and knitted blue tie. During a 16-game winning streak, the 1954 New York Giants wore the same clothes in each game and refused to let them be cleaned for fear that their good fortune might be washed away with the dirt. Losing often produces the opposite effect. Several Oakland A's players, for example, went out and bought new street clothes in an attempt to break a fourteen game losing streak.

Baseball's superstitions, like most everything else, change over time. Many of the rituals and beliefs of early baseball are no longer observed. In the 1920s and 1930s sportswriters reported that a player who tripped en route to the field would often retrace his steps and carefully walk over the stumbling block for "insurance." A century ago players spent time on and off the field intently looking for items that would bring them luck. To find a hairpin on the street, for example, assured a batter of hitting safely in that day's game. Today few women wear hairpins—a good reason the belief has died out. To catch sight of a white horse or a wagon-load of barrels were also good omens. In 1904 the manager of the New York Giants, John McGraw, hired a driver with a team of white horses to drive past the Polo Grounds around the time his players were arriving at the ballpark. He knew that if his players saw white horses, they'd have more confidence and that could only help them during the game. Belief in the power of white horses survived in a few backwaters until the 1960s. A gray haired manager of a team I played for in Drummondville, Quebec, would drive around the countryside before important games and during the playoffs looking for a white horse. When he was successful, he would announce it to everyone in the clubhouse.

One belief that appears to have died out recently is a taboo about crossed bats. Some of my Latino teammates in the 1960s took it seriously. I can still recall one Dominican player becoming agitated when another player tossed a bat from the batting cage and it landed on top of his bat. He believed that the top bat might steal hits from the lower one. In his view, bats contained a finite number of hits, a sort of baseball "image of limited good." It was once commonly believed that when the hits in a bat were used up no amount of good hitting would produce any more. Hall of Famer Honus Wagner believed each bat contained only 100 hits. Regardless of the quality of the bat, he would discard it after its 100th hit. This belief would have little relevance today, in the era of light bats with thin handles—so thin that the typical modern bat is lucky to survive a dozen hits without being broken. Other superstitions about bats do survive, however. Position players on the Class A Asheville Tourists, for example, would not let pitchers touch or swing their bats, not even to warm up. Poor-hitting players, as most pitchers are, were said to pollute or weaken the bats.

UNCERTAINTY AND MAGIC

The best evidence that players turn to rituals, taboos, and fetishes to control chance and uncertainty is found in their uneven application. They are associated mainly with pitching and hitting—the activities with the highest degree of chance—and not fielding. I met only one player who had any ritual in connection with fielding, and he was an error prone shortstop. Unlike hitting and pitching, a fielder has almost complete control over the outcome of his performance. Once a ball has been hit in his direction, no one can intervene and ruin his chances of catching it for an out (except in the unlikely event of two fielders colliding). Compared with the pitcher or the hitter, the fielder has little to worry about. He knows that, in better than 9.7 times out of 10, he will execute his task flawlessly. With odds like that there is little need for ritual.

Clearly, the rituals of American ballplayers are not unlike that of the Trobriand Islanders studied by Malinowski many years ago.[5] In professional baseball, fielding is the equiva-

lent of the inner lagoon while hitting and pitching are like the open sea.

While Malinowski helps us understand how ballplayers respond to chance and uncertainty, behavioral psychologist B. F. Skinner sheds light on why personal rituals get established in the first place.[6] With a few grains of seed Skinner could get pigeons to do anything he wanted. He merely waited for the desired behavior (e.g. pecking) and then rewarded it with some food. Skinner then decided to see what would happen if pigeons were rewarded with food pellets regularly, every fifteen seconds, regardless of what they did. He found that the birds associate the arrival of the food with a particular action, such as tucking their head under a wing or walking in clockwise circles. About ten seconds after the arrival of the last pellet, a bird would begin doing whatever it associated with getting the food and keep doing it until the next pellet arrived. In short, the pigeons behaved as if their actions made the food appear. They learned to associate particular behaviors with the reward of being given seed.

Ballplayers also associate a reward—successful performance—with prior behavior. If a player touches his crucifix and then gets a hit, he may decide the gesture was responsible for his good fortune and touch his crucifix the next time he comes to the plate. If he gets another hit, the chances are good that he will touch his crucifix each time he bats. Unlike pigeons, however, most ballplayers are quicker to change their rituals once they no longer seem to work. Skinner found that once a pigeon associated one of its actions with the arrival of food or water, only sporadic rewards were necessary to keep the ritual going. One pigeon, believing that hopping from side to side brought pellets into its feeding cup, hopped ten thousand times without a pellet before finally giving up. But, then, didn't Wade Boggs eat chicken before every game, through slumps and good times, for seventeen years.

Obviously the rituals and superstitions of baseball do not make a pitch travel faster or a batted ball find the gaps between the fielders, nor do the Trobriand rituals calm the seas or bring fish. What both do, however, is give their practitioners a sense of control, with that added confidence, at no cost. And we all know how important that is. If you really believe eating chicken or hopping over the foul lines will make you a better hitter, it probably will.

NOTES

1.   Mandel, *Major Dreams, Minor Leagues,* 156.

2.   Stouffer, *The American Soldier.*

3.   Sports Illustrated . . . , 48.

4.   Allen, "The Superstitions of Baseball Players," 104.

5.   Malinowski, B. *Magic, Science and Religion and Other Essays.*

6.   Skinner, B. F. *Behavior of Organisms: An Experimental Analysis;* Skinner, B. F. *Science and Human Behavior.*

BIBLIOGRAPHY

Malinowski, B. *Magic, Science and Religion and Other Essays.* Glencoe, IL, 1948.

Mandel, Brett. *Minor Player, Major Dreams.* Lincoln, Nebraska: University of Nebraska Press, 1997.

Skinner, B. F. *Behavior of Organisms: An Experimental Analysis.* D. Appleton-Century Co., 1938.

Skinner, B. F. *Science and Human Behavior.* New York: Macmillan, 1953.

Stouffer, Samuel. *The American Soldier.* New York: J. Wiley, 1965.

Torrez, Danielle Gagnon. *High Inside: Memoirs of a Baseball Wife.* New York: G. P. Putnam's Sons, 1983.

Body Ritual among the Nacirema

Horace Miner

Until the advent of modern technological medicine in the twentieth century, most health-related practices around the world were deeply embedded in religious ritual. Even today, many in American society believe in the power of religious ritual to heal them or protect them from disease. This topic is covered more fully in Part Four of this book. However, this essay is included here because it focuses on the many magical rituals of the Nacirema rather than on the context of their culture or changes within it.

In this essay, a classic in the anthropological literature, Miner shows that the Nacirema are, in fact, obsessed with their health and the performance of rituals that they hope will preserve and enhance it. Such rituals permeate most aspects of their daily life. Miner focuses on a central Naceriman notion: the idea that the body is always in a constant state of decay and that this can be slowed, if not completely arrested, through the correct performance of ritual.

As you read, consider these questions:

1. How do the body rituals of the Nacirema compare with other body rituals you may be familiar with?
2. Can these rituals exist in a society dominated by science?
3. If an anthropological description of a society is not recognized by members of that society, is it wrong?

Anthropologists have become so familiar with the diversity of ways different peoples behave in similar situations that they are not apt to be surprised by even the most exotic customs. In fact, if all of the logically possible combinations of behavior have not been found somewhere in the world, anthropologists are apt to suspect that they must be present in some yet undescribed tribe. . . . In this light, the magical beliefs and practices of the Nacirema present such unusual aspects that it seems desirable to describe them as an example of the extremes to which human behavior can go. The Nacirema are a North American group living in the territory between the Canadian Cree, the Yaqui and Tarahumare of Mexico, and the Carib and Arawak of the Antilles. Little is known of their origin, although tradition states that they came from the east. . . .

Nacirema culture is characterized by a highly developed market economy which has evolved in a rich natural habitat. While much of the people's time is devoted to economic pursuits, a large part of the fruits of these labors and a considerable portion of the day are spent in ritual activity. The focus of this activity is the human body, the appearance and health of which loom as a dominant concern in the ethos of the people. While such a concern is certainly not unusual, its ceremonial aspects and associated philosophy are unique.

The fundamental belief underlying the whole system appears to be that the human body is ugly and that its natural tendency is to debility and disease. Incarcerated in such a body, man's only hope is to avert these characteristics through the use of the powerful influences of ritual and ceremony and every household has one or more shrines devoted to this purpose. The rituals associated with the shrine are not family ceremonies but are private and secret. The rites are normally only discussed with children, and then only during the period when they are being initiated into these mysteries. I was able, however, to establish sufficient rapport with the natives to examine these shrines and to have the rituals described to me.

The focal point of the shrine is a box or chest which is built into the wall. In this chest are kept the many charms and magical potions without which no native believes he could live. These preparations are secured from a variety of specialized practitioners. The most powerful of these are the medicine men, whose assistance must be rewarded with substantial gifts. However, the medicine men do not provide

Reproduced by permission of the American Anthropological Association from *American Anthropologist* 58:2 (1956), 503–507.

the curative potions for their clients, but decide what the ingredients should be and then write them down in an ancient and secret language. This writing is understood only by the medicine men and by the herbalists who, for another gift, provide the required charm. The charm is not disposed of after it has served its purpose, but is placed in the charm-box of the household shrine.

Beneath the charm-box is a small font. Each day every member of the family, in succession, enters the shrine room, bows his head before the charm-box, mingles different sorts of holy water in the font, and proceeds with a brief rite of ablution. The holy waters are secured from the Water Temple of the community, where the priests conduct elaborate ceremonies to make the liquid ritually pure.

In the hierarchy of magical practitioners, and below the medicine men in prestige, are specialists whose designation is best translated "holy-mouth-men." The Nacirema have an almost pathological horror of and fascination with the mouth, the condition of which is believed to have a supernatural influence on all social relationships. Were it not for the rituals of the mouth, they believe that their teeth would fall out, their gums bleed, their jaws shrink, their friends desert them, and their lovers reject them.

The daily body ritual performed by everyone includes a mouth-rite, but in addition, the people seek out a holy-mouth-man once or twice a year. These practitioners have an impressive set of paraphernalia, consisting of a variety of augers, awls, probes, and prods. The use of these objects in the exorcism of the evils of the mouth involves almost unbelievable ritual torture of the client. The holy-mouth-man opens the client's mouth and, using the above mentioned tools, enlarges any holes which decay may have created in the teeth. Magical materials are put into those holes. In the clients view, the purpose of these ministrations is to arrest decay and to draw friends. The extremely sacred and traditional character of the rite is evident in the fact that the natives return to the holy-mouth-men year after year, despite the fact that their teeth continue to decay. It is to be hoped that, when a thorough study of the Nacirema is made, there will be careful inquiry into the personality structure of these people. One has but to watch the gleam in the eye of a holy-mouth-man, as he jabs an awl into an exposed nerve, to suspect that a certain amount of sadism is involved. If this can be established, a very interesting pattern emerges, for most of the population shows definite masochistic tendencies. For example, a portion of the daily body ritual performed only by men involves scraping and lacerating the surface of the face with a sharp instrument. Special women's rites are performed only four times during each lunar month, but what they lack in frequency is made up in barbarity. As part of this ceremony, women bake their heads in small ovens for about an hour. The theoretically interesting point is that what seems to be a preponderantly masochistic people have developed sadistic specialists. The medicine men have an imposing temple, or *latipsoh*, in every community of any size.

The more elaborate ceremonies required to treat very sick patients can only be performed at this temple. These ceremonies involve not only the priests who perform miracles, but a permanent group of vestal maidens who move sedately about the temple chambers in distinctive costume and headdress.

The *latipsoh* ceremonies are so harsh that it is phenomenal that a fair proportion of the really sick natives who enter the temple ever recover. Despite this fact, sick adults are not only willing but eager to undergo the protracted ritual purification, if they can afford to do so. No matter how ill the supplicant or how grave the emergency, the guardians of many temples will not admit a client if he cannot give a rich gift to the custodian. Even after one has gained admission and survived the ceremonies, the guardians will not permit the neophyte to leave until he makes still another gift.

The supplicant entering the temple is first stripped of all his or her clothes. Psychological shock results from the fact that body secrecy is suddenly lost upon entry into the *latipsoh*. A man whose own wife has never seen him in an excretory act suddenly finds himself naked and assisted by a vestal maiden while he performs his natural functions into a sacred vessel. This sort of ceremonial treatment is necessitated by the fact that the excreta are used by a diviner to ascertain the course and nature of the client's sickness. Female clients, on the other hand, find their naked bodies are subjected to the scrutiny, manipulation, and prodding of the medicine men. The fact that these temple ceremonies may not cure, and may even kill the neophyte, in no way decreases the people's faith in the medicine men.

In conclusion, mention must be made of certain practices which have their base in native esthetics but which depend upon the pervasive aversion to the natural body and its functions. There are ritual fasts to make fat people thin and ceremonial feasts to make thin people fat. Still other rites are used to make women's breasts larger if they are small, and smaller if they are large. General dissatisfaction with breast shape is symbolized in the fact that the ideal form is virtually outside the range of human variation. A few women afflicted with almost inhuman hyper mammary development are so idolized that they make a handsome living by simply going from village to village and permitting the natives to stare at them for a fee. Our review of the ritual life of the Nacirema has certainly shown them to be a magic-ridden people. It is hard to understand how they have managed to exist so long under the burdens which they have imposed upon themselves. But even such exotic customs as these take on real meaning when they are viewed with the insight provided by Malinowski when he wrote:

> Looking from far and above, from our high places of safety in the developed civilization, it is easy to see all the crudity and irrelevance of magic. But without its power and guidance early man could not have mastered his practical difficulties as he has done, nor could man have advanced to the higher stages of civilization.

PART THREE

Journeys of the Soul

Different cultures deal with death in radically different ways. In modern America, death is sanitized. The dead are largely invisible and we are shocked by displays of human bones. This, however, was not the case in Christian European cultures. There, as in this picture from the Charnel House in Hallstatt, Austria, the bones of the dead were often displayed and sometimes used to decorate places of worship.

8

Altered States

In the vast majority of the world's religions, at least some people experience states of religious ecstasy. Under such altered states of consciousness, they are filled with God's spirit, experience brightly colored hallucinations, "speak in tongues," or have other manifestations of trance states. In most cases, these experiences are understood as confirming the fundamental truths of their religious beliefs and their understanding of the world. As you read the essays in this section, keep the following points in mind:

- The use of drugs (including alcohol) as part of religion, though hardly universal, is extremely common around the world. It is not an accident that some of the best beer and finest distilled spirits are produced by European religious communities. Traditional Jews are instructed by the Talmud that on the feast of Purim they should get so drunk that they cannot tell the difference between the blessing of the holiday's hero and the cursing of its villain. Other religious traditions sanction the use of drugs of all sorts. Many of these are powerful mind-altering substances, as shown by Baker in his essay on datwa use among the Chumash.

- The religious use of drugs is particularly common in the Americas, especially in the tropics. There is some debate over why this is the case. Most authors argue that evolution produced a greater variety of hallucinogens in the Americas than in Europe, Africa, and Asia. Others, such as Wade Davis, in the essay presented here, suggest that cultural rather than ecological factors are responsible for the difference.

- Some people are certainly more susceptible than others to religious trance, and some are more susceptible to drugs. However, context is almost always much more powerful in shaping religious experience than the specific method used to create an altered state. As demonstrated in Baker's essay, religious experiences are shaped by the expectations of the individual undergoing the experience and the setting in which the experience takes place. People's bodies may react somewhat differently to drugs, but under similar circumstances users report similar experiences. An experience that may be interpreted as religious if it happens within the confines of a religious ritual or setting might be interpreted as a frightening but meaningless hallucination or hedonistic pleasure if it happens outside of that setting.

- J. D. Lewis-Williams's reinterpretation of San rock painting provides us with insight into religious experience. Clearly people from different religious traditions experience different things in trance, but all their experiences tend to have the same structure. Visually, trance experiences generally start with phosphenes or entopics. These are visual designs produced by the central nervous system as an individual slips into trance. As ecstatic states deepen, individuals organize these designs into shining, shimmering figures from their personal histories and cultures. In deep trance, people often experience bodily transformations including elongation of body parts, transformation into animal form, flight, and many other sensations.

- Many of the most ethnographically spectacular examples of states of religious ecstasy involve the use of drugs. However, drugs are not required to create altered-state experiences. In fact, nondrug methods—such as prolonged dancing to a driving beat, singing, fasting, meditation, bodily manipulation (including ceremonies during which individuals beat themselves or are cut, dragged, or have other things done to their bodies)—are almost certainly more common than those involving hallucinogens. People using nondrug methods may have religious experiences that are as profoundly hallucinogenic as experiences involving drug use. Though the ravers described in the essay by Scott R. Hutson may use various drugs, including "Ecstasy," much of their experience is probably created by loud music and dance. Similarly, the "Oneness" Pentecostals described by Elaine J. Lawless use no drugs but have profound religious experiences.

- Different religious traditions differ in how much they emphasize the experience of religious ecstasy. In some traditions, it may be extremely widespread, perhaps even required of members. The "Oneness" Pentecostal church is a good example of this. In such churches, people are considered members only if they have had the public experience of being "filled with the Holy Ghost" and "speaking in tongues." In other traditions, ecstatic religious experiences may be rare. Protestant denominations such as the Lutherans and Episcopalians accept that valid states of religious ecstasy are possible but do little to encourage ecstatic states among their members.

Hallucinogenic Plants and Their Use in Traditional Societies

Wade Davis

In this essay, author Wade Davis gives us a brief tour of the worldwide use of hallucinogens in traditional societies. Davis points out that hallucinogens are used for religious purposes in a very large number of societies and that traditional peoples must have avidly and enthusiastically searched for hallucinogenic plants and studied their preparation.

Davis also notes the difficulty of linking particular hallucinogens to particular effects. A hallucinogen alters the mind. However, the way in which the mind is altered, the effect the drug has, and the way the experience is understood are dependent on an individual's culture and the setting in which the drug is taken. Like so much else in religion, context is central to the experience.

We include this essay because it is an impressive and accurate catalog of the religious use of hallucinogens. However, you should be aware that Davis is a controversial author and some of his claims are suspect. For example, his notions about the use of hallucinogens in European witchcraft are interesting but rest on controversial data, and his comparison of Amerindian and African cultures is overgeneralized.

As you read, consider these questions:
1. What are the major differences between drug use in traditional societies and drug use in modern societies?
2. What are some of the methods used by traditional societies for taking hallucinogenic drugs?
3. What do "set" and "setting" mean when talking about the use of hallucinogenic drugs?

The passionate desire which leads man to flee from the monotony of everyday life has made him instinctively discover strange substances. He has done so, even where nature has been most niggardly in producing them and where the products seem very far from possessing the properties which would enable him to satisfy this desire.

Thus early in this century did Lewis Lewin, perhaps the preeminent pioneer in the study of psychoactive drugs, describe the primal search that led to man's discovery of hallucinogens. Strictly speaking, a hallucinogen is any chemical substance that distorts the senses and produces hallucinations—perceptions or experiences that depart dramatically from ordinary reality. Today we know these substances variously as psychotomimetics (psychosis mimickers), psychotaraxics (mind disturbers) and psychedelics (mind manifesters); dry terms which quite inadequately describe the remarkable effects they have on the human mind. These effects are varied but they frequently include a dreamlike state marked by dramatic alterations "in the sphere of experience, in the perception of reality, changes even of space and time and in consciousness of self. They invariably induce a series of visual hallucinations, often in kaleidoscopic movement, and usually in indescribably brilliant and rich colours, frequently accompanied by auditory and other hallucinations"—tactile, olfactory, and temporal. Indeed the effects are so unearthly, so unreal that most hallucinogenic plants early acquired a sacred place in indigenous cultures. In rare cases, they were worshipped as gods incarnate.

The pharmacological activity of the hallucinogens is due to a relatively small number of types of chemical compounds. While modern chemistry has been able in most cases successfully to duplicate these substances, or even manipulate their chemical structures to create novel synthetic forms, virtually all hallucinogens have their origins in plants. (One immediate exception that comes to mind is the New World toad, *Bufo marinus,* but the evidence that this animal was used for its psychoactive properties is far from complete.)

Within the plant kingdom the hallucinogens occur only among the evolutionarily advanced flowering plants and in one division—the fungi—of the more primitive spore bearers. Most hallucinogens are alkaloids, a family of perhaps 5,000 complex organic molecules that also account for the biological activity of most toxic and medicinal plants. These active compounds may be found in the various concentrations in different parts of the plant—roots, leaves, seeds, bark and/or flowers—and they may be absorbed by the human body in a number of ways, as is evident in the wide variety of folk preparations. Hallucinogens may be smoked or snuffed, swallowed fresh or dried, drunk in decoctions and infusions, absorbed directly through the skin, placed in wounds or administered as enemas.

To date about 120 hallucinogenic plants have been identified worldwide. On first glance, given that estimates of the total number of plant species range as high as 800,000, this appears to be a relatively small number. However, it grows in significance when compared to the total number of species used as food. Perhaps 3,000 species of plants have been regularly consumed by some people at some period of history, but today only 150 remain important enough to enter world commerce. Of these a mere 12–15, mostly domesticated cereals, keep us alive.

In exploring his ambient vegetation for hallucinogenic plants, man has shown extraordinary ingenuity, and in experimenting with them all the signs of pharmacological genius. He has also quite evidently taken great personal risks. Peyote *(Lophophora williamsii),* for example, has as many as 30 active constituents, mostly alkaloids, and is exceedingly bitter, not unlike most deadly poisonous plants. Yet the Huichol, Tarahumara and numerous other peoples of Mexico and the American Southwest discovered that sundried and eaten whole the cactus produces spectacular psychoactive effects.

With similar tenacity, the Mazatec of Oaxaca discovered amongst a mushroom flora that contained many deadly species as many as 10 that were hallucinogenic. These they believed had ridden to earth upon thunderbolts, and were reverently gathered at the time of the new moon. Elsewhere in Oaxaca, the seeds of the morning glory *(Rivea corymbosa)* were crushed and prepared as a decoction known at one time as ololiuqui—the sacred preparation of the Aztec, and one that we now realize contained alkaloids closely related to LSD, a potent synthetic hallucinogen. In Peru, the bitter mescaline-rich cactus *Trichocereus pachanoi* became the basis of the San Pedro curative cults of the northern Andes. Here the preferred form of administration is the decoction, a tea served up at the long nocturnal ceremonies during which time the patients' problems were diagnosed. At dawn they would be sent on the long pilgrimages high into the mountains to bathe in the healing waters of a number of sacred lakes.

Lowland South America has provided several exceedingly important and chemically fascinating hallucinogenic preparations, notably the intoxicating yopo *(Anadenanthera peregrina)* and ebene *(Virola calophylla, V. calophylloidea, V. theiodora)* snuffs of the upper Orinoco of Venezuela and adjacent Brazil and the ayahuasca-caapi-yagé complex *(Banisteriopsis caapi)* found commonly among the rainforest peoples of the Northwest Amazon. Yopo is prepared from the seeds of a tall forest tree which are roasted gently and then ground into a fine powder, which is then mixed with some alkaline substance, often the ashes of certain leaves. Ebene is prepared from the blood red resin of certain trees in the nutmeg family. Preparations vary but frequently the bark is stripped from the tree and slowly heated to allow the resin to collect in a small earthenware pot where it is boiled down into a thick paste, which in turn is sundried and powdered along with the leaves of other plants. Ayahuasca comes from the rasped bark of a forest liana which is carefully heated in water, again with a number of admixture plants, until a thick decoction is obtained. All three products are violently hallu-

cinogenic and it is of some significance that they all contain a number of subsidiary plants that, in ways not yet fully understood, intensify or lengthen the psychoactive effects of the principal ingredients. This is an important feature of many folk preparations and it is due in part to the fact that different chemical compounds in relatively small concentrations may effectively potentiate each other, producing powerful synergistic effects—a biochemical version of the whole being greater than the sum of its parts. The awareness of these properties is evidence of the impressive chemical and botanical knowledge of the traditional peoples.

In the Old World may be found some of the most novel means of administering hallucinogens. In southern Africa, the Bushmen of Dobe, Botswana, absorb the active constituents of the plant kwashi *(Pancratium trianthum)* by incising the scalp and rubbing the juice of an onion-like bulb into the open wound. The fly agaric *(Amanita muscaria),* a psychoactive mushroom used in Siberia, may be toasted on a fire or made into a decoction with reindeer milk and wild blueberries. In this rare instance the active principals pass through the body unaltered, and the psychoactive urine of the intoxicated individual may be consumed by the others. Certain European hallucinogens—notably the solanaceous belladonna *(Atropa belladonna),* henbane *(Hyoscyamus niger),* mandrake *(Mandragora officinarum)* and datura *(Datura metel)*—are topically active; that is the active principals are absorbed through the skin. We now know, for example, that much of the behavior associated with the medieval witches is as readily attributable to these drugs as to any spiritual communion with the diabolic. The witches commonly rubbed their bodies with hallucinogenic ointments. A particularly efficient means of self-administering the drug for women is through the moist tissue of the vagina; the witches broomstick or staff was considered the most effective applicator. Our own popular image of the haggard woman on a broomstick comes from the medieval belief that the witches rode their staffs each midnight to the sabbat, the orgiastic assembly of demons and sorcerers. In fact, it now appears that their journey was not through space but across the hallucinatory landscape of their minds.

There is in the worldwide distribution of the hallucinogenic plants a pronounced and significant discrepancy that has only inadequately been accounted for but which serves to illustrate a critical feature of their role in traditional societies. Of the 120 or more such plants found to date, over 100 are native to the Americas; the Old World has contributed a mere 15–20 species. How might this be explained? To be sure it is in part an artifact of the emphasis of academic research. A good many of these plants have entered the literature due to the efforts of Professor R. E. Schultes and his colleagues at the Harvard Botanical Museum and elsewhere, and their interest has predominantly been in the New World. Yet were the hallucinogenic plants a dominant feature of traditional cultures in Africa and Eurasia, surely they would have shown up in the extensive ethnographic literature and in the journals of traders and missionaries. With few notable exceptions, they don't. Nor is this discrepancy due to floristic peculiarities. The rainforests of West Africa and Southeast Asia, in particular, are exceedingly rich and diverse. Moreover, the peoples of these regions have most successfully explored them for pharmacologically active compounds for use both as medicines and poisons. In fact, as much as any other material trait the manipulation of toxic plants remains a consistent theme throughout sub-Saharan African cultures. The Amerindians, for their part, were certainly no strangers to plant toxins which they commonly exploited as fish, arrow and dart poisons. Yet it is a singular fact that while the peoples of Africa consistently used these toxic preparations on each other, the Amerindian almost never did. And while the Amerindian successfully explored his forest for hallucinogens, the African did not. This suggests the critical fact that the use of any pharmacologically active plant—remembering that the difference between hallucinogen, medicine and poison is often a matter of dosage—is firmly rooted in culture. If the peoples of Africa did not explore their environment for psychoactive drugs, surely it is because they felt no need to. In many Amerindian societies the use of plant hallucinogens lies at the very heart of traditional life.

To begin to understand the role that these powerful plants play in these societies, however, it is essential to place the drugs themselves in proper context. For one, the pharmacologically active compounds do not produce uniform effects. On the contrary, any psychoactive drug has within it a completely ambivalent potential for good or evil, order or chaos. Pharmacologically it induces a certain condition, but that condition is mere raw material to be worked by particular cultural or psychological forces and expectations. This is what our own medical experts call the "set and setting" of any drug experience. *Set* in these terms is the individual's expectation of what the drug will do to him; *setting* is the environment—both physical and social—in which the drug is taken. This may be illustrated by an example from our own country. In the northwest rainforests of Oregon are a native species of hallucinogenic mushrooms. Those who go out into the forest deliberately intending to ingest these mushrooms generally experience a pleasant intoxication. Those who inadvertently consume them while foraging for edible mushrooms invariably end up in the poison unit of the nearest hospital. The mushroom itself has not changed.

Similarly the hallucinogenic plants consumed by the Amerindian induce a powerful but neutral stimulation of the imagination; they create a template, as it were, upon which cultural beliefs and forces may be amplified a thousand times. What the individual sees in the visions is dependent not on the drug but on other factors—the mood and setting of the group, the physical and mental states of the participants, his own expectations based on a rich repository of tribal lore and, above all in Indian societies, the authority, knowledge and experience of the leader of the ceremony. The role of this figure—be it man or woman, shaman, curandero, paye, maestro or brujo—is pivotal. It is he who places the protective cloak of ritual about the participants. It is he who tackles the bombardment of visual and auditory stimuli and gives them order. It is he who must interpret a complex body of belief, reading the power in leaves and the meaning in stones, who must skillfully balance the forces of the universe and guide the play of the winds. The ceremonial use of hallucinogenic plants by the Amerindian is (most often) a collective journey into the unconscious. It is not necessarily, and in fact rarely is, a pleasant or an easy journey. It is wondrous and it may be terrifying. But above all it is purposeful.

The Amerindian enters the realm of the hallucinogenic visions not out of boredom, or to relieve an individual's restless anxiety, but rather to fulfill some collective need of the group. In the Amazon, for example, hallucinogens are taken to divine the future, track the paths of enemies, ensure the fidelity of women, diagnose and treat diseases. The Huichol in Mexico eat their peyote at the completion of long arduous pilgrimages in order that they may experience in life the journey of the soul of the dead to the underworld. The Amahuaca Indians of Peru drink yage that the nature of the forest animals and plants may be revealed to their apprentices. In eastern North America during puberty rites, the Algonquin confined adolescents to a longhouse for two weeks and fed them a beverage based in part on datura. During the extended intoxication and subsequent amnesia—a pharmacological feature of this drug—the young boys forgot what it was to be a child so that they might learn what it meant to be a man. But whatever the ostensible purpose of the hallucinogenic journey, the Amerindian imbibes his plants in a highly structured manner that places a ritualistic framework of order around their use. Moreover the experience is explicitly sought for positive ends. It is not a means of escaping from an uncertain existence; rather it is perceived as a means of contribution to the welfare of all one's people.

The Old Woman and Her Gifts:
Pharmacological Bases of the Chumash Use of *Datura*[1]

John R. Baker

Traditional peoples were often very adept at the use of hallucinogenic plants to achieve altered states of consciousness. The Chumash, described in this essay, are a good example. The Chumash used the hallucinogen *Datura* for a wide variety of purposes. Some uses were specifically religious, such as the quest for a supernatural guardian or a vision. However, other uses of the plant were more strictly medical. *Datura* was also used in setting bones and in treating hemorrhoids.

Baker approaches his subject from a medical perspective. He explains not only what the Chumash did with *Datura* but also how the drug's principal chemical constituents operate in the body. The key active constituents of *Datura* are scopolamine and atropine. These drugs are used in Western society both for medicinal and nonmedicinal purposes.

In America, most people consider the use of hallucinogens a highly individual experience. However, in many traditional societies people have more standard, predictable experiences. The author explains why this is so, with reference to *Datura*, by introducing the ideas of *set* and *setting*. Set is the basic physiological characteristics of the individual. Setting is the context, both physical and psychological, in which the drug is taken. Setting is more important than set in determining *Datura* experience. This means that a group of individuals who have similar preparation for taking the drug and take it under similar circumstances will likely have similar experiences.

As you read, consider these questions:

1. There are several reasons Chumash took *Datura*. What were they, and what role did *Datura* play in Chumash culture?
2. What are the clinical effects of *Datura,* and how do they relate to patterns of *Datura* usage?
3. How does dosage affect the use and effects of the drug?

Then Momoy took a bowl and put some water in it—then she washed her hands in the water and gave it to her

grandson to drink. He drank the water and then began to get dizzy. "I'm sleepy, grandmother!" he said. "Go to bed, and take careful note of what you dream," she said. The boy went to bed and slept for three days, and when he awoke the old woman asked him what he had dreamed (from a Chumash myth, related in Blackburn 1974b: 283).

INTRODUCTION

It is a truism that hunting and gathering groups, who typically inhabit a particular region for a long period of time, consequently have ample opportunity to learn about the plant and animal resources available to them. Some of these resources will come to be exploited for their nutritional value, others for their usefulness in constructing shelters, weapons, and the various implements which are used to survive in a particular environment. Still other resources may be used for less tangible ends, including healing and religious purposes. Occasionally, a group may discover a resource whose properties they find so exceptional that it comes to play a central role in that culture. Such was the case with the Chumash use of the plant *Datura*.

The use of *Datura* preparations has been documented across a wide area of North and South America (Gayton 1928). The Chumash Indians of Southern California, however, seem to have developed an exceptionally close relationship to the plant: "In the sense that Native American medicine is integrally involved with religious beliefs and practice, datura . . . probably was the single most important medicinal plant of the Chumash" (Timbrook 1987: 174).

Although the culture of the Chumash is now extinct, and much about them is still shrouded in mystery, recent analyses of previously unpublished field notes have taught us much about this fascinating group. In this paper, I will present some details of Chumash culture that have been revealed especially during the last three decades, following which I shall discuss the various Chumash uses of the plant they called *momoy* (and which the Spanish knew as *toloache*). I shall then consider the most important of these uses in light of our current understanding of the pharmacology of the plant's primary psychoactive alkaloids. This will make it possible to consider why *Datura* is such an effective means for treating certain afflictions and for attaining culturally desirable altered states of consciousness. . . .

[In a six-page section, Baker describes Chumash society and history. The Chumash were a series of foraging groups

John R. Baker, "The Old Woman and Her Gifts: Pharmacological Bases of the Chumash Use of Datura." *curare: Journal of Ethnomedicine and Transcultural Psychiatry* 17:2 (1994, 253–276. Revised by author for this edition. Reprinted with permission.

in central Southern California. They lived in villages of between 50 and 500 permanent inhabitants and were led by a hereditary chief. Compared to other foraging groups, they had relatively high population densities and relatively complex political organization. The Chumash encountered Europeans in the 16th century. In the 18th and 19th centuries they experienced extremely harsh conditions under the rule of Spanish Franciscan missionaries. This reduced their numbers from between 15,000 and 20,000 to fewer than 2,500. Today about 3,000 people claim some Chumash ancestry, but the last Chumash speaker died in 1965.—Editors]

THE CHUMASH USE OF *DATURA*

Because the culture of the Chumash was so quickly eradicated, scholars long knew little about its non-material aspects. Kroeber succinctly summed up the situation during the first half of this century: "It must be plainly stated, in fact, that our ignorance is almost complete on Chumash religion, on the side of ceremony as well as belief and tradition" (1925: 567). Since that time, however, a number of publications based primarily on the fieldwork of John P. Harrington[2] have increased our knowledge and cast much light upon the Chumash use of *Datura*.

In the cosmology of the Chumash, the world was originally inhabited by the First People, a group of supernatural entities whose social order closely paralleled that of the Chumash themselves. One of these was an old woman named *Momoy*, a wealthy widow who was generally depicted as living apart from the others and having the power to at least partially see the future and thus to warn people of the consequences of their actions. Others could share this ability by drinking water in which she had washed her hands. *Momoy* plays a central role in several Chumash myths, but does not seem to figure in the myths of any other California Indian group (Blackburn 1974b).[3]

The First People were transformed into birds, mammals, and plants as a result of a primeval flood. *Momoy* became the *Datura* plant—which the Chumash also called *momoy*—at the same time retaining many of her characteristics. Like the old woman which it derived from, *Datura* played a central role in Chumash culture, while its pattern of use differed from that of other California groups.

There were three principle reasons why the Chumash ingested *Datura*: 1. to establish contact with a supernatural guardian; 2. for visionary purposes; and 3. in cases of emergency (including medical reasons). By far the most important of these was the first (Applegate 1975). Like other tribes in south Central California, the Chumash believed that a person benefited greatly from acquiring an *'atɨshwɨn,* a dream helper. Among the Chumash, this dream helper was usually an animal, occasionally a personified natural force or a *ghost,* but was never an inanimate object (Applegate 1978). Generally, the Indians of California thought there were three ways in which a person could establish a relationship with a dream

helper: 1. through drugs; 2. through such ascetic practices as fasting and night-bathing; and 3. through a spontaneous event (Applegate 1978). The Chumash, however, solely recognized the first path. In their eyes, an *'atɨshwɨn* could only be acquired by ingesting *Datura*.[4] This exclusivistic attitude towards access to the supernatural was reflected in other aspects of the Chumash pattern of *Datura* use. Many of the neighboring tribes who used *Datura* restricted this to men alone, limited the time of year during which the plant could be used (usually the winter or early spring; Applegate 1978), and/or limited the number of times persons might use the plant. In addition, *Datura* use often took place in special locations outside of the villages. In contrast, *Datura* use among the Chumash was open to both men and women and could occur at any time (provided the requisite preparations had taken place). Individuals were allowed to use the plant as often as they saw fit, and they could take it right in their own village (Applegate 1975).

The Chumash universe was one in which supernatural forces controlled nature and influenced human activity (Walker and Hudson 1993). These powers could in turn be controlled and manipulated by persons possessing great supernatural power. The acquisition of this power was "always the purpose of an individual's first *Datura* experience" (Applegate 1975: 8), which took place when he or she was an adolescent, i.e., after puberty but before marriage and the onset of sexual activity. The decision to ingest the plant was an individual one, and persons were not required to do so; since, however, success in most activities depended upon having an *'atɨshwɨn,* and since this relationship could only be established via *Datura*, it seems likely that most of the Chumash—at least those who enjoyed a high social status—did elect to use the plant. An initiate was required to adhere to stringent dietary restrictions for twenty-one days before being given the drug. The first infusion was usually administered by a paid specialist (called a *'alŝukaẙayič* "one who causes intoxication," among the Ventureño) whose most important qualification was his skill in preparing the plant. However, relatives could also prepare the plant for this occasion (Applegate 1975).

Boys would always be initiated alone, while girls might occasionally be initiated in a group. The particulars of the process appear to have differed from village to village. In Ventura, a person's initial *Datura* experience was often administered and supervised by five old men. Following ingestion of an infusion of the root (considered the most potent part of the plant), the initiate would become dizzy and begin to tremble. The *'alŝukaẙayič* would then instruct the initiate to sleep and dream. The resulting state usually lasted from 18–24 hours, during which at least one of the five *'alŝukaẙayič* was always present. When the initiate began to revive, one of the *'alŝukaẙayič* might sing to him or her, after which all five would ask about and then interpret the initiate's experiences. They also used this opportunity to lecture the initiate on moral issues (Applegate 1975).

While a person might turn to a *'alŝukaẙayič* when he or she wanted to use *Datura* again, subsequent usage (which also occurred on an individual basis) frequently entailed preparations made by a relative instead. Reasons for retaking *Datura* included strengthening the bond with one's dream helper, the acquisition of additional dream helpers, and the accumulation of supernatural power in general. Women used the plant to help them become immune to danger and attain courage, especially for childbirth (Applegate 1975). Sometimes a person ingested *Datura* for a highly specific purpose (e.g., to ask for skill in fishing; Hudson et al. 1978); alternately, a person might ask for such power after having taken *Datura* for another reason. Like ordinary persons, shamans would use *Datura* for purposes of acquiring or augmenting their power; in contrast to others, however, they would also turn to the plant when they wished to ascertain the cause and cure of an illness (Applegate 1975).

A person who ingested *Datura* for visionary purposes might do so in order to communicate with the spirit of a beloved person who had died, or to obtain a glimpse of his or her own future. *Datura* could also be used to locate lost objects. Harrington reported an example of a man who took *Datura* so that he could find his lost *tomol* (Hudson et al. 1978: 152). Persons who wished to improve their social status would take *Datura* to learn their true name, for a knowledge of this name was a prerequisite for prosperity (Applegate 1975).

Regardless of whether *momoy* was consulted for purposes of acquiring supernatural power or to obtain visions, careful ritual preparation was required. These preparations represented a symbolic reversal of normal behavior and emphasized the extraordinary nature of the impending inebriation (Applegate 1978). It seems likely that at least some of these restrictions also had effects upon the physiological and the psychological states of the individual. The dietary rules enjoined a person from consuming grease and meat. Sweet items and salt might also be avoided for a time. A period of sexual abstinence both before and after the experience was mandatory. The degree to which these restrictions were to be followed was a function of the amount of power a person wished to acquire: the more power a person was striving for, the longer the period of abstinence and the greater the restrictions (Applegate 1975). Thus, the initiatory use prior to the beginning of sexual activity—which was the most important *Datura* session of a person's life—not only represented the transition from childhood to adulthood, but also entailed the longest period of pre-session sexual abstinence which most persons would likely ever know. The prohibition against eating meat may have reflected the fact that many of the *'atishwɨn* were animals, although physiological reasons probably also played a role (see below). Other taboos included not allowing menstruating women to use the plant. "Consumptives" (persons suffering from tuberculosis) were cautioned to avoid *Datura* because of "the excess of blood in their chests" (Applegate 1975: 9).

In contrast to these rigidly structured patterns of use, the "emergency" use of *Datura* to counteract sudden misfortune did not entail as many restrictions. Since such use typically occurred as a direct response to an unanticipated event, the dietary and sexual restrictions associated with it could only be applied *ex post facto*. As a result, these applications did not have the same import; they were viewed as a cure, and not as an attempt to acquire permanent supernatural power (Applegate 1975).

Emergency uses included ingesting *Datura* to ward off misfortune and to prevent soul loss. The Chumash believed that certain omens presaged a person's death; taking *Datura* could help to avert the event. They also believed that the soul was an eternal entity which could function independently of the physical body. If a person's soul was seen wandering about, this was taken as a sign of that person's impending death. The individual would then be advised to take *Datura* in an effort to deter the soul from permanently straying from the body (Applegate 1975; Blackburn 1974b).

As a medicinal plant (in a more restricted sense), *Datura* was administered as an anesthesia when setting bones and was ingested when treating bruises and wounds. *Datura* was taken internally to "freshen the blood" and to treat alcohol-induced hangovers (a post-contact innovation) and applied externally to treat hemorrhoids (Walker and Hudson 1993).

These many uses do not imply that the Chumash were unaware of *momoy*'s more lethal side. Deaths occasionally occurred following *Datura* ingestion (Applegate 1975). One common belief which demonstrates their knowledge of the dangers of *momoy* was that a rattlesnake which had decided in advance to kill someone (rather than simply striking in self-defense) would suck the juice from a *Datura* root prior to the attack, which would then invariably be lethal. Sorcerers too were known to use the plant as an admixture to their poisons (Applegate 1975). On the other hand, a person who succumbed after voluntarily using *Datura* was held to be responsible for his or her own death. One explanation that might be offered was that the person had not observed the proper dietary and sexual taboos prior to ingesting the plant; another possibility was that the person may have "lost the trail" back to the everyday world. But it was also believed that a person who consulted *momoy* might make a conscious decision not to return, especially when he or she had desired to see the dead (Applegate 1975). This may be related to the Chumash belief that the last function of the *'atishwɨn* was to help their protégé reach *ŝimilaqŝa*, the land of the dead. According to the Chumash, this lay west across the ocean, and reaching it required a soul to cross a narrow and unsteady bridge. Persons who had not acquired a dream helper could not complete this journey, and fell instead into the water below (Blackburn 1974b: 226–229).

THE BOTANY AND PHARMACOLOGY OF *DATURA*

Datura is a term which Linnaeus derived from the Hindu word *dhatura*, or *dutra* (Safford 1920). This term is now used to refer to a solanaceous genus encompassing species found throughout the Old and New Worlds. . . .

[In this section, Baker describes the chemistry and effects of *Datura*. We have deleted some of the more technical passages.—Editors]

Datura spp. are and have been used for such varied purposes as divination (Rätsch and Probst 1985; Dobkin de Rios 1990), initiation (Safford 1920; Johnston 1972), love magic (Rätsch and Probst 1985; Rätsch 1990), treatment of a wide range of ailments (Dutt 1980; Moerman 1986), and as a poison (Ardila and Moreno 1991). The toxic potential of *Datura* is great, and reports of poisoning following accidental and intentional ingestion of the plant are common in the literature (Dieckhöfer et al. 1971; Gowdy 1972; Siegel 1976; Hall et al. 1978; Hanna et al. 1992). Utilization of *Datura* preparations has been documented in Asia (Dutt 1980; Schultes and Hofmann 1980), Africa (Johnston 1972), and Europe (Hansen 1988); the most widespread use of *Datura,* however, occurred in the Americas (Gayton 1928; Yarnell 1959; Schultes 1972, 1979; Litzinger 1981; Plowman 1981). Gayton (1928) characterized the use of *Datura* throughout North and South America (she included species now subsumed within the genus *Brugmansia;* cf. Plowman 1981) as a single trait within a larger "narcotic complex." Gayton argued that this trait developed in "Middle America" and diffused outward towards the north and south.[5] Remarkably, and in spite of the extensive pan-American (and cosmopolitan) use of the plant, she concluded that: "There is no quality intrinsic to the drug itself that makes it sacred, or especially suitable for initiation rites, or use by a priesthood" (1928: 60).

In fact, however, the widespread utilization of *Datura,* and the variety of uses which the Chumash found for the plant, suggests that precisely the opposite is the case, and indeed plants of the genus *Datura* produce a constellation of alkaloids whose effects almost predispose them for use in medicinal, initiatory, and divinatory contexts. The use of these plants for hallucinatory purposes has been well documented (Lewin 1980; Schultes and Hofmann 1980; Hansen 1988; Rätsch 1990) and attests to the abilities of their psychoactive constituents to induce profound altered states of consciousness. . . .

Low doses (0.4–1.0 mg orally) of either atropine or scopolamine are sufficient to inhibit secretions of the nose, throat, bronchi, and sweat glands; relax the smooth muscle tone; affect the heart rate; reduce the secretion of digestive juices; and induce bronchodilation (Greenblatt and Shader 1973; Ali-Melkkilä et al. 1993). The resulting symptoms include dry mouth, dry skin, decreased bowel sounds, tachycardia, hyperthermia, hypertension, flushing or rash, dysphagia, and dysphonia. Higher doses can also produce constipation, blurred vision, and local anesthetic reactions (Greenblatt and Shader 1973). These peripheral effects explain the appropriateness of the Chumash use of *Datura* as an anodyne for treating bruises and wounds, and as an external treatment for hemorrhoids. The inhibitory effects upon mucous secretions and gastrointestinal motility also suggest that there may be palpable reasons why certain types of food were avoided prior to and following *Datura* ingestion.

Both atropine and scopolamine also affect the central nervous system, although the two differ in their dose-dependent effects. Scopolamine can produce sedation and amnesia in doses of 1.0 mg. or less, while atropine will typically not elicit such effects until dosage levels reach 3.0 mg or more (Greenblatt and Shader 1973).[6] These effects explain the efficacy of using *Datura* preparations as an anesthesia when setting bones.

Scopolamine is the predominant psychoactive tropane alkaloid in most *Datura* spp. (Schultes and Hofmann 1980), including *Datura wrightii* (Spurná et al. 1981), and is the alkaloid primarily responsible for the central nervous system effects of the plant. Since modern pharmacological research typically investigates the effects of individual alkaloids rather than plant extracts, the following discussion will primarily focus on work with scopolamine. This notwithstanding, it is important to note that plant preparations will usually have somewhat different effects than scopolamine compounds alone due both to the presence of other alkaloids and to possible synergistic interactions between scopolamine and these. It must also be kept in mind that different plants of the same species—and different parts of the same plant—can differ greatly with respect to the relative amounts of each of the principle tropane alkaloids, and thus it can be expected that the phenomenological effects of the preparations made from them will differ as well. What is more, the potency of a particular plant can vary throughout the year, a fact of which many California Indian groups were well aware (Applegate 1975). These qualifications notwithstanding, it will be apparent from the discussion below that the effects of scopolamine do indeed account for many of the symptoms of *Datura* inebriation.

Scopolamine has been found to affect a person's ability to visually track objects. Subjects administered scopolamine before attempting to follow randomly generated stimuli tend to become slower and more inexact in their saccadic eye movements, and their eyes tend to drift away from the stimuli once they have tracked them (Oliva et al. 1993). Since saccadic eye movements are necessary for the maintenance of the visual field (Evans and Piggins 1963), disturbances of these movements can effect a partial break with the external world by undermining a person's ability to accurately acquire visual data. This shift away from normal visual perception can be exacerbated by the abilities of both atropine and scopolamine to affect the smooth muscles which control accommodation of the eye. The resulting clinical symptom is known as cycloplegia, and primarily affects near-sightedness; i.e., a person cannot focus upon objects that are close at hand, but has little or no difficulty seeing objects that are farther away (cf. Safer and Allen 1971). Higher doses of scopolamine produce visual hallucinations.

In addition to the ability of scopolamine to affect visual perception, oral ingestion of scopolamine has also been found to enhance the occurrence of auditory hallucinations (Warburton et al. 1985). This effect may result from scopolamine's ability to produce a "twilight" condition (see below) similar to the hypnagogic state experienced while passing from wakefulness to sleep. In this liminal state, the authors noted, previously acquired information can become accessible to awareness in the form of images, phantasies, and hallucinations. The increased suggestibility of the scopolamine state might also play a role in evoking the hallucinations (Warburton et al. 1985). . . .

Higher doses of scopolamine produce a state of global amnesia in which no memory is retained of events which transpire during the acute phase of the drug effects. The retention and retrieval of previously learned material is not affected (Safer and Allen 1971). This ability of scopolamine (and *Datura*) to induce a submissive, amnesic state has been exploited for illicit purposes for centuries (Emboden 1979; Rätsch 1990). Often, such use simply entailed drugging a person into unconsciousness. Somewhat lower doses, on the other hand, produce a less extreme state in which a person is able to act more or less normally and can draw upon previously acquired information, although they will typically remember nothing of the events which occur while under the influence of the drug. Criminals in Columbia use *Datura* extracts as well as pure scopolamine preparations to induce such an intermediate state, during which, e.g., they suggest to their victims that they withdraw money from their bank accounts; the victims, who become markedly submissive, subsequently cannot remember what they have done (Ardila and Moreno 1991).

For decades, western physicians employed scopolamine to induce a "twilight sleep" and amnesia during parturition. Following an injection of the drug, a woman would not be able to recall the pain of giving birth—or even the process itself. Moreover, she did not recall the birth process. In recent years, however, the severe side-effects (dryness of mouth, restlessness, post partum depression in both mother and infant, and—when used in higher doses—delirium), the availability of more suitable drugs, and the desire of many mothers to remain conscious during labor have largely led to the abandonment of scopolamine in the delivery room (Bonica 1969; Plantevin 1973). Scopolamine also enjoyed a brief period of popularity earlier in this century as a potential "truth serum" for interrogation purposes, but such use was curtailed for both ethical and practical reasons (MacDonald 1969).

Still higher doses of scopolamine and *Datura* preparations (including those presumably utilized by the Chumash for initiatory purposes) produce a state in which the subject is completely oblivious to outside stimuli. A series of experiments during the 1950s explored the clinical possibilities of this condition. Researchers administered high doses of atropine (32–212 mg. intramuscular) to induce a brief (4–6 hour) "atropine coma" in psychiatric patients. The patients averaged twenty such sessions, some as often as six sessions

a week (Forrer and Miller 1958). The authors reported beneficial results with this therapy, and also noted that a colleague had achieved similar effects using scopolamine instead of atropine. Although they stated that their experience was limited, they did note their impression that "the post-coma period may be ideal for psychotherapeutic efforts" (1958: 458).[7]

The effects of scopolamine are strongly subject to environmental influence (Safer and Allen 1971). Use of the drug in ambient temperatures that are higher than body temperature (36.0–37.0°C) accentuate scopolamine's effects upon the central nervous system. The loss of just one night's sleep prior to ingestion can also markedly increase the effects of scopolamine, as can interactions with other drugs. On the other hand, Safer and Allen (1971) cited unpublished data indicating that in normal subjects, the central effects of scopolamine are essentially independent of at least some personality factors. Thus, scopolamine appears to be a drug in which the "setting"—the circumstances (including the physiological state of the individual using the drug) under which it is consumed—may play a somewhat greater role than the "set"—the basic psychological characteristics of the individual (cf. Leary et al. 1964). If this is this case, then this would suggest that the central effects of the drug are relatively uniform from person to person, especially when it is ingested following a standardized period of preparation and within a traditional framework of use.

DISCUSSION

It is clear that the Chumash use of *Datura* was based upon a thorough empirical knowledge of the effects of the plant. Unfortunately, information as to dosage levels is lacking. On the other hand, in the absence of plant specimens, the notorious variability in the amounts of substances present in plants would preclude detailed statements about dosage levels even if such data was available. However, it is possible to make some broad estimates of the relative dosage levels which the Chumash probably used to achieve certain ends. The discussion which follows will consider the probable dosages used as well as certain aspects of this use.

As we have seen, the effects of *Datura* preparations are dose-dependent and can be influenced by both pre-session preparation and environmental factors. The many uses to which the Chumash put the plant, the fact that it had been incorporated into their mythology (Blackburn 1974b), and the presence of specialists who often prepared and administered the plant indicates that the Chumash had long used *Datura* and hence had ample opportunity to learn to discriminate between the effects of different doses. Thus, it seems likely that when taken internally as an anodyne for treating wounds and bruises, and when applied externally to treat such disorders as hemorrhoids, the doses administered were substantially lower than those used for visionary or initiatory purposes. Anesthesic use, e.g., for setting broken bones, probably entailed intermediate doses. On the other hand, members of certain neighboring groups sometimes used *Datura* to deliberately induce a stupor lasting several days after they had been severely wounded, following which their recovery would be far advanced (Applegate 1975), and it is possible that such a practice might have existed among the Chumash as well. Without a better understanding of the nature of the Chumash concept of "freshening the blood" (Walker and Hudson 1993), it is difficult to conjecture what dosage levels might have been used for this purpose. Since, however, drinking sea water was considered the most effective means to this end, it is probable that the doses of *Datura*, used for the same purpose were relatively low. It seems reasonable to assume that the post-contact use of *Datura* to treat hangovers also involved low doses.

In contrast to these medicinal usages, initiation clearly involved very high doses of *Datura*. Applegate (1975) reported that an initiate would sleep for 18–24 hours or even longer; meanwhile, persons experienced in the use, preparation, and administration of *Datura* would monitor the initiate both during and after the session. It was, moreover, expected that a period of unusual behavior would follow the "coma." After fully recovering consciousness, the 'alŝukaẏayič would ask the imbiber about his or her experience and also utilize this period to instill moral values into the initiate. This regimen is strongly reminiscent of the work of Forrer and Miller with "atropine coma" (see above) and their suggestion that the period following the coma "may be ideal for psychotherapeutic efforts" (1958: 458).

No detailed descriptions are available of the procedures involved when *Datura* was used for visionary purposes. Doses low enough to allow a person to continue to function in the consensual world are sufficient to produce visual and auditory hallucinations, and may have been considered adequate for this purpose. On the other hand, since visionary usage necessitated the same types of preparation as initiatory usage, and since the intention was to gain access to the supernatural world, it seems more likely that doses high enough to produce a "*Datura* coma" (or at least a state of "twilight sleep") were utilized. If this interpretation is correct, then the primary difference between visionary use and use to acquire an 'atishwin, or dream helper, may have been essentially a question of *intent*. Thus, while basic personality variables of an individual might have little effect upon a *Datura* session (Safer and Allen 1971), the short-term "set" could have a great influence. Since scopolamine has little impact upon the ability to access previously acquired material, those cognitive and affective concerns which had led a person to use the plant and which had in all likelihood been contemplated many times during the preparatory period would not be barred from becoming manifest during the inebriated state. The hypersuggestibility which is typical of *Datura* inebriation (cf. Warburton et al. 1985) would have helped ensure that this material would emerge while the plant was exerting its effects. In addition, a person's initial experience would have presumably involved some anxious expectations as to what exactly *Momoy* was like and what she would reveal, while subsequent usage would have been anticipated and interpreted against the framework provided by previous session(s) and hence would have taken place for more specific purposes.

As mentioned above, the dietary regimen which preceded and followed *Datura* ingestion presumably affected the physiological as well as the psychological states of the individual. While there may have been tangible reasons why, for example, certain foods were to be avoided, the restrictions also served to focus attention on the impending session, and the cultural expectations surrounding use of the plant would certainly have helped sharpen a person's awareness of his or her intentions. On the other hand, many of the "emergency" uses of the plant, such as anodyne and anesthetic uses, likely involved lower doses, and hence were not as likely to produce untoward physical side-effects. Since, however, the inhibitory effects of high amounts of tropane alkaloids on gastrointestinal motility are pronounced and prolonged (Innes and Nickerson 1975), at least some of the dietary restrictions following *Datura* use (see Walker and Hudson 1993) probably had an empirical basis.

The Chumash were very pragmatic in their attitudes towards *Datura*. Their society, as we have seen, was highly stratified, but some mobility was possible. One way to increase status was through *momoy*. Since the Chumash believed that *Datura* use was essential for acquiring an 'atishwin, their liberal rules regulating use of the plant permitted an individual considerable latitude in deciding how much power he or she might wish to acquire, and thus how many encounters with *Momoy* that person was willing to undergo. While *Datura* use among the Chumash was not mandatory, it was vital to a person's success in life—and in the afterlife. Thus, it seems likely that most persons, and especially those of higher status, did in fact use the plant, most of them more than once. Cultural attitudes, however, also taught people to control their use, for the Chumash believed moderate ingestion of *Datura* promoted individual well-being; while too frequent use of *momoy* was said to result in personality changes, including antisocial behavior (Applegate 1975). Shamans, for example, who ingested *Datura* repeatedly to gain numerous dream helpers and acquire the charm stones (Yates 1889) which provided the basis of much of their power, often lived apart from others. While shamans could use their supernatural powers to cure illnesses, they were often hired by chiefs and other high status individuals to *cause* sickness or death. Thus, there was an inherent ambivalence about their presence and their role in society, which was tied to the fact that their social status was based upon acquired power and thus lacked the moral authority which could only come through birth (Blackburn 1974b). Of course, it is an open question whether shamans were considered antisocial because they used *Datura* so frequently, or whether frequent use was considered to produce antisocial behavior because it was an attribute of shamanism. Since, however, the effects of scopolamine become more pronounced with age (Sunderland et al. 1986; Flicker et al. 1992), it is possible that older shamans, who had acquired both experience and renown, may have even been more likely to exhibit erratic behavior than their younger cohorts and thus might have especially revered and feared.

The individualistic use of *Datura* may have also been a reflection of more practical considerations. Since *Datura* can cause delirium and delusional behavior, the cultural preference for using *Datura* on an individual basis would certainly have made it easier for others to deal with any erratic behaviors which might have arisen. This would be especially useful with men, who were stronger and whose training had inculcated them with more aggressive values than women. Since girls presumably posed less of a risk of harming themselves or others, they could be initiated in groups, and occasionally were.

The constant presence of an experienced adult during a person's first *Datura* session would have helped ameliorate anxieties about the experience, and certainly helped to ensure a positive outcome. In addition to enabling a person to acquire their first dream helper, this initial session taught respect for the powers of the plant as well as the cultural rules surrounding its use. As we have seen, initiates were instructed to sleep and dream after being given *momoy*, and would do so for a day or more. This indicates that a very high dose was administered on this occasion. Such dosage levels, combined with the unpredictability of plant preparations and the possibility that an initiate might be inherently oversensitive to the potent alkaloids produced by the plant, made the likelihood of occasional lethal overdoses all but certain. Of course, most initiates survived their first encounter with *Datura*, and in doing so they would take with them a respect for its powers which would probably make them err on the side of safety when estimating dosage levels for future sessions, especially in view of the prevalent attitude that lethal overdoses were the responsibility of the person who had ingested the plant.

As mentioned above, the Chumash use of *Datura* was based upon a long history of using the plant. They were aware that the root was the most potent part of the plant. They had a detailed awareness of its dose-dependent effects. A ritualistic framework was in place which managed the use of the plant and channeled the experiences it evoked in culturally-prescribed directions (cf. Dobkin de Rios and Smith 1977). This framework included a well-defined set of practical pre- and post-session behaviors as well as rules which ensured that experienced persons would oversee a person's first experience with the drug. Thus, the patterns of *Datura* use that the Chumash had developed, refined, and transmitted over generations made it possible for them to constructively exploit the effects of this very potent plant.

It has been speculated that the rock paintings of the Chumash were at least in part related to their use of *Datura* (Ap-

plegate 1975; Grant 1993). Blackburn (cited in Applegate 1975: 15) has suggested that many of the images in these paintings resemble phosphenes, the types of patterns that can be seen when a person gently presses a finger against his or her closed eyelids.[8] While it is quite likely that the Chumash did indeed represent their *Datura* experiences in this way, another effect of *Datura* upon vision which could also be interpreted within a supernatural context has been overlooked. As discussed above, one of the peripheral effects of tropane alkaloids on vision is excessive pupillary dilation (mydriasis). This causes photophobia, an increased sensitivity to light. Moreover, visual accommodation is affected in such a way that a person can clearly see distant objects, while close-up objects (including one's own body) are blurred. Since the quest for supernatural power entails a symbolic reversal of everyday life (Applegate 1978), the Chumash may have interpreted the heightened sensitivity to light and the inability to clearly see oneself—even though objects farther away than arm's length appear as they normally do—as an indication of the plant's ability to transport a person from the everyday world to the supernatural domain. These visual disturbances can appear even when relatively low doses of *Datura* are used, and would have provided a trenchant reminder of *Momoy*'s power even when she was used for medicinal purposes. Moreover, the fact that these visual symptoms are among the last to wear off after administration of the plant might also underscore the distance between the supernatural world and the world of everyday life.

It should now be clear that in spite of the well-deserved reputation of *Datura* as a dangerous plant, there is considerable variation in the effects it produces. Through time, many societies, including the Chumash, learned how to exploit these effects for their own ends. Native American societies and other groups use and have used preparations of *Datura* as well as other solanaceous plants to treat asthma and related respiratory disorders, wounds and bruises, snakebites, mouth and throat sores, and a wide variety of other ailments (Moerman 1986). As discussed above, many of these uses probably involved relatively low doses of the plant. Higher doses, which induce a transient amnesic state in which the individual is highly open to suggestion, fits well with the intent of initiation rituals, which a person enters as a youth and exits as an adult.[9]

The Chumash use of *Datura* provides us with an excellent example of how, when properly employed, even potentially lethal plants can be of great value to the individuals and groups who utilize them. But what could lead persons to explore the properties of such plants in the first place? In the view advanced by Weil (1972) and Siegel (1989), the human urge to alter consciousness reflects an innate biological drive. Evidence for this view can be found in the fact that almost every society in the world has culturally approved methods for inducing altered states of consciousness (Bourguignon 1973). Like the framework which the Chumash imposed upon their use of *Datura,* similar ritual frameworks in other cultures provide a safe context for the individual to explore the worlds within while furnishing culturally sanctioned interpretations of his or her experiences. In this way, dissociative states such as those induced by *Datura* can be exploited to ensure both individual and group stability (Ludwig 1983). The social integration provided by such culturally regulated systems of initiation as that of the Chumash stands in sharp contrast to the situation in most western societies, which have few initiation rituals and lack culturally accepted models for using most types of drugs, in spite of the predilection of many of their citizens to do so (cf. Grob and Dobkin de Rios 1992).

Of course, exploring the inner world, even within the comparative safety provided by a culturally accepted ritual framework, can be a perilous task, for what a person ultimately finds there is that which they have brought with them. In this sense, the Chumash were no different from us. The Chumash turned to *Momoy* so that they could acquire some of her power. What an individual then did with that power was determined by personal as well as cultural factors. The Chumash were aware of the dangers of *Momoy*—and with the dangers which dwelled in themselves. This may be clearly seen in their belief (Applegate 1978) that God sent the white man to punish the Chumash for having misused the supernatural powers which they had acquired—powers that came through the use of *Datura*. The lessons of the Chumash are also appropriate for today: clear intent, moderation, and respect for the worlds within.

NOTES

1. The author would like to thank Robert López for his comments on an earlier version of this paper and Kelly Macone for technical support.

2. John Peabody Harrington was a staff member of the Bureau of American Ethnology who spent years doing fieldwork among the Indians of California, and in particular among the Chumash. Harrington amassed thousand of pages of notes on the Chumash which are now a part of the Smithsonian Museum's collection (cf. Mills & Brickfield 1986).

3. Laird (1974) has reported a behavior that suggests that this mythological element might have been more widespread: the Chemeheuvi (a group who lived in the inland area southeast of the Chumash) would address *Datura* as "old woman" when collecting its root for visionary use.

4. The Chumash were also known to have ingested ants to induce a hallucinogenic state, a practice found among other California groups as well (Blackburn 1976). Such use, however, appears to have been essentially curative in nature (Walker & Hudson 1993), and it is not known whether the Chumash used ants to acquire an *'atishwin.*

5. The widespread use of the Spanish term *toloache* to refer to *Datura* supports this view. The word is derived from the Aztec *toloatzin* ("inclined-head"), a reference to the position of the seed capsules (Safford 1920: 549).

6. This difference helps explain why, for example, the effects of relatively scopolamine-rich *Datura* spp. contrast with those of such related nichtshades as *Atropa* spp., whose primary psychoactive component is atropine: "scopolamine can produce hallucinations in tolerable doses, whereas near toxic doses of atropine are required before hallucinations are experienced" (Schultes 1979: 150).

7. In what may be the largest reported dose of atropine to be survived, Alexander et al. (1946) describe the accidental administration of 1.0 gram (oral) to a patient who was admitted to the hospital for abdominal pain. The patient entered a coma which lasted 40 hours, followed by a similarly long period of delusional behavior. It took two weeks for the patient to fully recover.

8. Personal experimentation with an infusion of *Datura stramonium* leaves produced (in addition to the usual peripheral symptoms of reduced secretory activity and associated effects) a condition in which closing the eyes revealed several small objects that appeared to swirl or flicker against a uniformly dark background. These objects resembled some of the more abstract images that the Chumash produced (and which at that time I had not yet seen).

9. One extreme example of such a ritual is the "huskanawing" initiation ritual of the Algonquin, which involved sequestering the initiates for eighteen to twenty days, during which elders repeatedly gave them a preparation which included *Datura stramonium*. The aim was for the initiates to "unlive their former lives, and commence men by forgetting that they ever have been boys" (Beverly, cited in Safford 1920: 559).

REFERENCES

Alexander, E. Jr., D. P. Morris., and R. L. Eslick. 1946. Atropine Poisoning. *New England Journal of Medicine* 234: 258–59.

Ali-Melkkilä, T., J. Kanto., and E. Iisalo. 1993. Pharmacokinetics and Related Pharmacodynamics of Anticholinergic Drugs. *Acta Anaesthesiologica Scandinavica* 37: 633–42.

Applegate, R. B. 1975. The Datura Cult Among the Chumash. *Journal of California Anthropology* 2: 6–17.

———. 1978 *Atishwin: The Dream Helper in South-Central California.* Socorro, NM.

Ardila, A. and C. Moreno. 1991. Scopolamine Intoxication as a Model of Transient Global Amnesia. *Brain and Cognition* 15: 236–45.

Baumhoff, M. A. 1978. Environmental Background. *Handbook of North American Indians. Volume 8: California.* Edited by R. F. Heizer, pp. 16–24. Washington, D.C.

Bean, L. J. 1974. Social Organization in Native California. In *Antap: California Indian Political and Economic Organization.* Edited by L. J. Bean and T. F. King, pp. 13–34. Ramona, CA.

Birdsall, N. J. M., C. A. M. Curtis., P. Eveleigh., E. C. Hulme., E. K. Pedder., D. Poyner., and M. Wheatley. 1988. Muscarinic Receptor Subtypes and the Selectivity of Agonists and Antagonists. *Pharmacology* 37: 22–31.

Blackburn, Th. C. 1974a. Ceremonial Integration and Social Interaction in Aboriginal California. in *'Antap: California Indian Political and Economic Organization.* Edited by L. J. Bean and Th. F. King, pp. 95–110. Ramona, CA.

————. 1974b. *Chumash Oral Traditions: A Cultural Analysis.* Doctoral Dissertation Department of Anthropology, University of California, Los Angeles.

————. 1976. A Query Regarding the Possible Hallucinogenic Effects of Ant Ingestion in South-Central California. *Journal of California Anthropology* 3: 78–81.

Bonica, J. J. 1969. *Principles and Practice of Obstetric Analgesia and Anesthesia.* Philadelphia.

Bonner, T. I., N. J. Buckley, A. C. Young., and M. R. Brann. 1987. Identification of a Family of Muscarinic Acetylcholine Receptor Genes. *Science* 237: 527–32.

Bourguignon, E. 1973. Introduction: A Framework for the Comparative Study of Altered States of Consciousness, in *Religion, Altered States of Consciousness, and Social Change.* Edited by E. Bourguignon, pp. 3–35. Columbus.

Brown, A. K. 1967. The Aboriginal Population of the Santa Barbara Channel. *Reports of the University of California Archaeological Survey,* Berkeley 69: 1–99.

Buhot, M. C., M. Soffie., and B. Poucet. 1989. Scopolamine affects the cognitive processes involved in selective object exploration more than locomotor activity. *Psychobiology* 17: 409–17.

Castillo, E. D. 1978. The Impact of Euro-American Exploration and Settlement. In *Handbook of North American Indians. Volume 8: California.* Edited by R. F. Heizer, pp. 99–127. Washington, D.C.

Cook, S. F. 1978. Historical Demography. In *Handbook of North American Indians, Volume 8: California.* Edited by R. F. Heizer, pp. 91–98. Washington, D.C.

Cook, S. F. and R. F. Heizer. 1965. The Quantitative Approach to the Relation between Population and Settlement Size. *Reports of the University of California Archaeological Survey Berkeley* 64: 1–97.

Coombs, G. and F. Plog. 1974. Chumash Baptism: An Ecological Perspective. In *Antap: California Indian Political and Economic Organization.* Edited by L. J. Bean and Th. F. King, pp. 137–153. Ramona: CA.

Curran, H., V. F. Schifano., and Malcolm Lader. 1991. Models of memory dysfunction? A comparison of the effects of scopolamine and lorazepam on memory, psychomotor performance and mood. *Psychopharmacology* 103: 83–90.

Curtis, F. 1965. The Glen Annie Canyon Site (SBa-142): A Case for Sedentary Village Life. In *Archaeological Survey Annual Report* 7. Edited by D. S. Miller, pp. 1–18. Los Angeles.

Dieckhöfer, K., Th. Vogel and J. Meyer-Lindenberg. 1971. Datura stramonium als Rauschmittel. *Der Nervenarzt* 42: 431–37.

Dobkin de Rios, M. 1990. *Hallucinogens: Cross-Cultural Perspectives.* Bridport.

Dobkin de Rios, M. and D. E. Smith. 1977. The Function of Drug Rituals in Human Society: Continuities and Changes. *Journal of Psychedelic Drugs* 9: 269–75.

Dutt, U. C. 1980. *The Materia Medica of the Hindus.* Varanasi.

Elsasser, A. B. 1978. Development of Regional Prehistoric Cultures. In *Handbook of North American Indians, Volume 8: California.* Edited by R. F. Heizer, pp. 37–57. Washington, D.C.

Emboden, W. 1979. *Narcotic Plants.* New York.

Eschmeyer, W. N. 1983. *A Field Guide to Pacific Fishes of North America.* Boston.

Evans, C. R. and D. J. Piggins. 1963. A Comparison of the Behaviour of Geometrical Shapes When Viewed Under Conditions of Steady Fixation, and With Apparatus for Producing a Stabilised Retinal Image. *British Journal of Physiological Optics* 20: 1–13.

Evans, W. C. and M. Wellendorf. 1959. The Alkaloids of the Roots of Datura. *Journal of the Chemical Society:* 1406–09.

Flicker, Ch., Steven H. F., and M. Serby. 1992. Hypersensitivity to scopolamine in the elderly. *Psychopharmacology* 107: 437–41.

Forrer, G. R. and J. J. Miller. 1958. Atropine Coma: A Somatic Therapy in Psychiatry. *American Journal of Psychiatry* 115: 455–58.

Gardner, L. 1965. The Surviving Chumash. In *Archaeological Survey Annual Report* 7. Edited by D. S. Miller, pp. 277–302. Los Angeles.

Gayton, A. H. 1928. *The Narcotic Plant Datura in Aboriginal American Culture.* Doctoral Dissertation Department of Anthropology, University of California. Berkeley.

Gowdy, J. M. 1972. Stramonium Intoxication. *Journal of the American Medical Association* 221: 585–87.

Grant, C. 1978a. Chumash: Introduction. In *Handbook of North American Indians, Volume 8: California.* Edited by R. F. Heizer, pp. 505–08. Washington, D.C.

————. 1978b. Eastern Coastal Chumash. In *Handbook of North American Indians. Volume 8: California.* Edited by R. F. Heizer, pp. 509–19. Washington, D.C.

————. 1978c. Interior Chumash. In *Handbook of North American Indians. Volume 8: California.* Edited by R. F. Heizer, pp. 530–34. Washington, D.C.

————. 1978d. Island Chumash. In *Handbook of North American Indians. Volume 8: California.* Edited by R. F. Heizer, pp. 524–29. Washington, D.C.

————. 1993. *The Rock Paintings of the Chumash.* Santa Barbara.

Greenblatt, D. J. and R. I. Shader. 1973. Anticholinergics. *New England Journal of Medicine* 288: 1215–19.

Greenwood, R. S. 1978. Obispeño and Purismeño Chumash. In *Handbook of North American Indians. Volume 8: California.* Edited by R. F. Heizer, pp. 520–23.

Grob, Ch., and M. Dobkin de Rios. 1992. Adolescent Drug Use in Cross-Cultural Perspective. *Journal of Drug Issues* 22: 121–38.

Hall, R. C. W., B. Pfefferbaum., Earl R. Gardner., S. K. Stickney., and M. Perl. 1978. Intoxication with Angel's Trumpet: Anticholinergic Delirium and Hallucinosis. *Journal of Psychedelic Drugs* 10: 251–53.

Hammer, R. and A. Giachetti. 1982. Muscarinic Receptor Subtypes: M1 and M2 Biochemical and Functional Characterization. *Life Sciences* 31: 2991–98.

Hanna, J. P., J. M. Schmidley and W. E. Braselton, Jr. 1992. *Datura* Delirium. *Clinical Neuropharmacology* 15: 109–13.

Hansen, H. A. 1988. *Der Hexengarten.* München.

Heizer, R. F. 1941. A Californian Messianic Movement of 1801 Among the Chumash. *American Anthropologist* 43: 128–29.

Hester, T. R. 1978. Salinan. *Handbook of North American Indians. Volume 8: California.* Edited by R. F. Heizer, pp. 500–04. Washington, D.C.

Hickman, J. C. (ed). 1993. *The Jepson Manual: Higher Plants of California.* Berkeley.

Hudson, T., J. Timbrook., and M. Rempe (eds.) 1978. *TOMOL: Chumash Watercraft as Described in the Ethnographic Notes of John P. Harrington.* Socorro. NM.

Innes, I. R. and M. Nickerson. 1975. Atropine, Scopolamine, and Related Antimuscarinic Drugs. In *The Pharmacological Basis of Therapeutics.* Edited by L. S. Goodman and A. Gilman, pp. 514–32. New York.

Izquierdo, I. 1989. Mechanism of action of scopolamine as an amnestic. *Trends in Pharmacological Sciences* 10: 175–77.

Johnston, Th. F. 1972. *Datura fastuosa:* Its Use in Tsonga Girls' Initiation. *Economic Botany* 26: 340–51.

King, Ch. B. 1969. Map I: Approximate 1760 Chumash Village Locations and Populations. *Archaeological Survey Annual Report* 11. Edited by T. F. King, J. P. Carpenter and N. N. Leonard III p. 3. Los Angeles.

———. 1978. Protohistoric and Historic Archeology. In *Handbook of North American Indians, Volume 8: California*. Edited by R. F. Heizer, pp. 58–68. Washington, D.C.

King, L. B. 1969. The Medea Creek Cemetery (LAn-243): An Investigation of Social Organization from Mortuary Practices. *Archaeological Survey Annual Report* 11. Edited by T. F. King, J. P. Carpenter and N. N. Leonard III, pp. 23–68. Los Angeles.

King, Th. F. 1974. The Evolution of Status Ascription Around San Francisco Bay. *Antap: California Indian Political and Economic Organization*. Edited by L. J. Bean and T. F. King, pp. 35–53. Ramona, CA.

Kroeber, A. L. 1925. *Handbook of the Indians of California*. Bureau of American Ethnology. Washington, D.C.

Laird, C. 1974. Chemeheuvi Religious Beliefs and Practices. *Journal of California Anthropology* 1: 19–25.

Lampe, K. F. and M. A. McCann. 1985. *AMA Handbook of Poisonous and Injurious Plants*. Chicago.

Landberg, L. C. W. 1965. The Chumash Indians of Southern California. *Southwest Museum Papers* 19. Los Angeles.

Larson, D. O., J. R. Johnston., and J. C. Michaelsen. 1994. Missionization among the Coastal Chumash of Central California: A Study of Risk Minimization Strategies. *American Anthropologist* 96: 263–99.

Leary, T., R. Metzner., and R. Alpert. 1964. *The Psychedelic Experience*. Secaucus, NJ.

Lewin, L. 1980. *Phantastica: die betäubenden und erregenden Genussmittel* (second edition, enlarged). Linden.

Litzinger, W. J. 1981. Ceramic Evidence for Prehistoric *Datura* Use in North America. *Journal of Ethnopharmacology* 4: 57–74.

Ludwig, A. M. 1983. The Psychological Functions of Dissociation. *American Journal of Clinical Hypnosis* 26: 93–99.

Lydon, R. G. and S. Nakajima. 1992. Differential Effects of Scopolamine on Working and Reference Memory Depend Upon Level of Training. *Pharmacology Biochemistry and Behavior* 43: 645–50.

MacDonald, J. M. 1969. *Psychiatry and the Criminal*. Springfield, IL.

Merriam, C. H. 1967. Ethnographic Notes on California Indian Tribes II. Ethnological Notes on Northern and Southern California Indian Tribes. (compiled and edited by R. F. Heizer), *Reports of the University of California Archaeological Survey,* 68 (II): 161–256.

Miller, B. W. 1988. *Chumash: A Picture of Their World*. Los Osos, CA.

Mills, E. L. and A. J. Brickfield. (eds.). 1986. *The Papers of John Peabody Harrington in the Smithsonian Institution 1907–1957: Volume Three, A Guide to the Field Notes: Native American History, Language and Culture of Southern California/Basin,* White Plains, NY.

Mino, Y. 1994. Identical Amino Acid Sequence of Ferredoxin from *Datura metel* and *D. Innoxia*. *Phytochemistry* 35: 385–87.

Moerman, D. E. 1986. Medicinal Plants of North America. *University of Michigan Museum of Anthropology Technical Reports* 19 (two volumes). Ann Arbor.

Molchan, S. E., R. A. Martinez., J. L. Hill., H. J. Weingartner., K. Thompson., B. Vitiello., and T. Sunderland. 1992. Increased cognitive sensitivity to scopolamine with age and a perspective on the scopolamine model. *Brain Research Reviews* 17: 215–26.

Molinengo, L. 1993. The Action of Scopolamine on Retrieval and Memory Storage in Rats Evaluated in the Staircase Maze. *Behavioral and Neural Biology* 59: 18–24.

Nuotto, E. 1983. Psychomotor, Physiological and Cognitive Effects of Scopolamine and Ephedrine in Healthy Man. *European Journal of Clinical Pharmacology* 24: 603–09.

Oliva, G. A., M. P. Bucci., and R. Fioravanti. 1993. Impairment of Saccadic Eye Movements by Scopolamine Treatment. *Perceptual and Motor Skills* 76: 159–67.

Plantevin, O. M. 1973. *Analgesia and Anesthesia in Obstetrics*. London.

Plowman, T. 1981. Brugmansia (Baum-Datura) in Südamerika. In *Rausch und Realität*. Edited by G. Völger, pp. 436–443. Köln.

Powell, J. W. 1891. Indian Linguistic Families of America North of Mexico. *Seventh Annual Report of the Bureau of American Ethnology for 1885–86,* pp. 7–42. Washington.

Rätsch, Ch. 1990. *Pflanzen der Liebe*. Bern.

Rätsch, Ch. and H. J. Probst. 1985. Xtohk'uh: Zur Ethnobotanik der Datura-Arten bei den Maya in Yucatan. *Ethnologia Americana* 21: 1137–40.

Rupniak, N. M. J., N. A. Samson., M. J. Steventon., and S. D. Iversen. 1991. Induction of Cognitive Impairment by Scopolamine and Noncholinergic Agents in Rhesus Monkeys. *Life Sciences* 48: 893–99.

Safer, D. J. and R. P. Allen. 1971. The Central Effects of Scopolamine in Man. *Biological Psychiatry* 3: 347–55.

Safford, W. E. 1920 Daturas of the Old World and New: An Account of Their Narcotic Properties and Their Use in Oracular and Initiatory Ceremonies. *Annual Report of the Smithsonian Institution,* pp. 537–67.

Schultes, R. E. 1972. An Overview of Hallucinogens in the Western Hemisphere. In *Flesh of the Gods*. Edited by P. T. Furst, pp. 3–54. Prospect Heights, IL: Waveland (reissued 1990).

———. 1979. Solanaceous hallucinogens and their role in the development of New World cultures. In *The Biology and Taxonomy of the Solanaceae*. Edited by J. G. Hawkes, R. N. Lester and A. D. Skelding, pp. 137–60. London.

Schultes, R. E. and A. Hofmann. 1980. *Pflanzen der Götter*. Bern.

Siegel, R. K. 1976. Herbal Intoxication. *Journal of the American Medical Association*. 236: 473–76.

———. 1989. *Intoxication: Life in Pursuit of Artificial Paradise*. New York.

Siklós, B. 1993. *Datura* Rituals in the Vajramahabhairava-Tantra. *curare* 16: 71–76.

Spurnä, V., V. Sovová., E. Jirmanovä., and A. Sustäcková. 1981. Chromosomal Characteristics and Occurrence of Main Alkaloids in *Datura stramonium* and *Datura wrightii*. *Planta medica* 41: 366–73.

Sunderland, T., P. N. Tariot., H. Weingartner., D. L. Murphy., P. A. Newhouse, E. A. Mueller., and R. M. Cohen. 1986. Pharmacologic Modeling of Alzheimer's Disease. *Progress in Neuro-Psychopharmacology and Biological Psychiatry* 10: 599–610.

Symon, David E. and Laurence A. R. Haegi. 1991. Datura (Solanaceae) is a New World Genus. In *Solanaceae III: Taxonomy, Chemistry, Evolution* Edited by J. G. Hawkes, R. N. Lester, M. Nee, and N. Estrada, pp. 197–210. Surrey.

Timbrook, Jan. 1987. Virtuous Herbs: Plants in Chumash Medicine. *Journal of Ethnobiology* 7: 171–80.

———. 1990. Ethnobotany of Chumash Indians, California. Based on Collections by John P. Harrington. *Economic Botany* 44: 236–53.

Wada, S., T. Yoshimitsu., N. Koga., H. Yamada., K. Oguri., and H. Yoshimura. 1991. Metabolism *in vivo* of the tropane alkaloid, scopolamine, in several mammalian species. *Xenobiotica* 21: 1289–1300.

Walker, P. L. and T. Hudson. 1993. *Chumash Healing.* Banning, CA.

Wallace, W. J. 1955. A Suggested Chronology for Southern California Coastal Archaeology. *Southwestern Journal of Anthropology* 11: 214–30.

———. 1978. Post-Pleistocene Archeology, 9000 to 2000 B.C. in *Handbook of North American Indians. Volume 8: California.* Edited by R. F. Heizer, pp. 25–36. Washington, D.C.

Warburton, D. M., K. Wesnes, J. Edwards., and D. Larrad. 1985. Scopolamine and the Sensory Conditioning of Hallucinations. *Neuropsychobiology* 14: 198–202.

Watson, S. and D. Girdlestone. 1993. Tips Receptor Nomenclature Supplement 1993. *Trends in Pharmacological Sciences.*

Weil, A. 1972. *The Natural Mind.* Boston.

Weingartner, H. 1985. Models of Memory Dysfunctions. *Annals of the New York Academy of Sciences* 444: 359–69.

Yarnell, R. A. 1959. Prehistoric Pueblo Use of Datura. *El Palacio* 66: 176–78.

Yates, L. G. 1889. Charm Stones. *Annual Report of the Board of Regents of the Smithsonian Institution for the Year Ending June 30, 1886, Part I,* pp. 296–305. Washington.

Cognitive and Optical Illusions in San Rock Art Research[1]

J. D. Lewis-Williams

Many of us are familiar with the cave paintings of Europe and the petroglyphs and petrograms of the American West. In this essay, J. D. Lewis-Williams examines some of the rock art of South Africa. He argues that attempts to understand these paintings as accurate depictions of ancient life are misguided and that Western scholars tend to misinterpret rock art because they see it as being similar to the European tradition of art. Lewis-Williams suggests that the only accurate way to interpret such art is with regard to the ethnography of the people who created it. Seen in this light, it is clear that San rock art does not depict the material world of ancient people, but rather the hallucinogenic experiences of their medicine men.

Lewis-Williams argues that the curious effects seen in rock art—the elongation of limbs, the presence of rays extending from the bodies of people, cross-thatching, and other geometric forms—are not caused by the artists' inability to depict reality accurately. Instead, they are best explained as attempts by the artists to re-create the experience of moving into ecstatic states. Some elements of the paintings are phosphenes, or entopics: they are re-creations of optical effects caused by the central nervous system as the body moves into trance. Other elements are theriantropes,

images that combine aspects of humans and animals and, in this case, show the hallucinogenic transformation of the shaman into a spirit animal. Elements showing elongated arms or legs depict tactile hallucinations experienced while in trance.

Interpreting rock art as representations of hallucination may be foreign to Western art criticism, but it is supported by ethnographic work done with the San. Understood in this manner, the San rock paintings give us a rare glimpse into the experience of people entering into states of religious ecstasy—and also has implications for understanding of the Paleolithic art. Paleolithic rock art in many places around the world shows the same features as San rock art, as does some of the religious art of the European Middle Ages and Renaissance. Similarly, American psychedelic art of 1960s and 1970s has features that are strikingly reminiscent of those shown in the San rock paintings.

As you read, consider these questions:

1. What are "phosphenes" and what do they have to do with the trance state?
2. Why does the author claim that San art is shamanic?
3. What factors must be taken into consideration when interpreting rock art?

Lewis-Williams, "Cognitive & Optical Illusions in San Rock Art Research," *Current Anthropology* 27:2 (Apr. 1986): 171–78. Reprinted by permission of the author and The University of Chicago Press.

✳

A decade and a half ago Inskeep (1971:101) distinguished between "learning about" and "learning from" the San rock art of southern Africa.[2] Pursuing the second of these two courses, writers claim to have detected artefacts such as fur-lined leggings (Lee and Woodhouse 1970:105), practices such as an eland-jumping sport (Woodhouse 1969), hunting equipment such as game nets (Vinnicombe 1976:fig. 204; Parkington 1984:170; Manhire, Parkington, and Yates n.d.), and concepts such as zoomorphic spirits of the dead (Pager 1975:56–67; Lee and Woodhouse 1964). None of these had been previously suspected, and there is little or no ethnographic evidence for them. This approach has for many years constituted a substantial portion of southern African rock art research. Inskeep, however, also made the point that, before we can learn from the art, we must first learn about it, and since he wrote we have done so. Numerical inventories have provided a more precise account of the subject matter (e.g., Pager 1971; Lewis-Williams 1974; Vinnicombe 1976); the age is better, though still not adequately, understood (Thackeray 1983); and we have some insight into the meaning of the art and its place in San society (e.g., Vinnicombe 1976; Lewis-Williams 1982).

Undoubtedly, there is still much more to be learned, but, taking up Inskeep's cautionary point, I argue that what we already know about art in general and San rock art in particular has placed constraints on what we may expect to learn from it. In the first place, the possibility of deriving from San art information of the kind I have exemplified is posited on the assumption that the paintings are an accurate record of Stone Age life and thought which affords glimpses of the lives lived by the people whose stone artefacts archaeologists dig up. No art, however, communicates as directly as this. Without a verbal commentary of some sort it is impossible to know the meaning intended by a painter or sculptor even in one's own culture; some explanatory accompaniment is essential for unambiguous interpretation (Gombrich 1982). One cannot, for instance, infer the meaning of Rodin's *Age of Bronze* from the statue alone or guess that his *Thinker* surmounts the *Gates of Hell* and is contemplating that infernal region's horrors. It is, then, even less likely that we can discover the meaning of art from foreign cultures without some guidance from its makers. Finding it difficult to conceive of artistic conventions different from their own, some observers suffer from the cognitive illusion that alien works were created in terms of the conventions with which they are acquainted. One consequence of this illusion is that, in trying to learn about the San from southern African rock art, they reduce strange and otherwise inexplicable depictions to familiar objects. In the same way that Breuil reduced the "signs" of Palaeolithic art to traps, huts, and so forth, they infer literal explanations for enigmatic paintings. They believe, incorrectly, that this is the safest, simplest, and most reasonable course. In fairness, I must add that, given the literalist view, many of these supposed explanations appear persuasive, but the belief that art transcends language

and culture in its capacity to communicate ideas or even the nature of unfamiliar objects is simply incorrect. Art may move us, but it does not communicate.

In addition to problems with the communicative power of art in general, San art in particular is such as to diminish even further the possibility of extracting ethnographic data. San rock art portrays not only objects and practices from the "real" world but also metaphors, symbols, and hallucinations associated with or derived from the trance experience of San medicine men, or shamans (Huffman 1983; Lewis-Williams 1980, 1981a, b, 1983, 1984a; Maggs and Sealy 1983; Manhire, Parkington, and Yates n.d.). It is, indeed, essentially shamanic. Some painted hallucinations are iconic in that they depict real items such as animals and bows and arrows; others, phosphenes or form-constants, are "nonrealistic," being produced entirely by the human nervous system; yet others combine and associate iconic and noniconic forms in ways yet to be unravelled. Once the existence of at least some such depictions is allowed, it becomes impossible to infer artefacts and practices not already known from the ethnography, for we have no way of telling, apart from the ethnography, if puzzling paintings relate to the "real" world or to the hallucinatory one. We cannot be sure if the paintings of fur-lined leggings, eland-jumping, net hunting, and so on are indeed what they appear to be. What we know about San art restricts what we can learn from it.

These problems with the interpretation of San rock art recall the well-known optical illusion which can be seen as either a rabbit or a duck. Once they have viewed the drawing as a rabbit, many people find it difficult to make it "about face" so that the rabbit's ears become a duck's bill. Similarly, some students have believed for so long and so unquestioningly that San rock art is an intelligible record of San daily life with a small admixture of "mythical" depictions that they cannot see it as principally symbolic and hallucinatory. However, once disabused of their preconceptions, viewers find that the art radically changes form; the leggings, eland-jumping, and so forth, disappear and something quite different appears in their place.

Research should therefore be directed at ascertaining what kinds of information can be extracted from the art and what kinds cannot. Such a programme entails, amongst other things, testing the shamanic explanation against a wide range of paintings which have been considered literal depictions. It is insufficient simply to assert the shamanic explanation's comprehensiveness; each type of painting must be explained, and each explanation must be supported by verifiable San beliefs and practices. The value and power of the shamanic explanation will be demonstrated, at least in part, by the number of persuasive reinterpretations which can be sustained under these rigorous conditions. This task, of course, depends largely on the availability and the reliability of San ethnography. Fortunately, we need have qualms on neither of these points. Some highly significant remarks on specific paintings and on trance performance were collected

FIGURE 1 Rock painting of men apparently crossing a rope bridge, Natal Drakenberg. Scale in this and all other figures is in centimeters. *Source:* Lewis-Williams, "Cognitive and Optical Illusions in San Rock Art Research."

in 1873 from a Maluti San informant (Orpen 1874). Also in the 1870s the Bleek family compiled a much more extensive collection of /Xam folklore (e.g., Bleek 1935, 1936). In the 20th century numerous anthropologists have studied the Kalahari San (e.g., Biesele 1975; Lee 1968; Marshall 1969). Comparison of these three sources shows that, despite linguistic differences and wide separation in time and space, many rituals, beliefs, symbols, and metaphors were common to all San groups (Lewis-Williams and Biesele 1978; Lewis-Williams 1980, 1981*a*). It is on these commonalities that my argument is based.

To show that even some very convincing examples of "learning from the art" can, from a different viewpoint, change as the rabbit changes into a duck, I start with a well-known painting from the Ndedema Gorge (fig. 1) which, as far as I am aware, has been universally seen as evidence for the construction of bridges (Pager 1971:225, 1975:63; Willcox 1984:197; Woodhouse 1979:70) and, one must assume, their use by accomplished San funambulists. Though writers do not cite it, there is only the most tenuous ethnographic evidence to support this view. Orpen (1874:10) was told that the Maluti San "formerly knew how to make things of stone over rivers, on which they crossed." His informant seems, however, to have been referring to stepping stones rather than rope bridges. In contrast to this literalist interpretation,

I explore the possibility that the shamanic explanation explains the painting and in doing so directs attention to and elucidates numerous details which the literal view overlooks or ignores. Even if the San did construct rope bridges, this painting is better explained in another way altogether.

The relevance of the shamanic explanation is suggested first by the clapping figures to the left of and also below the "bridge." At a San trance dance, women sing and clap the rhythm of "medicine songs" believed to be imbued with a supernatural potency (for more detailed accounts of the trance dance, see Lee 1967, 1968; Marshall 1969; Biesele 1975, 1978; Katz 1982). This potency, which also resides in the stomachs of the medicine men themselves, is activated by the women's songs and the men's dancing. When it eventually "boils," the men enter the altered state of consciousness we call trance. At this point southern San medicine men frequently suffered a nasal haemorrhage and rubbed the blood on their patients in the belief that its odour would keep evil and sickness at bay (Arbousset 1846:247; Bleek 1935:12, 13, 19–20, 34; Orpen 1874:10). At least three of the figures crossing the "bridge" are bleeding from the nose in the manner of medicine men. Another feature associated with medicine dances is the flywhisk carried by four of the figures on the "bridge." Today the !Kung like to dance with these whisks, and Marshall (1969:358) had the impression that they were largely reserved for dances (see also Lee 1967:31). The apparently anomalous depiction of flywhisks along with bows is explained by the San belief that "medicine men of the game" were able to control and hunt animals while in trance (Bleek 1935:36–37, 39, 41, 44–46, 47; 1936:132). Dancing and hunting are, in this way, related activities; all too often the depiction, in one way or another, of hunting has been taken to preclude a hallucinatory interpretation. Indeed, all these features—clapping women, nasal bleeding, flywhisks, and bows—commonly appear in paintings of medicine dances and other trance compositions (e.g., Lewis-Williams 1981a:figs. 19, 20, 21, 23, 1981b:figs. 1, 2; 1983:figs. 16, 18, 19, 20, 21, 22, 64, 68).

The details to which I have so far drawn attention are observable by anyone at a trance dance. A second category of features is hallucinatory or conceptual and "observable" only by people in trance. For instance, when a man enters trance his spirit is "seen" to leave his body through a hole in the top of the head. The spirit then performs the various tasks undertaken by people in this condition: controlling antelope, curing the sick, visiting distant camps, and so forth. One of the bleeding figures on the "bridge" has two long lines emanating from the top of his head, as do trance figures in many other paintings (e.g., Lewis-Williams 1981a:figs. 22, 24, 30, 31, 38; 1982:fig. 3; 1983:figs. 20, 21). These lines probably depict the spirit leaving on extracorporeal travel.

Another visionary feature is represented below the "bridge," where there are at least four trance-buck. Woodhouse (1978:20), separating this group from the "bridge" paintings, has offered a Eurocentric interpretation: "Flying creatures, some with human characteristics, pay homage to a central figure." Pager (1971:344), on the other hand, notes the "uniformity of headgear" between the male figure in this group and those crossing the "bridge" and rightly concludes that they are all part of the same composition, a conclusion supported by the colour and condition of the paint. Though these "winged buck" have been interpreted as spirits of the dead (Pager 1971:343; Woodhouse 1979:98), the shamanic explanation accounts for more of their features by explicitly San, not Western, beliefs. When a medicine man enters trance he is believed sometimes to fuse with the animal potency he possesses. A !Kung man, for instance, told Wiessner (personal communication; Wiessner and Larson 1979) that he saw himself as the antelope he had tried to kill when he first obtained potency. In the art, therianthropic figures combining antelope and human characteristics are often shown with other features, such as nasal bleeding, which link them to trance performance, and Orpen's (1874:2, 10) southern San informant stated that the paintings of men with antelope heads depicted medicine men (Lewis-Williams 1980). The type of "headgear" to which Pager draws attention (if it is indeed a realistic portrayal) is shown on an unequivocal medicine man painted at another site (Pager 1975:41). This figure, surrounded by clapping women, holds

two flywhisks and dances in a bending-forward posture said to be occasioned by painfully boiling potency in a trance dancer's stomach. Other therianthropes and trance-buck are drawn with their arms in a distinctive backward position which some medicine men adopt when they are asking God to put potency into their bodies. Some of the depictions in this category also have "streamers" emanating from the back of the neck or from between the shoulder blades, as do the trance-buck in figure 1. These "streamers" are occasionally difficult to distinguish from arms in the backward posture. It is from the nape of the neck that medicine men expel the sickness they remove from their patients. Expelled sickness can be "seen" only by people in trance, and this fact, together with other considerations, suggests that trance-buck and therianthropes depict hallucinations of men transformed by potency (Lewis-Williams 1981a:75–100; 1984b:246).

The combination in figure 1 of observable features of the San trance dance (flywhisks, nasal bleeding, clapping women, and the arms-back posture) and ethnographically verifiable San hallucinations (the spirit leaving the body and trance-buck) therefore clearly indicates that, whatever the "bridge" may be, the painting has some connection with trance performance. Even if we could go no farther, we should already have good reason to doubt the depiction of a bridge. Fortunately, we are able to propose an alternative explanation.

This explanation starts with the transformation of medicine men in trance to which I have already referred. Evidence for the nature of some such transformations comes from Katz's (1982:235–37) work among the !Kung San of the Kalahari. He asked medicine men and men who had never experienced trance to draw pictures of themselves. Those who had never entered trance produced simple stick figures like that in figure 2a. The trancers, in contrast, drew zigzags and spirals which seem to bear no resemblance to a human body. One informant said that the long zigzags in figure 2d were his spinal cord and the shorter, adjacent zigzags his body. Katz (p. 236) finds these forms "reminiscent of the description of rapidly boiling and rising num [potency]." People in trance experience a variety of bodily sensations which include pain or a sensation of heat which starts in the stomach and rises up the spine (Katz 1982:45). If the zigzags are, as Katz suggests, an attempt to portray this physical experience, we may call the drawings somatogenic depictions of medicine men.

Whilst Katz is probably right, an additional suggestion about the origin of the zigzags can be made. Neurological work conducted independently of rock art research has shown that, in an early stage of trance, subjects "see" a variety of geometric forms including zigzags, grids, vortexes, and dots (Siegel 1977; Siegel and Jarvik 1975). These phosphenes (form-constants) are produced by certain stimulations of the central nervous system and are therefore, unlike many of the hallucinations experienced in later stages of trance, not culturally controlled (Lewis-Williams 1985).

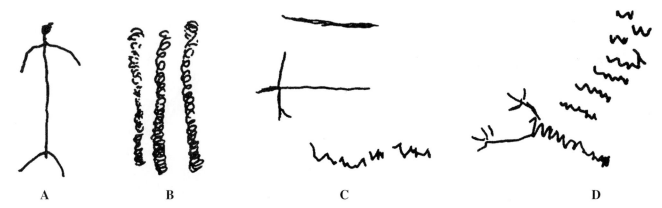

A   B   C   D

FIGURE 2 Self-portrait by !Kung informants (after Katz 198:237): *a*, by a man who had never experienced trance; *b–d*, by medicine man. *Source:* Lewis-Williams, "Cognitive and Optical Illusions in San Rock Art Research."

Similar phosphenes are reported from all over the world because the central nervous system is common to all men (e.g., Hedges 1983); some phosphenes are familiar to migraine sufferers, for that condition similarly affects the nervous system (Richards 1971). The close similarity between zigzag phosphenes and the drawings done by Katz's medicine men suggests strongly that the men were identifying themselves with the phosphenes they "saw" in trance. For the San, trance is a profound experience which expresses itself not merely in the mind but also in and through the body. Medicine men emphasise "the central importance of fluid psychological processes and transitions that break out of the body's ordinary anatomical boundaries" (Katz 1982:235). As their statements and their drawings show, their self-image is determined more by this fluidity of inner states than by external anatomical criteria: as their potency "boils," their body becomes fluid, parts of it separate, and parts are transformed. Phosphenes too are fluid, constantly shimmering, moving, expanding, and contracting. It is therefore understandable that medicine men should discern an analogy between what they see and what they feel. In the end, they *are* what they see and what they feel, and their drawings are derived from both the visual and the somatic effects of trance.

A connection between these hallucinations and San rock art is demonstrated by paintings such as those in figure 3. The recorder (Rudner 1959) of figure 3*a* regarded it as enigmatic, but it has subsequently been interpreted as clouds, rain, and lightning (Woodhouse 1985:53). However, the zigzag line joining the human figures casts serious doubt on this view: neither clouds nor rain nor lightning behave in this way. It seems more likely that this phosphene represents potency and the way it flows from person to person. Furthermore, another zigzag attached to the figure on the left is probably a transformed arm. The large zigzag form above the human figures may, like figure 2*d*, be a man whose potency has "boiled" and whose body has transcended ordinary boundaries. The lines in figure 3*b* have also been reduced to unconvincing literalism: Goodall (1959:32) sees the painting as

"a man handling snakes," an unlikely circumstance indeed among the San. An interesting aspect of this painting is that the figure appears to be grasping one of the lines. Human figures grasping nonrealistic lines are, in fact, not uncommon (e.g., Lewis-Williams 1981*b*:figs. 1 and 2; Pager 1975:79, 80; Vinnicombe 1976:fig. 240). Control or manipulation of potency is part of San trance experience, and it is this ability that is probably depicted. I am indebted to Aron Mazel for drawing my attention to an even clearer combination of phosphenes with the human body (fig. 3*c*). Here the neck and legs of the figure are phosphenic zigzags. The close similarity between paintings like these and the drawings made by Katz's informants suggests that they depict people associated in various ways with phosphenes rather than observable phenomena. Although such phosphenes are far more common in the rock engravings, they appear in the paintings more frequently than has been supposed. Because writers reduce the painted phosphenic zigzags, dots, grids, **U** shapes, and so on, to readily comprehensible depictions of body paint, decorations on karosses, clouds, rain, and even doodles, they have passed unnoticed. The recognition of these phosphenes and associated transformations in the art allows us now to reinterpret the "bridge."

This new interpretation is suggested first by those trance-buck which have elongated, backward-extended "arms" covered with long "hairs" (e.g., Pager 1971:381, nos. 5, 18, 35, 36, 38, 40, 44, 45; 1975:57, 62, 64, 81, 85). The example in figure 4 is on a large fallen stone some metres to the left of figure 1. Like many trance-buck, it has blood falling from its nose. The "hairs" on this and other hallucinatory forms are probably somatogenic; people who have experienced trance report a tingling or prickling sensation on various parts of the body including the outside of the arms. Katz's (1982:46) informants spoke of this sensation along the spine, and Bleek's (1935:2, 23) informants claimed that "lion's hair" grew on the back of a man in trance—a feature often painted. Among the San, the tingling sensation is interpreted as the growth of hair and transformation into an

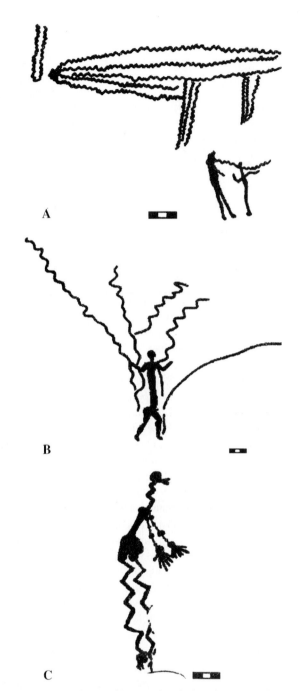

A

B

C

FIGURE 3 Southern African rock paintings incorporating phosphenes: *a,* Western Province (after Rudner 1959); *b,* Zimbabwe (after Goodall 1959: fig. 13); *c,* Natal Drakensberg (after a photograph by A. Mazel). *Source:* Lewis-Williams, "Cognitive and Optical Illusions in San Rock Art Research."

FIGURE 4 Rock painting of a trance-buck, Natal Drakensberg. *Source:* Lewis-Williams, "Cognitive and Optical Illusions in San Rock Art Research."

"bridge" is in fact two transformed medicine men with their hirsute arms extended towards each other and merging.

Further aspects of the painting also appear in a new light. The elongation of the "arms" is probably another somatogenic feature; people in trance often experience attenuation of their limbs. Many San paintings depict markedly elongated human figures. Though this aspect of the art has been interpreted as stylistic or as an attempt on the part of a diminutive people to represent themselves as tall (Woodhouse 1979:114), it more probably depicts a somatic experience of trance. Figure 5, for example, shows markedly elongated figures in typical trancing postures—arms back, bending forward, and hands placed on the chest. Furthermore, the "pegs" now become bodies without legs (cf. fig. 5) and with heads facing inwards. In any event, the heads face in the wrong direction to function usefully as the heads of pegs securing a rope bridge. Such a radical alteration of the human body is, as Katz's informants' drawings show, well within the bounds of San trance experience and, unlike a bridge, is concordant with the other visual and somatogenic hallucinations I have noted. Indeed, this view unites the apparently diverse features of the painting in a single coherent explanation which is rooted in San ethnography. All the concepts this interpretation incorporates are related and verifiable San beliefs about trance. I shall therefore henceforth refer to the "bridge" and certain other visual and somatogenic hallucinations by the neologism "trance-formed" medicine men.

Other paintings supposedly depicting rope bridges, ladders, nets, and so on, will eventually have to be examined in the light of this new understanding. For the present, I mention only two, both painted at a site known as "the bridge" near Harare, Zimbabwe. Because they are painted within a few centimetres of each other, they must be regarded as a single instance rather than two separate ones. Goodall (1959:44, pl. 21) sees each as "a humorous scene" and believes they show "people in comical attitudes trying to cross

animal. More importantly, the "hairs" on the trance-buck's arms are clearly similar to the "hairs" on the "bridge." Indeed, comparison of the "arms" of hirsute trance-buck with the "ropes" of the "bridge" demonstrates beyond reasonable doubt that they are two expressions of the same concept. The

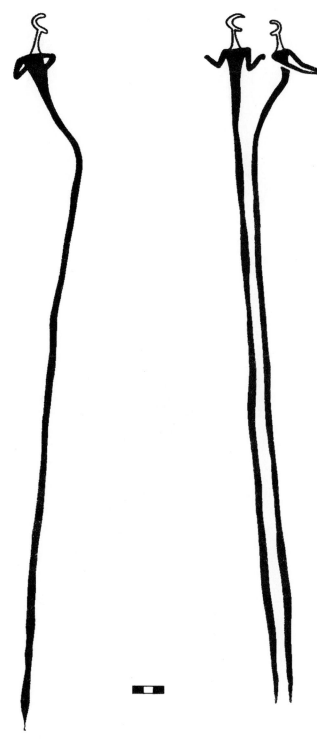

FIGURE 5 Rock painting of elongated human figures in trancing postures, eastern Orange Free State. *Source:* Lewis-Williams, "Cognitive and Optical Illusions in San Rock Art Research."

a river over rope bridges. The water is indicated by short dashes, and a snake with ears rises from the river." The dashes are, however, better interpreted as swarms of bees, especially as they are shown entering or leaving trees (Pager

1971:352; Huffman 1983; Woodhouse 1984:13–15). Bees are associated with the trance dance, and the modern !Kung like to dance at the time of year when the bees are swarming because they believe they can harness their potency for a particularly efficacious dance (Edwin Wilmsen, personal communication). This relationship is depicted in a painting in the northeastern Cape which shows a trance dance with bees swarming above (Lewis-Williams 1981*b:*fig. 1; 1983: fig. 16), though the relationship between the dancers and the bees should be seen as symbolic rather than in terms of Western perspective. The eared snake which Goodall mentions is likewise probably associated with trance; these fantastic serpents sometimes bleed from the nose as medicine men do (e.g., Lewis-Williams 1981*a:*fig. 23; Johnson and Maggs 1979:fig. 51; Lee and Woodhouse 1970:figs. D35, 208). In addition to the two features Goodall notes, there are others which confirm the view that this is a trance scene. These include the kneeling posture of many figures, lines emanating from the heads of some, and lines extending from the shoulders of six figures.

A remaining problem is why human figures in these paintings appear to be running or crawling on the extended arms of trance-formed medicine men. In trying to explain this feature we must again acknowledge that we still know little about San concepts of perspective and composition. It is, of course, wrong to assume that San artists entertained Western ideas of perspective. In fact, Western perspective is entirely unknown to most preliterate artists. San "scenes" were therefore probably composed according to conventions unknown in Western art. It is possible that no fixed relationships, as understood by Westerners, are intended in San "scenes": the "scenes" may portray figures individually and even in different temporal dimensions and therefore not capture an instant in the manner of a photograph, a peculiarly Western concept. Many of the relationships which Westerners see in San rock art may be no more than optical illusions.

Though we are still far from a clear understanding of the relationship depicted in figure 1 and in the Zimbabwean painting, it is worth noting that these are not the only depictions of men or animals apparently walking or running along "bridges" or lines (e.g., Pager 1975:57, 77, 79, 81, 84; Lewis-Williams 1981*b;* figs. 1, 2, 3). In some paintings the line is patently nonrealistic in one part, where it may be shown entering and leaving the bodies of antelope, while in another it may be held by a man as if it were a rope. I have argued that many of these lines represent the potency activated and harnessed by medicine men (Lewis-Williams 1981*b*), but they will have to be reexamined in the light of the new understanding given in this paper. If Katz is correct in thinking that the zigzags drawn by his informants are boiling potency and, at the same time, a medicine man's body, it is certainty possible that some of the painted lines are also men identifying themselves or others with potency. A more specific interpretation of the relationship in figure 1 may be that it expresses the San belief that men in trance pool their experience and protect one another with their potency: the more potency that is "boiling" and being transmitted from one man to another, the more efficacious the trance. Medicine men hold and embrace one another to facilitate transmission of potency. The men apparently running on the arms of the trance-formed medicine men may therefore be deriving power from them, though not in any strict temporal or spatial sense. The real relationship is probably entirely conceptual and the one suggested by Western perspective an illusion, but we have a long way to go before we can be more precise.

In the meantime we can use the new interpretation of figure 1 to throw light on other curious paintings of which I briefly discuss one (fig. 6a). It is one of three similar paintings close to one another on a large fallen rock at Giant's Castle, Natal Drakensberg. It has been seen as two drums or pots connected, for unexplained reasons, by thongs. However, comparison of the supposed drums or pots with certain paintings of kaross-clad therianthropes (e.g., fig. 6b; see also Lewis-Williams 1983:pl. 76) suggests that they are in fact the lower parts of a pair of legs. In addition to general shape, the so-called drums or pots have three features in common with the legs of some therianthropes. First, both have white dots above the calves and at the ankles; secondly, both are frequently outlined on one side with white paint; and, lastly, both terminate in the same way at the lower extremity. This last feature may be intended to indicate hoofs rather than feet, because many such therianthropes have clear antelope hocks and hoofs. Until now it has been impossible to accept that the two forms are what they appear to be—the legs of therianthropes—but a drawing such as figure 2d shows that the absence of a normal body does not vitiate this identification: Katz's informant drew feet and legs and then indicated the rest of the body by phosphenes.

Support for this interpretation of figure 6a comes again from trance-buck. The two in figure 6c have "wings" or arms with pendant attachments which have been thought to represent feathers. The paintings may indeed depict a combination of antelope and avian forms, because flight is a San metaphor for trance experience. But the general form of the "wings" is very like the "thongs" in figure 6a. While some therianthropic medicine men have "hairs" on their arms which resemble the "hairs" of the "bridge" in figure 1, others have more substantial, hanging lines which resemble the lines hanging from the "thongs" in figure 6a. Figure 6a, therefore, is probably another trance-formed medicine man. In this instance, the legs are fairly clear, but the rest of the body has been entirely trance-formed. Although they are at first glance very different, the "drums" and the "bridge" are cognate forms. This conclusion opens up a wide-ranging discussion of many other paintings the meanings of which have been considered self-evident.

The aim of this paper is not merely to show that the supposed depictions of bridges and drums are better interpreted as visual and somatogenic hallucinations of San medicine

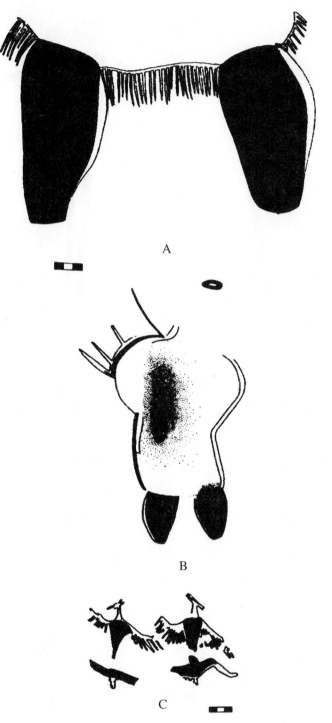

FIGURE 6 *a,* trance-formed medicine man, Giant's Castle, Natal Drakensberg; *b,* rock painting of a kaross-clad figure, Giant's Castle, Natal Drakensberg; *c,* two trance-buck (after Pager 1975:52). *Source:* Lewis-Williams, "Cognitive and Optical Illusions in San Rock Art Research."

men but, by probing the essence of the art, to argue the more general point that expectations of learning about San material culture and beliefs from the art alone are too sanguine. If such diverse depictions as "bridges" and "drums" can be explained by San beliefs about trance performance, it is clearly wrong to suppose that the art speaks directly to Western viewers to reveal an intelligible panorama of Stone Age life. Before we err in reducing unfamiliar paintings to objects known to Westerners, we should see if they are adequately explained by San beliefs, concepts, and practices. When there is no ethnographic evidence for an artefact or practice, let alone a belief, over and above apparent depiction in the art, the hallucinatory and symbolic nature of many paintings precludes inference that such objects or practices existed. The art may, of course, direct archaeologists to examine unexplored ethnography or to seek confirmation in their excavations where this is possible. At best the art may be a source of hypotheses, certainly not confirmation of them.

This conclusion may appear discouraging, even obscurantist, to those who use rock art as an ethnographic record. Yet it seems undeniable that, because they have misunderstood the very nature of the art, their approach often comprises little more than ad hoc inductions. Perhaps it was such work that caused Inskeep (1978:85), some years after distinguishing between "learning about" and "learning from" rock art, to call the southern African art "a rich and entrancing storehouse of information . . . that is not easily tapped." His despair can be allayed only by finding a key to the "storehouse." That key is San ethnography—though using it is no simple matter (Lewis-Williams 1977, 1980, n.d.). As authentic San beliefs and practices are more carefully and extensively deployed in rock art research, many reinterpretations will probably result and more and more of the art will be seen to be associated with medicine men and their hallucinatory experiences. With such a change in perspective, many rabbits will turn out to be ducks. But in these cases, the ducks are the artists' real intention; the rabbits are merely illusions.

NOTES

1. © 1986 by The Wenner-Gren Foundation for Anthropological Research, all rights reserved 0011-3204/86/2702-0007$1.00. I am grateful to colleagues who commented on earlier versions of this paper. It was first presented in 1984 at the Second Drakensberg Rock Art Colloquium. Denise Gelling and Pam Farrow typed successive drafts. The illustrations were prepared by Paul den Hoed. Aron Mazel kindly permitted reproduction of figure 3c. The research was funded by the University of the Witwatersrand and the Human Sciences Research Council.

2. The San (Bushman) hunter-gatherers formerly lived throughout southern Africa. The more southerly groups, such as the /Xam of the Cape Province and the Maluti San of what is now Lesotho, became extinct towards the end of the 19th century; only those, like the !Kung, who live in the Kalahari Desert of Namibia and Botswana have survived (Lewis-Williams 1982:fig. 1). Almost all the abundant rock art of southern Africa was produced by the San, but those surviving in the Kalahari have no tradition of painting. The Kalahari people nevertheless still hold many of the beliefs and perform many of the rituals that were part of the lives of the southern painters (Lewis-Williams 1981a, 1982; Lewis-Williams and Biesele 1978).

REFERENCES CITED

Arbousset, T. 1846. *Narrative of an exploratory tour of the Cape of Good Hope.* Cape Town: Robertson.

Biesele, M. 1975. Folklore and ritual of !Kung hunter-gathers. Ph.D. diss., Harvard University, Cambridge, Mass.

———. 1978. Sapience and scarce resources: Communication systems of the !Kung and other foragers. *Social Science Information* 17:921–47.

Bleek, D. F. 1935. Beliefs and customs of the /Xam Bushmen. Part 7. Sorcerors. *Bantu Studies* 9:1–47.

———. 1936. Beliefs and customs of the /Xam Bushmen. Part 8. More about sorcerors and charms. *Bantu Studies* 10:131–62.

Gombrich, E. H. 1982. *The image and the eye.* Oxford: Phaidon.

Goodall, E. 1959. "Rock paintings in Mashonaland," in *Prehistoric rock art of the Federation of Rhodesia and Nyasaland.* Edited by R. Summers, pp. 3–111. Salisbury: National Publications Trust.

Hedges, K. 1983. "The shamanic origins of art," in *Ancient images on stone.* Edited by J. A. Van Tilburg, pp. 46–59. Los Angeles: Institute of Archaeology, University of California.

Huffman, T. N. 1983. The trance hypothesis and the rock art of Zimbabwe. *South African Archaeological Society, Goodwin Series* 4:49–53.

Inskeep, R. R. 1971. "The future of rock art studies in southern Africa," in *Rock paintings of southern Africa.* Edited by M. Schoonraad, pp. 101–4. South African Association for the Advancement of Science, Special Issue 2.

———. 1978. *The peopling of southern Africa.* London: David Philip.

Johnson, T., and T. Maggs. 1979. *Major rock paintings of southern Africa.* Cape Town: Philip.

Katz, R. 1982. *Boiling energy: Community healing among the Kalahari !Kung.* Cambridge: Harvard University Press.

Lee, D. N., and H. C. Woodhouse. 1964. Rock paintings of flying buck. *South African Archaeological Bulletin* 19:71–74.

———. 1970. *Art on the rocks of southern Africa.* Cape Town: Purnell.

Lee, R. B. 1967. Trance cure of the !Kung Bushmen. *Natural History* 76 (9):31–37.

———. 1968. "The sociology of !Kung Bushman trance performance," in *Trance and possession states.* Edited by R. Prince, pp. 35–54. Montreal: R. M. Bucke Memorial Society.

Lewis-Williams, J. D. 1974. Superpositioning in a sample of rock paintings from the Barkly East District. *South African Archaeological Bulletin* 29:93–103.

———. 1977. Ezeljagdspoort revisited: New light on an enigmatic rock painting. *South African Archaeological Bulletin* 32:165–69.

———. 1980. Ethnography and iconography: Aspects of southern San thought and art. *Man* 15:467–82.

———. 1981a. *Believing and seeing: Symbolic meanings in southern San rock paintings.* London: Academic Press.

———. 1981b. The thin red line: Southern San notions and rock paintings of supernatural potency. *South African Archaeological Bulletin* 36:5–13.

———. 1982. The social and economic context of southern San rock art. *Current Anthropology* 23:429–49.

———. 1983. *The rock art of southern Africa.* Cambridge: Cambridge University Press.

———. 1984a. "Ideological continuities in prehistoric southern Africa: The evidence of rock art," in *Past and present in hunter-gatherer studies.* Edited by C. Schrire, pp. 225–52. New York: Academic Press.

———. 1984b. Reply [to H. C. Woodhouse on the social context of southern African rock art]. *Current Anthropology* 25:246–48.

———. 1985. The San artistic achievement. *African Arts* 18(3):54–59.

———. n.d. "People of the eland": An archaeo-linguistic crux. MS.

Lewis-Williams, J. D., and M. Biesele. 1978. Eland hunting rituals among northern and southern San groups: Striking similarities. *Africa* 48:117–34.

Maggs, T. M. O'C., and J. Sealy. 1983. Elephants in boxes. *South African Archaeological Society, Goodwin Series* 4:44–48.

Manhire, A. H., J. Parkington, and R. Yates. n.d. Nets and fully re-curved bows: Rock paintings and hunting methods in the western Cape. *World Archaeology.* In press.

Marshall, L. 1969. The medicine dance of the !Kung Bushmen. *Africa* 39:347–81.

Orpen, J. M. 1874. A glimpse into the mythology of the Maluti Bushmen. *Cape Monthly Magazine, n.s.,* 9(49):1–13.

Prager, H. 1971. *Ndedema.* Graz: Akademische Druck- und Verlagsanstalt.

———. 1975. *Stone Age myth and magic.* Graz: Akademische Druck- und Verlagsanstalt.

Parkington, J. E. 1984. "Soaqua and Bushmen: Hunters and robbers," in *Past and present in hunter-gatherer studies.* Edited by C. Schrire, pp. 151–74. New York: Academic Press.

Richards, W. 1971. The fortification illusions of migraines. *Scientific American* 224:89–94.

Rudner, J. 1959. Cover design. *South African Archaeological Bulletin* 14(54).

Siegel, R. K. 1977. Hallucinations. *Scientific American* 237:132–40.

Siegel, R. K., and M. E. Jarvik. 1975. "Drug-induced hallucinations in animals and man," in *Hallucinations: Behavior, experience, and theory.* Edited by R. K. Siegel and L. J. West, pp. 81–161. New York: Wiley.

Thackeray, A. I. 1983. Dating the rock art of southern Africa. *South African Archaeological Society, Goodwin Series* 4:21–26.

Vinnicombe, P. 1976. *People of the eland.* Pietermaritzburg: Natal University Press.

Wiessner, P., and F. T. Larson. 1979. "Mother! Sing loudly for me!": The annotated dialogue of a Basarwa healer in trance. *Botswana Notes and Records* 11:25–31.

Willcox, A. R. 1984. *The rock art of Africa.* Johannesburg: Macmillan.

Woodhouse, H. C. 1969. Rock paintings of "eland-fighting" and "eland-jumping." *South African Archaeological Bulletin* 94:63–65.

———. 1978. *Rock art.* (Pride of South Africa 25.) Cape Town: Purnell.

———. 1979. *The Bushman art of southern Africa.* Cape Town: Purnell.

———. 1984. *When animals were people.* Johannesburg: van Rensburg.

———. 1985. Elephants in the rain? *South African Archaeological Bulletin* 40:53–54.

The Rave:
Spiritual Healing in Modern Western Subcultures

Scott R. Hutson

We generally think of religious experiences as happening within the context of some religious tradition. However, people often describe the experience of going to concerts or other large events as religious. In this essay, Scott R. Hutson wonders if participating in a rave really does have the same characteristics as other, more conventional forms of religious experience.

Hutson points out that ravers achieve ecstatic states through a combination of factors, including the use of the drug Ecstasy, driving trance music, and dance. They are led on this journey by a DJ who has many of the classic characteristics of a shaman. United by an ideology of peace, love, unity, and respect (PLUR), ravers achieve the state that anthropologist Victor Turner, in his studies of religious ritual, has called *communitas*. In this state, the social boundaries between individuals dissolve and people experience transcendence.

Hutson's analysis of the rave takes him far and wide. He compares the rave experience not only to other modern American experiences, such as following the Grateful Dead or participating in the Rainbow Nation, but also to the spiritual journeys of the Huichol of Mexico and the experi-

"The Rave: Spiritual Healing in Modern Western Subcultures," by Scott R. Hutson, *Anthropological Quarterly* 73 (2000), 35–49. Reprinted with permission of George Washington University.

ences of Charismatic Christians in the United States. In the end, he concludes that while the rave may be criticized on many levels, it is not simply a hedonistic party, but an ecstatic experience filled with meaning and myth for its participants.

As you read, consider these questions:
1. What is "spiritual healing" and how does it relate to altered states of consciousness?
2. How is the role of a DJ at a rave similar to the role of a shaman in traditional cultures?
3. Other than drugs, what are the factors that contribute to an altered state of consciousness at a rave?

Ever had an experience that makes you sit up and re-evaluate all your ideas, thoughts and incidents in your life?[1]

INTRODUCTION

The question above was voiced by a young man who had just returned from a rave: a dance party, usually all night long, featuring loud "techno"[2] music, also called electronica, in which participants often reach ecstatic states, occasionally with the help of drugs.[3] Initially, in the late 1980s, when they first appeared in Britain, raves were underground events, taking place in makeshift and occasionally secretive venues such as warehouses and outdoor fields. By the mid-1990s analysts could comment that "the scale is huge and ever increasing" (McRobbie 1994: 168). Fully licensed and often held in nightclubs, raves now penetrated to the center of British youth culture. Combined attendance at dance events in Great Britain in 1993 reached 50 million, which was substantially more than at "sporting events, cinemas, and all the 'live' arts combined" (Thornton 1995: 15). Commercially, the 1993 British rave market brought in approximately $2.7 billion (Thornton 1995: 15). In Germany nearly two million youngsters and post-adolescents united in the so-called "rave nation" of the mid-1990s (Richard and Kruger 1998). Following this initial north European florescence, rave hot spots emerged around the world at Rimini (Italy), Ko Phangan (Thailand), the Balearic Islands (Spain), Goa (India), and coastal Mozambique. Though they have never been as popular in the United States as in Great Britain, raves have been a fixture in San Francisco, Los Angeles, and New York since the early 1990s and some of techno music's strongest roots are in Detroit and Chicago.

Raves today are remarkably diversified. In fact, in places like London where raves have their deepest roots, the rave "scene" has fragmented into many successor sub-scenes, usually centered on divergent varieties of techno music,

such as Big Beat or Drum $'n Bass. Raves in the traditional sense—semi-legal and located in factories and outdoors—are rare. Nevertheless, rave's various offshoots all feature what I believe are the critical elements of rave: dance music, long duration, and ecstatic experience. As in London, most all-night dance parties in U.S. cities with a long tradition of raves have blended into the regular nightclub scene and are no longer called raves. However, in smaller cities and especially in the Midwest (Champion 1998) and the Southeast, raves in the traditional sense are alive and well.[4]

Demographically, most people who attend raves—often called "ravers"—are between the ages of 15 and 25, thus making rave a "youth" subculture (see Epstein 1998). The socioeconomic and ethnic backgrounds of ravers are not nearly so predictable as their ages. For example, early raves in Great Britain attracted people of various backgrounds, mostly from the working classes (Reynolds 1998a: 64). This socially mixed tradition continues today in most urban venues. At the other extreme, in the midwestern United States, for example, most ravers are white and middle class. Though slightly more males than females attend raves, the organizers, producers, and musicians behind the rave scene are predominantly male (McRobbie 1994: 168; Tomlinson 1998: 198; Reynolds 1998a: 274; Richard and Kruger 1998: 169).

Much of the academic discourse on raves focuses on the rave as a hedonistic, temporary escape from reality. Writers who support this position argue from a "neoconservative" (Foster 1985: 2), postmodern perspective that emphasizes the prominence of nostalgia and meaninglessness in modern amusements. Though I find this view of the rave both plausible and informative, I argue that it is incomplete because it ignores the poignant and meaningful spiritual experiences that ravers say they get from raves. In this article I attend to discourses in which ravers claim that raves are therapeutic. Based on these testimonials, the rave can be conceptualized as a form of healing comparable both to shamanic, ecstatic healing documented in ethnographies of small-scale non-western societies, and to spiritual experiences in modern western subcultures. Our understanding of the rave, previously approached from a cultural studies or communications studies perspective, might therefore benefit from a perspective attuned to anthropological discussions of shamanism and spirituality.

[In a two-page section "Notes on Method," Hutson notes that a substantial part of this article is based on Internet sources: email and posted testimonials. He discusses the strengths and weaknesses of such sources and concludes that although some distortion may be present, most such communication is genuine and similar to face-to-face communication, which can also be distorted. He also notes that anthropologists tend to take ethnographic information on religion very seriously if it comes from small-scale, preliterate societies but dismiss accounts of religious experience and healing from Western culture as "psychobabble." He argues that although critical analysis is essential, it misses opportunities for understanding.—Editors]

ACADEMIC AND "NATIVE" PERSPECTIVES ON THE RAVE: MEANING, SPIRITUALITY, HEALING

The postmodern approach views the rave as a culture of abandonment, disengagement, and disappearance. To Fredric Jameson (1984: 60, 64), postmodernism is typified by the disappearance of the subject. Lack of subjectivity at raves is said to be reflected in the style of dance (Rushkoff 1994: 121; McKay 1996: 110; Russell 1993: 128–129), the relative anonymity of the DJ (disc jockey), the nature of the music (Tagg 1994; Reynolds 1998a: 254; Melechi 1993: 34), the ego-reducing effects of Ecstasy (the most prominent drug at raves, known chemically as "3, 4 methylene-dioxy-metamphetamine" [MDMA] [Saunders 1995][5]), and the occurrence of raves in out-of-the-way places at times when the rest of the population sleeps (Melechi 1993: 33–34; Rietveld 1993). Ravers fill the void of subjectivity with a collage of fragments, the archetypal form of postmodernist expression (Jameson 1984: 64). Fragmentation is seen in the DJ's sampling of various past and present styles of music (Connor 1997: 207; Reynolds 1998a: 41–45). Such bricolage of older styles exemplifies Jameson's idea that, with the decline of the high modernist ideology of style, the producers of culture have nowhere to turn but the past (1984: 65). Informed by this perspective, some argue that the first raves in London were simulacra of past all-night disco extravaganzas at tourist nightclubs in the Balearic Islands of the Mediterranean (Reynolds 1998a: 58–59; Melechi 1993: 30; Russell 1993: 119). Finally, the rave experience is said to be hyperreal in the sense that a multiplicity of surfaces replaces singularity of depth (Jameson 1984: 62). Due to the sensory overload of throbbing music, exotic lighting, exhaustive dance, and sensation-stimulating drugs, the rave becomes a mega-surface that gratifies a relentless and intense desire for pleasure.

Reynolds (1998b: 90), an authoritative rave journalist, summarizes the postmodern interpretation elegantly: rave culture is "geared towards fascination rather than meaning, sensation rather than sensibility; creating an appetite for impossible states of hypersimulation." I find the postmodern approach deficient precisely because it fails to acknowledge meaning. Baudrillard believes that in the postmodern world of simulacra, meaning is exterminated (1988: 10): the joy of Disneyland, raves, and similar amusements lies not in their intellectual stimulation, but in their ability to satisfy, on a purely sensory level, our voracious appetite for surfaces. Once the surfaces are rendered meaningless, interpretation stops. As a result, such interpretations are not very deep (Bruner 1994) and certainly not "thick" (Geertz 1973). The studies cited above do not consider the complex ways in which symbols and surfaces connect, intersect, and/or conflict with the praxis of the real human beings who construct and consume them. Their lives are certainly not meaningless, yet those who write about the rave rarely solicit the voices and experiences of people who actually go to raves.

As an exemplar of the idea that the rave is indeed a very meaningful experience to many of those who attend, I quote a raver named Megan:

> The rave is my church. It is a ritual to perform. I hold it sacred to my perpetuality . . . we in the rave are a congregation—it is up to us to help each other, to help people reach heaven. . . . After every rave, I walk out having seen my soul and its place in eternity.[6]

Megan's statement exemplifies the religiosity of the rave. The analogy between rave and religion manifests itself at various sites. In Nashville a club known as the Church hosted raves by the name of "Friday Night Mass." Thornton (1995: 90) reports on a rave in Great Britain that was held inside a church; the DJs operated from the altar. In an introduction to rave culture Brian Behlendorf refers to the DJ as "high priest."[7] Saunders' London informants refer to the drug Ecstasy as the holy sacrament (Saunders 1995). One raver, commenting on a rave in Orlando, said that the DJ did not just make him boogey, he made him "see God."[8]

Noticing the similarities between raves and Christian spirituality, Matthew Fox and Chris Brain, sponsored by the Episcopal church in Sheffield, UK, have fused traditional services with raves in an effort to increase youth church membership (Reynolds 1998a: 242). Brain's services, known colloquially as "Planetary Mass," feature ambient house music, nightclub-style lighting, and video screens with computer generated graphics.[9] In the United States a similar hybrid ceremony, also called Planetary Mass, takes place in the Grace Cathedral, San Francisco (p. 316).

Robin Green and other ravers disapprove of organized religion's attempts to co-opt the rave experience. According to Green,

> raves should influence people metaphysically outside of the religious sphere. In actual effect, this is the creation of a . . . religion without theological foundation or unified expression.[10]

Another raver claimed

> [On Sunday morning after the rave] I see people headed off to church dressed in their Sunday best and I just have to smile because I know that last night on the dance floor I felt closer to God than their church with all its doctrines and double standards will ever bring them.[11]

Rave is thus seen by some as a more "direct" form of spirituality than organized religion.

The ravers' own explanation of why they interpret their experiences in spiritual terms centers around the concept of "technoshamanism." The term was coined by Fraser Clark, who helped organize two prominent London dance clubs, UFO and Megatripolis, and edited *Evolution,* an underground magazine focusing on the culture of house music in London (Rushkoff 1994: 121). Technoshamanism refers to the DJ's role as "harmonic navigator," "in charge of the group mood/mind." The DJ "senses when it's time to lift the mood, take it down, etc., just as the shaman did in the good ol' tribal days."[12] In other words, through a tapestry of mind-bending music, the DJ is said to take the dancers on an overnight journey, with one finger on the pulse of the adventure and the other on the turntables[13] (Rushkoff 1994: 123; Thornton 1995: 65; McKay 1996: 111). Though such a description of the technoshaman does not match all of Eliade's criteria for the definition of shamanism (the technoshaman, for example does not appear to control "helper spirits"), the DJ's mastery of the techniques of ecstasy qualify him/her as a shaman in the more general sense of Eliade's definition (Eliade 1964: 4–6).

With the help of the DJ's ecstatic techniques, ravers like Edward Lantz claim to enter "areas of consciousness not necessarily related to everyday 'real' world experiences."[14] Though Ecstasy enables altered states of consciousness, drugs are not necessary (Reynolds 1998a: 9). In this sense, raves are similar to the trance dances of the Dobe Ju/'hoansi, which do not involve any mind-altering substances. In both cases, altered states of consciousness are stimulated by a combination of upbeat rhythmic drumming, exhaustive all night dancing, and flickering light (Lee 1967; Katz 1982). One raver remarked that techno music itself (especially genres like Goa and the suitably named "trance") is enough to cause an ecstatic experience without even dancing: "It's the only music that lifts you out of your body without putting something down your throat first."[15] According to another raver, techno music returns to you "the human ability to dream while awake."[16] The experiences recorded by ravers in ecstasy, specifically flying, also recall shamanic experiences documented ethnographically. In one particular trip San Francisco promoter Mark Heley claims to have visited the dead and transformed into a puma and then an eagle (Rushkoff 1994: 140), recalling the type of peregrinations that shamans all over the world experience as part of initiation (Eliade 1964).

Much more than a fantasy simulacrum, the altered states of consciousness that are part of the technoshamanistic journey are said to heal: according to an anonymous raver, "Our means of healing and growth is ritual celebration, where we gather once in a while to expand our consciousness and celebrate life with rhythm and dance."[17] Ravers most often attest to healing of a psychological sort, as the above quote on consciousness expansion implies. The technoshamanistic journey is said to bring calm: "After the trip, when we finally arrive back home, the inner peace and contentment we so deeply desired settles our restlessness."[18] Raves restore "general feelings of happiness and grooviness . . . raving brings me up when I'm down."[19] Themes of self-empowerment are also common in raver's reflections on their journeys: according to raver Sean Case. "The goal of the techno journey is for people to see themselves without the crushing ego, to know the possibilities of the self."[20]

> It is through dance that I have found transcendence. Music has taught me to fly using wings I never knew I had. It is through music and dance that my soul is free to soar amongst the heavens . . . allowing a clearer vision of the world that I am creating.[21]

Because the rave experience is so often described in religious and spiritual terms, and because the type of healing is of the spirit as opposed to the body, I refer to the type of healing discussed above as "spiritual healing."

Raver testimony of "spiritual healing" also bears a family resemblance to experiences of evangelical conversion. There is a long history of evangelical conversion in North America, of which the exemplary form appeared in the British colonies during the Great Awakening of the 1740s. The testimony of Nathan Cole of Connecticut serves as an early example of Great Awakening conversions (Cole 1970). After hearing itinerant preacher George Whitefield, Cole felt doomed to Hell and endured two years of misery and inner turmoil. Finally, God appeared to Cole, precipitating an unearthly disembodiment: "Now while my soul was viewing God, my fleshy part was working imaginations and saw many things which I will omit to tell." After the moment of conversion, Cole writes, "My heart and soul were filled as full as they could hold with joy and sorrow: now I perfectly felt truth . . . and all the air was love." Other accounts of conversion show that those in crisis were not as lonely as Cole, receiving support from small, like-minded congregations (Calhoon 1994). Though evangelical conversion since the eighteenth century has become much more peripheral and, according to Brushman (1970: xi), "commonly disdained," the structure of conversion remains approximately the same. Ethnographers of southern Baptist communities Susan Harding (1987) and Carol Greenhouse (1986) note that, similar to Cole's crisis, a period of questioning accompanied by a sense of being "lost" often precedes the conversion. Conversion, which may take years or minutes, replaces emptiness with a therapeutic sense of comfort, meaning, and purpose.

Three aspects of Evangelical conversions like that of Cole resemble raver testimony: 1) raw, personal emotions of a spiritual nature, unstructured by the norms of the church; 2) out-of-body experience, sometimes involving hallucinations that bring the convert close to God; and 3) healing and mental hygiene experienced after conversion. Despite such resemblances there are two major differences between spiritual healing at raves and evangelical conversion. The first of these differences has to do with context. Despite the raw, personal emotion associated with evangelical healing, the conversion takes place in an institutionalized context. In the Great Awakening a clergy devoted to the spiritual revival's advancement placed conversion in a commanding intellectual and theological structure (Brushman 1970: 67). In Baptist communities of the 1980s conversion was contextualized through hell-fire-and-brimstone preaching (Harding 1987) and close attention to the scripture (Greenhouse 1987: 75). Furthermore, fundamentalists of the 1980s were part of a community that, by giving witness of God's grace to the unconverted, provided those in crisis with a normalizing structure. As I will demonstrate below, raves do have a doctrine, codified as "Peace, Love, Unity, Respect" (PLUR) which is reinforced by exemplary behavior at raves and testimonial witnessing on the Internet. Nevertheless, the institutional context of rave spirituality is not nearly as serious, perhaps because eternal salvation is not at stake. PLUR is a four-word slogan not nearly so well developed or thorough, as evangelical theology. Also, passive witnesses on the Internet cannot compare to ponderous, hell-fire-and-brimstone preaching nor the extended, face-to-face witnessing that characterizes evangelism.

The second difference has to do with the process of transformation. For evangelical Christians, a burdensome period of guilt and despair, characterized with deep intellectual questioning, precedes salvation and transformation and is triggered by a crisis. Though disillusionment with society often precedes the positive spiritual transformation at a rave, the process of transformation, which I will discuss below, is usually neither painful nor triggered by personal crisis. Also, conversion is such an important milestone for evangelicals that it is called a second birth. Though rave experiences are remarkable, they occur frequently and are not as biographically salient as birth itself.

PHYSIOLOGICAL AND SYMBOLIC PROCESSES OF HEALING

The previous section provided native testimony on technoshamanism and how the technoshamanistic voyage releases anxieties, builds self-empowerment, and brings peace and contentment. In this section I discuss physiological and symbolic processes that, though not described by ravers themselves, might also contribute to the "spiritual healing" that ravers claim to undergo.

Flashing lights, dancing, and repetitive percussion, each of which are prominent features of the rave, may physiologically produce altered states of consciousness. Walter and Walter (1949: 63) note that rhythmic light can cause visual sensations (color, pattern, or movement) unrelated to the stimulus, non-visual sensations of kinaesthetic (swaying, spinning, jumping, vertigo) and cutaneous (prickling, tingling) varieties, emotional and physiological experiences (fear, anger, disgust, confusion, fatigue, pleasure), hallucinations, epileptic seizures and "clinical psychopathic states." Lights that flash to the rhythm of the music and other elaborate visual effects, such as spinning lasers and wall projections of fractals, are frequent components of raves in both areas of my participant observation.

Dancing is an important physiological factor because it is a motor activity. Extended rhythmic dancing and bodily movement brings on physical exhaustion, vertigo, hyperventilation, and other physiological conditions that may alter consciousness (Lee 1967: 33; Rouget 1985: 118). Csikszentmihalyi (1975: 43) argues that dancing and other forms of play are intrinsically stimulating because they produce a holistic sensation of total involvement—a sensation that he calls "flow." Dance as flow merges the act with the awareness of the act, producing self-forgetfulness, a loss of self-consciousness, transcendence of individuality, and fusion with the world (p. 49).

With regard to repetitive percussion, Andrew Neher argues that trance states and unusual behavior observed ethnographically in ceremonies involving drums result primarily from the effects of rhythmic drumming on the central nervous system. Neher found observations from laboratory studies on the effects of rhythmic stimulation and accounts of stimulation from anthropological drum ceremonies and found that the responses, which included unusual perceptions and hallucinations, were comparable. Neher believes that stimulation is the result of auditory driving: that the sensory and motor areas of the brain not normally affected are activated through the stimulation of the sensory area being stimulated—in this case the ear. Neher notes that drums are most successful as auditory stimulants because the sound of the drum contains many frequencies. Because "different sound frequencies are transmitted along different nerve pathways in the brain," the sound of a drum should stimulate a larger area in the brain. Furthermore, drum beats with main rhythms accompanied by slightly different reinforcing rhythms produce the strongest responses. Under Neher's criteria, techno music would be extremely successful in promoting auditory driving because percussion is a major feature of techno and because techno tracks have at least three complementary rhythms.[22] In their own testimonies ravers state that music is a key to their journey.

Michael Harner (1990: 50–51) has seized upon Neher's study to support his claim that the drum and the rattle are the basic tool for evoking and maintaining altered states of consciousness. Other scholars question the universality of Neher's results. Gibert Rouget (1985), who reviewed an encyclopedic range of ethnographically documented ceremonies involving spirit possession, found that drums are not always used to initiate altered states of consciousness. This and the common observation that two people react very differently to the same music at the same event within the same culture lead Rouget to conclude that music does not have any straightforward physiological affect on consciousness. Rouget does not deny the importance of music; he simply cautions us not to generalize its specific effects. In considering Rouget's critique, it is important to remember that spirit possession is a specific altered state of consciousness not described by ravers. Nevertheless, none of the aspects discussed above—flashing light, dancing, music—is a necessary condition for altered states of consciousness. However, when combined, as at a rave, they are more likely to have an effect: "rhythmic stimulation in more than one sensory mode aids the response" (Neher 1962: 155).

The physiological interpretation does not explain the rave as a social event. If an altered state of consciousness is the only prerequisite to "spiritual healing," why do young people go to the trouble of attending raves when they could attain an ecstatic state more easily by staying at home and taking drugs? To begin to understand how raves might "heal"—how they create a framework for therapeutic spiritual transformations—requires close attention to the symbols surrounding the rave and embellishing ravers' descriptions of their voyages. Much of the symbolism has to do with idealized versions of small scale "primitive communities." One rave website is decorated with pictures of people wearing loincloths, headdresses, and bodypaint, and holding spears.[23] The official Ibiza rave website is cluttered with images of Native American masks.[24] Music is often described as "tribal," and one genre of rave music is called "jungle." At some raves, like those sponsored by the New Moon collective or the Gateway collective, pagan altars are set up, sacred images from "primitive" cultures decorate the walls, and rituals of cleansing are performed over the turntables and the dance floor.[25]

A second theme at raves is futurism. Renegade Records, which feature drum 'n bass producers Future Forces, claims to market "future beats for future people." Eklectic, a weekly San Francisco drum 'n bass club, subtitles itself "San Francisco Futurism," and decorates its fliers with what its organizers call "neo-Tokyo" fashion: women enhanced with space-age graffiti. The name of the DJ/producer/artist responsible for the neo-Tokyo style, UFO!, highlights a prevalent motif of futurism—outer space. Among the most common outer space icons, which range from planets to fantasy space ships to actual satellites and satellite dishes, is the friendly extra-terrestrial. Anthropomorphic, neotonized, with massive forehead and long, slender eyes angled together in "V" formation, this friendly martian icon appears in a range of places—T-shirts, fliers, music videos, album cover art—and is the symbol of drum 'n bass record label Liquid Sky. The rave scene is also futuristic in that it embraces advanced technology. Production of techno music is an almost entirely digital affair, requiring thousands of dollars of synthesizers, samplers, mixers, and computers. It is no coincidence that the wide variety of rave musics are referred to collectively as "techno" or "electronica." Ravers are also savvy Internet users who design websites, who engineer webcasts of live events, and whose attentions have been targeted directly by Internet firms such as Gomo mail and Eradio. Futurism also shows in the preference for sans seriph, machine-like fonts and abstract, geometric, digital imagery.

The juxtaposition of primitives and martians appears to exemplify the random, superficial play of postmodern cultural expression. However, I argue that the predominance of these two genres of symbolism—future and primitive—is

neither random nor meaningless. Both genres share a sense of distance from and disdain for the present age and reveal an attraction to alternative possibilities. Fondness for distant societies is in fact an explicit feature of rave discourse. Raver Jason Parsons yearns for "a memory of a time before cement cages and aloof societies; a humanity that was part of the world, not apart from it."[26] For raver Chris Newhard the journey involves reuniting with "the ancestors."[27] For others, the rave is about going back to ancient history (Rushkoff 1994: 120). According to raver Sean Casey,

> techno [music] brings us back to our roots . . . [it] sings to a very visceral ancient part of us deep down inside. It draws from the "reptilian" brain, past our egos and beckons us to dance with abandon.[28]

For just about everybody, the return to tribal roots is characterized by total unity and harmony, a "vibe" of collectivization.

Together, idealization of the past and interest in the future creates the incendiary combination of 1) what is seen as a model society (the past), and 2) the prospect of such a society's reenactment (the future). This combination recalls what Eliade (1960) has termed the "myth of eternal return": the nostalgic desire to return to an original, primordial time and place—a paradise. The blend of characteristics that informs the ravers' conception of the primitive experience— the destination of the technoshamanistic voyage—resembles many features of this primordial paradise. A paradise is a timeless land of perfect and total joy, a pre-sexual age of innocence where there is no social discord, no differentiation between the self and other.[29] There is little doubt that raves are joyful, even hyperjoyful. Raves are timeless in the sense that they are long and that they occur in the interstices—the "carnivalesque inversion" (Reynolds 1998a: 66)—of normal time, in that dark void where most of the population is asleep. Ravers describe how time stops.[30]

Perhaps the most important element of the raver's paradise is non-differentiation. Non-differentiation, unity, solidarity, and similar themes figure prominently in raver discourse. Explaining Unity, the third pillar of the rave motto PLUR (Peace Love Unity Respect), the mission statement of Cloudfactory, a San Francisco rave collective, states that

> we all share a lot in common, regardless of age, gender, race, [sexual] orientation, whatevah. We all need other people. Though we may have differences, we all arise from the same source.[31]

According to raver Mike Brown, you could have dance music and laser lighting, but it is not a rave unless it is unified.[32] In short, "We rave because boundaries must be broken."[33]

> What matters is the inclusive gestures that recognize the groove across cultures, whether technologically literate or aboriginal.[34]

Further statements about inclusiveness at raves indicate that transcendence of individual identity brings ravers to a therapeutic, non-differentiated state of being, in unity with the gods and the world.

> Once purified, you can join in the dance of the celestial beings within the kingdom of the ultimate and enjoy the freedom of existing anywhere.[35]

According to raver Charlene Ma, if a rave is successful, it all "melds into one cosmic soup and everything is one and you can't separate the music or the moves or which came first."[36] Drawing on quantum physics, an anonymous raver states that "the dancing gives a sense of oneness as we all become part of the same uncertainty wave equation."[37] Raver Alice Braley claims that

> The effect is to align the physical, mental, and emotional bodies with the oneness of All That Is. This results in a downflow of force from above . . . [which] causes vivification and definite illumination.[38]

Rushkoff (1994: 120) writes enthusiastically that ravers are "phase locked": by being on the same drugs, on the same nocturnal schedule, and under the same music, they have reached complete synchronicity. Organic and familial metaphors are also used to express the sense of unity and re-unification. The group of friends one makes at a rave is often referred to as a family.[39] To quote raver Jason Page,

> Throw yourself in the winds of transformation and sow the seeds for a new world—one where the family is together again, when people respect and care for each other as a community—an organism.

The sense of unity that ravers claim to attain resembles communitas (Turner 1967: 96): Raves blend homogeneity and comradeship in a moment in and out of time. Just as Turner wrote that communitas feeds the spirit, one raver claimed that raves nurture the soul.[40] The feeding of the spirit is what might make the rave so therapeutic. By crossing over into a communitas state, rave culture dissipates the tension of entering a world of wage slavery, underemployment, and shrinking opportunity. Thus, by manipulating symbols of tribalism, ravers enter communitas where they reaffirm what they say the world ought to be—liberation, freedom, union, communion, harmony, warmth, peace, love, family, euphoria, bliss, happiness, godliness, and health. They confront with renewed vigor what they say the world actually is—violence, fear, hatred, racism, poverty, injustice, hunger, greed, performance, achievement, competition, enterprise, judgment, division, comparison, differentiation, distinction, distraction, isolation, impotence, and alienation.[41] In other words, the rave, like most "authentic" rituals, successfully unifies the "ought" and the "is" through symbols and experience.

Communitas cannot be a permanent state, however, because structure and social differentiation are necessary to maintain the physical body. Without the allocation of roles and resources, the division of labor, the organized, restrained, rational considerations necessary to meet daily needs would not be met (Turner 1967, cited by Myerhoff 1974: 246). This may explain why few permanent raver communities exist, despite the abundant chatter about forming a new world (see below). One raver/DJ even recognizes the inevitability of the return to structure: "raves are good because they don't happen all the time."[42]

To complete the description and explanation of rave transformation, I would like to contrast the experiences described above with the very similar phenomenon of group consciousness induced at Grateful Dead concerts. Citing Victor Turner, Robert Sardiello (1994: 129–131) states that Grateful Dead concerts are secular rituals which "symbolically separate individuals in both space and time from their ordinary social lives." Both Deadheads (loyal fans of the Grateful Dead) and ravers refer to their events as escapes from reality. According to Anthony Pearson (1987: 419),

> large numbers of Deadheads report a psychic connection with the band, often reporting Jungianlike synchronicities and other esoteric phenomena in the concert setting.

The altered states of consciousness recounted by Deadheads, referred to alternatively as hypnosis and catharsis, seem quite similar to transformations described by ravers. Grateful Dead drummer Mickey Hart acknowledges these ecstatic states induced at concerts, stating "we've got transformation going on here" (quoted in Pearson 1987: 419).

Pearson notes that drug use is high at Grateful Dead concerts, but, as I argue with regard to similar drugs at raves, Pearson (p. 426) argues that drug use cannot be simply viewed as the cause of the cognitive experiences reported by Deadheads. Rather, he believes that the Grateful Dead concert experience is triggered by feelings of psychic connection between band and audience (see also Sardiello 1994: 128). Audience members often feel that the band played a particular song because of the way it relates to a specific problem or situation in their lives. Or, a poignant Grateful Dead lyric may simultaneously coincide with a fan's own, unrelated thought, causing the fan to assume a causal connection between the two. The connection between Deadhead and band recalls the shamanic connection between raver and DJ. Sardiello (pp. 124–126) adds a symbolic interpretation to Pearson's psychic explanation. Omnipresent symbols such as tie-dyed T-shirts and colorful icons of skeletons, roses, and dancing bears work to unify the audience and create a shared text with mythical and philosophical meaning. Though neither Sardiello nor Pearson discusses the physiological mechanisms I propose for altered states of consciousness among ravers, the symbolic aspects and ritual nature of Grateful Dead concerts closely resemble raves and produce a similar ethos of communality.

SUBCULTURAL CAPITAL

It is difficult to accept ravers' statements about non-differentiation, unity, and oneness because a certain "political economy" underlies the rave scene. Thornton (1995) points out in her ethnography of club cultures that, despite the mantras of unity and collectivity, there is noticeable selectivity and exclusivity in the rave scene, based on a scale of hipness. Unable to compete with adults for occupational status, but in many cases still supported by parents, young ravers derive self esteem by competing for what Thornton calls subcultural capital, a concept founded in Bourdieu's notions of cultural and symbolic capital (Bourdieu 1977, 1984). Hierarchies of prestige and standards of authenticity develop based on familiarity with the latest music, the latest slang, the latest fashions (Appadurai 1986: 44–45). Those who make a living from subcultures—connoisseurs of rave authenticity such as club owners, promoters, and professional DJs—must uphold such hierarchies of subcultural capital in order to be successful. For example, to attract the best crowd, a club owner must be selective about which DJs can perform and who can enter the club (Thornton 1995: 102–105). The resulting exclusivity conflicts with the language of unity. Even London's first raves, held at the club Shoom, were restricted to a small clique (including some celebrities), despite an ethos of love, peace, and unity (Reynolds, 1998a: 61). Though Thornton's research might not apply to the many raves organized outside the club scene and its selective door policies, it certainly demonstrates the presence of difference and distinction within the rave.

This contradiction between the egalitarian unity claimed by ravers and the hierarchical divisions documented by Thornton can be reconciled by conceptualizing the rave as a temporal process. I believe that the rave process can be understood as a sort of journey, a term which ravers also use to characterize their events. The distinctions of hipness that Thornton observes best characterize the behavior behind the *organization* of a rave—when decisions are made as to which DJs are given the chance to spin, who gets on the guest list of a club, or who gets invited to secretive events—and possibly at the *beginning* of raves—when bouncers might be selective about who they let into a club and when egos may interfere with the proper vibe of Peace, Love, Unity, and Respect (PLUR). To repeat, many of these distinctions only pertain to raves held in nightclubs. After these distinctions have been made and the technoshamanistic journey progresses, remaining differences are slowly eliminated through dance, drugs, and other rituals that transform structures of subcultural capital into antistructure. Specifically, egos can be shed and inhibitions erased by MDMA, which is renowned as a harmony inducing drug (Saunders 1995; McRobbie 1995; Redhead 1993). Also, ravers suggest that dancing to trance music can bind communities together.[43] Similarly, Rietveld states that you can lose yourself in "the anonymity of fellow ravers and in blinding music" (1993: 69). Dance, as a technique of ecstasy, becomes a portal to transformation.

Maintaining the hypothesis that the rave experience is much like Eliade's myth of the eternal return, I believe that the rave journey can be fruitfully compared with a classic journey in the anthropological literature. The pilgrimage to Wirikuta made by the Huichol of Mexico is interpreted by Barbara Myerhoff (1974) as an enactment of Eliade's myth. On their journeys the Huichol and the ravers become one with the world. Barriers between young and old, male and female, and leader and follower are broken. A specific Huichol ritual for achieving oneness in which pilgrims connect with each other by each tying a knot on a string and then burning the string has a parallel in a ritual performed at raves sponsored by the New Moon collective and Gateway collective. At these raves the organizers set up an altar on the dance floor and each raver contributes an item to the altar. The altar becomes an objectification of the community and in contributing to the altar, the raver disconnects from the self and connects to the whole. Also, Wirikuta is a primordial place of origins that is very similar to the primitive tribal village described by ravers. Both destinations are viewed as places where ancestors dwell and places of origins from which human history has diverged. In the case of the Huichol the distinction between human and divine is erased. The rave scene also contains references to identify with gods: the DJ is referred to as god[44] and ravers can become gods, as in the Keoki track "Caterpillar,"[45] the name of which appropriately signifies the possibility of metamorphosis. Also, ravers claim to see the gods at the end of their journey and come closer to the gods than any other worldly experience could bring them. Finally, the journey to the lost homeland is said to bring positive spiritual transformations in both groups. Like those who return from raves with positive spiritual transformations, Huichol who endure the peyote hunt achieve unity and community, their highest religious goal, and are reassured through visions (Myerhoff 1974) that the world is a happy place. According to one raver, the "project" of the rave journey is also to visualize a world whose people are happy and healthy.[46] In sum, both ravers and the Huichol receive hopeful visions[47] of why life is good in the midst of disjointed times.

THE RAVE IN CONTEXT

The rave subculture also resembles other North American subcultures that emphasize spiritual healing and alternative spirituality, such as followers of New Age Channels, the Rainbow People, and cults like the Divine Light Mission. A major point of social or academic commentary on therapeutic activities like channeling and attending raves is the dynamic between individual healing and social improvement. The consciousness movement, of which channeling is one of the most controversial offshoots, is said to have arisen "out of a pervasive dissatisfaction with the quality of personal relations" (Lasch 1979: 27). An individualist and privatist movement emphasizing personal improvement, the consciousness movement "advises people not to make too large an investment in love and friendship, to avoid excessive dependence on others" (p. 27). Channels, who use altered states of consciousness to contact spirits or to "experience spiritual energy from other times and dimensions" (Brown 1997: viii), are also intensely individualistic, sharing a deep mistrust of churches and society as a whole (p. 123). Channels, like the ravers quoted above, feel that their spirituality is more authentic than the spirituality of organized religion. However, the channels' resistance to community organizations exists only on a local, pragmatic level. The concept of a global community, an abstract world universal enough to transcend race, class, and nationality, is a goal toward which many channels claim passionate commitment (p. 124). The Internet has become the primary locus for such community building among channels, and the sense of togetherness fostered by the net is deeply felt (p. 125). However, Brown adds a patent critique of this form of virtual community: channels do not "walk their talk." They fail to address any of the practical, day-to-day concerns of an actual community, such as who will supply water, run hospitals, capture criminals, and collect garbage.

Just like new age channels, many ravers appear to be committed to a global village blind to age, race, sex, and class. One raver desires "that through the rave ritual we can use technology to bring the people of the world together in peace by means of dance."[48] According to raver Robert Jesse, "during our shared moments of ecstatic joy, we explore who we are and we advance visions of our harmonious planet."[49] Despite the rhetoric of communal harmony, ravers, like channels, do not work toward creating such a community. Aside from

> a few disparate groups . . . [demonstrating] for the right to carry on getting out of their heads and dancing to weird music on weekends (McKay 1996: 104),

there is almost no political activism in the rave scene. Ravers do little more than attend late night and early morning parties in out-of-the-way places;[50] visions of future unity and global communities remain visions (Hesmondhalgh 1995). When ravers say that "We can only improve the society if we improve ourselves first,"[51] or that "consciousness unfolds and expands itself slowly from the individual to a group awareness,"[52] they sound very much like the channel who said

> We have to have inner communication to figure out who we are first, then those communities that we want can really happen (Brown 1997: 124).

The Rainbow Family is also dedicated to the creation of a cooperative, egalitarian, and utopian community (Niman 1997). However, whereas rave and new age utopias remain virtual, the Rainbow Family creates real, though temporary, utopias at their various national and regional Gatherings. Usually over the course of a month the Rainbow Family works to transform park land into actual communities with fully functional infrastructures (kitchens, latrines, infirmaries, childcare). In such a "Temporary Autonomous Zone," everybody is welcome, from yuppies to the homeless, and no money is required. The Rainbow Family enacts a working model of multiculturalism, a society whose differences are celebrated and unity achieved (Niman 1997: 99).

Perhaps at the far end of the spectrum of community building we find cults such as the Divine Light Mission, whose members completely renounce previous beliefs, communities (friends, family), and jobs and devote their lives to the preservation and outreach of their cult (Galanter 1989). Though these communities are often totalizing, raves and cults have some things in common. Cults involve spiritual highs and altered states of consciousness, and are highly popular among youths reacting against the uncertainties of the transition to adult society (Hexham and Poewe 1986). As in the rave, the experience of community is a cornerstone of the cult experience. In his study of the Divine Light Mission Galanter (1989: 10) noticed that the more people affiliated themselves with the cult, the more relief they received. Relief reinforces the members' involvement in the group and attachment to the group's principles. However, Galanter (pp. 5–7) argues that psychological processes cause the cult members to affiliate with the cult community, whereas I have made an explicitly cultural case for the positive transformations ravers say they undergo. Furthermore, the process of group attachment in cults is circular and self-reinforcing, so that involvement in the cult grows to dominate the cult members' lives. In contrast, ravers detach from their "group" when the rave event comes to an end in the early morning. Though such regular detachment from raves might be expected to produce frustrated feelings of interruption, testimonies of ravers instead reveal satisfaction and excitement about reuniting under the same principles of PLUR the next weekend. Perhaps permanent utopias are not viable, as Turner and others suggest, and that the superficiality of rave "community" reflects that condition.

Niman's ethnography of the Rainbow Family highlights a second commentary. Like ravers, the Rainbow Family has conscious roots in the revival of primitivism, paganism, and tribalism (1997: 37). Those who attend Rainbow Gatherings often mimic and alter Native American culture and religious rituals, believing that what they contrive is the real thing. Teepees, sweat lodges, pipe ceremonies, medicine bags, and feathers are central features of the gathering. Rather than dismissing such "fakelore" as inauthentic Indian culture, it might be better, to call it simply Rainbow culture (Niman 1997). Such a move puts us in line with Bruner (1994), who argues with Baudrillard that scholars should not criticize authenticity in the sense of fidelity to an original model because all cultures are caught in a process of copying and reinventing themselves. Instead, scholars should attend to authenticity as it is constructed by informants, particularly when competing segments of society call it into question in the context of uneven power relations (p. 408). With regard to power relations, the Rainbow practice of borrowing Native American customs might reflect a form of cultural imperialism that has powerfully negative consequences, and it is on this basis that a critique of authenticity should be considered. As Niman cogently argues, Rainbow impersonations of Indians trivialize Native American practices such that these practices lose their force. The impersonations consequently undermine attempts by Native Americans to affirm their own identities and thwart legal battles to preserve religious freedom. Though ravers also use Native American symbols, I argue that they are not as complicit in the unintentional cannibalization and trivialization of Native American culture because fakelore is comparatively limited within rave culture and located in highly fragmented contexts. The spiritual aspect of raves does not include conscious mimicry of Native American ceremonies. Unlike some New Age healing procedures, for example, rave rituals do not imitate Native American ceremonies, dress, orations, or props. I am aware of no raves that use Native paraphernalia like sweat lodges or medicine bags. I know of no DJs who, like new age shamans, take Native American names. Fakelore is most often limited to the use of Native American-inspired icons in two-dimensional, decorative contexts, sometimes tongue-in-cheek, and often heavily diluted by other motifs, futuristic and otherwise.

CONCLUSION

The critique of fakelore foregrounds a key question of this article: whether or not the technoshaman is a real shaman or just a plastic medicine man. Some commentators see the rave as a meaningless simulacrum. For some young people, raves are a form of entertainment not taken as seriously as a religious experience. Nevertheless, this does not eliminate the fact that for many people, the rave is spiritual and highly meaningful (Reynolds 1998a: 9). Based on the testimonials presented here, raves increase self esteem, release fears and anxieties, bring inner peace, and improve consciousness, among other things. When an informant claims that "Last night a DJ saved my life," it is reasonable to accept that this is "spiritual healing." I have elucidated the ritual framework for this therapeutic effect by attending to physiological factors as well as symbols and metaphors that dominate rave discourse. With the help of the DJ, ravers embark on an overnight journey to a primitive paradise where individuality is left behind and communitas is achieved. At their destination ravers claim to find a world of harmony, equality, and communality; a place similar to humanity in its early tribal stage, according to ravers, but diametrically opposed to the modern world. Reynolds (1998b: 86) points out that the myth of unity is just a myth; indeed, as seen in the previous section, ravers can be criticized for not following through on their goals of community building. But as the Huichol example makes clear, myths are powerful. The enactment of the myth of eternal return—a symbolic return to the primordial place where life is as it should be—invigorates the ravers, allowing them to face the sobriety and te-

dium of daily life, at least until the next rave. The rave experience might be highly symbolic, but these symbols are fashioned and imbued with such meaning that they far surpass the empty, touristic, simulacra that some academic commentators consider them to be.

NOTES

Acknowledgments. I would like to thank Byron Hamann, Megan Mooney, Michael Brown, Beth Conklin, and James Hutson for commenting on this paper. A preliminary version was read at the 97th Annual Meeting of the American Anthropological Association, December 2–6, 1998. Philadelphia.

1. David King, "Why 'Goa Trance?'" in www.third-eye.org.uk/trip/why.html [Internet]. 7 May 1997 [cited 22 October 1997].

2. Techno music includes various forms of pre-recorded dance music mixed by disc jockeys, though it can be produced live. Electronica is a more recent term coined by U.S. media and record companies. The various forms on sub-genres of techno change rapidly: many of the genres that were popular five years ago no longer exist or have evolved into new genres with their own names. Some of the genres of techno that were popular at the time of my research include house, trance, drum 'n bass, speed garage, trip hop, and big beat.

3. For an insider definition, see Brian Behlendorf, "The official alt.raveFAQ," in www.hyperreal.com/raves/altraveFAQ.html# [Internet]. May 8, 1994 [cited 3 November 1997]. Hyperreal is the largest and oldest Internet resource for rave music and culture.

4. Though similar to early 1990s raves, these late 1990s raves have many of their own peculiar features, as Champion (1998) elegantly documents.

5. See also Mike Brown, "Techno Music and Raves FAQ," in http://www.hyperreal.com/-mike/pub/altraveFAQ.html [Internet]. 1 December 1995 [cited 7 November 1996].

6. Megan, "Coup d'Academe.html," in www.hyperreal.org/raves/spirit/ [Internet]. [cited 16 November 1997].

7. Brian Behlendorf, "The official alt.raveFAQ," in www.hyperreal.com/raves/altraveFAQ.html# [Internet]. 8 May 1994 [cited 3 November 1997].

8. Anonymous, "DJ_Journeys.html," in www.hyperreal.org/raves/spirit/technoshamanism [Internet]. 29 February 1996 [cited 2 December 1997].

9. Bob, "Rave_Mass.html," in www.hyperreal.org/raves/spirit/culture [Internet]. 28 November 1995 [cited 10 December 1997].

10. Robin Green, No title. In www.hyperreal.org/raves/spirit/history [Internet]. [cited 4 January 1998].

11. "Beautiful_Visions.html," in www.hyperreal.org/spirit/vibes [Internet]. [cited 17 November 1997].

12. "Fraser Clark, "Technoshamanism_Definitions.html," in www. hyperreal.org/raves/spirit/technoshamanism [Internet]. 24 May 1995 [cited 8 December 1997].

13. Brian Behlendorf, "The official alt.raveFAQ," in www. hyperreal.com/raves/altraveFAQ.html# [Internet]. 8 May 1994 [cited 3 November 1997], and Anonymous, "Perfect_ Party.html," in www.hyperreal.org/raves/spirit/hopeful [Internet]. [cited 16 November 1997].

14. Edward Lantz, "Otherworlds_Experience," in www.hyperreal. org/raves/spirit/technoshamanism [Internet]. [Cited 2 December 1997].

15. Zazgooeya, "Why 'Goa Trance?'" in www.third-eye.org.uk/ trip/why.html [Internet]. [cited 24 October 1997].

16. Jake Barnes, "Why 'Goa Trance?'" in www.third-eye.org.uk/ trip/why.html [Internet]. [cited 24 October 1997].

17. Omananda@geocities.com, "Goa trance," in www.hyperreal. org/raves/spirit/technoshamanism [Internet]. 16 May 1993 [cited 22 November 1997].

18. Omananda@geocities.com, "Goa trance," in www.hyperreal. org/raves/spirit/technoshamanism [Internet]. 16 May 1993 [cited 22 November 1997].

19. Noah   Raford,   "Dance_for_tomorrow.html,"   in   www. hyperreal.org/raves/spirit/hopeful [Internet]. [cited 11 January 1998].

20. Sean Casey, "Techno_and_raving.html." in www.hyperreal. org/raves/spirit/technoshamanism [Internet]. 28 December 1994 [cited 10 December 1997].

21. Glenn Fajardo, "Dance_to_Transcendance.html," in www. hyperreal.org/raves/spirit/hopeful [Internet]. 15 February 1997 [cited 11 January 1998].

22. Usually, snare drum, base drum, cymbal, and often keyboard and synthetic bass each contribute separate but aligned rhythms. Bass drum usually supplies the main rhythm.

23. Glenn Fajardo, "Dance_to_Transcendance.htm," in www. hyperreal.org/raves/spirit/hopeful [Internet]. 15 February 1997 [cited 11 January 1998].

24. See the Ibiza website at www.the-tribe.com/main.html [Internet]. [cited 7 November 1997].

25. Ann, "The New Moon Altar," in www.hyperreal.org/raves/ newmoon/altar [Internet]. August 1997 [cited 22 October 1997].

26. Jason Parsons, "Vibe.Tribe.html," in www.hyperreal.org/raves/ spirit/hopeful [Internet]. 23 August 1996 [cited 4 January 1997].

27. Niehls Mayer, "Burning Man 95-Nevada.html," in www. hyperreal.org/raves/spirit/testimonials [Internet]. 27 September 1995 [cited 17 November 1997].

28. Sean Casey, "Techno_and_raving.htm," in www.hyperreal.org/ raves/spirit/technoshamanism [Internet]. 28 December 1994 [cited 10 December 1997].

29. The rave might even compare to the primordial state of being in the womb, where maturity, individuation, and separation have not yet occurred. The rave also matches the sensory experience of being in the womb. Raves are dark, humid (due to mist makers), and warm (due to sweating dancers), while the dance beat replicates the mother's heartbeat.

30. Jason Parsons, "Vibe.Tribe.html," in www.hyperreal.org/raves/ spirit/hopeful [Internet]. 23 August 1996 [cited 4 January 1997].

31. Brad Finley, 1995. "We are all connected," in www.cloudfactory.org [Internet]. 12 December 1995 [cited 2 December 1997].

32. Mike Brown, "Techno Music and Raves FAQ," in http// www.hyperreal.com/-mike/pub/altraveFAQ.html [Internet]. 1 December 1995 [cited 7 November 1996].

33. Salami and Komotion International, "Why you are here," in www.cloudfactory.org [Internet]. 12 December 1995 [cited 2 December 1997].

34. A. Lopez, 1994. "Techno_Subculture.html. in www.hyperreal. org/raves/spirit/technoshamanism [Internet]. 27 December 1994 [cited 22 October 1997].

35. Omananda@geocities.com. 1993. "Goa trance," in www. hyperreal.org/raves/spirit/technoshamanism [Internet]. 16 May 1993 [cited 22 November 1997].

36. Charlene Ma, "Telepathic message," in www.hyperreal.org/ raves/spirit/technoshamanism [Internet]. 19 September 1996 [cited 3 November 1997].

37. Lee, "Physics_and_raving.html," in www.hyperreal.org/raves/ spirit/technoshamanism [Internet]. 12 May 1995 [cited 10 December 1997].

38. Alice Braley, "House Music and Planetary Healing," in www.cloudfactory.org [Internet]. 12 December 1995 [cited 2 December 1997].

39. Jason Page, Untitled, in DCRaves listserv [Listserv]. 17 November 1997 [cited 13 November 1997]. Available at DCRaves@American.edu.

40. Omananda@geocities.com, "Goa trance," in www.hyperreal. org/raves/spirit/technoshamanism [Internet]. 16 May 1993 [cited 22 November 1997].

41. All of these terms appear in raver characterizations of the two worlds.

42. Interview conducted November 1997.

43. Erich Schneider, "Technoshamanism_Definitions.html: Why don't we start with a definition," in www.hyperreal.org/ raves/spirit/technoshamanism [Internet]. 24 May 1995 [cited 8 December 1997].

44. See liner notes in Doc Martin. 1994. *UrbMix Volume I: Flammable Liquid.* Planet Earth compact disk P50105-2.

45. Superstar DJ Keoki, 1995. *Caterpillar.* Moonshine Music compact disk MM 88419.

46. Robert Jesse, "The Monk in Europe," in www.hyperreal.org/raves/spirit/testimonials/ [Internet]. 16 May 1993 [cited 22 October 1997].

47. Anonymous, "Hopeful visions," in www.hyperreal.org/raves/spirit/hopeful [Internet]. [cited 16 November 1997].

48. *Cyberpun@wam.umd.edu* "Technopagan_Raveprayer.html," in www.hyperreal.org/raves/spirit/technoshamanism [Internet]. 28 December 1994 [cited 3 November 1997].

49. Robert Jesse. "The Monk in Europe," in www.hyperreal.org/raves/spirit/testimonials/ [Internet]. 16 May 1993 [cited 22 October 1997].

50. Most collectives, such as the New Moon Collective, San Francisco (www.hyperreal.org/raves/newmoon), Daydream Collective, Eugene OR (www.hyperreal.org/raves/daydream), Friends and Family collective, San Francisco (www.basestation.com/fnf), and Catalyst Effusion, Toronto (announced on an email message posted to the DCRaves listserv, 18 November 1997), in fact do nothing more than organize parties.

51. Salami and Komotion International, "Why you are here," in www.cloudfactory.org [Internet]. 12 December 1995 [cited 2 December 1997].

52. Omananda@geocities.com, "Goa trance," in www.hyperreal.org/raves/spirit/technoshamanism [Internet]. 16 May 1993 [cited 22 November 1997].

53. DeZKLR, "Positively Deep," in DCRaves listserv [List-serv]. 9 November 1997 [cited 1 December 1997]. Available at DCRaves@American.edu.

REFERENCES CITED

Appadurai, Arjun. 1986. *The social life of things: Commodities in cultural perspective.* Cambridge: Cambridge University Press.

Baudrillard, Jean. 1988. *America.* London: Verso.

Bourdieu, Pierre. 1977. *Outline of a theory of practice.* Cambridge: Cambridge University Press.

———. 1984. *Distinction: A social critique of the judgment of taste.* Cambridge MA: Harvard University Press.

Brown, Michael F. 1997. *The channeling zone: American spirituality in an anxious age.* Cambridge MA: Harvard University Press.

Bruner, Edward M. 1994. Abraham Lincoln as authentic reproduction: A critique of postmodernism. *American Anthropologist* 96(2): 397–415.

Brushman, Richard, ed. 1970. *The Great Awakening: Documents on the revival of religion, 1740–1745.* New York: Atheneum.

Calhoon, Robert. 1994. The evangelical persuasion. In *Religion in a revolutionary age,* ed. R. Hoffman and P. Albert. Charlottesville: University Press of Virginia.

Champion, Sarah. 1998. Fear and loathing in Wisconsin. In *The clubcultures reader,* ed. S. Redhead, with D. Wynne and J. O'Connor. Oxford: Blackwell.

Cole, Nathan. 1970[1741]. Conversion: The spiritual travels of Nathan Cole. In *The Great Awakening: Documents on the revival of religion, 1740–1745,* ed. R. Brushman. New York: Atheneum.

Connor, Steve. 1997. *Postmodernist culture: An introduction to theories of the contemporary,* 2d ed. London: Blackwell.

Csikszentmihalyi, Mihalyi. 1975. Play and intrinsic rewards. *Journal of Humanistic Psychology* 15(3): 41–63.

Danforth, Loring. 1989. *Firewalking and religious healing: The Anastenaria of Greece and the American firewalking movement.* Princeton NJ: Princeton University Press.

Dery, Mark. 1994. Flame wars. In *Flame wars: The discourse of cyberculture,* ed. M. Dery. Durham NC: Duke University Press.

Dibbell, Julian. 1994. A rape in cyberspace: or, how an evil clown, a Haitian trickster spirit, two wizards, and a cast of dozens turned a database into a society. In *Flame wars: The discourse of cyberculture,* ed. M. Dery. Durham NC: Duke University Press.

Eliade, Mircea. 1960. The yearning for paradise in primitive tradition. In *Myth and mythmaking,* ed. H. A. Murray. New York: Braziller.

———. 1964. *Shamanism: Archaic techniques of ecstasy.* Princeton NJ: Princeton University Press.

Epstein, Jonathan S. 1998. Introduction: Generation X, youth culture, and identity. In *Youth culture: Identity in a postmodern world,* ed. J. Epstein. Oxford: Blackwell.

Fischer, Michael M. K. 1999. Worlding cyberspace: Toward a critical ethnography in time, space, and theory. *Critical anthropology now: Unexpected contexts, shifting constituencies, changing agendas.* ed. George E. Marcus. Santa Fe NM: School of American Research Press.

Foster, Hal. 1985. *Recodings.* Port Townsend WA: Bay Press.

Galanter, Marc. 1989. *Cults: Faith, healing, and conversion.* New York: Oxford University Press.

Geertz, Clifford. 1973. Thick description: Toward an interpretive theory of culture. In *The interpretation of cultures.* New York: Basic Books.

Gotcher, J. Michael, and Ellen Kanervo. 1997. Perceptions and uses of electronic mail. *Social Science Computer Review* 15(2): 145–158.

Greenhouse, Carol J. 1986. *Praying for justice.* Ithaca NY: Cornell University Press.

Hakken, David. 1999. *Cyborg@cyberspace?* New York: Routledge.

Harding, Susan F. 1987. Convicted by the Holy Spirit: The rhetoric of fundamental. Baptist Conversion. *American Ethnologist* 14(1): 167–181.

Harner, Michael. 1990. *The way of the shaman.* New York: Harper and Row.

Hesmondhalgh, David. 1995. Technoprophecy: A response to Tagg. *Popular Music* 14(2): 261–263.

Hexham, Irving, and Karla Poewe. 1986. *Understanding cults and new religions.* Grand Rapids MI: William Beerdsman.

Jameson, Fredric. 1984. Postmodernism, or the cultural logic of late capitalism. *New Left Review* (196): 53–92.

Joralemon, Donald. 1990. The selling of the shaman and the problem of informant legitimacy? *Journal of Anthropological Research* 46: 105–118.

Katz, Richard. 1982. Accepting "boiling energy." *Ethos* 10(4): 344–368.

Lasch, Christopher. 1979. *The culture of narcissism: American life in an age of diminishing expectations.* New York: W. W. Norton.

Lee, Richard. 1967. Trance cure of the !Kung Bushman. *Natural History* 76(9): 31–37.

Marcus, George E., and Michael M. K. Fisher. 1986. *Anthropology as cultural critique: An experimental moment in the human sciences.* Chicago IL: University of Chicago Press.

McKay, George. 1996. *Senseless acts of beauty: Cultures of resistance since the sixties.* London: Verso.

McRobbie, Angela. 1994. *Postmodernism and popular culture.* London: Routledge.

Melechi, Antonio. 1993. The ecstasy of disappearance. In *Rave off: Politics and deviance in contemporary youth culture.* ed. Steve Redhead. Aldershot: Avebury.

Myerhoff, Barbara. 1974. *Peyote hunt: The sacred journey of the Huichol Indians.* Ithaca NY: Cornell University Press.

Neher, Andrew. 1962. A physiological explanation of unusual behavior in ceremonies involving drums. *Human Biology* 4: 151–160.

Niman, Michael I. 1997. *People of the rainbow: A nomadic utopia.* Knoxville: University of Tennessee Press.

Pearson, Anthony. 1987. The Grateful Dead phenomenon: An ethnomethodological approach. *Youth and Society* 18(4): 418–432.

Redhead, Steve. 1993. The politics of ecstasy. In *Rave off: Politics and deviance in contemporary youth culture,* ed. Steve Redhead. Aldershot: Avebury.

Reynolds, Simon. 1998a. *Generation ecstasy: Into the world of techno and rave culture.* Boston MA: Little, Brown and Company.

———. 1998b. Rave culture: Living dream or living death? In *The clubcultures reader,* ed. Steve Redhead, with D. Wynne and J. O'Connor. Oxford: Blackwell.

Richard, Birgit, and Heinz Hermann Kruger. 1998. Ravers' paradise?: German youth cultures in the 1960s. In *Cool places: Geographies of youth cultures,* ed. Tracey Skelton and Gill Valentine. London: Routledge.

Rietveld, Hillegonda. 1993. Living the dream. In *Rave off: Politics and deviance in contemporary youth culture,* ed. Steve Redhead. Aldershot: Avebury.

Rouget, Gilbert. 1985. *Music and trance.* Chicago IL: University of Chicago Press.

Rushkoff, Douglas. 1994. *Cyberia: Life in the trenches of hyperspace.* New York: Harper Collins.

Russell, Kristian. 1993. Lysergia suburbia. In *Rave off: Politics and deviance in contemporary youth culture,* ed. Steve Redhead. Aldershot: Avebury.

Saunders, Nicholas. 1995. *Ecstasy and the dance culture.* London: Turnaround.

Sardiello, Robert. 1994. Secular rituals in popular culture: A case for Grateful Dead concerts and Dead Head identity. In *Adolescents and their music,* ed. Jonathan S. Epstein. New York: Garland Publishing.

Tagg, Philip. 1994. From refrain to rave: the decline of figure and the rise of ground. *Popular Music* 13(2): 209–222.

Thornton, Sarah. 1995. *Club cultures: Music media and subcultural capital.* Cambridge: Polity Press.

Tomlinson, Lori. 1998. "This ain't no disco" . . . or is it? Youth culture and the rave phenomenon. In *Youth culture: Identity in a postmodern world,* ed. J. Epstein. Oxford: Blackwell.

Turkle, Sherry. 1995. *Life on the screen.* New York: Simon and Schuster.

Turner, Victor. 1967, *The ritual process: Structure and anti-structure.* Chicago IL: Aldine.

Walter, V. J., and W. G. Walter. 1949. The central effects of rhythmic sensory stimulation. *Electroencephalography and Clinical Neurophysiology* 1: 57–86.

"The Night I Got the Holy Ghost . . .": Holy Ghost Narratives and the Pentecostal Conversion Process

Elaine J. Lawless

"The Night I Got the Holy Ghost . . ." by Elaine J. Lawless, *Western Folkore* 47 (1988), 1–20. Copyright © 1988 California Folklore Society.

In this essay, Elaine Lawless explores the religious experience of women in "Oneness" Pentecostal churches. One element of these churches is that conversion requires that worshipers become filled with the Holy Ghost. Those hoping to receive the Holy Ghost "tarry" at the alter—that is, they move forward during the church service and engage in fervent prayer until they fall into a trance, stretching out their arms, crying, shouting, and moaning.

One necessary component of these trances is glossolalia, "speaking in tongues." Glossolalia is a common feature of some religious trances and is known from many religious traditions. During glossolalia, individuals appear to lose control of their voices and speak nonsense syllables in the pattern of their language. "Oneness" Pentecostalists take a particular passage from Acts in the Bible as the source for their belief that true conversion requires "speaking in tongues." They and some other Christians claim that people experiencing glossolalia are speaking in a foreign or ancient language. However, no objective study has ever shown this to be the case.

In addition to describing the religious trances of believers, Lawless notes that church members' stories of their religious experiences all follow a similar pattern. Such narratives focus on experiences leading up to the trance and on feelings afterward but include very little information about the trance itself. She speculates that these stories are an integral part of church membership. Because they follow a particular form, they confirm each individual's proper religious experience and shape the experience of the newcomer. In many cultures, a trance experience is desirable yet inspires both awe and fear. As in other societies, the narratives provide a framework within which individuals can have a predictable and controllable religious experience.

As you read, consider these questions:

1. Why are conversion rituals and narratives important?
2. What are the main components of a "Holy Ghost" service?
3. What does it mean to "get the Holy Ghost"?

In a typical Pentecostal religious service in the central and southern states, a female member of the congregation might stand during the testimony slot of the service and give the following testimony:

> *Tonight I'm glad I know the Lord*
> *And glad he's kept me all these years*
> *I've walked with the Lord forty-eight years*
> *I've been saved*
> *Been covered with the precious Holy Ghost.*
> *Since the Fourth of July, forty-eight years*
> *Since I received the Holy Ghost*
> *Since I tarried long and hard*
> *Since that blessed spirit*
> *Swept over me*
> *Covered me*
> *Since I was covered with the precious Holy Ghost.*
> *I'm so glad for the peace and the power*
> *Because I know it makes no difference*
> *What comes our way*
> *He can provide our needs.*
> • • •
> *When I was out in sin*
> *I was miserable.*
> *But you know when I found the Lord*
> *I found peace and joy*
> *I was so glad when my sister-in-law said to me*
> *Said, "Why don't you go to church with us tonight."*
> *You know, I went that night*
> *And I really got conviction*
> *The Lord really tugged at my heart*
> *And that was Wednesday night.*
> *On Saturday night, I went back again*
> *And I got saved, Hallelujah.*
> *I found the Lord*

> *And he came right into my heart*
> *Filled my soul*
> *Let me know*
> *He'd be there for me.*
> *You know, that's the happiest time of my life.*
> *When I found him.*
> *Found the love and joy and peace*
> *That he bestows*
> *Down inside*
> *Right in our hearts.*[1]

Similarly, while sitting at the dinner table with family and friends, another woman might be heard telling the following story:

> Well, I can't remember who the man was who was holding the revival, but it was the last night and they said, "Now, if you've come all of this time just come forth tonight. This may be the night you'll receive the Holy Ghost." And I was kind of disgusted like and I thought: I'll go because it is the last night and if the Lord comes I'm not ready. And I went up and kneeled down. Then I really honestly prayed, you know, and all at once I felt this glow just move into me, you know [gestures with arms extended, makes swooping gesture to indicate the glow moving into her body], and I just, if I ever shouted in my life, it was that night and I was sitting straight on the floor, you know, and then I *knew* I had the baptism.

Both of these accounts are testimonies about the women's experience with the Holy Ghost; in some ways they are narrative reenactments of the conversion experience and of speaking in tongues. The narratives are typical of the kind of re-counting of religious experience one might hear both in the context of a Pentecostal service and in the religious community at large. For Pentecostals who have determined that a Holy Ghost encounter, complete with tongue-speaking, is a mandatory component of conversion and salvation, the narrative accounts of that experience have come to constitute an important function in the complete conversion process. Further, both the performance of the conversion ritual and the narrative accounts of that conversion serve to guide the religious experience of subsequent conversions.

This examination of traditional religious experience and speech is based on work with southern and midwestern Anglo-American Pentecostals who are called "Oneness" or "Jesus Only" Pentecostals because they do not acknowledge the standard trinitarian concept of God the Father, the Son, and the Holy Spirit as three separate components of the Godhead; rather, they believe God and Jesus are one and the same (hence, the "Jesus Only" and the "Oneness"). The Pentecostal churches represented in this paper are small, largely autonomous churches; as religious folk groups, the members of these churches determine for themselves which traditional beliefs and practices will form the basis for their religious services. Styles of religious genres, prayers, testimonies, healing rituals, sermons, and service structure are determined strictly at the local level. Almost every service has clearly identifiable segments: music, healing, testifying, and preaching. In this religious context, most of the religious performances are folkloric in nature; that is, they are developed and colored by the religious convictions of the group and maintained in time and space through oral transmission, imitation, and audience critique. This paper deals primarily with one type of testimony that is given both by new members and by those of long standing about their Holy Ghost experience. Within the appropriate context of the testimony "slot" of the service, members will tell about their supernatural experience to the full congregation. This "testimony" seems as necessary to the survival and understanding of the belief in Holy Ghost experiences as do the experiences themselves.

In my work with fundamentalist Pentecostal groups in the Midwest, I have focused largely on the religious experiences and verbal performances of the women involved in this religion. This attention to women is appropriate because women make up the largest segment of the Pentecostal religious population, because their ecstatic participation in the religious services is very active and often surpasses that of the male membership, and because I believe that the women constitute a religious folk group which shares verbal repertoires and a worldview based on their female experiences in the context of their midwestern lives and their devotion to their religion.[2] Even when males have the authority in the churches, even when they are present in the services, and even when they, too, participate in the services, there is a distinctive difference between their verbal expertise and performance orientation and that of the women.

My work in this area has led to several observations about the gender-based differences in both transcendent religious experiences and in the testimonials recounting those experiences. Women have substantially more dramatic encounters with the Holy Ghost and more often speak in tongues than men do. Female narrative accounts of these religious experiences, too, are more fully developed and delivered more often in all contexts than those told by males. We can make sense of these facts by pointing out that Pentecostals accept the premise that women are more "spiritual" and "religious" than men are.[3] Both men and women in the group agree that women are more likely to be "filled" with the Holy Ghost, more likely to go into trance, more likely to "shout" and dance "in the spirit," and are more likely to "fallout," that is, fall on the floor in a spiritual faint. Because women are perceived to be closer to nature, in a sense, and more likely to exhibit emotions and uninhibited behavior, they are thought to be more tuned to the world of God and spirits; they are equally susceptible, of course, to the control of the devil!

In all of my fieldwork, I have seen very few males actually "shout" or dance "in the spirit," or go into trance and speak in tongues. Without exception, male conversions are modest facsimiles of the typical female experience. Similarly, male testimonies are brief, more analytical, less emotional, and less articulate about the conversion experience itself, although all males in the religion, both pastors and laymembers, consider normative the picture of conversion and transcendent religious experience painted by the women's performance and their narrative accounts. Two male testimonies indicate the gender-based differences evident in the recounting of the Holy Ghost experience:

I praise the Lord tonight
Because he made the way
And gave me another privilege
To stand up and witness for him.
I thank him
Because one time he picked me up out of sin
And started me in the right way.
I thank him for the Holy Ghost
And for the joy of finding it in the service.
You know, there's no other peace or joy
Or any other thing but is in the Lord.
I love him tonight
I love to serve him

———————

I want to thank the Lord tonight
For the privilege of being in his house
It's just wonderful to come out
And be with God's people
Have God down in their soul
It just makes you want to
Go on and live for him.
One of these days we can make it over there
It'll be just wonderful
No more headaches
No more pain for this old body.
Go on and live for Jesus
You pray for me that I'll do his will.

It is important to note that I have presented these testimonies verbatim and in their entirety. Men, in general, offer extremely short, brief testimonies, often delivered in a sharp, quick manner without details of the transcendent encounter and without any exhibition of emotion. When I ask men about their nonparticipation in the dancing, crying, and shouting they invariably point to those behaviors as "sissy" or appropriate for females, even though the theological premises of the religion stipulate that *all* converts must have such an encounter. Most often, after a male's conversion, it is assumed that his experience was adequate. Similarly, even though the men's narrative accounts do not show evidence of a transcendent experience, they are not deemed insufficient or inappropriate.

Several factors might suggest why this is so. First, because there are so few males in membership in many of these churches, the women, pleased to see their menfolk join, dare not ask them to perform in a particular manner. In fact, female critique of male behavior on any level in this cultural arena is prohibited. Second, the wildly dramatic behaviors of crying, shouting, twirling about in circles, or falling to the floor are recognized by all as more "appropriate" for women than for men. While it is acceptable for men to behave in these ways in this context, it is also understood that most of them are not likely to do so. Third, the God-given authority of the males in this culture—in the home, in the community, in the church—dictates a kind of protective leniency for them in "proving" their saved status. And, finally, because men do not think of themselves as being as spiritual as women, they relinquish this space and its activity largely to the women.

It makes sense, then, that the ritual conversion experiences, the Holy Ghost encounters, the tongue-speaking, and the narrative recounting of these transcendent events by Pentecostal *women* would serve as the models for such encounters. A female's experience will more closely delineate the parameters of Holy Ghost encounters than would a male's. Likewise, their narratives about the encounters serve to define and articulate the ritual to both males and females in subsequent conversions. It can be argued that it is the *female* transcendent religious experience that formulates, articulates, and preserves Pentecostal conversion beliefs. The experiences of the women and the narrative accounts of their experiences serve the religious community well in outlining the significant aspects of such an encounter with the supernatural.

Requirements for conversion into the fundamentalist "Oneness" Pentecostal denomination are based on a strict theological construct based on observable criteria. In order to know you have been saved and in order to become a member of the group (i.e., the group knows you are saved), the requirements are that the convert must experience in public display *two* baptisms: a water baptism, in the form of complete submersion following a claim of conversion, and a "spirit" baptism, which is a public demonstration of an "encounter" with the Holy Ghost, an act that is accompanied by characteristic paralinguistic features and a mandatory "speaking in tongues."[4] This second experience with the Holy Ghost embodies and reinforces the belief of the group that the Holy Ghost as a spirit may be encountered on a personal level, and that such an encounter is recognizable to all through the "evidence of the tongues." Further, within this belief system, tongue-speaking has come to be equated with salvation. The belief that salvation has been achieved and heaven is attainable only after a display of tongue-speaking (spirit baptism) is, in fact, the distinguishing characteristic of certain Pentecostal sects, including "Oneness." Charles Parham, one of the first Pentecostal preachers, preached that all Christians should experience what the praying group in "the upper room" had experienced as related in Acts 2:1–4:[5]

[1]And when the day of Pentecost was fully come
they were all with one accord in one place,
[2]And suddenly there came a sound from heaven as
of a rushing mighty wind, and it filled all the
house where they were sitting.
[3]And there appeared unto them cloven tongues like
as of fire, and it sat upon each of them.
[4]And they were all filled with the Holy Ghost,
and began to speak with other tongues, as the
Spirit gave them utterance.

The subsequent narratives concerning the spirit baptism perhaps are not stipulated as required components of the conversion process; yet the focus on these narratives emphasizes the importance of rendering the experience into a narrative account and suggests the evocative power of the narratives to shape subsequent experience.[6]

The public display aspect of the "Pentecostal experience" obviously places excessive pressure on all converts to "perform" a kind of conversion ritual, for salvation is not assured until the congregation has been convinced of this supernatural encounter. Pentecostals have developed, therefore, a traditional, ritualized procedure for this public display "performance."[7] Although not all elements will be exhibited in any one conversion performance, each display will and must contain enough of the anticipated elements to convey the message to the audience that what they are viewing is, in fact, an encounter with the supernatural. Within the religiocultural context, this ritual has become standardized; variation is possible, but unique performances risk conveying an erroneous message, the most dangerous of which is the possibility that the initiate has been "possessed" by the devil rather than "filled" with the Holy Ghost. As a check, certain members of the group are recognized as possessing the "gift of discernment" and are believed to be able to spot deficient or Satan-induced performances.[8]

Observers of a Pentecostal Holy Ghost experience largely view the experience from behind the performer. An observer who has attended a large number of Pentecostal services will, after a time, learn to anticipate which persons are most likely to "go forward" to seek such an experience based on their behavior at their pew during the service. Characteristic behavior, which may begin early in the service, may include crying, either in a visibly agonizing manner or silently weeping at their seat. Pre-conversion behavior often includes the raising of one or both hands to the ceiling, waving them palms up; may include "shouts" from the pew; or may include kneeling at the pew and praying with bowed head. All of these behaviors will be noted by the persons in charge of the service and will be interpreted to mean that the person wishes to seek the experience of the Holy Ghost. Often the leaders will acknowledge such behavior by physically going to the person, extending their hand, and leading the initiate to the front of the church to kneel or stand with hands outstretched. At other times, the leader will only verbally invite those persons in the congregation who are feeling a desire to "seek the Holy Ghost" to "step out and come forward," promising to meet the initiates as they reach the altar. When the initiates reach the front of the room, then, much of the experience is observable to the audience only from behind. The outstretched arms are, of course, visible; audible crying, shouts, moans can be heard; often the initiate is surrounded by several acolytes who may "lay hands" on the person's body—his or her shoulder or forehead, her back—or may take one of the uplifted hands; at times the agonized face may be visible for a moment. Long sessions of praying with the seeker at the altar, termed "tarrying," often follow the person's initial indications of an interest in joining the group.[9]

The newcomer is expected to kneel and pray, cry, raise his or her hands in full submission, and wait for the spirit to fill the body. For some, the tarrying lasts only through one religious meeting; for others, the tarrying may last through every night of a two week revival; for still others, the tarrying may actually occur, intermittently, over several months or years, before the person actually "gets the Holy Ghost" and converts.

Congregational support for the proselyte is generally sympathetic and is manifested in the form of constant encouragement, as each saved person in the group has a religious obligation to save as many newcomers as possible. In general, there is active respect for the problems of the one who tarries; most members recognize that the tarrying sinner is having difficulty giving his or her all to Christ and giving in to the Holy Ghost. They firmly believe anybody can receive the Holy Ghost, but the will to submit is, obviously, of the utmost importance. All inhibitions must be overcome before one can be filled with the Holy Ghost and speak in tongues. This all seems reasonable enough to those who may not be participants in such a religion: you would have to let go of your inhibitions to become the center of such a public exhibition. While the members may understand this natural reticence on some unconscious level, the articulation of the problem is never in such pragmatic terms, but rather is couched in terms of one's spiritual reluctance, one's inability to totally give up all things "of this world" and to devote one's life to Jesus in a consummate manner. On a very human level, however, the members recognize just how difficult such a commitment can be; their encouragement, then, remains gentle but constant; the pressure to conform is very real and the rewards of hugs and pats after the conversion are reassuring and reaffirming.

Ideally, since this public display must be witnessed by the group members, one initiate at a time gains "center stage" at the front of the room and begins to whirl about and speak in tongues. Yet, in reality, several initiates may be overlapping in the stages of their conversion behaviors. When the seeking person begins to "get the Holy Ghost," the crowd around disperses to a degree, allowing the initiate to sway or twirl around and around in the ecstatic semi-trance state that is customary in these experiences. At this point the initiate's shouting may increase and with the increased intensity of the moment, the convert may begin to "speak in tongues." Others around the initiate may also begin to shout and speak in tongues. At the conclusion of this often very dramatic and emotional performance the initiate—now well on the way to becoming a member—may collapse in a faint on the floor, may kneel and place his or her head on the altar bench, or may sit on a pew with another member or the pastor encouraging and hugging them. All of this has been performed to the accompaniment of loud music and singing by the congregation, always a vital part of the Pentecostal religious service. Although each seeker receives much attention from the leaders and their appointed assistants, several such performances may actually occur simultaneously or in a staggered manner during the conclusion of one service. Without raising the issue of whether or not these experiences are "real" or whether or not the new converts have actually encountered the supernatural, the more appropriate point is that for all the observers in attendance (whether outsiders such as myself or a member of the group), the description above constitutes basically what the audience can *see* and *hear* happening. Only the participant *knows* what has happened physiologically and emotionally.

Based on what they have seen and what they have heard, the Pentecostal audience interprets the observed phenomena to mean that the initiate has had a supernatural experience; the evidence is manifested in the glossolalia. It appears, however, that in addition to water baptism, one more component of the conversion process is necessary. The evidence of the Holy Ghost experience, and the conversion, are not actually complete until a narrative recounting of the experience is delivered by the one who experienced it. The observers need to be told what has happened to the performer; that is, the narrative recounting of the experience functions to articulate the belief. Appropriately, within the Pentecostal tradition, a framework exists not only for the experience itself, but also for a recounting of the Holy Ghost Experience—frameworks for both content and for expression. That is, a traditional "testimony" frame exists for recounting the experience, and a specific "slot" exists within the religious service in which to recount the Holy Ghost experience—to the *same* audience which observed the experience itself. New converts are expected to stand up during the appropriate "testimony service" and relate their Holy Ghost Experience narrative. Although testimonies in the "testimony slot" of the religious service take on many different and various forms, when a new convert stands and states "I want to give my testimony," often this indicates that she is about to relate the story of her conversion, which will include her Holy Ghost encounter. Audience members respond in a manner that indicates that they may have heard this narrative before but are eager to hear it again.

This is not, however, the only time a convert will tell this story. She may tell it within family situations, community contexts, and in "witnessing" situations where she has now taken on the role of proselytizer. Over some amount of time, the narrative becomes molded into a formulaic text that has been predicated by other similar Holy Ghost encounter narratives within this religious folk group.

Each re-telling of the event becomes an event itself.[10] Pentecostals tell and re-tell their personal encounter stories, constantly reaffirming that a spiritual encounter did, in fact, take place. Within the context of the Pentecostal religion, the group members in the religious service create in a very collective, perhaps even communal way,[11] the appropriate story of a spiritual encounter, molding and re-creating the story, telling and re-telling it, only cautiously adding or subtracting elements, until not only is an "appropriate" conversion story created for all to draw upon for their own personal "testimony," but a story that, in fact, actually prescribes the conversion experience of future initiates.[12] This might be termed the experiential power of Holy Ghost narratives; such an approach would explain the formulaic, predictable nature of both the narratives and the Holy Ghost encounters. The narratives serve as a control, too, on a potentially chaotic religious experience and serve to construct and preserve a Pentecostal belief in spirit possession.

Daniel Batson and W. Larry Ventis have attempted to outline the phenomenology of religious experience based on the work of Husserl, Merleau-Ponty, and Piaget.[13] Drawing first on Piaget, they suggest that cognitive structures formulate the conceptual dimensions on which we scale our experiences, the frameworks on which our "reality is woven," allowing us to compare one experience with another. Language, they argue, is the technique we use most frequently to influence the experiences of others: "It is hard to deny that religious language is capable of facilitating creative religious experience" for both the speaker and the listener.[14]

Batson and Ventis lament the fact that they know of no studies that directly address the question of the effect of religious language on religious experience. The present essay addresses this important issue. Here we see religious experience and language joined and rejoined in different configurations. Experience and performance formulate one set of "realities," while, through language, narrative accounts suggest a different and more complex "reality." Visibly, we can observe only the wild behaviors, recognized, perhaps, as evidence of a religious experience; but proof that the experience has been *transcendent* can be transmitted only through language. As Batson suggests, one Gestalt has been substituted for another.[15] A religious experience is now understood to have been an encounter with the Holy Ghost.

Importantly, converts learn how to ritually display a supernatural encounter by watching other performances, and they learn appropriate ways to tell their own conversion stories by listening to other conversion stories. The conversion accounts, in the form of Holy Ghost narratives, constitute a reiterative authentication of the original experience. My suggestions are cautious ones, because I do not question whether or not Pentecostals actually have supernatural encounters with the Holy Ghost. What is most important is that this group has determined what is to be viewed as "real" when experienced and described in the proper manner; that is, the encounter and the narrative re-enactment have both become ritualized aspects of the conversion process.[16]

The stories Pentecostal women tell about their supernatural encounters are memorates that embody their religious beliefs. The narratives nearly always acknowledge the fearful aspect of such an encounter, describe what the woman felt when she allowed the Holy Ghost to "fill her up," the ac-

tion that followed that submission, usually tongue speaking or "shouting," and a final sense of euphoria.[17] The formulaic aspects of these testimonies will be evident in the examples that follow; both the structural and componential similarities are striking. Significantly, not all the following stories are from a single Pentecostal church. This supports the argument that Pentecostals as a religious group form a community. Pentecostals hear other Pentecostal testimonies at their own church, as well as at the many meetings they attend at other like-minded churches; conversion stories may occur in services, in homes, and in interviews with collectors such as myself. In most contexts, they remain consistent in content, while their actual delivery may be modified to fit the context.

Conversion stories and encounters with the Holy Ghost have a formulaic quality that suggests their collective creation and their oral traditional nature. Striking repetition of various elements, such as the coldness of the baptism water or the presence of a blinding light, occur in many of the narratives.[18]

The first two stories below are from two women in Indiana who attend different churches and do not know one another.

Holy Ghost Experience #1:

When I was nine years old and we lived over in Sanders when I was nine years old, I got baptized there at Sanders church and got the Holy Ghost, spoke in tongues on my own one night. We went to church and it was cold, about zero, walked down the railroad and went there and I was baptized and got the Holy Ghost. And we came home walked all the way home and I had long hair which that was their belief that you had to have long hair at that time. On the way home my hair froze real hard but it never even give me a cold.

When you are baptized then you feel that the sins you were in, you were born in sin, everybody's born in sin, every human being is born in this world in sin, and when you get baptized you feel it is gone. You have such a sweet quiet feeling you feel like you feel the spirit over you, feel it's gone and then the Bible says to be baptized and receive the gift of the Holy Ghost. It says you shall, it don't say you may or you could, the Bible says that if you are baptized in Jesus' name then you *shall* receive the gift of the Holy Ghost. Then, when I was baptized I *knowed* I should, I *knowed* I would, because the Bible says you shall, so I went back the next night, me just nine years old, *knowing* all this because I had been taught, you know, in our church, they taught us that we had to have the Holy Ghost, so I went back the next night and just so happened in our prayers and you know other people always go up and help you, they go up and pray too, and there is always someone there that is really spiritual enough that you can feel the spirit from them working with you, maybe some maybe not everybody but there will be somebody and after a while you start speaking, that is, if you are really interested and you mean what you did, lay aside all sins you have, lay aside all sins. I don't care what you do you've got to promise the Lord right there, I'm not going to do that sin ever again.

And then you will speak with tongues. You will speak and you won't be able to help it and that's what I did on that day. I didn't know what I said. I didn't know what it was going to be like, but I'll never forget the night I got the Holy Ghost I saw a light off to the left of me and I felt just a beautiful light and a beautiful feeling and then I started speaking once I saw this light. And it just rolled out like, just like, you know, and then I felt good, way better than even when I was baptized. I felt like that now I can make it.

Holy Ghost Experience #2:

I was sitting upstairs in the church we had then and I had my two children up there on the bench. And they was coming up there and said, "Oh, your husband's getting the Holy Ghost come down here," and when I walked into that room it was just full of light, a radiant light in that room and some of the brothers was praying with my husband. When I opened the door, I guess God planned this for me to see, but my husband was just knocked backwards just like somebody knocked him down, because the power of God was so strong.

Now, when I received the baptism of the Holy Ghost I felt I was a little hard to convert, you know, and I kept telling myself, "well, I guess I'll just have to give it up," because I had tarried for so long.

Well, I can't remember who the man was who was holding the revival, but it was the last night and they said, "Now, if you've come all of this time just come forth tonight. This may be the night you'll receive the Holy Ghost." And I was kind of disgusted like and I thought, "I'll go because it is the last night and if the Lord comes I'm not ready." And I went up and kneeled down. Then I really honestly prayed, you know, and all at once I felt this glow just move into me, you know, [gestures with arms extended, makes swooping gesture to indicate the glow moving into her body], and I just, if I ever shouted in my life, it was that night and I was sitting straight on the floor, you know, and then I *knew* I had the baptism.

At first glance, these testimonies about the Holy Ghost experience may not appear to be all that similar. However, I should like to point out several of the typical characteristics of these stories that are consistent in Holy Ghost stories, illustrating their formulaic nature with further examples.

Most Holy Ghost experience stories begin with a reference to the age of the informant at the time of the experience. The age of nine is so consistently a part of these stories, it points to an esoteric notion of that age as being the appropriate age of accountability. To say that nine was the year of your Holy Ghost encounter is to indicate that you have conformed to conventional expectations. The second most popular age for the Holy Ghost experience is less specific but is that of a very young mother. Many stories make reference to the babies the young mothers must contend with in the church service; often a part of the story is the concern for who will take care of the children if the mother needs to go up front and pray. Holy Ghost experience stories generally contain concrete details about the time of year, the physical characteristics of the church building in which the experience occurred, names of other people involved in getting the initiate to church, names of other people involved in getting the initiate to church, references to the specific type

of service, almost always a revival service with mention of the evangelist preaching the revival. In many of the stories the narrator indicates her reluctance to participate in the loud shouting services, perhaps openly criticizing such behavior at first; this is followed with a realization that they have accepted the religion as "real" and desire active participation in it.

My girlfriend and I when we first entered into this Pentecostal church, this is kinda going back, I remember seeing the people raising their hands and speaking in tongues and one little lady shouting and we sat back there and I would just laugh, because I thought this was really unreal. And when I seen these people clapping their hands and raising their hands to worship the Lord, I thought this is, you know, this is really out of place for them to do this in church. Church is to come and sit still. The second night after that I came back because I thought I would laugh again. And I realized it was more than just watching people and they really did have something that they were expressing and that it was real. I knew there was something there and I knew it was right.

All of the above is in anticipation of the description of the experience event itself. Even after the proselyte has decided to participate, however, there may be expressed in the narratives the initial fear that accompanied the decision to go forward and seek the Holy Ghost. Most narratives include detailed descriptions of wanting to go to the altar; of other people being up there; of praying fervently; of lifting up of hands; of seeing a light or feeling a glow move into their body; and, finally, of shouting or speaking in tongues, which is followed by a sense of euphoria, which the believers call "getting a blessing." Although any or all of these elements may be present, the ones most noticeably absent are specific, concrete details of the tongue-speaking experience itself. In many of the narratives, in fact, that experience may be encapsulated in the words "and then I got the Holy Ghost." This may be followed by "and spoke in tongues" or "and began to shout" or "and then I knew I had the baptism," but the details of the actual supernatural experience are minimal, the most specific narratives being those which describe a glow that enters the body or the vision of a light.

As active participants in the effort to solicit a personal encounter with a supernatural spirit, Pentecostal women have imbued that experience with an appropriate dose of awe and fear. At the same time as they long for the cathartic "blessing" that accompanies such an uninhibited spiritual experience, they also express reluctance and apprehension. The consistent elements of the Holy Ghost narratives focus on the collective view of the supernatural encounter as awe-inspiring and aid the women in coming to terms with the single most important religious experience of their lives. It is important to note that the narratives rely heavily on concrete detail in some aspects but remain illusionary in terms of the actual supernatural encounter. The narratives do *not* linger on the actual moment on the supernatural encounter except to associate it with a pleasurable, non-apprehensive association with light and warmth; the supernatural encounter is merely the nexus between the apprehensions that precede it and the euphoria that follows. The clear, concrete details of the solicitation of the spirit and the ecstatic descriptions of the release that follow it are the more important elements of the narratives because they are conceivably attainable. By maintaining the illusive characteristics of the encounter itself, all subsequent encounters, if they conform to the "code" outlined in the collective "Holy Ghost Narrative" will be deemed appropriate for salvation by those watching. This allows for the necessarily "ineffable" quality of the actual moment of union with the supernatural.

The body of Holy Ghost narratives dictate what the fearful initiate will actually encounter when he or she approaches the altar. Supernatural encounters are by their very nature awe-ful and fear-inspiring. Humankind has always been fascinated with encounters with the supernatural, on either secular or sacred grounds. What *is* a supernatural encounter like? In many cases it is unsolicited and undesirable, largely because it causes disquiet at the very least and pure horror at the opposite end of the spectrum. Encounters with God, angels, saints, the Virgin Mary, prophets, Jesus Christ, the Devil, various spirits, or embodiments of any of these spiritual "beings" or others particular to the belief system of any group, whether solicited or not, are for the most part approached with awe and trembling. Active pursuit of a supernatural encounter, through drugs, fasting, prayer or other means, never fully loses its potential for invoking fear and suggesting danger, and that certainly is the case with Pentecostals. The supernatural encounter is much desired but is, at the same time, feared and met with apprehension. By outlining what is expected to happen, the narratives actually ensure that the anticipated aspects do occur and that unexpected ones do *not* occur; thus, they not only chart appropriate experience, but serve to eliminate the fear-invoking personality of an inappropriate experience. The Holy Ghost narratives of Pentecostal women operate to strip the experience of its most terrifying aspects and replace them with conceivable and pleasurable components, such as light and warmth.

The importance of the Holy Ghost narrative, complete with apprehensions and verbalized fears, becomes clear as we realize that the narrator suggests to her audience, "I know you are afraid because I have been there and I was afraid, too." Sometimes this communal approbation of the fearful aspects completely obscures the supernatural experience itself as in this testimony:

> I'd say I tarried probably two months before I received it, and *I don't remember receiving it.* I was real happy about it, but *it wasn't what I expected.* I thought I might fly away and when I got it I didn't know what it was and I had a fear of it. I didn't know what it was about and when they said go get it it was scary and a couple of times I almost got it and got up and prayed and left. I wouldn't stay with it because I didn't know what would happen to me. But when I did speak in tongues I do

remember that on the way home if someone would ask me something it would never come out in English. I could never respond until the next morning in the English language. It wasn't there. *The next morning I was all right.* [emphases mine]

In describing group notions of reality, Burkart Holzner has suggested: "the uncertainty of action is tolerable only within a framework of certainties, the most basic of which is the shared actuality of real things experienced in the moment of acting."[19] In the case of a Holy Ghost encounter, the narrative serves to elaborate a framework of certainty which incorporates the personal supernatural experience of each individual as well as the re-enactment of a communally shared experience. The power of the religious word is so potent as to allow for each submissive proselyte to potentially encounter all that the narrative suggests, although each individual may encounter fewer or more of the available supernatural elements that might be associated with an encounter with the Holy Ghost of God. The narratives set up a potential for the experience, one that excises from the solicitation of spirits its unknown power, while simultaneously providing, in the retelling of the story, the proof needed for assuring salvation for one individual and the framework of the experience for another. The completed conversion process for this Pentecostal sect, then, has three components: a water baptism, a personal but public encounter with the Holy Ghost which must include the verbal glossolalia, and the subsequent narrative re-construction of that spiritual encounter. For a conversion to be felicitous, all the necessary and appropriate conditions must be met and then recounted.

The speech event describes the lights visible to the performer, the glowing feeling that filled her body, the feeling of ecstasy and satisfaction that followed the "enfilling." These are necessary but invisible components of the event; they must be articulated verbally because they are hidden to the observer, the critical audience. Even more importantly, the belief that tongue-speaking is "the evidence of the Holy Ghost" must be articulated and interpreted for the audience in order for the entire experience to reinforce the belief system.

In an earlier article on a Pentecostal female's testimonies, I illustrated how a woman who testifies loud and long could actually gain temporary control of a Pentecostal service.[20] This article illustrates yet another aspect of female spiritual power and control in the Pentecostal religion. While it is true that men generally have both power and authority in this male dominated religion, this examination of Holy Ghost encounters and their narrative counterparts illustrates how the religious participation of women actually articulates and dictates the very nature of transcendent experience, the critical foundation of this religious denomination.

NOTES

1. The narratives used in this paper were collected from Pentecostals in Indiana (1980–81) and in Missouri (1984). Names of informants and church names have been changed to protect

their privacy; however, names of actual towns and states have been retained. I wish to acknowledge support from the University of Missouri in the form of a Summer Fellowship Grant in 1984 and the National Endowment for the Humanities for a Summer Fellowship Grant in 1986. For general information on Pentecostals, see Robert Mapes Anderson, *Vision of the Disinherited* (New York, 1970); William Clements, "The American Folk Church in Northeast Arkansas," *Journal of the Folklore Institute* 15 (1978):161–180; W. J. Hollenweger, *The Pentecostals* (Minneapolis, 1972); and John T. Nichol, *Pentecostalism* (New York, 1966).

2. Compare the work of Barbara Epstein, *The Politics of Domesticity: Women, Evangelism and Temperance in Nineteenth-Century America* (Middletown, Conn., 1981).

3. See Sherry Ortner, "Is Female to Male as Nature is to Culture?" in *Women, Culture and Society,* ed. Michelle Rosaldo and Louise Lamphere, 67–88 (Stanford, 1974).

4. See Felicitas Goodman, *Speaking in Tongues* (Chicago, 1972); William Samarin, *Tongues of Men and Angels* (New York, 1972); and Lawless, "What Did She Say?" An Application of Peirce's General Theory of Signs to Glossolalia in the Pentecostal Religion," *Folklore Forum* 13 (1980): 23–39. See also Harvey Cox's excellent volume, *The Seduction of the Spirit* (New York, 1978).

   The connection between tongue-speaking and salvation had not always been the case, however. Compare the roles of tongues in nineteenth-century camp-meeting revivalism in Dickson Bruce's *And They All Sang Hallelujah: Plain-Folk Camp Meeting Religion, 1800–1845* (Knoxville, 1974) with the development of the neo-Pentecostalism or Charismatic movement among mainline protestants and Catholics as traced in David Harrell, Jr., *All Things Are Possible* (Bloomington, 1975). See also Martin E. Marty, *A Nation of Behavers* (Chicago, 1976).

   There are many accounts of camp-meeting activities. See, for example, William James, *The Varieties of Religious Experience* (New York, 1936 [first published in 1902]); Bruce, *And They All Sang Hallelujah;* and B. A. Weisberger, *They Gathered at the River* (Chicago, 1958).

5. See Vinson Synan, *The Holiness-Pentecostal Movement in the United States* (Grand Rapids, 1971), for an account of Charles Parham and the first "Pentecostals."

6. The power of language to influence thought and action stems largely from applications of the work of B. L. Whorf. See *Language, Thought and Reality* (Cambridge, Mass., 1956). For such an application to the religious experience, see Clements, "Ritual Expectation in Pentecostal Healing Experience," *Western Folklore* 40 (1981): 139–148.

7. I am, of course, using the term "performance" in the manner outlined by Richard Bauman in *Verbal Art as Performance* (Rowley, Mass., 1977).

8. I Corinthians 12:8–10 lists the nine gifts of the spirit: wisdom, knowledge, faith, healing, working of miracles, prophecy, discerning of spirits, diverse kinds of tongues, and interpretation of tongues.

9. See Marion Dearman, "Christ and Conformity: A Study of Pentecostal Values," *Journal for the Scientific Study of Religion* 13 (1974): 87–104; Lawless, "Brothers and Sisters: Pentecostals as a Folk Group," *Western Folklore* 43 (1983): 83–104; and Clements, "Conversion and Communitas," *Western Folklore* 35 (1976): 35–45.

10. See Peter L. Berger and Thomas Luckmann, *The Social Construction of Reality* (New York, 1966).

11. See F. B. Gummere, *The Beginnings of Poetry* (New York, 1901).

12. Compare Brett Sutton, "Language, Vision, Myth: The Primitive Baptist Experience of Grace," in *Holding Onto the Land and the Lord,* ed. R. L. Hall and C. B. Stack (Athens, GA, 1982); and Stephen Crites, "The Narrative Quality of Experience," *Journal of the American Academy of Religion* 39 (1971): 291–311.

13. C. Daniel Batson and W. Larry Ventis, *The Religious Experience: A Social-Psychological Perspective* (New York, 1982).

14. Batson, 125.

15. Ibid. 71.

16. See Berger and Luckmann, 50–52.

17. Compare Epstein.

18. Compare these accounts with those collected by Mircea Eliade, *The Two and The One* (London, 1965). See also Kenneth M. George, "'I Still Got It': The Conversion Narrative of John C. Sherfey," M. A. Thesis. University of North Carolina at Chapel Hill, 1978; and Jeff Todd Titon and Kenneth George, "Testimonies," *Alcheringa/Ethnopoetics* 4 (1978): 68–83.

19. B. Holzner, *Reality Construction in Society* (Cambridge, Mass., 1968), 114.

20. See Elaine J. Lawless, "Shouting for the Lord: The Power of Women's Speech in the Pentecostal Service," *Journal of American Folklore* 96 (1983): 433–457.

9

Death and Funerals

Essays in This Section:

Death and what happens after death have probably been a concern for humans since we became aware of our mortality. Death is an unescapable fact of life. Because death is one of the few boundaries the living cannot cross, attempts to deal with death have typically been rooted in supernatural belief systems. As you read the essays in this section, keep the following points in mind:

- An individual's death is not simply an exit; it is an event that breaks social, political, and economic bonds. As such, it is a transition from one status (living member of society) to another status, such as ancestor, spirit, or even minor deity.

- Death is a cultural event that is acted out in mortuary rituals. Many such rituals help usher the deceased into a new status and location. They also typically reflect the values and beliefs of society. Both of these factors are evident in the first two essays in this section.

- In the first essay in this section, Richard Gill examines "the American way of death." In the 1950s and 1960s, the U.S. funeral industry was strongly criticized for promoting lavish death rituals. Today, most American funerals are extremely simple, and practices such as cremation are increasingly popular. Gill considers how changing funeral practices reflect changes in American understandings of life and death.

- In the second essay, Beth Conklin discusses a custom that will strike most readers as unusual. Until fairly recent times, the Wari' of western Brazil practiced mortuary cannibalism, cooking and eating all or part of the body of their dead group members. Conklin explains how this cannibalism reflects and undergirds the Wari' people's understandings of themselves and their relationship to the natural world.

- The final two essays in this section explore how death is linked with status. Shalinsky and Glascock show how cultural values are reflected in rituals surrounding the deaths of people who have become socially marginalized. They demonstrate that in many societies around the world it is acceptable to kill or hasten the death of people who—because of age, infirmity, or physical deformity—are perceived as no longer belonging to their society. In particular, infants and the aged are marginalized and disposed of in times of social or economic stress.

- Similarly, Choi discusses how widows in Hindu society were viewed as marginal people after their husbands died. With no place in society, they were encouraged, or sometimes forced, to perform suttee—to burn themselves to death on their husband's funeral pyre.

Whatever Happened to the
American Way of Death?

Richard T. Gill

In this essay Gill uses the changing concerns with death and memorializing the dead as a device for commenting on social change in American society. The article begins with a commentary on Jessica Mitford's book *The American Way of Death,* in which Mitford exposed the practices of funeral directors and mortuary owners, who, she claimed, unscrupulously invented ways to drive up the costs of funerals and enhance their profits. Gill argues that Mitford's critique of American funerals was really a criticism of nineteenth-century Victorian burial practices, which began to decline after World War I. He claims that recent trends in American burial practices— increasing cremation rates, less money spent on graves and monuments, the kind of thing of which Mitford would have approved—are actually a reflection of the growing trend for short-term, self-centered thinking in American society.

Gill argues that people in the nineteenth century believed in the idea of progress and worked to better the world for their children and grandchildren. One way this long-term thinking was expressed was in funeral memorials. Victorians wanted future generations to remember them and their work. Today, Gill argues, as our life spans increase, Americans focus more on themselves, and when they think of the future it is in terms of what their personal needs will be. He says that Americans' ability to "envision the future beyond [their] personal lives is shrinking," and what happens after them is of little consequence to them. One result of this is that more and more people do not care what happens to their bodies after they die and are not interested in memorializing themselves. However, Gill also claims that this "temporal myopia" has resulted in a host of social ills and a general lack of interest in the world that will be inherited by our children.

As you read, consider these questions:

1. How have American burial customs changed over the last two hundred years?
2. What do changes in burial customs and practices tell us about society in general?
3. How do you want your remains to be dealt with after you die? How does this reflect your own views about your life, your passing, and relatives you leave behind?

A few decades ago, we knew perfectly well what to make of the American way of death. It was overly sentimentalized, highly commercialized, and, above all, excessively expensive. We knew all this because our British friends, both visitors and expatriates, had told us so. The first major assault was Evelyn Waugh's 1948 novel, *The Loved One.* The next was Jessica Mitford's 1963 best-seller, *The American Way of Death* (which is now being revised by its author). Mitford, like Waugh, did have some fun with the barbarities of the American funeral establishment, but her tone and purpose were far more serious than his. Her quarry was precisely "the vast majority of ethical undertakers." And it was the very definition of "ethical" in the undertaking business that she found deeply offensive.

As an important example, Mitford cited the Forest Lawn Memorial Park of Southern California. Forest Lawn was admittedly a somewhat extreme case, but she pointed out that its creator (Hubert Eaton) "has probably had more influence on trends in the modern cemetery industry than any other human being." A paragraph or two at random easily conveys her view of the ethical product of this "dean of cemetery operators":

> Wandering through Whispering Pines, Everlasting Love, Kindly Light and Babyland, with its encircling heart-shaped motor road, I learned that each section of Forest Lawn is zoned and named according to the price of burial plots. Medium-priced graves range from $434.50 in Haven of Peace to $599.50 in Triumphant Faith to $649.50 in Ascension. The cheapest is $308 in Brotherly Love—for even this commodity comes high at Forest Lawn.

Or again:

> There are statues, tons of them, some designed to tug at the heartstrings: "Little Duck Mother," "Little Pals," "Look, Mommy!", others with a different appeal, partially draped Venuses, seminude Enchantresses, the reproduction of Michelangelo's David, to which Forest Lawn has affixed a fig leaf, giving it a surprisingly indecent appearance.

How gross it all was! And what was most indecent about this whole tasteless exercise was the amount of money being devoted to it. According to Mitford's calculations, the United States in 1960 was spending more on funerals than on all of higher education; also more than on conservation and the development of natural resources, police protection, fire protection, or even the estimated cost of providing medical care for Americans 65 or older under a (then still-in-the-future) federal medical insurance program. The "American way of death" was an outrage and an obscenity!

UP IN SMOKE

Mitford's book—rather like Rachel Carson's *Silent Spring*—was a shocker and may, indeed, have had some slight influence on subsequent developments. For the pattern of funerary practice in the United States has been changing quite significantly in recent decades. The change over the post–World War II period as a whole suggests that Waugh and Mitford were rather like army generals fighting the last war. The next war in the area of American funeral customs is likely to be the very opposite of the one in which they were so wittily engaged.

Take, for example, the matter of funeral expenses relative to Gross Domestic Product (GDP). Mitford calculated these in 1960 at around $2 billion or roughly 0.4 percent of U.S. national income. Based on figures for Current Consumption Expenditures, the U.S. Bureau of Economic Analysis arrives at a somewhat lower figure for funeral and burial expenses for 1960: $1,494 million in current dollars and $6,943 million in 1987 dollars. In real terms, this represents 0.35 percent of 1960 GDP. Whichever number is more "realistic," the downward trend of the Bureau of Economic Analysis's estimates is so dramatic as to be undeniable. By 1993, funeral and burial expenses as a percentage of GDP had fallen to 0.15 percent, or well under one-half the 1960 number. . . . Similarly, funerary costs per individual death as a percentage of per capita income in 1993 were also less than one-half what they were in 1960.

Most dramatic of all perhaps has been the rapid increase in cremation as compared to earth burial. Mitford was all for cremation, which was well suited to achieve the "objectives of economy and simplicity." It was a strong part of her argument that in the United States this desirable practice was stubbornly resisted by both clergy and profit-hungry funeral directors and was extremely rare (only 3.56 percent of American deaths in 1960).

The cremation rate began to change in the 1960s, reaching nearly 20 percent by 1993, and is projected to rise above 30 percent by 2010. (See Table 1.) The rapidity of the change in what one would assume to be a very basic social ritual is striking. Whatever the "American way of death" was in 1960, it is obviously becoming something radically different as we head into the twenty-first century.

GOING OUT OF BUSINESS

The changing character of American funerary practice is, moreover, noted by increasing numbers of historians and sociologists, as well as by funeral directors, cemetery superintendents, and others with a direct financial stake in burial practices. Already in the 1970s, in his book *Passing: The Vision of Death in America,* Charles O. Jackson could speak of the "extreme nature of our withdrawal from the dead" and could assert, as his "central point," that "in the present century, Americans have steadily moved to reduce the degree of time and resources which they must provide the dead."

TABLE 1 Cremation Rate, United States, 1960–2010

Year	Percent
1960	3.56
1965	3.87
1970	4.58
1975	6.55
1980	9.74
1985	13.81
1990	17.0
1993	19.8
Projected	
1994	20.8
2000	25.6
2010	32.5

Source: Cremation Association of North America (CANA).

Similarly, in his 1991 book about the history of American cemeteries *(The Last Great Necessity),* David Charles Sloan could note that "growing numbers of Americans are turning away from the customs of burial and memorialization." He further observed that

> as the twenty-first century approaches the cemetery remains in crisis. Americans are more willing to discuss death today than before, but they are also more willing to cremate the dead, scatter their remains, and memorialize them with a poem or tree. . . . New cemeteries are usually unwelcome in the neighborhoods of America. In the nineteenth century, residents gathered in the thousands to celebrate the formation of a new cemetery. Today protesters lobby legislators to forbid their creation or expansion.

And if the protesters don't prevent the establishment of a new cemetery, it is likely very shortly to become the object of vandalism. Sloan admits that such "vandalism has always existed. . . . The rampage of youngsters through a cemetery was a rare, but not unknown, occurrence in the nineteenth century." Today, however, such vandalism has become a "major issue": "The violence to gravestones, mausoleums, flowers, and other objects in today's cemetery has become endemic."

Nor are today's funeral directors, cemeterians, and monument makers unaware of the drastic changes taking place. In a 1995 handout from the death-care industry, one cemeterian notes ruefully that "the average citizen is somehow losing interest in memorialization." The rich and famous get their memorials all right, but "we are losing the appeal at the everyday level." For their part, monument makers, writing in their trade publication, *Stone in America,* note the implications of the "dramatic rise in cremation," which has been "accompanied by a corresponding fall in the popularity of monuments; after all, the very materiality of monuments inherently contradicts the de-materiality of cremation. Left with the ashes, survivors wonder how to dispose of the one who has disappeared."

Cremation has also obviously affected the funeral directors, usually in a negative way. One New Hampshire funeral director describes what is happening in the industry:

> The industry continues to consolidate. As cremation rates rise, many funeral homes are becoming less profitable. To survive, they cut down on staff, quality of services, and [they are] not putting capital back into their business. Many are selling out now while the cremation rate is still low.

Another notes that such issues as "the rise of hybrid, non-traditional funeralization, low-cost cremation, and increased governmental intervention and regulation" clearly "affect profitability." The challenge is to adjust to these complex and difficult trends.

Reading the literature that emanates from various branches of the death-care industry in the 1990s, one gets little sense of the optimism and ebullience that must have motivated entrepreneurs like Hubert Eaton of Forest Lawn fame to promote the "runaway growth" of the U.S. cemetery business earlier in this century. The mood is now defensive, puzzled, wary of the future. Certainly, there is little if any sense of an industry that has the consumer comfortably and tidily in its pocket. The public has changed. Consumers are beginning to abandon their old ways and to adopt the death-care arrangements favored by Mitford and her fellow critics.

REVERSING THE NINETEENTH-CENTURY TREND

But do we ourselves favor these new arrangements? Should we? What is the real significance of this dramatic change in our burial rites and rituals over the past several decades? To understand what is really going on here, one has to have at least some historical appreciation of how funerary practices in the United States have been changing not just over the past few decades but over the last two or three centuries. The important points for our purposes are two: (1) During the nineteenth century, there was a very strong increase in the ceremonies, expenses, and material attentions paid to the dead in the United States. (2) During our present century, at least from World War I on, though with some short-term and local variations, there was a decrease in the amount of attention paid to, and memorialization of, our dead.

Essentially, American cemeteries have gone through a complex evolution over time from frontier and domestic homestead graves, to the rural cemeteries of the nineteenth century, to the lawn park cemeteries of the late nineteenth century, to the memorial park cemeteries beginning around the time of the First World War and continuing on to the present. Needless to say, all these different practices overlap to a greater or lesser degree, and today, of course, we would have to make room for various styles of crematoria.

Now, it was in nineteenth-century America, particularly with the rural cemetery movement, that memorialization of the dead in a this-worldly context took on truly robust proportions. In the earlier Puritan world, physical death meant impermanence and decay. The majority of graves had no permanent markers. What was truly important, the immortality of the soul, was not of this world. It was thus only in the nineteenth century that we began to get the elaborate, Victorian funeral, and this, in fact, began to fade in the World War I era.

Interestingly, the example chosen by Waugh, and underlined by Mitford, to prove excessive American attention to the dead—Eaton's Forest Lawn—can actually be used to exemplify the beginnings of the American withdrawal from the nineteenth-century commitment to the dead. Forest Lawn was the prototype of the memorial park cemetery, and, although Eaton's stated aim was to celebrate the memorialization of the dead (as, indeed, the name of the park suggested), it was done in such a way as to rob death of any particular individuality. Thus, while statuary and art work were to be abundant, individual and family memorials were to be flush against the ground.

This practice of minimizing the attention given to individual and family graves has increased over the years. During very recent decades, the withdrawal of interest in memorializing the dead through elaborate funeral services, tombs, statuary, and the like has only intensified. We have noted the decline in funeral expenses relative to GDP and per capita incomes. Cremation is notable not only because it is a less expensive way of disposing of the dead but also because it conveys a sense of the impermanence of the deceased and, indeed, by implication, of memories of the deceased.

Since both Waugh and Mitford gave California a certain pride of place in their discussion of American funerary mores, it is interesting to observe that California now ranks among the top states in the percent of cremations. In fact, the Pacific coast states as a group in 1993 had more than double the overall U.S. ratio of cremations to deaths (41.78 percent versus 19.78 percent), and their projected percentage for the year 2010 is a dramatic 58.52 percent. In Hawaii, uncasketed deaths, which are particularly inexpensive and may involve no funeral service whatsoever, already account for nearly one-half of all deaths statewide.

In the late nineteenth and early twentieth centuries, the public insisted on memorializing the individual deceased, sometimes over the opposition of cemetery directors. Today, the more common battle is over how to get the funeral industry to provide ever cheaper means of disposing of one's loved ones. In short, the public attitude to the memorialization of the dead in America has changed radically. Rewritten today, *The American Way of Death* would, one would have to expect, be a totally different book.

THE IDEA OF PROGRESS

What are the reasons for the growing reversal of what we now might well think of not as the "American" but as the "Victorian" way of death?

One general hypothesis frequently advanced to explain America's current turn away from elaborate funeral rites and memorials is the increasing secularization of modern society. There are many ways in which the growing secularity of our interests and concerns might affect our attitudes toward the dead. Various commentators have suggested that, as our faith is an afterlife has begun to diminish, our fear of death has grown. Consequently, we tend to avoid death, turn it over to funeral directors, prettify the corpse, leave the maintenance of the grave to an impersonal "perpetual care" arrangement, and so on. Also, it could be argued that our increasing involvement in things of this world has lowered the priority given to caring for the dead, making it compete, as one funeral analyst suggested, with "trips to France" or other consumer goodies.

Again, there is almost certainly some truth in such explanations, but definitely not the whole truth. For while these explanations may have something to say about the retreat from death and dying during the past 75 years, they fail rather badly with respect to what happened in the previous hundred years, from say, 1820 to 1920. In the nineteenth century, we became a much more secular society than we had been a century or two before, but this development, far from lessening our interest in the memorialization of the dead, led to a general increase in the time, attention, and money spent on funerals, graves, and monuments. Why secularization should produce this result in the nineteenth and early twentieth centuries and the exact opposite result in the present era is a question that must be answered before we can even hope to evaluate today's "American way of death."

The answer is to be found in the two ways in which secularization expressed itself in the nineteenth century. The dominant secular notion of this period was the Idea of Progress. This notion was secular, first, in that it emphasized earthly concerns rather than the life to come. But it was also secular in another sense of that term. And here we have to note that the word "secular" has, in fact, two quite different meanings. So far, we have used the word to emphasize a this-worldly, as opposed to other-worldly, focus. But it can also be used to denote periods of time and, in particular, to suggest very long periods of time. As a dictionary definition (fourth meaning) reads: "lasting for an age or ages; continuing for a long time or from age to age." Economists regularly use the word in this sense to distinguish long-run trends from, say, business cycles or other short-run phenomena. At the end of the Great Depression, for example, some economists worried about the possibility of "secular stagnation," meaning that the long-run drift of the economy over time might be in the direction of increasing unemployment, excess capacity, and so on.

Now, the key from our point of view is that the late-nineteenth-century Idea of Progress was secular in both senses. It dealt with this world, and it dealt with it in terms of very extensive, long-run future time. It was, to play with words a bit, a secular secular idea. This is to be distinguished from a short-run secular idea or what might be called a myopic secular idea. The latter would involve an emphasis on things of this world but only with respect to immediate or relatively near-occurring developments.

Time-horizons can be long or short. In the nineteenth-century Idea of Progress, they were very long. Today, they have become notably shorter. Thus, in the past 75 years or so, our society, while becoming increasingly secular in a this-worldly sense, has become very unsecular in terms of time-horizons. The near-term dominates in a way that would hardly have been imaginable at the turn of the century.

GENERATIONAL SOLIPSISM

This growing temporal myopia of contemporary American society has, in fact, been noted elsewhere: in books about business behavior; in discussions of the national debt; in comments about the decline in personal savings; in analyses of the breakdown of the family, the growth of crime, the increasing incidence of illegitimacy; and, of course, in general comments about the "now" generation and about our apparent need for "immediate gratification" in all aspects of life.

These developments are very basic, and could hardly fail to affect our attitudes to the dead and especially to the memorialization of the dead. At the deepest level, and in terms of psychological motivation, nineteenth-century believers in the Idea of Progress envisioned the future (posterity) as giving meaning and vindication to the present. These believers could take satisfaction—in some cases, their greatest satisfaction—in the thought that their children and heirs would live richer, better, and happier lives than they themselves had. These same individuals would also certainly imagine their children and heirs as thinking of them and remembering them, perhaps even being a little grateful to them, for having helped bring about this beneficial outcome. Their stake in the future was real and important and essentially took the form of being remembered—i.e., memorialized in one way or another.

Neither the rotting graves of the Puritans nor the disposable ashes of today's crematoria would have satisfied those in the late nineteenth and early twentieth centuries who were in important respects living for the future. As they passed the torch on to their children and heirs, they wanted to be remembered—remembered in this world and, ideally, for generations to come.

Today, however, we no longer actually pass the torch to our children in the way it was done in earlier eras. We live too long for that. By the time we get ready to pass the torch, our children are middle-aged or, in some cases, already elderly themselves. The number of Americans 85 and older is increasing at an astonishing rate, exceeded only by the rate of increase of our centenarians. In this sense, our own individual lives are extending further and further into the future. This means that, other things being equal, when we today think of the future, it often tends to be in terms of what our own personal needs are likely to be—social security, Medicare, nursing homes, and the like. Meanwhile, the priority given children in our national life, as measured by everything from poverty rates to broken homes to latchkey children to illegitimacy, has fallen drastically in recent decades.

In other words, our ability to envision the future beyond our own personal lives is shrinking rapidly. Here is where we come to the particularly short-term, myopic thinking so characteristic of today's American society and, in many respects, intrinsic to any highly technological, complex, and rapidly changing society. It is hard enough to see what will be happening to the world (and to us personally) a few years down the road; to try to imagine what the world will be like long after we have departed the scene is futile. Who can possibly imagine what America will be like in 50 or 100 years, let alone the vast stretches of future posterity that were the source of pleasure and comfort to the great Progress dreamers of the nineteenth century?

To put the difference in a nutshell: In the nineteenth century, and perhaps up to World War I or so, Americans thought that they knew the general shape of things to come. Therefore, they could live imaginatively in the world that would exist after they themselves were dead. In the twentieth century, or at least during the past 60 or 70 years, Americans find it more and more difficult to envision what life will be like after they have departed from the scene. This is because their departures are coming later and later in life, and, at the same time, their ability to imagine, figure out, and in any way take comfort from the distant future has been steadily diminishing.

The result today is that: (a) each generation tends to think more of itself than of other generations, previous or subsequent; and (b) individuals increasingly care very little about what happens to their bodies after they have shuffled off this mortal coil. Or to phrase it a bit more carefully: What difference does it make what happens to your remains in this earthly context? For as faith in a long-run terrestrial future is diminishing steadily, so now many Americans are turning to what is essentially a pre-modern approach (i.e., evangelical religion). And this approach, should it become more and more wide-spread, could easily represent a rejection of the whole Progress enterprise. For then, as in our earlier history, the only thing that would really matter would be the immortality of the soul. Markers and monuments would, once again, become irrelevant.

AFTER WE'RE GONE

Presumably, by the standards of our earlier post-war critics, all the recent changes in our funerary rituals should be considered improvements. We are now being much more prudent, sensible, and modest, much more like our Anglo-Saxon cousins. And we are certainly now spending far, far more on federal medical care for the elderly than on burying (or cremating) the dead. Very good news, apparently.

I myself am much less sure about all of this. Or, at least, I would argue that the current movement toward lessening, or even abandoning, the memorialization of our dead is a reflection of deeper forces in society, and that these deeper forces, far from being uniformly healthy and benign, may well pose a serious threat to our future national well-being.

Of course, it is very nice that we are all, or most of us, living longer. Despite the horror stories we hear of nursing-home debilitation, incontinence, paralysis, wheelchairs, tubes, respirators, and so on, most of us, given the choice, prefer to live longer rather than shorter lives, and most of us, furthermore, enjoy reasonably good health until near the end.

It is a rather different matter, however, when we come to consider our increasingly shorter time-horizons. I believe that our current lack of interest in the dead is related to our increasing lack of interest in the welfare of children. That is, both reflect a given generation's interest in its own well-being over the course of its own life-span, and a general lack of interest in the future that will be inherited by one's children. Temporal myopia is almost certainly responsible for many social pathologies—increased crime, illegitimacy, failing school performance, and, very probably, the increasing breakdown of the traditional American family. It is, in fact, almost surely no accident that an unprecedented celebration of the American family and a very much increased emphasis on memorialization of the dead occurred together during the late nineteenth and early twentieth centuries. Arguably, both can be regarded as incidental to the morality embodied in the Idea of Progress.

Thus our new funeral practices indicate that our priorities have changed not only with respect to the dead but also with respect to the children and grandchildren who will live after us. Apparently, the only thing that matters is what happens in this world and in this world now. The future after we are gone is a blank. Forget about it. Live your life for yourself. All the rest is basically incomprehensible.

This new approach is not, of course, universal. Two recent examples of memorialization that quickly come to mind are the Vietnam Memorial and the quilt dedicated to those who have died of AIDS. Still, the general drift of things is quite clear, and the point to be stressed is that our newly limited time-horizons seem to fail most seriously when it comes to our children. These, more than the dead, appear to be the real sacrificial lambs of late-twentieth-century America.

So, before we congratulate ourselves too much on the increased rationality of the now emerging "American way of death," perhaps we should wonder whether there are any steps that might be taken to modify the underlying conditions that have made this approach seem so attractive. A renewed interest in what happens to this physical and material world of ours after we have departed the scene may be crucial. If this renewal leads to the occasional funeral procession or even monument, perhaps that would not be too great a price to pay for the ancillary benefits that might well accrue.

"Thus Are Our Bodies, Thus Was Our Custom": Mortuary Cannibalism in an Amazonian Society

Beth A. Conklin

In American society, most of the dead are disposed of through burial or cremation. However, methods for the disposal of corpses are typically related to a people's general beliefs about what happens after death. In this essay Beth Conklin discusses the Wari' custom of mortuary cannibalism, and explains the cultural logic of the practice in terms of Wari' expressions of grief and mourning and their concepts of human-animal regeneration.

Most accounts of cannibalism have focused on *exocannibalism,* the eating of enemies, which has been typically explained as an act of domination and aggression. But that doesn't explain the custom of eating a departed loved one. Theories of mortuary cannibalism, primarily drawn from Melanesia, have generally explained the practice as a means of acquiring the energy or personal attributes of the dead person. Many systems of Amazonian cannibalism, however, view mortuary cannibalism as a means of altering relations between the living and the dead. As Conklin relates, the Wari' do not conceptualize their practices as a means of recycling the energies of the dead but rather as a service to the dead person and their close surviving kin.

For the Wari', eating the dead is an act of respect. People do not eat their own family members; rather, one is expected to consume the roasted flesh of one's *affines,* or relations by marriage. Dying individuals fear being left in the ground to rot and prefer the idea of being incorporated into their friends' bodies. So at one level, consuming a corpse is an act that honors dead relatives. Further, the Wari' believe that prolonged grieving is not healthy for the living and they try to destroy all reminders of the deceased. They avoid using the dead person's name, burn the dead person's house, and give away the person's possessions. Similarly, the practice of dismembering and roasting a corpse, or cremating it, destroys the physical remains so that they will no longer serve as a reminder of the loved one.

Most importantly, the practice of mortuary cannibalism is related to Wari' beliefs about hunting and the death and regeneration of animals. Wari' believe that the spirits of the dead reside in a beautiful underwater underworld but can return to earth as white-lipped peccaries. Spirits of the recently dead can lead peccary herds to their relatives' hunting areas, or can offer themselves as a gift of food to their families. When a peccary is killed, a shaman looks into its eyes to identify the human spirit inside. Thus a peccary

death is also the visit of a beloved ancestor. In Wari' society, death and mortuary cannibalism set the stage for an act of creation that reflects the relationship between humans and game animals. The central theme of the Wari' funeral and mourning rites is the regeneration of ancestors as peccaries. For Wari' mourners, a corpse's dismemberment and roasting reflects this human-to-animal transformation.

As you read, consider these questions:

1. What is meant by the terms *endocannibalism* and *exocannibalism*?
2. How does this study challenge some of the existing interpretations of cannibalism?
3. What are the various meanings of "eating" in Wari' society, and what does this mean for the interpretation of mortuary cannibalism?

The Wari'[1] (Pakaa Nova) are an indigenous population of about 1,500 people who live in the western Brazilian rain forest, in the state of Rondônia near the Bolivian border. Until the 1960s, they disposed of nearly all their dead by consuming substantial amounts of corpses' body substances. All Wari' elders living today took part in or witnessed mortuary cannibalism, and their recollections offer an opportunity to view cannibalism from the perspectives of those who participated in it. This article explores the question of why cannibalism was the preferred means for disposing of the dead, emphasizing indigenous interpretations of the logic and meanings of cannibalism.

From a cross-cultural perspective, Wari' customs appear unusual in several respects. In most other societies, mortuary cannibalism involved the consumption of only small amounts of a corpse's body substances, which typically were ingested by a dead person's consanguineal kin.[2] Among the Wari', however, the dead person's affines ideally consumed all of the roasted flesh, brains, heart, liver, and—sometimes—the ground bones. Cannibalism was the preferred treatment for all Wari' corpses, except in a few circumstances in which bodies were cremated.

The Wari' practiced both exocannibalism (the eating of enemies and social outsiders) and endocannibalism (the eating of members of one's own group) but considered the two forms of anthropophagy to have little in common. The eating of enemies, which will not be examined in detail here,[3] involved overt expressions of hostility: enemy body parts were abused and treated disrespectfully, and the freshly roasted flesh was eaten off the bone *ak karawa,* "like animal meat" (see Vilaça 1992:47–130). In contrast, the very different customs of mortuary cannibalism expressed honor and respect for the dead.

This article focuses on how mortuary cannibalism fit into Wari' experiences of grief and mourning. My approach traces themes emphasized by contemporary Wari' in reflecting on their past participation in cannibalistic funerals. The question "Why did you eat the dead?" tended to draw a limited range of responses. The most common reply was *"je' kwerexi',"* "Thus was our custom."[4] This statement should be taken seriously; for many Wari', cannibalism was simply the norm; for reasons I discuss in this article, it was considered to be the most respectful way to treat a human body. Beyond this, when older people reflected on deeper, personal motives, they tended to link cannibalism to a process of achieving emotional detachment from memories of the dead: "When we ate the body, we did not think longingly [*ko-romikat*] about the dead much." Numerous middle-aged and elderly people—of both sexes and in various villages—independently offered the explanation that cannibalism altered memories and the emotions of grief in ways that helped them deal with the loss of a loved one. Elders were bemused and at times rather irritated by anthropologists' singular obsession with the eating of bodies, for they insisted that cannibalism cannot be understood apart from the entire complex of mortuary rites and mourning behaviors aimed at reshaping emotional and spiritual relations between the living and the dead.

To understand cannibalism's role in mourning, I propose to show that Wari' practices reflected two concepts of widespread salience in lowland South America: the idea of the human body as a locus of physically constituted social relationships and social identity, and ideas about human-nonhuman reciprocity. These concepts merged in a yearlong series of traditional mourning rites that focused on actual and symbolic transformations of a dead person's body, from human to animal form. Cannibalism was a powerful element in a social process of mourning structured around images of ancestors' regeneration as animals with ongoing, life-supporting relations to their living relatives.

Wari' testimonies concerning the affective dimensions of cannibalism are unusual in the ethnographic literature, for we have few detailed accounts of cannibalism from the viewpoint of its practitioners. Most peoples who formerly practiced it no longer do so, leaving few individuals able or willing to speak to personal experiences of people-eating. Perhaps because of this, anthropological analyses of cannibalism have tended to focus mostly on the level of societal systems of meaning and symbolism. Cannibalism as praxis is poorly understood. This is particularly striking in the case of mortuary cannibalism: although it is, by definition, a cultural response to a fellow group member's death, we know little about how the socially constituted symbols of mortuary cannibalism relate to emotions and fit into individuals' lived experiences of coming to terms with a relative's death. Wari' recollections offer insights into one people's experiences. . . .

[We have deleted a 600-word section in which Conklin conducts a review of various theoretical attempts to explain cannibalism. She argues that most theorists have tended to explain cannibalism as an antisocial or oral-aggressive act because most of the literature on cannibalism has focused on the eating of enemies and outsiders (exocannibalism). Little effort has been expended in the study of eating members of one's own group, or endocannibalism.

Conklin states that studies of mortuary cannibalism demonstrate that those who practice endocannibalism may be motivated by the need for social integration rather than by aggression. She cites several studies that argue that cannibalism can symbolize social order and the regeneration of life-giving forces.—Editors]

Wari' mortuary customs reflect complex social and symbolic systems about which a great deal more can be said than is possible in this article. I refer interested readers to the works of other anthropologists who have studied Wari' society (Mason 1977; Von Graeve 1972, 1989) and the puzzle of Wari' anthropophagy (Meireles 1986; Vilaça 1989, 1992). Meireles has examined the role of cannibalism in defining self-other relations in the construction of Wari' personhood and emphasized the symbolism of fire as mediator of human-nonhuman relations. Vilaça presented symbolic-structuralist interpretations of both exo- and endocannibalism, with special attention to affinal relations, festivals, and origin myths related to anthropophagy. Her analysis has focused on Wari' conceptions of the social universe as structured around oppositions and reciprocal exchanges between predators and prey. Symbolic oppositions between the categories of *Wari'* ("we, people") and *karawa* ("animals") recur in Wari' ideology and rituals at multiple levels: humans vs. animals, Wari' vs. non-Wari', consanguines vs. affines, the living vs. the dead. Vilaça (1992:291) has emphasized that mortuary cannibalism symbolically associated the dead person with the category of prey and identified the living Wari' with the category of predators.

My analysis complements Vilaça's and Meireles's interpretations by situating cannibalism in relation to three other dimensions of Wari' experience: social processes of mourning, body concepts, and the regenerative imagery of ancestors' transformations into animals. To examine relationships among the social, symbolic, and ritual systems, I first describe the ethnographic context and mortuary rites and discuss why the Wari' case does not fit the major materialist and psychogenic models proposed to explain cannibalism elsewhere. I then examine social and psychological dimensions of Wari' body concepts to show why the corpse's destruction by cannibalism or cremation was considered essential. Finally, I explore Wari' ideas about human-animal relations that suggest an answer to the question of why the Wari' preferred cannibalism rather than cremation.

ETHNOGRAPHIC CONTEXT

The Wari' speak a language in the Chapakuran language family isolate. They entered permanent relations with Brazilian national society between 1956 and 1969, when the former national Indian agency, the S.P.I. (Serviço de Proteção aos Índios), sponsored a series of pacification expeditions that terminated Wari' autonomy. The Wari' now reside in eight major villages in indigenous reserves along tributaries of the Mamoré and Madeira Rivers in the municipality of Guajará-Mirim, Rondônia. Prior to the contact they had no canoes and inhabited interfluvial (terra firme) areas of the rain forest, away from the larger rivers. Today, as in the past, subsistence depends on slash-and-burn farming, hunting, fishing, and foraging. Maize is the principal staple crop, and hunting is the most socially valued food-getting activity.

Precontact villages typically were comprised of about thirty people living in several nuclear family households. Contemporary Wari' communities are administered by FUNAI (Fundação Nacional do Índio), the Brazilian government Indian agency, whose policies of population concentration and sedentarization have disrupted traditional settlement patterns and social organization. Today's villages, of 80–400 people, are located at nontraditional sites near major rivers or roads accessible to transportation to town.

Wari' society is staunchly egalitarian, and social relations are characterized by a high degree of flexibility. Leadership is ephemeral; there are no "chiefs," and no formal positions of political authority above the household level. Mason (1977) categorized Wari' kinship terminology as a Crow/Omaha–type system. Wari' kin groups are ego-centered bilateral kindreds; there are no lineages, and no internal segregation based on age grades or ceremonial activities. Precontact postmarital residence was flexible, with couples free to live near either spouse's bilateral kin after initial matrilocal bride service. Of central importance for understanding mortuary customs is the role of affinity as the strongest organizing principle in Wari' society. Alliances among families related by marriage[5] are important in food sharing, mutual aid, funeral duties and, in the past, were one basis for war alliances. Wari' society is by no means conflict-free, but most decision making is consensual, and the general tenor of social relations emphasizes mutuality and reciprocity among kin, affines, and allies.

The precontact Wari' were divided into named, territorially based subgroups (Oro Nao', Oro Eo', Oro At, Oro Mon, Oro Waram, and Oro Waram-Xijein) that were the largest social units with which individuals identified. A subgroup's members were committed to peaceful coexistence and cooperation in warfare and emergencies. Amicable relations among the villages in a subgroup were affirmed and maintained by festival exchanges, including celebrations called hüroroin and tamara that are models for the human-nonhuman alliance exchanges represented in mortuary cannibalism.

After the first peaceful contacts with outsiders were established in the Rio Dois Irmãos area in 1956, government (S.P.I.) agents and New Tribes missionaries witnessed several anthropophagous funerals. Most of the Wari' population entered contact in 1961–62. News of Wari' funerary cannibalism became public knowledge in early 1962, when an S.P.I. agent sold his eyewitness account to a São Paulo newspaper (Folha de São Paulo 1962). In response, a competing paper sent journalists to the Rio Negro-Ocaia contact site, where they photographed dismemberment and roasting at a child's funeral (de Carvalho 1962). Brazilian anthropologists and S.P.I. officials convinced the paper not to publish these photographs and attempted to use the ensuing publicity to call public attention to the tragic situation of the recently contacted Wari' (Cruzeiro 1962:123–125).

Contact with the pacification teams introduced devastating epidemics of measles, influenza, tuberculosis, and other cosmopolitan diseases. Within two or three years of contact, approximately 60 percent of the precontact population was dead. Chronically ill, psychologically traumatized, and unable to hunt or plant crops, the survivors became extremely dependent on outsiders for food and medical care. Missionaries and government agents manipulated this dependency to put an end to cannibalism by threatening to withhold food and medicines from those who continued to eat the dead. They insisted that corpses be buried instead. At each of the three major contact sites, Wari' initially resisted this forced change to burial.

The deadly epidemics, however, created another reason to abandon cannibalism: traditional illness concepts could not explain the unfamiliar maladies, and so people listened when missionaries told them that the new diseases were spread by eating infected corpses. Wari' began burying people who died of illness (the great majority of early postcontact deaths), but, for a while, they continued to cannibalize those whose deaths were attributed to accidents, sorcery, and other nondisease causes. Families carried corpses into the forest, to be roasted away from outsiders' eyes. However, these efforts at deception ultimately failed, and by the end of 1962 or early 1963, nearly everyone had abandoned cannibalism altogether. (The exception was a group of about thirty Oro Mon who lived autonomously until 1969.) Today, all Wari' follow Western customs of burying corpses in cemeteries in the forest.[6]

No anthropologist has witnessed Wari' anthropophagy, and many data presented here are based on retrospective reconstructions. My primary sources are the testimonies of numerous older Wari' who say that they participated in or observed mortuary cannibalism. During two years of medical anthropological field work in 1985–87, I interviewed all 198 families in the communities of Santo André, Ribeirao, Lage, Tanajura, and Rio Negro-Ocaia (85 percent of the total Wari' population). Interviews with adults of both sexes, aimed at collecting genealogies and mortality and morbidity histories, often led to discussions of personal experiences with relatives' deaths and funerals. I observed aspects of contemporary mourning behavior, including ritual wailing and the handling of a corpse, but no one died in a village where I was present, and I attended no burials or complete funerals. Santo André, a community of 190 people, was my principal residence, and I discussed issues treated in this article with all the elders and many middle-aged people there. The most detailed information and insights came from several key informants: three men and two women between ages 60 and 75, two men in their 50s, and a man and woman in their early 40s. Most Santo André residents are descendants of the precontact Rio Dois Irmãos area population, and this article describes this group's practices, which differed only in minor details from other Wari' communities.

The Wari' do not conform to Arens' (1979) assertions that alleged cannibals seldom acknowledge eating anyone and that cannibalism is primarily a symbol of inhumanity and barbarism projected upon enemies, neighbors, and uncivilized "others." Wari' anthropophagy is not merely alleged by outsiders; Wari' themselves freely affirm practicing it in the past, even though they are aware that outsiders consider it barbaric. I found no one who denied that corpses customarily were cannibalized; numerous elders spoke openly of eating human flesh. Independent descriptions of particular funerals were internally consistent and corresponded to reports by New Tribes missionaries and S.P.I. agents who observed cannibalism in the early postcontact period. By any reasonable standards for the documentation of past events not witnessed by an ethnographer, there is no question that the Wari' ate their dead.

TRADITIONAL FUNERALS

Today, as in the past, funerals generally take place in the house of a senior kinsman of the deceased.[7] The household's sleeping platform (or raised floor) is removed to permit mourners to crowd together under the palm-thatch roof. Two loosely defined groups have prescribed roles at funerals. The first is the *iri' nari*[8] ("true kin," or close sanguines and the spouse). Wari' define consanguinity in terms of shared blood and classify spouses as consanguines by virtue of sexual transfers of body fluids that create shared blood. Between spouses, it is said, "there is only one body" (*xika pe' na kwere*). Linked to the deceased by shared body substance, the iri' nari are the principal mourners. From the time of biological death until the body is disposed of, they remain nearest the corpse, holding it in their arms and crying.

The second group of mourners, *nari paxi* ("those who are like kin but not truly related"), most properly consists of the dead person's own affines and affines of the deceased's close kin, but the term is extended to include all non-consanguines attending the funeral. Close affines are responsible for the work of funerals: female affines prepare maize *chicha* (a sweet, unfermented drink) and maize *pamonha* (dense, unleavened bread) to feed visitors, and male affines (ideally, the dead person's brothers-in-law or sons-in-law) serve as messengers summoning people to the funeral. They prepare and dispose of the corpse and funeral apparatus and look out for the welfare of emotionally distraught mourners.

In traditional funerals, the iri' nari sat together, apart from other mourners. In contemporary funerals, the spatial division is less marked, but close kin remain nearest the corpse. All mourners press close together around the body, leaning on each other's shoulders and wailing. Death wails are of several types, including wordless crying, the singing of kinship terms for the deceased, and a more structured keening called *aka pijim* ("to cry to speak"), in which mourners recount memories of the deceased, singing of shared experiences and the person's life history, deeds, and kindnesses. (On Amazonian ritual lament, see Briggs 1992; Graham 1986; Seeger 1987; Urban 1988, 1991.) From the moment of death until the funeral's end, everyone joins in a ceaseless, high-pitched keening that sends a haunting mantra of collective grief reverberating off the surrounding forest.

The dead person's humanity and social connections are repeatedly affirmed in funeral actions directed at the corpse itself, which is the constant focus of attention. Corpses are never left to lie alone. From the moment of death until the body is disposed of, grieving kin constantly cradle the corpse in their arms, hugging it, pressing their own bodies against it. Desire for physical contact can be so intense that, according to several Santo André residents, there was a funeral a few years ago where the corpse was in danger of being pulled apart by distraught kin struggling to embrace it. Finally, a senior kinsman enforced order by mandating that only one person at a time could hold the body.

Numerous funeral actions express mourners' self-identification with the dead person's physical state and desires to join the deceased in death. Any loss of consciousness, such as fainting, is considered a form of death. In one common funeral practice, close relatives "die" (*mi' pin*) by lying one on top of the other, in stacks of three or four people with the corpse on top. When someone faints from the suffocating press of bodies, he or she is pulled out of the pile and someone else joins the pile, in a process repeated again and again. In a 1986 funeral, people piled into the homemade coffin, embracing the corpse on top.

In traditional funerals, the male affine helpers constructed the ritual firewood bundle and roasting rack. Ideally, these were made of roofbeams, decorated with feathers and painted with red annatto (*urucú, Bixa orellana*). A beam was taken from each house in the dead person's village, leaving the thatched roofs sagging in visible expression of death's violation of the community's integrity. Funerals for infants were less elaborate; regular, undecorated firewood was used. When preparations were completed, the helpers lit the fire, spread clean mats on the ground, and dismembered the body, using a new bamboo arrow tip. Internal organs were removed first, and the heart and liver were wrapped in leaves to be roasted. Body parts considered inedible, including the hair, nails, genitals, intestines, and other entrails, were burned. The helpers then severed the head, removed the brains, cut the limbs at the joints, and placed the body parts on the roasting rack. Young children's body parts were wrapped in leaves in the manner used to roast small fish and soft foods.

Several elders recalled that the most emotionally difficult event in a funeral was the moment when the corpse was taken from its relatives' arms to be dismembered. As the body was cut, wailing and hysterical expressions of grief reached a fevered pitch. Up to this moment, funeral activities had been dominated by mourners' expressions of physical and affective attachments to the dead person's body. Dismemberment represented a radical alteration of the corpse and mourners' relations to it, a graphic severing of the attachments represented in the body. According to these elders, it was dismemberment, not cannibalism, that provoked the most intense emotional dissonance. Once the corpse had been cut, eating it was considered the most respectful possible treatment, for reasons discussed below.

The dead person's close consanguines (iri' nari) did not eat the corpse. Consumption of a close consanguine or spouse's flesh is strongly prohibited, because eating a close relative (with whom one shared body substance) would be tantamount to eating one's own flesh, or autocannibalism. It is believed to be fatal.[9]

The nari paxi, affines and other non-kin, were responsible for consuming the corpse; they are sometimes referred to as ko kao' ("those who ate"). In a married person's funeral, those who consumed the body typically included the dead person's spouse's siblings, spouse's parents, spouse's parents' siblings, and the deceased's children's spouses, as well as these individuals' own close consanguines. Unmarried people typically were eaten by their siblings' spouses, siblings' spouses' siblings, their parents' siblings' spouses, and these individuals' close kin. Thus, Wari' cannibalized members of the families from which their bilateral consanguines had taken marriage partners. Meireles (1986) noted that cannibalism restrictions generally coincided with incest prohibitions.

Cannibalism was a primary obligation of affinity. Adult men were obliged to eat their close affines; refusal to do so would have insulted the dead person's family. Women were not required to participate in cannibalism but did so at their own discretion.[10] Distinctions of generation, age, or gender were largely irrelevant: male and female adults and adolescents consumed corpses of all ages and both sexes. Men's and women's corpses were treated almost identically.

Roasting usually commenced in the late afternoon and eating usually began at dusk. The dead person's closest kin divided the well-roasted brains, heart, and liver into small pieces, placed the pieces on clean mats, and called the others to begin eating. The affines (nari paxi) did not descend greedily upon the flesh but hung back, crying and expressing reluctance to eat; only after repeated insistence by the dead person's close kin (iri' nari) did they accept the flesh. The iri' nari then prepared the other body parts by removing the flesh

from the bones and dividing it into small pieces. They usually arranged these on a mat along with pieces of roasted maize bread (pamonha); in some funerals, they placed the flesh in a conical clay pot and handed pieces to the eaters, cradling the pot in their laps in the affectionate position used to hold someone's head in repose or during illness. In marked contrast to the aggressive, disrespectful treatment of enemies' flesh in exocannibalism, funeral eaters did not touch the flesh with their hands but held it delicately on thin splinters like cocktail toothpicks. They ate very slowly, alternately crying and eating. There appears to have been no special significance attached to ingesting particular body parts, and no pattern determining who ate which portions.

The ideal was to consume all of the flesh, heart, liver, and brains; in practice, the amount actually eaten depended on the degree of the corpse's decay. It is considered imperative that corpses not be disposed of (by cannibalism, cremation, or burial) until all important relatives have arrived at the funeral, seen the body, and participated in the wailing eulogies. The length of time before a body was roasted traditionally varied according to the dead person's age, status, and social ties: the older and more socially prominent the deceased, the longer the delay in roasting. Before the contact, when villages were scattered over a wide territory, most adults were not roasted until two or three days after death, when decay was well-advanced.

It was considered important to consume as much flesh as possible. When, however, flesh was too putrid to stomach—as it usually was in the case of adult corpses—the eaters forced themselves to swallow small pieces from various body parts, then cremated the rest. The ideal of total consumption was realized mainly in funerals for infants and young children who, having few social ties of their own, were roasted within a day or so of their deaths and eaten entirely. Complete consumption also appears to have occurred for some terminally ill elders whose relatives gathered and commenced wailing long before biological death. In most adult and adolescent funerals, however, most of the flesh probably was burned rather than eaten.

Consumption of the corpse continued until dawn, at which time any remaining flesh was cremated. Treatment of bones varied. Sometimes they were ground into meal, mixed with honey, and consumed. In other cases, especially in the Rio Dois Irmãos area, the bones were burned, pulverized, and buried. In all cases, the clay pots, mats, roasting rack, and funeral fire remains were burned, pounded to dust, and buried in situ by the male affine helpers. The helpers then swept the earth to eradicate all traces of the funeral and replaced the household sleeping platform over the spot where the ashes were buried. . . .

[In the 650-word section deleted here, Conklin discusses the argument that cannibalism is practiced for nutritional reasons. She agrees that cannibalism could provide supplemental protein and calcium, but cites dietary studies that show the Wari' do not suffer from food shortages and that their diets are nutritionally adequate. In other words, there is no nutritional reason for the practice.

Conklin also revisits the question of whether endocannibalism is an expression of hostility or mediated tension between groups related by marriage. She states that her informants rejected the notion that their mortuary customs expressed hostility. They said that aggression has no place at funerals and that people who did not love the deceased are barred from attending the funeral. Conklin also states that she found little evidence of hostility between groups of affinal kin and that affinal tension among the Wari' is no greater than that found in noncannibalistic societies.—Editors]

AFFINITY AND EXCHANGE

Vilaça has emphasized the importance of mortuary cannibalism as a marker of Wari' affines' relations to one another: "The funeral rite . . . reveals, through the opposition between those who eat together [comensais] and those who do not [não-comensais], the opposition cognates/affines. In the interior of Wari' society, cannibalism constructs and identifies affinity" (1992:293).

Vilaça (1992:293) also observed that Wari' affinal cannibalism reflected a recurrent theme in South American mythology, identified by Lévi-Strauss in The Raw and the Cooked (1969): the characterization of affines (the "takers" of women) as real or potential cannibal prey. Besides the Wari', the Yanomámi also practice affinal cannibalism, consuming their affines' ground bones (Albert 1985). Sixteenth-century Tupinambá exocannibalism involved another kind of affinal cannibalism: a war captive was married to a Tupinambá woman (making him an affine to her kin) before being killed and eaten (Staden 1928[1557]). In the cosmology of the Araweté of central Brazil (who bury their dead), cannibalism is seen as a transformative mechanism for creating affinal ties between humans and divinities: when Araweté die, the gods consume the human spirits (making them into beings like themselves), then rejuvenate and marry them (Viveiros de Castro 1992). Viveiros de Castro has observed that among the Araweté, Tupinambá, Yanomami, and Pakaa Nova (Wari'), cannibalism "links affines or transforms into affines those whom it links" (1992:259).[11]

Wari' affinal cannibalism might suggest a Lévi-Straussian model of exchanges of cooked meat (human flesh) for "raw" (virgin, fecund) women given in marriage (Lévi-Strauss 1969). As in many societies, eating is a Wari' metaphor for sexual intercourse, and there are obvious parallels between affinal exchanges of human flesh in funerals and the frequent exchanges of meat (which men give to female affines) and fish (which women give to male affines) that mark affinity in everyday life. From a structuralist perspective, Wari' mortuary cannibalism resonates with exchanges of meat and marriage partners, but Wari' do not see it that way. Everyone with whom I raised this issue rejected

an equation of cannibalism with exchanges of sexual partners or food; some found the suggestion insulting. Sexual and reproductive imagery has little place in Wari' mortuary practices, in marked contrast to its prominence in many other societies' mortuary rites (Bloch and Parry 1982), and in Melanesian endocannibalism practices linked to elaborate ideas about male and female body substances (see Gillison 1983; Poole 1983).

From an emic point of view, what was important in cannibalistic Wari' funerals was not the exchange of substance (human flesh) but the exchange of services. Disposal of the body is a primary obligation of affinity, a service performed out of respect for the dead person and his or her family. When asked why it was the affines who ate the corpse, Wari' elders invariably replied that the affines ate it because somebody had to eat it, and the dead person's consanguines (iri' nari) could not do so (because of the prohibition against eating the flesh of someone related to oneself by shared biological substance). In addition, a number of people asserted that one simply does not feel like eating anything when grieving intensely. Eating, particularly meat-eating, expresses happiness and social integration. Symbolic oppositions between sadness and oral activity (eating, drinking, singing, shouting) are numerous: adults eat little during close kin's illnesses, consume nothing at their funerals, and eat little while mourning. People considered it irrational to suggest eating flesh at a close relative's funeral.

By Wari' logic, these cultural assumptions definitively precluded cannibalism by consanguines. The task thus fell to affines, who were the only clearly defined social group that had close social ties to the dead person's family but did not share their intimate biological and affective ties to the deceased.[12] Affinal cannibalism was a matter of pragmatism.

It was also a matter of politics. Mortuary services are central in marking, strengthening, and reconstituting affinal ties after a death. Funerals draw extended families together as does no other event, and they are the most prominent occasion (aside from mixita fights) when affines act as discrete groups in complementary opposition to one another. In fulfilling mortuary obligations, including disposal of the corpse, Wari' families linked by marriage affirm continuing commitments that transcend the lifetime of any individual member.

If one accepts this indigenous view of the disposal of corpses (whether by burial, cannibalism, or cremation) as a service rendered to the family of the deceased, assigning this task to affines does not appear particularly unusual cross-culturally. In native Amazonian societies, affines perform burial and other funeral duties among the Cashinahua (Kensinger, in press), Canela (W. Crocker, in press), and Shavante (Maybury-Lewis 1974:281). Among the Munducurú (Murphy 1960:72) and Kagwahiv (Kracke 1978:13), these tasks fall to members of the opposite moiety, the group from which the dead person's moiety takes marriage partners. Wari' mortuary cannibalism fit this pattern of delegating mortuary tasks to affines and reflected the associations between affinity and cannibalism found in other lowland South American societies' myths and cosmologies. But this does not explain why Wari' actually *ate* their affines, whereas other peoples with similar conceptual systems did not. In this article, the question to be addressed is not why the Wari' ate their affines, but why cannibalism was the preferred treatment for human corpses.

EATING AS AN ACT OF RESPECT

Pleasing the dead by consuming their bodies is a recurrent theme in Wari' discussions of mortuary cannibalism: the dead wanted to be eaten, or at least cremated, and not to have done either would have given offense. For dying individuals, the idea of being incorporated into fellow tribesmembers' bodies apparently had considerably more appeal than the alternative of being left to rot in the ground alone.[13] One man told of his great-aunt (FFZ) who, on her deathbed, summoned him and his father (normally expected to cry rather than eat at her funeral) and asked them, as a favor, to join in consuming her body. In contrast to Western views of eating as an act of objectification and domination of the thing consumed, eating can express respect and sympathy in Wari' culture, especially in contrast to the alternative of burial. The ground is considered "dirty" and polluting. Adults who take pride in their bodies do not sit in the dirt, ritual objects must not touch the earth, and people avoid spilling food on the ground. These values influence attitudes towards burial in the earth, which informants often described as not only dirty, but also "wet" and "cold." Respectful treatment for human remains is dry and warm; the only traditional space for respectful burial was beneath household sleeping platforms, where small fires burned almost constantly, keeping the earth warm as well as dry. This is where funeral ashes were interred in the past and where placentae and miscarried fetuses continue to be buried. Before the contact, burial in the forest expressed dishonor and normally occurred in only one context: if a woman suffered multiple stillbirths or neonatal deaths, her family might request a male affine to bury her dead infant in an anthill or in wet earth beside a stream to discourage her future babies from dying and risking similarly unpleasant treatment.

In contrast to the disrespect manifest in burial, eating can be a sympathetic act, as shown in this story about the Maize Spirit *(Jaminain Mapak)* told by a Santo André man. The story explains why one should not leave maize lying on the ground:

> Long ago, a man was walking to his field carrying a basket of maize seeds to plant. A maize kernel fell to the ground on the path. The man did not see it and went on. The maize seed began to cry like a child. Another man came along and found it crying on the ground. He picked it up and ate it. In doing so, he *saved* it, showing that he felt sympathy [*xiram pa'*] for it. The man who ate the seed planted his field and it yielded great

quantities of maize. The man who had left the seed on the ground planted his field, but nothing grew.

This parable demonstrates Wari' ideas that abandoning a spirit-being to lie on the forest floor connotes disrespect, whereas eating it expresses respect. Eating can be an act of compassion that pleases the thing consumed so that it bestows abundance on the eater.

Similar ideas about eating as an expression of respect for the eaten are evident in food taboos associated with *jami karawa,* animals whose spirits have human form (see Conklin 1989:336–350). Spirits never die, and when a hunter kills a jami karawa animal, its spirit assumes a new animal body. However, animal spirits cannot complete their transitions to new physical bodies as long as portions of their former bodies remain. To avoid provoking spirits' wrath, one must quickly roast and eat jami karawa. Animal spirits are offended by the killing and disrespectful treatment of their bodies, not by the eating of their flesh. On the contrary, eating demonstrates respect, especially in contrast to the alternative of abandoning uneaten body parts on or in the ground.

Several funeral customs expressed these values of honoring the dead by preventing their body substances from being lost to the earth. When corpses were cut, a close kinsman of the deceased sometimes lay face down, supporting the corpse on his back during the butchering, so that its fluids would spill onto his own body rather than onto the ground. Similarly, elders recalled that young children's corpses had much fat that dripped as they roasted; to prevent it from falling into the fire, a child's grieving parents and grandparents would catch the fat in a clay pot and smear it over their own heads and bodies as they cried. Mortuary cannibalism expressed similar compassion for the dead by saving their body substances from abandonment to the earth and, instead, incorporating them into a living person's body.

In the early postcontact period, many Wari' found the forced change to burial repulsive. One Santo André man told of his father's death, which occurred soon after outsiders had put an end to cannibalism. Unhappy with the prospect of being buried, the dying man requested that, as an approximation of traditional practices, his corpse be dismembered and the pieces placed in a large ceramic cooking pot to be buried by his affines. Even today, burial continues to be a source of covert dissatisfaction among some elders, who still view burial as a less loving way to treat a human body than cannibalism or cremation. They consider the body's persistence problematic for close kin, whose attachments to the dead require attenuation and transformation. . . .

[We have deleted a short section here called "Attachments to the Socially Constructed Body," in which Conklin shows how the Wari' conceptualized the link between one's body and social relations. The Wari' believe that relatives share body substances, especially blood. In this way kin relations are understood as a network that physically links individuals into an organic unity. Further, the Wari' believe that a person's behavior and personality characteristics are determined by their body substances, especially the heart and blood. Thus when Conklin asked about someone's behavior, the answer was typically something like "his flesh is like that." Consequently, whereas Westerners view a corpse as an empty shell, to the Wari' a corpse still houses a person's identity and a host of social relations and interpersonal bonds.—Editors]

DETACHMENT AND DESTRUCTION

Gradual detachment from thinking about and remembering the dead is considered a desirable social goal, for prolonged sadness *(tomi xaxa)* is believed to endanger individual health and productivity. The negative psycho-emotional process of grieving is described with the verb *koromikat*, which refers to the negative experience of nostalgia: missing, remembering, and thinking longingly about a lost or distant object (usually a kinsperson, lover, or friend). Wari' emphasize vision and hearing as primary sources of knowledge and stimuli to memory. Because the sight of material objects evokes memories, they consider it essential to destroy or transform all tangible reminders of the dead. They burn a dead person's house and personal possessions and burn, discard, or give away crops planted by the deceased. Less-easily destroyed modern possessions, such as kettles, machetes, and shotguns, usually are given to nonrelatives. Neighbors often change their houses' appearance by altering doorways and paths, and close kin cut their hair. People traditionally have avoided using dead people's names or kin referents, although in speaking to outsiders they have recently relaxed name avoidances.

The cultural rationale for these practices reflects two concerns: banishing ghosts, and removing stimuli that evoke memories of the dead.[14] Vilaça has noted:

> According to the Wari', the destruction by fire of all reminders of the deceased is, in the first place, a protection against the sadness that is felt upon seeing something that belonged to the deceased or that was touched, used or made by him; but it is also a way to avoid the coming of the ghost. [1992:228]

These dual concerns are consistent with the two primary objectives identified in cross-cultural analyses of death rites: to remove the deceased from the world of the living to the symbolic world of the dead, and to facilitate survivors' acceptance of the death and the consequent alteration of social life without the dead person (Bloch and Parry 1982:4). With regard to separating the dead from the living, the destruction of material traces is believed to lessen the tendency of ghosts *(jima)* to return to earth. Jima generally do not cause illness, but they do frighten people, and, in the days following a death, the jima of the recently deceased may try to carry kin away for companionship in death. Destroying possessions and altering appearances confuse jima so that, unable to find their former homes and companions, they return

to the otherworld of the dead. Some people also suggested that the smoke surrounding roasting corpses obscured and confused the vision of jima who returned during their own funerals.

Banishing spirits, or liberating spirits from their physical bodies, has been cited as a motive for cannibalism in some other lowland South American societies (Albert 1985; Clastres 1974:316; Dole 1974:306; Ramos 1990:196; Zerries 1960). Meireles asserted that the explanation for Wari' cannibalism was "based in the idea that the dead person's soul must be banished, at the risk of afflicting the living" (Meireles 1986:427). Vilaça (1992:233, 243, 262) has interpreted roasting as a dissociative mechanism required for spirits' liberation from their bodies and full transition to the afterlife.[15] This idea is clear in Wari' food taboos that require quick consumption of certain game animals to liberate the animal spirits from their bodies (Conklin 1989:345–346; Vilaça 1992:70), but it appears to be of limited relevance in explaining cannibalism. None of my informants spontaneously suggested that eating the dead liberated spirits or prevented their return. Rather, when asked if it had that effect, some agreed that it might. Others insisted that cannibalism had nothing to do with banishing spirits. As evidence, they cited the fact, which no one disputed, that the ghosts (jima) of people who are buried today do not return to wander the earth any more frequently than those who were cannibalized or cremated.

As Vilaça (1989:378) noted, the desire to dissociate body from spirit fails to explain the preference for cannibalism over cremation, except insofar as Wari' view the acts of cooking and eating as implicit in the act of making fire.[16] Because Wari' view cremation and cannibalism as equally effective in separating spirits from their bodies and from the world of the living, the preference for cannibalism must be explained in other terms.

REMEMBERING AND THE BODY

Wari' discussions of reasons for destroying corpses and possessions emphasized the need to remove reminders in order to help mourners stop dwelling on thoughts of the dead. In a cross-cultural study of grief and mourning, Rosenblatt et al. suggested that tie-breaking and "finalizing" acts (such as ghost fears, taboos on names of the dead, and destruction of personal property) facilitate survivors' transitions to new social roles:

> [I]n a long-term relationship such as marriage, innumerable behaviors appropriate to the relationship become associated with stimuli (sights, sounds, odors, textures) in the environment of the relationship. When death . . . makes it necessary to treat the relationship as ended and to develop new patterns of behavior, these stimuli inhibit the change, because they elicit old dispositions. To facilitate change, tie-breaking practices that eliminate or alter these stimuli seem to be of great value. [1976:67–68]

Battaglia has highlighted the cultural value ascribed to acts of "forgetting as a willed transformation of memory" (1991:3) in Melanesian mortuary rites that transform materially constituted aspects of the dead person's former social identity and replace them with new images. The importance that Wari' ascribe to the destruction of reminders and processual alteration of memories and images of the dead was evident in the ritual called *ton ho'* ("the sweeping"), practiced today in an attenuated form (see Vilaça 1992:227–229; for parallels among the Canela, see Crocker and Crocker 1994:121). For several months after a death, senior Wari' consanguines, especially kin of the same sex as the deceased, make repeated trips to the forest to seek out all places associated with the dead person's memory: the place where a hunter made a blind to wait for deer, sites where a woman fished or felled a fruit tree, a favorite log where the dead person liked to sit. At each spot, the kinsperson cuts the vegetation in a wide circle, burns the brush, and sweeps over the burned circle. Elders said that, while doing this, they thought intensely about the dead person, recalling and honoring events of his or her life. Afterward, the burning and sweeping have definitively altered sentiments associated with each place so that "there is not much sadness there."

The imperative to destroy tangible elements traditionally extended to the corpse itself. Given the strength of Wari' ideas about the body's social construction and the physical bases of social relatedness, it is understandable that corpses are powerful reminders.[17] A number of individuals commented that today, when people are buried rather than eaten, their thoughts return again and again to images of the body lying under its mound of earth. A Santo André father who had recently buried a young son tried to explain this to me, saying:

> I don't know if you can understand this, because you have never had a child die. But for a parent, when your child dies, it is a very sad thing to put his body in the earth. It is cold in the earth. We keep remembering our child, lying there, cold. We remember and we are sad. In the old days when the others ate the body, we did not think about [koromikat] his body much. We did not think about our child so much, and we were not so sad.

The emotional potency of mourners' subjective attachments to the dead and their physical bodies is one of the keys to understanding Wari' cannibalism.[18]

In traditional funerals, mourners' dramatic manifestations of physical identification with the dead person's body were followed by a dramatic sundering of these bonds, beginning with the corpse's dismemberment. Cutting and roasting or cremating the body initiated a processual disassembling of physical objectifications of social identity and social relations. Although Wari' considered cannibalism and cremation equally effective ways of severing ties between human bodies and spirits, they considered cannibalism more effective in attenuating affective attachments. Cannibalism

initiated and facilitated the construction of a new relationship between the living and the dead by evoking images of the dead person's regeneration in animal form, and human-animal reciprocity, in which endocannibalism was the mythic balance to human hunting.

PREDATION AND RECIPROCITY

Wari' myth traces the origin of endocannibalism to the establishment of mutual predator-prey relations between hunters and animals. A story called *Pinom* is a variation of a widespread Amazonian mythic theme of the origins of cooking fire (see, for example, Lévi-Strauss 1969; Overing 1986; Wilbert and Simoneau 1990:111–133). (For analysis of the Wari' *Pinom* myth, see Meireles 1986; Vilaça 1989, 1992.) The Wari' version tells how mortuary cannibalism originated as the consequence of the theft of fire, which originally was possessed by an avaricious old woman who ate children raw. Violating Wari' principles of egalitarian sharing, this cannibal-crone let people temporarily use her fire only in exchange for large payments of firewood and fish. Without fire, Wari' could not farm, could not roast and eat maize or fish (most game animals did not yet exist), and had to subsist on raw forest fruits and hearts of palm.

Finally, two boys managed to outwit the old woman and steal her fire. They and the other Wari' escaped by climbing a liana into the sky, but the old woman pursued them. At the last moment, a piranha came to their rescue and cut the vine. The cannibal-crone fell into her own fire below, and from her burning body emerged the carnivores: jaguars, ocelots, and *orotapan* (an unidentified carnivore, probably wolf or fox). In Wari' cosmology, jaguars not only kill and eat humans but also transform themselves into other animal spirits that cause illness by capturing and eating human spirits. Other animals, including birds, monkeys, deer, and tapir, originated when the Wari' turned into animals in order to jump from the sky back to earth, and some decided to remain animals. People and animals thus share a common origin. The myth highlights Wari' ideas about the balance of human-animal opposition: game animals came into existence, but people became prey for jaguars and animal spirit predators.

The origin of endocannibalism is attributed to parallel events in this myth's second part. The two boys turned into birds to carry the fire to earth, but a man named Pinom killed them and selfishly kept the fire to himself. Others could only watch hungrily while Pinom's family alone was able to cook food. Finally, a shaman tricked Pinom, captured the cooking fire, and shared it with everyone, thereby allowing the Wari' to become a hunting and farming society. Outwitted and enraged, Pinom told the Wari': "Now you will have to roast your children!"

This is interpreted as the mythic origin of endocannibalism, even though Pinom did not specify eating the dead, or affines' roles in it. Although most Wari' are now familiar with Christian concepts of sin and retribution, no one interpreted Pinom's dictum as a terrible punishment for human misdeeds. Instead, informants saw endocannibalism as a natural balance to humanity's acquisition of fire: the price for gaining fire to roast (and eat) animals was to be roasted (and eaten) oneself.

Reciprocity in relations between humans and animals is a common cross-cultural concept, especially among native American peoples whose survival depends on hunting and fishing. Sanday identified this idea as a recurrent theme in native North American myths about the origins of cannibalism and suggested that it reflected the following logic: "There is a reciprocal relationship between the eater and the eaten. Just as animals are hunted, so are humans; whoever wants to get food must become food" (1986:38–39). Notions of balanced, reciprocal, human-animal predation are central in Wari' cosmology and eschatology. Mortuary cannibalism reflected ideas of a human-nonhuman alliance predicated on reciprocal predation between living people and the spirits of animals and ancestors.

AFTERLIFE AND ALLIANCE

In Wari' visions of the afterlife, the spirits of the dead reside under the waters of deep rivers and lakes. The ancestors appear as they did in life, but everyone is strong, beautiful, and free of deformity, disease, and infirmity. The ancestors' social world resembles precontact Wari' society, with villages, houses, fields, and intervillage festival exchanges. Life is easy and crops grow abundantly, but all food is vegetarian; there is no hunting or fishing because all animals have human forms underwater.

In this underworld, the Wari' ancestors are allied and intermarried with a neighboring indigenous group called "Water spirits" (*jami kom*). The Water spirits appear human, but they are not Wari' ancestors and have never lived on earth as ordinary people. Rather, they are primal forces that control human death, animal fertility, and destructive storms. Their leader is a giant with huge genitalia named Towira Towira (*towira* means "testicle"), who resembles the masters of animals and other mythic figures common in lowland South American cosmologies (see, for example, Reichel-Dolmatoff 1971:80–86; Zerries 1954). Towira Towira is master of the entire underworld; all its inhabitants, including Wari' ancestors, are called jami kom.

Wari' believe that when ancestral spirits emerge from the water, they assume the bodies of white-lipped peccaries (*Tayassu pecari),* a wild, pig-like animal that roams in large herds.[19] In everyday speech, *jami mijak,* "white-lipped peccary spirit," is one of the most common ways of referring to the dead. The nonancestral Water spirits (Towira Towira's tribe) also can become white-lipped peccaries but more commonly appear as fish, especially as masses of small, easily killed fish that appear unpredictably in the flooded forest's shallow waters.

The Wari' cosmological system reflects a typically Amazonian view of cycles of reciprocal transformation and exchange between humans and animals (see, for example, Pollock 1992, in press; Reichel-Dolmatoff 1971). What is unusual about the Wari' case is that it links these ideas to an elaborate system of real cannibalism, framed in terms of symbolic and psychological rationales not previously examined in the mortuary cannibalism literature.

At the core of Wari' spiritual concerns is the idea of an alliance between Wari' society and the Water spirits (comprised of both Wari' ancestors and Towira Towira's tribe). This is envisioned as a cyclic festival exchange identical to the earthly hüroroin and tamara festivals that affirm and reproduce amicable relations among Wari' villages. These alliance-marking rituals are structured around dramatizations of antagonistic oppositions between a host village and visitors from another community. Hüroroin culminate in the hosts' symbolic killing of male visitors by inducing an unconscious state called *itam* that is explicitly equated with death by predation (hunting or warfare).[20] The hosts revive the visitors from this "death" with a warm water bath, symbol of birth and rebirth. Revival of the slain "prey" distinguishes this "killing" by itam from mere hunting or warfare. In a process parallel to shamanic initiation (in which an animal spirit kills and revives the initiate), the hüroroin festival's symbolic killing and revival create a bond between the killer and the killed, such that the two transcend their opposition and become allies. Role reversals are inherent in festival exchanges: the first party's visitor/prey usually later sponsor a festival at which the first party's host/killers become the visitor/prey who are "killed."

Wari' relations with the Water spirits are conceived in identical terms, as festival exchanges in which the terrestrial and underwater societies alternate in the roles of predators (hosts) and prey (visitors), enacting a reciprocity reducible to an eminently egalitarian proposition: "We'll let you kill us if you let us kill you." The Water spirits fulfill their side of this arrangement by visiting earth as white-lipped peccaries and fish that sing tamara songs, dance, and allow Wari' to kill and eat them.[21] Wari' reciprocate at the moment of biological death, when human spirits allow themselves to be killed by the Water spirits. This occurs when a dying person's spirit (jami-) journeys to the underworld and becomes a guest at the hüroroin party that is always in progress there. The hosts, Towira Towira and his wife, offer maize beer. If the spirit accepts, it enters itam and "dies" underwater; on earth, the person's physical body dies. As in terrestrial alliance festivals, Towira Towira later bathes the spirit and resuscitates it. He then paints it with black *genipapo* dye (*Genipa americana),* marking the dead person's new identity as a Water spirit.[22]

Each society benefits from this arrangement. Humans provide the Water spirit society with new members who marry and bear children, enhancing the reproduction of Water spirit society. The Water spirits provide the living

Wari' with life-sustaining animal food. For Wari', this exchange not only reproduces the primary human-nonhuman relations of their cosmology but also promises an enhancement of ecological resources important to their subsistence. White-lipped peccaries and fish are the only food animals encountered in dense concentrations in this environment; aside from the scarce and easily over-hunted tapir, they can yield the greatest quantities of animal food in return for the least expenditure of time and effort. Although they are relatively easy to kill when encountered, their appearance is highly unpredictable.[23] Given this combination of uncertainty and high potential productivity, it is not surprising that Wari' rituals focus on enhancing relations with peccaries and fish.

The mythic origin of the Wari' alliance with the Water spirits is recounted in a story called *Orotapan*,[24] which tells of how Wari', who used to be the Water spirits' prey, became their allies instead. As allies, they gained the right to kill Water spirits (as peccaries and fish) in return for submitting to being killed by them (at the time of biological death) and subsequently hunted, as peccaries, by the living. Three elements central to Wari' socio-ecological security originated in this myth: the festivals of intervillage alliance that ensure peace among neighbors, humans' postmortem transformations to peccaries (which ally the human and the nonhuman), and the songs that summon peccaries and fish to earth.

In the story of *Orotapan* (see note 24), the power to hunt and eat the ancestors/Water spirits (as peccaries and fish) is balanced by humans' destiny to become peccaries to be hunted and eaten. This is a reprise of themes from the myth of *Pinom*, in which the power to hunt and eat animals was balanced by the imperative for humans to become meat to be eaten, as corpses consumed in endocannibalism. Whereas the *Pinom* story emphasizes the primal balance between human and animal predation, the myth of *Orotapan* concerns the creation of cultural institutions that transform potentially antagonistic, antisocial, predator-prey relations into cooperative, security-enhancing alliances. The alliance festivals' symbolic predation substituted for the real killing and eating of humans by animals in a precultural era. By accepting this human place in the universe, alternating between the position of eaters and the eaten, Wari' gained the animal spirits' powers of predation.

The power to summon their ancestral/Water spirit allies to come to earth as animals is at the core of the sacred in Wari' life. In a precontact ritual that continues today in at least one community, villagers gather at night, before communal hunting or fishing expeditions, to sing the songs from the *Orotapan* myth that invite the Water spirits to earth. People avoid speaking of this music's power; I learned of it only because, after the one occasion when I heard the spirit-summoning songs sung collectively, the peccaries appeared early the next morning for the first time in several months. The herd passed just outside the village, and nine white-lippeds were killed—three times as many as on any day in the previous two years at Santo André. The entire community ceased work to feast on this bounty of meat, a tangible embodiment of the human-nonhuman alliance.

HUNTING THE ANCESTORS

In contrast to Durkheimian views of death as a rupture in the social fabric to be mended, native Amazonian systems often treat death, not as discontinuity, but as essential for the continuation of social life (Viveiros de Castro 1992:255; see Graham 1995). The Wari' case offers a prime example of death treated as a creative moment, a productive context for extending and renegotiating social ties that regenerate the cycle of human-animal exchanges.

Human death is necessary to the reproduction of the peccaries and fish upon which Wari' subsistence and survival depend, and the perpetuation of Wari'–Water spirit cooperation depends on the bonds of affection that link the recently deceased to their living kin. Only the recently dead, who still remember their terrestrial kin and are remembered by them, maintain active exchange relations with the living. The spirits of the recently dead send or lead the peccary herd to their living relatives' hunting territories, or send their allies, the fish. When ancestors appear as peccaries, they approach hunters who are their own kin and offer their bodies to be shot to feed their living relatives. Before butchering, a shaman is supposed to look at each peccary carcass to identify the human spirit inside. Today, people are lax about this; sometimes shamans are summoned to view peccaries, sometimes they are not. A peccary spirit usually is identified as being a close consanguine, or occasionally an affine, of the hunter who shot it.

Wari' see nothing odd about hunting their own relatives, as I learned from a conversation that took place the day after two white-lipped peccaries were slain. An elderly shaman was chatting with a young widower still saddened by his wife's death two years earlier. The shaman mentioned that he had talked to the roasting peccaries (who were killed by the deceased wife's patrilateral parallel cousin) and that one turned out to be the dead wife. "Is that so?" responded the young man. "Is it all right in the water?" "She's fine," the shaman replied. "With the peccaries, she took a peccary husband and has a peccary baby." "That's nice," was the widower's only comment.

Eavesdropping while eating fruit nearby, I nearly choked. "Hey!" I exclaimed. "Doesn't that make you sad? Aren't you sad that your wife's cousin killed her yesterday and that you ate her today?" The young man looked perplexed at my outburst, then replied, "No; why should I be sad? He just killed her body; she isn't angry. Her children are eating meat. It doesn't hurt her; she just will have another body. Why should I be sad? The ancestors are happy that we have meat to eat."

To Wari', the idea that some of the animals they eat are beloved kin is neither morbid nor repulsive, but a natural extension of familial food giving, a concrete manifestation of the ancestors' continuing concern for their families on earth.

There are numerous stories of encounters with peccaries that were interpreted as gifts of food sent by specific ancestors. One man told me that in the 1970s, when his mother was dying, she told her family that she would send the peccaries three days after her death. True to promise, on the third night, the herd thundered into the village, stampeding under elevated houses, sending women and children screaming while men scrambled for their shotguns. Most deaths are not followed by such immediate drama, but all peccary killings are potentially interpretable as visits from the ancestors. Each new death strengthens and reproduces the Water spirits' ties to the world of the living. . . .

[In a brief section called "Final Rites," Conklin describes the final stage of the Wari' funerary process. Near the first anniversary of the death, mourners conduct a final ritual hunt deep in the forest. During the mourning period, kin of the deceased withdraw from most of their subsistence and social activities. However, when senior members of the family decide it is time for mourning to end, family members depart on this extended hunt. Killing a white-lipped peccary indicates that the deceased is fully integrated into life in the afterworld and, remembering their loved ones on earth, has sent the peccary as a gift to feed them. Returning to the village with their game, the mourners hold one last feast in memory of the deceased. After this final expression of sorrow and remembrance, the elders declare the period of mourning over and the mourners resume their normal social lives.—Editors]

EATING THE DEAD

Viewed in the context of the yearlong series of traditional mourning rites structured around the dead person's transition to white-lipped peccary, the roasting and eating of the corpse appears as a first, symbolic marker of this change. Consistent with Hertz's (1960[1907]:34, 58) insight that transformations of the corpse often parallel changes happening to the dead person's spirit, Wari' envisioned that at the moment when the cutting of the corpse commenced at the earthly funeral, Towira Towira began to bathe and resuscitate the spirit underwater.[25] This resuscitation made the deceased into a Water spirit who eventually would return to earth as a peccary. For terrestrial mourners, the corpse's dismemberment and roasting evoked this human-to-animal transformation.

"When we made the big fire and placed the body there, it was as if the dead person became a white-lipped peccary [ak ka mijak pin na]," explained a male elder of Santo André. Switching to Portuguese, he emphasized, "It appeared to be peccary [parece queixada]." As mourners watched a beloved relative's corpse being dismembered, roasted, and eaten, the sight must have graphically impressed upon them both the death's finality and the dead person's future identity as a peccary that would feed the living. Dismembering the body that is the focus of so many notions of personhood and related-

ness made a dramatic symbolic statement about the dead person's divorce from human society, and imminent change from living meat eater to animal meat to be eaten. Cannibalism appears to have been the preferred method for disposing of the dead because eating (as opposed to cremation) not only destroyed the corpse but also affirmed the dead individual's eventual regeneration as an immortal animal.

Cannibalism made a symbolic statement about the eaters as well as the eaten. At the same time that it evoked images of the dead as peccaries, numerous prior aspects of funeral rites and mourning behavior emphasized the humanity and social identity of the eaten, explicitly rejecting any equation of human flesh with animal flesh. Thus, when mourners roasted and ate human flesh, they themselves were cast as carnivores, identified with the animal powers of predation traced to the Pinom and Orotapan myths. Funeral decorations recalled these associations: firewood and roasting racks were adorned with feathers of vultures and scarlet macaws (Orotapan's sacred bird), and firewood was tied with "fire vine" (makuri xe'), a liana associated with warfare and predatory powers linked to the Water spirits and the jaguar-cannibal in the myth of Pinom.

Eating the dead identified Wari' society as a whole with the transcendent powers of their allies, the immortal Water spirits. Cannibalism evoked and enacted the human position in this relationship, the alternation between the positions of meat-eater and meat to be eaten. Bloch (1992) has argued that a wide variety of religious and political rituals is structured around a quasi-universal dynamic: the transformation of individuals from prey/victims into hunter/killers. This theme, which is explicit in the origin myths of Pinom and Orotapan, was the central image underlying the traditional Wari' mortuary ritual sequence. The death rites moved living mourners from the position of being victims of the Water spirit forces of death to becoming hunters of Water spirits embodied as animals. At the same time, as was consistent with the egalitarian reciprocity that permeates Wari' social arrangements, the rites also enacted the reverse dynamic, marking humans' postmortem destiny to become animals, transformed from eaters into the eaten.

MOURNING AND TRANSFORMATION

The image of the dead as peccaries dominates Wari' visions of death and the afterlife. The ancestors' return as peccaries is a powerful negation of death's finality. It promises not only reunion after death but also contacts during life through encounters with the herd that are the only interactions that ordinary people (nonshamans) have with their deceased kin. This is not just an abstract religious notion but a moving experience for the many individuals who have interpreted encounters with peccaries as visits from dead relatives.

Cannibalism represented a dramatic affirmation of this human-to-animal transformation, an affirmation of the interdependency of human mortality and animal fertility. Thematic links between death and regeneration are prominent in many societies' mortuary rites (Bloch and Parry 1982; Metcalf and Huntington 1991), and the psychological importance of ideas about the continuity of life after death is widely recognized (see Lifton 1979). The Wari' preference for cannibalism as a way to dispose of human corpses reflected the intersection between these psychological-spiritual concerns, cast in images of human spirits' regeneration as peccaries, and cultural concepts of the human body's social meanings. As a focus of social identity and psycho-emotional ties between the living and the dead, the dead person's body served as the primary locus for the playing out of transformations of mourners' memories, images, and emotions related to the deceased. Beginning with the corpse's dismemberment, roasting, and eating, and proceeding through the memory-altering "sweeping" ritual (ton ho') to the final hunt (hwet mao) and feast, the mourning rites posited a processual transmutation of socially projected images of the dead person's body. The rites aimed to move mourners from experiences of loss, embodied in images of the deceased as corpse, to acceptance of the death as part of a regenerative cycle, embodied in images of the deceased rejuvenated as an animal.

It is difficult to assess, retrospectively, the extent to which the ritual transformations that operated on the level of the culturally constructed person also operated on the level of the individual. However, contemporary Wari' emphases on cannibalism's psychological significance, as an act that facilitated mourners' detachment from all-consuming memories of the dead, and elders' expressions of emotional dissonance concerning burial, suggest that many people found the body's destruction by cannibalism meaningful in personal experiences of grief and mourning. The eating of the dead was one powerful element in a social process of mourning understood to have eased the experience of coming to terms with a loved one's death. By casting the dead in the image of the animals they would become, cannibalism overlaid images of the deceased as corpse with new images of the deceased as an animal with ongoing relations to its living kin. It affirmed the transmutation of specific kinship ties between the living and the dead into a general enhancement of life-supporting relations between humans and animals. In essence, cannibalism was the dead person's first offering of self as food.

CONCLUSION

The explanation for Wari' mortuary cannibalism cannot be reduced to a single, simple function, for it reflected a complex amalgam of myth, eschatology, ideas about the human body, and social, psychological, and ecological concerns. Extending Lévi-Strauss's (1977:65) observation about myth, these are best understood as "an *interrelation* of several explanatory levels." As a central symbol in the rites of mourning, cannibalism presented a powerful, symbolic con-

densation of beliefs about life's continuity after death, affirmed in the ancestors' regeneration as animals. Mortuary cannibalism's symbolic potency derived from its evocation of multiple dimensions of the social and ecological relations in which Wari' perceive their security to be grounded. In the rites of mourning, human-nonhuman oppositions merged in what Sanday (1986:226) has called a "ritual of reconciliation" that transformed unpredictable ecological and social constraints into a meaningful conceptual order. Much anthropological discourse on cannibalism has tended to treat cultural-symbolic and ecological interpretations as mutually exclusive paradigms, but, explored in indigenous terms, the Wari' system is a symbiosis of social and ecological concerns that must be considered holistically. The material motivations associated with endocannibalism were not biological needs for protein from human flesh, but concerns with structuring cultural meanings in regard to human-animal relations that were essential, not just to subsistence but to the entire social order.

In contrast to views of anthropophagy as the ultimately antisocial act, the act of eating the dead affirmed and reproduced the bases of Wari' society. Endocannibalism was mythically linked to the origins of culture and the festival exchanges that transform potentially antagonistic relations into cooperative alliances between neighboring villages, and between humans and the nonhuman forces of death and animal fertility. As mortuary rites renewed the primary spiritual relations of the Wari' universe, so they also revitalized relations on the social plane with the gathering of affines in support of the dead person's family. Wari' cannibalism involved not the recycling of vital energies or body substances, but the renewal of vital institutions of socio-ecological security.

A Wari' elder recalled that shortly after the contact, a missionary lectured him, saying, "Eating is for animals. People are not animals, people are not meat to be eaten." In Western thought, the revulsion that cannibalism provokes is related to its apparent blurring of distinctions between humans and animals, in treating human substance like animal meat. For Wari', however, the magic of existence lies in the commonality of human and animal identities, in the movements between the human and nonhuman worlds embodied in the recognition through cannibalism of human participation in both poles of the dynamic of eating and being eaten.

NOTES

Acknowledgments. My primary debt is to the people of Santo André and other Wari' communities who shared with me their understandings and experiences of death and mourning. Field research in Brazil in 1985–87 was carried out with authorization from the CNPq and FUNAI and supported by fellowships from the Fulbright Commission and the Inter-American Foundation and a grant-in-aid from The Wenner-Gren Foundation for Anthropological Research. A Charlotte Newcombe Fellowship supported dissertation writing, and funding from the

Wenner-Gren Foundation allowed me to return to Brazil in the summer of 1991 to check my interpretations and obtain additional data. A Vanderbilt University Research Council small grant facilitated bibliographic research. Among the many Brazilian colleagues who aided this project, special thanks are owed to Julio Cezar Melatti and Martin Ibañez-Novion, who sponsored my research under the auspices of the Department of Anthropology at the Universidade de Brasília; Dídimo Graciliano de Oliveira of FUNAI/Guajará-Miri'm, who offered logistical support; and Aparecida Vilaça, whose insights and friendship have enriched my studies. For helpful comments on earlier versions of this paper, I am grateful to Debbora Battaglia, Brent Berlin, Michael Brown, Gertrude Dole, Frederick Dunn, Laura Graham, Thomas Gregor, Patricia Lyon, Lynn Morgan, Donald Pollock, Edward Schieffelin, and James Trostle.

1. The final syllable is stressed in all Wari' words. *Wari'* is pronounced "wa-REE," ending in a glottal stop. On the Wari' language, see Everett and Kern (in press) and Everett (in press).

2. Most reports of endocannibalism involve eating only small bits of flesh from specific body parts (the typical Melanesian pattern) or consuming only the ashes of cremated bones, which appears to have been the most widespread Amazonian pattern (see Dole 1974; Meireles 1986; Zerries 1960). In lowland South America, consumption of substantial amounts of fellow tribesmembers' boiled or roasted flesh has been reported among the Guayakí of Paraguay (Clastres 1974) and Panoan peoples along the Peru-Brazil border (Dole 1974; Kensinger, in press).

3. In excluding exocannibalism from this discussion, I do not mean to imply that it had no relation to mortuary cannibalism. Vilaça (1992:289–294) has emphasized that Wari' cannibalism of both enemies and affines expressed a broad "cannibal logic" of reversibility in the positions of predator and prey in Wari' relations to social others. Erikson (1986), Overing (1986), and Viveiros de Castro (1992) have noted that the traditional anthropological distinction between exo- and endocannibalism blurs in the face of the complex forms of cannibalism envisioned in lowland South American myths, cosmologies, and rituals.

4. All translations of Wari' oral texts are my own, as are all translations of written texts (with foreign titles).

5. Extensive incest prohibitions promote dispersed affinal alliances (Meireles 1986:273), and families generally intermarry with two or more different groups of affines. At the same time, there is an emphasis on repeating as well as proliferating affinal ties by taking spouses from families already linked by previous marriages.

6. The Wari' traditionally practiced cremation as an alternative way to dispose of corpses whose flesh was considered dangerous to eat because it was contaminated by specific disease conditions. Corpses were cremated, not eaten, when they had pus in their lungs, or symptoms resembling liver disorders (ascites and cirrhosis). The outsiders who suppressed Wari' cannibalism, however, did not present cremation as an option, perhaps because cremation is discouraged in Latin American Catholicism.

7. For more detailed discussions of funeral practices and variations, see Conklin (1989:407–417) and Vilaça (1992:208–221). Funerals for people who died in massacres and epidemics often deviated from normal patterns. When a village had been attacked, or a person killed close to home, Wari' sometimes feared that the assassin(s) would return. In such cases, they dispensed with much of the usual ceremony and quickly roasted and consumed the corpse(s). The mass death and social chaos of the contact-era epidemics brought similar disruptions of funeral practices, including painful episodes in which corpses were abandoned, and subsequently ravaged by vultures, because the survivors were too sick to cut the large amounts of firewood needed for roasting or cremation.

8. *Nari* is a verb meaning "to be related." The proper nominative designations for consanguines and affines, respectively, are *iri' ka-nari* and *oro-ka-nari paxi*. In this text, I follow Vilaça (1992) in using simplified verbal forms, iri' nari and nari paxi. Similarly, mixita, ton ho' and hwet mao are verbs; the nominative designations are *ka-mixita-wa, ka-ton ho'-wa,* and *ka-hwet mao-wa.*

9. This antihomeopathic idea recurs in Wari' shamanism and ethnomedicine. A shaman shares body substance with his animal spirit companion and falls violently ill if he eats that animal's flesh. Similarly, certain illnesses are attributed to ingesting substances that are similar to one's own body substance, but in a more potent, incompatible state (Conklin 1989:302–312). Corpses' flesh and body fluids, transformed by putrefaction, are considered dangerous only when ingested by their close consanguines. When eaten by affines and non-kin, roasted flesh is not believed to cause illness, although it is regarded as polluting.

10. Most women in the Rio Dois Irmãos region said that they participated in mortuary cannibalism. In the Rio Negro-Ocaia region, many women said that they did not eat human flesh because they disliked its stench. Vilaça (1992:216–217) cited one senior man who also claimed never to have eaten the dead. In addition, some women who usually participated in cannibalism told of decisions not to eat a specific affine's corpse because they felt too close, emotionally, to the dead person. Men were expected to perform impassively the duty of consuming the corpse, regardless of their feelings of intimacy with the deceased or the revulsion provoked by the smell and taste of decayed flesh.

11. In a provocative discussion that is beyond the scope of this article, Albert (1985) and Overing (1986) have discussed associations between affinity and images of cannibalism among the Yanomami and Piaroa, respectively, in relation to issues of social harmony, violence, warfare, and the internal dynamics of endogamous, egalitarian societies. Carneiro da Cunha and Viveiros de Castro (1985) have addressed related dynamics of vengeance and reciprocity in Tupinambá exocannibalism.

12. A similar rationale shaped affines' roles in euthanasia: when an elderly person suffering from a terminal illness wished to die, he or she summoned a male affine to perform the killing. Funerals were only one of several contexts in which Wari' traditionally called upon affines to perform such services.

13. A horror of burial, and preference for being cannibalized or cremated, has been reported among Panoans (Erikson 1986:198), Yanomami (Lima Figueiredo 1939:44), Guayakí (Clastres 1974:319), and Tupinambá war captives (Viveiros de Castro 1992:289–290).

14. Efforts to extinguish material traces of the dead are widespread in lowland South America. Especially common are name avoidances and the destruction of dead people's houses and personal property (see, for example, Albert 1985; Gregor 1977:264; Jackson 1983:200; Kracke 1981:262; Métraux 1947). The dual rationales of discouraging ghosts from returning to their homes, and removing reminders that cause sadness to the bereaved, are recurrent themes. Kracke commented that among the Kagwahiv, these two different rationales are given "so interchangeably that it almost seems as if they are different ways of phrasing the same thing" (1988:213–214).

15. According to Vilaça, "Only after the body is roasted and devoured, is the *jam* [spirit] of the deceased bathed under the water, and [it] passes to full living in the world of the dead" (1992:247).

16. Vilaça has emphasized that "for the Wari' culinary preparation (which is initiated with the cutting of the prey) and devouring are interrelated and indissociable processes. The cadaver is roasted in the fire that, in its origin, is cooking fire (see the myth of *Pinom*). In this sense the cadaver is prepared as prey and should be ingested as such" (1992:263).

17. Viveiros de Castro (1992:213) has noted Tupi ideas of a connection between the persistence of a corpse's flesh and the persistence of memories linking the dead and the living.

18. Vilaça's Wari' informants echoed these sentiments. She cited one man's explanation: " 'If we bury, we think about where he [the deceased] walked, where he worked; we think about his skin being there in the earth still. With the fire it is good, it finishes all the body, we don't think more' " (Vilaça 1992:265).

19. White-lipped peccaries are prominent in native American myths and rituals, from Mexico south to the Argentinian Chaco (see Donkin 1985:83–94; Sowls 1984:185–187). They often are considered closely related to people. In *The Raw and the Cooked*, Lévi-Strauss (1969:84) identified peccaries as an intermediary between jaguars (the quintessential animal predators) and human beings.

20. Hüroroin parties are structured around oppositions between a host community and visitors from elsewhere who sing and dance for their hosts. Male visitors stage dramatic raids on the hosts' village, destroy property, and perform parodies of sexual intercourse with host women. Hosts punish these transgressions by forcing the visitors to drink and vomit vast quantities of maize beer. With repeated vomiting, some lose consciousness and enter itam, in which they bleed from the mouth and experience involuntary muscular contractions that force the body into a rigid fetal position. When this occurs, the party's sponsor cries, "I've killed my prey!" (*"Pa' pin' inain watamata!"*). Submission to the physically painful "death" of itam affirms both a man's physical stamina and his trust in the allies who care for and revive him (see Conklin 1989:148–154; Vilaça 1992:186–191).

21. Metaphors of reciprocity pervade relations to the peccaries, just as precontact party hosts sent their guests home bearing gifts, Wari' hunters traditionally gave presents to the spirits of slain white-lipped peccaries, and occasionally do so today. Before butchering, a peccary carcass is surrounded with items such as bows and arrows, baskets, chicha, shotguns, clothing, and cigarettes. The peccary is told to carry the "images" (jami-) of these items home and tell fellow Water spirits that they, too, will be given gifts when they visit the Wari'.

22. Pollock (in press) has described strikingly similar eschatological beliefs among the Kulina of Acre, Brazil. At death, Kulina spirits journey to the underworld and receive a ritual welcome from their ancestors who, as white-lipped peccaries, fall upon the spirit and consume it. Like Wari', Kulina believe that the ancestors return to earth as white-lipped peccaries that are hunted by living people. Unlike Wari', the Kulina system carries this cycle one step further: white-lipped peccary meat becomes the souls of Kulina babies.

23. Kiltie observed that "[w]hite-lippeds are distinctive among all the terrestrial herbivorous mammals in neotropical rain forests in being the only species that forms large herds, which may include over 100 individuals" (1980:542). Hunting white-lipped peccaries is an unpredictable business, for the herds range over huge territories, never lingering long in one place and disappearing for weeks or months at a time. However, when the herd does appear, it offers relatively easy targets and multiple kills are common, making white-lipped peccaries the single most important terrestrial game in the diets of the Wari' and many other native Amazonians. Fishing involves similar patterns of high potential yield with a high quotient of procurement uncertainty; in the flooded forest, dense concentrations of huge numbers of small, easily-caught fish occasionally appear, quite unpredictably, in the fluctuating waters of temporary streams and ponds.

24. In the myth called *Orotapan* or *Hujin,* Towira Towira appears as an *orotapan* carnivore and as a white-lipped peccary named Wem Parom, who established the original alliance. Here is a summary of key events in this myth:

> A man named Hujin fell into a river and was eaten by Orotapan, the Water Spirits' leader. After eating Hujin, Orotapan threw his bones in the air and made his flesh whole again so that he could devour him again. Orotapan did this over and over, until a shaman reached into the water, caught Hujin's bones and pulled him out. However, Hujin's spirit remained captive to the Water Spirits, compelled to return every day to their underwater realm. Orotapan changed into a white-lipped peccary named Wem Parom and challenged Hujin to a musical duel. Hujin won this contest by becoming the first human to master the art of songmaking, which the Wari' consider the highest of artistic accomplishments. By this supremely cultural act, he ceased to be the spirits' prey and gained the status of an equal capable of entering an alliance with the spirits. Wem Parom sent his son, in the form of a fish, to Hujin's village to receive gifts of food marking the establishment of amicable relations. Hujin then invited the Water Spirits to a party at his earthly

village and instructed his own people to make large quantities of beer and new bows and arrows. The Water spirit guests came as white-lipped peccaries who sang, danced, drank all of their hosts' beer, and ran around breaking clay pots and destroying houses. Hujin and his kinsmen shot and killed the peccaries. From their bodies emerged the scarlet macaw, which is sacred to Orotapan. Hujin, who had shamanic powers, then looked at each peccary carcass, identified its spirit, and told his people whether it was a Wari' ancestor or a nonancestral Water spirit. It was then that the Wari' learned of their own postmortem fate to be killed by Towira Towira and become peccaries hunted by the living.

For other versions and analysis of this myth, see Vilaça 1992:255–262.

25. Although the spirit was believed to be revived when its corpse was dismembered and roasted, this revival does not appear to have been contingent on the corpse's being eaten. Several individuals described scenarios in which a spirit, revived when its corpse was cut, returned to earth and saw its own, still uneaten body roasting. Without exception, informants asserted that Towira Towira revived all spirits alike, regardless of whether their corpses were cannibalized, cremated, or buried. Vilaça (1992:265) has suggested that, since the change to burial, Wari' have come to see the rotting of the corpse as a kind of natural "cooking" that substitutes for the roasting at traditional funerals.

REFERENCES CITED

Acosta Saignes, Miguel
   1961   Estudios de Etnologia Antigua de Venezuela. (Studies of Early Ethnology of Venezuela.) Caracas, Venezuela: Universidad Central de Venezuela.
Albert, Bruce
   1985   Temps du sang, temps de cendres. Représentation de la maladie, système rituel et espace politique chez les Yanomami du Sud-est (Amazonie Brésilienne). (Time of Blood, Time of Ashes, Representation of Illness, Ritual System and Political Space among the Southeastern Yanomami [Brazilian Amazon].) Ph.D. dissertation, Université de Paris X.
Arens, William
   1979   The Man-Eating Myth: Anthropology and Anthropophagy. New York: Oxford University Press.
Battaglia, Debbora
   1991   The Body in the Gift: Memory and Forgetting in Sabarl Mortuary Exchange. American Ethnologist 19:3–18.
Berlin, Elois Ann, and E. K. Markell
   1977   An Assessment of the Nutritional and Health Status of an Aguaruna Jívaro Community. Amazonas, Peru. Ecology of Food and Nutrition 6:69–81.
Bloch, Maurice
   1992   Prey into Hunter: The Politics of Religious Experience. New York: Cambridge University Press.
Bloch, Maurice, and Jonathan Parry, eds.
   1982   Death and the Regeneration of Life. New York: Cambridge University Press.

Briggs, Charles
   1992   "Since I Am a Woman, I Will Chastise My Relatives": Gender, Reported Speech, and the (Re)production of Social Relations in Warao Ritual Wailing. American Ethnologist 19:337–361.
Carneiro da Cunha, Manuela, and Eduardo B. Viveiros de Castro
   1985   Vingança e temporalidade: Os Tupinambás. (Vengeance and Temporality: The Tupinambá.) Journal de la Société des Américanistes (Paris) 71:191–208.
de Carvalho, Bernardino
   1962   Pakaanovas: Antropófagos da Amazônia. (Pakaa Nova: Cannibals of Amazônia.) O Cruzeiro (São Paulo) February 10:118–124.
Chagnon, Napoleon A., and Raymond B. Hames
   1979   Protein Deficiency as a Cause of Tribal Warfare in Amazonia: New Data. Science 203:910–913.
Clastres, Pierre
   1974   Guayakí Cannibalism. P. Lyon, trans. In Native South Americans: Ethnology of the Least Known Continent. Patricia J. Lyon, ed. Pp. 309–321. Boston: Little, Brown.
Conklin, Beth A.
   1989   Images of Health, Illness and Death Among the Wari' (Pakaas Novos) of Rondônia, Brazil. Ph.D. dissertation, University of California at San Francisco and Berkeley.
Crocker, J. Christopher
   1977   The Mirrored Self: Identity and Ritual Inversion among the Eastern Bororo. Ethnology 16(2):129–145.
Crocker, William H.
   In press Canela Relationships with Ghosts: This-Worldly or Other-Worldly Empowerment. Latin American Anthropology Review.
Crocker, William, and Jean Crocker
   1994   The Canela: Bonding through Kinship, Ritual, and Sex. New York: Harcourt Brace.
Cruzeiro, O
   1962   Pakaanovas. (Pakaa Nova.) O Cruzeiro (São Paulo), March 23:152–160.
Dole, Gertrude E.
   1974   Endocannibalism among the Amahuaca Indians. In Native South Americans: Ethnology of the Least Known Continent. Patricia J. Lyon, ed. Pp. 302–308. Boston: Little, Brown.
Donkin, R. A.
   1985   The Peccary. Transactions of the American Philosophical Society, 75. Philadelphia: The American Philosophical Society.
Dufour, Darna L.
   1983   Nutrition in the Northwest Amazon. In Adaptive Responses of Native Amazonians. Raymond B. Hames and William T. Vickers, ed. Pp. 329–355. San Francisco: Academic Press.
Erikson, Philippe
   1986   Altérité, tatouage, et anthropophagie chez les Pano. (Alterity, Tattooing, and Cannibalism among Panoans.) Journal de la Société des Américanistes Paris 72:185–210.
Everett, Daniel L.
   In press Wari' Morphology. In the Handbook of Morphology. Andréw Spencer and Arnold Zwicky, eds. London: Basil-Blackwell.

Everett, Daniel L., and Barbara Kern
In press The Wari' Language of Western Brazil (Pacaas Novos). London: Routledge.

Folha de São Paulo
1962 Sertanista não conseguiu impedir que os Índios devorassem a menina morta. (Government Indian Agent Did Not Manage to Prevent the Indians from Devouring the Dead Girl.) Folha de São Paulo, January 13.

Freud, Sigmund
1981[1913] Totem and Taboo. In The Standard Edition of the Complete Psychological Works of Sigmund Freud, 14. James Strachey, ed. Pp. 100–155. London: The Hogarth Press and The Institute of Psychoanalysis.

Gillison, Gillian
1983 Cannibalism among Women in the Eastern Highlands of Papua New Guinea. In The Ethnography of Cannibalism. Paula Brown and Donald Tuzin, eds. Pp. 33–50. Washington, DC: Society for Psychological Anthropology.

Graham, Laura
1986 Three Modes of Shavante Vocal Expression: Wailing, Collective Singing, and Political Oratory. In Native South American Discourse. Joel Sherzer and Greg Urban, eds. Pp. 83–118. New York: Mouton de Gruyter.
1995 Performing Dreams: Discourses of Immortality among the Xavante of Brazil. Austin: University of Texas Press, in press.

Gregor, Thomas
1977 Mehinaku: The Drama of Daily Life in a Brazilian Village. Chicago: University of Chicago Press.

Harner, Michael
1977 The Ecological Basis for Aztec Sacrifice. American Ethnologist 4:117–135.

Harris, Marvin
1977 Cannibalism and Kings: The Origins of Cultures. New York: Random House.
1985 The Sacred Cow and the Abominable Pig. New York: Random House.

Hertz, Robert
1960[1907] Death and the Right Hand. Glencoe, IL: Free Press.

Jackson, Jean E.
1983 The Fish People: Linguistic Exogamy and Tukanoan Identity in Northwest Amazonia. New York: Cambridge University Press.

Kensinger, Kenneth M.
1991 A Body of Knowledge, or, the Body Knows. Expedition (University of Pennsylvania Museum) 33(3):37–45.
In press Disposing of the Dead in Cashinahua Society. Latin American Anthropology Review.

Kiltie, Richard A.
1980 More on Amazon Cultural Ecology. Current Anthropology 21:541–544.

Kracke, Waud
1978 Force and Persuasion: Leadership in an Amazonian Society. Chicago: University of Chicago Press.
1981 Kagwahiv Mourning: Dreams of a Bereaved Father. Ethos 9:258–275.

1988 Kagwahiv Mourning II: Ghosts, Grief, and Reminiscences. Ethos 16:209–222.

Lévi-Strauss, Claude
1969 The Raw and the Cooked. New York: Harper & Row.
1977 Structural Anthropology, 2. New York: Basic Books.

Lewis, I. M.
1986 Religion in Context: Cults and Charisma. New York: Cambridge University Press.

Lifton, Robert J.
1979 The Broken Connection: On Death and the Continuity of Life. New York: Simon & Schuster.

Lima Figueiredo, José
1939 Indios do Brasil. (Indians of Brazil.) Brasiliana (São Paulo), 5th ser., 163.

Lindenbaum, Shirley
1979 Kuru Sorcery. Palo Alto, CA: Mayfield.

Mason, Alan
1977 Oranao Social Structure. Ph.D. dissertation, University of California at Davis.

da Matta, Roberto
1979 The Apinayé Relationship System: Terminology and Ideology. In Dialectical Societies: The Gê and Bororo of Central Brazil. David Maybury-Lewis, ed. Pp. 83–127. Cambridge, MA: Harvard University Press.

Maybury-Lewis, David
1974 Akwe-Shavante Society. New York: Oxford University Press.

Meigs, Anna
1984 Food, Sex and Pollution: A New Guinea Religion. New Brunswick, NJ: Rutgers University Press.

Meireles, Denise Maldi
1986 Os Pakaas-Novos. (The Pakaa Nova.) Master's thesis, Universidade de Brasília, Brazil.

Melatti, Julio Cezar
1979 The Relationship System of the Krahó. In Dialectical Societies: The Gê and Bororo of Central Brazil. David Maybury-Lewis, ed. Pp. 46–79. Cambridge, MA: Harvard University Press.

Métraux, Alfred
1947 Mourning Rites and Burial Forms of the South American Indians. América Indígena 7(1):7–44.

Metcalf, Peter, and Richard Huntington
1991 Celebrations of Death: The Anthropology of Mortuary Ritual. 2nd ed. New York: Cambridge University Press.

Milton, Katharine
1984 Protein and Carbohydrate Resources of the Makú Indians of Northwestern Amazonia. American Anthropologist 86:7–27.

Murphy, Robert
1960 Headhunter's Heritage. Berkeley: University of California Press.

Overing, Joanna
1986 Images of Cannibalism, Death and Domination in a "Non Violent" Society. Journal de la Société des Américanistes (Paris) 72:133–156.

Pollock, Donald
1992 Culina Shamanism: Gender, Power and Knowledge. In Portals of Power: Shamanism among South American

Indians. E. Jean Langdon and Gerhard Baer, eds. Pp. 25–40. Albuquerque: University of New Mexico Press.

In press Death and the Afterdeath among the Kulina. Latin American Anthropology Review.

Poole, Fitz John Porter

1983   Cannibals, Tricksters, and Witches: Anthropophagic Images aAmong Bimin-Kuskusmin. *In* The Ethnography of Cannibalism. Paula Brown and Donald Tuzin, eds. Pp. 6–32. Washington, DC: Society for Psychological Anthropology.

Ramos, Alcida Rita

1990   Memórias Sanumá: Espaço e tempo em uma sociedade Yanomami. (Sanumá Memories: Space and Time in a Yanomami Society.) São Paulo: Editora Marco Zero.

Reichel-Dolmatoff, Gerardo

1971   Amazonian Cosmos. Chicago: University of Chicago Press.

Rosaldo, Renato

1989   Culture and Truth: The Remaking of Social Analysis. Boston: Beacon Press.

Rosenblatt, Paul C., R. Patricia Walsh, and Douglas A. Jackson

1976   Grief and Mourning in Cross-Cultural Perspective. New Haven, CT: HRAF Press.

Sagan, Eli

1974   Cannibalism: Human Aggression and Cultural Form. San Francisco: Harper & Row.

Sanday, Peggy Reeves

1986   Divine Hunger: Cannibalism as a Cultural System. New York: Cambridge University Press.

Seeger, Anthony

1987   Why Suyá Sing: A Musical Anthropology of an Amazonian People. New York: Cambridge University Press.

Seeger, Anthony, Roberto da Matta, and E. B. Viveiros de Castro

1979   A construção da pessoa nas sociedades indígenas brasileiras. (The Construction of the Person in Brazilian Indigenous Societies.) Boletim do Museu Nacional (Rio de Janeiro), Antropologia (n.s.) 32:2–19.

Sowls, Lyle K.

1984   The Peccaries. Tucson: The University of Arizona Press.

Staden, Hans

1928[1557]   Hans Staden: The True History of His Captivity, 1557. Malcolm Letts, ed. London: George Routledge & Sons.

Turner, Terence S.

1980   The Social Skin. *In* Not by Work Alone. Jeremy Cherfas and Roger Lewin, eds. Pp. 112–140. Beverly Hills, CA: Sage Publications.

Urban, Greg

1988   Ritual Wailing in Amerindian Brazil. American Anthropologist 90:385–400.

1991   A Discourse-Centered Approach to Culture. Austin: University of Texas Press.

Vilaça, Aparecida

1989   Comendo como gente: Formas do canibalismo Wari' (Pakaa Nova). (Eating like People: Forms of Wari' Cannibalism.) Master's thesis. Museu Nacional, Universidade Federal do Rio de Janeiro.

1992   Comendo como gente: Formas do canibalismo Wari'. (Eating like People: Forms of Wari' Cannibalism.) Rio de Janeiro: Editora UFRJ (Universidade Federal do Rio de Janeiro).

Viveiros de Castro, Eduardo B.

1992   From the Enemy's Point of View. Chicago: University of Chicago Press.

Von Graeve, Bernard

1972   Protective Intervention and Interethnic Relations: A Study of Domination on the Brazilian Frontier. Ph.D. dissertation, University of Toronto.

1989   The Pacaa Nova: Clash of Cultures on the Brazilian Frontier, Peterborough, Canada: Broadview Press.

Wilbert, Johannes, and Karin Simoneau

1990   Folk Literature of the Yanomami Indians. Los Angeles: UCLA Latin American Center Publications.

Zerries, Otto

1954   Wild-und Buschgeister in Südamerika. (Wild- and Bush-spirits in South America.) Studien zur Kulturkunde, 11. Wiesbaden, Germany: F. Steiner.

1960   Endocanibalismo en la América del Sur. (Endocannibalism in South America.) Revista do Museu Paulista (São Paulo), n.s., 12:125–175.

Killing Infants and the Aged
in Nonindustrial Societies:
Removing the Liminal

Audrey Shalinsky

Anthony Glascock

When is a person not a person? If a being is not a person, how should we consider their death? The killing of the very young or very old in times of social or environmental stress has been documented in many societies throughout the world. In this essay, Shalinsky and Glascock examine these killings using Victor Turner's notion of liminality (see Turner's essay in section 7), the state of being between or outside recognized categories. Shalinsky and Glascock argue that killing infants and the elderly is sometimes deemed socially acceptable because infants and the elderly are at times classified as liminal beings, on the periphery of humanity.

In general, infants might be classified as liminal if they suffer from a birth defect or are part of a multiple birth, if the birth circumstances are unusual, or if one of the parents is socially unacceptable. In other words, babies might be killed if they are biologically or socially abnormal. The aged may also be classified as liminal, particularly if they are sick and not expected to recover or they are so old that others believe they "should" be dead. Cross-cultural studies have found that in most societies some people live long enough to reach a stage where they are regarded as a liability. People at this stage are often separated physically and socially from the larger group, and when their social group becomes nonsupportive their death is hastened. Elderly people who become incapacitated are particularly vulnerable. They are similar to "abnormal" infants and may be separated from the larger group and killed, although hastening the death of the decrepit is more common than outright homicide.

The final paragraph of the essay points out that the fate of the liminal is an issue in American society too. In particular, debates over abortion and the right to die provide closer-to-home examples of arguments concerning the value of those who are liminal.

As you read, consider these questions:

1. In many cultures, infanticide (the killing of infants) is not considered murder. Why is this, and how do these cultures make a distinction between the two?

2. How can environmental changes affect why some aged are seen as "alive" or "dead"?

3. How do the practices of killing infants or the aged in nonindustrial societies compare to issues of abortion and euthanasia in Western societies?

In nonindustrial societies infants and the aged are sometimes killed in order to reduce stress from the environment or fluctuations in the workload. Eskimos are well-known for this, but in fact the ethnographic record shows dozens of other societies that engage in this practice. People from the Arctic to the Tropics, when they perceive a societal threat, may decide to kill expendable persons, thereby stabilizing their conditions.[1] The expendable persons are virtually always the very young or the very old. These persons are on the borders of life, on the borders of society. They are not quite full social persons. In other words, they are liminal. This article examines these liminal people. In particular, it asks how they move across the border from human to nonhuman and the role of rites in this passage.[2]

Life stages are delimited by rites of passage, which include the processual phases, separation from old status, transition or liminal phase, and reincorporation into society at the new status.[3] These rituals transform people from one position or category into another. They help each person become something new, and they involve group recognition of the process of transformation. Individuals in the ritual process of passage often are killed symbolically and then reborn symbolically into the new status position.[4] Anthropologists working from this perspective have also indicated that categories of people may be defined as permanently in a liminal condition, that is, permanently between or outside of recognized status positions.[5]

Victor Turner, who emphasized and developed the concept of liminality, noted that the symbolism attached to liminal personae is complex and modeled on biological process.[6] Thus the individual who is liminal may be marked with symbols of birth and death simultaneously. Though Turner does not state this, one might infer that birth and death processes themselves are, in some sense, liminal times

Reprinted from *The Social Science Journal* 25:3, Audrey Shalinsky & Anthony Glascock, "Killing Infants & the Aged in Nonindustrial Societies: Removing the Liminal," 277–287, copyright © 1988, with permission from Elsevier Science.

in which the person is on the edge of the life cycle itself. According to Mary Douglas, the boundaries of categories are imbued with power and mystery. They may be viewed as sources of danger or threats to orderly conceptions.[7] If newborns and the dying are liminal, they also could be perceived as threats to the social order, and thus, under some circumstances, they would be liable to elimination. This article contends that it is precisely those defined as liminal who will be killed at times of environmental or economic stress.

Decisionmaking about life and death is a twofold process that serves to define and redefine individuals under changing circumstances. First, individuals may be moved in social perception from positions of normal social being to liminal, interstitial, or outsider positions. They may be locked into such positions and not be allowed to achieve normal social personhood in the perception of others. Second, these people are killed under specific socioeconomic conditions that coincide with the time they are viewed as liminal. These socioeconomic conditions may in fact precipitate the imposition of liminality.

INFANTS AS PRE-SOCIAL PERSONS

In *The Ritual Process,* Turner speaks of a "widely prevalent social tendency either to make what falls outside the norm a matter of concern for the widest recognized group or to destroy the exceptional."[8] Applying this to the life cycle process leads to the conclusion that the normal healthy adult would provide a standard by which other categories of individuals are judged. Those who do not meet the standard—the old who are past the standard, the young who are incapable of achieving the standard, the physically, mentally or socially aberrant who fall to either side of the standard—are vulnerable to elevation as sacred objects, or equally vulnerable to their own destruction, two possibilities which may not be mutually exclusive.

The classic example of elevation to sacred status is found in the work of E. E. Evans-Pritchard on the Nuer.[9] According to Evans-Pritchard, twins are elevated to the sacred because they are symbolically associated with birds. Birds are products of multiple births and creatures "of the above" and "children of God." "Twinship presents the paradoxes that what is physically doubled is structurally single and what is mystically one is empiri'cally two."[10] In many societies, twins are mediational figures; somehow like animals, somehow like the deity. As such they exemplify liminality, because in regards to different categories they are both and neither, betwixt and between. Though some societies elevate multiple birth children to sacred status, many societies have the practice of killing one or all of these children.[11]

Turner himself does little with the notion that the liminal may become viewed as permanently outside human status and liable to be killed. However, the ethnographic record indicates in explanations of infanticide that infants appear to be extremely susceptible to placement in exceptional categories, with the consequence that infanticide is common. Infanticide is found in high percentages in various samples of societies ranging from 53% to 76%, even to 91%.[12] Leigh Minturn and Jerry Stashak who report the low figure, also state that "Reports of infanticide are so ubiquitous over time and place that we assume that some unwanted children are killed or allowed to die in virtually all societies."[13]

Minturn and Stashak hypothesize that infants that are killed are regarded as beings that are not yet full social members of their communities. They further state that for all societies in their sample in which infanticide occurred, infants were killed before the birth ceremony, a rite of passage which they view as establishing the social recognition of the infant as a fully human member of the group.[14] Though Minturn and Stashak are correct that the birth ceremony marks the acknowledgment of full human potential, they do not emphasize the prior period as one characterized by liminality. However, the period from birth to social acknowledgment can readily be compared to the liminal transition in ritual process. At birth, the baby separates from the mother, from darkness, from the state of the unborn, a state which may be likened to death. Perhaps birth itself should be compared to passage through a tunnel, a metaphor that has also been used to describe the lengthy liminal processes.[15] Clearly, this part resembles the separation phase in rites of passage. After the separation of birth when the child is liminal, its fate hangs in the balance. It may be allowed to progress into full social person status or it may not. Under certain conditions discussed below, the infant is perceived as having characteristics that permanently place it into an outsider category, and then it is usually killed. Placement in the outsider category is facilitated because of the close linkage between liminality and outsiderhood, the condition of being placed outside the structural arrangements of a given social system.[16]

Characteristics that lead to placement in the outsider category include both biological and social abnormalities. One holocultural study of infanticide listed the following motivations for infanticide based on HRAF materials: (1) viability of the infant or multiple births is a reason for infanticide in 63% of the sample where infanticide occurs: (2) irregular paternity is a reason for 46%; and (3) the mother's decision that she does not want the infant is a reason in 29%.[17]

Minturn and Stashak generally agree with these types of motivations for infanticide. They report that in their sample, illegitimate children are particularly likely to be killed if the father is socially unacceptable, e.g., mixed ancestry, slave, or rapist. Children of these fathers bridge bounded social categories and are thus liminal. Minturn and Stashak also report that one or all of infants of multiple births are killed in 40% of their sample's societies that practice infanticide, and ill or deformed infants in 53%. In 20%, healthy and legitimate infants may be killed if the birth is abnormal or extraordinary, breech, or premature; if the infant is born with teeth, defecates during birth, or is ill-omened; if the mother had bad dreams; if it was the wrong time of day or month, and so forth. Again, these children seem to bridge categories that should remain separate. The children born under these conditions or with the characteristics mentioned are frequently regarded as children of mixed parentage: animal and human, or evil spirit and human.

Minturn and Stashak mention the killing of "excess" children in 23% of the societies that practice infanticide in their sample. Excess is flexibly defined as too many children in the family, or a child too close in age to the older sibling (mother is still nursing). These reasons for infanticide clearly relate to the family economic circumstances, food supply, or labor requirements, which links to the ecological-economic model of expendability mentioned earlier. Minturn and Stashak also mention that mothers may decide to kill infants for their own reasons, especially that the mothers' age is somehow unusual (too old or too young).[18] The finding is consistent with the interpretation here. In these cases, the mother herself would cross unacceptable categories of the life cycle if the baby were allowed to live. She who has become too old a woman cannot give birth, nor can she who is still herself a child.

It is significant that abnormality can be social or biological. Indeed, the social and biological may be perceived as inextricably mixed together. An example illustrates: an ethnographer notes that an infant with a physical deformity is killed at birth. When questioned, informants state that the infant had a spirit father, and so the child is killed. This is a case of irregular paternity, biological deformity, and supernatural agency.[19] Clearly, the infant has been perceived as "betwixt and between" and then has been moved to permanent outsiderhood status and killed.

Whereas some biological deformities may affect the viability of the child, some physical attributes mentioned as reasons for infanticide, such as birthmarks, infants with teeth, or too much hair, would not affect survival. The cultural definition of extraordinary thus may allow for the fluctuating elimination of infants in response to stressful conditions, especially as experienced by the mother. When a child lacks an appropriate father or mother, or even if there are too many other children, the child may be defined as abnormal because it can never achieve social personhood under those conditions. The society makes use of its symbolic processes and places the child in the realm of the extraordinary which must be killed.

Deliberate killing is the primary technique of infanticide indicated in 71% of societies where infanticide is practiced. In only 27% of these societies will an infant be neglected and abandoned until it dies. It appears that once the decision is made, it is accomplished quickly and deliberately.[20] Further, the decision and the deed seem to be nontraumatic, because it is not a "real" person who is killed. Evidence for the nontraumatic nature of the event comes from the contrasting treatment of infants, who are nonsocial persons, and the victims of homicide, who are full social persons. In cases of homicide, sanctions are usually severe and most often involve death of the accused through execution or revenge by the kin group. A unit larger than the immediate family is involved. The sanctions imposed on the practitioners of abortion and infanticide were frequently not specified in HRAF materials but when described were limited to material fine, physical punishment, and, rarely, ostracism.[21] Infanticide appears to concern the family, especially the mother, and not, at least directly, any larger societal unit.

Infants whose potential for full social personhood has been defined away are invisible to the group. This is another feature of liminality. Thus, because of invisibility, their elimination does not have to be hidden or explained away. A social group recognizes only those in structurally visible categories. Therefore, the dead infant's body is disposed of without questions. The HRAF is weak here, and many societies lack information on the disposal of the body. However, 24% specify disposal in a place only used for infanticide victims, and only 7% indicate secret disposal. Twenty percent indicate that secrecy is not necessary, and information on 10 societies specifies that there is no censure of any activities related to infanticide.[22]

In a study of infanticide during the Middle Ages in England, Barbara Kellum states that there was an attitude that the killing of an infant was less than homicide.[23] In the Middle Ages, a time of severe socioeconomic stress, women had little control over their status and few opportunities to participate independently in the economic system. Marriages were often merely public announcements of betrothal followed by cohabitation without much social or legal sanction. Sometimes one or both partners were involved in other marriages. This and the large number of desertions led to a large number of unsupported children, both legitimate and illegitimate. The mother of an illegitimate child suffered not only the burden of supporting the child herself but also a fine and a social stigma for bearing a bastard. In addition to the economic hardship of supporting children, there was a perception that until baptism children were inherently evil. The mother was considered tainted and was excluded from the Church until the infant was baptized. Nursing babies were even viewed as parasites because they drank the "white blood" of the mother. Kellum concludes that strain on the women from economic stress combined with the social perception of children as evil resulted in fairly prevalent infanticide. The elimination of the infant would at once alleviate the stress, erase the social stigma, and allow a woman to maintain her relationship to her own family and their continued economic support.

Infanticide was usually carried out at birth despite the belief that this condemned the infant's soul to hell. Unbaptized infants were considered to be in the devil's power and in danger of being traded for changelings by fairi'es. That is, fairi'es would substitute other beings in the semblance of children for the real children. One method of detecting a changeling was to place it over a fire; changelings were expected to scream, whereas human babies were thought to remain silent. Because changelings could be killed with impunity, this might account for the number of infants who burned to death during this period. Kellum also reports the large number of infant drownings, which may point to tests of witchcraft, because it was commonly believed water would not receive a witch.

As in the ethnographic record, Kellum's analysis again shows how easily unbaptized infants, obviously liminal, are equated with witches and changelings, nonhuman and traditional outsiderhood categories. The redefinition of infants in social perception is associated with expendability. Minturn and Stashak suggest that many of the motivations for infanticide are mother-centered. Killing the baby may protect the mother from social sanction. A deformed or weak infant or multiple births may have less viability; an unusual birth may weaken the mother. The decision of the mother may well reflect her socioeconomic situation. Infants placed in extraordinary categories are likely candidates for elimination. Societies apparently perceive overall benefit to the mother and the group from infanticide.

THE AGED AS POST-SOCIAL PERSONS

Thanatologists maintain that death should not be viewed simply as an event corresponding to the biological death of an individual. There is frequently a period of dying during which the behavior of the affected person and his/her social network shifts. The nature of these behavioral changes has been used to define a period of social or psychological death in which the individual "has accepted the notion that he is 'as good as dead' or that he is, for all practical purposes, dead, in that his social role has ceased."[24] The period of dying incorporated liminal process and placement in an outsider category. Metaphorically, just as in birth, death may be likened to passage. Individuals who relate out-of-body experiences when they are legally dead describe movement through a corridor or tunnel to a light. The same metaphor of passage is found in liminal process.[25] Richard Huntington and Peter Metcalf note that the binary opposition alive–dead is mediated by the liminal process, dying.[26]

Anthony Glascock and Robert Braden suggest that social death is comprised of three major components.[27] First, a separation of the dying individual from others occurs. Clearly, this component is similar to the disengagement from previous status in an individual about to move through a rite of passage. Second, the behavior in relation to the dying person gradually comes to increasingly resemble the treatment of a corpse. Third, there is the gradual self-perceived recognition on the part of the dying person that he is no longer socially alive. The gradual changes in behavior and attitude of the person and the group mark the liminal period of transition. When the dying views himself as a corpse and is viewed and treated appropriately to that condition, the person has become an outsider. Status transition has been achieved, and

the individual is placed in what might be termed a position of post-personhood. Indeed, this position may accelerate the biological death.[28] Symbolic killing is part of many ritualized transitions, but in the case of post-personhood, the group may actually hasten death. Symbolic killing becomes real.

The earliest analysis of social death within anthropology is found in the work of W. H. R. Rivers. He argued that many cultures believe in a stage of life which is in between living and dead. He argued that this transitional stage complicates the notion of a dichotomous life and death. He writes of Melanesian culture that:

> It is true that the word *mate* is used for a dead man, but it is also used for a person who is seriously ill and likely to die, and also often for a person who is healthy but so old that from the native point of view, if he is not dead, he ought to be.[29]

Rivers argued that the category which he was attempting to delimit was culturally recognized, that it included the dead and the old who were extremely aged or incapacitated, and that members in this category were clearly differentiated from normal healthy members of the population.

In the 1940s, Leo Simmons conducted a systematic cross-cultural study of aging in 71 primitive societies. Simmons' work contained valuable insight into the process of dying.

> Among all people a point is reached in aging at which any further usefulness appears to be over, and the incumbent is regarded as a living liability. "Senility" may be a suitable label for this. Other terms among primitive people are the "over-aged," the "useless stage," the "sleeping period," "the age grade of the dying," and the "already dead."[30]

Simmons argued that this final stage of the life cycle is found in all primitive societies and is clearly distinguishable from normal life. He stated that people at this stage are separated emotionally and often physically from the larger social group. Rivers and Simmons thus confirm the existence of the transitional stage, which has been termed decrepitude.[31] Decrepitude is that stage in which individuals are perceived as incapacitated by age, illness, or a combination of these to a degree that they are living liabilities to the social group. Family and friends do not interact with the individual, food is denied (why feed a person who is dead?), funeral rites are planned and even begun, mourning begins. It would seem that once again, the old enter a phase of liminality. Like infants, they too may be pushed into outsider positions and killed. The proposition that in nonindustrial societies death is characterized by a process of liminality similar to ritual transition can be tested indirectly through an examination of beliefs in an afterlife. If dying is a kind of liminality, one would expect that death results in movement to another existence, another status position. Using the HRAF Probability Sample Files, Glascock and Braden found that 52 of 55 societies with data have the belief that death is a transition from one stage to another.[32] The belief that death is an endpoint or void did not occur as a primary attitude. Though religious systems may provide several answers about what occurs after death, no informant in the sample societies responded that after death there is nothing.

Analysis also indicates that "dying" is not simply illness. The belief that illness can be cured is found for all PSF societies with data available. Further, 40 societies indicate that a distinction is made between an ill person and a dying person. In other words, there are three different social categories: the normal healthy individual, the ill individual, and the dying individual. Each category may transit into the others in ways that parallel ritualized status changes. However, once in the category of dying, there appears not to be the possibility of return to the other categories. The logical outcome, movement to afterlife status, appears a foregone conclusion marked by behavior associated with social death.

Gerontological research has shown that approximately 26% of societies in the PSF make a distinction between intact and decrepit aged.[33] In these societies some marker— linguistic, behavioral, or ritual, is present to divide old -people into these two categories. The distinction may be present in more societies than has been reported, since researchers have not been aware that such a distinction might exist and therefore have failed to look for it. Changes in the definition of the old parallel liminal process and placement in the outsider category. Decrepit is equated with dead, which is equivalent to outsider, not a normal living group member.

The significance of the intact–decrepit distinction relative to social death is that each category is treated with specific behavior by other group members. Generally, there are three major treatment patterns for the aged in nonindustrial societies: (1) supportive, (2) nondeath hastening (nonsupportive treatment that does not lead to death), and (3) death hastening treatment that leads directly to the death of the old. The treatment patterns are not distributed in a random fashion; supportive treatment is directed at the intact aged. When a group perceives that a person moves from intact to decrepit, a change in treatment occurs. The group becomes nonsupportive, and in a majority of cases, the behavior of the group hastens death.

Death hastening, which includes withholding food or medical treatment, social isolation, abandonment, and direct killing, is found in 36% of the sample societies. Generally, non-supportive behavior is more common than supportive, contradicting the familiar belief that old people in most societies are given support and that the prolongation of life is always sought. The skewing toward nonsupportive behavior is found even though in every society in which this behavior occurs, there are stated attitudes of respect toward the old.

Nonsupportive treatment of the aged and, in particular, death hastening behavior, are related directly to the movement of the elderly from the intact to decrepit categories. Of the 22 societies in which the intact–decrepit distinction is found, only two do not have some form of death hastening behavior. Consistent with results from previous work by other anthropologists, the findings show that old people are supported until they become burdens, at which time they are defined as decrepit or socially dead. They are then not fed, not medically treated, isolated, abandoned, or killed. The changes in actual or perceived health therefore lead directly to the change in treatment. While defined as intact, the elderly are seen as making an important contribution to the social group's well-being and are supported. Once illness, actual or perceived, occurs, the definition changes, and at some point the time arrives when the best thing for all concerned is to hasten the death of the decrepit one. Once a person is defined as entering the transition process, he is, in fact, no longer a social person, and the implementation of death hastening behavior appears to be nontraumatic. As with infants, the transition process is associated with environmental and economic conditions such that the old person is perceived as nonviable and a liability. The death and rebirth symbolism used in life crisis rituals is played out here in reality. Perhaps this ultimate transition between life and death provides the model for the other ritual transitions.

The classic example of death hastening behavior occurs among the Eskimo. Old male and female Eskimos are equally supported and cared for by their families and other community members. They are accorded respect and prestige. The support lessens rapidly once the old people's children leave the household, or when the person has become incapacitated to the degree that he is a burden to the community.

> They suffer a marked reduction in both respect and affection when they are no longer able to make a useful contribution. As they grow older and are increasingly immobilized by age, disease, and the like, they are transformed into neglected dependents without influence and without consideration. In short, old age has become a crisis.[34]

The aged attempt in various ways to delay the definition of decrepit, but finally "at the point where the elderly become a drain on the resources of the community, the practical bent of the Eskimo asserts itself forcefully. To alleviate the burden of infirmity, the old people are done away with."[35] Another example comes from the Yanomamo of northern Brazil. Hans Becker reports, "If members of the tribe are very old or so seriously ill that in spite of all efforts to cure them, they are no longer able to take part in joint migration, they are killed, [or] . . . the very weak old people are walled up alive in a cave."[36] Among the Lapps of northern Norway, the distinction between intact and decrepit is stated most succinctly. "The Konkama Lapps have little respect for old people if combined with physical or mental weakness. But youths do not joke with or show disrespect to seniors who are still physically and mentally vigorous."[37] The lack of respect is not the only non-supportive treatment. "Decrepit Lapps were often killed by their young relatives with their consent."[38] Among the Tiwi, an Australian aborigine group, "The method was to dig a hole in the ground in some lonely place, put the old woman in the hole and fill it with earth until only her head was showing."[39]

The common denominator in these examples is the change in actual or perceived health. The emphasis on perceived health is crucial. Aged individuals who are defined as decrepit may sometimes show no change in physical appearance or physical or mental capabilities during the transition from intact to decrepit. Instead of changes in the old, there may be changes in the physical or social surroundings that bring about the change in the perceived health status of the aged. In other words, the situation in which the aged find themselves changes. Drought, seasonal mobility requirements, decreased food supply, or increased population in the area are examples of environmental or economic circumstances that might lead to a redefinition of some of the aged. These changes would precipitate a change in attitude by the group. The old would be judged more harshly as burdens rather than contributors. Consequently, the category of decrepit old and the associated nonsupportive treatment may not be present at all times, but may only occur for short periods at widely scattered intervals. The existence of the status-changing mechanism including liminal process which normally takes place during ritual transitions is transferred on these scattered occasions to deal with the old.

The lessons of liminality drawn from the ethnographic record for nonindustrial societies touch many points in modern Western society. Abortion has been the most controversial single political issue in the United States since the Supreme Court decided *Roe versus Wade* in 1973. Treatment of defective newborn babies flared into controversy in the Baby Doe case in 1982. Whether or not to maintain life support to Karen Quinlan, a comatose victim of a drug overdose, provoked intense legal, religious, and ethical debate. Surgical transplantation of human organs, now at a level of thousands per year, requires the harvest of healthy organs from the newly dead and the nearly dead. Finally, the belief that the suffering elderly have a right to die has moved from a passive response of withholding medical treatment to a more active response. Certain physicians in the Netherlands administer lethal doses to cause death. All of these Western instances have their parallels in nonindustrial societies.

APPENDIX A: LIST OF SOCIETIES IN THE PROBABILITY SAMPLE FILES

Amhara, Andamans, Annamese, Aranda, Aymara, Azande, Bemba, Blackfoot, Bororo, Bush Negroes, Cagaba, Chukchee, Copper Eskimos, Cuna, Dogon, Ganda, Garo, Greeks, Hausa, Hopi, Iban, Ifugao, Iri'sh, Iroquois, Kanuri, Kapauka, Klamath, Korea, Kurd, Lapps, Lau, Lozi, Malays, Masai, Mataco, Mundurucu, Ojibwa, Ona, Pawnee, Pygmies, Santal, Senussi, Serbia, Shluh, Sinhalese, Somali,

Tarahumara, Tikopia, Tiv, Toradja, Truk, Tupinamba, Turi, Tzeltal, Wolof, Yakut, Yanoama.

These societies are distributed around the world and are of varying degrees of complexity. The standard PSF has 60 societies, but as in most studies, here some had to be eliminated when information on the necessary topics was not available. This list also includes six substitutions of comparable societies not in the standard PSF.

NOTES

1. Anthony Glascock and Susan Feinman, "Social Asset or Social Burden: An Analysis of the Treatment of the Aged in Non-Industrial Societies," in *Dimensions: Aging, Culture, and Health,* edited by Christine Fry (New York: Praeger, 1981), pp. 13–31.

2. This material was originally presented in 1983 at the annual meeting of the American Anthropological Association. The sample of societies used for holocultural studies by University of Wyoming researchers are listed in Appendix A. Categories from the Human Relations Area Files, collections of ethnographic materials catalogued for statistical comparative purposes, provided the data base from which codes were constructed. Since some of the research questions included the relationship between infants or old people and ecological, economic, and social characteristics, G. P. Murdock's *Ethnographic Atlas* was used, because it provides the major encyclopedia of cultural traits on which cross-cultural hypotheses are tested. G. P. Murdock, "Ethnographic Atlas: A Summary," *Ethnology* 6 (1967): 109–236; G. P. Murdock, *Outline of World Cultures* (New Haven, CT: Human Relations Area Files, 1975).

   Pretest sampling consisted of at least 30 societies chosen at random from the HRAF with the limitations that societies had to be available in the HRAF files at the University of Wyoming and they could not be any of the 60 societies included within Naroll's Probability Sample Files, since these were selected for final hypothesis testing. Raoul Naroll, Winston Alnot, Janice Caplan, Judith Hansen, Jeanne Maxant, and Nancy Schmidt, "Standard Ethnographic Sample," *Current Anthropology* 11 (1970): 235–248 and Raoul Naroll, Gary Michik, and Frada Naroll, *Worldwide Theory Testing* (New Haven, CT: Human Relations Area Files, Inc.).

   On the basis of the pretest sampling, coding schemes were devised that primarily concerned the definition of personhood and the treatment of various categories of persons. Many of the codes resulted in nominal data, and thus only the Chi-square test of significance could be used. The significance level of 0.10 was used in final hypothesis testing. In both pretesting and final testing, two sophisticated and one naïve coder independently coded the data. The naïve coder was not aware of the hypotheses that were tested. Discrepancies in coding were settled by majority or by joint reexamination of the data. The holocultural studies by other researchers should be consulted for information regarding their methodology.

3. Arnold Van Gennep, *The Rites of Passage* (Chicago: University of Chicago Press, 1960).

4. Victor W. Turner, *The Forest of Symbols* (Ithaca, NY: Cornell University Press, 1967), p. 99.

5. Victor W. Turner, *Dramas, Fields, and Metaphors* (Ithaca, NY: Cornell University Press, 1974), p. 233.

6. Turner, *The Forest of Symbols.*

7. Mary Douglas, *Purity and Danger* (London: Routledge and Kegan Paul, 1966).

8. Victor W. Turner, *The Ritual Process* (Ithaca, NY: Cornell University Press, 1966), p. 49.

9. E. E. Evans-Pritchard, *Nuer Religion* (Oxford: Clarendon Press, 1956).

10. Turner, *The Ritual Process,* p. 45.

11. Leigh Minturn and Jerry Stashak, "Infanticide as a Terminal Abortion Procedure." Paper presented at the Annual Meeting for the Society for Cross-Cultural Research, Syracuse, New York, 1980.

12. The low percentage is from Minturn and Stashak, 1980. The middle range percentage is reported in William Divale and Marvin Harris, "Population, Warfare, and the Male Supremacist Complex," *American Anthropologist* 78 (1976): 521–538 and Martin Whyte, "Cross-Cultural Codes Dealing with the Relative Status of Women," *Ethnology* 17 (1978): 211–237. The high percentage is reported in Mary Feathers. "A Holocultural Study of Abortion and Infanticide," Master's Thesis, Department of Anthropology, University of Wyoming (1983).

13. Minturn and Stashak, p. 7.

14. Ibid., pp. 5, 8.

15. Victor W. Turner, "Variations on a Theme of Liminality," in *Secular Ritual,* edited by Sally Falk Moore and Barbara Myerhoff (Assen, The Netherlands: Van Gorcum, 1977), p. 37.

16. Turner, *Dramas, Fields, and Metaphors,* p. 233.

17. Feathers, "A Holocultural Study of Abortion and Infanticide."

18. Minturn and Stashak, pp. 9–10.

19. Feathers, p. 64.

20. Ibid., pp. 55–56.

21. Ibid., p. 71.

22. Ibid., p. 58.

23. Barbara Kellum, "Infanticide in England in the Later Middle Ages," *The History of Childhood Quarterly* 1 (1974): 167–188.

24. Richard Kalish, "Life and Death: Dividing the Indivisible," *Social Science and Medicine* 2 (1968): 254.

25. Turner, "Variations on a Theme of Liminality," p. 37.

26. Richard Huntington and Peter Metcalf, *Celebrations of Death: The Anthropology of Mortuary Ritual* (Cambridge: Cambridge University Press, 1979).

27. Anthony Glascock and Robert Braden, "Transitions of Being: Death and Dying in Cross-Cultural Perspective." Paper presented at the Annual Meeting of the American Anthropological Association, Los Angeles, California (1981).

28. Robert Blauner, "Death and Social Structure," in *Middle Age and Aging,* edited by Bernice Neugarten (Chicago: University of Chicago Press, 1968), pp. 532–534, and Wilbur Watson, "The Aging Sick and the Near Dead: A Study of Some Distinguishing Characteristics and Social Effects," *Omega* 7 (1976): 119–121.

29. W. H. R. Rivers, *Psychology and Ethnology* (London: Kegan Paul, 1926), p. 40.

30. Leo Simmons, "Aging in Pre-Industrial Societies," in *Handbook of Social Gerontology,* edited by Clark Tibbits (Chicago: University of Chicago Press, 1960), p. 87.

31. Anthony Glascock and Susan Feinman, "A Holocultural Analysis of Old Age," *Comparative Social Research* 3 (1980): 311–332; Glascock and Feinman, "Social Asset or Social Burden" (1981), pp. 13–31.

32. Glascock and Braden, "Transitions of Being."

33. Glascock and Feinman, "A Holocultural Analysis of Old Age."

34. D. Lee Guemple, "Human Resource Management: The Dilemma of the Aging Eskimo," *Sociological Symposium* 2 (1969): 65.

35. Ibid., p. 69.

36. Hans Becker, *The Surara and Pakidai: Two Yanomamo Tribes in Northwest Brazil* (Hamburg: Museum für Völkerkunde Mitterlunger, 1960), pp. 153–154.

37. Robert Pehrson, *The Bilateral Network of Social Relations in Konkama, Lapp District* (Bloomington: Indiana University Press, 1957), p. 34.

38. Bjorn Collinder, *The Lapps* (Princeton, NJ: Princeton University Press, 1949), p. 134.

39. C. W. M. Hart, "Fieldwork among the Tiwi 1928–1929," in *Being an Anthropologist: Fieldwork in Eleven Cultures,* edited by George Spindler (New York: Holt, Rinehart and Winston, 1970), pp. 142–163.

Origins and Realities of Suttee in Hinduism

Dong Sull Choi

As a prelude to a discussion of the practice of *suttee,* or the self-immolation of Hindu widows, Choi's article begins with a brief discussion of some well-known forms of ritual suicide. Choi shows that the sacrifice of a widow at her husband's funeral was not limited to India but was practiced in many parts of the world in ancient times. Additionally, the practice of suttee is not sanctioned by the Vedas, and no mention of it appears before 400 B.C. The practice appears to only have become popular after 400 A.D.

In traditional Hindu culture a woman had little place in society after the death of her husband. Abandoned by her husband's family and ignored by her friends, a widow would finish her life as a virtual slave in her own household. One alternative was that she could achieve honor by throwing herself into her husband's funeral pyre. In fact, Choi says that by the seventh century suttee was regarded as a solemn religious duty and it became a popular belief that a voluntary act of suttee would ensure that a woman's family would spend their afterlife in paradise. Although Hindu literature celebrates cases of women who gladly threw themselves on their husband's funeral pyres, most documented cases of suttee describe funeral participants forcing the woman into the fire. Although legislation prohibiting suttee was first passed in 1829, and no legal case of suttee has occurred since 1861, the practice still persists—particularly in the Indian state of Rajasthan, where it has become a political issue for Indian feminists.

Choi's article closes with a list of the ten reasons most commonly proposed to explain the practice of suttee. Whether any one reason is sufficient to explain the practice is up to debate. However, the custom clearly fits with the argument advanced in the essay on killing infants and the aged, for in traditional Indian culture women became liminal individuals upon the deaths of their husbands. Because they no longer had a strong social position, they became expendable in the beliefs of people in some segments of Hindu society.

As you read, consider these questions:
1. What is suttee and what are its origins and history?
2. What is "Karma" and how does it relate to the Indian practice of suttee?
3. What are the various reasons that have been proposed to explain the existence of suttee?

"Origins and Realities of Suttee in Hinduism," revised, by Dong Sull Choi. Original essay published in *Comparative Civilizations Review* 36 (1997), 38–53. Revised for this edition by author. Used by permission of the author & ISCSC.

For the Western observer, the Indian practice of "suttee" (widow-burning), the Japanese "harakiri'" (ritual suicide by disemboweling), and the Jain performance of nonresistant death from starvation—all these acts are not only difficult to comprehend but also even shocking and appalling. In Judeo-Christian tradition, suicide for any motive or purpose is not generally deemed acceptable, for God alone as the Creator and judge of man is entrusted with the ultimate power over life and death.

Yet from the time of Marco Polo (1254–1324), probably the greatest medieval traveler, until well into the nineteenth century, a number of Christian missionaries and Western travelers in the Indian subcontinent mentioned suttee they had witnessed. These men watched the Hindu suttee in deep horror but with great admiration, for the unbelievably superhuman heroism and dignity shown by the women involved. In Japan, the tradition of ritual suicide called harakiri' has existed for more than a millennium and constitutes one of the most fascinating cultural aspects in Japanese history. The suicides of samurai warriors during the Tokugawa shogunate (1603–1867) in particular, and of kamikaze pilots during the Second World War (1941–1945), are part of a tradition unique to the Japanese cultural mentality. In Jainism, various instances of death from starvation are found in the canons of the Svetambara sect, most of which are modeled on the spiritual career of the legendary Khandaga Kaccayana,[1] a disciple of Vardhamana Mahavira (599–527 B.C.), the founder of Jainism, who led an extremely ascetic life and died of slow starvation.

Ritual human sacrifice has always been carried out with noble intentions and, more significantly, has been performed on religious motivation. It is generally believed that the victims' deaths were the most direct means of achieving the desired goals, whether this was the restoration of the cosmic order or the reunion of man with the gods, and these sacrifices were normally accompanied by elaborate rituals. Human sacrifice was generally performed with a firm belief in an existence beyond the grave that was somewhat similar to the life on this planet. This paper examines and explores the origins, development, and realities of Hindu self-immolation called "suttee," or widow-burning.

The position of the widow in Hindu society is one of the most important and fascinating topics the historian of women must discuss and elucidate. The death of a loving husband is painful and agonizing in itself, whatever the circumstances, but apart from the anguish of bereavement, widows in Hindu society have had to bear an additional burden of humiliation and ignominy of every kind. Widows are so unfortunate and miserable that they are frequently under-reported in census figures, because other members of the family are unwilling to admit that a widow, particularly a young widow, resides under the same roof with them. Under the law of "karma" (cause and effect), the fundamental pillar of Hindu faith, everything one does in this life determines one's destiny in future existences. To put it differently, a Hindu's present life is the direct result of accrued past karma. Pain, suffering, and all sorts of calamities are therefore regarded by Hindus not as afflictions imposed by a certain divine being or by the actions of the individuals, but as the result of people's evil deeds or achievements in past lives. Based on this law of karma, it has been argued that because misfortune is the result of sins of previous lives, widows may be blamed for their husbands' deaths.[2]

Ram Mohan Roy (1772–1833), popularly known as the "Father of Modern India," said, "Widows are left only three modes of conduct to pursue after the death of their husbands. First, to live a miserable life as a complete slave to others, without indulging any hope of support from another husband. Secondly, to walk in the paths of unrighteousness for their maintenance and independence. Thirdly, to die on the funeral pyre of their husbands, loaded with applause and honor of their neighbors."[3]

It is not hard to see why death following her husband might be preferred to miserable widowhood. Widows were regarded as ill-omened and inauspicious, barred from festivities and denied all sorts of comforts and pleasures. Even singing, dancing, laughter, and entertainment were completely taboo to them. The widow should not eat more than one very plain meal a day, should not sleep on a bed, should perform the most menial tasks, should leave the house only to go to the temple, should wear nothing but the drabbest clothes, and should keep out of sight at festivals because she was considered unlucky to everyone except probably her own children. Perhaps the most unbearable and humiliating of all for a high-caste woman was having to have her head shaved monthly by an untouchable male barber.[4] All these instructions were required for the sake of her husband's "atman" (individual soul) and to prevent herself from being reborn as a female animal.[5]

According to an article published in Calcutta's *Telegraph* in October 1987, a widow confessed that she had been rebuked for trying to hug her twelve-year-old beloved son on his "upanayana" (thread ceremony). The Manu-smrti, one of Hindu scriptures, prohibits the widow from touching her boy, which was supposed to pollute the child. A widowed mother, as an inauspicious woman, is not customarily permitted to be presented at—much less participate in—the sacred ceremonies of her own son's or daughter's marriage.[6] The Hindu scripture Shuddhitattva says, "All the actions of a woman should be the same as that of her husband. If her husband is happy, she should be happy, if he is sad she should be sad, and if he is dead she should also die. Such a wife is called 'pativrata.'"[7] Again Parasara Samhita declares, "She who follows her husband in death dwells in heaven for as many years as there are hairs on the human body—that is, thirty-five million years."[8] In traditional

Hindu society, the remaining days of a widow were regarded as a "waiting period" to be spent in prayer and preparation to be eventually reunited with her husband when she met her own death. Under the circumstances, it is hardly surprising to see that a woman often preferred to burn herself to death along with her husband's corpse.

Suttee is the anglicized orthography for the Sanscrit *sati*, the Hindu rite of suicide of widows by self-immolation. The word is derived from *Sati* (wife of Shiva), who committed suicide because of an insult to which her husband had been subjected by Daksha (her own father). The term was extended to mean the "true wife" who remains faithful to the memory of her husband by not marrying again. Indian tradition holds chastity, purity, and self-sacrificing loyalty to the husband as the highest virtues for women, and consequently there is no denying the fact that a woman was willing to give up her life on the death of the husband as proof of unyielding fidelity. Strictly speaking, there are two different spellings with two different meanings. English chronicles used *suttee* and *sati*, the former meaning "the rite of immolation," and the latter "the woman who immolates herself." Some scholars, however, do not distinguish between the two words, asserting that both of these words have two meanings at the same time. So they use both terms by turns, without distinguishing their meanings.[9]

The custom of the sacrifice of the widow at the funeral of her husband was not limited to India alone; it was widely practiced in many parts of the world from ancient times. In China, for instance, the custom of self-immolation is often reported from an early date, and it survived even much longer than in India. Dating from the Shang dynasty (1523–1027 B.C.), large-scale burials of living with the royal dead have been disclosed by recent archaeological investigations. In China, when a widow chose to die in order to follow her husband to heaven, people took her corpse out in a great procession as a token of respect.[10] The Egyptian Pharaoh Amenhotep II (1450–1425 B.C.) of the eighteenth dynasty was accompanied to the other world by four of his most favorite wives.[11] As late as the tenth century A.D., in pagan Poland wives often died with their husbands. Arab travelers reported that in southern Russia, if a man had three wives, the favorite one would be the first strangled and then burned on her husband's funeral pyre.[12]

Exactly when the practice of suttee in India began is a matter of much speculation. There is no evidence that it was ever practiced among the invading Indo-Aryans; they only buried a few main material possessions with a dead man. Nor is there any record in the Vedas that shows it had Vedic sanction. One of the funeral hymns of the Rig-veda reveals that in the early obsequial ceremonies the widow lay down for a while beside her dead husband on the unlit pyre, with his bow placed in her hand. Then she was allowed to marry the dead man's brother and continue to produce children by so-called "niyoga," or levirate.[13] Why the custom of suttee was not performed during the Vedic period is not known. As some scholars assert, probably Vedic Aryan conquerors found themselves in the serious minority in India and felt it absolutely necessary to increase their population in order to secure their political and military ascendancy over the native Dravidians—and consequently thought it would be much better and wiser to urge widows to live and multiply the population by remarriage, instead of allowing them to be burnt.[14]

Whatever the reasons may have been, it is indisputable that there was no trace of suttee custom down to about 400 B.C. Again, the Brahmanic literature, ranging from about 1500 to 700 B.C., is completely silent on that practice. Suttee is not found in the Buddhist literature, either. If that custom had been practiced in the days of Gautama Buddha (563–483 B.C.), we feel quite certain that this staunchly pacifist sage would have launched a vigorous crusade against the barbarous custom. As the founder of one of the world's most charitable and peace-loving religions, the Buddha even opposed animal sacrifices to gods. Thus we can safely conclude that the custom was not prevailing in 500 B.C. among Kshatriya caste circles, to which the Buddha belonged.[15]

The first instances of suttee are found in the Hindu epic poem, the Mahabharata, from about 400 B.C. Probably the longest of all world's epic poems, the Mahabharata is made up of 110,000 couplets, or 220,000 lines—about seven times the length of the *Illiad* and the *Odyssey* combined, or 30 times the size of John Milton's *Paradise Lost*. It was compiled from about 400 B.C. to 400 A.D., even though the events in the stories may have occurred much earlier. This great epic Scripture, however, contains only a few cases of suttee. The story of Madri is most noteworthy and impressive. In her case, the assembled people try their best to dissuade her from her determination. Unmoved by their persuasion and arguments, Madri insists that she is resolved to die with her husband, firstly because she was the cause of his death, secondly because it would be impossible for her to control her strong passions, and thirdly because it might be difficult for her to treat evenly and fairly her sons and stepsons.[16]

The Mausala-parvan of the Mahabharata reveals an instance in which all four wives of Vasudeva (father of Krishna)—Devaki, Bhadra, Rohini, and Madira—are voluntarily burned with their husband at the same time in his pyre.[17] On hearing the news of Krishna's death, which occurred far away from their home in Hastinapura, five of his wives—Rukumini, Gandhari, Haimavati, Sahya, and Jabavali—all immolate themselves on a pyre (of course, without their husband's body).[18] It can safely be said that these three cases were the earliest available records to be found in the Hindu Scriptures.

As mentioned earlier, there prevailed a belief in prehistoric times that in the next world the life and personal needs of the dead are somewhat similar to those in this life. If therefore became a faithful duty or responsibility of surviving family members to provide the deceased with main necessities he used while alive in this world. In the case of death of an important figure, it was desirable that his usual

paraphernalia should be forwarded along with him. He would certainly need wives, servants, and horses in the next world, and it would therefore be not only necessary but also desirable to kill these all, and burn or bury them with him. Such a belief might partly have helped give rise to the custom of burning or burying the man along with his wife.[19] The dearest relation to a man is his wife, and consequently the visitations of a dead man's ghost were popularly attributed to his desire to be united with his beloved wife. It is no wonder people tried to lessen these dreaded visitations by burning or burying the woman with her husband's remains.[20]

The earliest historical instance of suttee probably is the case in Greek chronicles describing the burning of a wife of the Indian general Keteus, who was killed in 316 B.C. while fighting Antigonus, a general for Alexander the Great (356–323 B.C.).[21] The two wives of Keteus were very anxious to accompany their husband on the funeral pyre, but as the elder one was with child, the younger one alone was allowed to carry out her wish. Greek writers tell us that she was led to the funeral pyre by her brother, and she was gleeful and thankful even when her body was enveloped with flames. Some Greek historians report that the custom of suttee was widely prevalent among the Kathia tribes of the Punjab.[22] According to the Indian historian Upendra Thakur, during his campaign in Punjab, the Agalassai kingdom was helplessly routed by Alexander the Great, but survivors, said to number 20,000, set fire to their capital and cast themselves with all their wives and children into the flames.[23] This practice of mass suicide called "Jauhar" can be traced back to 1000 B.C., where a whole tribe or kingdom, including men and women, become extinct in a matter of hours to avoid the horrors of captivity and slaughter after defeat.[24]

From about 400 A.D., the suttee custom began to become gradually popular and prevalent in a significant way. A number of Hindu scriptures, such as the Vatsyayana, Bhasa, Kalidasa, and Sudraka, record the practice. In the Vatsyayana, we find out how clever dancing girls won over their lovers by swearing that they would immolate themselves on their funeral pyres.[25]

Turning to historic cases of the period, the Indian chronicles report that the wife of general Goparaja, who was killed in 510 A.D. while fighting for his kingdom against the Hunas, burned herself on her husband's funeral pyre.[26] King Harsha's mother chose to predecease her husband in 606 A.D. by committing herself to flames, when it was declared that there was no chance of her husband's recovery from incurable ailment.[27] According to the smrti writers, by the sixth and seventh centuries A.D., the life of a widow apart from her husband was unequivocally condemned as sinful, and it was indeed declared preferable that she mount the husband's funeral pyre. From that time onward the performance of suttee was regarded as a solemn religious duty, and the ideal of voluntary immolation was a religiously sanctified martyrdom. It was believed that through the act of suttee her husband, her husband's family, her mother's family, and her father's family would be in paradise for 35 million years, no matter how sinful they all had been.[28]

Historical evidence shows that the suttee custom was at first restricted to the wives of Kshatriya caste—wives of princes and warriors—but with the passage of time the widows of even weavers, barbers, masons, and others of lower castes adopted the practice. Probably the characteristic that most sets Hindu faith apart from all other religions is its unique system of social stratification, called "varna," or caste. Traditionally Hindu society had been divided into four distinct castes: Brahmin (priest), Kshatriya (warrior), Vaishya (merchant), and Shudra (laborer). In addition, there is the fifth caste, or outcaste, known as popularly "untouchable," which Mahatma Gandhi (1869–1948) called "Harijan," meaning literally "children of God." According to Robert Charles Zaehner (1913–1974), an international authority on eastern religions at Oxford University, there are over 250,000 castes or subcastes coexisting in India today. Numerous caste restrictions or taboos apply to all aspects of everyday life in terms of food, clothing, occupation, marriage, social interactions, civil rights, and dwellings, to say nothing of religious duties and responsibilities. The fact that suttee practice was prevalent first among the warrior circles is not difficult to understand. Fighting tribes are generally very jealous of their women and often prefer to kill them rather than take the risk of their going astray after their husbands' deaths on the battlefield.[29]

The Padma-prana writings, which deal mainly with theistic themes on the creation, destruction, and re-creation of the universe, also advocate suttee and detail the ceremonial procedure of the rite as it was then (in 1000 A.D.) already established. In his religious classic, *Hindu World*,[30] Benjamin Walker describes two kinds of suttee. One is *saha-marana*, "co-dying," in which a widow immolates herself on the same funeral pyre as that on which her husband's corpse is cremated. The other is *anu-marana*, "after-dying," in which the widow dies not on the funeral pyre of her husband, but later, on a pile lit with the embers preserved from the husband's pyre. This takes place in case the widow is in an "impure" state, for instance, menstruating (when seven days are allowed to pass after the cessation of the flow), or pregnant (when sixty days are allowed to pass after the birth of the child).

We have already observed that suttee was originally a Kshatriya custom. It is noteworthy to see that although the Padma-prana extols the suttee custom, it expressly prohibits Brahmin women from immolating themselves. Here one very logical question arises. If self-immolation promises salvation and 35-million-year bliss in heaven, why are they, as the highest-caste women, to be excluded from this extraordinarily matchless privilege? The Hindu scriptures have provided no convincing clue or explanation to this important and curious question. In her recent work *Sati: Widow Burning in India,* the Indian journalist-scholar Sakuntala Narasimhan (1940–   ) writes: "Two explanations are commonly put

forth for this—one is that chicanery and motives of selfishness induced the Brahmins to exempt their own women from a fiery death; the other is that immolations originated not as a religious rite for salvation but as a political device among the nobility and warrior classes, to ensure that the 'purity' of their women was not violated by the invading armies. Sati, therefore, in all likelihood began as a Kshatriya practice and gradually spread to the other caste."[31] One anonymous writer puts forward another explanation: "the Brahmins, by virtue of their lifelong study and recitation of the sacred verses, acquired so much merit that they did not need their women to burn themselves in order to 'pull them out towards heaven.' "[32] But some later texts of Hindu scriptures soon began to praise the virtues of immolation for the Brahmin widows, too. The Brahmin community was originally accustomed to pride itself on following the most ascetic and self-denying code of life, and eventually it began to feel that it should not allow itself to be outdistanced by the Kshatriyas in the custom of suttee. Both Indian and British chronicles show that the Brahmin widow must be always burnt along with her husband's remains on the same pyre.[33]

But most of the early historical references to suttee are in foreign travelers' accounts. The famous Venetian traveler Niccolo de' Conti (1395–1469) reports that as many as 3,000 wives and concubines of the king of Vijayanagara in the southern India were pledged to immolate themselves to death on his pyre. In Southern India, at the time of a king's death not only his wives and concubines but also his ministers and palace servants were often burned to death. Archaeological findings reveal that the Vijayanagara empire set up a number of suttee stones in order to commemorate these superhuman practices.[34] The Moroccan Muslim peregrinator Allah Muhammad ibn Batutah (1304–1378), probably the most far-ranging traveler of the medieval age, is said to have fallen into a faint on witnessing a suttee rite in Bombay. (In 24 years, ibn Batutah traveled over 75,000 miles, covering territories equivalent to about 44 modern countries scattering in three continents of Africa, Europe, and Asia.[35]) Francois Bernier (c. 1660), the widely traveled French physician of the seventeenth century, told a heartrending story of a twelve-year-old widow being burnt at Lahore, Punjab, in spite of her desperate screaming and struggles.[36] Again we read an extremely lamentable story, reported in 1796, in which a wife was fastened to her husband's funeral pyre. When night fell, it was raining and the woman escaped. But her disappearance was discovered later, and the villagers began to search every house for her. When she was captured and dragged from her hiding place, she desperately pleaded to be spared from death. But her own son insisted that she plunge herself on the funeral pyre because he feared losing his caste and suffering everlasting humiliation. When his mother still refused, he and some of the other villagers bound her hands and feet and hurled her into the flames.[37]

The Muslims, who first established their foothold in western India in 711 A.D., tried to restrain suttee practice by instituting a permit system, in which the widow should declare to become a suttee of her own free will. But the system was not successful and became a mere formality due to the pressure from their relations.[38] The only region where the anti-suttee movement was successful was Goa, on the Malabar Coast of west India. The first Portuguese governor Afonso de Albuquerque (1453–1515) captured Goa in 1510, and at the zenith of its prosperity (1575–1675) Goa became the administrative headquarters of Portugal's Asian empire. The Portuguese under Albuquerque's administration (1510–1515) took stern action and completely rooted out the inhuman practice.[39]

Seen as a percentage of the population, the number of women immolated on their husbands' pyres may be insignificant, but it is not the numbers but the significance associated with the beliefs glorifying the rite that is the main issue. When the practice of suttee gained its widest popularity, perhaps one in every thousand women on a nationwide basis ascended her husband's funeral pyre. However, in the case of the warrior families of Rajputana (today Rajasthan), known as traditionally suttee's greatest stronghold of all Indian states, the rate may have been as high as 10 percent.[40] The Bengal area, originally taken by the British soldier Robert Clive (1725–1774) in 1757 from the Mogul Muslim rulers, saw the largest number of suttee immolations performed in the three decades preceding the Suttee Abolition Act of 1829. According to statistics prepared by the British colonial government, for instance, a total of 8,036 incidents of widow-burning had taken place in the period of only 13 years, from 1815, the year when official figures became available on suttee, to 1828, the last year before suttee was legally prohibited.[41] This figure shows that the percentage of suttee among the women of Bengal was much higher than that of Bombay or Madras, or even Benares, the greatest mecca of Hindu orthodoxy.

The British, who first set foot on Indian soil on August 24, 1608, in the name of the East India Company (chartered in 1600), took no decisive measure on suttee for some two centuries, until Christian missionaries and social reformers launched serious crusades against this practice. One of the significant watersheds in the history of suttee came on November 8, 1829, when the British governor-general Lord William Bentinck (r. 1828–1835) inaugurated legal campaigns against suttee on the ground of humanitarian principles. *The Reformer,* a weekly publication journal in Calcutta, acclaimed Lord Bentinck's enactment as one of the "noblest triumphs ever achieved in the cause of humanity." The editorial went on to proclaim, "No longer shall legalized murder stalk through the land, blasting the fair forms of those beings whom heaven gave us for our comfort and solace through the pilgrimage of life."[42] Although this epoch-making legal action could not eradicate such a deep-rooted religious custom overnight, and indeed suttee deaths continued to take place in many remote regions in India well into the twentieth century, there is no denying the fact that Lord

Bentinck's act set a noticeable precedent for government intervention into some of the religion's most sacred ritual practices.

Although no case of public legal suttee has occurred since 1861, the custom still lingers today, particularly in Rajasthan. Some Hindu women still believe it is their duty to follow their husbands to the grave, and have tried to immolate themselves on their husbands' funeral pyre, but most have been prevented from achieving their goal by their relatives, friends, or the police. Having failed in this attempt, some of them locked themselves up in a room and committed suicide by burning their saris. Rajasthan has seen the largest number of suttee incidents in the last 150 years, and it has also one of the lowest literacy rates in India today. Only one in ten urban women is literate, and for rural women the illiteracy rate is still higher. In contrast, the state of Kerala, where the largest Christian population resides, has the highest literacy for women, at 65.7 percent.[43]

Recently, one of the most sensational incidents of suttee took place in Deorala, a small village about a 90-minute drive from the state capital Jaipur of Rajasthan. On September 4, 1987, a twenty-four-year-old young man by the name of Maal Singh died suddenly from a malady that was diagnosed as acute gastroenteritis or burst appendix. Some source says that he committed suicide by poisoning because he had recently failed the second time in his examination for admission to medical school. One of his cousins was then studying medicine, and Maal Singh was planning on going to medical college. At the time of his death, he had a beautiful, well-educated wife named Roop Kanwar, only eighteen years old, to whom Maal Singh had been married for less than eight months. The day after Singh's death, Kanwar, now a widow, dressed in bridal finery, walked at the head of the funeral procession to the center of the village, ascended the funeral pyre in the presence of a crowd numbering some 4,000 people, and immolated herself in the flames with her husband.[44]

This suttee and the events following in its wake brought about nationwide hot debate among political, social, and religious circles and were covered substantially in the international press. Although a total of 40 cases of suttee-style deaths were officially reported since August 15, 1947, when India became an independent and secular republic, none of these incidents caused the anger, horror, and disgust, or invited the controversy and mass media attention, that the Roop Kanwar's case created. Some national newspapers reacted to the suttee with horrified headlines ("Barbaric Tradition Comes Alive"; "Festive 'Chunri' Veils Monstrous Deed").[45] On October 1, 1987, the government promulgated the Rajasthan Suttee Ordinance, which made the glorification of suttee through the observance of public rituals a criminal offense. Under this ordinance, any action aiding or abetting suttee became punishable by death. As one might expect, strong voices were also raised in the defense of suttee by orthodox and conservative Hindu groups. Swami Niranjan Dev

Teerth, one of the most powerful and staunch advocates of suttee, calling the ordinance "a great insult to democracy," insisted that Article 25 of the Indian constitution guarantees freedom of religion and that the government had no right to forbid a religious practice.[46] One week later, on October 8, 1987, some 70,000 pro-suttee demonstrators turned up in the streets of Jaipur, carrying saffron banners and chanting "As long as the moon and sun survive, Roop Kanwar's name will remain alive too."[47]

What made Kanwar's suttee such a profound and sensational news was the activism and concern of women themselves. Now the world has changed in a significant way. Professor Veena Talwar Oldenburg's comment on this issue is persuasive: "Arguably, the Roop Kanwar case has coverted the idea that a woman can become (an alleged) sati—and be glorified for it—from a residual quasi-religious theme into a critical political issue on which women's voices were heard for the very first time."[48] The important fact to be considered here is that in the colonial period it was the men who debated and dealt with the issue, such as social reformers headed by Ram Mohan Roy (1772–1833), Christian missionaries headed by William Carey (1761–1834), and British government officials. And later the East India Company (1600–1858) eventually legislated to root out the practice in 1829. But now the women, not the men, had the initiative and handled the issue. Feminists were now united, demonstrated their concerted power, and denounced the rite and other inhuman crimes against women with one voice. For them, suttee as an issue was already abolished and declared illegal by law 158 years ago (in 1829) by Lord William Bentinck, then governor-general of the East British Company. To them, the practice of suttee was a humiliating legacy of the past, and something like a museum piece. The question is why this evil practice was to be still allowed to persist.

Mahatma Gandhi (1869–1948), one of India's foremost spiritual and political leaders, commented on a suttee incident back in 1931, tracing the genesis of the self-immolation of wives to male chauvinism, when he said: "If the wife has to prove her loyalty and undivided devotion to her husband, so has the husband to prove his allegiance and devotion to his wife. Yet, we have never heard of a husband mounting the funeral pyre of his deceased wife. It may therefore be taken for granted that the practice of the widow immolating herself at the death of the husband had its origins in superstitions, ignorance, and blind egotism of man."[49]

Let me conclude by mentioning the ten most common reasons given for the custom of suttee: (1) To express woman's fidelity to her husband. As mentioned before, a Hindu woman's absolute loyalty, purity, and chastity to her husband are the highest ideals in Hindu culture. Thus it is a logical and pious duty to give up her life on the death of her husband as proof of fidelity to her husband. (2) To ensure eternal heavenly bliss. It was thought that a woman on ascending the funeral pyre of her husband is capable of bestowing 35 million years of heavenly bliss for her husband and herself. (3) To continue to possess the wife in the next world. One of the most pervasive ancient beliefs is that a man's possessions could be forwarded with him for use in the next world if they were burned or buried with him. Hindus considered a man's wife to be his most important possession. (4) Compulsion (force). Evidence shows that most women who performed suttee were forced to by Brahmins, family members, villagers, or tradition. According to reports of Christian missionaries and foreign travelers, most women performed suttee against their will. They were drugged or carried forcibly to the pyre, tied to the logs, held down by means of long poles to prevent escape. (5) To escape from miserable widowhood. To the orthodox Hindu family, a widow was ill-luck incarnate. If the widow was young and childless, she was all the more calamitous, since she was a husbandless, barren, and menstruating female animal. Her presence in itself caused contamination, her glance was poisonous, her voice was a curse, and her very existence after the death of her husband was perilous and brought misfortune and woe to all her relatives. Shunned by all (even her former servants and housemaids), left in isolation and subject to scorn and abuse, it is no wonder that she was willing to choose suttee. To some even a painful death by fire was much preferable to the living hell of widowhood. It has been said by some scholars that there is no more miserable and unfortunate life in the whole range of human experience than that of the Hindu widow. (6) To relieve relatives of a burden to support the widow. Generally speaking, relatives did not want to be burdened with the heavy responsibility of having to support a widow. The concept of helping others in Hindu culture is quite different from that of the West. Because they believe in the doctrine of karma (cause and effect), they regard pain, suffering, and any other sort of misfortune as the direct result of the person's own sinful life in past existence. Even sons did not want to support their widowed mothers for fear of losing their present caste status. (7) To honor and deify the victim. On September 18, 1987, the *Jansatta*, a paper with a large circulation, carried this editorial comment: "One in a million widows resolves to become a sati, and it is only natural that her self-sacrifice should become the center of people's devotion and worship."[50] Right after her suttee, Roop Kanwar had already become exalted and deified in the eyes of orthodox Hindu believers in the state of Rajasthan. (8) To alleviate male jealousy. This applied particularly in Kshatriya circles or warriors. As already observed, the suttee custom was originally a creation of fighting races, and then spread to all other social classes. Warlike tribes were extremely jealous of their women and often killed them before going to the battlefield. They were jealous at the thought of leaving their beautiful wives behind after their death for others to enjoy. (9) To prevent the widow from disgracing the family. Sometimes an unwilling widow was forcibly burned to death by relatives who feared she might eventually misbehave and bring shame or ignomiy to the family. Given the many restrictions and taboos the widow lived under, it was believed difficult for her to live as a good family member. (10) To immortalize the victim's fame. The Vijayanagara empire (1336–1565), the last of India's greatest kingdoms, set up a number of suttee stones on which were inscribed accolades to the heroic virtue and superhuman fortitude of women who had performed suttee. Also, in some Hindu houses, the handmarks of women who ascended the funeral pyres of their husbands were left imprinted on walls with turmeric paste.[51]

NOTES

1. Christopher Key Chapple, *Nonviolence to Animals, Earth and Self in Asian Traditions* (Albany: State University of New York Press, 1993), p. 102.

2. Leigh Minturn, *Sita's Daughters* (New York: Oxford University Press, 1993), p. 221.

3. Iqbal Singh, *Ram Mohan Roy: A Biographical Enquiry into the Making of Modern India* (Delhi: Asia Publishing House, 1983), p. 19.

4. A. L. Basham, *The Wonder that was India* (New Delhi: Rupa, 1990), pp. 188–189; Benjamin Walker, *Hindu World* (New Delhi: Munshiram Monoharlal, 1983), p. 601.

5. Leigh Minturn, p. 222.

6. Sakuntala Narasimhan, *Sati: Widow Burning in India* (New York: Doubleday Dell, 1992), p. 39.

7. Quoted from Sakuntala Narasimhan, p. 11.

8. Ibid.

9. John Stratton Hawley, ed., *Sati, the Blessing and the Curse* (New York: Oxford University Press, 1994), pp. 3, 11–15.

10. A. S. Altekar, *The Position of Women in Hindu Civilization* (Delhi: Motilal Banarsidass, 1987), p. 116.

11. Nigel Davies, *Human Sacrifice in History and Today* (New York: Dorset Press, 1988), p. 103.

12. Ibid., p. 104.

13. A. S. Altekar, pp. 143–150.

14. Ibid., p. 118.

15. Ibid., p. 119.

16. Ibid., p. 120.

17. Ibid.

18. Ibid.

19. Ibid., p. 116.

20. Ibid.

21. Benjamin Walker, p. 461.

22. Ibid.

23. Upendra Thakur, *The History of Suicide in India* (New Delhi: Munshiram Monoharlal, 1963), p. 139.

24. Nigel Davies, p. 102.

25. A. S. Altekar, p. 123.

26. Ibid.

27. Ibid.

28. Leigh Minturn, p. 229.

29. A. S. Atekar, p. 116.

30. Benjamin Walker, p. 462.

31. Sakuntala Narasimhan, p. 20.

32. Ibid.

33. A. S. Atekar, p. 129.

34. A. L. Basham, p. 189.

35. Benjamin Walker, p. 463; Ross E. Dudd, *The Adventures of Ibn Batutah* (Berkeley: University of California Press, 1989), pp. 1–3.

36. Benjamin Walker, p. 464.

37. Ibid.

38. Ibid.; Stanley Wolpert, *A New History of India* (New York: Oxford University Press, 1993), p. 105.

39. Benjamin Walker, p. 464.

40. A. S. Atekar, p. 138.

41. Ibid., p. 139; Sakuntala Narasimhan, p. 115.

42. Sakuntala Narasimhan, p. 71.

43. Ibid., p. 56.

44. John Stratton Hawley, p. 7; Sakuntala Narasimhan, p. 2.

45. *Indian Express,* September 11, 1987, p. 5; *Hindustan Times,* September 17, 1987, p. 1.

46. Sakuntala Narasimhan, p. 4.

47. Ibid., p. 5; John Stratton Hawley, p. 4.

48. John Stratton Hawley, p. 101.

49. Quoted from Sakuntala Narasimhan, p. 57.

50. Ibid., p. 4.

51. Benjamin Walker, p. 465.

PART FOUR
Sickness and Health

Sickness and health have been important concerns of religions everywhere. Until the development of technological medicine in the last century, treatments that had elements we would consider spiritual or magical were dominant throughout the world. Despite the success of technological medicine, traditional medicines continue to be popular as the Botanica in San Antonio, Texas shows.

10

Healing

At first glance, it might seem odd to have a section on healing in a book on religion. When most of us think of sickness and health, we think of technology and science rather than religion and ritual. However, for most of the history of humanity, the ways of understanding and treating disease have been primarily religious. In our own culture, many hospitals are administered by religious organizations. As you read the essays in this section, keep the following points in mind:

- Modern technological medicine is a very recent historical development. Many of the medicines we take for granted were discovered relatively recently. Antibiotics, for example, were discovered early in the twentieth century but were not in common use until World War II. Even as "traditional" a drug as aspirin was developed only in the 1890s (although plants containing chemical compounds related to its main ingredient, acetylsalicylic acid, have been in use since ancient times). Before this era, much of Western medicine was religious. For example, in medieval Europe, holy names were written on paper and worn by pregnant women or carved into apples and eaten.[1] They were literally cured by the Word. Blistering was a popular medical treatment of the nineteenth century. Doctors believed that the body could house only one infirmity at a time. Therefore if the skin were burnt with acid, hot plasters, or hot pokers, other diseases could be forced from the body. Techniques such as these are gone today, but the continued popularity of psychic, magical, and religious treatment of disease in America attests to the power of belief in the connection between religion and illness.

- Religious medicine persists alongside technological medicine because the two ask fundamentally different questions and prescribe different treatments. Technological medicine strives to treat symptoms of disease through laboratory-tested procedures. Doctors are not much concerned with why an individual got a disease. They might wonder how an individual got a disease, or they might be curious about patterns of contagion. Some treatments address issues of the patient's lifestyle. However, modern doctors are unlikely to see disease as being the result of an individual's having broken rules, moral principles, or social conventions. Religious medicine, on the other hand, starts precisely with these social and spiritual factors, seeing them as the fundamental underlying causes of disease. Traditional practitioners may prescribe drugs, but, as Wolf Roder points out in the first essay in this section, they link the effectiveness of such treatment to spiritual rather than chemical properties.

- One of the most basic aspects of any disease treatment is building a model of how an individual got ill and the actions the healer is taking to make them well. This is true even in technological medicine. Few of us have ever actually seen germs, but we believe these invisible creatures invade our bodies and make us ill, and we think that doctors are able to make drugs that attack germs and make us healthy. As Krassner points out in her essay on curanderismo, a Latin American system of folk healing, building such a model and naming and explaining illness is a key element in causing a cure.

- The notion of a culture-bound syndrome is a basic part of the anthropology of disease. A culture-bound syndrome is a set of symptoms that are given a name by members of a specific culture, but do not correspond to any disease identified by technological medicine. Sometimes, these are simply diseases with physiological causes that are simply unknown to technological medicine. *Kuru* is a good example of such a disease. Kuru is an extremely slow acting virus that causes psychosis and death among groups in New Guinea that traditionally practiced cannibalism. More often, such culture-bound diseases have no known organic cause and are psychological rather than physiological. Essays in this section by Putsch and Lazar explore culture-bound diseases in widely dispersed ethnographic settings. They point out that understanding local conceptions of the origins and treatment of a disease may be fundamental to obtaining its cure.

• Like so much else about culture, the ways in which we understand sickness are often tied to the social and political structures in which we live. Both symptoms of disease and understandings about how these are caused are altered by cultural factors. For example, in classic studies done in the 1950s, Opler and Singer and Fantl and Shiro[2] showed that Irish

schizophrenics tended to be obsessed with guilt, often for acts they did not commit, while Italian schizophrenics tended to act out their fantasies. The final essay in this section, by Alean Al-Krenawi compares male and female Bedouin-Arab understandings of mental disease. Al-Krenawi shows that women and men understand their afflictions differently and that these differences are linked to female and male positions within the social and political structure of Bedouin-Arab society.

NOTES

1. Jocelyn Wogan-Browne, "The Apple's Message: Some Post-Conquest Hagiographic Accounts of Textual Transmission." in A. J. Minnis, ed. *Late Medieval Religious Texts and Their Transmission: Essays in Honour of A. I. Doyle* (Cambridge: Cambridge University Press, 1994).

2. M. K. Opler and J. L. Singer, "Ethnic Differences in Behavior and Psychopathology: Italian and Irish," *International Journal of Social Psychology* 1 (1956):11–17; B. Fantl and J. Shiro, "Cultural Variables in the Behavior Patterns of Symptom Formation of 15 Irish and 15 Italian Schizophrenics," *International Journal of Social Psychiatry* 4 (1959):245–253.

Magic, Medicine, and Metaphysics in Nigeria

Wolf Roder

In terms of its ability to cure many specific diseases, twenty-first-century technological medicine is much more powerful than traditional medicines (both Western and non-Western). No one individual or group ever developed drugs as effective as antibiotics or procedures such as the heart transplant. Despite this, belief in and use of traditional forms of medicine and healing remains strong among many people in the United States and in places such as Nigeria, where it plays an important cultural role despite the availability of technological medicine.

In this essay, Wolf Roder argues that the reason for the continued success of traditional techniques of healing is that technological and traditional healing address fundamentally different issues. As Roder points out, to view traditional healing as simply another form of medicine is to miss the point. Traditional healing operates on a metaphysical and spiritual plane. Technological medicine operates on a biological and chemical level. While some traditional medications may have real chemical actions, the understanding of those who use them is that any physiological effect of such drugs is secondary to the effect of the rituals and prayers that accompany them.

Somewhat less convincingly, Roder argues that a critical reason for the continued success of magical practices is that technological medicine was first introduced by missionaries who, incorrectly, made it appear that their ability to provide such medicine was the result of the strength of their god. This conflated religion, medicine, and colonialism in the eyes of Nigerians. Such origins certainly made technological medicine appear as an outside and alien force, perhaps one to be resisted but it is not a very powerful argument for the persistence of belief in magical practices. If we extended the argument to wealthy countries, we would have to claim that psychic healers remain popular in Europe and America because, in these places, a relatively large percentage of hospitals are run by religious orders.

As you read, consider these questions:

1. What is meant by the term *witchdoctor* in this chapter, and what kinds of problems do witchdoctors attempt to solve?
2. Why was the introduction of Western medicine into much of Africa seen as a religious system rather than a scientific system?
3. Are there parallels between witchcraft beliefs in Africa and spiritual beliefs in Western society? If so, what are they?

"Magic, Medicine and Metaphysics in Nigeria" by Wolf Roder. *Skeptical Inquirer* 15 (1991) 290–295. Used by permission of the Skeptical Inquirer.

Throughout Africa the rhinoceros is being hunted to extinction because its ground horn is believed to restore potency to old men. Also, the belief in witchcraft and traditional medicine flourishes despite modern medicine and Western education, which, as a standard development text puts it, "releases people from the bonds of superstition, enabling them to act rationally rather than traditionally. . . ." (Barnett (1989:138). In fact, formal education and medicine have had very little influence on the firm belief that all illnesses and other misfortunes are caused by witchcraft perpetrated by evil persons and that only magical traditional medicines can defend the individual against disaster.[1]

Modern biochemical medicine is well received and widely used by all sections of society. Health services for Africans were introduced by Christian missionaries during the colonial period, and until independence most hospitals were run by missionaries. Today many doctors trained in countries of European culture are joined by medical experts educated at the university teaching hospitals founded in Africa since independence. In Nigeria such doctors in private practice are the preferred providers because of their superior access to imported medicines and drugs. Unfortunately many people can still not afford their services or, in remote rural areas, find them inaccessible.

The person who consults a Western M.D. will also consult a traditional healer, who may be referred to as a "witchdoctor" or "herbalist" (*babalawa* in Yoruba, *boka* in Hausa). The focus of such consultation is not the physical disease but an attempt to find out why the person fell ill. The concept is that an enemy, i.e., a witch, because of envy or malice or as the result of a real or fancied slight, has used sorcery to cause the illness. The witchdoctor—the healer who defends against witches—will find the culprit by various methods of divination and will take countermeasures. These can take many forms, of which an herbal concoction is only one. At his best, the healer may help reach a compromise and settle a rift or dispute between two antagonists.

The role of the witchdoctor, diviner, traditional healer, or herbalist is clearly different from that of the medical doctor. The witchdoctor is dealing with metaphysical issues beyond the ken of biology, chemistry, or reason. To call traditional medicine an alternative form of health care, as some social scientists have done in an attempt to be fair-minded, seems to miss the point. The witchdoctor's role is akin to that of a priest or a pastor who prays with patients in Western hospitals.

To call such practitioners herbalists also seems mistaken, for many courses of action other than herbs are used. The term appears to have arisen shortly after the beginning of the colonial period at the turn of the last century. In precolonial times, witch-finding often led to persecution, trial by ordeal, execution, and other forms of violence, and sometimes to protracted disputes dividing communities. Colonial authorities outlawed the practice of witch-finding, to the dismay of Africans who felt themselves helplessly confronting the forces of evil. Thus, the milder forms of witch-doctoring were allowed to reappear or persist in the name of herbal native medicine. That the efficacy of the concoction is not in the herbs themselves has been shown by scientific investigation. Biologists and chemists who have tried to examine traditional herbal remedies have found it exceedingly difficult to find consistency of prescription not only between practitioners but in cases treated by the same traditional healer. Besides, the witchdoctor may tell the inquirer quite openly that the effect is not in the drink but in the incantation.

This is not to say that some remedies may not have a physical effect. Ceslaus Prazan (1977) describes two about which he found widespread independent agreement among the Duka people regarding their preparation and use. Hot vapor of an infusion of the bark of the *hano* tree *(Bostoellia dalzieli)* inhaled under a cloth hood was prescribed for headache. He also reported that ground root of the *gwandar daji* tree *(Anona senegalensis)* mixed into food would help common stomach ills. For many other herbals he found little or no agreement even within the small community he studied.

A remedy against sorcery may take many forms. A potion or powder may contain mineral, vegetable, or animal matter, with the ash of various things featured prominently. The concoction may be ingested or infused into the body through an incision. Other means of using the witchdoctor's product might involve burying it in a designated place at a specific time with a prescribed ritual. It may require sprinkling it in the livingroom or bedroom or even the office of the victim or the putative enemy witch. It may have to be used in the bath water, or as a soap. It may even be a treated commercial soap. The remedy may have to be worn as a ring, bracelet, or amulet. Sacrificial animals are widely prescribed, e.g., chickens, goats, or sheep with blood or body parts becoming part of the remedy or ritual. Finally, the making of most remedies involves ritual incantations, and these alone may be recommended in some cases.

Among Muslims in Nigeria a potion made from the ink with which appropriate verses from the Koran have been written is widely accepted as good for many problems. The ink is soluble, and the Koranic verses are brushed onto a smooth board and washed off; then the water is taken internally. No local village market would be complete without its booth of learned *malamai* (Koranic teachers; singular, *malam*) to deal with problems brought to them.

The use of witchdoctors is by no means confined to cases of physical illness. For the achievement of all sorts of desirable ends the use of the supernatural powers of witchcraft appears necessary. Farmers use these methods to ensure good crops, to defend their harvests against vermin, or to promote the multiplication of stock. Fishermen use them to attract fish into their nets, or to identify persons they believe can turn themselves into marauding crocodiles. Hunters use charms to make themselves invisible to game. In married love and in dalliance or to ensure fertility the right traditional medicine is indispensable. Nor is this kind of sorcery confined to the traditional sector of life and the economy. To gain promotion in the workplace or at school, to win a court case, to secure an appointment, or to assure success in a business venture requires medicine. No candidate would enter a civil service or university examination without the necessary charm. Sports teams have their official witchdoctors.

Riches in particular are thought to be achieved only through sorcery. In consequence, people who are exceptionally successful in their communities may find themselves accused of sorcery, or at least talked about in this vein. Fear of being thought of as using "wealthmagic" (*lukudi* in Yoruba) may persuade people to hide or bury their savings—that is, unless they own strong counter magic. Such idling of resources hinders economic development, which cries out for the productive investment of capital.

Why is the belief in witchcraft and magic so widespread in Africa despite the enormous headway made by education and health services since independence? My preferred hypothesis is that it has to do with the way these services were brought to Africa. For most of the colonial period and certainly until the end of World War II, education and health services for Africans were the exclusive province of Christian missions. To some extent they were grudgingly subsidized by governments in need of literate clerical workers and other civil servants, but management and curriculum remained firmly in religious hands. What we tend to think of as "Western civilization" was thus not presented as a rational-logical system and approach to life, but rather as a superior gift from a truer god. Health was achieved not through biology and chemistry, but by the grace of Christ. Other ideas were muddled together with Christianity, the "superiority" of the white man, "proper" dress to cover up the correct body parts, monogamy and marriage customs, the "right" names for children, i.e., biblical and European. To go to school meant to become Christian, and Christianity was valued as an attribute of the sophisticated, literate person.

Traditional African concepts usually recognized an ultimate god in control of the universe, whom the missionaries could reinterpret to their own view. More recent African religious traditions revolved around the souls or spirits of each person's ancestors, who were understood to guard and care for their descendants as they had in life. With the coming of a broader national society and the mixing of many ethnic groups in cities, the particular ancestor-divinities of the village needed to be subordinated to a more universalistic faith. The missions of the conquerors supplied one such faith; in the northern parts of Nigeria, Islam represents another. What the missions failed to instill was an understanding and respect for rationality, science, and logic.

While it is difficult to summon ancestors in a strange town far from family and homestead, witchcraft requires the services of a local practitioner who understands the local forces and counter remedies. Witchcraft is a concrete explanation of particular events—death, illness, lack of rain, a car crash. It offers a precise reason that a disaster happened at a particular time and to the particular person together with instructions to combat the evil. A rationalist might explain it as random chance, but to a believer that merely begs the question. Explanations offered by Christian or Muslim were akin to the African understanding of witchcraft. The priest or pastor will preach of the devil and about the evil that lurks in the human heart and that must be cast out. Africans were quick to recognize that the Bible too speaks of witchcraft, sorcery, and evil spirits—did not Jesus himself cast them out? When mainline missionary churches refused to incorporate ideas of witchcraft and spirits directly, Africans founded their own. In Nigeria these include the Brotherhood of Cross and Star, the Celestial Church, and the Church of the Cherubim and Seraphim.

Support for belief in witchcraft and its remedies is extraordinarily widespread and persistent in African societies. This is true even among the elite, who in this context may be thought of as all who have enough income to afford a private car in running condition and have at least a secondary school education (Oyedipe 1979). It is consequently difficult to find anyone who does not subscribe to at least part of this belief system. Healers will be quick to cite testimonials from satisfied customers or point to uncontrolled cases of success. Since the newspapers widely and sensationally report accusations and court cases involving witchcraft, the questioned healer may reach for a magazine or newspaper clipping as evidence of his qualifications. Oyedipe (1979) reports several such experiences. In a society where the judge may be assumed to take the existence of witchcraft for granted, the claim that the whole idea is a gross superstition can be no defense against such an accusation (Ojo 1978).

Persons more familiar with Euro-American culture may point out that Africans do not stand alone. Oyedipe (1980:9) writes: "Africans . . . are not the only people with belief systems and metaphysics." He goes on to cite the White Eagle Lodge, the Rosicrucians, and the Theosophists as examples of belief in spirits in the prestigious Euro-American culture realm, and points out that covens of witchcraft may be found in the West. He appears to be especially impressed with the efficacy of the Transcendental Meditation (Oyedipe 1982). Magic shows also help. After all, if a magician can saw a person in half, there must be something to it.

Successful healers are not bound by rigid convention. They may well couch their findings in medical terminology. They may speak of infection, of parasites entering the body, or of a deficiency in the blood. The examination as well may take on an aura of a medical checkup, with white coat, stethoscope, and all. Some herbalists have taken to dispensing available Western medicines, such as aspirin and antibi-

otics. It is particularly the latter development that has encouraged social scientists to defend the practice of herbalism. In a society where proper medical care is frequently unavailable or beyond the reach of the poor, it may be held that any treatment is better than none at all.

In the West a distinction is often made between standard, official, or liberal religion, on the one hand, and far-out claims of pseudoscience and the paranormal, on the other. In Nigeria this distinction would be very difficult to make. Christian and Islamic ideas are thoroughly mixed with traditional beliefs in the evil forces of persons both living and dead. There is a rich continuum, from missionary teaching, through independent churches and traditional concepts about the spirits of ancestors, to belief in witches and other evil. To separate religion from superstition would present considerable conceptual obstacles. One would have to take on the entire gamut.

A way of summing up the Nigerian situation is to point out that African society is much closer in time than ours is to its traditional roots. Many paranormal beliefs in our society are shown on examination to have deep roots in folklore and mythology, e.g., the ancient practices of astrology, dowsing, and the expectations of werewolves. Such paranormal ideas have persisted despite rationalism, which has its roots as far back as the Renaissance, unless we wish to trace it back to the ancient Greeks. Rationalistic materialism was introduced to Africa only about a hundred years ago, and then very imperfectly by those least qualified to do so.

NOTE

1. Almost any anthropological or sociological text reporting field work in Africa will discuss traditional beliefs and witchcraft.

REFERENCES

Ademuwagun, Z. A., ed. 1979. *African Therapeutic Systems* (Waltham, Mass.: Brandeis University Press). This is an accessible work devoted to the topic.

Barnett, Tony. 1989. *Social and Economic Development: An Introduction* (New York: Guildford Press).

Ojo, J. D. 1978. The place of supernatural powers in the criminal law with particular reference to Nigeria. *Nigerian Behavioral Sciences Journal,* 1.

Oyedipe, Francis P. A. 1979. The ambivalence of the Nigerian elite in metaphysical matters. *Proceedings of the Nigerian Anthropological and Sociological Association, Annual Conference.*

—. 1980. Pointers to verification in metaphysical aspects of traditional healing in the Kainji Lake Basin, Nigeria. Paper presented at the Tenth International Congress of Tropical Medicine and Malaria, Manila (Philippines), November 9–15.

—. 1982. Corruption, personality, and transcendental meditation in Nigeria. Paper presented at the Nigerian Anthropological and Sociological Association, Annual Conference.

Prazan, Ceslaus. 1977. *The Dukkatoa of Northwest Nigeria* (Pittsburgh: Duquesne University Press).

Effective Features of Therapy from the Healer's Perspective: A Study of Curanderismo*

Madelyn Krassner, M.S.W.

Curanderismo is the traditional system of curing found in many Mexican and Mexican-American communities. Curanderismo is particularly popular in Texas and the southwest United States. However, as Mexican-Americans have increasingly spread throughout the United States, curanderismo has spread with them. Curanderismo is rooted in the historic experience of many Mexicans and Mexican-Americans, merging Spanish, Native American, and African elements with some characteristics of populist and charismatic Christianity. It is most common among the poor in both cities and rural areas, but it is probably true that there is someone, usually an older woman, who knows some of the techniques of curanderismo in most Mexican-American families.

Madelyn Krassner's essay on curanderismo provides insight into the nature of traditional curing around the world. In the first part of her essay, she reviews some of the features of traditional curing that are present in many different cultures. These include the faith of both the healers and their patients, the bond of trust established between the two, the heightened emotional state of the patient, the process of naming the illness, the power of suggestion, and the medical effects of various traditional drugs and herbs.

The second half of the essay is particularly powerful. In it, Krassner reports the findings of her interviews with five curanderos and curanderas. In their own words, these healers describe how they came to practice curanderismo, how clients are referred to them, their process for diagnosis and evaluation, and the ways in which they cure.

Within limits, curanderismo works because it provides clients with a convincing myth—an explanation of how they got sick and how they will get well. It creates an empathetic relationship between healer and patient, and makes effective use of the patient's (and healer's) beliefs. In many ways, the more technological medicine used by medical doctors does just these same things.

As you read, consider these questions:
1. What are the important similarities and differences between curanderismo and Western medicine?
2. What are some of the typical illnesses treated by curanderos and curanderas? What are the perceived causes of these illnesses?

"Effective Features of Therapy from the Healer's Perspective: A Study of Curanderismo" by Madelyn Krassner in *Smith College Studies in Social Work* 1986 56(3), 159–183. Reprinted by permission of Smith College.

3. How is the healer-patient relationship in the curandero/curandera system important to the curing process?

Psychotherapeutic healing exists in various cultures of the world. Each society contains built-in sources of stress and conflict which are relieved in societally determined ways. Techniques of healing evolve with unique manifestations in concurrence with the cultural context. This study aims to examine "curanderismo," a form of therapeutic healing existing in a relatively insulated sub-culture of Mexican-Americans in the southwest. The study explores the beliefs, features and practices of curanderismo as the healers themselves view them. Specifically, the study aims to shed light on the essential features of the "therapeutic process" as seen by the healers in the initial phase of treatment. In addition to investigation into salient features of therapy, the study explores and describes elements of traditional Mexican-American beliefs. With increased knowledge of a culture, a therapist can better meet the needs of a patient whatever the form of treatment used.

Studies investigating the under-utilization of mental health services by Hispanic-Americans in the United States have shown that the services offered are often unavailable or inappropriate for this minority group (Edgarton & Karno, 1969; Karno & Morales, 1971). The need to bridge the gaps in knowledge about people in the United States of Mexican descent seems apparent. There are few studies of curanderismo. Ideally for maximal health care, curanderos and medical practitioners would consult with one another and refer patients to one another when the needs of a patient would be best met by a particular approach. Unfortunately, there is now little collaboration between the systems. More referrals occur from curanderos to medical practitioners than in the reverse. Thus there is a need for increased knowledge in the dominant culture about the values and practices of these folk healers.

THE ORIGIN AND NATURE OF CURANDERISMO

Ackerknecht (1971) points out that disease, especially that viewed as derived from sorcery or taboo violation, is an expression of social tensions. Disease and its healer thus play a social role particular to each culture (Kiev, 1968; Ackerknecht, 1971). Certain therapeutic techniques are found in a variety of cultures, although each has its own preferences based on theories of causation of disease:

> If you believe that your sickness is caused by the loss of your soul, then you want techniques that will successfully retrieve your soul . . . if you believe that your sickness is caused by childhood experiences, then you want a therapist who will explore these experiences and not take a ritual to look for a lost soul (Torrey, 1972, p. 79).

In the curanderos world view, disease is viewed as both a personal and social phenomenon, caused either by the punitive action of God or the malevolence of others (Kiev, 1968). . . .

The folk medical system of curanderismo blends New World beliefs (15th and 16th century European medicine and theories about the humors) and the customs of the Indian heritage, which go back to the precursors of the Aztec empire and the earlier civilizations of the Olmec, Toltec, Zapotec and Mayan (Fox-Baker, 1981; Belasso, 1967; Kiev, 1968; Trotter & Chavira, 1980; Rose, 1978). The interinfluence of Indians and Spaniards has been involved in the medicine of both groups for so long that the original source of many elements is unclear (Senter, 1947).

Martinez and Martin (1966) outline prominent disease concepts in folk-beliefs of Spanish and Hispanic-American origins. These concepts as outlined in the study are mal ojo (evil eye), empacho (surfeit), and susto (magical fright), caida de mollera (fallen fontane) and mal puesto (hex). Based on exploratory interviews with 75 Mexican-American housewives living in a housing project near the business district of a large Southwestern city, the study reported that 97% know about these five diseases and 85% knew about the symptoms and etiology. Two thirds felt that doctors do not know how to treat these problems because of lack of knowledge, faith or understanding. The findings of this study confirmed that belief in folk illness and use of folk healers continue to be widespread among urbanized Mexican-Americans while not precluding reliance upon physicians and medical services.

Trotter and Chavira (1980) contacted and interviewed some 60 healers in the Mexican-American community and identified seven types: parteras, who deliver babies; sobadores, who give massages; yerberas, who prescribe herbal remedies; card readers; espiritistas or spiritists; espiritualistas, spiritualists or mediums who hold seances; and curanderos whose healing knowledge usually overlap several specialized areas including both natural and magico-religious folk medicine. For the purpose of the study, curanderos interviewed were defined as individuals who are recognized in the community as having the ability to heal, who work "full time" as healers and who hold a theoretical stance described in their study (i.e., those who manipulate the supernatural as well as the physical world).

Findings of the study revealed that one of the key problems that the curandero deals with is in identifying the nature of the causal agent for a particular illness. For example, the disturbance in the balance between hot and cold are connected with the ingestion of particular foods or herbs (Rose, 1978). Kelly (1965) notes that treatment in curanderismo is a function of the determined cause of illness:

> Therapy varies with the supposed cause . . . "unnatural" afflictions generally call for a certain amount of esoteric treatment, i.e. curative "sweeping" or "cleansing." Certain elements strongly reminiscent of Roman Catholic ritual are prominent such as prayers, lighted candles, signs of the cross, and incense. Natural illness calls for direct, matter-of-fact treatment such as sucking, massage and rubbing (pp. 24–25).

Like Kiev (1968), Trotter and Chavira (1980) found that there is much less dichotomizing of physical and social problems within curanderismo than within the medical care system.

Trotter and Chavira (1980) presented curanderismo as encompassing three health levels: physical or material; mental; and spiritual or supernatural. Curanderos interviewed worked on all levels. Each level involves a different type of folk-medicine practice. The level of the physical or material, the natural folk medicine, includes natural healing techniques such as herbal remedies, purgatives, application of oils, poultices, regulation of diet, massage, cuppings and patent medicines. The mental level, the magico-religious folk medicine, employs psychological techniques involving the effects of magical and symbolic religious rituals, such as confession in form of consultation; prayers; offering candles to specific saints; visiting shrines; suggestion through verbal communication and/or through the use of symbolic objects and rituals to help convey a mental message; and social reintegration through family involvement. The supernatural level, also magico-religious folk medicine, includes the spiritual and/or the parapsychological realm such as spiritual healing which involves the intercession of saints, prayers, and religious healing rituals, and psychic phenomena.

It is widely confirmed in the literature that an essential element in understanding the general order of existence for the Mexican-American is understanding the influence of Catholicism. Curanderos regard the person's religious faith as an essential part of the curing process. Bach-y-Rita (1982) contends that, in the Mexican-American view, the will of God is frequently invoked as the cause of illness and suffering as well as the source of cure in which the healer is only God's helper. This influence is evident in the prayers used in treatment and by the incidence of healers claiming to have powers through God or a Saint (Rose, 1978).

There has been little in-depth research of the curanderos themselves (Alegria, Guerra, Martinez & Meyer, 1977), nor has there been any consensus about the incorporation of this traditional medical system into the scientific system. The technique and approach employed by the curandero has also been observed to depend on the effects of acculturation and anglicization (Rose, 1978). Studies by June Macklin (1978) and Alegria et al. (1977) address the maladies treated by the folk psychiatrist. Alegria et al. (1977) found that the bulk of the curers' practice include a range of complaints from anxiety and depression to unspecified pain and gastrointestinal problems. Macklin's study (1978) addresses the flexibility of the folk healer to use both traditional and "scientific" medicine. The person seeking help does not expect the healer to treat major medical emergencies.

The concept of the "gift of healing" (el don) allows the healer to practice particularly in the "supernatural" or spiritual area (Trotter and Chavira, 1980). The "don" could be a gift from God or an inborn trait and/or a developed ability. According to Alegria et al. (1977), a "medium" in a "spiritual center" may inform the curer that he/she has been chosen by the divine will to follow a curing vocation. Mediums/spiritualists who specialize in healing and those curanderos who work in the spiritual realm make use of an "x-ray clarivendencia" for diagnosis. In other words, they "look into someone to see the sickness within them" (Kearney, 1974, p. 21).

The training process among curanderos varies (Kiev, 1968). Alegria et al. (1977) described the curers' entry into the profession, delineating several routes. These routes may include current practice as a continuation of an activity learned beginning in childhood and/or adolescence within the family environment or an apprenticeship outside of the family. Some healers are restrained from practice because of familial role and may return to practice motivated by a specific event or may undergo a period of instruction at a "spiritual center." There are those who have experiential training begun by a "divine inspiration." Routes of entry affect the healing practices:

> Some individuals learn by explicit instruction while others learn by observation and imitation. The use of herbs, an important element of the healer's therapeutic practice, was most often reported to represent a tradition acquired from another curer or family member. In this particular realm, however, some curers make use of books (edited in Mexico) to supplement the knowledge gained through personal experience or directly inherited from other curers. The situation is similar in respect to oraciones (prayers), which the curer often uses during ritual procedures. Some of the prayers are orthodox Catholic prayers learned as part of the curer's religious training; others are unorthodox mixtures of Catholic and folk tradition (Alegria et al. [1977], pp. 1355–1356).

Kiev (1968) also points out the curanderos vary highly in "traditional" educational background; quite often they are illiterate.

The curandero's "office" may consist simply of a room or corner of the home in which the curandero lives. There may be a waiting area as well as a room for private consultation. The curing environment may vary greatly as to how elaborately it is decorated. Often there may be religious icons and/or objects used in Catholic ritual such as candles, holy water, beads, and incense (Kiev, 1968).

Certain culturally established symbols reinforce the patient's image of the healer as a help-giver and authority figure. In the initial contact the help seeker's overall expectations of help are enhanced by the therapeutic setting and evaluation procedure. Alegria et al. (1977) describe ways that the curanderos appeal to their patients:

> All the home settings share the same personal atmosphere, which is to be contrasted to their medical equivalents. The curers all practice in the community they serve. In this respect they are completely integrated with their clients. In addition to sharing their clients' geographic location, the curers share their patients' class, background, language, and religion as well as system of disease classification. In contrast to physicians, the curers frequently treat members of their immediate and extended families (p. 1356).

The therapeutic effect of the "temple in the home" with its religious icons and aspects of catholic ritual, such as candles, holy water, and incense, undoubtedly increases the patient's willingness to cooperate and expectation of relief (Kiev, 1968; Torrey, 1972). Torrey (1972) also discusses the value of the setting to the healer, drawing a comparison between the setting of the therapist in modern society (scientific model) and the setting of the curandero. The "office" and "formal professional attire" is comparable to the "temple in the home" and "religious symbolism" in making the psychotherapist and the curandero respectively in command of the power that comes from the patient's response to the setting and symbolism. This respect undoubtedly increases the patient's willingness to cooperate and expectation of relief (Kiev, 1968).

EFFECTIVE FEATURES OF "THERAPEUTIC HEALING"

In his anthology of cross-cultural studies in shamanistic traditions ranging from Kenya to South Texas, Kiev (1968) delineates some "universal therapeutic techniques." These include: the faith of native healers in their system; emotional aspects of psychotherapy; the role of group forces; influence of therapist; and psychological catharsis. The literature highlights other fundamental features such as a shared world view of healer and help seeker; a warm personal relationship between them; high prestige of the healer; expectant hope of the people seeking help; and the power of suggestion. Discussion of the role of trance, possession and endogenous mechanisms is also addressed (Meyer, Blum & Cull, 1981).

From a cross-cultural analysis, Torrey (1972) and Kiev (1968) draw out components of psychotherapy as most important for effectiveness. These components include: 1) The therapist and patient sharing a world-view; 2) the therapist having personal qualities deemed therapeutic in the culture; 3) the therapist raising the patient's expectations; and 4) the therapist demonstrating command over therapeutic techniques. These components are considered as feeding into a main therapeutic force: suggestion (Meyer, Blum & Cull, 1981).

The initial contact is considered important. Frank et al. (1978) discusses the relief a patient feels as soon as they call for help, thereby resolving their indecision as to whether or not to seek help. Patients may fear they are insane and/or fear that nothing can be done. Often people seek therapy because of symptoms and "demoralization." The initial interview can serve to increase a person's morale and combat demoralization.

As an important factor in increasing faith and expectations and the likelihood of a successful outcome of treatment is the induction of the patient into the process of being cured. Salzman (1984) writes that the utilization of the patient's positive powers and will to cooperate and participate enhances the therapeutic process. Bergman (1981) discusses the rituals of indoctrination as important in creating for the patient an atmosphere of expectancy to be cured. Whether it is a person's connection with God achieved through association with an idealized healer or his connection to a scientific theory, faith is an important factor (Kearney, 1974).

In the initial stage of treatment most often the healer will be given some explanation as to their understanding of the presenting distress. Torrey (1972) and Bergman (1981) also make the point that "naming" what is wrong with the patient in itself has a therapeutic effect. The diagnoses also enable individuals to express their conflicts and symptoms in culturally standardized ways. Kearney (1974) points out that the identification of the magical nature of the illness by the healer is what the invalid seeking help from the Mexican spiritualist already suspects.

Studies reviewed by Hoen-Saric (1978) discuss ways in which a person comes to a healer with a heightened level of suggestibility. Through stimulation and rituals there can be an unfreezing of attitudes. Heightened emotional arousal is said to affect attitude change. Either through rituals such as chanting or prayers, or those in psychoanalysis such as the "aha experience," when the sudden explanation or insight clarifies for the patient the cause of his suffering, a sudden dramatic change can occur. Persuasion, confession and suggestion are all used by the curandero (Kiev, 1968; Torrey, 1972).

For example, the objective of "magical procedures" used by the shaman or curandero in the cure of susto (anxiety/depression) is the recapture of the soul. Gillin (1948) describes a case history of the treatment procedures. The curer first diagnoses the malady. In the second case the curer elicits a "confession" and "psycho-social history" and information on events leading up to the susto. Included in the treatment are features of emotional catharsis; transference to the curer; prescription of herbal medicine; ceremonies that involve friends and family; and attention fixed on goals outside the self. Such folk healing is widely practiced in this country (Meyer, Blum & Cull, 1981), making use of ancient herbal remedies tested in use over time (Fox-Baker, 1981).

In sum, effective features of therapy have been presented based on examining aspects of different forms of therapy in cross-cultural practices. Some of the ingredients considered effective are: faith (this aspect may be contributed to by the healing setting, referral system and the healers' personal qualities, training and practices); the relationship between the healer and the patient and the emotional components of this relationship; emotional arousal; a sense of mastery; naming the illness; the power of suggestion; and lastly the pharmacologic effects of drugs or herbal remedies.

The conceptual system by which healing practices are formed is closely linked to cultural world views. Thus the western-scientific orientation of the dominant culture in the United States supports a form of therapy including a long verbal investigation of the self with the goals of personal insight and greater social adjustment. Within the practice of curanderismo, there is an adherence to traditional Mexican-American spiritual and religious beliefs. The goals of treatment, relief of suffering and social reintegration, are therefore reached through manipulation in a spiritual religious realm. . . .

[In a five-page section removed from this edition, Krassner discusses her meth-odology, her choice of sample, and her data-collection techniques.

Krassner wanted to investigate how healers understand the effective elements of their craft. She conducted in-depth interviews with five Mexican-American curanderos. The interviews focused particularly upon the initial phase of contact between curandero and patient, including how the patient was referred to the curer, the evaluation of the patient, and the mutual expectations of patient and curandero. She anticipated finding that curanderismo had features similar to psychotherapy.

For this study, Krassner chose members of the Mexican-American community in and around San Antonio, Texas, who were well-established healers and had been residents in the United States at least ten years. She had some difficulty finding curanderos to interview, but of the seven she asked, five—three women and two men—agreed.

Krassner used an open-ended questionnaire in her interviews and focused on the questions of faith, emotional arousal, and expectations that she discussed earlier in the paper. The interviews were conducted in both Spanish and English and in a variety of settings. Some interviews were tape-recorded, others were transcribed from notes.—Editors]

FINDINGS

Respondents' Characteristics and Training

The curanderos interviewed were all of the lower-middle socio-economic background. Two of the curanderos spoke strictly Spanish; three were bilingual. Four spoke primarily Spanish with clientele who were almost exclusively Mexican-American. The curandera at the Ecumenical Center stated that she worked with a mixture of Hispanic and Anglo clients and used both Spanish and English. Two curanderos were illiterate, one was semi-literate and two were literate. The respondents were three females, ages 45, 70 and 77 years and two males ages 58 and 75.

The process by which the respondents became healers varied among the five. Two of the respondents said they had begun their careers at the age of eight or nine years learning methods of healing from an older relative. In these two cases the respondents were taught by a maternal grandmother. One curandera was also instructed by two aunts. One respondent stated he began the practice of healing at the age of fifteen. When asked how he got started he commented about the process shared by all but one of the respondents:

> Healing skills run in my family. Just the way a father who is a doctor may want his son to be a doctor. . . . Well my family is like that. I learned watching my grandfather. Also, I've learned certain things by the experience of watching people. When people come to me for advice I know what to tell them because of my experience.

One of the curanderas interviewed described her healing as accomplished by relinquishing herself to the spirit El Nino Fidencio. Unlike the other curanderos interviewed, she did not report any "apprenticeship."

> About 43 years ago I became ill. I was told to pray and have faith in El Nino Fidencio. I did so and became cured. From then on, I was motivated to heal others, and it seemed that I was able to heal through the spirit of El Nino. . . . Three years after I began healing, I got a sign from God who appeared to me in a cloud. This confirmed my vocation as a healer.

The other curanderos also acknowledged inspiration and "power" to heal as coming from God. Three of the curanderos mentioned a "divine inspiration" or a sign from God. In two cases it was reported as a voice "confirming or ordaining" the individual to become a healer.

Two of the curanderos continued their training later in life by studying under some established teachers of hypnosis and/or spiritual healing. One curandera, in addition to the teaching of a grandmother and aunts, considers her master's degree in theology and her doctorate of ministry as a part of her training. The level of formal schooling of the other respondents was unknown to the investigator.

Setting and Referral Process

Culture and socio-economic variables are critical in understanding the manner and method by which a patient gets to the healer. The referral system to curanderos differed markedly from that of the formal medical system.

Four of the five curanderos live in the community of their clientele. One of the respondents practiced at a religious healing/counseling center called the Ecumenical Center. All curanderos had clients who came from surrounding areas as well as some from other cities and states.

Two of the curanderos met with patients in their living rooms. There were some comfortable chairs and a table somewhere along the wall with some religious objects, for instance, a picture of a saint or Christ, also candles and rosary beads. One curandero had a separate room similarly ornamented in a trailer home where he lived. Outside under an awning was his waiting area with several flat wooden benches.

One curandera had a small chapel "spiritual center" next to her home the size and shape of a large garage. There was an altar with candles, rosary beads, flowers and a large picture of El Nino Fidencio who was her healing "Don." One curandera worked through an established institution called The Ecumenical Center, a modern-looking building with wall-to-wall carpeting, glass, chrome, desks, comfortable chairs in offices where the "pastoral counselors" worked. This woman considered herself a "pastoral counselor" at the Ecumenical Center as well as a curandera in her own home. She reported healing sessions with people in her home.

None of the respondents advertised their services (with exception of the curandera at the Ecumenical Center). In response to a question regarding how the patients come to the healer, all reported that the referral system is by "word-of-mouth." As one healer stated:

> I heal one person and that person's family members may also come to me with their problems . . . they may tell a neighbor who tells another friend. Sometimes people will come from miles and miles away having heard of someone who was healed . . .

Another curandero stated:

> I take it for granted that people tell one another about a cure. . . . Sometimes people come from long distances. . . . Sometimes they seem to know more about me than I know myself.

Very often clients don't call or ask to be seen at a set "appointment" time. There is an acceptance of a "drop in" system, although it seemed that the respondents preferred to be contacted in advance. The respondents stated that they will generally see a client when they appear, unless they are too tired, sick or otherwise occupied. One curandera, in a joking manner, responded to the author's inquiry if patients call to ask for a "healing session."

> Call?! No, that would be nice. Actually they sometimes come in a caravan. . . . Especially if they have come some distance. It always seems patients will appear one after another for a time and then weeks will go by and I'll have very few . . .

The curandera who worked through the Ecumenical Center had hours regular to the institution. One of the curanderas very definitely stated that "she only works on Sunday, Monday, Wednesday and Friday." The older curanderos discussed a decrease in work hours due to their own health problems.

The investigator discovered herbolarias in San Antonio's west side to be a source of referral to the local curanderos. Respondents acknowledged that some of their patients came to them through the local herbolaria. One curandera interviewed owned a small herbal shop herself.

Another curandero related that while most of the clients came to him having heard of him through the community, there are times when there is a "tough case" the curanderos will consult with one another or send a person to another curandero. When asked if the healer did not feel that they could help the client would they refer the person to another healer or a physician, all five respondents stated that they would refer the client to an M.D. One curandero stated that he prefers to see clients after they had been to an M.D. because he treats only mental and spiritual problems. Three of the curanderos said they would treat most all types of illnesses including cancer. However, as one curandera stated:

> If I don't think I can help them, I tell them immediately to go where they can get help.

Fees/Gratuity for Therapy

As the majority of clients who come to a curandero are of a lower socioeconomic status, fees or gratuities are in accordance with this factor. Three of the five respondents stated that they never charge. One of the curanderos said he has a $5.00 fee, which people usually are cognizant of before they arrive (by word of mouth). All curanderos said they would heal somebody regardless of money available. One curandera was paid through the Ecumenical Center where clients are seen on a sliding fee scale determined according to "means." Fees vary from $1.00 to $70.00 per session. However, the healing she did at home was not charged for. All curanderos received gifts and favors from clientele. As one curandera stated:

> . . . the power I have to heal is a gift from God. I do it out of love and responsibility so I never would charge. People seem to want to give a gift or an offering or return the favor . . .

Cause of Illness

All the curanderos interviewed stated that the "causes" of illness were many and the ways in which they were treated would depend upon what caused them. All made reference to cause of illness on different levels: physical, mental or supernatural. One curandera verbalized what seemed to be a premise by which all practiced and made reference to:

> There are forces/energy of good and evil. Sometimes, people get sick because of the type of thoughts the person has—they can attract infirmities. With a negative thought one attracts the bad; with positive thoughts one can attract the good.

Another curandero explained:

> People have "energy" and the brain can be used as a transmitter of energy. One is able to transmit energy from eyes to a body. For example, in "mal ojo" (evil eye), a person with "strong vision" cannot admire a child or object without touching it lest he inflict the evil eye which causes the person to become ill. . . . They may have insomnia, crying spells, diarrhea, fever or a headache.

The curanderos interviewed heal both illnesses with natural causes. Those "natural" illnesses were reported to have "natural cures" such as herbal remedies, purgatives, applications of oil or ashes, massage or patent medicines as well as some ritual cures (oraciones, prayers) and suggestive cures (through verbal communication and/or use of symbolic objects). The curanderos all acknowledged that some "natural" illnesses were beyond their "healing power"; with these illnesses the curandero would refer the person to a physician. Some examples given were in the case of gall stones, broken bones and advanced stages of cancer.

The curanderos made reference to several of the folk illnesses identifying them as either a "naturally caused" illness or a supernatural one. One curandero explained "susto" (soul loss). All said they had treated "susto."

> Susto is caused by a sudden scare/fright, for example if the person saw an animal, had an accident or got traumatic news. The event causes the soul to leave the body and the cure involves taking out the fear.

Empacho was mentioned by two of the curanderos as caused by eating a "sticky" food "such as a tortilla that isn't cooked well, banana or cheese." The food is believed to cling to the intestinal wall.

The supernaturally caused illnesses are those most commonly initiated by evil spirits or by witches. The curanderos all made reference to "brujeria" (witchcraft) or "mal hex" and possession. The cures included primarily specific rituals performed or prescribed by the healer or manipulation by the healer on a psychic plane.

Some illnesses were understood to be on an emotional/mental level. The curanderos referred to marital problems and other such difficulties. All of the curanderos said that they sometimes gave advice to these people after listening to them tell of their problems.

Diagnosis/Evaluation

The curanderos interviewed varied in their responses to questions asked about the diagnostic/evaluation process. All acknowledged that the amount of time spent with each individual/family who came with a problem would vary depending on the difficulty. The general range was somewhere between one half hour and four hours.

The curanderos interviewed all worked on the three "levels" delineated by Trotter and Chavira (1980): the physical, mental and spiritual. However, it seemed that each of the respondents worked primarily on one of the three levels. The diagnostic process was carried out on three levels. While none of the respondents verbalized the delineation of the evaluation process as such, responses indicated that each worked with a greater orientation toward one of the levels.

All respondents discussed the "expectations" of the patient to the healer in a similar manner. There was a common theme reported, that patients came expecting the healer to heal them. Also, all confirmed that their role involved determining the illness/infirmity and doing whatever possible for the person. All referred to "advice giving" as both expected by the patient and as part of the curative process.

One curandera responded to my questioning about the "expectations" of the patient stating that:

> Some people come to me for the wrong reasons. I only cure with good intentions. For example, a woman might come because she wants more control over her husband. I tell her I won't help her with this.

The curanderos seemed to conduct their interviews according to the source of the problem stated. With the exception of the curandera-medium, the initial process generally began with the person telling their troubles.

One curandero who worked primarily on the physical level used mainly herbal remedies. He resembled a small-town country doctor. While he treated people from far away, the majority of his clientele came from the immediate vicinity and he stated that he sometimes knew whole families of patients he treated. This curandero described the "evaluation" phase as:

> . . . people come to me. I know what their problem is because they complain to me and tell me what is bothering them. I also study them and by observing the person, I can often see what the cause of the illness is. I sometimes talk with the person's family members, mothers, sisters and brothers, aunts to find out. . . . Sometimes the person comes with their whole family. I can determine if the problem is caused by witchcraft. This I can tell by "sweeping" the person with an egg or a lemon. If a "spot" appears on the lemon or egg it is "brujeria" (witchcraft). This requires a different sort of cure.

Another curandera described the process similarly, although no mention was made of the egg or lemon. She added that she also asks questions:

> I ask them questions following along with what they tell me. For example, they may tell me the problem and I will find out when it started and what happened. If it goes back to an earlier time, I will find out about it . . . very often it does or it could be a family problem. I can usually tell about the problem by observing the person's aura (energy flow around upper body) and often I can see when there is a change or disturbance in the energy flow. . . . I usually see right away what the problem is, but I help them to figure it out for themselves. It is worth more that way.

Two of the curanderos described a "trance-like" state they put themselves into, sometimes in the presence of the person and sometimes not. In this "trance" both reported "seeing the soul-body" of the person. These curanderos stated that the infirmity will show itself on this image either by a change in the color or by taking on a shape or form. Both also acknowledged listening to the person tell of their problems and observing the person and their aura (energy field). One explained:

> I can tell a lot from sitting with the person and observing them . . . even from person's facial expression, the lines in their face, their movement and the shape of their hands. . . . I can tell if they are angry or resenting something . . . also what type of person they are . . . if they are perfectionistic, etc.

The other of the curanderos who described the diagnostic process as "seeing" the infirmity explained:

> When the problem is on a mental/emotional level, it often appears as a cloudy ball above someone's head. In place of a clarity in the aura, everything is intertwined. People tell me about the illness. I then go into a trance. . . . I can control and focus my own mind. I ask God to help me; to give me the power to help the person. I ask God to help me to see what the infirmity is. After I have asked God, I count backwards from five and enter the trance state. . . . Each illness appears in a different way. . . . I can see it when I'm in this trance. For example, I was able to see a cancer as tiny pinhead size dots, some diseases or tumors appear with different colors. If it is witchcraft or susto I can tell because it will present in different ways. I can see a word or an animal . . . with susto I can often see the thing that caused the fright.

Two of the curanderos commented on abilities to heal a person when the person was not physically present. Both generally treated people who came to them in person; however they responded that given a name and age they are able to heal while in a "trance." One explained:

> I can make contact with the person on a different level. I am not working in the material level. The problem appears on the person's soul body and I can work by manipulating the energy toward healing.

The other explained the process similarly adding that:

> People may come once with a problem. After that they don't necessarily have to come again, rather they can call me (by phone) and I'm able to work on them from a distance.

One curandera interviewed worked as a medium/spiritualist, relinquishing her body to a folk saint/healer called El Nino Fidencio. This curander acknowledged that she listened to people, observed their aura and manner. In explaining how she determined the problem she remarked:

> I don't determine the infirmity myself. . . . El Nino enters my body and knows the problem and directs me to carry out the treatment. He has knowledge of herbs and ritual cures. . . . Also when people need advice, El Nino speaks through me.

Curative Factors

The healers were asked what factors they thought were important in the cure. Specifically, healers were asked if they gave the patients a name or "cohesive myth" as to the healers impression of the problem. The curanderos interviewed all confirmed that the most important factor in the cure was that the person have faith they will be healed. One curandero summarized:

> The person must trust the healer and have faith in God. The curandero must be reassuring, that is very important.

Another responded similarly and added:

> What the healer tells the patient is very important. Healers must be careful about what they say. It is like conditioning. If you grow up and someone tells you every day to put a coat on because it is cold outside, you will begin to do that. People need encouragement to get better.

One curandera said that she attempts to change people's attitudes:

> I believe that people attract good or bad. With negative thoughts illness can be attracted—that is, when the problem is mental/emotional. So I try to change the person's attitude. If the problem is physical or supernatural, a different cure is involved. In that case I work on a spiritual level. For example, I can concentrate on the image of the infirmity (physical) as I see it and imagine its cure. If it is possession of "brujeria" (witchcraft) then a ritual is done. Often I work at night when the person is sleeping. That is the best time.

The curanderos in different ways communicated that illness and health have a great deal to do with the psyche. The curanderos (including but with variation in style of the curandera-medium) all maintained some sense of power to manipulate forces of healing. In the case of three of the curanderos, the manipulation was described in terms of "energies." In other words, healing was a way of attracting or sending the healing energy. Faith in God or a Don is an important factor for the healer to be able to use themselves. One curandera explained:

> We all have this energy—the energy flows through you. We can use this energy to heal. God gives us everything to survive on this planet. Even the plants/herbs can be used to heal. One just needs to learn how to use them.

One curandera in discussion of the use of healing "energy" stated:

> I use my hands and eyes to heal. I don't need to actually touch the people. I can just send the energy through my hands and thoughts. I pray silently or aloud. When I feel it is O.K., I massage the person. At this time I might sing a healing song or oracion. I don't always use touch. It comes like an intuition—I'll ask the person if they would like that. I am never refused. I can only heal when my hands are warm.

Rituals seemed to be an important part of the curing process. All acknowledged them to be a necessary part of the cure. In describing cures for specific ailments such as "folk illnesses," prayers/oraciones were included as a part of a prescribed ritual cure. One curandera explained the rituals and prayers as:

> . . . increasing the faith of the person. I go along with the person's belief. They may expect me to light a candle and say prayers. I think that my style varies with what each person seems to need. Also, I think my acceptance of them helps them.

One curandera described the rituals involved in curing the folk illnesses of susto, mal de ojo and empacho. Others mentioned them and explained some similar curing procedures. In summary, the following important features were included by the curandera in her description of the cure:

> If someone comes for a cure of susto, I first listen to them tell me of the fright. With branches of a particular type of tree, I cleanse them (seeping) of the negative energies. A cross/symbols are made on the ground, also a tea is brewed with particular herbs and a ring of gold. A ritual is performed. The more severe the fright, the more days the cure may take. For cure of mal de ojo, cleansing (sweeping) with an egg is important. Curing empacho involves rubbing oil and ashes with a bar of soap on the small of a person's back and a particular form of massage.

The curanderos communicated an acceptance of people coming to them for help. They acknowledged using themselves in treatment either by actively asking questions, listening and observing, giving advice, using themselves as a channel for the healing powers from God or a Don and/or helping the person to heal themselves. Depending on the presenting difficulty, direct advice is sometimes given. The wisdom to give advice was acknowledged by some to have come from "experience," by others, from God or a Don.

One curandera discussed the effects of the healer's relationship to God:

> If the person feels guilty about something, I can help them to pray for forgiveness and work out their guilt. People often confess to me and let out their troubles. I think there is some good in this catharsis.

One of the curanderos acknowledged that having patience is an important factor in the helping process:

> Everyone takes a different approach. Some people get healed in their own time—when they are ready and not just when I am ready. It is in God's time and that is an important thing to remember.

Family members were reported to often accompany an individual who seeks help from a curandero. Family members may be included in the treatment.

Four of the curanderos acknowledged use of herbal remedies in the curing process. Some examples of specific herbs for different problems were given. While it seemed that there was specialized knowledge of herb use, this was not an area widely explored in the interviews. One curandero explained a factor possibly affecting all:

> There is a law against using herbal cures. Only doctors can use "medicines" so we have to be very careful when it comes to this . . . I am not a doctor.

The curandera/medium mentioned some herbal brews used/recommended in healing. When asked what herbs they were she answered that they were the ones that El Nino Fidencio had knowledge of.

All of the curanderos stated that they will tell the person something about what they feel is wrong with the person within the initial encounter. Three stated that they always tell the patient their impression. One curandero stated:

> I give feedback but I am careful about what I say because anything that would not be encouraging the person to overcome their problem might not be helpful.

Another curandera remarked:

> The patient often knows what the problem is. I give them a sense about their problem using their own words. Sometimes a person needs to be told they are sick if they don't know why they have a problem. Often I go along with their own idea of a problem.

Thus all felt that the "cohesive myth" was an important curative factor.

DISCUSSION

This study was undertaken to investigate effective features of therapeutic healing from the perspective of a sample of curanderos. Findings of the study suggest that there are some basic commonalities in healing practices across different cultures. Anthropological literature addresses the relationship of culture to healing practices. Professional and folk cultures shape the illness and therapeutic experiences in distinct ways. A health system, as Kleinman (1980) states, can only be fully appreciated by examining the external factors including political, economic, social-structural, historical and environmental.

The referral process in any system serves to increase trust and expectations of the clients. The curanderos interviewed generally relied on a word-of-mouth referral system dependent on efficacy reported by the clients themselves. Those people who seek help from a psychiatrist will most likely place their faith in the "scientific" system. In the traditional Mexican-American community, the healers are known to the clientele and faith in the system is built through testimonial. In contrast to the curandero's system, expertise in psychiatry is validated by a "scientific" training process, and relatively little importance is placed on the patient-reported efficacy of the healer.

The curanderos interviewed acknowledged faith as an essential and possibly the most important ingredient of treatment. It follows that the particular referral system in the traditional Mexican-American culture inspires that faith. The residence of the curanderos were generally in the community of their patients. The personal characteristics of the respondents, their training and attitude toward healing contributes to the increased faith of their patients.

As noted by Meyer, Blum and Cull (1981), healers are often viewed as having special powers and knowledge. The respondents interviewed discussed their techniques and tools as gifts of God or Saint. They confirmed that the power to heal comes with the ability to mediate God's power. In this way the patients benefit by the healer's association with the ideal. The trust is thus increased by the fact that the healer is closely identified with religious beliefs. The gratuity system reported by the majority of respondents was a part of the general attitude that curanderismo is a vocation or "calling." The process of training by apprenticeship, observation and inspiration was reported and confirmed in the literature.

In the majority culture, the psychiatric referral system, the "set fee" and fee negotiation and other characteristics of the expert-professional healer model prevail. Salzman's models (1984) place the psychiatrist in the category of the "skilled, detached scientist" who functions as a specialist or as an expert in a partnership relationship in which the healer is supportive and understanding. The curandero fits more into the model of the wise, magical healer. Among the curanderos, it seemed that all but one utilized some "supra-natural" mechanism for diagnosis. It seems evident that the Mexican-American clientele, with a lower socio-economic status and cultural value placed on externality would have greater faith in a system of healing in which there is greater acceptance of spiritual conviction and authority. As Madsen (1964) states, the belief in God and spirituality overrides all; there is no preoccupation with "control" over the natural world as in science.

Like most psychiatrists, curanderos also described a general practice of listening to the patient's and/or family's account of the presenting difficulty including some history of the problem. The curandero may also meet the identified patient's family and/or live in the community of the patient.

Curative factors acknowledged in the literature are contained in the first contact described by the curanderos. As acknowledged by Frank et al. (1978), the culturally established symbols of the healer as an authority-figure increase the patient's faith and expectancy. In the diagnostic process, the curanderos discussed their acceptance of the patients. Some commented specifically on techniques or rituals that either increased the patient's faith or at the least decreased anxiety. The healer is able to communicate an acceptance and understanding without fear or discouragement. The curanderos also acknowledged empathy, commenting that they had ways in which they could determine and understand the patient's problem/suffering. However, the curanderos generally described faith rather than relationship as the most essential ingredient in treatment.

The role of catharsis and suggestion or persuasion, while not directly addressed as "curative factors" by the healers interviewed, seemed to be present. The non-judgmental stance of the healers may contribute to a generalized "corrective emotional experience." Also not directly commented on, but nonetheless a present factor, was the influence of mastery. The patient's perceptions of success in treatment could be achieved by the healer's communications.

The findings of this study raise some important considerations for any clinical healing practitioners. The myths and beliefs of a culture inform the conceptual system which defines health and illness as well as how individuals are supposed to feel and behave. Perhaps this study in essence describes an inherent human need to create an understanding of our existence. Health systems evolve in all societies, serving to relieve suffering as well as to integrate the "misfit" or "maladapted" into society. Those beliefs held by the dominant culture become designated as "truths," while other beliefs are considered as uniformed, primitive or aberrant.

There is little question that the psychotherapist and the curandero use very different lenses through which to view health and illness. People seeking help may view their difficulties through a lens quite different from the healer. However, ideally the healer meets the patient with emphatic understanding of his/her experience. Generally, in the healing process the healer lends the patient a lens through which to view the illness, and the treatment becomes an outgrowth of the healer's beliefs. The process, including the giving of a cohesive myth or name of the malady, becomes an agent for cure. Whatever the healer understands as the basis for illness, it becomes a way that the healer can approach the patient in an integrated, organized way.

There is value in knowledge of the system and beliefs embodied in curanderismo. Understanding other world views and perspectives can assist the clinician in the dominant culture to approach a client or clinician from another culture with appropriate understanding to meet the needs of people seeking help. Healing practices have evolved in all societies and will continue to exist as long as there is the need. They will evolve to fit the culture in which they arise. Optimal health care in the ideal form would be flexible enough to integrate a variety of world views in a multicultural society such as exists in the United States.

NOTE

*This article is based upon a thesis, submitted in partial fulfillment of the requirements for the degree of Master of Social Work, Smith College School for Social Work, 1985.

REFERENCES

Ackerknecht, E. 1971. *Medicine and ethnology: Selected essays.* H. Walser and H. Koelbing (Ed.). Baltimore: The Johns Hopkins Press.

Alegria, D., Guerra, E., Martinez, C. and Meyer, G. 1977. El hospital invisible: A study of curanderismo. *Archives of General Psychiatry,* 34, 1354–1357.

Bach-y-Rita, G. 1982. The Mexican American: Religious and cultural influences. In R. Becerra, M. Karno and J. Escobar (Eds.), *Mental health and Hispanic Americans: Clinical perspectives* (pp. 29–40). New York: Grune and Statton.

Belasso, G. 1967. The history of psychiatry in Mexico. *National Institute of Neurology,* Mexico City, Mexico.

Bergman, R. 1981. The physician and the folk healer. In G. Meyer, K. Blum and J. Cull (Eds.), *Folk medicine and herbal healing.* Springfield: Charles C. Thomas.

Edgarton, R. and Karno, M. 1969. Perception of mental illness in a Mexican-American community. *Archives of General Psychiatry,* 20, 233–238.

Ekholm, G. F. 1964. Transpacific contacts. In J. D. Jennings and E. Norbeck (Eds.), *Prehistoric man in the new world* (pp. 489–510). Chicago: University of Chicago Press.

Fox-Baker, J. 1981. Mexico: Folk medicine, magic and mind molding. In G. Meyer, K. Blum and J. Cull (Eds.), *Folk medicine and herbal healing* (pp. 121–131). Springfield: Charles C. Thomas.

Frank, J., Hoehn-Saric, R., Imboer, S., Liberman, B. and Stone, A. 1978. *Effective ingredients of successful psychotherapy.* New York: Bruner/Mazel, Inc.

Gillin, J. 1948. Magic fright. *Psychiatry,* 11, 387–400.

Hadingham, E. 1984. *Early man and the cosmos.* Norman: University of Oklahoma Press.

Hoehn-Saric, R. 1978. Emotional arousal, attitude change and psychotherapy. In J. Frank, P. Hoehn-Saric, S. Imber, B. Liberman, A. Stone. *Effective ingredients of successful psychotherapy* (pp. 73–106). New York: Bruner/Mazel, Inc.

Hollis, F. and Woods, M. E. 1981. *Casework—a psychosocial therapy* (3rd ed.). New York: Random House.

Karno, M. and Morales, A. 1971. A community mental health service for Mexican-Americans in a metropolis. *Comprehensive Psychiatry,* 12, 116–121.

Kearney, M. 1974. Spiritualist healing in Mexico. In P. Morley and R. Wallis (Eds.), *Culture and curing anthropological perspectives on traditional medical beliefs and practices* (pp. 19–39). USA: University of Pittsburgh Press.

Kelly, I. 1965. *Folk practices in North Mexico.* Austin: University of Texas Press.

Kiev, A. 1968. *Curanderismo: Mexican-American folk psychiatry.* New York: The Free Press.

Kleinman, A. 1980. *Patients and healers in the context of culture.* Berkeley: University of California Press.

Macklin, J. 1978. Curanderismo and espiritismo: complementary approaches to traditional mental health services. In S. West and J. Macklin (Eds.), *The Chicano experience* (pp. 207–226). Boulder: Westview Press, Inc.

Madsen, W. 1964. *The Mexican-Americans of South Texas.* New York: Holt, Rinehart.

Martinez, C. 1981. Chicanos and curanderismo and the healing tradition. In G. Meyer, K. Blum and J. Cull (Eds.), *Folk medicine and herbal healing* (pp. 114–120). Springfield: Charles C. Thomas.

Martinez, C. and Martin, H. W. 1966. Folk diseases among urban Mexican-Americans. *J.A.M.A.,* 196, 1987–1094.

Meyer, G., Blum, K. and Cull, J. (Eds.), 1981. *Folk medicine and herbal healing.* Springfield: Charles C. Thomas.

Northen, H. 1982. *Clinical social work.* New York: Columbia University Press.

Rose, L. 1978. *Disease beliefs in Mexican-American communities.* San Francisco: R & E Research Assoc.

Salzman, L. 1984. Change and the therapeutic process. In M. Meyers (Ed.), *Cures by psychotherapy: What effects change?* (pp. 103–117). New York: Praeger Publishers.

Senter, D. 1947. Witches and psychiatrists. *Psychiatry,* 10, 49–56.

Sue, D. W. 1981. *Counseling the culturally different: Theory and practice.* New York: John Wiley & Sons.

Torrey, E. F. 1972. *The mind game: Witchdoctors and psychiatrists.* New York: Bantam Books, Emerson Hall Publishers.

—. 1969. The case for the indigenous therapist. *Archives of General Psychiatry,* 20, 365–373.

Trotter, R. and Chavira, J. 1980. Curanderismo: An emic theoretic perspective of Mexican-American folk medicine. *Medical Anthropology,* 423–487.

Ghost Illness:
A Cross-Cultural Experience with the Expression of a Non-Western Tradition in Clinical Practice

Robert W. Putsch III, M.D.

Culture-bound syndromes have been of interest to both anthropologists and medical personnel for many years. A culture-bound syndrome is a disease that is recognized by members of a specific culture, but does not correspond exactly to any disease recognized by modern technological medicine. Some well-known examples of culture-bound syndromes are *amok* and *koro,* both found in Malaysia. Individuals with *amok* experience a period of intense brooding followed by violent behavior aimed at people or objects (hence, "running amok"). Men with *koro* experience intense fear that their penises will recede into their bodies, possibly resulting in their deaths.

In this essay, Robert W. Putsch III describes three cases of ghost illness from widely separated cultures: the Navajo, the Salish, and the Hmong. Though specific symptoms and understanding differ, in each case, sufferers believe that their physical symptoms are brought about by the appearance of a recently deceased relative and that such an appearance portends their own death. For each case, Putsch compares the native understanding of the problem with a Western psychiatric understanding and shows how medical practitioners used native understandings to help these patients. Importantly, he notes that patients experienced enormous psychological and emotional benefits, even though in some cases their physiological symptoms actually got worse.

Putsch concludes that these examples of ghost illness suggest a universal human problem: in all cultures, the mortality rate of those who are left behind when a spouse or other close relative dies is higher than for those who have not experienced such a loss. Notions of ghost illness and traditions of songs, offerings, and ceremonies to cure it are ways that human societies have addressed this fundamental problem. It is clear that health professionals can better serve the needs of people of different cultures by recognizing culturally specific manifestations of ghost illness and working at least partially within traditional frameworks to cure it. It is less clear that modern technological medicine has provided more successful treatments to death resulting from bereavement than various traditional medicines.

"Ghost Illness: A Cross-cultural Experience with the Expression of a Non-Western Tradition in Clinical Practice" by Robert W. Putsch III in *American Indian and Alaska Native Health Research* 2:2, 6–26. Reproduced by permission of the National Center for American Indian Mental Health Research.

As you read, consider these questions:
1. What is "ghost illness," and how are the three cases described in this chapter similar? How are they different?
2. Some cultures interpret dreams about dead relatives as negative, others interpret them as positive. Why?
3. Why is it important for Western health care professionals working in non-Western cultures to know about the belief systems of their patients?

It is twelve days since we buried you.
We feed you again, and give you new clothes.
This is all we will feed and clothe you.
Now go to the other side.
We will stay on our side.
Don't seek us and we won't seek you.
Don't yearn for your relatives.
    don't call for us . . .

—A Lahu funery prayer
(Lewis and Lewis, 1984, p. 192)

Go. Go straight ahead
Do not take anyone with you.
Do not look back.
When you reach your destination,
    talk for us.
Tell them not to trouble us.
Or not to come here
    and take anyone else away.

—A Cree funery prayer
(Dusenberry, 1962, p. 96)

Writings on death and dying focus heavily on the problems experienced by dying individuals and those who care for them; the survivors of death in a family have received far less attention. Death and dying pose serious problems for surviving family members. Beliefs and practices regarding death and the dead have had a profound effect on the behaviors surrounding illness, and in many groups have led to traditions in which patients and/or family members may perceive a sickness as being connected in various ways to someone who has died (often family member). This traditional stance regarding connections between the dead and the etiology of illness will be referred to as "ghost illness" in this paper.

Ghost illness appears to be a culture-bound syndrome. Spirits or "ghosts" may be viewed as being directly or indirectly linked to the etiology of an event, accident, or illness, and this may occur irrespective of biomedical etiologic views. Western languages lack formal terminology for ghost illness, and the parallel beliefs and behaviors are masked by and hidden within Western social fabric as well as the paradigms of Western psychiatry and medicine. In contrast, specific terminology for ghost illnesses not only exists in many non-Western cultures, but the terms coexist with extensive and elaborate means of dealing with the problem.

The recurring theme that the dead may take someone with them is illustrated by the funery prayers at the beginning of this paper. These two tribal groups expressed similar fears in prayers addressed to the dead.

Don't seek us and we won't seek you.
Don't yearn for your relatives.
  don't call for us . . .

—A Lahu funery prayer
(Lewis and Lewis, 1984, p. 192)

Tell them not to trouble us.
Or not to come here
  and take anyone else away.

—A Cree funery prayer
(Dusenberry, 1962, p. 96)

Since epidemiology informs us of a high rate of mortality during bereavement, these prayers and myths have a basis in fact. Additionally, there is real and symbolic evidence of an associated self-destructive impulse in the bereavement period. Thus it is that the psycholinguistic response of anxiety, dread, and fear of death in another is based on reality. We will observe the clinical significance of these themes in the three cases of "ghost illness" which follow. Each of the individuals to be presented had interacting somatic as well as psychosomatic components to their experience of illness, depression, and anxiety. In each instance, however, their views were directly tied to special, culture-bound beliefs and to the emergence of hallucinations and/or dreams of deceased relatives.

This paper reviews three patients who come from cultures which have well-documented views regarding illness caused by the dead. The patients are Navajo, Salish (a Northwest coastal group) and Hmong (a hill tribe in Laos, Thailand and China). Concern over burial, ghosts, and ghost sickness is well known in the Navajo (Haile, 1938; Levy, 1981). The religious/therapeutic expression of this concern is seen in multiple Navajo healing ceremonials that belong to the evil chasing or ghost way chant groups. Both the Salish (Ahern, 1973; Collins, 1980) and Hmong (Chindarsi, 1978) people have ancestral religious process, and both groups have ceremonial means to deal with ancestral interference and ambivalence. All three of the individuals to be discussed sought help from Western trained physicians for physical complaints. Following the cases, there is a discussion of the ghost illness tradition in the broad context of experience and beliefs relating to death and dying.

CASE 1—A NAVAJO WOMAN WITH GHOST ILLNESS

Date of Onset	Problem List
May, 1977	1) Bilateral accessory breasts
1972	2) Infertility, 5 years duration, resolved 1977
July, 1977	3) Post-partum depression, family problems

This 27-year-old Navajo woman was seen in an emergency room two months after the birth of her first child, a daughter. She complained of painless swelling in both axillae which had begun during the eighth month of her pregnancy. Earlier, her family physician had advised her that the swellings were caused by the enlargement of accessory breast tissue, and he had counseled her to avoid breast feeding in an attempt to prevent further enlargement. She had complied, but in spite of this precaution, the tissue failed to recede during the post-partum period.

Her pregnancy had ended a five-year problem with infertility. She was perplexed by the developments that followed delivery. "We waited so long . . . I should be happy, but I'm not . . . I've been having crying spells, and I get mad over anything." In addition, she had developed difficulty sleeping, had lost interest in her usual activities, and noted a markedly diminished libido. She had argued with her husband over minor issues, and on two separate occasions, she became angry and "took off in the car." "I found myself driving 80 to 90 mph, headed for the Navajo reservation . . . it really scared me, I was going 80 right through last night." Fright generated by this driving episode had precipitated a Sunday morning emergency room visit.

The patient presented two major concerns. One involved the lumps under her arms; although she acknowledged that these were accessory breast tissue and not cancer, the patient found herself worrying about "looking ugly" and about dying. Her second concern was of "losing her mind"; she explained this fear by referring to "not caring about anything" and to her "crazy driving." Additionally, she mentioned a brother who was a binge drinker, often threatened people (especially her mother), and was judged by the family to be uncontrollable and "out of his mind." "I'm afraid I'll get like that."

During the months following the birth of her first child, the patient had experienced repetitive disturbing dreams. She began dreaming about having an operation and had noted the sudden resurgence of an old, recurring dream of her deceased father. The dream of her father had a special meaning for her: "Whenever I dream him, it makes me feel like I'm going to do something crazy." She immediately gave "driving fast again" as an example of what she meant. While her original dreams about her father occurred prior to her marriage, the dreams had suddenly reemerged, increasing in frequency during the post-partum period. Her father had died suddenly six years earlier under circumstances in which she was "with him the whole time." She had raised the issue of details surrounding her father's death after the interviewer made a comment about a possible Navajo interpretation of her dreams: "sometimes this kind of dream means that the dreamer thinks that something bad is going to happen, occasionally Navajos refer to dreams like that as *Ch'iidi dreams*." (*Ch'iidi* is a term that relates to ghost-related materials, places, dreams, or visitations. It has become the slang term for "crazy.")

The patient felt it was necessary to explain her concern in some detail. Six and one-half years previously, she had assisted in the delivery of her youngest brother at home; it was her mother's last pregnancy. The placenta had become stuck, and she had to take her mother to the nearest health clinic. She returned home alone in the truck to find that her father had suddenly become ill. "It turned out that he had a ruptured appendix. I went straight back to the clinic . . . they still had my mother, and they sent us to the hospital (a 175-mile trip by ambulance). Later the doctors said it had gone too far. He died when they tried to operate on him." When the patient subsequently developed nightmares about her father, her mother insisted that the patient needed a ceremonial to rid her of the malignant influence of the father's spirit. The patient's mother felt that the patient was somehow tied to the father's death. The patient had discussed the need for this ceremonial with her husband. "But," she stated, "he doesn't believe in it."

There were other problems. The patient had experienced irritability, decreased interest in daily activities, and inability to relate well to her husband since the birth of their child. Additionally, she noted that references to her as "La India" by her husband's Spanish speaking family were now very upsetting. "Why do they call me The Indian? They know my name, why don't they use it?" In the past, the patient and her husband had experienced difficulties when they entered the environment of each other's homes. For this reason, they were purposively living away from both families, and had been supportive of each other when at either in-law's home. Until her husband's brief layoff at work, they had been doing well.

The patient and her husband had participated in Navajo ceremonials on numerous occasions. Her family and friends had occasionally stated that it "wasn't right" for the husband to help Navajo ceremonials. She was convinced that her successful pregnancy was the direct result of treatment by a female ceremonialist on the reservation a few months before becoming pregnant. On her husband's side, she had agreed to the christening of her daughter via the Catholic church. Her husband's family had used traditional healers and had an awareness of the special folk knowledge of Curanderismo. The husband's aunt, for instance, was regarded as a *bruja* (witch) by the rest of the family, and a number of family problems had been ascribed to her malevolence.

An Approach to Treatment

The therapy, outlined below, was designed to simultaneously account for both the traditional views of the illness and the biomedical problems the patient was experiencing.

1) Arrangements were made for a cosmetic surgery evaluation, and the patient was advised to wait a sufficient period to be certain that the effect of her pregnancy on her breasts was maximally resolved.

2) Diagnostic measures were undertaken to ensure that there was no other endocrinologic problems contributing to the prolonged post-partum depression. (This included an evaluation for post-partum hypothyroidism.)

3) Lengthy discussions were undertaken regarding the couple's disparate beliefs and backgrounds. Each spouse had made prior concessions to the other's backgrounds; however, their beliefs and ethnic differences had become an issue during this period of stress. The patient viewed her problem from a distinctly Navajo point of view. At one point, she explained her behavior by directly stating that her father "was making me do these things, he's the one who makes me do it." In fact, this view was shared by her mother, who had discussed the need for a ceremonial repeatedly, by mail and over the phone. The patient was not a Christian, and after the birth of their daughter had participated in a Catholic christening without "really believing it." Her husband and his family had been unhappy over her failure to participate fully in Catholicism, but they were pleased by her participation in the christening. The difference between believing in things and respecting them was reviewed. The patient's husband eventually agreed that it was necessary to respect his wife's views and to deal with the dreams "in a Navajo way."

4) The couple decided to attack the problem of the dreams first. Their first decision to have a ceremonial done dovetailed with the need for the patient to await any spontaneous regression of the massively developed accessory breast tissue and her husband's layoff. (He was off work at the time, and the ceremony would require a week-long trip to the reservation.)

Discussion

This case is a classic example of the ghost illness process. The individual views the experience both as an assault and as a means of explaining the death wish and associated behavior. To the patient, the dreams were concrete evidence that she was going to die (actually, be killed). This was the reason for her quick association between reckless driving and the dream (literally, "he is making me do it"). She was not assuming responsibility for the actions at any level; the problem was one of intrusion of an external force. The patient's view is in concert with that described by Kaplan and Johnson (1974).

> In ghost sickness, the patient is a victim of the malevolence of others . . . we have speculated that, since in fact there is no ghost, the symptoms derive from the patient's own beliefs and attitudes. The social definition of the illness is that of an evil attack on the good. In the curing process, the community ranges itself on the side of the victim and musters its strength for his support. (p. 219)

According to Western theory, the ghost of the father was a projection of a death wish growing out of the patient's frustration with her accessory breasts, fear of surgery, postpartum depression, and anger at her husband. While the Western explanation psychologizes about the ghost experience, the Navajo explanation concretizes it. The ghost is real, an essential part of the etiology of the problem.

The patient had explained her fears about "going crazy" via discussion of her brother's behavior. Part of her perception of craziness had to do with being "out of control" and part had to do with "thinking about dying." Both were attributes that the family had ascribed to her brother at one time or another. At one point, her family blamed his drinking on marital discord and witchcraft. Although they had sought therapeutic help for him through traditional means (the traditional Navajo pollen way) and through the Native American Church, the brother's drinking had persisted. The family felt that her brother had no control over his behavior, and his behavior, like her own, had become destructive.

Historically, there was little room for "natural death" among the Navajo. Everyone was thought to die as the result of some malevolence, and the reference (except for death in old age which is sought for) was to being "killed." Psycholinguistically, the culture has given very little attention to the existence of death as a natural and inevitable event; one gets "killed," and the evidence for this recurs with such regularity among the Navajo that it helps to underscore the patient's views of the events described above. As a result, self-destructive behavior is not logically seen as self-destructive. The Navajo often view self-destructive behavior as the fault of someone else, or as the result of "being driven to it." The patient's view was not idiosyncratic. There was evidence of family agreement on this point; "He (the father) is driving you to it."

Her mother's response included the suggestion that she would assist the patient by arranging for a ceremonial, and a request that the patient return home to live and to help out. The patient reacted to these suggestions with ambiguity. She did not like either the pressure to return home or the uneasiness associated with not complying. Keep in mind that this mother suggested that the patient had some connection with the father's death. This suggestion may have sounded unusual to the reader. However, establishing blame for a death is not an uncommon circumstance among the Navajo. The mother's accusatory suggestion that a connection existed between the daughter's actions and the father's death is interesting from the point of view of family dynamics. The author has observed the same accusation after the death of a parent in other clinical situations. The effect on the child is profound and frequently ties the child in a highly ambivalent fashion to the surviving parent.

The ceremonial provided a solution to the dream and established a compromise with the mother. Having made the decision to undertake the ceremonial, the couple verbalized a series of plans to handle their remaining difficulties. By

Western psychologizing standards, the dreams and the patient's interpretation of them were clearly projections of her anxiety and depression. Her own view differed, the threat seemed all too real. Toward the end of an interview, the question was asked again with a slightly different approach: "What does your mother say is causing these troubles?" There was no hesitation; "She says my father is making me do it." Her mother had not focused on the patient's marital problems, financial troubles, being isolated in a mountain town, or the new baby. The patient's decision to focus on the ceremonial becomes all the more clear and reasonable when seen in this context. This initial step appeared to be necessary in order to remove the threat and to reestablish her role as an active mother and wife.

CASE 2—A SALISH WOMAN WITH GHOST ILLNESS

Date of Onset	Problem List
Summer/Fall 1976	1) Rheumatoid arthritis
Longstanding	2) Diabetes mellitus, insulin dependent
Longstanding	3) Obesity
1976	4) Positive tuberculin, treated with isoniazid (INH)
	a) Hepatitis related to INH therapy
Summer, 1976	5) Depression
Longstanding	6) Asymptomatic diverticulosis

This middle-aged woman was referred for the evaluation of diffuse arthritic complaints. Two and one-half months prior to her hospitalization, she had developed recurrent problems with early morning stiffness and aching of the proximal interphalangeal joints of her hands. She became progressively unable to care for herself during the six-week period immediately preceding hospitalization. She required assistance dressing, eating, and bathing. Two weeks prior to her admission, she became almost entirely dependent upon the help of others. Physical examination in a referring clinic did not explain the severity of her illness. Her laboratory evaluation had been negative. At the time of her admission to the hospital, she was a remarkably disabled woman; walked with a shuffle, shoulders forward, stooped over, and with her arms folded across her chest. Her evaluation in the hospital supported the referring clinic's view; there was a disparity between her laboratory evaluation and physical examination on the one hand, and her severely incapacitated state on the other.

The patient's history was unusual. She dated the onset of her illness to a specific date in the preceding fall, the morning after she experienced a visit by her deceased father. "I felt a bump against the bed and I thought, 'I wonder what my husband is doing on that side of the bed.' I felt the bump again, I opened my eyes and my father was standing there.

He had on his tie, and looked the same as when we buried him . . ." The patient insisted that she was awake at the time, and stated that her father spoke and made her the special gift of a Salish spirit song.

A later part of the interview included an account of an associated episode which she felt may have contributed to her illness. She stated that her arthritis may have been caused by her failure to be properly "brushed off" after participating in a healing ceremony. This incident had occurred about three months prior to her admission, and the ceremony was being done for an individual who had multiple arthritic complaints. The patient hypothesized that the spirit that was causing the arthritic individual's illness had "come off" and somehow had been transferred to herself. (Brushing off healers and participants in healing practices is a common practice used by Salish groups. It is aimed at preventing dangerous spirits from sticking to others during and after the healing process.)

The patient had acted on the basis of her Salish beliefs and disparate Salish interpretations of her sickness. She had sought the assistance of different healers from a number of different Salish groups. Multiple attempts at dealing with her problems had been unsuccessful. At one point, she was treated during a service in the Indian Shaker Church. "They saw the spirit, and took it off me." However, the healer in charge of the service noted that the "whole church seemed to be rocking and upset," and because "he felt the spirit was too powerful, he put it back on me the next morning—I'm telling you that I never felt so bad as I did when that man put that thing back on me." At least two other medicine men had attempted to deal with her, and the therapy had failed. Subsequently, one of the medicine men suggested that she needed to see a Western physician because the illness was not responding. In an attempt to put the spiritual aspect of her illness into perspective, the patient described earlier illnesses of similar nature. "I've lost my soul a number of times." As an example, she reported becoming ill after the death of her father 18 months earlier. During his funeral she had an impulse to "jump in his grave," and two weeks later was "still feeling real bad." She was treated by a medicine man who "told me that I had lost my soul in the graveyard . . . that it had been standing out there in the rain and cold all that time." His therapy involved retrieving her soul. She then described a second episode of a "spirit sickness" and in doing so revealed a longer history of arthritic complaints. Six years earlier she had developed pains in her arms, shoulders, and neck for a period of three or four weeks following an episode in which she had inadvertently unearthed some snakes while clearing an area for a new home. "The spirits from those snakes wrapped around my arms and shoulder, and the medicine man had to take them off before I got better."

An Approach to Treatment

According to Salish tradition, dreams of the dead may portend illness or even death, or might indicate that the spirit has laid claim on the dreamer. The following suggestion was made to the patient: "Your story gives me the idea that you have been thinking of someone's death." She immediately replied, "I told my mother that if these symptoms don't clear by spring, I'd go with my father's spirit." The Salish ancestral religion demands respect and recognition of the dead by gifts and prayers (Amoss, 1978; Collins, 1980; Jilck, 1974). In circumstances in which someone believes that they are being made ill by a spirit, there is a perceived threat of soul loss, or even death.

> In the 1950's, the Lummi . . . (Salish) . . . would still attribute chronic illness during Winter time to possession by a spirit demanding the patient to sing it song as a new dancer; all owners of spirit songs were assumed to become possessed in Winter and to suffer an illness treatable only by singing and dancing. (Jilek, 1974, p. 34)

Although the patient had already been a dancer, she was convinced of the need to "bring out" her father's song. Additionally, according to the Salish tradition, a spirit might bother one of the living because the spirit lacks something. A frequent interpretation is that the living have something that belongs to the dead, or that some goods are needed by the dead. This can be objectified and returned to the dead by way of a ceremonial burning. The patient denied that she might have something that belonged to her father. However, after initiation of discussions about her beliefs and concerns, she improved remarkably, became more mobile and active, and began to care for herself.

In addition, the patient and her mother had been discussing the need to have a memorial service for the father. The service was to be held near the second anniversary of his death, the period when the deceased father's spirit would cease wandering and become less of a threat to the living. The patient feared dying in the period before the anniversary of this death. Her interviews involved discussion of the memorial, family members' opinion about it, disagreements between herself and her siblings, and the relationships between the surviving family members. Eventually, she was given direct encouragement to complete the ceremonial. She then announced her plans to undertake the singing of her father's song, and to complete his memorial service. Prior to her discharge she asked if I would see her mother who, she said, had the same trouble. Her mother was hallucinating her father "all the time," and refused to believe that he was really gone.

During the months following discharge from the hospital, the patient's rheumatoid arthritis worsened, and the evolution of the arthritic changes revealed typical physical findings with the additional supportive laboratory evidence. Six weeks later, at a follow-up appointment, she had marked progression, with swelling of the synovium over the metacarpophalangeal joints becoming quite noticeable, increased weakness of her grip, etc. In contrast, her mental status had improved remarkably. She had made a commitment to return to work. She was taking care of herself and

her mother. Her appearance and activities suggested a remarkable reversal in her anxiety and morbid ideation.

Discussion

A number of issues seemed clear: (a) Choosing between
competing, traditional explanations of her illness, the patient
had interpreted the onset of her symptoms as a sign that she
had been singled out by her father's spirit and that she, or
someone else was threatened with imminent death. (b) The
patient's problems with unresolved grief were shared with
her mother, and both women came to the conclusion that
someone was going to die. The daughter initially had feared
her own death, and later both women came to the conclusion
that it was an ill grandchild who was threatened. (c) Both
were filled with anxiety, and had severe bereavement problems. (d) The daughter's grief reaction was likely exacerbated by the emergence of her rheumatoid arthritis.

The mother's denial of her husband's death made her reluctant to participate in the memorial service. The service
would be an irrevocable sign and recognition that many
decades of marriage had come to an end, and that her husband was indeed gone. The therapeutic suggestions were
specifically designed to meet the circumstances. The patient
was encouraged to sing her father's spirit song, to give
something up, and to help with the ceremonial process. The
mother was encouraged to participate in the memorial service. The service was successfully held two months later,
and the patient participated with vigor in spite of severe
problems with active rheumatoid arthritis.

CASE 3—A HMONG REFUGEE WITH GHOST ILLNESS

Date of Onset	Problem List
September 1976	1) Headaches, sleep disorder
Longstanding	2) Amebiasis, hookworm
10/31/77	3) Miscarriage
1975	4) Refugee, monolingual

The patient is a 19-year old, monolingual Hmong woman.
She was born in the north central highlands of Laos,
schooled for a short period of time in a Catholic school, and
fled Laos after her parents were killed. She immigrated to the
United States from a Thai refugee camp when she was 17
years old and married a young Hmong refugee shortly after
arriving in the United States. The two had met in Thailand.

The month following her immigration to the United
States, she developed severe headaches which occurred one
to three times per week, and occasionally lasted 24 to 48
hours. The headaches were predominantly left-sided, and
were associated with nausea and occasional vomiting. She
had often awakened with a headache, but she had not experienced an aura, or visual symptoms. Neither aspirin nor
prescribed medication had provided any relief. Her

headaches seemed to respond only to sleep. She denied a
past medical history of trauma, seizures, or other neurologic
symptoms. She did recall a pattern of infrequent headaches
dating from her early teens, headaches that occurred during
times of stress.

Her recent efforts to sleep off the headaches had often
caused her to stay home and miss her English classes. She
had been seen acutely at least eight times in emergency
rooms and clinics over a 15-month period. The physicians
involved had recorded a variety of impressions of her problem: migraine, cluster headaches, and on "tension, acclima-
tization, and adjustment problems." Extensive neurologic
evaluations had been unrevealing, and empirical therapy for
tension headaches, migraine, and (later) cluster headaches
had been unsuccessful.

In October, 1977, the patient had a miscarriage. Her
headache pattern had persisted throughout her two months
of pregnancy, and thereafter. She was reevaluated for
headaches in January of 1978 and part of the inquiry focused on her sleep patterns and dreams. She reported severely disturbed sleep and recurrent nightmares in which
she saw her deceased parents: "She sees her mother and father . . . sometimes her father's face comes towards her . . .
it comes right at her." She would awaken screaming and her
husband reported that she often made references to death at
these times: "Sometimes, she wakes up saying she's going
to die." Referring to the dream and the father's image, the
husband said, "She thinks he's going to take her with him.
. . ." She had been experiencing a similar dream pattern since
the onset of the symptomatology. Severe headache episodes
were always preceded by the dreams.

An Approach to Treatment

The nature of the dream was discussed in some detail. The
patient's reaction to the dream—specifically, that her father
was "coming after her . . . going to take her with him"—represents a universal interpretive option regarding such
dreams. It is important to recognize that the patient's problems with her dreaming were not idiosyncratic. A night-long
Hmong funery prayer known as Sersai makes a direct reference to both illnesses caused by ghosts and the relationship
between death and dreams. A translation of part of the
prayer as used for a family that had lost their father is as
follows:

"If you do not want to remain healthy and prosperous it
does not matter, but if you want to you must give charity to
your father by giving him three joss sticks, and three
amounts of paper money. . . . For years and years there has
been no sickness. This year the sickness came this way and
then come to this house. . . . This year sickness came to the
roof and came to the bedroom. The first time it came to the
roof and later it came to our bodies. He did not want to die
but Si Yong the ghost used Chijier to touch his heart. If he
touches anybody with Chijier, that person must die. . . ."

(*CHIJIER* is a kind of illness which the Hmong believe belongs to *SI YONG,* the ghost.)

> The old man had a nightmare last night. He dreamed that he trod on the ghost flower. He dreamed that he rode the ghost horse. He dreamed that he stepped in the grave . . . The old man did not want to die but the ghost up in the sky world blew the pipe. They blew it in the sky world and blew it along the way, and then blew it at the house of the old and then the soul of the old man went with the ghost and he died . . .
> (Chindarsi, 1978, p. 150).

Once again we find the theme of the dead calling for, or returning for the living. It had significant meaning for this patient. Interviews with the patient and her husband evolved as follows:

1. To begin with, the couple was encouraged to discuss the religious practices and beliefs of their parents and grandparents. This was a natural extension of an earlier discussion of details regarding the patient's origins, early experience, family members, etc. The parents on both sides had practiced ancestral worship and the discussion focused on what they "would have thought" about the dreams. The couple's response was clear: the dream meant that the wife was threatened. The couple insisted that they were not aware of a solution.

2. To the patient, the dreams represented a direct threat that within the context of Hmong beliefs, the spirit(s) needed to be neutralized (via gifts, prayers, by showing respect, and the like). For these reasons, a separate discussion was then undertaken; it focused on generalities regarding the ancestral aspects of celebrations and ceremonial meals, or gifts. The couple was given an example of a family who had prepared meals and gifts, and offered prayers to their ancestors during a time of trouble. It was not pointed out that these practices were often viewed as helpful to the participants, and that in the face of need, similar offerings and prayers could be undertaken any time of the year.

3. The couple protested, "We've heard about those things, but we don't believe them." "We're Catholic, we both went to Catholic school, and we don't know about those things . . ." (Their combined exposure to Catholicism had been less than 20 months.) In a concrete sense, being Catholic implied immunity to the patient's interpretations of the dreams and was viewed as an effort to avoid unpleasant, threatening explanations of the dreams. Additionally, their statements about their Catholic backgrounds were viewed as attempts to avoid being labeled as different. The discussion then focused on the difference between knowing about things and believing them. They both knew about the beliefs and the point was made that the wife's interpretations of the dreams were very similar to those she attributed to her parents and her grandmother.

4. The patient and her husband were encouraged to discuss the matter further with the family members and with some older Hmong people that they respected and trusted.

Diagnosis and Treatment in the Community

Initially, the couple approached an older brother of the patient. His initial reaction was similar to their own: he stated that "as a Catholic," he did not know enough to make a decision. All three decided to discuss the matter with an uncle, and thus began to involve the entire family. Within 48 hours, a number of relatives and other Hmong refugees gathered, a meal was prepared along with gifts and prayers for the deceased relatives. A diagnosis had emerged: the family had decided that the patient's problems were due to failure to seek parental permission for her marriage. Since the husband's parents were also deceased and he had no relatives in the United States, the wife's family and other members of the Hmong community assumed primary responsibility for preparing the meal.

The patient and her husband were seen in a follow-up visit. They were delighted with the outcome; she had become cheerful, animated, and involved. She remained headache-free for a six-month period after the meal. After six months had passed, she developed a problem with anxiety associated with a second pregnancy. However, neither the dreams nor the headaches recurred. The patient did report a dream two week after the meal. She dreamed that she was visited by the deceased mother of her husband. The older woman made a sign of respect to the patient and voiced approval of both the patient and her marriage.

Discussion

A number of questions have been raised about this case. Does this illness have a unified etiology? Was there more to it than the dreams and associated meanings? Why insist on the term ghost illness? The patient had experienced multiple traumatic events and complicated changes, which included the experience of war, the killing of her parents, flight from Laos, refugee camps, immigration, marriage in the absence of family support, and an early miscarriage. The patient was isolated from the community at large by language, lack of knowledge of the society, and the like. Certainly these were all valid features of her problem, and they existed in the face of what appeared to be prior underlying problems with tension and occasional headaches whenever she was under pressure (evidenced by the problems she experienced in younger years). According to Western psychology, the sum of her difficulties could be viewed as creating high levels of anxiety and depression. A Western solution would focus on helping her explore and work out those difficulties. However, Hmong tradition lacks a similar formulation of this sort of problem; there is no Hmong term for anxiety or depression.

Therapeutically, the decision was made to separate out the concrete fears associated with the dream interpretation—literally, the perceived threat of death. The ceremonial therapy was aimed at the dreams. The more complex issues of the young woman's character and personality structure, and of her status as a monolingual parentless refugee and a newlywed with a recent miscarriage would remain. The patient's dream-related fears and associated ideation about dying may return, but they are likely to do so only in response to a new set of circumstances. Should ghost dreams recur, the meaning of her reaction to them will be partially dependent upon her circumstance at the time. In this case, the term "ghost illness" describes the traditional view of the cause and potential effect of the dreams. Discussion of Southeast Asian traditions about the dead provided a specific means of communicating about the illness and associated fears. It also established a basis for a partial solution within the context of the beliefs involved.

The meal provided by relatives and the Hmong community neutralized the patient's dreams and dread. By participating, she dealt with her own and her husband's identity in a new, threatening, and difficult place. The therapeutic activity was undertaken with the full knowledge and support of a group and can be viewed as displacing a series of fears and concerns onto a process that had powerful meanings to the patient. In addition, the therapeutic process directly diminished her sense of isolation. The process mobilized the concern and acceptance of a small Hmong community. As in many other therapeutic actions, the patient was forced to make a decision regarding her beliefs—but that is not unusual.

The therapeutic role of the physician was undertaken without a detailed knowledge of Hmong beliefs; that is, without detailed knowledge of terminology, practices, and the like. As is evident from the history, the patient and extended family managed to fill in many of the gaps regarding a solution to the problem.

GHOST ILLNESS AND HUMAN EXPERIENCE AND BELIEFS

In order to place the previous three cases and the mythology of the ghost illness tradition in a broader perspective of human experience, this paper will next discuss the prevalence of the ghost illness phenomena. It will be linked to: (a) the epidemiology of human experience with death in family members, (b) the impulse to die during bereavement, and (c) beliefs regarding hallucinations, dreams, and recurrent thoughts of the dead.

Ghost illness is well known in many North American Indian groups. For instance, the Mohave have had a rich terminology for the problem that includes real ghost illness, ghost contamination, ghost alien diseases, and fore-ordained ghost disease (Devereau, 1969). By Mohave definition, illness may erupt from dreaming of dead family members, by direct contamination with the dead, by violation of funeral practice, by witchcraft killings, by contact with twins, and so on. The Mohave have attached ghost-related causes to a wide variety of somatic illnesses. (One must recall that the mind/body separation that exists in Western biomedical paradigms does not exist for many members of groups like the Mohave. The same applies to a large number of human groups, perhaps the majority.)

Similar beliefs are widespread among American Indian groups, although there may be wide variation in specific rules and mythology. For example, there is anthropologic literature describing concern over interference by the dead in diverse groups such as the Sioux (Powers, 1986), Comanchee (Jones, 1972), Tewa (Ortiz, 1969), Eskimo (Spencer, 1969), and Salish-speaking people (Amoss, 1978; Jilek, 1974). An active ancestral religion exists for the Salish tribes in the Northwest, forms the basis for current practices in their "Smoke House" tradition, and has been incorporated in syncretic fashion into their newer Indian Shaker religion. The dead are appeased by gifts and prayers, help may be sought from the dead, and lost or stolen souls can be located. These practices have the capacity to help the living receive strength, power, and aid from the dead. They are also designed to protect believers from potential malevolence on the part of the dead.

Experience with the dead is broadly represented in the anthropologic literature. The dead may play a role in the religion, healing practices, and beliefs of Chinese (Ahern, 1973), Pacific Indian groups (Johnson, 1981; Sharp, 1982; Lazar, 1985), the Thai (Tambiah, 1980), African peoples (Bohannan, 1960) and in India (Kakar, 1982). One can find ceremonial means of dealing with alien spirits, ancestors, and animistic representatives of human spirits. The purposes of these ceremonial processes range from obtaining direct assistance, blessing, or protection from the dead, to obtaining advice on how to deal with or drive off a malignant spirit. Interestingly, ghosts have either served the needs of the living or harmed them in a uniquely human fashion. Illness, or even conflict between individuals, may be attributed to malevolent spirits (Shore, 1978). The view "that death is an end of consciousness and of the person's involvement with the world of the living" has been described as a Western "ethnocentric assumption," which is contrasted with the view of "some Melanesian people . . . (who) . . . assume that a ghost has consciousness, that it is aware of the effects of its death on its survivors and on mundane events, and that it is capable of contacting those who are still living" (Counts, 1984, p. 101–102).

HUMAN EXPERIENCE WITH DEATH IN FAMILY MEMBERS

The epidemiologic basis for reactions to a death and dying are brought into sharp focus by a number of striking studies of mortality among the immediate survivors of a death in the family. In 1969, Rees (1967) reported on the mortality of bereavement among 903 close relatives (widows and family members) in Wales. Over 12% of widowed individuals died within one year of losing a spouse. Widowers died at the rate of 19% and widows at the rate of 8.5%. Overall, these rates represented a seven-fold increase in death when the bereaved group were compared with a matched control group from the same community. There was additional evidence that the remainder of the family was also at increased risk (primarily siblings and children).

In another study of 4,486 widowers in England (Young & Wallis, 1963), mortality was found to exceed that of a control group by 40% in the first six months of bereavement. Helzing and Szklo (1982), suggested that only male widows were at increased risk, and found that broad statistical analysis of a widowed group of 4,302 persons failed to support increased risk during the period of bereavement. In contrast to this finding, Karrio, Koskenvuo, and Rita (1987), did a prospective study of 95,647 widowed persons in Finland, and found striking increases in risk during the first year of widowhood. Additionally, high mortality rates among the widowed were clearly demonstrated in statistics based on all deaths in the United States between 1949 and 1951. Kraus and Lilienfeld (1959), demonstrated that death rates for widowed individuals ranged from 4 times greater to more than 10 times the rates in married individuals of the same age. Remarkably, this study showed that widowed individuals are at increased risk from a wide variety of diseases. These included tuberculosis, vascular lesions of the central nervous system, heart disease, arteriosclerotic disease, hypertension with heart disease, as well as accidents and suicide.

An excess mortality rate extends beyond the first year of loss, and the figures begin to provide a real basis for the widespread human dread of the death of another human. Mythology, religion, and popular ideas regarding death focus on the notion that one death may follow another. These myths and beliefs codify actual human experience. Assuming that similar patterns have held over the centuries, actual survivor experience of increased risk has provided a direct basis for the dread of death of another. The survivors sense the threat, which at times is coupled with their own impulse to die.

THE IMPULSE TO DIE DURING BEREAVEMENT

The impulse to die at the time of another's death is symbolically and concretely represented by the Hindu practice of Suttee, in which a widow would throw herself on the funeral pyre of her husband. Whether one views Suttee as an individual impulse or a sociocultural expectation secondary to the pressure of others, the outcome is the same. If the act of Suttee is solely secondary to group pressures, customs, and enforceable expectations, then the widow becomes a scapegoat for the group.

The suicide impulse of bereavement provides an additional tie between the dead and survivors of the experience. Referring again to the study by Kraus and Lilienfeld (1959), they proposed three hypotheses to explain the high frequency of death among the surviving widowed individuals. The first two hypotheses deal with the notion that marriage mates may select individuals with comparable high-risk illness and inabilities, or may be mutually exposed to environmental or infectious factors which lead to early death. The third hypothesis deals with the issues of "grief, the new worries and responsibilities, alterations in the diet, work regime . . . frequently reduced economic condition," and the like.

Human emotions are strongly tied to experience within the family and community. In cross-cultural clinical settings, one may find patients who have had direct experience with preparations for burial, sewing clothing from the deceased, choosing burial goods, digging the grave, burial of the dead, and even the washing of ancestral bones for reburial (Ahern, 1973; Collins, 1980). In this regard, death in many societies and families provokes a level of direct personal involvement that may not be true for Westernized people. There is nothing to suggest that the practice of burying one's own dead is necessarily good or bad for the survivors. The point is that different practices and beliefs dictate different perceptions of death as a reality. In addition, some individuals and groups have a higher frequency of experience with death in immediate family members. Our experience with American Indian patients, for instance, shows a remarkable incidence of direct and frequently recent experience with death. The experiences necessarily mold the individuals' reactions and thoughts when threatened by illness or adverse life events.

HALLUCINATIONS AND DREAMS OF THE DEAD

Patients may report or experience dreams or hallucinations of the dead during a state of physiologic and/or psychologic disruption. The emergence of troubles from a variety of sources may provoke concern over death. This is especially true in patients with disrupted family process, anxiety states, or depression. The process may also arise with any circumstance that gives rise to aggressive and/or destructive impulses, even impulses towards self-destruction.

Dreams of the dead may be associated with a variety of reactions on the part of the dreamer, although the patient may not explain the event by the kind of formulas used by modern psychology. It is important to recall that the dreams are often viewed as real events, real in the sense that the ghost or the spirit is real. The commonly-shared belief that dreams portend trouble leads to a sense of dread on the part of the dreamer or the dreamer's family. Dreams of the dead are associated with a high frequency of sleep disruption and may provide direct evidence of anxiety and/or depressive patterns. For these reasons, it is essential to obtain sleep histories and dream patterns from patients whose cultures have historic involvement with ancestral beliefs. The clinician should recognize that such dreams of death or the dead may be equivalent to seeing the dead in a waking state. Four points must be made in this regard.

First, the patient may describe a waking experience as a dream and attribute it to a non-waking state. This is often done to avoid the sequelae of appearing to be unbalanced, insane, or even dangerous. (Anyone who reports seeing the dead in a waking state is likely to be avoided by others and may be regarded as unusual, dangerous, or even psychotic. This is a universal phenomena except in those groups that have formally sanctioned the activity by making it an expectation).

Second, the patients often project their own dread of hallucination (or dream) to the listener and may withhold or alter the description of the experience. This is often explained in terms of "not wanting to put a burden on someone else."

Third, many societies, especially those that have not developed or depended upon a written language, have paid extensive attention to dreaming, and to the important implication dreams hold for the living. Individuals from these societies must be dealt with in a fashion that takes their dreaming patterns into accounts, especially as their dreams may help to explain their own explanations of disrupted health or life patterns.

Fourth, patients from backgrounds that include extensive magical-religious beliefs and/or lack a written language, may sense that dreams are causative. That is, they may believe that speaking about dreams may literally cause trouble.

In 1971, Rees reported on the "hallucinations of widowhood." He interviewed 293 widowed individuals in a Welsh community and inquired about visual, tactile, or auditory hallucinations of the dead. He included those experiences he termed "illusions (sense of presence)" of the dead spouse. Of the 293 people interviewed, he reported that 137 (49.7%) had post-bereavement hallucinations. Many of these hallucinations lasted for years; at the time of interview, 106 people (36.1%) still had hallucinations. It is important to recognize that Rees did not include experiences reported to have occurred at night, or on retiring in the evening; for the purposes of his study, Rees regarded all these instances as dreams, not hallucination. In addition, he did not count instances in which individuals reported an experience and then rationalized about it, for example, saying they had seen the deceased in "their mind's eye."

In Rees' study, the incidence of post-bereavement hallucinations increased with the duration of marriage, tended to disappear with time, were relatively common occurrences, and generally remained a secret which the survivor had not previously revealed to a professional. The information remained a "folk" issue. Although 33% of the women, and 12% of the men had disclosed their experiences to others, none had reported them to a physician, and only one person out of 137 had spoken with a member of the clergy regarding the experience. Rees felt that most of his patients were helped by the experiences and that the hallucinations served a useful purpose.

Rees felt he lacked evidence that religious beliefs played a role in the frequency of these experiences. The majority of his subjects were Christians of either Anglican or Welsh Methodist denominations, and 49% denied a religious affiliation. Rees' findings are not unique to individuals of Celtic descent. In 1958, Marris reported interviews with 72 widows in Southeastern London and found that 50% had experienced hallucinations or illusions of the dead spouse. Additionally, in 1969, Yamamoto and colleagues reported interviews with 20 widows in Tokyo and found that 90% of them reported feeling the presence of the dead spouse.

Note that none of the cited reports involved investigation of situations in which the hallucinations or dreams appeared to be playing a role in the individual's state of health. They do, however, establish the existence of human experience with hallucinatory phenomena after bereavement. The first case in this paper illustrated a relationship between ghost dreams and suicidal ideation. Similar dreams, ruminations and hallucination of the dead have been reported to the author in suicidal American Indian patients, survivors of suicide in Alaska Native families, and by unsuccessful suicides. For all of these reasons, assessments of mental status in American Indian patients should take interactions with the dead (dreams, ruminations, and hallucinations) into careful account.

To the Western mind, waking hallucinations of the dead, seeing, hearing, talking to, being touched by, or sensing the presence of the dead, are considered projections of the living individual who reports the experience. It is important to recognize that this Western tradition is not shared on a universal basis. Patient views and reactions to experiences with the dead must be assessed with great care, since either the individual's explanation or explanations provided by his culture may be in discord with a view based on Western psychology. In clinical settings, these experiences most often involve deceased relatives or friends, and less frequently someone whose identity is not clear.

SUMMARY

There is no cross-cultural normal or abnormal set to which one can refer when dreams and hallucinations of the dead occur. One must judge hallucinations and dreams of the dead in the context of an individual's life history and circumstances. Patients may present these experiences as being protective, comforting, or threatening. Clinical findings parallel Spiro's (1953) description of the multiple human attributes of ghosts. Presentations which indicate pathology or difficulties for the patient are highly varied.

It is not necessary for a dream or hallucination to fill the patient with dread. For example, a professed sense of comfort and ease regarding auditory hallucinatory experiences with a deceased son were presented by an Irish woman. She refused to change her residence because she feared she would lose contact with him. She stated that if she moved, her son would no longer be able to find and communicate with her. Her family felt that the experiences represented her excuse for refusing to deal with the need to change residences. An Eskimo patient reported that hunting dreams involving his deceased brother indicated that a good hunting season lay before him. He was simultaneously excited and anxious to report this knowledge. In my view, the dreams represented evidence of the patient's return to a positive outlook after a long illness and successful surgery. Prior to surgery he had experienced dreams of the dead which had filled him with dread (Putsch, in press). Terminally ill patients may report comforting dreams of the dead in preparation for their own demise.

The tradition of ghost illness reminds us that the interpretation of illness is dependent upon belief systems. Any illness can provoke concerns over loss and death, and may result in the patient having an interaction with the dead. When patients with special beliefs interface with Western medicine, failure to take their beliefs and concerns into account may lead to an inability to either understand or resolve a significant clinical problem. Accommodation to disparate beliefs often requires that solutions fit the context of the patient's beliefs system and simultaneously deal with both the Western and non-Western traditions.

REFERENCES

Ahern, E. (1973). *The cult of the dead in a Chinese village.* Stanford, CA: Stanford University Press.

Amoss, P. (1978). *Coast Salish Spirit Dancing: The survival of an ancestral religion.* Seattle, WA: University of Washington Press.

Bohannan, P. (Ed.) (1960). *African homicide and suicide.* Princeton, Princeton University Press.

Chindarsi, N. (1978). *The religion of the Hmong Njua.* Bangkok, Thailand: Siam Society.

Collins, J. M. (1980). *Valley of the spirits: The Upper Skagit Indians of western Washington.* Seattle, WA: University of Washington Press.

Counts, D. R., & Counts, D. A. (1984). Aspects of dying in northwest New Britain. *Omega, 14,* 101–111.

Devereux, G. (1969). *Mohave ethnopsychiatry: The psychic disturbances of an Indian tribe.* Washington, DC: Smithsonian Institution Press.

Dusenberry, V. (1962). *The Montana Cree: A study in religious persistence.* Uppsalu, Sweden: Almqvist and Wiksell.

Haile, B. (1938). *Origin legend of the Navajo enemy way.* New Haven, CT: Yale University Publications in Anthropology, Number 17, Yale University Press.

Helsing, K. J., & Szklo, M. (1981). Mortality after bereavement. *American Journal of Epidemiology, 114,* 41–52.

Jilek, W. (1974). *Salish mental health and culture change.* Toronto, Ontario: Reinhardt and Winston of Canada. Reprinted as *Indian healing: Shamanic ceremonialism in the Pacific Northwest today.* Surrey, BC: Hancock House, 1982.

Johnson, P. L. (1981). When dying is better than living: Female suicide among the Gainj of Papua New Guinea. *Ethnology, 20,* 325–334.

Jones, D. E. (1972). *Sanapia, Comanche medicine woman.* New York, NY: Holt, Rinehart & Winston.

Kakar, S. (1982). *Shamans, mystics and doctors. A psychological inquiry into Indian and its healing traditions.* Boston, MA: Beacon Press.

Kaplan, B., & Johnson, D. (1974). The social meaning of Navajo psychopathology and psychotherapy. In A. Kiev (Ed.), *Magic, faith, and healing* (pp. 203–209). New York, NY: Free Press.

Karrio, J., Koskenvuo, M., & Rita, H. (1987). Mortality after bereavement: A prospective study of 95,647 widowed persons. *American Journal of Public Health, 77,* 283–287.

Kraus, A. S., & Lilienfeld, A. M. (1959). Some epidemiologic aspects of the high mortality rate in the young widowed group. *Journal of Chronic Diseases, 10,* 207–217.

Lazar, I. (1985). Ma'i Aitu: Culture bound illnesses in a Samoan migrant community. *Oceania, 55,* 151–181.

Levy, J. E. (1981). Navajos. In A. Harwood (Ed.), *Ethnicity & medical care* (pp. 337–396). Cambridge, MA: Harvard University Press.

Lewis, P., & Lewis, L. (1984). *Peoples of the Golden Triangle.* New York, NY: Thames and Hudson.

Marris, P. (1958). Widows and their families. *Institute of Community Studies,* Vol. 3. London, England: Routledge and Kegan Paul.

Opler, M. E. (1969). *Apache odyssey: A journey between two worlds.* New York, NY: Holt, Rinehart, and Winston.

Ortiz, A. (1969). *The Tewa world.* Chicago, IL & London, England: The University of Chicago Press.

Powers, M. N. (1986). *Oglala women.* Chicago, IL & London, England: The University of Chicago Press.

Putsch, R. W. (In press). Language in cross-cultural care. In Walker, J. K., Hurst, J. W., and Hall, W. D. (Eds.), *Clinical methods,* (3rd ed.). Boston, MA & London, England: Butterworths.

Rees, W. D. (1967). Mortality of bereavement. *British Medical Journal, 4,* 13–16.

Rees, W. D. (1971). The hallucinations of widowhood. *British Medical Journal, 4,* 37–41.

Sharp, P. T. (1982). Ghosts, witches, sickness and death: The traditional interpretation of injury and disease in a rural area of Papua New Guinea. *Papua New Guinea Medical Journal, 25,* 108–115.

Shore, B. (1978). Ghosts and government: A structural analysis of alternative institutions for conflict management in Samoa. *Man* (NS), 13, 175–199.

Spencer, R. F. (1969). *The North Alaskan Eskimo.* Washington, DC: Smithsonian Institution Press.

Spiro, M. E. (1953). Ghosts: An anthropological inquiry into learning and perception. *Journal of Abnormal and Social Psychology, 48,* 376–82.

Tambiah, S. J. (1980). *Buddhism and the spirit cults in Northeast Thailand.* Cambridge, MA: Cambridge University Press.

Yamamoto, J., Okonogi, K., Iwasaki, T., & Yoshimura, S. (1969). Mourning in Japan. *American Journal of Psychiatry, 125,* 1660–1665.

Young, M., Benjamin, B., & Wallis, C. (1963). The mortality of widowers. *Lancet, 2,* 454–456.

Culture-Bound Illnesses in a Samoan Migrant Community

Ineke M. Lazar

The essay by Putsch explores the role of cultural-bound syndromes in dealing with grief and bereavement. In this essay, Lazar shows how such syndromes can also be involved in the maintenance of social norms.

In the Samoan community in Los Angeles, women sometimes experience *ma I aitu,* a ghost sickness during which they become briefly possessed by an *aitu,* a spirit from among the dead of their family. Symptoms of such an attack include violent behavior and vomiting, following which the woman speaks in the voice of the *aitu,* who frequently is male.

Lazar argues that such spirit possession has two distinct functions in the Samoan community. First, it is considered punishment for the violation of social norms such as wearing "flashy clothing" or "standing while eating." Second, women in the Samoan migrant community face hard lives and, compared to men, are limited in their outlets for stress release. Having *ma I aitu* allows for a period of socially sanctioned release. The ceremonies surrounding the curing of the disease make the individual feel like a more important member of their family unit.

Lazar's essay shows that what the practitioners of technological medicine might call a mental disorder plays an important role in the maintenance of the Samoan way of life in this migrant community. Further, because this illness provides a socially sanctioned method of stress release, contracting the disease might be a partially conscious decision on the part of the afflicted. The eminent and controversial psychiatrist Thomas Szasz has made some similar arguments about the Western understanding of mental illness.[1]

As you read, consider these questions:

1. What is the difference between supernatural and natural causes of disease?
2. How do Samoans in Los Angeles perceive the cause of mental illnesses, and what steps do they take to cure them?
3. What are the perceived causes of ghost illness, and why are women more prone to this disease than men?

1. Thomas Szasz, *The Myth of Mental Illness: Foundations of a Theory of Personal Conduct* (New York: Paul B. Hoeber, 1961).

"Culture-bound Illnesses in a Samoan Migrant Community" by Ineke M. Lazar, *Oceania* 55:3 (1985). Reprinted with permission.

The urbanization experience of Samoans on the West Coast during the past two decades provides an unusual example of a non-Western village people who have retained their traditional values after migration. A steady stream of immigrants bringing traditional Samoan customs and values to mainland Samoan communities in effect helps balance the encroaching pervasive influences of mainstream American society. The result in Los Angeles is an active and viable community. Many migrants still live in a virtual Samoan world, which is readily identifiable yet little understood by the surrounding non-Samoan population.

The Los Angeles community is the single largest Samoan settlement in the continental United States. Informal estimates have placed the size of the Samoan population in Southern California at between 20,000 and 40,000 [Hayes and Levin 1984]. Because of migration and natural increase, the present size of this population is probably even higher.

There is no clearly demarcated geographical area in Los Angeles recognized as Samoan. However, Samoans interact primarily with each other instead of with *palagis* (whites) or other cultural groups. This measure of social isolation as well as continuous exchange within the Samoan population help to maintain and perpetuate a deep sense of commitment to *Fa'a Samoa* (the Samoan way of life).

This paper discusses the perpetuation of traditional concepts of health and disease among Samoan migrants in the Los Angeles harbor area and the manner in which these concepts contribute to the maintenance of certain core values and ways of behavior. The central intent is to show the effects of *aitu* (ghost-spirits) beliefs, which serve as covert (not explicitly recognized) control mechanisms for appropriate role behavior. Accordingly, a person who deviates from his or her expected role performance can anticipate an unpleasant visitation from an aitu, the spirit of a departed kin, who will punish the living in the form of a variety of illnesses.

Data are predominantly based on repeated interviews with three *taulasea* (Samoan therapists) and eight key Samoan women informants. Samoans do not readily discuss aitu beliefs with outsiders. There is little motivation to talk about events which may cause discomfort or create an apparent threat to one's well-being. As one informant stated: "If you talk about an aitu today, you are going to see one tonight . . . they might punish me."

The use of a questionnaire and tape recorder was not possible. An informal, friendly setting became a more accepted format for gaining information. Because of the sensitivity in this area of inquiry, adequate quantification of aitu-related illnesses concerning the entire community was not possible.

DISEASE CLASSIFICATION AND TREATMENT

Concepts of cause are part of the ideational system reflecting the cognitive orientations of members of the community. In order to understand indigenous causality concepts, I make a distinction between supernatural and natural etiological categories of disease. I follow Seijas' "supernatural" and "non-supernatural" categories (1973: 545). In this sense, supernatural refers to those explanations that place the origin of disease in suprasensible forces (i.e., aitu) that cannot be directly observed. Natural explanations are based entirely on observable cause-and-effect relationships (i.e., injury as a result of a car accident). Native classification of a particular illness can, however, include both natural and supernatural concepts, when the former is intensified by the activities of aitu. This is often the case with prolonged or terminal illnesses, where neither modern medicine nor indigenous practitioners are able to cure the patient. The lack of recovery is then attributed to aitu intervention.

Natural Explanations

Natural etiologies are restricted to diseases that do not stem from the machinations of aitu. Whether the patient seeks aid from an indigenous practitioner or a Western doctor, the emphasis is on the relief of symptoms. For treatment of a somatic condition, a Samoan will often go to a *foma'i,* an indigenous practitioner who treats natural illnesses using massage and herbs.

Diagnosis is of minor importance, for the etiology of the illness is clearly recognized. For example, there is an obvious causal relationship between falling down stairs and hurting one's back.

Samoans do not recognize mental illness as a personality disorder. Clement argues:

> The Samoan concepts of mental illness tend to focus upon states of feeling brought about by adverse circumstances and outside forces (aitu) rather than abnormalities in the personality. (1974: 91)
>
> Samoan concepts imply that mental problems (other than those caused by brain damage) are an understandable reaction to contemporary pressures impinging upon the person. (1974: 100)

Kennedy distinguishes between Western and non-Western conceptions of mental disorders on the basis of evaluation of "abnormal" behavior. He notes that behavior patterns labeled neuroses or "character disorders" in the West are in other societies regarded as within the normal range (1974: 1173).

There is, however, a Samoan term, *ma'i valea,* which translates as "mad," "insane," or "stupid" (Milner 1978:

312). Samoans in Los Angeles use the term for two distinct conditions: (1) organic conditions (brain damage at birth, and head injuries suffered in fights and accidents), which are deemed permanent and held to be incurable, and (2) deviant behaviors (use of narcotics, and transgression of social etiquette), which are believed to be temporary and curable by a change in behavior patterns.

The distinction between temporary ma'i valea and aitu illnesses is in the cause and effect of a set of symptoms. A person with ma'i valea knowingly violated social rules and his or her behavior is immediately recognized and classified by that label. Causality is specific to the condition, and responsibility for such behavior resides with the deviant individual. Ma'i valea can be eliminated by a change in behavior. The etiology of an aitu illness, on the other hand, is ascribed post facto.

Supernatural Explanations

Ma'i aitu, a Samoan term literally meaning "ghost sickness," is caused by the intervention of supernatural entities. Etic functional equivalents range from physiological to mental disorders. Such disorders can affect anyone in the community. Samoan etiology for aitu-related illnesses is in the form of post hoc rationalizations. They are the recognition that the patient or a member of his family has not behaved properly. Among Samoan migrants who tend to uphold traditional values in Los Angeles, supernatural causality predominates and embraces not only concepts of health and illness, but misfortunes in general. An aitu, consequently, may even cause economic problems, a breakdown in family relations, or a string of "bad luck."

A *taulasea* (indigenous therapist) specializes mainly in aitu-related illnesses and treats them using *va'i aitu* (spirit medicine), *pule* (supernatural power), and *folo* (massage).

Illnesses may or may not involve spirit possession. Two-way communication is possible in some cases where the causing spirit is believed to be present in the body of the patient. Field data indicate a variety of cases in which the spirit was manifested by possession. These include a special form of ma'i aitu that women are subject to, which will be described later, and *fa'alia* (visions, hallucinations). Fa'alia are spontaneous dissociational states which can occur among both men and women. In most cases, these states are precipitated by a stressful life event.

Possession is also associated with *ma'i tafafo* (shouting and talking to oneself), *ma'i ulu* (extreme headaches, which may lead to a loss of consciousness), and *mata paia* (eye conditions). In the later case, the sore eyes are caused by aitu who "poked" into the patient's eyes. In treatment, the aim of the taulasea is to "drive out" the spirit.

Other aitu illnesses are those in which the causing agent is not perceived to be present in the body of the afflicted individual. In such cases, supernatural causality is validated through social mechanisms such as gossip, accusations, or public confessions. As part of the treatment, taulasea use one-way communication with the aitu who is believed to be responsible for the ailment. This is accomplished in the form of "praying" and reciting magical sentences. When asked specifically, taulasea replied that they "prayed to Christ." Other informants argue that taulasea "worship devils." Treatment includes the whole person, both body and mind. My observations in the community suggest that the social etiology of an illness alleviates the patient's guilt for his/her physical incapacity and possible social misconduct. Physical therapy is aimed at relieving bodily discomfort.

The etiology of an aitu illness is ascribed post facto. The error in behavior and social relations will be revealed during diagnosis. Responsibility for the illness may be beyond the patients' control, for misconduct could have been committed by another member of the family. The point is clearly demonstrated in illnesses of children. Manava tata (infantile diarrhea) is often perceived as a supernatural warning or punishment for the mortal behavior of the parents (Epling and Siliga 1967:141).

Disease categories classified as ma'i aitu among Samoans are not necessarily recognized as bona fide conditions by Western doctors. Consequently, modern medicine is often not able to effect a cure for those conditions to which the label applies. A common complaint in the Los Angeles community is that "Samoan illnesses do not show up on X-rays. So, the doctor does not know what to do." However, a person suffering from ma'i aitu manifests symptoms that are clearly recognized by Samoan therapists as particular illnesses, requiring special treatment.

There is an interplay between natural and supernatural constructs indicating a measure of assimilation to Western medical concepts of disease. Modern nosology, "sugar diabetes," is accepted, but its etiology is substituted by indigenous conceptions of supernatural punishment.

The Social Dimensions of Aitu Illnesses

Illness may be the result of a family member's transgression of social norms, which is then reflected in aitu retribution. The episode of illness is frequently utilized as a means to achieve social cohesion and integration within the *aiga* (extended family), the basic Samoan social unit. Aigas range in size from 50 to 500 individuals, and members of an aiga tend to live in households in adjacent apartment dwellings. It is to the aiga that a member must look for socially sanctioned support for his or her individual behavior. A Samoan, therefore, owes his first loyalty to his aiga. It is unthinkable that he should turn away needy relatives if they approach him for help or solace. This system of mutual help and kinship interdependency is constantly reinforced by family gatherings. The basic Samoan values of reciprocity, hospitality, sharing, and mutual aid are especially evident during times of crisis, such as funerals and other communal events. At these times, Samoan identity is strongest.

At the first sign of illness members of the patient's family usually apply "home remedies" (*fofo* with *fanu'u*, massage with coconut oil, or herbal concoctions). If the illness is prolonged or becomes severe, the aiga will decide whether to consult a taulasea.

Proper behavior is thought to be a way of avoiding aitu punishment. Samoans know the kinds of behavior, commission or omission, that may lead to aitu retribution. Predominant emic causal categories include: neglect of a relative; disobedience or disrespect to parents, older relatives, and matai; improper behavior, such as "flashy clothing," "letting your hair down at funerals," "standing while eating," etc.; breaking a promise to a relative; and not contributing enough material goods to aiga events such as weddings and funerals.

The social etiology of the illness may be known beforehand or learned during the cure. A child's sickness is often immediately attributed to aitu punishment for the father's failure to abide by proper behavioral rules. If it is a case in which investigation is needed, affinal relationships with both the living and deceased are examined to determine the fault.

MA'I AITU

Symptoms of one specific form of ma'i aitu resemble those of hysterical psychosis. Field data indicate that this particular form of ma'i aitu is mainly confined to Samoan women and seems to be related to role stress in the male-dominated community.

The linkage between culture and certain mental disorders has been suggested in anthropological literature. The study of such disorders is not only significant in the determination of pathoplastic features of mental illness but can also shed light on stress points and susceptibility groups in a particular society. Following psychiatric theory, it is assumed that anxiety producing stress can be a predisposing factor for mental illness. The present study is concerned with role choices available to men and women as possible bases for differential responses to anxiety.

Role Expectations and Performance

In the two major areas of community social intercourse in Los Angeles, the family and the church, male dominance prevails. In individual households and aiga settings, older males exert control. Cultural expectations require women to be obedient, respectful, work hard about the house, and remain properly reticent in the presence of outsiders. One of the difficulties in obtaining data was that I could seldom interview a woman without the presence of her husband or other male family members. The major responsibility of a married woman is to serve her husband. Although a mother asserts a good deal of control over younger children, she is supposed to be naïve about worldly matters and occupy herself with housekeeping affairs. It is highly desirable for a woman to have many children, for a large family is considered a "blessing." Among Samoan migrant women, this is not always by choice. A woman would not consciously think of deviating from prescribed conduct. Conformity is the result of a long process of training.

This training begins in childhood. Girls are required to be more submissive, while boys are permitted expressions of aggressive behavior (i.e., fights).

When a girl marries, she is subject to the demands of both her own aiga and that of her husband. The husband is always served meals first and usually eats separately from his wife and children. Traditional Samoan women are economically and socially dependent on their husbands. They are burdened with domestic labor, child care, and cooking. A family of eight to ten children is not uncommon.

Samoan migrant women's roles vis-à-vis those of men are also subordinate at the community level. Owing to the diminution of the *matai* (family chief) system on the mainland, ministers have assumed a great deal of power, as the churches have become the center of community life. Within the church organizational hierarchy, all the leadership positions are occupied by males. Women's organizations, such as Women's Fellowship, under the leadership of male ministers, deacons, and lay preachers, are burdened with fund-raising activities (i.e., bingo games, sales of Samoan food delicacies). Women are, however, excluded from business meetings in the church.

Community organizations in Los Angeles, such as the Samoan Community Council, the Samoan Chiefs Association, and the Samoan Homeowners Association, are controlled by men. Women fill only clerical positions and are excluded from decision-making processes. The isolation of women from a significant part of social life sharply limits their access to authority and power within the community.

Expression of Emotions

In the Samoan migrant community differential sex role expectations correspond to culturally accepted modes of expressing emotions. Women are permitted to express emotions of unhappiness, sadness, sorrow, feeling low, and dislike directly and through withdrawal, being uncooperative and so forth, but not *ita* (hate, strong anger). Women are always expected to keep their composure: "She (the woman) has to keep it all inside. Anger can't be shown on the face. You always have to keep a smile, even if you are raging mad." By contrast, men are able and frequently expected to exhibit open hostility, aggressive and violent behavior *(ma'i ita),* which can, in severe cases, even lead to homicide.

Women also have fewer ways of reducing anxiety. They are barred from drinking in public (although some drink heavily at home when their husbands are away). Further, women lack experience in developing strong bonds with females outside their own aiga. By contrast, men take on a more public role and participate in a multitude of social activities away from the family.

Thus, because of differing role expectations, women experience a greater amount of stress than men, and are prone to ma'i aitu. However, when discussing probabilities of specific occurrences of ma'i aitu, one must take personality variables, organic predisposition, and other situational factors into consideration.

Course of Illness

The symptomatology of ma'i aitu follows a prescribed cultural pattern. Without obvious warning, a woman displays stereotyped shaking and convulsive movements. At the onset, she may also exhibit a violent behavior, including spitting, kicking, biting and screaming. In such cases, several people (up to four adult males) are needed to "hold the woman down." As the attack continues, the eyes dilate accompanied by frequent bouts of vomiting. Behavior is always consistent and predictable.

Ma'i aitu is validated by both the aiga and taulasea. The mode of therapy differs from practitioner to practitioner, for each has his/her own "secret" va'i aitu (spirit medicine). One taulasea uses the Amvilega plant, a type of weed, the root of which is ground up. Plants in use are not native to California and must be brought in from Samoa by visiting relatives.

After the medicine is administered, there is a dramatic alteration in bodily movements, speech, voice and facial expressions. The patient usually takes on the personality and speaking manner of the possessing aitu. These are predominantly male figures. Samoans believe that through possession the spirit communicates with the living in order to give explicit instructions concerning a family matter. The appearance of behavioral features suggests role reversal. In a deep male voice of authority, the aitu states "why he is in the woman." The taulasea usually attempts to identify the possessing spirit and ask "how to make up."

Because of the ingredients in va'i aitu and extensive physical activity, the patient will fall into a deep sleep lasting up to fourteen hours. When she wakes up, her eyes are "all bloodshot." The patient is amnesiac for the period of ma'i aitu. The aiga will relate the event to her in great detail. The final phase of recovery, *fa'alanu,* lasts three days. During the final phase, the aitu can still cause harm to both patient and therapist. Danger is removed through ritual bathing and cleansing. Although much care is taken to ensure proper recovery, ma'i aitu may be recurrent.

Once a woman has ma'i aitu, normal role expectations are suspended. She is constantly watched and cared for by her aiga and the taulasea. The patient becomes the center of attention and alofa (love). Regardless of the social etiology of the episode, at the individual level the woman is made to feel a valued member of her aiga.

Discussion

Among Samoan migrants in Los Angeles, ma'i aitu appears to be a culture-bound disorder, which, in anthropological literature, most writers explain by a single theme. However, ma'i aitu cannot be adequately explained with a single framework. Themes such as role stress, the lack of available role choices, psychological and social deprivation in the female role, the psycho-therapeutic aspects of dissociational states, and the fear of illness as a social control mechanism are all present in varying degrees. Certain patterns concerning "self-perceived" role stress, the "conscious" choice to play the sick role, and "economic deprivation" are absent.

According to Devereux, there are emotionally disturbed persons in whom the unconscious segment of their ethnic personality has not become so disorganized as to incite them to wholesale rebellion against all social norms. While they are genuinely ill, such persons tend to borrow from their culture the means of implementing their subjective derangement in a conventional way (1956: 36).

Hirsh and Hollender make a distinction between "culturally sanctioned hysteria" and "true psychosis." The first is considered "legitimate or normal" within the cultural context because it is "recurrent, learned, predictable in form, and acceptable" (1969: 81). Among Samoan migrant women the distinction may not be applicable. While ma'i aitu fits the description of a "culture-bound" disorder, its symptomatology is that of a "true psychosis."

SUMMARY AND CONCLUSION

The traditional Samoan as a social being receives and maintains his/her identity through continuous participation in the family. Dominant Samoan values demand that the individual conform to group ideals. Aitu illnesses are highly instrumental in maintaining group cohesion and alleviating culturally produced stresses and strains. Women experience a greater amount of role stress than men and have fewer avenues open for them for the alleviation of anxiety and stress. In the Los Angeles Samoan community, ma'i aitu among women is one culturally patterned way of coping. While they are possessed, women release tension through role reversal (taking on a male authority figure), which is a culturally permissible temporary behavior pattern. Organic predispositions to ma'i aitu would be difficult to determine.

Samoan etiology and nosology of mental illness do not include personality disorders. The concept closest to mental illness is ma'i valea, which, however, encompasses only organic psychosis and social deviance. Visions, hallucinations, talking to oneself, temporary states of withdrawal, and possession are not culturally defined as abnormalities. Even though they are perceived as normal within the community, these behavior patterns do reflect symptoms of mental illness. I conclude that Samoan mental disorders are variants of basic psychopathological states with a culturally acceptable label. Hence, the efficacy of community mental health services for the Samoan community largely depends on an in-depth understanding of the patients' cultural background on the part of the health care provider.

REFERENCES

Clement, Dorothy Cay
   1974   *Samoan Concepts of Mental Illness and Treatment.* Ph.D. dissertation, Anthropology Dept., University of California, Irvine.
Devereux, George
   1956   Normal and abnormal: The key problem of psychiatric anthropology. *In* J. B. Casagrande and T. Gladwin (eds.), *Some Uses of Anthropology: Theoretical and Applied.* Washington, D.C.: Anthropological Society of Washington.
Epling, P. J., and Nofo Siliga
   1967   Notes on infantile diarrhoea in American Samoa. *Journal of Tropical Pediatrics* 3: 139–149.
Hayes, Geoffrey R., and Michael J. Levin
   1984   How many Samoans? An evaluation of the 1980 census count of Samoans in the United States. *Asian and Pacific Census Forum* 10(4): 1–4, 10–14, 16.
Hirsh, Steve J., and M. H. Hollender
   1969   Hysterical psychosis: Clarification of the concept. *American Journal of Psychiatry* 125: 81–87.
Kennedy, John G.
   1974   Cultural psychiatry. *In* J. J. Honigmann (ed.), *Handbook of Social and Cultural Anthropology.* Chicago: Rand McNally.
Milner, G. B.
   1978   *Samoan Dictionary: Samoan-English, English-Samoan.* Manila: Samoan Free Press.
Seijas, H.
   1973   An approach to the study of the medical aspects of culture. *Current Anthropology* 14: 544–545.

Explanations of Mental Health Symptoms
by the Bedouin-Arabs of the Negev

Alean Al-Krenawi

The ways in which we understand diseases may be intimately linked to the social forms in which we live. In this essay Alean Al-Krenawi shows that although the Bedouin-Arabs living in the Negev desert in Israel have access to modern technological medicine and do make frequent use of it, they overwhelmingly understand their mental diseases in supernatural terms. Al-Krenawi, himself the first Bedouin-Arab psychiatric social worker in Israel, tries to give readers an inside view of mental illness from the Bedouin point of view.

Though both Bedouin men and women perceive mental illness as being caused by supernatural means, the particulars of their understandings vary widely. Men are likely to see their afflictions as punishment for sins they have committed. Women almost universally relate their problems to sorcery, usually performed by other members of their household. According to Al-Krenawi, this is the result of the differences in social position between men and women. Bedouin-Arab society is highly patriarchal. Men have relatively great freedom and understand themselves as the primary actors of society. Hence, they understand their diseases as being caused by their actions. Women, on the other hand, are severely constrained by their social roles. Many are junior wives in polygynous households and have little freedom of action. They tend to understand themselves as being acted upon. Consequently, they understand their mental illnesses as caused by the actions of jealous or evil outsiders. The disease understandings of both men and women thus reflect their place in Bedouin-Arab society and the relative amount of freedom and power that comes with it.

Al-Krenawi's essay reminds us of the importance of context in understanding and treating disease. Most of the doctors treating Bedouin patients come from a different culture. Many are Eastern European immigrants with no knowledge of Bedouin culture and little understanding of their patients' lives or ways of thinking. Thus, the effectiveness of the therapies they prescribe are limited.

As you read, consider these questions:
1. What are some of the problems that could emerge when Western psychologists without knowledge of Bedouin-Arab culture attempt to counsel Bedouin-Arabs?

2. What are the four basic types of Arab Negev Bedouin traditional healers, and what are the functions of each?
3. Male and female Bedouin-Arabs have different perceptions about the cause of mental disorders. Why is this?

INTRODUCTION

It has often been reported that cultural differences affect the ability of mental health practitioners to diagnose and treat patients' problems (Al-Krenawi et al., 1996; Al-Krenawi et al., 1994; Bravo & Grob, 1989; Budman et al., 1992; Chiu, 1994; Schwartz, 1985; Wessels, 1985). Several scholars have observed frequent miscommunication when practitioners are unfamiliar with their patient's culture (Al-Krenawi et al., 1994; Creyghton, 1977; Eisenbruch, 1991; Kortmann, 1987). Moreover, recent research has questioned whether Western psychiatric classification can be applied to all cultures, since it is so strongly grounded on the symptoms of patients from Western cultural backgrounds (Al-Issa, 1970, 1977, 1990; Budman et al., 1992; Cervantes et al., 1989; El Sayed et al., 1986; Meleis & La Faver, 1984; Prince & Tcheng-Laroche, 1987).

Since symptoms may be coded and communicated in the language of the culture, it is the task of practitioners to decode the symbolic expressions and explanations given by their patients (Bilu & Witztum, 1995; Gaines, 1992). The existence of divergent explanatory models of human suffering stemming from different symbolic realities has been presented as a major source of practitioner-patient incompatibility in multi-cultural settings (Beger & Luckman, 1967; Kleinman & Good, 1985).

An explanatory model is a symbolic representation of distress applied to a particular case of human suffering or illness. It is a culturally based, cognitive attempt to cope with questions regarding the etiology, onset, manifestations, treatment and prognosis of the particular illness or suffering (Good & Good, 1986; Marsella, 1993). All human societies frame the bodily and behavioral manifestations of sickness and distress within the contours of some symbolic map (Bilu & Witztum, 1993; Obeysekere, 1970). This shift from immediate experience to symbolic representation is universal. The symbolic representation of distress is grounded in a wider cosmological context: in the symbolic reality (Budman et al., 1992; Kleinman, 1980).

A. Al-Krenawi "Explanations of Mental Health Symptoms by the Bedouin-Arabs of the Negev" *International Journal of Social Psychiatry* 45:1 (1999), 56–64. Copyright © 1999 International Journal of Social Psychiatry. Reprinted by permission of Sage Publications Ltd.

In modern, secular societies the epistemological shift from cosmology to psychology as the symbolic reality in which the representation of suffering is situated has been characterized by the mushrooming of increasingly intricate symbolic maps of the mind. Western representatives of distress tend to be inner oriented, minutely and meticulously mapping hitherto unacknowledged or unconscious intrapsychic states with landmarks designated as "motivations," "affects," "conflicts," "complexes," and so forth. These modern, scientifically informed representations—theories, conceptual models, schema, and the like—provide idioms for articulating a wide variety of distressful experiences in Western oriented societies (Bilu & Witztum, 1995; Good, 1994).

In many non-Western societies, the symbolic representations from which idioms of distress are derived tend to be grounded in external realities, which are often ultrahuman and metaphysical (Al-Krenawi & Graham, 1997; Ben-Ezer, 1992; El-Islam, 1975, 1980; Kiev, 1972; Leff, 1981; Pliskin, 1987). Designated as myth, magic, mysticism, and religion, they identify and map entities and forces with special ontological status—for example, divine energy, moral sins, demons, and sorcery—as agents of affliction and empowerment (Bilu & Witztum, 1995; Parson & Wekely, 1991).

This study examines how a sample of Bedouin-Arab psychiatric patients explain their mental health symptoms.

THE BEDOUIN-ARAB OF THE NEGEV

Although originally applied only to those who herded camel, the term "Bedouin" has come to be applied as the general name for all Arabic-speaking, nomadic tribes in the Middle East (Kay, 1978). The Bedouin-Arab have lived in the Negev region for two millennia (*Hebrew Encyclopaedia,* 1954). As a single, unique national, linguistic, political, and geographic entity, the Negev Bedouin-Arab are distinct from other non-Bedouin-Arab communities in Israel, and distinct from, although related to, Bedouin-Arab communities in other countries in the Middle East (Abu-Khusa, 1994).

Traditionally the Bedouin-Arab were a nomadic people, but today they are undergoing a rapid and dramatic process of sedenterization. Of the Negev's 120,000, 40% now live in villages, while 60% live in unrecognized villages (Al-Krenawi & Graham, 1997). This process notwithstanding, Bedouin-Arab culture remains "high context" (Al-Krenawi & Graham, 1997). "High context" cultures emphasize the collective over the individual and have a relatively slow pace of social change and high sense of social stability (Hall, 1981). In Bedouin-Arab society, as in other "high context" societies, the individual remains embedded in the collective identity. The family is particularly important to the homologous interrelationship between the individual and group, as well as between the social and economic status of the individual family members. Tribes remain important to this population's self-identity, particularly as social support and so-

cial control networks (Abu-Khusa, 1994; Al-Aref, 1934; Marks, 1974).

BEDOUIN-ARABS AND PSYCHIATRY

Bedouin-Arabs grow up as a part of a collective in which the individual's first commitment is to his/her nuclear and extended family (Al-Krenawi & Graham, 1997). An individual's illness is regarded as a problem of the entire family and help-seeking often becomes a collaborative family effort (Al-Krenawi, 1995). Given the convergence of tradition and modernity in the Bedouin-Arab society of the Negev, most families make simultaneous use of modern and traditional healing systems. Before, during, and after treatment by a Western trained physician, they often consult with traditional healers in the community who treat physical and mental health problems in their own ways (Al-Krenawi & Graham, 1997).

The Bedouin-Arab of the Negev consult four types of traditional healers: 1) The *Khatib* or *Hajjab* are male healers who produce amulets that are worn on the body to ward off evil spirits. This tradition is usually passed down from father to son, provided that the latter is perceived as having sufficient literacy and community acceptance. 2) The *Dervish* treat mental illness using a variety of religious and cultural rituals. Both males and females can become a *Dervish* by receiving a *baraka,* which is a kind of emotional breakdown that is perceived as a blessing from God and endorsed by a recognized *Dervish.* 3) The *Moalj Bel* Koran, or Koranic healer, works on the basis of religious principles derived from the Koran and treats patients who have been attacked by evil-spirits. All *Moalj Bel* Koran are men and most have some form of post-secondary education (Al-Krenawi & Graham, in press). Koranic healing has gained popularity recently with the revival of Islam throughout the Muslim world. 4) The *Al-Fataha* is a fortune-teller, who is usually consulted about psycho-social problems and uses coffee grains to reveal any secret the patient may have. The role is usually passed down from mother to daughter (Al-Krenawi, 1995; Al-Krenawi et al., 1996). All four types of healers tend to attribute illness to supernatural powers. These healers are consulted both by males and females.

METHODOLOGY

Sample

The study was conducted in the psychiatric clinic of the Soroka Medical Centre, the main hospital in the Negev region of Israel. Of the nearly 250,000 people in Soroka's catchment area, 120,000 are Bedouin-Arabs (Al-Krenawi & Graham, 1997; Al-Krenawi et al., 1994). Most of the patients reach the clinic through referral: by a general practitioner, a family physician working in a community primary-care clinic, a doctor or intern at the emergency room of

Soroka Hospital, or a private physician. They are generally referred with somatic symptoms for which no physical explanation has been found.

The sample consisted of 60 newly referred Bedouin-Arab patients, 36 (60%) females and 24 (40%) males. All of them presented their difficulties through one or more bodily complaints (*colo bogaa,* or somatization). All of them were Muslims, of varying degrees of religiosity. Fifty (83.3%) were diagnosed as neurotic and 10 (16.6%) as psychotic. Fifteen (25%) were unmarried, 1 (1.7%) widowed, 37 (61.6%) married, and 7 (11.6%) divorced. The males ranged in age from 16 to 61 (mean 30.25), the females from 17 to 80 (mean 35.30). The males had 0 to 15 years (mean 3.88) of schooling, the females 0 to 10 (mean 1.86). An ANOVA revealed a significant difference in their education of $[F(1,58) = 23.3, p<0.0001, MSE = 15.795]$. Twelve (50%) of the males were employed and 12 (50%) were unemployed. All the females were housewives who did not work outside the home.

Data Collection and Procedure

All the patients were interviewed in the clinic's waiting room before they met the psychiatrist and again two weeks later, in order to determine the rate of premature termination. The interviews were conducted by the author—the first Bedouin-Arab psychiatric social worker in Israel, and for over eleven years the coordinator of the mental health services for the Bedouin-Arab of the Negev in the Soroka Hospital mental health clinic. The interviews were conducted over a three-month period using a semi-structured, open-ended questionnaire designed for the study and prepared in the Bedouin-Arab dialect. The questions were aimed at examining the patients' perceptions and explanations of their symptoms. Using the emic approach aimed at understanding culture specific concepts, knowledge and techniques from within the context where the phenomena occur (Lum, 1992; Pike, 1967), the researcher was able to understand the patients' explanations of their symptoms from their own perspective.

In addition, background information and diagnoses were gathered from the patients' medical files, which the author read with the patients' and psychiatrists' consent.

Findings and Discussion

All the patients, regardless of education, social class, and diagnosis, perceived their symptoms as caused by some supernatural power: God's will, evil-spirits, or sorcery. None of them made conventional medical attributions. Their families, who were involved in their treatment, corroborated their perceptions. A similar view of the etiology of mental illness has been reported among Arabs in other parts of the Middle East (Caliph, 1989; El-Islam & Abu Dagga, 1992; Haj-Yahia, 1995; Sanua, 1979; West, 1987). The belief in these evil-spirits is deeply rooted in pre-Islamic Arab culture (Al-Shatti, 1977). The evil-spirits are mentioned in the

Koran and accepted within the tradition of Islam (Korna, Surah Al-Hijr, v. 28–40).

Males and females viewed the causes of their symptoms somewhat differently. Seven (29.2% of 24) of the males said that their symptoms were caused by God's will *[Mn Allah]* and explained them as God's punishment *(Aqab Mn Allah)* for some sin they had committed; 16 (66.6%) believed their symptoms had been caused by the actions of evil-spirits; and one (4%) explained his symptoms as the product of sorcery. In contrast, 35 of the 36 females in the sample (97.2%) attributed their symptoms to sorcery—shr—and one to both sorcery and evil-spirits $[X(sup2) = 259; df = 5; p < 0.0001]$.

The explanatory model which was used by the Bedouin-Arab patients in the present study is based on naturalistic and personalistic theories (Cf. Foster, 1976; Littlewood, 1988). The male explanatory model is both supernatural and personalistic. God and evil spirits are both supernatural forces, while God's action is seen as a punishment for an act that the sufferer had himself perpetuated. Moreover, in Islam, evil-spirits are regarded as tools in God's hand to punish the sinful (Al-Krenawi et al., 1996; El-Shamay, 1977).

The explanation thus encompasses both external and internal loci of control. The internal locus of control is evident in the shame and self-blame that led the majority of male subjects to explain their symptoms as punishment. For example, as one male patient confessed: "Last Ramadan [the *Muslim* holy month, when purity of action is expected] I had sex with a prostitute; a few months later, I felt that I committed a sin that made God angry with me."

The female explanatory model is also a combined model, but it joins super-natural agents with social ones. Sorcery is a supernatural force in that it is accomplished through the actions of evil spirits (Al-Sabaie, 1989; El-Islam, 1982; El-Islam & Ahmed, 1971; Sanua, 1979; Sebai, 1981); it is a natural force in that human beings are required to activate the evil spirits to effect the sorcery. A person who wants to use sorcery against another approaches a sorcerer (a *sahar* in Arabic). As Bali (1993) explains it, the sorcerer promises to do bad deeds to satisfy the evil spirits, and the evil spirits promise to help the healer carry out the sorcery. Also in contrast to the male explanatory model, the female model reflects an entirely external locus of control. In most cases, another woman in the nuclear or extended family is believed to have initiated the sorcery.

The combination of social and supernatural forces in the women's explanatory model is reflected in the following two statements by women in the sample: a) *"Soanh Ale Ma Becafan mn Allah,"* which means, "They [in the feminine inflection] did *amaal* [amaal is the term for what the sorcerer does] on me, those who are not afraid of God"; and b) *"Tharti Askatah wa slaat Qalbah, Wa clatah ma egdar Ishofna,"* meaning "My husband's second wife gave him something to drink, and she gained his heart; he cannot see me and my children." The second quotation is consistent with Al-Dramdash's (1991) finding that one of the aims of sorcery among Arab-Muslim peoples is to cause family disputes, as well as with the tendency among Arabs in some communities to blame female sorcery for male sexual dysfunction (Al-Issa, 1989; Al-Alooji, 1964; Bazzoui & Al-Issa, 1966).

The patients' explanations probably have several sources. To begin with, all the patients, both male and female, had prior experience with traditional healers in their community (Al-Krenawi & Graham, 1996a, 1996b). Not only did the traditional healers' understandings of their symptoms probably influence their explanations; but since the Bedouin-Arab patients share the same world view as their healers, their explanatory model is also likely to be similar (Frank, 1973; Torrey, 1986).

To some extent, the attributions seem to have been related to the individual's education. The males who attributed their symptoms to God had up to ten years of schooling, while those who attributed their symptoms to evil spirits had less education. Most of the female patients (26, or 72%), who universally attributed their illness to sorcery, had no formal schooling and were illiterate.

More broadly, the differing explanatory models may be seen as the product of the differential roles and status of the males and females in Bedouin-Arab culture, much as is the disparity in their schooling. Bedouin-Arab social structure is patriarchal, with men exercising the authority in the household, the economy, and the policy (Al-Krenawi, 1996; Kacen et al., 1992). Sons have higher status than daughters in the family (Al-Abbadi, 1973; Habash, 1977; Kacen et al., 1992) and the male's dominance remains unchallenged, as do the cultural prohibitions against women obtaining higher education and having careers outside of the home comparable to men's. Bedouin-Arab women are at a structural disadvantage in both the family and society (Mass & Al-Krenawi, 1994).

The male explanatory model seems to reflect men's dominant role in Bedouin-Arab society, and men's relative freedom to act as they wish. The acceptance of personal responsibility for their symptoms by about a third of the males implies their perception of self-efficacy in affecting their surroundings and what happens to them.

The females' explanatory model reflects the personal and social difficulties women face in a society that subjects them to rigid restrictions and leaves them little opportunity for either action or expression. In adolescence, Bedouin girls are closely guarded by their families. If a girl is suspected of being in love with a man, her family may punish her physically and will undoubtedly impose strict restrictions on her freedom of movement and communication. As adults, their social status is strongly contingent upon being married and rearing children, especially boys. Moreover, to the distress of many Bedouin-Arab women, polygamy is still a common practice, even among the young and the well-educated (Al-Krenawi et al., 1997).

Their attribution of their symptoms to sorcery—initiated by another female in the nuclear or extended family—appears to be their way of coping with distressing events over which they have little or no control. It is a traditional and accepted attribution, common to women throughout the Arab world (Al-Saati, 1984; Bar-Zvi, 1988; Dickson, 1949; Doughty, 1936), which enables them to express their feelings of anger and hatred towards the women whom they perceive as rivals or otherwise hostile.

Placing the blame on a single external source reflects their socially based lack of self-efficacy and lack of opportunity for action. It also enables them to avert having to contemplate a multiplicity of causes that are beyond their ability to rectify. These suggestions are in keeping with Al-Saati's (1984) observation that sorcery is the weapon of the weak in traditional Arab societies and with Whiting's (1977) point that sorcery is useful in meeting problems posed by the environment for which no satisfactory realistic solutions are provided by the culture. They are similarly consistent with Crapanzano's (1973) view of possession as "an idiom of articulating a certain range of experience" (p. 10), with Boddy's (1989) and Wernber's (1989) view of possession as a strategy of expressing emotional difficulties and/or as a way of thwarting danger and cleansing the domestic domain, and with Favret-Saada's (1989) understanding of sorcery as a symbolic system producing specific social and psychological effects.

CONCLUDING REMARKS

The explanatory models of the Bedouin-Arab patients in this study are clearly very different from those of Western psychiatry and psychology. When a Bedouin-Arab patient reaches a Western mental health clinic, two different explanatory models thus come together in the therapeutic encounter (Budman et al. 1992; Kleinman, 1980). One, represented by the mental health practitioner, is derived from a medical reality. The other, represented by the patient, is derived from a cultural and religious reality.

Yet like other Bedouin-Arabs of the Negev, most of the patients in this study were treated by Jewish Israeli psychiatrists, unfamiliar with their language, culture, social structure, religion, and perceptions of illness and mental health problems. Many of them were treated by recent arrivals to Israel from the former Soviet Union, whose understanding of the Bedouin-Arabs' culture is even more limited than that of long term Israelis.

Because of the huge cultural gap and widely different explanatory models, 50% of the patients terminated their treatment after two sessions. This is much the same as the percentage of Asian American and Hispanic people who terminate their use of mental health services in North America after only one or two sessions (Sue & Zane, 1987).

This high rate of very premature termination raises questions about the validity of the diagnosis and treatment of the

Bedouin-Arab patients in Israel. As Chiu (1994) and Budman et al. (1992) point out, limited understanding by mental health providers of the patient's cultural background can lead to misdiagnosis and inappropriate treatment. The findings of this study emphasize the need for mental health practitioners to be aware of their patients' understandings of mental and physical illness and of the culture and belief systems in which those understandings are anchored.

REFERENCES

Abu-Khusa, A. (1994) The Tribes of Beer-Sheva. Amman: Al-Matbaha Al-Wataniah (in Arabic).

Al-Abbadi, A. U. (1973) The Bedouin Woman. Amman: Al-Maktabah Al-Wataniah (in Arabic).

Al-Alooji, A. H. (1964) The Knotted Husband. Baghdad: As'ad Press.

Al-Aref, A. (1934) The Bedouin Tribes in Beer-Sheva District. Jerusalem: Bostnai Publishing (in Hebrew).

Al-Dramdash, H. (1991) The Koran as a Treatment Tool for People Who Are Attacked by Satan. Cairo: Daar Wali Al-Islameh (in Arabic).

Al-Issa, I. (1990) Culture and Mental Illness in Algeria. International Journal of Social Psychiatry, 36(3), 230–240.

Al-Issa, I. (1989) Psychiatry in Algeria. Psychiatric Bulletin, 13, 240–245.

Al-Issa, I. (1977) Social and Cultural Aspects of Hallucinations. Psychological Bulletin, 84, 570–587.

Al-Issa, I. (1970) Culture and symptoms. In Symptoms of Psychopathology: A Handbook (ed. C. Costello) (pp. 27–45). New York: John Wiley & Sons.

Al-Krenawi, A. (1996) Group Work with Bedouin Widows of the Negev in a Medical Clinic. Affilia: Journal of Women and Social Work, 15(3), 303–318.

Al-Krenawi, A., & Graham, J. R. (1997) Spirit Possession and Exorcism in the Treatment of a Bedouin Psychiatric Patient. Clinical Journal of Social Work, 25(2), 211–222.

Al-Krenawi, A., & Graham, J. R. (1996a) Tackling Mental Illness: Roles for Old and New Disciplines. World Health Forum, 127(3), 246–248.

Al-Krenawi, A., & Graham, J. R. (1996b) Social Work and Traditional Healing Rituals among the Bedouin of the Negev, Israel. International Social Work, 39(2), 13–21.

Al-Krenawi, A., Graham, J. R., & Al-Krenawi, S. (1997) Social Work Practice with Polygamous Families. Child and Adolescent Social Work Journal, 14(6), 445–458.

Al-Krenawi, A., Graham, J. R., & Maoz, B. (1996) The Healing Significance of the Negev's Bedouin Dervish. Social Science and Medicine, 43(1), 13–21.

Al-Krenawi, A. (1995) A Study of Dual Use of Modern and Traditional Mental Health Systems by the Bedouin-Arab of the Negev. Unpublished Ph.D. dissertation, University of Toronto.

Al-Krenawi, A., Maoz, B., & Riecher, B. (1994) Familial and Cultural Issues in the Brief Strategic Treatment of Israeli Bedouin. Family Systems Medicine, 12(4), 415–425.

Al-Krenawi, A., & Graham, J. R. (In Press) Social Work and Koranic Mental Health Healers. International Social Work.

Al-Saati, S. H. (1984) The Cultural Barriers and the Rural Egyptian Woman. In Conference about the Woman and the Development of the State (pp. 37–45). Cairo: Al-Markz Alk-Iqlimi Al-Arabi (in Arabic).

Al-Sabaie, A. (1989) Psychiatry in Saudi Arabia: Cultural Perspectives. Transcultural Psychiatric Research Review, 26(4), 245–262.

Al-Shatti, A. S. (1977) The pre-Islamic Medicine. Cairo: Moassat Al-Matbbat Al-Haditha (in Arabic).

Bali, W. A. (1993) Protection from the Sorcerers and the Spirits. Jeddah: Maktabat Al-Shabah (in Arabic).

Bar-Zvi, S. (1988) Old Tradition and Customs among the Negev Bedouin. In The Bedouin (eds. Y. Iani & A. Aorean) (pp. 358–369). Sede Boker: Ben-Gurion University of the Negev (in Hebrew).

Bazzoui, W., & Al-Issa, I. (1966) Psychiatry in Iraq. British Journal of Psychiatry, 112, 827–832.

Beger, P. L., & Luckmann, T. (1967) The Social Construction of Reality: A Treatise in the Sociology of Knowledge. New York: Anchor Books.

Ben-Ezer, G. (1992) Migration and Absorption of Ethiopian Jews in Israel. Jerusalem: Mass Press (in Hebrew).

Bilu, U., & Witztum, E. (1993) Working with Jewish Ultra-Orthodox Patients: Guidelines for a Culturally Sensitive Therapy. Culture, Medicine, and Psychiatry, 17, 197–233.

Bilu, Y., & Witztum, E. (1995) Between Sacred and Medical Realities: Culturally Sensitive Therapy with Jewish Ultra-Orthodox Patients. Science in Context, 8(1), 159–173.

Boddy, J. (1989) Wombs and Alien Spirits: Women, Men, and the Zar Cult in Northern Sudan. Wisconsin: The University of Wisconsin Press.

Bravo, G., & Grob, C. (1989) Shamans, Sacraments, and Psychiatrists. Journal of Psychoactive Drugs, 21(1) 123–128.

Budman, C. L., Lipson, J. G., & Meleis, A. I. (1992) The Cultural Consultant in Mental Health Care: The Case of an Arab Adolescent. American Journal of Orthopsychiatry, 62(3), 359–370.

Caliph, A. M. (1989) Belief and Attitudes of Egyptian Students Related to Mental Illness. Egyptian Journal of Psychology, 11(3), 103–117 (in Arabic).

Cervantes, R. C., Salgado de Snyder, V. N., & Padilla, A. M. (1989) Post-Traumatic Stress in Immigrants from Central America and Mexico. Hospital and Community Psychiatry, 40(6), 615–619.

Chiu, T. L. (1994) The Challenges Faced by Psychiatrists and Other Mental Health Professionals Working in a Multicultural Setting. The International Journal of Social Psychiatry, 40(1), 161–174.

Crapanzano, V. (1973) The Hamadsha: A Study in Moroccan Ethnopsychiatry. Berkeley: University of California Press.

Creyghton, M. (1977) Communication between Peasant and Doctor in Tunisia. Social Science and Medicine, 11(5), 319–324.

Dickson, H. R. P. (1949) The Arab of the Desert: Bedouin Life in Kuwait and Saudi Arabia. London: Allen & Unwin.

Doughty, C. M. (1936) Travels in the Arabian Desert, vol. 2. New York: Dover Publications.

Eisenbruch, M. (1991) From Post-Traumatic Stress Disorder to Cultural Bereavement: Diagnosis of Southeast Asian Refugees. Social Science and Medicine, 33(6), 673–680.

El-Islam, M. F. (1982) Arabic Cultural Psychiatry. Transcultural Psychiatric Research Review, 19(1), 5–24.

El-Islam, M. F. (1980) Symptom Onset and Involution of Delusions. The International Journal of Social Psychiatry, 15, 157–160.

El-Islam, M. F. (1975) Culture Bound Neurosis in Qatari Women. The International Journal of Social Psychiatry, 10(1), 25–29.

El-Islam, M. F., & Abu-Dagga, S. (1992) Lay Explanation of Symptoms of Mental Ill Health in Kuwait. The International Journal of Social Psychiatry, 38(2), 150–156.

El-Islam, M. F., & Ahmed, S. A. (1971) Traditional Interpretation and Treatment of Mental Illness in an Arab Psychiatric Clinic. Journal of Cross-Cultural Psychology, 2, 301–307.

El-Sayed, S. M., Maghraby, M., & Hafeiz, H. B. (1986) Psychiatric Diagnosis Categories in Saudi Arabia. Acta Psychiatrica Scandinavica, 74(6), 553–554.

El-Shamy, H. (1977) The Supernatural Belief-Practice System in the Contemporary Folk Culture of Egypt. Mimeographed. Bloomington, IN: Folklore Publication Group Monograph Series.

Favret-Saada, J. (1989) Unbewitching as Therapy. American Ethnologist, 16(1), 40–56.

Foster, G. M. (1976) Disease Etiologies in non-Western Medical Systems. American Anthropology, 78, 773–782.

Frank, J. D. (1973) Persuasian and Healing. New York: Schocken.

Gaines, A. D. (1992) From DSM-I to III-R: Voices of Self, Mastery and the Other: A Cultural Constructivist Reading of U.S. Psychiatric Classification. Social Science and Medicine, 35(1), 3–24.

Good, B. J., & Good, M. J. (1986) The Cultural Context of Diagnosis and Therapy: A View From Medical Anthropology. In Medical Health Research and Practice in Minority Communities: Development of Culturally Sensitive Training Programs (eds. M. Miranda & H. Kitano) (pp. 1–28). Washington, DC: DHHS Publication.

Good, J. (1994) Medicine, Rationality, and Experience. Cambridge: Cambridge University Press.

Habash, A. (1977) Changes and Modernisation in the Arab Family. Jerusalem: The Institute for Work and Welfare (in Hebrew).

Haj-Yahia, M. (1995) Towards Culturally Sensitive Intervention with Arab Families in Israel. Contemporary Family Therapy, 17(4), 42–46.

Hall, E. (1981) Beyond Culture. Garden City, New York: Doubleday.

Hebrew Encyclopaedia (1954) Vol. 7. (pp. 624–630). Tel-Aviv: Reshafim Press (in Hebrew).

Kacen, L., Anson, J., Nir, S., & Linveh, N. (1992) Group Work with the Bedouin Population of the Negev. Social Work with Groups, 15(2/3), 81–94.

Kay, S. (1978) The Bedouin. New York: Crane Russak.

Kiev, A. (1972) Transcultural Psychiatry. New York: Free Press.

Kleinman, A. (1980) Patients and Healers in the Context of Culture. Berkeley: University of California Press.

Kleinman, A., & Good, B. (Eds.) (1985) Culture and Depression. Berkeley: University of California Press.

Kortmann, F. (1987) Problems in Communication in Transcultural Psychiatry. Acta Psychiatrica Scandinavica, 75, 562–570.

Leff, J. (1981) Psychiatry around the Globe: A Transcultural View. New York: Marcel Dekker.

Littlewood, R. (1988) From Vice to Madness: The Semantics of Naturalistic and Personalistic Understandings in Trinidadian Local Medicine. Social Science and Medicine, 27(2), 129–148.

Lum, D. (1992) Social Work Practice and People of Color. Monterey, CA: Brooks/Cole Publishing Company.

Marks, E. (1974) The Bedouin Society in the Negev, Tel-Aviv: Reshafim Press (in Hebrew).

Marsella, A. (1993) Counseling and Psychotherapy with Japan American: Cross-Cultural Consideration. American Journal of Orthopsychiatry, 63(2), 200–208.

Mass, M., & Al-Krenawi, A. (1994) When a Man Encounters a Woman, Satan Is also Present: Clinical Relationships in Bedouin Society. American Journal of Orthopsychiatry, 64(3), 357–367.

Meleis, A., & La Faver, C. (1984) The Arab American and Psychiatric Care. Perspectives in Psychiatric Care, 22(2), 72–80.

Obeyesekere, G. (1970) The Idiom of Demonic Possession: A Case Study. Social Science and Medicine, 14(1), 97–111.

Parson, C. F. F., & Wekely, F. (1991) Idioms of Distress Somatic Responses of Distress in Every Day Life. Culture, Medicine, and Psychiatry, 15, 111–113.

Pike, K. (1967) Language in Relation to a Unified Theory of the Structure of Human Behaviour. (2nd ed.). Paris: Mouton & Co.

Pliskin, K. I. (1987) Silent Boundaries: Cultural Constraints on Sickness and Diagnosis of Iranians in Israel. New Haven, CT: Yale University Press.

Prince, R., & Tcheng-Laroche, F. (1987) Culture-Bound Syndrome and International Disease Classifications. Culture, Medicine and Psychiatry, 11(3), 3–19.

Sanua, V. D. (1979) Psychological Intervention in the Arab World: A Review of Folk Treatment. Transcultural Psychiatric Research Review, 16, 205–208.

Schwartz, D. (1985) Caribbean Folk Beliefs and Western Psychiatry. Journal of Psychosocial Nursing and Mental Health Services, 23(11), 26–30.

Sebai, Z. A. (1981) The Health of the Family in a Changing Arabia: A Case Study of Primary Health Care. Riyadh: Tihama Publication.

Sue, S., & Zane, N. (1987) The Role of Culture and Cultural Techniques in Psychotherapy: A Critique and Reformulation. American Psychologist, 42(1), 37–45.

Torrey, E. F. (1986) Witchdoctors and Psychiatrists. Northvale, N.J.: Jason Aronson.

Werbner, R. (1989) Ritual Passage, Sacred Journey: The Process and Organisation of Religious Movement. Washington, DC: Smithsonian Inst. Press.

Wessels, W. H. (1985) The Traditional Healer and Psychiatry. Australian and New Zealand Journal of Psychiatry, 19(3), 283–286.

West, J. (1987) Psychotherapy in the Eastern Province of Saudi Arabia. Psychotherapy, 24(1), 105–107.

Whiting, B. B. (1977) Paiute Sorcery: Sickness and Social Control. In Culture, Disease, and Healing (ed. D. Landy) (pp. 210–218). New York: Macmillan Publishing Co., Inc.

11

Bewitching

For those of us who are scientifically minded, the notion that one individual can bewitch another, causing them disease or misfortune, seems fanciful or absolutely irrational. Yet our current scientific understanding of disease is quite recent and is based on large-scale statistical studies. How many of us have ever seen a germ? How many can claim to understand why disease or bad luck plagues one individual but another person seems to go from success to success? In cultures all over the world, people answer these questions through accusations of witchcraft and sorcery or through belief in possession. Many people in the United States believe in these as well. The essays in this section all deal with different aspects of witchcraft and possession beliefs as they are expressed in different parts of the world. As you read the essays in this section, keep the following points in mind:

- Beliefs about witchcraft and possession can be found in most societies, including the United States. However, these beliefs and the ways in which they are expressed can vary dramatically. Though possession can be viewed positively (as is the case with possession by the Holy Ghost in some Christian Pentecostal churches and the trance states of shamans—see sections 10 and 6), the essays in this section focus on cases of malignant possession and show how these cases, defined as possession in their original contexts, can be seen as manifestations of psychiatric problems such as depression, acute anxiety, and schizophrenia. Furthermore, the essays demonstrate the effectiveness of indigenous systems of healing in treating these cases when Western psychiatric interventions are not culturally appropriate.

- When people are under stress, whether from disease or from social and economic disruption, they search for ways to understand their problems. Once they

find a model for understanding that seems convincing to them, they generally cling to it tenaciously, even if it is demonstrably wrong. People get their models for such understanding from their cultural contexts: the models are articulated by the key institutions and individuals that surround them. These factors have a profound effect on how people understand their place in the world. Ronald Johnson provides an outstanding example of this in his essay on those who claim to have recovered repressed memories of childhood sexual abuse, been kidnapped by space aliens, and the young women afflicted during the Salem witch hunts. In each case, he shows how people's unease or unhappiness was shaped and explained for them by ministers, therapists, and others. These explanations then became fundamental to the identities of those who were seeking relief and became very difficult to supplant, even when it was shown that the explanations were in error.

- In a famous 1934 essay "Anthropology and the Abnormal,"[1] the great American anthropologist Ruth Benedict argued that the notions of normal and abnormal are purely culturally relative: characteristics that might identify a person as schizophrenic in American society are taken as perfectly normal ways of behaving in another. Benedict overstated her case. It is clear that major forms of mental illness are recognized cross-culturally. However, the ways in which members of different cultures understand particular symptoms may vary enormously. Characteristics that might be diagnosed as various forms of neurosis by American clinicians may be understood as evidence of bewitchment or possession by shamans in other culture. Joseph Tobin and Joan Friedman's essay about a Hmong refugee is a case in point. They argue that although this individual was considered abnormal by both members of his own culture and American therapists, treatment by a Hmong shaman was effective because it fit the individual's understanding of his condition. Treatment by a Western-trained therapist would not likely be as useful.

• It is clear that the threat of bewitching can also be used to extract money or compliance from individuals. Peter Wogan provides a personal contemporary account of this aspect of witchcraft in Ecuador. He shows how witch beliefs in the area persist because of the association of witch books with governmental and Catholic Church archives.

NOTE

1. Ruth Benedict, "Anthropology and the Abnormal," *Journal of General Psychology* 10, no. 2 (1934): 59–82.

Parallels between Recollections of Repressed Childhood Sex Abuse, Kidnappings by Space Aliens, and the 1692 Salem Witch Hunts

Ronald C. Johnson

In the 1980s in the United States, there was a nationwide satanic abuse scare, driven by books such as *Michelle Remembers* and sensationalized television programs. Reputations were ruined and people were jailed based on the recovered memories of "victims" of this abuse. Looking back now, it is widely accepted that there was virtually no evidence for the claims of satanic conspiracies, child sex abuse, sacrifice, and cannibalism that were spread by the popular media. In fact, it is recognized now that most of the accounts of satanic abuse were confabulated—that is they were the product of therapy sessions, self-help books, and support groups in which people were seeking psychological help.

In this essay, Ronald Johnson, a professor of psychology, examines the psychological processes by which memories of satanic childhood sexual abuse were created in supposedly therapeutic settings with counselors and ministers, and then demonstrates how this process has been repeated with those who claim to have been abducted by aliens. Similarly, his examination of the Salem witch trials of 1692 show that the experiences of the young women whose accusations fueled the trials paralleled those of people who claim to have been victims of satanic abuse or alien abduction. In all cases the claims come from people who are unhappy and feel that something is wrong. They go to a minister or therapist for help and under this guidance begin to "recall" previously unknown details of abuse or kidnapping. Participation in group therapy sessions or interaction with others who suffer the same problems helps create even more "memories," which are validated by the therapist, support group, and even the general public.

As you read, consider these questions:

1. The author compares recollections of childhood sexual abuse, alien abductions, and witch hunts. What are the parallels and what do these have in common?
2. What is the "satanic abuse conspiracy"? How does it relate to claims of alien abductions?

"Parallels Between Recollections of Repressed Childhood Sex Abuse, Kidnappings by Space Aliens, and the 1692 Salem Witch Hunts" by Richard C. Johnson, *Issues in Child Abuse Accusations* 6:1 (1994), 41–47. Reprinted by permission of the Institute for Psychological Therapies, Northfield, MN.

3. How can those making claims of childhood sexual abuse or alien abductions come to firmly believe that these events occurred when in fact they did not?

RECOVERED MEMORIES OF REPRESSED CHILDHOOD ABUSE

The topic of recovered memories has been extensively covered in the popular media and in professional meetings and literature. An American Psychological Society (APS) symposium in San Diego in 1992, an article in the *APS Observer* (July, 1992), and a comprehensive paper (Loftus, 1993) dealt with the validity of claims of recovered memories of childhood sexual abuse. Elizabeth Loftus and John Briere debated the topic at the 1993 American Psychological Association convention in August. Few topics in psychology have created as much controversy and polarization.

The debate is over whether reports of "recovered" memories are based on memories of actual events or are a result of confabulation evoked by therapists, survivor books, television shows, or other sources. As Wakefield and Underwager (1992) report, in many cases where the accused parents are aware of their adult child's therapy program, the book, *The Courage to Heal* (Bass & Davis, 1988), was used.

"The Courage to Heal"

This book (Bass & Davis, 1988) is sometimes referred to as the "Bible" of the survivor movement. Here are some quotes:

> Often the knowledge that you were abused starts with a tiny feeling, an intuition. It's important to trust that inner voice and work from there. Assume your feelings are valid. So far, no one we've talked to thought she might have been abused, and then later discovered that she hadn't been (p. 22).

> If you told someone about what was happening to you, they probably ignored you, said you made it up, or told you to forget it. They may have blamed you. Your reality was denied or twisted and you felt crazy (p. 58).

> Many survivors suppress all memories of what happened to them as children. Those who do not forget the actual incidents often forget how it felt at the time. Remembering is the process of getting back both memory and feeling (p. 58).

Recovering occluded memories (those blocked from the surface) is not like remembering with the conscious mind. Often the memories are vague and dreamlike, as if they're being seen from far away (p. 72).

If you don't remember your abuse, you are not alone. Many women don't have memories, and some never get memories. This doesn't mean they weren't abused (p. 81).

If you don't have any memory of it, it can be hard to believe the abuse really happened. You may feel insecure about trusting your intuition and want "proof" of your abuse. This is a very natural desire, but it is not always one that can be met (p. 82).

One practical way to validate your abuse is to look at your life. If you see the effects of abuse and then, as you begin the healing process, you see your behavior change, even slightly, you can trust that your belief is sound (p. 88).

(In the "For counselors" section). *Believe the survivor.* You must believe that your client was sexually abused, even if she sometimes doubts it herself. Doubting is part of the process of coming to terms with abuse. Your client needs you to stay steady in the belief that she was abused. Joining a client in doubt would be like joining a suicidal client in her belief that suicide is the best way out. . . . If a client is unsure that she was abused but thinks she might have been, work as though she was. So far, among the hundreds of women we've talked to and the hundreds more we've heard about, not one has suspected she might have been abused, explored it and determined that she wasn't (p. 347).

Working in a group is the only helpful therapy I've gotten in my whole life, and I've been in therapy since I was six years old. That's forty-one years. Being in a group is better than being with a therapist because other survivors really understand—they weren't *taught* to understand. And hearing other people's stories has sparked things in my memory. I can see myself coming in and out of groups for years, maybe for my whole life. Group support is fantastic (p. 463).

Ritual abuse (often called satanic ritual abuse or SRA) is a special form of childhood sexual abuse. In SRA there are allegations of satan worship, torture, ritual sacrifice of animals and humans, and cannibalism along with the sexual abuse. Many mental health and police professionals believe that satanic ritual abuse exists and is frequent. Bass and Davis are convinced of its reality:

"This isn't an isolated thing that only happened to me. I traced it back in my little town three generations. And it happens in other towns too. It's happening to kids today. I've had more than a hundred calls about ritual abuse. It's starting to break into the papers. And people are starting to believe it." . . . Ritual abuse is surfacing now because we've started to talk openly about the sexual abuse of children. More and more adults are remembering what happened to them when they were young (p. 419).

The book, *Michelle Remembers* (Smith & Pazder, 1980), seems to have triggered the flood of claims of ritual abuse. This book was written by Smith (the victim) along with Pazder, her therapist, whom she later married. Since then,

there have been a variety of books, magazine articles, and talk show presentations featuring ritual abuse "survivors."

The Paul Ingram Case

Probably the best single description of a case of alleged satanic ritual abuse is in "Remembering Satan" (Wright, 1993). (Also see Ofshe, 1992.) Paul Ingram was a policeman and also a member of Pentecostal sect. The case began when fellow police officers questioned him following his two daughters' accusation of sexual molestation. The allegations began following a Pentecostal retreat for girls, and Pentecostal church officials, especially an assistant pastor, John Bratun, had much to do with the events that followed. (One of Ingram's daughters had also read a book on the topic.)

Ingram denied any memory of sexually abusing his daughters but said that his daughters wouldn't lie, so that he might be "repressing" his memory of the abuse. Next, two other persons were accused of sexual molestation by one of the daughters. With the help of his interviewers, Ingram began to remember the events and came up with recollections of the involvement of the two persons who also were charged. Pastor Bratun helped Ingram develop a technique for remembering and soon Ingram began to have memories of people in robes gathered around a fire, with one of them cutting the heart out of a black cat. (The daughters, to this point, had said nothing about satanic rites.) A son was brought in for questioning and eventually recalled being plagued by a witch, being bound and gagged, and being forced to commit fellatio.

Ingram's wife was accused of sex abuse by the daughters. A son, interviewed in Nevada, recalled seeing his mother having sex with his father and one of the two other accused men while the other accused person masturbated. Mrs. Ingram could not recall the event at first, but eventually did so.

The daughters now recalled satanic rites, animal sacrifice, being tortured by being burned, and being cut with knives, and one of them recalled the sacrifice of a human infant. One of the daughters charged that her father forced her to have sexual intercourse with goats and dogs and took photos of the intercourse.

At Paul Ingram's trial one of the daughters described approximately 25 infant sacrifices and claimed that she had been impregnated and then aborted with the abortus being cut up and rubbed all over her body. Paul Ingram cooperated with the prosecution at his own trial. However, some of the testimony was so strange that an outside consultant, Dr. Richard Ofshe, was brought in by the police.

Ingram claimed to be able to recall the events described by his daughters by using the memory technique that Pastor Bratun assured him would bring him only the truth. Dr. Ofshe decided to test Ingram by making a new accusation— that he had forced a daughter to have sex with one of his sons. Ingram had only vague memories, but was told to pray on it. His memories became more clear at a second meeting. Dr. Ofshe brought up the same scenario to one of the daughters, who denied it. A third meeting with Ingram resulted in a full and complete confession.

Paul Ingram, after praying and visualizing (developing mental pictures that then can be put into words) with Pastor Bratun produced a list of ten other alleged cult members—all present or former employees of the sheriff's office. Charges of satanic ritual abuse faded away. Ingram pleaded guilty to six counts of rape. Charges against the other two accused persons were dropped. A daughter charged that approximately 30 satanists controlled the county government and that there had been a cover-up. Paul Ingram, who began to have doubts about his memories of satanic rites before sentencing, is now serving a 20-year prison term.

The Satanic Abuse Conspiracy

A recent book, *Out of Darkness: Exploring Satanism and Ritual Abuse* (edited by Sakheim & Devine, 1992), addresses events such as those in the Paul Ingram case. Although Sakheim and Devine note the need for skepticism, most of the contributors accept the existence of a vast conspiracy of satanic abuse. For example, Greaves (1992) evaluated alternative hypotheses concerning claims of satanic cult activity and stated that they were gravely wanting. He asserts that survivors' memories cannot be a result of having read of or heard of other accounts of abuse since most survivors profess not to have read anything concerning the topic and no single book or movie contains the material reported by even a single patient. However, contrary to Greaves' assertion, the Ingram daughters' accounts mirror those of *Michelle's Secret* (Smith & Pazder, 1980) and *Satan's Underground* (Stratford, 1988) and at least one of the daughters had read *Satan's Underground* (Wright, 1993, May 24, p. 80).

Greaves cites the *Necronomicon* (Schlangecraft, Inc., 1977) as a major source in supporting the belief in ritual satanic abuse. However, the *Necronomicon* has a strange history and its acceptance as anything but a hoax indicates, at the least, a lack of exposure to literature. H. P. Lovecraft wrote a large number of short stories, novelettes, and novels about decaying New England families, most of them in the region around the imaginary Massachusetts town of Arkham. The equally imaginary Miskatonic University was located in Arkham and there—in the locked shelves—was the *Necronomicon,* a book on satanism to be treated cautiously, since reading it could drive one mad. Schlangecraft, Inc. (obviously a somewhat obscene pseudonym based on Lovecraft's name) decided to fill the gap and produce the book. It is now accepted as real, by Greaves and also by some law enforcement officials (see Terry, 1987).

The one skeptic in Sakheim and Devine's book is Kenneth Lanning (1992) from the FBI's Behavior Science Unit at Quantico, Virginia. His unwillingness to accept the claims of widespread ritual abuse has led to the accusation that he is a satanist (p. 110). (Lanning notes other instances of unfounded fears—for example, the belief that hundreds of thousands of missing children have been abducted each year. All but a few hundred were runaways or involved in parental disputes over child custody and only about a quarter of these may have been abducted by strangers.) In discussing ritual abuse Lanning observes:

> The most significant crimes being alleged that do not seem to be true are the human sacrifice and cannibalism. In none of the multidimensional child sex ring cases of which the author is aware have bodies of the murder victims been found—in spite of major excavations where the abuse victims had claimed the bodies were located. . . . Not only no bodies found, but also, more important, there is no physical evidence that a murder took place. Many of those not in law enforcement do not understand that, while it is possible to get rid of a body, it is much more difficult to get rid of the physical evidence that a murder took place, especially a human sacrifice involving sex, blood, and mutilation (p. 130).

> The large number of people telling the same story is, in fact, the biggest reason to doubt these stories. It is simply too difficult for that many people to commit so many horrendous crimes as part of an organized conspiracy. Two or three people murder a couple of children in a few communities as part of a ritual, and nobody finds out? Possible. Thousands of people do the same thing to tens of thousands of victims over many years? Not likely. Hundreds of communities all over America are run by mayors, police departments, and community leaders who are practicing satanists and who regularly murder and eat people? Not likely (p. 131).

> If a group of individuals degenerate to the point of engaging in human sacrifice and cannibalism, that would most likely be the beginning of the end for such a group. The odds are that someone in the group would have a problem with such acts and be unable to maintain the secret (p. 132).

KIDNAPPINGS BY SPACE ALIENS

The controversy about repressed childhood abuse and ritual abuse is over whether these reports are reality based or are a result of confabulation evoked by therapists, religious leaders, survivors' groups, books, or other sources. The claims of abductions by space aliens are relevant to this debate since the way the memory for the alien abduction is uncovered closely resembles how memories of early sexual abuse and ritual abuse develop.

While having been kidnapped by space aliens is not yet a part of the Diagnostic and Statistical Manual, treatment of these victims is a growth industry in some therapeutic circles. Dr. John E. Mack, a full professor at Harvard Medical School, has written a review article (Mack, 1992), and is writing a book on the abduction experience. He claims that "between several hundred thousand to more than 3,000,000 adults in the United States alone have had an abduction experience" (Mack, 1992, p. 10). He states:

> Many abductees have been forced to go "underground," keeping the information of what they have been through to themselves until, with considerable fear and courage, they

venture forward to contact someone who they hope is capable of helping them (p. 10).

. . . experiencers are more likely to have self-diagnosed their conditions as being UFO or abduction-related through a grapevine of connections. This generally begins with a friend or colleague to whom they have confided their experiences and questions and who then refers them to a book dealing with the subject or to a lay person or professional associated with UFOs or otherwise involved in the UFO network (p. 10).

UFO-related abductions affect powerfully the lives of experiencers. Some abductees feel as if they have been living a second, secret life that they have denied or kept out of consciousness, separate from their everyday experiences, even though they know or suspect that what they have been through is of great significance. When the memories of what they have been through are relived, especially under hypnosis, feelings are expressed of terror, rage, and grief as intense as any I have encountered as a psychiatrist (p. 11).

I watch carefully for what I call signs of "ontological shock." This is demonstrated by a certain sadness, even tearing, which represents the impact of the undoing of the experiencer's denial ("I have treated them as dreams" or "I was hoping, doctor that you would tell me I was crazy"), leaving them with the bleak realization that what they have experienced actually occurred and that reality as they have defined it is forever altered. It is an existential moment brought about primarily by my indicating familiarity with the details of their story from other cases, thus distinguishing what they have been through from dreams, fantasies, or psychological symptoms (p. 12).

In most, but not all, cases the person wishes to go further with the exploration of what he or she usually feels has been, if not a lifelong process, an area of their lives that has been troubling, burdensome, and mysterious. Further curiosity has usually been aroused in the session, and the experiencers want to know "what has been happening to me," as if to reclaim their lives. I discuss with them the possible pain and distress they will almost inevitably encounter if they explore further (pp. 12–13).

. . . abductees usually feel, in addition, that they have been instructed not to, or forbidden to, remember their experiences. Sometimes they are told that this is for their own protection . . . (p. 13).

Mack says much more, but these quotations demonstrate that there are parallels between becoming aware of early sexual abuse, including ritual abuse, and becoming aware of having been kidnapped by space aliens. *Communion: A True Story* (Strieber, 1987), widely read in UFO circles, includes descriptions of space alien activity that appear to involve sexual assault (e.g., on p. 115, Strieber has his mouth forced open, something stuffed into it, brushed his teeth afterward) and the possible creation of alien-human hybrids (p. 227–278).

A recent article on abductions by space aliens (Judge, 1993) begins with the case history of Catherine. "Catherine

is an alleged UFO abductee. She believes that alien creatures have kidnapped her countless times since she was a child, taken her aboard a flying saucer, and sexually abused her for breeding purposes. Her story is not unique" (Judge, 1993, p. 26). The article goes on to describe the experiences of John Mack's abductees:

Most of the abduction stories Mack hears from his patients are similar to Catherine's. In a typical scenario, the victim is taken from his or her environment—in most cases, from bed while asleep or shortly after spotting a UFO—by small, humanoid creatures who are able to pass through walls and windows. The person is then taken aboard a spaceship—usually a saucer with bright lights—where he or she is disrobed and subjected to medical procedures, including sperm removal from males and pregnancy tests on females. Often the abductee is shown images of global destruction; many describe an enormous room containing rows of incubators that hold fetuses that resemble hybrids of humans and aliens. After the abduction the victim is returned to the site of the abduction with virtually no recall of the incident and sometimes bearing small scars. The aliens—or visitors, as some abductees call them— often force them to forget the abduction episode or plant bogus "screen memories" to replace the traumatic events. Later hypnosis or another incident—seeing aliens portrayed on television, for example—may trigger memories (Judge, 1993, p. 26).

THE SALEM WITCH TRIALS

Both the claims of satanic ritual abuse and abductions by space aliens have similarities to the Salem witchcraft trials. Almost certainly the definitive work on devil worship in Salem Village (the town of Salem was almost completely unaffected) in Massachusetts in 1692 in Starkey's *The Devil in Massachusetts* (1949).

The sufferers generally were adolescent girls. Starkey points out the dullness of their lives, their relatively low status, the fact that their lives were "on hold" until they married, the general public interest in witchcraft, the willingness of the clergy (the psychotherapists of that era) to believe their claims, their "contagious" influences on one another's claims of victimization, their increased status that resulted from these claims, and the validation of their claims from community support that led to the deaths of many of those whom they accused.

Many women, and a few men, were hanged and one man was pressed to death as a result of accusations of witchcraft made against them by adolescent girls. This evidence brought against the convicted witches was spectral evidence. The accusers "saw" events, such as witches flying to satanic rituals in the Reverend Parris's orchard, "saw" evil spirits at the witchcraft trials, and "felt" the strength of these spirits as they choked their victims while in the act of accusing the witches persecuting them.

As Starkey notes (1949, p. 251), Salem Village was "so odd a site for God to choose as the battleground between heaven and hell." The infestation of witches began in the Reverend Parris's own kitchen, where Tabitha, a Black slave, informed a group of adolescent girls on the art of magic. Among the visitors to Tabitha's kitchen was Ann Putnam. Her mother, a semi-invalid, had persons she regarded as enemies in Salem. Ann was very close to her mother. Ann first, then other young women, accused persons (almost all women) residing in Salem village of witchcraft. The idea of witchcraft was in the air; four children in Boston had been bewitched six years earlier and it took the work of four ministers, including the redoubtable Cotton Mather, and the hanging of the witch, to restore the children to normalcy. Mather's book on the topic had wide circulation and the Reverend Parris is known to have had a copy (Starkey, 1949, pp. 21–22). The symptoms experienced by the young women of Salem Village were the same as those earlier experienced by the children in Boston. Starkey also notes other means by which these young women could develop parallel sets of symptoms to earlier cases and to one another.

Some of the accused managed to escape, but of those tried, all were convicted and all put to death except (as the accusations spread) those who were willing to turn "state's evidence" and testify against others. Notably pious persons, such as Rebecca Nourse, died by hanging.

The young women afflicted by witches were sought out as witch-finders by other communities, but began to suffer defeats. They identified Robert Calef as a witch; he began suit against them for defamation of character, and they fell silent (Starkey, 1949, p. 195). At Ipswich they met an old woman and had the convulsions that identified her as a witch, but the people of Ipswich ignored them. The same kind of spiritual messages that had identified witches told Mary Herrick that the wife of John Hale, a very prominent minister, was invading her dreams (Starkey, pp. 223–225). Other witch finders accused the wife of Governor Phips of being a witch (Starkey, pp. 232–233), and even Cotton Mather, Massachusetts' leading theologian, was accused (Starkey, p. 265).

Respected citizens began to question the witchcraft proceedings. Judge Richard Pike wrote Judge Jonathan Corwin (one of the panel of judges hearing the witchcraft cases) arguing that trial procedures were questionable. Thomas Brattle, a wealthy Boston merchant, circulated an open letter stating that it was disgraceful that magistrates based their judgments on common gossip, irresponsible "confessions" and the pretensions of the afflicted girls. Neighbors who earlier feared to speak, lest they, too, be accused, petitioned for the release of persons accused of witchcraft (Starkey, 1949, pp. 216–220). Dutch theologians in the former New Amsterdam, by then renamed New York, were questioned by Joseph Dudley, a former deputy governor of Massachusetts. They denied that spectral evidence (on which all convictions rested) could be trusted (Starkey, 1949, pp. 238–240).

Governor Phips had equivocated, but the spread of accusations (including those against his wife), expressions of doubt by leading citizens, and the Dutch theologians' denial of the validity of spectral evidence, led him to change the rules. Spectral evidence was not allowed and 49 of the 52 persons scheduled for trial were not tried. Three were tried and convicted. Judge Stoughton signed their death warrants as well as those of five previously convicted witches but Governor Phips reprieved them all. Some remained in prison for some time, since they had to pay their room-and-board before release, but eventually all who survived imprisonment were released. Despite the wholesale jail delivery of witches, the previously afflicted young women no longer manifested their seizures or other symptoms. They no longer had a responsive audience.

Some of the judges, such as Samuel Sewall, admitted error, which others such as Stoughton and Hathorne (grandfather of Nathaniel Hawthorne, who wrote of these events in "Goodman Brown") did not. Reparations were made to surviving witches and children of those killed. Starkey notes:

> Massachusetts had come out of its delusion not without honor. There had been misery, injustice, bloodshed, but at the worst nothing on such a scale as had in the recent past been suffered in witch-hunts in England, on the Continent, and in Sweden. In comparison with historical precedents, the panic in Massachusetts had been distinguished less by its violence than by the pertinacity with which sanity had struggled for domination from the first and by which it had finally prevailed (Starkey, p. 291).

DISCUSSION

The similarity between claims of recovered memories of childhood sexual abuse, satanic ritual abuse, and abductions by space aliens are clear. The same sequence of events occurs. The person claiming that such events have transpired (1) is unhappy and feels that "something is wrong," (2) with the aid of a therapist, begins to recall the details of the abuse or kidnapping, (3) further therapy, along with interaction with fellow sufferers, evokes ever more memories which are, in turn, (4) validated by the therapist, the support group of fellow sufferers, and the general community.

The events in Salem Village followed a similar pattern. The girls led relatively low-status and boring lives until they became involved in allegations of witchcraft. They were influenced by the Black slave, Tabitha, and the allegations were supported by the clergy (the psychotherapists of that era). The allegations gained them much attention. Under the influence of each other (the local survivors' group), the clergy, and the general community, the allegations grew and more people were accused. As with today's "survivors," the influence of therapists and the group support and encouragement resulted in ever increasing and elaborate allegations.

The belief in the infestation of witches in Salem Village illustrates that when presented with information concerning strange events, each person has a point where disbelief sets in. In Salem, when the governor's wife was accused, when leading citizens expressed doubt, and when the Dutch theologians denied the validity of spectral evidence, attitudes changed and the witch hunts were over.

For most people today the point of doubt is reached well before believing that 3,000,000 Americans have been kidnapped by space aliens, sometimes with repeat abductions between one therapy session and the next. For many, that point is reached well before accepting the belief that there is a nationwide conspiracy of satanists who sacrifice thousands of victims without detection—over twice as many as the victims of known murders (Lanning, 1932, p. 131). For others, the point of disbelief is reached at the point where people claim sexual abuse on the basis of evidence of the sort accepted as valid by Bass and Davis (1988).

The events in Salem occurred when the original charter of the Commonwealth was revised, putting an end to the theocracy, King Philip's Indian war against the colonists had been moderately successful, and at a more local level, family feuds festered. Times were bad, and the residents of Salem village were a close, tight, dysfunctional family. The problem erupted in Salem but spread, possibly because Salem's problems were, to a degree, the problems of all residents of Massachusetts (they did not spread to other colonies). As Starkey points out, the citizens of Massachusetts did manage to come to terms with reality, express their remorse, and make restitution.

We, too, are living in times of social change and of personal feelings of powerlessness. May we do as well as the citizens of Massachusetts in coming to terms with the reality of the claims of recovered childhood sexual abuse and satanic ritual abuse.

REFERENCES

APS Observer (1992). Remembering "repressed" abuse. *APS Observer,* pp. 6–7.

Bass, E., & Davis, L. (1988). *The courage to heal.* New York: Random House.

Greaves, G. B. (1992). Alternative hypotheses regarding claims of satanic cult activity. A critical analysis. In D. K. Sakheim, & S. F. Devine (Eds.), *Out of darkness: Exploring satanism and ritual abuse.* (pp. 45–72). New York: Lexington Books.

Judge, M. G. (1993). The outer limits of the soul. *Common Boundary,* 11(4), 24–33.

Lanning, K. V. (1992). A law enforcement perspective on allegations of ritual abuse. In D. K. Sakheim, & S. E. Devine (Eds.), *Out of darkness: Exploring satanism and ritual abuse.* (pp. 109–146). New York: Lexington Books.

Loftus, E. F. (1993). The reality of repressed memories. *American Psychologist,* 48, 518–537.

Mack, J. E. (1992, July-August). Helping abductees. *I.U.R.,* pp. 11–15, 20. (Available from *International Ufological Reporter,* 2457 W. Paterson Drive, Chicago, IL 60659).

Ofshe, R. J. (1992). Inadvertent hypnosis during interrogation: False confession due to dissociative state; misidentified multiple personality and the satanic cult hypothesis. *The International Journal of Clinical and Experimental Hypnosis,* 40(3), 125–156.

Sakheim, D. K., & Devine, S. F. (Eds.), (1992). *Out of darkness: Exploring satanism and ritual abuse.* New York: Lexington Books.

Schlangecraft, Inc. (1979). *Necronomicon.* (Edited by Simon). New York: Avon Books.

Smith, M., & Pazder, L. (1980). *Michelle remembers.* New York: Congdon and Lattes.

Starkey, M. L. (1949). *The devil in Massachusetts.* New York: Time Incorporated.

Stratford, L. (1988). *Satan's underground.* Eugene, Oregon: Harvest House.

Streiber, W. (1987). *Communion: A true story.* New York: Avon.

Terry, M. (1987). *The ultimate evil: An investigation of Americas most dangerous satanic cult.* Garden City, NY: Doubleday.

Wakefield, H. W., & Underwager, R. (1992). Recovered memories of alleged sexual abuse: Lawsuits against parents. *Behavioral Sciences and the Law,* 10, 483–507.

Wright, L. (1993, May 17 & 24). Remembering satan. Parts I and II. *New Yorker,* pp. 60–81 & pp. 54–76.

Spirits, Shamans, and Nightmare Death: Survivor Stress in a Hmong Refugee

Joseph Jay Tobin, Ph.D.

Joan Friedman, M.S.W.

In this essay, Tobin and Friedman describe the case of a young Hmong man who suffered from acute anxiety and depression after fleeing his homeland and being resettled in the United States. The article is a clear example of how illness may be defined dramatically differently depending on the cultural context. In this case the article demonstrates how illness can be understood as a spiritual or supernatural problem, and how shamanic therapies can be beneficial to such patients.

The article describes the case of Vang, a Hmong soldier who fought for the Americans during the Vietnam War. When the war ended, many Hmong had to flee the victorious Vietnamese army. After three years of fighting, in which he lost most of his family and friends, and a year and a half in a Thai refugee camp, Vang and his family were resettled in Chicago. After a few months, as they struggled to adapt to life in their new country, Vang began to have nightmares in which spirits sat on his chest and made him unable to breathe or call for help. Vang became afraid to go to sleep and increasingly anxious that these spirits would kill him. Because of the divide between Hmong and American culture, Vang's friends decided that referral to the community mental health center or a psychiatrist would not be effective. Instead they contacted a Hmong shaman, who came to his house to treat him.

An American psychiatrist would have diagnosed Vang as suffering from acute anxiety and depression caused by survivor's guilt (common in those who survive extremely traumatic circumstances). The shaman announced that Vang's problems were caused by the spirits of the apartment's previous tenants. Vang accepted this and added that because he did not perform the proper rituals for his parents when they died, their spirits could not follow his family and protect them as a family's ancestral spirits should. The shaman then performed a series of rituals designed to prevent the spirits from following Vang. After this ceremony Vang was able to resume his normal activities.

Tobin and Friedman's account reminds us that illness can be defined very differently in different cultural contexts

and that to be effective, treatment must fit the worldview of the patient. Conventional Western therapies probably would not have been effective for Vang, but when the symptoms of his anxiety attacks were redefined and treated in Hmong spiritual terms, his symptoms disappeared and Vang was able to resume his normal life.

As you read, consider these questions:
1. What is "survivor guilt" and how might it be expressed in Hmong refugees?
2. What is "sudden death syndrome" and what are the various hypotheses to explain it?
3. How do shamans deal with patients who are experiencing traumatic dreams?

In a comprehensive review of scholarship on refugee mental health issues, Cohon[4] has pointed out that, since the "new" refugees are largely non-Western (Asian and African) and thus in crucial ways unlike the "traditional" European and Cuban refugees whose cases are reported in the literature, we cannot yet know to what extent "traditional" theorists of refugee stress, mental illness, and treatment will turn out to be applicable in the future. In an attempt to apply some of these traditional (but still vital) theories to a new refugee, we shall present the case of Vang Xiong, a 22-year-old Hmong soldier, who was resettled in Chicago by Travelers and Immigrants Aid in 1980, and who experienced what the Hmong call a spirit problem, and what we call an acute mental health crisis, shortly after his arrival in America. We will use Vang Xiong's case to explore the interaction of war, flight, and relocation stresses in a "new" refugee, to document the presence in a Southeast Asian refugee of the kind of survivor guilt previously reported chiefly in World War II Holocaust survivors, to examine the interplay of precipitating stressful events with the individual's premorbid personality, and to indicate the need for non-Western treatments for non-Western diseases.

We have chosen Vang Xiong's case in particular not only because it provides elegant testimony to the sophistication and skill of a traditional healer and the efficacy of culturally appropriate (even if, by our standards, unorthodox) counseling, but also because we believe this case can teach us about the "Hmong sudden death syndrome," a problem that is currently threatening the lives of the Hmong in America and baffling American pathologists and epidemiologists.

THE CASE OF VANG XIONG

From the moment he stepped off the plane in Chicago, how strange America must have seemed to Vang Xiong: Mrs. Smith, his American sponsor, so unlike Hmong women as she stepped forward to shake his hand, to speak directly to him, and, in the course of the next week, to drive him and his wife and baby through the city in search of an apartment. Uptown, his Chicago neighborhood, crowded with buildings and people and cars, so unlike his mountain village in Laos. American teenage girls, necking with their boyfriends on the street, so unlike Hmong women, who are married at 15 but are publicly discreet at any age. And social security offices, welfare checks, and social workers, so unlike the clan system of mutual aid in which he grew up, took strength, and found meaning and direction.

When Vang was born 22 years ago, life for the Hmong, the highlanders of Laos, was stable and predictable. In those days, Vang Xiong and his countrymen lived as Hmong had lived for centuries—farming, raising cattle, practicing animism and polygamy, and living a life largely isolated from the modern world. During the 1970s, life for the Hmong drastically changed as they became involved in the Southeast Asian wars, fighting on the side of the Americans, saving downed American pilots, and sustaining casualty rates ten times as high as the American units in Southeast Asia. As the older men were killed, younger ones took their place, and thus Vang Xiong became a soldier at age 15. Eventually, the Americans withdrew; South Vietnam, Cambodia, and Laos fell; and the Hmong were left behind to fight the communists alone, without air support or new weapons and ammunition. Vang Xiong and his people spent the last half of the decade on the run. In one battle with communist troops, 20 of the 45 men in Vang's squadron were killed.

In 1978, after three years of fighting and running, Vang and his wife and new baby fled Laos, leaving their homeland, friends, and relatives behind. Their trek through the jungles was arduous; one old woman in their group grew too weak to walk, and had to be left on the trail. As Vang's group crossed the Mekong on small rafts, they looked back to shore and saw another group of Hmong, waiting for boats, fall under a communist machine gun attack. After a year and a half of languishing in a Thai refugee camp, Vang Xiong's name was called, and he and his family were taken first to a transit center in Bangkok, and then on to Chicago.

Spirit Possession

Vang and his family seemed to do well their first few months in Chicago. They learned to use public transportation and to shop on their own, and Vang made some progress learning English. Then, five months after their arrival, the Xiongs, with the help of their sponsor, moved into a more conveniently located apartment. Vang could not sleep the first night in the apartment,

nor the second, nor the third. After three nights of sleeping very little, Vang came to see his resettlement worker, a young bilingual Hmong man named Moua Lee. Vang told Moua that the first night he woke suddenly, short of breath, from a dream in which a cat was sitting on his chest. The second night, the room suddenly grew darker, and a figure, like a large black dog, came to his bed and sat on his chest. He could not push the dog off and he grew quickly and dangerously short of breath. The third night, a tall, white-skinned female spirit came into his bedroom from the kitchen and lay on top of him. Her weight made it increasingly difficult for him to breathe, and as he grew frantic and tried to call out he could manage but a whisper. He attempted to turn onto his side, but found he was pinned down. After 15 minutes, the spirit left him, and he awoke, screaming.

Vang told Moua Lee he was afraid to return to the apartment at night, afraid to fall asleep, afraid he would die during the night, or that the spirit would make it so that he and his wife could never have another child. He told Moua that once, when he was 15, he had had a similar attack; that several times, back in Laos, his elder brother had been visited by a similar spirit; and that his brother was subsequently unable to father children due to his wife's miscarriages and infertility. Moua Lee listened carefully to Vang Xiong's story, and was very concerned. He asked Vang to return to his office later in the day, assuring him that he would find some way to help. Moua then sought the advice of his agency's mental health specialist. They considered providing counseling themselves to Vang Xiong, but felt they lacked the expertise for so complex and potentially dangerous a case. They considered referring Vang to the community mental health center, or to a private psychiatrist, but worried that even with a bilingual translator, the huge cultural gap between Vang and the therapist would make successful treatment unlikely. In the end, they decided to call on the services of Mrs. Thor, a 50-year-old Hmong woman who is widely respected in Chicago's Hmong community as a shaman.

A Shaman's Cure

That evening, Vang Xiong was visited in his apartment by Mrs. Thor, who began by asking Vang to tell her what was wrong. She listened to his story, asked a few questions, and then told him she thought she could help. She gathered the Xiong family around the dining room table, upon which she placed some candles alongside many plates of food that Vang's wife had prepared. Mrs. Thor lit the candles, and then began a chant that Vang and his wife knew was an attempt to communicate with spirits. Ten minutes or so after Mrs. Thor had begun chanting, she was so intensely involved in her work that Vang and his family felt free to talk to each other, and to walk about the room without fear of distracting her. Approximately one hour after she had begun, Mrs. Thor completed her chanting, announcing that she knew what was wrong. She said that she had learned from her spirit that the figures in Vang's dreams who lay on his chest and who made it so difficult for him to breathe were the souls of the apartment's previous tenants, who had apparently moved out so abruptly they had left their souls behind. Mrs. Thor constructed a cloak out of newspaper for Vang to wear. She then cut the cloak in two, and burned the pieces, sending the spirits on their way with the smoke. She also had Vang crawl through a hoop, and then between two knives, telling him that these maneuvers would make it very hard for spirits to follow. Following these brief ceremonies, the food prepared by Vang's wife was enjoyed by all. The leftover meats were given in payment to Mrs. Thor, and she left, assuring Vang Xiong that his troubles with spirits were over.

There is much that is familiar and much that is very exotic about Mrs. Thor's treatment of Vang Xiong. Her use of incense, candles, and newspaper; her trance-like chanting; her interpretations in terms of spirits; and, last but not least, her willingness to make a house call are strikingly unlike therapeutic approaches we are used to in the West. But we should not let the exoticness of Mrs. Thor, of Vang Xiong, and of people like the Hmong interfere with our appreciation of the transcultural, universal aspects of anguish and cure. In many ways Mrs. Thor functioned in a manner analogous to that of Western psychotherapists. She presented herself to Vang Xiong as a specialist, a professional with long years of training and experience in dealing with similar cases. She showed compassion, but maintained a professional detachment, neither pitying nor scorning her patient. She avoided making premature diagnoses; she offered herself as the chief instrument of cure, relying on her ability to get in touch with a hidden world (in her terms, with spirits; in Western terms, with unconscious thoughts) to interpret Vang Xiong's unique circumstances. As is so often the case in Western therapy, her ability to help her patient understand (become conscious of) mysterious (unconscious) forces proved to be the key to the cure.

Mrs. Thor interpreted Vang Xiong's nightmares and night breathing difficulties as, literally, spiritual problems. And since Vang Xiong, like Mrs. Thor, and indeed like virtually all Hmong, believes in spirits, her interpretations and ministrations on his behalf were intelligible, desired, and ultimately successful. But how are those of us who do not believe in spirits (American or Hmong) to view Vang Xiong's illness and cure? Cultural relativism requires that we acknowledge and respect beliefs that differ from our own, but not that we necessarily subscribe to these beliefs. We can appreciate Mrs. Thor's skill and recommend her to our Hmong clients without agreeing with her understanding of what underlies her clients' suffering, or why her cures work.

TRAUMA REACTIONS IN REFUGEES

Being unlike the Hmong in not believing in spirits, but like them in our need to explain, to give meaning to apparently inexplicable and troubling phenomena such as Vang Xiong's sleep disturbance, we can understand Vang's suffering as a result of emotional stress. To nonbelievers, Mrs. Thor's explanations ring true only metaphorically; automatically we substitute for her word "spirit" something we believe in: "unconscious processes." Viewed from this perspective, Vang Xiong's case is instructive not just as a recording of an exotic, non-Western cure for an exotic, non-Western disease,

but as a prototypical example of a refugee mental health crisis. We can see in Vang's symptoms and in his story evidence of the trauma and the survivor's guilt that burden many, if not all, refugees.

Clearly, there are several serious events in Vang's recent past that would be consistent with a diagnosis of "trauma neurosis"[4] or "stress response syndrome."[4,9] The kind of combat experiences Vang endured as a teenager are capable of producing a stress reaction called "combat fatigue," and it is by no means uncommon for combat veterans to suffer from flashbacks and other nightmares even several years after they last saw action.[8] In addition to being a combat veteran, Vang, like all his fellow Hmong in America, is a disaster victim, a survivor of a holocaust that has seen perhaps 200,000 (out of a population of approximately 500,000) Hmong die. It is well documented that victims of disasters, whether natural or man-made, frequently suffer from either immediate or delayed trauma reactions.[9,24] And, finally, the kind of dislocation that confronted Vang as he moved from Laos to America is known frequently to produce a relatively benign form of trauma reaction in refugees, immigrants, and temporary sojourners, called "culture shock."[7,17,20]

In this light, we can see Vang's sleeping and breathing difficulties as symptoms of the anxiety, depression, and paranoia that threaten all victims of trauma and extreme stress.[21] Anxiety and paranoia are apparent in Vang's belief that "something" attacked him in his bed. Vang's female American sponsor was convinced that Vang's dreams, and thus his anxiety and paranoia, were focused on her, that she was the white female spirit who attacked him. She was so convinced that she became afraid to see Vang, fearing she might further provoke hostile feelings. We believe it is more likely that Vang's dream of a white woman lying on him was an expression of his feelings not specifically about his sponsor but about Americans in general, an expression not so much of hostility as of anxiety: How was he to live (breathe) in this strange land among these strange people?

It has been argued that since we so often find in recent refugees a constellation of acute anxiety, depression, and mild paranoia, we should classify these cases not according to their dominant symptom (for example, as paranoid schizophrenia or depressive neurosis) but rather as a distinctive malady, "the trauma syndrome" (or "the stress response syndrome"), a condition that has a clearly identifiable precipitating cause and a relatively bright prognosis compared to the more chronic and incapacitating conditions it mimics.[4,13] Following this logic, we can speculate that, although Vang Xiong's symptoms seemed quite severe, and the delusional and paranoid quality of Vang's "dreams" might have led the staff of an American mental health center to conclude that he needed aggressive chemotherapeutic intervention if not institutionalization, in fact Vang Xiong was probably not as ill as he looked and his prospects for rapid recovery not so bleak as they might have seemed. In this light the rapidity and apparent thoroughness of Vang's cure became less surprising. We believe Mrs. Thor alleviated Vang Xiong's symptoms by providing cathartic release and sympathetic reassurance to a man suffering from an acutely developed and well circumscribed anxiety reaction.

Though we agree with arguments for the validity of the trauma syndrome as a diagnostic category, with the suggestion that trauma syndrome sufferers' dysfunctions tend to be self-limiting,[4,14] and with the therapeutic rule of thumb of doing less rather than more in these cases,[4] we must be careful lest the "trauma syndrome," "survivor syndrome," "stress response syndrome," and similar diagnoses of refugee mental problems lead us to underestimate the severity or complexity of an individual refugee's emotional condition. We must not let our clients' refugee status, and our sympathetic awareness of the trauma they have recently endured, obscure underlying, chronic pathology. We must be on guard lest our belief that the majority of refugees showing signs of mental illness will get better without our aggressive intervention prevent us from responding appropriately to the plight of the few who urgently need professional care.

SURVIVOR GUILT

Mental health professionals who worked closely with survivors of the Nazi Holocaust have found, not surprisingly, that many of the survivors had lingering, often severe emotional problems. In addition to the depression, anxiety, and paranoia that are generally associated with trauma neuroses, many of the Holocaust survivors were found to be suffering from guilt and self-loathing.[2,10,15] Upon being freed from persecution and returned to society, many of these victims experienced their new-found comfort, safety, and modest reparation payments as undeserved rewards; some felt that they had no right to be alive, much less to live well, while so many others had died in their places.[2]

Applying some of the insights of the Holocaust literature to the plight of the Southeast Asian refugees, we can view Vang Xiong's emotional crisis (his breathing and sleeping disorder) as the result not so much of what he suffered as of what he did not suffer, of what he was spared. Just as some survivors of the Nazi concentration camps have been reported to say, "Why should I live while others died?" so Vang Xiong, through his symptoms, seemed to be saying, "Why should I sleep comfortably here in America while the people I left behind suffer? How can I claim the right to breathe when so many of my relatives and countrymen breathe no more back in Laos?" Working with Hmong (and Cambodian) refugees, we often hear, "I should have stayed and fought and died," and "I shouldn't be alive while better men than me, like my elder brother, are dead." Their individual ambivalence about surviving is mirrored by the ambivalence of the Hmong in America as a people about having fled, and exacerbated by a sometimes bitter debate among the Hmong leaders about the merits of building lives in America versus preparing to return to fight to reclaim the homeland.

STRESSES, PAST AND PRESENT

To suggest that Vang Xiong's sleeping and breathing problems were caused by trauma and survivor guilt is to offer only a partial explanation. As survivors, all of the Hmong in America are confronted with guilt, with trauma, and with grief and loss. Yet most of them are able to deal with the pain of their recent memories and the challenge of living in a new culture without being overwhelmed by either guilt or spirits. To understand Vang's case more fully we must ask what made him more vulnerable than most of his countrymen to traumatic memories and survival guilt?

Some months after his dramatic recovery, we asked Vang, "Why you? There are one thousand Hmong living in Chicago. Why did the spirits choose to attack you?" His answer proved to be most revealing:

> This most recent attack in Chicago was not the first encounter my family and I have had with this type of spirit, a spirit we call *Chia*. My brother and I endured similar attacks about six years ago back in Laos. We are susceptible to such attacks because we didn't follow all of the mourning rituals we should have when our parents died. Because we didn't properly honor their memories we have lost contact with their spirits, and thus we are left with no one to protect us from evil spirits. Without our parents' spirits to aid us, we will always be susceptible to spirit attacks. I had hoped flying so far in a plane to come to America would protect me, but it turns out spirits can follow even this far.

Clearly, a central theme in Vang Xiong's life has been the struggle to come to grips with the deaths of others. In his 22 years of life Vang has survived and mourned the deaths of his parents, of fellow soldiers, of other Hmong with whom he fled, of brothers and sisters and nieces and nephews left behind in Laos, and, indeed, of his land, his people, and his culture. When Vang described the battle in which 20 of his squadron died, his eyes filled with tears, and his voice fell to an intense whisper:

> Suddenly, there was gunfire. An ambush. Bodies fell to the ground all around me. Blood flowed into the ground at my feet. I stepped across my friends' bodies to flee.

Survivor guilt is equally evident in Vang's account of his flight, with his wife and infant, from Laos in 1978:

> There were 74 people in the group we fled with. We walked through the jungle for five days. We knew the communist patrols were all around us. Many in the group demanded we leave our infant behind, that we kill her, because they feared her crying at night would give us all away. We refused, and quieted her with opium. An old woman among us grew too weak to walk. Her sons took turns carrying her on their backs for three days, but finally they were forced to leave her behind, to leave her on the trail with just a bowl of rice, for the Communists were getting closer and our pace was too slow. Finally, we reached the Mekong. Several of the men in our group swam across and returned some hours later with a few small boats. We boarded the boats, and just as we got out into open water we heard shots on shore. We saw another group of perhaps 50 Hmong waiting for boats by the river

bank being shot at with machine guns. Men and women and children fell to the ground. Blood was everywhere. Most, if not all, in that group were killed.

We can distill from Vang's case a general principle of mental illness in refugees. Although a precipitating cause of a refugee mental health crisis generally can be found in the trauma associated with migration, a more careful analysis of the refugee's life and mental functioning prior to the move will often reveal chronic neurotic patterns, lifelong susceptibilities that emerge under the pressure of the refugee experience.[14,18] There are undoubtedly some people in any culture strong enough to maintain emotional stability under conditions of great stress. There are others who were noticeably unstable or borderline even before becoming refugees. And there are a great many people who are able to function when life is relatively benevolent, or at least predictable, but who succumb to the pressure of life as refugees. Vang seems to fit into this last category. The grief, separation, and survivor guilt brought on by his combat experiences, his flight from Laos, and his resettlement in the United States reawakened anxiety and guilt that originated in childhood, with his unresolved mourning of his parents' death.[2,12] In this light, Vang's sleep and breathing disturbance may be seen not as an isolated reaction to trauma, but as an acute attack of a chronic condition, a response to stress that is consistent with lifelong themes and tensions.

A year after his nights of terror and his session with Mrs. Thor, Vang Xiong reported no further trouble with spirits, nightmares, or night breathing. His second child was now six months old. Vang was still struggling to learn English, and was increasingly depressed and anxious about not being able to find a job. He still thought frequently of Laos, and worried about the relatives he left behind. Two and a half years after fleeing to Thailand, Vang continued to second-guess his decision to leave his homeland:

> I feel I left too early but also too late. If I had known, in 1975, how bad the fighting would become in the next few years, I would have left then. But, on the other hand, when I think of my brothers and sisters and their children back in Laos I feel I should not have left at all. I will never forgive myself for leaving them.

NIGHTMARE DEATH

His uncertain situation and anxieties notwithstanding, Vang Xiong has fared better than many of the Hmong who have come to America. Some have not survived at all. Twenty-five Hmong* refugees, all but one a young or middle-aged male, have died inexplicably and suddenly in their sleep. Perhaps their deaths are unrelated to Vang's nightmare attacks. But there is much to suggest that Vang may be a survivor of a "Hmong sudden death syndrome." Vang's age, life history, and symptoms are very like those of many of the victims. In each of the reported cases of the Hmong sudden death syndrome the story has been similar: an apparently healthy Hmong man went to bed feeling well, and died suddenly during the night. In many of these cases there are reports that labored breathing, screams, and tossing in bed immediately preceded death. Autopsies were performed, but no probable cause of death could be established.

Twenty-five mysterious deaths among the approximately 50,000 Hmong refugees in America is a startlingly high figure, so doctors at Federal Centers for Disease Control have begun a careful investigation. So far, the epidemiologists and pathologists in Atlanta, like the local medical examiners in Los Angeles, Minneapolis, Portland, and Des Moines, are baffled. Many Hmong believe the deaths are caused by poison gas they say was used against them by the communists as they fled. Medical authorities refute this explanation by pointing out that chemical and biological agents would affect women and children as well as men; that "nerve gas" and mycotoxins have immediate, rather than delayed effects; and that no tissue damage shows up in the autopsies. Most medical authorities also tend to discount psychological explanations, suggestions that the sudden deaths may be a reaction to emotional stress, or even a form of unconscious suicide. But, in the absence of physical findings, psychological factors must be considered. Based on Vang Xiong's case, we would like to offer two hypotheses (which are by no means mutually exclusive) that link the Hmong sudden deaths to nightmares like Vang's, suggesting that these nightmares may function either as a cause of death or as a side effect of the causative factor.

There are several accounts in the medical and anthropological literature of "psychological" causes of death, including voodoo (death by suggestion),[1,3] anniversary reactions and other examples of loss of will to live (death by unconscious suicide), and nightmare deaths.[5,6] The nightmare deaths are of the most interest to us here. Descriptions in the literature of *bangungut*, which is also known as "Oriental nightmare death," are strikingly similar to accounts of the deaths of the Hmong in the United States, and indeed to Vang Xiong's spirit attack. *Bangungut*, which is a Tagalog phrase meaning, literally, "nightmare," affects young, apparently healthy men.[11,16,19] The young men go to sleep, usually after eating a heavy meal, then either never wake up, or scream in their sleep just before dying. Survivors of *bangungut* attacks report nightmares, including some accounts of incubi sitting on their chests. The word incubus comes from the Latin word for nightmare, and its use in English dates back to the Middle Ages, when it was commonly believed, and recognized by the ecclesiastical and civil laws, that evil spirits could cause death by lying on a sleeping

---

*It is worth nothing that, in addition to the 25 Hmong, eight other Laotians, as well as one refugee from Kampuchea and four from Vietnam, had also died under similar circumstances, as of December 1981, according to the Centers for Disease Control's *Morbidity and Mortality Weekly Report,* Dec. 4, 1981, 30(47):582. Since that time, there have continued to be reports of such deaths among Hmong and other Southeast Asian immigrants in the U.S.A.

person's chest and thereby squeezing out his or her breath. The incubi were generally of the opposite sex to the sleeper (male incubi properly are called succubi), and thought to seek sexual intercourse with their victim.[6]

Our first hypothesis is thus that the Hmong sudden death syndrome may be caused by nightmares or, more specifically, that nightmares, perhaps of incubi, may precipitate death through an as yet poorly understood mechanism. The victims of the sudden death syndrome, of course, can tell us nothing of their nightmares, nor of their emotional condition immediately preceding death. But the case of Vang Xiong, as a possible survivor of the process that killed the others, may provide the basis for some speculation on this phenomenon. If the trauma and survivor guilt expressed in Vang Xiong's nightmares similarly torment other Hmong, can these feelings of anxiety, depression, paranoia, and guilt be strong enough to drive a man to seek death, to seek release in the psychological confusion of the middle of the night? The suggestion here is that the Hmong deaths may be a form of unconscious suicide mediated by a loss of self-respect, a loss of feelings of control over one's life, and a loss of will to live in such anxious circumstances. Hmong men would be more susceptible than women to feelings of guilt, since in their culture it is the man's role to protect his family and homeland, and to feelings of lingering trauma, since the men, as soldiers, usually had more direct contact with death.

Vang Xiong's case not only provides clues to a possible motive for what may be essentially suicidal death, but insight into a possible means of death as well. Vang's nightmares, his fantasies of a spirit sitting on his chest and interfering with his breathing, provide us with a phenomenological understanding of the meaning of sleep, dreams, and breathing for the Hmong. We can see in Vang's story that Hmong believe that some dreams (and especially nightmares) are caused by evil spirits, that these evil spirits prey on people who have been made vulnerable through sins of omission or commission, and that spirits have the power to interfere with physiological functions, notably fertility and breathing. Vang Xiong's case suggests that, just as Americans tend to experience anxiety and guilt as aches of the stomach, head, or back, Hmong are likely to experience their psychological discomfort as a spiritual attack—in some cases, specifically as a threat to their ability to breathe.

We have so far focused our speculations on nightmares as a possible cause of night breathing problems and even, perhaps, of sudden death. A second possibility is that such nightmares are related to breathing not as a cause, but as an effect. It has been known since Freud's 1905 *Interpretation of Dreams* that internal and external stimuli are often incorporated by the sleeping mind into the night's dreams. For example, a man who wishes to remain asleep may incorporate his alarm clock's ringing into his dream as a school bell, or an upset stomach may lead to a dream of being poisoned. Following this line of thought, we can suggest that, whatever the cause of the Hmong sudden deaths (guilt, infection, diet,

nerve gas), among its pathological effects the syndrome produces a shortness or loss of breath, which the sleeping mind visualizes as a dream of an incubus squeezing out one's air. Vang's vision of a spirit interfering with his ability to breathe can thus be interpreted as his sleeping mind's metaphorical description of his body's physiological condition. If Vang is indeed a survivor of the same process that killed the other Hmong, his dreaming descriptions of feeling a heavy weight preventing adequate respiration provide insight into the mechanism and perhaps even the cause of death.

CONCLUSION

Vang Xiong's sleepless nights in his new Chicago apartment can tell us something about the Hmong, about spiritual illness, about shamans' cures, about refugee mental health, and perhaps about an exotic and mysterious illness that has killed 25 Hmong in America. While the hypotheses we have offered about the Hmong sudden death syndrome are highly speculative and in need of further investigation, we believe Vang Xiong's case has significance as a documentation of the presence in a Southeast Asian refugee of the kind of survivor guilt that has previously been described chiefly in survivors of the Nazi Holocaust and the atomic bombings of World War II. It suggests that all refugees who survive cataclysmic events may be burdened by guilt to a greater degree than has generally been acknowledged. The particular vulnerability of a population that has experienced, in rapid succession, personal trauma and cultural disorientation requires special attention on the part of mental health researchers and clinicians.

REFERENCES

1. Arieti, S. 1959. American Handbook of Psychiatry. Basic Books, New York.
2. Berger, D. 1977. The survivor syndrome: A problem of nosology and treatment. Amer. J. Psychother. 31:238–251.
3. Cannon, W. 1942. 'Voodoo' Death. Amer. Anthropol. 44(2): 169–178.
4. Cohon, D. 1981. Psychological adaptation and dysfunction among refugees. Inter. Migration Rev. 15:255–274.
5. Devereux, G. 1980. Pathogenic dreams in non-Western societies. *In* Basic Problems in Ethnopsychiatry, G. Devereux, ed. University of Chicago Press, Chicago.
6. Freeman, D. 1967. Shaman and incubus. *In* Psychoanalytic Study of Society, W. Muensterberger and S. Axelrad, eds. International Universities Press, New York.
7. Garza-Guerrero, A. 1974. Culture shock: Its mourning and the vicissitudes of identity. J. Amer. Psychoanal. Assoc. 22: 408–429.
8. Grinker, R., and Spiegel, J. 1945. Men Under Stress. Blakiston, Philadelphia.
9. Horowitz, M. 1976. Stress Response Syndromes. Aronson, New York.
10. Krystal, H. 1966. Massive Psychic Trauma. International Universities Press, New York.

11. Larsen, N. 1955. The men with deadly dreams. Sat. Evening Post 228:20.
12. Lifton, R. 1963. Death in Life: Survivors of Hiroshima. Random House, New York.
13. Meszaros, A. 1961. Types of displacement reactions among the post-revolution Hungarian immigrants. Canad. Psychiat. Assoc. J. 6:9–19.
14. Murphy, H. 1977. Migration, culture, and mental health. Psychol. Med. 9:677–684.
15. Nederland, W. 1968. Clinical observations on the survivor syndrome. Inter. J. Psychoanal. 49:313.
16. Nolasco, J. 1957. An inquiry into "bangungut." Arch. Intern. Med. 99:905–912.

17. Oberg, K. 1954. Culture Shock. Bobbs-Merrill, Indianapolis.
18. Pedersen, S. 1949. Psychopathological reactions to extreme social displacements. Psychoanal. Rev. 36:344–354.
19. Sta, Cruz, J. 1931. The pathology of "bangungut." J. Phillipine Med. Assoc. 27:476-481.
20. Spradley, J., and Phillips, M. 1972. Culture and stress: A quantitative analysis. Amer. Anthropol. 74(3):518–527.
21. Tyhurst, I. 1951. Displacement and migration: A study in social psychiatry. Amer. J. Psychiat. 101:561–568.
22. Wolfenstein, M. 1957. Disasters: A Psychological Essay. Free Press, Glencoe, Ill.

Magical Literacy:
Encountering a Witch's Book in Ecuador

Peter Wogan

In Wogan's essay about a witch's book in Ecuador, we learn some Andean beliefs about witchcraft and how it is practiced. Additionally, Wogan explains why people in Salasaca, who understand that the witch books are a scam to extort money, still take San Gonzalo and his witch book seriously.

Wogan opens his essay by outlining some theories advanced to explain why indigenous people around the world have often linked magical properties to Western alphabetic writing. Wogan relies on one such explanation—that writing is a reflection of class and power—but adds to that thought by proposing that the Salasacans' belief in the magical power of San Gonzalo's witch book is a result of the integration of their witchcraft beliefs with their ideas about personal names and their experiences with the Ecuadorian Civil Registry and Catholic Church Archives.

Indigenous people in Ecuador associate their name with their individual essence. The most important archives where people's names are recorded and preserved are the Ecuadorian Civil Registry and the archives of the Catholic Church. These archives are controlled by the two most powerful groups in Ecuador, the ruling families who run the government and the Catholic Church. The Civil Registry is where births, marriages, and deaths are recorded, and where one can acquire legal documents such as birth certificates. The Catholic Church also keeps large books recording birth dates, baptisms, confirmations, marriages,

and funerals, all organized by name and date. Consequently, Wogan proposes that people still fear San Gonzalo's witch books because they still believe witchcraft is the cause of unusual misfortune—and the witch books, which contain people's names and the amount that was paid to cast the spell on them, correspond to the government and Church archival records where peoples' lives and fates are recorded.

As you read, consider these questions:
1. What are the relationships among church, literacy, and power in Ecuador?
2. What are the three major explanations for literacy as power?
3. How does the witch book function in regards to literacy and power?

Since the period of European exploration to the present, and in every major area of the world, indigenous peoples have been reported to equate Western alphabetic writing with "magical" power, comparing writing to indigenous shamanism, witchcraft, and ritual methods for contacting supernatural spirits and foretelling the future. Such reports come from sources as diverse as Christopher Columbus and Thomas Harriot in the New World, nineteenth-century missionaries in Africa and Australia, and contemporary anthropologists working in South America and Melanesia.[1] In scholarly accounts the following explanations for these sorts

"Magical Literacy: Encountering a Witch's Book in Ecuador," by Peter Wogan, *Anthropological Quarterly* 71:4 (Oct. 1988), 186–201. Reprinted by permission of George Washington University.

of beliefs in magical literacy have been offered: 1) writing is an incomprehensible novelty; 2) writing is related to indigenous beliefs; and 3) writing symbolizes social groups and their power. What follows is a review of these previous accounts, with suggestions about how they might be improved. The article then focuses ethnographically on a specific case of magical literacy in Ecuador, where I encountered witchcraft based on a written book of names. By correlating this witchcraft with an indigenous group's specific experiences with archival literacy, the article contributes to understanding of magical literacy. A secondary advantage to the case I examine is that it involves a personal encounter with witchcraft (finding my own name in the witch's book); due to its obviously secretive nature, witchcraft has rarely been reported in depth in the Andean ethnographic literature (see Bolton 1974: 200). . . .

[To conserve space we have deleted here a section called "Major Explanations for Magical Literacy" (1,100 words and four footnotes). In this section Wogan discusses three major explanations for magical literacy: (1) writing is an incomprehensible novelty that causes nonliterate people to react with awe and fear; (2) writing is related to indigenous analogs, that is, writing may be considered magical when it corresponds to indigenous beliefs such as shamanism and witchcraft; (3) writing symbolizes Westerners and may be treated as a symbol of their power. Wogan proposes a fourth explanation that he develops in this essay: that magical beliefs reflect actual experiences with textual power. He uses elements of the second and third explanations above but rejects the first because the society in which he works is literate.—Editors]

WITCHCRAFT AND WRITING: A WITCH-SAINT'S BOOK

Salasaca is a 14-square-kilometer village of approximately 12,000 Quichua-speaking Indians, located south of Quito in the Andean region of Ecuador. Although most Salasaca families are dependent on subsistence agricultural production, as of recent decades many also seek outside income sources, particularly weaving sales and seasonal labor. Salasaca contact with the Catholic church has intensified since 1945, when a group of nuns started a permanent mission in Salasaca: this date marks the construction of a church in Salasaca, the initiation of regular mass and catechism services, and the beginning of formal education in Salasaca itself. Although writing has been almost exclusively controlled since the colonial period by Spanish-speaking blancos (whites), especially church and state officials, today most young Salasacas are bilingual in Spanish and Quichua, and they acquire basic literacy skills through (minimally) primary school education. Salasaca now has eight schools, including a high school, and the student population has been steadily growing. Still, school teachers, clergy, and state officials are usually whites, and interethnic relations are often marked by hostility and mistrust (see Whitten 1981).

Although San Gonzalo is the patron saint of a large Catholic church, the Salasacas say he is a "witch-saint" who kills people with a book of written names. San Gonzalo is represented by two statues: the statue outside the big church in Ambato, the provincial capital near Salasaca, and the small, one-foot copy of this statue maintained in a private residence. Apart from the difference in size, the two statues are identical: in both cases San Gonzalo is depicted as a monk with a harrowing, blank expression, blood trickling from his nose and ears, and a sword stabbed to the hilt in his upper back. The difference is that the San Gonzalo statue outside the church is supposed to be the church's official patron saint, especially according to local whites, whereas the small statue is the "witch-saint" who kills people. Both statues are incarnations of the same saint, but the small statue is used for witchcraft purposes: hence the small statue is actually controlled by a group of non-church-affiliated whites, who keep the statue in their private residence. These San Gonzalo "owners" (fundadora, Sp.; santoyuj, Q.) are two sisters from a lower-class white family: they are "owners" in the sense that they maintain the statue in their home, receive clients, and perform the ritual duties that activate San Gonzalo's witchcraft powers.[2]

The clients, who pay the San Gonzalo owners to have an enemy harmed or killed, are usually indigenous groups from the countryside surrounding Ambato (that is, Chibuleo, Pillahuín), as well as working-class or peasant whites. I concentrate here on the Salasacas' experiences with San Gonzalo.[3] The main reason for putting someone else's name in the book is envy or a personal conflict. For example, a Salasaca man told me that San Gonzalo's witchcraft explained why his weaving business suddenly fell apart. Within a short period of time, he lost most of his usual tapestry orders, he was robbed of a large sum of money while travelling, and he was forced to sell off some lands to pay his bills. Although he did not specify who did this to him, he said somebody must have put his name in San Gonzalo's book because of "envy" (envidiashca munda), the most common term used to describe others' witchcraft motivations. "Envy" was also mentioned in stories about interpersonal conflicts, such as the wife who told me that her husband had fallen sick because of witchcraft initiated by his jealous ex-girlfriend, and others who related bitter stories about fighting with their neighbors over property boundaries. Thus, San Gonzalo never kills people arbitrarily or on his own initiative: the killing or suffering is carried out through San Gonzalo, but always at the behest of some individual client. In some cases, the client may also visit a local witch, who will contact the statue owners on his or her behalf. There is, in short, a triad of collaborators responsible for the witchcraft: 1) San Gonzalo, the saint himself, 2) the San Gonzalo owners, that is, the owners of the small statue or the books, and 3) the individual client, that is, the victim's enemy, or the witch representing the client.

There are also various ritual objects and verbal formulae that activate San Gonzalo's powers. The client (or the witch representing the client) usually brings the saint owner some of the designated victim's personal items, such as clothes, hair, photographs, or sand from the victim's footprint. Similar to other witchcraft found throughout the world, these items are thought of as the embodiment of the victim's personhood (Salasacas say they represent the person's "soul," *alma espíritu, sami*), and they become the physical basis for the witch's attack. In addition, the San Gonzalo owner lights candles beside the statue every Tuesday and Friday night, and, with a personal article and the written name (see below), prays to San Gonzalo.[4] Usually the client gives the owner a package of candles, and while saying the prayers, the owner burns a candle. When these candles are completely burned up, the victim, whose soul is represented by the candle flame, should be dead.

However, the single most critical aspect of San Gonzalo's power is a large book, where the owner writes the victim's name. The personal articles vary and may even be omitted, but Salasacas say that if the person's name were not entered in the book, nothing would happen to the intended victim. On the basis of the book, which is placed beside the candles and other items during the prayers, San Gonzalo pursues the victim's soul (*almada perseguin*), making the victim burn up and eventually die or at least suffer misfortune.[5] This book's importance is further demonstrated by the belief that you can avoid death if you have your name removed from the book in time. To do this, the victim goes to the Ambato house of San Gonzalo and tells the saint owner his/her name and the (approximate) date on which he/she first became sick. The owner then looks up the victim's name in the books under that date, and, for a price, removes the name, either crossing or cutting out the name, or pulling the entire page out of the book. This procedure for name removal is quite expensive, costing as much as $200, about four months' wages.[6] The fact that removal of the written name effects a cure demonstrates the book's central role in this witchcraft.

Salasacas do not normally visit San Gonzalo to check through the books unless they have reason to suspect their names are entered there. They become suspicious when they experience sudden reversals of fortune or a persistent sickness that can not be cured by either Western doctors or indigenous healers (*jambicguna*). In most cases such suspicions of witchcraft are confirmed or established during a guinea pig-entrail diagnosis by an indigenous healer, who tells you that, if you want to get better, you have to get your name removed from the book in Ambato.

To give a fuller sense of how this witchcraft works, I will describe my own experience in finding my name in the witch-saint's book.

A PERSONAL ENCOUNTER WITH SAN GONZALO'S BOOK

Most Salasacas were understandably vague about the exact nature of San Gonzalo's book: revealing intimate knowledge of San Gonzalo can create the impression that you have engaged in this witchcraft yourself, so it's always safer to say as little as possible on the subject. As a result, many people understandably gave evasive answers or simply said they did not know anything at all about San Gonzalo. Fortunately, though, I did eventually make some headway with my inquiries. One thing that helped was my speaking in Salasaca Quichua. This put me into an unusual category of human being, perhaps something like "a strange but friendly foreigner": nobody was ever going to mistake me for a Salasaca, but my Quichua almost always bolstered the level of trust (*confianza*) in personal relationships. Over time, I also formed stronger, more intimate bonds with certain people through the course of normal social interaction, such as sharing meals and exchanging gifts, and, especially, by forming godparent relations. These finally gave me a true, comprehensible place in this kinship-based society.[7] This sort of improved rapport naturally facilitated all areas of my investigation, but no more so than with the highly sensitive topic of witchcraft. Once I had learned the basic story about San Gonzalo from a very close godparent, I went to other friends and acquaintances and told them what I already had heard, exploring what they were willing to confirm, disconfirm, or add to the story.[8] Especially since I already knew part of the story, these people were usually willing to talk with me about San Gonzalo's activities, albeit in rather general terms. Little by little, then, I learned about San Gonzalo, until the accounts eventually started to exhibit consensus.

For a long time I only heard these second-hand accounts, without ever actually getting to see the San Gonzalo books or the statue myself. I did not customarily ask friends to take me to see San Gonzalo, except some of my closest friends. They unfortunately truly did not know where to find the house; and I thought that, even if someone were to take me to the house, I would never get to see the books anyway. I therefore more or less resigned myself to never actually seeing the San Gonzalo books and statue . . . which made me all the more excited when, on a subsequent fieldwork trip in 1997, one of my Salasaca friends suddenly volunteered to take me to see San Gonzalo. Naturally I leapt at this opportunity to verify what I had heard about San Gonzalo and to follow up on some of my remaining questions. To give a fuller sense of San Gonzalo's witchcraft, below I describe what I witnessed during this visit with my Salasaca friend, a literate, middleaged farmer and weaver whom I will call Jorge.

On an early Sunday afternoon Jorge and I took a bus to the San Gonzalo owner's house on the outskirts of Ambato, just off the main road between Ambato and Salasaca. When we arrived, the owner was sitting on a street corner with a group of men passing around bottles of liquor. Judging by their dress, the neighborhood, and exclusive use of Spanish, I would think of these people as working-class whites. The owner was a middle-aged, small-framed woman, with missing front teeth and an affable manner. She warmly greeted Jorge in Spanish, exclaiming, "How have you been? Where have you been hiding? It's so great to see you. . . ." Clearly she had known Jorge for some time, though Jorge had told me earlier that he never engaged in witchcraft himself, that he only learned about San Gonzalo's methods when other people tried to put spells on him.

After showing Jorge and me her new, modest house, the owner led us across the street to a one-room shop, where she sold things like liquor, soda, matches, toilet paper, and candy. While a cheap radio blasted Spanish music and the group of friends carried on at the doorstep, we sat inside the store on a wooden bench and talked with the owner. When Jorge finally told the owner that we wanted to "have a look at the candle" *(una vista a la vela),* she instructed us each to buy a candle (in her store) and rub ourselves with it. Next we were told to write our names with a needle in the side of the candle. The owner then lit the candles and, examining the flame, she told us what the candle revealed about our fates. She first asked me if I was married. When I replied "yes," she asked whether I had had a girlfriend before getting married, to which I again replied affirmatively. The owner then announced that my ex-girlfriend was envious and trying to do me harm, that she was the one responsible for my suffering. She said the pain would start in my stomach and legs (I agreed that my stomach did not feel very good) and eventually spread to my whole body, turning into a grave illness. To my Salasaca friend, she said that he had had a conflict with a neighbor over land, and that now a nearby witch *(brujo)* was trying to harm him. Neither Jorge nor I said much in response to our diagnoses; we just agreed that this was bad news and that we should do something about it.

When we then asked to see San Gonzalo, from a locked cabinet the owner brought out a one-foot statue of San Gonzalo, which very closely resembled the official statue outside the church in Ambato. Jorge also asked about the books, saying he would like to see if his name was in there by any chance. Neither Jorge nor I had any reason to think that our names were actually in the San Gonzalo books, but Jorge knew that I expressly wanted to see the books. As we noted to each other in Quichua when left alone for a moment, the woman obviously did not mind revealing details about San Gonzalo, since she had already shown us the statue. In fact, the owner did not seem surprised by our request: she simply instructed her teenage daughter, who had entered the store by this point, to get the books from their house across the street. With nine notebooks brought back by the daughter, Jorge and I searched for our names for about twenty minutes, giving me a good chance to examine the books in detail. These were ordinary school notebooks, filled with names on the left side of the page, followed by the words "black mass" *(misa negra)* and prices that ranged from $20 to about $200.[9] My friend said that the lower prices must have been from books made several years ago; in fact, the higher prices were listed in the newest looking notebooks. All the writing was done in the same hand, neat and orderly. Each line had only one name, and there was a blank line between each name. Some of the name lines, however, had

been cut out with a pair of scissors; the owner explained that those lines were removed because the victim paid the price listed, which was also the price paid by the initial client (whose name was not listed).

After about twenty minutes, Jorge and I started getting ready to leave, without having found our names, but then the owner said she would bring us one more book to check. This book was much more impressive than the school notebooks: it was a foot high, heavy, and made with sturdy, blue covers and large, lined pages. We again searched without finding our names, but then the daughter asked us for the book so she could look more carefully. Within a few minutes the daughter pointed to a page where she had found my friend's name, with a price listed at $160, as well as my own name, priced at $200. As Jorge and I studied our written names with a mixture of shock and skepticism, we were told by the owner that this was a very serious matter, that our lives were in danger, and that we should pay the money right away to get our names removed from the book. She also said that if we paid, we would get back the personal article left there, which might be sand from a footprint or a piece of clothing. When pressed for more information about the article, she said we probably wouldn't be able to recognize it anyway, because we'd just get the remaining ashes.

For various reasons, I chose not to pay for the name removal: promising I would come back later with the cash, I simply paid a small fee ($3) for the look at the candle and books, and left without ever returning. Jorge left together with me, insisting he didn't need to pay anything because I had already paid for both of us. While I wouldn't have ruled out witchcraft in principle, there were contradictions and alternative explanations in this particular case that convinced me not to pay for the name removal. First, there was the general problem of motivation: I could not believe that my ex-girlfriend had come all the way from the United States to put my name in the witch's book, especially since we had parted on good terms over seven years earlier. This just was not plausible, and, for that matter, I could not think of anybody in the area who wanted me dead or hurt. Then there was the suspicious way in which my name was found in the book. It did not seem like a coincidence that I had first written my name in the candle, and that my written name appeared in the book that had been kept in a separate room. In other words, my guess was that the owners (most likely the daughter) had read my name off the candle, written it in the book in the other room, and then brought the book to me. These suspicions seemed confirmed by the fact that no lines were skipped between my name and the surrounding names (indicating mine was written in recently), and the fact that the owner's daughter located my own name for me.

Moreover, this skeptical interpretation was immediately affirmed by Jorge as we walked back to the bus stop. While I was still debating whether I should share my suspicions with him, he himself declared that it had all been a scam. He said they must have written our names on the spot; in fact, he was sure of this because he did not write his actual name in the candle, yet this other, false surname showed up in the book. He laughingly said they were just trying to rip us off, but that we had been even better at fooling them. And when I got home to my Salasaca family that night and told them what happened, they came to the same conclusions, saying the owners were just trying to get a gringo's money.

In this case, the Salasacas were echoing the views of many Ambato whites, who, if they had heard of San Gonzalo's witchcraft at all (many had not), told me that it was just an exploitative scam (*estafa, engaño*), a way to make money off the ignorance of the Indians. Indeed, as I was well aware, this interpretation is explicitly declared on a sign next to the church's San Gonzalo statue, which says:

> Respected devotee of San Gonzalo, please do not allow yourself to be fooled by the exploiters (*no se deje engañar por los explotadores*) that want to create surprises. God is the only one who cures and saves. God is the only giver of all good things. Devotion to San Gonzalo is for good and not for evil. Do not let them fool you if they say that your name is written somewhere else.[10]

It is not that these Ambato whites reject the concept of saints' miracles or witchcraft, just that they would not accept this particular witchcraft. As far as most white residents of Ambato are concerned, San Gonzalo is a martyr and a bona fide Catholic saint.[11]

With all of this in mind, I decided not to return to have my name removed from the book, for better or worse. But where does this leave San Gonzalo and the Salasacas? Is it that easy to unmask and explain away this witchcraft as a simple, exploitative fraud? For the reasons outlined in the next section, I would say the answer is "no": attitudes toward San Gonzalo are more complicated than either sheer rejection or blind acceptance.

DEEP, AMBIVALENT BELIEFS

This skepticism notwithstanding, a number of things make it clear that San Gonzalo's witchcraft is taken very seriously by the Salasacas. First of all, most Salasacas still say they believe that San Gonzalo can and does kill people, and some Salasacas *do* pay these extremely high prices to have names removed from and entered in the book. For example, one of the San Gonzalo owners caught by the police in 1996 reported that she generally charged $150 to have the name removed from the book, though that price was often lowered to around $100.[12] Even to pay $100 in 1996, which equaled about four months' wages, would be a major sacrifice, showing that at least some Salasacas deeply believe in San Gonzalo's powers.

And even those who saw my experience with San Gonzalo as fraudulent exploitation still believed in this witchcraft at another level. The Salasaca friends who told me that I was just being tricked by the owners were, nonetheless, concerned that I had given them my real name. They said I should have given them another name, so that my name would not appear in the book, as Jorge did; and they were relieved when I pointed out that my real English name is not the same as what I told the owner in Spanish. There is no contradiction between this disbelief with regard to my individual experience and their continued belief in San Gonzalo's witchcraft as a whole (per Evans-Pritchard's classic study of witchcraft). Of course at a certain point such empirical failings or alternative explanations may become overwhelmingly embarrassing to the whole system, throwing it into question, but that crisis point had apparently not been reached by my Salasaca friends. Even my more skeptical friends never referred to San Gonzalo as a "stick saint" (*caspi santo*), the insult term reserved for saints who supposedly have no powers.[13] I would characterize most Salasacas, then, as having a healthy skepticism about San Gonzalo's witchcraft, while still taking it quite seriously.

But perhaps the best illustration of the depth of beliefs in San Gonzalo's witchcraft is his continual regeneration in the face of repeated attempts to kill him off. It turns out that San Gonzalo often gets killed, only to resume his witchcraft business a few months later. These San Gonzalo rebirths are worth chronicling not only because they demonstrate the depth of beliefs in San Gonzalo, but also because they reveal complex Salasaca attitudes toward San Gonzalo.

One of the most famous of these incidents occurred around 1992, when a Salasaca woman protested the stipulated fee—$100, a very large sum—for the removal of her name from San Gonzalo's book. When the owner would not lower the price, the Salasaca woman complained openly at a Salasaca community meeting about the prices being charged by the San Gonzalo owner. As noted earlier, witchcraft is understandably a non-public subject, but, in this case, once the silence was broken by this woman, others started to openly complain about San Gonzalo, creating a chorus of angry resentment. They eventually took their complaints to the president of UNIS (Unión Indígena de Salasacas), a community government organization, who went into Ambato to negotiate a compromise with the saint owners, but the owners still refused to lower the price or turn over the books. Later, responding to calls by UNIS leaders on the local loudspeakers, a large, angry group of Salasacas returned to Ambato to get San Gonzalo by force. Against the protests of the saint owners, the crowd forced its way into the house and removed the San Gonzalo statue, books, and victims' personal belongings. The Ambato police, who had arrived by this point, would not allow these items to be taken back to Salasaca, so they were temporarily stored in the Ambato hospital. About four days later, hundreds of Salasacas and other local Indians came to the hospital to witness the public destruction of San Gonzalo. The UNIS president stood on a balcony, displaying some of the books and personal articles that were found. As the crowd cheered, all of these materials were thrown on the ground, doused with gasoline, and burned. Witnesses say that the books, rather than burning in an ordinary way, exploded in flames at intervals, then sat quietly, then burst into flames all over again. The San Gonzalo statue, however, would not burn, supposedly because of its special witch-saint powers, so it was brought back to the central plaza in Salasaca, where it was chopped with axes into small pieces and finally burned. The fact that the Salasacas were so concerned with getting rid of San Gonzalo, even risking their personal safety by marching into a white family's house in Ambato, clearly demonstrates that they take this witchcraft quite seriously.

Most Salasacas I talked with seemed proud of their destruction of San Gonzalo in 1992, crediting themselves with having put an end to his long reign of terror over the surrounding countryside. But while impressive, the Salasaca victory over San Gonzalo was only temporary. San Gonzalo obviously later regenerated himself: after all, I saw him in 1997 with my friend Jorge, and, in fact, I was also able to visit a resurrected San Gonzalo in 1994, when I first arrived in Ecuador. To find the San Gonzalo house in 1994 I simply went to the Miraculous Medallion church in Ambato, and began talking with an old woman selling candles near the church steps. After gathering that I wanted to see San Gonzalo (the witch-saint), the woman called over a young boy, who told me to start walking down the block by myself, that is, so that we would not be seen leaving the church together. The boy caught up with me at the next block, then guided me to a small house about three blocks behind the church. In a bare outer room I sat in a wooden chair and talked with a woman sitting behind a desk like a secretary. She indicated that San Gonzalo was in the next room (because I could not pay the high fee required, I never got to see the books or the statue that day). When I asked whether San Gonzalo had not been destroyed earlier by the Salasacas, she acknowledged the incident, but said the statue was put back together with the pieces that were left in Salasaca, so now he was fine. It turned out, then, that San Gonzalo was not dead after all.

And in 1996, after I had returned to the U.S., two sisters were again arrested and imprisoned for running a San Gonzalo operation. In an article that appeared in the Ambato newspaper, one of the sisters described a San Gonzalo operation very much like what I had heard about. The article reported, for example, the following familiar details:

> When the victim had just barely arrived, they asked his name, and wrote it down in a black book without the patient realizing it; in this way, later they could say that, in fact, his name was in the book all along. . . . In the book of black masses, appear the names of the victims and the amount that they have to pay to save themselves from the witchcraft.[14]

According to the article, this business was recently started by a woman who was imitating the success of the Camana sisters, the owners I visited in 1997:

> Margoht Heredia said that she started out as an intermediary for the witches of the name Camana, from the Banos Road. They saw that the business was profitable and put up her own

consultation room on the corner of Tomas Sevilla and Darquea Streets.

Margoht Heredia was thrown in jail but, just a year later, my Salasaca friend Jorge and I found an active, open-for-business San Gonzalo operation in Ambato, run by the Camana sisters who had inspired Ms. Heredia's satellite operation.

When I pointed out during my 1997 visit that San Gonzalo was still doing harm in Ambato, some Salasacas acknowledged that they heard the witch-saint was back in town, that he apparently was not killed in 1992 after all. They lamented that, as a powerful witch-saint, San Gonzalo will probably continue to relocate and regenerate himself in the future; judging by San Gonzalo's many recent resurrections, this seems like a reliable prediction. In fact, beyond the turbulent 1992–97 years, San Gonzalo has a long history of narrowly escaping angry mobs or getting destroyed, only to resurrect himself again shortly afterwards. People say that in the 1940s San Gonzalo was kept in a house on the outskirts of Ambato, where the Bella Vista stadium now stands, but he later had to escape with his owners just before an angry mob could burn him. He was then resettled next to the Plaza Ovina marketplace, on the other side of Ambato, but yet again, sometime in the 1980s, he was forced to escape, this time to a marketplace near the River Ambato, not too far from the center of Ambato. The San Gonzalo house I found in 1994 was in a separate location, closer to the town center, so obviously the witch-saint had moved again. These were the moves that I was told about or personally witnessed, but, given their frequency and Salasacas' reluctance to reveal publicly very detailed knowledge about San Gonzalo, I would not be surprised if the witch-saint had moved several other times during the course of this century.[15]

This history of resurrections reveals a highly complex—conflictive, ambivalent, but intense and ongoing—relationship between the Salasacas (and others) and San Gonzalo. On the one hand, many Salasacas want to rid themselves of the witch-saint, showing deep anger and resentment toward his tyranny. At this larger, community level, they have even taken strong measures to rid themselves of San Gonzalo once and for all. On the other hand, many individuals obviously continue to go back to see San Gonzalo, whether to have their names removed or enter others' names, which allows the saint to regenerate (with the help of the San Gonzalo owners, of course). If these Salasaca individuals did not believe in San Gonzalo's witchcraft, they could simply stop going to see the saint, allowing the witchcraft business to die its own natural death. An opportune moment for this sort of moratorium would be immediately after the burning of all the books, when the old accounts and grievances between individuals are wiped out. Yet this has not happened, nor does it seem likely to happen anytime soon, raising the question of San Gonzalo's continual appeal. To be so feared, despised, and yet continuously regenerated, clearly San Gonzalo must have deep meaning for the Salasacas. What, then, is the meaning or the function that San Gonzalo serves?

While there are numerous theories explaining witchcraft in general, ranging from functionalist to intellectualist to symbolic accounts, these theories do not explain the specific meaning of San Gonzalo's book: they still do not tell us why Salasaca witchcraft should take this particular form as opposed to anything else. This is not a minor problem: the book is so central to San Gonzalo's witchcraft that it cannot be dismissed as an irrelevant, arbitrary detail. While pressing to uncover literacy's specific meaning for the Salasacas, I will now employ certain aspects of previously offered explanations for magical literacy, and suggest a separate but complementary approach that more precisely explains the specific meaning of San Gonzalo's book.

THE WITCH'S COMMENTARY ON WHITE POWER

San Gonzalo is clearly associated with the whites and their power. San Gonzalo's book possesses the ultimate power of life and death, and, especially since the Salasacas always have the option to visit indigenous witches, it is significant that the San Gonzalo owners are literate, Spanish-speaking whites, and that San Gonzalo is a Catholic saint from a white church in Ambato. On this basis alone it would be safe to say that San Gonzalo's book symbolizes white identity and power. The exact aspects of the power represented by San Gonzalo will be more precisely identified below, but, for the moment, this power can be glossed as the traditional power held by middle- and upper-class whites in political, economic, social, and textual realms. Of course, given the rigid class system, not all whites are equally powerful: hence many poor white farmers visit San Gonzalo, in addition to indigenous groups like the Salasacas. However, as a starting point for analysis, the generalized term "white power" will be used here.

San Gonzalo's book, as an image of white power, is borrowed by Salasaca individuals as an instrument in their interpersonal conflicts. The book is also helpful, though, in allowing the Salasacas as a group to comprehend, reflect, and comment on white power. Like a myth or some other symbolic form, this witchcraft-by-book allows the Salasaca community to contemplate their own relation to white power and domination. San Gonzalo's witchcraft is like a story the Salasacas tell themselves about their relation with white power, or, perhaps better stated, their own anthropology of the Other, their own social theory. While this may sound like an overly intellectualized interpretation, we have to keep in mind that Salasaca witchcraft addresses a very real, nontrivial question: how to understand and come to terms with white power and domination? For the Salasacas, who confront this power differential almost every day on diverse levels, this is a pressing, important question, one that addresses a major contradiction in the social order. As much as anything else in the Salasacas' universe, this is the sort of ambiguous, troublesome social predicament that calls for explanation. Also,

this witchcraft is integrally connected to individuals' physical and emotional experiences, so obviously this theorizing is not being carried out at a purely abstract level.

What commentary, then, does San Gonzalo provide on white power? First, San Gonzalo beliefs clearly acknowledge whites' power, rather than disregarding it. In addition, that power is being criticized: San Gonzalo is, after all, a witch and an ally of the devil, the source of all evil and immoral behavior; San Gonzalo's book is used to kill people; and the Salasacas have repeatedly tried to rid themselves of this witchcraft. In short, San Gonzalo is deemed evil, which means white power is also morally condemned in the Salasacas' eyes, similar to the devil pacts that Taussig (1980) says contain a moral critique of new economic modes of exchange.

But feelings about San Gonzalo are more complex than a purely negative commentary. From the patient's perspective, for example, you could say that San Gonzalo saves people; his book has the power to cure illness, if you can just get your name out in time. In this sense, San Gonzalo is like other Salasaca saints who both help and punish you, especially if you do not properly honor them. For example, a friend told me that, after deciding not to sponsor a fiesta for the Santísima Cruz saint from the Chilcapamba section of Salasaca, that same week he tripped and hurt his arm. Later he almost choked on a piece of meat, which he interpreted as the saint's punishment for not sponsoring the fiesta (he therefore decided to sponsor the fiesta). Similarly, if you promise but do not go to the Teligote fiesta in honor of San Antonio, you and/or your animals will suffer. On the other hand, these saints award benefits—especially a better harvest and healthy cattle—to those who honor them with payment, ideally including a full fiesta, which can cost between $500–$1000. San Gonzalo, too, will punish someone who does not provide the required payment; but, if you do as instructed, San Gonzalo cures you.

San Gonzalo, however, exceeds the normal level of a saint's vindictiveness, since he causes major suffering and death, and his works are primarily focused on hurting other people. This is why people refer to San Gonzalo as a "witch-saint" (brujosanto), whereas the others are simply called "saint" (santo). Also, San Gonzalo cures people only in the negative sense of withdrawing his own witchcraft; he does not do miraculous cures like San Antonio, for example, who can cure you in exchange for a candle and small cash offering. For that matter, San Gonzalo also surpasses the vindictiveness of other witches, since his prices are exploitatively high, which the Salasacas resent. San Gonzalo—and, by extension, white power—is therefore essentially seen as morally wrong and exploitative.

In periodically trying to rid itself of the saint, the Salasaca community as a whole shows it does not accept this white power and exploitation. On the other hand, this white power has not been eliminated since it proves helpful to individuals in their interpersonal conflicts. White power, then, is accepted begrudgingly, but hardly fatalistically. Salasacas wish to live without this power, but must accept it as long as their own witchcraft conflicts persist. The attempts to eliminate San Gonzalo therefore represent a double critique of white power and Salasaca witchcraft, against both of which the Salasacas chafe. This is important to keep in mind, for the emphasis on resistance to domination can easily blind us to the complex nature of such beliefs, including their internal critique.[16] Similarly, I want to stress that San Gonzalo beliefs are only one aspect of the Salasacas' responses to literacy. Other responses—which cannot be analyzed here—include a book of names used by God to determine death dates, and lists used to contact deceased relatives during the Day of the Dead. If we considered these other responses, including more practical mastery of literacy skills, we would find an even more complex, fuller range of Salasaca reactions to literacy and white power.

There are several advantages to this writing-as-symbol approach, starting, above all, with the fact that it provides a fuller, more specific (albeit not final) answer to the question of why there is a book of names. Furthermore, in answering this question in terms of an indigenous critique of white power, this approach provides a window on Salasaca perspectives on ethnicity and domination. This is important, because, whereas other symbolic forms like ritual, myth, devil pacts, and millenarianism have been extensively studied, the window provided by magical writing has rarely been gazed through by anthropologists. Another advantage is this approach counteracts the evolutionary assumption, described above, that magical literacy beliefs will inevitably disappear when writing is understood; this symbolic approach can make better sense of magical literacy beliefs that continue despite extensive contact with literacy.

Still, these advantages notwithstanding, central questions remain unanswered: why choose writing as a symbol for these groups and their power as opposed to any number of other objects—or, for that matter, phrases, gestures, or other behavior—that could be used? If a symbol of white power is needed, why not use distinctive dress, speech, ritual, technology, or anything else? Again, why a book of names? And what exactly is the power that the Salasacas are responding to? The problem is that the symbolic-critique approach can never answer these questions about the specific meaning of literacy until it starts to consider the native group's specific, actual experiences with writing. That is, we should not disregard, as too often happens, the way magical beliefs are also literally about literacy, not just symbols of something else.[17] Developing this fourth line of argument, below I show that Salasaca literacy beliefs derive from specific literacy practices and native understanding of power relations.[18]

SPECIFIC ARCHIVAL SOURCES FOR SAN GONZALO

There are various possible textual sources for the beliefs in San Gonzalo, including the following types of writing that the Salasacas have had contact with: land titles, taxes, documents for legal disputes, state documentation, church documentation, the Bible, newspapers, educational materials, literacy campaigns, and scientific investigators' writings. If we considered this long list, we would not reach many conclusions: this list, ranging from legal disputes to anthropologists' notes, does not rule out much of anything. The list can be narrowed down, though, by isolating the sources that most closely correspond—in function, appearance, and content—to San Gonzalo's book, allowing us to make much more precise linkages between San Gonzalo and the Salasacas' experiences with white power. The key correspondence, above all, is the archival function. San Gonzalo's book is a type of archival literacy. Writing is used to store information for extended periods of time, to systematically organize this information, and to selectively retrieve it at later dates. This archival function is facilitated by name lists contained in large books organized by date of entry, which allows retrieval by name or date. As I will show below, this archival function is most fully paralleled in state and church documentation, and land titles. Furthermore, the Salasacas have had extensive contact in the twentieth century with these archival sources; the archives are maintained by whites, and they all impinge on important aspects of Salasaca life. They are therefore the most probable source of San Gonzalo beliefs.[19] In concentrating on archival literacy, I am following Joanne Rappaport's work on Andean literacy, particularly her emphasis on legal writing: "It is more properly within the legal document . . . that the impact of literacy among Andean native peoples is most clearly evident" (Rappaport 1994: 272).[20]

The Salasacas have had extensive contact with the Ecuadorian state through the Civil Registry (Registro Civil). Since its creation in 1901 the Salasacas have been officially required to visit the Civil Registry to obtain certificates of birth, marriage, and death, and, since 1965, to obtain personal identification cards (Flores Freire 1987: 8–9). According to the Salasacas and some Civil Registry officials, enforcement of these rules was previously lax, but, at least within the past several decades (especially after the Civil Registry Reform Law of 1966), most Salasacas have consistently visited the Civil Registry. These visits are required by a tight system of interlocking authorization requirements: for example, a state birth certificate is required for a child's baptism, communion, school enrollment, and to obtain an identification card. The Civil Registry is clearly an archive organized by name and date. All of the Civil Registry forms are saved in the local office in large books organized by year, with separate books for birth, marriage, and death. Clients who need updated copies of their certificates come to the Civil Registry office and have the form searched for under the appropriate year and name.

Throughout the country's history, the Catholic Church has also kept records for births (baptisms), marriages, and deaths, as well as, more recently, confirmations. Following the religious ceremony, the priest or sacristan fills out small forms with the basic information (that is, names of parents, godparents, godchild, date, name of priest). Before these forms are sent to the provincial archbishop's office, the information is copied into large books (for example, Libro de Partidas Bautismales) with vertical columns. Whenever someone needs to retrieve a copy of his certificate (most commonly a baptism record for confirmation or marriage), s/he visits the local church and has that certificate searched for according to the date of the ceremony and the names of the participants.

Finally, though less systematically employed than the Civil Registry and church archives, land titles are maintained in archives kept by local "notary publics" (notario, escribano). Since most Salasacas simply keep land inheritance within their family (bilaterally and equally among parents' children), many have not felt the need for any legal writing to insure title to their land. Nor has the community held common land titles (these may have been lost in an earthquake in the eighteenth century). However, some form of land writing has been used by those who buy land outside of the family, those who wish greater security for their land, and those who need legal title to get a bank loan (all of these situations are increasingly common). In some cases, though less frequently these days, the buyer and seller simply obtain a land contract written up by non-official whites, usually a neighbor or godparent relation; alternatively, the contract is written (or typed) by a notary public in a nearby city. In the latter case records are archived in the office of the notary public. For example, the "first notary public" of Pelileo has 407 books of such records, dating from 1910 to 1973, when she took this office and inherited these books from the previous "first notary" of Pelileo. If necessary, Salasacas can return to this notary (or the other two Pelileo notaries) to have papers searched for under the date of the original land sale and names of the seller or buyer. Salasacas certainly see these notary books as important archives: as one friend put it, "If by some chance we lose our land writing, it will be there, archived, in the old book" (De repente achpa papilda chingachiqui, chibi saquirin, archivashca, ruculibrubi).

In all three cases, then, an archive is maintained by whites, and Salasacas regularly use the archive to retrieve information by name and date, closely paralleling San Gonzalo's book. The correspondence is even more precise in terms of writing materials: all three archives as well as San Gonzalo's book (and the list of souls and God's book), are written with black ink on white, lined paper. This writing corresponds most closely to a special type of lined, numbered paper, literally called "numbered paper" (papel numerado, Spanish), which has been used throughout the century for Civil Registry certificates and land titles.[22] "Numbered paper" was used for certificates from the Civil Registry's inception in 1901 until 1985, when other types of paper were introduced.[23] Until 1985 any client who wanted a certificate from the Civil Registry first had to buy a sheet of "numbered paper" in a bookstore and bring it back to the

Civil Registry. There, an official used it to type up the certificate. In many cases, the Salasaca client then had physically to carry the certificate to a church or school official, as described above. To this day, land titles are also made up on "numbered paper," which is supplied by the notary publics; once again, the Salasacas have physical contact with this lined paper, since they receive a copy of the title and carefully store it in their homes.

In sum, the Salasacas have had extended, even tactile contact with "numbered paper."[24] The church, on the other hand, does not use "numbered paper," nor does it usually give clients any papers to take home. However, the church books for retrieving records are written on white, lined paper, and, before 1955, the church used lined paper instead of standardized forms. The church writing is also done in black ink.[25]

These similarities—in terms of archival function and writing materials—therefore suggest that the most likely sources for San Gonzalo beliefs are the church and state documents, as well as the land titles. San Gonzalo's book and these three sources (as opposed to other candidates) use almost identical materials: white, lined paper and black ink; furthermore, there is a clear archival function in each case. Given the great consistency among these types of writing, it seems fair to say that San Gonzalo's book draws upon these associations, rather than just being used as a more or less arbitrary symbol for white power. Furthermore, the power represented and criticized by San Gonzalo is church and state bureaucracy, rather than capitalist structures or anything else. Since these bureaucratic aspects are not usually considered in analyses of indigenous reactions to dominant society, these witchcraft beliefs shed greater light on indigenous perspectives. They allow us to see exactly what the Salasacas focus on in their interactions with white power, as well as how they critically evaluate that power.

NAMING PRACTICES

To explain San Gonzalo's specific focus on writing, one could also say, as in the second explanation above, that writing corresponds to—and is equated with—indigenous beliefs and practices.[26] In the Salasaca case, names are equated with individual essence, influencing perceptions of written lists of names like San Gonzalo's book.[27]

One example is the Salasaca practice of naming children rucu and vija, which translate as "old man" and "old woman," respectively. That is, a child who has the same full name as his or her parents or grandparents of the same sex will be called "old man" or "old woman" by family members (it is quite surprising and confusing the first time you hear a one-year-old baby called "old man"!).[28] These children are given the same personal names as their elders as a way of honoring and remembering them, with the understanding that a rucu/vija child will carry much of the personality of his or her elder namesake. People say, for example, that a *rucu* will have the heart and thoughts of his father *(libre shunguda apan, paibug yuyida charinga)*, increasing the father and son's chances for harmonious relations.[29]

The same principle of name-personality connection is found in other areas. Two people who share the same first name, for example, may refer (often jokingly) to each other as tocayo, which lightheartedly implies some sort of personality or kinship connection. And, partly because of the lack of specificity in personal and family names, most Salasacas are actually best known by colorful nicknames such as Guinea Pig Face *(cuy cara),* Bishop *(obispo),* and Rabbit *(conejo).* The nicknames usually center on some identifiable characteristic—often a weak spot—of the person in question. There are no rules about creating nicknames, but many are coined when a group of males weave together day after day—in other words, in a social situation among friends and kin. Once again, the (nick)name captures personal essence. Finally, a similar principle operates when healers name mountains in order to call upon their powers, when they call patients' names in order to get their souls to come back into their bodies, or when living relatives call dead relatives' names to send them back to the afterlife after Day of the Dead ceremonies. For the Salasacas the name is therefore equated with personal essence, whether of a child, a sick person, a dead relative, or a mountain. This naming principle is, in short, an indigenous analog that makes Salasacas predisposed to focus their magical literacy on lists of names. That is, since the Salasacas themselves equate the name with personal essence, they are predisposed to accept the idea that a written name can represent and kill one's soul.

On the other hand, since the Salasacas have the option to reject writing-witchcraft in favor of other witchcraft methods, further explanation is required to account for San Gonzalo's appeal. For the full answer, we have to return to the previous point about social/textual power: there has to be something powerful about those white, literate naming practices to compel the Salasacas to incorporate them into their witchcraft. That power seems to be writing's ability to define individual existence. As various studies (see Foster 1991: 244–248) have shown, ostensibly innocuous records—birth certificates, census records, registrations—actually construct identities, so that, ultimately, one's very existence is defined by state records. For example, in 1995 the Ecuadorian government encouraged citizens who had not done so to register themselves at the Civil Registry, waging a campaign primarily through a flood of television commercials informing viewers that the usual registration fees were being temporarily waived. The commercial's main character, an animated toucan, perfectly captured the significance of state documentation when he flatly told viewers that, "If a child is not registered, it's as if he didn't exist" *(si el niño no está inscrito es como si no existiera).* That is, an individual's existence is only real to the state insofar as that person's name is located in the archives. The Salasacas are reminded of this

every time they return for another Civil Registry certificate (for baptism, marriage, schooling), forced to prove that they still exist in the records. This system is perhaps best captured in the insomnia scene in García Márquez's *One Hundred Years of Solitude* (1967:138; my translation), where archival writing is parodied in these terms:

> At the entrance to the road into the swamp, they had put up a sign that said "Macondo" and a larger one on the main street that said "God Exists." In all the houses, keys to memorizing objects and feelings had been written. But the system demanded so much vigilance and moral strength that many succumbed to the spell of an imaginary reality, one invented by themselves, which was less practical but more comforting to them.

Despite their lack of literacy skills, the Salasacas have long understood this "imaginary reality" created by writing. They are particularly concerned with archival records from the Civil Registry and church, where names are officially given. The church naming is particularly important: hence the Quichua word for the baptismal naming is shutichina, literally, "too make the name," whereas the naming at the Civil Registry is simply known as asentachina, from the Spanish verb asentar, "to note down." From the perspective of the Catholic Church, the naming is also critically important, as baptism is the rite of passage that brings the child into the Christian community; echoing church teaching, Salasacas say that a non-baptized child is a "pagan-savage" *(auca)* or "devil's child" *(diablobug huahua).* The Salasacas are therefore concerned with San Gonzalo's written lists of names because of their own equation between name and essence, which corresponds to church and state textual practices. . . .

[We have here deleted a brief section called "Writing as a Western Fetish," where Wogan argues that white Ecuadorians consider writing prestigious, a view that is reinforced by the Catholic Church and state authorities through schooling and the extensive social documentation required of citizens in Ecuador. He concludes that the focus on magic among the indigenous people of Salasaca is a reflection of the exalted view of writing held by white Ecuadorians.—Editors]

CONCLUSION

As an example of magical literacy, I have explored the sources of Salasaca beliefs in San Gonzalo's textual witchcraft. By comparing function (archival literacy), materials (black ink on white, lined paper), degree of contact and importance (extensive contact throughout this century, government and church authorizations), and correspondence with Salasaca beliefs (naming), I narrowed down the likely sources for San Gonzalo's book to church and state registration, and land titles. Because these three archives semble San Gonzalo's book more closely than other types of writing known to the Salasacas, they most likely serve as prototypical models for the witch's book. This is not to deny that other literacy practices may also be associated with San Gonzalo's power, but only to highlight these three types of archival literacy as the most important inspirations for San Gonzalo beliefs. Although the Salasacas have less frequent dealings with land titles than Civil Registry and church documentation, and the land titles are not directly concerned with naming, the land titles are included in this "top-three list" because of their obvious importance for a family's survival.

Beyond treating literacy as a symbol of outside power, I have tried to demonstrate that a group's actual experiences with writing can shed light on their magical beliefs. While the white Ecuadorians have presumably fetishized writing, the Salasacas' San Gonzalo beliefs do not merely reflect this emphasis, but have focused on specific, important aspects of literacy's power as judged by their own standards. All these approaches to magical literacy build on each other: I have used the argument about indigenous analogs (though with a focus on naming rather than shamanism, unlike previous studies), and I agree that writing serves as a symbol of whites' power. My concern, though, is to show how focusing on actual experiences of textual power helps to account for beliefs in magical literacy.

NOTES

Acknowledgments. For their careful readings of this text I am grateful to Judith Irvine, Joanne Rappaport, Richard Parmentier, David Sutton, and the anonymous reviewers for *Anthropological Quarterly.* I also greatly appreciate support provided by the Mellon Fellowship Program and a 1997 Jane's Travel Grant, from Brandeis University's Latin American Studies Program.

1. Although the following list is not exhaustive, it includes some of the authors who have either provided numerous historical examples of such reactions to writing and/or analyses of these reactions: Axtell (1985); Bhabha (1985); Bledsoe and Robey (1993); Gebhart-Sayer (1985); Galb (1963); Goody (1968: 205; 1987: 131–132); Gow (1990); Guss (1986; 1996); Harbsmeier (1988: 253–56); Helms (1988: 183); Hill and Wright (1988: 92–93); Holbek (1989); Hugh-Jones (1989); Kulick and Stroud (1990); Léry (1990 [1580]): 134–135; Lévy-Bruhl (1923: 368); Meggitt (1968); (1982); Perrin (1985); Platt (1992, 1997); Rappaport (1987, 1990); Rescaniere (1972); Seed (1991); Street (1987); Wachtel (1973: 42–47); Wogan (1994). The following authors provide three or more (as many as ten) examples of such reactions to writing: Gelb (1963); Harbsmeier (1988: 253–256); Helms (1988: 183); Holbek (1989); Lévy-Bruhl (1923: 368); Seed (1991: 19); Wogan (1994: 408–409).

2. Some people told me there are various San Gonzalo owners, but, because of my experience with the Camana sisters, I primarily refer to them below. Also, although the small statue is usually used for witchcraft, I have heard of a few cases in the past where witches and other individuals prayed to the church statue to have witchcraft done.

3. San Gonzalo's fame is so great, at least in certain networks, that Ecuadorians also sometimes come from as far away as the coast (one day by bus), or the northern capital, Quito (four hours by bus), for a consultation with the witch-saint. An Ambato taxi driver told me that, during the past three decades, he had often taken visitors from distant cities to see San Gonzalo. On the other hand, most middle-class whites I talked to in Quito had never heard of San Gonzalo. San Gonzalo is also sometimes referred to as "San Gonzalez," but I retain the more common term here.

4. The owner's prayers are often characterized as "calling your name" *(cambug shutida cayan)* and compared to indigenous witches who call their victims' names in order to catch and harm them.

5. Although some say that San Gonzalo's victims may just go crazy or become drunkards, most say they die without any intermediate, lesser punishments.

6. Some Salasacas say that, when the victim returns to Salasaca, he or she gets purified by a healer, and they have the paper burned; further details were not forthcoming.

7. On Ecuadorian indigenous preferences for foreign godparents, see Belote and Belote (1977).

8. Despite the power differential in our relationship, the Salasacas were perfectly capable of declining to answer my questions if they were not interested or willing. For a useful discussion of fieldwork power dynamics and ethics in Ecuador, see Weiss (1993); on "dissembling behavior" among the Coaiquer, see Ehrenreich (1985).

9. No one name seemed to be repeated. Since I did not recognize any of these names, I could not discern any pattern in the types of people listed (for example, how sick they were or what sort of sickness they had).

10. A newspaper report (*El Heraldo,* July 18, 1996, p. 1) also referred to the witchcraft as a "scam" *(estafa),* and described similarly devious methods for getting the victim's name in the book. This report is discussed further below.

11. However, San Gonzalo is not listed in Delaney's *Dictionary of Saints* (1980).

12. This was reported in the Ambato daily newspaper: "Curanderos indígenas cómplices de brujas" (Indigenous healers accomplices to witches), *El Heraldo,* July 18, 1996, p. 1.

13. For example, some refer to the small saint in the Chilcapamba Valley of Salasaca, Cruz Santísima Santo, as a worthless "stick saint."

14. "Curanderos indígenas cómplices de brujas," (Indigenous healers accomplices to witches), *El Heraldo,* July 18, 1996, p. 1.

15. Elders told me that San Gonzalo has always existed, that even their grandparents talked about him, so he has clearly been around since at least the turn of the century. For obvious reasons, no historical documentation of this witchcraft exists, so it is hard to know more about San Gonzalo apart from what people remember.

16. Here I follow Brown (1991), who has made this cautionary point with regard to millenarian movements and internal critiques of sorcery.

17. This problem exists, more generally, with any symbolic approaches that stray too far from social realities and native, conscious explanations. Most immediately relevant is Taussig (1980), whose own model did not match his ethnographic material.

18. This sort of approach to magical literacy beliefs has previously been used in several studies of writing associated with religious specialists, who monopolize supernatural contact and writing skills. One of the fullest (article-length) accounts is Bledsoe and Robey (1993), but see also Gelb (1963).

19. Tax records are also stored in archives and the Salasacas are deeply worried by any threat of taxes. Other authors (Sánchez Parga 1983; Valarezo 1991) have mentioned taxes as the source of magical literacy beliefs in Ecuador. This explanation does not work well for the Salasacas, who have essentially avoided paying taxes in this century because of indigenous exemptions for land taxes, their lack of official land titles (see below), and the absence of other municipal services like sewage that could be taxed.

20. See Rappaport (1987, 1990, 1994) and Platt (1992, 1997). Platt (1992: 136) has argued that the "myth of the archive has also struck firm roots in the modern consciousness of the Andean 'people called indians.' "

21. The Quichua term for "numbered paper" is *hila rurashca papil,* that is, paper made with lines.

22. More recently, from 1985–1995, the standard Registro Civil paper became a type of blank, bond paper *(papel bon),* and in 1996 the Registro Civil started using special, standardized forms.

23. The Registro Civil books for certificates contain forms, but not numbered, lined paper *(papel numerado).* These forms, which also follow a linear format, with dotted lines where the information is to be entered, have not changed much since 1901, except that since 1966 the birth certificate forms have a section where the child's fingerprint is entered.

24. In terms of the importance of black ink, it is significant that, in referring to the writing up of a land title, you can say "ña binda yanaquiga," "now it's been well taken care of," or, literally, "it's become very black." The distinction between type and script does not appear to be particularly significant for the Salasacas, though some note that typed documents are nicer and clearer than handwritten ones.

25. For examples of this approach, see Axtell (1985); Goody (1968: 201–205; 1987: 131–132); Gow (1990); Hill and Wright (1988: 92–93); Kulick and Stroud (1990); Meggit (1968); Platt (1992); Perrin (1985).

26. Of course belief in the power of names is not limited to Salasaca or the Andes (others report Ecuadorian indigenous groups that rarely give full names to outsiders and frequently change children's names), but is found in many parts of the world (for example, Sutton 1997).

27. A child usually goes exclusively by the *ruca/vija* name until he or she is about 14 years old, at which point the name becomes embarrassing.

28. The connection is said to be stronger for males than females because the males share more name components across generations.

29. See Guss (1986); Harbsmeier (1988); Rappaport (1987: 47); Wogan (1994: 420).

REFERENCES CITED

Axtell, James. 1985. *The invasion within: The contest of cultures in colonial North America.* Oxford: Oxford University Press.

Belote, Jim and Linda Smith Belote. 1977. The limitation of obligation in Saraguro kinship. In *Andean kinship and marriage,* ed. Ralph Bolton and Enrique Mayer. Washington DC: American Anthropological Association.

Bhabha, Homi. 1985. Signs taken for wonders: Questions of ambivalence and authority under a tree outside Delhi, May 1817. In *Europe and its Other,* ed. Francis Barker, Peter Hulme, Margaret Iverson, and Diana Loxley. Proceedings of the Essex Conference on the Sociology of Literature, 1984. Essex: University of Essex Press.

Bledsoe, Caroline H. and Kenneth M. Robe. 1993. Arabic literacy and secrecy among the Mende of Sierra Leone. In *Cross-cultural approaches to literacy,* ed. Brian V. Street. Cambridge: Cambridge University Press.

Bolton, Ralph. 1974. To kill a thief: A Kallawaya sorcery session in the Lake Titicaca region of Peru. *Anthropos* 69: 191–215.

Brotherston, Gordon. 1979. *Image of the New World: The American continent portrayed in native texts.* London: Thames and Hudson.

Brotherston, Gordon. 1981. A controversial guide to the language of America, 1643. In 1642: *Literature and power in the seventeenth century,* ed. Francis Barker, Jay Bernsetein, John Coombes, Peter Hulme, Jennifer Stone, and Jon Stratton. Proceedings of the Essex Conference on the Sociology of Literature. Essex: University of Essex Press.

Brown, Michael F. 1991. Beyond resistance: A comparative study of utopian renewal in Amazonia. *Ethnohistory* 38: 388–413.

Butt Colson, Audrey. 1971. Hallelujah among the Patamona Indians. *Anthropologica* 28: 25–58.

Certeau, Michael de. 1988. *The writing of history.* Trans. by Tom Conley. New York: Columbia University Press.

Collins, James. 1995. Literacy and literacies. *Annual Review of Anthropology* 24: 75–93.

Delaney, John J. 1980. *Dictionary of saints.* Garden City NY: Doubleday.

Ehrenreich, Jeffrey. 1985. Isolation, retreat and secrecy: Dissembling behavior among the Coaiquer Indians. In *Political anthropology in Ecuador: Perspectives from indigenous cultures,* ed. Jeffrey Ehrenreich, Albany NY: Society for Latin American Anthropology.

Evans-Pritchard, E. E. 1976 [1937]. *Witchcraft, oracles, and magic among the Azande.* Oxford: Clarendon Press.

Flores Freire, Fanny. 1987. *Organización administrativa del Registro Civil en la provincia del Tungurahua.* Thesis, Facultad de Ciencias Administrativas, Universidad Técnica de Ambato, Ambato, Ecuador.

Foster, Robert. 1991. Making national cultures in the global ecumene. *Annual Review of Anthropology* 20: 235-260.

García Márquez, Gabriel. 1967. *Cien años de soledad,* 4th ed. Madrid: Ediciones Cátedra.

Gebhart-Sayer, Angelika. 1985. The geometric designs of the Shipibo-Conibo in ritual context. *Journal of Latin American Lore* 11: 143–175.

Gelb, I. J. 1963 [1952]. *A study of writing.* Chicago IL: University of Chicago Press.

Goody, Jack. 1968. Restricted literacy in northern Ghana. In *Literacy in traditional societies,* ed. Jack Goody. Cambridge: Cambridge University Press.

Goody, Jack. 1987. *Interface between the written and the oral.* Cambridge: Cambridge University Press.

Graff, Harvey. 1987. *Legacies of literacy: Continuities and contradictions in western culture and society.* Bloomington: Indiana University Press.

Gow, Peter. 1990. Could Sangama read? The origin of writing among the Piro of eastern Peru. *History and Anthropology* 5: 87–103.

Guss, David M. 1986. Keeping it oral: A Yekuana ethnology. *American Ethnologist* 13: 413–429.

Guss, David M. 1996. Reading the Mesa: An interview with Eduardo Calderón. In *The book: Spiritual instrument,* ed. Jerome Rothenberg and David Guss. New York: Ganary Books.

Harbsmeier, Michael. 1985. Early travels to Europe: Some remarks on the magic of writing. In *Europe and its other,* ed. Francis Barker, Peter Hulme, Margaret Iverson, and Diana Loxley. Proceedings of the Essex Conference on the Sociology of Literature, 1984. Essex: University of Essex Press.

Harbsmeier, Michael. 1988. Inventions of writing. In *State and society: The emergence and development of social hierarchy and political centralization,* ed. John Gledhill, Barbara Bender, and Mogens T. Larsen. London: Unwin Hyman.

Harbsmeier, Michael. 1989. Writing and the Other: Travellers' literacy, or Towards an archeology of orality. In *Literacy and society,* ed. Karen Schousboe and Mogens Trolle Larsen. Copenhagen, Denmark: Akademisk Forlag.

Harriot, Thomas. 1972 [1590]. *A briefe and true report of the new found land of Virginia.* New York: Dover.

Helms, Mary W. 1988. *Ulysses' sail: An ethnographic odyssey of power, knowledge, and geographical distance.* Princeton NJ: Princeton University Press.

Hill, Jonathan D., and Robin M. Wright. 1988. Time, narrative, and ritual: Historical interpretations from an Amazonian society. In *Rethinking history and myth: Indigenous South American perspectives on the past,* ed. Jonathan D. Hill. Urbana: University of Illinois Press.

Holbek, Bengt. 1989. What the illiterate think of writing. In *Literacy and society,* ed. Karen Schousboe and Mogens Trolle Larsen. Denmark, Copenhagen: Akademisk Forlag.

Hugh-Jones, Stephen. 1989. Waríbi and the white men: History and myth in northwest Amazonia. In *History and ethnicity,* ed. Elizabeth Tonkin, Malcolm Chapman, and Maryon McDonald. London: Routledge.

Jackson, Jean E. 1995. "Déja entendu": The liminal qualities of anthropological fieldnotes. In *Representation in ethnography,* ed. John Van Maanen. London: Sage.

Kulick, Don, and Christopher Stroud. 1990. Christianity, cargo and ideas of self: Patterns of literacy in a Papua New Guinean village. *Man* 25: 286–304.

Léry, Jean de. 1990 [1580]. *History of a voyage to the land of Brazil, otherwise called America.* Trans. by Janet Whatley. Berkeley: University of California Press.

Lévy-Bruhl, Lucien. 1923. *Primitive mentality.* Trans. by Lilian A. Clare. New York: Macmillan Co.

Meggitt, M. 1968. Uses of literacy in New Guinea and Melanesia. In *Literacy in traditional societies,* ed. Jack Goody. Cambridge: Cambridge University Press.

Mignolo, Walter D. 1992. When speaking was not good enough: Illiterates, barbarians, savages, and cannibals. In *Amerindian images and the legacy of Columbus,* ed. René Jara and Nicholas Spadaccini. Minneapolis: University of Minnesota Press.

Mignolo, Walter D. 1995. *The darker side of the Renaissance: Literacy, territoriality, and colonization.* Ann Arbor: University of Michigan Press.

Olson, David. 1994. *The world on paper: The conceptual and cognitive implications of writing and reading.* Cambridge: Cambridge University Press.

Perrin, Michel. 1985. "Savage" points of view on writing. In *Myth and the imaginary in the New World,* ed. Edmundo Magaña and Peter Mason. Dordrecht, Netherlands: Centro de Estudios y Documentatión Latinoamericanos.

Platt, Tristan. 1992. Writing, shamanism and identity or voices from Abya-Yala. *History Workshop Journal* 34: 132–147.

Platt, Tristan. 1997. The sound of light: Emergent communication through Quechua shamanic dialogue. In *Creating context in Andean cultures,* ed. Rosaleen Howard-Malverde. London: Oxford University Press.

Rappaport, Joanne. 1987. Mythic images, historical thought and printed texts: The Páez and the written word. *Journal of Anthropological Research* 43: 43–61.

Rappaport, Joanne. 1990. *Politics of memory: Native historical interpretations in the Columbian Andes.* Cambridge: Cambridge University Press.

Rappaport, Joanne. 1994. *Cumbe reborn: An Andean ethnography of history.* Chicago IL: University of Chicago Press.

Rescaniere, A. Ortiz. 1972. El mito de la escuela. In *Ideología mesiánica del mundo andino,* ed. Juan Ossio A. Lima: Colección Biblioteca de Antropólogía.

Sánchez Parga, José. 1983. Estado y alfabetización. *Ecuador Debate* 2: 59–71.

Seed, Patricia. 1991. "Failing to marvel": Atahualpa's encounter with the word. *Latin American Research Review* 26: 7–33.

Street, Brian V. 1987. Orality and literacy as ideological constructions: Some problems in cross-cultural studies. *Culture and History* 2: 7–30.

Sutton, David E. 1997. Local names, foreign claims: Family inheritance and national heritage on a Greek island. *American Ethnologist* 24: 837–852.

Taussig, Michael. 1980. *The devil and commodity fetishism in South America.* Chapel Hill: University of North Carolina Press.

Tylor, E. B. 1923. *Anthropology: An introduction to the study of man and civilization.* New York: D. Appleton.

Valarezo, Galo Ramón. 1991. Ese secreto poder de la escritura. In Indios: Una reflexión sobre el levantamiento indígena de 1990, ed. Ileana Alme ida. Quito: Abya Yala.

Wachtel, Nathan. 1973. La visión de los vencidos: La conquista española en el folklore indígena. In *Ideología mesiánica del mundo andino,* ed. Juan M. Ossio. Lima: Ignacio Prado Pastor.

Weiss, Wendy A. 1993. "Gringo . . . gringita." *Anthropological Quarterly* 66: 187–196.

Whitten, Norman, Jr. 1981. Introduction. In *Cultural transformations and ethnicity in modern Ecuador,* ed. Norman E. Whitten, Jr. Urbana: University of Illinois Press.

Wogan, Peter. 1994. Perceptions of European literacy in early contact situations. *Ethnohistory* 41: 407–421.

PART FIVE

New Religious Movements

New religions are constantly emerging. A good example of this is the serpent-handling churches of Appalachia. The Holiness Churches were founded by a traveling preacher named George Hensley in the 1920s. Taking a passage of The Gospel According to Mark literally, Hensley taught that God mandates believers to pick up poisonous snakes during worship. Today, there are snake-handling churches in many states and the group is believed to have an active membership of about 5,000.

12

New Religious Movements

Religion is a model of meaning. That is to say, religions provide individuals with a sense of the value and meaning of their lives. These, however, are dependent on the context of society. As society changes, old meanings change. And as this happens, religions change as well. Thus, new religions and new understandings of older religions are constantly emerging. The essays in this section give examples of new and changing religious traditions. As you read the essays in this section, keep the following points in mind:

- While it is in no way clear that all religions have the same origins, there are common patterns in the development of new religions. In his classic essay "Revitalization Movements," Anthony F. C. Wallace proposes a general model for such origins. He argues that societies undergo periods of normality and periods of stress. In periods of extreme stress, people's internal model of their society no longer functions. Prophets arise—proposing new formulations of society. Their messages may be so compelling to people under stress that new religions may form around these charismatic leaders and societies may undergo profound change.

- The social and intellectual backgrounds to religious change are various. However, new religions always emerge from the historical context of other religions. One way this is clearly visible is in theological conflicts within religious traditions. For example, Christianity originated in Judaism, but Jews and Christians split over the identity of Jesus. Similarly, in the fifteenth and sixteenth centuries Catholic priests led theological disputes with their mother Church that led to the Protestant Reformation.

- Conflicts over doctrine sometimes take the form of revelation. Individuals claiming personal experience

of the divine are sometimes able to build followings around their messages and personal leadership. Examples of this type of movement are legion in the history of Christianity. For example, in the late eighteenth century Ann Lee began to preach that she was the incarnation of Jesus Christ and founded the United Believers in Christ's Second Appearing, or Shakers. In the early nineteenth century, Joseph Smith began to preach that the angel Moroni appeared to him with golden tablets on which were inscribed the Book of Mormon. Smith founded the very successful movement now called the Church of Latter-Day Saints, or Mormons. Similarly, William Miller became famous in the 1840s for predicting the return of Jesus based on his calculations in the Old Testament and founded a movement that became the Seventh-Day Adventist Church. A recent example of the different paths that new religious movements can take is the revival of interest in witchcraft, or Wicca, which developed largely from within Christianity (most of the books from which Wiccans draw their practice were authored by people from European and American Christian backgrounds) but is based on goddess and nature worship. The essay in this section by Scarboro and Luck examines the beliefs of members of a coven called Ravenwood outside of Atlanta, Georgia.

- The emergence of new religious movements might seem to be an idiosyncratic, random process, but religious beliefs are usually tightly woven into the fabric of a society. Religious innovation is often preceded by social and technological change. The Protestant Reformation, for example, was fueled by a desire to translate the Bible into vernacular languages, aided by a new technology, the printing press, which made mass production of the book possible. It was accompanied by the decline of feudalism and the increasing importance of urban classes.

- The connection between society and religion can also be seen in religious movements that have political objectives. Juergensmeyer's essay on Christian violence in America examines the Christian Identity Movement, whose leaders use biblical passages to infuse their followers with a radical and racist political viewpoint. Leaders of this movement find biblical justification for stockpiling weapons and murdering both specifically chosen and random victims associated with causes or ethnic groups they oppose. More benignly, Lee's essay on *Taipūcam* in Malaysia shows that a religious ritual can be a critical element in ethnic and political identity. For the Tamil minority in Kuala Lumpur, Taipūcam is a celebration and reaffirmation of their identity. It also both demonstrates and solidifies political power.

- Social, technological, and political forces as well the personalities and revelations of individual leaders lead to the constant reinterpretation and reshaping of religion. The essay by Williamson and Pollio, a good example of such reshaping, examines serpent-handling churches of the southeastern United States whose congregations focus on a passage in the New Testament that they believe literally instructs them to handle venomous serpents and drink poison when "God moves upon them" during worship services. Although this passage has been in the Christian Bible for over fifteen centuries, it is only since the rise of the Pentecostal movement in the early twentieth century that some people have felt compelled to take the passage literally.

- Sometimes it seems as if events within religions should create greater changes than they in fact do. The failure of religious prophecy is a good example of this. It would seem that the failure of key prophecies should be enough to discredit a religion, but there are many cases where it has not had that effect. For example, the Jehovah's Witnesses Watchtower Society has repeatedly prophesied the end of the world (in 1878, 1881, 1910, 1914, 1918, 1920, 1925, and 1975). Joseph Smith, founder of the Latter-Day Saints, prophesied the coming of the Lord for 1891. The failure of these prophesies obviously did not cause the decline of these religions. The final essay in this section tracks the failure of the Lubavitch understanding that their leader, Menachem Schneerson, was the messiah. One might have expected that Schneerson's death in 1994 would have discredited this belief, but most Lubavitchers continue to revere Schneerson, and the group has prospered in the years since his death.

Revitalization Movements

Anthony F. C. Wallace

In this classic essay, Anthony F. C. Wallace proposes a general model for the origins of all religions. His essential idea is that societies undergo periods of normality and periods of stress. In periods of extreme stress, people's internal model of their society—what Wallace calls their "mazeway"—no longer functions. Under such circumstances, prophets arise proposing new formulations of society, either by changing people's understanding of their society, by changing the society, or both. Religions are formed around these charismatic individuals.

Wallace argues societies under stress experience a pattern of stages: steady state, increased stress, cultural distortion, revitalization, and the emergence of a new steady state. He focuses on the period of revitalization, the time when new religions emerge. Wallace identifies six phases in the emergence of a new religion: mazeway reformulation, communication, organization, adaptation, cultural transformation, and routinization. He argues that all successful religions pass through these phases. Wallace also attempts to classify religious movements based upon key principles of their beliefs and the methods by which they propose to put those beliefs into action.

There are numerous difficulties in Wallace's model. Wallace wrote in an era when most anthropologists understood societies as self-contained, homogeneous, and slowly changing. Today, these assumptions are in doubt. Boundaries between societies are porous. Societies are often riven by internal conflict, and driven by changing circumstances. Religious movements are more likely to be found in some subset of a society rather than an entire society. And religion seems to be an increasingly powerful force in the world rather than a diminishing one. Despite these problems, Wallace's general notions about the origins of religion and his ideas that religious movements start with prophecy, communication, and organization have withstood the test of time.

As you read, consider these questions:
1. Why do revitalization movements emerge under certain social circumstances and not under others?
2. What are the six stages of the emergence of a new religion, and what are the major features of each?
3. What is the role of a prophet in a revitalization movement?

Reproduced by permission of the American Anthropological Association from *American Anthropologist* 58:2 (1956) 406–419.

INTRODUCTION

Behavioral scientists have described many instances of attempted and sometimes successful innovation of whole cultural systems, or at least substantial portions of such systems. Various rubrics are employed, the rubric depending on the discipline and the theoretical orientation of the researcher, and on salient local characteristics of the cases he has chosen for study. "Nativistic movement," "reform movement," "cargo cult," "religious revival," "messianic movement," "utopian community," "sect formation," "mass movement," "social movement," "revolution," "charismatic movement," are some of the commonly used labels. This paper suggests that all these phenomena of major cultural-system innovation are characterized by a uniform process, for which I propose the term "revitalization." The body of the paper is devoted to two ends: (1) an introductory statement of the concept of revitalization, and (2) an outline of certain uniformly-found processual dimensions of revitalization movements. . . .

[In two paragraphs, Wallace notes that his work is based on library and archival sources, includes many different groups, and is in an intermediate stage.—Editors]

THE CONCEPT OF REVITALIZATION

A revitalization movement is defined as a deliberate, organized, conscious effort by members of a society to construct a more satisfying culture. Revitalization is thus, from a cultural standpoint, a special kind of culture change phenomenon: the persons involved in the process of revitalization must perceive their culture, or some major areas of it, as a system (whether accurately or not); they must feel that this cultural system is unsatisfactory; and they must innovate not merely discrete items, but a new cultural system, specifying new relationships as well as, in some cases, new traits. The classic processes of culture change (evolution, drift, diffusion, historical change, acculturation) all produce changes in cultures as systems; however, they do not depend on deliberate intent by members of a society, but rather on a gradual chain-reaction effect: introducing A induces change in B; changing B affects C; when C shifts, A is modified; this involves D . . . and so on *ad infinitum.* This process continues for years, generations, centuries, millennia, and its pervasiveness has led many cultural theorists to regard culture change as essentially a slow, chain-like, self-contained procession of superorganic inevitabilities. In revitalization movements, however, A, B, C, D, E . . . N are shifted into a new *Gestalt* abruptly and simultaneously in intent; and frequently within a few years the new plan is put into effect by the participants in the movement. We may note in passing that Keesing's assessment of the literature on culture change (1953), while it does not deal explicitly with the theoretical issue of chain-effects versus revitalization, discusses both types. Barnett (1953) frankly confines his discussion to innovations of limited scope in the context of chains of events in acceptance and rejection. As Mead has suggested, cultures *can* change within one generation (Mead 1955); and the process by which such transformations occur is the revitalization process.

The term "revitalization" implies an organismic analogy.[1] This analogy is, in fact, an integral part of the concept of revitalization. A human society is here regarded as a definite kind of organism, and its culture is conceived as those patterns of learned behavior which certain "parts" of the social organism or system (individual persons and groups of persons) characteristically display. A corollary of the organismic analogy is the principle of homeostasis: that a society will work, by means of coordinated actions (including "cultural" actions) by all or some of its parts, to preserve its own integrity by maintaining a minimally fluctuating, life-supporting matrix for its individual members, and will, under stress, take emergency measures to preserve the constancy of this matrix. Stress is defined as a condition in which some part, or the whole, of the social organism is threatened with more or less serious damage. The perception of stress, particularly of increasing stress, can be viewed as the common denominator of the panel of "drives" or "instincts" in every psychological theory.

As I am using the organismic analogy, the total system which constitutes a society includes as significant parts not only persons and groups with their respective patterns of behavior, but also literally the cells and organs of which the persons are composed. Indeed, one can argue that the system includes nonhuman as well as human subsystems. Stress on one level is stress on all levels. For example, lowering of sugar level (hunger) in the fluid matrix of the body cells of one group of persons in a society is a stress in the society as a whole. This holistic view of society as organism integrated from cell to nation depends on the assumption that society, as an organization of living matter, is definable as a network of intercommunication. Events on one subsystem level must affect other subsystems (cellular vis-à-vis institutional, personal vis-à-vis societal) at least as information; in this view, social organization exists to the degree that events in one subsystem are information to other subsystems.

There is one crucial difference between the principles of social organization and that of the individual person: a society's parts are very widely interchangeable, a person's only slightly so. The central nervous system cells, for example, perform many functions of coordinating information and executing adaptive action which other cells cannot do. A society, on the other hand, has a multiple-replacement capacity, such that many persons can perform the analogous information-coordination and executive functions on behalf of society-as-organism. Furthermore, that regularity of patterned behavior which we call culture depends relatively more on the ability of constituent units autonomously to perceive the system of

which they are a part, to receive and transmit information, and to act in accordance with the necessities of the system, than on any all-embracing central administration which stimulates specialized parts to perform their function.

It is therefore functionally necessary for every person in society to maintain a mental image of the society and its culture, as well as of his own body and its behavioral regularities, in order to act in ways which reduce stress at all levels of the system. The person does, in fact, maintain such an image. This mental image I have called "the mazeway," since as a model of the cell-body-personality-nature-culture-society system or field, organized by the individual's own experience, it includes perceptions of both the maze of physical objects of the environment (internal and external, human and nonhuman) and also of the ways in which this maze can be manipulated by the self and others in order to minimize stress. The mazeway is nature, society, culture, personality, and body image, as seen by one person. Hallowell (1955) and Wallace (1955 and 1956) offer extended discussions of the mazeway and the related concepts of self, world view, and behavioral environment.

We may now see more clearly what "revitalization movements" revitalize. Whenever an individual who is under chronic, physiologically measurable stress, receives repeated information which indicates that his mazeway does not lead to action which reduces the level of stress, he must choose between maintaining his present mazeway and tolerating the stress, or changing the mazeway in an attempt to reduce the stress. Changing the mazeway involves changing the total *Gestalt* of his image of self, society, and culture, of nature and body, and of ways of action. It may also be necessary to make changes in the "real" system in order to bring mazeway and "reality" into congruence. The effort to work a change in mazeway and "real" system together so as to permit more effective stress reduction is the effort at revitalization; and the collaboration of a number of persons in such an effort is called a revitalization movement.

The term revitalization movement thus denotes a very large class of phenomena. Other terms are employed in the existing literature to denote what I would call subclasses, distinguished by a miscellany of criteria. "Nativistic movements," for example, are revitalization movements characterized by strong emphasis on the elimination of alien persons, customs, values, and/or material from the mazeway (Linton 1943). "Revivalistic" movements emphasize the institution of customs, values, and even aspects of nature which are thought to have been in the mazeway of previous generations but are not now present (Mooney 1892–93). "Cargo cults" emphasize the importation of alien values, customs, and materiel into the mazeway, these things being expected to arrive as a ship's cargo as for example in the Vailala Madness (Williams 1923, 1934). "Vitalistic movements" emphasize the importation of alien elements into the mazeway but do not necessarily invoke ship and cargo as the mechanism.[2] "Millenarian movements" emphasize mazeway transformation in an apocalyptic world transformation engineered by the supernatural. "Messianic movements" emphasize the participation of a divine savior in human flesh in the mazeway transformation (Wallis 1918, 1943). These and parallel terms do not denote mutually exclusive categories, for a given revitalization movement may be nativistic, millenarian, messianic, and revivalistic all at once; and it may (in fact, usually does) display ambivalence with respect to nativistic, revivalistic, and importation themes.

Revitalization movements are evidently not unusual phenomena, but are recurrent features in human history. Probably few men have lived who have not been involved in an instance of the revitalization process. They are, furthermore, of profound historical importance. Both Christianity and Mohammedanism, and possibly Buddhism as well, originated in revitalization movements. Most denominational and sectarian groups and orders budded or split off after failure to revitalize a traditional institution. One can ask whether a large proportion of religious phenomena have not originated in personality transformation dreams or visions characteristic of the revitalization process. Myths, legends, and rituals may be relics, either of the manifest content of vision-dreams or of the doctrines and history of revival and import cults, the circumstances of whose origin have been distorted and forgotten, and whose connection with dream states is now ignored. Myths in particular have long been noted to possess a dream-like quality, and have been more or less speculatively interpreted according to the principles of symptomatic dream interpretation. It is tempting to suggest that myths and, often, even legends, read like dreams because they *were* dreams when they were first told. It is tempting to argue further that culture heroes represent a condensation of the figures of the prophet and of the supernatural being of whom he dreamed.

In fact, it can be argued that all organized religions are relics of old revitalization movements, surviving in routinized form in stabilized cultures, and that religious phenomena per se originated (if it is permissible still in this day and age to talk about the "origins" of major elements of culture) in the revitalization process—i.e., in visions of a new way of life by individuals under extreme stress.

THE PROCESSUAL STRUCTURE

[In a brief passage, Wallace discusses his methodology, called "event-analysis."—Editors]

. . . The structure of the revitalization process, in cases where the full course is run, consists of five somewhat overlapping stages: 1. Steady State; 2. Period of Individual Stress; 3. Period of Cultural Distortion; 4. Period of Revitalization (in which occur the functions of mazeway reformulation, communication, organization, adaptation, cultural transformation, and routinization), and finally, 5. New Steady State. These stages are described briefly in the following sections.

I. Steady State

For the vast majority of the population, culturally recognized techniques for satisfying needs operate with such efficiency that chronic stress within the system varies within tolerable limits. Some severe but still tolerable stress may remain general in the population, and a fairly constant incidence of persons under, for them, intolerable stress may employ "deviant" techniques (e.g., psychotics). Gradual modification or even rapid substitution of techniques for satisfying some needs may occur without disturbing the steady state, as long as (1) the techniques for satisfying other needs are not seriously interfered with, and (2) abandonment of a given technique for reducing one need in favor of a more efficient technique does not leave other needs, which the first technique was also instrumental in satisfying, without any prospect of satisfaction.

II. The Period of Increased Individual Stress

Over a number of years, individual members of a population (which may be "primitive" or "civilized," either a whole society or a class, caste, religious, occupational, acculturational, or other definable social group) experience increasingly severe stress as a result of the decreasing efficiency of certain stress-reduction techniques. The culture may remain essentially unchanged or it may undergo considerable changes, but in either case there is continuous diminution in its efficiency in satisfying needs. The agencies responsible for interference with the efficiency of a cultural system are various: climatic, floral and faunal change; military defeat; political subordination; extreme pressure toward acculturation resulting in internal cultural conflict; economic distress; epidemics; and so on. The situation is often, but not necessarily, one of acculturation, and the acculturating agents may or may not be representatives of Western European cultures. While the individual can tolerate a moderate degree of increased stress and still maintain the habitual way of behavior, a point is reached at which some alternative way must be considered. Initial consideration of a substitute way is likely, however, to increase stress because it arouses anxiety over the possibility that the substitute way will be even less effective than the original, and that it may also actively interfere with the execution of other ways. In other words, it poses the threat of mazeway disintegration. Furthermore, admission that a major technique is worthless is extremely threatening because it implies that the whole mazeway system may be inadequate.

III. The Period of Cultural Distortion

The prolonged experience of stress, produced by failure of need satisfaction techniques and by anxiety over the prospect of changing behavior patterns, is responded to differently by different people. Rigid persons apparently prefer to tolerate high levels of chronic stress rather than make systematic adaptive changes in the mazeway. More flexible persons try out various limited mazeway changes in their personal lives, attempting to reduce stress by addition or substitution of mazeway elements with more or less concern for the *Gestalt* of the system. Some persons turn to psychodynamically regressive innovations; the regressive response empirically exhibits itself in increasing incidences of such things as alcoholism, extreme passivity and indolence, the development of highly ambivalent dependency relationships, intragroup violence, disregard of kinship and sexual mores, irresponsibility in public officials, states of depression and self-reproach, and probably a variety of psychosomatic and neurotic disorders. Some of these regressive action systems become, in effect, new cultural patterns.

In this phase, the culture is internally distorted; the elements are not harmoniously related but are mutually inconsistent and interfering. For this reason alone, stress continues to rise. "Regressive" behavior, as defined by the society, will arouse considerable guilt and hence increase stress level or at least maintain it at a high point; and the general process of piecemeal cultural substitution will multiply situations of mutual conflict and misunderstanding, which in turn increase stress-level again.

Finally, as the inadequacy of existing ways of acting to reduce stress becomes more and more evident, and as the internal incongruities of the mazeway are perceived, symptoms of anxiety over the loss of a meaningful way of life also become evident: disillusionment with the mazeway, and apathy toward problems of adaptation, set in.

IV. The Period of Revitalization

This process of deterioration can, if not checked, lead to the death of the society. Population may fall even to the point of extinction as a result of increasing death rates and decreasing birth rates; the society may be defeated in war, invaded, its population dispersed and its customs suppressed; factional disputes may nibble away areas and segments of the population. But these dire events are not infrequently forestalled, or at least postponed, by a revitalization movement. Many such movements are religious in character, and such religious revitalization movements must perform at least six major tasks:

1. Mazeway Reformulation.   Whether the movement is religious or secular, the reformulation of the mazeway generally seems to depend on a restructuring of elements and subsystems which have already attained currency in the society and may even be in use, and which are known to the person who is to become the prophet or leader. The occasion of their combination in a form which constitutes an internally consistent structure, and of their acceptance by the prophet as a guide to action, is abrupt and dramatic, usually occurring as a moment of insight, a brief period of realization of relationships and opportunities. These moments are

often called inspiration or revelation. The reformulation also seems normally to occur in its initial form in the mind of a single person rather than to grow directly out of group deliberations.

With a few exceptions, every religious revitalization movement with which I am acquainted has been originally conceived in one or several hallucinatory visions by a single individual. A supernatural being appears to the prophet-to-be, explains his own and his society's troubles as being entirely or partly a result of the violation of certain rules, and promises individual and social revitalization if the injunctions are followed and the rituals practiced, but personal and social catastrophe if they are not. These dreams express: 1. the dreamer's wish for a satisfying parental figure (the supernatural, guardian-spirit content), 2. world-destruction fantasies (the apocalyptic, millennial content), 3. feelings of guilt and anxiety (the moral content), and 4. longings for the establishment of an ideal state of stable and satisfying human and supernatural relations (the restitution fantasy or Utopian content). In a sense, such a dream also functions almost as a funeral ritual: the "dead" way of life is recognized as dead; interest shifts to a god, the community, and a new way. A new mazeway *Gestalt* is presented, with more or less innovation in details of content. The prophet feels a need to tell others of his experience, and may have definite feelings of missionary or messianic obligation. Generally he shows evidence of a radical inner change in personality soon after the vision experience: a remission of old and chronic physical complaints, a more active and purposeful way of life, greater confidence in interpersonal relations, the dropping of deep-seated habits like alcoholism. Hence we may call these visions "personality transformation dreams." Where there is no vision (as with John Wesley), there occurs a similarly brief and dramatic moment of insight, revelation, or inspiration, which functions in most respects like the vision in being the occasion of a new synthesis of values and meanings. . . .

[In five long paragraphs, Wallace speculates on the nature and origins of prophetic visions. He argues that they are dreamlike but happen in a waking state, they frequently work personality transformations on those who have them, and they are often analogous to the process of becoming a shaman. Some prophets were suffering from mental disorders before their experiences, but prophets are unlike mental patients. Schizophrenics believe they are God, prophets only that they have encountered God. Prophets maintain their personal identity, but schizophrenics lose theirs. Wallace concludes that religious visionary experience is not part of mental disorder but, in fact, may cure mental disorder.— Editors]

2. Communication.   The dreamer undertakes to preach his revelations to people, in an evangelistic or messianic spirit; he becomes a prophet. The doctrinal and behavioral injunctions which he preaches carry two fundamental motifs: that the convert will come under the care and protection of certain supernatural beings; and that both he and his society will benefit materially from an identification with some definable new cultural system (whether a revived culture or a cargo culture, or a syncretism of both, as is usually the case). The preaching may take many forms (e.g., mass exhortation vs. quiet individual persuasion) and may be directed at various sorts of audiences (e.g., the elite vs. the downtrodden). As he gathers disciples, these assume much of the responsibility for communicating the "good word," and communication remains one of the primary activities of the movement during later phases of organization.

3. Organization.   Converts are made by the prophet. Some undergo hysterical seizures induced by suggestion in a crowd situation; some experience an ecstatic vision in private circumstances; some are convinced by more or less rational arguments, some by considerations of expediency and opportunity. A small clique of special disciples (often including a few already influential men) clusters about the prophet and an embryonic campaign organization develops with three orders of personnel: the prophet; the disciples; and the followers. Frequently the action program from here on is effectively administered in large part by a political rather than a religious leadership. Like the prophet, many of the converts undergo a revitalizing personality transformation.

Max Weber's concept of "charismatic leadership" well describes the type of leader-follower relationship characteristic of revitalization movement organizations (1947). The fundamental element of the vision, as I have indicated above, is the entrance of the visionary into an intense relationship with a supernatural being. This relationship, furthermore, is one in which the prophet accepts the leadership, succor, and dominance of the supernatural. Many followers of a prophet, especially the disciples, also have ecstatic revelatory experiences; but they and all sincere followers who have not had a personal revelation also enter into a parallel relationship to the prophet: as God is to the prophet, so (almost) is the prophet to his followers. The relationship of the follower to the prophet is in all probability determined by the displacement of transference dependency wishes onto his image; he is regarded as an uncanny person, of unquestionable authority in one or more spheres of leadership, sanctioned by the supernatural. Max Weber denotes this quality of uncanny authority and moral ascendency in a leader as charisma. Followers defer to the charismatic leader not because of his status in an existing authority structure but because of a fascinating personal "power," often ascribed to supernatural sources and validated in successful performance, akin to the "mana" or "orenda" of ethnological literature. The charismatic leader thus is not merely permitted but expected to phrase his call for adherents as a demand to perform a duty to a power higher than human. Weber correctly points out that the "routinization" of charisma is a critical issue in movement organization, since

unless this "power" is distributed to other personnel in a stable institutional structure, the movement itself is liable to die with the death or failure of individual prophet, king, or war lord.

Weber, however, is essentially discussing a quality of leadership, and one which is found in contexts other than that of revitalization movements. In consequence, his generalizations do not deal with the revitalization formula itself, but rather with the nature of the relationship of the early adherents to their prophet. Furthermore, there is a serious ambiguity in Weber's use of the charisma concept. Weber seems to have been uncertain whether to regard it as an unusual quality in the leader which is recognized and rationalized by his adherents, or whether to regard it as a quality ascribed to the leader by followers and hence as being a quality of their relationship to him, determined both by the observed and the observer in the perceptual transaction. We have used it to denote the libidinal relationship which Freud described in *Group Psychology and the Analysis of the Ego* (1922).

It would appear that the emotional appeal of the new doctrine to both the prophet and his followers is in considerable part based on its immediate satisfaction of a need to find a supremely powerful and potentially benevolent leader. For both the prophet and his followers, this wish is gratified in fantasy (subjectively real, of course); but the follower's fantasy is directed toward the person of the prophet, to whom are attributed charismatic properties of leadership (Weber 1946, 1947).

4. Adaptation.   The movement is a revolutionary organization and almost inevitably will encounter some resistance. Resistance may in some cases be slight and fleeting but more commonly is determined and resourceful, and is held either by a powerful faction within the society or by agents of a dominant foreign society. The movement may therefore have to use various strategies of adaptation: doctrinal modification; political and diplomatic maneuver; and force. These strategies are not mutually exclusive nor, once chosen, are they necessarily maintained through the life of the movement. In most instances the original doctrine is continuously modified by the prophet, who responds to various criticisms and affirmations by adding to, emphasizing, playing down, and eliminating selected elements of the original visions. This reworking makes the new doctrine more acceptable to special interest groups, may give it a better "fit" to the population's cultural and personality patterns, and may take account of the changes occurring in the general milieu. In instances where organized hostility to the movement develops, a crystallization of counter-hostility against unbelievers frequently occurs, and emphasis shifts from cultivation of the ideal to combat against the unbeliever.

5. Cultural Transformation.   As the whole or a controlling portion of the population comes to accept the new religion with its various injunctions, a noticeable social revitalization occurs, signalized by the reduction of the personal deterioration symptoms of individuals, by extensive cultural changes, and by an enthusiastic embarkation on some organized program of group action. This group program may, however, be more or less realistic and more or less adaptive: some programs are literally suicidal; others represent well conceived and successful projects of further social, political, or economic reform; some fail, not through any deficiency in conception and execution, but because circumstances made defeat inevitable.

6. Routinization.   If the group action program in nonritual spheres is effective in reducing stress-generating situations, it becomes established as normal in various economic, social, and political institutions and customs. Rarely does the movement organization assert or maintain a totalitarian control over all aspects of the transformed culture; more usually, once the desired transformation has occurred, the organization contracts and maintains responsibility only for the preservation of doctrine and the performance of ritual (i.e., it becomes a church). With the mere passage of time, this poses the problems of "routinization" which Max Weber discusses at length (Weber 1946, 1947).

V. The New Steady State

Once cultural transformation has been accomplished and the new cultural system has proved itself viable, and once the movement organization has solved its problems of routinization, a new steady state may be said to exist. The culture of this state will probably be different in pattern, organization or *Gestalt*, as well as in traits, from the earlier steady state; it will be different from that of the period of cultural distortion.

VARIETIES AND DIMENSIONS OF VARIATION

I will discuss four of the many possible variations: the choice of identification; the choice of secular and religious means; nativism; and the success-failure continuum.

1. Choice of Identification

Three varieties have been distinguished already on the basis of differences in choice of identification: movements which profess to *revive* a traditional culture now fallen into desuetude; movements which profess to *import* a foreign cultural system; and movements which profess neither revival nor importation, but conceive that the desired cultural endstate, which has never been enjoyed by ancestors or foreigners, will be realized for the first time in a future *Utopia*. The Ghost Dance, the Xosa Revival, and the Boxer Rebellion are examples of professedly revivalistic movements; the Vailala Madness (and other cargo cults) and the Taiping Rebellion

are examples of professedly importation movements. Some formulations like Ikhnaton's monotheistic cult in old Egypt and many Utopian programs, deny any substantial debt to the past or to the foreigner, but conceive their ideology to be something new under the sun, and its culture to belong to the future.

These varieties, however, are ideal types. A few movements do correspond rather closely to one type or another but many are obvious mixtures. Handsome Lake, for instance, consciously recognized both revival and importation themes in his doctrine. It is easy to demonstrate that avowedly revival movements are never entirely what they claim to be, for the image of the ancient culture to be revived is distorted by historical ignorance and by the presence of imported and innovative elements. Importation movements, with professed intentions to abandon the ancestral ways, manage to leave elements of the ancestral culture intact, if unrecognized, in large areas of experience. And movements which claim to present an absolutely new conception of culture are obviously blinding themselves to the fact that almost everything in the new system has been modeled after traditional or imported elements or both. Although almost every revitalization movement embodies in its proposed new cultural system large quantities of both traditional and imported cultural material, for some reason each movement tends to profess either no identification at all, a traditional orientation, or foreign orientation. This suggests that the choice of identification is the solution of a problem of double ambivalence: both the traditional and the foreign model are regarded both positively and negatively.

Culture areas seem to have characteristic ways of handling the identification problem. The cargo fantasy, although it can be found outside the Melanesian area, seems to be particularly at home there; South American Indian prophets frequently preached of a migration to a heaven-on-earth free of Spaniards and other evils, but the promised-land fantasy is known elsewhere; North American Indian prophets most commonly emphasized the revival of the old culture by ritual and moral purification, but pure revival ideas exist in other regions too. Structural "necessity" or situational factors associated with culture area may be responsible. The contrast between native–white relationships in North America (a "revival" area) and Melanesia (an "importation" area) may be associated with the fact that American Indians north of Mexico were never enslaved on a large scale, forced to work on plantations, or levied for labor in lieu of taxes, whereas Melanesians were often subjected to more direct coercion by foreign police power. The Melanesian response has been an identification with the aggressor (vide Bettelheim 1947). On the other hand, the American Indians have been less dominated as individuals by whites, even under defeat and injustice. Their response to this different situation has by and large been an identification with a happier past. This would suggest that an important variable in choice of identification is the degree of domination exerted by a foreign society, and that import-oriented revitalization movements will not develop until an extremely high degree of domination is reached.

2. The Choice of Secular and Religious Means

There are two variables involved here: the amount of secular action which takes place in a movement, and the amount of religious action. Secular action is here defined as the manipulation of human relationships; religious action as the manipulation of relationships between human and supernatural beings. No revitalization movement can, by definition, be truly nonsecular, but some can be relatively less religious than others, and movements can change in emphasis depending on changing circumstances. There is a tendency, which is implicit in the earlier discussion of stages, for movements to become more political in emphasis, and to act through secular rather than religious institutions, as problems of organization, adaptation, and routinization become more pressing. The Taiping Rebellion, for instance, began as religiously-preoccupied movements; opposition by the Manchu dynasty and by foreign powers forced it to become more and more political and military in orientation.

A few "purely" political movements like the Hebertist faction during the French Revolution, and the Russian communist movement and its derivatives, have been officially atheistic, but the quality of doctrine and of leader–follower relationships is so similar, at least on superficial inspection, to religious doctrine and human–supernatural relations, that one wonders whether it is not a distinction without a difference. Communist movements are commonly asserted to have the quality of religious movements, despite their failure to appeal to a supernatural community, and such things as the development of a Marxist gospel with elaborate exegesis, the embalming of Lenin, and the concern with conversion, confession, and moral purity (as defined by the movement) have the earmarks of religion. The Communist Revolution of 1917 in Russia was almost typical in structure of religious revitalization movements: there was a very sick society, prophets appealed to a revered authority (Marx), apocalyptic and Utopian fantasies were preached, and missionary fervor animated the leaders. Furthermore, many social and political reform movements, while not atheistic, act through secular rather than religious media and invoke religious sanction only in a perfunctory way. I do not wish to elaborate the discussion at this time, however, beyond the point of suggesting again that the obvious distinctions between religious and secular movements may conceal fundamental similarities of socio-cultural process and of psychodynamics, and that while all secular prophets have not had personality transformation visions, some probably have, and others have had a similar experience in ideological conversion.

Human affairs around the world seem more and more commonly to be decided without reference to supernatural powers. It is an interesting question whether mankind can profitably dispense with the essential element of the religious revitalization process before reaching a Utopia without stress or strain. While religious movements may involve crude and powerful emotions and irrational fantasies of interaction with nonexistent beings, and can occasionally lead to unfortunate practical consequences in human relations, the same fantasies and emotions could lead to even more unfortunate practical consequences for world peace and human welfare when directed toward people improperly perceived and toward organs of political action and cultural ideologies. The answer would seem to be that as fewer and fewer men make use of the religious displacement process, there will have to be a corresponding reduction of the incidence and severity of transference neuroses, or human relationships will be increasingly contaminated by character disorders, neurotic acting out, and paranoid deification of political leaders and ideologies.

3. Nativism

Because a major part of the program of many revitalization movements has been to expel the persons or customs of foreign invaders or overlords, they have been widely called "nativistic movements." However, the amount of nativistic activity in movements is variable. Some movements—the cargo cults, for instance—are antinativistic from a cultural standpoint but nativistic from a personnel standpoint. Handsome Lake was only mildly nativistic; he sought for an accommodation of cultures and personalities rather than expulsion, and favored entry of certain types of white persons and culture-content. Still, many of the classic revivalistic movements have been vigorously nativistic, in the ambivalent way discussed earlier. Thus nativism is a dimension of variation rather than an elemental property of revitalization movements.

A further complication is introduced by the fact that the nativistic component of a revitalization movement not uncommonly is very low at the time of conception, but increases sharply after the movement enters the adaptation stage. Initial doctrinal formulations emphasize love, cooperation, understanding, and the prophet and his disciples expect the powers-that-be to be reasonable and accepting. When these powers interfere with the movement, the response is apt to take the form of an increased nativistic component in the doctrine. Here again, situational factors are important for an understanding of the course and character of the movement.

4. Success and Failure

The outline of stages as given earlier is properly applicable to a revitalization movement which is completely successful. Many movements are abortive; their progress is arrested at some intermediate point. This raises a taxonomic question: how many stages should the movement achieve in order to qualify for inclusion in the category? Logically, as long as the original conception is a doctrine of revitalization by culture change, there should be no requisite number of stages. Practically, we have selected only movements which passed the first three stages (conception, communication, and organization) and entered the fourth (adaptation). This means that the bulk of our information on success and failure will deal with circumstances of relatively late adaptation, rather than with such matters as initial blockage of communication and interference with organization.

Two major but not unrelated variables seem to be very important in determining the fate of any given movement: the relative "realism" of the doctrine; and the amount of force exerted against the organization by its opponents. "Realism" is a difficult concept to define without invoking the concept of success or failure, and unless it can be so defined, is of no use as a variable explanatory of success or failure. Nor can one use the criterion of conventionality of perception, since revitalization movements are by definition unconventional. While a great deal of doctrine in every movement (and, indeed, in every person's mazeway) is extremely unrealistic in that predictions of events made on the basis of its assumptions will prove to be more or less in error, there is only one sphere of behavior in which such error is fatal to the success of a revitalization movement: prediction of the outcome of conflict situations. If the organization cannot predict successfully the consequences of its own moves and of its opponents' moves in a power struggle, its demise is very likely. If, on the other hand, it is canny about conflict, or if the amount of resistance is low, it can be extremely "unrealistic" and extremely unconventional in other matters without running much risk of early collapse. In other words, probability of failure would seem to be negatively correlated with degree of realism in conflict situations, and directly correlated with amount of resistance. Where conflict-realism is high and resistance is low, the movement is bound to achieve the phase of routinization. Whether its culture will be viable for long beyond this point, however, will depend on whether its mazeway formulations lead to actions which maintain a low level of stress.

SUMMARY

This programmatic paper outlines the concepts, assumptions, and initial findings of a comparative study of religious revitalization movements. Revitalization movements are defined as deliberate, conscious, organized efforts by members of a society to create a more satisfying culture. The revitalization movement as a general type of event occurs under two conditions: high stress for individual members of the society, and disillusionment with a distorted cultural *Gestalt*. The movement follows a series of functional stages: mazeway reformulation, communication, organization, adaptation, cultural transformation, and routinization. Movements vary along several dimensions, of which choice of identification, relative degree of religious and secular emphasis, na-

tivism, and success or failure are discussed here. The movement is usually conceived in a prophet's revelatory visions, which provide for him a satisfying relationship to the supernatural and outline a new way of life under divine sanction. Followers achieve similar satisfaction of dependency needs in the charismatic relationship. It is suggested that the historical origin of a great proportion of religious phenomena has been in revitalization movements.

NOTES

1. This article is not the place to present a general discussion of the notions of order and field, function and equilibrium, the organismic analogy, the concept of homeostasis, and certain ideas from cybernetics, learning and perception, and the physiology of stress, which would be necessary to justify and fully elucidate the assumptions on which the revitalization hypothesis is based. See however, Wallace 1953, 1955, and 1956 for further development of the holistic view and more extended discussions of the mazeway concept.

2. After we had coined the term "revitalization movement," we discovered that Marian Smith in an article on the Indian Shakers (Smith 1954) uses the closely related term "vitalistic movements" ("a vitalistic movement may be defined as 'any conscious, organized attempt on the part of a society's members to incorporate in its culture selected aspects of another culture in contact with it' "). However, she uses this term for what I would call nonnativistic revitalization movements with importation (rather than revivalistic) emphasis.

BIBLIOGRAPHY

Barnett, H. G.
    1953   Innovation: The Basis of Culture Change. New York.
Bettelheim, B.
    1947   Individual and Mass Behavior in Extreme Situations. In Newcomb, Hartley, et al., eds., Readings in Social Psychology. New York.
Cantril, Hadley
    1941   The Psychology of Social Movements. New York.
Deardorff, M. H.
    1951   The Religion of Handsome Lake: Its Origin and Development. In Symposium on Local Diversity in Iroquois Culture, edited by W. N. Fenton, Bureau of American Ethnology Bulletin 149:79-107. Washington.
Eggan, Fred
    1954   Social Anthropology and the Method of Controlled Comparison. American Anthropologist 56:743-63.
Freud, Sigmund
    1922   Group Psychology and the Analysis of the Ego. London.
Fromm, Erich
    1951   The Forgotten Language. New York.
Hallowell, A. I.
    1955   The Self and Its Behavioral Environment. In A. I. Hallowell, Culture and Experience. Philadelphia.
Hoffer, A., H. Osmond, and J. Smythies
    1954   Schizophrenia: A New Approach. II. Result of a Year's Research. Journal of Mental Science, 100:29–45.

James, William
    1902   Varieties of Religious Experience. New York.
Keesing, Felix M.
    1953   Culture Change: An Analysis and Bibliography of Anthropological Sources to 1952. Stanford.
Knox, R. A.
    1950   Enthusiasm: A Chapter in the History of Religion, with Special Reference to the XVII and XVIII Centuries. Oxford.
Linton, Ralph
    1943   Nativistic Movements. American Anthropologist 45:230–40.
Lowe, Warner L.
    1953   Psychodynamics in Religious Delusions and Hallucinations. American Journal of Psychotherapy 7:454–62.
Mead, Margaret
    1954   Nativistic Cults as Laboratories for Studying Closed and Open Systems. Paper read at annual meeting of the American Anthropological Association.
    1955   How Fast Can Man Change? Address presented to Frankford Friends Forum, Philadelphia, 4 Dec. 1955.
Mooney, James
    1892–93   The Ghost Dance Religion. Bureau of American Ethnology Annual Report. Washington.
Parker, Arthur
    1913   The Code of Handsome Lake, the Seneca Prophet. New York State Museum Bulletin 163. Albany.
Sargant, William
    1949   Some Cultural Group Abreactive Techniques and Their Relation to Modern Treatments. Proceedings of the Royal Society of Medicine 42:367–74.
    1951   The Mechanism of Conversion. British Medical Journal 2:311 et seq.
Schwartz, Theodore
    1954   The Changing Structure of the Manus Nativistic Movement. Paper read at annual meeting of the American Anthropological Association.

Smith, Marian
    1954   Shamanism in the Shaker Religion of Northwest America. Man, August 1954, #181.
Steward, Julian N.
    1953   Evolution and Process. In A. L. Kroeber, ed., Anthropology Today. Chicago.
Voget, Fred W.
    1954   Reformative Tendencies in American Indian Nativistic Cults. Paper read at annual meeting of the American Anthropological Association.
Wallace, Anthony F. C.
    1952a   Handsome Lake and the Great Revival in the West. American Quarterly, Summer: 149–65.
    1952b   Halliday Jackson's Journal to the Seneca Indians, 1798–1800. Pennsylvania History 19: Nos. 2 and 3.
    1953   A Science of Human Behavior. Explorations No. 3.
    1955   The Disruption of the Individual's Identification with His Culture in Disasters and Other Extreme Situations. Paper read at National Research Council, Committee on Disaster Studies, Conference on Theories of Human Behavior in Extreme Situations, Vassar College.
    1956   The Mazeway. Explorations No. 6. In press.
Wallis, Wilson D.
    1918   Messiahs—Christian and Pagan. Boston.
    1943   Messiahs—Their Role in Civilization. Washington.
Weber, Max
    1930   The Protestant Ethic and the Spirit of Capitalism. Translated by Talcott Parsons. New York.
    1946   From Max Weber: Essays in Sociology. Translated and edited by H. Gerth and C. W. Mills. New York.
    1947   The Theory of Social and Economic Organization. Translated and edited by A. M. Henderson and Talcott Parsons. New York.
Williams, F. E.
    1923   The Vailala Madness and the Destruction of Native Ceremonies in the Gulf Division. Port Moresby: Territory of Papua, Anthropology Report No. 4.
    1934   The Vailala Madness in Retrospect. In Essays Presented to C. G. Seligman. London.

The Goddess and Power:
Witchcraft and Religion in America

Allen Scarboro

Philip Andrew Luck

Along with the growth in Christian fundamentalism in the United States, there has been a parallel development of a women-centered, goddess- and nature-worshiping movement called Wicca. In this essay Scarboro and Luck seek to discover why Wicca beliefs appeal to contemporary Americans and provide some insights into the contemporary practice of Wicca derived from their study of the Ravenwood coven in Atlanta, Georgia.

Through interviews with coven members and participation in rites, Scarboro and Luck were able to form some hypotheses explaining why some people are attracted to the practice of Wicca. They propose that women are drawn to the practice of Wicca because the movement is largely led by women and is goddess-centered. This is in contrast to Christianity, where the metaphors for the Divine are all male and the church leadership positions are held by men. Also, many women apparently feel an affinity to Wicca practices and the Wiccan movement's incorporation of women's attitudes and experiences that they did not experience in the Christian churches in which they were raised.

Scarboro and Luck also point out that Wicca practitioners worship nature as a manifestation of the Divine, in contrast to the Christian notion of God's separateness from the world. Wiccans see and feel the Divine in the natural world around them, experiencing the presence of the Divine in an immediate, personal way that is not possible in Christianity. Wicca rites are also open and participative. Any initiated witch is a priestess of Wicca. One doesn't need an intermediary priest or minister to allow one access to the Divine.

Unlike Christian churches that teach there is but one path to God, Wicca practitioners are open to theological truths and ritual practices from other religious traditions. Consequently, Scarboro and Luck claim that those who practice Wicca feel an involvement and "empowerment" that is central to their religious experience. This empowerment is particularly evident in witches' practice of magic, through which they believe they can control the world around them.

Finally, Scarboro and Luck point out that many sociologists of religion believe that people in the modern world have become disenchanted—that is, they have lost the ability to make moral sense of their lives. Witches, in contrast, live in a world with spirits, fairies, and gods of the elements—which provides a way for people who do not like their existence to "remythologize" their lives.

As you read, consider these questions:

1. Wiccan religions have strongly developed notions of feminine supernatural power. What are the implications for this among its followers and in American Society?
2. Wicca absorbs ideas and concepts from other religions. How does this compare to modern Christianity?
3. What are the critical differences between Wicca and Christianity? What are the implications of these differences for Wiccans?

INTRODUCTION: WITCHCRAFT IN THE UNITED STATES

Among the efflorescence of contemporary American religious revival, several religious streams variant to mainstream American faith and practice have emerged. In addition to the vigour of enthusiastic charismatic and Pentecostal communities, with their roots in an earlier period of American religious history, one notes the growth, for example, of non-denominational churches, of American Islamic communities, of Buddhist, Sikh, Hindu and other Eastern practices, of the Unification Church and Scientology, and of New Age movements, native American traditions, Vodou, Santeria and the occult (Melton, 1984; Brown, 1991; Musser, 1991; Murphy, 1993; Truzzi, 1993).

Amid this religious plethora, Wicca or Witchcraft has an important place.[1] Some estimate that the United States holds 100,000 practising witches (Melton, 1984: 464). Alongside initiated witches, perhaps as many as 500,000 Americans participate in pagan ceremonies, in radical faery practices, and in other activities akin to witchcraft.[2]

"The Goddess and Power: Witchcraft and Religion in America" by A. Scarboro & P.A. Luck, (1997) *Journal of Contemporary Religion* 12:1, 69–79. Reprinted by permission of the authors and Taylor & Francis Ltd., http://www.tandf.co.uk/journals.

Wicca is a woman-centred, goddess-worshipping, nature-affirming, participative, this-worldly-oriented religion. Since witchcraft is clearly deviant from the contemporary American scene, how do we account for the attraction of Wicca? What is the appeal of witchcraft to contemporary Americans? Furthermore, what does Wicca offer to the wider American religious tradition? What should the scientific study of religion learn from witchcraft?

RESEARCH STRATEGY

These questions formed the groundwork for a year-long participant-observation study of Ravenwood, a large coven in Atlanta, Georgia. Ravenwood, organised in 1976 by Lady Sintana (Candace Huntsman), has from its inception adopted a role as a 'teaching coven,' i.e. devoted to making Wicca available to a wider public, and to training priestesses and priests for the 'Old Religion.' Although the number of Ravenwood initiates has varied, a core group of approximately 50 members were active in the coven in 1991–1992; another 50 people participated in some rituals, in classes offered by the coven, and in other activities. While most Ravenwood participants live in the greater Atlanta area, some come to rituals from as far away as Birmingham, Alabama, or Columbia, South Carolina.

Ravenwood became the locus of close scrutiny from October 1991 to August 1992 by Allen Scarboro and two colleagues, Nancy Campbell, a clinical psychologist, and Shirley Stave, a literary theorist.[3] After receiving consent from the Ravenwood High Priestess, Lady Sintana, and other coven members, several research strategies were employed. Early in the research, a loosely structured, open-ended questionnaire was mailed to all members of a list (*n* = 67) of Ravenwood initiates and neophytes.[4] The questionnaire asked for demographic data and for a 'free-write' response to the prompt: In what ways is Wicca important to you? Forty-five completed questionnaires were returned and analysed. In addition, the researchers reviewed two 'Books of Shadows' (journals kept by individual witches recording their spiritual and ritual experiences), coven records, and journals kept by several neophytes approaching and completing their initiations.

Extensive semi-structured interviews were conducted with a sample of associates and members of the coven. The interview schedule included such areas as a religious involvement history, family background, means of making contact with and becoming involved in Wicca, development within Wicca, contact with other pagan and Wiccan groups, doubts about witchcraft, and degree of openness about involvement with witchcraft. The sample interviewed included neophytes (non-initiates), newly initiated witches ("first degree witches"), more experienced witches ("second degree witches" who are authorised to teach coven classes), elder members ("third degree witches" who had "devoted themselves full time to the Craft"). These interviews typically extended over a period of time stretching from 2 to 6 hours.

Lady Sintana and other important coven elders were interviewed more extensively, over a period of several months. In addition, several group interviews were conducted. These interviews, which included between four and seven coven members and lasted from 3 to 6 hours, focused on the history of Ravenwood, on the role and practice of magic, on the relationships among Ravenwood and other—both Wiccan and pagan—groups, on coven leadership and on the oral tradition of the coven.

Over a period of a year, starting in October, 1991, at least two members of the original research team attended each coven ritual, including the more formal sabbats[5] and the less formal esbats, or "moons." In addition, team members attended the classes which the coven offered for neophytes interested in the traditional 'year and a day' of study in preparation for initiation.

While the research strategy was multi-staged, the goal was to come to an understanding of who the Ravenwood witches were, what they did as witches, and what meaning their practice of witchcraft held for the members of the group. From this research, several motifs emerge in response to the questions that guided our investigation.

MOTIFS OF BELIEF AND PRACTICE

First, Wicca as practised at Ravenwood is a goddess-centred religion. While Ravenwood witches affirm that the divine itself may transcend issues of gender or sex, indeed of personhood at all, they also affirm that the goddess is the primordial metaphor for apprehending the divine. That is, the goddess makes the divine present and available to experience.

Within American culture with its religious roots firmly in the Christian tradition of god the father, where male metaphors frame our thinking about and experience of the divine, the goddess presents a strikingly different set of images. While Christian theology in its sophisticated form may argue that god transcends those male metaphors traditionally associated with 'Him,' both popular Christian piety and Christian ritual and congregational life are enmeshed in those male images. Many Ravenwood witches come to witchcraft from earlier involvements with Christian denominations. As they describe their religious journeys, they recount their discomfort with both the Old Testament god and the Christian god the father. Witches describe both the Old Testament god and the traditional god the father as presenting images of the divinity as distant, stern, judging, vengeful, universal, associated with the Law and abstract standards of justice, standing over against the human—which they see as mainstays of Christian prayer life, of Christian religious texts, of Christian practice.

What Rosemary Radford Ruether calls the "public theology" (Ruether, 1984: 265) of the Western Christian tradition echoes more formal theological writings. In both the public and the formal traditions,

The subordination of woman to man is replicated in the symbolic universe in the imagery of divine-human relations. God is imagined as a great patriarch over against the earth or Creation, imaged in female terms . . . Divine–human relations in the macrocosm are also reflected in the microcosm of the human being . . . as images of the hierarchy of the 'masculine' over the 'feminine.' (Ruether, 1984: 266)

An implication of this public theology is, according to John Wilson, that women are seen as "something 'totally other,' impossible to identify with or enter into a normal relationship with" (Wilson, 1978: 264), because they differ essentially from attributes that reflect the divine. Nancy T. Ammerman (1987; 1990) finds that the current rapid growth of American fundamentalism is linked to such sentiments which underscore traditional gender roles and their religious legitimations. For women and men striving to develop models of divinity which support newer gender roles, "Goddess symbolism is spiritually uplifting, for it legitimates female power . . . in contrast with the usual images . . . of women as . . . seductive or sinful" (Roof, 1993: 143).

The goddess celebrated at Ravenwood brings with her a very different set of characteristics. One striking difference is the goddess's multiplicity. She shows herself through an almost limitless array of faces. Ravenwood witches see and experience the goddess through many mythic threads through a range of guises, as maid, mother, crone, as creatrix, nurturer, destroyer, as daughter, wife, mother, as distant and elusive, as well as intimate and close. The goddess's very multiplicity distinguishes her sharply from the deities of the Western monotheistic traditions. Her multiplicity opens her to a wide variety of modes of apprehension, and makes each of those modes holy and pregnant with significance. Rather than the restricting 'One Way' of many conservative Christians, the goddess affirms multiple ways of being in the world, a multiplicity which has increasingly come to characterise modern life.

As an important consequence of the goddess's multiplicity, women and women's experiences are hallowed and brought into the centre of religious sensibility. As many feminist Christian thinkers have pointed out, the maleness of the Christian god has marginalised and devalued women: god the father and god the son have told women that their primary religious roles are always subordinate to those of men (see Trible, 1978; Ruether, 1983; Fiorenza, 1994). For example, the sex of god the son still frames the Roman Catholic Church's insistence that the priesthood is open only to men, that women's role in the Church is to serve, to adore, to stand for purity and restraint.

The goddess, on the other hand, valorises women. She presents herself as maid, as mother, as crone, in relationships as well as alone. With the goddess, women's concerns and experiences, throughout the life cycle and in their many roles, find an echo and an affirmation in the divine. Furthermore, the goddess's many faces present her moving through the life cycle, rather than being caught static in any one role.

The goddess enters puberty and menarche, she ages and she grieves.

The goddess's multiplicity not only valorises women, but it also affirms women's physicality, their sensuality, their sexuality. Through the goddess, women's bodies are hallowed and brought into the centre of religious experience, not—as in the Christian myth—as the site of sin ("through Eve all have sinned"), but rather as the locus of celebration.

Ravenwood witches also affirm that the divine always presents itself through images of balance and harmony. Although Wicca is goddess-centred, the multiple quality of the divine is also experienced through male guises. Alongside the goddess is the god. The central act in Wiccan circle ritual is the divine marriage, the conjunction of the chalice and the sword. In Wiccan ritual, the priestess and the priest enact a symbolic marriage—a *hierogamos*—between the goddess and the god, between the priestess and the priest, between each witch and her or his peers. In the Great Rite, as this meeting of chalice and sword is called, the divine female and the divine male act both together and discretely. Just as the divine presents itself through multiple female forms, so too does it present itself through multiple male forms: the hunter, the worker, the child, the son, the consort, the old man. Here, too, we find a valorisation of multiplicity, of the holy's epiphanic presence in the many roles and masks through which we live our lives. However, the male god at Ravenwood is never the distant, disconnected, totally other often found in traditional accounts of Christian thought.

At Ravenwood, Wiccan myth and practice affirm both male and female, both man and woman, as integrated into life in this world, into life as process, into life as always limned by death and rebirth. In their celebration of a goddess-centred religion expressed through balance and harmony, the Ravenwood witches embrace a religious commitment which is in marked variance to traditional American Christianity.

Secondly, Ravenwood witches affirm a radically immanent divine. Wicca counters the traditional Western notion of a radically transcendent god, one 'totally other' to humans and the world. Many argue that the Christian god is separate from his creation, thus privileging the non-visible world as more 'real' than the visible one. This notion gives priority to the non-empirical and to the spiritual. Within that conception, for example, the body is often seen as a snare for the soul. Witchcraft, on the other hand, celebrates a divine at one with the world.

For Wicca, the divine is found in nature, in the paths of the stars and the changes of the moon, in 'rabbit-tracks in the snow,' in the ceaseless run and turn of the tides. The goddess is in the world, in nature, rather than separate from the world. Here again, the goddess is known through her connectedness rather than through her transcendence. The goddess peeps through woodland leaves, through the lives of animals, through the round of the seasons. To find the goddess, one need not deny the world, but rather embrace it. The world itself is holy, not fallen and corrupted.

The immanence of the goddess in the world includes her immanence in us: we and the goddess are one. That is, humans living their daily lives are living the goddess. Our lives act out the goddess. As we are born, as we eat and sleep, and go about our everyday tasks, as we marry and bear children, as we age and die, we are the goddess. We and the goddess are one. Our lives are lived in the presence of the goddess, through her and with her. We need not escape the world, need not deny ourselves nor our bodies, to reach the divine. Our bodies become vehicles and agencies of the divine. Whatever is human is at the same time divine.

The radical immanence of the goddess has two important consequences. On the one hand, Ravenwood witches assert the holiness of nature. Ecological concerns come naturally to witches. Nature is neither a chaotic force to be tamed, nor a morally neutral field on which humans play or over which they are given dominion. Rather, nature is the divine, and we and nature are one. In this point, Wicca is similar to many native American religions which see the earth itself as holy, as the mother of us all. Like ecologists, witches understand that to love your mother is to love the earth, that care for the earth is care for the self and for the divine.

On the other hand, since the divine is immanent in human lives and bodies, we are held strongly responsible. Wiccan ethics are the ethics of responsibility, rather than an ethics of sin or guilt. Our acts are ours alone, they have consequences, and we alone are held to account for our acts and their consequences. Our acts are not judged against some universal abstract standard or against a law of 'thou shalts' and 'thou shalt nots,' but against their consequences. Here, too, Wicca presents a religious path at variance with much of traditional American Christianity, but one in tune with the lived experiences of many contemporary Americans.

Thirdly, attuned to the Ravenwood witches' emphasis on a radically immanent goddess at the centre of their religion, is their participative religious ritual. Every initiated witch is priestess or priest of Wicca, without the need for an intermediary to permit access to the divine. Each witch is empowered to act with and in the divine. Priestly Christian religions require an ordained official to conduct religious services or a body to define, defend, and transmit a canonical set of texts, beliefs and practices. Wicca, on the other hand, asserts that each person has immediate and effective connections to the divine. This ease of connection to the divine is similar to the early Gnostic sects which believed that each practitioner had direct access to the holy (see Pagels, 1979). Likewise, any Wiccan priestess or priest can call the divine into the ritual circle, can stand in the presence of—in fact, stand in—the divine.

At Ravenwood, the priestly functions (e.g. presiding at ritual) circulate among all the initiates; in 'pagan' circles at Ravenwood, even non-initiated neophytes conduct esbats.[6] In Wicca, religious office is not restricted like a scarce resource, but is available to each initiate.

Just as religious office is available to all, Wiccan ritual is participative. Everyone in the circle joins in the activity: all initiates participate in creating the sacred space for the ritual, everyone participates in the chants, dance, cakes and wine, the greeting and farewell to the spirits attending.

Ravenwood ritual has no audience: everyone is an actor, empowered to act with and in the divine space and time of ritual. Unlike the serried rows of worshippers in most mainline Protestant congregations who listen to the minister and the choir, Ravenwood witches are not auditors, but are instead each co-creators of the ritual. Ritual at Ravenwood acts out a non-hierarchical religious practice, one of immediacy and immanence, of the worshipper as active agent rather than as passive recipient. While charismatic and Pentecostal American Protestants have reasserted the immediate in Christian worship, much of American religious practice defines the appropriate posture of the religious practitioner as one of need and insufficiency. Wicca stresses that the practitioner is one with the divine—underscoring the practitioner's fullness and sufficiency. Here, again, Wicca valorises religion as active, as personal, as participative, characteristics that attract seekers who search for a way to affirm their richness and value, rather than to descry their emptiness and need.

Finally, the Wiccan stance at Ravenwood of theological openness challenges a more traditional American Christian notion of religious exclusivity. Typically, Americans are asked by religious bodies to make a choice of a single faith and a single practice: 'join this church' because it offers the only road to salvation; other churches or religions are, either explicitly or implicitly, seen as false, in error, or inadequate. While this pattern of choosing the 'one true faith' is most characteristic of conservative religious bodies, the theme of exclusivity runs throughout American Christianity.

This theme has a subsidiary motif: other religious traditions, especially non-Christian ones, have little or nothing of importance to offer religiously. In its more extreme expressions, this theme of religious particularity and exclusivity paints other religious traditions as diabolic or as perverse (see, for example, Pagels, 1995). Wicca stands in sharp contrast to this theme. Ravenwood witches talk about Wicca as one path among many to the goddess or to religious truth. They ask of seekers, "Does this path work for you? Is it the right path?—If not," they continue, "find one that does work for you." Such a posture is in concordance with the Wiccan notion of the multiplicity and immanence of the divine. Rather than attempt to corral the divine into any given human structure, Ravenwood witches look for its presence throughout all traditions and practices.

In the same way that Ravenwood witches do not argue for restricting the divine to any single practice, they are open to theological or spiritual truths within other religious traditions. For example, the Hindu notion of *karma* has been easily, almost seamlessly, grafted onto the Wiccan notion of ethical responsibility. Likewise, Ravenwood witches may include ritual practices from other traditions, such as a Zen chant or African drumming, within Wiccan ritual. Ravenwood witches then pose another challenge to traditional American Christianity through their openness to religious heterodoxy, variety and tolerance. The path of the goddess, they say, is a wide path with room for many travellers.

What is the appeal of Wicca to the witches at Ravenwood? Ravenwood practice and belief embrace life itself, in its variety and complexity, its mystery and contingency, as holy. Wicca affirms those lives which its practitioners act out in their everyday surroundings, affirms that those lives, in all their particularities and differences, are parts of a cosmic whole. Wicca assures the witch that she participates fully and wholly in cosmic processes, and affirms that the self is captain of its own journey, responsible to its actions and to the meaning that undergirds the universe. Wicca underscores our connectedness and our value in the face of a world increasingly fragmented and perplexing. As a witch, the individual is validated within a community of difference, rather than judged against an external and de-contextualised standard. As a witch, a Ravenwood initiate joins others in their uniqueness, in a life of joyful celebration of the multiple gifts of the Goddess and the responsibility to live in a multiphonic harmony with cosmic strains.

WITCHCRAFT AND THE SOCIOLOGY OF RELIGION

As we review these themes by distinguishing Wicca from mainstream American religions, we note two major issues of particular interest for sociologists, particularly for sociologists of religion. First, Robbins & Anthony (1990), among other contemporary sociologists of religion, criticise much of the writings in the area of sociology of religion over the last century as having fallen in the thrall of a too-narrow understanding of religion. Robbins and Anthony argue that the sociology of religion has been dominated by an understanding growing out of Max Weber's (1976) modernization thesis, especially as interpreted by such theorists as Peter Berger (1967) or Clifford Geertz (1979). This understanding, which has dominated sociologists' thinking about contemporary religion, focuses on the meaning-giving function of religion, its gnomic character, to use Berger's term popularised in his *Sacred Canopy* (see Berger, 1967). When one takes the meaning-giving function of religion as primary, then it comes as no surprise that sociologists keep predicting religion's demise in the modern world and that they have been caught by surprise by the rise over the last 30 years of fundamentalist religions in America (see Lechner, 1990).

It is interesting to note that two recent works on witchcraft follow the strategy of analysing witchcraft primarily in terms of its meaning-giving. Even though Carlo Ginzburg titles his analysis of European witchcraft between the fourteenth and seventeenth centuries *Ecstasies* (Ginsburg, 1991), he sets as his goal a "deciphering" of the esoteric meaning of the Craft and its practice. For him, witchcraft codes a nomic structure for dealing with marginality. T. M. Luhrmann's (1989) ac-count of contemporary English witchcraft and occult practices ends up focusing on practitioners' commitment to ideas which they find compelling. One can almost hear Weber whisper to each author: "seek the meaning-giving function."

James Beckford joins Robbins and Anthony in urging us to recover the role of power in religion, claiming that "empowerment . . . [is] a core element of contemporary religious experience" (Beckford, 1990: 58). As we review the Wiccan critique of mainstream religion, the Wiccan emphasis on power becomes more telling. With the radical immanence of the divine, with the priesthood of all initiates, with the participative role of all celebrants of ritual, Wicca's empowerment of its practitioners becomes evident. This role of empowerment becomes even clearer when we note the role of magic in witchcraft—that the witch wills herself into the world. Wicca's emphasis on empowerment through magical action is underscored as we remember the second half of the word witchcraft. That is, Wicca is a craft, a set of activities to be practised. These practices are perceived to have demonstrable effects both on the practitioner and on her world. Wicca, while it does provide a gnomic function, cannot be understood without an emphasis in its function of empowerment. The Wiccan notion of the witch's empowerment is summed up in the Wiccan Rede. The Rede is a set of instructions, a knitting together of the sense of Wicca, and a warning. According to the Rede, "An ye harm none, do what ye will" (Scarboro et al., 1994: 47). With the caution that the witch must do no harm, the Rede asserts that the only limit to a witch's possibility is her will.

The second major issue also touches on a strand from Weber's work. For Weber, the primary metaphor for modernisation and the modern world is "disenchantment" (Weber, 1946: 148). A word once enchanted has become merely mundane. Bellah et al.'s magisterial *Habits of the Heart* (1985), among other works, explores the effects of this disenchantment on American life. The authors of *Habits* fret that the tension between individualism and commitment has heightened to a point where Americans have lost the language needed to make moral sense of their lives. Weber's sociological vision of the disenchanted modern sensibility is paralleled not only in works such as Bellah et al.'s but also in the works of Weber's contemporaries among Protestant theologians, such as Rudolf Bultmann (1951–1955), John A. T. Robinson (1963), and Paul Tillich (1955, 1957). They attempted to retrieve the salience of current Protestant commitment through a method which Bultmann called demythologisation—retelling Biblical and Christian stories denuded from their mythic trappings.

The authors of *Habits,* among many others, have traced out some effects of this demythologising and disenchantment in American society. They conclude with a call for a "reconstitution of the social world," largely through the reappropriation of what they call communities of memory, collectivities organised around a "second language" of narratives which re-locate individuals within larger communal stories. While they do not call this reappropriation a 're-mythologisation,' such a term seems fitting. Wicca participates in such a remythologisation: witches live in a world again peopled by sprites, faeries, elementals and gods, incorporating in wind, earth, fire and water. A Wiccan circle opens with an invocation of the spirits to renew their participation in the affairs of humans and the circle concludes with a farewell to these spirits.

When witches look at society outside Wicca, they see a world bereft of stories. They respond to this lack in ritual, in the belief in the goddess, her multiplicity and her immanence, in a natural world resacralised, that is, through narratives of enchantment. Wicca is an attempt at these communities of memory, communities which re-attach individuals into a resacralised world peopled by powerful actors, communities that attempt to put the *Habits'* 'second language' into practice.

CONCLUSION: WICCA, THE SOCIOLOGY OF RELIGION, AND RELIGIOUS PRACTICE

Witchcraft, rather than being seen as a marginal, trivial new age phenomenon, holds important lessons for sociologists, and for those concerned with the state both of contemporary American religion and of where American society may be going. Witches call on sociologists to re-see the role of power in the religious life of individuals and collectivities. Wiccan practice revives both personal empowerment and the creation of communities of memory shaped by narratives of the natural and social world's empowerment. Witchcraft also offers an antidote to a narrow, de-personalised picture of nature; Wicca acts out an image of nature imbued with cosmic character and significance, a nature rescued from the mundane. Furthermore, witches remind sociologists of the possibilities of a social world ripe with multiplicity rather than one organised and normalised through a monolithic nomic order that brings all society's members into one hegemonic structure. They assert a playful response to a routinised social world, a response that cultivates imagination and creativity of action, rather than resignation and despair.

For contemporary mainstream American religion, Wicca draws a new image of the congregant and believer. In witchcraft, the witch embodies an active engagement rather than a passive religious stance of *ennui,* an embodiment in favour of a stance open to newness and personal expression. In its support of a transgendered divine, Wicca calls for a rethinking of our inheritance of masculinised notions of god and the transcendent in favour of multiplicity and immanence. Here, Wicca puts forth models for sacralising life and experience which embraces a wider conception of human possibility and responsibility than is currently available in mainstream thinking. Finally, in a society experiencing increasing tension between its history and its increasingly multicultural character, Wicca offers a religious model

of tolerance—indeed, of celebration—of difference and multiplicity.

ACKNOWLEDGMENTS

An earlier draft of this paper was presented at the 1995 annual meetings of the Georgia Sociological Association (GSA). We are grateful for the helpful discussions at the GSA and for the contributions offered by Cheryl Scarboro, Frances Coker, and anonymous reviewers. Without the assistance of the Witches of Ravenwood, particularly Lady Sintana, this project would not have been possible; we are continually in their debt.

NOTES

1. American witches use the terms 'witchcraft' and 'Wicca' interchangeably. By using 'witchcraft,' they stress the connections between contemporary groups of witches and earlier practitioners of witchcraft, including medieval European witches (see e.g. Murray, *The Witchcult in Western Europe,* 1953). They use 'Wicca' to point out the connection between contemporary witches and the herbalists and 'wise women' in traditional European society. 'Wicca' and 'Witch' are connected etymologically; our informants (see below) offer a folk etymology which traces the term 'witch' to 'Wicca,' which they explicate to mean 'wise woman' (see also Sjoo & Mor, 1987: 203).

2. The growth of witchcraft in the United States has occurred in a context of growth in other, similar religious expressions. Witches differentiate themselves from pagans, a closely allied group, on two primary criteria. First, witches claim to be the direct inheritors and practitioners of the 'Old Religion.' That is, they claim an unbroken descent from earlier Wiccan groups. For example, the high priestess of each Wiccan coven claims a genealogy of initiation reaching back for generations. Secondly, in order to be a witch, not just a pagan, a person must undertake at least 'a year and a day' of instruction from an initiated witch and then undergo an initiation supervised by a high priestess into a coven.

3. See Scarboro et al., 1994: ix–xii, 183–192 for a fuller discussion of the research strategy.

4. Neophytes are people who have expressed an interest in Wicca and who may be attending classes offered by the coven, i.e. classes required for initiation, but who have not committed themselves to witchcraft by participating in the ritual of initiation. Initiates have completed at least 'a year and a day' of classes, have sought initiation, have been accepted by the high priestess and other coven leaders, and have undergone initiation. Each initiate is a priestess or priest of Wicca.

5. Sabbats are the eight festivals marking the solar year, including, e.g. Hallowmas (31 October, the Wiccan New Year) and Beltane (1 May, spring fertility festival). Esbats, which mark each new moon, are more relaxed festivals. At Ravenwood, esbats are often celebrated in pagan rather than more formal Wiccan rituals.

6. For clarification of 'pagan,' see footnote 2.

REFERENCES

Ammerman, N. T. *Bible Believers: Fundamentalists in the Modern World.* New Brunswick, NJ: Rutgers University Press, 1987.

Ammerman, N. T. *Baptist Battles: Social Change and Religious Conflict in the Southern Baptist Convention.* New Brunswick: Rutgers University Press, 1990.

Beckford, J. A. "Religion and Power," in Robbins, T., & Anthony, D. (eds.), *In God We Trust: New Patterns of Religious Pluralism in America.* 2nd ed. New Brunswick: Transaction, 1990: 43–60.

Bellah, R. N., Madsen, R., Sullivan, W. M., Swidler, A., & Tipton, S. M. *Habits of the Heart: Individualism and Commitment in American Life.* Berkeley, CA: University of California Press, 1985.

Berger, P. *The Sacred Canopy: Elements of a Sociological Theory of Religion.* New York: Doubleday, 1967.

Brown, K. M. *Mama Lola: A Vodou Priestess in Brooklyn.* Berkeley: University of California Press, 1991.

Bultmann, R. *Theology of the New Testament,* trans. K. Grobel. New York: Charles Scribner's Sons, 1951–1955.

Fiorenza, E. S. *In Memory of Her: A Feminist Theological Reconstruction of Christian Origins,* 10th anniversary edn. New York: Crossword, 1994.

Geertz, C. "Religion as a Cultural System," in Lessa, W. A., & Vogt, E. Z. (eds.), *Reader in Comparative Religion: An Anthropological Approach.* New York: HarperCollins, 1979: 78–89.

Ginzburg, C. *Ecstasies: Deciphering the Witches' Sabbath,* 4th ed., trans. by Raymond Rosenthal. New York: Penguin, 1991.

Lechner, F. J. "Fundamentalism Revisited," in Robbins, T., & Anthony, D. (eds.), *In Gods We Trust: New Patterns of Religious Pluralism in America,* 2nd ed. New Brunswick: Transaction, 1990: 77–98.

Luhrmann, T. M. *Persuasions of the Witch's Craft: Ritual Magic in Contemporary England.* Cambridge: Harvard University Press, 1989.

Melton, J. G. "Modern Alternative Religions in the West," in Hinnells, J. R. (ed.), *A Handbook of Living Religions.* London: Penguin, 1984: 455–474.

Murphy, J. M. *Santeria: African Spirits in America.* Boston: Beacon Press, 1993.

Murray, M. *The Witchcult in Western Europe.* New York: Oxford University Press, 1953.

Musser, D. W. "What's New in American Religion?" Paper presented at Berry College, Rome, Georgia. April 1, 1991.

Pagels, E. *The Gnostic Gospels.* New York: Random House, 1979.

Pagels, E. *The Origin of Satan.* New York: Random House, 1995.

Robbins, T. & Anthony, D. "Introduction: Conflict and Change in American Religions," in Robbins, T., & Anthony, D. (eds.), *In Gods We Trust: New Patterns of Religious Pluralism in America,* 2nd ed. New Brunswick: Transaction, 1990: 3–41.

Robinson, J. A. T. *Honest to God.* Philadelphia: Westminster Press, 1963.

Roof, W. C. *A Generation of Seekers: The Spiritual Journeys of the Baby Boom Generation.* San Francisco: Harper, 1993.

Ruether, R. R. *Sexism and God-Talk: Toward a Feminist Theology.* Boston: Beacon Press, 1983.

Ruether, R. R. "The Feminist Critique in Religious Studies," in McNamara, P. H. (ed.), *Religion: North American Style,* 2nd ed. Belmont: Wadsworth Publishing. 1984: 265–273.

Scarboro, A., Campbell, N., & Stave, S. *Living Witchcraft: A Contemporary American Coven.* Westport: Praeger, 1994.

Sjoo, M. & Mor, B. *The Great Cosmic Mother: Rediscovering the Religion of the Earth.* San Francisco: Harper & Row, 1987.

Starhawk. *The Spiral Dance: A Rebirth of the Ancient Religion of the Great Goddess,* 10th anniversary ed. San Francisco: Harper & Row, 1989.

Tillich, P. *Biblical Religion and the Search for Ultimate Reality.* Chicago: University of Chicago Press, 1955.

Tillich, P. *Systematic Theology: Existence and the Christ,* Vol. 1. Chicago: University of Chicago Press, 1957.

Trible, P. *God and the Rhetoric of Sexuality.* Philadelphia: Fortress Press 1978.

Truzzi, M. "The Occult Revival as Popular Culture: Some Observations on the Old and the Nouveau Witch," in Lehmann, A. C., & Myers, J. E. (eds.), *Magic, Witchcraft, and Religion: An Anthropological Study of the Supernatural,* 3rd ed. Mountain View, CA: Mayfield, 1993.

Weber, M. "Science as a Vocation," in Gerth, H. H., & Mills, C. W. (eds.), *From Max Weber: Essays in Sociology.* New York: Oxford University Press, 1946: 129–156.

Weber, M. *The Protestant Ethic and the Spirit of Capitalism,* trans. T. Parsons, introduction by A. Giddens. London: Unwin, 1976.

Wilson, J. *Religion in American Society: The Effective Presence.* Englewood Cliffs: Prentice-Hall, 1978.

Christian Violence in America

Mark Juergensmeyer

Although people in the United States typically associate religious violence with the Islamic countries of the Middle

Mark Juergensmeyer, "Christian Violence in America" from *Annals of the American Academy of Political and Social Science* Vol. 558 (July 1998) 88–100, copyright © 1998 by American Academy of Political and Social Science. Reprinted by Permission of Sage Publications, Inc.

East and, to a lesser degree, with Hindus and Sikhs in India, Juergensmeyer's essay examines the religiously motivated violence perpetrated by Americans who are members of various militant Christian militia movements. The members of these movements are followers of what is called *reconstruction theology* and *Christian Identity theology.* As Juergensmeyer demonstrates, members of these movements justify their use of terroristic violence through their claims that Satan is controlling American political and social institutions and that he must be opposed by any means possible. In particular, followers of these movements have focused on creating paramilitary training camps and on the issue of abortion. They have bombed abortion clinics and murdered medical personnel who worked in clinics where abortions were performed.

This violent crusade is directed by leaders who found inspiration for their actions in the writings of the twentieth-century Lutheran theologians Dietrich Bonhoeffer and Reinhold Niebuhr. Both men argued that a Christian acting for the sake of justice could use violence, and that righteous force was sometimes necessary to deter larger acts of violence or injustice. However, Bonhoeffer and Niebuhr were writing in the context of the Second World War and combatting Nazi Germany. Leaders of the violent Christian movements compare the government of the United States to Nazi Germany and insist that only a biblically based political system can be just.

Reconstruction theology is a branch of "dominion theology," which asserts that Christians must reassert the dominion of God over all things. Two of Dominion theology's leading spokesmen are the Reverend Jerry Falwell and Pat Robertson. Reconstruction theology is at the extreme right wing of dominion theology. Leaders of the movement do not believe in the American separation of church and state and would like to start a Christian revolution that would result in a Christian theocratic government based on biblical law.

Christian Identity theology is based on a somewhat different set of principles. Christian Identity theology has been the basis for some of the white supremacist militia movements in the United States such as the Aryan Nation and Posse Comitatus. Followers of this theology generally have an even more extreme view of the government and religion than those who subscribe to reconstruction theology. Those who endorse Christian Identity theology generally distrust the mainstream Christian denominations because they are too "liberal," and they long for a state governed by religious law. They are typically white supremacists, anti-Semitic, and believe the government of the United States is totally corrupt and run by Jews. The members of these movements believe that they are God's soldiers in a secret war against satanic forces allied with the United States and the United Nations and that it is their God-given mission to battle these forces. They see themselves as engaged in a great struggle against forces of evil that act through the institutions of the U.S. government, United Nations, International Monetary Fund, and other such organizations.

As you read, consider these questions:

1. What is the logic that some Christians use to justify violent actions against others?

2. Some conservative Christians believe that the dominion of God must be asserted over all things. What implications does this have for government, policy, and political activism in the United States?

3. What is the "Christian Identity movement" and what are their ideas about church and state?

The Islamic Revolution in Iran in 1978 heralded a new kind of religiously motivated political violence and protest, a wave of disaffection from modern forms of secular political authority throughout the world that ultimately reached American shores. Writing in 1993, I could characterize this as largely a Third World, postcolonial phenomenon (Juergensmeyer 1993, 19–20). As the millennium approaches, however, this wave of antimodernism has increasingly come to such industrialized and thoroughly modern countries as Japan, which suffered a nerve gas attack in Tokyo subways by the Aum Shinrikyo religious movement; France, where militant supporters of the Islamic Party in Algeria have placed bombs in Parisian subways; and, perhaps most surprising, the United States, where the bombing of the World Trade Center, attacks on abortion clinics and the killing of abortion clinic staff, and the destruction of the Oklahoma City federal building are chilling examples of assaults on the legitimacy of modern social and political institutions.

The examples of Christian militancy in America are especially noteworthy, for they present a religious perception of warfare and struggle in what is perhaps the most modern of twentieth-century societies. It is not totally uncharacteristic of Christianity to have a violent side, of course: the bloody history of the faith—the Crusades, the Inquisition, and the holy wars—has provided images as disturbing as those provided by Islam, Hinduism, or Sikhism. What is significant about the recent forms of Christian violence is not so much the violence as the ideology that lies behind it: the perception that the secular social and political order of America is caught up in satanic conspiracies of spiritual and personal control. These perceived plots provide Christian activists with reasons for using violent means.

The social history of Christianity and theological positions based ultimately on the Bible provide legitimacy for the worldviews of a variety of contemporary Christian subcultures. Some of them emerged from mainstream denominations; others are fiercely independent from traditional forms of organized Christianity. In the case of recent attacks on abortion clinics, the theological justification and the social vision associated with it are firmly rooted in Protestant reformation theology. Such is the position of the Reverend Michael Bray, for instance. He is a Lutheran pastor who has been convicted of a series of abortion clinic attacks and defends the use of lethal weapons against abortion clinic staff.

ABORTION CLINIC BOMBINGS

The Reverend Bray recalled that it was "a cold February night" in 1984 when he and a friend drove a yellow Honda from his home in Bowie to nearby Dover, Delaware. The trunk of the car held a cargo of ominous supplies: a cinder block to break a window, cans of gasoline to pour in and around a building, and rags and matches to ignite the flames. The road to Delaware was foggy that night, and the bridge across the Chesapeake Bay was icy. The car skidded and a minor accident occurred, but the pair was determined to forge ahead. "Before daybreak," Bray recalled, "the only abortion chamber in Dover was gutted by fire and put out of the business of butchering babies" (Bray 1994, 9). The following year, Bray and two other defendants stood trial for destroying seven abortion facilities in Delaware, Maryland, Virginia, and the District of Columbia, totaling over $1 million in damages. He was convicted of these charges and served time in prison until 15 May 1989.

When I talked with the Reverend Bray in his suburban home in Bowie in April 1996, there was nothing sinister or intensely fanatical about him. He was a cheerful, charming, handsome man in his early forties who liked to be called Mike. Hardly the image of an ignorant, narrowminded fundamentalist, Mike Bray enjoyed a glass of wine before dinner and talked knowledgeably about theology and political ideas (Bray 1996).

It was a demeanor quite different from his public posture. As a leader in the Defensive Action movement, he advocated the use of violence in anti-abortion activities, and his attacks on abortion clinics were considered extreme even by members of the pro-life movement. The same has been said of his writings. Bray publishes one of the country's most militant Christian newsletters, *Capitol Area Christian News,* which focuses on abortion, homosexuality, and what Bray regards as the Clinton administration's pathological abuse of government power.

Bray was the spokesman for two activists who were convicted of murderous assaults on abortion clinic staffs. On 29 July 1994, Bray's friend, the Reverend Paul Hill, killed Dr. John Britton and his volunteer escort, James Barrett, as they drove up to the Ladies Center, an abortion clinic in Pensacola, Florida. Several years earlier, another member of Bray's network of associates, Rachelle ("Shelly") Shannon, a housewife from rural Oregon, confessed to a string of abortion clinic bombings as well as being convicted of attempted murder for shooting and wounding Dr. George Tiller as he drove away from his clinic in Wichita, Kansas. Bray wrote the definitive book on the ethical justification for anti-abortion violence, *A Time to Kill,* which defended his own acts of terrorism, the murders committed by Hill, and the attempted murders committed by Shannon (Bray 1994). Yet, in person, the Reverend Michael Bray was in many ways an attractive and interesting man.

Mike Bray had always been active, he told me, having been raised in a family focused on sports, church activities, and military life. His father was a naval officer who served at nearby Annapolis, and Mike grew up expecting to follow in his father's military footsteps. An athletic hero in high school, he took the most popular girl in class to the senior prom. Her name was Kathy Lee, and later she became an actress and a nationally televised talk show host, receiving top billing on her own daytime show with Regis Philbin. Mike's own career was marked by less obvious attributes of success. He attended Annapolis for a year and then dropped out, living what he described as a "prodigal" life. He searched for religion as a solution to his malaise and was for a time tempted by the Mormons, but then the mother of his old girlfriend, Kathy Lee, steered him toward Billy Graham and the bornagain experience of evangelical Christianity. Mike was converted and went to Colorado to study in a Baptist Bible college and seminary.

Yet Bray never quite rejected the Lutheranism of his upbringing. So when he returned to Bowie, he rejoined his childhood church and became the assistant pastor. When the national Lutheran churches merged, Bray led a faction of the local church that objected to what it regarded as the national church's abandonment of the principle of scriptural literalism. Seeing himself as a crusader, Mike and his group of 10 families split off and formed their own Reformed Lutheran church in 1984, an independent group affiliated with the national Association of Free Lutheran Congregations. Over 10 years later, Bray's church remained a circle of about fifty people without its own church building. The church operated out of Bray's suburban home: Bray remodeled the garage into a classroom for a Christian elementary school, where he and his wife taught a small group of students.

Increasingly, Mike Bray's real occupation became social activism. Supported by his wife, members of the church, and his volunteer associate pastor, Michael Colvin—who held a Ph.D. in classics from Indiana University and worked in the federal health care administration—Mike and his followers launched several anti-abortion crusades and tapped into a growing national network of like-minded Christian activists.

They became consumed by the idea that the federal government—particularly the attorney general, whom Mike called "Janet Waco Reno"—was involved in a massive plot to undermine individual freedom and moral values. He saw American society as being in a state of utter depravity, over which its elected officials presided with an almost satanic disregard for truth and human life. He viewed President Clinton and other politicians as latter-day Hitlers, and the Nazi image pervaded Bray's understanding of how ethically minded people should respond to such a threat. Regarding the activities that led to his prison conviction, Bray had "no regrets." "Whatever I did," he said, "it was worth it."

According to Bray, we live in a situation "comparable to Nazi Germany," a state of hidden warfare. The comforts of modern society have lulled the populace into a lack of awareness of the situation, and Bray was convinced that if there were some dramatic event, such as economic collapse or social chaos, the demonic role of the government would be revealed, and people would have "the strength and the zeal to take up arms" in a revolutionary struggle. What he envisioned as the outcome of that struggle was the establishment of a new moral order in America, one based on biblical law and a spiritual, rather than a secular, social compact.

Until this new moral order was established, Bray and others like him who were aware of what was going on and had the moral courage to resist it were compelled to take action. According to Bray, he had the right to defend innocent "unborn children," even by use of force, whether it involved "destroying the facilities that they are regularly killed in, or taking the life of one who is murdering them." By the latter, Bray meant killing doctors and other clinical staff involved in performing abortions.

When I suggested that such violent actions were tantamount to acting as both judge and executioner, Bray demurred. Although he did not deny that a religious authority had the right to pronounce judgment over those who broke the moral law, he explained that his actions in attacking abortion clinics and the actions of his friend, the Reverend Paul Hill, in killing abortion doctors were essentially defensive rather than punitive acts. According to Bray, "There is a difference between taking a retired abortionist and executing him, and killing a practicing abortionist who is regularly killing babies." The first act is, in Bray's view, retributive; the other, defensive. According to Bray, the attacks that he and Hill committed were not so much aimed at punishing the clinics and the abortionists for their actions as at preventing them from "killing babies," as Bray put it.

APPROPRIATING BONHOEFFER AND NIEBUHR

Bray found support for his position in actions undertaken during the Nazi regime in Europe. His theological hero in this regard was the German theologian and Lutheran pastor Dietrich Bonhoeffer. Bonhoeffer abruptly terminated his privileged research position at Union Theological Seminary in New York City in order to return to Germany and clandestinely join a plot to assassinate Hitler. The plot was uncovered before it could be carried out, and Bonhoeffer, the brilliant young ethical theorist, was hanged by the Nazis shortly before the end of the war. His image of martyrdom and his theological writings have lived on, however, and Bonhoeffer is often cited by moral theorists as an example of how Christians can undertake violent actions for a just cause and how occasionally Christians are compelled to break laws for a higher purpose.

These are positions also held by one of Bonhoeffer's colleagues at Union Theological Seminary, Reinhold Niebuhr, whom Bray similarly admired. Often touted as one of the greatest Protestant theologians of the twentieth century, Niebuhr wrestled with one of Christianity's oldest ethical problems: when is it permissible to use force—even vio-

lence—in behalf of a righteous cause? Niebuhr began his career as a pacifist, but in time grudgingly began to accept the position that a Christian, acting for the sake of justice, could be violent (Niebuhr 1932, 1942).

Niebuhr showed the relevance of just war theory to contemporary social struggles in the twentieth century by relating this classic idea—a notion first stated by Cicero and later developed by Ambrose and Augustine—to what he regarded as the Christian requirement to fulfill social justice. Viewing the world through the lens of "realism," Niebuhr was impressed that moral suasion was not sufficient to combat injustices, especially when they are buttressed by corporate and state power. For this reason, he explained in a seminal essay, "Why the Christian Church Is Not Pacifist" (1940), it was at times necessary to abandon nonviolence in favor of a more forceful solution. Building his case on Augustine's understanding of original sin, Niebuhr argued that righteous force was sometimes necessary to extirpate injustice and subdue evil within a sinful world, and that small strategic acts of violence were occasionally necessary to deter large acts of violence and injustice. If violence is to be used in such situations, Niebuhr explained, it must be used sparingly and as swiftly and as skillfully "as a surgeon's knife" (1932, 134).

Bray borrowed this theological logic for justifying violence from Niebuhr and Bonhoeffer, but where Bray radically differed from these thinkers was in his interpretation of the contemporary political situation that made the application of the logic credible. In a conceptual sleight of hand that Bonhoeffer would have regarded as inconceivable, Bray compared America's democratic state with Nazism. In a manner that would have sent Niebuhr reeling, Bray insisted that only a biblically based religious politics, rather than a secular one, was capable of dispensing social justice. Both of these positions would be rejected not only by these but also by most other theologians within the mainstream of Protestant thought.

Bonhoeffer and Niebuhr, like most modern theologians, accepted the principle of the separation of church and state. They felt the separation was necessary for the integrity of both institutions. Niebuhr was especially wary of what he called "moralism," the intrusion of religious or other ideological values into the political calculations of statecraft.

RECONSTRUCTION THEOLOGY

To support his ideas about religious politics, therefore, Bray had to look beyond mainstream Protestant thought. He found intellectual company in a group of recent writers associated with dominion theology, the theological position that Christianity must reassert the dominion of God over all things, including secular politics and society. This point of view—well articulated by such rightwing Protestant spokespersons as the Reverend Jerry Falwell and Pat Robertson—has led to a burst of social and political activism on the Christian Right in the 1980s and 1990s.

The Christian anti-abortion movement is permeated with dominion theology ideas. Randall Terry, the founder of the militant anti-abortion organization Operation Rescue, writes for the dominion magazine *Crosswinds* and has signed its Manifesto for the Christian Church, which asserts that America should "function as a Christian nation." The manifesto opposes such "social moral evils" of secular society as abortion on demand, fornication, homosexuality, sexual entertainment, state usurpation of parental rights and God-given liberties, statist-collectivist theft from citizens through devaluation of their money and redistribution of their wealth, and evolutionism taught as a monopoly viewpoint in the public schools (Berlet 1996, 8).

At the extreme right-wing of dominion theology is a relatively obscure theological movement that Mike Bray has found particularly appealing: a movement known as reconstructionist theology, whose exponents long to create a Christian theocratic state. Leaders of this movement trace their ideas to Cornelius Van Til, a twentieth-century Presbyterian professor of theology at Princeton Seminary who took seriously the sixteenth-century ideas of the Reformation theologian John Calvin regarding the necessity for presupposing the authority of God in all worldly matters. Followers of Van Til, including his former students, the Reverend Greg Bahnsen and Rousas John Rushdoony, and Rushdoony's son-in-law, Gary North, have adopted this presuppositionalism as a doctrine, with all its implications about the role of religion in political life.

Reconstructionist writers have regarded the history of Protestant politics since the early years of the Reformation as having taken a bad turn, and they were especially unhappy with the Enlightenment formulation of church-state separation. They felt that it was necessary to "reconstruct" Christian society by turning to the Bible as the basis for a nation's law and social order. To propagate their views, the reconstructionists established an Institute for Christian Economics in Tyler, Texas, and published a steady stream of literature on the theological justification for interjecting Christian ideas into economic, legal, and political life (for example, Rushdoony 1973).

According to the most prolific reconstructionist writer, Gary North, it was "the moral obligation of Christians to recapture every institution for Jesus Christ" (North 1984, 267). This was especially so in the United States, where secular law as construed by the Supreme Court and defended by liberal politicians has taken what Rushdoony and others regard as a decidedly un-Christian direction, particularly in matters regarding abortion and homosexuality. What the reconstructionists ultimately wanted, however, was much more than the rejection of secularism. Like other dominion theologians, they utilized the biblical concept of dominion, reasoning further that Christians, as the new chosen people of God, were destined to dominate the world.

The reconstructionists have a postmillennial view of history. That is, they believe that Christ will return to earth only after the thousand years of religious rule that characterizes the Christian idea of the millennium, and therefore Christians have an obligation to provide the political and social conditions that would make Christ's return possible. Premillennialists, on the other hand, hold the view that the thousand years of Christendom can come only after Christ returns, an event that will occur in a cataclysmic moment of world history, and therefore they tend to be much less active politically. Postmillennial followers of reconstructionist theology such as Mike Bray, dominion theologians such as Pat Robertson, and many of the leaders of the politically active Christian Coalition believe that a Christian kingdom can be established on earth before Christ's return, and they take seriously the idea of Christian society and the eruption of religious politics that would make biblical code the law of the land.

In our conversation, Bray insisted that the idea of a society based on Christian morality was not a new one, and he emphasized they "are" in "reconstruction." Although Bray rejected the idea of a pope, he appreciated much of the Roman Catholic church's social teachings and greatly admired the tradition of canon law.

Only recently in history, he observed, had the political order not been based on religious concepts. For that reason, Bray labeled himself an "antidisestablishmentarian." He was deeply serious about his commitment to bring such religious politics into power. He imagined that it was possible, under the right conditions, for a Christian revolution to sweep across the country, bringing in its wake constitutional changes that would allow for biblical law to be the basis of social legislation. Failing that, Bray envisaged a new federalism in America that would allow individual states to experiment with religious politics on their own. When I asked Bray which state might be ready for such an experiment, he hesitated and then offered the names of Louisiana and Mississippi, or, he added, "maybe one of the Dakotas."

CHRISTIAN IDENTITY

A somewhat different set of theological justifications lay in the background of another anti-abortion activist, Eric Robert Rudolph. Rudolph was the subject of a well-publicized manhunt by the Federal Bureau of Investigation early in 1998 for his alleged role in bombing abortion clinics in Birmingham, Alabama, and Atlanta, Georgia; blasting a gay bar in Atlanta; and exploding a bomb at the 1996 Atlanta Olympics. He subscribed to the theology of Christian Identity. The thinking of Christian Identity has been part of the background of such movements as the Posse Comitatus, the Order, the Aryan Nation, the supporters of Randy Weaver at Ruby Ridge, Herbert Armstrong's Worldwide Church of God, and the Freeman Compound. It also has been popular in many militia movements throughout the United States.

Christian Identity ideas were most likely a part of the thinking of Timothy McVeigh, the convicted bomber of the Oklahoma City federal building. McVeigh was exposed to Identity thinking through the Michigan militia with which he was once associated and which had a strong Christian Identity flavoring, and through his visits to the Christian Identity encampment, Elohim City, on the Oklahoma-Arkansas border. He also imbibed Christian Identity ideas through the book *The Turner Diaries* (Macdonald 1978), which he treated virtually as a bible and which was strongly influenced by Christian Identity ideas.

McVeigh had distributed *The Turner Diaries* at rallies and had contacted the author shortly before the Oklahoma City blast. A copy of the book was found in his car when it was intercepted leaving Oklahoma City within an hour of the attack. The anti-Semitic novel, which was written by William Pierce under the pseudonym Andrew Macdonald, tells the story of the encroachment of government control in America and the resistance by a guerrilla band known as the Order, which attacked government buildings using a modus operandi almost exactly the same as the one McVeigh used in destroying the Oklahoma City federal building.

Pierce, who received a Ph.D. from the University of Colorado and for a time taught physics at Oregon State University, once served as a writer for the American Nazi Party and in 1984 proclaimed himself the founder of a new religious group, the Cosmotheist Community (Solnin 1995, 8). Although Pierce denied affiliation with the Christian Identity movement, he knew the literature well, and his own teachings were virtually synonymous with those associated with the movement.

Pierce, like many members of the Christian Identity militia groups, distrusted ordinary Christian churches for their liberalism and lack of courage. He claimed that in the future described in his novel, the "Jewish takeover" of the Christian church would be "virtually complete" (Macdonald 1978, 64). The members of the fictional Order in his novel were characterized as being intensely religious, having undergone an initiation similar to that of joining a monastic order. The narrator in the novel tells of being required to take an oath, "a mighty Oath, a moving Oath that shook me to my bones and raised the hair on the back of my neck" (Macdonald 1978, 73). With this oath the members of the Order were spiritually armed to be "bearers of the Faith" in a godless world (Macdonald 1978, 74). According to Pierce, such missionary efforts were necessary because of the mind-set of secularism that had been imposed on American society as a result of an elaborate conspiracy orchestrated by Jews and liberals who were hell-bent on depriving Christian society of its spiritual moorings. In formulating his own version of this view, McVeigh had read Pierce and *The Turner Diaries;* Pierce, in turn, had read thinkers associated with Christian Identity.

Although the writers associated with the Christian Identity movement distrusted most modern churches, they railed against the separation of church and state—or, rather, religion and state—and longed for a new society governed by religious law. They were strongly anti-Semitic, held an apocalyptic view of history, and possessed an even more conspiratorial view of government than the reconstructionists. Christian Identity originated in the movement of British Israelism in the nineteenth century. According to John Wilson, whose central work, *Lectures on Our Israelitish Origin,* brought the message to a large British and Irish middle-class audience, Jesus had been an Aryan, not a Semite; the migrating Israelite tribes from the northern kingdom of Israel were in fact blue-eyed Aryans themselves who somehow ended up in the British Isles; and the "Lost Sheep of the House of Israel" were none other than present-day Englishmen (Barkun 1994, 7). Adherents of this theory hold that those people who claim to be Jews are imposters—according to one variation of the theory, they are aliens from outer space—who pretend to be Jews in order to assert their superiority in a scheme to control the world. Their plot is allegedly supported by the secret Protestant order of Freemasons.

British Israelism came to the United States in the twentieth century through the teachings of the evangelist Gerald L. K. Smith and the writings of William Cameron, who was the publicist for the famous automobile magnate, Henry Ford (Zeskind 1986, 12). Ford himself supported many of Cameron's views and published a book of anti-Semitic essays written by Cameron but attributed to Ford, *The International Jew: The World's Foremost Problem.* Central to Cameron's thought were the necessity of the Anglo-Saxon race in the United States to retain its purity and political dominance, and the need to establish a biblical basis for governance. These ideas were developed into the Christian Identity movement in America by Bertram Comparet, a deputy district attorney in San Diego, and Wesley Swift, a Ku Klux Klan member who founded the Church of Jesus Christ-Christian in 1946. This church was the basis for the Christian Defense League, organized by Bill Gale at his ranch in Mariposa, California, in the 1960s, a movement that spawned both the Posse Comitatus and the Aryan Nation (Zeskind 1986, 14).

In the 1980s and 1990s, the largest concentration of Christian Identity groups has been in Idaho—centered on the Aryan Nation's compound near Hayden Lake—and in the southern Midwest near the Oklahoma-Arkansas-Missouri borders. In that location, a Christian Identity group called the Covenant, the Sword, and the Arm of the Lord established a 224-acre community and a paramilitary school which it named the Endtime Overcomer Survival Training School (Zeskind 1986, 45). Nearby, Christian Identity minister Steven Millar and former Nazi Party member Glenn Miller established Elohim City, whose members stockpiled weapons and prepared themselves for "a Branch Davidian-type raid" by the U.S. government's Bureau of Alcohol, Tobacco and Firearms (Baumgarten 1995, 17). It was this Christian Identity encampment that Timothy McVeigh visited shortly before the Oklahoma City federal building blast.

The American incarnation of the Christian Identity movement contained many of its British counterpart's paranoid views, updated to suit the social anxieties of many contemporary Americans. For instance, in the American version, the United Nations and the Democratic Party were alleged to be accomplices in a Jewish Freemason conspiracy to control the world and deprive individuals of their freedom. According to a 1982 Identity pamphlet, Jews were described as "parasites and vultures," who controlled the world through international banking (Mohr 1982). The establishment of the International Monetary Fund, the introduction of magnetized credit cards, and the establishment of paper money not backed by gold or silver were the final steps in "Satan's Plan" (Aho 1990, 91). Gun control was also an important issue to Christian Identity supporters, since they believed that Jewish, U.N., and liberal conspirators intended to remove the last possibilities of rebellion against their centralized power by depriving individuals of the weapons they might use to defend themselves or free their countrymen from a tyrannical state. The views of Timothy McVeigh, although less obviously Christian and anti-Semitic than most Christian Identity teachings, otherwise fit precisely the paradigm of Christian Identity thought.

THE HIDDEN WAR

The world as envisioned by both reconstructionist theology and Christian Identity was a world at war. Identity preachers cited the biblical accounts of Michael the Archangel's destruction of the offspring of evil to point to a hidden, albeit "cosmic war" between the forces of darkness and the forces of light (Aho 1990, 85). "There is murder going on," Mike Bray explained, "which we have to stop." In the Christian Identity view of the world, the struggle was a secret war between colossal evil forces allied with U.N., U.S., and other government powers, on the one hand, and a small band of the enlightened few who recognized these invisible enemies for what they were—in their view, satanic powers—and were sufficiently courageous to battle against them. Although Bray rejected much of Christian Identity's conspiratorial view of the world and specifically decried its anti-Semitism, he did appreciate its commitment to struggle against secular forms of evil and its insistence on the need for a Christian social order. Both Christian Identity and reconstructionist thought yearned for a version of American politics rooted in Christian values and biblical law.

As Mike Bray explained, the destruction of abortion clinics was not the result of a personal vendetta against agencies with which he and others have had moral differences, but the consequences of a grand religious vision. His actions were part of a great crusade conducted by a Christian subculture in America that has seen itself at war with the larger society and, to some extent, victimized by it. Armed with the theological explanations of reconstruction and Christian Identity, this subculture has seen itself justified in its violent responses to what it perceives as a violent repression waged by secular (and, in some versions of this perception, Jewish)

agents of a satanic force. Mike Bray and his network of associates around the country saw themselves engaged in violence not for its own sake but as a response to the institutional violence of what they regarded as a repressive secular state. When he poured gasoline on rags and ignited fires to demolish abortion clinics, therefore, Mike Bray was firing the opening salvos in what he envisaged to be a great defensive Christian struggle against the secular state, a contest between the forces of spiritual truth and secular darkness, in which the moral character of America as a righteous nation hung in the balance.

In this regard, the Reverend Bray joined a legion of religious activists from Algeria to Idaho who have come to hate secular governments with an almost transcendent passion, and dream of revolutionary changes that will establish a godly social order in the rubble of what the citizens of most secular societies regard as modern, egalitarian democracies. Their enemies seem to most of us to be benign and banal: modern secular leaders and such symbols of prosperity and authority as international airlines and the World Trade Center.

The logic of their ideological religious view is, although difficult to comprehend, profound, for it contains a fundamental critique of the world's postEnlightenment secular culture and politics.

After years of waiting in history's wings, religion has renewed its claim to be an ideology of public order in a dramatic fashion: violently. In the United States, as in other parts of the world, religion's renewed political presence is accompanied by violence in part because of the nature of religion and its claims of power over life and death. In part, the violence is due to the nature of secular politics, which bases its own legitimacy on the currency of weapons and can be challenged successfully only on a level of force. In part, it is due to the nature of violence itself. Violence is a destructive display of power, and in a time when competing groups are attempting to assert their strength, the power of violence becomes a valuable political commodity. At the very least, the proponents of a religious ideology of social control such as those American activists associated with the ideas of reconstruction theology and Christian Identity have to remind the populace of the godly power that makes their ideologies potent. At their destructive worst, they create incidents of violence on God's behalf.

REFERENCES

Aho, James. 1990. The Politics of Righteousness: Idaho Christian Patriotism. Seattle: University of Washington Press.

Barkun, Michael. 1994. Religion and the Racist Right: The Origins of the Christian Identity Movement. Chapel Hill: University of North Carolina Press.

Baumgarten, Gerald. 1995. Paranoia as Patriotism: Far-Right Influences on the Militia Movement. New York: AntiDefamation League.

Berlet, Chip. 1996. John Salvi, Abortion Clinic Violence, and Catholic Right Conspiracism. Somerville, MA: Political Research Associates.

Bray, Michael. 1994. A Time to Kill: A Study Concerning the Use of Force and Abortion. Portland, OR: Advocates for Life.

———. 1996. Interview by author. Bowie, MD, 25 Apr. 1996.

Juergensmeyer, Mark. 1993. The New Cold War? Religious Nationalism Confronts the Secular State. Berkeley: University of California Press.

Macdonald, Andrew [William Pierce]. 1978. The Turner Diaries. Arlington, VA: Alliance National Vanguard Books.

Mohr, Gordon "Jack." 1982. Know Your Enemies. N.p.

Niebuhr, Reinhold. 1932. Moral Man and Immoral Society. New York: Scribner's.

———. 1940. Why the Christian Church Is Not Pacifist. London: Student Christian Movement Press.

———. 1942. The Nature and Destiny of Man. New York: Scribner's.

North, Gary. 1984. Backward, Christian Soldiers? An Action Manual for Christian Reconstruction. Tyler, TX: Institute for Christian Economics.

Rushdoony, Rousas John. 1973. Institutes of Biblical Law. Nutley, NJ: Craig Press.

Solnin, Amy C. 1995. William L. Pierce: Novelist of Hate. New York: Anti-Defamation League.

Zeskind, Leonard. 1986. The "Christian Identity" Movement: Analyzing Its Theological Rationalization for Racist and Anti-Semitic Violence. New York: National Council of Churches of Christ in the U.S.A., Division of Church and Society.

Taipūcam in Malaysia:
Ecstasy and Identity in a Tamil Hindu Festival

Raymond L. M. Lee

The festival of Taipūcam is vividly described in this essay by Raymond L. M. Lee. Taipūcam is celebrated by the Tamil Hindu minority living in largely Muslim Malaysia. During the festival, participants enter into deep states of trance. Their bodies are pierced by hooks and spears, and they carry shoulder harnesses called Kavadis up more than 200 steps to a shrine in a cave outside of Kuala Lumpur, the capital of Malaysia.

Lee argues that in order to understand the rapidly increasing popularity of this festival, one must understand the position of Tamils in both Hindu and Malaysian society. The Tamils number about 60 million in Southern India and Sri Lanka but they are a relatively small minority in Malaysia. They arrived as menial laborers and plantation workers and have traditionally occupied the low rungs of society. Further, they are largely lower caste within Hinduism. So, they occupy low social and religious positions.

It is in the context of the Tamil struggle for both personal and political power that Taipūcam takes on significance. Through their acts of penitence, individual participants believe they gain great spiritual power. Because they are lower caste, and most of the priests officiating at the ceremony are not Brahmins, this power opposes that of the traditional Hindu leadership. Further, despite their low status, the Tamil have engaged in a long-running insurrection in Malaysia and

have become increasingly important in Malaysian politics. The mass demonstration of Tamil presence at the festival and the close identification of the festival with Tamil political leadership, manifest and consolidate political power. Thus Taipūcam is a political and social festival as well as a religious one, and its celebration is linked to the changing fortunes of the Tamil minority community in Malaysia.

As you read, consider the following questions:

1. What role does the ritual of Taipūcam play in establishing Tamil identity in Malaysia?
2. What is the meaning of Taipūcam to those who go through it?
3. What roles does trance play in successfully participating in Taipūcam?

Religious revivalism has been a significant event in Malaysia during the decade 1977–1987 (Nagata 1984; Ackerman and Lee 1988). Among Indian Hindus in Malaysia, this revivalism has facilitated a growing interest in Hindu scriptures, temple worship, and organisational activities (Lee and Rajoo 1987). Hindu religious festivals are attracting larger crowds every year, especially the south Indian celebration of *Taipūcam*.[1] This festival represents the annual climax of Murukaṇ worship in Malaysia. It occurs in the Tamil month of *Tai* (January–February) when the full moon conjoins the star constellation *pūcam*. The festival is most noted for the extravagant displays of penance, particularly the carrying of *kāvaṭi*, wooden or metal arches mounted on the shoulders of devotees and often attached to sharp hooks dug into their skin.

The roots of the ritualistic ordeal can be found in the myth associated with the demon, Iṭampan, who was defeated by Murukaṉ and later became his loyal disciple (Clothey 1978: 119; Shulman 1980: 48). According to the myth, Iṭampan had survived Murukaṉ's slaughter of the Cūr demons and spent his time performing *śraddha* rites for his departed companions. The sage Agastya was impressed by Iṭampan's behaviour and thought he was sufficiently reliable to carry two hills to Poṭikai, the abode of Śiva. Using the staff of Brahmā as a pole and snakes as ropes, Iṭampan carried the hills like a *kāvaṭi* until he reached Palani. He rested his burden there but when he attempted to lift them again, he discovered that they were stuck to the ground. To trace the cause of this problem, he climbed one of the hills only to encounter the youthful Murukaṉ who claimed the hills as his own. A fight ensued which resulted in Iṭampan's demise, but Murukaṉ restored the demon to life upon the pleading of Agastya and the demon's wife. The ever grateful Iṭampan became Murukaṉ's faithful servant and requested that whoever offers vows to his master be blessed. *Kāvaṭi* carriers are, therefore, thought to be re-enacting Iṭampan's submission to Murukaṉ.

The ecstatic worship of Murukaṉ continues to be observed not only in Palani and other towns in Tamil Nadu, but also at Kataragama in Sri Lanka where Murukaṉ is worshipped as Skanda (Obeyesekere 1977, 1978). In Malaysia *Taipūcam* is celebrated with much pomp and fanfare at many Murukaṉ temples, particularly at the Waterfall temple in Penang and the Batu Caves shrine in Kuala Lumpur. Of these two centres, the one in Kuala Lumpur attracts the largest crowds and receives the widest publicity. Each year the media reports an increasing number of devotees, pilgrims and tourists at the Batu Caves shrine. In 1987 800,000 people were estimated to have attended the festival at Batu Caves. This shrine has been a major pilgrimage and worship centre for Murukaṉ devotees in Malaysia since the end of the last century. Batu Caves is a limestone outcrop about two square miles in circumference and located approximately five miles north of the city centre. There are at least five caves of varying sizes that have been transformed into Hindu shrines or recreational sites. The central shrine, dedicated to Murukaṉ, is found in the largest cave which rises more than 300 feet above the ground and is reached by an ascent of 272 concrete steps. Two other shrines dedicated to Gaṇēśa and Nāga are located at the bottom of the steps. As a god that is associated with the *kuṟñci* or hill tract (Clothey 1978: 24), it is not surprising that the Murukaṉ shrine is housed in an elevated limestone cave. For devotees living in Kuala Lumpur, a city built on a flat estuary surrounded by distant hills, Batu Caves is indeed an ideal location for easy access to the worship of a popular south Indian hill deity.

TAMIL IDENTITY IN MALAYSIA

The specific meanings of *Taipūcam* cannot be isolated from the wider historical developments in the Malaysian Tamil community. The emigration of Tamils to Malaysia has been well documented (Sandhu 1969; Arasaratnam 1970). South Indian Tamils constitute about 80 per cent of the one million Indians living in peninsular Malaysia today.[2] As the largest Indian sub-ethnic group in Malaysia, south Indian Tamils have maintained a distinct identity from the other groups originating from the subcontinent. Most south Indian Tamils arrived in colonial Malaya as labourers under the *kangany* system, working mainly in the rubber plantations or railways. Their isolation on the plantations not only implies an encapsulated social existence but also limited social mobility in relation to the other ethnic groups (Jain 1970; Wiebe and Mariappan 1978). Because of south Indian Tamil concentration in the rubber estates, a stereotype has emerged of the Tamil as a low caste, uneducated, dirty labourer.

Despite this unflattering image, many Tamils have continuously sought to enhance their social standing through involvement in political and religious activities. Before World War II, Tamil identity was most vigorously expressed in the activities of the Tamil Reform Association (TRA), an organisation founded in 1931 that was heavily influenced by the Dravidian nationalist ideologies of E. V. Ramasamy Naicker and the Self-Respect League of Madras. Originating in the Ahampadiyar Sangam of Singapore (a depressed caste society) in the late 1920s, the TRA was initially concerned with the problems of caste prejudice, Brahmin dominance, and various issues related to education, health and marriage. It also advocated bans on *kāvaṭi*, fire-walking, blood sacrifices, and other practices perceived as retarding the progress of Hinduism. The members of TRA were mainly Tamil journalists, businessmen, and school teachers whose efforts at reform were gradually transformed into a sense of moral trusteeship for the Tamils in Malaya (Ampalavanar 1969, 1972).

The TRA continued to foster new meanings of Tamil identity until the Japanese invasion of Malaya in 1941, when its activities were eclipsed by the mobilisation of the Japanese-sponsored Indian National Army. After the war there were renewed efforts at heightening Tamil consciousness, especially with the formation of various Tamil literary and cultural organisations under the leadership of Tamil journalists, lawyers and teachers. In 1951 a Tamil Representative Council was formed as an umbrella body for these cultural movements. As a demonstration of its concern for Tamil unity, the Council promoted the Tamil harvest festival of *Taiponkal* to distinguish it from *Tipāvali* which was thought to suggest north Indian cultural hegemony (Arasaratnam 1970: 129; Ampalavanar 1981: 34).

This trend in Tamil cultural awareness was complemented by a growing interest in Śaiva siddhānta, a body of religious teachings derived from the works of several Tamil saints. In the 1950s and 1960s, several religious movements were established under the inspiration of Ramanathan Chettiyar of Madras to disseminate siddhānta teachings of Malaysian Tamils. The momentum generated by these events has not abated, for even as recently as 1980 a Śaiva siddhānta organisation was formed in Kuala Lumpur with the help of the Śaiva Siddhānta Church of Hawaii. In addition to these developments, various Śaivite scholars and dignitaries from Tamil Nadu are frequently invited to give lectures in Malaysia. The renewed focus on Śaivism, spawned by the post-war Tamil cultural revival, offers a powerful alternative to the Sanskritic tradition generally associated with the Hinduism of north India.

Politically, Tamils did not secure dominant positions in the Malaysian Indian Congress (MIC—the Indian component of the Malaysian coalition government) until the mid-1950s. In 1936 a Central Indian Association of Malaya was formed but its leading members were Malayalis (Stenson 1980: 45). The MIC which was established in 1946 was initially controlled by some north Indians (Ampalavanar 1981). As has been suggested by Stenson (1980: 177), the Tamils' rise to power in the MIC was facilitated partly by the post-war Tamil cultural movements.[3] However, this leadership comprised mainly higher caste and propertied Tamils. After the death in 1979 of V. Manickavasagam, the sixth MIC president, a new leadership pattern emerged that was more populist in rhetoric and style. Manickavasagam's successor was S. Samy Vellu whose political exhortations were suggestively aimed at cultivating Tamil respectability through tough and firm actions. It is in this context of a change from an elitist to a populist MIC leadership that Tamil identity and its association with various religious practices can be better understood.

THE FESTIVAL OF FRENZIED PENANCE

Taipūcam is usually celebrated for three consecutive days in early February. The second day of the festival, when the carrying of *kāvaṭi* reaches its peak, is a public holiday in four of the 11 states in peninsular Malaysia. Hundreds of Indian pilgrims arriving in chartered buses converge on Batu Caves a day or so before the festival, crowding into tents in the temple grounds. A temple official has estimated that at least 80 per cent of them are from rubber plantations outside Kuala Lumpur and in other states. The normally quiet temple grounds at Batu Caves are turned into a kaleidoscope of noise, colour, heat, and smells that can produce an overwhelmingly narcotic effect on the devotees. The bazaar-like atmosphere, with several hundred stalls offering a varied range of consumer items, and the colourful performances of *kāvaṭi* carriers suggest that the quiet fulfillment of an individual vow (*veṇṭutalai*) to Murukaṇ achieves its full meaning in the blatantly loud celebration of *Taipūcam*.

The Śrī Mahā Māriyamman temple in Kuala Lumpur is responsible for the initial preparations for *Taipūcam* since it directly controls the Murukaṇ shrine at Batu Caves. *Upayam* (endowment) members of the temple provide a variety of services to devotees. For example, the railway *upayam* provides rail transport to and from the cave shrine at a reduced rate, the merchant *upayam* provides free camphor, coconuts,

sandalwood paste, ashes, and so on. But not all services are offered gratis by the temple. Ear-piercing, head-shaving, and *arccaṇai* (offerings) services are performed by temple staff upon payment by devotees. Space for more than 500 stalls is advertised in the local Tamil newspapers a few weeks before the festival. A few days before the main event, all competitors gather at Batu Caves to place their identity cards into a box for a lottery draw to determine the assignment of stalls.[4] Individuals who provide free medical services, free food and drinks, and devotional singing are usually given stalls without charge. Penitents are required to pay M$ 5 a person for the entitlement to traverse the path and the steps leading to the Murukaṇ shrine. According to the temple's estimates, the money collected from these sources and individual donations amount to more than M$ 200,000 every year.[5]

Pre-festive preparations also include the recruitment of 60 to 70 *paṇṭāram* priests to administer to the needs of devotees and penitents. This is the responsibility of the chief *paṇṭāram* at the Murukaṇ shrine. For this occasion, he recruits *paṇṭāram* priests from Hindu temples throughout Malaysia and other non-Brahmin priests trained by local Hindu organisations. He generally pays each priest M$ 50 to M$ 60 as wages. In addition these priests receive free transport, food, clothing, and accommodation. The non-Brahmin *paṇṭāram* is the major religious functionary at *Taipūcam* because the festival is largely celebrated by non-Brahmins and devotees from the lower castes. Brahmin priests would regard it as ritually polluting if they have to administer to hundreds of non-Brahmins on this occasion.

Day One

The first day of *Taipūcam* is marked by the pre-dawn performance of the *viśeṣa pūjā* at the Śrī Mahā Māriyamman temple. This *pūjā* comprises a special *abiṣekam* or the ceremonial bathing of the Murakaṇ image with nine items: water, milk, *pañcāmirtam* (a fruit dish made from jackfruit, mango, banana, grape, and orange), coconut juice, ghee, honey, ashes, sandalwood paste, and rose water. This ritual is performed by a Brahmin priest who recites the *abiṣekam mantra* as he washes the image. The *abiṣekam* is open to public viewing. Upon the completion of this ceremony, a yellow curtain is drawn around the image which is then adorned with silk, jewellery and garlands. The curtains are parted and a lamp known as the *alaṅkāram tīpam* is waved three times before the image. This is followed by a similar waving of seven silver items: *kumbam* (pot), *kuṭai* (umbrella), *alavadham* (leaf), *viciri* (fan), *vencāmaram* (fan), *koṭi* (flag), *kaṇṇāṭi* (mirror). As these items are waved, the priest recites the 108 names of Murukaṇ. When the recitation ends, on *ōtuvār* (hymn singer) sings some verses from the Tevāram. The priest then offers a tray of flowers to the image while reciting the 108 names. He performs the *alaṅkāram tīpam* and offers the flames to the devotees. *Prasādam* comprising *vibhūti* (ashes), *tīrttam* (blessed water), *kuṅkuman* (a red powder), sandalwood paste, and flowers are distributed to the devotees.

Individual devotees with requests for blessings from Murukaṉ approach the priest for *arccaṉai*. After the performance of *arccaṉai* the images of Murukaṉ and his consorts, Vaḷḷi and Devasenā, are carried around the temple three times in a clockwise direction. The circumambulation ceremony is accompanied by musicians playing traditional instruments. The images are mounted on a silver chariot and more *arccaṉai* are performed. From this moment on, the *paṇṭāram* priests take over as the chariot, pulled by two bulls and a few devotees, leaves the temple grounds. At 6 AM before the chariot departs for Batu Caves, *tīrttam* is sprinkled on the devotees and coconuts are broken in front of the chariot. The journey from the temple to Batu Caves takes nearly five hours as the chariot makes its way through several main streets in downtown Kuala Lumpur, followed by a large crowd of devotees. Early morning traffic is brought to a standstill as the procession winds it way to Batu Caves.

An the Sentul section of Kuala Lumpur, about three miles from Batu Caves, the chariot stops at some shops with banana trees tied to the two ends of the front door.[6] This is to signify that the shops are owned by Hindus who wish to receive *darśan* (blessing by sight) from Murukaṉ. Other Hindus living in the area congregate at these shops to receive *darśan* and request *arccaṉai*. The procession makes one more stop in Sentul at the Śrī Taṇṭāyutapāṇi temple where the resident *paṇṭāram* performs more *arccaṉai* for devotees. The chariot arrives at Batu Caves in the late hours of the morning and the images are promptly installed at the Swami Mandapam below the cave shrine. The chief *paṇṭāram* waves lamps, distributes *prasādam,* and performs *arccaṉai*. The *vēl* (lance) of Murukaṉ is removed from the chariot and carried into the cave shrine.

In the evening the temple grounds at Batu Caves resemble a carnival with many stalls opened for business and a small amusement park attracting crowds of children. The stalls sell an assortment of items ranging from sweets, drinks and food to cosmetics, paintings, books and tapes. The stalls set up by Hindu organisations distribute pamphlets advertising their activities and sell hagiographic literature of their gurus. The public is treated to Tamil movies, *bhajan* performances, and speeches given by itinerant Hindu ascetics from India. Many young MIC workers take this opportunity to sell MIED lottery tickets to the public.[7] In the midst of all these transactions, a few penitents carrying *kāvaṭi* ascend the steps into the cave to fulfil their vows to Murukaṉ.

Day Two

Before dawn many penitents gather at the Batu Caves river, about half a mile from the shrine, to wash themselves in preparation for carrying *kāvaṭi*. Some of them take a quick dip in the polluted river, but most prefer to pour on themselves buckets of water mixed with turmeric, lime and flowers from four large tanks installed on the right bank of the river. Each penitent is usually surrounded by a small group of friends and relatives as he or she is initiated into trance by an older experienced *kāvaṭi* carrier. Nearby under a shed, a group of young devotees sing devotional songs to help facilitate trance in the penitents. The tunes of these songs are derived largely from popular Hindi and Tamil movies, but the lyrics comprise chants of Murukaṉ. Male penitents wear only a waist cloth *(vēṣṭi)* in one of three colours: white, yellow, red. Some wear colourful turbans and embroidered sashes to signify possession by the guardian deity Muṉīśvaraṉ or Muṉiyāṇṭi. Female penitents are dressed in saris or pantsuits. Many penitents wear bell anklets on both ankles which amplify the rhythm of their dance movements.

Penitents who have entered trance are pierced with hooks, needles and skewers *(alaku),* measuring from six inches to more than three feet in length, in their backs, cheeks, tongues, and chests. These sharp implements are attached to a wooden or metal arch mounted on the penitent's shoulders and secured firmly around his waist. Not all penitents, however, endure these acts of self-mortification; some merely carry unobtrusive and sparsely decorated *kāvaṭi* without perforating their flesh with sharp metal objects. Generally, more male penitents perform self-mortification than female penitents.[8] The temple grounds reverberate with cries of *vēl, vēl* and *arōhara* (a salutation to Śiva) as supporters lend encouragement to *kāvaṭi* carriers dancing their way to the cave shrine. The supporters surround the penitent in a circle to give him space to dance and at the same time keep onlookers at a safe distance from flailing arms and sharp metal. The better organised supporters, dressed uniformly in logo-embroidered T-shirts, blue jeans and sun caps, come prepared with whistles and ropes for crowd control. Many of them beat long bongo drums to maintain the rhythm of *kāvaṭi* dancing. Occasionally, some supporters may spontaneously fall into a trance, twitching and jerking as though infected by the ecstatic mood of their *kāvaṭi*-carrying colleagues. These individuals are quickly held down by their friends and removed from the scene to be revived elsewhere. Rare cases of spontaneous mediumship may occur in which an entranced penitent makes predictions or gives advice based on the claim that the outpourings are derived from a recognised deity. Many onlookers approach the medium for blessings and forecasting, while the supporters prevent photographers from taking pictures of the medium.

At least ten types of *kāvaṭi* are observed in the procession of penitents to the cave shrine. The most common is *pāl kāvaṭi* which is milk offering in small metal containers covered at the mouth with a banana leaf and a yellow cloth. *Pāl kāvaṭi* is required of all penitents because it is a product of the cow, a sacred animal, and therefore a symbol of fertility, purity and prosperity. The containers of milk are hung on the ends of *kāvaṭi* arches or on hooks inserted into the penitent's body. Some supporters carry the containers for penitents who are busily engaged in various acts of self-mortification. Some female penitents merely carry large pots of milk on their heads or shoulders without exhibiting the lurid flamboyance of their male counterparts.

Another common *kāvaṭi* is *vēl kāvaṭi* which is either a short needle in the shape of a lance pierced through the penitent's tongue, or a long arrow-tipped skewer pierced through one or both cheeks. The *vēl* is the lance of Murukaṉ given to him by Śakti to destroy demons. Other *kāvaṭi* that are worn on the penitent's body or placed on the arch are *puṣpam* (flowers), *mayil iṟaku* (peacock feathers), and *pavalam* (beads or gem stones) *kāvaṭi*. Some *kāvaṭi* are carried on the head such as *kalaca kāvaṭi* which is made from betel leaves in the shape of a *gopuram* (temple tower) and carried as an offering for Gaṇeśa, or *cantaṉam kāvaṭi* which is made of sandalwood paste in the shape of a *gopuram* with limes hanging from it. *Kāvaṭi* that are carried by hand include *agni kāvaṭi* or pots of fire placed on top of *vēppilai* leaves, and *paṉṉīr kāvaṭi* or pots of jasmine scented water. *Agni kāvaṭi* is usually carried as an offering for Śakti, sometimes by penitents whose family members have been cured of smallpox or chickenpox. *Karumpu kāvaṭi* is carried by married couples whose wish for a child has been granted. The head-shaven child is placed in a cloth tied to the centre of a long cane. The husband holds the front end of the cane, the wife the rear end, and together they carry their child up 272 steps to show their gratitude to Murukaṉ. Married couples usually perform *karumpu kāvaṭi* before sunrise to avoid the crowds.[9]

Kāvaṭi is not only restricted to the carrying of ashes and elaborate contraptions. Some penitents, both male and female, carried by their supporters shoot brightly decorated wooden arrows into the air to re-enact Murukaṉ's destruction of the *asura* demons. Penitents who are possessed by the deity, Maṭurai Vīraṉ, walk on several large knives held by their supporters. Those who are possessed by Muṉīśvaraṉ or Muṉiyāṇṭi smoke cigars and flagellate themselves, or may even pull a chariot connected with ropes to hooks and skewers in their backs. These penitents usually end their journey at the Swami Mandapam because of the physical and technical difficulties in dragging the chariot up into the cave shrine. Penitents who claim possession by Kaḷī cut their tongues. Possession by the monkey deity Hanumān, is manifested in the penitent's enactment of simian-like behaviour, such as jumping around and scratching the body vigorously.

Many penitents who carry *kāvaṭi* are not Indians. Over the years many Chinese have been observed participating in this ritualistic ordeal. Some Europeans have returned to Batu Caves for several consecutive years to carry *kāvaṭi*. Few Malay penitents are seen at this festival because as Muslims they are discouraged from participating in what Islamic religious officials would consider a pagan celebration.[10]

Darśan of the Murukaṉ image is given at 8 AM on the river banks. The Brahmin priest performs *abiṣekam*, after which *darśan* is given and the image is returned to the Swami Mandapam. By 11 AM the route from the river to the cave shrine is packed with an endless stream of *kāvaṭi* penitents. The crowd is thickest from 11 AM to 1 PM because carrying *kāvaṭi* at this time is regarded as most auspicious when the sun is at its highest point. Not only does the penitent gain additional merit from suffering the increased heat of the sun, but he also enjoys the opportunity to perform sun worship (*cūryanamaskāram*). As the crowd begins swelling, leading politicians from the MIC make speeches extolling the virtues of Hinduism and Tamil achievements in Malaysia.[11] They harangue the crowd from the balcony of a building situated near the steps leading to the cave shrine. Devotees making their way to the shrine at this hour run a gauntlet of pickpockets, lost children, frenzied penitents, and 'eve teasers.'[12] They also have to wade their way through individual entrepreneurs selling *arccaṉai* items in plastic bags. For M\$ 1 a devotee can purchase an *arccaṉai* bag containing a coconut, several bananas, a few pieces of camphor, betel leaves and nuts, and some ashes.

Most devotees and penitents are expected to pay homage to the image of Iṭampaṉ, located on the left corner of the entrance arch, as they make their way into the main cavern. But many of them are not even aware of the image as they eagerly struggle toward the Murukaṉ shrine. Nevertheless, it is believed that the spirit of Iṭampaṉ helps penitents maintain their momentum in their sacred journey to the central shrine. Inside the main cave the mood of the crowd is softened by the cool air circulating within the cavernous opening which can accommodate more than a thousand people at any one time. The cave is brightly lit by electric bulbs and two large fires fed by camphor from the devotees. The main activities are concentrated on the Murukaṉ shrine, a white-tiled structure located in a small opening on the left side of the cave. Upon reaching their final destination, the penitents carrying *kāvaṭi* dance vigorously in front of the shrine before falling exhausted to the ground. It is believed that if the milk offering rises and flows out of the pots carried by the penitents, it is a sign that Murukaṉ is pleased with them.[13] All sharp implements are removed from the penitents' bodies and they are revived with gentle slaps and shakes. Milk in the pots is first offered to Murukaṉ, then to the penitents' supporters and other devotees. With the arches removed from their bodies, the sweating penitents trudge their way down the 272 steps to the bottom of the cave. Devotees who wish to have *arccaṉai* performed buy a M\$ 1 ticket from a priest stationed at the shrine. They hand their offerings and tickets to another priest who performs *arccaṉai* and returns some of the blessed items to them. Having completed their worship, some devotees may strive for more merit by giving alms to families of beggars grouped in one corner of the cave.[14] Some devotees offer gifts of live chickens to the temple. Because of the prohibition of public blood sacrifices, these chickens are kept alive in a cage in the centre of the cave and later sold or given away.

By late afternoon the crowds thin out and the stalls close up. The temple grounds resemble a deserted fair, strewn with rubbish and saturated with a spent atmosphere. The devotees, penitents, tourists, politicians, and ethnographers have gone, leaving the temple grounds silent until the next *Taipūcam* celebrations.

Day Three

At 8 AM the *vēl* is brought down from the shrine to the Swami Mandapam. The return journey of the images to the Srī Mahā Māriyamman temple begins at 10 AM. The procession accompanied by traditional musicians stops at the Sentul artisan quarters. The images are removed from the chariot and mounted on a platform under a shed beside a large field. Devotees approach the images for *darśan*, prayers and *arccaṇai*. At noon yellow curtains are drawn around the images and the gods are allowed to rest until 3 PM. The *paṇṭāram* priest performs *abiṣekam* and hangs fresh garlands on the Murukaṉ image, after which the curtains are opened and the public allowed to receive *darśan* and request *arccaṇai*. Interaction between the images and the public continues until 6:30 PM. The images are re-mounted on the chariot and the procession moves on uninterrupted to the temple. Two weeks after *Taipūcam*, various items donated by devotees to the temple are auctioned and the proceeds amounting to more than M$ 20,000 go into the temple's treasury.

KĀVAṬI: THE PROCESS OF PENANCE

Kāvaṭi is the focus of *Taipūcam* where men and women reciprocate the favours of Murukaṉ by enduring a ritualistic ordeal once a year for three consecutive years or for life. Experiencing the ordeal demonstrates the lowly, mortal status of human beings whose dependence on the gods is guaranteed through ritualistic appeasement and submission. Yet the penitents must prepare themselves for submission, to condition their flesh and spirit to a threshold beyond human pain. In a sense, preparing for *kāvaṭi* is a temporary renunciation of the world. For several weeks the penitents distance themselves from other people and train their thoughts on Murukaṉ in order to attain the consciousness required for discharging their spiritual obligations. Some older, experienced men and women organize these preparations on their own. They may serve as spiritual guides to younger penitents, especially those who are carrying *kāvaṭi* for the first time. Younger penitents usually seek the tutelage of temple priests or individual laymen through their networks of relatives and friends. The spiritual guides may vary in their methods of preparation but all penitents are required to perform several types of austerities (*tapas, viratam*) for a period lasting from a week to 48 days. *Tapas* is generally a private affair, per-

formed mainly at home and away from the gaze of others. It is intended to reinforce the penitents' personal relationship with Murukaṉ.

The Performance of Austerities

In following the rules of *tapas*, the penitents observe a strict regimen of daily fasting, prayer, and sexual abstinence until they complete their vows at *Taipūcam*. They are expected to rise before dawn, take a cold bath, clean the prayer room, pray, and perform *ārati* (waving of lights) before an image or a picture of Murukaṉ. If possible, they recite the Murukaṉ Stōtre while praying. These verses are available in English transliterations for penitents who do not read Tamil or Sanskrit. Two more prayers, at 12 PM and after sunset, are performed along with food offerings to Murukaṉ. Penitents are discouraged from sleeping in comfort—they sleep on a hard cement floor, using a piece of wood as a pillow. Although they are advised to limit their social relations and to maintain silence, they are permitted to continue their daily routines at home and at work. The length of abstinence varies from individual to individual but it is not expected to exceed 48 days. Generally, the more significant the vows the longer the period of abstinence.

Fasting is regarded as essential for conditioning the body and mind to endure the ordeal of *kāvaṭi*. Upon wakening in the morning, the penitents drink a glass of water or milk containing *tulasī* (basil) leaves. Aside from its medicinal value, *tulasī* is considered a sacred plant that is often used in ritual offerings.[15] No food or drink is taken for the rest of the day until the early evening. Penitents are encouraged to cook their own food, usually a bland mixture of rice and vegetables, to avoid pollution by other people. Consumption of meat is strictly prohibited. In families which observe the fast with the penitents, food is cooked in separate utensils and served individually to maintain ritual purity.

During this period of *tapas*, the penitents spend their spare time constructing the *kāvaṭi* arches following the instructions of friends, relatives and experienced laymen. There is a strong preference for fixing collapsible metal arches which can be dismantled and kept for another occasion. Some penitents prefer to rent readymade arches for as much as M$ 200 a day. Others may pay their friends or relatives to make the arches. Generally, the size of the arch provides a proportional measure of the importance of vows: the larger the arch the more important the vow.

The spiritual advisor, usually an older Indian male, plays a pivotal role in *tapas*. In most cases he does not accept cash payment for his services but only gifts of food and consumer items. Several days before *Taipūcam*, the advisor summons the penitents under his tutelage to his home where he performs *pūjā*, recites *mantra*, and sings devotional songs. He attempts to create a conducive atmosphere for trance by encouraging collective participation in these spiritual exercises over several meetings. He puts into motion the psychological processes of imitation and suggestion that are necessary for inducing trance in the penitents. When he is satisfied that his charges are mentally and physically ready, he initiates them into trance. Those who are not ready are instructed to intensify their *tapas* or to stop altogether. It is believed that if an advisor allows ill-prepared penitents to carry *kāvaṭi* he will incur the wrath of Murukaṉ.

On the day of *Taipūcam*, the advisor meets the penitents on the banks of the Batu Caves river. While the penitents take their ritual baths by the water tanks, the advisor performs *pūjā*, cuts lime, and waves *ārati* before a picture of Murukaṉ. More *pūjā* are performed when the penitents appear dripping wet before him. They clasp their hands in a posture of prayer, close their eyes and concentrate on Murukaṉ, while the advisor smears ashes on their chests, backs, arms, necks, and foreheads. As the supporters sing devotional songs and chant *vēl*, *vēl*, the advisor burns *cāmpirāṇi* (benzoic) and waves the fumes to be inhaled by the penitents. When they show initial signs of trance by moving rhythmically forward and backward, he applies ashes on their foreheads at a point between the eyes *(netrikaṉ)* and rubs it. Most penitents lose consciousness at this moment and the advisor inserts needles and skewers into their bodies.[16] If a penitent bleeds or cries out in pain, the advisor will stop the piercing and instruct him not to continue because he has no blessings from Murukaṉ or he has not observed his fast properly. When the piercing is completed, limes are fixed to the sharp ends of the skewers or hung on hooks attached to the penitents' torsos.[17] The advisor pats the penitents' cheeks gently, bringing them to a le *vēl* of consciousness sufficient for carrying *kāvaṭi* to the shrine. He accompanies his charges into the cave to complete his spiritual responsibility. After the penitents dance in front of the Murukaṉ shrine, the advisor massages their foreheads making them unconscious while he removes all sharp objects from their bodies. The exhausted penitents are revived and instructed to go home, wash, pray, and sleep. In the evening they are required to pray at the nearest Hindu temple and to continue their fast for another three days.

No penitent would consider his spiritual task completed without paying homage to Iṭampan. Food offerings to Iṭampan, known as Iṭampan *pūjā*, are made on the third day after *Taipūcam*. The offerings comprise cooked curry chicken, rice, beer, and a cigar. All these items are placed on a banana leaf. After the offerings are made, water is sprinkled on the food to 'cleanse' it for human consumption. The penitents eat the food first, then offer it to their friends and relatives. Male penitents offer food only to other males. Female penitents cannot give or receive food from others because of their ritually impure status. They feed themselves individually. When the feast is over, the leftovers are wrapped in a banana leaf, placed in a plastic bag and thrown into a river or a drain with flowing water as final offerings to Iṭampan.

The steps leading to the induction of trance at *Taipūcam* have been interpreted by psychologists as classic methods in altering states of consciousness (Ward 1984). However, the alternation between sensory deprivation during *tapas* and sensory bombardment during *kāvaṭi* preparation does not necessarily comprise a sufficient condition for explaining the penitent's mental state of *Taipūcam*. This state of mind is not merely an end result of specific ritual techniques but a manifestation of a religious tradition that emphasises a debt bondage between gods and men, and the penalties that are incurred if debt remained unpaid. A case study of a female penitent will illustrate the importance of this debt relationship.

A Case Study

The subject of this case study is Selvarani, a university student in her twenties.[18] She claimed that in 1985 her mother fell seriously ill and could not move. At that time she was preparing for a major examination that would determine her entry into university. The stress was too much to bear. She made a private vow to Murukaṉ that she would carry *pāl kāvaṭi* if her mother got well and she passed the examination. As it happened, her wishes were fulfilled. She reported this to her father who expressed great concern about her vow and insisted that they seek the help of Mr. Gopal, a 55-year-old retired soldier and a spiritual advisor to many penitents. He instructed her to fast for a week before *Taipūcam* and to perform *tapas* similar to the practices described above. Her family gave her moral support by fasting with her.

On the third day of her fast, she went with her parents to Mr. Gopal's house where seven other penitents had gathered. Mr. Gopal had summoned them to perform collective *pūjā* and to test their abilities to enter into trance. Selvarani was surprised at his intentions because she had assumed that carrying *pāl kāvaṭi* without self-mortification did not require trance. Mr. Gopal, however, insisted that entering a trance was a prerequisite to the proper performance of *kāvaṭi*. The thought of becoming entranced made Selvarani extremely nervous, but she felt she could not back out of her obligations. Mr. Gopal ushered the penitents into his prayer room where he performed *ārati* and led them in singing devotional songs. Selvarani reported that 'there was something in the atmosphere around us,' referring to a highly charged sense of spirituality and religious camaraderie perpetrated by rhythmic chanting and singing. Mr. Gopal initiated the seven penitents into trance quite effortlessly before turning his attention to Selvarani. He held her back, touched her forehead, and began singing while the others clapped their hands and chanted *vēl*, *vēl*. She said she felt cold and could not open her eyes. Her legs felt glued to the floor. Mr. Gopal instructed her to open her eyes and told her she had *aruḷ* (divine grace), but she had to concentrate more to achieve trance.

On the fifth day of her fast, she went into trance after Mr. Gopal touched her forehead. She said she felt a chill in her legs, a little dizzy, and as though she were enveloped in darkness. Then she lost consciousness. After Mr. Gopal revived her, he instructed her to meet him by the Batu Caves river on *Taipūcam* at 4 AM and he would bring her the *kāvaṭi* arch. Selvarani admitted that she felt apprehensive and nervous. She prayed that Murukaṉ would accept her *kāvaṭi*. Any mishaps in carrying *kāvaṭi* was interpreted as Murukaṉ's displeasure and a bad omen for her family. On the appointed day, she awoke at 3 AM, prayed and asked for her parents' blessings. Accompanied by her family, she arrived at the river banks to meet Mr. Gopal who was nowhere to be seen. She witnessed many penitents preparing for trance and self-mortification. She said she was terribly frightened. She waited until the break of dawn and there was still no sign of Mr. Gopal. By that time she claimed she began to feel a sense of excitement and eagerness to carry *kāvaṭi*. Mr. Gopal finally showed up at 8:30 AM with a decorated wooden arch for Selvarani. She later learned from her father that he had arranged for Mr. Gopal to come almost five hours late, in order to give her time to adjust to the surroundings and to prepare mentally for her spiritual task.

After the initial preparations, Mr. Gopal applied ashes on her forehead, neck and hands, while her family formed a circle around her chanting *vēl, vēl*. At this junction she closed her eyes and concentrated on Murukaṉ. She felt a sudden chill in her body and felt as if she was struck by brightly coloured lights. She lost consciousness but was quickly revived by Mr. Gopal who mounted the arch on her shoulders. She said she was not fully conscious and experienced little vision on her left and right. Mr. Gopal directed her to the Swami Mandapam to bow to the image of Murukaṉ before she climbed the steps into the cave shrine. On reaching her final destination, she felt a great sense of elation and burst into tears. Mr. Gopal touched her forehead, made her unconscious and removed her arch. Later he revived her and gave her milk to drink. She went home exhausted, took a bath and promptly fell asleep. The following day she went to the Sentul artisan quarters to offer a jasmine garland to Murukaṉ. Three days after *Taipūcam* her family performed Iṭampan *pūjā*, but they did not invite friends and relatives. As a gesture of her gratitude, Selvarani gave Mr. Gopal a chicken, fruits and some cloth.

This case study suggests the complex interaction between fear and obligation in the act of penance. Selvarani's *raison d'être* for carrying *kāvaṭi* was not simple gratitude for wishes fulfilled but the worrisome concern that gratitude was not shown at all. It is as though Murukaṉ will not accept a private whisper of thanks but only a grand display of penance. That was probably the reason for her father's anxious reaction to her confession: vows to Murukaṉ cannot be casually taken without a sense of fear. Only by fearing Murukaṉ's powers can one discharge his religious obligations, otherwise the god is merely taken for granted and his role in human affairs moribund. Thus, Selvarani's initiation into trance was a test of her relationship with Murukaṉ. If she experienced trance, it was a sign that Murukaṉ was satisfied with her spiritual commitments. Trance was an opportunity

for controlling fear that arose from her uncertainties about Murukaṉ's emotions. By observing the actions of other penitents and heeding the persuasions of Mr. Gopal, Selvarani executed the procedures necessary for altering her mental state, a state that she found disconcerting initially but later accepted as essential for transcending the baser emotions.

THE MEANINGS OF *TAIPŪCAM*

The social significance of *Taipūcam* can, according to Babb (1976), be discerned at two levels. At the individual level, the penitent carries *kāvaṭi* as an expression of self-worth or, as Babb puts it, 'to engage in an act of ritual self-creation' (ibid.: 18). At the collective level, *Taipūcam* hypostatises the group through the performance of various *pūjā* and reasserts Murukaṉ as a god of the Tamil community. While the juxtaposition of the individual and collective modes at *Taipūcam* tells us something about Tamil society, it also raises the question of how individualism is fostered through the relationship between gods, demons and men; and the problem of Tamil religious integration in a society where they are a minority.

Gods, Demons and Men

In the Tamil puranic myths *(Talapurāṇam)*, the relationship between gods and men is often articulated through the notion of *bhakti*: unquestioning devotion to the deities that is expected to result in earthly rewards or divine salvation. *Bhakti* as spiritual oblation produces in devotees the submissive behaviour required to elicit remunerative responses from the gods. *Bhakti* in this sense encourages individualism or a type of egoism that links personal acts of devotion to the acquisition of appropriate gains either in the present or the hereafter. This relationship in the Tamil myths also applies to that between gods and demons. Both men and demons stand in an inferior relationship to the gods, but when demons are destroyed they have the opportunity to be elevated to the status of devotee. This is possible because the destruction of a demon at the hands of a god is a non-polluting sacrifice. The impure status of a demon negates the pollution implied in a sacrificial act. As an object of sacrifice, the demon becomes a devotee rewarded with more power and promised more satiation of his desires. This pattern of sacrificial death and rebirth produces an individualistic lust for power, while the rejection of this power through self-sacrifice is more difficult to achieve (Shulman 1980: 317–46).

The myth of Iṭampan clearly illustrates this moral message. The deaths of Iṭampan's companions, as sacrifices to Murukaṉ, resulted in their ascent into heaven, whereas Iṭampan was deprived of this chance because of his survival. There is no indication that Iṭampan was prepared to lay down his life for Murukaṉ, yet he was willing to sacrifice himself in defending the hills for Agastya. Iṭampan's death at the hands of Murukaṉ was his rebirth as the god's devotee. Iṭampan's initial loyalty was not to Murukaṇ, but to Agastya. It was only because of his death and eventual resurrection that his devotion was transferred to Murukaṇ.

The story of Iṭampan provides an attractive model for men to follow, men who strive for power and earthly gains. In the myth, Iṭampan's self-sacrifice does not result in the complete suppression of his ego. Although he is linked spiritually to Murukaṇ, he continues to maintain a revitalised but separate self. Similarly, penitents at *Taipūcam* re-enacting the devotion of Iṭampan are not really attempting to vanquish their egos. Rather, the acts of self-mortification in carrying *kāvaṭi* demonstrate the power inherent in an individual who fulfills his obligations to his god. As such, the penitent's ego is not denied but emphasised as a vehicle for the accomplishment of vows.

The power sought by penitents to facilitate their fulfilment of vows is initially experienced through the performance of *tapas*. While austerities are undertaken to purify the body and mind, they are believed to produce 'internal heat' which are sources of spiritual power necessary for carrying *kāvaṭi*. The penitents demonstrate this power by various acts of self-mortification. As they are pierced and hooked with sharp objects, no cries of pain emanate from their lips. No blood flows out of the punctures in their bodies. These are the physical signs that the penitents have accumulated sufficient power from *tapas*. The spiritual signs of power comprise the penitents' ability to enter into trance. As they become familiar with the procedures leading to trance, the level of power within them is believed to amplify. In their terms, Murukaṇ has showered them with *aruḷ*. Trance also symbolises the death of the old self, just as the demonic self of Iṭampan was destroyed by Murukaṇ. All penitents are expected to die this symbolic death, otherwise their *kāvaṭi* is meaningless. Their revival at the end of *kāvaṭi* is akin to Iṭampan's resurrection, a symbol of rebirth imbued with the power of Murukaṇ's grace.

As a tale of power through devotion, the myth of Iṭampan provides the symbolic framework for the promotion of the type of religious individualism described by Babb (1976). The individualism implied in these pursuits does not necessarily conflict with the tenets of *bhakti* that prescribe self-efforts in devotional worship. Each penitent taking vows in private must exert his own energy in experiencing the discomforts and pains associated with *kāvaṭi*. For many penitents, *bhakti* is also construed as an obligation because their wishes were fulfilled prior to the performance of *kāvaṭi*. This does not mean that there was no devotion before their wishes were granted, but that carrying *kāvaṭi* demonstrates greater devotion as religious dues. In other words, obligation, sacrifice and power are the interlinking motives of *kāvaṭi*. Nowhere is this theme better conveyed than the explanation of one informant that more people are carrying *kāvaṭi* because problems in life keep increasing. His assertion suggests that individualistic quests for power multiply with the greater uncertainties resulting from social change.

The ideal of self-sacrifice for union with Murukaṇ is farthest from the minds of the penitents. In 1975 a monk from the Divine Life Society, a nonsectarian Hindu organisation, attempted to articulate this ideal by carrying *kāvaṭi* containing only vessels of milk in stark contrast to the self-mortification of other penitents. His example has not been successfully emulated, as grander and more elaborate acts of self-mortification are observed at *Taipūcam* every year. The concern for power continues to hold supreme.

Caste, Identity and Politics

If the enhancement of individual power is an underlying theme of *kāvaṭi*, its social equivalent is the expression of Tamil Hindu identity centering on the worship of Murukaṇ. Devotion to Murukaṇ is inextricably intertwined with Tamil self-consciousness. According to Clothey (1978: 108), 'Murukaṇ is often called the "god of Tamil," the "god of the Pāṇṭiyas," and "lord of the Palni Hills" and other phrases associating him with Tamil Nadu.' Even Tamil politicians in India have fused the divine status of Murukaṇ with the political identity of the Dravida Munnetra Kalakam (DMK) which comprises the government of Tamil Nadu (ibid. 1978: 116). Tamil politicians in Malaysia have yet to make this claim explicitly, but their presence at *Taipūcam* in Batu Caves every year conveys a similar message: the god of the DMK is also the god of the MIC.

As a god of war, Murukaṇ's status is consistently associated with the destruction of demons. Although this image of Murukaṇ is especially emphasised at the *Skanda Ṣaṣṭi* festival (October–November) (Clothey 1969), his war-like characteristics are beginning to be given more expression at *Taipūcam*. The shooting of arrows, previously not performed at *Taipūcam*, has recently become a popular ritual among penitents at Batu Caves. It is as though the warriorhood of Murukaṇ is present at all festivals dedicated to him, and *Taipūcam* is not deemed complete if his martial aspects are not given due attention. Alongside this demonstration of Murukaṇ's power are the trance enactments of penitents claiming possession by deities noted for their ferocity and bloodthirstiness. These acts have become more frequent at *Taipūcam* even though the festival is not dedicated to these deities.[19] These possession rituals suggest that there is an increasing emphasis on the display of naked power, particularly power associated with violence as symbolically represented by arrows, whips and knives.

Most of the penitents are non-Brahmins and from the lower castes. Temple officials recognise that *Taipūcam* at Batu Caves is almost purely a non-Brahmin affair. The toleration of possession rituals by the non-Brahminical village gods (*gramadevata*) is undoubtedly related to this recognition. These lower deities do not have the same status as Murukaṇ, but the non-Brahmin, lower caste composition of the crowd tends to attenuate this status gap. Penitents who have made vows to the village gods do not separate themselves

from the Murukaṉ devotees. They intermingle with the Murukaṉ devotees and move undaunted toward the same shrine,
as though they have individually assigned a higher but liminal status to the *gramadevata* for the day.

The overall non-Brahmin dominance of the festival suggests that the manipulation of Tamil Hindu identity in
Malaysia is not strictly the domain of a Brahminical priestly
caste; rather, it is the domain of politicians, religious groups,
and individual laymen. The preparation of penitents for
kāvaṭi under the guidance of laymen suggests that *tapas* is
not a centralised religious activity but depends on the interpretive whims of individual advisors. This looseness in religious interpretation is also evident in the selection of hymns
and chants for inducing trance, most of which are not derived from devotional songs but from the music scores of
popular films. There is no overt condemnation of these religious innovations. On the contrary, a competitive demand
for ostentatious displays of penance promotes the trend toward innovation.

As a non-Brahminical vehicle to the projection of Tamil
identity, *Taipūcam* is indeed the antithesis of Srinivas'
model of Sanskritisation, the ideal of upward mobility by
cultural imitation of higher castes (Srinivas 1966). The
Brahmin religious functionaries play a minor role in the festival. The main events are focused on the performances of
the non-Brahmin penitents. The invocation of the *gramadevata* and the almost rabid obsession with self-mortification
point toward a non-scriptural, experiential approach to status establishment. Through their acts of self-mortification
and possession by the *gramadevata,* the penitents are indirectly rejecting the Sanskritic models of Hindu identity. One
may even speak of the 'plebianisation' of Tamil Hindu identity at *Taipūcam,* in the sense of a rediscovery of the village
roots of the festival. The increasing emphasis on a baroque,
uninhibited style of penance seems to signal the advent of a
Tamil superciliousness toward Brahminical and Sanskritic
definitions of Hinduism.

The context of this change can be related to political cur-
rents in Malaysia. As an ethnic minority without strong economic and political niches in Malaysian society, the Tamils
have limited clout in the expression and pursuit of their interests. The present political leadership of the Tamil community is non-Brahmin, comprising members from middle-
and lower-ranking caste groups. Through their close alliance
with the dominant Malay political leadership, the Tamil political elite is able to negotiate the survival of the Tamil
community and the advancement of its interests. The political patronage derived from this alliance is extended to the
rest of the Tamil community, thus strengthening the position
of the Tamil politicians as important power-brokers in the
ethnic mosaic of Malaysian society. The sheer weight of this
patronage and the strong MIC connections of the Śrī Mahā
Māriyammaṉ temple suggest that the emerging definitions of
Hinduism will be heavily influenced by the non-Brahminical
pact of temple bureaucrats and Tamil politicians.

CONCLUSION

In an era of competing religious revivalisms, it is inevitable
that politicians and temple officials will play a greater role in
sponsoring public festivals for a more avid expression of
Tamil Hindu identity. The contemporary celebration of
Taipūcam in Malaysia, with its significantly non-Sanskritic
features, connotes the plausibility of an inchoate Hindu identity shaped by power-wielders with mass appeal to a largely
non-Brahmin Tamil population. This process of religious developments does not necessarily imply a decreasing influence of the Sanskritic paradigm in Malaysian Hinduism. The
Sanskritic paradigm continues to mold Malaysian Indians'
definitions of Hinduism through the activities of various
Vedanta organisations, but it comprises a source of tension
with the Tamil models of Hinduism. As one of these models,
Taipūcam appeals to a broad section of the non-Brahmin
Tamil population and will continue to influence the public
perception of popular Hinduism in Malaysia.

NOTES

1. The data were obtained at the 1987 *Taipūcam* festival in Batu
   Caves, Kuala Lumpur. Additional research on Tamil Hinduism, ethnicity, and politics was accomplished with the help
   of the following individuals to whom I am most grateful: R.
   Rajoo, T. Neelavani, G. Kalaiyarasi, and D. Subrahmaniam.

2. The other Indian sub-ethnic groups are Malayalis, Telugus,
   Sri Lankan Tamils, Bengalis, Gujaratis, Punjabis, Sindhis, and
   Pakistanis. As an ethnic group, Indians comprise about 10 per
   cent of the population in peninsular Malaysia. The other ethnic groups are Malays (55.3 per cent), Chinese (33.8 per
   cent), Others (Eurasians, aborigines, Europeans—0.7 per
   cent) (1980 Population Census of Malaysia).

3. The MIC leadership in the 1950s was dominated by south Indian Tamils. Their traditional rivals, the Sri Lankan Tamils
   who had occupied important political positions in the pre-war
   years, were excluded from the higher ranks of the MIC.

4. All Malaysian citizens are required to carry government-
   issued identity cards.

5. In 1987, US$ 1 was equivalent to M$ 2.50.

6. The Sentul section of Kuala Lumpur was formerly the residential quarters of Malayan Railways employees, many of whom
   were Indians. Present-day Sentul is still heavily populated by
   Indians.

7. MIED or the Maju Institute of Educational Development is an
   educational fund sponsored by the MIC. At the 1987
   Taipūcam festival, nearly 20,000 MIED lottery tickets were
   sold at M$ 2 a ticket.

8. Some of my informants have observed that the number of female penitents performing self-mortification is increasing
   every year.

9. Another type of *kāvaṭi* that is popular in Tamil Nadu, but not
   in Malaysia, is *maccam kāvaṭi* or fish offering that is usually

performed by fishermen. Dead fish are placed in a pot filled with water but allegedly become alive after the offering has been made to Murukaṇ. The fish are released into a pond.

10. An informant related to me the case of three Malay brothers who carried *kāvaṭi* for three successive years, hoping that their gravely ill father would recover. A Muslim official *(kadi)* in Kuala Lumpur accused them of committing apostasy. Because their father eventually recovered from the illness, the brothers completed their vow at the Waterfall temple in Penang, away from the watchful gaze of the *kadi*.

11. MIC politicians are invited to *Taipūcam* every year because of their alleged connections with the Śrī Mahā Māriyamman temple. The temple is said to be controlled by the non-Brahmin Mukkulatór caste cluster comprising the Kaḷḷar, Ahamuḍiyar and Maṟavar. Samy Vellu, a Kaḷḷar, is linked to this temple by virtue of his caste background.

12. 'Eve teasers' is an Indian term referring to lecherous individuals who pinch women's privates in thick crowds where their identities are safely concealed.

13. Alternatively, milk flows out of the pots because of the constant shaking perpetrated by the penitents' vigorous movements and the extreme heat of the day.

14. Beggars are usually given one-cent coins by devotees who buy 80 to 90 of them for a dollar from money changers in the cave.

15. There are two types of the *tulasī* plant. The black *tulasī* is believed to represent Śiva and the green *tulasī* Śakti. Leaves from both plants are used in the drink.

16. A spiritual advisor informed me that it is not difficult inserting needles and skewers into the penitents' bodies because their flesh becomes softened from the long period of fasting.

17. Limes are not only sacred fruits but also believed to be cooling agents for neutralising the heat generated by *tapas* (Babb 1975; Beck 1969).

18. All names in this case study are pseudonyms.

19. Temple officials claim that they have absolutely no control over how penitents should behave at the festival. Most of them turn a blind eye to these possession rituals.

REFERENCES

Ackerman, Susan and Raymond L. M. Lee. 1988. *Heaven in transition: Non-Muslim religious innovation and ethnic identity in Malaysia.* Honolulu: University of Hawaii Press.

Ampalavanar, R. 1969. Aspects of leadership of the Indian community in Malaya in the period 1920–41. *Tamil oli* 8: 79–95.

———. 1972. Class, caste and ethnicism among urban Indians in Malaya, 1920–1941. *Nusantara* 2: 209–36.

———. 1981. *The Indian minority and political change in Malaya, 1945–1957.* Kuala Lumpur: Oxford University Press.

Arasaratnam, S. 1970. *Indians in Malaysia and Singapore.* London: Oxford University Press.

Babb, Lawrence. 1975. *The divine hierarchy.* New York: Columbia University Press.

———. 1976. *Thaipusam in Singapore: Religious individualism in a hierarchical culture.* Sociology Working Paper No. 49, University of Singapore.

The Phenomenology of Religious Serpent Handling: A Rationale and Thematic Study of Extemporaneous Sermons

W. Paul Williamson

Howard R. Pollio

Most explanations of serpent handling in Holiness-Pentecostal groups in the southeastern United States conclude that the practice serves a psychiatric/emotional function, helping the serpent handlers deal with the frustrations

"The phenomenology of religious serpent handling: a rationale and thematic study of extemporaneous sermons" by W. Paul Williamson & Howard R. Pollio, *Journal for the Scientific Study of Religion* 38:2 (June 1999), 203–218. Copyright © Blackwell Publishing. Reprinted with permission.

and disappointments of their lives, or as a form of compensation for some individual psychopathology. In this essay Williamson and Pollio examine serpent handling from the perspective of its practitioners, and elicit the personal meanings that serpent handlers assign to their activities.

What the researchers discovered is that central to serpent handling is a feeling that participants described as feeling God "moving upon" them. This personal experience with God is described as being more pleasurable than sex, drugs, or alcohol. Second, along with the pleasure of feeling God working through them is an intense awareness of death that enhances their feelings of life's vitality and God's power. The participants in this study all felt separate from those who did not handle serpents. They described themselves as being favored by God or sanctioned as true believers by the experience of serpent handling. Finally, serpent handlers speak of their experiences in a way that indicates they have acquired a kind of spiritual meaning that is beyond rational understanding. These people feel that a truth has been revealed to them in their worship services that would otherwise have been unattainable and is beyond rational understanding.

From their sermons it is clear that those who take up serpents believe that they are empowered with spiritual understanding and that they have a specialness to God that others do not possess. The practice of these rites results in feelings of an indescribable "joy." Serpent handling is a physical as well as emotional experience for the people who practice it. Serpent-handling rites legitimate their religious beliefs, give them a feeling of specialness to God, allow participants to confront death and receive an increased sense of vitality, and create a physical sensation of euphoria.

As you read, consider these questions:
1. Various studies have proposed a variety of explanations or interpretations of serpent handling. What are these, and how do they differ?
2. What are the five major themes associated with serpent handling identified in this study?
3. Several methodologies have been used to study serpent handling. What are these, and what insights can each reveal?

An interesting ritual of certain religious sects in the southeastern United States is that of serpent handling. In a typical worship service, members of these Holiness-Pentecostal groups practice a specific passage from the King James Bible and take up poisonous serpents as obedient believers of God (Burton 1993; Kimbrough 1995). This ritual derives from a literal reading of Mark 16 in which the faithful are instructed to "take up serpents" in the name of Jesus.[1] As an impelling religious rite, serpent handling has not escaped the attention of the popular media or investigation by some social scientists (Hood 1998). Unfortunately, most analyses of this practice tend to decontextualize it as pathological or to characterize it in functional terms, that is, as mitigating the difficulties of life. For example, La Barre (1962/1992), a psychoanalytically trained anthropologist, cast his unfortunate subject, Beauregard Barefoot, as a compulsive snake handler who attempted through ritual to resolve the sexual conflicts of his childhood life. In a doctoral dissertation,

S. M. Kane (1979) focused largely upon an experienced serpent handler whose "obsession" with the practice was interpreted to be an unconscious drama linked to a repressed oedipal conflict and its related guilt. Not all dynamic interpretations of serpent handling, however, view it as pathological. Hood and Kimbrough (1995), for example, suggest that, within serpent-handling practice, the symbolism of the serpent is not necessarily rooted simply in sexual repression but also concerns themes of death and resurrection. Though this characterization helps to mitigate more traditional dynamic renditions, pathological traces still persist in many theoretical interpretations of this observance. . . .

[In a 500-word passage, the authors continue to briefly review interpretations of serpent handling. They mention studies that focus on cathartic psychological effects of serpent handling and the ways in which people successfully handled snakes as well as studies that analyzed serpent handling as "a safety valve for many of the frustrations of life" (Gerrard 1968). Such explanations do not account for the personal meanings of serpent handling for ritual participants. This study uses phenomenological interpretation to access those meanings.

In an 1,800-word section titled "Methodological and Philosophical Rationale," the authors describe phenomenological interpretation based on the collection and analysis of first-person descriptions of experiences from participants. These are analyzed by dividing them into units expressing meaning. Such units are then transformed into personal statements and the personal statements into a thematic description that presents the meaning of the experience for all participants.

This methodology derives from three philosophical traditions: phenomenology, existentialism, and hermeneutics. These traditions emphasize everyday experience, personal meanings, and language.

Bracketing and group interpretation were used to prevent the personal biases of the researchers from unduly influencing the results. In bracketing, researchers's encounters with the phenomenon of interest are interpreted to make them mindful of the meanings they bring to the research. In group interpretation, textual data is read aloud and its meanings thematized within a group. At the University of Tennessee, Knoxville, where this research was done, numerous procedures are used to improve the objectivity of group interpretation. These include bracketing, including participants of diverse backgrounds to produce multiple interpretations, requiring participants to show where they find meanings in the text, shared responsibility for the results, and the requirement that interpretations must be agreed upon unanimously.

The authors continue by describing a hermeneutic interpretive circle, a system in which interpretations of a passage or a remark are compared to interpretations of the entire text, which are then used to further interpret the passage or remark. This technique can be used to produce a "global meaning" to improve researchers' understanding of a phenomenon as experienced in different contexts. This has been compared to a piece of music played in different keys—though the notes are altered, the melody continues to be recognizable.

The extemporaneous sermons of serpent handlers legitimate their experiences for fellow believers. Such sermons are part of an oral tradition that connects individual serpent handlers with their congregations through interactions and feedback. As such, they are rich sources for analysis and have an immediacy of experience lacking in other sources.—Editors]

THE PRESENT STUDY

Since the purpose of the present study is to provide a descriptive understanding of the phenomenon of religious serpent handling from the perspective of its practitioners, spontaneous sermons produced during ongoing worship services were collected and analyzed on the basis of phenomenological interpretation. The present set of sermons all took place during services at times when serpents were handled or just thereafter. To collect these sermons, a serpent-handling congregation in northern Georgia was attended on various occasions from January 1995 through March 1996. During this period, segments of the services which included extemporaneous sermons were audiotaped by permission. From the tapings, 18 sermons that were most descriptive of serpent handling were selected for study. All 11 of the preachers were male and included the pastor and various self-acclaimed ministers who had practiced the "sign" the night of their sermons.[2] All sermons were impromptu and free associative in nature, lasting from a few minutes to an hour in length. Each sermon was carefully transcribed verbatim, and the resulting text was submitted for thematic analysis to the interpretive research group with concern for specific passages descriptive of serpent handling.

Since most sermons were relatively brief, lasting from five to 10 minutes, themes were not required to appear in each sermon, as is the usual requirement for interpretive analysis (e.g., see Thompson et al. 1989). For present purposes, it seemed reasonable to require themes to have been noted in over 75% of the sermons considered. In addition, any given thematic meaning defining the experience of serpent handling, derived from this procedure, could not be contradicted by the content of any sermon in order for it to be considered as critical to the meaning of the overall practice. The final results were presented to the interpretive research group at which time the thematic analysis of the texts was found to be both plausible and enlightening to the experience of religious serpent handling.

RESULTS

Interpretive analysis of the various sermons indicated that the experience of religious serpent handling is an embodied event emerging from the context of Pentecostal worship. In addition to serpent handling, each service includes intense preaching, singing, shouting, dancing, glossolalia, and prayer, all of which illustrate the emotional expressiveness of Pentecostalism (Synan 1997; McCauley 1995). From this context of ongoing activities, the phenomenon of serpent handling emerges in relation to a particular awareness of the body that serves to affect the meaning of the event for the person. The body is the modality through which the handlers experience this sacred world and God (see McGuire 1990).

From the present analysis of sermons, five themes were noted to characterize the first-person experience of serpent handling . . . serpent handling emerges as a [Gestalt-type] pattern of themes related to experiences of the body which, in turn, serves to ground the themes in corporeal existence and to provide a context within which they are understood. All themes are felt in the body, not thought and represented, and the experience is direct and unreflected. . . . Relationships among and between themes are fluid within the experience of serpent handling; all, however, are consequential to the central theme of God moving on the believer. Each of the major themes and subthemes of the experience is outlined below with brief excerpts from various sermons to illustrate its sources.

Theme I

Being moved . . . the feeling of God. Central to the activity of handling serpents is the experience of God moving upon the person. Within the context of a service, many activities take place: praying for the sick, singing fervent songs, dancing to intense music, and preaching of personal convictions; however it is agreed that no one goes inside the serpent box without first feeling God move in a convincing way. How that moving is discerned differs from individual to individual, although each of the preachers emphasized the need to feel God move personally before any attempt to take up a serpent. Their words clearly describe this powerful experience:[3]

> The Lord moved on us while we was a cleaning them serpent boxes and got to handling them and everything . . . Brother, once you get into this, and get a little taste of this victory . . . how sweet it is . . . there's just one way to go . . . and that's straight ahead! (I1).
>
> The TV news reporter wanted me to come outside and talk to him, and he began to ask about taking up serpents . . . That lady, she asked about the women that took up serpents in here, what kind of training they had . . . laughter . . . They think there's a gimmick to it. Brother B, I don't care what the Lord does, somebody's going to look for a gimmick, Brother B, a slight of hand or something. I said, "Hey, there ain't no kind of training to do it," Sister C. I said, "The best thing to do is get down on your knees and cry out to God, push your plate back for three or four days till you find the answer." And when you find the answer, that begins to get on you . . . Brother D, when you began to praise the Lord, and that begins to get upon you. And when it gets on you, you can't wipe it off of you. That begins to get upon you, you can't walk out from under it, and you know that the Lord's moving on you, then that's the time to do that. (E2).

The experience of anointment—or feeling the Lord move—is curious, and preachers describe it in various ways. In terms of personal manifestation, some descriptions openly shared its bodily affect when being moved to handle; others were more secretive and did not describe it directly. As will be shown, the experience of feeling God move upon the person is linked to other themes that emerge.

Theme II

"Life"/"death" . . . the feeling of vitality. In their preaching, the ministers regularly addressed and affirmed the reality of death. On many visits to serpent-handling services, a caution often heard from the pulpit was "There's death in that box"; hence, life takes on a certain vitality, becoming more pronounced and accentuated in its sacred confrontation with death. Some of the preachers handled serpents as they preached and expressed a full awareness of the potential for death as present. In addition, the experience of being bitten holds meaningful interpretations that range from lack of congregational prayer in the course of handling, to personal disobedience when told by God to put the serpent down, to God's wisdom in using the incident as a testimony to unbelievers in revealing the genuine danger and divine protection afforded those who obey his word.

Two particular preachers experienced serpent bites at the times of their sermons: one was bitten only minutes beforehand, the other was struck between sermons while singing a song. If bitten, the consensus was that survival is in God's hand; no mention of medical intervention was made in either case. The following are a few examples that illustrate clearly their consciousness of death and its implications:

> But Boys, I don't care about this old flesh. Boys, I'll keep taking up serpents cause the Bible says, "The signs shall follow them that believe" . . . It ain't nothing more than a shortcut to the other side. (B1).

> Immediately after being bitten: Through these serpent, bites, he'll take care of us . . . Don't worry about me. Don't cry over me when I leave this world. Rejoice. I'm gonna be with Jesus. (G1).

> I'd love to take that serpent up, if God moves . . . If he don't, I'm just gonna leave him right there in the box. Amen, Thank God. One end of it's got a head, and the other one's got a tail . . . and that head part's what's gonna bite. (A4).

As indicated by their words, these men experienced a full awareness of potential death related to their practice, and yet there was a vitality emerging within the confrontation that they "love" (A4) to experience. As the Spirit moves, they reach inside the serpent box and experience the vitality of spiritual life overcoming death within a sacred community and locale.

Theme III

"Us"/"them" . . . the feeling of specialness. The preachers made constant reference to themselves as "us" and to others who did not handle serpents as "them." Such distinctions included "we"/"they," "God's children"/"the world," and "ours"/"theirs." In each case, they experienced themselves as favored by God and sanctioned as true believers by virtue of their obedience to the mandate of serpent handling. As a pattern, the "us"/"them" theme emerged as figural in terms of three subthemes, each lending a feeling of specialness to the "us" group.

Subtheme A: Obedience. Those obeying the scriptural mandate to take up serpents experience themselves as having crossed over a line to full obedience and thus becoming recipients of the blessing and favor that follow. On the other hand, the "them" group will not believe or obey—hence they fail to merit God's blessing and may be eternally lost. True believers, however, make the ultimate sacrifice and live in full obedience to God.

> Jesus said, "These signs shall follow them that believe." And, if you believe it, Boys, you're gonna do it. And if you don't do it, I believe it with all my heart that you'll die and go to hell. (B1).

> No matter what it takes, I'm gonna do what the Lord wants me to do. (K1).

> The Bible says, "They shall take up serpents." Honey, it means what it says, and says what it means . . . It won't change for me. It won't change for you, Amen, thank God . . . Some folks, Amen, thank God, they go in around, thank God, where they preach you can get there any way. Amen, thank God. But we're gonna have to go the Bible way. Amen, thank God. The word of God's right. (A3).

Subtheme B: The Sign of True Believers. The sermons indicate that serpent handling is considered a literal indicator of God's genuine people. An analogy shared in one sermon likened the Bible to the map book of a trucker. It may indeed show the route to a destination; however, highway signs are needed along the road to confirm the validity of the map. Hence, serpent handling confirms the word of God in the life of the believer and publicly indicates the rightness of his (the preacher's) walk. More importantly, the sign is an indicator of how God can richly bless people if they believe and fully obey the biblical command. Such a meaning is implied in an excerpt that follows a reprimand to an overly zealous TV crew for disrespectful conduct and obtrusive maneuvers while filming serpent-handling activities:

> When people see the Lord move on you, then they can say they've seen something move. Whenever I began to see this, I didn't see them people handling them snakes. What I seen, I seen God moving in them. I seen the Lord moving in people . . . you come up here and you just handle that snake just to be handling that snake, that, don't prove nothing . . . If the Lord's moving on you, thank God, somebody can see that, and they'll know there's something real about that. When I seen that move on them, I wanted that. It wasn't so much handling that snake. That wasn't it, thank God, but I wanted to see the Lord move . . . and I wanted to feel the goodness of God. I didn't

care nothing about handling that snake, but I wanted to feel that . . . that moved on them. (A6).

It is not simply the handling of serpents that is the sign of distinction—in fact some preachers expressed an awareness that counterfeiters may occasionally handle serpents with success. What is of more significance is the manifest power of God upon the handler which is felt to be the true mark transcending even the act itself so as to become the distinguishing feature of belief.

There's more to this than just handling a serpent. It ain't nothing to handle a snake, but it takes a believer to take up serpents . . . I've seen homosexuals handle snakes. That ain't no big thing. But when the power of God gets into it, when the power of God gets into it, then it's gonna edify. It's gonna edify. (K1).

Subtheme C: The Established versus the "Sugar-Coated."

Those of the in-group, qualified by obedience and performance of the signs, see themselves as spiritually mature and "established" in the word. They boldly stand without compromise for what the Bible says regarding signs of the believers. On the other hand, they experience their counterparts as preferring and settling for a "watered-down" or "sugar-coated" gospel that cultivates immaturity and unbelief. Of course, the mature stand fast in belief and practice all of God's Word:

I'm surprised some of the churches ain't got rubber snakes in them. Amen, thank God. I am. I'm surprised. They try to imitate every other way. They do! The devil, amen thank God, he'll try anything and everything to counterfeit for everything the Lord's got . . . He's a counterfeiter. The true thing's gonna stand. (A3).

God's children is gonna be standing. Brother, He said when He'd come back He'd find faith on the earth. Somebody's gonna be standing and doing that word. (H1).

Some of them try to say that . . . I don't believe that like that. I don't see that like that . . . You know what? People has sugar-coated this thing around trying to please to somebody . . . sugarcoated. We've had to pet people, amen thank God, we've had to pamper them . . . Just give them the word. (A1).

As a group, serpent handlers characterize themselves as fully obeying the Bible, manifesting the sign of true believers, and being firmly established in the truth of God's Word without compromise. When handling serpents, these three qualities lend a unique feeling of specialness—as an "us" group privileged by God.

Theme IV: The Power of True Knowing

Although the actual words "true knowing" did not appear in the various sermons, they convey an idea that the following three subthemes harmonize to compose. Serpent handlers, especially those new to the practice, speak of their experiences in such a way as to indicate a kind of ineffable knowl-

edge or meaning that surpasses rational understanding; that is, they have encountered true knowledge and are convinced of its impact on their lives. The three subthemes that define this theme are:

Subtheme A: True Knowledge of Being "Somebody."

Although this subtheme is similar to the "Us"/"Them" theme, the manner in which it appeared in the sermons was distinct. The feeling of specialness associated with the "Us"/"Them" theme involves a sense of achievement centered about a decided obedience to the Bible—a manifest enactment of the sign and a visceral stance for the "truth." In the present subtheme, true knowledge of being "somebody" is recognized by virtue of one's acceptance by God. Where the former is earned by personal effort and achievement through obedience, the latter is consequence to unmerited grace, a part of the experience where one feels lifted from insignificance by a power greater than the self—a humble feeling that one is "somebody" based upon his connection to God. The preachers indicated quite positive self-perceptions in their sermons, but always in relation to God's merciful favor and not to themselves.

Somebody said, "Preacher . . . ," said, "you act like you're better than somebody." I am! Hey, I'm a child of the King! I'm better than any sinner man that walks the streets. Do you hear me now? I'm not any better than my brothers and sisters . . . now you follow what I'm saying . . . I'm not lifting handler's name up. I'm lifting God up. (F1).

Let me express something to you tonight. God never took the time to make a nobody. I've said that repeatedly. God never took the time to make a nobody, and you are a somebody. Everybody here is a somebody in the sight of God. (J1).

Subtheme B: True Knowledge of "Understanding."

Preachers who handled serpents reported that God had broadened their "understanding" of truth and had revealed the real way of life to them that would otherwise have been inaccessible. They also spoke of such revelation as an ongoing process:

I want to stand up and thank the Lord for everything he's done for me. God moves on you and more everyday. He doesn't leave you in the dark. He opens your understanding. I want to thank God for that. You know, he'll move you on up and in. (D1).

We might back up . . . We might just get disgusted, "Well, I ain't gonna go back around those snake-handlers no more." You better stay in the Truth. You better not hear that devil . . . You better stay in the Truth. If God has put you into the Truth, you better stay there. (C1).

Thank God. I said He blessed me tonight. If you knowed what I knowed, you'd raise your hands and you'd thank Him tonight. (K1).

Subtheme C: True Knowledge of the "Good Way."

In their sermons, the preachers did not speak of "good" as describing their own personal dispositions, but rather as characterizing their changed way of life as revealed by God. They viewed their present lives as serpent handlers as the "good way" in comparison to their former ways in the world:

> Oh . . . this is a good way. This is the best thing that could ever happen to you. (A3).

> This is a good way. That's what this thing is founded on. It's on love and nothing else. (K1).

> The Lord moved on us while we was a cleaning them serpent boxes and got to handling them and everything . . . and it came to me, Brother pastor, there ain't no way back . . . There ain't no looking back . . . There ain't nothing back there . . . Brother, once you get into this, and get a little taste of this victory . . . how sweet it is . . . there's just one way to go . . . and that's straight ahead! (I1).

Those who handle serpents report experiencing a unique kind of power that only true knowledge can give: knowledge of a personal significance made possible by God, enlightenment concerning hidden spiritual truth, and the good life to experience while on earth.

Theme V: "Joy Unspeakable"

In reference to their experiences of serpent handling, preachers spoke of "joy unspeakable" that accompanied the remarkable event. Many acknowledged prior experience with "worldly" activities including alcohol, drugs, sex, etc., although the pleasure deriving from such experiences had no comparison to the ultimate joy found in the practice of their religion. The joyful feelings, however, were almost always attributed to the experience of God while handling rather than to the act of handling the serpent itself.

> This feeling that you got . . . the world didn't give it to you, Brother name. Amen. This Holy Ghost you got, the world didn't give it to you . . . If folks—people would have told me 30 years ago that I'd be handling rattlesnakes, I'd told them they was crazy . . . But this feeling that comes on you . . . I tell you, it'll make you do some strange things . . . Joy unspeakable and full of glory. (A6).

> I was trying to describe to my son, Amen, glory to God, when he was by the house the other day, I said, "Son," I said, "I want to tell you it's a wonderful feeling to take up a serpent" . . . But you can't explain it. You can't tell me how it feels. I've got to experience it for myself. (F1).

When a handler takes up a serpent as moved by the spirit of God, there is an ineffable sense of joy accompanying it that transcends any found in the world. It is this unspeakable joy that connects with, and to, the other themes and captures the apex of the serpent handling experience.

DISCUSSION

The phenomenon of serpent handling may be described as an experience of the body being moved upon by a pattern of special meanings within the context of Pentecostal worship.

When feeling a particular moving of God in or on his body, the person takes up the serpent within that sacred context, consciously confronts death and thereby comes to encounter a renewed vitality in his present spiritual life. In taking up the serpent, the person feels a particular specialness to God that gives him distinction from all others who refuse the scriptural mandate. In addition, the person experiences an empowerment of true knowledge that is reflected in a transformed significance of self, in spiritual understanding, and in an enlightenment of the good way of life reserved to those who take up serpents. Finally, the experience of taking up serpents culminates in a "joy unspeakable and full of glory," an ineffable feeling that escapes precise description but was sometimes referred to as "a bubbling in my soul" (A4). The phenomenon of religious serpent handling is a powerful, direct body experience charged with personal and religious meaning for the people who engage in this practice.

It is significant to note that since the collection of this data, one of the preachers (Preacher K), a well-renowned minister in the tradition, was fatally bitten by a timber rattler while preaching in a revival service, October 3, 1998. The 34-year-old preacher refused the offer of medical aid and died within several minutes of the inflicted bite. Of further interest is the fact that his 28-year-old wife had also died from a rattlesnake bite received during a serpent-handling homecoming service only three years earlier. Fewer than 80 such deaths have been documented in this century (Hood 1998), whereas these two fatalities appear to be the first husband/wife deaths recorded in the history of this tradition.[4] What appears on the one hand to be tragedy to the secular world is underscored on the other to be an affirmation of the rich meaning this tradition holds for those who live (and die) in the faith—a meaning we hope this study helps to illuminate more fully.

Based on information contained in the present set of sermons, the ritual of religious serpent handling is undertaken only after the person experiences a movement of God on the corporeal body. Often referred to as "the anointing," handlers reported an unmistakable body sensation that provides a sense of knowing when it is time to reach for a serpent inside the box or from another person. It is felt by some to be compelling in the sense that "you can't wipe it off of you . . . and . . . you can't walk out from under it" (E2). For others, the moving of God is not so commanding as to usurp personal will; indeed, for these individuals, it requires them to "learn to yield ourselves to God so we'll know when to move" (F1). When the anointing does move upon the handler, however, it relieves worry and fear about the immediate situation. As God is felt to move upon the body, the serpent handler loses personal concern for danger and feels fully prepared to obey God in fulfilling the biblical mandate to take up serpents.

It seems probable that the most compelling theme to emerge in these sermons is the handler's awareness of life and death, and the subsequent feeling of vitality it provides.

Within a context made sacred by scripture, serpent handlers are very much aware of the reality and potentiality of death through the presence of poisonous serpents. In fact, Preacher K told in his sermon of a revival he had attended in Kentucky where another believer prophesied to him that he would "have the fangs laid to you." He recalled that, earlier the same week, he had hunted and caught several rattlesnakes for worship services without being harmed, yet he later sat in the evening service of the revival replaying in his mind the words of the so-called prophet, wrestling with the possibility of their truth. Feeling God move upon him, however, he felt courage enough to pray silently, "Lord, I'm gonna find out if it was you speaking through the man." Obeying the Spirit, he took up serpents that very night, despite the warning of injury and possible death, without any bodily harm. Commenting on the "victory" God gave him over the serpent, he declared, "The devil can't do nothing God won't let him do" (K1).

Rather than deny the reality of death, the serpent handler confronts it openly when he feels the moving of God to take up the poisonous serpent. It is through this very act that the embodied feeling of God negates the fear of death for the handler—hence the threat of death is transcended and gives way to a vitality of spiritual life that is experienced as an ineffable kind of "joy unspeakable and full of glory" (A6). Given the powerful, spiritual meaning of this experience, as it relates to death, there is left little wonder that Preacher K continued in the tradition after the loss of his wife—or that other believers, including Preacher K's parents, continue now in the faith after the fact of his own death. Indeed, it was no great surprise when one of the authors watched the faithful of the tradition respond to the moving of God and take up poisonous serpents once again, this time at Preacher K's graveside service. In this otherwise somber context, the stark reality of death was confronted and transcended once more on the basis of a meaningful religious experience that bridges for them the temporal with the eternal. Those who had gathered for the service left knowing that Preacher K's death was much less a loss than a far greater victory attained through the literal practice of his faith.

Through the literal taking up of a serpent comes an awareness of feeling kinship with a select group special to God, for it is indeed the consequence of a decided obedience to His Word. It is "us" who are willing to fully comply with all the express words of Jesus—not "them" who pick and choose from among scriptures what is appealing and conducive to their compromising way of life. In the words of one preacher:

> They take out what sounds good to them, but Jesus told John, said, "Take ye it and eat it," talking about that little book . . . But when it begins to cut down deep they back up and they don't want it . . . Boys, it don't change for me. It don't change for you. The word of God means what it says, and it says what it means. (H1) Membership in this favored group is also marked by the very fact that they take up serpents—a sign

made visible not only by the virtue of taking them up, but also by a notable manifestation of God's Spirit upon the believer in a very convincing way. The group who practices all the mandates of scripture further knows itself to be selected because of a spiritual maturity not found among those who do not. In fact, concerning those who had once stood strong on the doctrine of serpent-handling but have since weakened, another handler declares, "They ain't stable. They ain't rooted. They ain't grounded . . . They are just like a ship out on the sea, and they're tossed about by every wind of doctrine" (A3). Serpent handlers, by their complete devotion to the scripture, see themselves as a unique group given to full obedience that is honored by God. This awareness, however, is not prideful: "You get exalted, and God can't do nothing. But if you get down on them knees and cry out to God, we'll see God move" (G1). Indeed, the road to God is paved with humility.

In the experience of handling serpents, there comes a certain power of true knowledge. The handler no longer feels himself to be an unworthy creation of God but one who comes to a knowledge of being graced and valued by God, and deemed worthy to participate in the signs of true believers. In fact, it is felt that no matter "how little you feel like you are, how big you think you are, God still can use you" (A1)—if only one has an obedient heart. Through practicing the signs, the handler discovers a deeper revelation of spiritual knowledge that has been found in no other way. After handling his first serpent, one young man stated, "You don't know the way until He shows you the way. You can't do when you're ignorant" (D2). The knowledge of the best possible life to live is one that knows the fulness of God through following the signs; even in the most difficult of times, "this thing will do you to depend upon" (E2).

It has been through the practice of religious serpent handling that these persons have become aware of such knowledge as this which has changed their lives in such profound ways. This theme of true knowledge weaves together with all others discussed above and contributes to indescribable feelings of joy, blessedness, gladness, goodness, peace, victory, wonder, and greatness, all of which transcend any others experienced from pleasures in the corporeal world and are "better felt than told." Hence the structured pattern of themes found to emerge from the sermons concerning serpent handling is directly felt by these practitioners as an embodied experience directly connected in meaningful ways to their complete religious tradition—including, most especially, their understanding of life and death.

The structure and meaning of religious serpent handling emerging from the present analysis seems appropriate and plausible for the texts studied; however, the use of extemporaneous sermons may be thought to present some limitations. One possible limitation might be that all participants in this study were preachers whereas all who handle serpents are not. Despite this, it should be remembered that preachers circumscribe and predicate the religious language used by others to interpret and legitimate their experiences within the tradition. A second possible limitation is that sermons given in the context of worship tended to reflect certain rhetorical devices often lacking in precise descriptions. For example: What is it like to experience "joy unspeakable and full of glory" (A4)? What does it mean to "know that the Lord's moving on you" (E2)? In the context of ongoing worship, there was no opportunity to query for further clarification of such descriptions as these, as might be done in an interview. On the other hand, given the direct experience of serpent handling just as sermons were given—or immediately beforehand—it would be difficult to ascertain how much descriptive material might be lost in such belated interviews well distanced by time from the actual phenomenon of experience. Nonetheless, these concerns should be considered in evaluating present results.

In addition to its substantive findings, the present study would seem to have some implications for psychological research. First of all, contemporary psychology continues to pursue an objective, or third-person, perspective in which theoretical neutrality is meant to free the researcher from bias and help him/her to discover "objective truth" about the subject of investigation. Since truth, but most especially religious truth, may be thought of as perspectival, it seems unnecessary to maintain an outsider approach to religious phenomena, and an important contribution of a phenomenological approach might be to shift psychological inquiry from a strict third-person perspective toward one in which the first-person perspective is recognized. Thus, in addition to observing religious serpent-handling practices from a distance, as objective psychology would do, phenomenological interpretation allows the researcher to see the world as the religious practitioner sees it, unaffected (as far as possible) by theories external to the context of the practitioner's belief and experience. In this blending of perspectives, a more complete picture of the phenomenon, a more exacting truth of religious serpent handling than would be otherwise possible, is likely to emerge. As Wulff (1998) has suggested, discovering the richness of religious experience requires the inclusion of such methodological approaches that are qualitative in nature.

Given present findings, further study of religious serpent handling would seem warranted. Although the structure of meaning described by the present analysis seems illuminating and substantiated by relevant texts, it would be interesting to conduct direct phenomenological interviews with serpent handlers and collect additional descriptions of personal experiences. Since extensive field research has noted that approximately 30%–35% of handlers are women, it also would seem necessary to include female participants, as well as handlers from different geographical locations.[5] In such an endeavor, care could be also given to include nonpreaching believers who have taken up serpents. It may be that the same structure of experience found in extemporaneous sermons, or a similar variation, would emerge from such dialogic encounters.

In addition to these possibilities, future interviews should provide an opportunity for issues surrounding the specific experience of anointing to be raised. Although present sermons characterized the anointing—God moving on the person—as a prerequisite to handling, additional conversations with handlers have suggested that serpents can be handled "by faith alone." Such an issue could prove a fruitful one for rich descriptions during an interview. Given the suspicion of serpent handlers toward "outsiders," phenomenological interviews would require time to develop personal relationships within the serpent handling community, although the outcome of such a study should fully justify the investment made. After all—in the words of one serpent handler—"This is the best thing that could ever happen to you" (A3). If this is so, then further investigation with phenomenological methods could well bring it to light.

NOTES

We would like to thank Ralph W. Hood, Jr., and the anonymous reviewers for their helpful remarks and suggestions on previous drafts of this article. This article is based on research that served as a foundation for the doctoral dissertation of W. Paul Williamson. Portions of this article were presented at the annual meeting of the Society for the Scientific Study of Religion, Nashville, Tennessee, November 1996.

1. The actual passage is found in St. Mark 16: 17–18: "And these signs shall follow them that believe; In my name shall they cast out devils; they shall speak with new tongues; They shall take up serpents; and if they drink any deadly thing, it shall not hurt them; they shall lay hands on the sick, and they shall recover."

2. Within the serpent-handling sects we have researched, women are not allowed to preach in services, although they are permitted and sometimes encouraged to give brief testimonials—hence no women are represented in this study.

3. Citations from protocols are referenced by a letter assigned to each preacher, followed by a number identifying which sermon contained the quote. Some preachers gave more than one sermon.

4. Hood (1998) credits Kimbrough (1995) who relies largely upon Kane (1979) for the most complete documentation of deaths from bites during the religious practice.

5. At the present time, we have attended serpent-handling churches in Alabama, Georgia, Kentucky, and West Virginia. Future research plans include visits to other congregations in eastern Kentucky, North Carolina, Tennessee, and Indiana.

REFERENCES

Burton, T. 1993. *Serpent handling believers.* Knoxville: University of Tennessee Press.

Gerrard, N. L. 1968. *The serpent handling religions of West Virginia.* Trans-Action 5(6): 22–28.

Hood, R. W., Jr. 1998. When the spirit maims and kills: Social psychological considerations of the history of serpent-handling sects and the narrative of handlers. *International Journal for the Psychology of Religion* 8(2): 71–96.

Hood, R. W., Jr., and D. L. Kimbrough. 1995. Serpent-handling Holiness sects: Theoretical considerations. *Journal for the Scientific Study of Religion* 34(3): 311–22.

Kane, S. M. 1979. Snake handlers of Southern Appalachia. Unpublished doctoral dissertation, Princeton University.

Kimbrough, D. L. 1995. *Taking up serpents.* Chapel Hill: University of North Carolina Press.

La Barre, W. 1962/1992. *They shall take up serpents: Psychology of the Southern snake-handling cult.* Prospect Heights, IL: Waveland Press.

McCauley, D. V. 1995. *Appalachian mountain religion.* Chicago: University of Illinois Press.

McGuire, M. B. 1990. Religion and body: Rematerializing the human body in the social sciences of religion. *Journal for the Scientific Study of Religion* 29(3): 283–96.

Synan, V. 1997. *The Holiness-Pentecostal tradition: Charismatic movements of the twentieth century.* Grand Rapids, MI: Wm. B. Eerdmans Publishing Co.

Thompson, J. T., W. B. Locander, and H. R. Pollio. 1989. Putting consumer experience back into consumer research: The philosophy and method of existential-phenomenology. *Journal of Consumer Research* 16(9): 133–46.

Wulff, D. M. 1998. Does the psychology of religion have a future? *Psychology of Religion Newsletter: American Psychological Association Division* 36 23(4): 1–9.

Lubavitch:
A Contemporary Messianic Movement

Simon Dein

What happens to a religious movement when its beliefs fail? when, by any objective standard, its predictions are clearly not fulfilled? Common sense suggests that the movement will suffer, that members will look for other paths of devotion. However, as Simon Dein shows in this article, common sense is frequently wrong. The disappointment of expectations and failure of prophecy do not always have a negative effect on a movement, and the story of the Lubavitchers is a case in point.

The Lubavitchers are a subgroup of Hasids, who are themselves a subgroup of Orthodox Judaism. The Lubavitchers are characterized by their belief in the imminent coming of a messiah and their devotion to a righteous and miraculous leader, called a *Zaddik*. From the 1950s to the mid 1990s, the Lubavitch leader was Menachem Schneerson. In the 1980s and early 1990s, Lubavitchers became increasingly devoted to the idea that Schneerson was the messiah. Schneerson did not claim to be the messiah, but he did nothing to dispel this belief. However, his death in 1994 left his followers in a quandary. Clearly the messiah has not yet come.

Faced with such a crisis, Lubavitchers did not disappear. If anything, the group has grown since Schneerson's death. Dein attributes their success to a series of factors, including the strength, closeness, and intensity of the Lubavitch community and the ability of Lubavitchers to reinterpret their understanding of Schneerson. The experience of the Lubavitchers is a testimony to the resilience of religious belief. To believers, even the most seemingly objectively false understandings and prophecies can be accommodated through a combination of reinterpretation of the message, accepting blame for the failure of the message, or insisting that the event has occurred in the spiritual rather than the physical world. All of these tactics represent both change and continuity in religious tradition.

As you read, consider these questions:

1. When prophecy fails, there are two basic interpretations or responses. What are they and what factors contribute to the interpretation?
2. What are the major features of Hasidism and Lubavitch?
3. What are the Lubavitch explanations for the "failed prophecy"?

INTRODUCTION

A belief in the advent of the Messiah is an integral part of Jewish belief. As the great Jewish philosopher Maimonides states in his Twelfth Principle of Faith: "I believe with complete faith in the coming of the Messiah, even though he should tarry, nevertheless I shall await his coming every day." The history of Judaism is replete with examples of "false messianism," personalities who were credited with

"Lubavitch: a Contempory Messianic Movement" by Dein, S. (1997) *Journal of Contemporary Religion* 12:2, 191–204. Reprinted by permission of the author and Taylor & Francis Ltd., http://www.tandf.co.uk/journals.

being the messiah (Sharot, 1982). Included among these are Simeon Bar Kochba (2nd century), David Alroy (12th century) and Abraham Abulafia (13th century). Often these messianic episodes ended in severe disillusionment, when the supposed messiah died or failed to reveal his messianic status for other reasons. Perhaps the best example of this is the case of Sabbatai Sevi (1626–1676). Sevi was a manic depressive with messianic delusions. His messianic claims and antinomian acts swept the Jewish Diaspora with promises of immediate redemption. He aroused great hopes in Jews across the world. These soon ended as the would-be messiah converted to Islam (Scholem, 1973; Littlewood, 1995; Littlewood & Dein, 1995). When Sevi converted to Islam, some followers returned to rabbinical Judaism. Others converted to Islam or Christianity.

Religious groups deal with failed prophecy in different ways. In a recent paper in this journal, Stark (1996: 137) asserts that "Other things being equal, failed prophesies are harmful for religious movements. Although prophesies may arouse a great deal of excitement and attract many new followers beforehand, the subsequent disappointment usually more than offsets these benefits."

Failure of empirical doctrines, such as the advent of the messiah, may lead to serious problems for religious groups as exemplified by recent events among Jehovah's Witnesses where there was a marked decline in missionary activity and conversion rates following failed prophecy that the world would end in 1975 (Singelenberg, 1989; Stark & Iannaccone, 1997). However, Festinger et al. (1956) suggested conditions under which the opposite effect would follow failed prophecy, i.e. the intensification of religious belief and proselytisation:

> Man's resourcefulness goes beyond simply protecting a belief. Suppose an individual believes something with his whole heart; suppose further that he has a commitment to this belief, but he has taken irrevocable actions because of it; finally suppose that he is presented with evidence, unequivocal and undeniable evidence, that his belief is wrong: What will happen? The individual will frequently emerge, not only unshaken, but even more convinced of the truth of his beliefs than ever before. Indeed, he may even show a new fervour about convincing and converting other people to his view. (Festinger et al., 1956; 3)

Festinger argued that in order for such a process to occur, there must be firm conviction; there must be public commitment to this conviction; the conviction must be amenable to unequivocal disconfirmation; such unequivocal disconfirmation must occur and, lastly, social support must be available to the believer subsequent to the disconfirmation. The believer does not pursue his or her faith in isolation and is involved in the community of individuals who hold the same beliefs. This community serves as an important source of social support, when the beliefs are challenged. Even if the believer has doubts, he or she only has to look to the community to be reminded that others still believe. Similarly, Shupe

(1981) points out that it is not unfulfilled prophecy *per se* that irrevocably disillusions believers, but rather the social conditions in which such disconfirmations are received that determine the ultimate impact on faith. Festinger's theory has been confirmed in a number of historical instances [Hughes (1954) among Montanists; Sears (1924) among Millerites] and also in field observations (Festinger et al., 1956) and quasi-experimental situations.

Melton (1985) pointed out that although one or more prophecies may be important to a group, they will be set within a complex set of beliefs and interpersonal relationships. Groups do not generally disintegrate after an error of prediction. Attention must be paid to the larger belief structure of the group and the role that the belief structure plays in the life of the believers. In relation to failed prophecy, Zymunt (1972) proposes three modes of adaptation. First, they may acknowledge the error of dating, in other words the members of the group have miscalculated the date for the millennium. Secondly, the blame for failure may be shifted to some force either within or outside the group which has interfered with the cosmic plan. Last, and one of the most common ways of adaptation, is to claim that the event occurred not on the material level, but on the spiritual level. The prophecy had, indeed, been fulfilled, it was only that it could not be readily seen. A good example of this was in relation to Joanna Southcott who after her failure to deliver a male messianic child, claims were made that the child was born, but was taken up to heaven (see Hopkins, 1982).

This paper reports on a contemporary messianic movement among a group of Hasidic Jews called Lubavitch. For many years Lubavitcher Hasidim have held that their leader Menachem Schneerson, the Rebbe, is the Messiah and that redemption is imminent. However, the Rebbe died in June of 1994 and the prophecy that he had indeed been the Messiah had clearly not been confirmed so far. He was childless and left no successors.

FOUNDATIONS OF HASIDISM

Lubavitch is a worldwide movement of Hasidic Jews whose centre is in New York where its leader, the seventh Lubavitcher Rebbe, resided until his death in June 1994. This paper concentrates on the Stamford Hill community which is an offshoot of this larger community in New York. Hasidism emerged as a Jewish pietistic movement in the eighteenth century in Eastern Europe. Its founder was the Baal Shem Tov. It taught that every present moment was a moment of redemption for the individual, leading to ultimate consummation for the whole. Every individual, whatever his status or capacity, could be caught up in the redemptive process. All he needed was a heart willing to cleave to God and enter into communion with him. It emphasised the idea of Devekut, i.e. that one should always be attached to God at all times and one's thoughts should always be on him (Epstein, 1959).

Hasidism singled out the inner state of the worshipper, rather than his understanding of the tradition, as the primary value in the service of God. It encouraged prayer recited with exalted joy and in a state of ecstatic fervour in which man forgets self and all his surroundings, and concentrates all his thoughts and feelings on union with God. A unique facet of Hasidism and the way in which Hasidism differs from other ultra-Orthodox groups in the idea of the *Zaddik* or *Rebbe,* a perfectly righteous man who is the spiritual leader of the group. The concept of *Zaddik* was introduced by the successor of the Baal Shem Tov, Rabbi Dov Baer of Meserich (1710–1771). The *Zaddik* was believed to work miracles and act as a channel for divine energy to flow into this world. Hasidim sought the *Zaddik*'s blessings for all their undertakings and told many stories about his wonderful deeds.

The Hasidic movement spread rapidly in Poland and was introduced to Lithuania by Rabbi Schneur Zalman (1746–1813) who founded the Lubavitch movement there (named after the town in Russia where the movement started). Throughout the nineteenth century Lubavitch battled under the banner of Hasidism to secure economic and political benefits for Jews. The vast majority of Lubavitchers were wiped out in the Holocaust. The 6th Lubavitcher Rebbe, Rabbi Joseph Isaac Schneerson (1880–1950) organised communities outside Russia. In the 1940s the movement settled in New York. Today Lubavitch exists on a worldwide basis, the main centres being New York, London, Antwerp, Jerusalem and Tel Aviv.

It is important to emphasise that although Hasidism is often referred to as a sect within Judaism, they are not a sect in the true sense. Never did the Hasidim secede from the main body of traditional Judaism. The Hasidim are simply a group of Orthodox Jews who emphasise a different aspect of the tradition. Originally, they emphasized feelings over and above intellect. As Hasidism spread, it ceased to be a religion of protest and came closer to institutionalised orthodoxy. Today, the meticulous following of Talmudic norms and the study of Torah are the main ideals of religious life for Hasidism. Hasidic Jews share a great deal with other ultra-Orthodox groups. What differentiates them is their doctrine of the *Zaddik* which sets clear boundaries between Hasidim and non-Hasidim.

Lubavitch is just one of a number of Hasidic groups in the UK. The others include Satmar, Visnitz, Braslav and Gur. They are all ultra-Orthodox groups. What distinguishes Lubavitch from the other groups is their attempt to bring non-orthodox Jews back to orthodoxy. It also emphasises the study of mystical concepts by all, not just a scholarly or religious élite. Satmar Hasidism arose in Transylvania in the decades immediately preceding the Holocaust and rose to prominence primarily in the post-war years. It is identified with the personality of Yoel Teitelbaum (1888–1979). The movement is largely based in Williamsburg in New York. This Rebbe was known for his unswerving and increasingly bitter opposition to Zionism, the state of Israel and all forms of Judaism which differed from his own ultra-Orthodox way of life. When the Satmar Rebbe died in 1979, some of the mourners compared the event to the Holocaust. The current Satmar Rebbe still expresses dismay at the willingness of Lubavitchers to interact with secular Jews and chides Lubavitchers for their belief that their leader is the messiah.

THE STAMFORD HILL COMMUNITY

Stamford Hill is an area of three square miles in North London. The population consists of Hasidic Jews, West Indians, and a number of Irish and Cypriot families. At present, there are about 200 Lubavitch families living there. The number of families rises every year. One explanation for this is the emphasis placed by Lubavitch on activity related to penitence (about 60% of the current Stamford Hill community are converts from non-Orthodox Judaism, i.e. non-Orthodox Jews who have become orthodox). Much of the work of the Lubavitcher rabbis involves mass campaigns to bring stray Jews back to Orthodoxy and to prepare for the advent of the Messiah. These include large meetings where rabbis preach, *Mezuzot* (encased scrolls of the Torah) campaigns (trying to ensure that all Jews have Kosher *Mezuzot* on their doors) and the *Mitzvah* (good deed) tank, a lorry going around the streets of Stamford Hill calling in male Jews to perform religious activities, such as laying *Tefillen* (phyllacteries).

The community is very close-knit and members have multiple social ties to other members of the community. There is a strong sense of community expressed by Lubavitchers and several people cited this as a reason for joining the movement. As one rabbi stated: "Lubavitch gives me a strong sense of belonging. When something goes wrong there is always support available even from people whom you do not know very well."

Men wear the traditional Hasidic clothing, black coats and black Homburgs. Married women wear a *Sheitel* (wig) with their hair cropped short. Hasidic residence, family life and education are strictly determined by Talmudic law. There are fixed rituals for living one's daily life according to Talmudic teachings. Life centres around festival days, the most important day of the week being *Shabbat,* the day of rest. The community affairs are guided primarily by religious considerations. So strong are the religious sentiments that not only religious affairs, but secular activities as well are controlled and directed by religious prescription and authority.

The community is largely isolated from the outside world. Mixing with *Goyim* (non-Jews) is minimal, except for business purposes. The justification for not mixing with non-Jews among the ultra-Orthodox is that through friendship and intimacies, the temptation to stray from the law could become irresistible and thus the self-imposed segregation is seen as a precaution. There is strong gender segregation in the community. The domestic role of women is stressed. About 25% of the men are rabbis, the others work as administrators, book keepers and shop keepers. Many of the women teach in local Jewish schools. Unmarried men and women of adult age are forbidden to mix. Even from childhood, boys and girls are taught separately. It would be forbidden for a man to visit a married woman alone. The Lubavitch explain this segregation as a protection of the sanctity of the family.

THE REBBE

The current Rebbe, Menachem Mendel Schneerson, has been described by Lubavitchers as "the most phenomenal Jewish personality of our time" (Lubavitch publications, 1989). Until his death in 1994 from a massive stroke, he resided in Brooklyn at his residence "770" and never left there for 40 years until his death. He was born in Nikolaev in Russia in 1902 and became a Torah Prodigy (a young person with an exceptionally good knowledge of the Torah). He was fluent in 10 languages and had a degree in Electrical Engineering from the Sorbonne. He became leader of Lubavitch in 1951. Lubavitchers recount many miraculous stories about him. It was claimed that he slept for an hour a day and fasted for 3 days a week. He was attributed with the ability to communicate with the soul of the deceased Sixth Lubavitcher Rebbe and meditated at his graveside on a weekly basis. He was seen by his followers as having the power to predict miraculous events.

Lubavitchers refer to him in everyday conversation with great frequency, and discuss his teachings, directives, and extraordinary powers of perception and wisdom. Where possible, his discourses were transmitted to Lubavitcher communities around the World, and, on the Sabbath and holy days when broadcasting was forbidden, those present attempted to memorise his words and pass them on to their communities. He was a spiritual guide of the Lubavitch community in all matters. For several years prior to his death, he rarely held private audiences, but each Sunday morning in Brooklyn several thousand people visited "770" for a ceremony called "Dollars" at which he distributed a dollar to everyone who visited him. He also gave them a blessing. Many people wrote to him about various matters, such as health, divorce, marriage and business. There are many stories in the Stamford Hill community of his miraculous abilities:

> Mr Levey had a disabled son and was keen to find for him a *Shidduch* (arranged marriage). He visited the Lubavitcher Rebbe in Brooklyn to help him with this. The Rebbe gave him two dollars, one for himself and one to take to Israel. He did not understand why he had a dollar for Israel but his wife told him to take it to Israel. He did this and, while sitting on a bus in Tel Aviv, he spoke to the man next to him. This man asked him why he had come to Tel Aviv and, when he recounted his tale, the man collapsed on the floor in shock. When he came round, he asked him what had happened. This man himself

stated that he had a disabled daughter for whom he wanted to arrange a *Shidduch*. He himself had gone to see the Lubavitcher Rebbe who had also given him two dollars, one for himself and one for Israel. He had brought this dollar to Israel. Subsequently, the son and daughter met and married (see Dein 1992 for further accounts of miracles in the community).

I have been conducting ethnographic fieldwork in the Stamford Hill community over the last 4 years. During this period, I interviewed a large number of people about Messianic ideas and observed their responses to failed prophecy.

THE MESSIAH CAMPAIGN IN STAMFORD HILL

The topic of *Moshiach* has always been an important topic of discussion among Lubavitchers. Over the past few years, there has been an escalating interest in the advent of *Moshiach* (the Messiah) in the Stamford Hill community. In the early 1980s Lubavitch began a "We-want-*Moshiach*" campaign to popularise the belief that the arrival of the Messiah was imminent. The campaign increased in momentum over the next few years, with frequent advertisements appearing in Jewish newspapers about the topic of *Moshiach*. One popular advert entitled "Draw your own conclusion" stated,

> These are amazing times. The Iron Curtain has crumbled. Iraq is humbled. The people of Israel emerge from under a rainstorm of murderous missiles. An entire beleaguered population is airlifted to safety overnight. A tidal wave of Russian Jews reaches Israel. Nations around the world turn to democracy. Plus countless other amazing developments that are taking place in front of our eyes. Any of these phenomena by itself is enough to boggle the mind. Connect them all together and a pattern emerges that cannot be ignored. The Lubavitcher Rebbe emphasises that these remarkable events are merely a prelude to the final redemption. The era of *Moshiach* is upon us. Learn about it. Be part of it. All you have to do is to open your eyes. Inevitably, you will draw your own conclusion.

Although the Rebbe never openly encouraged Messianic expectation, he did little to condemn it. A number of public statements were made by the Rebbe in relation to *Moshiach*. Although *Moshiach* was always a favourite topic of discourse for the Rebbe, on April 11, 1991, the contents of his discourse changed from his usual discourse to an injunction: "What more can I do to motivate the entire Jewish people to actually bring about the coming of *Moshiach*. All that I can possibly do is to give the matter over to you now, immediately. I have done whatever I can: from now on you must do whatever you can."

Lubavitchers were stunned by this injunction and started organising teachings and directives about the Messianic redemption. The Rebbe's talks on *Moshiach* were published and classes were organised to teach Messianic topics. *Moshiach* became a major topic of discussion. Soon Lubavitchers talked of the Rebbe himself being *Moshiach*.

Shortly afterwards, the Rebbe not only spoke about yearning for the coming of *Moshiach,* but also about his imminent arrival: "*Moshiach*'s coming is no longer a dream of a distant future, but an imminent reality which will very shortly become manifest" (April 1991).

In September 1991, the Rebbe stated that only if Jews believed with absolute certainty that the Messiah would come as redeemer, would such an event occur. When the Jewish New Year was approaching, he said, "When the divine service of the Jewish people over the centuries is considered as a whole, everything that is necessary to bring about redemption has been accomplished. There is no valid explanation for the continuance of the exile."

The Rebbe's statement had a profound effect on the Stamford Hill Lubavitchers. *Moshiach* became a major topic of conversation, as was life after the redemption. Issues, such as the types of food permitted after the redemption, were commonplace. One discussion centred around whether people would still have bodies at this time. After a short time, Lubavitchers discussed not just the imminent arrival of *Moshiach,* but that the Rebbe himself was *Moshiach.* There was the publication of books and seminars relating to Messianic topics and special Messiah Awareness Days were held in Stamford Hill. One Rabbi stated:

> Today, only one person fulfils the criteria for *Moshiach.* This is the Lubavitcher Rebbe. If pressed, all Lubavitchers will say he is *Moshiach.* There is no other candidate. We are nearly out of our predicament now. Many miraculous things are happening, such as the fall of Communism. Redemption is not yet here but we are in the beginnings of it. There is some debate among Lubavitchers concerning the *Moshiach* campaign. What is the best way to conduct it? Some say we should not say the Rebbe is *Moshiach.* I disagree with this. I feel that Lubavitchers must say that the Rebbe is *Moshiach.* I personally feel one cannot talk about one without the other. If you are seriously minded, there is nothing wrong with saying the Rebbe is *Moshiach.* It will not turn people off.

There was a split in the movement between those members who thought that they should publicly announce that the Rebbe was the Messiah and those who strongly disagreed with this. As the Messiah campaign grew in intensity, other ultra-orthodox Jewish groups who were not sympathetic to the Lubavitch cause publicly criticised Lubavitch. In February 1992, an article appeared in *The Times* newspaper describing the response of Rabbi Shach, himself an eminent Rabbi, to Lubavitchers' claims that their leader was the Messiah. He branded the Lubavitcher Rebbe as a heretic who harboured Messianic pretensions.

In March 1992, the Rebbe suffered a stroke which rendered him speechless and paralysed on the right-hand side. Despite his profound incapacity to look after himself, his followers described the stroke as "mild." Following this, he was unable to give "Dollars," but his followers continued to write to him for blessings. His secretary would read the letters to him and he would gesticulate an answer by moving his head up or down. In Brooklyn, he would be seen frequently, but unpredictably at prayer services, sometimes twice a day and sometimes less than once a week. In order to ensure that his followers would be present when he came out, his followers carried *"Moshiach"* bleepers. When he came on to the platform of the Synagogue in Crown Heights, a message would be flashed up on the bleeper "M H M is on the platform" (meaning Melech Ha Moshiach— King Moshiach).

In April 1993, a *"Moshiach* Awareness" caravan tour was held in Stamford Hill. A motorcade of three specially prepared caravans known as "Mitzvah Tanks" embarked on a grand tour around Britain to provide information about the concept of *Moshiach,* and its significance for Jewish life and belief. It was launched by the Mayor of Hackney, while a Hasidic band offered musical entertainment. A public discussion was held in the grounds of Lubavitch House in Stamford Hill which focused on a number of Messianic issues, including one talk entitled "Taking the first steps towards miracle making."

Discourse relating to the Messiah increased rapidly in Stamford Hill from about 1993. Although some Lubavitchers were reluctant to publicly admit it, most privately believed that their leader, Menachem Schneerson was the Messiah and they were waiting for him to reveal himself. In fact, in 1993, a group of women in Brooklyn prepared to crown the Rebbe. There was much excitement in the Stamford Hill community and many people spoke of the Messiah being in our midst and of the redemption being imminent.

MESSIANIC BELIEF AND THE REBBE'S ILLNESS

In Stamford Hill, the Rebbe's illness was frequently discussed. Publicly, Lubavitchers stated that the Rebbe would recover, that his stroke was a significant event which would usher in the Messianic era. Talk of the *Moshiach* increased and the fact that the Rebbe could not talk did nothing to detract Lubavitchers from the Messianic belief. There was increased discourse about more *Moshiach* meetings, advertisements and books about Messianic topics. Belief that the Rebbe was *Moshiach* intensified.

A number of explanations were given for the Rebbe's illness, often based *post hoc* on biblical and Talmudic sources. They deployed the writings of Maimonides to argue that the Rebbe himself had chosen to become ill and had taken on the suffering of the Jewish people. It was a process he had to go through before revealing himself. He was, as Maimonides had described, "A man of pains and acquainted with sickness. Indeed he has borne our sickness and endured our pains (Isaiah, Chapter 52–53)." Rabbi Rabin explained how he could be healed:

> The soul of the Rebbe represents a group soul of the Jewish people. His suffering represents the suffering of every Jew.

Just like a body and a head, the Rebbe is the head of the Jewish body. The two cannot exist independently. If the body is sick it can give rise to a headache. If the brain does not work, how can the body function? If every Jew did not perform good deeds the Jewish body would become sick and, in turn, the Rebbe. If all Jews perform these deeds the Rebbe will recover.

Lubavitchers attempted to restore the health of the Rebbe by the recitation of Psalms. Every day Lubavitchers were encouraged to say extra Psalms. Shortly after his first stroke, a *Sefer Torah* (scroll containing the text of the Torah) was written in New York and every Lubavitcher was asked to donate £1 towards a letter. The aim of writing this was to perfect the Rebbe's soul and, in turn, his body. This was explained to me in the following way:

All Jewish souls are tied to the Rebbe's soul. In the Torah there are 600,000 words (328,000 complete words and 272,000 incomplete words). In the world there are 600,000 general souls (each divides up into many more souls). These general souls are linked to the Rebbe's soul. By writing a perfect Torah, the Rebbe's soul becomes perfect again and this will affect his body. The Rebbe must first undergo a descent into the realms of evil to redeem the souls of the sinners. This descent on the spiritual plain is associated with physical sickness.

Alas, however, the Rebbe had another stroke in March 1994, almost 2 years after the first. This time he was rendered comatose. From the time of his stroke on March 10, 1994, until his death on June 12, 1994, he was on a ventilator and never regained consciousness. There was much consternation in the Stamford Hill community and the Rebbe's sickness was the focal talking point. Despite various newspaper reports alleging that the Rebbe was "brain dead" or "without brain function," his followers continued declaring him to be the *Moshiach*. When questioned about the meaning of the Rebbe's stroke, the answers given were *Moshiach*, and "we are on the threshold of the Messianic era." Messianic propaganda increased in intensity. Extra meetings were held where Psalms were said. Thousands of followers slept in the hospital where the Rebbe lay, reciting Psalms in the hope that he would arise.

During this period, I interviewed several Lubavitchers about his illness. Although no-one publicly discussed the possibility that he could die and who his successor would be (the Rebbe had no children to succeed him), privately, several people admitted their concerns about his possible death. One person said, "I know the Rebbe is a great man, but he is human after all and he is about 90 years of age. I think he could die. I hope, for the sake of Lubavitch, that he does not but we must face this possibility. If he dies, how will Lubavitchers account for his death and what will happen to the Messianic belief?"

Publicly, however, the "party line" was that this illness signified the imminent arrival of the Messianic era and forthcoming redemption. Rabbi Rabin stated:

The Rebbe is now in a state of concealment. The Jews could not see Moses on Mount Sinai and thought he was dead. They built the golden calf and had a vision of him lying dead on a bier, whereas he was in fact alive and in a state of concealment. The Rebbe is in a state of *Chinoplet,* a trancelike state where the soul leaves the body. The soul of the Rebbe has to go down to lower realms to drag up the souls of the sinners. He must do this before he declares himself as *Moshiach.* The spiritual energy required to bring *Moshiach* is very great and his body is depleted of energy. It is only now that we have the medical technology to keep him alive. We should not be sad. The attitude to adopt is one of *Simha* (joy). We are of course sad that the Rebbe is suffering but must be joyful that he is undergoing the process of transformation to reveal himself as Moshiach.

Even though Hasidim emphasise joy in the face of adversity, during the 3 months leading up to his death, people were very subdued. A notice was distributed to Lubavitch House relating to how people should act at this time. It emphasised that Lubavitchers should learn the Rebbe's teachings, perform good deeds, give charity and support their neighbours, and recite Psalms. Even when the Rebbe was comatose and attached to a ventilator, his followers continued to write for blessings. His secretary would stand over his sick bed and read them to him. New miracle stories appeared, such as the one below which was circulated around the community shortly before the Rebbe's death.

Dr Fink, one of the Rebbe's physicians, was traveling up to a hill in New York. The car in front of him had a trailer attached. Suddenly the trailer came loose and started to roll backwards. Dr Fink saw a vision of the Rebbe in front of his car, holding the trailer up, giving the physician enough time to escape. It is reported that Dr Fink had never met the Rebbe before he went into a coma.

Every day, faxes were received from Beth Israel Hospital in New York, documenting the Rebbe's medical condition. Slight improvements were taken as signs of imminent recovery and ascension to the Messianic role. Over the last weeks of his life, his medical condition deteriorated considerably. In May 1994, he had pneumonia from which he recovered, and several days before his death, he had a cardiac arrest and was resuscitated. Still his followers did not give up hope and claimed that he would get up from his sick bed and proclaim he was the Messiah.

MESSIANIC BELIEF AFTER THE REBBE'S DEATH

However, prophesised recovery was not to be the case. The Rebbe died on 12 June, 1994. His death was reported in the major tabloids, on the radio and television. *The Times* newspaper reported the event as follows:

The death of the Rebbe, Menachem Schneerson, seventh leader of the Lubavitcher Rabbinic Dynasty, brings to a close a remarkable career which culminated in his followers' claim that he was about to be revealed as the Messiah. His face, with its piercing blue eyes and black Fedora, was familiar throughout with photographs in thousands of shops, offices and homes in the Jewish world. During his 55-year stewardship, the Lubavitch movement was transformed from a practically moribund branch of Hasidism to a powerful and international movement, deploying all the resources of modern communication technology to spread its message.

A message was faxed from the Rebbe's residence "770" to the Stamford Hill community at the time of the Rebbe's death. This said, "Blessed be the divine judge," meaning that God had ordained that the Rebbe should die.

I arrived at Lubavitch House several hours after the Rebbe had died, having heard the news on a local radio station. The atmosphere was subdued. I was struck by the small number of people there and was told that most of the community had, at very short notice, flown to New York for the funeral. Some were praying, others saying *Tehillim* (Psalms), while other Lubavitchers stood in groups talking. I could see no-one crying. After an hour, more and more people assembled in the Synagogue. I was able to discuss with them what had happened. There was a distinct lack of leadership, no-one knew exactly how to proceed.

"Do we sit *Shiva?*" (7 days of ritual mourning), asked one man. "The Rebbe is not our immediate family." Some answered that it was necessary to sit *Shiva* for several hours only, others suggested a day and others said a week. Everyone agreed that, at the time of the funeral, they would do *Keriah* (rending garments) and someone was appointed to perform this task.

As the day proceeded, more and more people assembled in the Synagogue and attempts were made to link Lubavitch House by satellite with NBC, the American news channel, which was due to broadcast the funeral live.

Right up to his funeral, there was still a feeling of hope expressed by those present. "The Rebbe could still arise and proclaim himself as *Moshiach*," said one student. With this hope in mind, a group of Lubavitchers read *Tehillim* loudly. About an hour before the funeral, a commentary on Genesis 49 was distributed, describing how just as Judah is being buried, he will arise, implying the same thing would occur with the Rebbe:

> Jacob says the time will come when the Kingship of the House of David will appear in its lowest, deepest end and Judah, no longer strong as a lion, but femininely weak, and one will think it has reached its final stage where Judah's virility will almost have disappeared and then—just then— when the undertakers of World history will already have ordered the coffin for Judah's body apparently coming to its end, it will manfully arise and to it all the weak of the Nations will come.

With the room full to the brim with Lubavitchers, some stood reciting Psalms, some observed the funeral procession by satellite, and yet others tore their clothes. On satellite, a group of Lubavitchers could be seen dancing and singing in anticipation of his resurrection and the imminent redemption. Suddenly, one man shouted he could hear the *Shofar* (ram's horn) which announced the arrival of *Moshiach*. After the burial, some Lubavitchers left, others continued to say *Tehillim*.

The following morning, everyone was asking why he had died and what it meant for the arrival of *Moshiach* and the future of Lubavitch. Two days after his death, a statement was made by a spokesman for the Lubavitch movement which emphasised how much good work had been done by the Rebbe and how Lubavitchers now had the job of bringing forth the coming of the redemption. In it, he stated,

> By sharing with us his vision, his hopes and his promise, and by making us active participants in the perfection of God's world, the Rebbe has empowered us in the way that every parent can hope to empower his or her children. Handicapped as we are now with the loss of his physical presence . . . , we rededicate ourselves to continue to accomplish that which our beloved Rebbe taught through his life's work for a humanity uplifted by good and a world sanctified and redeemed by God.

I discussed his death with a number of people in the community. Several themes emerged from these discussions. Many Lubavitchers expressed the idea that he would be resurrected. Most emphasised that he still had a major presence in the world and that, without the hindrance of his physical body, his spiritual presence was even greater. Everyone expressed a feeling that they must continue, and hope and pray for the Messianic arrival and redemption. However, very soon, the overwhelming feeling in the community was that the Rebbe would resurrect very soon and that the redemption would arrive. I spoke to one 18-year-old Lubavitcher who stated:

> All Lubavitchers believe the Rebbe is *Moshiach*. We still believe this. It is not impossible that the Rebbe will be resurrected. The Rebbe has great power now. His spiritual presence is even greater now in all the world. People still write to him for a blessing, although, of course, they do not get a reply but there is a response. Things are happening.

The conversation centred around how and when he would be resurrected. Some Lubavitchers, however, admitted that they had been wrong. One Rabbi said:

> Concerning *Moshiach:* up till now we thought that we knew the script, the series of events that were going to happen in the process of the revelation of *Moshiach*. The Rebbe never actually told us a script, but we thought we should make it up. Now we realise we do not know the script. We should try to understand that this is not surprising. The coming of *Moshiach* is the drawing of the infinite into the finite, this is very difficult. It is quite beyond ordinary reason. It is understandable we do not know the steps which led to this.

Following his death, Lubavitchers started to fly out to the Rebbe's tomb. Today, queues of people wait in line to deposit small pieces of paper on the tomb with requests for a blessing written on them. Others write to the Rebbe's secretary with their request. He takes them to the tomb and reads them to the Rebbe. There is a growing number of miracle stories about people who have visited his grave. For instance, "Mr Rubin was in great financial despair recently having gone bankrupt. He went to the *Ohel* (Rebbe's tomb) and left a request for a blessing to save his business. Shortly after he returned home, he unexpectedly received a letter from a distant relative informing him that they were willing to give him money to save his business."

It is now almost 2 years since the Rebbe's death. Even now, in Stamford Hill, people are talking about the Rebbe still being *Moshiach*. Although some people publicly announce this, the organisation running Lubavitch has stated that people should not say this in public on account of reactions of other people. Lubavitchers in Stamford Hill seem to be getting on with their everyday life. They still talk about the Rebbe's influence in their life. For many, the belief that the Rebbe is the *Moshiach* has not in any way decreased, even following his death. For some, it has, in fact, intensified.

CONCLUSIONS

The observations presented above do present some confirmation of Festinger's theory of cognitive dissonance. What is particularly interesting about the community is how well people have adapted to the fact that they are without a leader. To my knowledge, no-one left Lubavitch when the Rebbe died, although one Lubavitcher developed a severe depressive illness. These findings are corroborated by Shaffir (1995) in Brooklyn who found evidence of belief intensification amongst American Lubavitchers. Although there are some political tensions in the movement, generally people carry on with their everyday lives still waiting for the Messiah and the redemption which they still believe is imminent.

Different religious groups deal with failed prophecy in different ways. For some, there is intensification of belief and activity. This has been the case among Lubavitchers. The following statement was published in Lubavitch magazine in August 1994:

> Some antagonists had initially predicted a diminishing of Lubavitch activity after the Rebbe's passing, or even a complete breakdown and collapse of Lubavitch. Thank God, the doomsayers were proven false, and their bad predictions did not materialise. On the contrary, we are witnessing a worldwide spur of new activities, projects and institutions established in the Rebbe's honour.

What factors account for the ability of Lubavitchers to deal with this failed messianism is mentioned above, the Stamford Hill Lubavitcher community is very close-knit. Generally, members have multiple social ties to other members. At times of crisis, Lubavitchers receive a lot of social support from other members of the community. These strong interpersonal attachments help to maintain religious commitments and prevent members leaving the group following failed messianism.

Lubavitchers have coped with this failed prophecy by appealing to a number of rationalisations which not only preserve, but enhance their commitment to messianic prophecy. Several members stated that although the Rebbe was a potential messiah, the generation did not possess enough merit to warrant his coming, i.e. it was their fault. Another explanation was that it is only God who knows when the messiah will arrive. Lubavitchers thought that they knew the script, but were wrong. Men cannot know God's intentions.

However, one of the most common explanations was that even though the Rebbe was dead, without the hindrance of his physical body, he was, in fact, more powerful spiritually and was better able to bring on the coming redemption. Melton (1985) argues that if a prediction fails, the members of the group do not abandon the movement, but aim to resolve the dissonance while relying on the "unfalsifiable beliefs out of which religious thought worlds are constructed and within that context believers can engage in a reaffirmation of basic faith and make a reappraisal of their predicament." The empirical testable belief that the Rebbe is the messiah changes into a supernatural unfalsifiable belief that he is more powerful in the spiritual worlds. As the Rebbe stated after the death of his predecessor,

> And the Alter Rebbe (first Lubavitcher Rebbe) explains, that the Zohar also means to say that the Zaddik is present in this physical world more than during his life on this world. He also tells us that after the departure of the Neshemo (soul) from this world, the Neshemo of the Zaddik generates more strength and more Koach (power) to his devoted disciples (Chabad Newsletter, September 1994).

Why do some groups persist following failed prophecy and others break up? As mentioned, one factor may be the level of social support. However, another factor may be that religious groups can withstand one episode of failed prophecy, but successive episodes in close proximity may cause members to leave. There is some empirical evidence for this. Following the failed prophecy by Millerites that the second coming would occur on April 23, 1843, there was some disappointment, but this soon gave rise to renewed confidence and fervour and as one Millerite stated, "We looked for it too soon, that was all" (Sears, 1924). A new date of December 31, 1843, was chosen, but again, there was no second coming. There was some disillusionment, but again there was a resurgence of fervour. However, when another date of October 22, 1844, was selected, and it came and went without any sign of anything happening, the movement withered and died. It took 18 months of disconfirmation for the movement to disintegrate. The early disconfirmations led to an intensification of belief as dissonance theory would suggest.

There is a need for further research in this area. As the year 2000 rapidly approaches, we may expect the arrival of new millennial groups some expecting the end of the world to come or the Messiah to reveal himself. A close eye should be kept on these movements to examine whether or not the above hypotheses are confirmed.

REFERENCES

Chabad Newsletter, September 1994.

Dein, S. "Letters to the Rebbe: Millennium, Messianism & Medicine Amongst the Lubavitch of Stamford Hill, London." *International Journal of Social Psychiatry* 38(4), 1992: 262–272.

Epstein, I. *Judaism.* Harmondsworth: Penguin, 1959.

Festinger, L., Riecken, H. W. & Schachter, S. *When Prophecy Fails.* New York: Harper & Row, 1956.

Hopkins, J. K. *A Woman to Deliver Her People.* Austin, Texas, University of Texas Press, 1982.

Hughes, P. *A Popular History of the Catholic Church.* New York: Doubleday, 1954.

Littlewood, R. "Psychopathology and Religious Innovation: An Historical Instance," in Bhugra, D., *Psychiatry and Religion.* London: Routledge, 1995: 116–136.

Littlewood, R. & Dein, S. "The Effectiveness of Word: Religion and Healing Among the Lubavitch of Stamford Hill." *Culture, Medicine and Psychiatry* 1, 1995: 339–383.

Melton, J. G. "Spiritualization and Reaffirmation: What Really Happens When Prophecy Fails." *American Studies* 26(2), 1985: 82.

Nichol, F. D. *The Midnight Cry.* Washington DC: Review & Herald Publishing Company, 1994.

Scholem, G. *Sabbatai Zevi.* London: Routledge, 1973.

Sears, C. E. *Days of Delusion—A Strange Bit of History.* Boston: Houghton Mifflin, 1924.

Shaffir, W. "When Prophecy Is Not Validated: Explaining the Unexpected in Messianic Campaign." *The Jewish Journal of Sociology* 37(2), Dec 1995: 119–136.

Sharot, S. *Messianism, Mysticism & Magic.* Chapel Hill: University of N. Carolina Press, 1982.

Shupe, A. D. *Six Perspectives on New Religions: A Case Study Approach.* New York: E. Mellen Press, 1981.

Singelenberg, R. " 'It Separated the Wheat from the Chaff': The '1975' Prophesy & Its Impact on Dutch Jehovah's Witnesses." *Sociological Analysis* 50, 1989: 23–40.

Stark, R. "Why Religious Movements Succeed or Fail: A Revised General Model." *Journal of Contemporary Religion* 11(2), May 1996: 133–146.

Stark, R. & Iannaccone, L. R. "Why the Jehovah's Witnesses are Growing so Rapidly." *Journal of Contemporary Religion* 12(2), 1997: 133–157.

Zymunt, J. F. "When Prophecies Fail." *American Behavioural Scientist* 16, 1972: 245–268.

PART SIX
World Religions

The Blue Mosque in Istanbul was built by Sultan Ahmet I in the early seventeenth century and is one of the best known religious structures in the world. It was built opposite the Hagia Sophie, a massive church built in the sixth century. Most of the world's population is either Hindu, Buddhist, Jewish, Christian, or Muslim.

This final part of the book consists of essays we have written to describe five of the world's numerically largest and historically most significant religions: Hinduism, Buddhism, Judaism, Islam, and Christianity. There are three reasons why such a section is particularly important. First, understanding different large-scale religious traditions helps in understanding an increasingly multireligious American society. Second, the large-scale religions provide context and points of comparison for beliefs and practices described elsewhere in this book. Third, small-scale religions are disappearing, and these five religions play an increasingly larger role in the cultures of the world.

To begin with, our society is increasingly a religious mosaic. Not only are more people actively practicing their religion than at any other time in the past half century, but the number of religions that are widely practiced in America has grown.[1] Many religious traditions have been present in the United States since the earliest days of the nation. However, until the end of the nineteenth century, Christians thoroughly dominated this country's economy and society. In the twentieth century, as a result of large-scale immigration from Europe, Jews came to have a substantial role in American culture. In the last fifty years, there has been a great wave of immigration from Africa, Asia, and Latin America. These immigrants have brought their religions. As a result, Islam, Hinduism, and Buddhism are more and more present in American society. Christians still dominate American society, but members of other groups will certainly have larger roles in the future. Thus, understanding the traditions and beliefs of various religions is critical to understanding how American culture is changing.

Second, the other essays in this book have focused on specific practices, ideas, and beliefs within both large and small religious groups. The essays in this part provide additional context within which these practices can be understood. Reading general descriptions of these large-scale religions helps us understand the role that particular religious practices and beliefs play within a broader tradition. It also helps us see parallels between these traditions and many of the smaller religions described in other essays.

It is important for us to point out that the religions described in Part Six—Christianity, Judaism, Buddhism, Hinduism, and Islam—are not set apart because they are better, more logical, or more highly evolved than others. There is no objective evidence that this is the case. In fact, a key reason for reading about both large- and small-scale religious traditions is to note that although their stories, beliefs, and practices differ enormously, they all contain the same basic elements: the stories and myths themselves, a belief in something supernatural, a series of symbols and the rituals in which they are used, special practitioners who perform the actions of religion for the benefit of others, the means for some members to have direct experiences of the supernatural, and histories of change.

A third critical reason to focus on these mass religions is that they have been expanding extremely rapidly. Like language and many other aspects of culture, religious variety has declined markedly in the past hundred years and continues to decline. At the turn of the twentieth century, small-scale religions, perhaps numbering in the thousands, were practiced by small, relatively isolated ethnic groups around the world. By the turn of the twenty-first century, many of these religions had disappeared or were practiced by a mere handful of people. Both push and pull factors are responsible for this state of affairs.

People have been pushed into the large religions through the active efforts of missionaries. This is particularly true of Christianity and Islam. Subgroups of both of these religions have actively searched for converts, especially in Africa and Latin America. In many cases, these missionary efforts have been underwritten by governments in Europe (in the first half of the twentieth century) and in the Middle East (in the second half of the twentieth century). In some cases, during the colonial era in the first half of the twentieth century, church attendance was required of colonial subjects. Those who did not convert faced severe penalties.

For many reasons, the large religions often were powerfully attractive to members of smaller religious groups. In some cases they offered direct and evident benefits. Churches ran schools and medical clinics and offered these services preferentially to their members. Gifts of food, clothing, and wealth of all kinds flowed from missionaries to people they favored. Governments and businesses employed people who spoke, read, and wrote European languages fluently, and often such training was available only through missionary schools.

Beyond these benefits, individuals had other reasons to seek membership in larger religions. As communications improved, contact among members of different ethnic groups increased. In these circumstances, membership in a common religious group, with a shared set of beliefs, ethical principles, values, and, in the case of Islam, language, could unite people across ethnic divides. In parts of West Africa, for example, Islam, with its strict ethical system for commercial transactions, became a critical factor enabling merchants to bridge their differences. Additionally, members of some small religions were stigmatized as "primitive" and joined large religions to escape that labeling. The result of these factors is that within the past century, vast numbers of people have left their traditional religious practices for Christianity and Islam.

In some ways, the success of the large religions has unquestionably resulted in greater homogeneity of religious belief and culture around the world. This is particularly the case because certain subgroups, such as the Catholic Church and the Saudi Wahaabite Muslims, have been more influential in missionary activity than others. Despite this, religious diversity is constantly created as people combine their older practices with new religions or improvise new ones. For example, Christian missionaries were very successful in Africa in the past century. Many Africans are members of churches that conduct their ceremonies and rituals in ways that would be familiar to most American Christians (although they do often use styles of song and dress drawn from African culture). However, there are also many churches that would be less familiar to Americans—churches like the Winner's Church and the Redeemed Christian Church, both in Nigeria, the Maximum Miracle Centre in Kenya, the apocalyptic Movement for the Restoration of the Ten Commandments of God, in Uganda, and the Christian Kimbanguist Church in Congo. These churches often incorporate elements of preexisting local belief and ritual into their practice of Christianity. Some of these churches are very large. For example, the Kimbanguists claim between 5 and 10 million members. The Winner's Church has branches in thirty-two African countries and recently built a 50,000-seat auditorium in Otta, Nigeria. By comparison, the number of Christian Scientists, an influential American group, is believed to be between 150,000 and 300,000

In our essays in Part Six, we present brief and balanced introductions to each religion. In the anthropological tradition of cultural relativism, we neither praise nor criticize any of them. These essays are, of course, only brief descriptions of the religions they cover. Each of these traditions is old, rich, and detailed. A short essay can give only the most rudimentary information about them. We urge you to read about them in greater depth.

Anthropology has traditionally been concerned with documenting and explaining small groups and their practices. It has generally paid far less attention to large-scale society. However, in the current world, a firm understanding of the basic elements of the large-scale religions is essential to a thorough anthropology of religion.

NOTE

1. Roger Finke and Rodney Stark, *The Churching of America: Winners and Losers in Our Religious Economy* (New Brunswick, N.J.: Rutgers University Press, 1992).

13

Hinduism

Describing Hinduism, perhaps the world's oldest religion, presents special problems not found in explaining the other religions covered in this part of the book. For starters, there is the word *Hinduism* itself. The word *Hindu* has its origins in the ancient Persian word for "river" and was used for centuries to describe the inhabitants of India (as well as Pakistan and Bangladesh) without referring to religion. In English, the word *Hinduism* seems to have been first used to describe a religion in the 1820s. Before the mid nineteenth century, the people who we today would call Hindus did not use that name to refer to their religious practices. Many people today reject the terms *Hindu* and *Hinduism* as impositions of the British colonial government. They prefer to call their religion *Sanatana Dharma*, which can be translated as "Eternal Law" or "Eternal Religion."

To further complicate matters, Hinduism includes an enormous variety of beliefs. While Judaism, Christianity, Islam, and Buddhism are all diverse traditions that include many different practices, their complexity pales before that of Hinduism. Within Hinduism there are not only a great many sacred texts but ideas that seem absolutely at odds with each other. For example, some Hindus believe that there are many gods, perhaps millions of them; others do not believe in devotion to gods at all. Some believe that god and human are the same; others believe that there is a radical separation between god and human. Some believe that the physical world is real; others think it is an illusion. This diversity is possible because one of the fundamental tenets of Hinduism is that there is no single correct pathway to religious understanding. Instead, there are a great many ways of finding religious truth.

THE HISTORICAL DEVELOPMENT OF HINDUISM

Unlike the other religions discussed in this part of the book, Hinduism has no single founding figure. Though it is generally considered to be the world's oldest religion, its founding dates, the identities of its original sages, as well as the origins of its key beliefs are all hotly contested. However, some knowledge of the early history of India helps in understanding the origins and development of Hinduism.

Harappan Civilization

India is home to one of the great early civilizations. In the 1920s, archaeologists discovered the remains of ancient cities in the Indus River valley. Excavations revealed that an enormous civilization began to emerge there 4,500 years

ago. At its height the Harappan civilization covered perhaps half a million square miles (about the size of modern-day Pakistan) and included cities with populations of up to 50,000. One unusual feature of Harappan cities is that running water seems to have played an important role in their design. There were toilets flushed by running water as well as prominent large public baths. The great bath at a site called Mohenjo-Daro, constructed more than four thousand years ago, is certainly the largest, oldest public bathing structure yet discovered. The prominent use of water and the large amounts of labor spent on constructing plumbing systems may have had religious importance. Many modern Hindu practices stress issues of purity and pollution, and many rituals involve bathing and other uses of water. It is possible (though a long way from proven) that modern Hindu practices had Harappan antecedents.

There is a great deal of archaeological evidence about Harappan religious beliefs. For example, one image commonly found at Harappan sites is of a man, with horns on his head, sitting in a position that in the modern world is associated with certain forms of Hindu meditation. There are also small pillars that seem to be symbols of male sexuality. Stones of similar shape are considered holy objects in some forms of Hinduism today. In addition to these examples, many Harappan objects have been interpreted as charms, amulets, and other ritual items. The Harappan civilization was literate, and many examples of Harappan writing have been found. Harappan script remains undeciphered, but some scholars have argued that many writings are religious texts. It thus appears that there is some relationship between the religious beliefs of ancient Harappans and modern Hindus, but the exact nature of this relationship and the degree to which modern beliefs are similar to ancient ones is unknown.

Aryan Invasions?

It seems clear that around 2000 B.C.E. the Harappan civilization became strongly influenced by outside forces. Since the nineteenth century, most scholars have believed that India was invaded and conquered by a people who called themselves Aryans who spread out from southeastern Europe to occupy a region stretching from north central Europe, through the Middle East and Persia to India. Much of the evidence supporting this view of history is linguistic, based on underlying similarities in languages as diverse as Sanskrit, Hindi, Greek, Latin, and German. However, new genetic data suggesting that upper-caste Indians are more related to Europeans than are lower-caste Indians[1] might also support the theory. According to the Aryan Invasion interpretation, the invaders quickly suppressed those they conquered, making them servants and slaves. The religion and lore of the Aryans replaced that of earlier peoples. Additionally, the fact that class divisions based on skin color rapidly developed during this period might be due to the Aryans being lighter skinned than the conquered.

The Aryan Invasion interpretation of history has come under much fire in recent decades. Detractors point out that there is little evidence of invasion in the archaeological record. The pattern of tools, weapons, and other artifacts of outside origin corresponds more to slow diffusion than to conquest and replacement. Further, the Vedas, sacred books of Indian religion generally understood as Aryan in origin, contain little that links them to any ancient homeland other than the Indian subcontinent.

The academic arguments about the Aryan invasion are tied up in issues of nationalism, racism, and colonialism. The notion of light-skinned invaders suppressing dark-skinned indigenous inhabitants certainly fit well with the racist ideologies common in Europe in the nineteenth and early twentieth centuries. Promoting the idea that historically light-skinned people had dominated darker-skinned people was also beneficial to the British colonizers of India. It is equally the case that the notion that Indian civilization (and Hinduism) has entirely Indian origins is useful to those who want to argue against "foreign" practices and promote Indian nationalism.

Given the great distance in time and the difficulties of archaeological interpretation, it is unlikely that we will ever be able to resolve the difficulties posed by the Aryan Invasion theory. It is clear, however, that Indian language, religion, and social structure are related to those of people found throughout Europe and the Middle East. It is further clear that the earliest written Indian sacred literature, the Vedas, date from a time after the city-sites of Harappan culture had been abandoned and that the language of the Vedas, the stories they tell, and the rituals they prescribe, are related to those of other peoples throughout the Middle East and Europe. It is to this sacred literature we now turn.

THE SACRED LITERATURE OF HINDUISM

Hindus possess no single book like the Jewish or Christian Bibles or the Qur'an. Instead there is a voluminous sacred literature. Different elements of this literature are considered critical by different groups within Hinduism. Some of the best-known elements of Hindu sacred literature are the Vedas, the Law of Manu, the Epics, and the Puranas. Each of these is described below.

The Vedas

The Vedas are the most ancient of the Hindu texts, probably committed to writing between 1500 and 1200 B.C.E. There are four separate Vedas, and, as we shall see, three additional elements are attached to each of these. Thus, Vedic literature, taken as a totality, consists of sixteen elements.

The four Vedas—the Rigveda, Yarjurveda, Samaveda, and Atharvaveda—consist of collections of hymns to the ancient gods. Of these the Rigveda is best known. It consists of songs and poems from which, in ancient times, chief priests drew their worship. The other Vedas are additional groups of songs and poems used by other priests.

The gods extolled in the Vedas are not associated with modern-day Hindu practice. Instead, they are connected with features of the natural world or human virtues. Some examples are Agni, the god of fire; Indra, a god associated with war and rain; Mitra, the god of honor; and Usas, the god of the dawn. The critical rituals described in the Vedas are fire sacrifices. The notion behind them is that Agni, the god of fire, conveys messages and sacrifices to the other gods. Those who make generous sacrificial offerings will be rewarded by the gods.

One important aspect of Vedic literature is the *soma* ritual. Soma was a drink made by crushing the stems of the soma plant. Imbibing it produced ecstatic, possibly hallucinogenic, states. No one has yet identified the soma plant; the Vedas say it is of heavenly origin. As part of sacrificial rituals, the juice of the soma plant was extracted and mixed with water and milk. Then a portion of the juice was offered to the gods and the remainder was drunk by the priests and the individual who commissioned the sacrificial ritual. The soma ritual is similar to the *haoma* ritual found in ancient Persian religions, particularly Zoroastrianism, and probably indicates a historic link between these traditions.

Literature "Attached" to the Vedas

The Vedas were complete by about 1200 B.C.E. In the eight hundred years that followed, three additional types of text became attached to each of the four Vedas. These are the Brahmanas (written down between 900 and 700 B.C.E.), the Aranyakas (composed about 700 B.C.E.), and the Upanishads (recorded between 1000 and 400 B.C.E.). Each of these contains a particular sort of information.

The Brahmanas are collections of commentaries in which scholars interpret the origins, meaning, and significance of the hymns of ritual and sacrifice of the Vedas. They provide guidance in the correct performance of sacrifice and the proper ways to chant hymns.

The Aranyakas, or "Books of the Forest," contain information that was probably concerned with secret rituals intended to be carried out by initiates to the priesthood. These people may have lived as hermits in the forest or have performed the rituals described in the Aranyakas in the forest, away from the eyes of the uninitiated.

The final section of the Vedas, the Upanishads, is among the best known of all Hindu literature. The earliest parts of the Upanishads may be as much as three thousand years old. The word *upanishad* means "session." Its implication is that the Upanishads contain wisdom gained by listening to great teachers. The Upanishads are among the most powerful spiritual literature in the world and include several of the elements that outsiders often associate with Hindu thought.

The key teaching of the Upanishads is that there is a single, ultimate reality in the universe. They call this reality *Brahman* (not to be confused with *Brahmin,* which means "priest"). Brahman pervades everything, is the ultimate essence of everything, and animates all existence in the universe. Everything that is, is a manifestation of Brahman.

A second critical concept is the notion of *atman.* Atman is that element of Brahman contained in all things. It is the ultimate individual essence of an individual (or indeed of any object). Hindus sometimes translate *atman* as "soul." Atman is the force that animates the existence of individual people as well as other living and nonliving things. However, atman is a manifestation of Brahman. Therefore, one can achieve knowledge of Brahman, of the ultimate, by turning inward to discover the transcendent reality within each individual.

In addition to the ideas of Brahman and atman, the Upanishads also introduce and explore the interrelated ideas of reincarnation, karma, samsara, and moksha. The Upanishads portray Brahman as eternal, unchanging, and divine. The world we live in, however, is subject to constant change and is therefore imperfect. Birth, life, death, and rebirth are all part of this changing and imperfect world, as is all suffering and pain. In Hindu thought, the constant process of change and the misery it necessarily entails is referred to as *samsara,* or reincarnation. The goal of a spiritual life is to liberate oneself from the cycle of life, death, and rebirth, moving away from samsara toward the perfection of Brahman. This movement is understood as liberating and is called *moksha.*

The ideas of samsara and moksha are closely linked to the ideas of karma and reincarnation. The literal meaning of *karma* is "action." However, the principle behind it is much more complicated than this. Karma is the notion that every action (or thought) in the world is both caused by and the cause of other actions. Both good and bad come to an individual as a result of their actions in previous lives. Good actions earn benefits in the future, evil actions lead to future harm. This can be interpreted in either a deterministic or an individualistic sense. On the one hand, through our actions and thoughts we determine both the good and the bad aspects of our future. On the other hand, our present-day actions and thoughts (and the good or ill that befalls us) were determined by our past actions and thoughts.

The effects of karma percolate not only through our present life but through our future lives as well. The Upanishads maintain that the atman is born over and over again. Just as an individual human sheds clothes and puts on new ones, so too the atman sheds one form of existence, one body, only to put on a new one. In Hindu thought, individual identity is not maintained through reincarnation. Only atman and karma pass from life to life. That is, the animating principle and the positive or negative weight of one's actions are reincarnated. This means it is useless to wonder who (or what) individuals were in their past lives. But at the same time, it is certain that their social position as well as their fortune, for good or ill, is the result of the actions or karma of their past lives.

The ideas of karma, samsara, and moksha are closely linked. Ultimately karma creates samsara. Individuals may be reincarnated to higher or lower social stations (or even to nonhuman form) depending on their karma. However, the ultimate goal is not to be rewarded by better and better lives. Rather it is the release of the atman from the cycle of karma and samsara and the achievement of moksha through the union of atman and Brahman.

It is important to note that although these basic ideas inform almost all Hindu worship and practice, the Upanishads are very abstract and difficult texts. They are intended for scholars and spiritual masters, not for the average person. Most Hindus believe in the notions of karma, samsara, moksha, and reincarnation, but very few give their religious lives over to the study of the Upanishads or the contemplation of Brahman and atman. Popular forms of religious devotion are much more likely to center on the veneration of particular deities.

The Manu-smrti, or Code of Manu

Manu, in Hindu sacred narrative, was the first man and the lawgiver. The Manu-smrti, or Code of Manu, may have had its origins as long as 3,500 years ago, but in its current form it dates to the first century B.C.E. Unlike the Vedas and their associated literature, the Manu-smrti deals with the specific duties and obligations of individual members of society. It is an enormously influential document because it divides Indian society into social classes (varnas—"colors" or castes; these are described more fully later in this essay) and specifies in detail the *dharma,* or duties, of the members of each of these groups.

In addition to descriptions of caste, the Manu-smrti includes many rules about purity and pollution that are linked to caste membership. These rules concern the particular jobs that can be held by members of different groups, as well as who can prepare food for whom, and who can eat with whom. Moreover, many passages specify proper relations between husband and wife as well as correct behavior for members of both sexes. By modern standards, many of these regulations seem particularly oppressive. For example, chapter five of the Manu-smrti includes the following verses: "By a girl, by a young woman, or even by an aged one, nothing must be done independently, even in her own house. In childhood a female must be subject to her father, in youth to her husband, when her lord is dead to her sons; a woman must never be independent" (V 147–148) and "A faithful wife, who desires to dwell (after death) with her husband, must never do anything that might displease him who took her hand, whether he be alive or dead" (V 156).

This last verse is generally understood as prohibiting the re-marriage of widows.

Because the society envisioned by the authors of the Manu-smrti is extremely hierarchical and bound by many detailed rules, the code of Manu presents enormous difficulties for current-day thinkers who tend to stress the equality of women and men as well as the equal rights of all people in society. Nonetheless, the Manu-smrti remains an extremely important document, and its words both reflect and inspire much of social conduct in India.

The Epics and the Puranas

The Vedas and their associated literature as well as the Manu-smrti are literary works aimed at the scholarly and initiates to the priesthood. The epics and the Puranas are stories that express the values of the other Hindu literature and are written (and told) in forms that are accessible to most people. The epics and Puranas are among the most famous and best loved of Hindu sacred narratives, and some of them are popular among non-Hindus as well.

There are two epics: the Mahabharata and the Ramayana. One particular part of the Mahabharata (actually eighteen chapters of book 6), the Bhagavadgita, is particularly famous both inside and outside of India. Most groups of Hindus count eighteen Puranas. These are lengthy texts that recount the stories, legends, and genealogies surrounding individual gods and heros of the Hindu pantheon.

The Mahabharata is possibly the world's longest religious text. It consists of more than a hundred thousand stanzas of poetry written in Sanskrit. Scholars believe that some elements of the Mahabharata may be more than three thousand years old, but the epic was written down in its current form about 350 B.C.E.

At its most basic level, the Mahabharata tells the story of an internecine war. Two groups of first cousins, the Pandavas and the Dhartarashtras, battle each other for possession of their ancestral kingdom, Bharata, located somewhere on the Ganges River in northern India. However, the story is extremely complex for several reasons. First, there is a very large number of characters involved, and this allows for many subplots and twists of narrative. Second, one of the sets of cousins (the Pandavas) is associated with (and ultimately aided by) the gods, whereas the other set (the Dhartarashtras) are closely identified with demons and the enemies of the gods. Third, although the Pandavas ultimately vanquish the Dhartarashtras, this is not a simple tale of the triumph of good over evil. Both sides are confronted by numerous ethical dilemmas, and though the Pandavas win the war, they pay a terrible price for that victory and their leader remains convinced of the war's wrongfulness.

The most famous element of the Mahabharata is the Bhagavadgita. These chapters concern one of the Pandavas princes, Arjuna, and his mentor and charioteer, Krishna Vasudeva. The Bhagavadgita is written as a dialogue between these (and several other) characters. It is set on the eve of a critical battle between the Pandavas and Dhartarashtras. Prince Arjuna despairs, considering the battle and the close family relationships among those on different sides, saying that he can see only evil in the destruction of his enemies. Rather than kill, Arjuna proposes to allow himself to be killed. Krishna Vasudeva responds to Arjuna's despair by revealing that he is, in fact, an incarnation of the god Vishnu and that he will instruct Arjuna in the proper understanding of the tasks before him. In particular, Krishna reminds Arjuna that both his own atman and that of his enemy are eternal and only appear to live and die, and, further, that as a member of his particular social group (a kashatrya) he achieves his highest purpose by fulfilling his duties and fighting. He must not shy from the fight but fulfill his duty with faith and without concern for personal gain.

The Bhagavadgita goes on to expound on the meaning and practice of Hindu theology. Throughout the Bhagavadgita, Krishna is portrayed as a wise and companionate mentor deeply concerned with the affairs of humanity. Though the Bhagavadgita is ultimately concerned with Brahman, the supreme power of the universe, it images Brahman through Krishna, who thus becomes, for many Hindus, a central image of the divine.

The Ramayana (romance of Rama) is the second epic. It is much shorter than the Mahabharata, and the story it tells is less complex. It primarily concerns the prince Rama and his wife Sita. Rama and Sita are portrayed as wise and holy people who faithfully follow their dharma. Rama is the eldest son of the king. But his stepmother conspires to have her son, Bharata, named king instead. This is done, and Rama is sent into exile in the forest for fourteen years. Sita follows him, along with his half brother Lakshamana. In the forest, Rama and Lakshamana busy themselves by destroying the rakshasas, evil demons. However, this angers Ravana, the evil king of Lanka, who kidnaps Sita and imprisons her in Lanka. Rama and Lakshamana try many ways to defeat Ravana and get Sita back, but only succeed after forming an alliance with the monkey king and his general Hanuman. Together Rama, Lakshamana, and the monkey army led by Hanuman defeat Ravana and free Sita, but Rama will not take Sita back until she proves her fidelity in a series of tests. Rama becomes king, but Sita is exiled to the forest where she bears him two sons. When these come of age, the family is reunified, but Sita calls upon the earth goddess to testify to her innocence of any wrong. The earth goddess appears and she and Sita are swallowed by the earth as a mark of their holiness.

For many Hindus, the Ramayana is an extraordinarily powerful story. Devotion to Rama and Sita are widespread, and rituals and plays that reenact the Ramayana are frequently performed throughout India to large audiences. Rama and Sita appear as the epitome of humanity, the perfect role models. They are faithful, courageous, and bound to devotion and duty. The reign of Rama is thought of as a utopian era. Indian politicians frequently refer to their efforts in terms of the restoration of the time of Rama.

VARNA: THE CASTE SYSTEM

Casteism, or discrimination against individuals based on caste, is now illegal in India, and the Indian constitution has abolished the status of "untouchable." Despite these facts, castes have been central to the organization of Hindu society for at least three thousand years and remain salient categories today. The two elements of the caste system, varna and jati, are related in complex ways.

The varnas, as described in the Rigveda, correspond to the social classes. *Varna* literally means "color," and some scholars argue that this system originated as a result of the Aryan invasions: Invaders became members of prestigious varnas while the conquered were subjugated as menial workers and worse. Whatever the truth of that hypothesis, Hindu religion teaches that the origins of varna come from the god Purusha, the primal being. In the Vedas, Purusha creates humanity from an act of self-division. However, not all humans are created in the same fashion. Instead, five different varnas are created: the head of Purusha gives rise to the brahmans, the priestly, poet-writer class; the shoulders and arms give rise to the kshatriyas, or kingly and warrior class; the thighs give rise to vaishyas, or merchants and landowners; the feet give rise to the shudras, or peasant and laborer class; and the fifth group is the polluted workers. Technically, people in the fifth group are not members of a varna. They are frequently called "untouchables," but in the late twentieth century they came to be called dalit, harijan, or scheduled castes. About one-quarter of India's population are members of this group.

Although the varnas are the major divisions of society, individuals experience their position in the caste system through their jati. Jati (the term is from the Sanskrit word for "birth") are endogamous occupational groups. Individuals are born into a jati, and the jati is part of a varna. There are only five Varna but several thousand jati. In theory, at least, an individual can become a member of a jati only by birth, and jatis are firmly identified with varnas. Therefore, one can be a member of a varna only through birth. In practice, however, people often dispute the assignment of jati to particular varna, arguing, for example, that though their jati has been widely believed to be vaishya, this is a misinterpretation and it is actually kshatriya. Thus, although the system is in theory static, in practice it can be dynamic.

Members of the first three varnas—the brahman, kshatriya, and vaishya—as adults are referred to as the "twice born" or *dvija*. This refers, not to reincarnation, but rather to a coming-of-age ceremony called the Upanayanam (thread ceremony). After this ceremony, individuals become full members of their varnas and are entitled to read and study the sacred literature. Upanayanam ceremonies may be held for both boys and girls, but boys' ceremonies are more common than girls' ceremonies.

Varnas embody a theory of multigenesis. Those who believe in varnas believe that different groups of human beings have different origins (for example, from the head or thighs of Purusha) and that the members of each varna have special, essential qualities, or *guna*. For example, brahmans are identified with the color white and with the qualities of purity, truthfulness, and detachment; shudras are associated with the color black and with solidity, dullness, and inertia.

If humans are of different origins and have different qualities, it is only logical that different rules apply to different groups of humans. One critical way this is expressed is through the notion of dharma, or duty. Many aspects of dharma are specified by the Code of Manu.

An individual receives their dharma as a member of a varna. A dharma is a set of rules concerning many aspects of life, particularly what occupation individuals may follow, which rituals they may participate in, whom they may eat with, and who may prepare their food. Purity and pollution are critical concerns of dharma. In general, it is held that members of upper varnas are polluted by contact with members of the lower varnas. Dharma rules are designed to prevent this contact and specify rituals of purification that must be performed when, despite the rules, contact occurs.

The idea of reincarnation provides a critical bulwark supporting dharma. We have noted that karma follows an individual through their many lives, determining their status as well as fortune and misfortune. One critical way individuals accumulate good karma is by adhering to the dharma of their varna. People who faithfully follow their varna's dharma can expect to improve their position in the varna system in their next lives. Because the end goal of reincarnation is not to become a brahman but rather to escape the cycle of samsara all together, this rule of the action of dharma is applicable to all Hindus, brahman as well as shudra or dalit.

VARIETIES OF HINDU RELIGIOUS PRACTICE

Although all Hindus tend to agree that the goal of spirituality is moksha, or liberation, they disagree on exactly what that is and on how it is best achieved. However, these disagreements are of a different nature than those among many groups within other religious traditions. Whereas many religious traditions demand obedience to a particular teaching and pronounce alternative pathways anathema, Hindus believe that there are many different ways to achieve moksha and that different ways are appropriate to different people. It is broadly accepted that there are three different ways to practice Hinduism. These are referred to as *margas,* or paths. They are karma marga, jnana marga, and bhakti marga. In addition to these, there may be others less widely recognized.

Most Hindus further believe that progress toward moksha is difficult to achieve through self-instruction. Instead, there is an emphasis on teachers or gurus. Gurus are individuals who are understood to have achieved great progress toward moksha. Some are considered to be the living embodiments of profound spiritual truth. Gurus help individuals along their spiritual journey, promoting and prescribing particular spiritual disciplines. Service, devotion, and obedience to gurus is a fundamental part of Hinduism.

Karma Marga

Karma marga is the path of duty. In the Bhagavadgita, Krishna observes that even though action leads to suffering, for humans there is really no possibility of inaction—therefore individuals' goals should be to achieve action that cleanses the mind and cultivates selfless devotion to the spiritual. Followers of karma marga attempt to achieve such action through the fulfillment of the ritual and lifestyle requirements laid out in the Code of Manu. Even though the Code of Manu includes a great many specific instructions covering all aspects of life, many of these are hard to practice in the modern world. Indeed, some might have been very hard to follow in any historic era. Despite this, many devout Hindus attempt to observe them fully.

High ethical standards as well as specific duties are enjoined upon those who follow karma marga. Of these, perhaps the most critical is strict obedience to the dietary rules and social regulations of one's varna. Another important duty is the Shraddha ceremony. This ritual is performed periodically to ensure the passage of the dead from lower to higher realms. Only men may perform the Shraddha, and this is one reason why great importance is placed on the birth of sons in Hindu families. Other karma marga obligations are sacrifices to deities, daily rituals to honor the sun, and careful maintenance of the hearth fire.

Observance of the critical rites of passage are also of particular importance. Hindus practice anywhere from 12 to 40 rites of passage, but the most frequent number is 16. These are divided into rituals done before a child is born, rituals of birth, those of childhood and education, and those of marriage and death. Some examples of these ceremonies are the *pumsavana* ritual to ensure the birth of a male child, the *annaprasana* marking the child's first solid food, the *upanayana* coming of age ceremony for members of the brahman, kahatriya, and vaishya varnas, and the *samavartana* marking the ending of student life.

Jnana Marga

Few non-Hindus have much interest in discovering and obeying the Code of Manu as demanded by karma marga. On the other hand, jnana marga (the way of knowledge) has drawn much interest in the West. The yogic practice of different body postures as well as many popular forms of meditation and beliefs about chakras are all parts of jnana marga.

In Hinduism, jnana marga is considered an intellectual pathway to moksha, suitable for only those who have the time and discipline to cultivate their mind and their senses. Its goal is to use the power of the mind, focused and magnified by study and meditation, to perceive the ultimate changeless reality behind the vicissitudes of daily life and thus fully realize the universal nature of Brahman. There is no single way to achieve this end. Instead, jnana marga includes many individual teachers (both current and historical) and well as a variety of philosophical schools and styles of study.

Traditionally, all systems of knowledge within jnana marga are classified into six *darshans,* or philosophical systems: the Nyaya, Vaisheshika, Sankhya, Yoga, Purva-Mimansa, and Vedanta systems. There are strong similarities among these systems of thought, and the goal of each is to achieve moksha. However, each makes somewhat different assumptions about the nature of reality and prescribes different sorts of learning and action to achieve moksha. For example, the Sankhya system is dualistic. Its thinkers understand existence as consisting of *prakriti* (matter) and *purusha* (self). On the other hand, the Vedanta system is strongly monistic. Its teaching, called *advaita,* holds that a single unchanging reality (Brahman) underlies all apparent variation.

Yoga is an important term in Hinduism. Its literal meaning is "yoking" or "union." It can be used to describe any sort of path an individual takes toward spiritual knowledge, but it also specifically refers to one of the six *darshans* and the practices associated with it. The yoga darshan has been extremely influential. Originally, yoga was tied to a philosophy similar to that of Sankhya darshan, holding that the goal of discipline was to achieve the release of self *(purusha)* from matter *(prakriti)*. However, yoga darshan developed a distinct series of practices, called *astanga yoga* (eight-membered yoga), to achieve this end. The practice of yoga has been taken up by members of the other darshans as well as by those following different margas and non-Hindus who believe that these practices confer both intellectual and health benefits.

In astanga yoga, the eight steps of yoga proceed from preparation to the achievement of *samadhi,* a state of total consciousness in which the individual is connected to the absolute. The first stage of yoga is called *yama* and is characterized by restraint. Individuals are focused away from the self. *Ahimsa,* the doctrine of causing no hurt to living beings that is behind the Hindu taboo against animal slaughter, is a characteristic of this first stage. The second stage is called *niyama* (observance) and is characterized by study and devotion to god. *Asana* (seat), the third stage, is the mastery of a series of postures intended to enhance meditation. The fourth stage is *pranayama* (breath control), learning different patterns of breathing to enhance meditation. *Pratyahara* (withdrawal) comes next. It involves learning to focus attention away from the senses and toward the mind. This is followed by *dharana* (holding on), where the goal is to concentrate exclusively on a single object or idea. The seventh and eighth stages of yoga are states of consciousness that Hindus believe can be achieved by the practice of the first six stages. They are *dhyana* (concentrated meditation) and *samadhi* (self-collectedness). These are spiritual states that involve the total loss of the self and the merging of the self with the single object or idea chosen in the *dharana,* the sixth stage.

There are many different styles and practices of yoga. Followers of different styles use different posture, breathing, and meditation techniques, and have different philosophical understandings. Two of the most influential styles are hatha yoga and laya yoga. Practitioners of hatha yoga focus on breathing techniques and a series of postures called *asanas,* as well as the stretches and balancing exercises necessary to achieve these. The most famous posture is the *padmasana,* or lotus position. Laya yoga involves understanding the body as incorporating a vast number of *chakras,* or psychic energy centers. The five critical chakras are located in a line extending from the base of the spinal column to the top of the skull. Followers of laya yoga believe that a kind of spiritual energy called *kundalini,* usually visualized as a coiled serpent, lies at the base of the spine. The purpose of laya yoga is to cause this energy to move upward through the chakras until, when the *kundalini* reaches the highest chakra, the practitioner experiences *samadhi.*

Bhakti Marga

The third pathway in Hinduism is called bhakti marga, the pathway of devotion. Like karma marga, bhakti marga has great appeal within India but much less outside. The key element of bhakti marga is selfless devotion to specific, individual gods. According to tradition, the number of gods and goddesses in Hinduism is set at 330 million. Of course, no comprehensive listing of these deities has ever been made. The key purpose of this very high number is to emphasize that there are a virtually limitless number of manifestations of the divine. However, Hinduism is also a good example of the general principle that the difference between monotheism (belief in one god) and polytheism (belief in many gods) is often more apparent than real. Despite the plethora of deities, most Hindus understand these as different manifestations of each other rather than as existing completely independently. Ultimately, all are dependent on Brahman, the force that both is and animates everything. Thus, in a sense, all 330 million gods are a single god.

The Trimurti.   The word *trimurti* comes from the Sanskrit for "three forms." Though this notion bears little relationship to the Christian concept of trinity, it does capture the idea that a single god may present itself in many different guises. The trimurti are the three principal gods of Hinduism: Brahma, Vishnu, and Shiva. A great many (if not all) of the other gods are either manifestations of these three or in some way related to them. For example, the extremely popular elephant-headed god, Ganesh, who is credited with the particular ability to remove obstacles, is the son of Shiva.

Brahma (not to be confused with Brahman) is generally believed to be the oldest god of the trimurti. He is the god who created the universe. Despite this, Brahma is rarely worshiped in India and there are only three temples dedicated to this god.

Vishnu, on the other hand, is probably the most popular of the three gods. He is associated with love, benevolence, the restoration of the moral order, and the preservation of humankind. A critical characteristic of Vishnu is that throughout history he periodically appears in physical form, and in different guises, to aid humankind by correcting evil or bringing good. These appearances of Vishnu are referred to as "avatars." For example, Vishnu appears first as the fish Matsya, then as the tortoise Kurma. Each time he appears, humanity is saved (or the gods themselves are saved) from a catastrophe. Ten avatars of Vishnu are recognized by most Hindus, but some groups recognize more.

By far the best known of the avatars of Vishnu are Rama, the hero of the Ramayana; Buddha, the historic personage Siddhartha Gautama, founder of Buddhism; and Krishna, the hero of the Bhagavadgita. The inclusion of Buddha is particularly interesting because it shows how Hinduism was able to expand to encompass Buddhism as a legitimate spiritual pathway. The fact that the extremely popular figures Krishna and Rama are avatars of Vishnu makes this deity perhaps the best beloved of all Hindu gods.

Hindus believe that nine of the ten avatars of Vishnu have already appeared, the most recent being Krishna. The tenth avatar is Kalki, who will appear at the end of the current age (called the Kali Yuga), exterminating evil, bringing an end to the age itself, and ushering in an age of enlightenment (called the Satya Yuga) that will be characterized by the perfect following of dharma. However, the Hindu notion of time is cyclical, and Satya Yuga is not a permanent state such as is established by the coming of God's Kingdom in Judaism, Christianity, and Islam. Instead, the Satya Yuga is inevitably followed by ages in which evil increases. The Kali Yuga is destined to return. Each complete cycle, from Satya Yuga to Kali Yuga (passing through the ages between these), takes twelve thoussnd years and there are many thousands of such cycles.

The third deity of the trimurti is Shiva, the god of destruction. Shiva is perhaps the most difficult of the gods for non-Hindus to understand. This is because Shiva calls to mind complex and contradictory images. He is at the same time the god of death, disease, and destruction as well as the god of sexuality, reproduction, and dance. Shiva's consort, Parvati, personifies the divine power of femininity, but she is also understood as Kali, a bloodthirsty female figure generally pictured dancing with a chain of human skulls around her neck.

Shiva Nataraja (Shiva, Lord of the Dance) is one of the best known and most common of Hindu sculptures. While it is found in many variations, most Shiva Nataraja sculptures have common characteristics that provide insight into

Shiva's nature. In these sculptures, Shiva is portrayed with four arms. Statues with multiple arms are common in Hindu sculpture. The arms are not meant as literal representations of the deities. Rather, each arm represents a particular characteristic of the deity. In the case of Shiva Nataraja, one of the arms holds a drum, which symbolizes the rhythm of creation and Shiva's creative power. A second arm holds the flame of destruction, a vivid reminder of Shiva's power to destroy and the fact that all creation leads ultimately to death and destruction. With a third arm, Shiva points to his raised foot, indicating that all must join him in the dance of creation and destruction (or alternatively, that all must worship at his feet). With the last of his four hands, Shiva makes a conventional gesture that means "Have no fear." Finally, one of Shiva's feet is raised in the dance, but the other rests on the back of the dwarf-demon Apasmara, who represents human ego and ignorance of the true nature of reality.

The lingam and yoni are a second conventional representation of Shiva and his consort Parvati. These sculptures represent the male and female sex organs, respectively. They are usually highly stylized. The yoni, representing the vagina, usually forms the base of the lingam, which represents the erect penis. Lingam and yoni sculptures are symbolic of the creative (and destructive) forces of the universe. They are a common object of veneration on altars in homes as well as in temples.

VENERATION OF CATTLE

The veneration of cattle plays an important part in both Hindu beliefs and anthropology. It is well known that cattle are considered sacred among Hindus. Cattle are allowed to roam freely, they are frequently decorated for holidays, and there are specific laws against slaughter of cattle in many parts of India. Many students of anthropology are also aware that in the 1960s, Marvin Harris, a well-known anthropologist, argued that the Hindu ban on cattle killing could be explained without reference to Hindu religious beliefs.[2] Briefly, Harris argued that plows pulled by cattle and cattle byproducts such as milk, dung, and urine were vital to the traditional rural Indian economy. If cows were slaughtered for food during times of hardship, people would be fed in the short term but the long-term result would be widespread famine. Under these dire circumstances, the best way to protect cattle, and hence avoid disaster, was to encourage religious beliefs that equated the killing of cattle with evil. This analysis became famous and was one prototype for ecological, economic, and functional analyses of many other social phenomena.

Regardless of the value we place on Harris's analysis, it is true that Hinduism takes a strong position on cattle. First, the ban on cattle slaughter is part of the general doctrine of *ahimsa*, causing no hurt to living beings. It is not only cattle that are protected by *ahimsa* but other animals as well. Hindu temples often contain imagery that represents divinities as snakes and monkeys, as well as cattle. Some deities, such as the elephant-headed Ganesh, combine both human and animal characteristics.

Beyond ahimsa, cattle do have a special place in Hinduism. The Rigveda identifies cows with goddesses and with the mother of the gods. Cow products—milk, curd, butter, dung, and urine—all have special roles in religious ritual. For Hindus, the most sacred place on earth, the source of the Ganges River, is referred to as *Gaumukh,* or "The Cow's Mouth." A famous hymn to cattle, found in the Atharaveda, begins:

> Worship to thee, springing to life, and worship to thee when born. Worship, O Cow, to thy tail-hair, and to thy hooves and to thy form! Hitherward we invite with prayer the Cow who pours a thousand streams. By whom the heaven, by whom the earth, by whom these waters are preserved.[3]

Gurudeva, a popular spokesman for current-day Hinduism, says:

> The cow represents life and the sustenance of life. It also represents our soul, our obstinate intellect and unruly emotions. But the cow supersedes us because it is so giving, taking nothing but grass and grain. It gives and gives and gives, as does the liberated soul give and give and give. The cow is so vital to life, the virtual sustainer of life for humans. If you lived in a village and had only cows and no other domestic animals or agricultural pursuits, you and your family could survive with the butter, the cream, yogurt, ghee and milk. The cow is a complete ecology, a gentle creature and a symbol of abundance.[4]

Despite all of this, there is no specific cow deity, and statues of cows (as opposed to bulls) are rarely found in temples.

FESTIVALS

Because Hinduism is so diverse and there are so many manifestations of God, the number of festivals celebrated is very high. In fact, there is probably no day of the year when a festival is not celebrated by some Hindu group. Most festivals involve public processions during which one or more statues of gods are taken from their temples and paraded through the streets. The statues are often accompanied by elephants, holy people and performers of various kinds. The atmosphere on such occasions is usually joyous and like a carnival. For Hindus, to witness such a spectacle is to receive the blessing of the god being celebrated.

In addition to local holidays, seven festivals are celebrated by most Hindus. These festivals are set to dates in lunar calendars. However, there are several such calendars in use in India, which accounts for the fact that different holidays are considered new year celebrations in different parts of India. One new year celebration, Divali, is held in October and celebrated with lights and gifts. It is followed by Siva Ratri, a festival to honor the god Shiva, in November or December.

Holi, one of the biggest festivals of the year, is also a new year holiday in many places. It occurs in early spring

(February/March). Holi, whether new year or not, is a celebration of spring and fertility. It is often characterized by feasting, sexual license, and riotous behavior. One way people celebrate Holi is by throwing water and colored powder on each other.

The holidays of Krishna Jayanti and Rakhi Bandham both fall in the Hindu month of Sravana, corresponding to July or August. The first of these is a celebration of Krishna's birthday. The second honors the ties between brothers and sisters. At Rakhi Bandham women tie thread around their brothers' wrists, symbolizing sisters' attachment to their brothers and brothers' protection of their sisters.

Ganesa Caturthi, held in August or September, honors Ganesh, the elephant-headed god. The key act of the festival is the immersion of images of Ganesh in bodies of water. Though this festival has been celebrated for several hundred years, it became popular in the late nineteenth century as a vehicle for protest against British colonial rule. It still retains some political importance and often includes speeches, displays, and demonstrations promoting Indian nationalism.

Dassera, the last of the seven festivals, is held for ten days in September or October and celebrates the story of the Ramayana. In many parts of India, the festival features professional and amateur groups that reenact the story. On the last day of the festival, it is common for young men and boys to dress as characters from the story and reenact the battle in which Rama defeats the evil Ravana.

HINDUISM AND THE MODERN WORLD

When Europeans began trading directly with India in the early 1500s, they brought their religion and culture. However, these had little influence until military victories brought India under British control in the eighteenth and nineteenth centuries. In the time since then, Indian, European, and American culture and history have become increasingly enmeshed. British rule, Christian missionary influence, and the experiences of many Hindus outside of India changed Hinduism, driving some practices to virtual extinction and modifying others. For example, the British outlawed Sati, the practice of a woman throwing herself (or being thrown) onto the funeral pyre of her deceased husband (see Dong Sull Choi's essay in section 9). The British also eliminated the Thugs, a confederacy of professional assassins and devotees of Kali who preyed on travelers, ritually murdering then robbing them. More far reaching changes, however, were philosophical, and in this area it is likely that Hinduism has had greater impact on Western beliefs than these latter have had on Hinduism.

The thinking of Ram Mohun Roy (1772–1833) is a good early example of the ways in which Christianity influenced Hindu thinking. Roy, a frequent employee of the British East India Company, was deeply affected by Christianity in general and Unitarianism in particular. He promoted the idea that all religions were different expressions of the same universal truth and that this truth was best understood through rigid monotheism. Roy translated the Upanishads and Vedas into Hindi, Bengali, and English and founded the Brahmo Samaj, a religious society based around Hindu writings but Protestant worship styles. The Brahmo Samaj was very influential among intellectuals but had little effect on most Indians.

Like Roy, Sri Ramakrishna (1836–86) also promoted the belief that all religions were pathways to a single absolute truth. However, unlike Roy, Ramakrishna was a priest, a devotee of Kali who was subject to frequent ecstatic religious experiences. In addition to visions of Kali and Krishna, Ramakrishna also had visions of Muhammad and Jesus. Ramakrishna's key disciple, Vivekananda (1863–1902), played a critical role in spreading his ideas. Vivekananda was originally a member of the Brahmo Samaj but left it to follow Ramakrishna. After Ramakrishna's death, Vivekananda traveled widely in Europe and America promoting Hindu spiritual knowledge. He established the Ramakrishna Mission in India as well as the Vedanta Society in New York and Ramakrishna centers throughout the world. Many European and American intellectuals frequented these centers, and today there are Ramakrishna centers in many major American and European cities.

Mohandas Gandhi (1869–1948) was one of the best known and most important religious figures of the twentieth century, not only in India but throughout the world. Ghandi was from a jati belonging to the vaishyas varna. He studied law in England, where he was deeply influenced by both his communications with the great Russian author Leo Tolstoy and European intellectuals who were particularly interested in Hinduism. He was unable to find employment when he returned to India in 1891, so he took a job in South Africa, where he remained for twenty-one years. There, he had dramatic, firsthand experiences of racism and oppression. When he came back to India in 1915, he was determined to work for Indian independence by peaceful means.

In the years between Gandhi's return to India and his death by assassination in 1948, Gandhi became firmly linked with the political tactics of nonviolence and passive resistance. His deployment of these against the British government was a critical component of the Indian independence movement. Gandhi promoted the idea of *satyagraha,* "holding fast to the truth." For him, the essence of this truth was the universal oneness of all people. He believed that harmony and nonviolence should be the result of this oneness. For Gandhi, *satyagraha* also implied that although the original occupational varnas of classic Hinduism were acceptable, the social status of the untouchables was not. Gandhi promoted the abolition of untouchable status and renamed untouchables "Harijan" (children of God). However, this name is now rejected as patronizing by many members of this group, who prefer to be called the dalits (the oppressed).

Gandhi's tactics of nonviolence, his espousal of the unity of humankind, his ascetic lifestyle, and ultimately his tragic death made him a icon of peace, tolerance, and nonviolence throughout the world. He had a profound effect on other movements of oppressed people, particularly the civil rights movement in the United States in the 1950s and 1960s. His work on behalf of oppressed peoples raised awareness of Hinduism throughout the world.

In the years since Indian Independence and Gandhi's death, Hinduism has become an increasingly powerful force both inside and outside of India. However, the meaning and importance of this influence is very different in India and in the rest of the world. While in the rest of the world the spiritual dimension of Hinduism has been predominant, in India Hinduism has been an extremely powerful political force. Gandhi himself was assassinated by militant Hindu nationalists. His crime? Promoting tolerance toward Muslims. Numerous Indian political organizations, particularly the RSS (Rastriya Svayam-Sevak Sangh) and the BJP (Bharatiya Janata Party) promote the notion of India as a Hindu religious state and resistance to Muslim, Christian, and secularist ideology. Most members of the RSS and BJP are not violent, but both of these organizations have been involved in violence against Muslims and members of other minority communities in India. In the past twenty years, the BJP has been increasingly successful in Indian national politics. Since the 1990s, coalitions led by the BJP or with prominent BJP participation have often been in the majority in governing the nation. It was during a BJP-led government in 1998 that India began testing nuclear weapons. Members of the BJP have marked these tests with celebrations, setting off firecrackers and handing out sweets.[5] Another Hindu nationalist organization, the VHP (Vishva Hindu Parishad), announced plans to commemorate the site of the nuclear tests by building a temple.

In most places outside of India, the message of Hinduism has focused on the universal and has had little to do with nationalism. Holy people such as Vivekananda and Ghandi have been followed by many others. A large number of gurus, holy people, and organizations promote Hindu worship and practice through the world. One of the best known of these is ISKCON, the International Society for Krishna Consciousness, founded by Swami Bhaktivedanta Prabhupada (1896–1977). ISKCON was founded in New York in 1968 and gained enormous publicity (mostly negative) throughout the late 1960s and 1970s when groups of devotees (called Hare Krishnas) could be seen chanting, dancing, and asking for donations in public places throughout the United States. In the past two decades, ISKCON has greatly lessened its public presence but still thrives, operating vegetarian restaurants, farms, communities, schools, and other facilities in ninety countries worldwide. The many other Hindu groups that have been particularly active in the United States and other wealthy nations include the Transcendental Meditation Movement started by Maharishi Mahesh Yogi (1911   ), and the Siddha Yoga movement founded by Swami Muktananda (1908–1982).

In addition to these popular forms of Hinduism designed to appeal to Indians and non-Indians alike, increasing emigration of people from India to the wealthy nations has created a worldwide Hindu diaspora. Hindus in the United States constitute a small percentage of the total population, but their numbers have increased rapidly in recent years. In the 1970s there were probably fewer then 100,000 Hindus in the United States. Today the U.S. Hindu population is estimated to be between 1 and 1.5 million, and there are more than 150 Hindu temples.[6] These numbers, the continued high level of Indian migration to the United States, as well as the active efforts of many temples ensure that Hindu thought will play an important role in the future.

NOTES

1. Ananthasivamy Anil, "Written in Blood," *New Scientist.* 170 n. 2291 (2001) 17.

2. Marvin Harris, "The Cultural Ecology of India's Sacred Cattle," *Current Anthropology* 7, no. 1 (1966): 51–59.

3. "In Praise of the Cow," in *The Hindu Tradition*, Ainslie T. Embree, ed. (New York: Vintage, 1966), 39–41.

4. "Nine Questions of Hinduism," downloaded from Hinduism Online, the website of The Saiva Siddhantu Church. www.himalayanacademy.com/basics/nineq.

5. "India's Ruling Party Celebrates Nuclear Tests Despite Protests," *Boston Globe,* Sept. 15, 1999.

6. Jacob Neusner, ed., *World Religions in America: An Introduction* (Louisville, Ky.: Westminster/John Knox Press, 1994), 196.

14

Buddhism

Buddhism began as a dissident movement within Hinduism in the sixth century B.C.E. This movement was based on the teachings of Siddhartha Gautama, who was later given the title *Buddha*—the "awakened" or "enlightened one." Siddhartha rejected the authority of the Vedas and the caste system. In its first few hundred years the movement gained great popularity in India. By the third century B.C.E. missionaries had spread Buddhism into neighboring Asian countries, particularly southeast Asia, China, Korea, and Japan. Today, there are more than 300 million followers of Buddhism.

THE LIFE OF SIDDHARTHA GAUTAMA (563–483 B.C.E.)

The traditional story of the life and teachings of Buddha was preserved as oral tradition for several hundred years before being written down in the first century B.C.E. A text called the *Tripitaka* (Three Baskets) is considered to be the earliest record of the Buddha's life, although it is difficult to distinguish historical fact from legend. According to the *Tripitaka*, Siddhartha was born about 2,500 years ago in what is today Nepal. The Buddha's father, Suddhodana, was a chieftain of the Sakya clan and a member of the kshatriya (warrior) caste. Legend has it that before Siddhartha was born, Maya, his mother, dreamed that a white elephant entered her womb. Hindu priests interpreted this dream to mean that she would bear a son who would become a great leader and teacher. At Siddhartha's birth a Hindu sage supposedly recognized signs on his body that indicated his future greatness. His mother died soon after his birth, and Siddhartha was raised by his mother's sister, who became his father's second wife.

After Gautama's birth, a Hindu sage predicted that he would become either a great king or, if he ever saw human suffering, a great religious teacher. Because his father did not wish Gautama to follow a religious life, he sought to shelter his son from the pain and suffering in the world. So Gautama was raised surrounded by luxury and beauty. At 19 he married his cousin and they had a son.

Despite his family, power, and wealth, Gautama was dissatisfied. As Gautama matured he became aware of the ugliness of the real world. The turning point in his life came when he was 29. According to tradition, four sights precipitated Gautama's spiritual crises. First he saw a bedraggled old man leaning on a cane as he walked past. The second sight was of a sick man, in great pain, who was incontinent and had soiled himself. The third sight was of a decaying corpse being carried to a funeral pyre. And finally, the fourth was an ascetic monk in a yellow robe who had renounced the world to find spiritual peace. These sights plunged Gautama into a profound crisis of faith and it became impossible for him to continue his life of luxury. He began what is called the "great renunciation," leaving his home and family in search of a solution to the problem of human suffering.

Initially, Gautama sought the answers to his questions in the study of Hindu philosophy and meditation. When this provided no satisfaction, he turned to extreme asceticism. Gautama joined a group of five Hindu monks who taught him techniques of self-denial. For six years Gautama practiced self-deprivation and self-torture. Legend has it that he practiced fasting until he could live on a grain of rice a day and became so thin he could touch his spine through his stomach. At one point Gautama became so weak that his companions thought he had died. Gautama also quit bathing and let filth accumulate on his body. He wore garments that irritated his body and slept on beds of thorns. However, after six years of these disciplines Gautama came to believe that self-torture would not provide the answers he sought and decided to eat and drink normally again. His five companions were repulsed by this decision and abandoned him in disgust.

During his recuperation Gautama decided to seek a middle ground between the paths he had attempted. One day, in the small North Indian town of Uruvela (now called Bodh Gaya or Mahabodhi), he sat down under a fig tree and decided not to leave until he had received enlightenment. It was here that Gautama encountered the personification of evil, the demon Mara. Mara attempted to deflect Siddhartha's search for truth by subjecting him to a series of temptations. First, Mara told Siddhartha that his cousin, an old enemy, had led a revolt at home imprisoning his father and taking his wife. Siddhartha remained impassive. Next, Mara produced several beautiful goddesses who attempted to seduce Siddhartha, but he ignored them. Finally, Mara summoned a series of demons who threatened Siddhartha and tried to terrify him. But Siddhartha sat unmoved and, placing his right hand on the ground, produced a thundering noise that confused Mara and the demons and caused them to flee.

With Mara defeated, Siddhartha spent the rest of the night meditating, achieving deeper and deeper levels of consciousness. While in this profound meditative trance, Siddhartha reviewed his past lives and this led him to understand the cycle of rebirth and the reasons for it. This insight led him to finally understand the riddle of human suffering and the path by which this suffering could be eliminated.

Thus as the new day dawned Siddhartha achieved enlightenment and became the Buddha. The tree under which Gautama received enlightenment became known as the *Bodhi* tree (tree of knowledge). The tree itself became a symbol of Buddhism and a site of pilgrimage. While the original and several subsequent trees were destroyed, many Buddhist temples have trees believed to be descendent from the original Bodhi tree. One such tree, planted in 1881, grows at the site of Gautama's enlightenment in Bodha Gaya today.

Initially, Buddha was unsure about what to do with his newfound knowledge, and he meditated for several weeks on the knowledge he had attained and whether he should communicate these cosmic truths, this dharma, to others. Although Buddha realized that humans differed in their capacity to understand the dharma, he decided that it was his responsibility to communicate his discovery. Buddha first sought out the five Hindu companions who had previously abandoned him. He found them in the holy city of Varanasi (colonial Benares) at a place called Deer Park and preached his first discourse to them in which he outlined his Four Noble Truths. Today this first sermon is known as the "Setting in Motion of the Wheel of Truth," and the wheel has become the symbol of Buddhism. The five ascetics initially resisted Buddha's message, but his sincerity eventually won them over and these five formed the core of Buddha's disciples and founded the first *sangha,* or monastic order.

Buddha was about 35 when he achieved enlightenment, and he spent the rest of his life teaching his growing band of followers. Unlike orthodox Hindus who made caste distinctions based on spiritual purity, Buddha preached that all people could find the same enlightenment he had experienced, and once one joined the sangha, caste distinctions ceased to matter. Buddha's message was so compelling that he soon had sixty *arhats* (saints)—disciples who had attained enlightenment. Buddha enjoined them to travel over the world to spread his message while he remained in India. Ultimately, monasteries were built for Buddha and members of his sangha in virtually every major Indian city.

Initially Buddha's movement was dominated by men, but his cousin and close companion Ananda argued the case for allowing women into Buddha's following. Buddha hesitated at first, but then relented and allowed women to form an order of nuns. According to tradition, Buddha's stepmother and wife were the first women to join this order.

The role of women in Buddhism has been a source of tension throughout Buddhist history. Although Buddha approved of a monastic order for women, women have been associated with lust and seduction and portrayed as a threat to the spiritual welfare of men. On the other hand, married women have been portrayed as the foundation of the family in their role as mothers. This tension remains today. Because women are idealized as the foundation of the household, they are seen as unable to pursue the fundamental Buddhist goal of detachment. However, when women have left their homes to join monastic orders they have been accused of causing the disintegration of the family. Nonetheless women have joined convents since the time of Buddha.

Buddhist nuns usually live in their own convents or have their own cloistered quarters when they share a monastic community with men. Like men they shave their heads, and they wear the same robes as their male associates. Buddhist nuns in particular are respected for the services they provide to the less fortunate.

Buddha's mission lasted for forty-five years. He reportedly died at the age of 80 after eating spoiled pork. The picture of him that can be gleaned from the accounts of his life is of a man of great compassion. Buddha sought to discover the causes of human suffering and spent the greater portion of his life teaching a path by which people could free themselves from suffering.

BUDDHA'S TEACHINGS

Buddha was raised in the Hindu religion and taught his followers in those terms. Like Hinduism, Buddhism teaches that individuals (or their qualities) are reincarnated a great many times on their path to enlightenment and liberation. Both Hindus and Buddhists believe in the illusory nature of the physical world and both believe there is no single path to enlightenment. However Buddha made several very significant breaks with Hinduism. He rejected the authority of the Code of Manu, the caste system, and the centrality of Brahman priests. For Buddhists, karma is not earned by following the dharma of one's caste, but through following Buddha's teachings. Whereas Hindus believe there are three paths by which one can free oneself from the reincarnation cycle (karma marga, jnana marga, and bhakti marga; see pages 420–422, Buddha taught that only jnana marga, contemplation, and meditation was effective but there were many paths within jnana marga. Buddha also maintained that the individual soul (the Hindu atman) did not exist. He taught that what is called a soul is a combination of five elements: body, feelings, perceptions, will, and consciousness. It is this combination of traits, which forms the personality, that is caught up in a cycle of deaths and rebirths. For Buddha, liberation from this cycle did not mean the uniting of atman with Brahman as in Hinduism. He preached that the path to enlightenment was opened by the extinction of *tanha,* the craving for physical or material pleasure through the cultivation of a detached, contemplative state of mind.

Buddha replaced the Hindu notions of caste, and spiritual purity with the dharma (cosmic truth), which he summarized in his Four Noble Truths. These principles form the foundation of Buddhist philosophy. The First Truth is that nothing is permanent. All things are in process of never-ending change. This impermanence, or *anicca,* leads humans to a state of *dukkha,* which can be translated as dissatisfaction, suffering, anxiety, frustration, or misery.

The Second Truth is that humans live in this unsatisfactory state of mind because of *tanha,* the desire for material possessions and intellectual and emotional gratification. According to Buddha, people delude themselves into thinking that peace of mind or fulfillment can come from possessions or relationships. They do not realize that because nothing is permanent the things they think will make their lives complete are actually temporary and thus the cause of more suffering.

The Third Truth follows from the second: tranquility can come only by banishing *tanha*. Inner peace can be achieved only by eliminating the craving to achieve satisfaction through external means, such as the accumulation of material things.

The Fourth Truth is that self-fulfillment can be found only by following the Middle Way. He argued that those searching for truth should avoid the extremes of self-gratification and self-mortification. Buddha had tried both paths and found no peace. He insisted that these two paths are degrading and vulgar and lead nowhere. Instead, he urged his followers to pursue the Middle Way by living within the day-to-day practices he called the Noble Eightfold Path. These are:

- *Right understanding.* Believing the Four Noble Truths.
- *Right intention.* Once one accepts the Four Noble Truths, one must renounce worldly life and follow the Eightfold Path.
- *Right speech.* One must act with compassion and consideration for others and not lie or be verbally abusive.
- *Right conduct.* One must respect others and refrain from stealing, hurting other people, committing adultery, and using intoxicating substances.
- *Right occupation.* One must not engage in jobs or other activities that violate elements of the Eightfold Path.
- *Right endeavor.* One must attempt to do good and stay away from evil.
- *Right contemplation.* One must learn to control one's mind so that emotions are not allowed to disturb one's inner calm.
- *Right concentration.* If one follows the other principles, one can reach a state of mental control and concentration that is beyond reason. Ultimately, this leads to enlightenment and nirvana.

Nirvana means literally "to extinguish a flame," like blowing out a candle. Buddha taught that those who follow the Eightfold Path will ultimately achieve a state of nirvana, where they finally shed *tanha,* the desires that tie them to life and the craving for existence. *Tanha,* remember, is the source of human suffering, or *dukkha.* Once *tanha* is eliminated, a person is freed from the cycle of birth, life, death, and rebirth. Thus the goal of Buddhist practice is not the salvation of a soul or going to heaven, but rather release from

the cycle of life and the suffering that goes with it. But nirvana is not a state of annihilation. It is the end of all transitory states, a final, peaceful bliss that ends *annica,* the individual's constant cycle of change. As Buddha described it:

> There is, monks, that plane where there is neither extension nor . . . motion nor the plane of infinite ether . . . nor that of neither-perception-nor-non-perception, neither this world nor another, neither the moon nor the sun. Here, monks, I say that there is no coming or going or remaining or deceasing or uprising, for this is itself without support, without continuance, without mental object—this is itself the end of suffering.[1]

THE DEVELOPMENT AND SPREAD OF BUDDHISM

At the time of Buddha's death, his followers were found principally in India and Nepal. The sect remained small until about two hundred years later, when it became predominant in India and spread into Southeast Asia under the patronage of one of the great emperors of India, Asoka (d. 238 B.C.E.). Asoka, who ruled from 268 to 238 B.C.E., converted to Buddhism in 297 B.C.E. and put the power and influence of his throne into spreading his new faith throughout his empire. Asoka sent Buddhist missionaries westward, possibly as far as Syria and Greece, south to Sri Lanka, and eastward to Burma. From Burma, Buddhism continued to spread into Laos, Thailand, and Cambodia in succeeding centuries. By the first century C.E., Buddhism had reached China. It is fortunate for Buddhists that Asoka's zeal led to the spread of Buddhism throughout Southeast Asia, because a few hundred years later a resurgent Hinduism, and then Islamic conquest of India in the eighth century C.E., virtually eliminated the religion in India.

Buddhism spread throughout China in the early fifth century C.E. when Chinese leaders adopted the religion and Buddhist monks began to translate scriptures into Chinese. Buddhism survived several periods of persecution at the hands of different emperors during the fourth and fifth centuries, then experienced a flourescence in the sixth century during the reign of the Emperor Wen. Wen considered himself a disciple of Buddha, and during his reign envoys carried the religion to Korea and Japan. Buddhism became the state religion of Japan during the eighth century and, together with Shinto, remains popular in Japan today.

Buddhism spread to Tibet in the 600s but did not become widespread there until a century later. The history of Tibetan Buddhism is one of intense political rivalries between competing factions. This struggle for dominance was resolved in the seventeenth century by a Mongol chieftain who awarded Tibet to the Dalai Lama, who became the country's spiritual and political leader. Many Americans today are aware of Tibetan Buddhism because of media attention to the Dalai Lama. Additionally, numerous American celebrities have spoken out supporting Tibet's political resistance to occupation by China since 1959.

DIVISIONS OF BUDDHISM

Buddhist tradition maintains that a council was convened immediately after Buddha's death in 483 B.C.E. At this council his followers attempted to set down an authoritative version of his teachings and establish a set of rules to govern the monastic orders. But this council failed to bring unity to the movement. A second council called in 390 B.C.E. resulted in a schism over Buddhist doctrine that led to the two main divisions in Buddhism today. The smaller and more orthodox group formed in this split was the *Hinayana.* Today the dominant faction of this branch is the Theravada (tradition of the elders) school of Buddhism. The larger and more liberal faction was the Mahasanghika (Great Sangha) or Mahayana Buddhists. Further councils were held in the third and first centuries B.C.E. during which the Tripitaka, or Buddhist canon, was completed. The Tripitaka consists of three collections of material: the Vinayana Pitaka, the rules of the Buddhist monastic orders; the Sutta Pitaka, dialogues between Buddha and his disciples; and the Abhidhamma Pitaka, metaphysical teachings.

Theravada Buddhism is the more conservative of the two main groups. Because of the devotion and discipline required to emulate the life of Buddha and the discipline necessary to achieve nirvana, monks, with their shaven heads, yellow robes, and begging bowls, are the central figures in Theravada Buddhism. Monks rise at daybreak, wash, light a candle before an image of Buddha, and pray. After morning prayers they leave the monastery, begging bowl in hand, accepting whatever food offerings are provided by devout laypeople. They then return to the sangha for breakfast and then join their brothers for prayer and silent meditation. The last meal of the day is at midday, and the afternoon is spent studying scripture and meditating. There is one final assembly at sunset, then the monks' day ends.

To achieve a state of nirvana, everyone must sooner or later renounce their worldly lives and join a sangha. The alternative is to be caught up in the eternal cycle of rebirth. However, devout Theravada Buddhists who cannot join a monastery can still earn spiritual merit by supporting their local monasteries and providing food for the monks who have devoted their lives to the monastic disciplines. Laypeople hope that in another life they will be able to join a monastery and pursue their own spiritual advancement, but most people do not make a permanent commitment to the monastic life. It is common for monks to leave the sangha and return to it at different points in their lives. In fact, many young men become monks as a rite of passage from youth to adulthood, leave the monastery after a few years of study, and do not return until the end of their lives.

The physical embodiment of Theravada Buddhism is the *wat,* or monastic compound, which contains a hall for prayer, meditation, and instruction. Other buildings within the wat are the monks' quarters, and towers known as *stupas,* or pagodas. Some stupas house sacred relics of Buddha, but in general they are places of meditation and worship for both monks and lay Buddhists.

All Buddhists revere Buddha as a great teacher. However, when Theravada Buddhists speak of Buddha they are referring strictly to the man, who by practicing detachment pioneered the quest for nirvana. Theravada Buddhists believe that anyone can follow the path Buddha set out and attain the same spiritual liberation through their own efforts.

Mahayana Buddhism is the more liberal of the two sects. One of the obvious differences between Mahayana and Theravada Buddhists is that the former do not regard entering monastic life as a necessary precondition for achieving nirvana. Anyone can achieve enlightenment, in the Mahayana view. Less obvious but equally important is the different view of Buddha that is held by Mahayana Buddhists. Mahayana Buddhists believe that Siddhartha was the physical incarnation of an eternal "Buddha essence" that exists for the spiritual liberation of human beings. Thus, some Mahayana sects have deified Siddhartha, contrary to Theravada practice. Similarly, many Mahayana Buddhists revere *bodhisattvas,* "future Buddhas." Mahayana Buddhists reason that if Siddhartha was a physical incarnation of an eternal force or presence, then there must be other such incarnations too. Bodhisattvas are individuals who reach nirvana, are reborn beyond this world, but retain an interest in helping those who remain. They exist in another dimension but can appear to people who need their help. They are spirit teacher-saviors who act as guides for people who pray to them and request their help in reaching nirvana.

The variety of Mahayana Buddhist sects is so great that we will attempt to describe only a few of the largest movements. One of the most popular branches of Mahayana Buddhism is the Pure Land sect, which has a large following in China and Japan. The Pure Land school originated in China in the fifth century. The emphasis of this sect is salvation through faith in the bodhisattva Amitabha. According to tradition, Amitabha was a Chinese king who became a monk and at death became a bodhisattva. Because of his compassion and the strength of his spiritual merit, he was able to create a place called Sukhavati (western paradise), the Pure Land. According to members of the Pure Land sect, those who worship Amitabha, lead a virtuous life, and recite Amitabha's name will be reborn in his Pure Land where they can continue working toward nirvana without the distractions of human life on earth.

Whereas some groups emphasize the monastic life and discipline, others the devotion to bodhisattvas, there have always been Buddhist groups that argue that spiritual truths are achieved through meditation and flashes of insight. These groups cite Buddha's experience under the Bodhi tree in support of this view. The most important of these Buddhist sects is Ch'an (Zen) Buddhism. Practitioners of Zen believe that it is only through meditation and strict physical and mental discipline that one's Buddha essence will be revealed.

Ch'an Buddhism traces its beginnings to an Indian monk named Bodhidharma, who is said to have come to China in about 470 to begin his meditation school. One of the basic principles in Zen Buddhism is the notion of inner enlightenment that is achieved through meditation. One popular saying in the movement is "If you meet the Buddha, kill him." This saying reinforces the belief that enlightenment is an inner process that people have to achieve on their own from their own experience; it cannot be given by someone else. Prayers, temples, scripture, and good works, though popular, are all irrelevant to this goal. One good illustration of this attitude about religious paraphernalia is a cartoon that shows a monk warming himself on a cold morning. He has chopped up a statue of Buddha for firewood and is raising his robe to warm his buttocks.[2]

The basic Zen technique for reaching enlightenment is sitting meditation called zazen. In Zen monasteries, zazen is normally practiced for several hours every day, morning and evening. One simply sits in silence, back straight, body still, quieting the mind and focusing on the moment. With practice, one can enter a state of awareness in which one's inner nature is revealed.

Logic and reason are distrusted in Zen because they hinder one from grasping the inner truths that are beyond human logic. Thus teachers of Zen often use techniques to help their pupils surpass the limits of logic. One of the most common of these techniques is the use of riddles or statements called *koans*. The koan is a question that cannot be answered using logic. Students of Zen first meditate and when their minds are clear the teacher gives them a koan. It is hoped that while the student meditates upon the question a flash of enlightenment will lead the student to the truth that is beyond their reason. A well-known koan is "What is the sound of one hand clapping?" Another is "Why did the monk Bodhidharma come from the West?" An appropriate response might be "the bush in the garden" or to take off one's shoe. Obviously these are not logical answers to the questions. The point of the exercise is to push beyond the barriers of logic to realize the Buddha essence, or nature within. Zen masters may even kick or slap their students to try to break their hold on reason.

Manual labor is also important in Zen training. Silent work in the monastery kitchen and garden or cleaning are techniques to promote silent meditation coupled with the direct experience of the physical world. In Zen philosophy, words are barriers that keep us from knowing the true nature of things.

The final branch of Mahayana Buddhism to be discussed in this section is Tantric Buddhism, which is practiced in Tibet, Nepal, Bhutan, and Mongolia. This form of Buddhism is called Tantric Buddhism because of its use of *tantras,* or manuals that contain magical words and spells that are believed to aid the quest for positive rebirth and enlightenment. When Buddhism was introduced into Tibet by Indian missionaries in the seventh century, it mixed with the local shamanic beliefs of the time. Thus Tantric Buddhism is an esoteric mix of magical beliefs, ritual symbolism, and practice. In particular, it differs from other forms of Buddhism in that it challenges the original doctrine of detachment from the world and physical pleasure. In early practice the tantras taught that the body could be be used to reach enlightenment, and Buddhist Tantrists used sex, the most potent of the passions, as a means to liberation. For the Tantric practioner, enlightenment is the experience of oneness when a person unites all opposites. Sex is a powerful experience of the union of opposites, and Tantric Buddhism uses sexual imagery and, in an earlier time, sexual practices to work toward enlightenment. Those who practice Tantric Buddhism believe that, rather than trying to eliminate passion, one should stimulate sexual energy, learn to control it, and direct it toward enlightenment.

Inflaming the passions to work toward enlightenment is a dangerous path to tread. Much of the Tantric literature was written in a code called "twilight language," which a layperson could not read. Students of this technique had to study under the close supervision of a Tantric master called a *lama,* the Tibetan translation of the Hindu word *guru.* By the early twelfth century, some of the more controversial practices, especially those sexual practices that violated conventional Buddhist morality, were restricted to marriage or in other ways legitimized. But the sexual imagery in Tantric Buddhism still remains vivid, and it is common to see images of Buddhas and bodhisattvas depicted in sexual embraces.

A common belief in Tantric Buddhism is that certain lamas are reincarnations of earlier lamas who are the manifestations of bodhisattvas. The Dalai Lama, for example, is considered to be an incarnation of Avalokiteshvara, the heavenly bodhisattva of compassion. When an important lama dies, his reincarnation is sought out and trained. The thirteenth Dalai Lama died in 1933. In 1936, following numerous signs, three delegations of monks disguised as traders left Lhasa to search for the next Dalai Lama. They identified a 2-year-old boy, Tentzin Gyatso (born Lhamo Dhondrub) in the village of Taktser in Eastern Tibet who seemed to fill the omens. After passing numerous tests, the child was brought to Lhasa and affirmed as the fourteenth Dalai Lama.[3]

Practitioners of Tantric Buddhism must master numerous yoga stages and ritual practices before they can achieve enlightenment. Wisdom and the help of bodhisattvas are acquired through the long repetition of three classes of ritual behavior. These are *mudra, mantra,* and *mandala.* Mudras are symbolic hand gestures. For example, statues of Buddha often show him sitting cross-legged with his right hand pointing up, palm facing out, in the mudra of blessing. It is common for adherents to chant while making a series of mudras.

Mantras are sound formulas that can be chanted or written to convey spiritual power and wisdom from the bodhisattvas. One of the most common mantras in Tantric Buddhism is *Om mani padme hum,* which means "Om—the jewel—oh lotus—ah!" The jewel in this phrase is the divine Buddha nature and the lotus is the everyday world. Thus the mantra helps teach the practitioner that the enlightened person understands that the everyday world is the same as Buddha nature. There is also sexual imagery in the chant in that it also refers to the sexual union of male and female powers. Drums, trumpets, and cymbals often accompany these deep, slow, chants and can add to their hypnotic effect.

Mandalas are geometrical designs that are diagrams of the sacred cosmos, and they are often used as aids in meditation. A common form is a design that contains squares nested in circles, and they often depict arrangements of Buddhas and bodhisattvas.

In their training, Tibetan monks go through thousands of repetitions of these ritual exercises. By performing these rituals a person is gradually able to identify with a particular bodhisattva who will help them reach the goal of enlightenment.

Another feature of Tibetan Buddhism is the prayer wheel, a cylinder mounted on a pole. Inside the cylinder are pieces of paper on which are written prayers. Tibetans believe that spinning the cylinder is similar to reciting the prayers. Some people carry small prayer wheels that they spin as they go about their daily business. Prayer wheels at temples are often much larger and are pushed or pulled by the devout who visit to pray. Buddhist prayer flags follow the same principle. The flags are inscribed with prayers that are offered as the wind blows through them.

The Tibetan form of Buddhism also uses certain ritual objects, such as trumpets made from human thighbones or bowls made from decorated human skulls, to help believers accept and get over their fear of death. Paintings or figures of terrifying demons have a similar purpose.

RELICS, PILGRIMAGES, AND HOLY DAYS

Since Buddha's death, relics of his body such as teeth, pieces of bone, and hair have been enshrined in stupas or pagodas throughout the East. Every temple has a stupa. When worshipers enter a temple, they circle the stupa three times and then pray in front of it. This practice is believed to bring spiritual merit. Laypersons as well as monks travel to these shrines to meditate and make offerings of food or flowers. Even if you cannot devote yourself to the monastic life, your temple offerings, contributions to building a stupa, support of monks, and other devotional acts can bring you spiritual merit that may lead to a better rebirth.

Pilgrimages to holy places associated with Buddha's life can also bring a believer spiritual merit. In particular, Buddha's birthplace, the Bodhi tree where he received enlightenment, Deer Park where he first preached, and the place where he died are destinations for millions of Buddhist pilgrims each year.

Because there are many types of Buddhism, there are also a variety of holy days, and Theravada Buddhists often celebrate festivals on different days than Mahayana Buddhists. Some festivals are recognized by most Buddhists. New Year is celebrated in April and lasts three days. This carnival-like holiday is a time of cleaning and reorganizing for the new year, and also a time to visit a local temple and rededicate oneself to a Buddhist life. Buddha's birthday is celebrated on April 8 in China and Japan and on the last full moon of May in Southeast Asia. Flower festivals are held in Buddhist temples on Buddha's birthday, and there also may be processions of Buddha images through the streets. On this day Theravada Buddhists not only celebrate his birthday but also commemorate his enlightenment and entry into nirvana. Mahayana Buddhists celebrate Buddha's enlightenment on Bodhi Day, December 8, and his death and entry into nirvana on February 15.

The Bon Festival, or festival of Souls, in July or August is a time when Buddhists celebrate the memory of lost loved ones and believe the spirits of the dead come to visit their homes. Families provide gifts of food for the spirits during this time, and during the middle of the month priests perform rituals designed to comfort the dead. Theravada Buddhists celebrate the Dharma-chakka festival on the first full moon in July to commemorate Buddha's first sermon to the five Hindu companions in Deer Park. Finally, Theravada Buddhists celebrate the Dharma-vijaya, or Robe Offering ceremony, which celebrates Asoka's commission of the first Buddhist missionaries. Laypeople present new yellow robes to local monks, and there is a public feast and display of the new robes. The festival ends with the presentation of a "great robe," one that has been made in a single night. This commemorates the actions of Buddha's mother, who upon hearing that he was renouncing his worldly life is supposed to have woven his first robe in one night.

CONTEMPORARY BUDDHISM

Buddhism remains an active and vital force in the world. Historically, Buddhism has been principally located in Asian countries. However, while most Buddhists still live in Asia, the religion suffered severe setbacks there after World War II. Buddhism, among other religions, was suppressed in China after the Communist takeover in 1948 and Tibetan Buddhism was severely repressed after the Chinese takeover of that country in 1950. While Chinese government restrictions on religion have eased in the past twenty years, conditions remain difficult for Buddhists in China and Tibet. Successful missionary efforts by Christians has diminished the numbers of Buddhists in some places. For example, in South Korea, a traditionally Buddhist country, about one quarter of the population is now Christian. Despite this, Buddhism remains strong throughout Asia and, in the past fifty years, Buddhist missionary outreach has steadily increased. Buddhist shrines and temples are found all over the world, and the world population of Buddhists is growing.

Buddhism came to the United States with Asian immigrants in the nineteenth century. However, American interest in Buddhism greatly increased after World War II. Then, scholars such as D. T. Suzuki and poets and writers such as Jack Kerouac, Allen Watts, Allen Ginsberg, and Gary Snyder were inspired by Buddhist ideas and brought them to a mainstream audience. Buddhist influence in the United States increased again as large numbers of refugees from Vietnam, Cambodia, and Laos fled to the United States after the war in Vietnam. In recent years still more Buddhists have been drawn by opportunities in technology and education. Today, most American urban centers support large communities of Buddhists, whose message of nonviolence, compassion, and social responsibility has attracted American converts. The Buddhist magazine *Tricycle* has a directory that lists Buddhist centers across North America.

Tibetan Buddhism has also established communities of believers in many places in the United States. Exhibits of Tibetan Buddhist art are regularly displayed, and several recent popular movies have dealt with aspects of Tibetan life and religion. Thus many young Americans are familiar with some aspects of Buddhism.

NOTES

1. *Buddhist Texts Through the Ages,* ed. Edward Conze (New York: Philosophical Library, 1954), 94–95.

2. Lewis M. Hople and Mark R. Woodward, *Religions of the World,* 2nd ed. (New York: Prentice Hall, 1998), 151.

3. Claude B. Levenson, *The Dalai Lama: A Biography* (New Delhi, Oxford University Press, 1999), 47–57.

15

Judaism

Judaism is a complex mix of religious practices, ethnic identity, and history. Today there are roughly 20 million followers of Judaism. However, being a Jew is more than practicing a set of religious rituals. Many Jews do not actively practice their religion but have a Jewish ethnic identity. Jewish ethnicity is not a uniform complex of traits. Travel to Israel today and you will find an incredible mix of people with diverse cultural, linguistic, and religious backgrounds. In a religious sense, what makes people Jewish is that they believe they have made a living covenant with their creator, they acknowledge this one God, and they follow God's laws as revealed in the *Torah*. Though religious practices may differ, the center of Jewish belief is that there is one God, that God works through historical events, and that God made a historical covenant with the Jews, making them God's chosen people (though the meaning of this often heard phrase is controversial).

The largest number of Jews, 6 million, reside in the United States. There are another 4 million Jews in Israel and about 1.5 million in Russia. Although many religions have larger followings, Judaism was critically influential in the foundation of Christianity and Islam. Thus Judaism directly or indirectly has an influence on the majority of people who are practitioners of the principal world religions, and to understand those religions a background in Judaism is essential.

SACRED LITERATURE

Judaism is inextricably linked with its sacred literature. The Hebrew Bible, or *Tanakh* (called the Old Testament by Christians), traces Jewish history back about four thousand years. Although published as a single volume, the Tanakh is made up of individual sections. These are the *Torah* (Teachings), *Nevi'im* (Prophets), and *Kethuvim* (Writings). This complete collection of writings is called Tanakh because *TANAKH* is an acronym derived from the first syllable of each section.

The five books of the Torah (Genesis, Exodus, Leviticus, Numbers, and Deuteronomy) form the core of the Hebrew Bible and are also called the *Pentateuch,* or "five scrolls." The Torah is the most significant body of Jewish literature. It describes the relationship between God and the cosmos and humans. The Torah outlines the laws of conduct that help define a Jewish lifestyle and provides the rules upon which Jewish ritual activity is based. According to the Torah, God is the creator of the heavens and earth. God is just and merciful, but he is also jealous and punishes those who violate his commandments. A Jew is free to choose

what actions he or she takes, but God holds a person accountable for their choices. The purpose of a Jew's life is to serve God through piety, reverence for life, and service to others. Jews believe they are God's chosen people only because they accepted the conditions set forth for them in the Torah, not because of some arbitrary favoritism on God's part.

The Torah also includes some of the best-known stories in the Western world, including the stories of creation, Adam and Eve, Noah, and the Tower of Babel. It recounts the history of the Jews, starting with the patriarch of the Israelites, Abraham, his son Isaac, and grandson Jacob. The life of Moses the lawgiver and his brother Aaron, who started the priesthood, are described in the Torah, as is the history of the Israelites from their flight from Egypt under the leadership of Moses to their arrival in the land of the Canaanites. Legend attributes authorship of the Torah to Moses, although scholars today believe it was written by several authors over a period of hundreds of years.

Prophets is the second part of the Tanakh and is named for those who spoke to the Jewish people in God's name. The books of the prophets are Joshua, Judges, Samuel (I), Samuel (II), Kings (I), Kings (II), Isaiah, Jeremiah, Ezekiel, and the twelve minor prophets Hosea, Joel, Amos, Obadiah, Jonah, Micah, Nahum, Habakkuk, Zephaniah, Haggai, Zechariah, and Malachi. Prophets gives us an account of the history of the Israelite kingdom from the settlement of Canaan to its fall in the sixth century B.C.E. Prophets also expands on the importance of Jewish moral conduct and obedience to God through the visionary preaching of individual prophets. For example, Amos 5:21–24:

> I hate, I despise your feasts, and I take no delight in your solemn assemblies. . . . Take away from me the noise of your songs; to the melody of your harps I will not listen. But let justice roll down like waters, and righteousness like an ever-flowing stream.

The last part of the Tanakh—the Kethuvim (Writings)—contains proverbs, psalms, poetry, and short stories. The sections of the Kethuvim are Psalms, Proverbs, Job, Ruth, Lamentations, Ecclesiastes, Song of Solomon, Ezra, Nehemiah, Esther, Chronicles I, and Chronicles II. If you are unfamiliar with this section of the Bible and sit down to read it, you will be surprised at how many elements of popular songs, poetry, and sayings in Western literature are derived from the Kethuvim. The Psalms provide many of the basic prayers and hymns used in Jewish and Christian worship. The book of Proverbs is a collection of maxims, humor, and sayings, many of which sound just as true today as when they were written. For example, "Wisdom builds her own house, but folly with her own hands tears it down (14:1)." Or Proverbs 11:24: "One man gives freely, yet grows all the richer; another withholds what he should give, and only suffers want." Finally, there is the love poetry in Song of Solomon.

One striking feature of the Writings is that the authors of the various works address problems facing humanity in general, not just those faced by Jews. The story of Job, for example, confronts the paradox of why good people may suffer while the wicked prosper. In the Book of Ecclesiastes the author deals with the meaning, or meaninglessness, of life. No matter what a person does in life, rich or poor, wise or fool, wicked or good, death is the common fate of all:

> What profit hath a man of all his labor which he taketh under the sun? One generation passeth away, and another generation commeth: but the earth abideth for ever. (Ecclesiastes 1:3–4) There is no remembrance of the wise more than of the fool for ever; seething that which now is in the days to come shall all be forgotten. And how dieth the wise man? As the fool. (Ecclesiastes 2:16)

It is also in Ecclesiastes, chapter 3, that one finds the famous line "For everything there is a season and a time for every matter under heaven."

The stories, laws, and events described in the Tanakh were orally transmitted from generation to generation for centuries. Some of these traditions may have been put into writing as early as 1000 B.C.E., but the oldest Jewish manuscripts that have so far been discovered are the Dead Sea Scrolls, which date back to the second century B.C.E.

The historical accuracy of the Tanakh is uncertain. Although many places and people discussed in it were real, few biblical accounts can be substantiated through archaeology or historical records. For example, other than the Torah, there is no evidence that Abraham and Moses were real individuals. There is no physical or documentary evidence for events such as Moses' parting of the Red Sea, or Joshua felling the walls of Jericho with a ram's horn trumpet and a shout from his men. Other stories such as the Flood, Garden of Eden, and Tower of Babel are derived from earlier Mesopotamian legends. However, whatever its historical accuracy, there is no questioning the power and spiritual significance of the Tanakh. Try to imagine Christianity without the Old Testament. For example, the Gospel of Matthew begins with a recitation of Jesus' ancestry, tracing his forebearers back to critical Jewish figures including Abraham, David, and Solomon. Christians view Jesus as fulfilling prophesies from Isaiah and other writings in the Tanakh. Compilers of the earliest books of the New Testament, who were Jews, frequently brought stories of Jesus' life into line with such prophecies. Specific events in the story of Jesus relate to aspects of Jewish ritual and practice of two thousand years ago. Jesus enters Jerusalem for a Jewish religious festival, disputes with members of different Jewish factions, and most scholars believe that the Last Supper was a Seder, an essential part of the celebration of Passover.

In addition to its religious importance, Tanakh has had enormous political importance. Crusaders of the Middle Ages, Reformers, revolutionaries, and conservatives of the European enlightenment, Civil War abolitionists, members of modern day liberation struggles, and many others have looked to its words. And it is critical to understanding modern political struggles in the Middle East.

HISTORICAL BACKGROUND

Jewish history goes back four thousand years but can be divided into two periods. The dividing line between these epochs is the destruction of Jerusalem, the razing of the second Temple, and subsequent dispersion of Jews throughout the Roman Empire between 70 and 132 C.E. Before this time, Judaism had been primarily a temple-based religion in which the central role was played by members of a priestly caste and critical rituals involved animal sacrifice at the Temple in Jerusalem. After the destruction of the Temple and the dispersal of the population, Jews had to develop new ways to ensure the survival of their beliefs. Their response was the elaboration of Rabbinical Judaism, a form of worship that had come into existence during the Babylonian captivity almost six hundred years prior. Rabbinic Judaism could be practiced in the home or synagogue anywhere in the world. Most Jewish beliefs and rituals practiced today developed from this form of Judaism.

According to the Torah, Jewish history begins about 2000 B.C.E. when the ancestors of modern Jews were members of nomadic tribes living in the Middle East under the leadership of the patriarch Abraham, his son Isaac, his grandson Jacob, and Jacob's twelve sons. Some scholars have argued that Abraham was not a real individual and that Isaac and the rest were tribal chiefs, not direct descendants of a tribal patriarch. But whatever the historical truth, it is written in the Torah that God made a pact with Abraham promising him and his descendants a permanent home in the land of the Canaanites, (territory that now comprises Israel, the West Bank, Gaza, Jordan, and the southern portions of Syria and Lebanon). In return, Abraham and his male descendants must be circumcised as a sign of their covenant with God. Famine forced Jacob and his family to emigrate to Egypt, where the Jews lived peacefully for centuries. They were ultimately enslaved by the Egyptians about the year 1300 B.C.E., but were liberated from slavery by a leader named Moses.

According to tradition, Moses was a Jew who was raised by an Egyptian royal family and fled Egypt after killing an Egyptian who mistreated an Israelite slave. One day while tending his father-in-law's herds, Moses saw a bush burning but not being consumed in the flames. When he approached the bush, the voice of God commanded him to return to

Egypt and lead his people out of slavery. When the pharaoh rejected Moses' request to let the Jews leave Egypt, the Egyptians were struck by ten successive plagues, the last being the death of all firstborn sons. Only Jewish families were spared, because they had marked their doors with the sacrificial blood of a lamb. Because the Angel of Death passed over the Jewish children, this event is commemorated as the night of Passover in the festival of *Pesach.* Moses then led his people out of Egypt to the Sinai Peninsula.

The Books of Exodus and Numbers recount in detail the story of the forty-year migration to the promised land. The most significant event during this period was the journey to Mount Horeb, also called Mount Sinai, which Moses ascended to speak with God. After several days Moses descended the mountain carrying stone tablets inscribed with the commandments of God. These are the familiar Ten Commandments described in Exodus 20. (Jews traditionally believe that God outlined 613 commandments in the Torah, not just Moses' ten.) The Book of Exodus also describes how Jews constructed a portable shrine, or tabernacle, within which was a chest containing the stone tablets. During their journey, Moses was able to communicate with God in this shrine.

One notable feature of the journey described in Exodus is Moses' attempts to get his followers to have unquestioning faith in God. On numerous occasions, the Israelites worship other Gods or disbelieve God's directions. Critically, when the Israelites reach the border of Canaan, they doubt their ability to conquer it and refuse to enter the land despite God's assurance that they will be successful. They are punished for their disobedience: God decrees that none of the generation then living will enter Canaan. Instead, they are condemned to wander the desert for forty years. It is only under Moses' successor Joshua that the Jews enter the promised land of Canaan.

When the Jews crossed the Jordan River, they encountered a people called the Philistines, who also desired to occupy the land of the Canaanites. Jews, Philistines, and Canaanites fought for more than two hundred years until the Jewish tribes under the leadership of King David captured Jerusalem and occupied parts of Palestine in the eleventh century B.C.E. David's son Solomon built the First Temple in Jerusalem and consolidated all religious activities at this temple. However, the unified Jewish state did not last long. After the death of Solomon the northern tribes rebelled and the kingdom was split in two. The northern section was called Israel, the southern Judah. Assyrians conquered Israel in 721 B.C.E. Judah carried on for about one hundred years longer before being conquered by the Babylonians. In 586 B.C.E., the Babylonian king Nebuchadnezzar II destroyed Solomon's temple, tore down the walls of Jerusalem, and carried off most of the Jews into exile in Babylonia (modern-day Iraq).

The Babylonian exile (586–38 B.C.E.) was a traumatic period in Jewish history. Summarizing the grief of this period, it is written, "By the rivers of Babylon, there we sat down, and wept, when we remembered Zion" (Psalm 137). How-

ever, it was also a time of dramatic changes in religious practices. With the temple destroyed, state-level rituals came to an end, replaced by a new emphasis on the written word and a new form of worship. During the Babylonian exile, Jews began to meet weekly and to discuss scripture and pray. What developed was the Sabbath service of worship in a *synagogue,* a Greek term meaning a meeting place or assembly. With the synagogue appeared the *rabbi,* or Jewish religious teacher, and Jewish religious life began to revolve around elements of the Torah, which was being codified at this time. Thus the roots of modern Judaism began during the period of the Babylonian exile.

Seventy years after the destruction of the First Temple, the Persian king Cyrus the Great conquered Babylonia and allowed the Jews to return to Jerusalem. This began an era called the Second Temple Period. Two Babylonian Jews, Ezra and Nehemiah, returned to Jerusalem and inaugurated a new theocratic Jewish state. The Second Temple was completed in 515 B.C.E.; its western wall, called the Wailing Wall, still stands today. However, not all Jews returned to Israel. During the Second Temple Period, Jews who had remained in Babylonia finished compiling the Torah, and a thriving Jewish community remained in Babylonia for centuries.

Some parts of the Tanakh, particularly Daniel and Job, were probably written at the time of the Babylonian captivity and show the influence of Zoroastrianism, which originated in what is now Iran. Ideas concerning the nature of God, and the concepts of heaven, hell, judgment, and a cosmic battle between good and evil appear to be elements borrowed from Zoroastrian thinking.

In Jewish theology before the Babylonian captivity God encompassed both good and evil. However, in Zoroastrianism good and evil are personified as opposing forces: Ahura Mazda and Ahriman. Ahura Mazda represents the principles of righteousness and truth, whereas Ahriman is embodiment of evil, and there is an ongoing battle between these two forces. Zoroastrianism also focuses on the notions of heaven, hell, and individual judgment. The Book of Daniel with its apocalyptic vision and message of final judgment seems to follow Zoroastrian thinking. Similarly, the Book of Job first introduces the character of Satan and pits him against God in a contest between good and evil. The timing and content of these books indicates to biblical scholars today that Zoroastrianism influenced Jewish thinking during this period.

Additionally, in the post-exile period, Zoroastrian-influenced ideas about life after death emerge. Pre-exile Jews believed that the dead lead a shadowy existence in the underworld (called *Sheol* in Hebrew and *Hades* in Greek). However, factions of post-exile Jews focused on the Zoroastrian notion of a final battle. They believed that prior to the cosmic battle and the age of righteousness, a powerful Messiah was to appear. The mission of this human but God-appointed figure was to establish a kingdom in Israel and prepare for God's intervention and final judgment. Clearly, such ideas had a powerful influence on Christian thought.

Alexander the Great conquered Palestine in 332 B.C.E., bringing Greek influence to the area. Jews lived peacefully under Greek rule, adapting to Greek customs such as sports, theaters, and libraries, until the reign of King Antiochus IV (175–164). Antiochus tried to force the hellenization of Jews and hasten their assimilation into Greek life, by establishing policies such as a prohibition against Jews' keeping the Sabbath and owning copies of the Torah. In addition Antiochus tried to force Jews to worship Zeus. The attempts to force these Greek changes on Jewish society ultimately failed. A revolt ignited when an elderly Jew named Mattathias killed an official who tried to force him to make a sacrifice to the Greek god Zeus. Under the leadership of Mattathias's son Judas Maccabeus, Jews reconquered Jerusalem in 165 B.C.E. and reestablished Jewish worship in the Temple. The Maccabean revolt is remembered today in the Jewish festival of Hanukkah. One hundred years later (63 B.C.E.) the Roman general Pompey, who was stationed in Syria, was asked to arbitrate a bloody dispute between feuding Jewish factions. Instead of mediating the dispute, he occupied Palestine and claimed it as a new Roman province.

In this early period of Greco-Roman history, Hellenistic culture had a strong influence on Jewish thought. During this time, the Books of Ruth, Esther, Jonah, Job, and Ecclesiastes appeared and the Greek translations of Hebrew scriptures (the *Septuagint*) were completed.

During the Roman occupation of Palestine, several Jewish groups gained some measure of recognition. Among these were the Essenes, the Sadducees, the Pharisees, and the Zealots. The Essenes were a monastic group who practiced nonviolence and lived a communal celibate life, isolated from the rest of Jewish society. The Essenes described themselves as "sons of light," and it is thought that they believed they were preparing for the time when the Messiah would arrive and God would destroy the old, evil order. The Dead Sea Scrolls, scrolls containing nearly all of the books of Hebrew scripture, were found in caves above a community called Qumran between 1947 and 1955. It is possible that these scrolls were part of the library of the Essenes, hidden from the Romans during the rebellion that began in 66 C.E. The Sadducees were another faction that gained prominence at this time. They were members of priestly families who were in charge of the Temple and wealthy businessmen who lived primarily in Jerusalem. The Sadducees were very traditional in that they viewed the Torah as sacred and did not accept other books or oral traditions. The Pharisees were considered the most pious of the groups, and their members came from all classes. While the Sadducees focused on the Temple and Temple worship, the Pharisees emphasized daily religious practice as well as the observance of religious laws and traditions. The Pharisees were less conservative than the Sadducees in that they accepted a wider body of scripture and oral traditions as canon. A final faction, the Zealots, were uncompromising in their opposition to Roman rule of Palestine. The Zealots interpreted the messianic prophecies of the time to mean that the Messiah would be a war leader who would lead the forces that would defeat the Romans and restore Jewish political rule in Palestine.

The Jews rose in rebellion against Roman rule in 66 C.E. After some initial successes, the rebellion faltered against the power of the Roman legions sent to suppress it. Jerusalem was sacked, the inhabitants were slaughtered or driven into the countryside, and the Second Temple was destroyed. This event was a turning point in the Jewish faith. The destruction of the Second Temple ended the power of the priesthood. There was no longer anywhere for them to practice their rituals, the Romans forbade them to rebuild, and the Jewish population of Jerusalem was dispersed. One consequence of the Temple's destruction was that Judaism began to develop in a new direction. Without a temple and a formal priesthood to run it, a greater emphasis was placed on Scripture and scriptural interpretation. Consequently, in 90 C.E., about twenty years after the destruction of the Temple, a group of prominent rabbis met in the city of Jabneh to decide which religious books would be recognized with the Torah as sacred literature. The inclusion of several books of the Writings, such as the Song of Solomon and Ecclesiastes, was controversial. However, agreement was finally reached and the document we now call the Hebrew Bible reached its final form.

A second revolt against Rome followed in the years 132–135. When the Romans were initially driven from Jerusalem, the leader of the rebellion, Bar Kokhba, was hailed as the Messiah. However, after three years of fighting, the Romans crushed the rebellion, destroyed Jerusalem, and dispersed the Jewish population, who were forbidden from reentering the city. Jews who had remained in Israel after the destruction of the Temple were finally forced to flee in a diaspora that scattered Jewish families around the Mediterranean. However, with an agreed-upon body of Scripture that could be copied and taken anywhere, Rabbinical Judaism flourished. Additionally, the messianic movement that formed around the teachings of Jesus of Nazareth, later to become Christianity, helped spread the teachings of the Tanakh and keep them alive during the diaspora.

Without the temple and priests, rabbis became teachers and religious decision makers. In addition to studying the Tanakh, the rabbis began to interpret biblical teachings in light of contemporary events and values. This process of study and interpretation was called *midrash* and produced two types of material, *halakah* (discussions of law and legal decisions) and *haggadah* (history and folklore). This process of midrash created a large body of legal and spiritual literature known as the "oral torah." About 200 C.E. a scholar named Judah the Prince completed an edition of the oral Torah which thereafter became known as the *Mishna*.

Because the Tanakh is a closed document, subject to interpretation but not revision, the Mishna became the basic body of material for rabbinic studies. In about 500 C.E., the Mishna and accumulated commentaries (called the *Gemara*) were organized into the *Talmud.* Today this collection of commentaries and interpretations of Scripture complements the Hebrew Bible as a source of authority. The Talmud is a vast amount of material. In the Talmud, rabbis have added centuries' worth of insight and discussions of problems of scriptural interpretation and religious life.

In a sense the Talmud is open-ended, for religious controversies and new theological ideas have continued to arise and create new discussions over the centuries. No single opinion has dominated this ongoing discussion of the Torah, and rabbis have often disagreed in their interpretations. This constant revision and interweaving of historical commentaries allows the introduction of new ideas into the religion. For example, the concept of the soul is not found in the Tanakh but was introduced in the Talmud.

After the diaspora of 135 C.E., Jews settled throughout the Mediterranean world and flourished, especially in Iraq, Egypt, and, by the ninth century, Spain. The Babylonian Jewish community, which dated back to the period of the Babylonian exile, became a leading center of Jewish life and thought. Even after the Muslim conquest of Baghdad in the late 600s, Jewish intellectual and religious life flourished. Jews were treated benignly under Islamic rule because, like Christians, they were "people of the Book," and Muslims, like Jews, trace the foundation of their faith to Abraham. Throughout the Islamic Middle East, Jews prospered.

Under Islamic rule, Jewish intellectual life also flourished. Islamic countries were far ahead of Christian Europe in the development of medicine, philosophy, mathematics, and the arts. Jews living in Muslim countries benefited from this climate of creativity and toleration. Muslim Spain, in particular, was the source of many great Jewish physicians, scholars, philosophers, and poets. For example, perhaps the greatest medieval Jewish philosopher was *Moses Maimonides.* Maimonides was born in Córdoba, Spain, in 1135 and distinguished himself as a scholar at an early age, studying Jewish and Greek philosophy and medicine. He began his first major work, a commentary on the Mishna, at the age of 23. Driven from Spain by a fanatical Islamic sect that conquered Córdoba in 1148, Maimonides' family searched for a new home in Morocco, and then Palestine, and finally settled outside of Cairo in Egypt where Jews were free to openly practice their faith. When his father and brother died soon after arriving in Egypt, Maimonides was left with the task of supporting his family. Out of economic necessity, Maimonides turned to the practice of medicine. His reputation as a physician grew so rapidly that he ultimately was given the position of physician to the sultan Saladin. At the same time he became a leading member of the Jewish community and continued to write commentaries on Judaism. Some of his most important works were his commentaries on the Mishna, which were completed when he was 33; the *Mishne Torah,* a review of Jewish law and doctrines; and his most important work, the *Moreh Nevukhim* (A Guide to the Perplexed), which he started in 1176 and completed fifteen years later. In this latter work Maimonides issued a plea for a more rational approach to Judaism and tried to integrate his studies in science, philosophy, and religion. Maimonides wrote this book in Arabic, but it was soon translated into Hebrew, Latin, and later most other European languages. Maimonides' influence spread far beyond Judaism. His work, translated into Latin, was influential in the work of many of the great Christian philosophers of the medieval period. Maimonides died in 1204. He was buried in Tiberias in modern day Israel, and his grave continues to be a shrine today.

Jews in Christian countries often had more difficult lives than Jews in Muslim lands. The Christian Crusades, initiated by Pope Innocent II in 1096, started a period of widespread persecution of Jews in Europe. By the end of the fifteenth century, Jews had been expelled from or made unwelcome in virtually every western European nation. Edward I expelled Jews from England in 1290. King Phillip of France drove the Jews from his country in 1306. However, one of the most traumatic events for European Jews was their expulsion from Spain, where Jews had lived for more than one thousand years, in 1492. Life for European Jews deteriorated further in 1555 when a papal decree authorized the segregation of Jews into *ghettos,* sections of cities that were walled in and locked at night to minimize contact between Jews and Christians.

Many Jewish refugees found safety in the Muslim territories of the Ottoman Empire. Jewish refugees from Spain and Portugal who settled in Ottoman territory became known as Sephardic Jews. Other refugees turned to eastern Europe. Poland in particular became a haven for the Jews driven from western Europe. By the end of the sixteenth century there were an estimated half million Jews in Poland, and by the early seventeenth century it had become the major center of Jewish life. Jews in eastern Europe became known as Ashkenazi Jews. Their language was Yiddish, a combination of German and Hebrew.

KABBALAH AND HASIDISM

During the Middle Ages there was a renewed interest in Jewish mysticism and mystical literature called *Kabbalah.* A common assumption of Jewish mystics was that the Tanakh was written in code and could be interpreted only by those who had broken the code. The key for interpretation of the texts was *gematria,* the transposing of words into numbers. For example, *aleph,* the first letter of the Hebrew alphabet, would be given a value of 1; the second letter, *beth,* a 2; and so on. In this way the letters could be added up and patterns between number combinations could be found. Common messages discovered in this manner typically had to do with the divine origin of the world, God's care of the Jews, and the arrival of the Messiah. For example, Genesis 18:2 tells the story of angels visiting Abraham. The text does not name the three angels, but kabbalists claimed the names must be *Michael, Gabriel,* and *Raphael.* They "decoded" these names by adding the totals of the numbers in the letters in the phrase "behold, three men stood in front of him": 701. The numerical value of the names Michael, Gabriel, and Raphael is also 701. Therefore, the Kabbalists concluded that these were the names of the angels who visited Abraham.[1] The most famous book of the Kabbalah was the *Zohar* (Splendor) written by Rabbi Moses de León in about 1280. The book instructs the devout kabbalist on such topics as the nature of God, the creation of humans and angels, and the nature of evil.

During the sixteenth century the most influential of the Jewish mystics was Isaac Luria. Luria claimed that the creation of the world occurred when God beamed divine light into ten vessels. Some of these containers shattered because they could not bear the intensity of the light, and the breaking of the vessels scattered particles of evil as well as fragments of this divine force into the world. According to Luria only the arrival of the Messiah will bring *tikkun,* the repair of this situation, and thus end the evil in the world. Although God would decide when this will happen, humans have the responsibility to prepare for the Messiah's coming by following purification rituals, prayer, and strict adherence to the Torah.

In the seventeenth century, conditions for Jews changed drastically for the worse in Poland and eastern Europe. The Cossack peasants of the Ukraine rebelled against Polish rule in 1648. Associating Jews with their Roman Catholic rulers, the Russian Orthodox Cossacks carried out terrible massacres against Polish Jews. As the stability and prosperity enjoyed by Jews in Poland fell apart, and persecution increased, a wave of Jewish mysticism swept across eighteenth-century Ukraine and Poland. This was called *Hasidism,* which means "devotion" or "piety" and was led by a healer and teacher named Israel Ben Eliezer (1700–1760) or, more affectionately, Baal Shem Tov (Good Master of the Holy Name). Baal Shem Tov taught that the Divine could be found everywhere, and everyone was capable of the highest levels of enlightenment. According to Hasidic teachers, God is in the midst of even the most mundane tasks. Eating, drinking, and even working can become holy acts if carried out in the name of God. Followers of Baal Shem Tov entered ecstatic states during their worship services, finding God in the midst of the Polish ghettos. Hasidism spread rapidly until nearly half of all eastern European Jews followed Hasidic teachings.

The expansion of Hasidic teachings is credited to Dov Ber, who stressed the importance of the *tzaddik,* or *rebbe,* an enlightened teacher. Ber encouraged Hasidic Jews to follow a tzaddik, because the teacher's personal relationship with God meant that his prayers would be more powerful than their own. This form of charismatic leadership, and the position of tzaddik, is often hereditary in Hasidic groups today and remains one of the central elements of modern Hasidism. Today Hasidic groups are Ultra-Orthodox Jews who adhere rigidly to an extremely conservative lifestyle and in-

terpretation of the Torah. They live and marry within their own closed communties and avoid contact with other Jews as well as Gentiles. Although most Jews today are not Hasidic, groups like the Lubavitchers in New York City are respected for their spirituality and knowledge of the Torah. At the same time, Hasidic groups are also condemned for their narrow-mindedness and intolerance of others.

THE HOLOCAUST

For most Europeans and Americans, the Holocaust, or *Shoah* (Hebrew for "extermination"), is the defining act of evil in the twentieth century. The Nazi government's systematic murder of almost 12 million people, including 6 million European Jews, is the most horrifying event in Western history.

Adolf Hitler became chancellor of Germany in 1933. Working with his followers in the National Socialist (Nazi) Party he quickly set out to turn Germany into a dictatorship, bolstering his support by blaming Jews for all of Germany's post–First World War problems. Beginning in 1935, German Jews saw their businesses and assets confiscated and were deprived of their legal and economic rights. The Nuremburg laws of 1935 stripped Jews of their citizenship. Virtually every synagogue in Germany was vandalized or destroyed in the Kristallnacht (Night of Broken Glass) pogrom of 1938. Austrian Jews suffered the same fate when Hitler annexed Austria in 1938.

By 1939 Jews could not attend public schools, own their own land or businesses, visit a library, park, or museum, or associate with non-Jews. Hundreds of thousands of Jews tried to flee Europe, but few countries would accept Jewish refugees. The U.S. government attempted to broker a deal for the systematic emigration of Jews, but that effort fell apart in 1939 when Hitler invaded Poland, then Belgium, Holland, and France. Although about 160,000 Jews were admitted into the United States and thousands more escaped to British Palestine, by 1940 about 11 to 12 million Jewish people were under Nazi control. These Jews were forbidden to use public transportation or telephones, and all of them over 6 years of age were required to wear a badge or armband with a yellow Star of David.

As World War II began, the Nazis began to deport Jews from Western Europe to Poland, and confined Polish Jews into walled ghettos. When German armies moved eastward into Poland, the Balkan States, and the Soviet Union, death squads known as *Einsatzgruppen* (action groups) were created to slaughter Jews and other "undesirables" such as Gypsies and Slavic peoples, whom the Germans considered subhuman. Although the world witnessed several instances of mass murder in the twentieth century, the scale of the Germans' mass slaughter of civilians is still difficult to comprehend. The populations of whole towns were rounded up and shot, then buried in mass graves. For example, 34,000 were killed at Babi Yar and 32,000 at Vilna. At the Wannsee

Conference in January 1942, Nazi bureaucrats met to discuss how to more efficiently conduct their program for the "final solution" to the problem of the Jews. It was decided to evacuate Jews from all over occupied Europe to extermination camps in the east, and within the year the first death camps were in operation. Jews were transported to the extermination camps in cattle cars from all over Europe. There, the elderly and children were immediately gassed in industrial-sized gas chambers; able-bodied men and women were worked to death as slaves. Perhaps as many as 4 million people were put to death in camps such as Auschwitz, Treblinka, and Sobibor. During the course of the war the Nazis murdered a total of about 5.7 million Jews.

The governments of some countries tried to protect their Jewish citizens, and individuals all over Europe risked their own lives to shelter Jewish friends or help them escape. But overall, the rest of the world watched in silence and many Europeans were happy to cooperate with the Nazis. Even the Allied forces took no special action to save Jews in the camps during the war. Winston Churchill urged bombing the gas chambers, but he had no support from members of his own cabinet or the United States. Those who survived the camps were liberated when Allied armies pushed the Germans back in the spring of 1945. In all, about one-third of the world population of Jews were killed in the Holocaust.

ZIONISM

After the Second World War, knowledge of the Holocaust created widespread sympathy for the suffering of the Jewish people and gave strength to the *Zionist* movement. Zionism, which started in the late nineteenth century, was a movement dedicated to the creation of a Jewish homeland. It was not a religious movement but rather an attempt to found a country where Jews could live free from persecution.

By the nineteenth century the Jewish population of western Europe had assimilated, more or less, into mainstream society. However, anti-Jewish sentiment remained strong. In France, these feelings were exposed in 1894 by the Dreyfus affair. In that year, Alfred Dreyfus, a captain in the French army, was accused of giving away French military secrets during the Franco-Prussian War. The accusations were dubious, but Dreyfus was convicted and sentenced to life imprisonment. During the course of Dreyfus's trial, anti-Jewish feeling was widely expressed, not just against Dreyfus but against Jews in general. Dreyfus's conviction was invalidated in 1899, but it demonstrated the hostility that existed toward Jews in western Europe. The desire to return to Zion (site of the Jerusalem Temples) has long been a theme in Jewish prayers; but after Dreyfus, Zionism became an organized political movement under the guidance of Theodor Herzl, a journalist from Vienna who believed that Jews would receive fair treatment only when they had their own homeland. In the early 1900s, Jews started buying land

and building settlements in Palestine. By 1920, about fifty thousand Jews had moved to Palestine.

During World War I, Britain issued the Balfour Declaration of 1917. This declaration stated British support for Jewish settlements in Palestine after the defeat of Turkey, an ally of Germany. Limited immigration occurred when the Ottoman Empire broke up at the end of the First World War and Palestine became a British protectorate. However, the protests of Muslims and Arab Christians who opposed large numbers of Jewish immigrants entering the country convinced the British government to pass a law restricting immigration to Palestine. In 1939, Jewish immigration to Palestine was limited to fifteen thousand people per year for five years. Unfortunately, this act and similar immigration restrictions in the United States trapped Jews in Europe precisely when Nazi Germany was rising to power and immeasurably increased the death toll of Jews during the Second World War.

After World War II, when the details of the Holocaust became widely known, the United Nations partitioned British Palestine into two areas, one to be governed by Jews and the other by Arabs. When the British left Palestine in May 1948, Israel immediately proclaimed its statehood and declared the Law of Return, which invited all Jews to resettle in their homeland. However, Israel was almost instantly attacked by its Arab neighbors and in the course of the war that followed Israel occupied a good portion of the land originally slated for Arab settlement. Israel has had to face the continuing hostility of its Arab neighbors, and has had to fight several wars to preserve itself. The occupation of Palestinian territory in 1948 and again after the Arab-Israeli War of 1967, including parts of Old Jerusalem, has continued to fuel the bitterness between Israel and the surrounding Arab countries. Governance of the city of Jerusalem, administration of the Palestinian areas of the West Bank of the Jordan River, and the displacement of Palestinian refugees all are serious sources of tension between Arabs and Israelis today.

As if the hostility from neighboring countries were not enough, there is also tension between factions within Israel. Some Ashkenazi Jews from Eastern Europe, who founded Israel, tend to view themselves as superior to settlers from other areas such as Asia and Africa. Additionally, Ultra-Orthodox Jews wield considerable political influence although they represent only about 15 percent of the population. They insist on a strict adherence to religious laws and rituals that are not followed by most Jews. Additionally, there is wide disagreement over treatment of the Palestinian minority within Israel.

CONTEMPORARY JUDAISM: SACRED PRACTICES

To be a Jew is not simply to hold a set of beliefs; it is a way of living. The Ten Commandments are at the heart of Jewish life, but there are many more laws and customs that direct Jews' behavior.

At the heart of all forms of Judaism is *Shabbat*, the Sabbath. Recalling the day of rest God took after six days of divine labor, Shabbat is a day of prayer and relaxation. This day begins at sunset each Friday and ends at sunset Saturday. Shabbat begins with the lighting of candles by the women of the house. The best food of the week typically is served at the Friday evening meal, which is accompanied by a series of blessings; first over the Shabbat candles, then the children present then the wine, and finally the bread.

Synagogue worship on Shabbat became common during the Babylonian exile, and today religious Jews attend services on Friday evening or Saturday morning. There are public and private prayers during the service, singing and reading of passages from the Torah, and in more liberal congregations there may be discussion of the passages that are read. In Hasidic congregations there is an emphasis on the intensity of prayers, and people sway as they pray to induce an ecstatic state of communion with God. Traditionally, because Shabbat is a day of rest, many activities are prohibited. People are forbidden to light or extinguish fires or electric lights, use electric appliances, cook, ride in automobiles, smoke, perform any transaction involving money, or perform any manual labor (though any of these is permitted in the case of life threatening emergency). The degree to which Jews today follow these prohibitions varies enormously.

RELIGIOUS FESTIVALS

Just as the week is sanctified by the weekly festival of Shabbat, so too the year is marked by a series of holy days. Many Jewish holy days originated at an earlier time when the lives of most Jews followed the agricultural seasons. However, additional holy days have been added to commemorate important events in Jewish history. Because the dates of Jewish festivals are calculated using the traditional Jewish lunar calendar, their dates on the Gregorian calendar that most others use vary somewhat from year to year.

Rosh Hashanah, the Jewish New Year, is celebrated on the first two days of the seventh month in the Jewish calendar, around the time of the fall equinox. Rosh Hashanah is also known as the Day of Remembrance or Day of Judgment, for it celebrates the creation of the world, and it begins a ten-day period of self-examination and penitence. It is a time for Jews to medidate on their responsibilities as God's chosen people. The most important symbol of the festival is the *shofar*, the ram's-horn trumpet. During the month before Rosh Hashanah the shofar is sounded at the beginning of each day's synagogue service to remind people that they stand before God. The sound of the shofar calls Jews to a spiritual awakening like that Moses received on Mount Sinai. The shofar is also sounded during the service on New Year's Day as prescribed in Numbers 29:1, and for the following ten days until the start of the most sacred Jewish holy day, Yom Kippur.

Yom Kippur, the Day of Atonement, is a time when Jews renew their sacred covenant with God. This day is typically passed in prayer and strict fasting, and many devout Jews spend it at their synagogue. Like all Jewish holidays, Yom Kippur runs from sundown to sundown. An evening service is followed by services that last throughout the following day and include readings from the Tanakh and prayers of penitence. Congregations also confess their sins as a group and ask for forgiveness. Memorial prayers for those who have died, called *yiskor* (from the Hebrew for "let him remember"), may also be offered.

On Yom Kippur, prayers ask for atonement for sins committed between people and God. It is also customary to atone for wrongs committed against another person but the Talmud teaches that such sins can not be pardoned through prayer but only through seeking reconciliation with the person who has been wronged.

Rosh Hashana and Yom Kippur are called the High Holy Days, and even the most secular Jews celebrate these two festivals.

Five days after the conclusion of Yom Kippur is the fall harvest festival of *Sukkot*, also called the Feast of Booths. Long ago it was common for families to sleep outdoors in their fields during the harvest season. This allowed them to stretch their workday and protect their harvest. The small sleeping shed (*sukkah*) that was built in the fields became part of the harvest celebration and eventually came to symbolize the ancient Israelites' wandering in the desert before they entered Canaan. Today Jews build a light wooden shelter and decorate this structure with branches and fruits to suggest the bounty of the earth. Participants hold the *lulav*, a bundle made of a palm branch, myrtle, and willow twigs, in one hand, and the *etrog*, a citrus fruit, in the other hand and wave them together toward the four cardinal directions, earth, and sky, praising God as the center of creation. Sukkot is followed immediately by *simhat Torah* (day of rejoicing in the Torah). This day marks the end of the yearly cycle of Torah reading, which starts with Genesis and ends with the final chapters of Deuteronomy where Moses dies and Joshua leads the Israelites into Canaan, and the cycle of Torah readings begins anew.

Hanukkah, the Festival of Lights, is an early-winter celebration that occurs at the darkest time of the year, near the winter solstice. Although the modern emphasis in this festival is often on the victory of the Maccabean rebels over the forces of Antiochus IV in 165 B.C.E., this festival commemorates the rededication of the Second Temple of Jersulaem three years after its desecration by Antiochus IV. Antiochus had tried to force Jews to offer sacrifices to Zeus and desecrated their temples, thus inciting the rebellion that was led by Judas Maccabaeus. According to tradition, when Jews rededicated the Temple they had only enough oil to keep a lamp burning for one day but the lamp miraculously burned for eight days, the period required to make and consecrate new temple oil. Consequently, over an eight-day period families gather each night, light a candle on a nine-branched candelabra called a *hanukia*, and play games, such as gambling for nuts or chocolate coins with a *dreidel*. Each night over this eight-day period one more candle is lit on the hanukia until on the last night of the festival all are burning. In the United States it is also common for those celebrating Hanukkah to exchange gifts because the festival falls near the Christian celebration of Christmas and most Jewish parents want their children to enjoy the season even if they do not celebrate the birth of Jesus.

Following Hanukkah is *Tu B'Shevat,* a festival held in late January or early February that welcomes spring and is celebrated in Israel by the planting of trees. Tu B'Shevat is a minor holiday, but in Israel it has become popular because it symbolizes reclaiming land from the desert.

Purim is a festival that occurs during the full moon in the month before spring. Purim commemorates events described in the Book of Esther. The story tells of how Queen Esther and her uncle Mordecai save their people when the evil royal minister Haman plots to have Mordecai executed and his people slaughtered. Esther thwarts Haman's plan and her husband, the king, orders Haman's execution on the gallows Haman had built for Mordecai. This festival is marked by reading from the Book of Esther and costume plays that reenact the story. Traditionally, this was a festival in which Jews exchanged gifts of portions of food. Drinking to the point of complete intoxication was also a part of this feast, but this element has now fallen out of common practice.

The weeklong festival of *Pesach,* or Passover, occurs in March or April. It celebrates the liberation of the Jews from slavery in Egypt and the sparing of the Jews' firstborn sons on the eve of the Exodus. According to Jewish tradition, the tenth plague predicted by Moses—the death of all firstborn sons—finally forced the pharaoh to relent and free the Israelites. However, Jews were spared from this plague because they slaughtered lambs and marked their doors with the blood so that the Angel of Death passed by their houses. They then roasted the lamb and ate it with bitter herbs and bread. The tenth plague was so terrible that the pharaoh finally agreed to let the Jews go. They departed in such haste that they didn't have time for the bread to rise, so they ate unleavened bread. The major event of Passover is a memorial meal called the *Seder,* in which the story of the Jews' Exodus from Egypt is reenacted with the eating of several symbolic foods while the story of their liberation is read. In particular, unleavened bread called *matzah* and bitter herbs such as horseradish are eaten at the beginning of the meal. The matzah is to remind participants of the urgency of the Jews' departure, and the herbs are a reminder of the bitterness of slavery. Other foods that are part of the Seder include *haroset,* a sweet mix of fruit and nuts that symbolizes both the mortar used by slaves in their labors and the sweetness of freedom, and parsley dipped in salt water. The salt water is a reminder of the slaves' tears, and the parsley represents the renewal of life in the spring.

Fifty days after Passover is the summer festival of *Shavuot.* Originally a summer grain harvest festival in which offerings from the harvest were brought to the Temple, the celebration now commemorates God's gift of the commandments to Moses.

Nine weeks after Shavuot is a day of fasting called *Tisha be'Av* (ninth day in the month of Av). This is a solemn day for remembering the destruction of the First and Second Temples. According to tradition, several other disastrous events have occurred on the ninth of Av, including the decree that Jews would wander in the wilderness for forty years, the battle that ended the Jewish revolt against Rome in 135, and, in 136, the construction of a pagan temple in Jerusalem and the expulsion of all Jews from the city.

Other important holidays of more recent origin are *Yom Hashoah,* or Holocaust Day. Yom Hashoah commemorates the Holocaust and its victims and is observed on April 19 or 20. This day is considered the anniversary date of the beginning of the Warsaw Ghetto Uprising of 1943. Finally, there is also Israeli Independence day, *Yom Haatzma-ut.* This day celebrates the day Israel declared itself a sovereign state—May 14, 1948.

DIETARY AND RELIGIOUS PRACTICES

Jews have been concerned with the ritual purity of food since the religion's earliest days, and many Jews, especially Orthodox Jews, follow the dietary instructions spelled out in the Book of Leviticus. The term *kosher,* which means "ritually correct," especially applies to food preparation and consumption. Pork and shellfish are forbidden foods. Poultry is kosher, but the only ritually acceptable meats are those from animals with cloven hoofs that chew their cuds, such as cows, goats, and sheep. Meat is also kosher only if it has been butchered in the traditional way by an authorized Jewish butcher and great care has been taken to make sure all blood is drained from the animal before its meat is cooked and eaten. Meat and dairy products cannot be eaten together, and kosher households use separate pots and pans and dishes to make sure the two are kept separate.

It is customary for many Jews to pray at dawn, noon, and dusk. Covering one's head is a way of showing respect to God in Judaism, and most Jewish men wear a skullcap called a *kipah* to show their reverence when praying. Women may cover their heads with a scarf. Orthodox men, however, typically keep their heads covered with a hat at all times. Orthodox men may also wear *t'fillin,* or phylacteries. These are two small leather boxes containing the words of one the most important Jewish prayers, which is based on Deuteronomy (6:4–9). It says:

> Hear O Israel; the LORD our God, the Lord is one. And thou shalt love the Lord thy God with all thy heart, and with all thy soul, and with all thy might. And these words which I command thee this day, shall be upon thy heart; . . . And thou shalt bind them for a sign upon thy hand, and they shall be for frontlets between thine eyes. And thou shalt write them upon the doorposts of thy house, and upon thy gates.

In order to literally act out this prayer, these men tie one of the phylacteries to their forehead with leather straps and secure the other to the upper left arm by straps wound down the arm and around the hand. This practice also signifies that God's commandments are in the mind and heart of the person at prayer. Traditional men also typically wear a *talit,* or prayer shawl. The shawl is usually white with dark stripes and fringes, and men wear it over their heads and shoulders when at prayer to signify humility. Also following the passage in Deuteronomy, many Jewish homes have a *mezuzah,* a small container that holds scriptural verses and is attached to the entrance to a home or in a doorway of an interior room. When walking past a *mezuzah,* a devout Jew touches it as a reminder of God and his laws.

Judaism also has a number of rituals that deal with birth and sexuality. Circumcision is a sign of a Jewish man's pact with God, and in a ceremony called a *bris,* baby boys are ritually circumcised when they are 8 days old. Orthodox Jews consider women ritually unclean during their menstrual periods and for seven days afterward. They are not to engage in sexual relations during this time, and at the end of this period women immerse themselves in a special bath that purifies them called a *mikvah.* Puberty is marked with a coming-of-age ceremony called a *b'nei mitzvah.* The *bar mitzvah,* which means a "son of the commandment," is conducted for boys when they are 13. Boys typically undergo religious instruction before this time and are called upon to read a portion of the Torah in Hebrew. Afterward, there is usually a party to celebrate a young man's acceptance into the religious community. Most American Jewish congregations conduct an identical ceremony for girls called a *bat mitzvah.*

DIVISIONS WITHIN JUDAISM

As with the other religions described in this book, a wide variety of groups and practices fall under the heading of Judaism. In the United States and Canada, Jewish groups are divided into Modern Orthodox, Ultra-Orthodox, Reform, Conservative, and Reconstructionist. Reform, Conservative, and Reconstructionist groups are less represented throughout the rest of the world, although their influence on world Judaism is powerful.

Modern Orthodox Jews are those who strive to live by the letter of the commandments and laws spelled out in Tanakh and Talmud. In Orthodox Judaism such commandments and laws are immutable and the sole basis for religious observance (though there is much discussion about how the commandments and laws are properly interpreted). Modern Orthodox Jews believe in integration with the rest of society and participate fully in the life of the broader Jewish and non-Jewish community.

Ultra-Orthodox Jews on the other hand, generally try to isolate themselves from the outside world. Some Ultra-Orthodox groups, such as the Lubavitch Hasidim live in fairly closed religious communities but have embraced modern technology and use websites to spread their message around the world. Ultra-Orthodox Jews often have distinctive styles of appearance. Men leave their beards untrimmed and the hair in front of their ears uncut in response to a command in Leviticus. They often wear black coats and pants with a black hat, a style that originated in Poland in the eighteenth century.

Despite these differences, Modern Orthodox and Ultra-Orthodox Jews have several traits in common. For instance, both segregate men and women during synagogue services and neither permits music. Men keep their heads covered at all times (either with a hat or a kippah (skullcap) and married women generally cover their heads outside of their homes as an expression of modesty. Orthodox families follow dietary laws strictly and adhere to the rules that prohibit work on Shabbat. Prohibited work includes cooking, driving, making a phone call, or turning on a light.

Some Orthodox families have Gentile friends who will come over on the Sabbath to perform small chores such as turning out lights for them. In Israel, Orthodoxy is the official form of Judaism and Orthodox rabbis wield considerable political power. However, although they are highly visible, only a tenth of the population is Ultra-Orthodox. In the United States they constitute a much smaller percentage of the Jewish population.

Reform Judaism is, in a matter of speaking, the opposite of Orthodox Judaism. The movement began in Germany at the turn of the nineteenth century and was a product of the European Enlightenment. With the opening of the European ghettos, many Jews began to question restrictive traditions such as the dietary laws, services in Hebrew, and the necessity of wearing special garments that set them apart as Jews. The Reform movement was an attempt to modernize Judaism and make it relevant to European Jews who were entering mainstream European life. Toward that end, Reform Jews modified or even abandoned many traditional Jewish practices. In imitation of Protestant Christian churches, for example, the Shabbat service was shortened and translated from Hebrew to German and other European languages. Synagogues added choirs and organ music, and references to the return to Zion, the return of the Messiah, and Temple sacrifices were eliminated from the services. In Reform synagogues, men and women sat together, and tallit and t'fillin were not required. Work was permitted on the Sabbath and the dietary laws were declared obsolete. Men and women received more equal treatment in Reform Judaism, and Israel Jacobson (1768–1828) pioneered the bat mitzvah ceremony for young women as an equivalent to the bar mitzvah for young men.

Rabbi Abraham Geiger was a leading philosopher of the nineteenth-century Reform movement. He argued that the essence of Judaism was belief in one God for all humankind, in the practice of ethical principles that were eternally valid, and in Judaism being a living, constantly developing faith. A German emigrant, Rabbi Isaac Mayer Wise (1819–1900), was a leading figure in the spread of the Reform movement in the United States, which began in 1841. Wise authored a revised prayer book and helped establish Hebrew Union College for the education of Reform rabbis in 1875.

In 1937, several principles of the original Reform movement were revised in a conference of American Reform rabbis. These rabbis issued a document endorsing the use of traditional customs and ceremonies and the use of Hebrew in religious services. In the second half of the twentieth century, the central organization of Reform rabbis continued to consider new issues such as the inclusion of single parents (in the nineteenth century the Reform movement had rejected Orthodox laws governing marriage and divorce), the inclusion of women rabbis, and homosexuality.

There is a fundamental philosophical difference between Reform and Orthodox theology. Whereas Orthodox Jews regard their religion as being revealed by God and spelled out in the Tanakh and Talmud, and attempt to conform their lives as closely as possible to that ancient code, Reform Jews believe that Judaism needs to evolve and adapt to be relevant in a continually changing society. One of the original goals of the Reform movement was to modernize Judaism and make it relevant to modern life. It is not surprising that Reform Judaism is the most popular form of Judaism in the United States or that Reform Jews have led the way in establishing interfaith dialogues with non-Jewish organizations. However, Reform Judaism is not fully accepted in Israel and the authority of non-Orthodox rabbis is not recognized there. Converts to Reform Judaism are not accepted as Jews in Israel, where the officially recognized religious practice is Orthodox.

Conservative Judaism is the second-largest branch of Judaism in the United States. It is attractive to many people because it has forged a position between Orthodox and Reform Judaism. Followers of Conservative Judaism accept traditional rabbinical teachings and leadership, such as conducting services in Hebrew, but they also believe that religions and societies change and that religious beliefs and practices may need to be revised to be relevant to modern life. The Conservative movement was led by Zacharias Frankel (1801–1875), a German Jew who believed that the changes proposed by the Reform movement in the 1840s were too radical. He refused to accept that traditional religious customs had no relevance in the modern world and sought middle ground between the Orthodox and Reform positions.

Following Orthodox practice, Conservative Jews maintain a belief in the sacredness of the Sabbath and respect traditional dietary rules. However, they have also embraced numerous changes, such as driving to worship services on the Sabbath and the ordination of women as rabbis, but these changes are not forced—individual congregations have the right to accept or reject proposed changes. Like the Reform movement, Conservative Judaism has enjoyed a great deal of success in the United States.

The newest and smallest branch of Judaism is Reconstructionist Judaism. The founder of Reconstruction Judaism was a Lithuanian-born American rabbi named Mordecai Kaplan (1881–1983). Kaplan was probably the most influential Jewish American thinker in the second half of the twentieth century. In 1922 he established the Society for the Advancement of Judaism, which later became the center of the Reconstructionist movement.

Kaplan's philosophical ideals were influenced by secularism and rationalism. He outlined his ideas in a 1934 book titled *Judaism as a Civilization: Toward the Reconstruction of American Jewish Life*. He did not believe in the literal accuracy of the Bible and taught that Judaism needed to adapt to modern-day realities. For example, Kaplan wrote: "as long as Jews adhered to the traditional conception of Torah as supernaturally revealed, they would not be amenable to any constructive adjustment of Judaism that was needed to render it viable in a non-Jewish environment."[2] Kaplan created a new prayer book, deleting such things as derogatory references to women and Gentiles, and passages describing God punishing people with natural phenomena. At the same time, he encouraged Jews to become familiar with as many elements of traditional Judaism as possible, but allowed them to interpret these elements individually. Although Reconstruction Judaism has a small number of followers, Kaplan's ideas have been very influential in the Reform and Conservative branches of Judaism.

JEWS IN THE MODERN WORLD

The Jewish community today is located primarily in three places: the former Soviet Union, Israel, and the United States. While different processes remain in each of these three centers, the general trend has been toward increasing secularization and a growing gulf between Ultra-Orthodox and other Jews.

In the states of the former Soviet Union, Jews have become highly secularized. From the 1930s until the collapse of communism in the late 1980s, the Soviet government specifically banned the teaching of Jewish religion and culture. The result was the creation of two generations of people who were ethnically Jewish (and required to carry identity papers stating this fact) but knew little of Jewish religion or culture. With the collapse of communism, Jews in the former Soviet Union are more easily able to practice their religion; however, they have also faced economic collapse and a rising tide of anti-Semitism. One result of this has been steady emigration of former Soviet Jews to the United States, Israel, and Western Europe. In all three areas, they now form important elements of the Jewish community, but they are generally not very religious.

Israel was founded as a Jewish state, but its founders were highly secular. One result of this is a tension in Israeli life between religion and national identity. For most Israelis, national identity is much more important than religion and the sense of Israeli identity is not tied to any religious practices. Most Israelis are secular Jews who maintain Jewish cultural identity but rarely engage the religious practices of Judaism. However, Israel is also home to a large population of Ultra-Orthodox Jews and the political parties that represent these Jews play important roles in the governance of the state. For such Jews, Israeli identity, Israeli national boundaries, and Jewish religious practice are inexorably mixed. The differences between the Ultra-Orthodox understanding of the meaning of the Israeli state and that held by most secular Israelis creates intense political conflict. This was shown tragically when an Ultra-Orthodox Jew assassinated Israeli Prime Minister Yitzhak Rabin in 1995.

The situation of Jews in the United States is also very complex. A high percentage of the Jews who emigrated to the United States in the late nineteenth and early twentieth centuries believed firmly in the notion of the American melting pot. Members of Reform and Conservative congregations in particular attempted to minimize differences between themselves and their non-Jewish neighbors. In some cases, in the Reform movement, this went as far as holding Shabbat services on Sunday rather than Saturday. In the nineteenth century and the first half of the twentieth century these effects were not particularly successful. American anti-Semitism was strong; quotas and restrictions kept Jews separated from non-Jews and limited their participation in American social and political life. However, in the years since World War II, Jews have been much more fully accepted into American life. Although anti-Semitism still exists, its role in American society is greatly reduced. The level of American acceptance of the Jewish community was shown dramatically in 2000 when a presidential ticket with an openly Jewish senator running for Vice President received the majority of the popular vote (though, of course, not the majority of electoral votes). The wide acceptance of Jews in America also poses a threat to the survival of the Jewish community. As Jews have become more accepted by their neighbors, rates of intermarriage between Jews and non-Jews have soared and rates of synagogue membership have declined. One good index of this is the relative strength

of the Conservative and Reform movement. Throughout most of the twentieth century, most American Jews belonged to the Conservative movement, but the number of Conservative Jews has actually declined in recent years and now the Reform movement represents the largest block of American Jews.

While most Jews in America have become increasingly secular, the Ultra-Orthodox Hassidic movements have grown as well. While these movements represent only a small fraction of American Jewry, both their size and importance has been increasing. Part of the increase has been fueled by the immigration of Ultra-Orthodox Jews from Eastern Europe, but much is the result of previously secular Jews joining Ultra-Orthodox groups. Unlike other Jewish groups, many Ultra-Orthodox groups are proselytizing. Members of Ultra-Orthodox groups spend enormous amounts of time and energy trying to convince members of other Jewish groups to move toward Ultra-Orthodoxy. For example, one group, the Chabad Lubavitch movement, maintains facilities at over 2,700 institutions, mostly universities, worldwide. While the number of their followers in most places is quite small, they hope to grow through outreach to other Jews. The emergence of the Ultra-Orthodox as a powerful force has led to increasing tensions between them and members of other Jewish communities.

Thus, at the beginning of Judaism's fifth millennium, the great challenges facing the Jewish community include dealing with the growth of secularism that threatens the identities and beliefs that have sustained Jews through thousands of years of persecution while at the same time coping with the increasing divide between secular and religious Jews.

NOTES

1. Lewis M. Hopfe and Mark R. Woodward. *Religions of the World,* 7th ed. (Upper Saddle River: Prentice Hall, 1998), 278.

2. Quoted in Mary Pat Fisher, *Living Religions,* 5th ed. (Upper Saddle River: Prentice Hall, 2002), 279.

16

Christianity

Christianity, which developed out of Judaism in the first century C.E., is based on the life, teachings, death, and Resurrection of Jesus of Nazareth, who was born in Roman Palestine approximately two thousand years ago. It the world's largest religion, with close to 2 billion followers. About one-third of the world's people claim to be Christian, and Christianity is spread over a larger geographic region than any other religion. Originating in the Mediterranean, it quickly spread to Europe, which became the center of Christianity for almost two thousand years. Today, however, the demographic center of Christianity has shifted to Latin America, Africa, and Asia. Given this geographical diversity, Christianity has become incredibly diverse and encompasses more than 22,000 separate sects and denominations. The largest divisions within Christianity are the Roman Catholic Church, the Eastern Orthodox Church, and the Protestant denominations.

The basic components of Christianity include the belief that Jesus, whose title *Christ* means "Anointed One," was the son of God, that he came to redeem humankind's sins, and that after he was crucified he was resurrected from the dead and ascended into heaven. Most Christians believe that a person has one life on earth and that after death God will judge their fate for eternity, committing them to either heaven or hell. Although different Christian groups have different ideas about concepts such as salvation, and conduct their worship services differently, all teach that the path to spiritual salvation is to accept Jesus as one's redeemer, or savior, before God.

HISTORICAL BACKGROUND

Christianity began as a movement within Judaism in the first century C.E. during the height of the Roman Empire, which at that time included areas of Europe, North Africa, and the Middle East. The Roman general Pompey annexed Palestine for Rome in 63 B.C.E. Thus, Jesus lived and preached as a Jew in Roman-occupied Palestine in a time when many Jews expected the arrival of a messiah who would liberate them from Roman oppression. During Jesus' lifetime, several Jewish groups competed for power within the Jewish community and influence with the Romans. The political climate in which Jesus carried out his mission, and ultimately his fate, was defined by these groups. They were the Sadducees, the Pharisees, and the Zealots.

The Sadducees were the most prominent of the three factions. The Jewish high religion at this time was unlike Judaism today. It was based around worship and sacrifice at the Temple in Jerusalem. The Sadducees were members of priestly families who were in charge of the Temple and wealthy merchants who were leaders of the Jewish community in Jerusalem. As community leaders they had to mediate between the Roman authorities and the Jewish population. The Sadducees were conservative in that they viewed the Torah as sacred and did not accept other books or oral traditions.

The Pharisees, on the other hand, came from all classes. While the Sadducees focused on the Temple and Temple worship, the Pharisees emphasized daily religious practice and the observance of religious laws and traditions. Though they were considered the most pious of the three groups, the Pharisees were less conservative than the Sadducees in that they accepted a wider body of Scripture and oral traditions. When the New Testament Gospels talk about Jesus debating with men in the Temple or preaching to elders in synagogues, they are describing Jesus' disputes with Sadducees and Pharisees. Although Jesus is depicted as challenging the priests in the Temple in the New Testament, the Gospels identify his chief opponents as the Pharisees.

A final faction, the Zealots, were in favor of military opposition to the Romans in Palestine. Although the notion that a messiah would appear to destroy evil and rescue the devout was common among Jews at this time, the Zealots believed that the Messiah would be a war leader who would drive the Romans from Palestine and restore the Jewish kingdom. Jews of this period believed that the Messiah would appear during a time of great oppression, and the Zealots believed that Roman rule was this time.

There are only brief mentions of Jesus and Christians in works of classical authors of the first century C.E. such as Josephus, Tacitus, and Suetonius. Most of what we know about the life of Jesus and his teachings is derived from the Gospels, the first four books of the Christian Bible—Matthew, Mark, Luke, and John.

It is not known exactly when Jesus was born. The Gospels of Matthew and Luke place his birth in Bethlehem, although some scholars suggest that he was born in or near Nazareth. The Gospel of Matthew states that the birth of Jesus occurred in the years prior to the death of Herod the Great in 4 B.C.E., while Luke describes Jesus' birth in the context of a Roman census that occurred in 6–7 C.E. The best estimate of most scholars is that Jesus was probably born between 6 and 4 B.C.E. His mother is called Mary in the Gospels, and his father is said to be a carpenter named Joseph. The Gospel of Matthew (13:55–56) mentions Jesus' brothers and sisters, but they are not discussed in any detail.

In fact, the Gospels provide virtually no information about Jesus' childhood or young adulthood until he began preaching in his late twenties.

The Gospel narratives begin to describe Jesus' life in more detail starting with his baptism by John the Baptist in the Jordan River. Roman rule in Israel had caused considerable social, economic, and political stress. Apocalyptic messages of a new world or social order were common as a result of this stress. John was a messianic prophet who preached from the Book of Isaiah in the Hebrew bible (Tanakh) and predicted the imminent arrival of the Kingdom of God. John had developed a large following in Judea, attracting large crowds and devoted disciples. He encouraged his followers to repent their sins and be spiritually purified by immersion in the Jordan River. Jesus' encounter with John, described in Mark 1, Matthew 3, and Luke 3, was a defining moment in his life and the start of his ministry.

After his baptism, Jesus went into the wilderness to fast for forty days and to contemplate his ministry. There, according to the Gospels (Mark 1, Matthew 4), Jesus was tempted by Satan to use his powers for worldly gain, but he rejected these temptations and returned to Galilee to start preaching.

The Gospels do not clearly indicate the length of Jesus' ministry. Matthew, Mark, and Luke suggest that it was just one year, capped by the visit to Jerusalem that resulted in his crucifixion. John's description of Jesus' ministry indicates that Jesus preached for a couple of years and that he visited Jerusalem several times as he traveled through the regions of Galilee and Judea.

As presented in the Gospels, Jesus' teachings were organized around a few fundamental principles. One of these centered on the themes of a loving God and kindness to others. Another central theme was the arrival of the Kingdom of God. The Gospels, however, are ambiguous on the timing of the Kingdom. They indicate both that this event was imminent and that in Jesus the Kingdom had arrived. In either event, Jesus instructed his followers to forsake material gains on earth and focus on eternal life in heaven. Jesus' message was compelling enough that he gathered a group of disciples who gave up their previous ways of life to follow him.

Jesus' disciples recognized him as the Messiah, but characters in the Gospels also call him Rabbi and Prophet. He calls himself "Son of Man," a title taken from a passage in Daniel in the Tanakh that describes a dream or vision foretelling the coming of a messiah-like figure:

> I saw in the night visions, and, behold, one like the son of man came with the clouds of heaven . . . and there was given him dominion, and glory, and a kingdom that all people, nations and languages, should serve him: his dominion is an everlasting dominion, which shall not pass away. (Daniel 7:13–14)

Jesus' ministry consisted primarily of teaching and healing. One of his most common methods of teaching was to tell parables. Parables are simple stories involving common events and situations that illustrate particular morals and principles. For example, one well-known parable is that of the prodigal son, described in Luke 15. Luke says that a group of Pharisees criticized Jesus for eating with "sinners." In answer to this, Jesus tells the story of the prodigal son: A man has two sons. The younger son asks for his inheritance, travels to a "far country" and "squanders" it. When a famine breaks out, the young man finds himself starving. He decides to return home and beg his father's forgiveness. His father welcomes him with open arms and calls for a feast to be held in his honor. The man's older son, who has dutifully remained home working for his father, resents the welcome given his younger brother and refuses to join the party. His father rebukes the elder son, saying: "It was fitting to make merry and be glad, for this your brother was dead, and is alive; he was lost, and is found." The message Jesus is delivering to his critics is that he welcomes sinners because, like the younger son, they have been lost, and by coming to Jesus they are found again.

Jesus had to walk a fine line between the Jewish authorities, and the Romans. In the end, he probably offended them both equally. A famous example of the complexity of Jesus' teachings occurred when a group of Pharisees asked him if it was lawful to pay taxes to Rome. Aware that they were trying to trick him, he asked them to bring him tax money. When they showed him the coins, Jesus asked, "Whose likeness and inscription is this?" They answered "Caesar's." Jesus answered them: "Render therefore to Caesar the things that are Caesar's, and to God the things that are God's" (Matthew 22:17–21). In the context of Roman Palestine this was a particularly ambiguous and complex response. It seems to suggest that citizens should pay taxes, but it is also true that many protesters against Roman rule insisted that nothing in Palestine belonged to Caesar because everything belonged to God. Thus, it could just as easily be interpreted as meaning that one should not pay taxes.

Some of Jesus' behaviors were radical for his time and violated Jewish standards of behavior. He touched lepers and the sick, ate with people of all social classes. Jesus also welcomed women from all walks of life in his movement, a significant departure from the patriarchal Jewish society in which he lived. Love and compassion for all were common elements in his teachings. For example, following Jewish scripture he stated that the two greatest commandments were "You should love the Lord your God with all your heart, and with all your soul, and with all your mind" and "You shall love your neighbor as yourself" (Matthew 22:37–39).

The Gospels report that Jesus performed many miracles. These included restoring sight to the blind, calming storms, restoring sanity to the insane, expelling demons, raising people from the dead, and healing the sick, lame, and paralyzed. In one famous case Jesus is said to have fed four thousand people with seven (five, in Matthew) loaves of bread and a few fish (Mark 8:1–10, Matthew 15:32–39).

According to the Gospels, the radical nature of Jesus' teachings brought him into conflict with both Jewish and Roman authorities in Palestine. The final week of his life began when he and his followers went to Jerusalem for the Passover feast. Because the Temple in Jerusalem was the center of Jewish ritual life, it was common for Jewish pilgrims to travel there for the celebration. The Gospels describe Jesus' entrance to Jerusalem as triumphant and report that he was greeted by the shouts and cries of the multitudes who accepted him (Jesus' procession into the city is now commemorated by Christians as Palm Sunday). Jesus seems to have spent his time in Jerusalem talking with his followers, teaching, and engaging in religious debates with the priests in the Temple. In one visit to the Temple, Jesus drove out those who sold animals for sacrifice, saying: "It is written, My house shall be a house of prayer; but you have made it a den of robbers" (Luke 19:46).

On Thursday evening, Jesus ate a Passover meal with his disciples, the famous Last Supper. During this meal Jesus shared bread and wine with his followers. What he is recorded as saying at this time has formed the basis of the Christian practice of Communion, the most important ritual for the majority of Christian groups. This moment is described in the Gospel of Matthew in the following way:

> Now as they were eating, Jesus took bread, and blessed, and broke it, and gave it to the disciples and said "Take, eat; this is my body." And he took a cup, and when he had given thanks he gave it to them, saying, "Drink of it, all of you; for this is my blood of the covenant, which is poured out for many for the forgiveness of sins. I tell you I shall not drink again of this fruit of the vine until that day when I drink it new with you in my Father's kingdom." (Matthew 26:26–29)

Jesus and three of his disciples then went to pray in the Garden of Gethsemane at the Mount of Olives. Jesus was betrayed by Judas, one of his disciples, and taken away by Temple guards for interrogation. On Friday morning he was questioned by Joseph Caiaphas in the Jewish high court. Jesus was asked if he was the Christ, the Son of God. His response was: "You have said so. But I tell you, hereafter you will see the Son of man seated at the right hand of power, and coming on the clouds of heaven" (Matthew 27:64). Jesus' statement was proclaimed blasphemy, punishable by death, and the next day he was handed over for trial before Pontius Pilate, the Roman procurator (governor) of Judea. According to the Gospels, Pilate asked Jesus if he was the King of the Jews. Jesus' response once again was "You have said so" (Matthew 27:11). Pilate ultimately convicted Jesus for the crime of sedition and ordered him executed. Jesus was taken to a hill and crucified on a wooden cross, a traditional form of Roman execution. According to the Gospel accounts, he was on the cross for several hours and died in the afternoon. The exact date for this event is not known, but it is believed to have occurred on a Friday, on either the 14th or 15th day of the Hebrew month of Nisin in the year 29 or 30 C.E.

Jesus' body was wrapped in a shroud and placed in the tomb of one of his wealthy followers, Joseph of Arimathea. A large stone was positioned to seal the opening. Two days later, on Sunday, some women came to the tomb to care for the body and prepare it for its proper final burial. According to the Gospels the stone had been rolled away and the tomb was empty. This is the central event in the Gospel stories, for in it lies proof of Jesus' divinity and his promise of triumph over death for those who believe in him.

The event is described differently in each Gospel. In Matthew, Mary Magdalene and Mary the mother of James went to see the tomb and were greeted by an angel who opened the tomb and told them that Jesus had risen. As the women returned to tell the disciples, Jesus met them and instructed them to tell his followers to meet him in Galilee (Matthew 28:1–10). In Mark, the women see that the tomb is open and in the tomb meet a young man dressed in a white robe who tells them that Jesus is risen and that his disciples should meet him in Galilee (Mark 16:1–8). Luke says that when the women entered the open tomb, they met two men in dazzling apparel who asked them, "Why do you seek the living among the dead?" The women returned to tell the disciples, but the disciples did not believe them until two of them encountered Jesus on the road outside of Jerusalem. When they returned to tell the disciples that they had seen Jesus, he reappeared before the assembled disciples and ate a piece of fish to prove to them he was real (Luke 24:1–43). In John 20 and 21, Mary saw two angels sitting in the tomb and then turned around and saw Jesus, although she did not recognize him at first and supposed that he was the gardener. Jesus asked her not to hold him, explaining that he had not yet "ascended to the Father" (John 20:17). Jesus appeared to the disciples later that day. In all, John says that Jesus revealed himself three times to his disciples after he was crucified, the last time in the company of Judas, who had betrayed Jesus and then in remorse committed suicide. Whatever the exact events, the Resurrection story, celebrated at Easter, has become the central feature of Christianity.

THE EARLY CHRISTIAN MOVEMENT

Although Jesus' followers despaired after the Crucifixion, stories of his Resurrection created new life for the movement. During these times, early followers struggled to derive meaning from the events of Jesus' life and place them into a framework of Jewish thought and tradition. The Gospel of Matthew, for example, opens with a recitation of Jesus' ancestry beginning with Abraham.

The stories and sightings of Jesus after his death convinced many of his followers that he was the Son of God, and they began to refer to him as the Messiah who had fulfilled biblical prophecies. Many left Jerusalem to preach in other areas of Palestine. Most Jews, however, did not accept Jesus as the Messiah, and a theological rift developed between those Jews who believed in Jesus and those who did not.

One aggressive persecutor of early followers of Jesus was a Pharisee named Saul. According to the Book of Acts (9:3–5), Saul was on his way to Damascus seeking out followers of Jesus when a voice spoke to him from a heavenly light and instructed him to carry the message of Jesus. Following this conversion experience, Saul was baptized and took the name Paul. He is perhaps the most influential and well known of the early Christian leaders. His letters, or "Epistles," were among the first documents to be widely read in early Christian churches.

Between the years 45 and 62 C.E., Paul traveled extensively through Asia Minor, Greece, and Rome, tirelessly spreading the message of the new movement. His message to Jews was that the birth, death, and Resurrection of Jesus fulfilled biblical prophecy. But more importantly, Paul was responsible for opening the "Jesus movement" to Gentiles. Before Paul, the story of a Jew claiming to be the Jewish Messiah had little impact outside of Jewish society in Palestine. As Paul spread his message that Jesus came to redeem all of humankind, and began founding churches around the Mediterranean, the movement began to grow.

The process of including non-Jews in the movement was critical to the movement's survival, but also controversial, and increasingly separated the followers of Jesus from their Jewish roots. Paul taught that Jesus' Crucifixion redeemed humankind from sin. Salvation, in Paul's view, was a gift of divine grace not achieved by moral behavior and following Mosaic law. This divergence from traditional Jewish thought created great contention among Church members, particularly James, the brother of Jesus and the head of the Jerusalem church. Paul was arrested in Jerusalem in 56 C.E., imprisoned in Caesarea for two years, then sent to Rome, where he died sometime after the year 60 C.E. Peter and James, two other critical members of this movement, died in the late 60s.

Although there was a clear division between followers of Jesus and more orthodox Jews by the end of the first century C.E., the break between early Christians and Jews was not total. Like Jews, early Christians read from the Hebrew Bible, but they discussed these Scriptures in light of their understanding of Jesus' life. They focused on passages that emphasized the coming of the Messiah and identified Jesus as the agent of salvation. The Book of Psalms was adopted into Christian worship directly from the Tanakh, and congregations discussed stories concerning the important events in the life of Jesus such as his baptism, Crucifixion, and Resurrection. These oral narratives about Jesus were written down around the end of the first century C.E. However, the collection that we know today as the New Testament was not finalized in the form familiar to contemporary Christians until near the end of the fourth century. Early Christian congregations also read the letters of Paul in their worship services.

Baptism, popularized by John the Baptist, also continued with new emphasis and form. Originally it was practiced as full immersion in the Jordan River, but as the movement grew, variations such as sprinkling or pouring water on the head of the convert became increasingly popular. However, unlike baptism today, which is practiced as an initiation into Christian life, baptism in the early Church was typically done at the end of life because it was believed to cleanse one completely of sin. Another important practice was Communion—a ritual re-creation of the last supper of Jesus with his disciples in which the congregation shares bread and wine, which Jesus referred to as his body and blood.

The structure of the Jewish/Christian Church was not clearly defined during the first century C.E. Authority within the movement was invested in the kinsmen of Jesus and those he had chosen as apostles. The church in Jerusalem was the mother church. As long as the apostles were alive, there were living, authoritative voices to answer questions about Jesus and decide theological questions.

The early followers of Jesus believed that the Kingdom of God was immediately at hand, and because of this they saw no need for a more permanent organization. However, as time passed and the first generation of leaders of the Jesus movement died, the questions of who held organizational and theological authority became more important. By the end of the first century, there developed a new interest in establishing an organizational structure for the movement, choosing a standard form of worship, and establishing canonical literature. The early churches founded by the apostles had been led by elders (Greek *presbyteroi*, "priests") or overseers (*episkopoi*, "bishops") assisted by attendants (*diakonoi*, "deacons"). These were the leaders of individual congregations and had the responsibilities of preaching and administering baptisms and the Eucharist. In this early movement, bishops were elected by their congregations, but by 100 C.E. a clear distinction between the laity and clergy had emerged. Authority was increasingly invested in the bishops of large cities. By the end of the second century, the bishop of Rome was considered to be more important than others. The supremacy of Rome rested on the assertion that Jesus had named the apostle Peter as the foundation of the church, and Peter had handed his authority to the bishops of Rome. Ultimately, the bishop of Rome was given the title *pope* and held supreme authority over the Christian Church until the great rift between eastern and western churches in 1054.

Once the problems of institutional authority within the movement had been resolved, Church leaders had to deal with problems of scriptural authority. Christians had inherited more or less without debate the Hebrew Bible as the Word of God, but this was no longer viewed as God's final Word to his people. As in Judaism, oral traditions were very important to first-century Christians. Used during services, these stories were a popular way of teaching the story of Jesus' words and actions and were probably held in higher regard than the written Word. Documents, however, provided some measure of protection against unauthorized material entering into the accepted body of tradition, and by about 150 C.E. the Gospels of Matthew, Mark, and Luke were in use in Rome. The Gospel of John was controversial and did not gain wide acceptance until later. Letters of the apostles and especially Paul's epistles were also in wide circulation by 90 C.E.

Throughout this era, Christians were viewed with suspicion and sometimes persecuted for a variety of reasons. Accusations against them included violation of Judaic social and dietary laws, revolution against Roman rule, refusal to acknowledge or participate in official Roman religious events and rituals, and sexual immorality. As the movement increased in numbers and strength, persecution of Christians also increased, although early persecutions were limited to Christians in Rome. For example, when a fire destroyed much of Rome in 64 C.E., the emperor Nero blamed Christians and killed large numbers of them as scapegoats. In another incident, Emperor Domitian (81–96 C.E.) issued an edict requiring Roman citizens to worship him as divine. Many Christians saw this as idolatry and suffered harsh punishment or death as the result of their refusal to follow this injunction. In the third century, Roman emperors ordered empire-wide persecutions, seeing Christianity as a threat to Roman authority and preservation of the empire. The emperor Diocletian (284–305 C.E.) ordered Christian churches, books, and artifacts destroyed. Despite these famous exceptions, the Roman Empire generally tolerated religious diversity; throughout most of the years under Roman rule, Christians were not persecuted.

Constantine (306–337 C.E.) was the first European emperor to openly support Christianity. His Edict of Milan, issued in the year 313, officially recognized the right of Christianity to exist, and in 325 he convened the Council of Niceae in an effort to unify church doctrine. Christianity became the official religion of the Roman Empire under the reign of Theodosius (379–395 C.E.). After this, all other religions in the empire were suppressed. By the end of the fifth century, Christianity was the faith of the majority of the peoples in the Roman Empire.

DIVISIONS IN EARLY CHRISTIANITY

One common idea about the early Christian movement was that there was a fellowship of followers all united in one set of beliefs and practices and that divisions within Christianity came later. This is not really true. From the outset, as the Christian movement gained popularity, there were theological disagreements about who Jesus was and what he taught. Marcionism and Gnosticism are two prominent examples of these early divisions.

Many bishops and theologians considered Marcionism one of the most dangerous early deviations from the Church they were fighting to establish. Marcion was reportedly the son of a bishop and raised as a Christian. He believed that it was his mission to proclaim the "truth" and began teaching his views in Rome sometime around 138 C.E. Marcion believed that the Church had twisted the gospel by including elements of Judaism. Recalling the words of Jesus that a good tree cannot bring forth evil fruit, Marcion taught that humans and the world they live in were the work of an evil being he called the Demiurge. He proposed that the laws of Judaism were created to worship this Demiurge. In contrast to the Demiurge, there was a second God hidden from humans until the appearance of Jesus. This God was a God of love. Out of mercy, seeing the miserable plight of humans, he revealed himself in Christ. The Christ, therefore, was pure spirit and not of the world created by the Demiurge. To escape the rule of the Demiurge, humans needed to have faith in God's love. Marcion's movement became very popular in Rome and lasted for several centuries before being finally extinguished by the established Church.

Though not as focused as the Marcionists, the Gnostic movement was also influential in the second century. The term *Gnostic* is derived from a Greek word *gnosis* meaning "secret knowledge." Gnostics believed that Jesus taught secret knowledge to his disciples and that a person who obtained this knowledge could develop a level of spiritual enlightenment equal to Jesus'. This claim was controversial in early Christianity because if people could become the spiritual equals of Jesus, there would be no need for priests and bishops to run churches and direct their worship—all that would be needed was a guide to the secret knowledge that Jesus had taught the apostles.

Gnostic teachers taught that Jesus was a spiritual being who appeared in different ways to different people. The author of the Gnostic manuscript *The Acts of John,* for example, wrote that Jesus never blinked or left footprints. A fundamental consequence of the notion that Jesus was a spiritual being was that he could not really have been crucified nor could he reappear in solid form. Thus, Jesus' Resurrection appearances must have been spiritual rather than material experiences. Jesus, according to the Gnostic teachings, was to be experienced by enlightened followers through dreams, visions, and trances, not encountered in some new life after death. Gnostic theologians also unsettled the established Church officials by claiming that God was a duality, both male and female. In Gnostic manuscripts God is presented as our father and mother.

Gnostics were considered heretics by orthodox Church members and great lengths were taken to suppress Gnostic teachings. These efforts were so successful that until the discovery of a collection of fifty-two Gnostic manuscripts in 1945, called the Nag Hammadi manuscripts, virtually all that scholars knew of Gnosticism was derived from the writings of second-century critics of Gnosticism. In fact, a number of Christian practices developed in reaction to Gnosticism and Marcionism. For example, the canonization of New Testament Scripture and the emphasis on the authority of bishops were early responses to the spread of Gnostic teachings and literature.

Early orthodox Christian leaders also found it necessary to convene councils to resolve theological debates and codify the basic tenets of the new faith. The first of these was the Council of Nicaea, convened by Constantine in the year 325. The councils issued official statements or creeds that clarified issues of controversy. Creeds had to be unambiguous and simple enough for followers to memorize. Perhaps the most famous of them became known as the Apostles' Creed, and appeared in its first form in about 340 C.E. The teaching of creeds became a form of pledge of allegiance to the Church. Look at the Catholic version of the Apostles' Creed, for example, and see how it is a direct refutation of elements of Gnostic Christianity and Marcionism:

> I believe in God Almighty, maker of Heaven and Earth, and in Jesus Christ, His only son, our Lord, who was conceived by the Holy Ghost, born of the Virgin Mary, suffered under Pontius Pilate, was crucified, dead, and buried; He descended into hell; the third day He rose again from the dead; He ascended into Heaven, sitteth at the right hand of God the Father Almighty; From thence He shall come to judge the living and the dead. I believe in the Holy Ghost, the Holy Catholic Church, the communion of saints, the forgiveness of sins, the resurrection of the body, and life everlasting.

To pledge that one believes that Jesus was born by Mary, crucified by Pilate, and physically resurrected contradicts the fundamental beliefs of Gnostics and Marcionists.

MONASTICISM

Along with the consolidation of Church structure and bureaucracy, by the fourth century the monastic movement was beginning to develop. Monastic disciplines began as a way of achieving spiritual purity through isolation and self-denial in order to develop a more perfect love of God. The first monks were individuals who rejected their everyday lives and moved into caves in the deserts of Syria and Egypt. They sought isolation and an ascetic lifestyle as part of their quest for spirituality.

These early desert communities were created to regulate the physical life of their members more than they were concerned with spiritual development. Basically, monasteries were places where people dedicated themselves to lives of manual labor, prayer, fasting, and, in some cases, scholarship. Some of the best minds of the medieval period were produced in monastic communities. Jerome (345?–420), for example, translated Hebrew and Greek manuscripts into Latin to create the Vulgate Bible, the Bible used in the Roman Catholic Church for almost 1,500 years.

The first great Western monastic movement, the Benedictine Order, was founded in Italy by Benedict of Nursia (c.480–c.547). Benedict was born into a wealthy Roman family but abandoned that lifestyle to live in a cave. Eventually he began to attract followers and built a monastery on the top of Monte Cassino near Rome.

Benedict created a set of rules to govern monastic life. Known collectively as the Rule of Saint Benedict, this document became the founding guide for all future Western monastic orders. Benedict's rules provide detailed instructions for the workings of a monastery, the duties of officials, the worship of God, the punishment of erring monks, and a variety of additional regulations. Every facet of monastic life is specified. The Benedictine Rule encouraged days spent in manual labor interrupted periodically for prayer. The goal was to focus the monks' lives on prayer, meditation, and spiritual contemplation that they might live a purely spiritual life dedicated to poverty, chastity, and obedience to the abbot of the monastery.

Monastic life provided several key elements in the culture of the Christian world. For example, because a monk's day depended on strictly scheduled activities, keeping track of time beyond simply noting the position of the sun became crucial and led to the development of a standardized calendar. The calendar was needed in order to synchronize the celebrations of the New Year and especially Easter throughout the Christian world. The monastic emphasis on celibacy, derived from the life of Jesus and the apostle Paul, neither of whom ever married, also popularized the notion that sexuality was not conducive to a spiritual life.

Benedictine monks spread Christianity throughout western Europe, and with the fall of the Roman Empire and Europe's descent into the Dark Ages (roughly 450–1000 C.E.), monasteries became the leading centers of philosophical thought and learning. Some of the great works of classical Greece and Rome are available to us today because European monks copied these manuscripts and preserved them in their libraries.

Numerous additional monastic orders developed in Europe. Two of these were the Franciscan Order, which was founded by Saint Francis of Assisi (1181–1226) in 1209 and is most noted for service to the needy, and the Dominican Order, founded by Domingo de Guzman (c. 1170–1221) in 1216 and noted for its missionary work. The most notable Dominican thinker was Thomas Aquinas (1225–1274), who wrote extensively on the relationship between faith and reason.

MEDIEVAL CHRISTIANITY: DIVISION BETWEEN EASTERN AND WESTERN CHURCHES

The emperor Constantine established Constantinople (also known as Byzantium and later still as Istanbul, Turkey) as the new capital of the Roman Empire in the year 330. This move led to increasing differences between the Eastern and Western portions of the Christian world. Most of the great thinkers of the early Church were from Asia Minor and North Africa, and the various councils that established official doctrine were typically held in or near Constantinople. Although the councils were convened to bring unity to the

Church, they also were tied to political issues and struggles for power. Eastern and Western Christians became bitterly divided over certain political and theological issues.

One of the largest conflicts dividing East and West was the authority of the pope in Rome. The great cities of the eastern Roman Empire all had powerful bishops known as patriarchs. Although Constantinople was the political capital of the empire, its patriarch did not have power over the patriarchs of other large cities. In the West the principal city was Rome, and the bishop of Rome, the pope, was already the leader of the Western Church. When the bishop of Rome claimed jurisdiction over all of Christendom, the Eastern patriarchs refused to accept his authority. By the fifth century, this led to schism between the Western and Eastern Churches.

The division between East and West was geographical, political, and theological. After the capital of the Roman Empire was moved to Constantinople, the Western half of the Empire continued to decline. The Western Church, centered in Rome, became an increasingly important actor in European political affairs and a center of relative stability in an area that was full of political turmoil. On the other hand, the Eastern Church, centered in Constantinople, developed in a more stable political climate. Consequently, the Eastern Church was more concerned with issues of ritual and theology than with acting as a political power broker. Further, unlike the bishop of Rome, who was always regarded as having power and authority over the bishops of the West, the patriarchs of the East were of equal status.

In addition to issues of organization and papal authority, disagreements over ritual and theology also separated East and West. For example, in the West baptism was performed by sprinkling water on the initiate; in the East this was done by immersion. Celibacy was required of priests in the West; in the East, patriarchs could marry before ordination. Finally, Latin was the language of the Western Church, whereas services were conducted in Greek in the East.

In 1054 C.E. the leaders of the two factions of East and West excommunicated each other and created a rift between the Churches that exists to this day. The official reason for the split was a disagreement over the origin of the Holy Spirit. Church scholars in the West claimed that the Holy Spirit came from both God the Father and God the Son, whereas Eastern theologians argued that it came only from the Father. The underlying reasons for the split, however, were the authority of the pope and increasing cultural differences between East and West.

REFORMATION AND RESPONSE

Starting in the 1300s and accelerating in the fifteenth century, several trends began to emerge that contributed to calls for reform of the Catholic Church. A major factor in England, for example, was the move of the papacy from Rome to Avignon, France, from 1309 to 1417. France was England's hereditary enemy, and the English crown and church refused to support a French pope who was a puppet of the King of France. Other factors that challenged Church dominance were the emergence of autonomous states that claimed jurisdiction over the appointment of Church authorities, increasing literacy rates, a strong popular desire to read the Bible in the vernacular, and the emergence of a middle class that challenged the old feudal order. Additionally, it was widely believed that the Church was corrupt. Some factors that fueled this belief were the scriptural ignorance of the clergy, political maneuvering by Church authorities, and particularly the sale of indulgences.

In Catholic doctrine, the souls of those who are not unsalvageably evil go to purgatory, after death, where they are punished for their sins and perform acts of penance to purify themselves for eventual entry into heaven. To shorten time in purgatory for themselves (or in some cases, for those who are already there), Catholics can be granted indulgences for prayers and acts which are officially recognized by higher level church officials—pope, cardinals, archbishops, and bishops. Properly, indulgences were to be granted with the authority of the church for great acts of piety or specific deeds. In reality, in the late Middle Ages, the selling of indulgences had become a major profit-making business for Church officials and the trade in indulgences was widely viewed as an example of the corruption of the Church.

The foundation for the Protestant Reformation was laid by John Wycliffe (1328–1384), an English priest and Oxford professor of theology. His work influenced virtually every reform movement of the fifteenth and sixteenth centuries. Wycliffe was not a social reformer, but he believed fervently in the authority of the Gospels. The official position of the Catholic Church was that Scripture was not directly accessible to people but rather had to be interpreted by Church authorities. Further, they insisted that Church traditions such as papal infallibility and the veneration of saints held equal doctrinal standing with the Gospels. Wycliffe rejected these ideas, arguing fervently for the right of all people to read and interpret the Bible, and he opposed any Church doctrine or ritual practice that did not have a scriptural basis.

Wycliffe was not unique in this regard. Others before him, such as Willam of Ockham, had emphasized the authority of Scripture, but Wycliffe's focus was different. In Wycliffe's day, Bible reading was rare, even among the clergy. Few Bibles were available for public use, and those in circulation were in Latin. To make scripture available to all who could read it, Wycliffe risked his life and career to champion an English translation of the Bible. He argued that because Christ and the apostles had taught people in their own languages, it was appropriate to translate Scripture, and he was involved in the preparation of the first English Bible by 1380.

Wycliffe's ideas flourished at Oxford and his students spread his doctrine across Europe. One of the most famous of those influenced by Wycliffe was a Czech priest named Jan Hus (1369–1415). Hus was born at Husinetz in southern

Bohemia in 1369 and was ordained a priest in 1400. Although much of Wycliffe's work was banned by Church authorities, Hus translated Wycliffe's work into Czech and helped distribute it. Hus was an ardent reformer and publically commented on the corruption of the Church from his pulpit. Eventually, he was called to account for his support of Wycliffe's work, with the result that in 1409 Pope Alexander V forbade him from preaching and directed that Wycliffe's writings be burned. Hus protested these measures and was excommunicated on July 16, 1410. In November 1414 the Council of Constance was assembled and Hus was called to give an account of his doctrine. At Constance he was tried and condemned. He was to be burnt at the stake on July 6, 1415. This same council also condemned the work of Wycliffe, declared him a heretic, and ordered that his bones be removed from consecrated ground. In 1428, Wycliffe's remains were disinterred and burned, and the ashes were poured into the river Swift.

Although the ideas of Wycliffe and Hus were symptomatic of deep divisions within the Catholic Church, these divisions did not cause the breakup of the Church until a century later. The two people most closely associated with the Reformation of the sixteenth century were Martin Luther (1483–1546) and John Calvin (1509–1564). The English monarch Henry VIII also played a critical role.

Luther was born in Eisleben, Germany. He was the son of a miner, but despite this modest background he attended the Latin School in Mansfeld starting in 1488. In 1501, he began studying to become a lawyer. In 1505, however, he decided to enter the Augustinian monastery in Erfurt and was later ordained a Catholic priest. In the course of his studies, Luther became disenchanted with the fund-raising activities of the Church, especially the selling of indulgences, the purchase of masses for the dead to buy them merit in purgatory, and the commerce in saints' relics. In particular, Luther was troubled by the notion that one could buy spiritual salvation. His own belief was that God, through Jesus, offered salvation to sinners by his grace alone. He could find no scriptural basis for the notion that good works or the ritualized graces offered by the Catholic Church could earn a person salvation. As far as Luther was concerned, good works were the result of the flowering of faith, not the means by which a person bought salvation.

In 1517 Luther challenged the religious community to discuss these issues by nailing 95 points of debate (known as the 95 theses) on his church door in Wittenburg, Germany. In addition to questioning the sale of indulgences, Luther also questioned other aspects of Catholic doctrine, including the concept of transubstantiation, the extensive use of relics, and any other practice that was not specifically sanctioned by Scripture. Luther rejected the authority of the pope, bishops, and priests as intermediaries between the laity and God, and believed that any Christian could intercede with God on behalf of another. This doctrine was called the "priesthood of all believers." However, over time the phrase came to signify the Protestant view that clergy and laity were equal before God and that anyone who could read and interpret Scripture had the same authority as a priest.

Luther intended to raise important questions for public debate within the Catholic Church, not to separate from it. However, his criticisms led to the start of a court of inquisition, culminating in Luther's excommunication in 1521. Luther finalized the break with his clerical vows when he married the former nun Katharina von Bora in June 1525.

Although Luther was excommunicated, his statements and call for debate were widely read and quickly gained support. Many people supported Luther's reforms for religious reasons, but European rulers were also aware that a break with the Catholic Church would give them greater independence and that confiscating Church lands would give them greater wealth. These factors heightened the speed of the Reformation. The reform movement resulted in a split in the Western Church into the Roman Catholic Church and the first Protestant denominations.

John Calvin (1509–1564) (this is the Latinized form of his birth name, Jean Cauvin) was born to an upper-middle-class family in France. Before emerging as one of the preeminent figures of the Reformation, Calvin studied for the priesthood and showed an early inclination to pursue the study of Greek and Hebrew. However, exposed to the ideas of Luther while he was in Paris, Calvin became a reformer by 1533. On November 1, 1533, he delivered a speech in which he attacked the established Church and called for reforms. Rather than bringing about the reforms he sought, Calvin's speeches elicited a wave of anti-Protestant sentiment that forced him to flee France for his own safety. During the next few years, he sought refuge in various cities, but eventually settled in Geneva, Switzerland, a center of reformist thought.

Calvin's theology influenced many Protestant denominations. The principal tenets of Calvinism include a belief in the primacy of Scripture as an authority for doctrinal decisions, a belief in predestination, insistence that salvation is wholly accomplished through God's grace with no influence from good works, and a rejection of the Catholic Church hierarchy. Calvin believed that true Christianity had been corrupted by centuries of Church tradition, and he wrote a series of works that played a large role in shaping Protestantism. The fact that many of his writings emphasize education, hard work, and a frugal existence made his beliefs popular with the rising European middle class.

One of the principal ideas associated with Calvin is the concept of predestination. The Catholic Church taught that belief, good actions, and receiving the sacraments earn one God's grace. Following Luther, Calvin argued that human actions are insufficient to earn God's grace and the kingdom of heaven. Calvin believed that time is meaningless to God and that God knows all things. Consequently, whether an individual is to be granted admission to heaven or condemned to hell is known to God before their birth and not dependent on any actions that person might take in their life. For Calvin, a person's good works are a result of living a life of faith, not the ticket by which one gains entry into heaven. Even though the belief in predestination played an important role in the history of Protestantism, very few Protestant churches subscribe to it today.

Like Wycliffe and Luther, Calvin argued that the Bible is the ultimate authority in matters of faith and that power to interpret it lies with individuals, not with the priesthood. Thus, he denied the authority of the pope and other Catholic officials. Some movements that emerged out of Calvinism include the Presbyterian, Reformed, and Congregational Churches, and the Puritan movements in England and America.

The Reformation in England followed a slightly different path and achieved a different outcome. The Church of England, or Anglican Church, had its beginnings in 1533 when King Henry VIII pressured Parliament into naming him the head of the Catholic Church in England. This allowed Henry to appoint his own bishops, usurping the power of the pope. Henry's actions were taken in response to the pope's refusal to grant an annulment of his marriage to Catherine of Aragon. Henry was smitten with Catherine's lady in waiting, Anne Boleyn, and angry that Catherine had not born a male heir. The king requested an annulment on the grounds that his marriage to Catherine was invalid because she was his older brother Arthur's widow (when Arthur died prematurely, Henry had inherited both the throne and a queen). When the pope refused, Henry appointed his own bishop of Canterbury, Thomas Cranmer. Cranmer annulled Henry's marriage, and Henry and Anne Boleyn were secretly married in January 1533. Boleyn subsequently bore him a daughter, who became Queen Elizabeth the First (reigned 1559–1603).

Henry's actions set off a long battle between Catholics and reformers in England that lasted through the reign of Henry's daughter Elizabeth. The Anglican Church, which kept much of the ritual and structure of the Catholic Church but broke from Rome on important issues such as the authority of the pope and translating the Bible into English, was the result of this conflict.

Although many people left the Roman Catholic Church and became Protestants, many Catholics also sought reform but had no desire to leave the Church. The Council of Trent was convened in 1545 to deal with this call for reform. At Trent, the Catholic Church reaffirmed its position on a variety of issues. Seven sacraments were officially sanctioned: baptism, confirmation, communion, penance, marriage, last rites, and devotion to Holy orders. The Council also declared that salvation comes through faith, the veneration of saints, images, and relics, acts of mercy, and participation in the sacraments. Additionally, the Church claimed for itself the right to interpret Scripture and decreed that both Scripture and Church traditions were truths to guide the faithful.

The Catholic Church also reaffirmed its position on transubstantiation—the doctrine that the Communion wine and wafer literally transform into the blood and body of Christ during the rite of Communion. Also during this time, Ignatius Loyola started the Society of Jesus, or Jesuits, a militant missionary order known as the "soldiers of Christ." Jesuits played a key role in Catholic education and missionary work in the sixteenth and seventeenth centuries.

Once the Protestant reform movement was under way, it almost immediately began to fragment into several forms. The concept of the priesthood of all believers, in which anyone could interpret Scripture, played a key role in this process, which continues today. Within one hundred years after Luther's challenge to the Catholic Church, a variety of radical reform groups had emerged, each with its own view of what religious practices are sanctioned by Scripture. Many of these groups were persecuted, and some were declared illegal. For example, Puritans were persecuted by the Church of England.

The Anabaptists were one of the most notable radical groups. The ritual of baptism was a key flashpoint for some Church reformers. Catholics and most Protestants practice infant baptism. They baptize by sprinkling water on the heads of infants born to church members. Anabaptists rejected this form of baptism as having no scriptural basis. They practiced only full-immersion baptism with adults. In England and America the Baptists, Mennonites, Amish, and Hutterites are groups that derive from the Anabaptist tradition.

Increasing autonomy, nationalism, and political change accompanied the spread of Protestantism in Europe, and all of these factors helped fuel the break from Rome among the emerging European nations. In northern Europe, several variations of Protestantism emerged, eventually producing hundreds of denominations. In Catholic France, for example, the Huguenots were one of the Protestant groups that appeared in the 1500s. In Scotland a Protestant movement emerged under the leadership of John Knox in 1559 and eventually became the Presbyterian Church. Many European countries endorsed specific forms of Protestantism. For example, Sweden, Denmark, Norway, and most of Germany became Lutheran.

The founder of the Methodist movement was an Anglican preacher named John Wesley (1703–1791). This movement emerged in England in the mid eighteenth century and was popular among middle and lower classes. Methodist preachers traveled a "circuit" carrying the message to followers who were arranged into congregations called societies. It was not Wesley's intention to separate from the Church of England, but shortly after his death the movement formally separated from the Anglican Church over differences in doctrine. The Methodist movement also became popular in North America as English settlers moved westward.

British colonialism played a role in spreading many of the Protestant movements that had emerged from the Church of England. Some, such as the Nonconformists and Dissenters, left England to avoid persecution. The British Puritan movement of the late sixteenth century was of particular importance in the colonial history of the United States. The Puritans wanted to go further than the Church of England in separating themselves from the Catholic Church. They were called Puritans because they wanted to "purify" the Anglican Church of what they called "papist influence." Heavily influenced by the work of Wycliffe and Calvin, Puritans emphasized predestination, the authority of Scripture, and the importance of personal morality. Additionally, they wanted increased participation in Church leadership and to take away the power of the bishops who had control of the Anglican Church. The Puritans separated themselves from the Church of England to pursue their vision of a purified form of Christianity. One of these groups was the Pilgrims who emigrated to the Americas and founded Plymouth Colony in 1620. Eventually, these "Congregationalists" became the dominant group in the northern American colonies.

There was a great deal of social, political, and religious strife in England during the 1600s. In general, the middle class was Puritan and the upper-class gentry supported the Church of England. Ultimately, the Church of England was reestablished as the dominant religion and most of the radical movements disappeared. One that survived was the Society of Friends, or Quakers, founded by George Fox in 1648. The Quakers were controversial because they emphasized inward reflection and prayer and the equality of men and women, and generally did not participate in baptism and communion. Even today, Quaker worship services are often silent unless someone is moved to speak or pray out loud.

While much of Northern Europe adopted Protestant reform movements, Italy, France, Portugal, and Spain remained Roman Catholic and, through conquest, exported Catholicism to Mexico and Central and South America. It took a long time for the Catholic Church to come to terms with the Protestant movements. The Council of Trent defined Roman Catholic doctrine for centuries. However, by the mid twentieth century, it was evident to many in the Catholic leadership that reforms were needed to modernize the Church. Pope John XXIII convened the Second Vatican Council (often known as Vatican II) between 1962 and 1965. This council introduced a variety of reforms that were considered radical for their time and which many Catholics continue to debate. For example, throughout the history of the Roman Catholic Church mass had been conducted in Latin. The Second Vatican Council authorized the printing of Bibles in a variety of languages and gave permission for masses to be conducted in the native language of the congregation. Greater participation from the congregation was also encouraged, and there were attempts to reestablish bonds with other Christian groups. The Protestant and Eastern Orthodox Churches were recognized as other forms of true Christianity. The Council also acknowledged respect for other religions such as Judaism, Hinduism, Buddhism, and Islam, and officially declared that Jews were not responsible for the death of Jesus.

SACRED LITERATURE

Christian literature is composed of the Old and New Testaments. The Old Testament is the Tanakh, or the Hebrew Bible (see section 15). The New Testament is composed of twenty-seven works. First are the Gospels of Matthew, Mark, Luke, and John, which record the events in Jesus' ministry. The first three of these were written between 65 and 85 C.E., forty to fifty years after Jesus' death. Mark was the earliest, the first attempt to put the oral traditions about Jesus down in narrative form. The authors of Matthew and Luke borrow heavily from the account set down by the author of Mark. Because they are so similar, these first three Gospels, which all focus on the life and teachings of Jesus, are called the synoptic Gospels. The Gospel of John is believed to have been written slightly later, sometime between 90 and 100 C.E., and is quite different from the others. It deals with the relationship between Jesus and God, emphasizing that Jesus is the Son of God and the incarnation of God on earth.

The Gospels are followed by the Acts of the Apostles, written by the same author as the Gospel of Luke. Acts discusses the activities of the apostles after the execution of Jesus. In particular, just as the Gospel of Luke depicts Jesus' inescapable movement toward crucifixion in Jerusalem, Acts depicts Paul in a similar journey to sacrifice in Rome. Following Acts are the Epistles, letters written by Paul and other disciples. The Epistles are divided into two sets: the Pauline Epistles, whose authorship is attributed to Paul, and the catholic or "universal" Epistles addressed to all believers in Jesus. The Pauline letters were among the earliest documents shared by followers of Jesus. Some were written between 50 and 60 C.E.

The final piece in the New Testament is Revelation. Written around 100 C.E., Revelation depicts a series of visions in which evil and suffering are ultimately defeated by goodness. The language of Revelation is deliberately obscure, using a symbolism of numbers and images whose meaning may have been clear to early Christians but disguised from nonbelievers. However ambiguous, images such as the visions of heaven and the Four Horsemen of the Apocalypse have become common in Christian art and literature.

CHRISTIAN HOLIDAYS

The birth, death, and Resurrection of Jesus are central features of all forms of Christianity and are recognized in the celebrations of Christmas and Easter.

Christmas is a festival that celebrates the birth of Jesus. The date of his birth is not exactly known, and the earliest recorded celebration of Christmas was in December 326 C.E. One of the great Roman festivals was a harvest celebration, called the Saturnalia, that coincided with the winter solstice and was celebrated in late December. Pagan populations in Europe had mid-December harvest celebrations that included gift giving and decorations of greenery. The placement of and celebration of Christmas in December played an important role in displacing these non-Christian celebrations and practices.

Notions of Santa Claus and gift giving combine the gifting of European harvest festivals and veneration of Saint

Nicholas, a bishop of the fourth century known for his kindness and generosity. Christmas was one of the last Christian celebrations established. Today it is the most popular and widespread Christian festival, although Puritan groups of the American colonies and some sects today such as Jehovah's Witnesses rejected it as a pagan practice without scriptural basis. Additionally, the Eastern Orthodox churches do not celebrate Christmas. On January 6, Orthodox Christians celebrate Epiphany, or the day on which the baby Jesus was visited by the three Magi.

Easter is the commemoration of the Resurrection of Jesus. Easter is celebrated on the first Sunday after the first full moon following the spring equinox on March 21. Consequently, Easter falls between March 22 and April 25. Easter is a celebration of new life and coincides with many non-Christian rituals of spring. Some scholars suggest that the word *Easter* comes from the old English word *Eastre,* which may have been the name of a pagan goddess of spring or the name for the spring season. Some Eastern Orthodox Christians refer to Easter as Pascha, from the Hebrew word *Pesach,* or Passover. Easter coincides with the Jewish celebration because Jesus had come to Jerusalem for Passover. Thus the timing of the festival that commemorates his death and Resurrection is necessarily linked to that holiday.

Some Christians, particularly Catholics, Anglicans, and Episcopalians, observe Lent, a period of repentance and fasting that occurs during the forty days before Easter. This is a time of penance, and many observe a fast that limits the types or amount of food they consume. The observance of Lent is modeled after the period of forty days that Jesus spent in the wilderness after his baptism. Catholics and churches originating in western Europe generally mark the beginning of Lent with an Ash Wednesday service in which a priest traces a cross in ash on the foreheads of the faithful. In the Eastern Orthodox Church, Lent begins on the Monday before Ash Wednesday.

The last week of Lent is called Holy Week and is important in many parts of the Christian world, especially Latin America. The first day of Holy Week is Palm Sunday. This commemorates Jesus' entry into Jerusalem. The following Friday, Good Friday, commemorates the death of Jesus on the cross. Holy Week ends with Easter Sunday, a celebration of Jesus' rising from the dead.

Pentecost, which occurs fifty days after the Jewish Passover, commemorates a day described in the Book of Acts, when Jesus' followers were filled with the Holy Spirit and spoke in languages unknown to them. Christians celebrate the Day of Pentecost as the birth of the Christian Church, and in early Church practice it was the occasion for the baptism of new Church members.

Two feasts that are particularly important in the Eastern Orthodox Church are the Transfiguration and Assumption. The Transfiguration commemorates an event described in Mark 9, Matthew 17, and Luke 9. According to these Gospels, Jesus took three of his disciples to a mountain where he appeared to them bathed in light alongside Moses and Elijah. Thus, he was transfigured, revealing his divinity to them.

The Assumption of Mary is celebrated by Roman Catholics and members of the Eastern Orthodox Church. This feast celebrates Mary's acceptance into heaven after her death. There is no explicit mention of the Assumption in the New Testament, therefore most Protestant groups do not celebrate this holiday.

CHRISTIANITY TODAY

Christianity today can be divided into three main groups: Roman Catholic, Eastern Orthodox, and Protestants. Much of this essay has discussed the development of the Roman Catholic and Protestant churches, but the Eastern Orthodox Church has an equally long and complex history. Today there are fifteen self-governing Orthodox churches worldwide, each with its own leader known as a patriarch or archbishop. The Orthodox Church is composed of the Patriarchate of Constantinople, the Patriarchate of Alexandria, the Patriarchate of Antioch, the Patriarchate of Jerusalem, and a group of self-governing local churches in Russia, Serbia, Rumania, Bulgaria, Georgia, Cyprus, Greece, Poland, Albania, Finland, and the Czech Republic. The majority of Eastern Orthodox Christians live in Russia, Eastern Europe, Greece, and the Middle East.

The word *orthodox* means "correct or right belief," and over the last millennium the Orthodox churches have attempted to preserve what they believe to be the earliest form of Christianity. All fifteen church organizations within the Eastern Orthodox Church are autonomous and led by their own patriarch. There is no Orthodox pope, although the patriarch of Constantinople is the titular head of the Church. All churches are united in doctrine and sacramental observances. Any change that will affect all churches must be decided by a synod, a council of Church officials who work to reach a consensus on issues affecting the Church.

In addition to the Bible, devout Orthodox Christians study the writings of the saints of the Church. An important practice is "unceasing prayer"—the continual remembrance of God through the constant repetition of prayers. Orthodox Christians believe that the repetition of the name of Jesus brings purification of the heart and allows one to experience his presence in all things.

Another distinctive feature of Orthodox Christianity is its veneration of icons. These are paintings of Jesus, his mother Mary, and the saints. Icons are viewed as windows to the eternal, and some are reported to have great spiritual powers. Believers tap into this power by kissing the icon and praying before it.

In general, Eastern Orthodox beliefs are similar to those in Western Christianity, but the Orthodox Church has a different focus. In the West, there is an emphasis on the death of Jesus as an atonement for sin. Orthodox Christianity places more emphasis on the mystical relationship that one can experience with Christ.

The term *Protestant* refers to all non–Roman Catholic and non–Eastern Orthodox churches that originated in the sixteenth-century Reformation in Western Europe. Although the Protestant churches form a diverse collection, from the Anglican Church to silent Quaker meetings to Pentecostal groups whose members speak in tongues during services, certain themes are found in virtually all the Protestant groups. With the exception of the Anglican Church, Protestants emphasize the authority of Scripture over Church doctrine. Anglicans, like Catholics, give Church doctrine and traditions equal weight with Scripture, and believe that the Bible must be interpreted within the heritage of the Church. Although Protestants base their beliefs on biblical authority, there is disagreement over liberal and Fundamentalist interpretations of the Bible. Fundamentalists tend to take a literal interpretation of the Bible and events such as the virgin birth and miracles of Jesus, whereas liberal Protestants tend to interpret the Bible in terms of current scientific and historical knowledge.

Whether liberal or Fundamentalist, all Protestant groups place a strong emphasis on the belief that the one path to salvation is faith in God and accepting his Son Jesus as one's personal savior. Catholics, of course, also stress faith, but one must also participate in the sacraments, such as baptism and Communion, administered by a priest, to earn spiritual merit.

From the formal services of Episcopalians to the "holy rolling" of Pentecostal churches, mainstream Protestant denominations have developed a strong membership in the United States. There are more than 9 million Methodists, 7 million Lutherans, 4 million Presbyterians, and 2.5 million Episcopalians. Baptists are the largest block of American Protestants, and Southern Baptists are the largest division within the Baptist Church, with about 16 million members. In comparison, there are roughly 60 million Roman Catholics in the United States today, and about 2 million members of the Eastern Orthodox churches.

Among the most important trends in Christianity today are the increase in the total number of Christians and the increase in the percentage of Christians who live in the economically poor nations of Latin America, Africa, and Asia. By 2025, the world's population of Christians is expected to increase by more than half a billion, to more than 2.6 billion. Additionally, by that time more than 65 percent of the world's Christians (and 75 percent of the world's Catholics) will live in Latin America, Africa, and Asia.[1] This historical shift in population will have important consequences for Christianity. Historically, the Christian churches have been dominated by Europeans and North Americans. In the past half century, most of these churches have become more liberal, more inclusive, and more tolerant. There are certainly exceptions, but in general the churches in Latin America, Africa, and Asia have not followed these trends. Today,

these are some of the most conservative Christian groups. This implies that although Christians might be by far the most numerous group in the twenty-first century, they are also likely to be one of the most deeply divided groups. It remains to be seen how large religious organizations such as the Catholic and Anglican Churches will manage the increasingly deep divides between their liberal and conservative members.

NEW DENOMINATIONS AND CHRISTIAN FUNDAMENTALISM IN AMERICA

The sixteenth-century Protestants' focus on individual spiritual experience and the personal interpretation of Scripture encouraged the rise of many different denominations in the last five hundred years, and this process has continued to flourish in the United States. In America, the nineteenth century in particular was a time of tremendous religious creativity. For example, the Seventh-Day Adventist movement was founded in the 1840s by William Miller. Based on personal calculations derived from his study of the Bible, Miller predicted that Christ was going to return in 1843. He was convincing enough to enlist the aid of local ministers, and he traveled through the northeastern United States publicizing his viewpoint. When 1843 passed without the promised event, Miller reviewed his calculations, found several errors, and promised that October 24, 1844, was the real date for Christ's return. Despite the failure of his second prediction, Miller's movement continued to grow and Adventist congregations began to spring up in many states. Today there are more than 700,000 members of the Seventh-Day Adventist Church who believe that Jesus' return is imminent and who strive to keep a variety of the Old Testament laws, including holding services on Saturday, the Jewish day of worship.

Perhaps the best-documented religion to arise in the United States is the Church of Jesus Christ of Latter-day Saints, or Mormons, founded by Joseph Smith in the 1820s in New York state. Smith claimed that an angel had led him to golden plates buried near his home. After his discovery Smith spent two years translating the script on the plates (which he claimed was "reformed Egyptian") with the help of two "translation stones." Smith did not let anyone else see the plates while he was working, including his wife, who transcribed his translations from one side of a curtained partition while Smith dictated from the other. His Book of Mormon, published in 1830, was intended to supplement the Bible and announce God's most recent revelations. The Book of Mormon claims that a tribe of Israelites sailed to the Americas in 600 B.C.E. and built a new civilization. Jesus Christ visited these people after his Resurrection and organized a new church. But this Israelite community was torn by internal strife, and one group, the Lamanites, who were hunters and the ancestors of Native Americans, defeated the other faction, the Nephites, who were peaceful farmers. The last Nephite prophet was Mormon, who wrote his account of the history of the Israelites on golden tablets and gave them to his son Moroni. Moroni buried the plates, leaving them to be discovered by a man who could restore this true church. It was the angel Moroni who revealed the location of the tablets to Joseph Smith. The Latter Day Saints follow these revelations as set down by Smith.

The Mormons have a colorful history. Smith first moved his small band of followers to Ohio in 1831. Local hostility led to a move to Missouri, and in 1838 a third move to Illinois where the group settled in a town they named Nauvoo. Smith continued to receive revelations, including the command, in 1843, that God wanted men to have more than one wife. Nauvoo grew quickly into a prosperous community, and Smith declared himself King of the Kingdom of God, but his rule was short-lived—Smith was lynched by a mob on June 27, 1844. Smith's death led to a split in the movement, and some of his followers, along with members of his family, returned to Missouri. However, the majority of the group continued west under the leadership of Brigham Young. In 1849 they finally established their headquarters on the Great Salt Lake in what is today the State of Utah.

The Church of Latter-day Saints is now an international movement with around 8 million followers, most of whom live in the United States. The center of Mormon activity is still Salt Lake City, where a group of elderly men, called the Quorum of Twelve Apostles, manages the Church. The senior-most apostle is the Church's president, who still directs Church affairs through revelations from God. Mormons attend local chapels, which hold Sunday services. Rituals held in larger temples are kept secret from non-Mormons.

Mormons attach great importance to history, for two reasons. First, they believe that they can save the souls of deceased persons. Following one of Smith's original revelations, ancestors of present-day Mormons can be baptized into the Church with living persons standing in as a substitute for the dead. However, one must first establish a biological connection between the dead individual and a living Mormon: thus Mormons keep extensive genealogical records.

Second, history is part of the Church's claim to authority. The Mormons see themselves as the direct inheritors of God's latest messages to humankind through the tablets found by Joseph Smith and their Church leader's continuing revelations. This view of the world is based on the story of the Israelites' fleeing from Jerusalem, founding a civilization in the New World, seeing Christ, and establishing a new, "pure" Church. Although the Israelites were destroyed, they left the record of their history for Joseph Smith, the latter-day prophet, through whom God once again communicated with his people. It is Mormon history, therefore, that provides the rationale for accepting Joseph Smith as an authentic prophet. One implication of this understanding of history is that Native Americans as descendants of the Lamanites have special status. They are entitled to convert and become full members of the Church, a privilege that has only recently been granted to African Americans.

As discussed earlier, one arena of conflict between sixteenth-century Catholics and Protestants was that the Protestant rejection of doctrines or practices, such as the authority of the pope, that did not have a biblical justification. One result of this emphasis on Scripture was that many Protestant movements came to believe in biblical inerrancy— that the Bible cannot be wrong. However, with the advance of scientific knowledge in the nineteenth and twentieth centuries, the historical accuracy of many biblical stories and the relevance of specific laws, particularly those in the Hebrew Bible, were increasingly questioned. The older and more established Protestant denominations generally took a less literal interpretation of the Bible and tried to accommodate their teachings to changes in culture and knowledge. For example, Catholics and most Protestant denominations accept the biological work of Charles Darwin on the evolution of species. However, a variety of Christian movements have sprung up in the last century that have challenged the established denominations and demanded a return to what they believe are the fundamentals of Christian faith. Together these movements constitute the *Fundamentalism* movement.

One of the fastest-growing waves of fundamentalism is the Pentecostal movement, which began in Los Angeles in the early 1900s. A number of churches have grown out of the Pentecostal movement, including the Church of God, the Assemblies of God, and the Pentecostal Holiness Church. Pentecostal churches take their name from the day of Pentecost, described in Acts 2. On that day, according to the Book of Acts, Jesus' followers were visited by the Holy Spirit and manifested the ability to speak in languages unknown to them. Members of Pentecostal churches emphasize the expression of biblical "signs," such as speaking in tongues and faith healing, and believe in possession by the Holy Spirit.

Pentecostals rely more on lay clergy than on the seminary-trained professional priesthood of the established Protestant denominations, and they are biblical literalists. Some Holiness Churches in Tennessee and West Virginia, for example, refer to Mark 16:17–18 as justification for handling venomous snakes and drinking poison during their services. The fact that most church members can accomplish these feats without harm gives them an intense religious experience and, in their view, provides a demonstration of God's power.

For worshipers in Pentecostal churches, a service provides an opportunity to come into contact with the Holy Spirit. It is an intense and personal experience, which is one reason the Pentecostal movement has grown so quickly. However, it is precisely this emphasis on individual experience and the preaching of lay members that makes a general summary of the Pentecostal movement difficult. Any person who feels the inspiration can preach based on their individual reading of the Bible. Additionally, because of the focus on individual inspiration, virtually any person can decide to create their own church. There are thousands of such small churches in the United States. They are organized around the preaching and inspirational leadership of charismatic individuals who are able to build small local followings. Many of them meet in church members' homes to worship, home-school their children, and restrict much of their social interaction to the other members of their church.

Despite their inward focus, Christian Fundamentalists have become a powerful political force in the United States through organizations such as the Moral Majority. Because Fundamentalists believe that the United States should be a Christian society based on biblical principles, they have waged war on what they perceive as a tide of liberalism and secularism in American society. The battlegrounds have been issues such as the teaching of evolutionary theory in textbooks, school prayer, abortion, and the gay rights movement.

Starting as a small movement in ancient Palestine, Christianity has lasted two thousand years and spread all around the world. Christianity exists in the poorest countries and the richest. It has been used as an excuse for war and has stood firm as a force for peace. The diversity of belief and practices found among its millions of members makes it a vibrant and conflicted force in the world today.

NOTE

1. Philip Jenkins, "The Next Christianity," *Atlantic Monthly,* October 2002, 53–68.

17

Islam

Islam is the youngest of the three religions of the Judaeo-Christian and Islamic tradition. Its origins date to the life of Muhammad, 570–632 C.E. Islam developed in a social context that included Christian and Jewish communities as well as many people practicing traditional Arab religions. Islam incorporates the sacred writings and many of the beliefs of these communities. In addition, the development of Islam was strongly conditioned by Zoroastrianism, an ancient Persian religion that emphasized worship of a supreme god and portrayed the world as a battleground between good and evil.

A critical thing distinguishing Islam from Christianity and Judaism is its emphasis on the life and teaching of Muhammad. Muslims believe that biblical figures such as Abraham, Moses, the prophets, and Jesus received authentic communication from God, and that, as a result, the religious beliefs (and persons) of Jews and Christians are to be generally respected—they are "people of the Book." However, Muslims insist that the revelations contained in Jewish and Christian Bibles are incomplete, and that only through Muhammad was God's full revelation heard by humankind. Therefore, the words of Muhammad, contained in the sacred Qur'an, and the traditions surrounding him, referred to as the *Hadiths,* supersede all earlier revelations. Because of the centrality of Muhammad in Islamic belief and life, this account of Islam starts with his life.

THE LIFE OF MUHAMMAD

Muhammad was born to a powerful family in 570 in the Arabian city of Mecca. His grandfather seems to have occupied an important position among the *Quraysh,* the tribe that dominated social and political life in that city. Orphaned at a very early age, Muhammad was raised by his relatives and, though the reputation of his family was strong, his childhood was relatively impoverished.

The Mecca of Muhammad's childhood was a thriving center of commerce and religion. Pilgrims, members of various pre-Islamic religious traditions, came to see the Black Stone of Mecca. The Black Stone has been shown to be a meteorite, but many stories, legends, and beliefs have grown around it. By Muhammad's time, the Kaaba, a square shrine, had already been built around the Black Stone and filled with images of tribal gods. Pilgrims visited Mecca to give devotion to both the stone itself and these images. In addition to the Black Stone, there were several other holy sites in the city.

At the age of 25, Muhammad went to work as a caravan driver for a prosperous widow, Khadijah. Though Khadijah was about fifteen years older than he, they eventually married. Of their children, only one, Fatima, survived to adult-hood. But she was to play a critical role in the development of Islam after Muhammad's death.

As a merchant, Muhammad traveled throughout Arabia and was exposed to the religious communities and controversies of his era. These seem to have made a deep impression on him and drawn him to the possibility of a religion that would reconcile the differences among competing interpretations of God. At the age of 40, he began to spend long periods in solitary meditation, often traveling into the wilderness seeking spiritual guidance. In 611, Muhammad began to experience revelations. A darkness would overcome him, followed by a bright illuminating presence which he interpreted as the angel Gabriel. The presence repeatedly commanded Muhammad to "recite" the words given to him. These visions, and the recitations they produced, were to continue for the remainder of Muhammad's life.

In the context of Muhammad's revelations, the use of the word *recite* is extremely important. Muhammad understood the words to come directly from God. He was simply reciting a text that was outside of himself and had been given to him. Muslims believe that the words Muhammad spoke were the words of God, with no interpretation or alteration. Because they came from God, the words themselves are sacred.

Though Muhammad at first doubted his own revelation, he was convinced of its veracity by his wife Khadijah and other family members. The word *Muslim* means "one who submits [to God]." Thus, the members of Muhammad's family became the first Muslims.

Muhammad remained at Mecca and continued to proclaim his revelations. He gained converts, but his message also aroused strong opposition. His insistence that all prayer should be directed at a single, all-powerful God disturbed many powerful interests. Much Meccan wealth depended on commerce generated by pilgrimage. Muhammad's insistence that prayers to the idols in the Kaaba were wrong not only contradicted the beliefs of many, but attacked the source of their wealth as well. As a result, Muhammad and his followers were persecuted. By 615, some of his followers had fled for their lives. Problems for Muhammad increased with the death of his wife and uncle in 619, as he lost much of the political protection they had provided.

It was at this time that one of Muhammad's most important mystical experiences occurred. Sometime in 620, Muhammad, led by Gabriel and mounted on the white-winged beast Al-Buraq, experienced himself being transported from Mecca to "the farthest mosque" and thence toward heaven. As he experienced this ascent through seven heavens, he met with the great figures of Jewish and Christian literature, including Adam, Jesus and John, Joseph, Idris (Enoch), Aaron, Moses, and Abraham. Each of these greeted Muhammad as a prophet and either a son or a brother. Ultimately Gabriel ushered him into the presence of God.

Muhammad's account of the Night Voyage was critical for two reasons. First, for Muhammad it legitimated his role as prophet and confirmed his destiny as the final prophet of God. Second, though Muhammad did not specifically mention the city of Jerusalem as the site of the "farthest mosque," ever since the late seventh century Moslems have made this identification. The construction of the Dome of the Rock on the site of earlier Jewish temples around 690 C.E. confirmed the importance of Jerusalem to Muslim identity. Today, it is generally considered Islam's third holy city.

As the political situation in Mecca deteriorated, Muhammad and his followers searched for a solution. This came in the form of an invitation from the nearby city of Yathrib (later renamed Medina). A group from that city had become Muslims during a pilgrimage to Mecca several years earlier, and now they invited Muhammad to come to their city to teach and to settle political differences between contending factions. The migration of Muhammad and his followers to Yathrib in 622, known as the Hijrah, marked a turning point in Islam. The Muslim calendar begins with this date.

In Yathrib, Muhammad established his moral and political authority. In 624 he began a series of military campaigns that continued throughout the decade. These were at first directed against Muhammad's enemies within and around Yathrib, particularly members of the Jewish and Christian community. However, Muhammad's goal was to return to Mecca. Forces from Mecca and Yathrib fought repeatedly, with inconclusive results. But in 630, through a combination of battlefield victories and skillful diplomatic maneuvering, Muhammad and his followers returned in triumph to Mecca. Once in Mecca, Muhammad acted quickly to solidify his authority and claim religious sites. He affirmed the sanctity of existing sites such as the Kaaba and the Zamzam well, but destroyed all statues and other previous religious images associated with them and claimed the sites for Islam.

The years Muhammad spent in Yathrib were critical to the development of Islam. There, Muhammad first created a theocratic state. His prophecies concerned not only spiritual matters but politics as well. Muhammad cemented his leadership in Yathrib by seeking political alliances with neighboring chieftains and backing these alliances by marriage with members of their families. This pattern continued once Muhammad and his followers returned to Mecca. By the time of Muhammad's death, in 632, Mecca had become not only the most powerful religious center in its region, but a formidable political and military center as well.

ISLAMIC EXPANSION

Muhammad created a state held together by common beliefs and bonds of family. However, he left no male heir, so after his death the succession of leadership was hotly disputed. The first thirty years after Muhammad's death were a time of great violence and intrigue. The justice of the successions that took place during those years are still debated by Muslims, and the successions were the origin of the critical division between Sunni and Shiite Muslims.

Abu Bakr, Muhammad's father-in-law and close friend, became the first leader after Muhammad. He called himself Kahlifah (successor), which is most often transliterated into English as "caliph." In Islam, then, caliphs are successors to Muhammad. The position implies both religious and secular authority.

Abu Bakr ruled for only two years. He was followed by Umar and Uthman, then by Ali, who was both Muhammad's nephew and his son-in-law. All of these were assassinated as a result of disputes among factions within the *Quraysh* tribe. The *Quraysh,* a large tribe composed of ten clans, were the principal power in Mecca. Muhammad had been a member of one of the tribe's clans, the *Hashimites.* The *Umayyads,* led by Abu Sufyan, were another powerful clan, and after Muhammad's death they challenged his successors for the leadership of Islam. After the death of the fourth caliph, Ali, this challenge was successful. One of Ali's sons, Hasan, renounced his rights to the caliphate. The other, Husayn, was defeated on the battlefield. And in 661, Mu'awiyah, the son of Abu Sufyan, emerged as caliph and founder of the Umayyad dynasty.

Mu'awiyah had been governor of Syria, and his victory moved the center of Islamic rule from Mecca to Damascus. Syria had been a province of Rome and retained some of the administrative structure of the empire. It was probably this, combined with the dynamic new beliefs of Islam, that made the Syrian army under the Umayyads one of the most formidable fighting forces of its era. Between the early 660s and 715, Umayyad power was projected across the Mediterranean world. Major battles brought North Africa and much of the Middle East under Umayyad control. By 711, Muslim forces had begun the conquest of Spain and Islamization was well under way in Central Asia.

The Umayyads achieved their maximal expansion in the early 700s. The end of this era was marked by two dramatic losses. In 717 the Syrian army was defeated by the Byzantines, and in 732, Muslim expansion into western Europe was stopped in southern France at the Battle of Poitiers.

While the Umayyads successfully expanded Islam's reach, they were beset by problems, particularly palace intrigues and disputes between those who were born into Muslim families and those who had converted to Islam. These latter were taxed more heavily than those born Muslim and denied certain privileges. Attempts to rectify these problems, as well as disastrous military campaigns, led the empire into financial difficulties and created substantial unrest. This was exacerbated by an increasingly vitriolic debate over the proper exercise of Islam. Dissidents argued that the Umayyads were not proper caliphs—that they were administrative and political leaders only, lacking any spiritual legitimacy. Some argued that true spiritual leadership could come only from Muhammad's clan, the Hashimites, or from his direct descendants.

Opposition to Umayyad rule crystalized around the Abbasids, a family of Muhammad's Hashimite clan, but not one directly related to him. Between 747 and 750, under Abu al-Abbas, the head of the Abbasid family, a broad coalition of forces defeated the Umayyads. However, once in power, Abu turned on his allies, crushed them, and promoted the interests of his own family. To emphasize his determined effort to wipe out all opposition to his rule, Abu nicknamed himself *as-Saffah,* "the shedder of blood."

When Abu al-Abbas as-Saffah died in 754, he was succeeded by his brother al-Mansur, who distanced himself from his most extreme backers and moved his capital to Baghdad. Under al-Mansur and the caliphs who followed him, the Abbasid dynasty grew in strength and achievement. Baghdad became one of the largest and most powerful cities in the world.

The genius of the Abbasids was their ability to merge elements of different cultural traditions. Under their patronage, the arts flourished. Classics from ancient Greece and Persia were translated into Arabic. Critical advances were made in mathematics, philosophy, and literature. For example, the modern word *algorithm* comes from the name of the Abbasid scholar al-Khwarizmi (780–850), and the word *algebra* comes from the title of his principal work, *Kitab al-jabr wa al-muqabalah* (the book of restoring and simplification).

The height of Abassid power was reached by the late 800s. After this, though a caliph continued to reign in Baghdad, power became increasingly decentralized. The caliphate fell when the Mongols sacked Baghdad in 1258, but by that time the Islamic world had already fragmented into many contending centers of power.

Islamic lands eventually were unified again under the Ottoman Empire. The Ottomans, fleeing from the Mogul powers of Central Asia, began expanding into the Middle East in the eleventh and twelfth centuries. By the mid fifteenth century, they had conquered Constantinople (which they renamed Istanbul), and under the sixteenth-century emperor Suleyman the Magnificent (1495–1566) the Ottoman Empire became one of the largest and most powerful political entities in the world. Suleyman's reign, however, also marked the beginning of the empire's decline. In the years between the mid sixteenth century and the empire's eventual collapse in 1924, the power and importance of the empire diminished steadily. Islam continued to expand along trade routes, particularly to Indonesia and the southern Philippines, but the era of centralized Islamic power had ended.

MUSLIM BELIEFS AND PRACTICES

To a Muslim, the word *Islam* means submission to the will of God. The word itself is derived from the Arabic root *salema,* which also has connotations of peace, purity, and obedience. Muslims refer to God as Allah, but believe that Allah is the same as the God of Jewish and Christian tradition. Allah is thus best translated simply as "God." Muslim belief stresses the unity, power, and purity of God. They understand and experience God through their sacred literature, the Five Pillars of Islam, the celebration of holidays, as well as mystical religious experience.

Sacred Literature

The Qur'an. The most fundamental element of Islamic sacred literature is the Qur'an. It is the record of Muhammad's religious revelations. Muhammad believed that the angel Gabriel caused him to recite words that came directly from God and the word *Qur'an* is best translated "recitation." Muhammad himself was illiterate. He memorized the words and repeated them to his followers who wrote down his words to prevent their loss. Twenty years after his death, a council, under the leadership of the caliph Uthman, established a single, authoritative version of the work. Muslims believe that this version of the Qur'an is identical to its current form. Outsiders point out that technical problems in the Arabic script of that era as well as the lack of vowels suggests that there have been variations of the text. Nonetheless, scholars agree that the current form of the Qur'an is very close to the original.

Muslims believe that because the words of the Qur'an came directly from God (having passed through only the mouth of Muhammad), they have a special status. The Arabic words themselves are sacred; their recitation is a sacred duty that brings healing, protection, guidance, and knowledge. Translations of the Qur'an are brought about by human agency and therefore, though still holy, cannot have the same sacred quality as the original. Thus, believers are encouraged to memorize as much of the Qur'an in Arabic as they can and to pray in Arabic.

The Qur'an is arranged into 114 chapters, called *suras.* The first sura, called Fatiha (the opening), is brief. However, after Fatiha the suras are arranged in order of decreasing length so that the shortest suras come last. This order is, very roughly, the reverse of that in which they were revealed to Muhammad. Thus, the first and longest suras are sermons he preached late in his life; the last and shortest suras are his first revelations. Each sura has a name that comes from a predominant image it contains. The names are not necessarily indicative of the subject matter of the sura. Some sura names are "the Bee," "the Cave," "the Spider," "the Evident Smoke," and "the Star."

Textually, the Qur'an is written in rhyming verses called *ayah.* This form is most evident in the shortest suras. As the suras grow longer, rhyming is less evident. Because the Qur'an is the word of God, it is written in God's voice, frequently using the first-person plural "We." When Muhammad is speaking, his words are prefaced by the command

"Say," so that the reader might understand that although Muhammad is speaking, the words are God's. The Qur'an makes frequent reference to stories from the Jewish and Christian traditions but insists on its final authority. For Muslims, Jewish and Christian sacred texts are important but incomplete revelations of God; Muhammad's words and the Qur'an are God's final, perfect revelation.

SUNNAH AND THE HADITHS

Sunnah, which is sometimes translated as "well-trodden path," is the general term for "habit," "practice," or "customary procedure." It refers specifically to the practices, sayings, and living habits of the prophet Muhammad. These are most frequently expressed in Hadiths. *Hadith* is best translated as "to tell a happening." The Hadiths are sayings, observations, and accounts of the life of Muhammad and those closest to him. Most individual Hadiths are quite brief. For example, consider the following Hadith:

Narrated 'Umar bin Abi Salama:

I saw the Prophet offering prayers in a single garment in the house of Um-Salama and he had crossed its ends around his shoulders.[1]

Because Muhammad wrote nothing himself, all Hadiths were recorded by those around him. Each Hadith provides the name of its narrator (to prove its authenticity), any chain of individuals that might connect that narrator to the Prophet, and a simple statement about something Muhammad did. The example above is a very brief Hadith, but few are longer than two hundred words.

There are a great many Hadiths, and in the first three centuries after the death of Muhammad these were arranged into many different collections. Some of the best known are *Sahih Bukhari, Sahia Muslim,* and *Sunin Abu-Dawud.* Each is named after its compiler. Though Muslims accept the Qur'an as the indisputable Word of God, there is much debate among scholars both within and outside of Islam over the authenticity of the Hadiths. Different groups of Muslims may rely on different collections of Hadiths and emphasize different individual Hadiths.

Taken together, the Qur'an and the Hadiths are the source of both Islamic religious practice and Islamic jurisprudence (shari'ah). Shari'ah is intended to regulate the individual's conduct with regard to others, the state, their conscience, and God.

The Five Pillars

There are five elements of religious practice that are common to all Muslims. In fact, in many ways, a Muslim is simply an individual who attempts to practice the Five Pillars.

The Shahadah.   The first pillar of Islam is the Shahadah (testimony), a simple statement that affirms the unity of God and the role of Muhammad as his final messenger. In full, it states: "There is no God but God, and Muhammad is the prophet of God." The recitation of the Shahadah, once in a lifetime, with pure heart, is sufficient to make one a Muslim. However, the Shahadah is a constant presence in Islamic life. It is the first sentence whispered into a baby's ear. It is the last sentence a dying person is supposed to hear. It is repeated daily in prayer, and it is seen frequently in inscriptions inside mosques and over their doors.

Salat.   The second pillar is prayer. Muslims are called upon to pray five times each day: before dawn, just before noon, at midafternoon, at sunset, and at night. In Islamic communities, each time for prayer is announced by a muezzin, who from the minaret (tower) of the mosque chants, "God is most great. I testify that there is no God but God. I testify that Muhammad is the prophet of God. Come to prayer. Come to salvation. God is most great. There is no God but God" to each of the four directions. Today, many mosques have tape recordings and amplification systems that take the place of a human muezzin.

Before they participate in prayer, individuals must purify themselves through washing their hands, arms, neck, face, and feet. If water is unavailable, people may use sand to do the washing ritual.

Ideally, Muslims pray in groups, arranged behind a leader, called an imam. All face toward Mecca. Each of the five daily prayers requires a certain number of repetitions of key prayers, accompanied by a variety of body postures including standing, kneeling, and prostration. Though group prayer is preferred, individuals may pray alone if they are unable to join a group. Strictly speaking, no one is exempt from the requirement to pray. Even the sick must pray in bed.

While the five prayers are a daily requirement, Friday is a day of particular public prayer. Men may go to pray at the mosque at any time (in many places women may go as well, but their area is separate from the men's area). However, attendance at the mosque for Friday midafternoon prayers is a special obligation. At that time, in addition to the prayers required each afternoon, the imam may give a sermon. Mosques that have only small attendances throughout the week may be very crowded on Fridays.

Zakat.   Zakat is the duty of charity. Islam is a religion deeply concerned with social justice. The Qur'an and the Hadiths repeatedly urge the duty of charity on all Muslims. There are two elements to this duty. First, a good individual performs acts of charity "for your kin, for orphans, for the needy, for the wayfarer, for those who ask, and for the ransom of slaves."[2] Second, in addition to the general giving of charity, Muslims are enjoined to give a percentage of their total wealth in charity each year. The way this obligation is interpreted and how the money is collected varies from society to society. The expectations are that families will give anywhere from 2.5 to 10 percent of their total wealth.

Sawm. Like many other religions, Islam requires its adherents to participate in fasting. Each year, during the Islamic calendar month of Ramadan, all Muslims—except the sick, travelers, nursing mothers, and children—are expected to fast from the first light of day until after dark. The yearly fast commemorates Muhammad's first revelations of the Qur'an. Devout Muslims offer longer prayers each night of Ramadan, but the twenty-seventh night is particularly important. Called Laylat-al-Qadr, and sometimes translated as the "night of power," the twenty-seventh night is believed to mark the exact night Muhammad received his first revelation. Many Muslims will remain awake praying all night to mark this event and believe that during this night God determines the events of the world for the coming year.

Because the Islamic calendar is lunar, the date of Ramadan advances about eleven days each solar year. The result is that Ramadan gradually rotates around the seasons. Fasting always requires discipline, but when Ramadan occurs during the hottest times of the year, people experience greater discomfort.

The sharing of the fast during Ramadan unites Muslims as a people and separates them from non-Muslims among whom they might live. When the fast ends, on the first day of the month of Shawwal, people exchange gifts and celebrate a three-day holiday called Eid-al-Fitr, the feast of fast-breaking.

Hajj. The final pillar of Islam is the pilgrimage, or hajj. Mecca, and particularly the Kaaba, was a place of pilgrimage before Muhammad. Muhammad destroyed the tribal god images housed in the Kaaba but continued the tradition of pilgrimage. Each Muslim, if he or she can afford it, is expected to visit Mecca at least once during their lifetime. An individual who does so takes an honorary title, *hajjii* for men and *hajjiyah* for women, much respected in Muslim societies.

The hajj occurs during the twelfth month of the Islamic calendar, Zul-Hijja, and follows a prescribed ritual order. Pilgrims begin by visiting the Great Mosque at Mecca and circling the Kaaba seven times. They then proceed to a series of stops in Mina, Arafat, and Muzdalifa, all of which are locations in the desert near Mecca. Of the many ritual elements to the hajj, several of particular importance deserve special mention.

Tawaf: Making *Tawaf* is the act of circling the Kaaba seven times (in a counterclockwise direction). The Kaaba is located in the Great Mosque of Mecca, which can accommodate up to a half million worshipers at a single time. Pilgrims make *Tawaf* at the start, during the middle, and at the end of the hajj. Ideally the *Tawaf* should be the last thing a pilgrim does in Mecca.

Rami, the stoning of the pillars: Several times during the hajj, pilgrims collect small pebbles to throw at three stone pillars located at Mina. Worshipers throw the stones at each pillar in sets of seven. The pillars symbolize the devil, and stoning them represents human efforts to jettison evil and vice.

Eid-al-Adah: Muslims all over the world (not only those on the hajj) celebrate Eid-al-Adah on the tenth day of Zul-Hijja. This holiday commemorates Abraham's sacrifice. You may recall that a key story in the Jewish Bible is the sacrifice of Isaac. Abraham, the patriarch, is told to take his son, Isaac, and sacrifice him to God. Abraham complies, but at the last moment God provides an animal substitute, a ram, and Isaac is spared. Muslims believe that it was not Isaac who was to be sacrificed, but Abraham's other son, Ismael. They sacrifice an animal on the tenth day of Zul-Hijja to commemorate this event. For Muslims, this event is among the most important of the year. It symbolizes humankind's absolute submission to the will of God.

Sa'i: Pilgrims also reenact another critical episode of the story of Ismael and his mother, Hagar. In Islamic tradition, Abraham had two wives, Sara and Hagar.[3] Sara, the first wife, bore a son, Isaac. Hagar, the second, bore Ismael. As a result of Sara's jealousy, Hagar and Ismael were cast into the desert, where they wandered desperate for food and water. Ultimately, they were answered by an angel who provided a well of water and told Ismael that he would become a great nation. In performing the *Sa'i,* pilgrims symbolically repeat Hagar and Ismael's search for food and water by running seven times between two hills, called Safa and Marwah. At the conclusion of the *Sa'i,* pilgrims drink at the Zamzam well, which Muslims believe to be the miraculous well the angel provided for Hagar and Ismael.

Additional Holidays

The most important of the Muslim holidays are Eid al-Fitr (the breaking of the fast) and Eid al-Adah (the feast of sacrifice). As these are also elements of the Five Pillars of Islam, they have already been described above. In addition to these holidays, Muslims may also celebrate the New Year and the birthday of the prophet Muhammad. The New Year is the first day of the Islamic month of Muharram. It is also believed to mark the date of the Hijrah, Muhammad's movement from Mecca to Yathrib (Medina). Muhammad's birthday is celebrated on the twelfth day of the third Islamic month. There is considerable variation in the celebration of these holidays. Some Muslims consider Muhammad's birthday to be a modern innovation and do not celebrate it.

Jihad

Because of its connection with current-day militant groups, most Americans are probably familiar with the concept of jihad. The word *jihad* means "battle" or "fight" and is often translated as "holy war," though "struggle" might be more accurate. Traditionally, there are four types of jihad, though these may be combined: jihad by heart, by tongue, by hand, and by sword. The first of these refers to the spiritual struggle to purify one's own heart and one's own belief. The second and third refer to speaking out for justice and doing what is right according to Islamic law. They are also interpreted as a call to mission activity propagating the faith. The fourth refers to taking up arms against enemies of the faith. These enemies might be non-Muslims who refuse to convert to Islam or live under Islamic rule, or they might be Muslims whose practices are at variance with those declaring the jihad.

The universal conversion of humankind to Islam is an important goal for Muslims, but the degree to which this goal has been pursued and the means used to pursue it have varied greatly over time. In the early years of Islam, expansion was pursued through military means and calls of jihad were directed against non-Islamic communities, particularly Christian and Jewish communities that refused to accept Muslim rule. However, wars of expansion against non-Muslims, while important, have been the exception rather than the rule in Islamic history. Calls to jihad have been most often aimed at purification of one's own belief or suppression of rival parties within Islam.

Islamic Mysticism

As we have seen, the period of turmoil after the death of Muhammad ended with the emergence of the Umayyad dynasty, which became one of the most powerful political entities of the world during its era. Islamic power increased further under the Abbasids who followed them. The transformation of Islam from a small religious group to a large, wealthy, and powerful political state necessarily involved an increasing worldliness. Under the Umayyad and Abbasid caliphs, mainstream practice of Islam became increasingly formal. One early response to this was a call to a more spiritual, more mystical experience of God. In Arabic, mysticism is referred to as *tasawwuf,* which literally means "to dress in wool." The reference is to the asceticism of mystics who turn away from worldly wealth to pursue spiritual union with God. In English, Islamic mysticism is referred to as Sufism.

Sufism began in the early years of the Umayyad dynasty. Initially, most mystics concentrated on passages of the Qur'an dealing with the end of the world, and as a consequence were known as "those who weep." However, by the ninth century the focus of mysticism changed to the achievement of mystical union with God. For mystics of this era, the goal of worship was to achieve perfect and disinterested love of God, absolute love without hope of heaven or fear of hell. The sage most closely identified with these ideas was a woman named Rabi'ah al-'Adawiyah.

The mystical claim that individuals could achieve direct union with God often conflicted with the political prerogatives of the state and the religion of court clerics. One notable example of this was the tenth-century mystic Al-Hallaj. Al-Hallaj studied under Sufi masters, but against their wishes he traveled throughout the Islamic world preaching. Many followers were attracted by his belief that in moments of religious ecstasy personal identity is lost and union with God is achieved. However, this teaching also drew the attention of the political authorities, and Al-Hallaj

was suspected of fomenting rebellion. He was arrested on his return to Baghdad, reportedly for claiming, in a moment of religious ecstasy, that he was "the truth." The meaning of Al-Hallaj's words and actions were unclear and his imprisonment and trial long and complex. However, in 922, Al-Hallaj was tortured and executed. The beauty of his poetry, his martyrdom, and the grace with which he suffered it made Al-Hallaj a key figure for subsequent Islamic mystics.

Al-Ghazali was another critical figure in the development of mysticism. He was a scholar in eleventh-century Baghdad who left his prestigious post as chief professor to pursue a life of poverty and mystical devotion. Al-Ghazali is well known for two reasons. First, he wrote very widely on topics such as logic, theology, and jurisprudence as well as his own life experiences. Secondly, as a prestigious official in Baghdad he was able to forge a link between the political hierarchy and mysticism, thus increasing the acceptance of Sufism.

Many Sufi mystics and their followers lived in semi-monastic communities. Disciples gathered around a master in order to learn specific techniques of spiritual mastery and to live a sacred life. Other devotees remained in the lay community. These communities of believers are often referred to as *tariqua,* from the Arabic word for "road." In English this is generally glossed as "brotherhood." Many thousands of different brotherhoods have arisen since the twelfth century. Many of these were associated with specific places, occupational groups, or practices. Each group begins with a leader who claims spiritual descent from Muhammad and promotes the use of a technique for achieving religious ecstasy. These techniques have included the use of hallucinogenic drugs, repetition of mantras, physical exercise, whirling, and dancing. Because of these practices, and because members of brotherhoods often focused devotions on particular spiritual masters, the *tariqua* frequently suffered harsh criticism, and sometimes physical repression, from those whose approach to Islam was less mystical. Nonetheless, many large brotherhoods survive today. Among these are the Qadiriyah, founded in the twelfth century, Shadhiliyah and Mawlawiyah, both founded in the thirteenth century, and the more recent Tijaniya, founded in the eighteenth century.

Through its emphasis on divine love and the experience of the sacred, the Sufi movement has given the world some of its finest poetry and art. Some of the best-known Sufi poets are Hafiz (1325–1390), Jami (1414–1492), and Rumi, the founder of the Mawlawiyah order. Rumi, for example wrote:

Today, like every other day, we wake up empty
and frightened. Don't open the door to the study
and begin reading. Take down a musical instrument.
Let the beauty we love be what we do.
There are hundreds of ways to kneel and kiss the ground.[4]

SHIITE AND SUNNI IN ISLAM

There are many variations in Islamic beliefs and practices among different communities around the world. The largest division, however, is probably that between the Sunni and Shiite groups. This division originated in the decades immediately following the death of Muhammad and continues to be salient in the Islamic world today.

You will recall from the discussion earlier in this essay that between Muhammad's death in 632 and the emergence of the first Umayyad caliph in 661 there was strife over the leadership of Islam. Many Muslims felt that the successor to Muhammad should come from within his own family. For those who believed this, there was only one possible candidate: Ali, Muhammad's nephew and son-in-law. Ali did become caliph in 656, but his reign was short-lived; he was assassinated in 661 and Mu'awiyah became the first caliph of the Umayyad dynasty. One of Ali's two sons renounced the succession, but the other, Husayn, fought on against Umayyad rule. He was defeated and killed by Yazid, the second Umayyad caliph, at the battle of Karbala in 680.

For most Muslims, the definitive battlefield victory of the Umayyads and their subsequent success proved Umayyad caliphs were the rightful successors to Muhammad. These Muslims developed legal traditions and daily practices that they understood as based on *Sunnah*—habitual practice or tradition. They are known as Sunni Muslims. There are four different schools of religious law within Sunni Islam—the Hanifites, the Malikites, the Shafi'ites, and the Hanbalites—all with different interpretations of Islamic tradition. The vast majority of Muslims today are Sunni, and the center of Sunni power is represented by Saudi Arabia, which is home to the cities of Mecca and Medina.

When Husayn was defeated and the Umayyads solidified their power, the backers of Ali (called the Shi'a [faction of, or partisans of] Ali, hence Shiites) did not disappear. They formed a minority party within Islam, maintaining that the rightful place of Ali and his descendants had been usurped by the Umayyads. The Shiites rejected the rule of the Umayyad caliphs and their successors, instead promoting the rule of Ali and his successors. To distinguish themselves from the Umayyads, who called their leaders caliphs, the Shiites called their leaders imams, a word that, when used by non-Shiites, is an honorific title applied to leaders of mosques and scholars of Islam. Ali was the first imam. Most Shiites believe that Ali's line continued unbroken through eleven successors. The twelfth imam, Muhammed al-Mahdi, left no descendants. Indeed, believers claim that he did not die but rather disappeared in 878. Many Shiites believe that he was hidden by God in a secret realm from which he guides current-day imams and from which he will return, on judgment day, to establish justice on earth.

Early Shiite communities were located throughout the Muslim world but particularly in the area that is now Iraq. With the end of the Umayyad dynasty and the emergence of the Abbasids, members of these communities had hoped to establish the rule of Ali's descendants. But even though the Abbasid caliphs did originate from Muhammad's Hashimite clan of the Quraysh tribe, they rejected Ali's descendants,

and when the center of Abbasid power moved to Baghdad, the Shiites went into exile, principally in Iran, which is still the center of Shiite Islam.

Not all Shiite Muslims agreed with the notion that there were eleven successors to Ali. Some insisted that the line of succession was clear only up to Ja'far, the great-great-grandson of Ali and the sixth imam. Ja'far had a son, Isma'il, who died before Ja'far. Some Shiite Muslims believe that Ja'far's son Musa-al-Kazim became the seventh imam after his father's death, but Isma'ilite Muslims believe that Isma'il became the seventh imam. They believe that it was he who was hidden and will reappear at the last judgment. Isma'ilite Muslim communities exist in East Africa, Pakistan, India, and Yemen.

In many respects Shiite Islam is very similar to Sunni Islam. Like Sunnis, Shiite observance is based around the Qur'an, the Hadiths, and the Five Pillars of Islam. There are, however, key differences. The most notable of these is probably faith in the return of the hidden twelfth (or seventh) imam, but there are others. While Sunni Muslims respect and honor Islamic scholars and leaders of mosques, Shiites believe that certain imams are infallible and truly speak with the authority of god. Thus the role of imam is generally more powerful in Shiite than in Sunni communities. Unlike Sunni beliefs (but rather like Christian beliefs), Shiite beliefs have a strong thread of martyrdom and betrayal. For Shiites, Husayn, the son of Ali who was heroically martyred on the battlefield by the Umayyads, plays a key role. Each year on the anniversary of the battle of Karbala, the tenth of the month of Muharran, devout Shiites commemorate the death of Husayn. Additionally, the perceived betrayal of Ali by the Umayyads and of his descendants by the Abbasids colors the Shiite view of history.

OTHER VARIATIONS: BLACK MUSLIMS

One of the variations of Islam that is of particular interest to Americans is the Nation of Islam, frequently called the "Black Muslim" movement. The Nation of Islam is a black nationalist organization founded in the 1930s by W. D. Fard. Fard's origins are extremely obscure, but his followers believe he was born in Mecca in 1877. After Fard disappeared under mysterious circumstances in 1934, leadership of the movement passed to Elijah Muhammad (born Elijah Poole).

Fard and Muhammad taught their followers an eclectic religion that mixed bits of Islam with black nationalism and Pentecostal Christianity. While they promoted belief in and practice of the Five Pillars of Islam, their variety of Islam also included many idiosyncratic elements. For example, they taught that the original man, called Allah, created himself 76 trillion years ago. He then created men as well as the universe. He populated the earth with "Asiatic blackmen." The world, they claimed, exists in 25,000-year cycles. About 8,400 years into the current cycle, the evil "big head scientist" genetically engineered the "devil race," that is to say, white people. Through a complex history of war and destruction, the "devil race" used "tricknology"—lies and deception—to defeat, demoralize, and enslave the "Asiatic blackmen." The world wrought by the "devil race" can only end in universal destruction. However, a savior will appear (Fard himself, or Elijah Muhammad) to enlighten "Asiatic blackmen" and prepare them for salvation. At the time of judgment, an enormous wheel-shaped spaceship, the "mother plane," will arrive and incinerate everything except the righteous who have heeded Elijah Muhammad's message. These will be saved by black scientists and go on to populate a new, righteous world.

In the late 1950s and 1960s, the Nation of Islam's most prominent member was Malcolm X (born Malcolm Little). His eloquence, as well as his appeal to black pride, separatism, independence, and violence, won many converts to the Nation of Islam. But his success also aroused opposition within the organization. In 1964, Malcolm X split from the Nation of Islam, founding the Muslim Mosque Inc., his own religious organization. After a visit that same year to Mecca, he abandoned the more idiosyncratic elements of Fard and Elijah Muhammad's prophecies and began to promote an Islam more in keeping with that practiced throughout the world. Malcolm X was assassinated in 1965, a casualty of the conflict between his followers and those of the Nation of Islam.

Rivalries continued with the Black Muslim community. By the 1970s, the movement had split into two factions. One faction, under the leadership of Elijah Muhammad's son, formed the American Muslim Mission and continued to promote a form of Islam based on the international model. This organization continued until 1985, when it was dissolved and its members were encouraged to join the international Muslim community. A second faction coalesced under the leadership of Louis Farrakhan. It retained both the Nation of Islam name and belief in the teachings of Fard and Elijah Muhammad.

ISLAM IN THE LAST ONE HUNDRED YEARS

Islamic civilization expanded under the Umayyads, the Abbasids, and then the Ottoman Empire. However, by the late 1400s, major expansion had ceased. As Christian European culture grew more powerful in the sixteenth through nineteenth centuries, Muslim culture entered a period of comparatively little change. However, events in the twentieth century led to a resurgence of Islam that continues to this day. A thorough examination of modern Islam is well beyond the scope of this essay. However, several factors are important to discuss in relation to the expansion of Islam today.

The Collapse of Colonialism

By the end of the nineteenth century, European nations held most of the world under either direct colonization or political and economic domination. However, in the twentieth century European colonialism collapsed. The end of the colonial system benefited Islam in two ways. First, some of the colonized nations were Islamic, and independence brought to power governments more favorable to Islam. Second, in many places, such as West Africa, both Muslims and Christians had launched missionary efforts. Christianity was often tied to hated colonial powers, and resistance to colonialism frequently coalesced around Islam. This contributed to the growth of Islam throughout the twentieth century. The appeal of Islam continued into the years of the cold war, when many people in the former colonies saw Islam as a philosophical alternative to the dominant Christianity of the capitalist world and the official atheism of the communist world.

The Oil Economies

One hundred years ago, oil was of little importance in the world's economy. Today, it is an essential natural resource. Some of the world's largest oil reserves are found in the Middle East, in nations with Muslim majorities. Throughout much of the twentieth century, oil prices were low and this resource was of little benefit to oil-producing nations. However, in the 1970s, acting as a group, the oil-producing nations substantially raised the price of oil. In consequence from 1973 through the mid 1980s enormous amounts of money poured into these nations. The price of oil has fluctuated considerably in the last decade, but the presence of vast oil reserves in Muslim nations has continued to make these countries important players on the world stage.

The results of oil wealth have been substantial. Populations in oil-producing nations went from relative poverty to relative wealth in a short time. Money flowing into governments and religious organizations has been used to promote Islamic causes throughout the world. These include public relations efforts aimed at promoting Islam in wealthy industrialized nations, economic development in poor nations, and missionary efforts throughout the world.

Immigration of Muslims to Wealthy Nations

Since the mid twentieth century, large numbers of Muslims have left predominantly Muslim countries to seek prosperity and new lives in wealthy, industrialized nations. For example, there are now 4 to 5 million Muslims in France and almost 3 million Muslims in Germany. A recent survey estimates that 6 to 7 million people in the United States identify themselves as Muslims. Of these, about 2 million identify with one of the more than 1,200 mosques in this nation.[5] By comparison, the population of Saudi Arabia is about 20 million. Further, the Muslim population of traditionally non-Muslim nations is rising rapidly. As a result, Islam is increasingly a visible and important part of life throughout the world's wealthy nations. In the United States, for example, most cities with populations over a quarter million now have mosques. Almost all major universities have Muslim student associations. Islamic groups have increasingly important voices in politics and cultural affairs in the world's wealthiest nations.

Political Islam

Islam has also recently achieved prominence because of its heavy involvement in questions of politics, particularly in the Middle East, South Asia, and Indonesia. Most Americans are very aware of the conflict between the Muslim Palestinian Arabs and Israelis over land and political autonomy. This conflict involves history, religion, and passion on all sides. Many Americans (and others around the world) are vitally interested in the fate of Jerusalem and other sites holy to Jews, Muslims, and Christians. On all sides the conflict is partly animated by closely held religious beliefs, and some groups on all sides have been moved to violence partially by their understanding of religious duty.

The issues created by the conflict between Palestinians and Israelis are important, but there are other critical dilemmas in the Muslim world. As we have mentioned above, from the sixteenth century through most of the twentieth century, the pace of change was much more rapid in the European nations than in areas where majorities were Muslim. During that time, Europeans and North Americans developed enormous wealth and influence. In the last one hundred years, and particularly in the past fifty, enormous change and substantial wealth have come to predominantly Muslim nations, and with these have come social problems as well.

With rapid modernization, Muslims have had to confront issues of changing social forms and the enormous influence of non-Muslim cultures. Different leaders have drawn very different conclusions. Some nations have attempted to entirely separate religion from political and economic life. Perhaps the most outstanding example of this is Turkey. In the 1920s, under the leadership of Mustafa Kemal Ataturk, Turkey moved decisively toward secularization, abolishing religious courts and schools and other aspects of the public political presence of Islam. In most places, Muslim leaders and clerics have striven to find ways of living with the values of modern international capitalist culture while remaining true to those of Islam. In nations such as Syria, Indonesia, Malaysia, Iraq, Jordan, and Egypt, Islam plays an important role in politics but governments are secular. Still other nations, such as Iran, Sudan, and Saudi Arabia, have maintained governments based in religion and committed to the promulgation of religious law.

Because Islam is sometimes seen as providing an alternative to the policies of modernizing governments and globalization, it has attracted and catalyzed those with political and economic grievances against their governments, becoming a focus of those who reject modern values and long for a return to what they envision as a traditional lifestyle. In Muslim societies, clerics and other leaders have often called for a rejection of modern consumerist society, gender equality, democracy, and other aspects of Westernization. In some places, particularly Iran, these calls have been successful and revolutionary groups proclaiming the rejection of European values and a return to Islamic traditionalism have come to power, overthrowing secular governments. In many other nations, such groups are important in the political process, whether as members of the government, of the political opposition, or of banned but present parties.

Given the trends in the past hundred years, it is clear that Islam will play an important role in the economic and political future of the world. Exactly what that role will be is much less clear. Certainly no one "Muslim answer" will be found to the problems of governance and society. Muslims, much as the religious in all current societies, will have to determine how to live their beliefs in a complex and heterogeneous world.

NOTES

1. *Sahih Bukhairi* 1(8): 351.

2. Sura 2. Al-Baqara (The Cow): 177.

3. This story is recounted in Genesis 16.

4. *The Essential Rumi,* trans. Coleman Barks (San Franscisco: Harper, 1995), 36.

5. Ihsan Bagby, Paul M. Merl, and Brian T. Froehle, *The Mosque In America: A National Portrait* (Washington D.C.: Council on American-Islamic Relations, 2001), 3.

INDEX